THE LETTERS OF

T. S. ELIOT

VOLUME I

THE LETTERS OF

T. S. ELIOT

EDITED BY

VALERIE ELIOT

AND

HUGH HAUGHTON

VOLUME I

1898–1922

REVISED EDITION

GENERAL EDITOR

JOHN HAFFENDEN

Yale

UNIVERSITY PRESS

New Haven & London

First published in the
United States in 2011 by Yale University Press.
First published in
Great Britain in 2009 by Faber and Faber Limited.

Yale University Press books may be
purchased in quantity for educational, business, or
promotional use. For information, please e-mail sales.press@yale.edu
(U.S. office) or sales@yaleup.co.uk (U.K. office).

Printed in the United States of America.

Library of Congress Control Number: 2011928724
ISBN 978-0-300-17645-2 (hardcover: alk. paper)

A catalogue record for this book is available from the British Library.

This paper meets the requirements of
ANSI/NISO Z39.48-1992 (Permanence of Paper).

10 9 8 7 6 5 4 3 2 1

'The desire to write a letter, to put down what you don't want anybody else to see but the person you are writing to, but which you do not want to be destroyed, but perhaps hope may be preserved for complete strangers to read, is ineradicable. We want to confess ourselves in writing to a few friends, and we do not always want to feel that no one but those friends will ever read what we have written.'

from 'English Poets as Letter Writers',
an unpreserved lecture given by TSE
at Sprague Memorial Hall, Yale University,
23 November 1933.
This fragment was recorded by his brother.
(MS Houghton)

CONTENTS

ILLUSTRATIONS

10A Charlotte, the sister who painted his portrait. *Houghton Library MS Am 2560 (233)*

B His sister Marian. *Houghton Library MS Am 2560 (245)*

C At the front gate of 2635 on the morning after the cyclone of 27 May 1896, with his mother and, *left*, cousin Henrietta and sister Margaret. Marian is hidden. *Houghton Library MS Am 2560 (162)*

11A With his father, 1895. *Houghton Library MS Am 2560 (160)*

B And in 1898. *Houghton Library MS Am 2560 (154)*

12 TSE in his bedroom at St Louis, *c.*1900. *Collection Valerie Eliot*

13A With his cousins Abigail, Martha and Frederick Eliot. *Collection Valerie Eliot*

B At the piano, *c.*1899. *Houghton Library MS Am 2560 (170)*

C One of his father's cat drawings. *Collection Valerie Eliot*

14A His mother's bedroom at Locust Street. *Houghton Library MS Am 2560 (262)*

B Interior of the house at Eastern Point. *Houghton Library MS Am 2560 (260)*

15 Charlotte's oil portrait (18 x 23in) *c.*1900–1. TSE is reading a volume of his red Shakespeare set, which remains in his library. *Original in the possession of Theodora Eliot Smith. Houghton Library MS Am 2560 (172)*

16 Aged about twelve. *Houghton Library MS Am 2560 (171)*

17A The view from the Eliot home at Eastern Point. *Collection Valerie Eliot*

B TSE. *Houghton Library MS Am 2560 (179b)*

C Henry, 1895. *Houghton Library MS Am 2560 (236)*

18A 1907. *Houghton Library MS Am 2560 (177)*

B 1908. *Houghton Library MS Am 2560 (178)*

C On other occasions. *Houghton Library MS Am 2560 (179b, 188a)*

19A Henry (who is taking the photograph) with his parents at the breakfast table, 4446 Westminster Place, St Louis. *Houghton Library MS Am 2560 (235)*

B Henry. *Houghton Library MS Am 2560 (236)*

C TSE in 1910. *Houghton Library MS Am 2560 (179a)*

20 Sailing off the Dry Salvages.

Photographs 1, 2A and B, 3, 4B and C, 6, 7A and B, 8A and B, 9A and B, 10A, B and C, 11A and B, 13B, 14A and B, 15, 16, 17B and C, 18A, B and C, 19A, B and C, 21A and 23 are reproduced by permission of the Houghton Library, Harvard University.

ACKNOWLEDGEMENTS

I owe a special debt of gratitude to both Dr William H. Bond, formerly Librarian, and Rodney G. Dennis, Curator of Manuscripts, at the Houghton Library, Harvard University; to Dr Donald Gallup, bibliographer of Eliot and Pound, who has answered innumerable questions with grace; and to Matthew Evans with my editor, John Bodley, for their generous support and encouragement.

For permission to print letters and quote from copyright material, I wish to thank Alain Rivière (Alain-Fournier), Alastair Kershaw (Richard Aldington), Professor Charles W. Eliot (President Eliot), Mme Catherine Gide (André Gide), The Ezra Pound Literary Property Trust, and James Laughlin (Ezra Pound), The Bertrand Russell Estate and McMaster University (Bertrand Russell), Francis Wyndham (Sydney Schiff), Françoise Valéry (Paul Valéry), Harvard University Libraries (J. H. Woods).

I am grateful to Professor John Weightman for translating all letters in French, and to the following for help in various ways: Joan Bailey; Anne Olivier Bell; Kenneth Blackwell, McMaster University; Michael Harry Blechner, McFarlin Library, University of Tulsa; Mary Boccaccio, McKeldin Library, University of Maryland; Dr J. M. L. Booker, Lloyds Bank Archivist; Penelope Bulloch, Balliol College Library; William R. Cagle, Saundra Taylor, Lilly Library; Douglass Campbell; Dr Joseph Chiari; the late Marguerite Cohn; Joyce Crick; Arthur Crook; Roy Davids; Dr A. Deiss, General Secretariat, Swiss Medical Institutions; Giles de la Mare; Peter du Sautoy; Donald D. Eddy, Cornell University Library; Barclay Feather, Director of Libraries, Milton Academy; K. C. Gay, Lockwood Memorial Library, Buffalo; Herbert Gerwing, Special Collections, University of Victoria; Mrs Ghika; R. C. Giles, T. G. Mallinson, Highgate School; Robert Giroux; Sir Rupert Hart-Davis; Professor E. N. Hartley, Institute Archives, MIT; Cathy Henderson, Humanities Research Center, University of Texas; the late Robert Henderson; Dr Roger Highfield, Merton College Library; Robert W. Hill, New York Public Library (Manuscript Division); Penelope Hughes-Hallett; J. W. Hunt, Royal Military Academy, Sandhurst; Lord Hutchinson; Carolyn Jakeman; Professor Dorothy O. Johansen, Reed College, Portland, Oregon; William Jovanovich; Monique Kuntz, Bibliothèque Municipale,

Vichy; the staff of the London Library; Richard M. Ludwig, Princeton University Library; R. Russell Maylone, Northwestern University Library; Professor B. K. Matilal; Joe Mitchenson; Mary C. McGreenery, Harvard Alumni Records; Lord Quinton; Angela Raspin, London School of Economics; Benedict Read; Dr R. T. H. Redpath; Helene Ritzerfeld; Rosenbach Museum & Library; Anthony Rota; Samuel A. Sizer, Special Collections, University Libraries, University of Arkansas; Lola L. Szladits, Berg Collection; Theodora Eliot Smith; Kendon L. Stubbs, University of Virginia Library; Barbara Sturtevant; Elizabeth Stege Teleky, Joseph Regenstein Library, University of Chicago; Professor Kathleen Tillotson; Dr George Watson; the late Helen Willard; Professor David G. Williams; Patricia C. Willis, Beinecke Library, Yale University; Dr Daniel H. Woodward, Huntington Library.

It is a pleasure to record my heartfelt appreciation of the Faber team: Ron Costley, designer, Mark Massingham, typesetter, Jane Robertson, managing editor, Hazel Orme, copy-editor, and Gillian Bate, proof reader, who have combined their skills to produce such an elegant tribute to TSE in his centenary year.

1988

The acknowledgements above are those made by Valerie Eliot in the first edition of Volume 1. Sadly, a number of those mentioned are now deceased (as are some of those we will add below). The editors would like also to thank: Owen Barfield; H. Baugh; Jewel Spears Brooker; Robert Brown; Andrew Boxer; Ronald Bush; François Chapon; Mrs Charlton; Alan Clodd; the Literary Trustees of Walter de la Mare; J. P. G. Delaney; the estate of Geoffrey Faber; Toby Faber; Jennifer Formichelli; Mrs Burnham Finney; Estate of Enid Goldsmith; Herbert T. Greene; Warwick Gould; Michael Halls; Saskia Hamilton; Hal Hlavinka; Michael Hofmann; Michael Holroyd; Steven Isenberg; P. D. James; Iman Javadi; Emeline Jouvé; Paul Keegan; Kenneth A. Lohf; Jim McCue; Tessa Milne; Tim Munby; Mary Middleton Murry; Anne Owen; Craig Raine; Carol Rothkopt; Gerd Schmidt; Rev. Karl Schroeder, SJ; Ronald Schuchard; Jesse Cordes Selbin; Timothy and Marian Seldes; Prue Shaw; James Strachey; M. J. Tilby; François Valéry, Judith Robinson-Valéry; David Van Ness; Michael J. Walsh; Jemma Walton, J. Waterlow; Dave Watkins; Kieron Winn; Susan Wolfson; John Worthen and Michael Yeats. Special thanks go to Ron Costley, Donald Sommerville for his copy-editing, Jenny Overton for proofreading, Alison Worthington for indexing, and to Debbie Whitfield (PA to Mrs Eliot) for her commitment to this project.

We are grateful in addition to: Leslie Morris and Elizabeth A. Falsey (Houghton Library); Dr P. Kelly (National Library of Scotland); Robin Carlaw (Harvard University Archives); Eamon Dyas (News International); Moira A. Fitzgerald and Eva Guggemos (Beinecke Library, Yale); Thomas Lannon (New York Public Library); Molly Schwartzburg (Harry Ransom Research Center, University of Texas); Claire Nicholas-Walker (British Library); Thomas Whitehead (Temple University Libraries); Stephen Young (Regenstein Library, University of Chicago); Bibliothèque Littéraire Jacques Doucet; Bibliothèque Nationale, Paris; Bodleian Library, Oxford; University of Bonn Library; British Library; Bundesarchiv (German Federal Archives), Koblenz; Rare Books and Manuscripts Division, Butler Library, Columbia University, New York; University of California, Los Angeles; Fondazione Camillo Caetani, Rome; Clare College, Cambridge; Fondren Library, Woodson Research Center, Rice University; Galleria Nazionale d'Arte Moderna, Rome; Harvard University Archives; Special Collections, Isabella Stewart Gardner Museum, Boston, Mass.; Hornbake Library, University of Maryland; Special Collections, Keele University; Modern Archives Centre, King's College, Cambridge; Magdalene College, Cambridge; Marshall Library, Cambridge; Massachusetts Institute of Technology; Lockwood Memorial Library; University Library, Missouri History Museum; Morris Library, Southern Illinois University at Carbondale; Mugar Memorial Library, Boston University; National Library, Scotland; New College, Oxford; Pennsylvania University Library; Reading University Library; Real Academia de la Historia; Schiller-Nationalmuseum, Marbach am Neckar; Schweizerisches Literaturachiv (Swiss National Archives), Berne; University of Sussex Library; Trinity College, Cambridge; Trinity College, Dublin; University of Virginia Library; Washington University Library, St Louis, Missouri; Widener Library, Harvard University; Chapin Library, Williams College, Williamstown, Massachusetts; Yale University Archives.

2009

INTRODUCTION

At the time of our marriage in 1957 I was dismayed to learn that my husband had forbidden the future publication of his correspondence, because I appreciated its importance and fascination. As he often read aloud to me in the evenings – *Kim*, English and French poetry, Sherlock Holmes, *Pickwick Papers*, Uncle Remus – I took every opportunity to introduce a poet's letters, until, eventually, he burst out laughing, and said he would relent on condition that I did the selecting and editing.

When in 1965 I began my research – which was interrupted three years later in order to prepare the hitherto missing manuscript of *The Waste Land* – the material relating to this volume filled a single folder in TSE's desk, and many of today's collections of Eliot letters were still in the hands of their recipients.

The correspondence with Ottoline Morrell did not become available until 1975, and that with Mary Hutchinson until 1977. Very few of their replies have been preserved, and there are none from Brigit Patmore. Letters to Ezra Pound came together at Yale University in stages, except for the last cache, now at the Lilly Library, Indiana University, which was only released in 1982 after a legal dispute. Those to J. H. Woods were given by his widow to Professor David G. Williams, who kindly allowed me to have photostats in 1981. Several unknown early letters to Scofield Thayer were an exciting bonus last year, together with a fair number to Ivor and Dorothea Richards.

Bruce Richmond, like W. H. Auden, threw away letters once they had been answered, and it is known that TSE's to Lady Rothermere were not kept. I have been unable to trace his correspondence with Charles Whibley, J. M. Robertson or Frederic Manning, but fortunately there are some carbon copies.

On the deaths of his mother and brother, in 1929 and 1947, TSE recovered his correspondence with them and burnt a good part of it, together with their side, thus removing the family record of his final school year, his student days at Harvard and the period in Paris. Furthermore, in his mother's case, there is a gap between 23 August 1921 and 12 January 1926, for which she may be partly responsible, having written to him on 8 March 1924 to say that she had all his letters from the time he went to Milton, and supposed she ought to destroy part of them.[1]

*

As Charlotte Eliot was forty-five when TSE was born, his eldest sister, Ada, who was nineteen years his senior, seemed more like a mother to him. He enjoyed eavesdropping on his siblings' conversation, although Marian was inclined to say teasingly, 'Little pitchers have big ears.' This remark nettled him because at his dancing class one little girl had leaned heavily across him to hiss at another, 'Look at his ears!' Mortified, he went home and tied them to his head with string.

From his mother, who understood him well, he inherited an anxious, nervous temperament. His father, he felt, was inclined to leave too much to her – such as taking him to the tailor – but no doubt this was partly due to his deafness. When they parted for the last time at the end of his 1915 visit, TSE was convinced that his father thought him a failure. This memory always tormented him, so he was thankful that his mother lived to see him achieve some success.

*

I intended this first volume to run to the end of 1926, which seemed a natural break, and was a biographical span which showed his relationship with several lifelong friends, but the physical extent of the book would, in my publisher's opinion, have been too bulky for the reader's comfort. We hope, by publishing the second part next year, to restore the balance. However, the significance of the year 1922, in which *The Waste Land* was published and *The Criterion* began, requires no emphasis.

During the course of his correspondence with Emily Hale, between 1932 and 1947 – when Vivien died, after nine years in a mental home – TSE liked to think that his letters to her would be preserved and made public fifty years after they were dead. He was, however, 'disagreeably surprised' when she informed him in 1956 that she was giving the letters to Princeton University Library during their lifetime. It seemed to him 'that her disposing of the letters in that way at that time threw some light upon the kind of interest which she took, or had come to take, in these letters. *The Aspern Papers* in reverse.'

1 – Valerie Eliot was slightly mistaken here: there are some letters between Charlotte Eliot and TSE beginning in 1923 (the first from her is dated 29 March 1923, and the first to her is from mid-October 1923). See Volume 2.

On 24 January 1957 the Librarian wrote stating that the letters would remain sealed until fifty years from the death of the survivor [2020]. TSE's reaction was to ask a friend to incinerate Emily Hale's letters to him.

He had met her, the daughter of a Boston Unitarian minister, at Eleanor Hinkley's house in 1912, and before he left for Europe in 1914, he told her that he was in love with her. He had no reason to believe, from the way in which his declaration was received, that his feelings were returned 'in any degree whatever'. They exchanged a few letters, 'on a purely friendly basis', while he was up at Oxford.

In a private paper, written in the sixties, he continued: 'To explain my sudden marriage to Vivienne Haigh-Wood would require a good many words, and yet the explanation would probably remain unintelligible. I was still, as I came to believe a year later, in love with Miss Hale. I cannot however even make that assertion with any confidence: it may have been merely my reaction against my misery with Vivienne and desire to revert to an earlier situation. I was very immature for my age, very timid, very inexperienced. And I had a gnawing doubt, which I could not altogether conceal from myself, about my choice of a profession – that of a university teacher of philosophy. I had had three years in the Harvard Graduate School, at my father's expense, preparing to take my Doctorate in Philosophy: after which I should have found a post somewhere in a college or university. Yet my heart was not in the study, nor had I any confidence in my ability to distinguish myself in this profession. I must still have yearned to write poetry.

'Then in 1914 . . . my meeting with Ezra Pound changed my life. He was enthusiastic about my poems, and gave me such praise and encouragement as I had long since ceased to hope for. I was happier in England, even in wartime, than I had been in America: Pound urged me to stay . . . and encouraged me to write verse again. I think that all I wanted of Vivienne was a flirtation or a mild affair: I was too shy and unpractised to achieve either with anybody. I believe that I came to persuade myself that I was in love with her simply because I wanted to burn my boats and commit myself to staying in England. And she persuaded herself (also under the influence of Pound) that she would save the poet by keeping him in England.

'To her the marriage brought no happiness . . . to me, it brought the state of mind out of which came *The Waste Land*.'

VALERIE ELIOT

PREFACE TO THE REVISED EDITION

The publication of Volume 1 of *The Letters of T. S. Eliot*, edited by Valerie Eliot in 1988, covered the period of the poet's life down to the publication of *The Waste Land* in 1922, with the bulk of the letters dating from between August 1914, when Eliot arrived in England, and the end of 1922. Volumes covering the rest of his career were to have followed, and Valerie Eliot has continued to gather letters from her husband's correspondents and their families, from libraries in Britain and the USA, from the book trade, and from the archives of Faber & Faber. The remarkable scale and scope of Eliot's correspondence became increasingly clear, however, and as the materials grew more copious the publication of subsequent volumes was postponed, until eventually the edition had to be reconceived on a more ample scale.

*

Among the letters that have come to light, over the last twenty years, a good many date from the period covered by the first volume, and fill important gaps in the literary record. These now appear in this integrated revised edition, along with others originally excluded as being of minor interest, but which flesh out the story of Eliot's social life and literary career during these years. In all, the new edition contains some 200 new letters. These include important items of correspondence from Eliot to members of his family, while others illuminate his many friendships – with Mary Hutchinson, Wyndham Lewis, Aldous Huxley and Julian Huxley, the Sydney Schiffs and Virginia Woolf, as well as a wider cast of acquaintances and contacts. A few of the letters are straightforward arrangements to meet, but they help document Eliot's London life during the years when he was establishing himself as an intellectual presence and writing some of his greatest poems; and they add valuable information about the publication of his work, particularly that of *Ara Vos Prec* with John Rodker's Ovid Press in 1920, and *The Waste Land* in periodical and volume form in 1922. The cards and letters written during the gestation of *The Waste Land* from early 1921 to the end of 1922, though often brief and telegrammatic, are of enormous intrinsic importance, and they dramatise a crucial moment.

*

One of the strengths of the 1988 edition of Volume 1 came from Valerie Eliot's decision to include voices other than the poet's own, and in particular those of his family. The thirty-eight letters from Vivien Eliot are now supplemented by a further twenty, some written by her to Eliot's mother in parallel with Eliot's own letters. To the letters from Eliot's father in the original edition are now added two more, both addressed to Eliot's uncle, the Rev. Thomas Lamb Eliot; also included is a notable additional letter to Eliot from his mother.

Incorporating these additional letters into the original volume has involved several editorial adjustments: the text of the letters already published remains intact, but the annotation has been revised where necessary, and much additional annotation has been provided.

HUGH HAUGHTON

BIOGRAPHICAL COMMENTARY 1888–1922

1888 26 SEPTEMBER – Thomas Stearns Eliot, seventh child of Henry Ware Eliot and Charlotte Champe Stearns Eliot, born at 2635 Locust Street, St Louis, Missouri.

1894? His nursemaid, Annie Dunne, takes him to Mrs Lockwood's school. Spends summer holidays in Maine and at East Gloucester, Mass.

1897 Composes his first poem, four little verses, about the sadness of having to start school again every Monday morning.

1898 Goes as a day boy to Smith Academy.

1899 28 JANUARY to 19 FEBRUARY – Writes and illustrates in pencil fourteen numbers of 'A Weekly Magazine', *The Fireside*, containing 'Fiction, Gossip, Theatre, Jokes and all interesting'.

1904 Visits the St Louis World's Fair.

1905 JANUARY – Publishes in the *Smith Academy Record* 'The Birds of Prey'; FEBRUARY – 'A Fable for Feasters'; APRIL – 'A Tale of a Whale' and 'A Lyric'; JUNE – 'The Man Who was King'. Recites 'Standing upon the shore of all we know' on Graduation Day. 19 SEPTEMBER – TSE begins the academic year at Milton Academy, Milton, Mass.

1906 OCTOBER – Starts his freshman year at Harvard, lives at 52 Mount Auburn St. He studies Greek and English Literature, Elementary German, Medieval History and Constitutional Government. In DECEMBER he is put on probation for poor grades and 'for working at a lower rate than most Freshmen', although he has 'an excellent record of attendance'.

1907 26 FEBRUARY – TSE is relieved from probation. (He told his second wife that he 'loafed' for the first two years.) 24 MAY – The *Harvard Advocate* publishes 'Song': When we came home across the hill', and 3 JUNE 'If time and space, as Sages say', a slightly altered reprint of 'A Lyric'. OCTOBER – In his sophomore year he shares rooms with John Robinson and Howard Morris in 22 Russell Hall, and meets Conrad Aiken, who becomes his closest Harvard friend. He studies History of Ancient Art, French Prose and Poetry, German Prose and Poetry, Greek Literature, Greek Prose Composition, History of Ancient Philosophy and History of Modern Philosophy.

1908 OCTOBER – begins his junior year and lives at 25 Holyoke Street. He studies the Literary History of England and its relation to that of the Continent from the Beginning to Chaucer, and from Chaucer to Elizabeth; Tendencies of European Literature of the Renaissance; English Composition; Latin Literature – General View of Latin Poetry; Latin Literature – The Roman Novel. 13 NOVEMBER – The *Harvard Advocate* publishes 'Before Morning', 25 NOVEMBER 'Circe's Palace'. DECEMBER – In the *Advocate* Library TSE finds *The Symbolist Movement in Literature* by Arthur Symons, which he describes in 1920 as 'an introduction to wholly new feelings, as a revelation' . Ten years later he continues 'But for having read his book, I should not, in the year 1908, have heard of Laforgue or Rimbaud; I should probably not have begun to read Verlaine; and but for reading Verlaine, I should not have heard of Corbière.' It has 'affected the course of my life'.

1909 JANUARY – Joins the editorial board of the *Harvard Advocate*, which publishes 26 JANUARY 'Song: The moonflower opens to the moth' and 'On a Portrait', 7 MAY a review of *The Wine of the Puritans* by Van Wyck Brooks, 20 MAY 'The Point of View', 25 MAY 'Gentlemen and Seamen'. 30 JUNE – BA. OCTOBER – starts his senior year and lives at 42 Apley Court. Begins MA course in the Graduate School of Arts and Sciences with: Chaucer; the Drama in England from the Miracle Plays to the Closing of the Theatres; Studies in the Poets of the Romantic Period; Literary Criticism in France, with special reference to the Nineteenth Century (with Irving Babbitt); Studies in the History of Allegory; Philosophy of History – Ideals of Society, Religion, Art and Science in their historical development (with George Santayana); and Florentine Painting. A classmate introduces him to Pound's *Exultations* and *Personae*, with the comment 'this is up your street: you ought to like this', but TSE 'didn't really. It seemed to me rather fancy old-fashioned romantic stuff . . . I wasn't very much impressed by it.' 5 OCTOBER – The *Harvard Advocate* publishes his review of *Egoists* by James Huneker, and 12 NOVEMBER 'Nocturne'.

1910 12 JANUARY – The *Advocate* prints 'Humouresque' (after J. Laforgue), and 26 JANUARY 'Spleen'. FEBRUARY – Writes Part II of 'Portrait of a Lady'. MAY – TSE in Stillman Hospital with scarlet fever. 24 JUNE – Class of 1910 graduates. TSE reads the Class Ode: 'For the hour that is left us Fair Harvard, with thee', in Sanders Theater, and it is published in the local newspapers. OCTOBER – TSE goes to Paris to attend the Sorbonne and hear Henri Bergson's weekly philosophical lectures at the Collège de France. He is tutored by Alain-Fournier, and introduced to his brother-in-law, Jacques Rivière. At his *pension*, 151 bis rue St Jacques, he meets Jean Verdenal, a medical student, and they become very friendly. NOVEMBER – Writes Part I of 'Portrait of a Lady'.

1911 21 FEBRUARY – MA. APRIL – Pays his first visit to London, writes a poem, 'Interlude in London'. JULY – Leaves for Munich and Northern Italy. Completes the third 'Prelude' and the final version of 'Prufrock'. *c.* mid-SEPTEMBER – Leaves for America and East Gloucester. OCTOBER – Returns to the Harvard Graduate School to read for a doctorate in Philosophy. Lives at 16 Ash St. Aiken finds him 'perceptibly Europeanized'. Enrols in Professor Lanman's Indic Philology course, studies Sanskrit and reads Indian Philosophy with Professor Woods. NOVEMBER – Completes 'Portrait of a Lady'.

1912 Appointed Assistant in Philosophy. Meets and falls in love with Emily Hale. *The New Realism* by E. B. Holt and others is published and 'made a considerable stir in the philosophical departments of American universities', TSE wrote in 1935. The Six Realists 'were animated by a missionary zeal against the Hegelian Idealism which was the orthodox doctrine of the philosophical departments of American universities at the time, and which had begun to turn manifestly mouldy . . . the Six Realists were un-Teutonised, and on the whole anti-religious, which was refreshing; they were ascetically, even gloomily, scientific; and they professed considerable respect for Mr Bertrand Russell and his Cambridge friends. All this was to the good; but it must be admitted that the New Realism, like most pre-War philosophies, seems now as demoded as ladies' hats of the same period.'

1913 JUNE – Buys F. H. Bradley's *Appearance and Reality*. OCTOBER – Is appointed President of the University Philosophical Club. 15 DECEMBER – Pays Emma Wright Gibbs seven dollars for three hours' dancing lessons.

1914 27 MARCH – TSE meets and comes under the influence of Bertrand Russell, a Visiting Professor at Harvard. 31 MARCH – TSE, who is appointed a Sheldon Travelling Fellow in Philosophy for the academic year 1914/15, plans to spend it at Merton College, Oxford. 7 JULY – Passes through London on his way to a summer school in Marburg. 1 AUGUST – Germany declares war on Russia. 2 AUGUST – The course, due to start next day, is cancelled, and students are told they cannot leave for a fortnight. 16 AUGUST – TSE departs for Frankfurt, reaches London five days later. Stays at 28 Bedford Place, Russell Square, W.C.1. Early SEPTEMBER? – Writes 'Morning at the Window'. 22 SEPTEMBER – Meets Ezra Pound. OCTOBER – Runs into Bertrand Russell in New Oxford Street. 6 OCTOBER – Goes up to Merton College to study Aristotle under Harold Joachim. Pound sends Harriet Monroe 'Prufrock'. DECEMBER – TSE, Brand Blanshard and Karl Culpin spend a holiday together at Swanage in Dorset.

1915 JANUARY – Lives at 1 Gordon Street, Gordon Square. MARCH – Reads a paper on 'The Relativity of the Moral Judgement' in Russell's rooms at Trinity College, Cambridge. 24 APRIL – Tells Eleanor Hinkley that he has met some English girls 'with such amusing names', and one is called Vivien [Haigh-Wood], who is at that time living as a governess at 26 Malcolm Street, Cambridge. 2 MAY – Jean Verdenal is killed in the Dardanelles. JUNE – *Poetry* prints 'Prufrock'. 26 JUNE – TSE marries Vivienne Haigh-Wood at Hampstead Registry Office. JULY – Wyndham Lewis's magazine, *Blast*, prints 'Preludes' [I–IV] and 'Rhapsody on a Windy Night'. 24 JULY – TSE sails for America to join his parents at East Gloucester. Visits Harvard's Philosophy Department to discuss returning tor his degree. 21 AUGUST – Leaves for England, having decided his future lies there. SEPTEMBER – 'Portrait of a Lady' appears in *Others*. Russell offers the Eliots a room in his Bury Street flat. TSE begins teaching at High Wycombe Grammar School, lives at Sydney Cottage, Conegra Road, High Wycombe. OCTOBER – *Poetry* prints 'The Boston Evening Transcript', 'Aunt Helen' and 'Cousin Nancy'. NOVEMBER – *Catholic Anthology* is published.

1916 Early JANUARY – Russell takes Vivien to Torquay for a holiday and is succeeded after five days by TSE, whose first review for the *International Journal of Ethics* is published. TSE begins teaching at Highgate Junior School. 6 MARCH – Tells Professor Woods that he is sending his thesis in a few days. Late MARCH – The Eliots move to 18 Crawford Mansions, Crawford Street, W.1. TSE prepares to sail to America on 1 APRIL in order to take his *viva* at Harvard, but at the last minute his boat is delayed for five days and he cancels his plans. 2 APRIL – TSE and Pound see Yeats's Noh play, *At the Hawk's Well*, with Mischio Itow as the hawk and masks by Edmund Dulac, in Lady Cunard's drawing-room. 23 JUNE – Woods informs him that his thesis has been accepted 'without the least hesitation'. 24 JUNE – TSE's first contribution to the *New Statesman*. 21 AUGUST – The Eliots at Bosham cottage. 3 SEPTEMBER – Pound writes John Quinn that 'Eliot seems to be getting on all right (though he is producing very little, practically nothing)'. 6 SEPTEMBER – TSE tells Henry that he often feels that Prufrock 'is a swan song'. OCTOBER – Begins reviewing for *The Monist*. 3 OCTOBER to 12 DECEMBER Gives a course of six lectures on Modern French Literature at Ilkley, Yorkshire, and begins the first year of a three-year tutorial class on Modern English Literature at Southall on Monday evenings. 3 DECEMBER – TSE's first visit to Garsington. 5 DECEMBER – Tells Henry that he is giving up teaching at Christmas as he finds that he is 'losing in every way'.

1917 19 MARCH – Starts work in the Colonial and Foreign Department of Lloyds Bank. 6 APRIL – America declares war on Germany. MAY – Begins writing for the *Little Review*. JUNE – The Egoist Limited publishes *Prufrock and Other Observations*. Clive Bell takes a number of copies to a party at Garsington and distributes them among the Morrells, Mary Hutchinson, Aldous Huxley, Middleton Murry and others, including Katherine Mansfield who reads the title poem aloud. TSE appointed Assistant Editor of *The Egoist*. JULY – Reviews 'Reflections on Violence' by Georges Sorel, trans. with an introd. by T. E. Hulme, in *The Monist*. (His copy is dated MAY 1916). 28 SEPTEMBER – Begins a course of twenty-five Friday evening lectures on Victorian Literature at the County Secondary School, Sydenham. OCTOBER – Starts second year of his tutorial class in Modern English Literature.

1918 JANUARY – In New York Knopf publishes *Ezra Pound: His Metric and Poetry*, after the subject has supplied the title and made three deletions in the text. It is issued anonymously because, Pound tells Quinn, 'I want to boom Eliot and one can't have too obvious a ping-pong match at that sort of thing.' 9 JUNE – The Eliots at 31 West St, Marlow. 2 AUGUST – TSE cables Henry to inquire about his chances of a military or naval training commission if he returns to America. 5 AUGUST – Tells Lewis that he is trying to get into US Navy. 25 AUGUST – Writes Henry that he has had a medical examination and been passed fit for *limited* service. As Washington has forbidden 'any more commissions over here' he is applying to be an officer in the Quartermaster's or Interpreters' Corps, and has been collecting testimonials. 'It was a shock to both of us that Tom was graded so high in the medical exam,' Vivien writes earlier to Mary

Hutchinson. 'I did not realise until then how much I had *counted* on his being passed quite *UNFIT*. I can't understand it. He took a very strong certificate from our doctor, and had been *fearfully* ill over the weekend so that he was obviously in a wretched state.' 8 SEPTEMBER – Tells his father that he now needs three American testimonials. 11 SEPTEMBER – Afraid that TSE 'was likely to be took fer the Army', Pound tells Quinn that he went to the Embassy 'to point out that if it was a war for civilisation (not merely for democracy) it was folly to shoot or have shot one of the six or seven Americans capable of contributing to civilisation or understanding the word'. 11? SEPTEMBER – Pound sends Knopf TSE's manuscript of poems after putting it into shape, as TSE has no time. He thought early publication 'could strengthen TSE's position with the authorities'. Mid-SEPTEMBER – The Eliots let their Marlow house 'at a good rent'. OCTOBER – TSE begins his final Southall course on Elizabethan literature. *c.* 26 OCTOBER – Leaves bank as US Navy Intelligence has sent for him. 9 NOVEMBER – Returns to bank after official muddle and confusion. 10 NOVEMBER – Tells Jack Hutchinson 'this ends my patriotic endeavours'. 11 NOVEMBER – Armistice Day. 15 NOVEMBER – Visits Leonard and Virginia Woolf at Hogarth House to discuss the publication of his *Poems*. 27 NOVEMBER – TSE sent Order of Induction into Military Service of the United States from St Louis, and told to report to the Headquarters European Forces in London. 18 DECEMBER – Pound writes Quinn that he is afraid that TSE is 'in a bad way, back in his bank, but health in very shaky state. Doctor orders him not to write any prose for six months.'

1919 3 JANUARY – Henry Ware Eliot tells his brother that TSE is 'getting along now and has been advanced at the bank so that he is independent of me'. 7 JANUARY – TSE's father dies. 12 MARCH – He has been invited to become the Assistant Editor of *The Athenaeum*, TSE tells his mother. 6 APRIL – He informs Henry that he has declined the post. 4–14 MAY – TSE stays at the Hotel Constance, 23 Lancaster Gate, W.2. 11 MAY – The Eliots at Garsington. 12 MAY – Hogarth Press publishes *Poems*. 19 MAY – TSE is sent on a tour of the provinces by the bank 'for some weeks', returning at intervals. 9 JULY – TSE writes Quinn: [This] 'part of *Ulysses* [Scylla and Charybdis] . . . struck me as almost the finest I have read: I have lived on it ever since I read it.' 22 JULY – The Eliots accompany the Sacheverell Sitwells to the first night of Falla's *Three-Cornered Hat*, performed by Massine and the Ballets Russes. 9 AUGUST – TSE leaves for a walking tour in the Dordogne with Ezra Pound, returning on 31 AUGUST. Vivien records that he was 'very nice at first, depressed in the evening'. 29 SEPTEMBER – TSE meets Bruce Richmond, editor of the *Times Literary Supplement*, who admires his critical prose and invites him to write leading articles. 28 OCTOBER – Lectures on 'Poetry' under the auspices of the Arts League of Service in the Conference Hall, Westminster. 13 NOVEMBER – His first contribution, 'Ben Jonson', appears in the *TLS*. DECEMBER – *The Egoist* ceases publication.

1920 Early FEBRUARY – The Ovid Press publishes *Ara Vos Prec*. Late FEBRUARY – Knopf issues *Poems* in New York. 15 AUGUST – TSE meets James Joyce in Paris, and the following day leaves with Lewis for a painting and cycling holiday in northern France. 20 SEPTEMBER – The first mention of *The Waste Land* to his mother: 'I want a period of tranquillity to do a poem I have in mind.' 4 NOVEMBER – Methuen publishes *The Sacred Wood*. The current *Dial* contains his first contribution, 'The Possibility of a Poetic Drama'. Later that month the Eliots move to 9 Clarence Gate Gardens, N.W.1. 2 DECEMBER – Tells his mother that he is 'rather tired of [the essays] now, as I am so anxious to get on to new work, and I should more enjoy being praised if I were engaged on something which I thought better or more important. I think I shall be able to do so, soon.'

1921 SUNDAY 20 MARCH – TSE dines with the Woolfs and accompanies them to the Phoenix Society production of Congreve's *Love for Love* at the Lyric Theatre, Hammersmith, and on 24 APRIL, with Edgar Jepson, sees Sybil Thorndyke in *The Witch of Edmonton*. 9 MAY – He tells Quinn that he is 'wishful to finish' a long poem which is now 'partly on paper'. 10 JUNE – His mother, Marian and Henry arrive on the SS *Adriatic*, and occupy 9 Clarence Gate Gardens. TSE and Vivien move to 12 Wigmore Street. JULY – TSE and Scofield Thayer wonder if they can interest Lady Rothermere in establishing an international review, comprising the *Dial* in America and a new magazine edited by TSE in London, but by the beginning of August she has decided, partly for financial reasons, to confine herself to an English review. 16 AUGUST – TSE confides to Richard Aldington '*in strict confidence* that there is a possibility of a new literary venture' [*Criterion*]. 20 AUGUST – TSE's family return to America. Towards the end of SEPTEMBER TSE's health breaks down. He sees a specialist who orders him to have three months' complete rest and change, and the bank gives him leave. 15 OCTOBER – Goes to the Albemarle Hotel, Margate. Vivien joins him for part of the time. While there he decides to become a patient of Dr Vittoz in Lausanne. 12 NOVEMBER – Returns to London. 18 NOVEMBER – The Eliots go to Paris, and Pound sees some drafts of *The Waste Land*. 22? NOVEMBER – TSE leaves for Lausanne. Vivien remains in Paris. DECEMBER – TSE continues working on *The Waste Land*.

1922 2 JANUARY – TSE rejoins Vivien in Paris. Pound writes Quinn, 'Eliot came back from his Lausanne specialist looking O.K.; and with a damn good poem (19 pages) in his suitcase; same finished up here; and shd. be out in *Dial* soon, if Thayer isn't utterly nutty . . . About enough, Eliot's poem, to make the rest of us shut up shop' (21 FEB.). 12 JANUARY – TSE returns to London alone and succumbs to flu. Vivien goes to Lyons for about a week and plans to spend a few more days in Paris before following him. Mid-MARCH – Disturbed by reports from Aldington that TSE 'was going to pieces', Pound revives an earlier scheme to enable TSE to leave Lloyds Bank. Called 'Bel Esprit', the aim is to find thirty guarantors of £10 a year. 17 MAY – The Eliots at the Castle Hotel, Tunbridge Wells. TSE writes Ottoline Morrell that his forthcoming visit to Italy 'will just save me from another breakdown, which I felt was impending'. 20 MAY – TSE tells Gilbert Seldes that his mind is 'in a very deteriorated state, due to illness and worry'. Goes to Lugano for a fortnight. 11 JUNE – TSE dines with the Woolfs; Virginia records in her diary that he read *The Waste Land*. 'He sang it & chanted it, rhythmed it. It has great beauty & force of phrase: symmetry; & tensity.' JULY – He receives $200 from the Carnegie Fund of the US Authors' Club. Ottoline Morrell launches the Eliot Fellowship Fund which involves Virginia Woolf and Aldington. It continues, on and off, until December 1927. AUGUST – TSE judges the Lloyds Bank Short Story Competition, and a Satirical Poem on the Housing Problem or the Cost of Living. 7 SEPTEMBER – Quinn arranges with Seldes and Liveright that TSE will get the *Dial* award of $2,000. 15 OCTOBER – First number of the *Criterion*. It contains *The Waste Land*, which also appears in the *Dial*. 16 NOVEMBER – *Liverpool Post* accuses him of accepting £800 raised by admirers to enable him to leave Lloyds Bank, and then refusing to do so. 30 NOVEMBER – *Liverpool Post* publishes TSE's reply and apologises. 15 DECEMBER – Boni and Liveright publishes *The Waste Land* in New York. TSE inscribes a copy 'For Ezra Pound *il miglior fabbro*' [the better master].

ABBREVIATIONS AND SOURCES

PUBLISHED WORKS BY T. S. ELIOT

ASG	*After Strange Gods* (London: Faber & Faber, 1934)
AVP	*Ara Vos Prec* (London: The Ovid Press, 1920)
CP	*The Cocktail Party* (London: Faber & Faber, 1950)
CPP	*The Complete Poems and Plays of T. S. Eliot* (London: Faber & Faber, 1969)
EE	*Elizabethan Essays* (London: Faber & Faber, 1934)
FLA	*For Lancelot Andrewes: Essays on Style and Order* (London: Faber & Gwyer, 1928)
FR	*The Family Reunion* (London: Faber & Faber, 1939)
HJD	*Homage to John Dryden: Three Essays on Poetry of the Seventeenth Century* (London: The Hogarth Press, 1924)
KEPB	*Knowledge and Experience in the Philosophy of F. H. Bradley* (London: Faber & Faber, 1964; New York: Farrar, Straus & Company, 1964)
IMH	*Inventions of the March Hare: Poems 1909–1917*, ed. Christopher Ricks (London: Faber & Faber, 1996)
OPP	*On Poetry and Poets* (London: Faber & Faber, 1957; New York: Farrar, Straus & Cudahy, 1957)
P	*Poems* (London: The Hogarth Press, 1919)
P 1909–1925	*Poems 1909–1925* (London: Faber & Gwyer, 1925)
POO	*Prufrock and Other Observations* (London: The Egoist Press, 1917)
SA	*Sweeney Agonistes: Fragments of an Aristophanic Melodrama* (London: Faber & Faber, 1932)
SE	*Selected Essays: 1917–1932* (London: Faber & Faber, 1932; 3rd English edn., London and Boston: Faber & Faber, 1951)
SW	*The Sacred Wood: Essays on Poetry and Criticism* (London: Methuen & Co., 1920)
TCC	*To Criticize the Critic* (London: Faber & Faber, 1965; New York: Farrar, Straus & Giroux, 1965)

TUPUC	*The Use of Poetry and the Use of Criticism: Studies in the Relation of Criticism to Poetry in England* (London: Faber & Faber, 1933)
TWL	*The Waste Land* (1922, 1923)
TWL: Facs	*The Waste Land: A Facsimile and Transcript of the Original Drafts*, ed. Valerie Eliot (London: Faber & Faber, 1971; New York: Harcourt, Brace, Jovanovich, 1971)
VMP	*The Varieties of Metaphysical Poetry*, ed. Ronald Schuchard (London: Faber & Faber, 1993; New York: Harcourt Brace, 1994)

PERIODICALS AND PUBLISHERS

A.	*The Athenaeum* (see also *N&A*)
C.	*The Criterion*
F&G	Faber & Gwyer (publishers)
F&F	Faber & Faber (publishers)
IJE	*International Journal of Ethics*
N.	*The Nation*
N&A	*The Nation & The Athenaeum*
NC	*New Criterion*
NRF	*La Nouvelle Revue Française*
NS	*New Statesman*
TLS	*Times Literary Supplement*

PERSONS

AH	Aldous Huxley
BD	Bonamy Dobrée
BR	Bertrand Russell
CW	Charles Whibley
CWE	Charlotte Ware Eliot, TSE's mother
DHL	D. H. Lawrence
EP	Ezra Pound
EVE	(Esmé) Valerie Eliot
GCF	Geoffrey (Cust) Faber
HR	Herbert Read
HWE	Henry Ware Eliot (TSE's brother)
IPF	Irene Pearl Fassett (TSE's secretary)
JDH	John Davy Hayward
JJ	James Joyce

JMM	John Middleton Murry
LW	Leonard Woolf
MH	Mary Hutchinson
OM	Ottoline Morrell
RA	Richard Aldington
RC-S	Richard Cobden-Sanderson
SS	Sydney Schiff
TSE	T. S. Eliot
VHE	Vivien Haigh Eliot
VW	Virginia Woolf
WBY	W. B. Yeats
WL	Wyndham Lewis

ARCHIVE COLLECTIONS

Arkansas	Special Collections, University Libraries, University of Arkansas
BL	British Library, London
Beinecke	The Beinecke Rare Book and Manuscript Library, Yale University
Berg	Henry W. and Albert A. Berg Collection of English and American Literature, New York Public Library
Bodleian	The Bodleian Library, Oxford University
Bonn	Universitäts und Landesbibliothek, Bonn University
Buffalo	Lockwood Memorial Library, State University of New York at Buffalo
Bundesarchiv	German Federal Archives, Koblenz
Chicago	Special Collections, The Joseph Regenstein Library, University of Chicago
Cornell	Department of Rare Books, Olin Library, Cornell University
Fondren	Fondren Library, Woodson Research Center, Rice University
Gallup	Donald Gallup Papers, The Beinecke Rare Book and Manuscript Library, Yale University
Gardner Museum	Isabella Stewart Gardner Museum, Boston, Massachusetts
Harvard	University Archives, Harvard University
Hornbake	Hornbake Library, University of Maryland
Houghton	The Houghton Library, Harvard University
Huntington	Huntington Library, California

King's	Modern Archive Centre, King's College, Cambridge
Lilly	Lilly Library, Indiana University, Bloomington
LSE	British Library of Political and Economic Science, London School of Economics
McMaster	Mills Memorial Library, McMaster University. Hamilton, Ontario
Milton Academy	Milton, Massachusetts
MIT	The Weiner Papers Institute Archives, Massachusetts Institute of Technology, Cambridge, Mass.
Reed College	Portland, Oregon
Mugar	Mugar Memorial Library, Boston University
NYPL (MS)	New York Public Library (Manuscripts Division)
Northwestern	Special Collections, Northwestern University Library, Evanston, Illinois
Princeton	Department of Rare Books and Special Collections, Princeton University Library
Rosenbach	Rosenbach Museum and Library, Philadelphia, Pennsylvania
Texas	The Harry Ransom Humanities Research Center, University of Texas at Austin
Tulsa	Department of Special Collections, McFarlin Library, University of Tulsa, Oklahoma
UCLA	University of California at Los Angeles
Vichy	Bibliothèque Municipale, Vichy
Victoria	Special Collections, McPherson Library, University of Victoria, British Columbia
Virginia	Alderman Library, University of Virginia Library
Washington	Washington University Library, St Louis, Missouri
Williams College	Williamstown, Massachusetts

EDITORIAL NOTES

The source of each letter is indicated at the top right. CC indicates a carbon copy. Where no other source is shown it may be assumed that the original or a carbon copy is in the Valerie Eliot collection or at the Faber and Faber Archive.

del. deleted

MS manuscript

n. d. no date

PC postcard

sc. *scilicet*: namely

TS typescript

< > indicates a word or words brought in from another part of the letter.

Place of publication is London, unless otherwise stated.

Ampersands and squiggles have been replaced by 'and', except where they occur in correspondence with Ezra Pound.

Some obvious typing or manuscript errors have been silently corrected.

Dates have been standardised.

Some words and figures which were abbreviated have been expanded.

Punctuation has occasionally been adjusted.

Editorial insertions are indicated by square brackets.

Words both italicised and underlined signify double underlining in the original copy.

Where possible a biographical note accompanies the first letter to or from a correspondent. Where appropriate, this brief initial note will also refer the reader to the Glossary of Names at the end of the text.

Vivienne Eliot liked her husband and friends to spell her name Vivien; but as there is no consistency, it is printed as written.

26 September 1888 St Louis, Missouri

'Young Thomas (Stearns for his Grandfather) came forth at 7.45 this a.m. I like the name for your sake, and shall always feel as though *that* part of it was for you, though the prime cause was the other . . .'[1]

13 April 1943 Cambridge, Massachusetts

'When you were a tiny boy, learning to talk, you used to sound the rhythm of sentences without shaping words – the ups and downs of the thing you were trying to say. I used to answer you in kind, saying nothing yet conversing with you as we sat side by side on the stairs at 2635 Locust Street. And now you think the rhythm before the words in a new poem! . . . Such a dear little boy!'[2]

1 – Henry Ware Eliot to his elder brother, the Reverend Thomas Lamb Eliot (MS Houghton).
2 – Ada Eliot Sheffield (1869–1943), the first-born, in her last letter to TSE, written while she was dying of cancer (MS Valerie Eliot). She and TSE were intellectually close; he described her as the Mycroft to his Sherlock Holmes. She has in mind *The Music of Poetry* (1942): 'I know that a poem, or a passage of a poem, may tend to realize itself first as a particular rhythm before it reaches expression in words, and that this rhythm may bring to birth the idea and the image.'

THE LETTERS

1898–1922

1898

TO *His Father*[1] MS Houghton

Thurs. 23–24 June 1898 Gloucester[2] [Massachusetts]

Dear Papa,

It is very cool here when we get up – that is, indoors, outdoors it is just right. We have *no* sunflowers, there were two in the rosebed, and Marion weeded them up. I found the things in the upper tray of my trunk all knocked about. A microscope was broken and a box of butterflies and a spider.

Charlotte and I hunt for birds. She found a *empty* nest yesterday (23d). Marion, Margret (?) & Henry are going to Class-day.[3]

Yours Truly,
Tom.

1–Henry Ware Eliot; the other family members referred to are Marion, the fourth child and TSE's favourite sister; Charlotte, the third child; Margaret, the second child; and Henry, the fifth child and TSE's only brother, who was nine years his senior. See Glossary of Names.
2–From 1896 the family spent their summers in the house built by Henry Ware Eliot on land originally purchased in 1890 at Eastern Point, overlooking Gloucester Harbor. On earlier visits they had stayed at the Hawthorne Inn.
3–When ceremonies are held in schools or colleges to mark the graduation of the senior class.

1904–1910

TO *Charlotte Eliot Smith*[1] MS Houghton

August [1904] Oliver's Corner[2]
[Province of Quebec, Canada]

Dear Charlotte,

Hoping you are better,
At least enough to read my letter,
Which I have twisted into rhyme
To amuse you, I have taken time
To tell you of the happenings
Swimming, rowing, other things
With which I have the time been killing.
Wednesday morning, weather willing,
We after breakfast took a start,
Four of us, in a two horse cart
Together with a little luncheon,
Including things quite good to munch on,
To climb a mountain, quite a feat,
3000 ft., and in the heat.
To make a lengthy story short,
We did not take the path we ought,
And though we exerted all our powers,
It took us all of ~~two~~ three long hours
To reach the top, when, what a view,
Mount Washington, and Montreal too!
We took one hour down the road,
Then two hours more to our abode.
I suppose now I should desist,

1–Charlotte had married George Lawrence Smith, an architect, in Sept. 1903. Their daughter, Theodora, had been born on 25 July 1904. Charlotte studied at the St Louis and Boston Art Schools, specialising in sculpture. For her oil portrait of TSE, see Plate 15.

2–In 1903 TSE's uncle, Christopher Rhodes Eliot, had bought some land over the border in Canada, on Lake Memphremagog, as a site for a family camp. In the early years everyone slept under canvas.

2 TSE at fifteen

For I am needed to assist
In making a raft.
The family sends
To you their love and complimen's.
I must not close without once more a
Health to you and Theodora.

I am afraid this letter will not please you but I hope you will excuse your brother

Tom.

Charlotte C. Eliot[1] TO *the Head Master of Milton Academy*[2]

MS Milton Academy

27 March 1905 2635 Locust St, St Louis

My dear Mr Cobb,

I write to ask whether at Milton Academy you will take a boy who has passed his finals for Harvard. My son is sixteen years of age and will be seventeen the 26th of September. As a scholar his rank is high, but he has been growing rapidly, and for the sake of his physical well being we have felt that it might be better for him to wait a year before entering on his college career. If you have any provision for such cases, and can keep him employed without his going over the same ground, please let me know, and oblige

Yours very truly,
Charlotte C. Eliot
Mrs Henry W. Eliot

Tom passed his preliminaries with credits in two studies. Took Latin prize last year at Smith Academy.[3]

1 – Charlotte Champe Stearns Eliot, TSE's mother; see Glossary of Names.

2 – In Milton, Massachusetts. Richard Cobb was Head Master, 1904–10.

3 – From 1898 to 1905 TSE was a dayboy at Smith Academy, which his grandfather had founded. 'My memories of [it] are on the whole happy ones; and when, many years ago, I learned that the school had come to an end [in 1917], I felt that a link with the past had been painfully broken. It was a good school.' He recalled with gratitude Mr Hatch, his English master, who 'commended warmly my first poem ['A Lyric'], written as a class exercise, at the same time asking me suspiciously if I had had any help in writing it . . . Well! so far as I am educated, I must pay my first tribute to Smith Academy; if I had not been well taught there, I should have been unable to profit elsewhere . . . I remember it as a good school also because of the boys who were there with me: it seems to me that, for a school of small numbers, we were a well-mixed variety of local types' (from an Address delivered at Washington University, 9 June 1953). See 'American Literature and the American Language', *TCC*.

4 April 1905 2635 Locust St, St Louis

My dear Mr Cobb,

Your letter was received yesterday, and I enclose today a list of studies taken here which my son has prepared. He and I have examined the catalogue you sent, and Tom thinks he could make out a course partly scientific, and then there are elective studies like 'Advanced History, English and American'. Then he has had but two years of German, one with a poor teacher, and could resume that study, and drop French, in which he needs principally conversation. I should think he could drop Latin and Greek this year. He took the Latin prize last year at Smith Academy. His teacher informs him that in the Harvard preliminaries he received credit in French and English. He has always been a student, and read extensively in English literature, especially Shakespeare. He has read practically all of Shakespeare, whom he admires, and retains much in memory.

It is now partly in deference to his own wishes that we consider sending him to Milton. A friend suggests that he will be lonely there, because most of the boys have been there some years. I hope not, for although quiet and very dignified he is a most friendly boy, of sweet nature, and every inch a gentleman, withal very modest and unassuming, yet very self-reliant too.

We have lived twenty-five years on the old Eliot place, while all our friends have moved out, and Tom desires companionship of which he has been thus deprived.[1] I talk with him as I would with a man, which perhaps is not so good for him as if he had young people about him.

If you think that Tom can make out a course, and you advise and are willing to take him, I should like a decision very soon, as otherwise his room must be engaged for Harvard. He has been a faithful student and we are willing to have him wander a little from beaten paths this year and take a somewhat miscellaneous course.

His teacher here says he can enter Harvard next year without repeating his examinations. I will write to Mr Hart and inquire.

1 – TSE's remarkable grandfather, the Revd William Greenleaf Eliot, whom Dickens described as 'a gentleman of great worth and excellence' (*American Notes*, 1842), had been a Unitarian Minister of the First Congregational Church in St Louis, 1834–70; and his widow, Abby Adams, remained there although the area became a slum. Their son, TSE's father, stayed nearby out of loyalty.

I have gone somewhat into detail to assist you in making an early decision, as the number admitted into your school is limited, I judge, and I should like a place reserved in one of the cottages of the upper school.

Yours very truly
Charlotte C. Eliot
Mrs Henry W. Eliot

[In TSE's hand:]

I passed in June 1904, for Harvard:
4 Elementary English (a)
2 " French
4 " Latin
4 " Greek
2 " Algebra
2 Plane Geometry.
–
18 points.

I shall take in June, 1905:
2 Advanced Greek
2 " Latin
2 " French
4 " English (b)
2 Elementary Physics
2 " History (Greek and Roman)
–
14 points

Total 32 points.
German
History
Trig. and Phys.
Chem.

English: Hill's *Principles of Rhetoric*. Pancoast's *Introduction to English Literature*. Reading: *Othello*, *Golden Treasury*, *Macbeth*, Burke's Speech on Conciliation [with America, 1775], Milton's Minor Poems, Macaulay's 'Milton' and 'Addison'. Themes. Elocution.
Latin: Virgil's *Aeneid*, Books 3–12. I read Books I–II last year. Ovid 2000 lines. Cicero, Milo. Grammar. Composition based on Caesar.
Greek: I read Xenophon's *Anabasis* Books I–IV, with *Hellenica* at sight last year. *Iliad* I–III. Also Books IV–VI, VII and XVIII at sight. *Odyssey* selections. Xenophon at sight. Prose composition.

French: Fraser and Squairs' Grammar. Stone's *Grammaire Française*. Résumés in French of the authors read. Reading: *Horace*, Corneille; *Le Misanthrope*, Molière; *Andromaque*, Racine; *Zadig* and other tales, Voltaire; *Hernani, Les Misérables*, Hugo; *La Mare au Diable, La Petite Fadette*, Sand; *Five Tales* of Balzac; *Mademoiselle de la Seiglière*, Sandeau; *Athalie*, Racine; and others. Memorizing poetry.
History: Myers' *History of Greece* and *History of Rome*.
Physics: Wentworth and Hill's *Principles of Physics. Forty experiments.*

Thomas S. Eliot

7 April 1905 St Louis

My dear Mr Cobb,

I do not know whether in my last note I made it sufficiently explicit, that if after reading my letter and looking over my son's schedule, you approve of his entering Milton Academy, I desire to make formal application for his admission into one of the Upper School dormitory buildings.

Yours very truly
Charlotte C. Eliot

22 July 1905 Eastern Point, Gloucester

My dear Mr Cobb,

Your letter has just been forwarded to me from Saint Louis, which has caused delay in answering. My son's marks were 'B' in History, and 'C' in everything else except Physics, in which he was conditioned, receiving 'E'. This result was not unexpected, as he had in the latter study a poor teacher, who finally broke down with nervous prostration.

He would still greatly prefer to attend Milton Academy – I was, however, so discouraged by your last letter that I took steps to hire rooms at Cambridge. If Mr Eliot approves, however, I will see what steps can be taken to dispose of these (they are in a private house on Mt Auburn Street), provided you are still willing to take him on his 'one condition'. He had intended to take German this year, which is on your programme.

How early is it necessary for you to know results of my Cambridge inquiries regarding disposal of rooms?

Yours sincerely,
Charlotte C. Eliot

You are probably out of the city, but I address this to Milton.

23 July 1905 Eastern Point, Gloucester

My dear Mr Cobb,

I write a line to say that if you are still in Boston or Milton, my son and I will make an appointment to call on and confer with you. I want to be *sure* he can go to Milton Academy, before taking active steps to dispose of his rooms.

I greatly prefer to have him a year at a Preparatory School, rather than to enter college this year. I am officially informed that his certificate of admission will hold good next year, making up physics.

Yours sincerely
Charlotte C. Eliot
Mrs Henry W. Eliot

26 July 1905 Eastern Point, Gloucester

My dear Mr Cobb,

I have just learned from your secretary that you are out of town, but will return on the 1st of August. As soon thereafter as is convenient to you, Tom and I will visit Milton Academy, and confer with you. Mr Eliot writes that he approves of his going to Milton rather than Harvard this year, and thinks it will do him good. As soon as I have perfected arrangements with you, I will close matters at Cambridge.

Tom's certificate will admit him to college next year with only an examination in Physics, and any extra study will be a gain.

We should be happy to have you spend the day with us at Eastern Point, if you care for a fine view.

Yours sincerely,
Charlotte C. Eliot

28 August 1905 Eastern Point, Gloucester

My dear Mr Cobb,

I have been considering with my son-in-law, Mr Alfred Dwight Sheffield,[1] who has had considerable experience in past years in a Preparatory School, the best course of study for Tom to pursue at Milton Academy this coming year. Mr Sheffield thinks, and I agree with him, that it is better to take studies other than those in which he has passed his

1–Alfred Sheffield (1871–1961), husband of TSE's eldest sister, Ada. 'Shef' taught English for four years at University School, Cleveland, Ohio, before joining the editorial staff of *Webster's International Dictionary*.

examinations. This would exclude Latin, Greek and French, and perhaps English. Attendance at these courses would mean the reading again a second time much that he has already been over. This, Mr Sheffield believes, would induce a mental ennui. It certainly would not act as a stimulus.

Among the elective studies is Advanced History, upon which Tom could spend considerable time. Is this course *always* included in the curriculum, however small the number of students desiring to take it?

There are reasons why it would be better for Tom to take Chemistry at Milton than at Harvard. It would be more interesting and less technical and abstruse. Would it conflict with his Physics?

Physiography Tom does not care for, and I do not consider it worth while for a boy who reads and easily acquires general information.

As to the German, Tom is going through with Mr Bierwirth's *Thirty Lessons*,[1] and recalls much more than I expected – he could easily enter the Third Class were it desirable. German is still an open question.

Mr Sheffield, who is, I think, known to you, has offered to go to Milton on Saturday for an interview concerning Tom's studies, but I am loath to accept his kind offer as it would shorten his stay here by a day. I should like however, in any case, to visit Milton again and ascertain more definitely what programme of studies can be arranged without conflict; all that I have written is merely preliminary to a final interview.

I should like to ask two practical questions. I desire to know whether a student is allowed to keep his trunk in his room, and if so, should it be of such a height that it can be kept under the bed? Also does an advanced pupil require a 'swallow tail' evening suit for any occasion, or are tuxedo suits worn? I inquire because my son has not yet attained his full growth.

Please let me know how long before the opening of the fall term it will be best for me again to confer briefly with you.[2]

Very sincerely,
Charlotte C. Eliot

1–H. C. Bierwirth, *Beginning German: a series of lessons with an abstract of grammar* (1903). Bierwirth was Professor of German at Harvard.

2–She and TSE saw Mr Cobb on Sat., 16 Sept. The term began on the following Tuesday, with TSE being placed in Forbes House.

17 September 1905 [Eastern Point]

My dear Mr Cobb,

I have purchased Tom a low steamer trunk, and should like very much to have him able to keep it under his bed in his room, unless it is an infringement of rules to which Mrs Chase would object. As there are no closets in the rooms, I think clothes not in immediate use can be best kept from dust etc. in a trunk.

You need not answer this note except to Tom personally.

With kind regards to Mrs Cobb,

Sincerely yours,
C. C. Eliot

[end September 1905] Hotel Bellevue, Beacon St, Boston

My dear Mr Cobb,

I thought perhaps I had better explain to you just why Tom could not participate in football and other such strenuous sports, involving risk of strain. He has had a case of congenital rupture[1] which, our physician thinks, is *superficially* healed, but as the abdominal muscles there are weak, care must still be exercised. He participated in the gymnasium training at Smith Academy. I think, however, it would be well for your instructor to know exactly Tom's physical condition, and presume he examines each new pupil.

Tom has never fully realized until now, when he is almost the only fellow debarred from football, his physical limitations. We hope in a few years he will be entirely normal, but his rapid growth has rendered him less rugged, perhaps, although perfectly healthy. I hope he will soon be over his cold.

I know Tom will be particular about observing all rules.

With kind regards to yourself and Mrs Cobb,

Yours sincerely,
Charlotte C. Eliot

Should Tom ever be ill, which I do not apprehend, I should like to be informed by telegraph.

1–He remembered as a small boy asking his nurse why a naked child in a book was not wearing his truss, which he had assumed all boys wore (Valerie Eliot).

20 May 1906 2635 Locust St [St Louis]

My dear Mr Cobb,

Tom has written home requesting permission to swim in a quarry pond near the Academy. As this authority from parents is a new requirement, it conveys the impression that there is an element of danger, and Mr Eliot and I would like to know the conditions. We both have a prejudice against quarry ponds, partly because Mr Eliot's sister was drowned in one,[1] and also because every year the quarry ponds about the city prove fatal to boys bathing in or skating on them. This is partly due to the deep holes in the bottom rock. I suppose Milton boys never attempt diving in one. Mr Eliot says if the pond is stagnant, fed by rains, there is danger of typhoid. If fed by springs, the cold currents must be carefully avoided. Do boys use their own judgement as to the length of time to remain in the water?

A boy may be very careful himself, but the peril of a comrade endangers his rescuers. I have seen quarry ponds surrounded by steep rock that looked dangerous.

Although sorry to trouble you, we do not feel ready to accord Tom the required permission until we are better acquainted with conditions.[2]

Very cordially yours
C. C. Eliot

FROM *H. W. Eliot* TO *E. H. Wells*[3] MS Harvard

7 December 1906 The Hydraulic-Press Brick Company, Missouri Trust Building, St Louis

Dear Sir,

I thank you for your letter of the 4th containing information which I already had received from my son, who is sufficiently concerned therefore.[4] He did not know that English did not count. I am inclined to think that he has been permitted (with the assistance of his College advisors) to take courses all of which are difficult and require much outside

1–Abby Adams Eliot ('Ada') had drowned in 1864, aged sixteen, in a skating accident. TSE's eldest sister was named after her.

2–On the Head Master's reassurance, permission was given. He added that TSE seemed happier than he had been at first, and was mingling much more with his fellows (23 May).

3–E. H. Wells was Assistant Dean of Harvard College, 1905–7.

4–TSE had been placed on probation at the end of his first semester at Harvard. He later told Valerie Eliot that he 'loafed' for the first two years.

reading. I do not know if this can be remedied. When he comes home for the holidays I will discuss it with him.

Yours truly,
H. W. Eliot

TO *His Mother*[1] PC Houghton

Tuesday [1909] Port Clyde, Maine

My dear Mother

We have had very light and very warm weather: pleasant and lazy. This is only about twenty-five miles from North Haven.

Your aff. Son
Tom

FROM *His Mother* MS Houghton

3 April 1910 4446 Westminster Place,
[St Louis]

My dear Boy,

I was very glad indeed to receive your last letter,[2] and pleased with the success of your lecture. I am so much interested in every detail of your life, my only regret being that you have not time to write more fully. You have not yet told me your marks in the two remaining courses. Surely you must know by this time. I enclose a postal on which I hope you will write and mail.

I hope in your literary work you will receive early the recognition I strove for and failed. I should so have loved a college course, but was obliged to teach before I was nineteen. I graduated with high rank, 'a young lady of unusual brilliancy as a scholar' my old yellow testimonial says, but when I was set to teaching young children, my Trigonometry and Astronomy counted for naught, and I made a dead failure.

Shef[3] wrote early in the fall, that he thought before the end of the collegiate year your ideas would crystallize and you would know better the best direction for your literary activity. I have rather hoped you would

1–Addressed to Mrs H. W. Eliot, Eastern Point, Gloucester, Massachusetts.

2–None of TSE's letters to his parents from Milton Academy, Harvard or Paris has been preserved. After their mother's death, TSE told his brother on 25 May 1930 that he was 'glad to have the letters to make ashes of'.

3–He was about to become an instructor in rhetoric and composition at Wellesley College.

not specialize later on French literature. I suppose you will know better in June what you want to do next year. And you will have the literary judgment of able advisers probably. I cannot bear to think of your being alone in Paris, the very words give me a chill. English speaking countries seem so different from foreign. I do not admire the French nation, and have less confidence in individuals of that race than in English. I suppose I am not enough of a scholar to know what is termed the 'particular genius' of any people. I will enclose Henry's last letter, as you say you have not heard from him for so long. I wish you could live nearer together. But New York is more likely to be your destiny than Chicago.

You must be sure and secure tickets when the time comes for Father and me to hear your Ode.[1] Is it on Class Day, at Sanders? You know Henry had no tickets. Having a part may enable you to secure them. I am glad you know the Littles so well. They must be a fine family. Ed[2] was one of the nicest of Henry's friends. Poor fellow! he was very pathetic in his enfeebled condition.

I suppose you have been too busy to see Marian or Uncle Chris' family. And also too busy to write for the *Advocate*,[3] since you have sent no more copies.

Father will send your draft tomorrow. When is the Easter vacation?

Today has been typically April – showers and sunshine. We have a wood fire in the study. Father has had a little cold. He seems to tire easily. We are hoping Ada will come on in May to the Conference of Charities.[4] She thinks she must be at the Hotel several days. I hope then she will stay with us as long as possible – until we go.

I will not enclose the card – Please let me know without.

Your loving Mother

Hope the trip to New Haven will be pleasant. Father thinks before long you can take your deposit from Bank if you are to leave Cambridge.

1 – As Class Odist, TSE recited his tribute to 'Fair Harvard' in Sanders Theater on Graduation Day, 24 June (*Poems Written in Early Youth*).

2 – Edward Little (1881–1905), who died of tuberculosis, was co-illustrator with Frederick Hall of *Harvard Celebrities*. His brother Clarence (1888–1971), known as 'Pete', was a classmate of TSE.

3 – After the 'Ode', TSE did not contribute again until 1934.

4 – Ada was a member of the Massachusetts State Board of Charities, 1909–14. As a probation officer in New York City's prison, 1901–4, she had been known as 'the angel of the Tombs'.

Henry Ware Eliot TO *Thomas Lamb Eliot*[1]

MS[2] Reed College

12 May 1910 [St Louis]

Dear Bob,

The world wags and the end draws nigher.

Laus Deo.

I have not seen your Tom[3] lately but he is well and busy. My Tom is in hospital at Cambridge – probably scarlet fever which is epidemic in Boston. We have so much difficulty in getting information that Lottie goes to Boston tonight. Why don't folks think more of the feelings of absentees and give them the whole story! It is unfortunate just now as Tom is working so hard for his A.M. which is just in sight.[4]

Tis a parlous world.

Yr
H

In the autumn of 1910, TSE went to Paris for the academic year to attend the Sorbonne, and to hear the weekly lectures at the Collège de France by the philosopher Henri Bergson. Nearly fifty years later he said, 'I had at that time the idea of giving up English and trying to settle down and scrape along in Paris and gradually write French.' He left France in July 1911 to visit Munich and northern Italy, before returning to Harvard to work for his doctorate in philosophy.

1–Thomas Lamb Eliot (1841–1936), brother of TSE's father, was Pastor of the First Unitarian Society of Portland, Oregon, 1867–93; author of *The Radical Difference between Liberal Christianity and Orthodoxy*. See Earl M. Wilbur, *Thomas Lamb Eliot, 1841–1936* (Portland, 1937).

2–From a copy made by the recipient's granddaughter.

3–Thomas Dawes Eliot (1889–1973), who was to become Professor of Sociology at Northwestern University, 1924–54.

4–Although his illness was not serious, he was unable to sit his final examinations.

TO *Theodora Eliot Smith* MS Houghton

[Postmark 23 December 1910] [Paris]

LONCLE · TOM ·
· ET · LES · ENFANTS · DE · LA · FRANCE ·
SOUHAITENT · LA · BONNE · ANNÉE ·
· À · THEODORA ·

1911

TO *Theodora Eliot Smith* MS Houghton

[late February? 1911] Paris

My Dear Theodora,

Thank you very much for the nice letter that you sent me, and the Valentine of Puss in Boots. Have you the puss in the green boots still, and do you remember the story about him?

You must have been studying hard in order to be able to write so nicely. I have been studying too. But I often go out and walk in the Luxembourg Gardens, which is a sort of park like the Boston Public Gardens, or the park back down the hill from your home in Brookline, where you used to go. There is a pond there too, and the children play boats when it is not too cold. There are lots of boats and they sail right across the pond and right through the fountain and never upset. They spin tops and roll hoops. You would like the French children. I don't think they have as many playthings as the American children, but they seem quite happy. I see lots of them in the Champs Elysées (which is a long wide street) on Sunday afternoon, riding in little carts behind goats. But it is hard to talk to the little ones, because they don't talk French very well yet, and I don't either.

When they are older and go to school you see them walking out two by two, very quiet and proper, in a long line, with their teachers. They all wear black capes, and carry their schoolbooks on their backs underneath the capes, so that they all look as if they had big bumps on their backs. And they wear black pinafores, and have their legs bare all winter. But it is never very cold in Paris. It has not snowed here all winter, and the little steamboats go up and down the river like black flies: 'fly-boats', they call them.

Just about now you are having supper in America, and here, it is my bed time. Isn't that funny?

– With love to mother and father and all the dolls

Your
Uncle
TOM

TO *Eleanor Hinkley*[1] PC Houghton

[Postmark 24 March 1911] [Paris]

Dear Eleanor, I have been meaning to write a letter to thank you for your Christmas card, and I don't think that I did. I am not sure that this card will go through the American post. I have not seen this costume[2] on the street and I don't think it will be a success. Is the Cambridge season agreeable this year? I have no news from there.

Ever sincerely yours
T

Give my regards to Aunt Susie and Barbara.[3]

TO *Eleanor Hinkley* MS Houghton

26 April [1911] 151 bis rue Saint Jacques [Paris]

Dear Eleanor,

I just came back from London[4] last night, and found a pile of letters waiting for me, with yours sitting on the top. I mounted to my room to read them; then my friend the *femme de chambre* burst in to see me (after two weeks absence). She tells me I am getting fat. Also she had a store of news about everyone else in the house. Monsieur Dana[5] has gone to the Ecole Normale, where he has to rise every day at seven. This is a prime joke, and lasted for ten or twelve minutes. Monsieur Verdenal[6] has taken his room, because it is bigger than M. Verdenal's room, and gives upon the garden. Had I been out into the garden to see how the trees *poussent* [are growing]? So then I had to go into M. Verdenal's room to see how the garden did. Byplay at this point, because M. Verdenal was in the garden, and because I threw a lump of sugar at him. And a Monsieur *americain*

1–Eleanor Hinkley, TSE's cousin; see Glossary of Names.
2–It showed a model wearing *la jupe-culotte* (divided skirt) at the Auteuil races, where it continues, according to the caption, 'à égayer les habitués . . . qu'elle intrigue par la nouveauté de ses mystérieux dessous' ['to amuse the race-goers . . . intriguing them by the novelty of the mysterious under-garments'].
3–Eleanor's mother (sister of TSE's mother) and Eleanor's sister, Barbara (1889–1958), who in 1909 had married Edward Welch (1888–1948).
4–His first visit, always associated in his mind with the music of Herman Finck's 'In the Shadows' (1910), which was popular at the time.
5–Henry ('Harry') Dana (1881–1950): educated at Harvard, he had been a lecturer in English at the Sorbonne 1908–10. He was later dismissed from Columbia for pacifist activities.
6–Jean Verdenal, who was to be dedicatee of *Prufrock and Other Observations*: see Glossary of Names.

named Ladd has taken M. Verdenal's room. He does not speak French very well yet. He speaks as Monsieur spoke in November. (And I shortly heard Monsieur Ladd bawling through the hall '*A-vous monté mes trunks à l'attique?*'[1] – I settle the affair by crying out '*les malles au grenier!*'

But finally I read the letters, and enjoyed yours more than any. In fact I must compliment you on it – you have a gift for letter writing. This was quite different from any I have had all year. I have no news equally amusing to repay with. I feel rather guilty about that, I do: for Paris has burst out, during my absence, into full spring; and it is such a revelation that I feel that I ought to make it known. At London, one pretended that it was spring, and tried to coax the spring, and talk of the beautiful weather; but one continued to hibernate amongst the bricks.[2] And one looked through the windows, and the waiter brought in eggs and coffee, and the *Graphic* (which I conscientiously tried to read, to please them) and commented on the chauffeurs' strike[3] and all was very wintry and sedate. But here! –

But I was outdoors most of the time. I made a pilgrimage to Cricklewood.[4] 'Where *is* Cricklewood?' said an austere Englishman at the hotel. I produced a map and pointed to the silent evidence that Cricklewood exists. He pondered. 'But why go to Cricklewood?' he flashed out at length. Here I was triumphant. 'There is no reason!' I said. He had no more to say. But he *was* relieved (I am sure) when he found that I was American. He felt no longer responsible. But Cricklewood is mine. I discovered it. No one will go there again. It is like the sunken town in the

1–'Have you taken my trunks [*malles*] up to the attic [*grenier*]?'

2–'We hibernate among the bricks / And live across the window panes' ('Interlude in London', ll. 1–2, in *IMH*, 16).

3–Motor cab proprietors were seeking an increase in charges, which had remained unaltered since 1907, and their drivers were in dispute with them over the payment of petrol tax. Although the Home Secretary had appointed a commission to examine the grievances, drivers in London's West End went on strike on 15 Apr. To the public's delight, the horse cab came into its own again, *The Times* reporting two days later that 'the cab-driver with a silk hat reappeared after a long absence and some astonishing animals were to be seen between the shafts'.

4–Cricklewood, London N.W.2, 'was [then], I should think, part of the parish of Hendon but no more than a hamlet. It rose to fame owing to its position on the Edgware Road and the tavern there which became a tram stop' (John Betjeman to Valerie Eliot, 15 Mar. 1978). Though most of the places that TSE visited would form part of a regular tourist itinerary, his 'pilgrimage to Cricklewood' (like his visit to the City and Camberwell Work House) shows his independence of Baedeker. TSE's copy of Baedeker, *London and Environs* (1908), is at King's.

fairy story,[1] that rose just every May-day eve, and lived for an hour, and only one man saw it.*

<* *Note explanatory:* I suggest that if the Sayward family were English – well, they might live in Cricklewood.>

– I have just discussed my trip with the prim but nice English lady at the *pension*. She said 'And did you go through the Tower?' 'No!' 'Madame Tussaud's?' 'No!' 'Westminster Abbey?' 'No!' here I triumphed again – 'the Abbey was closed due to the coronation preparations!'[2] (This is a remark which, in a novel, would be 'flung back'). I then said – do you know

St Helens
St Stephens
St Bartholomew the Great
St Sepulchre
St Ethel[d]reda[3]

and finally – Camberwell Work House! And she knew none of these. 'I have it on you!' I cried (for I know her well enough for that). But she does not understand the American dialect.

– But at this point, lest you should give people the idea that I wasted my time! note that I have seen

National Gallery
Brit[ish] Mus[eum]
Wallace Collection (made notes!!)
S. Kensington[4] (in large part)
Cambridge University
Hampton Court
The Temple

1 – 'Germelshausen' by Friedrich Gerstäcker (1816–72) tells of a lost village, under Papal interdict, which appears for a day's revelry once every hundred years before sinking beneath the earth again. On 18 June 1936 TSE wrote to Lady Richmond 'East Coker was delightful, with a sort of Germelshausen effect'; and after publication of *East Coker* he wrote to H. S. Häussermann on 24 May 1940, 'I think that the imagery of the first section (though taken from the village itself) may have been influenced by recollections of *Germelshausen*, which I have not read for many years.'

2 – King George V was crowned on 22 June.

3 – St Helen's Bishopgate, St Stephen Walbrook, St Bartholomew the Great, West Smithfield, and St Sepulchre Old Bailey are churches in the City of London. The medieval Roman Catholic St Etheldreda is in Ely Place, Holborn. TSE's love of City churches is further in evidence in *TWL*, l. 264 (his note to that line refers to *The Proposed Demolition of Nineteen City Churches*), as well as in his pageant play *The Rock* (1934), staged on behalf of the 'Forty-Five Churches Fund of the Diocese of London'.

4 – The old name for the Victoria & Albert Museum (until 1899).

The City – Thoroughly
Whitechapel (note: Jews)[1]
St Pauls
et al.
also the Zoo (note: gave the apterix a bun)[2]

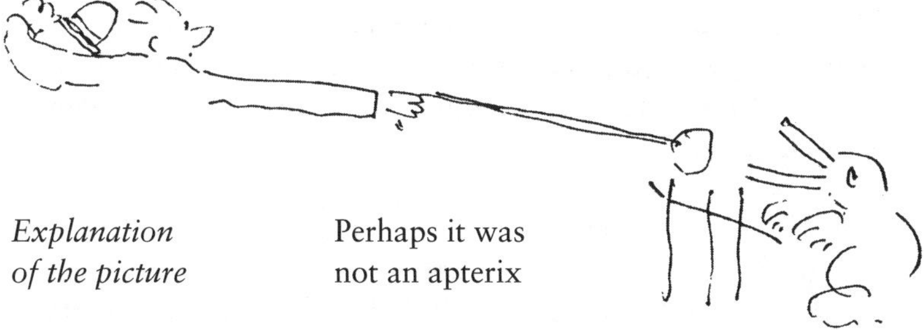

Explanation of the picture Perhaps it was not an apterix

And so I will close this spring letter which becomes more and more foolish. Do write again.

Thanking you in advance
Yours faithfully
Thos. S. Eliot

TO *Edward Forbes*[3] MS Harvard

22 May [1911] c/o Credit Lyonnais, 19 bvd des Italiens [Paris]

My dear Mr Forbes

I have just arranged with Alphonse-Picard that they should send you a copy of the Trocadero catalogue.[4] It appears to be a new edition. As for the Luxembourg, there is no catalogue. I suppose that the museum is conceived

1–By 1900 there were about 135,000 Jews in London, most of whom lived within the East End around the Whitechapel area. In *East London* (1898), the Christian missionary Henry Walker noted of Whitechapel, 'Here, in spite of the English-looking surroundings, [the stranger] is practically in a foreign land, so far as language and race are concerned. The people are neither French nor English, Germans nor Americans, but Jews.'
2–An apterix is 'A New Zealand bird, about the size of a goose, with merely rudimentary wings and no tail, called by the natives Kiwi' (OED). TSE wrote three reviews for the *Egoist* in 1918 under the pseudonym 'Apteryx', or 'T. S. Apteryx'.
3–Edward Forbes (1873–1969): collector and Harvard benefactor; Director of the Fogg Museum at Harvard, 1909–44. TSE had taken his course Fine Arts 20b in 1909–10.
4–Camille Enlart, *Le Musée de Sculpture Comparée du Trocadero* (1911).

to be never in a stable enough condition to warrant it.[1] There are three 'guides' containing selections (illustrations) of the sculptures only. If you would like them, let me know, but I judged them useless for museum purposes.

This is a long time since you wrote asking for the catalogues, and no doubt you thought that your letter was never received. Perhaps you have already obtained the catalogue through someone else, or perhaps the lack of it may have bothered you a great deal. In any case, I hope you will not attribute my delinquency to gross negligence, but rather to a fundamental failing of character. I have been known to procrastinate even longer.

I have enjoyed my winter very keenly, and have gained, I think, a great deal. My opinions on art, as well as other subjects, have modified radically. At Christmas I travelled for two weeks in France, and saw several things not often visited – including Poitiers, Angoulême, Toulouse, Albi, Moissac, and other places in the south west. My Easter vacation I spent in London. At present, I am commencing a series of trips to towns about Paris, and began last Sunday with Rouen.

After the middle of June I shall go to Munich for some time, to study German.[2] I hope to spend a few weeks, at least, in Italy.[3]

If you come to Europe this summer, I shall hope to see you. In case the catalogue does not arrive, send me word of it.

Please remember me to Mrs Forbes

Sincerely yours
Thomas Eliot.

FROM *Jean Verdenal* — MS Houghton

Dimanche [July? 1911] [Paris]

Mon cher ami,

Je suis impatient de vous voir trouver du papier à lettres en Bavière, et d'en recevoir un échantillon couvert de votre belle écriture avant que la

1–The Luxembourg Museum was devoted to works by living painters and sculptors. They remained there for ten years after the artist's death, and the best of them were then selected for the Louvre.

2–He left France in July 1911 for Munich and northern Italy before returning to Harvard for the autumn to work for his doctorate in philosophy. In a letter to Eudo Mason (21 Feb. 1936), he was to recall that most of 'The Love Song of J. Alfred Prufrock' was written 'in the summer of 1911 when I was in Munich'.

3–See TSE's 'Notes on Italy' (Houghton).

bière allemande n'ait engourdi votre esprit. Elle y aurait d'ailleurs de la peine, si lourde soit-elle, et nous voyons que quelques naturels du pays y échappèrent; l'histoire conte que le terrible Schopenhauer en était fort amateur. Il jouait aussi de la clarinette, mais c'était peut-être pour embêter ses voisins.[1] Voilà bien assez de choses pour nous rattacher à la vie. La volonté de vivre est mauvaise, cause de désirs et de peines mais la bière est appréciable – et l'on continue. O! Raison.

Je viens de lire hier soir la *Mère et l'Enfant* de Philippe,[2] quelle belle et bonne chose; blanche comme le pain et le lait, sans procédés, sans littérature. Il faut l'aimer, bien l'aimer pour la comprendre. J'ai compris à propos de ce bon Philippe tout ce qu'a d'inférieur la critique purement intellectuelle, un jour où j'ai entendu quelque Sorbonnard dire à propos de ses romans: 'Très intéressant! Comme il a bien *étudié* la vie des humbles.' Pauvre, pauvre ami, plus que toutes les misères, cette phrase lui eût été douloureuse. Avoir souffert, vécu chacune de ses lignes pour servir de sujet d'étude au professeur de littérature – qui n'y verra rien – tant il est vrai que c'est nous-mêmes que nous projetons sur toutes les choses extérieures. Il faudrait, en critique, réserver la raison à démolir, à cogner sur les faux bonshommes, à cogner dur pour mettre par terre les faiseurs, falsificateurs professionnels de l'art. Les bonnes choses restent à la lumière; il faut en parler pour les faire connaître, comme on prête un livre à un ami. Tout essai de démonstration par l'intelligence de la beauté d'une oeuvre d'art est, sans aucun doute, une contradiction. Monsieur Dana en tressaillerait derrière ses lorgnons d'or, mais c'est comme cela, le critique rationnel m'a toujours fait penser à l'enfant qui casse son jouet mécanique pour voir ce qu'il y a dedans. Et que dire des critiques scientifiques? Mais ceux-ci ne sont pas dangereux, ils sont trop embêtants et personne ne les lit.

Au revoir, mon vieux, je vous serre la pince cordialement.

Jean Verdenal.[3]

1 – The daily routine of Arthur Schopenhauer (1788–1860), author of *Die Welt als Wille und Vorstellung* (1819), involved a good intake of beer as well as clarinet practice. TSE later noted that his (and Verdenal's) literary hero Laforgue was fascinated by 'the Kantian pseudo-Buddhism of Schopenhauer' (*VMP*, 216).

2 – *La Mere et l'Enfant* (1900), by Charles-Louis Philippe (1874–1909). TSE's copy of this novel (Édition de la *NRF*, 4th edition), is inscribed 'T. S. Eliot / Paris / September 1911' (Houghton). In his preface to a translation of Philippe's *Bubu of Montparnasse*, TSE would praise the author's 'sincerity'; comparing him to Dickens and Dostoevsky, he called him 'perhaps the most faithful to the point of view of the humble and oppressed themselves . . . more their spokesman than their champion' (*Bubu of Montparnasse*, trans. Laurence Vail [Paris, 1932], 10).

3 – *Translation*: My dear friend, I am waiting impatiently to hear that you have found some notepaper in Bavaria, and to receive an example of it covered with your beautiful

FROM *Jean Verdenal* MS Houghton

[Mid-July 1911] 151 bis rue St Jacques, Paris

Mon cher ami,

Je reçois votre lettre[1] au moment où je vais quitter Paris pour aller quinze jours là-bas aux Pyrénées. Tout le monde a quitté déjà, à part Fellows;[2] et des figures de passage remplissent la maison; presque toutes repondent à l'étiquette 'vieille fille americaine'. Cela suffit.

Le spectacle de Paris ces jours-ci (fête du 14 juillet) était assez intéressant. C'est, avec les jours gras, la vraie fête de Paris, maintenant que l' 'antique renouveau des fêtes surannées ne fleurit plus aux vieux pavés du siècle dur'. Je crois même que l'expression artistique est plus parfaite qu'au Mardi gras, rien ne sonne de travers. Illuminations officielles, revue et cocardes, populo dansant; horribles orchestres dont les valses vous suggestionnent totalement; c'est une atmosphère chaude, poussiéreuse, suante sous un ciel ardent; c'est tricolore, commandé par l'État et les gens s'en donnent de rigoler. L'après-midi les gosses triomphent, les sales gosses à mirlitons; le soir il monte une excitation sensuelle qui va en grandissant; le cheveux des

---

handwriting, before German beer has dulled your wits. As a matter of fact, it would have some difficulty in doing so, and we see that even a few natives of the country escaped its effects; history tells us that the formidable Schopenhauer was a great beer-lover. He also played the clarinet, but perhaps that was just to annoy his neighbours. Such things are quite enough to make us cling to life. The will to live is evil, a source of desires and sufferings, but beer is not to be despised – and so we carry on. O Reason!

I have just read – only last evening – *Mother and Child* by Philippe, what a good and beautiful book; as wholesome as bread and milk, without artifice or rhetoric. To understand it, you have to like it, really like it. It was in connection with Philippe that I realised what is so unsatisfactory about purely intellectual criticism, one day when I overheard some Sorbonne professor saying about his novels: 'Very interesting! How well he has *studied* the lives of humble people.' Poor, good fellow, the remark would have hurt him more than the worst of his sad experiences. To have suffered and lived every line he wrote only to become a subject of study for a professor of literature – who will miss the point – so true it is that we project ourselves on to everything outside us. Reason, in criticism, should be reserved for demolishing, for hammering charlatans, for hammering phoneys and falsifiers of art until they are laid low. The good things stand out of their own accord; they have to be talked about to make them known, as you lend a book to a friend. Any attempt on the part of the intelligence to demonstrate the beauty of a work of art is, undoubtedly, a contradiction in terms. Monsieur Dana would shudder behind his gold *pince-nez* if he heard this, but it's true; a rationalistic critic always makes me think of a child breaking his clockwork toy to see what there is inside. As for scientific critics? But they are not dangerous; they are too boring and no one reads them.

Goodbye, my dear fellow, I shake you warmly by the hand. Jean Verdenal.

1 – TSE was staying at Pension Bürger, Luisenstrasse 50, Munich.

2 – Unidentified.

filles sont collés aux tempes de sueur; la roue des loteries tourne; la roue des chevaux de bois tourne entraînante, attirante de lumière, chaque oscillation des chevaux cambrant le torse souple des poules, une jambe bien prise est entrevue par la 'jupe fendue à la mode'; un souffle lourd et gras passe chaudement.

Toute cette manifestation extérieure répond bien, sans aucun doute, à l'actuelle tendance régnant dans le peuple de Paris. C'est, tendance peu élevée, matérialiste, mais je ne dirais pas grossière, car le peuple Parisien reste fin, sceptique et distingué malgré tout; dans les instants graves il saura être généreux, je crois. On peut considérer qu'il subit la même poussée que l'aristocratie au XVIIIe siècle. Vous rencontrerez constamment aujourd'hui le type 'ouvrier intelligent et instruit'; il ne croit plus aux vieilles histoires de jadis; beaucoup croient à la science (!) mais surtout beaucoup ont refoulé les bons élans intérieurs, attirés par le désir de raisonner. Sans doute la plupart restent de braves gens et de bons types, malgré tout, et intuitivement, mais leur système les condamne, logiquement. Vous entendez des gens du monde dire avec sourire que 'la demi-culture, la demi-science, le demi-intellectualisme ne leur donnera rien'. Mais, ô braves gens, est-ce que l'intellectualisme tout entier vous donnera beaucoup plus? Cependant que le positivisme (matérialisme mal déguisé) descend et se vulgarise, voici qu'une tendance vers l'Idée se montre dans l'Élite, chaque jour plus forte. Toute la fin du XIXe siècle en est pleine et la manifestation la plus marquée est sans doute dans la poésie moderne, puis dans la musique. La forme souvent prise est celle d'un retour au christianisme catholique ou évangélique galiléen. Quelle valeur y a-t-il dans les innombrables et diverses oeuvres ayant cet aspect? Quelles différences en effet! aperçues dès qu'on prend q[uel]ques noms (Verlaine, Huysmans, Barrès, Francis Jammes, Péguy, Bourget, Claudel, Le Cardonnel etc.).[1] Je fais cette salade exprès, pour montrer le tri à faire. Nous en recauserons si vous voulez. Il serait convenable de discerner en chacun ce qui revient à diverses causes: snobisme, intérêt, sincère repentir, defaut d'intelligence, croyance catholique et littérale du dogme, point de vue social (national, provincial, traditionnel, école), évocation du passé, procédé littéraire,

1–Paul Verlaine (1844–96), poet; Joris-Karl Huysmans (1848–1907), author of *À Rebours*; Maurice Barrès (1862–1923), nationalist intellectual and polemicist; Francis Jammes (1868–1938), poet; Charles Péguy (1873–1914), poet and Catholic nationalist, discussed by TSE in *NS* 8 (7 Oct. 1916); Paul Bourget (1852–1935), novelist, whose *Lazarine* was reviewed by TSE in *NS* 9 (25 Aug. 1917, unsigned); Paul Claudel (1868–1955), influential Catholic poet, dramatist and essayist, to whom TSE paid tribute (*Le Figaro Littéraire* 10, 5 Mar. 1955); Louis Le Cardonnel (1862–1936), religious poet.

pragmatisme, etc. Il convient surtout de dire pour chacun *en quelle mesure il peut influencer notre vie intérieure vers la connaissance du bien suprême.*

Mon vieux, je serai là en septembre, bien content de vous revoir; croyez à toute mon amitié.

Jean Verdenal

1) J'ai lu le *Mystère de la Charité de Jeanne d'Arc.*[1] J'aime surtout le récit que Madame Gervaise fait de la Passion (Bethléem et finit à Jérusalem). J. V.

2) Tâchez donc si possible d'entendre qq. chose de Wagner à Munich. J'étais l'autre jour au *Crépuscule* dirigé par Nikisch;[2] la fin est sans doute un des points les plus hauts où l'homme se soit élevé.

3) J'oubliais encore de vous dire que le semaine d'avant j'ai eu plusieurs fois le plaisir d'aller avec Prichard[3] boire de l'eau minérale et manger des haricots verts, en divers restaurants. Quelle âme belle et forte, mais un peu raide quand on ne la connaît pas encore.[4]

1–Charles Péguy, *Le Mystère de la Charité de Jeanne d'Arc* (1909). Much of Péguy's drama takes the form of a theological dialogue between Madame Gervaise and Jeanne. Mme Gervaise's meditation on the Passion includes: 'Vie commence à Bethlehem et finie à Jerusalem / Vie comprise entre Bethlehem et Jerusalem. / Vie inscrite entre Bethlehem et Jerusalem . . . / Vie commence à Bethlehem et qui ne finit pas à Jerusalem' (*Oeuvres poétiques complètes* [1975], 437).

2–The Hungarian Arthur Nikisch (1855–1922) became in 1895 principal conductor of both the Leipzig Gewandhaus Orchestra and the Berlin Philarmonic. *Götterdämmerung* ('The Twilight of the Gods') is the last opera in Wagner's tetralogy *The Ring of the Nibelungs*: TSE refers to the song of the Rheinmaidens in his notes to l. 266 of *TWL*.

3–Matthew Prichard (1865–1936), English aesthete who had become secretary to the Director of the Boston Museum of Fine Arts in 1902. Henry Eliot had given TSE an introduction to him.

4–*Translation*: My dear friend, I have received your letter just as I am on the point of leaving Paris to go down for a fortnight to the Pyrenees. Everyone has already gone, apart from Fellows; and the house is filled with ephemeral visitors, almost all corresponding to the label 'elderly American spinster'. No more need be said.

Paris has presented quite an interesting spectacle recently (14 July, Bastille Day). Together with the period around Shrove Tuesday, it is the true Parisian holiday, now that 'the antique renewal of age-old feast-days no longer flowers on the ancient cobblestones of this hard century'. I even believe that it takes a more artistic form than Shrove Tuesday; nothing is out of key. Official illuminations, march-past, patriotic rosettes, the common folk dancing in the streets; appalling bands playing overpoweringly emotional waltzes; the atmosphere is warm, dusty and sweaty, under a blazing sky; a tricolour, State-commissioned atmosphere, and the populace enjoys itself up to the hilt. In the afternoon, the children take over, wretched urchins blowing tin trumpets; the evening is filled with an ever-mounting sensual excitement; sweat makes the girls' hair stick to their temples; lottery wheels spin; a merry-go-round, attractively lit and alluring, also revolves, and with every jerk of the wooden horses, the whores brace their supple busts and a shapely leg can be glimpsed through the slit of a 'fashionably split skirt'; a heavy, sensuous gust flows warmly by.

FROM *Alain-Fournier*[1] MS Houghton

25 July 1911 2 rue Cassini [Paris]

Mon cher ami,

Combien je vous suis reconnaissant des renseignements que vous avez pris la peine de m'envoyer sur cette littérature anglaise que je connais si superficiellement et que je désirerais tant connaître!

—

All this outward demonstration corresponds, without doubt, to the present dominant tendency among the Parisian populace. Not being a very elevated tendency, it is materialistic, but I would not call it coarse, since your average Parisian, even so, remains subtle, sceptical and refined; in time of danger, he will, I believe, know how to behave generously. There is reason to think that the Parisian working class is undergoing the same evolution as the aristocracy in the eighteenth century. Today, you constantly come across examples of the 'educated, intelligent worker'; he no longer believes in the old stories dating from the past; many of them believe in science (!) but, what is more important, many have repressed their good inner impulses through a desire to think rationally. (No doubt, most of them remain nice people and decent fellows, intuitively and in spite of all this, but, logically, they are doomed by their system.) You can hear upper-class people remarking with a smile that 'semi-culture, semi-science and semi-intellectualism will bring them no advantage'. But, my dear, good people, will complete intellectualism give you much more? While positivism (materialism poorly disguised) spreads downwards through society, an aspiration towards the Idea can be seen growing daily stronger among the Elite. The end of the nineteenth century is permeated by it, and it shows itself most markedly, no doubt, in modern poetry, then in music. It frequently takes the form of a return to Christianity, whether Catholic or Galilean and evangelical. What value is there in the innumerable and varied works showing this feature? What differences appear, indeed, as soon as you think of a few names! (Verlaine, Huysmans, Barrès, Francis Jammes, Péguy, Bourget, Claudel, Le Cardonnel, etc.). I deliberately quote them at random to show the sorting out to be done. We'll talk about all this again some time, if you like. It would be appropriate to decide, in each case, how far various causes have operated: snobbishness, self-interest, sincere repentance, flawed intelligence, literal Catholic belief in the dogma, social attitudes (national, provincial, traditional, sectarian), harking back to the past, literary artifice, pragmatism, etc. But the main thing is to say, in the case of each, *how far he can influence our inner life towards the knowledge of the supreme good.*

My dear fellow, I shall be here in September, and very pleased to see you again; all friendly greetings. Jean Verdenal

1) I have read *The Mystery of the Charity of Joan of Arc.* I particularly liked Madame Gervaise's account of the Passion (Bethlehem and Jerusalem, life beginning at Bethlehem and ending in Jerusalem). J. V.

2) Try, if possible, to hear something by Wagner in Munich. I went the other day to the *Götterdämmerung*, conducted by Nikisch; the end must be one of the highest points ever reached by man.

3) Another thing I forgot to tell you is that, the previous week, I had the pleasure of going several times with Prichard to drink mineral water and eat French beans, in various restaurants. A fine, strong nature, but a little stiff until one gets to know him.

1–Henri-Alban Fournier (1886–1914): author, under the pseudonym Alain-Fournier, of *Le Grand Meaulnes* (1913). He tutored TSE in French language and literature, and made him recite passages from the classics. Fournier shared with his pupil his delight in Gide, Péguy,

Je vais me faire acheter, les uns après les autres, tous les livres que vous m'avez indiqués. Mais quand vais-je pouvoir les lire?

En ce moment j'achève le livre de Ford[1] que vous m'avez donné et où je trouve tant de fièvre et tant de pathétique beauté.

Durant quelques jours de vacances que j'ai pris à la campagne, j'ai achevé la lecture facile de *Catriona* de Stevenson. Je trouve là les qualités les plus françaises de subtilité, de grâce et d'héroisme, le talent de romancier le plus fin et le plus précis mis au service des aventures le plus délibérément invraisemblables . . .

Je suis aussi en train de lire le *Typhon* de Conrad que vous m'avez indiqué, et je vais acheter *Youth*.[2]

Je n'ai que peu de temps à vous consacrer aujourd'hui. Je veux seulement m'excuser de mon retard et remettre à plus tard une lettre plus importante.

Savez-vous que le jeune homme à qui je donnais des leçons de philosophie pour le bachot a été reçu avec 'mention' grace à des notes de philos. renversantes. 17/20 à l'oral. Le professeur l'a gardé près d'une demi-heure et lui a dit que depuis trois ans il n'avait pas mis une note aussi forte!

Voyez que, si je suis bon chroniqueur, je n'aurais pas été non plus trop mauvais professeur. N'importe, je crois que je ne me risquerais plus à vous donner des leçons de Philosophie. Tout au plus de français, si vous voulez, mais vous n'en avez guère besoin, si j'en juge par votre lettre.

Ce que vous me dites des Allemands m'intéresse infiniment. Moi qui étais internationaliste il y a quatre ou cinq ans, je partirais aujourd'hui bien volontiers contre eux. Et je crois que la majorité des Français est comme moi.

J'ai entendu dire déjà que leur architecture était parfois intéressante.

Je suis allé porter vos paquets de livres rue St Jacques, mais vous étiez déjà parti. Je suivrai vos instructions sur ce point, car, hélas, je ne serai pas à Paris au commencement de Septembre. Je pars le 26 août à Mirande (Gers) faire une période de manoeuvres de vingt-quatre jours.

—

Stendhal, Marivaux, and the novels of Dostoevsky in French translation. (On 11 Apr. 1911, TSE saw the first dramatisation of *The Brothers Karamazov*, adapted by Jacques Copeau and Jean Croué, at the Théâtre des Arts: see Nancy Hargrove, 'T. S. Eliot and the Parisian Theatre World, 1910–11', *South Atlantic Review* 66: 4, Autumn 2001.) TSE would remember Fournier's 'exquisite refinement, quiet humour and his great personal charm': see Robert Gibson, *The Quest of Alain-Fournier* (1953).

1–Possibly Ford Madox Ford's *Ladies Whose Bright Eyes: A Romance* (1911), which TSE later recommended to William Turner Levy as a 'treat in store' (*Affectionately T. S. Eliot*, 1968, 136), although the novelist did not change his name from Hueffer to Ford until 1919.

2–Igor Stravinsky recorded TSE saying in his later years that *Youth* and 'The End of the Tether' were 'the finest stories of their kind I know' (*Themes and Conclusions* [1972], 71).

Ne manquez pas de me tenir au courant de tout ce qui vous arrive et de tout ce qui vous intéresse et croyez-moi

Votre bien sympathiquement dévoué

Alain-Fournier

PS Lire quelque chose de moi dans la *Nouvelle Revue Française* de 1er Septembre.[1]

[On envelope] Un de mes amis désire savoir dans quelles parties de l'Allemagne on parle l'allemand le plus pur. Pourriez-vous le renseigner? Il désirerait résider dans la banlieue d'une ville agréable. A. F.[2]

1 – 'Portrait', *NRF* 3: 33 (1 Sept. 1911) – the last of Fournier's short stories – is a brief memoir of a school acquaintance who came to a tragic end.

2 – *Translation*: My dear friend, I am most grateful to you for the information you have taken the trouble to send me about English literature, a subject with which I am very superficially acquainted and that I would so much like to know more about.

I am going to order, in turn, all the books you mention. But when shall I be able to read them?

At the moment, I am finishing the book by Ford you gave me, and in which I find so much feverish emotion and heart-rending beauty.

During a few days' holiday in the country I finished Stevenson's *Catriona*, an easy book to read. I find in it the eminently French qualities of subtlety, grace and heroic feeling, together with the most delicate novelist's gift, put at the service of the most deliberately incredible adventures . . .

I am also busy reading *Typhoon* by Conrad, which you mentioned to me, and I am going to buy *Youth*.

I have only a little time to spare today. I merely wish to apologise for my delay in replying, while postponing the writing of a more substantial letter until later.

Would you believe it – the young man I was coaching in philosophy for the *baccalauréat* has passed with distinction thanks to some staggering philosophy marks? Seventeen out of twenty for the oral. The examiner kept him talking for half an hour and said he had not given anyone such a good mark for the last three years!

So you see, I may be a good story-teller, but I would not have been too bad a teacher either. Even so, I don't think I would ever again venture to give you philosophy lessons. French lessons, at a pinch, if you like, but, to judge by your letter, you hardly need any.

I am greatly interested by what you say about the Germans. Although I was an internationalist only four or five years ago, I would now very willingly march against them. And I think the majority of Frenchmen are like me.

I have been told that German architecture is not without interest.

I took your parcels of books to the rue Saint-Jacques, but you had already left. Tell me what I should do about them because, unfortunately, I shall not be in Paris at the beginning of September. I am leaving on 26 August for Mirande (Gers) to take part in manoeuvres lasting twenty-four days.

Don't fail to keep me informed of everything that happens to you or interests you, and believe me. Yours most truly, Alain-Fournier

PS You can read something by me in *La Nouvelle Revue Française* of 1 September.

[On envelope] One of my friends would like to know in which parts of Germany they speak the purest German. Could you tell him? He would like to stay on the outskirts of some pleasant town. A. F.

FROM *Jean Verdenal* MS Houghton

Mardi 17[1] Octobre [1911] [Paris]

Ne croyez pas que je vous oublie. Mais pour quelques semaines encore je travaille douze heures par jour. Sans grand espoir, je passe les diverses épreuves à quelque faible distance de ce qu'il faudrait pour réussir; je m'entends chaque jour répéter que je suis trop jeune. Je continue avec la vitesse acquise, assez fatigué mais excité heureusement comme il convient.

Excusez ma hâte à vous quitter. Votre lettre m'a fait plaisir; nous causerons un autre jour.

Cordialement je vous envoie mille choses affectueuses.

J. Verdenal

PS J'ai quelquefois déjeuné avec Prichard qui me semble engagé sur une mauvaise voie – 'artificielle' dirais-je – à propos de la morale (?)[2]

1 – Appears to be misdated '18 Octobre'. Tuesday was the 17th.

2 – *Translation*: Don't think I have forgotten you. But for a few more weeks I shall be working twelve hours a day. With no great hopes, I am sitting the various parts of the examination a little below the level required for success; every day I tell myself I am too young. I am maintaining the momentum, exhausted but appropriately exhilarated by the tension.

Excuse my haste in leaving you. I was pleased to have your letter; we will talk together some other time. Cordially, J. Verdenal

PS I have lunched occasionally with Prichard, who seems to me to be on the wrong course – an 'artificial' course, I should say, in relation to morality(?).

1912

FROM *Jean Verdenal* MS Houghton

Lundi 5 Février 1912 151 bis [rue St Jacques, Paris]

Cher ami,

L'abrutissement de ces derniers mois de galère m'a laissé bien paresseux. Depuis un mois mon concours est fini; suis nommé Interne provisoire et devrai recommencer le métier l'été prochain et l'automne. Zut. Enfin c'est un échelon. Mais recommencer encore à être asservi aux mêmes chinoiseries creuses que cet été, refréner toute émotion et toute, si petite fût-elle, lueur d'intelligence!

N'y pensons plus. Après ma dernière épreuve quelques semaines de vacances étaient imposées – repos béat en province dans la neutralité d'une bonne nourriture et de promenades réglées, avec le débouché sentimental de la vie de famille. Depuis quinze jours je suis à Paris et peu à peu reprends contact avec la vie, à tâtons, comme le conducteur de tramway raccroche le trolley au fil électrique. – Je ne sais trop à quoi me raccrocher – peu d'amis (mon meilleur ami est en voyage), pas de relations les ayant toutes plaquées volontairement depuis plusieurs mois, plus d'habitudes pour remplir le temps intelligemment, et la pluie tombe. Je me rabats sur mes bouquins – avec méfiance cependant – c'est très artificiel. Je sens de vagues nostalgies, et je mordrais facilement à n'importe quoi. Et ce qu'il faut avant tout éviter, c'est de faire exprès la course à un idéal artificiel. La musique va plus directement au fond de moi-même et j'en entends assez ces jours-ci (toujours Wagner surtout). Je commence à me reconnaître dans la Tétralogie. Chaque fois le drame s'éclaire et les passages obscurs prennent une signification. Tristan et Y., du premier coup vous émeuvent atrocement, et vous laissent aplati d'extase, avec une soif d'y revenir. Mais je bafouille, tout cela est confus et difficile, et impossible à raconter, nécessairement (sans cela on n'aurait pas éprouvé le besoin de le dire en musique). Tout de même, je serais heureux de savoir que vous entendez du Wagner vous aussi en Amérique, ainsi que du Franck si vous en avez l'occasion. C'est ce qui m'intéresse le plus pour le moment.

Je vois quelquefois Prichard, pour déjeuner dans un restaurant végétarien qui a l'air d'une boutique (c'en est une). On y mange des choses aux noms étranges comme ceux d'une religion inconnue; les initiés commandent sans la moindre gêne 'une protose aux poivrons', un 'nuttolène'. Ces noms de chimie organique répondent à des choses qui simulent la viande sans en être, comme il y a aussi des bouteilles de jus de raisin non fermenté simulant le vin. Je déteste ce genre de choses. Les végétariens sont des êtres dignes de louanges; on voit des habitués, des vieilles filles avant tout, des étudiantes étrangères, des préparateurs de quelque chose dans une faculté, des hyperboréens – ils ont la conscience d'accomplir un rite en mangeant leur lait caillé Bulgare; ce sont des convaincus qui démontrent aux autres qu' 'on peut fort bien se passer de viande'. C'est merveilleux de pouvoir s'emballer pour de semblables choses et cela dénote une grande âme. Ce bon Prichard raconte un peu toujours la même chose; cet homme qui prêche la vie et l'action est un des êtres les plus figés que je sache – parfois il dégage un peu d'ennui. Et cependant j'aime sa sincérité, son sens des verités vitales, sa bonté, quoique parfois appliquée à des choses inutiles (y a-t-il des choses inutiles?). Quand je parle plus d'une heure avec lui, j'ai un mal de tête. Ne trouvez-vous pas qu'il y a toujours une certaine *gêne* à l'écouter? Et puis par moments il expose mal, il embrouille physique et métaphysique (à propos des couleurs). L'absolu de certaines de ses affirmations m'agace un peu – eh! n'avons-nous pas assez déjà de systèmes. Je ne parviens pas à voir ce qu'il y a derrière, ce qui importe. Qu'est-ce que cache son visage anguleux, aux yeux petits mais profonds? Je ne crois pas que nous nous comprenions fort bien l'un l'autre, et notre amitié ne progresse pas. Je vous en reparlerai. (N'attribuez pas grande valeur à tous mes jugements actuels, soyez indulgent pour mon abrutissement en pensant que peut-être il est passager.)

Je suis flémard et déshabitué de tout effort intellectuel. Vingt fois, cher ami, depuis un mois j'ai voulu vous écrire, et n'ai pas la force de le réaliser. Cela devient inquiétant, cette mollesse. J'occupe votre petite chambre de l'an dernier, et j'aime que le lit soit dans un petit renfoncement, mais les dessins du papier (vous en souvient-il?) m'ont bien souvent exaspéré. Zut, je viens d'avoir l'idée de vous envoyer un tout petit bout de ce papier en question – au même instant je m'aperçois que l'idée n'est pas de moi et me vient d'une lettre de J. Laforgue,[1] et je n'en ferai rien. Je ne suis pas sûr d'avoir jamais eu une idée personnelle. Je voudrais n'avoir rien lu, ni rien entendu dire, jamais. Quand retrouverai-je un peu de cette spontanéité, de cette ardeur que j'avais (oh bien mal placée, cher ami, placée dans la science) que j'avais vers mes dix-huit ans? Je ne suis pas fait pour être mélancolique (et puis c'est

1 – 'What can I send you as a souvenir this time?' Laforgue asked his sister Marie in a letter of Sept. 1881. 'From the corner behind the chest of drawers in my room I have cut a piece of wallpaper. Treasure it' (*Oeuvres Complètes de Jules Laforgue* [Paris, 1925], IV, 13).

trop romantique), je ne sais guère agir; et si j'agis, (ô l'action, ô Bergson) je suis assez malin pour qu'un sincère regard vienne bientôt analyser la joie d'agir et la détruire. Il est vrai que mon action s'exerce à des métiers bizarres – si artificiels (comme apprendre de mémoire des descriptions de maladies, comme dessiner en couleurs des organes – ça c'est assez amusant, encore).

Toutes mes ardeurs, aujourd'hui vaines comme un feu d'artifice raté, pourront-elles un jour pleinement s'épanouir? L'espérance me reste encore, mon vieux, douce et grave, voilée encore et peut-être demain souriante . . .

Mon cher ami, nous ne sommes pas très loin, vous et moi, de la limite au dela de laquelle les êtres perdent, l'un l'autre, je ne sais quelle influence, quelle puissance d'émotion naissant à nouveau quand ils sont rapprochés. Ce n'est pas seulement le temps qui peut faire l'oubli – la *distance* (l'espace) y a une part qui est grande. Elle déjà pèse entre nous, sans doute (avouons le franchement) puisque des occupations stupides, et beaucoup de paresse ont tellement raréfié ma correspondance. Cela m'obsédait, (sur un plan peu conscient encore, émergeant parfois) que je ne vous aie pas écrit depuis plusieurs mois. Ceci excuse la longueur de cette lettre et son décousu. Ecrivez-moi de vos nouvelles, avec détails suggestifs, comme vous savez; secouez votre gracieuse nonchalance et donnez-moi un peu de temps volé à vos études – si indigne que j'en sois. Je ne vois pas trop quelle figure vous pouvez faire parmi tous ces Americains (il doit encore en rester là-bas, malgré tous ceux qui sont ici). J'oubliais de vous donner des nouvelles de la boîte – tout est absolument pareil (c'est la 2474me fois ce soir que je vois Madame Casaubon tenir sa serviette entre son menton et sa gorge pendant que ses mains ridées remuent la salade). Il y a votre philosophe Fuller.[1] C'est un homme charmant; bon garçon, aimable, très joyeux camarade avec tout le monde et plein d'anecdotes. J'ai cru longtemps que je ne pourrais rien en tirer mais je me suis trompé: nous faisons ensemble de la gymnastique suédoise tous les matins. En ce moment il est à Rome auprès de sa mère. Louise Rousselot se marie – avec un agrégé.

Cher ami, je vous serre la main.

Jean Verdenal

Je recopie cette phrase d'A. Gide[2] qui me plaît infiniment ces jours-ci:

'*Alternative* – Ou d'aller encore une fois, ô forêt pleine de mystère, jusqu'à ce lieu que je connais où, dans une eau morte et brunie, trempent et s'amollissent encore les feuilles des ans passés, les feuilles des printemps adorables.'

1–B. A. G. Fuller (1879–1956): later Professor of Philosophy at Harvard; author of *A History of Greek Philosophy* (1923).

2–The penultimate sentence of André Gide, *Paludes* (1895).

<Excusez l'écriture – l'orthographe, le style et les ratures – mais j'avais l'habitude de descendre parfois dans votre chambre en vieux veston, sans col et en pantoufles.>[1]

1 – *Translation*: Dear Friend, The drudgery of these last months as a galley-slave has left me feeling very lazy. My examination ended a month ago; I have been given a temporary appointment as houseman, and must begin work again next summer and autumn. Damn. Still, it's a step on the ladder. But to think of being in thrall to the same vacuous complexities as during last summer, and having to suppress all emotion and any glimmer of intelligence, however minute!

Let's forget about it. After the final session, I had to take a few weeks' holiday – blissful provincial rest in a neutral atmosphere of good food and regular walks, and with the sentimental release of family life. I have been in Paris for a fortnight, and am gradually re-establishing contact with life, tentatively, as a tram-driver fits the trolley-pole back on to the power-wire. I am at a loss to know what to hang on to – few friends (my best friend is away), no acquaintances, since I deliberately dropped them all some months ago, no habits with which to fill time intelligently, and the rain is coming down. I fall back upon my books – mistrustfully, however – the expedient is very artificial. I feel vague surges of melancholy and could easily get absorbed in anything. And what must be avoided above all is chasing deliberately after some artificial ideal. Music goes more directly to the core of my being, and I have been listening to it quite a lot recently (still mainly Wagner). I am beginning to get the hang of *The Ring*. Each time the plot becomes clearer and the obscure passages take on a meaning. *Tristan and Isolde* is terribly moving at the first hearing, and leaves you prostrate with ecstasy and thirsting to get back to it again. But I am not making much sense, it is all so confused and difficult, and impossible to put into words, and necessarily so (otherwise, no one would have felt the need to express it in music). However, I should be happy to know that you too are able to hear some Wagner in America, and something by Franck as well, if you get the opportunity. This is what I am most interested in at the moment.

I see Prichard occasionally for lunch in a vegetarian restaurant which looks like a shop (it is one). The dishes have strange names, like those of some unknown religion; initiates think nothing at all of ordering 'a *protose* of peppers', a 'nuttolène' [a type of vegetarian loaf]. These names, smacking of organic chemistry, correspond to substances which pretend to be meat without being so, just as there are bottles of unfermented grape-juice pretending to be wine. I hate this sort of thing. Vegetarians are praiseworthy people; there are *habitués* among them, elderly spinsters especially, foreign women-students, technicians from some university laboratory or other, and Hyperboreans – they are conscious of performing a rite as they consume their Bulgarian curds; they are convinced people, demonstrating to others that 'it is quite easy to do without meat'. It is wonderful to be able to enthuse about such things, and a sign of greatness of soul. The worthy Prichard's conversation is still more or less the same; although he preaches in favour of life and action, he is one of the most hidebound individuals I know – sometimes he can be ever so slightly boring. Yet I like his sincerity, his instinct for vital truths, and his goodness, although it is sometimes directed towards useless matters (are there useless matters?). If I talk with him for more than an hour, I am left with a headache. Don't you find listening to him always rather a *strain*? And then, at times, he expounds his ideas badly, mixing up physics and metaphysics (in connection with colours). The absolute nature of some of his assertions irritates me a little – well, haven't we enough systems already? I cannot see what lies behind them, what is important. His bony face, with its small, deep-set eyes hides what, exactly? I don't think we understand each other very well and our friendship is not progressing. I will tell you about it some other time. (Don't attach any great value to my present judgements; excuse my stupefied state with the thought that it is perhaps only temporary.)

FROM *Jean Verdenal* MS Houghton

Lundi 22 Avril 1912 [Paris]

Mon cher ami,

Une vivace ardeur de soleil de printemps m'a poussé aujourd'hui à sortir dans les bois. Le petit bateau m'a doucement conduit à Saint Cloud entre

—

I am feeling work-shy and have lost the habit of intellectual effort. Twenty times, my dear fellow, during the last month I have felt like writing to you, and haven't had the strength to do so. This listlessness is becoming rather worrying. I now occupy the little room that was yours last year, and I like having the bed in a little recess, but the pattern of the wallpaper (do you remember it?) often gets on my nerves. Damn. It occurred to me a moment ago to send you a little piece of wallpaper – then I immediately realised that the idea was not mine but that I had got it from a letter by J. Laforgue, so I will abstain. I am not sure of ever having had an idea that really belonged to me. I wish I had never read or heard anything, ever. When shall I recover a little of the spontaneity and enthusiasm that I had (oh, it was quite wrongly invested, dear friend, invested in science) that I had around the age of eighteen? I was not made to be a melancholic (anyway, melancholy is too romantic), and I have little gift for action; and if I act (O action, O Bergson), I am bright enough to take a sincere look at the joy of action and destroy it by analysis. It is true that action, in my case, is applied to bizarre, highly artificial practices (such as learning descriptions of diseases by heart or making coloured drawings of organs – the latter, actually, is quite amusing).

Will my enthusiasms, now as inoperative as damp squibs, ever be able to flower fully? The hope still remains with me, my dear fellow, a sweet and serious hope, as yet veiled but tomorrow, perhaps, wreathed in smiles . . .

My dear friend, we are not very far, you and I, from the point beyond which people lose that indefinable influence and emotive power over each other, which is reborn when they come together again. It is not only time which causes forgetfulness – distance (space) is an important factor. It is already, no doubt, making itself felt between us (let us admit this frankly), since my stupid occupations and considerable laziness have made my letters few and far between. I was bothered by the thought (sometimes only half-conscious, at other times fully so) that I had not written to you for several months. That is the excuse for the length of this letter and its disjointedness. Send me news of yourself, with evocative details, as you know how; shake off your elegant indolence and grant me a little time filched from your studies, however unworthy of it I may be. I cannot quite imagine what sort of figure you cut among all those Americans (there must still be some left in America, despite the number here). I had almost forgotten to give you news of the *pension* – everything is just the same (this evening, for the 2474th time, I shall see Madame Casaubon hold her napkin between her chin and her chest as her wrinkled hands mix the salad). Your philosopher, Fuller, is still here. He is a charming man; decent, likeable, hail-fellow-well-met with everyone, and full of stories. For a long time, I thought I would be able to make nothing of him, but I was wrong; we do Swedish exercises together every morning. At the moment, he is in Rome with his mother. Louise Rousselot is getting married – to an *agrégé*.

Dear friend, I shake your hand. Jean Verdenal

I am copying out here a sentence by André Gide, which has given me enormous pleasure during the last few days: 'The Alternative: – Or to go once more, O forest filled with mystery, to that place I know, where, in darkened, stagnant water, the leaves of bygone years are still steeping and softening – the leaves of adorable springtimes.'

Excuse the handwriting – the spelling, the style and the crossings out – but I was in the habit of sometimes coming down to your room in an old jacket, collarless and in slippers.

les claires et vertes rangées de jeunes feuilles tendres inondées de lumière. Là-bas la poussée printanière était moins éclatante, cristallisée dans les lignes artificielles des grandes allées; décor délicat, presque irréel et, dirais-je, féerique, si ce mot n'avait pas été employé à tort et à travers et déformé.

Alors, ce soir en rentrant j'ai pensé à vous écrire, parce que *vous* me fûtes particulièrement évoqué par le contact de ce paysage senti ensemble.* Excusez mon affreux papier, je n'ai que cela sous la main.

* *Note.* Le paysage n'a cependant que peu evoqué le bon Prichard et votre grand ami Child.[1]

Aucun événement special ne m'est arrivé depuis l'an dernier, et peut-être cependant le temps n'a pas été perdu. Je n'ai pas appris grand'chose, ni fait de nouvelles connaissances en Art. Mais j'ai pris conscience de la force de quelques-uns de mes élans; <J'écris en largeur, c'est moins gênant> je commence à avoir moins peur de la vie et à voir les vérités moins artificiellement. Je répète souvent les mêmes phrases qu'autrefois mais leur trouve un sens plus intense, plus cuisant. Je m'exprime très mal parce que cela n'est encore pas bien défini. Je suis comme si j'avais toujours vécu à l'aube et comme si bientot le soleil allait paraître. La lumière de mon monde intérieur change: des faces encore obscures s'éclairent (brilleront-elles jamais?). Je me sens plus jeune et plus mûr à la fois; j'étouffe dans le nonchalant découragement où j'ai vécu. Voici sans doute le prélude de quelque nouvelle course après l'absolu, et comme les autres fois on se laissera tromper.

Je suis assez intéressé par tout cela. Il est très net que l' 'idéal' est un *élan intérieur* et non une attraction du dehors puisqu'on peut être passionné sans objet. (Seulement nous n'en avons bien conscience que quand il rencontre quelque chose à quoi s'appliquer, tel un rayon de lumière quand il frappe un pan de mur.) Or les hommes tant qu'ils vivront en seront animés (puisque qu'il est inhérent à l'élan de la vie) et l'atteinte d'un but ne pourra l'assouvir puisqu'il préexiste à ce but. C'est ce qui

1) Nous fait croire à une finalité à la vie

2) Fait que cette finalité est inconnaissable.

Et nous avançons, nous avançons toujours.

Excusez mon bavardage, si ça vous embête, sautez par dessus et pardonnez-moi d'écrire au courant de la plume des idées qu'il faudrait vraiment au moins essayer de présenter avec plus de clarté. Ce n'est pas facile de se faire comprendre, et puis d'ailleurs ce n'est pas mon métier.

1 – Harrison Bird Child (1889–1944), later an American Episcopal priest, had been with TSE at Milton Academy and at Harvard (Class of 1911).

A propos, le cubisme est détruit par le futurisme qui proteste contre les musées, etc. et a fait une grande exposition chez Bernheim.[1] Voici des exemplaires de la nouvelle école, à moins qu'une autre encore n'apparaisse pendant que ma lettre traverse la mer. On est offusqué à notre époque par le manque de modestie des gens de lettres et des artistes qui créent des écoles nouvelles tous les six mois, et par leur faiblesse de se mettre à plusieurs pour lutter. Ce mélange de violence et de manque de force n'indique rien qui vaille et nous souffrons de ce que l'art ne soit pas au niveau de notre sensibilité.

Au revoir, mon vieux, écrivez-moi quand cela vous passera par la tête. J'espère que vous faites de belles choses là-bas, et que germent des fleurs radieuses.

Jean Verdenal[2]

1 – One of the first Futurist exhibitions outside Italy was held at the Bernheim-Jeune Gallery in Paris in Feb. 1912. The term 'Cubism', first used by Louis Vauxcelles in 1908, was applied to the work of Picasso and Braques, and by 1911 there were frequent references to a 'Cubist school' of painters.

2 – *Translation*: My dear friend, A persistent blaze of spring sunshine prompted me to go out into the woods today. The little boat carried me gently to Saint Cloud between translucent green rows of tender young leaves drenched in light. At Saint Cloud, the explosion of spring was less conspicuous, being crystallised into the artificial lines of the great avenues; it was a delicate, unreal scene, even fairy-like, I would say, if that word had not been too much bandied about and distorted.

So, this evening, when I got back, I thought of writing to you, because *you* were especially called to mind by the contact with a landscape we appreciated together.*

* *NB*. However, the landscape only faintly recalled the worthy Prichard and your great friend Child.

Nothing special has happened to me since last year, and yet the time has not, perhaps, been wasted. I haven't learned much or acquired any new knowledge of Art. But I have come to realise the strength of some of my aspirations; <I am writing straight across the sheet – it's less awkward> I am beginning to be less afraid of life and to see truths less artificially. I often repeat the same sentences as in the past, but their meaning now strikes me as being more intense, more excruciating. I am expressing myself very badly, because all this is not yet very clear in my mind. It is as if I had always lived before daybreak and the sun were just about to rise. The light in my inner world is changing: surfaces still dark are beginning to gleam (will they ever shine brightly?). I feel both younger and more mature; I am stifled by the listless discouragement in which I have been living. This is no doubt the prelude to some new pursuit of the absolute and, as on previous occasions, I shall be taken in.

I am quite interested by all this. It is very obvious that the 'ideal' is an *inner impulse* and not an attraction from outside, since it is possible to be passionate without an object. (However, we are only fully aware of the ideal when it encounters something to which it can apply itself, like a ray of light striking a patch of wall.) But men, as long as they exist, will be inspired by it (since it is inherent in the impulse of life itself) and it cannot be appeased by the achievement of any goal, since it existed before the goal. It is this which

1) Leads us to believe that life has a purpose

2) Makes that purpose unknowable.

And so we go forward, always further forward.

FROM *Jean Verdenal* MS Houghton

Le 26 Août 1912 [Paris]

Mon cher ami,

Depuis un mois rentré de vacances volontairement sportives et hygiéniques, 'bien douché, bien musclé', je mène la vie la plus occupée du monde dans un bel entraînement pour concours. Grande mobilisation de tout le peu de médecine que je sais, revue en grand de toutes les questions, astiquage: ce sont les préparatifs au combat; les jours passent dans ce bel entrain.

Et ce soir voici que, sonnant dix heures (toutes les cloches du quartier sonnent et presque en même temps une grêle assez loin bientôt écrasée par les coups plus espacés d'une cloche plus grave, vous en souvient-il?) voici que tout à coup je pense à vous pendant que sonnent dix heures. Et votre image est là devant moi, alors je vous écris ce petit mot. Puis vite, vite – bonsoir . . . là – je reviens au travail.

Jean Verdenal.

PS Ecrivez-moi quand vous pourrez, cela me fera plaisir. Hôtel-Dieu, place du Parvis, Notre-Dame.[1]

Excuse this blather; if it bores you, skip it and forgive me for putting down, just as they occur, ideas that I really ought to try at least to explain more clearly. It is not easy to make oneself understood, and besides it is not my line of business.

Incidentally, Cubism has been destroyed by Futurism, which protests against museums, etc. and has a big exhibition at Bernheim's. Such are the manifestations of the new school, unless yet another springs up while my letter is crossing the sea. One is shocked these days by the lack of modesty on the part of writers and artists who create new schools every six months, and by the weakness which makes them band together to fight. The mixture of violence and lack of strength is not a good omen and we suffer from the fact that art is not on a par with our sensibilities.

Goodbye, my dear fellow, write to me whenever the thought occurs to you. I hope you are doing splendid things in America, and that radiant blooms are germinating. Jean Verdenal.

1 – *Translation*: My dear friend, Back a month ago from an intentionally athletic and health-giving holiday, 'well-showered and with muscles in trim', I am now leading the busiest possible life to get myself perfectly in shape for the examination. Full mobilisation of every scrap of my meagre medical knowledge, general review of all questions, polishing up of details: such is the preparation for the battle to come; the days fly past as I labour away.

And then this evening, on the stroke of ten (all the bells in the area are ringing and, almost at the same time, comes a tinkling of fairly distant chimes, soon blotted out by the measured pealing of a deeper bell, do you remember?) suddenly I think of you as ten o'clock is striking. And your image is there in front of me, and so I am writing you this little note. But now, a hurried, very hurried good night . . . because I must get back to work. Jean Verdenal

PS Write to me when you can, I shall be pleased to hear from you. Hôtel-Dieu, place du Parvis, Notre Dame.

FROM *Jean Verdenal* PC Houghton

[Postmark 7 September 1912] Aubonne

Ca va mon vieux – Je voudrais tellement que [tu] serais avec moi. Aff Jean.[1]

FROM *Jean Verdenal* MS Houghton

Le 26 Décembre 1912 [Paris]

Mon cher ami,

J'arrive à la fin de cet ennuyeux concourse, la tête assez semblable à un grand magasin détenant tout ce qu'on veut pour bluffer le public. Dans un mois, j'espère avoir réussi et ne plus rien garder de l'encombrant étalage. Comme tout métier, la médecine ne retient que les connaissances qu'elle utilise. Il n'y faut rien chercher que de pratique. J'aurai ce métier. Par moments, cela m'irrite d'y être astreint; un certain orgueil intellectuel nous a déprécié la valeur d'avoir un métier. Et puis on a la peur d'y avoir perdu un temps réclamé par de plus graves problèmes. Prenons-le autrement: je tâcherai qu'il soit l'occupation appliquée, méticuleuse, la discipline nécessaire à ne point m'énerver ailleurs. Puisse cependant ma pensée progresser libre et mon coeur répondre aux appels de la vie . . .

Je me propose un plan régulier de culture philosophique et littéraire. Excusez mon ambition, mais je hais les amateurs. On en fourmille, car le public aime le clinquant; mais est-il étalage plus odieux que celui d'objets sacrés? Ne dédaignons pas la méthode. Je vous vois avec plaisir appliqué à des études sérieuses; votre goût délicat et votre clairvoyance y auront plus bel emploi qu'à des futilités. Je vous souhaite pour cetre année une ardeur souvent renouvelée – ardeur, flamme – mais c'est au coeur qu'en est la source et voici où nos voeux doivent être prudents. 'Amène sur moi les biens, ô Dieu, que je te les demande ou non, et écarte les maux quand même je te les demanderai.'

Au revoir, mon cher ami, et bien à vous.

J. Verdenal.

PS J'ai revu le bon Prichard qui m'a dit force opinions ridicules sur maintes oeuvres d'art, et répété des théories dont il ne sort guère. Il n'a pas, je crois, assez d'études philosophiques et scientifiques pour échapper aux charlatans.[2]

1 – *Translation*: How are you my friend – I wish so much that you could be with me. Affectionately, Jean.

2 – *Translation*: My dear friend, I am coming to the end of this boring examination, and my head is rather like a department store stocked with anything and everything to hoodwink the public. A month from now, I hope I shall have passed and can dispense with the

—

burdensome display. The medical profession, like any other, is only interested in knowledge it can make use of. No good looking to it for anything other than the practical. It is to be my profession. At times, I feel exasperated at being obliged to submit to it; a sort of intellectual pride causes us to underrate the value of having a profession. Also, there is the fear of having wasted time needed for more serious problems. But let us take a different view: I shall endeavour to make it into a conscientious, meticulous occupation and the discipline necessary to prevent me wasting nervous energy in other directions. I hope, however, that my thought will continue to develop freely and that my heart will respond to the calls of life . . .

I propose to give myself an organised scheme of literary and philosophical study. Forgive my ambition, but I detest amateurs. There is no lack of them, since the public is fond of the flashy; but what more disgusting display could there be than that of sacred objects. Let us not despise methodicalness. I see with pleasure that you are engaged in serious study; your delicate taste and perspicacity will be put to better use than in dealing with futile matters. I wish you, for the coming year, an oft-renewed ardour – ardour, flame – but its source is in the heart, and here it is that our wishes must be prudent. 'Bring good upon me, O Lord, whether I ask for it or not, and remove evil from me, even though I ask for it.'

Goodbye, my dear friend, and all best wishes. J. Verdenal.

PS I have seen the worthy Prichard again; he delivered himself of a mass of ridiculous opinions about a host of works of art, and repeated theories from which he more or less refuses to budge. He hasn't, I think, a sufficient grounding in philosophy and science to avoid being taken in by charlatans.

1913–1914

TO *Eleanor Hinkley* PC[1] Houghton

[Postmark 29 June 1913] Portland, Maine

This is sure one warm place. Am having photo snapped: if real good will send you one.

Yours etc
TSE

PS Going to have fortune told. If real nice will let you in on it.

TO *W. E. Hocking*[2] MS Houghton

10 October 1913 16 Ash St, Cambridge,
Massachusetts

My dear Professor Hocking

I am writing to you as a representative of the Harvard Philosophical Club. We are anxious to secure a speaker for our first open meeting of the year, which will take place on Friday evening the thirty-first of October. Would it be possible for you to come up to Cambridge and address us on that night? We feel that it would be very much to the interest of the club and the pleasure of the public if you could accept. As you are an old member of the club yourself I have no need to describe the sort of occasion that our public meetings are; I can only assure you of our appreciation in the case of your acceptance. The club, of course, defrays the expenses of speakers whom it invites from a distance. And if you cannot accept for this date, could you suggest some other time, either in November or December, or later in the year, when it might be possible for you to come?[3]

Very truly yours
Thomas S. Eliot
(President)

1–Entitled 'Quitcherkidin', the postcard shows a woman tickling a man with a long feather.
2–William E. Hocking (1873–1966), idealist follower of Josiah Royce; Professor of Philosophy at Yale, 1908–14; Harvard, 1914–43. Author of *The Meaning of God in Human Experience* (1912).
3–Hocking spoke on Bergson's Philosophy of Art, 5 Dec.

Stunt Show

Monday, February seventeen, at eight o'clock

"From ignorance our comfort flows."
— *Prior*

Songs	(a) "Ecstasy"	*Mrs. H. H. Beach*
	(b) "Julia's Garden"	*J. H. Rogers*
	(c) "Serenata"	*Tosti*

MISS EMILY HALE

"An Evening at the Bayham Badgers'" — *Dickens*

Mrs. Bayham Badger	MISS EVELYN BOLLES
Mr. Bayham Badger	MR. C. W. PUTNAM
Mr. Jarndyce	MR. G. H. HULL
Butler	MR. JOHN REMEY

"Rosamond and her Mother," (1813) — *Miss Edgeworth*

Rosamond	MISS ELIZABETH ALLEN
Her Mother	MISS ELEANOR HINKLEY

A Débutante Monologue, (1913)
"We're only asking Buds" — *Anon*

Débutante	MISS KATHARINE MUNRO

Intermission —— Auction

Songs	(a) "Mavourneen"	*Margaret Lang*
	(b) Old Air	
	(c) "May Morning"	*Denza*

MISS EMILY HALE

"Monsieur Marcel and his latest Marvel" — *E. Hinkley*

M. Marcel	MR. THOMAS. ELIOT
The Marvel	MISS AMY GOZZALDI
Assistant	MR. H. R. BOWSER

"Arnold Bennett choosing a Heroine" — *E. Hinkley*

The Actress	MISS LILIAN SMITH
The Sunday School Teacher	MISS MARION ELIOT
The Governess	MISS SARAH EVARTS
Arnold Bennet	MR. PHILIP ADAMS

"An Afternoon with Mr. Woodhouse" — *Jane Austen*

Mrs. Elton	MISS EMILY HALE
Emma	MISS E. HINKLEY
Mr. Woodhouse	MR. THOMAS ELIOT
Mr. Knightly	MR. TRACY PUTNAM
Butler	MR. JOHN REMEY

The Scenes from Miss Edgeworth, Jane Austen and Dickens, arranged by
MISS HINKLEY

Prompter, MISS ANNA GRISWOLD *Usher,* MISS PENELOPE NOYES
Artist and Property Manager, MRS. SOHIER WELCH

This was TSE's first dramatic appearance, in 1913, at one of the private theatricals given in the house of his aunt, Mrs Holmes Hinkley, for the benefit of The Cambridge Visiting Housekeeper, a scheme organised by Mrs Hinkley to train unskilled girls for domestic service. Eleanor Hinkley recorded that 'the scenes were laid in the parlor fireplace in a space no bigger than seven square feet, so that the actors could be seen by the audience in the next room, through a doorway that was four feet eight'. The guests consisted of relatives, friends of the cast, and neighbours.

TO *Professor W. E. Hocking* MS Houghton

7 December [1913] 16 Ash St

My dear Professor Hocking

I am writing just to remind you to send a note of your expenses either to me or to our treasurer, Mr A. A. Roback, 51 Mt. Auburn Street, whenever it is convenient to you.

I hope that you feel justified for the time and fatigue of coming up to address us – if you could have talked (as I did) with a number of the members afterwards you would realise our gratitude!

Sincerely yours
Thomas S. Eliot

FROM *Henry Ware Eliot* TO *Thomas Lamb Eliot*

MS Reed College

7 March 1914 [St Louis]

Dear Bob,

You must and I have written to Tom D.[1] It probably is a good thing to mix foreign blood with our effete New England people. Especially if it means brawn. It will prevent petering out.

I can't get up sympathy with Sex Hygiene. It is a questionable fad.

I do not approve of public instruction in Sexual relations. When I teach my children to avoid the Devil I don't begin by giving them a letter of introduction to him and his crowd. I hope that a cure for Syphilis will never be discovered. It is God's punishment for nastiness. Take it away and there will be more nastiness, and it will be necessary to emasculate our children to keep them clean.

So there!

Yr
H

1 – Unidentified, but probably Thomas Dawes Eliot.

FROM *His Father* MS Houghton

11 April 1914 [St Louis]

My dear Tom:

I am much pleased that you have rec[eive]d the Scholarship,[1] on ac[coun]t of the honor, as you couldn't get it unless you deserved it. You have never been a 'burden' to me, my dear fellow. A parent is always in debt to a son who has been as dutiful and affectionate as you have been.

Yrs.
P.

TO *The Secretary of the Bureau of Information, University of Marburg* MS Bundesarchiv[2]

15 June 1914 [London]

Dear Sir,

I have received the announcement of your summer courses, and should like to ask a few questions, if I may impose upon your courtesy.

1) Do the July and August courses cover the same ground, or is the latter more advanced?

2) As it is impossible for me to reach Marburg till the 10th or 11th of July, could I still join the July course?

3) Is it possible for a foreigner to attend lectures without attending every series?

If the two courses (July and August) cover the same ground, I will subscribe to the August course, though I shall be in Marburg in July.

Perhaps these questions are answered in your pamphlet, but you will forgive a foreigner his uncertainty. Would you be so good as to reply (in either English or German – I read the latter readily enough) to me care of the British Linen Bank, Threadneedle St, *London*, *England*.

Very sincerely yours
T. S. Eliot
(Sheldon travelling fellow, Harvard University).

1–On 31 Mar., the President and Fellows of Harvard University had appointed TSE a Sheldon Fellow in Philosophy for the academic year 1914–15. He planned to use this travelling award, worth $1000, at Merton College, Oxford, after attending a summer school in Marburg.

2–Eventually returned after being taken to the USA in German Captured Documents, container 189.

TO *Eleanor Hinkley* TS Houghton

[Postmark London 7 July 1914] [Crossing the Atlantic]

Dear Friend:

I thought that I would while away a weary hour by culling for you a few of the fruits of my excursion upon Neptune's empire. Free from the cares and irks of city life, indifferent to my whilom duties, I sit in my snug little cabin lazily watching the little clouds slip across the sky and the trunks slide across the floor. From my tiny round window I can see a flock of lovely birds dip and skim athwart the zenith (sparrows I believe – I am not much on ornithology). There are not a few interesting people among our company; many from the West. Some seventy, inspired by devotion to Art, join together in a University Tour (pronounced Tewer). There are about the same number of men and girls – 98 girls and 18 men,[1] so that we have great fun, especially when it comes to dancing to the sound of the captain's phonograph. There are diversions aplenty: shuffleboard, ringtoss, bridge, checkers, and limericks. Wednesday last we held a field day. Twould have given you keen delight to have seen me in the Pillow Fight, astride a pole, a pillow in each hand. The master of ceremonies was a real charming man, he introduced me as the champion of Russia. Some of his remarks were real witty and bright, for instance: 'We have here Mr Williams and Miss Williams in the driving contest. Mr Williams and Miss Williams are not related **yet**'. I was also entered in the Thread the Needle contest, with my partner, Miss Mildred Levi Of Newton, the belle of the boat. Then last night we held a concert, for somebody's benefit. Miss Mazie Smith sang us 'Good bye Summer good bye good bye'.[2]

Collected from various sources:

Well I never should have said you came from St Louis . . . Is Harvard going to be your college . . . How did you enjoy your visit to America? . . . Well I thought you were an Englishman . . . When I look at the water, heven, it 'eaves my stomach 'orrible . . . My but you do have *grand* thoughts! . . . why arn't **you** dancing? . . . Very pleased to meet you . . . My name's Calkins, Michigan 1914 . . . Aw I wish I'd known what was good for me and staid in Detroit Michigan, it's a long swim to the Irish coast . . . If I ever get to Liverpool I'm going to join the church . . . Ah no sir they don't make no trouble for me, they just lays where I put 'em and

1 – The figures are reproduced as TSE typed them.

2 – The refrain of a popular Edwardian ballad, 'To Angela . . . Goodbye', with words by G. J. Whyte-Melville (1821–78) and music by Paolo Tosti (1846–1916).

honly wants to be left quiet . . . Try the tripe and onions, its just lovely . . . Yes this genlmn knows I'm speakin gospel truth (pointing at me) he's connected with the buildin trades hisself, he knows how business is now, its Wilson and Bryan's[1] made all the trouble . . . &, &, &.

This is not a real letter, as I am not writing letters till I reach Marburg. Your letters baffled me completely, with the exception of the first, which I guessed at once. You would be amused at some of my attributions. Regards to the bunch in the little old burg.

[unsigned]

TO *Conrad Aiken*[2]

MS Huntington

19 July 1914

care Herr Superintendent Happich,
Luth. Kirchhof 1.
Marburg, a./d. Lahn, Germany

BLESS[3]

COLUMBO

BOLO BLUBUNG CUDJO

THE CHAPLAIN BRUTUS SQUIRTY PANSY

BLAST

THE BOSUN COUSIN HUGH THE COOK

PROF. DR. KRAPP

My dear Conrad

If you are in London, I am going to ask a serious favour of you. I should like <you!> to go to Murray's Agency, 23 Regent Street, and reclaim (by means of the authorisation which I enclose) the valise which I have left there, having previously found out, from the American Express Co. whether you can send it to me in Marburg. There is a blue suit in it, and as I am perhaps going to live with a Lutheran Herr Pfarrer, I want to be able to look *herrlich* [splendid] on Sundays. If you can send it, I will refund

1–President Woodrow Wilson (1856–1924) and his Secretary of State, W. J. Bryan (1860–1925).

2–Conrad Aiken, poet, novelist and critic: see Glossary of Names.

3–TSE was imitating WL's magazine *Blast* 1, which had appeared in June, and included a series of Blessings and Curses. Several of the characters here recur in TSE's Bolo poems. Aiken's memoir of TSE at Harvard and afterwards offers an account of the 'hilariously naughty *parerga*' about Bolo, Columbo and others: 'these admirable stanzas . . . were to continue for years as a sort of cynical counterpoint to the study of Sanskrit and the treatise on epistemology'.

you a money order at once. I think that the Am. Ex. told me it would cost about 6s. 6d. to send it. <The *card* in the leather holder ought perhaps to be redirected.> It is insured for storage in Murray's, but I don't know whether that insurance would cover a trip, and I should like to insure it between sending and receiving. It would be sent I suppose to the railroad station or the post office, <if possible?> as I don't know just when I shall leave this hôtel or just what my address will be. <Address: *care* Herr Superintendent Happich, Luth. Kirchhof 1.>

Marburg is charming, and I will write you more about it later, when I have seen more of the people. It seems a wonderfully civilised little place for its size: as you can get Abdulla's cigarettes and several kinds of tooth powder; and being all on the side of a steep hill, is very compact. The houses have beautiful unkempt gardens, with great waves – 'where tides of grass break into foam of flowers'![1] – of roses, in terraces looking out over the hills. Just now the Student *verbindungen* [societies] are very evident, as they are holding *fests* [celebrations] and parades, and their colours decorate all the houses; in a couple of weeks they will be gone. I think that this will be a very pleasant exile on the whole, – though I cannot look upon a summer in Germany as anything but an exile.

I called upon a Herr Professor this afternoon this is a very clear likeness of him – but he is a very good sort, and his wife is charming, though they neither have any conversation; and I was very much rattled, and wiped the sweat from my face as I stuttered every mistake in the language.

Belgium was a fatiguing trip in the hot weather. Bruges is charming if you like that sort of thing – very 'picturesque' – *malerisch*, but has a sort of post-putridity about it, the sort which infects small old towns and old things generally – Italy stinks the same way, except up in the lakes. The chimes are damnable – my hotel was opposite them, couldn't sleep – in

1–A. C. Swinburne, 'Laus Veneris', l. 55.

Ghent I was round the corner from them – in Antwerp I could lie in bed and look at them – in Brussels, which is a large modern town, very likeable and no sights to see – I slept. Flanders on the whole I don't care for; it is neither French nor German, and seems to combine some of the defects of both. Still, it is unique, and the paintings are *stunning*! only one (great) one in Ghent,[1] but *treasures* in Bruges and Antwerp and Brussels: Memling, van Eyck, Mastys, David, Breughel, Rubens – really great stuff. And I'm not in close sympathy with Flemish art either. <And O a wonderful *Crucifixion* of Antonello of Messina. There are *three* great *St Sebastians* (so far as I know):

1) Mantegna (Ca d'Oro)
2) Antonello of Messina (Bergamo)
3) Memling (Brussels)>[2]

I have written some *stuff* – about fifty lines, but I find it shamefully laboured, and am belabouring it more. If I can improve it at all I will send it you. If you write me Poste Restante I shall get it; and if you are in the country (or just off for the country) you must of course leave my luggage out of consideration. It is *not* essential to me. If you are not in the country or going to the country you might wait a few days, and I will send you an address. Meanwhile I will send you this to go to sleep on:

Now while Columbo and his men
Were drinking ice cream soda
In burst King Bolo's big black queen
That famous old breech l(oader).
Just then they rang the bell for lunch
And served up – Fried Hyenas;
And Columbo said 'Will you take tail?
Or just a bit of p(enis)?'

The bracketed portions we owe to the restorations of the editor, Prof. Dr Hasenpfeffer (Halle), with the assistance of his two inseparable friends, Dr Hans Frigger (the celebrated poet) and Herr Schnitzel (aus Wien). How much we owe to the hardwon intuition of this truly great scholar! The editor also justly observes: 'There seems to be a *double entendre* about the

1 – *The Adoration of the Mystic Lamb*, a polyptich by the van Eyck brothers, is the altarpiece of St Bavo's Cathedral.

2 – Andrea Mantegna (*c.*1431–1506) painted three versions of St Sebastian, the last of which is in the Ca d'Oro in Venice. A ribbon curling from a candle in its bottom right-hand corner bears the motto '*nihil nisi divinum stabile est; caetera fumus*' ('nothing is permanent unless divine; the rest is smoke'), quoted in the epigraph to TSE's poem 'Burbank with a Baedeker: Bleistein with a Cigar'. The St Sebastian in Bergamo is by Raphael (Antonello da Messina's is in the Staatliche Gemäldegalerie, Dresden); and Hans Memling's St Sebastian is in the Musée des Beaux-Arts, Brussels.

last two lines, but the fine flavour of the jest has not survived the centuries'. – Yet we hope that such genius as his may penetrate even this enigma. Was it really the custom to drink ice-cream soda just before lunch? Prof. Dr Hasenpfeffer insists that it was. Prof. Dr Krapp (Jena) believes that the phrase is euphemistic, and that they were really drinking SEIDLIDZ POWDER. See Krapp: STREITSCHRIFT GEGEN HASENPFEFFER.[1] I.xvii §367, also Hasenpfeffer: POLEMISCHES GEGEN KRAPP[2] I–II. 368ff. 490ff.

By the way, I find that I have only one (torn) pair of pajamas, and my dictionary does not give the word for them. *Que faire?* The dictionary, however, gives the German equivalent for *gracilent* and *pudibund. You* might do something with that, but I lack inspiration.[3] I really feel very constipated intellectually. Some people say that pain is necessary ('they learn in suffering' *etc*),[4] perhaps others that happiness is. Both beside the point, I think: what is necessary is a *certain kind* (could one but catch it!) of *tranquillity*, and *sometimes* pain does ~~buy~~ bring it. A kind of tranquillity which Dostoievsky ~~*must*~~ must <on second thoughts I delete the line> have known when he was writing his masterpieces at top-speed to keep from starving. But I have come to fancy that a perfectly commonplace happiness (such as I now find so attractive!) would be a great stimulus. For when you have all those little things you cease to fret about them, and have room for a sort of divine dissatisfaction and *goût* [taste] for the tragic which is quite harmless, *d'ailleurs* [moreover], and compatible with a bank account. I think perhaps that only the happy can appreciate the tragic, or that the tragic only exists for the happy. Anyhow, I have become a great friend of the *petites gens de l'histoire*,[5] materialist, even 'householder'. *Das ewig weibliche.*[6] –

Bien affectueusement
Tom.

1 – 'Disputation contra Hasenpfeffer'.

2 – 'Polemics contra Krapp'.

3 – 'Pudibund, in the clinging vine' ('Exequy', *TWL: Facs*, 102–3).

4 – 'He said: "Most wretched men / Are cradled into poetry by wrong, / They learn in suffering what they teach in song"' (P. B. Shelley, *Julian and Maddalo*, ll. 544–6).

5 – 'The humble people of history'.

6 – 'The Eternal Feminine' (Goethe, *Faust*, l. 12,110).

Be sure to let this matter alone if at all inconvenient, for I think that the agency will perhaps forward it themselves. If you did go there you could let them do it.

TO *Conrad Aiken* MS Huntington

25 July 1914 c/o Herr Supdt. Happich,
Luth. Kirchhof 1, Marburg a. Lahn

Dear Conrad,

I've written to Murray, who will forward the bag, so don't concern yourself. I hope you are happily stowed away in the country by this time. I find myself very well fixed here *chez* the Herr Pfarrer, his wife, and his daughter Hannah. The people are extremely kind, the quarters comfortable, the view from my windows (south) excellent – over roofs and hills – the house is on the side of the hill, and the hill is steep – the food is excellent – I find that I like German food! I like German people! and we have five meals a day. I stuff myself; the Frau Pfarrer thinks I don't eat enough. Then I swim (there are baths) or walk (there are beautiful walks among the woods) but not far, because I must always be back in time for the next meal.

I enclose some *stuff* – the *thing* I showed you some time ago, and some of the themes for the 'Descent from the Cross' or whatever I may call it.[1] I send them, even in their present form, because I am disappointed in them, and wonder whether I had better knock it off for a while – you will tell me what you think. Do you think that the *Love Song of St Sebastian* part is morbid, or forced? Then there will be an Insane Section, and another love song (of a happier sort) and a recurring piece quite in the French style beginning

'The married girl who lives across the street
Wraps her soul in orange-coloured robes of Chopinese.' –

Then a mystical section, – and a Fool-House section beginning

'Let us go to the masquerade and dance!
I am going as St John among the Rocks
Attired in my underwear and socks . . .'

1–Aiken later sold the poems enclosed in this letter. They were eventually printed in *IMH* from the drafts that TSE sent with those of *The Waste Land* to John Quinn in 1922. *The Descent from the Cross* (which appears to be the provisional title for the collection of poems he was writing at this time, including 'The Love Song of St Sebastian') refers to the central panel in Rubens's great triptych in Antwerp Cathedral, which TSE had recently seen.

Does it all seem very laboured and conscious? The S. Sebastian title I feel almost sure of; I have studied S. Sebastians – why should anyone paint a beautiful youth and stick him full of pins (or arrows) unless he felt a little as the hero of my verse? Only there's nothing homosexual about this – rather an important difference perhaps – but no one ever painted a female Sebastian, did they?[1] So I give this title *faute de mieux*.

Send me some verse, please. I am working up my Greek, mornings, and read *Logische Untersuchunger*[2] evenings. We rejoice that the war danger is over.

Affy.
T. S. E.

[ORIGINAL ENCLOSURES][3]

Oh little voices of the throats of men That come between the singer and the song Oh twisted little hands of men held up To rend the beautiful and curse the strong. Impatient tireless undirected feet! On what remote frontier of heaven and hell Shall time allow our divers ways to meet? Yet you do well to run the ways you run Yes you do well to keep the ways you keep And we who seek to measure joy and pain We blow against the wind and spit against the rain For what could be more real than sweat and dust and sun And what more sure than night and death and sleep?	} **Introduction. To be amplified at the end also.**

1–The OED's first record of the term 'homosexual' is in a translation of Richard von Krafft-Ebing's *Psychopathia Sexualis* (1892). This is followed by a quotation from Havelock Ellis (1897), and a reference by Bernard Shaw to 'The forty tolerated homosexual brothels of Berlin' (*NS* 21/22 Nov. 1914). St Sebastian became something of a homosexual icon in the late nineteenth century, as in Frederick Rolfe's sonnets about Guido Reni's 'St Sebastian' published in *The Artist* magazine (1891), and John Gray's 'Saint Sebastian: On a Picture' (1896). Likewise, Wilde's *The Picture of Dorian Gray* (1891) refers to 'medallions of many saints and martyrs, among whom was St Sebastian'. The first art-historical account of homoeroticism in representations of the saint was by Georges Eekhoud, 'Saint Sebastien dans la peinture', *Akdemus* 1 (15 Feb. 1909).
2–*Logische Untersuchunger* ['Logical Investigations'], (1900–1) by Edmund Husserl (1859–1938), Austrian founder of the philosophy of phenomenology. TSE's annotated copy of the 1913 edition, inscribed 'T. S. Eliot / Marburg 1914', is in the London Library.
3–TS Hornbake Library. For TSE's manuscript, see *IMH*, 75–9.

Appearances appearances he said
I have searched the world through dialectic ways
I have questioned restless nights and torpid days
And followed every by-way where it lead
And always find the same unvarièd
Interminable intolerable maze.
Contradiction is the debt you would collect
And still with contradiction are you paid
And while you do not know what else you seek
You shall have nothing other to expect.
Appearances appearances he said
And nowise real; unreal, and yet true;
Untrue, but real – of what are you afraid?
Hopeful of what? Whether you keep thanksgiving
Or pray for earth on tired body and head
This ~~truth~~ <word> is true on all ~~ways you keep~~ the paths you tread
As truth as truth need be (when all is said)
That if you find no truth among the living
You will not find much truth among the dead.
No other time than now, no other place ~~than~~ but here, he said.

He drew the shawl about him as he spoke
And dozed in his armchair till the morning broke.

finale to the foregoing

Across the window panes the plumes ~~the~~ of lilac swept
Stirred by the morning air
Across the floor the shadows crawled and crept
And as the thin <light> shivered through the trees
Around the muffled form they danced and leapt
They crawled about his shoulders and his knees
The[y] rested for a moment in his hair
Until the daylight drove them to their lair
And then sprang up a little damp dead breeze
That rattled at the window while he slept
And had those been human voices ~~at~~ in the chimneys
And at the shutters, and along the stair
You had not <known> whether they laughed or wept.

The Love Song of St Sebastian

Does this mean anything to you? I mean stand all about in a pool on the floor

I would come in a shirt of hair
I would come with a little lamp in the night
And sit at the foot of your stair
I would flog myself until I bled
And after hour on hour of prayer
And torture and delight
Until my blood should ring the ~~light~~ <lamp>
And glisten in the light
I should arise your neophyte
And then put out the light
~~And~~ <To> follow where you lead
To follow where your feet are white
In the darkness toward your bed
And where your gown is white
And against your gown your braided hair
Then you would take me in
Because I was hideous in your sight
You would take me in to your bed without shame
Because I should be dead
And when the morning came
Between your breasts should lie my head.

preterite! not present[1]

I would come with a towel in my hand
And bend your head ~~between~~ <below> my knees.
Your ears curl back in a certain way
Like no ones else in all the world
When all the world shall melt in the sun
Melt or freeze
I ~~should~~ <shall> remember how your ears were curled.
I ~~shall~~ <should> for a moment linger
And follow the curve with my finger
And your head between my knees
I think that at last you would understand
There would not be one word to say
You would love me because I should have strangled you
And because of my infam~~m~~y.
And I should love you the more because I had mangled you
And because you were no longer beautiful
To anyone but me.

NOT to rhyme with 'mammy'

1 – So, correctly, 'led'.

TO *Eleanor Hinkley* MS Houghton

26 July 1914 bei Herrn Suptdr. Happich,
Luth. Kirchhof 1, Marburg a. Lahn

Dear Eleanor

Mit freun[d]lichem Gruss aus Deutschland! [With friendly greetings from Germany!] Here I am, safely out of harm's way, settled in the bosom of the family of the Lutheran Pastor, and the church is right across the street. I have just been to church, and feel as good as gold. This will not be an exciting summer, but I think a pleasant one, though I hope you will not circulate any gossip about me and the Pastor's daughter. She is named Hannah. In the evening, when we gather about the lamp, and the Herr Pfarrer takes a nap and composes his thoughts, and the ladies sew needlework, then the Frau Pfarrer says 'Ach Hannah, spiel uns ein Stuck Beethoven', ['Oh, Hannah, play us a bit of Beethoven',] and Hannah spiels for 15 minutes. Hannah also sings, and can talk a little French and English (but she hasn't tried it on me). Then we read the paper, and discuss the Balkan Question, and the difference in climate between America and

1–Signs (above and right): NACH DER SCHÖNEN AUSSICHT [TO THE BEAUTIFUL VIEW]; BIER LOKAL [PUBLIC HOUSE]. HEUTE ABEND UM 8 UHR KUNSTLER-KONZERT [THIS EVENING AT 8 P.M. ARTISTS' CONCERT].

Deutschland. Altogether they are aw'f'ly good people, and we all eat a great deal. I feel that I am quite in darkest Germany. I have heard talked not a word of English since my arrival. This is a small town, but as small towns in Germany sometimes are, more a miniature compact city than a small town, as it has very good shops, and a cunning little street car that runs round the town on one track, and little narrow streets. You walk down the middle of the chief business street, and the street is about as wide as a very wide sidewalk, and on the sidewalks just two people can pass squeeze by (two Germans). As the town is very small, and the university numbers 2500, the students are much in evidence. Lately they have been having student *fests*, and the various clubs parade the streets in the evening carrying paper lanterns of their colours (usually three colours); and as they come winding down the steep narrow streets it makes a pretty sight. The houses are much decorated too; apparently each student hangs a flag of his club colours out of his own window. The students appear a little cub-like and uncouth, but are fearfully polite – I have always considered the Germans the politest people on earth. In fact everyone, servants, railroad employés, and all, are very obliging. From my window I have a beautiful view (there is a little grove – telegraph poles, I believe? I am not

THE BERLINER

strong in botany). The house is on the side of this steep hill, and my window looks out over the roofs toward distant hills on the other side of the Lahn valley. The country about is really quite charming, hilly and wooded, with nice walks, not too wild; a woody farming country, such as I like – I don't care for 'sublime' scenery, do you? Only one cannot walk far, or one would miss a meal; – for we have five a day. One is either just recovering from a meal or just preparing for one. As I was going out to swim the other day the Frau Superintendent (Superintendent seems to be a sort of *rector*) suggested that I had better eat some bread and sausage to fortify myself. Really, the food is very good; I had not supposed that I could like German food.

I shan't have anything very exciting to narrate this summer; this is as peaceful a life as one could well find. Perhaps I shall make some amusing acquaintances in my summer-school; the reception is next Sunday evening. They have excursions, just as in Cambridge, and I intend to participate in them. You must tell me about your Summer School and I will tell you of mine . . . I wrote to Walter Cook;[1] has he come to see you? I think that he will if the letter reaches him. Do you know Bill Greene,[2] or shall I send him an introduction to you? You would like him, I know; he is not *intense*, but he is very gentle and good and near-intellectual. He will be in Cambridge this winter.

1–Walter Cook (1888–1962), Harvard Class of 1911, archaeologist and teacher.

2–William C. Greene. See letter of 14 Oct. 1914. He had been at Harvard with TSE and Aiken, working alongside them on *The Advocate*, and went as a Rhodes Scholar to Oxford in 1912.

I wished that you had been on the boat; there were some amusing characters. Miss *Levi* was very attractive in her way. She is an Irish Roman Catholic Jew! Her mother was Irish. – There were several persons on the boat who claimed to come from Chestnut Hill[1] – 'but it's really Newton'. Sometimes it was Newton Highlands, – but I think every Newton had a representative. You should have seen us round the piano on the 4th July, singing 'Rally, rally round the Flag, Boys!'[2] They were awfully good people, some of them. Then there was Miss Bessie Wood, of Somerville (do you know her? She is a Saff.); everyone thought I was her nephew.

Affy
Tom.

TO *Eleanor Hinkley* PC Houghton

[Postmark 22 August 1914][3]

c/o British Linen Bank,
Threadneedle St, London

Dear Eleanor,

I have just got to London after being five days on the route. The Germans treated us royally, but we had to stay in Marburg two weeks without any outside communication, and did not feel very much at ease. I will write about it soon. Do write to me here.

Tom.

TO *His Mother* MS[4] Houghton

23 August 1914

28 Bedford Place, London

Dear Mother,

I hope that by this time you will have received the letter that I sent by the courtesy of Mr Bicker, to mail in Boston. I did not write during the two weeks after the outbreak of war, because I could obtain no certain information as to the probability of letters arriving, and hoped (as proved

1 – Chestnut Hill, Newton, Newton Highlands and Somerville were then suburbs of Boston.
2 – 'Rally Round the Flag, Boys' (1862), by George F. Root, was originally a rallying song for supporters of the Union, but was also sung in an adapted form by Confederate troops.
3 – Germany declared war on Russia on 1 Aug. 1914, and on France two days later. Germany's invasion of neutral Belgium on 4 Aug. provoked Britain to declare war on Germany the same day.
4 – From a copy in her hand.

to be the case) to be able to telegraph from London before any such letters could reach you. I did send one card (in German) asking for money – which proved unnecessary, and I hope that you received my cable of the 3rd of August.

I confess that I did feel a little doubtful of the advisability of remaining in Germany a day or two before war was declared against Russia; but it never entered my head that England would declare war too: and we all supposed that after the mobilization, we could (as proved the case for those of us who were Americans) slip away without difficulty. Besides, I had come to Germany *expressly*. The summer school was just opened that day, and I did not want to lose my summer for a scare. It was not until evening (August 2) when the pupils assembled that I appreciated the seriousness of our position. We were told it would be impossible to leave for a fortnight; that it would be impossible for the summer course to continue; but that to fill our time during the enforced stay various makeshift courses and conversation groups would be arranged. The director made a speech in which he cautioned us to be very careful, to avoid crowds, and not to talk in foreign languages in the street. By this time he had got us pretty well frightened of course, and no one was taking very keen interest in the proposed courses. The Russians, who knew they wouldn't get out anyway, were miserable and silent; there appeared to be only one Frenchman, the professor, who was also miserable; the English and Americans were talkative and excited. We made a list of names, and we tried to communicate with the consul at Frankfurt, and couldn't think of anything else to do, and disbanded for the evening. At first I was for taking the makeshift course, but as it gradually came upon me that I might need the money I decided to withdraw, and was subsequently glad I did. I had 20 marks cash; 10 went for the cable; next day I got 45 marks back which I had paid for the course; and subsequently, my $40 American Express checks proved to be good. But there were several days when I found my letter of credit useless, I feared that I might have to stay till my 40 marks would no longer get me over the frontier; for although I was not paying my board (they knew I could not) there was laundry every week, soap, haircuts etc. In the event, I had quite enough.

There was really no danger for us, but the suspense – penned up with no certain communications and no knowledge of when we could get out, and with only imperfect sympathy with the people we were among, (though we saw only German papers and felt that Germany was quite in the right); all this made a fortnight seem a month. There were eight or nine of us who used to gather every evening at the Kaiserhof, pool our misinformation and take heart from the fact that no one knew anything. Gradually the group dwindled; one man went to Berlin; one tried to get to Italy; at the end there were four of us, who hoped to reach Rotterdam together. As for the English, the women were all right, and are now getting away; as for the men, they stay'd in their houses, or went to the Poorhouse, where I suppose they are yet, – looked after sharply and getting board at seven and a half marks a week, but humanely treated. There was one Irishman, a very plucky chap, who managed to keep about, and joined us every evening. He came to the train to see us off. I suppose he is in the Poorhouse by this time; he had only 80 marks left.

When we made up our minds to leave, I did not know whether it would be possible to get to England or not, but there was a rumor (nothing was more than a rumor) that one could get money by having one's letter of credit viséd by a consul, and I thought I could throw myself on the consul at Rotterdam, in any case. Anything to get out of the country, even if we had to travel steerage (we were prepared for that). We left Marburg Sunday afternoon. The trip to Frankfurt is ordinarily an hour and a half. It took five hours. Mobilization ended, but they were still on the lookout for bombs. There were soldiers on the train, too, reservists. I shall never forget one woman's face as she tried to wave goodbye. I could not see his face; he was in the next compartment. I am sure she had no hope of seeing him again.

At Frankfurt we had to spend the night, and see the consul next day. Here there was good news; boats were moving to England. We have our passes viséd by the Dutch consul, and went on. We had taken a chance; it was not certain that we could get through Cologne by train; but the boats down the Rhine would have taken three days, and it was raining. Some went to Cologne. In the train we fell in with a man I had known in college, with his wife, and as we filled one compartment, had a pleasant day. Of course there was little enough to eat, as no dining cars were run. We reached Cologne at 10 p.m. after a change and a tedious wait. We made a good supper, and decided to press on the same night. So we tried to sleep with our heads on tables in the waiting room, and were very uncomfortable till 3 a.m., when we took our train. The train was crowded; Germans but some Americans; and we were packed in tight. We got underway late, just at daybreak. At 7 a.m. we had to change again, and had time for breakfast. There was another change; then another, and we reached the frontier about 3 p.m. We were very nervous, expecting to be searched, but they did not even open our bags; looked at our passes – '*Amerikaner – ach, schoen!*' ['American – oh fine!'] let us by.

It was a tremendous relief to be in neutral country; even the landscape seemed more peaceful. We reached Rotterdam at 10 p.m. and got the last room in the hotel. I slept very solid! We had to wait a day there; a most uninteresting shipping town. There two of our party got passages on a freighter for $100 apiece to Boston. The last man and I took a train for Flushing – changing twice – slept on the boat, an excellent boat; and got to London the following night. And that's all. The American pass does anything in Germany. They are making a strong bid for American sympathy.[1] I was treated with the greatest courtesy everywhere. As the German press offers only a very one sided view of affairs, it is safe to say that they are getting this sympathy from Americans in Germany. Besides, they are extremely hospitable and warmhearted; all the hosts of Americans in Marburg told them to stay and not to think of paying. The people in general are persuaded of the rightness of the German cause; so was I, to a certain extent, till I found that the English papers were making exact contradictions of the German. Germany is animated by an intense spirit, but I don't see how she can possibly win. They will do no harm to England; the waters as we approached were black with English warships. And Germany is putting forth every ounce of strength. '*Deutschland kaempft um das Existenz!*' ['Germany is fighting for her existence!'] they say and they are right. *But I think it is better that Germany should go.* London is full of Americans but I have not met any acquaintances yet.

[incomplete]

TO *Henry Eliot* — MS Houghton

Monday 7 September [1914][2]

28 Bedford Place, Russell Square,
London W.C.

My dear Henry,

I will ask my tailor to send you some samples at once, if he has any winter goods now; he could make you a suit to my measure; as he is a cash tailor he would have to have the money before you have the suit. I will pay him if you like, when the time comes.

1 – 'As soon as the panic that followed the outbreak of war had subsided, elaborate orders were issued that every courtesy should be shown to Americans, and all this week special trains have been running for their benefit from Munich, Frankfurt and other centres to Rotterdam and Flushing, where nothing was left undone which could give to the departing guests a favourable last impression of Germany' (*The Times*, 25 Aug. 1914).

2 – TSE put 'Monday 8 September'.

I fear that I have no interesting anecdotes of my adventures beyond what I have already imparted. I was interviewed by a reporter when I got here, but had nothing interesting to give him even had I been willing to communicate it. It is really much more interesting to be in London now than it was to be in Germany: the latter experience was much like the childhood's exasperation of being in an upper berth as the train passed through a large city. – In fact it was an intolerable bore. There, one was so far from any excitement and information that it was impossible to work; here in all the noise and rumour, I can work. The quarter where I live is rather foreign anyway, being composed exclusively of boarding houses, in rows, all exactly alike except for the fancy names on them; and now we are full up with Belgian and French refugees, whole families of them, of the well-to-do sort, with babies and nurses;[1] – we have just acquired a Swiss waiter instead of a German one who was very unpopular (one excited lady said 'what's to prevent him putting arsenic in our food?' I said 'Nothing! – he already puts blacking on my tan shoes') so I have been talking French and acquiring a war vocabulary. The noise hereabouts is like hell turned upside down. Hot weather, all windows open, many babies, pianos, street piano accordions, singers, hummers, whistlers. Every house has a gong: they all go off at seven o'clock, and other hours. Ten o'clock in the evening, quiet for a few minutes, then a couple of men with late editions burst into the street, roaring: GREAT GERMAN DISASTER![2] Everybody rushes to windows and doors, in every costume from evening clothes to pajamas; violent talking – English, American, French, Flemish, Russian, Spanish, Japanese; the papers are all sold in five minutes; then we settle down for another hour till the next extra appears: LIST OF ENGLISH DEAD AND WOUNDED. Meanwhile, a dreadful old woman, her skirt trailing on the street, sings 'the Rosary'[3] in front, and secures several pennies from windows and the housemaid resumes her conversation at the area gate.[4]

1 – See 'London, The City of Refuge': 'This invasion has turned London into a city where alien tongues can be heard everywhere. In omnibuses and trains, in the shops and theatres, one sees foreigners and one listens to foreign speech. One might almost suggest that London's motto should be, "Ici on parle Français", for in certain parts of the city the language of our allies is heard almost as frequently as our own. The bulk of London's French and Belgian guests are women and children, whose men are under arms . . .' (*The Times*, 10 Sept. 1914, 4).

2 – See 'Severe German Defeat', *The Times*, 8 Sept. 1914, 8: 'In an attack on the southern section of the Antwerp fortifications yesterday the Germans lost a thousand dead and retreated towards Vilevorde in a demoralized condition.'

3 – 'The Rosary' (*c.*1901): poem by Robert C. Rogers, music by Jennie P. Black.

4 – 'I am aware of the damp souls of housemaids / Sprouting despondently at area gates' ('Morning at the Window', 3–4).

I find it quite possible to work in this atmosphere. The noises of a city so large as London don't distract one much; they become attached to the city and depersonalise themselves. No doubt it will take me some time to become used to the quiet of Oxford. I like London better than before; it is foreign, but hospitable, or rather tolerant, and perhaps does not so demand to be understood as does Paris. Less jealous. I think I should love Paris now more than ever, if I could see her in these times. There seems to have come a wonderful calmness and fortitude over Paris, from what I hear; the spirit is very different from 1870. I have a great deal of confidence in the ultimate event; I am anxious that Germany should be beaten; but I think it is silly to hold up one's hands at German 'atrocities' and 'violations of neutrality'. The Germans are perfectly justified in violating Belgium – they are fighting for their existence – but the English are more than justified in turning to defend a treaty. But the Germans are bad diplomats. It is not against German 'crimes', but against German 'civilisation' – all this system of officers and professors – that I protest. But very useful to the world if kept in its place.

Yours affy
Tom

TO *Eleanor Hinkley* — MS Houghton

8 September [1914] — 28 Bedford Place, Russell Square

My dear Eleanor

Here I am in Shady Bloomsbury, the noisiest place in the world, a neighbourhood at present given over to artists, musicians, hackwriters, Americans, Russians, French, Belgians, Italians, Spaniards, and Japanese; formerly Germans also – these have now retired, including our waiter, a small inefficient person, but, as one lady observed, 'What's to prevent him putting arsenic in our tea?' A delightfully seedy part of town, with some interesting people in it, besides the Jones twins, who were next door for a few days, and Ann Van Ness[1] who is a few blocks away. I was quite glad to find her, she is very pleasant company, and ~~not at all uninteresting~~ quite interesting (that's better). Only I wish she wouldn't look like German allegorical paintings – e.g. POMONA blessing the DUKE of MECKLENBURGSTRELITZ, or something of that sort – because she hasn't really a German mind at all, but quite American. I was in to tea yesterday, and we went to walk afterwards, to the Regent's Park Zoo. The only other friend I have here now is my French friend of the steamer, just returned from Paris, who is also very interesting, in a different way – one of those people you sometimes meet who do not have much discursive conversation on a variety of topics, but occasionally surprise you by a remark of unusual penetration. But perhaps I do her an injustice, as she does talk pretty well – but it is more the latter that I notice. Anyway it is pleasant to be in contact with a French mind in a foreign city like this. I like London very well now – it has grown on me, and I grew quite homesick for it in Germany; and I have met several very agreeable Englishmen. Still I feel that I don't understand the English very well. I think that Keith[2] is really very English – and thoroughly so – and I always found him very baffling, though I like him very much. It seemed to me that I got to know him quite easily, and never got very much farther; and I am interested to see (this year) whether I shall find it so with all English; and whether the difficulty is simply that I consider him a bit conventional. I don't know just what conventionality is; it doesn't involve snobbishness, because I am a thorough snob myself; but I should have thought of it as perhaps the one quality which all my friends lacked. And I'm sure that if I did know what it was, among men, I should have to find out all over again with regard to women.

Perhaps when I learn how to take Englishmen, this brick wall will cease to trouble me. But it's ever so much easier to know what a Frenchman or an American is thinking about, than an Englishman. Perhaps partly that a Frenchman is so analytical and selfconscious that he dislikes to have anything going on inside him that he can't put into words, while an Englishman is content simply to live. And that's one of the qualities one counts as a virtue; the ease and lack of effort with which they take so much of life – that's the way they have been fighting in France – I should like to

1–Ann Van Ness (b. 1891), daughter of a Unitarian Minister.

2–Elmer D. Keith (1888–1965) graduated in 1910 from Yale, where he won the University poetry prize. A Rhodes Scholar at Oriel College, Oxford, 1910–13, he later worked at Harvard University Press.

be able to acquire something of that spirit. But on the other hand the French way has an intellectual honesty about it that the English very seldom attain to. So there you are.

I haven't said anything about the war yet. Of course (though no one believes me) I have no experiences of my own of much interest – nothing, that is, in the way of anecdotes, that are easy to tell – though the whole experience has been something which has left a very deep impression on me; having seen, I mean, how the people in the two countries have taken the affair, and the great moral earnestness on both sides. It has made it impossible for me to ~~take~~ adopt a wholly partizan attitude, or even to rejoice or despair wholeheartedly, though I should certainly want to fight against the Germans if at all. I cannot but wonder whether it all seems as awful at your distance as it does here. I doubt it. No war ever seemed so real to me as this: of course I have been to some of the towns about which they have been fighting; and I know that men I have known, including one of my best friends, must be fighting each other. So it's hard for me to write interestingly about the war.

I hope to hear that you have had a quiet summer, at best. Did Walter Cook ever call? If you have seen Harry [Child] let me know how he is, and that he is not starving himself.

Always affectionately
Tom

PS (After rereading). Please don't quote *Pomona*. It's perhaps a literary as well as a social mistake to write as one would talk. I apologise for the quality of this letter anyway.

TO *Conrad Aiken* — MS Huntington

30 September [1914] — Merton College, Oxford

Dear Conrad,

No, I'm still in London, but I go to the above address Tuesday. I reflect upon the fact that I neglected to add my address to my last. I wait till Tuesday because there is a possibility of dining at a Chinese restaurant Monday with Yeats,[1] – and the Pounds. Pound has been *on n'est pas plus*

1 – William Butler Yeats (1865–1939): Irish poet and playwright.

aimable,[1] and is going to print 'Prufrock' in *Poetry* and pay me for it.[2] He wants me to bring out a Vol. after the War. The devil of it is that I have done nothing good since J. A[lfred] P[rufrock] and writhe in impotence. The stuff I sent you is not good, is very forced in execution, though the idea was right, I think. Sometimes I think – if I could only get back to Paris. But I know I never will, for long. I must learn to talk English. Anyway, I'm in the worry way now. Too many minor considerations.[3] Does anything kill as petty worries do? And in America we worry all the time. That, in fact, is I think the great use of suffering, if it's *tragic* suffering – it takes you away from yourself – and petty suffering does exactly the reverse, and kills your inspiration. I think now that all my good stuff was done before I had begun to worry – three years ago. I sometimes think it would be better to be just a clerk in a post office with nothing to worry about – but the consciousness of having made a failure of one's life. Or a millionaire, ditto. The thing is to be able to look at one's life as if it were somebody's else – (I much prefer to say somebody else's). That is difficult in England, almost impossible in America. – But it may be all right in the long run, (if I can get over it), perhaps *tant mieux* [so much the better]. Anyway, I have been living a pleasant and useless life of late, and talking (bad) French too. I have dined several times with Armstrong[4] who is very good company. By the way, Pound is rather intelligent as a talker: his verse is well-meaning but touchingly incompetent; but his remarks are sometimes good. O conversation the staff of life shall I get any at Oxford? Everything *à pis*

1–'Pound couldn't have been kinder': TSE called on Ezra and Dorothy Pound (for EP, see Glossary of Names) at 5 Holland Place Chambers, Kensington, with an introduction from Aiken, on 22 Sept.
2–On this same day (30 Sept.), EP wrote to Harriet Monroe, editor of *Poetry*, telling her that 'The Love Song of J. Alfred Prufrock' was 'the best poem I have yet had or seen from an American. PRAY GOD IT BE NOT A SINGLE AND UNIQUE SUCCESS. He has taken it back to get it ready for the press and you shall have it in a few days.' EP sent the poem in Oct., writing 'Hope you'll get it *in* soon.' When Monroe demurred, he wrote: 'No, most emphatically I will not ask Eliot to write down to any audience whatsoever . . . Neither will I send you Eliot's address in order that he may be insulted' (9 Nov.). To further objections, he replied: '"Mr. Prufrock" does not "go off at the end". It is a portrait of failure, or of a character which fails, and it would be false art to make it end on a note of triumph. I disliked the paragraph about Hamlet, but it is an early and cherished bit and T. E. won't give it up, and as it is the only portion of the poem that most readers will like at first reading, I don't see that it will do much harm' (31 Jan. 1915). Finally he implored her (10 Apr.), '*Do* get on with that Eliot' (*Selected Letters of Ezra Pound 1907–1941*, ed. D. D. Paige, 1950). The poem was published in *Poetry* 6: 3 (June 1915).
3–'Oh, these minor considerations! . . .' ('First Caprice in North Cambridge', l. 11 (*IMH*).
4–Martin Armstrong (1882–1974), British author, was serving as a private in the 2nd Battalion, Artists' Rifles.

aller. Où se réfugier? [Everything's a stand-in. Where can one hide?] Anyway it's interesting to cut yourself to pieces once in a while, and wait to see if the fragments will sprout.

My war poem, for the $100 prize, entitled

UP BOYS AND AT 'EM!

Adapted to the tune of 'C. Columbo lived in Spain' and within the compass of the average male or female voice:

Now while our heroes were at sea
    They pass'd a German warship.
The captain pac'd the quarterdeck
    Parading in his corset.
What ho! they cry'd, we'll sink your ship!
    And so they up and sink'd her.
But the cabin boy was sav'd alive
    And bugger'd, in the sphincter.

Yours
Tom.

The poem was declined by several musical publishers on the ground that it paid too great a tribute to the charms of German youth to be acceptable to the English public. I acknowledg'd the force of the objection, but replied that it was only to be regarded as a punitive measure, and to show the readiness and devotion to duty of the British seaman.

I should find it very stimulating to have several women fall in love with me – several, because that makes the practical side less evident. And I should be very sorry for them, too. Do you think it possible, if I brought out the 'Inventions of the March Hare',[1] and gave a few lectures, at 5 p.m. with wax candles,[2] that I could become a sentimental Tommy.[3]

TO *The Chairman of the Committee on Sheldon Fellowships* — MS Harvard

2 October 1914 — Merton College, Oxford

Dear Professor Briggs,[4]

In accordance with the requirements I send my address, which will remain the same throughout the year. I had expected to go to Germany

1–This is the title, cancelled by TSE himself, on the flyleaf of the Berg Notebook (*IMH*, i).
2–A whimsical thrust at gatherings in Harold Monro's Poetry Bookshop.
3–Playing on his own name and J. M. Barrie's title, *Sentimental Tommy* (1896).
4–Professor L. B. R. Briggs (1855–1934), Dean of Harvard University, 1878–1934. In his article 'Donne in our Time', in *A Garland for John Donne*, ed. Theodore Spencer (1931),

for the spring term, but this will now evidently be impossible, so I shall remain here until the end of the year.

Very sincerely yours
Thomas S. Eliot

TO *J. H. Woods*[1]

MS Professor David G. Williams

5 October 1914

Merton College, Oxford

My dear Professor Woods,

I received your letter of the 22nd September by the last boat. I repent of having caused you such a mass of correspondence, and forward my apologies and thanks.

I am going up to Oxford tomorrow. I shall not forget your request, and will keep for your inspection any notes I may take or get; and if anything turns up that may be of immediate use to you I will see to having it copied. I believe that I told you that Joachim[2] expected to have no other pupils, but would go through the *Post*[*erior*]-*Anal*[*ytics*][3] and perhaps the *de Interp*[*retatione*] with me alone.

I have been plugging away at Hüsserl, and find it terribly hard, but very interesting; and I like very much what I think I understand of it. I have also broken ground by going through most of the *Metaphysics* for the first time in Greek.

I hope that you have had a restful as well as fruitful summer at Rockport.

Very sincerely
Thomas S. Eliot

If you hear anything of German universities being open for neutrals in the spring, I hope you will let me know, as we have no communication with Germany from here. But it would greatly surprise me to hear that work there was possible.

TSE was to recall how Briggs 'read, with great persuasiveness and charm, verses of Donne to the Freshmen at Harvard', which was 'enough to attract to private reading at least one Freshman who had already absorbed some of the Elizabethan dramatists, but who had not yet approached the metaphysicals'.

1–James Haughton Woods, Professor of Philosophy at Harvard, see Glossary of Names.

2–H. H. Joachim, philosophy tutor at Merton College, Oxford: see Glossary of Names.

3–TSE invoked 'the opening phrases of the *Posterior Analytics*' in 'The Perfect Critic' [II], *A.*, 23 July 1920; *SW*, 9.

TO *Eleanor Hinkley* TS Houghton

14 October 1914 Merton College, Oxford

My dear Eleanor:

A letter crossing one of yours can hardly be regarded as an answer to it, and so I am writing again. This is a good time for writing letters; I always have half an hour or so before breakfast. You see, we have to report to a roll call at ten minutes before eight – that is, rush across two quadrangles and sign one's name to a blank paper, and breakfast never seems to appear till about half past eight. The discipline is excellent practice in getting up early, at least; it is a great many years since I have made a practice of rising at quarter past seven, and please do not say that it will be very good for me, for I am sure that it will have not the slightest effect upon my character one way or another. There are a certain number of other regulations here, but I forgive that for the sake of being taken care of, as I hate having to look out for myself. You don't have to think about meals, and the day is pretty well divided up for you. I do not object to the boarding school discipline in the least – for a time. I suppose that everyone will want to know how I like Oxford, and of course I shall be quite unable to give an unqualified answer one way or another. I like it quite well enough to wish that I had come here earlier and spent two or three years; perhaps even before the end of my college course at home, for I am sure that I should have got more profit from both my work and my play. I think that I should have gotten along with the undergraduates better and made more friends than I made at Harvard, though I should be very sorry to have to give up those whom I did make. On the one hand I like the English very much, and on the other hand I don't think that I should ever feel at home in England, as I do for instance in France. Perhaps I admire the English more in some ways but find the French more congenial. I should always, I think, be aware of a certain sense of confinement in England, and repression; one puts up with it in one's native land, and is simply more conscious of it in a country in which one does not *have* to live. But even these qualifications ought to be qualified, and I do not want to give the impression that my admiration for Oxford is of a grudging sort. I only mean that Oxford is not intellectually stimulating – but that would be a good deal to ask of a university atmosphere. At least, if it isn't stimulating, it is relaxing, and that is a good deal in itself. It is a dreadful climate, I know, but one seems able to eat and sleep very well, and keep very healthy.

My only exercise so far has been walking. The country about here is beautifully adapted for long walks, as perhaps you know, and at the present time, at least, is not infested with automobiles. There is a dear little village named Cumnor, which perhaps you know, with low thatched cottages, where I have walked. I think that the English countryside is more beautiful than the French; at any rate the scenery seems more solid and massive, and the trees are bigger and more beautiful; the little villages more picturesque, if also dirtier. The middle class localities, the rows of semi-detached villas, are certainly far uglier than anything I can remember in France, and the middle class life must be more drab and dismal. I hope to take up a little rowing, if we can gather enough Americans and such English as are too-short-sighted to be acceptable for the Training corps. There will of course (I have just put on a new ribbon) be no regular sports here this year, as the university is too much depleted. We have about forty men up in this college, and that is more in proportion than Magdalen, for example; and all the able-bodied English will be worked in to the officers training corps. Doubtless some of them will get commissions later; so that by the end of the year, I am afraid, the university will be sensibly reduced even below its present numbers, which are about a third of the ordinary enrollment. Four recent Magdalen graduates have been killed already. I should have liked to have gone in to the training corps myself, for the sake of being able to take my exercise with the Englishmen, but they won't take a foreigner. It is not pleasant to think that if the Germans *did* get over here I should be obliged to sit still and not even look out of the window, but I suppose that the contingency is a remote one. Francis Thwing, by the way, says that he is having himself naturalised as an Englishman and is to join the corps; and he hopes to get a commission.[1] I certainly shall not go to that length. But one feels very much the strain of the present situation even in Oxford; and no doubt you do in America too. I hope that we may not have to stand another year of it.

Just now I am working on my great ten-reel cinema drama, EFFIE THE WAIF, with which I hope to provide funds for the visiting housekeeper. It is to be staged at vast expense, the first reel to be in the mountains of Wyoming, but I expect some difficulty in assembling all my actors, as for the role of SPIKE CASSIDY the reformed gambler, I want W. J. Bryan[2] <perhaps *Carl*[3] would do> and for that of SEEDY SAM, the blackmailer,

1 – Francis Butler-Thwing (1891–1964). After graduating from Harvard he spent a term at New College, Oxford, then entered Sandhurst Military College. Twice wounded in the war he retired, a captain in the Coldstream Guards, in 1922.

2 – W. J. Bryan (1860–1925), unsuccessful Democratic Presidential candidate, and Secretary of State under President Wilson, was an advocate of 'free silver'.

3 – Unidentified.

Pa Noyes,[1] and the others in proportion. Here is the scenario for the first reel:

MEDICINE HAT, Wyoming, Christmas Eve. Spike Cassidy, the most notorious gambling house proprietor in the county, (ever since the early death of his wife, his only good influence), returns from the saloon, where he has won all the money and shot a man, to find a small bundle on his doorstep. He stops and stoops. A feeble cry from the bundle – it squirms, it is warm, it is alive! He takes it tenderly in his arms. Large snow flakes begin to fall, the clock strikes twelve, and the small organ in the orchestra plays softly 'peace on earth, goodwill to men'.

Scene: YE POOR LITTLE MOTHERLESS BRAT.

REEL TWO

Spike, reformed by the sweet insidious influence of the child, has managed to make virtue pay, and is now mayor and the richest man in the county. Effie believes herself his daughter, is just returned from the convent in Paris where she has been receiving all the fixings that money can buy.

Scene: (Sitting on the arm of the old man's chair and patting his grey locks):

FATHER, WONT YOU TELL ME SOMETHING ABOUT MOTHER NOW?

SOME OTHER TIME, DEAR.

REEL THREE

But there is a canker in the rose. Seedy Sam, the partner of Spike's (now the Hon. Daniel Cassidy) early crimes, has returned, a ruined and desperate man, with his son Peter (a comic simpleton, this part to be taken by Raymond Smyth).[2]

Scene: YOUR DAUGHTER'S HAND FOR MY SON PETER. OR I DENOUNCE YOU FORTHWITH.

REEL FOUR

Walter Desborough (a good role for Tracy)[3] scion of one of Harlem's oldest and richest families, goes west to seek his fortune. His father has been swindled out of all his wealth, and has died of the shock. There is one property left – a mine, value unknown, near Medicine Hat, Wy. Walter leaves his weeping widowed mother to seek his fortune in new fields. As the canal boat carries him westward up the Erie he turns and gazes at the Statue of Liberty disappearing on the horizon (not strictly accurate geography, but a fine scene) –

1 – James Noyes, father of Eleanor Hinkley's close friend Penelope.

2 – Raymond Smyth (1888–1918), metallurgical engineer.

3 – Tracy Putnam (1894–1975), who became a physician.

Scene: CAN I WHO REALLY REMEMBER EVER FORGET?

In the next scene we are carried back to the stately manor where Gwendoline, Lady Chomleyumley, still mourns the loss of her infant daughter, torn from her at a tender age by her wicked brother-in-law. This is as much as I have completed, but you see its possibilities. I have not chosen any candidate for the role of Effie. Do you think that Ann Van Ness could fill it competently? By the way, before she left she said that she 'would be glad to hear from me'. I don't find myself particularly keen about writing to her. Not that I don't like her very much; but there are moments when I don't; and there are many people whom one likes to know very much up to a certain point – and you don't know where that point is until you hit it. Perhaps it is simply that I thought her father rather plebeian (I have cast him for a comic postman in EFFIE THE WAIF.) I don't know what you will think of me for talking this way.

I had a pleasant time in London, and saw several pleasant people. Do you remember Bertie Russell,[1] whom you admired? I met him on the street and found that he was living quite near me, and went and had tea with him.[2] As I expected, he is a pacifist,[3] but he talked very interestingly on the European situation. It was he who said that the Germans made the same mistakes in their warmaking that he had always found in their scholarship – where, said he, a German writer had always read every book under the sun except the one which counted: so in war they were careful to provide their soldiers with forceps for cutting barbed wire but managed their diplomacy in just such a way as to unite everybody against them. – He has a little apartment furnished in very good taste, not overcrowded, in fact almost preciously simple, with only one picture on the wall.

I will send Bill Greene a card. I hear, by the way, that he only got a fourth in Greats last summer – a great shock to everyone. Keith had a second, which is very good, and Bill was rather expected to secure a first. I mention this as possibly he may be a bit sensitive about it, so one can talk about other things.

I appreciate your Social Column of Births, Funerals, and Broken Hearts – it is rather an Agony column. I have nothing to offer in return but to continue my column of

1 – Bertrand Russell (see Glossary of Names) had lectured at Harvard in spring 1914.

2 – Russell was living at Russell Chambers, Bury Street, nr. the British Museum, just a short walk away from TSE's lodgings at 28 Bedford Place.

3 – Though not describing himself as a pacifist, Russell was a vocal conscientious objector.

BRILLIANTS

'Est-ce-vous dansez le verrry-mussstard?'

HOW did you learn to speak such good English? I'd never know you were a foreigner . . . Well I never! I thought all this time you were one of the Belgians! Bertha! this young man's a countryman of ours!

My nephew was in Germany and he had a terrible time. You see, he's a sort of literary young man, and he's very reticent. He's had a good education, and he loves his books, but he's so reticent I suppose they thought he was a spy. Well, as I wrote his mother, it's bad for his nervous system, but it'll be good for his moral character.

You can leave the curtain up, sir. It ud take a seven footer to look in your window. That ouse hoppisite? Ho, that's honly the warden's ouse, sir.

I am sure that you must have liked the Haven, even if Pete [Little] didn't recognise you, and it's awfully healthy. I hope that Emily [Hale][1] is not very tired and will have a good servant, as she speaks as if she were going to start in acting very soon. Tell me what you are going to do at Radcliffe[2] this Fall. I was surprised to find that girls attend the lectures here – come right into the college buildings, and attend the same lectures as the men. PS No one looks at them.

Affectionately
Tom
(signed)

PS I think I am the only man in this college who takes *cold* baths. BRILLIANT: 'Do you keep it hup all winter, Sir?'

TO *William C. Greene*[3]

MS Herbert T. Greene

[14 October 1914]

Junior Common Room,
Merton College, Oxford

Dear Bill

I presume you are now going through what I tried my hand at last year; teaching freshmen what they didn't want to know and what I didn't know myself. Since arriving here I have decided that I knew a number of things

1–TSE had met Emily Hale at Eleanor Hinkley's home in 1912 (both in Glossary of Names).
2–Radcliffe College (chartered in 1894): the women's college associated with Harvard.
3–William C. Greene (1890–1978), formerly a board member of the *Harvard Advocate* with TSE and Conrad Aiken. As a Rhodes Scholar at Balliol College, Oxford, in 1912, he was the first American to win the Newdigate Prize. Later Professor of Greek and Latin at Harvard.

which were not essential and was ignorant of a number of things which are. I wish now that I had taken a year – several years – here first and done my Harvard work later, instead of beginning my house at the roof. I have begun to entertain the highest respect for English methods of teaching in addition to the disapproval for our own which I had acquired through experience. I would give a great deal to have done the regular undergraduate course here. But I must make the best of it now. Oxford is a quiet and deserted place now, but, I expect, a better place to work in. At any rate, I find it exceedingly comfortable and delightful – and very 'foreign'.

I wonder how you will like Cambridge [Mass.] after three years absence. I am enclosing a card, in case you care to call upon my cousin [Eleanor Hinkley], who knows your brother and knows you by reputation at least. The address is 1 Berkeley Place, Cambridge (I have no small envelopes by me, so enclose it loose.)

I hear Conrad's book is out.[1] Remind him that he was to send me a copy, and tell him that he ought to write to me. E. D. Keith also.

I expect to be back in the summer. The war looks to keep up for a long time; if so we shall lose most even of the undergraduates whom we have.

I am glad that I chose Joachim, for I like him very much, and I imagine that he is the best philosopher here; though I think Prichard[2] is good. But I should hate to have to subsist *only* on the Oxford sort of philosophy.

Yours always
T. S. Eliot

TO *Norbert Wiener*[3] TS MIT

23 October 1914 Merton College, Oxford

Dear Wiener

I hear from an American here that you are back at Cambridge. If you should ever come up here (which I suppose not likely?) or if you are to be

1–Conrad Aiken, *Earth Triumphant and Other Tales in Verse* (1914).
2–H. A. Prichard (1871–1947), Fellow of Trinity College, Oxford, 1898–1924; White's Professor of Moral Philosophy, 1928–37; intuitionist moral philosopher; author of *Kant's Theory of Knowledge* (1909) and the influential essay 'Does Moral Philosophy Rest on a Mistake?' (1912).
3–Norbert Wiener (1894–1964), founder of Cybernetics; Professor of Mathematics at Massachusetts Institute of Technology, 1932–9. He gained his Harvard PhD at eighteen and was now a Sheldon Fellow, 1914–15, studying at Cambridge with BR and the mathematician G. H. Hardy.

about London during any of the vacations, I hope you will let me know. How are you getting on?

Sincerely,
T. S. Eliot

TO *Norbert Wiener* MS MIT

Tuesday [9? November 1914] Merton College, Oxford.

Dear Wiener,

I am glad to know that my letter reached you. I don't know just what I shall do in vacation, but should like to get hold of you. I was planning to retire somewhere in the country with books; travelling sounds expensive and one can't leave England anyway. Let me know what you are to do when you have decided.

I am doing my work under Joachim. I also have J. A. Smith,[1] who I imagine is unknown outside of Oxford. Bradley is seldom up, and never teaches. I should like to have a chance to meet him.[2]

You seem to be doing phil[osophy] rather than math[ematics].[3] I can't imagine what on earth you are doing with McTaggart,[4] unless you are reading Hegel or drinking whiskey.

Sincerely,
T. S. Eliot

1–J. A. Smith (1863–1939), Waynflete Professor of Moral and Metaphysical Philosophy, 1910–36; co-editor of the Oxford edition of Aristotle (12 vols, 1908–52); translator of *De Anima*.

2–F. H. Bradley (1846–1924), English Hegelian philosopher; Fellow of Merton College from 1870; and author of *Ethical Studies* (1876), *Appearance and Reality* (1893), and *Principles of Logic* (1922). TSE was never to meet him – Bradley had been suffering from poor health since 1871 and led a secluded life – but he went on to complete in 1916 his doctoral dissertation on him: *Knowledge and Experience in the Philosophy of F. H. Bradley* (1964). After his death, TSE called him 'the last survivor of the academic race of metaphysicians'.

3–Wiener had addressed the Cambridge discussion group The Heretics on 'Scepticism', 31 Oct.

4–John McTaggart Ellis McTaggart (1866–1925), Hegelian philosopher; Lecturer in Moral Sciences at Trinity College, Cambridge, 1897–1923; author of *Studies in the Hegelian Dialectic* (1896), *Some Dogmas on Religion* (1906), and *A Commentary on Hegel's Logic* (1910).

TO *J. H. Woods* MS Professor David G. Williams

9 November [1914] Merton College, Oxford

Dear Professor Woods,

I have promised to keep you *au courant*, but I do not quite know what I have to offer. I am following these courses of lectures, Joachim's on the *Ethics*, Collingwood's[1] (of Pembroke) on the *de Anima*,[2] and J. A. Smith's Logic. Joachim is reading the *Posterior Analytics* with myself and one other man (who is likely to get a commission in the new army by Christmas, so that I may possibly have J. to myself); and besides I have an hour a week conference with Joachim and Smith's 'Informals' which are quite informal indeed, as only one other man besides myself attends them. Smith's Lectures are interesting as representing the purest strain of old fashioned Hegelianism to be found in England, I believe, and a type of philosophy with which I had never come into contact. The *de Anima* course consists in reading, explaining, and commenting upon the text. Collingwood is a young person, but very good, I think. We use the Teubner text. C. likes Rodier's the best; better than Hicks. The course is to end with the term, and I fear that we shall not cover the whole of the three books. The other courses continue; and I see that Stewart is to have a course – a class, I mean – in the *Enneads* [of Plotinus].[3] I intend to go to this, and probably also to a course on the *Politics* [of Aristotle].

The course of Joachim's on the *Ethics* is particularly good. J. is perhaps the best lecturer here. He sticks pretty closely to the text, explaining other portions of Aristotle – especially parts of the *Organon*, when relevant. I find the abundance of cross references very useful.

1–R. G. Collingwood (1889–1943), Waynflete Professor of Moral and Metaphysical Philosophy, 1936–41. His books *The Principles of Art* (1938) and *The New Leviathan* (1942) are in TSE's library.

2–In his annotated copy of Aristotle, *De Anima* Libri III, ed. Guilelmus Biehl (Leipzig, 1911), TSE later wrote: 'Used in 1914–15 with notes made during R. G. Collingwood's *explication de texte*, and extracts from Pacius' commentary on the *De Anima* which Joachim made me read' (King's).

3–E. R. Dodds, in his autobiography *Missing Persons* (1977), traced his love of Plotinus back to the classes given by J. A. Stewart, author of *Notes on the Nichomachean Ethics of Aristotle* (1892) and *Plato's Doctrine of Ideas* (1909): 'The membership of the class was initially six, but as Stewart proved to be an unexciting teacher it quickly dropped to two. I was one of the two; the other was a young American lately arrived from the Graduate School at Harvard . . . Like me he was seriously interested in mystical experience. But what astonished me as I came to know him better was the wide knowledge of contemporary European literature, poetry in particular, which he gradually revealed. Then one day he confessed shyly that he had written some poems himself' (40).

The *Posterior Analytics* I find very difficult. I accompany it with the commentary of Zabarella,[1] which is remarkably good, and very minute, so that this reading takes most of my time. If there is a copy in the British Museum (and Pacius[2] also) I shall make good use of it during the vacation. If the Harvard library possesses a copy I hope that you will let me know, as I should consider it great good luck. J. A. Smith also said that he owed his knowledge of Aristotle chiefly to Zabarella.

I do not think that anyone would come to Oxford to seek for anything very original or subtle in philosophy, but the scholarship is very fine, and the teaching of philosophy, especially the historical side of philosophy, as a part of the training and equipment of an *honnête homme*, has aroused my keen admiration. For anyone who is going to teach the Oxford discipline is admirable. It has impressed upon my mind the value of two things: the value of personal instruction in small classes and individually, and the value of careful study of original texts in the original tongue – in contrast to the synoptic course.

I do not know whether any of my notes would be of the slightest use to you, but if either my notes on the *Ethics*, *de An.* or *Post-Anal.* would interest you I should be very glad indeed to typewrite them off for you. – Or if there are any books you wish to be looked up second-hand – I am sorry that nothing on the *Metaphysics* or on the later Platonic dialogues is offered this year. I believe that J. has some good notes on ZHθ[3] but I do not like to ask to borrow them.

Very sincerely yours
Thomas S. Eliot

TO *Conrad Aiken* — MS Huntington

16 November [1914] — [Merton College]

Dear Conrad

I was very glad to hear from you after the summer interval. But why are you 'slothful'? Are you satisfied to be in Cambridge at present? It would seem that there was nowhere else to go at present, unless you went to New York. I conclude that London is a pleasant place when the road to Paris is *gesperrt* [closed], and hope to pass several weeks there during the vacation.

1 – Giacomo Zabarella (1533–89) published a commentary on Aristotle's *Posterior Analytics* in 1582.
2 – Giulio Pace's edition of the *Organon* (1584).
3 – *Metaphysics* VII–IX.

University towns, my dear fellow, are the same all over the world; only they order these matters better in Oxford.[1] For intellectual stimulus, you will find it not in Oxford nor in Urbana Indiana (or is it Illinois).[2] Only the most matter of fact people could write verse here, I assure you. But life is pleasant in its way, and perhaps I also am contented and slothful, eating heartily, smoking, and rowing violently upon the river in a four oar,[3] and performing my intellectual stint each day. Oxford even at this time is peaceful, always elegiac. It is Alexandrine verse, nuts and wine. What else? Oh yes, I have had to buy a larger collar. What else should I say about Oxford, or about the war? Let us take them for granted.

I think that you criticise my verse too leniently. It still seems to me strained and intellectual. I know the kind of verse I want, and I know that this isn't it, and I know why. I shan't do anything that will satisfy me (as some of my old stuff *does* satisfy me – whether it be good or not) for years, I feel it more and more. Not in the life I have been leading for several years. And I don't know whether I want to. Why should one worry about that? I feel that such matters take care of themselves and have no dependence upon our planning –

> I can't say that I always understand
> My own meaning when I would be *very* fine
> But the fact is that I have nothing plann'd
> Except perhaps to be a moment merry –[4]

I have secured your book. I regret to tell you that I have seen no advertisements of it in England, *have* they taken any steps about that? Of course, it's a low time for poetry; but it would be an outrage if you did not get some good reviews in America. And they do take their time in reviewing verse, always. Could you not have it on sale at the Poetry Bookshop, at least? If you were over here it might be possible for you to give a reading there. You say nothing about your plans for next year, which I presume are affected by the war. Better wait till spring and see then –

Bien affectueusement
Th. Eliot

1–Cf. the opening of Sterne's *Tristram Shandy*: 'they order these matters better in France.'
2–Cf. 'Tell it not in Gath, Publish it not in the streets of Askelon' (2 Samuel 1. 20).
3–His crew, of which he was stroke, beat the only other four-oar that could be mustered in wartime Oxford. Later his prized pewter mug was stolen during a removal.
4–Byron, *Don Juan* IV v: 'I don't pretend that I quite understand / My own meaning when I would be *very* fine; / But the fact is that I have nothing planned, / Unless it were to be a moment merry.' In 1933 TSE wrote that he had thought of prefixing this stanza to *Ash-Wednesday* if ever it went into a second edition: 'There is some sound critical admonition in these lines' (*TUPUC* 30–1).

TO *Conrad Aiken* MS Huntington

Saturday 21 November [1914] Junior Common Room,
Merton College, Oxford

Dear Conrad,

Will you do me a great favour? I enclose a money order for $4. Will you go to Galvin, or to Howard in Cambridge, and order some red or pink roses, Killarney I suppose. I understand that Emily [Hale] is to act in the Cambridge Dramatic play which will be early in December – I suppose the 5th or the 12th; you will have to find out which date, if you can. I enclose a card; please put it in a small envelope and address it to her simply Miss Hale, 'Brattle Hall', and have the roses for the *Saturday* night performance. The name of the play is *Mrs Bumpstead-Leigh*.[1] If you can't find out when the play comes off, or if you can't find out without conspicuous inquiry, or if, as is quite possible, this reaches you too late, simply hold the money and send the flowers at Christmas. In that case the address is

5 Circuit Road,
Chestnut Hill.

I have lent your book to Scofield Thayer,[2] who has expressed himself quite enthusiastic over it. He thinks, as I do, that the title poem is decidedly the most successful and unusual.

Yours
Tom

TO *Eleanor Hinkley* MS Houghton

27 November 1914 Merton College

Dear Eleanor,

I regretted very much that I could not share your supper with you, but I was satisfied on the whole to have the letter for myself. I really feel quite as much *au courant* of Cambridge life as anyone can who has not yet learned the fox trot.[3] In the same mail with your letter came this picture, which I enclose without comment, to indicate my state of mind. I expect

1–*Mrs Bumpstead-Leigh* (1911) is a comedy by Harry James Smith (1880–1918).

2–Scofield Thayer, the future editor of *The Dial*, had known TSE at Milton Academy and Harvard, and was now studying philosophy at Magdalen College, Oxford. See Glossary of Names.

3–The foxtrot, invented by the vaudeville star Harry Fox in New York in the summer of 1914, was danced to ragtime music.

when I return to put myself into the hands of Lily[1] for a month of the strictest training: rise at six, run around Fresh Pond, bath, breakfast of one egg followed by ancle exercises for one hour, knee exercises one hour, and so on; and perhaps by the time I emerge I shall be able to appear in society without your having to blush for me. I was able to make use of the fox trot in a debate in the college common room a few evenings ago. The subject was 'Resolved that this society abhors the threatened Americanisation of Oxford'. I supported the negative: I pointed out to them frankly how much they owed to Amurrican culcher in the drayma (including the movies) in music, in the cocktail, and in the dance. And see, said I, what we the few Americans here are losing while we are bending our energies toward your uplift (building the city beautiful, as a young clergyman so aptly put it); we the outposts of progress are compelled to remain in ignorance of the fox trot. You will be interested to hear that my side won the debate by two votes.

Lily may have forgotten to tell you what struck me very much at the time, that the name of the druggist in whose shop we met was Jones. A really striking motive for EFFIE THE WAIF. How can I work it in? At present I am engaged in drilling and giving names to all the comic and villainous characters who fall in love with EFFIE, and all the villainous and comic characters who fall in love with WILFRED (the hero – his name was Walter, but I thought Wilfred better). As the drayma takes place chiefly on the plains (you must have either the plains or the desert if you expect a good pursuit) there is of course DANCING BEAR the chief of the Pottawottobottommies, a terrible fellow, given to drink, and no end treacherous. Then there is Traihi Sheik, the maharaja of Chowwannugger. You simply have to have either a red Indian or an East Indian, and I see no reason why you should not have both. They will be distinguished from each other by the fact that Bear wears feathers and a very old silk hat (for comic effect a red Indian is absolutely worthless without an old silk hat); while Traihi wears a turban and polo boots (he was at Christ Church): otherwise they are exactly alike, except perhaps that Traihi is a shade the more treacherous and given to drink of the two. The way I bring the latter in I consider especially ingenious. Guendolyne Lady Chumleyumley, who is really Effie's mother, though everybody has guessed it, has been getting lonelier and lonelier all alone in her baronial halls all alone with fifty-five devoted servants (to whom I have not yet given names, but who will all play some part); this process of increasing loneliness has been going on for

1 – Lily Jones, with her sister Pauline, taught dancing and was involved in the theatre.

eighteen years (Effie was lost at the age of one – the audience now computes Effie's age by a sum in higher mathematics similar to that by which I learned the age of my old flame Hannah in Germany). Finally she decides, having had no sleep throughout this time, eighteen years, that something must be done. She receives a tip that there is an old faquir in India who has been very successful in recovering lost umbrellas, etc. It was in India that Effie was stolen. Shall she return to these scenes, so painful to her memory?

If she had had more gumption she would probably have done so long before, but that would have spoiled everything. She arrives in India. Everyone wonders who the strange memsahib is, so liberal with backsheesh (here a street scene, with camels, monkeys (comic) and pythons), but who has never been seen to smile. (She has not smiled for eighteen years). Still beautiful, she has a troupe of comic and villainous lovers of her own, but she *will* remain faithful to the memory of her Adalbert – perhaps he too is still alive (of course he is: but he is still in captivity in Turkestan, where he works on the farm, and we won't get him out for several reels yet). Finally she interviews the faquir. After a lot of hocus pocus, he produces a crystal sphere into which she gazes. The next reel of course shows what she saw in the sphere: the whole history of the foul abduction of her husband and her babe from their station in Kashmeer, with the aid of a monkey, a cobra, and a man-eating tiger. I shall elaborate this later; the point is that she is finally shown Effie in her present position in the act of spurning Peter (Effie is going to be awfully good at spurning before she gets through). Here she faints dead away. Meanwhile Traihi Sheik has been hanging about in the ante room waiting to see the faquir about a matter of a purloined jewel which weighs ten pounds and has religious associations as well, has got tired of waiting, and bursts in just in time to look over her Ladyship's shoulder and catch a glimpse of Effie's face in the crystal. Of course it's all off at once. He turns to the audience, rolls his eyes and tears at his shirt in the usual oriental fashion to show passion.

SCENE: I WILL FIND HER IF SHE LIVES UPON THIS GLOBE. BE SHE PRINCESS OR BE SHE PEASANT MAID. I WILL MAKE HER MAHARANEE OF CHOWWANNUGGER.

I started to tell you all about Effie's lovers, and I hoped to do them up in one letter, but I shall have to postpone the rest. I will only briefly mention Karl Wurst, who works in the barber shop in Medecine Hat. You see, I thought it would be so novel and interesting to have a German spy, and it doesn't interfere with his business in the least to have him in love with Effie (he sees her waiting in the carryall while her so-called father the hon. Cassidy is being shaved: comic scene, Karl slices a bit off his ear while looking out of window at Effie). Of course Karl is really Lieutenant Prince Karl of Katzenkraut-Schwerin, occupied in doing some plans of the local gas-works.

This is nearly the end of the term. I am planning to spend a fortnight or so somewhere on the south coast with two friends – one an Amurrican, the other an Englishman, and then return to London, which I find has a strong attraction for one.

I think that you understand poor Harry [Child] exceedingly well, and you say some things which had not occurred to me. It's just because the whole thing seems so strained and forced, and yet that *given* the premisses, he carries out the programme with so much pluck and modesty and temperateness and sense, that he is particularly appealing and pathetic. And he is what a good many people engaged in religion are not, not because they have more sense or wisdom, but simply because they have not the fortitude or feeling. I feel a particular sympathy with him, because I know that I may have come very near to drifting (if you would use the word drift – err is perhaps better) into something rather similar, though with very different dogmas; it begins with having intelligence and not applying it to some subject matter which should be at once personal, and solid enough to let one's personality develop freely without allowing it to wander into freaks and vagaries. Anyway, I have had for several years a distrust of strong convictions in any theory or creed which can be formulated. One must have theories, but one need not believe in them! I wish I could see how it was going to end for Harry. I don't believe he has anything very serious on his conscience, but even two or three merely wasted years are something which such a man may never be able to forget or smile at.[1]

I haven't very many

BRILLIANTS

Scout (breaking a tumbler with his thumb before my very eyes):

Kind o' light for college use, aint they, sir?

I'm only a plain man, Effie, but I love you.

(Thanksgiving Day sermon): . . . And what are we, the young men of America, doing to help build the city of God? . . . (Silence, followed by breathing).

Affectionately
Tom

1 – TSE made a marginal line against this paragraph and wrote 'What syntax'.

You will be interested in Hawkes, one of the most attractive men (and the best scholar) in the college, who is engaged to a German girl, and doesn't want to go to fight in the least.[1] It seems a pity that he couldn't have broken his ancle last summer, instead of little Bulmer,[2] who I think regrets his incapacity. These things don't happen only in civil-war plays, you see.

TO *Norbert Wiener* TS MIT

[December 1914] Swanage, Dorsetshire

Dear Wiener,

Did you ever get a note from me? I addressed it to 'Malcolm' Street, but it occurred to me afterwards that you might have meant 'Magdalen St'[3] and I had misread it.[4] If you are in London any time during the vac. you will probably find me at the address below.

Sincerely,
T. S. Eliot

1 Gordon St
Gordon Square
W.C.

TO *Conrad Aiken* MS Huntington

31 December 1914 [London]

My dear Conrad,

Thank you very much for performing my commission so cleverly; I hope that it did not give you great inconvenience; and I hope that you will let

1–Frederick Hawkes (1892–1974) served in the war, after which he married his German fiancée. He ultimately became President of the College of Estate Management and Master of the Worshipful Company of Farmers.
2–John Legge Bulmer went up to Merton in 1913. As a second lieutenant in the 5th Oxford and Bucks. Light Infantry, he was reported missing, presumed killed, in action in France, on 3 May 1917, aged twenty-two.
3–Magdalene; Magdalen is the spelling used in Oxford.
4–He had been right the first time: on 7 Jan. 1915 he sent a postcard to Scofield Thayer, reading: 'I forgot to say that Wiener's address is 26 Malcolm St.' The postcard shows Rembrandt's *Le Philosophe en Méditation* (Louvre), with its spiral staircase, and to the right of the picture, TSE wrote: 'Something pour faire descendre la dame aux cheveux rouges. Moralité de [?] Toujours prêt' ['Something to make the lady with the red hair come down. Ready made morality'].

me know if there were any extra expenses in the way of express or messenger commissions; also let me know (to appease mere curiosity), how you informed yourself of the place and time.

I am back in London now till January 15, not at your old home, which had run down fearfully in cooking, but at a pension off Gordon Square,[1] in rather a nice street, where the houses are neither named nor painted. The inhabitants however are not interesting, but are mostly Americans – including two middlewestern professors and their families. We have six weeks vacation, of which I spent nearly three at the seashore [at Swanage] in Dorsetshire.

Oxford is all very well, but I come back to London with great relief. I like London, now. In Oxford I have the feeling that I am not quite alive – that my body is walking about with a bit of my brain inside it, and nothing else. As you know, I hate university towns and university people, who are the same everywhere, with pregnant wives, sprawling children, many books, and hideous pictures on the walls. I have decided to have no pictures on the walls, but I should like some good china. Of my own choosing: solid glowing colours, and a few Indian silks, and perhaps a terracotta by *Maillol*.[2] Outside I should have two bell pulls, viz –

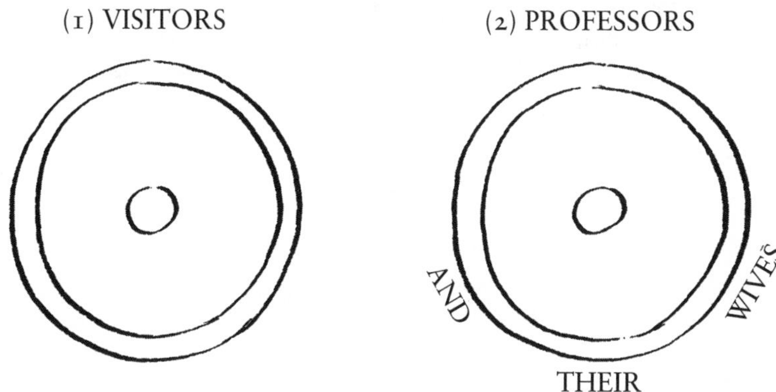

and the second should have no bell. Come let us desert our wives and fly to a land where there are no Medici prints, nothing but concubinage and conversation. That is my objection to Italian Art: the originals are all right, but I don't care for the reproductions.

Oxford is very pretty, but I don't like to be dead. I don't think I should stay there another year, in any case; but I should not mind being in

1 – At 1 Gordon Street.
2 – Aristide Maillol (1861–1944): French sculptor who specialised in classical female nudes.

London, to work at the British Museum. How much more self-conscious one is in a big city! Have you noticed it? Just at present this is an inconvenience, for I have been going through one of those nervous sexual attacks which I suffer from when alone in a city. Why I had almost none last fall I don't know – this is the worst since Paris. I never have them in the country. Wiener, like a great wonderful fat toad bloated with wisdom, has returned to Cambridge; Scofield Thayer, who has developed a good deal and promises to be a fine dilettante and talker if he loses all literary ambition, has also gone to Cambridge to see Santayana;[1] Pound and Russell I have not yet found; Armstrong is in camp in Putney, where I have written to him; and another man is in the country. So for a couple of days I have seen no one but the humble folk of the pension. I am very dependent upon women (I mean female society); and feel the deprivation at Oxford – one reason why I should not care to remain longer – but there, with the exercise and routine, the deprivation takes the form of numbness only; while in the city it is more lively and acute. One walks about the street with one's desires, and one's refinement rises up like a wall whenever opportunity approaches. I should be better off, I sometimes think, if I had disposed of my virginity and shyness several years ago: and indeed I still think sometimes that it would be well to do so before marriage.

I hope you will write soon and tell me about yourself. I think one's letters ought to be about oneself (I live up to this theory!) – what else is there to talk about? Letters should be indiscretions – otherwise they are simply official bulletins.

Always yours
Tom

1 – George Santayana, writer and philosopher: see Glossary of Names. On 15 Nov. he spoke at the Cambridge Heretics on 'An Interpretation of Transcendentalism'. In Mar. 1915 Thayer would address the Heretics on 'The Aesthetic Value of Orthodoxy'.

1915

TO *Eleanor Hinkley* MS Houghton

3 January 1915[1] London

Dear Eleanor,

Just a line to bear to you and yours the ringing greeting of friend to friend at the season of high festival – may the New Year (a baby face with golden promise fraught)[2] bring fulfilment of all desires and rare heart's ease.

I promised to tell you more of my heroines, but have only time for three of those particularly dead gone on our Wilfred. First there is

PAPRIKA!

Mexican dancer (pianola voluntary: 'Carmen').[3] This part is created for Amy.[4] Huge eyes and a stiletto. Easily offended. Does a dance with castanets. Rejected by Wilfred. Swears revenge, and is aided by her admirer DOMINGO and his band of banditti. She is to be one of our best eye-rollers. A more sympathetic part is that of

EARLY BIRD

Indian maiden. Proud, but noble. She has a wonderful prose style: *SHALL EARLY BIRD, DAUGHTER OF OOPALOOMPAH, CHIEF OF THE BOOZAWAYS DO OBEISANCE TO THE GREAT WHITE FATHER OF THE PALEFACES? NOT WHILE THE BISON STAMPS UPON THE PLAINS OF MY FOREFATHERS.*

She is engaged to Night Hawk, but throws him over when Wilfred appears. Later, she is killed while saving W.'s life.

There is a more cheerful part

1–Misdated 1914.

2–Cf. perhaps 'But soon – like any human life / The golden promise of whose dawn doth fail' (James Thomson, 'The Doom of a City I').

3–A popular 'Carmen Potpourri' from Bizet's opera *Carmen* was adapted for pianola.

4–Amy de Gozzaldi (d. 1981) – who had played the part of his wife Fanny to TSE's Lord Bantock in the Cambridge Social Dramatic Club production of Jerome K. Jerome's *Fanny and the Servant Problem* (1908), in 1912–13 – married Richard Hall (1889–1966), a classmate of TSE.

PEGOON

the Irish lass (pianola voluntary: 'Wearin' o' the Green'.[1] Tremendous applause in S. Boston) daughter of Mrs Flaherty, who runs the hash house. She has thirty-one cowboy admirers (I forgot to say the Paprika had thirty-one Mexican 'greaser' admirers – there is a battle later) headed by Grizzly Joe, a tremendous fellow with large feet (comic). Scene: in the hash house. thirty-one admirers eating pork and beans. Pegoon enters. thirty-one attempts to kiss her. Thirty-one slaps on the face (comic). Enter Wilfred. Evident admiration on the part of Pegoon. Evident jealousy on the part of the thirty-one. Grizzly Joe (so called because he once slew a bear by hugging it to death) challenges him to a wrestling match. Wilfred (very slender, with curly hair) knows jiu jitsu and throws Joe into the horse-trough. Splash (comic). Reconciliation.

BOYS, THIS YERE TENDERFOOT BEATS US ALL. SHAKE ON IT PARD!

The thirty-one help in several rescues, and Pegoon ultimately marries Joe.

I have just thought of a part for Frederic.[2] It is the

REV. HAMMOND AIGS

comic negro minister, of the 'come breddern' type. Beyond a tendency to gin, chicken-stealing and prayer, I have not elaborated his part. (Adalbert is still getting in the hay in Turkestan. A good part for Harvey).[3]

I have just been to a cubist tea. There were two cubist painters, a futurist novelist, a vorticist poet and his wife, a cubist lady black-and-white artist, another cubist lady, and a retired army officer who has been living in the east end and studying Japanese (now thinking of going to Central America to avoid rheumatism). We discussed poetry, art, religion, and the war, all in quite an intelligent way, I thought. On the way home was accosted by an elderly person in spectacles, who asked if it did not at once strike my eye that he was perfectly sober? I said yes; and he proceeded to inform me that he was a Scotchman, not a Scotchman from Scotland, but a Scotchman from Ceylon, and asked me if I could put him in the way of a job in the Electrical Way? Or in the Medical Way? The lords of the Admiralty, said he, educated him both as an Electrician and as a medico

1–'The Wearin' o' the Green' was an anonymous street-ballad of 1798 popularised by the playwright Dion Boucicault (1822–90) and recorded by John McCormack, *c.*1914.

2–TSE's cousin, the Revd Frederick May Eliot (1889–1958), graduated in 1911 from Harvard Divinity School and in 1915 became associate minister of the First Parish in Cambridge; later president of the American Unitarian Association.

3–George Harvey Hull (1879–1974), lawyer.

(yes, medico – you can see I've been to the grammar school, sir). Are ye an American, noo? Then I insist on shakin' hands with you, sir; I've been in America. From Boston? Then I'll shake hands again, I was in the north, too, in Toronto. – I thought his eloquence worth a sixpence (for bread and cheese, yes, and a cup o' cold water, as the parson says).

My Christmas day was passed very quietly; and dined with Norbert Wiener, who is a vegetarian, and the lightest eater I have ever seen.

This pension is not a very interesting one. There is Prof. Ellwood[1] and his family, from the University of Missouri (says my mother is one of his three dearest friends in St Louis), a Prof. Cajore and his wife from Colorado, with whom I talk about mathematics, of which I know nothing; Dr and Mrs Greever, just out of Harvard graduate school (Dept of English), Dr McLeod, ditto,[2] Miss Morgan, middle-aged English lady who likes to talk French, Mrs Nichols an elderly white rabbit with a very small timid daughter who plays solitaire when it rains, Mrs Cook and Miss Cook (New Zealand) with red hair who sleeps very late; Mr and Miss Mott his daughter, very mysterious, talk English with a slight German accent, and talk English *to eacher other* – Miss Mott rouges very badly in the evening; Miss Bosche (?) American art student who hates the Germans and is afraid of Zeppelins. – Not a very remarkable outfit, is it?

I have been passing my days at the British Museum library, with occasional walks, and tea when there is anyone to have it with. I like London – not that I don't like Oxford, as universities go, but I could never endure to live there – and London agrees with me – better in fact than the seashore did. I had a pleasant fortnight there however, with the most intelligent of the Englishmen at Merton,[3] and an American,[4] who, if not intelligent, was at least an excellent butt for discourse, as he defended with

1–Charles A. Ellwood (1873–1946) had founded in 1900 the Department of Sociology at the University of Missouri; later author of *Sociology and Modern Social Problems* (1935).

2–Gustave Greever and Malcolm McLeod were also Sheldon Travelling Fellows from Harvard.

3–Karl Culpin (1893–1917), of Anglo-German parentage, was TSE's closest friend at Merton. He went as an exhibitioner to Oxford from Doncaster Grammar School, taking a first in Modern History in 1915. His call-up was delayed owing to poor eyesight, but he became a second lieutenant in the Gloucestershire Regiment and died of wounds received in action, 15 May 1917.

4–Brand Blanshard (1892–1987) – Professor of Philosophy at Yale, 1945–61 – recalled how on this holiday, TSE 'sat at the dining room table each morning with a huge volume of Russell and Whitehead's *Principia Mathematica* propped open before him. He had a certain facility in dealing with its kind of symbols; he said that manipulating them gave him a curious sense of power' ('Eliot at Oxford', in *T. S. Eliot: Essays from the 'Southern Review'*, ed. James Olney [1988]).

great zeal all the great American fallacies, and exhibited all the typical American middle class confusion of thought – anxious to be broadminded (that is, to be vague), to have wide interests (that is to say, diffuse ones), to be tolerant (of the wrong things) etc., and very amiable, though I think he has come to regard me as an unscrupulous sophist – as I always took either the ultra conservative or the ultra radical view. But I think one can discuss the difference between ideas in process of development and ideas which have gone as far as they will ever go – and his (at twenty-three) were the latter, so I was myself the less tolerant.

BRILLIANTS

So you're one of the Harvard young men? And what is your home state, Mr Eliot?

From Effie the Waif:

'Welcome my lord and lady' cried old Blenkinsop the housekeeper, in her quavering silvery voice, 'Welcome back to East Lynne!'[1]

Affectionately
Tom

Do tell me all about your part in the 47 play.[2] Thank you much for the cards.

Did Bill Green[e] never come to call? I sent a card to him long ago (c/o Harv. Univ'y).

TO *Norbert Wiener* MS MIT

6 January 1915 1 Gordon St, Gordon Square, W.C.

Dear Wiener,

I am returning herewith the essay on relativism[3] and the paper on the rearrangement of integers.[4] The latter I have only glanced at, but I know that it would take me so long to puzzle the paper out that I had better return it at once in the hope that I may obtain a copy at some later date.

1–Mrs Henry Wood's best-selling sensation novel *East Lynne* (1861) enjoyed considerable success in a stage adaptation featuring the famous line 'Gone! And never called me mother!'

2–She was playing Margaret Westby in Mark W. Reed's farce, *In for Himself*.

3–'Relativism', *Journal of Philosophy, Psychology and Scientific Methods,* 11: 21 (8 Oct. 1914), 561–77.

4–'On a Method of Rearranging the Positive Integers in a Series of Ordinal Numbers Greater than That of Any Given Fundamental Sequence of Ω', *The Messenger of Mathematics* 43 (May 1913–Apr. 1914), 97–105.

You mentioned the 'Highest Good'[1] and the 'Synthetic Logic'[2] as the ones I may keep. There are two more – the Logic of Relations[3] and the Relative Position[4] – which have 'compliments of the author' written on the cover. As however you do not refer to them in your letter, pray let me know in case you wish these returned also. With many thanks.

The Relativism I cordially agree with, but nearly all of the subject matter I think we had already touched upon, at one time or another, in conversation. I hope that you will have reprints taken of it, in order that the doctrine may be promulgated. Such a doctrine can however, as it seems to me, be worked out, under different hands, with an infinite variety of detail. One can, I should think, be a relative idealist or a relative realist. What it seems to me to lend itself to most naturally, is a relative materialism – or at least this is the way in which my sympathies incline. The only way in which we can talk about the 'universe' at all, it seems to me, is with reference to the universe of physical science; or, in other words the mechanistic world is that to which one would tend to conform.[5]

In a sense, of course, all philosophising is a perversion of reality: for, in a sense, no philosophic theory makes any difference to practice. It has no working by which we can test it. It is an attempt to organise the confused and contradictory world of common sense, and an attempt which invariably meets with partial failure – and with partial success. It invariably involves cramming both feet into one shoe: almost every philosophy seems to begin as a revolt of common sense against some other theory, and ends – as it becomes itself more developed and approaches completeness – by itself becoming equally preposterous – to everyone but its author. The theories are certainly, all of them, implicit in the inexact experience of every day, but once extracted they make the world appear as strange as Bottom in his ass's head.

– These are all obvious remarks which I need not weary you with: but the upshot is (or would be if I continued till I had really expressed my meaning) that relativism, strictly interpreted, is not an antidote for the other systems: one can have a relative absolute if one likes, for it is all one

1–'The Highest Good', *Journal of Philosophy, Psychology and Scientific Methods* 11 (10 Sept. 1914), 512–20.

2–'Studies in Synthetic Logic', *Proceedings of the Cambridge Philosophical Society* 18 (1914), 14–28.

3–'A Simplification of the Logic of Relations', *Proceedings of the Cambridge Philosophical Society* 17 (1914), 387–90.

4–'A Contribution to the Theory of Relative Position', *Proceedings of the Cambridge Philosophical Society* 17 (1914), 441–9.

5–'He said, this universe is very clever / The scientists have laid it out on paper' (*IMH*, 71).

if one call the Absolute, Reality or Value. It does not exist for me, but I cannot say that it does not exist for Mr Bradley. And Mr Bradley may say that the Absolute is implied *for* me *in* my thought – and who is to be the referee?

Of course one cannot avoid metaphysics altogether, because nowhere can a sharp line be drawn – to draw a sharp line between metaphysics and common sense would itself be metaphysics and not common sense. But relativism does I think *suggest* this recommendation: not to pursue any theory to a conclusion, and to avoid complete consistency. Now the world of natural science may be unsatisfying, but after all it is the most satisfactory that we know, so far as it goes. And it is the only one which we must *all* accept. One cannot, of course, hope to separate Reality from Value. Some philosophies are only a play upon this ambiguity of the word Reality. In a way the most valuable is the most real, and the beauty of a work of art is in this way more real to me than its ultimate (or relatively ultimate) physical constituents. But one has got to neglect some aspects of the situation, and what relativism does, it seems to me, is to neglect *consciously* where realism protests that there is nothing to neglect, and idealism that it has neglected nothing. Thus I put, frankly arbitrarily, Reality and Value as opposite ends of a scale. Nowhere, of course, is either *utterly* absent. But I am content to say figuratively that the goal to which 'reality' strives is the world of the materialist. One is equally free to say that it 'strives' toward the other end too. Of course it does not get there, in either case.

I am quite ready to admit that the lesson of relativism is: to avoid philosophy and devote oneself to either *real* art or *real* science. (For philosophy is an unloved guest in either company). Still, this would be to draw a sharp line, and relativism preaches compromise. For *me*, as for Santayana, philosophy is chiefly literary criticism and conversation about life;[1] and you have the logic, which seems to me of great value. The only reason why relativism does not do away with philosophy altogether, after all, is that there is no such thing to abolish! There is art, and there is science. And there are works of art, and perhaps of science, which would never have occurred had not many people been under the impression that there was philosophy.

1–Though Santayana wrote literary as well as philosophical essays, and his *Three Philosophical Poets: Lucretius, Dante and Goethe* (1910) moves between literature and philosophy, he did not actually speak of philosophy as literary criticism. In 1922 he wrote, 'Criticism is something purely incidental – talk about talk – and to my mind has no serious value, except perhaps as an expression of the philosophy of the critic' (quoted in John McCormick, *George Santayana: A Biography* [1987], 247).

However, I took a piece of fairly technical philosophy for my thesis, and my relativism made me see so many sides to questions that I became hopelessly involved, and wrote a thesis perfectly unintelligible to anyone but myself; and so I wished to rewrite it. It's about Bradley's theory of judgment, and I think the second version will be entirely destructive. I shall attack first 'Reality' second 'Idea' or ideal content, and then try to show sufficient reason for attempting to get along without any theory of judgment whatsoever. In other words, there are many objects in the world (I say many, as if one could draw a sharp line, though in point of fact it is degree everywhere) which can be handled as things sufficiently for ordinary purposes, but not *exactly* enough to be subject matter for a science – no definition of judgment, that is, is formally either right or wrong; and it simply is a waste of time to define judgment at all.

Well, I think I have bored you with these commonplaces long enough. Do let me know if you wish the other papers back. I thank you for sending them to me.

I have given a card of introduction to you to a friend of mine Thayer, an American (Harvard '13) now in Oxford. I do not know whether you will find much in common, but he was anxious to meet you, and is intelligent. He is a friend and admirer of Santayana's.

Sincerely
Eliot

TO *Eleanor Hinkley* TS Houghton

[Postmark 27 January 1915] [Merton College, Oxford]

SCENE I[1]

Miss Elizabeth Biddy, her tiring woman

B: And saw you Master Frederick at the ball, miss?

E: Ay, that I did, Biddy, and I vow I believe there was none there to match him. With what an easy grace did he enter the room, dextrously advancing one foot before the other; how magisterially did he glance about him, as one who knew himself formed to set all female hearts in commotion, and yet aware of his own excellences and perfections would not acknowledge himself ~~aware~~ sensible that he was observed; how punctilious was his manner; how exact his dress; how informing

1 – This *jeu d'esprit* was prompted by the announcement of the engagement of his cousin the Revd Frederick Eliot to Elizabeth Lee.

his discourse; how aimiable and condescending his smile; how gay and sprightly his sallies, and yet all the while with a kind of sad gravity about him, as one accustomed to consideration of weighty matters, and who knew how to reprove and check any unseemly levity. I confess that when he did summon me to the Sir Roger de Coverly, my knees would scarce sustain me.

B: Fye, my lady, I do perceive your ladyship has taken a fancy to the gentleman.

E: Ah, Biddy, how shrewdly do you devine my thoughts! Tis true he has taken my fancy hugely.

B: I beseech you, miss, bestow not your heart so lightly. Tis not five years that he hath smiled upon you, and men are ever fickle creatures.

E: Tis justly you advise me Biddy. I have indeed some comeliness of feature; but whether he deems me worthy for his spouse, or whether he but toys with me, that I cannot tell. Blame rather the weakness of my sex, than the impetuosity of my blood, or the defect of my understanding, when I avow that I look upon him with aspiration of holy wedlock.

Enter Footman.

F: Master Frederick waits below, miss, and he bid me request of you that you dally not, for tis but fifteen minutes he can give you.

E: (aside) Oh my heart, how it flutters . . . Tell him I descend forthwith.

SCENE II

Miss Elizabeth Master Frederick

* * * * * * * * *

E: Oh la, Master Frederick, you men are such dissemblers, I vow there's no believing a one of you. Will you never ha' done a-plaguing a poor maid?

F: Miss Elizabeth, the devotion and ardour of my flame in the past is sufficient earnest and token guarantee of my constancy in the future, and any further hesitation upon your part would argue not that natural coyness and timidity which in the female appears so seemly, but rather a coldness of complexion and a defect of appreciation of my merits. Conscious as I am, and as I ought to be, of the honour I bestow, and of the exalted and difficult post which I propose that you should occupy, I yet am fully minded to make you my wife.

E: Then, Master Frederick, I will make no further conditions but own myself your willing slave and adorer. And still I admire much whether you have not learnt these blandishments and cunning wiles which bespeak such knowledge of the female heart, at the cost of those victims of whom perhaps your Elizabeth is not the last.

F: (*on one knee*) My Elizabeth!

(*Sensation among the old ladies in the front row*)

He rises, his boots creaking as he does so. 'There, that's settled'. *Looks at his watch.* 'Now I must be off to address a meeting of the Church Lads Brigade in Arlington'. *Starts to put on his rubbers.* 'Oh, I forgot'. *Advances f.c..* 'Permit me'. *Kisses her decorously in exact centre of left cheek.*

CURTAIN

TO *J. H. Woods*

MS Professor David G. Williams

28 January 1915 Merton College, Oxford

Dear Professor Woods,

I have not forgotten. I am sending you under separate cover the notes on Joachim's *Ethics* for the first term, including all that he has to say *up to* Book V. In script are the more important marginal notes, and the references of course are to Burnet's text.[1] I hope to send you Collingwood's notes within a fortnight. I hope that some small part of the notes will be of use to you.

My notes on the *Post-Anal.* and on Zabarella on the *de An.* are brief and marginal, or on interleaves, but I will put them in order for you.

I have written, at Mr Joachim's suggestion, to Mr R. P. Hardie of Edinburgh, who knows the resources of Italian booksellers, but have not yet had an answer.

I am continuing with Joachim's and Smith's lectures, and with Joachim's *Post-Anal.*, and am taking up a class in Plotinus with Stewart. I shall go to Smith's and I expect Stewart's informals as well. For Joachim I am now writing papers on Plato, and shall later write on Aristotle. He is much better on historical problems than on constructive philosophy I think, and is really almost a genius, with respect to Aristotle. In general philosophical discussion I did not often really 'get anywhere' with him, though this failure was due no doubt as much to my fatal disposition toward scepticism as to his Hegelianism. I find that I take so much keener enjoyment in criticism than in construction that I propose making a virtue of a vice and recasting my thesis with a mind to this limitation; as I find satisfaction only in the historical aspect of philosophy. I had great difficulty, even agony, with the first draft, owing to my attempt to reach a positive conclusion; and so I should like to

1–TSE's annotated copy of *The Ethics of Aristotle*, ed. John Burnet (1900), is in his library.

turn it into a criticism and valuation of the Bradleian metaphysic – for it seems to me that those best qualified for such tasks are those who have held a doctrine and no longer hold it. It is possible that I may prefer to remain here for the spring term, as I shall not be done with the commentaries within the next six weeks.

Very sincerely yours
Thomas S. Eliot

TO *Professor L. B. R. Briggs* MS Harvard

28 January 1915 Merton College

My dear Dean Briggs,

In accordance with the instructions of my letter, I offer respectfully this account of my work. I was in residence at this college for the first term of eight weeks from the 5th October to the 5th December. During this period I attended three sets of lectures, one on logic, the other two explanations of texts of Aristotle; I also participated in a small class reading the *Posterior Analytics* of Aristotle under my tutor Mr Joachim; and I attended the weekly discussion class of Professor J. A. Smith. I also brought once a week to Mr Joachim a short paper dealing with some one of the questions considered in the thesis which I hope to present for the degree of Ph.D. at Harvard; this paper we discussed always in detail; and I hope that at the end of the year Mr Joachim will be able to give a satisfactory report of this work and also of the work in his class. I have spent a large part of my time studying certain Italian commentaries upon Aristotle which he has recommended to me.

During the vacation I continued my reading, both during a fortnight in the country, and the rest of the period in London, where I devoted my time to the use of another commentary preserved in the British Museum.

The present term will continue much the same routine. Instead of one of the lecture courses (now completed) I pursue a class under Professor Stewart, reading Plotinus, and the essays which I carry to Mr Joachim are to be devoted to questions of criticism of Plato and Aristotle.

I had had some purpose of removing to Gottingen or Berlin for the spring term (from the latter part of April); but as I have become engrossed in the work I am doing here in Greek Philosophy, I shall probably continue as before. I have consulted Professor Woods upon this matter, and have been in communication with him throughout. Last summer was to have been spent in Germany, but soon after the outbreak of war the impossibility of securing money made it necessary to return to London.

I have the honour to remain
Very sincerely yours
Thomas S. Eliot

TO *Ezra Pound*[1] MS Beinecke

2 February [1915] Merton College

My dear Pound,

I am very glad to hear from you, and[2] it is certainly very kind of you to make these efforts[2] on my behalf. I enclose a copy of the Lady,[3] which seems cruder and awkwarder and more juvenile every time I copy it. The only ~~enrichment~~ enhancement which time has brought is the fact that by this time there are two or three other ladies who, if it is ever printed, may vie for the honour of having sat for it. It will please you, I hope, to hear that I had a Christmas card from the lady,[4] bearing the 'ringing greetings of friend to friend at this season of high festival'. It seems like old times.

I must thank you again for your introduction to the Dolmetsch family[5] – I passed one of the most delightful afternoons I have ever spent, in one of the most delightful households I have ever visited. You were quite right – there was no difficulty about the conversation, and I made friends with the extraordinary children in no time, and am wild to see them again. As for the dancing, they all danced (except the head of the family) for about an hour, I think, while I sat rapt. I have corresponded with [Wyndham] Lewis,[6] but his puritanical principles seem to bar my way to Publicity. I fear that King Bolo and his Big Black Kween will never burst into print.

1–Ezra Pound: see Glossary of Names.
2–Above these smudged words TSE added 'excuse tea', which he had spilt on them.
3–'Portrait of a Lady'.
4–Miss Adeleine Moffatt, the subject of the poem, lived behind the State House in Boston and invited selected Harvard undergraduates to tea. During a visit to London in 1927 she asked the Eliots to dine, offering 'a modest choice of dates to sacrifice yourselves on the altar of New England', but they were away.
5–Arnold Dolmetsch (1858–1940), musician and craftsman, who made early English musical instruments and revived the playing of them. The eldest of his four gifted children was then aged eight.
6–(Percy) Wyndham Lewis, writer and painter: see Glossary of Names. Though often difficult and cantankerous, he was greatly admired by TSE.

I understand that Priapism, Narcissism etc. are not approved of, and even so innocent a rhyme as

. . . pulled her stockings off
With a frightful cry of 'Hauptbahnhof!!'

is considered decadent.[1]

I have been reading some of your work lately. I enjoyed the article on the Vortex (please tell me who Kandinsky is).[2] I distrust and detest Aesthetics, when it cuts loose from the Object, and vapours in the void, but you have not done that. The closer one keeps to the Artist's discussion of his technique the better, I think, and the only kind of art worth talking about is the art one happens to like. There can be no contemplative or easychair aesthetics, I think; only the aesthetics of the person who is about to do something. I was fearful lest you should hitch it up to Bergson or James or some philosopher, and was relieved to find that Vorticism was not a philosophy.

I hope that your work is progressing satisfactorily. I probably shall not be in town again until March. I hope that Yeats will still be there. Please remember me to Mrs Pound.

Sincerely yours Thomas S. Eliot

I enclose one small verse. I know it is not good, but everything else I have done is worse. Besides, I am constipated and have a cold on the chest. Burn it.

SUPPRESSED COMPLEX[3]

She lay very still in bed with stubborn eyes
Holding her breath lest she begin to think.
I was a shadow upright in the corner
Dancing joyously in the firelight.

1–'Eliot has sent me Bullshit and the Ballad for Big Louise. They are excellent bits of scholarly ribaldry. I am longing to print them in *Blast*; but stick to my naif determination to have no "Words ending in –Uck, –Unt and –Ugger",' said WL to EP in Jan. 1915 (*Pound/Lewis: The Letters of Ezra Pound and Wyndham Lewis*, ed. Timothy Materer [1985], 8). For 'King Bolo and his Big Black Kween', see *IMH*, 315–21.

2–Wassily Kandinsky (1886–1944), Russian abstract painter and writer on art. EP had written that he thought WL 'a more significant artist than Kandinsky', adding that 'I have not yet seen enough of Kandinsky to use a stronger verb than "think"' ('Affirmations . . . II. Vorticism', *New Age* 16: 11 (14 Jan. 1915), 277–8; reprinted in *Ezra Pound and the Visual Arts*, ed. Harriet Zinnes (1980).

3–*IMH*, 54.

She stirred in her sleep and clutched the blanket
with her fingers
She was very pale and breathed hard.
When morning shook the long nasturtium creeper in
the tawny bowl
I passed joyously out through the window.

TO *Conrad Aiken* MS Huntington

25 February [1915] Merton College

My dear Conrad,

I was very much grieved to hear of your loss, though of course I had not known of your expectations.[1] But I hope that Jessie is well, and that John is thriving – you do not mention him.

I should think that you would be glad to leave Cambridge [Mass.] for a time at least. Even New York I should think you would prefer, if you have friends there, and unless the cost of living is appreciably higher. Italy I suppose is unlikely to take part in the war, and would be safe enough: but why not try Spain, if you can find a good place for babies? I suppose that one can secure fairly sanitary conditions in the large cities, and in Spain you would be remoter from this exhausting war talk.

I do not know my own plans for the future. Day before yesterday came a telegram from Harvard, notifying me of my renomination to my fellowship. But I do not know what I should do with it if I had it. Oxford I do not enjoy: the food and the climate are execrable, I suffer indigestion, constipation, and colds constantly; and the university atmosphere. If I could be allowed to stay in London and work at the Museum I should be content; but the War suffocates me, and I do not think that I should ever come to like England – a people which is satisfied with such disgusting food *is not* civilised. On the other hand I dread returning to Cambridge, and the nausea of factory whistles at seven and twelve o'clock (one doesn't mind it so much at night – one doesn't *see*, then) and the college bell, and the people in Cambridge whom one fights against and who absorb one all the same. The great need is to know one's own mind, and I don't know that: whether I want to get married, and have a family, and live in America all my life, and compromise and conceal my opinions and forfeit my independence for the sake of my children's future; or save my money and

1 – His second son had died at birth on 11 Feb.

retire at fifty to a table on the boulevard, regarding the world placidly through the fumes of an aperitif at 5 p.m. – How thin either life seems! And perhaps it is merely dyspepsia speaking. I suppose that I shall be forced to a decision in a few days, and if I have to be in Cambridge next winter I shall wish secretly that you remain; but I think you would do well to travel.

I will put one or two small verses into this letter. Pound is still trying to get two of my things into print.

Affectionately
TSE

The idea of a submarine world of clear green light – one would be attached to a rock and swayed in two directions – would one be happiest or most wretched at the turn of the tide?

SUPPRESSED COMPLEX[1]

She lay very still in bed with stubborn eyes
    Holding her breath lest she begin to think.
I was a shadow upright in the corner
    Dancing joyously in the firelight.

She stirred in her sleep and clutched the blanket with her fingers
    She was very pale and breathed hard.
When morning stirred the long nasturtium creeper in the tawny bowl
    I passed joyously out through the window.

AFTERNOON

The ladies who are interested in Assyrian art
Gather in the hall of the British Museum.
The faint perfume of last year's tailor suits
And the steam from drying rubber overshoes
And the green and purple feathers on their hats
Vanish in the sombre Sunday afternoon

As they fade beyond the Roman statuary,
Like amateur comedians across a lawn,
Towards the unconscious, the ineffable, the absolute.

1 – Aiken sold these two poems, copied on the first and third pages of a folded sheet now lost, but made typescript copies (Huntington); see *IMH*.

TO *J. H. Woods* MS Professor David G. Williams

2 March [1915] Merton College

Dear Professor Woods,

I have to thank you for two letters, as well as the cablegram, and I do not know how to thank you for your encouragement and interest. I presume that you have received my cable in reply.

I am still hesitating. I feel, in the first place, that there must be equally deserving and perhaps abler students in the department who would be benefited by a year abroad; and I should feel that perhaps it would be very unfair for me to stand in the way of a man of the grade say of Sen Gupta.[1] And particularly because there is no one piece of work which I should be completing or continuing. I do not feel that I should care to spend another year in Oxford, though I am not dissatisfied with this. Certainly I think that the alternatives seem to be limited to Germany and Italy. I should want to go where I could profitably continue work on Greek philosophy, and perhaps on other periods in the history of philosophy: for, as I said before, the historical and critical aspect is that which now appeals to me the most strongly. I mention Italy as the alternative to Germany, because it is as well to have alternatives at a time like the present; one does not know what may happen by next fall, and it might be that Italy would have more to offer. (I am hopeful, you see, that the Italians will be prudent enough to pursue their present policy of keeping both sides in doubt). But I really do not know what either country has to offer at present, and so cannot present a convincing programme.

Besides reasons of modesty, which are cogent enough, I am also urged by the feeling that it is time to take my degree, if I can, and start my *métier*. I do not know how cogent this feeling ought to be when a man has at least no one dependent on him.

I wait to receive further counsel from you, and it would interest me to know what other students are desirous of the appointment.

I owe you contrite apologies for my inexcusable delay in forwarding more notes. The fact is that my superfluous time has been going (with very meagre results) towards a paper I am to read before the Moral Science Club at Cambridge.[2] As I have chosen an ethical topic I feel some fear of

1–Dhirendra C. Gupta (d. 1956), attended Harvard 1909–12, then returned to India.

2–On 12 Mar., in Russell's rooms, he 'read a paper entitled The Relativity of the Moral Judgment in which he attempted to compromise between an absolute idealist position and a relativist view. In the course of the discussion which followed it became evident that he regarded value as in some sense dependent upon the feeling of a particular subject at a

rough treatment at the hands of Moore and his disciples.[1] But I hope that I can send you the *de Anima* notes by the 15th and follow them with the second section of the *Nic[omachean] E[thics]* notes, and my annotations on the *Post. Anal.* I hope that these will still be of some use to you.

In any case, I shall have to be in America this summer, and hope to see you and Mrs Woods at Rockport.

Yours very gratefully
Thomas S. Eliot

TO *Eleanor Hinkley* MS Houghton

21 Mars [March 1915] [London]

Dear Eleanor

I have really two of your letters to acknowledge and thank for, haven't I? as I have not really written a letter since the important announcement of Master Frederick's engagement. And that, I remember, was not long after Christmas, for I recollect as clearly as 'twere yesterday the shock of surprise when I saw the envelope ('Why the devil is Frederick writing to me?'); so I infer that I have written to you only once in two months or more.

There has really very little happened since. I am back in London now; and as the boarders are few, I have been promoted to the table with the delightful Miss Cook, from New Zealand, with red hair. Her first name is *Sheila*, and she likes pillow fights, and I must finish this page rapidly so that she won't look over my shoulder and see that I've written her name. She is now sitting on the sofa and reading fashion notes aloud to myself and two Harvard Ph.D's of the English department. My friend Miss Smart is still here, and there are also two Belgian ladies who say 'oh yesss!' to everything. That's about all of interest.

I have somewhat enlarged my acquaintance in Oxford society also. Do tell Aunt Susie that the Miss Rhyss' are the most charming persons I have met in Oxford – certainly the most *aristocratic*. They have invited me several times, usually to help entertain Belgians: though I am so

—

particular moment and in some sense not. Conversation was kept up till 11.30' (minutes of the Moral Science Club, Cambridge University Library). See also Jack Pitt, 'Russell and the Cambridge Moral Science Club', *Russell: The Journal of Russell Studies* 1: 2 (1981–2), 112.

1–G. E. Moore (1873–1958): philosopher; author of *Principia Ethica* (1903); Cambridge Apostle.

disaccustomed that when I find myself obliged to make conversation in French at a formal dinner party I break into a perspiration and eat nothing. I also made the cardinal blunder of addressing Sir John as *Mr* Rhys, under the impression that he was somebody else who edited something:[1] I have rectified the error in a distinct voice since.

Besides Belgians, there is a very pretty Miss Cobb <Mr Cobb is English> whose mother was a Bostonian (I don't know what her name was); the mother is an odd fluttering person who is evidently looking out for her daughter, and lays compliments very thick (I know this because I have seen her laying them on to other people); she never talks to me for five minutes without bringing out Julia Ward Howe,[2] whom she knew in Boston, and evidently considers a very illustrious person. – A very tiresome person, I should say, for all the anecdotes about her end by making her recite the 'Battle Hymn of the Republic' (like Mrs Leo Hunt[er]'s '[Ode to an] Expiring Frog')[3] which I always considered pure bombast. But Miss Cobb is very nice. Then there are the Petersens, a mother with three daughters. Unfortunately the beautiful one (really very beautiful indeed) is the younger one, aged sixteen or so; and, as in the *Taming of the Shrew*, the interests of the elder are consulted first. This is really a very nice girl however; she plays the fiddle and raises white rats, and we have lots in common – at least I shall have to take her punting next term. I should like English girls better if they were not so completely managed by their mothers – but perhaps it is merely that the ones I have met have been rather young.

I have met several very agreeable men this term, too. Two Irishmen, who have rather raised my opinion of that race, one or two new Englishmen, and several Indians, (whom on the whole I find more congenial than English – but Bertie Russell says they give him the creeps). As I have said already, I don't think there is any more *brains* here than at Harvard, but the average of culture is far higher. A cultivated aristocracy is sadly to seek even in England, but God knows it is <far> better here than in our Slater-ised society.[4] There is a marked difference I think even between Oxford

1–He had confused his host with Ernest Rhys (1859–1946), the editor of Everyman's Library. Sir John (1840–1915) was Principal of Jesus College and Professor of Celtic. His daughters were Myfanwy and Olwen.

2–Julia Ward Howe (1819–1910), American poet and social reformer; author of 'The Battle-Hymn of the Republic'.

3–Charles Dickens, *Pickwick Papers*, ch. xv: 'Can I view thee panting, lying / On thy stomach, without sighing; / Can I unmoved see thee dying / On a log, / Expiring frog!'

4–Samuel Slater (1768–1835), English-born founder of the American cotton manufacturing industry.

and Cambridge, where I have just been. Both at the Moral Science Club, where I read a paper, and at the Heretics (the leading literary society) the men impressed me by their resemblance to Harvard graduate school types; serious, industrious, narrow and plebeian. The more *brilliant* ones (one or two) more like the clever Jew undergraduate mind at Harvard; wide but disorderly reading, intense but confused thinking, and utter absence of background and balance and proportion. I should expect it to be accompanied by a philistine aristocracy. As I remember, Harry Child's friends were very attractive (three years ago), and there must be many other charming men at Trinity and King's; yet I think the centre of intelligence and the centre of society are probably farther apart at Cambridge than at Oxford. The temper of the place is *scientific*, whereas that of Oxford is *historical*; and history is a more aristocratic pursuit than natural science, and demands a more cultivated mind. Not that Bertie Russell is not an aristocrat, but not quite in that sense; he has a sensitive, but hardly a cultivated mind, and I begin to realise how unbalanced he is. I do enjoy him quite as much as any man I know; we had breakfast with him, and stayed talking with him one night till one o'clock; he talked very well about the war, and is wonderfully perceptive, but in some ways an immature mind: wonderfully set off in contrast by Santayana, (who was in Cambridge too).

Now I am back in London, the town of cubist teas, and find it more delightful and beautiful than ever. Also healthy, which Oxford is not.

Always affectionately
Tom

TO *Mrs Jack Gardner*[1] MS Gardner Museum

4 April [1915] Merton College [Oxford]

My dear Mrs Gardner,

I wonder if you would care for a brief word from London. I have been meaning to write to you for some time. Quite two months ago I think it may have been (or six weeks) I made the acquaintance (at a meeting of the Buddhist Society!) of a man who attracted me by a certain serenity of

1–Isabella Stewart Gardner (1840–1924), prominent Boston hostess and art collector, who bequeathed her Venetian-style house, Fenway Court, with its contents, to the city. Her guest book records two visits by TSE in 1912, on 16 Sept. and between 31 Oct. and 3 Nov.

manner, and by mentioning Mr Okakura.[1] His name was Henry Furst,[2] and as he said he was about to write to you, I asked him to write of me and my intentions. I am sorry not to have seen anything of him since; he said he was going to live at Marston, outside of Oxford; I was unable, during the time I remained in Oxford, to get out to him; and though I have written to him, (at a not very definite address), I have not had a reply. I breakfasted with him once. He showed me a photograph and a letter of poor Matt Prichard, of whom I had heard nothing whatever.[3] I did not realise that we had been so near to each other when the war broke out, he at Freiburg and I at Marburg. As I seem to have lost contact with Furst, and am not in touch with any other of Matt's friends, I should be more than indebted to you if you would let me have word about him: if he is eventually released, especially. Furst spoke of him as very happy, in being able to help other people in the camp. I can imagine its bringing out exclusively the best in his restless spirit; and now that I know that he is there, it seems to me the happiest and best and most appropriate thing for him at such a time as this: a certain curious symbolism about it.

The war is very real and very frightful to me, as I know the country and the people so recently. On the 14 Juillet I was in Brussels, having come from Ostende, Bruges, Ghent, and Antwerp. Two days later I was in Germany, and in a fortnight I wished myself well out of Germany. Not that the people were not very kind to me – the Germans have that hospitality and cordiality which characterises the less civilised peoples. And not that I wish the Germans to be crushed – but France is so important, and defeat would do the French so much harm! This alone outweighs any consideration of right and wrong in my mind. I found that Santayana takes a similar view. At Cambridge, where he has been living, (in hideous lodgings), I discovered him writing an article for the *New Republic* on Spanish feeling toward the war.[4] To turn from these dismal topics; I have been having a very interesting time in London – which grows upon me more and more: – there are at least a dozen people whom I like in London, and that is a great deal. I have been seeing a good deal of some

1–Okakura Kakuzo (1862–1913), Japanese scholar and writer; author of *The Book of Tea* (New York, 1906). From 1906 until his death he was Curator of Chinese and Japanese Art at the Boston Museum of Fine Arts. In 1910 he had taken TSE to meet Matisse.
2–Henry Furst (1893–1967), American journalist and translator of many books into Italian. He studied at Exeter College, Oxford, 1913–14.
3–Matthew Prichard, whom TSE had last seen in Munich in Sept. 1911, was interned by the Germans for the duration of the war. He had known Mrs Gardner since his Boston days, and they kept in touch when he left America in 1907.
4–George Santayana, 'Spanish Opinion on the War', *New Republic*, 10 Apr. 1915.

of the modern artists whom the war has so far spared. One of the most interesting of the radicals – Gaudier-Brzeska[1] – do you know of him? – is in the trenches, (as is the interesting T. E. Hulme);[2] cubism is still represented by Wyndham Lewis, by Jacob Epstein,[3] and a man whose work I like exceedingly, Edward Wadsworth.[4] There has been an exhibition – a very ill-assorted one – at the Goupil gallery:[5] Lewis had a fine canvas, Wadsworth two good woodcuts, Brzeska an interesting small marble, and nothing else of the slightest merit; unless one excepts Epstein's four things, which are certainly extraordinarily *habile* [clever], but did not please me, though once or twice his wood statues (one is painted red) give something suggesting the vigour of a central African image.

I do not know whether you have heard of a certain infamous soi-disant quarterly called *Blast*,[6] only one number of which has so far appeared. If the second ever does appear – it has been impending for two months – I am thinking of sending you a copy, on the supposition that you would not in America see it otherwise; because it might at least amuse you and incidentally because it promises to contain a few things of my own. There

1–Henri Gaudier-Brzeska (1891–1915), French sculptor, was killed in action two months later. EP wrote on him in 'Affirmations . . . V. Gaudier-Brzeska', *New Age* 16: 13 (Feb. 1915), and later in his *Gaudier-Brzeska: A Memoir* (1916).
2–T. E. Hulme (1883–1917), poet and critic, volunteered at the outbreak of war, serving in the trenches until being wounded in Apr. 1915. Back in Britain, he wrote 'War Notes' for the *New Age* (using the pseudonym 'North Staffs') in most weeks from Nov. 1915 to Feb. 1916. He returned to the front in May 1917 and was killed by a shell in Flanders on 28 Sept. Through his anti-romanticism and his dedication to the idea of 'original sin', Hulme exercised a considerable intellectual influence on English modernism. When HR edited his papers as *Speculations* (1924), TSE described him as 'classical, reactionary, and revolutionary', and as 'the forerunner of a new attitude of mind, which should be the twentieth-century mind' (*C.* 2: 9, Apr. 1924).
3–Jacob Epstein (1880–1959), American sculptor championed by EP and WL; naturalised British subject from 1907. He designed the tomb of Oscar Wilde in Père Lachaise, and his *Rock-Drill* was sculpted during his Vorticist period. In 1951 he was to execute a fine bronze head of TSE.
4–Edward Wadsworth (1889–1949), painter and printmaker, served as an intelligence officer with the Royal Naval Volunteer Reserve in the eastern Mediterranean. After being invalided home, he worked on naval camouflage. In 'Edward Wadsworth, Vorticist. An authorised appreciation', EP remarked: 'The vorticist movement is not less unanimous because its two best known painters, Mr. Lewis and Mr. Wadsworth, are quite different . . . Turbulent energy: repose. Anger: placidity, and so on' (*Egoist* 1: 16, 15 Aug. 1914).
5–The Second London Group Exhibition (Mar. 1915) included many of the Vorticists backed by EP, including WL, Epstein and Wadsworth. The Vorticists held their own exhibition at the Doré Gallery in July.
6–The second and final issue of *Blast*, in July 1915, contained the four 'Preludes' and 'Rhapsody on a Windy Night'.

will be some poems by a girl named Jessie Dismorr,[1] which I think might interest you.

I see the charming Bertie Russell from time to time; having in fact been to Cambridge recently . . . Of my work in Oxford there is little to say; it is satisfactory, but London is infinitely more attractive, and since I am in London now, I talk of that instead! The last time I was here I had the pleasure of meeting Yeats: he is now in Ireland, I believe because a play of Lady Gregory's is coming on at the Abbey.[2] I am hoping for his return – he is a very agreeable talker.

I remain, my dear Mrs Gardner, devotedly yours

Thomas S. Eliot

I was extraordinarily impressed by Flemish art, especially van Eyck –

TO *Ezra Pound* — TS Beinecke

15 April [1915] Merton College, Oxford

Dear Pound:

I hope that my delay in returning the manifesto[3] has not inconvenienced you. A number of criticisms have formed themselves in my head and disintegrated again during the course of the week. I think that a thing of the sort has to be written by one man, and cannot be made up like an Appropriation Bill to please the congressman from Louisiana and Dakotah. Doubtless the enlightened public will see the work of your hands, and I trust that you will keep the same order – i.e. an alphabetical taxis for all the names except your own.

How much is implied by the word Alliance? Is the alliance anything more than for the purposes of the manifesto? Of course I don't know the work of any of these men myself, but that doesn't matter. But I should like to know in what way this is to be promulgated and how followed up.

I have made only ~~one~~ <two> comment<s> in the text, and they can be easily erased. As to the rest, I should have liked a more crystallised

1 – Jessica Dismorr (1885–1939), English artist, had signed the Vorticist Manifesto in the first issue of *Blast* (20 June 1914), and contributed poems and notes to the second. She appears in William Roberts's painting *The Vorticists at the Restaurant de la Tour Eiffel, Spring 1915*.

2 – Lady Augusta Gregory (1852–1932), Irish playwright, folklorist and translator, had founded in 1903 (with WBY and J. M. Synge) the Abbey Theatre, Dublin. *Shanwalla* opened on 8 Apr.

3 – This manifesto was probably connected with EP's (anonymous) 'Preliminary Announcement of the College of Arts', *Egoist* 1: 21 (2 Nov. 1914), 413–14; reprinted as a leaflet in the same month. See *Letters of Ezra Pound*, 81–3.

statement of the function of the university and the need for an intellectual capital. The reference to the war does strike me as platitudinous, and I wonder if one could not get the thing said more concretely and immediately, without the use of such generalisations. <It wd be more irritating, too.> I mean, I like the mention of Stendhal, James, etc., and again in your article 'The Renaissance'[1] you succeed. If you pointed out the need to have our universities situated in and their life merged in the life of a metropolis; the pernicious influence of athletics, social helpfulness and sermons; if it could be mentioned that a university is not the same thing as a school of agriculture, but that America has schools of agriculture which are better and honester places than its universities; because they have a work to do which they can take seriously; and that the function of the university is not to turn out Culcher and Civic Pageants. At present, you see, I am more alarmed at the Americanisation than at the Prussianisation of our universities. The Germans have at least a few facts, and we have only words; they have Archaeologie and we have How to Appreciate the Hundred Best Paintings, the Maiden Aunt and the Social Worker. Something might be said (at another time) about the Evil Influence of Virginity on American Civilisation.

It might be pointed out <again and again> that literature has rights of its own which extend beyond Uplift and Recreation. Of course it is imprudent to sneer at the monopolisation of literature by women.

The Degradation of Women in American Society.

Pardon these ravings: I am suffering from the effects of a debauch and have done nothing but play tennis today, so I am not in a state to talk intelligently. I am likely to be coming up to town for the day on Friday or Saturday next, and should like to see you. Would you be in about tea time perhaps? Or would you be at Lewis's[2] on Saturday?

Yours ever
Th. Eliot

1–The second of three articles under this title, published in *Poetry* Feb., Mar. and May. TSE included them in his choice of *Literary Essays of Ezra Pound* (1954).

2–In his memoir *Blasting and Bombardiering* [1937], WL recounts his first meeting with TSE in EP's flat in Kensington at some time between June 1914 and July 1915. 'A sleek, tall, attractive transatlantic apparition – with a sort of Giaconda smile. I looked up one day from a brooding interval . . . And there, sitting down with a certain stealth, not above a couple of feet away from me, was the author of Prufrock – indeed, it was Prufrock himself: but a Prufrock to whom the mermaids would decidedly have sung . . . For this was a very attractive young Prufrock indeed, with an alert and dancing eye – *moqueur* to the marrow, bashfully ironic, blushfully *taquineur*. But still a Prufrock!' (282–3).

TO *Eleanor Hinkley* MS Houghton

24 April [1915] Merton College

Dear Eleanor,

This will be a short and rambling letter: take it simply as a sort of outlet, for when one returns from a place where one has a number of delightful friends to a place where one has very few, one turns to correspondence for relief. I admit that my preference of London to Oxford is partly the preference of health to indigestion, but as I acquire more friends in the city the difference between English metropolitan and provincial life presents itself more acutely; the latter is so much like *New* England, and the former quite unique. There are at least a dozen people in London whom I like exceedingly. I had lunch with Russell a few days ago, and he talked most brilliantly. (We walked along the Embankment afterwards. He said suddenly 'Do you remember what Mrs Elton's Christian name is?' 'No.' 'It is mentioned once – Harriet Smith says to Emma: "He calls her Augusta. How delightful!!"').[1]

I have been mostly among poets and artists, but I have also met a few ladies, and have even danced. The large hotels have dances on Saturday nights, to which one can go by paying or by taking dinner there. By being admitted to two dancing parties I have met several English girls, mostly about my own age, and especially two who are very good dancers. The English style of dancing is very stiff and old fashioned, and I terrified one poor girl (she is Spanish at that) by starting to dip in my one-step. The two I mentioned are more adaptable, and caught the American style very quickly. As they are emancipated Londoners I have been out to tea or dinner with them several times, and find them quite different from anything I have known at home or here. (I fear my previous generalisations were misleading – they do not seem to apply to London girls over twenty-five.) They are charmingly sophisticated (even 'disillusioned') without being hardened; and I confess to taking great pleasure in seeing women smoke, though for that matter I do not know any English girls who do not. These English girls have such amusing names – I have met two named 'Phyllis' – and one named 'Vivien'.[2]

1 – Jane Austen, *Emma* ch. 32. (The name is in fact used on three later occasions in the novel.)

2 – TSE met Vivien Haigh-Wood in Mar. 1915 at a lunch party in Scofield Thayer's rooms in Magdalen College, Oxford, after which they went punting and dancing: see Vivien Eliot in Glossary of Names.

I went very little to the theatre – saw *Fanny's First Play*[1] which I enjoyed very much – and have been to a few music-halls, and to the cinema with a most amusing French woman who is the only interesting acquaintance at my boarding house. There is a tall English Department Ph.D named Malcolm Macleod to whom I thought of giving an introduction to you, until he pronounced 'moustache' twice with the accent on the first syllable. Have you come across Bill Greene at all? It is not a serious loss if you have not.

I have had a card from Elmer Keith in regard to his engagement: very happy and sentimental. I told him that I was not surprised, because he would be an anomaly as a bachelor. I have looked into a crystal and seen them sitting side by side on a sofa, he reading Francis Thompson aloud, she darning socks. I have a premonition that she wears flannel waists and likes to hear him talk.

There is an interesting rumour about. Keith said that Ann Van Ness told him I was planning to work in the British Museum next winter. A few days later came a letter from Ann, saying that Keith had told her I was planning to work in the British Museum next winter. It seems to be quite settled.

I hope to have news of you before long. You have not told me much about your dramatics.

Affectionately
Tom

TO *J. H. Woods* — MS Professor David G. Williams

6 May [1915] — Merton College

Dear Professor Woods,

I enclose a letter from Mr Hardie, which reached me this morning. If you wish to accept his offer, I could bring the books myself, though I dare say they would be quite as well off by express.

As I have not heard from you for some time, I wonder if you have received two notes, two packages of lecture-notes, and a text of the *Organon*.

I hope you will let me know about next year, because, if I do not have a reappointment, financial conditions make it desirable for me to get as much assistant's work at Harvard as I can adequately perform in addition

1 – First performed in 1911, Shaw's *Fanny's First Play* had been revived in the spring of 1915 at the Kingsway Theatre, starring Henry Ainley and Miles Malleson.

to my own affairs – in case there is room for me. I certainly should not resign in the middle of the year.

I am attending the remainder of Joachim's *Ethics* lectures, some lectures by J. A. Smith on the Concept of Value, a short course by McDougall,[1] and am finishing the *Posterior Analytics*. I am writing papers for Joachim on Aristotle.

Oxford is very charming at this time of year and rather more healthy than at most times [of] year – I have found the climate (and the food!) very difficult.

Santayana is here now, I believe, though I have not been to see him yet.

Very sincerely
Thomas S. Eliot

On 26 June TSE married Vivienne Haigh-Wood at Hampstead Register Office in the presence of her aunt Lillia Symes and her close friend Lucy Thayer (cousin of TSE's friend Scofield Thayer). Their respective parents knew nothing of the wedding beforehand. Bride and groom were both stated to be twenty-six, although she had just turned twenty-seven. TSE was recorded as 'of no occupation' and living at 35 Greek Street, Soho. His father was described as a 'Brick Manufacturer', and Vivienne's father as an 'Artist (Painter)'.

Ezra Pound TO *Henry Ware Eliot* — TS Houghton

[Postmark 28 June 1915] London

Dear Sir,

Your son asked me to write this letter, I think he expects me to send you some sort of apologia for the literary life in general, and for London literary life in particular.

I can only cite my own case as proof that it is possible to exist by letters, not only by popular fiction but by unpopular writing, and I have gone

1–William McDougall (1871–1938), author of *Introduction to Social Psychology* (1908), was then Wilde Reader in Mental Philosophy at Oxford.

through difficulties which it seems needless for T.S.E. to encounter. I may as well be explicit. I came to London in 1908, for some years I have made enough to live on with some comfort. I knew no one when I came, I have written no fiction. I have indeed written scarcely anything save poetry, a few grave articles in the heavier reviews and a certain amount of current criticism.

T.S.E. begins in rather better position. I have already hammered the fact that he can write into [the] heads of four editors (e.g. 'Prufrock' in *Poetry* for June), the most intelligent of the editors needed no demonstration. *Poetry* pays rather well, there are of course other magazines with which it would be advisable for him to get in touch by his own initiative. <Also he should have made acquaintances at Oxford who might give him advantages which I did not have at the start.> If (or when) I succeed in organizing a weekly paper I should certainly take on your son. That event is however (at least for the present) so uncertain that one cannot count upon it solidly. And failing that he will hardly be able to make all his expenses right away at the start. On the other hand I am now much better off than if I had kept on my professorship in Indiana,[1] and I believe I am as well off as various of my friends who had plugged away at law, medicine, and preaching. At any rate I have had an infinitely more interesting life.

As to T.S.E.'s work, I think it the most interesting stuff that has appeared since my own first books, five years ago. Of the conceit of artists there is of course no end, but this letter is between ourselves and I see no reason to beat about the bush. I do not imagine that my name is known to you, or if it is it is merely a name, like another, appearing now and again in the newspapers. Stripped of a certain amount of flimsy notoriety we may say that I have brought something new into English poetry, that I have engineered a new school of verse now known in England, France and America, and incidentally that I have introduced certain young poets to the public. At least I am as closely in touch with what is being done here and in France as it is possible for a man to be, and when I make a criticism of your son's work it is not an amateur criticism. There are a certain number of young men doing good work, of one sort or another, I have in one place and another blamed or commended them. Edgar Lee Masters has just brought out a new book[2] which is, I believe, having a very great success, but Masters is an older man than T.S.E. and even his work seems to me less unusual.

1–EP had been an Instructor in Romance Languages at Wabash College, Crawfordville, 1907–8.

2–TSE thought Edgar Lee Masters's *Spoon River Anthology* (New York, 1915) 'not material of the first intensity' ('Reflections on Vers Libre', *NS* 8 [3 Mar. 1917], 518–19).

I don't know to what extent these critical minutiae ~~entertain~~[1] you, but I may as well set down my own thought as clearly as possible and you can take it or leave it. Apart from all question of 'inspiration' and 'star born genius' I should say that the arts, as the sciences, progress by infinitesimal stages, that each inventor does little more than make some slight, but revolutionizing change, alteration in the work of his predecessors. Browning[2] in his *Dramatis Personae* and in his *Men and Women* developed a form of poem which had lain dormant since Ovid's *Heroides* or since Theocritus. Ovid's poems are, to be sure, written as if they were letters, from Helen to Paris, from Paris to Oenone, etc. In Theocritus (IV. 2 I think) we have a monologue comparable to those of Browning (much more passionate, to be sure, but still comparable as a form).

The Anglo Saxon 'Seafarer' and Rihaku's 'Exile's Letter' are also poems of this sort.[3] Nevertheless Browning's poems came as a new thing in their day. In my own first book I tried to rid this sort of poem of all irrelevant discussion, of Browning's talk *about* this, that and the other, to confine my words strictly to what might have been the emotional speech of the character under such or such crisis. Browning had cast his poems mostly in Renaissance Italy, I cast mine in mediaeval Provence, which was a change without any essential difference. T.S.E. has gone farther and, begun with the much more difficult job of setting his 'personae' in modern life, with the discouragingly 'unpoetic' modern surroundings.

(For what my position is worth, I am willing to say this about him, in print, as soon as the right time comes, for the present I should be glad if you would keep it for family consumption, as the difficulties of an author having a certain number of friends in the same profession are not diminished by having them all know that he thinks much more highly of one than of all the rest.)

Robert Frost has, let us admit, done a book of New England eclogues.[4] (Incidentally, it was I who insisted or 'suggested' that he should do it. He brought me one or two poems that now appear in that book and spoke of more in the making, and he might have brought out the present book without meeting me. However I was one of the first critics to acclaim him and I certainly had some part in getting him to do that series of 'eclogues'.)

1–Word cancelled but not replaced.

2–Next five sentences crossed through, from 'Browning . . .' to '. . . in their day'.

3–EP's 'The seafarer' appeared in *Ripostes* (1912); his version of 'The Exile's Letter' in *Cathay* (1915).

4–Robert Frost, *North of Boston* (1914), which EP reviewed ('Modern Georgics', *Poetry* 5: 3, Dec. 1914), praising Frost for daring to write 'in the natural speech of New England', and calling the book 'a contribution to American literature' (*Selected Essays*, 384–6).

Still a set of provincial studies, local, a bit dull, is a very different thing from poetry which accepts the tone and difficulties of contemporary civilization.

Again with Masters, the work is rough, given the form of poem, it is much easier to do a series such as he has done than it is to bring in a sort of new element, which I think T.S.E. does and will do. His newer things show a great advance in workmanship.

Pardon this flood of detail. I suppose it reduces itself to this: there are a few noteworthy new poets, there are a dozen or so young men with charm, with temperaments, with excellent 'poetic' interiors, some of whom, most of whom seem to me likely to stay stuck plumb where they now are, for the rest of their natural lives (if they don't get fat headed and worse) simply because they 'ain't got the sense' to get on or to invent anything. (I beg you to accept this in the secrecy of the confessional, as I like several of these young men and have no desire for more quarrels than I now have on hand, and no desire to hurt people's feelings unduly, or unduly discourage them.) In some cases they suffer from a deficient culture, for which they cannot be held in any way responsible.

T.S.E. is (as the *Spectator* said of me some years since) 'that rare thing among modern poets, a scholar'.[1] That means not only an advantage in the initial sprint, it means much more: a chance of being able really to finish 'a long distance race', a chance of having matter and volume enough in one to keep on writing more and more interestingly, with increasing precision and development. Mental stamina . . . which I do not see in a number of the advertised writers of the passing year and moment.

As to his coming to London, anything else is a waste of time and energy. No one in London cares a hang what is written in America. After getting an American audience a man has to begin all over again here if he plans for an international hearing. He even begins at a disadvantage. London likes discovering her own gods. Again in a literary career mediocrity is worse than useless. Either a man goes in to go the whole hog or he had better take to selling soap and gents furnishings. The situation has been very well summed up in the sentence: 'Henry James stayed in Paris and read Turgenev and Flaubert, Mr Howells returned to America and read Henry James.'[2]

1 – The anonymous reviewer of *Exultations* went on to call EP 'too bookish and literary' (*The Spectator*, 11 Dec. 1909, 1001).

2 – 'Henry James went to France and read Tourgueneff. W. D. Howells stayed at home and read Henry James' (George Moore, *Confessions of a Young Man* [1888], 254–5).

Now on the practical side a writer making one thousand dollars per year here is, I should say much better off than if he were making five thousand a year in America. In fact so long as he can pay his board and washing and keep a decent coat on his back, he has all his luxuries free and has the most interesting life in the world at his disposal.

(Even if his career is to be half scholastic, any philological job of the first rank must start and get its orientation in the British Museum.)

As for American publication you have readier access, I think, to American magazines from this side of the water, whereas English publication is practically impossible for any man out of England unless he is fully established. (That is to say Kipling might live where he liked).

Again if a man is doing the fine thing and the rare thing, London is the only possible place for him to exist. Only here is there a disciplinary body of fine taste, of powerful writers who 'keep the editors under', who make it imperative that a publisher act in accordance, occasionally, with some dictates other than those of sheer commercialism.

I should, of course, advise T.S.E. to meet personally as many American editors of good standing as is possible, before he returns, and to work his American social connections to the utmost so as to have that anchor to westward. But still you may bear in mind that London imposes her acceptance of a man's work on all the English speaking world and that she accepts no other standard than her own . . . and after some lapse of years that of Paris. At any rate if T.S.E. is set on a literary career, this is the place to begin it and any other start would be very bad economy.

I expect to give him a trial run with the British reviewers this autumn. That is to say I shall give him the first eight or ten pages in an anthology which I expect to bring out this autumn unless war conditions prevent. I have merely the publishers' verbal agreement to print the book in September (which means according to publishers habits, possibly November).[1]

The last Anthology I brought out has provided a new word for France, England and America[2] and the battle of ink is still raging. The *Mercure de France* in the current number (June 1, 1915) is sufficiently excited to consider 'l'imagisme comme une preuve de la vitalité de la race anglaise.'[3] (Which it isn't). We have not, as they say 'renouvelé la poésie au bruit du

1 – *Catholic Anthology 1914–1915* (Nov. 1915), published in an edition of 500 copies, included 'The Love Song of J. Alfred Prufrock', 'Portrait of a Lady', 'The Boston Evening Transcript', 'Aunt Helen', and a new prose poem, 'Hysteria'.

2 – *Des Imagistes: An Anthology* (New York, 1914). The 'new word' was 'Imagism'.

3 – 'Imagism as a proof of the vitality of the English race.'

canon occidental'[1] we did the job before the war started and we are mostly Americans so the *race anglaise* has nothing much proved about it one way or the other. (Again I beg the secrecy of the confessional, for I have no desire that this last fact should be rubbed into the English publishers and reviewers, who won't like to be reminded of it.)

I don't know what more I can say except to repeat that I am very much interested in T.S.E.'s work and that if (or when) he comes back to London I shall continue to use such influence, as I have, in his behalf to get his work recognized. It has already excited the interest of several of the best critics of my acquaintance beside my own. As to the times and places of publication, of course a man who is not under the lash of necessity can do better than one who is. It is better to *begin* in the best magazines and at good rates. It is much better to sell one article at twenty pounds than thirty articles at one pound or than ten articles at two pounds.

It is better not to publish a book of poems until one has a book that will 'get through'. The amount of actually good work that is done, is so small that a few people more or less control the output, and with proper discretion, I think we may say that ordinary business conditions prevail. 'A man succeeds either by the scarceness or the abundance of his copy.' If he cares for the really fine thing and if his standard is decently high, it is only by the first road that he will attempt to go forward.

Sincerely yours

On reading this through it seems that I might add, that a literary man's income depends very much on how rigidly he insists on doing exactly what he himself wants to do. It depends on his connection, which he makes himself. It depends on the number of feuds that he takes on for the sake of his aesthetic beliefs. T.S.E. does not seem to be so pugnacious as I am and his course should be the smoother and swifter. Still, it *is* possible for a man to do exactly what he pleases, *and* live.

sincerely yours
Ezra Pound

As to exact sums, or the amount a man actually needs to begin on, I should think that if a fellow had five hundred dollars for the first year and two hundred and fifty for the second he ought to be able to make the rest of his keep and get decently started.

1 – 'renewed poetry to the noise of the western guns'.

TO *Henry Eliot*

MS Houghton

[Postmark 2 July 1915]

3 Compayne Gdns,[1] London N.W.

Dear Henry

You will have heard by this time of the surprising changes in my plans. You know, however, what I always wanted, and I am sure that it will seem natural enough to you. The only really surprising thing is that I should have had the force to attempt it, and when you know Vivien, I am sure that you will not be surprised at that either. I know that you will agree that the responsibility and independent action has been and will be just what I needed. Now my only concern is how I can make her perfectly happy, and I think I can do that by being myself infinitely more fully than I ever have been. I am much less suppressed, and more confident, than I ever have been.

Your letter came very opportunely. It showed that the family will be better prepared for my decision. I have given it to Vivien: she wanted to keep it. She likes you. I cannot tell you how much pleasure it gave me.

Now I am going to ask you to do something for me, in case you are in Boston or New York this summer. These are suggestions of Ezra Pound's, who has a very shrewd head, and has taken a very great interest in my prospects. There will be people to be seen in Boston and New York, editors with whom I might have some chance, and it might even be better, if you are on the spot, for you to see them than for me. As you are likeliest to be in Boston, the first thing is the *Atlantic Monthly*. Now Pound considers it important, whenever possible, to secure introductions to editors from people of better social position than themselves. In a paper of notes which he made out for me he says: 'Mrs Gardner ought to insist on the *Atlantic*'s making you their English representative. Sedgwick[2] would think it a score off me, whom he hates, to have someone here in touch with everything that I know'. I do not know how much Mrs G. can or will do in that quarter, but I am enclosing a letter of introduction to her, and I shall write to her at once about my affairs. I should like you to see Sedgwick, and find out if anything can be done.

My assets up to date are the poem you have seen, another long poem (earlier and inferior) which will be out presently in a small new publication called *Others* in New York,[3] which may be useful because it includes some

1–The Hampstead home of VHE's parents.

2–Ellery Sedgwick (1872–1960), a close friend of Isabella Stewart Gardner, bought the *Atlantic Monthly* in 1908 and edited it with great success for thirty years.

3–'Portrait of a Lady' appeared in the anthology *Others* I: 3 (Sept. 1915), 35–40.

of the people whom Amy Lowell and Houghton Mifflin are taking up, and the assurance of a dozen pages in an anthology like *Imagistes*, to be out in the autumn; with not the same people (except Pound) and including Masters, whom you may have heard of, as he first appeared. I also have on hand some rather second rate things which I may send to Mencken (the *Smart Set*).[1]

On second thoughts I enclose part of Pound's paper of notes. Besides *Century* and *Harpers*, I believe there is also the *Bookman*. Nothing needs to be done in Chicago, I believe. You know F. Hackett, who was in that paper in which you sometimes did reviews, don't you.[2] I believe he is now in New York, and he is an editor of the *New Republic*. That pays, and might be persuaded to take criticism, or little articles.[3] What I want is 1) to have these magazines mentioned know my name in some personal way. 2) to get some steady connection such as the writing of an 'English letter' or discussion of current French stuff. There is little of the latter now, but there is enough of the last year-or-two's produce which is unknown to America to provide matter for some time. James Huneker's[4] rot pays him, and I don't see why more intelligent writing should not be made to.

Forgive the exclusively practical tone of this letter. I feel more alive than I ever have before. We are anxious that mother and father should come over to see us, and I hope you will use your influence, as I do not want *anything* but possibly his business to interfere.

I want to send you her picture soon. Vivien is not very well at present, and this has knocked her out completely, so I do not want one taken yet.

I am hoping you will be able to settle in N.Y. or Boston soon.

Always affectionately
Tom

[In Vivien's hand:]

I have read this letter and I am sure we can depend on you to help us. I read the letter you wrote to Tom and liked it so much, and I almost feel I know you. I should like it if you will write to me.

Vivien S. Eliot

1–H. L. Mencken (1880–1956), journalist and critic, was co-editor (with George Jean Nathan) of *The Smart Set*, 1914–23.

2–Francis Hackett (1883–1962), Irish author, was editor of *The New Republic*, 1914–22.

3–TSE published no articles or reviews between 1909 and 1916.

4–James Huneker (1857–1921), American music critic, also wrote about art, literature and drama for the New York *Sun*, 1900–17. TSE had reviewed his book *Egoists* in *Harvard Advocate* 88: 1 (5 Oct. 1909), 16.

TO *Harriet Monroe*[1] MS Chicago

10 July 1915 3 Compayne Gdns

Dear Miss Monroe

I received your cheque for eight guineas[2] some days ago, and only unusual preoccupations prevented me from acknowledging it and thanking you at once.

The address at the head of the paper will always reach me, and I will notify you of any change.

Sincerely yours
T. Stearns-Eliot

TO *Mrs Jack Gardner* MS Gardner Museum

[10 July? 1915] 3 Compayne Gdns

My dear Mrs Gardner,

It gave me very great pleasure to hear from you, and to have so much that I am glad to hear about Prichard. I have heard a little from Furst, and a few weeks ago I saw Richard Fisher,[3] but your letter gives much more what is essential.

I have been meaning to write to you for some time about my affairs, but they were at first so indefinite, and later so precipitous, that now when I am revealing them, I suppose that some of the people to whom I shall write will suspect either that I have been very secretive, or very rash. You will know that I have been neither.

The enclosed clipping will disclose one piece of news.[4] You said once that marriage is the greatest test in the world. I know now that you were right, but now I welcome the test instead of dreading it. It is much more than a test of sweetness of temper, as people sometimes think; it is a test of the whole character and affects every action. This is what I have discovered. I know that saying this, more than anything I can tell you

1–Harriet Monroe: see Glossary of Names.
2–Payment for 'The Love Song of J. Alfred Prufrock', *Poetry* (June 1915).
3–Richard T. Fisher (1876–1934), forester, became Director of Harvard Forest, Petersham, Massachusetts.
4–*The Times* had announced the Eliots' marriage on 30 June: 'STEARNS-ELIOT: HAIGH-WOOD. On the 26 June, by special licence, Thomas Stearns-Eliot, youngest son of Mr. and Mrs. Henry Ware Eliot, of St Louis, Missouri, U.S.A., to Vivienne Haigh-Wood, only daughter of Mr. and Mrs. C. H. Haigh-Wood, of 3 Compayne Gardens, Hampstead.'

about Vivien, and about my happiness, will show you that I have done the best thing. But I hope that I may some day bring her to see you, or better still, that you will be coming again to London.

The last sentence will show you that I have changed my plans. This process has gone on parallel with the other, and has fitted into it wonderfully. Since I have been at Oxford I have, as you know, acquired a few literary connections in London, and made a few friends who have been very encouraging. This support has nourished a hope which I had entertained before; and I see a possibility of being able to express myself through literary channels; and this I prefer to the makeshift of professional philosophy. It is hard to make a foothold, but I felt that the work at Harvard was deadening me. And the prospect of [becoming] a professor at some provincial university in America is not stimulating!

I want to live in London, and if one is to do anything in literature this is the best place to be. It was a London friend – Ezra Pound – who got printed for me the poem which I sent you. So we plan to settle here. And I am looking for a position in some London school, to substitute throughout the war; and if I can get this, it will help me through the most trying period. If not, some other occupation, for it takes time to attain independence in a literary life.

This is a far greater responsibility than I have ever incurred before. Yet I feel much more competent to face it. I worry far less over it than over infinitesimal things in the past. But I realise its full seriousness. Had I come to America this summer – I do not now expect to do so – I should have been able to interview editors myself, first because a personal acquaintance is necessary in order to place contributions, second because I should like to be a regular 'foreign correspondent' for some periodical. As it is, I expect my brother to be in Boston and New York at some time during the summer, and in Boston I am going to ask him to see the *Atlantic Monthly*, and possibly Miss Lowell.[1] And as he will probably be in Boston a fortnight I am taking the liberty of giving him a letter to you, in order that he may get your advice, if happily you are at Green Hill,[2] and in order that he may have the privilege of meeting you.

Well, this is really all my news. I am very tired and very happy. I have a great many letters to write. I will send *Blast* – if it ever comes out! Do pardon the messiness of this letter; at present I find myself writing parts of

1–Amy Lowell (1874–1925), poet and critic.
2–Mrs Gardner's house in Brookline, Massachusetts.

letters, cramming them into my pocket and finishing them in railway stations or on the street.

Very sincerely yours,
Thomas Stearns Eliot

TO *J. H. Woods*

MS Professor David G. Williams

10 July 1915

3 Compayne Gdns

Dear Professor Woods,

I have been starting letters to you for the past three weeks, and have never had the time to finish them. I must first thank you for your efforts on my behalf, though I do not now regret their failure. I must also with apologies withdraw my application for an assistantship at Harvard. I shall be sending you a complete typewritten copy of my notes on Mr Joachim's Aristotle's *Ethics* course.

My reason for resigning is that I wish now to remain in London and engage in literary work. This may perhaps seem a surprising choice and is admittedly a great risk – still it is much worse to be deterred from anything by fear, and I shall try it out. It is what I wanted to do before. Now I have made a few professional connections and am anxious to start the battle, with an initial literary capital of eight guineas from *Poetry* in Chicago.

I wish also to tell you that on the 26th June I was married quite privately to Miss Vivien Haigh-Wood of London. Our marriage was hastened by events connected with the war.

I do not regret my time spent in the graduate school, and I pant to tell you particularly how much I enjoyed the Sañkya and Patañjali course. And I shall write to Professor Lanman in appreciation of his friendship and kindness.[1]

Pray accept my wishes for a restful summer for Mrs Woods and yourself at Rockport, and my expression of continued interest in the department.

Sincerely yours
Thomas Stearns Eliot

1–C. R. Lanman (1850–1941), Harvard authority on the ancient languages and culture of India, with whom TSE studied Sanskrit and Pali, 1911–13. He had helped to secure a travelling scholarship for TSE. He edited *The Sanskrit Reader*, TSE's copy of which, inscribed 'Cambridge 1912', is in his personal library. On 6 May 1912, Lanman gave TSE a Sanskrit edition of *The Twenty-Eight Upanishads* (Bombay, 1906), now at King's. Tipped in is Lanman's hand-written key including 'Bṛhadāraṇyaka, 220 (v. 1, 2, 3), Da-da-da = *dāmyata datta dayadhvam*'.

TO *Professor L. B. R. Briggs* MS Harvard

10 July 1915 3 Compayne Gdns

Dear Dean Briggs,

I must apologise for not having written sooner my final report on my work at Oxford. Unusual preoccupations have prevented me from attending to even very pressing correspondence.

During the second term I attended two courses of lectures, one by Mr H. H. Joachim, my tutor, and one by Professor J. A. Smith. I attended a small class reading a text of Plotinus with Professor J. A. Stewart, was engaged in reading an Aristotle text with Mr Joachim, and once a week brought Mr Joachim papers on the philosophy of Plato.

In the last term I continued attendance at lectures by Mr Joachim and Professor Smith, completed the reading of the text with Mr Joachim, and brought Mr Joachim weekly papers on the philosophy of Aristotle. He has, he tells me, written to Professor Woods some account of my work.[1]

I thoroughly appreciated the privilege of a year of study abroad, and at Oxford, and feel deeply grateful to the department and to the committee. I only wish that I could express my appreciation by my further work at Harvard, but changes in my plans have made that impossible. I have decided to remain in London, or at least in England, and attempt to engage in literary work, hoping to be able to find a position in a school at the same time.

I wish also to announce my marriage to Miss Vivien Haigh-Wood of London, on the 26th June. Our marriage was accelerated by events connected with the war.

Believe me to remain
yours faithfully
Thomas Stearns Eliot

1 – Joachim wrote on 18 June that TSE had 'worked most thoroughly and enthusiastically' and 'undoubtedly made good progress'; his essays showed 'the extent and solidity of his knowledge of Greek Philosophy'.

TO *His Father*[1] MS Hornbake

23 July 1915 3 Compayne Gdns

My dear Father,

I am writing the night before I sail. This letter I am going to leave with Vivien, and she is to send it to you, I have told her, in case anything happens to me before I arrive home. There is very little danger, I am sure. But if anything did happen, I want to feel that you, as well as her own family, would look after her future as much as you could from that side of the ocean.[2]

My one certain hope is that you will see that she gets the $5,000.00 insurance which you were so good to take out for me. She will need it. She will be in a most difficult position. Her own family are in very straitened circumstances owing to the war, and I know that her pride would make her want to earn her own living. This would be very hard for her at first, with the weight of my loss.

I have taken on a great responsibility. She has been ready to sacrifice everything for me. I am very very sorry that I have been forced to write so much about our affairs only, and that you know so little of her. But now that we have been married a month, I am *convinced* that she has been the one person for me. She has everything to give that I want, and she gives it. I owe her everything. I have married her on nothing, and she knew it and was willing, for my sake. She had nothing to gain by marrying me. I have imposed upon you very much, but upon her more, and I know you will help to make her life less difficult.

Your loving son
Tom.

She has not seen this.
I will seal it and give it her to keep in case of emergency.

1–This unposted letter was found among VHE's papers and sold by her brother after TSE's death.
2–The *Lusitania* had been sunk in May 1915. BR told OM that VHE understandably refused 'to go to see [TSE's] people, for fear of submarines' (*Autobiography*, II [1968], 54).

Vivien Eliot TO *Scofield Thayer* MS Beinecke

2 August 1915 3 Compayne Gdns

Dear Scofield,

Thanks very much for your cable – *and* for your gratters and invitation. Charmed as I should be to avail myself of the latter, I fear it is impossible at *present*. Tom has gone to America without me, and arrived yesterday. Rather unwise perhaps to leave so attractive a wife alone and to her own devices! However – I did not at all want to go – I am frightened of the voyage and the submarines – and preferred to remain and play my own little games alone. But all the Eliots appear to have an overwhelming desire to see me, and have written me such charming letters of welcome into their select family, that I am sure I *shall* have to go over very soon – probably in the spring, so I hope you will then repeat your invitation.

Do you remember my mentioning a studio flat which I rather hankered to take, while you were here? Well, Tom and I took it – furnished – and lived there for about three weeks before he went, and I kept it on another week after he had gone. It was a delightful place, I wish you could have seen it. I am here now for three days, and am then going to join Lucy [Thayer] at Thyme Cottage. Tom is supposed to be coming back by September 1st, and after we have had a second honeymoon! we shall have to set up a house or a flat of our own in London of course. It is very nice being Mrs Stearns-Eliot (notice the hyphen). I am very popular with Tom's friends – and who do you think in *particular*? No less a person than Bertrand Russell!! He is all over me, is Bertie, and I simply love him. I am dining with him next week. I see a good deal of the Pounds, of course, and between ourselves, find them rather boring. However, they are very nice to me, and seek me out a lot, so I suppose I should feel honoured! I was at the Savoy the other night, with two male friends who are consoling the grass widow, and I thought of you, Scofield, and that very nice dinner which cost you such an *awful lot* that we had there. You ought really to be over here now, just to think of the dinners in Soho we could do – and grass widows do seem, I find, to be so very *very* attractive, *much more* than spinsters! Now W H Y is that?

Butler-Thwing is in the *5th Lancers*! so is of course bullied[1] to death. But he has done well – it is a very crack regiment.

Perhaps you will see Tom while he is there – if so remember me kindly to him.

1 – Reading uncertain.

Have you seen the new *Blast*?

I am mentioned in it – as the Poet's Bride, and blessings are called down on my head.[1]

Do you remember that terrible dinner with [Wyndham] Lewis? Why on earth were you so cross? But what an impossible man! I hope you were amused at the 'lost woman' incident! I did that rather well.

Are you married yet? If not why not? If you can manage to refrain from marriage (it *is* catching I know!) do come over here before long and let us resume our childish acquaintance, and youthful prattle. I don't think I'm really keen on meeting you in U.S.A. London's far better – is it not so? Please answer this – this address will always find me.

Vivien S-E.

TO *Conrad Aiken* — MS Huntington

5 August [1915]

Eastern Point, Gloucester,
Massachusetts

My dear Conrad,

I wonder where you are. I should rejoice to hear that you are in Cambridge. If you are, let me know *at once!* I am here for a *limited engagement* – three weeks only. Have you heard my news? I was married on June 26 to Miss Vivien Haigh-Wood of London England. I mean to try to go back there to live, and have a job in a school for next year in point of fact; but I have agreed to my family's wish that I should complete my work and take my Ph.D., so it's not yet certain whether I stay this winter or return for it later. What I want is MONEY!$!£!! We are hard up! War!

BLAST
THE KAISER   ED. GREY[2]
THE AMERICAN AMBASSADORS (SÄMTLICH)[3]
THE DEMOCRATS

1 – Wyndham Lewis, in the 'Blasts and Blesses' section of *Blast* 2 (July 1915, 93), bestows his final blessings upon 'The Poet's Bride (June 28th)'.

2 – Sir Edward Grey, third baronet, later Viscount Grey of Fallodon (1862–1933); Liberal politician and Foreign Secretary, 1905–16.

3 – 'to a man': the US Ambassador Walter Hines Page was in dispute with the Foreign Office about the right of Americans to pursue 'neutral trade' at sea during wartime. Page's letter of 17 July and the ensuing correspondence were published as 'Rights of Neutrals at Sea', *The Times*, 4 Aug. 1915, 5.

BLESS

CONSTANTINOPLE[1]

T. S. ELIOT HARRIET[2]

GEN. BOBO GEN. BLOT[3]

Now tell me *your* news. I hear you have plunged into the *Atlantic.*[4] Good for it.

Yours
T. S. E.

TO *Scofield Thayer* MS Beinecke

Monday [9 August 1915] Eastern Point, Gloucester

My dear Scofield

It is very pleasant to hear from you after such a long silence broken only by the medium of the transatlantic cable.[5] Alas! a few miles can separate friends as effectually as an ocean. Heaven alone, if we concede it omniscience, is the guardian of the secrets of the future. This weekend I have promised to some relatives in Weston, and by next weekend I may be gone. I must always be one of the first to testify to your taste for hospitality, but in the limited time that I have, we should be obliged to meet, if at all, on neutral ground; if there is any likelihood of your coming to Boston next week, let me know.

I must confess that at the time I was surprised at the extent to which you were 'nettled'. You had never given me the impression that your interest in the lady was exclusive – or indeed in the slightest degree a pursuit: and as you did not give *her* this impression, I presumed that I had wounded your vanity rather than thwarted your passion. If I was in error, at least Time (let us say) is the anodyne of disappointment rather than the separation of friends.

Sincerely yours
Thomas Stearns Eliot

1 – During the Dardanelles Campaign, 1915, the fate of Constantinople was crucial to both Allies and the Germans.

2 – Harriet Monroe.

3 – In July, the US cruiser *Washington* had steamed to Haiti in response to a revolt of rebel troops under Dr Rosalvo Bobo. The rebels withdrew on the arrival of government forces under General Blot, but at the end of the month, after mass executions and riots, US forces invaded.

4 – Aiken's poem 'Rupert Brooke' was published in the *Atlantic Monthly* in July.

5 – Scofield Thayer's letter has not survived.

TO *J. H. Woods* MS Harvard

16 August [1915] Eastern Point, Gloucester

Dear Professor Woods,

I now expect to return to Cambridge in September. I have seen Professor Palmer,[1] and also Professor Perry,[2] who thinks that the difficulties of preparation while teaching school would be very great. My only compunction is toward the headmaster: I have given him five weeks notice, but he has lost a month through having engaged me.

Unfortunately I have just had word that my wife is very ill in London, so I must go at once, sailing Saturday. I do not anticipate that her illness will prevent my return before the opening of college; but if it is serious enough to detain me I will cable to you.

Sincerely yours
T. S. Eliot

Address as above until Saturday: after that 3 Compayne Gardens, London, N.W.

TO *J. H. Woods* MS Chicago

Monday [16 August 1915] Eastern Point [Gloucester]

Dear Professor Woods

I forgot to answer your questions. The first notes I copied myself; the last were a duplicate of a copy ordered by a friend for himself. So there was no expense involved. I shall bring back *de An.* and *Organon.*

R. P. Hardie[3] is an authority on Greek Philosophy and I believe professes at Edinburgh, whether in a school or at St Andrews I do not know; nor do I know how rich he is. I don't see why Harvard should not accept his offer; on the other hand I do not see any reason for his not taking the market price for the volumes.

Sincerely yours
T. S. Eliot

1–G. Herbert Palmer (1842–1933), Professor of Philosophy, with whom TSE studied History of Ancient Philosophy, 1907–8, and Ethics, 1912–13. Palmer later wrote that, though TSE had a mind of 'extraordinary power and sensitiveness', he 'allowed himself to be turned into weak aestheticism by the influence of certain literary cliques in London' (cited in Manju Jain, *T. S. Eliot and American Philosophy* (1992), 34).

2–Ralph Barton Perry (1876–1957), chairman of the Philosophy Department, Harvard, 1906–14.

3–R. P. Hardie (1864–1942), Professor of Philosophy at Edinburgh University.

TO *Scofield Thayer* MS Beinecke

4 September [1915] Eastbourne[1]

Dear Scofield

I have just returned to England after my brief visit to my family in Gloucester. Now that I detach myself from the excitement and fluster of a hurried trip, I regret very much not having seen you. And, though I could not have come, I realise that my letter was a very shabby one. It was certainly very kind of you to ask me to Edgartown,[2] and I really should have enjoyed seeing you. However, I do hope it will not be very long before you exhaust the limited resources of New York society, and return to your proper environment in London. When that happens, I look forward to seeing a good deal of you. I hope you will write and tell me your plans very soon. My address (anyhow till Christmas) will be care of Bertie Russell, 34 Russell Chambers, Bury Street, W.C. He is lending us his flat for a time.[3]

Do accept my regrets for a petty irritation which should have evaporated long before I wrote, and believe me

yours ever
Tom.

TO *His Father* MS Houghton

10 September [1915] c/o British Linen Bank,
Threadneedle St, London E.C.

My dear father,

I have written to mother by this mail, and you will see her letter.[4] I said that I felt that my great mistake was in hurrying home before I had got your letters, and so failing to get a balanced view of the situation; and

1 – The Eliots were having a belated honeymoon, following TSE's return from the US.

2 – Believing that the USA was about to enter the war, Thayer had abandoned his planned thesis on Aesthetics and left Oxford in the summer, returning home to Edgartown, Mass.

3 – Russell was allowing them to stay at his flat, and he was also there much of the time. Russell had first met VHE on 9 July 1915, two weeks after her marriage. He told OM by letter that VHE was 'light, vulgar, adventurous, full of life', and that 'she says she married [TSE] to stimulate him, but finds she can't do it' (Texas). On 2 Aug. VHE wrote to Thayer that she was 'popular with Tom's friends', particularly Russell: 'He is all over me, is Bertie, and I simply love him' (Beinecke). By the time TSE returned from the USA at the beginning of Sept., it was decided that the Eliots would move into the spare bedroom in Russell's Bury Street flat: they stayed there until Christmas 1915.

4 – Not preserved.

secondly in blundering into a change of plan which was unjustified and unnecessary.

I cannot say very much now, as I have been delayed in writing this and must get it off in a few minutes. I am thankful to have found High Wycombe[1] still open. Without Wellesley[2] too, we should have been almost entirely dependent upon you. I have put our position as clearly as I could. You will see that until January we shall be in urgent need of funds, and that we shall need some money very soon. We have planned a very economical mode of life, and Vivien's resourcefulness and forethought are inexhaustible. We are not planning how to make living easier: the question is how to live at all.

I know that I have made matters hard for you by the blunders of which I spoke. Had I avoided them, I am sure that you would have felt at ease. Nevertheless, I feel that I shall make matters right by returning to my original course.

Always your affectionate son
Tom

I shall write again in a few days.
Will you ask mother to send my clothes on as soon as she can?

TO *Bertrand Russell*[3] MS McMaster

11 September [1915]

8 Hartington Mansions,
Eastbourne, Sussex

Dear Mr Russell,

Your letter[4] coming on top of all your other kindnesses, has quite overwhelmed me. Such generosity and encouragement means a great deal to me at present, above all coming from you. I have been intending to write

1–For a salary of £140 a year with free dinners, TSE spent the winter term teaching French, mathematics, history, drawing and swimming at Wycombe Grammar School, High Wycombe.
2–Mary Whiton Calkins (1863–1930), Professor of Philosophy and Psychology at Wellesley College, had written to J. H. Woods on 17 June saying she wished to recommend TSE to her department for the purpose of directing 'small divisions of students in introduction courses in philosophy and psychology'. He was offered the post but declined it.
3–Bertrand Russell: see Glossary of Names.
4–Apparently not preserved. 'As they were desperately poor, I lent them one of the two bedrooms in my flat [in London], with the result that I saw a great deal of them. I was fond of them both, and endeavoured to help them in their troubles until I discovered that their troubles were what they enjoyed' (Russell, *Autobiography*, II, 19). TSE spent the weekdays at High Wycombe.

to you ever since I got here, but have had so many and such worrying American letters to write, that I have been quite exhausted each day when I have done them.

When you first spoke to me about the flat, I was too overpowered by such a generous offer to discuss the practical details. Vivien and I both feel very strongly that, although you speak of our staying until Christmas, we wish it to be part of the arrangement that we should vacate the flat at any moment should you need it exclusively to yourself. Circumstances might alter your plans, and then we cannot endure the thought that you should hesitate to let us know. We shall keep this possibility always in view, so that you may feel assured that your flat is your own at any moment you want to have it.

As to your coming to stay the night at the flat when I am not there, it would never have occurred to me to accept it under any other conditions. Such a concession to conventions never entered my head; it seems to me not only totally unnecessary, but also would destroy for me all the pleasure we take in the informality of the arrangement.[1]

I had been counting upon seeing you and having a talk with you in London before leaving for High Wycombe. Vivien understood from your letter that you would be staying Wednesday night in town, and it stupidly did not occur to me that you would be leaving so early Thursday as to prevent us seeing you. Otherwise we should not have consented to the arrangement to which we are now bound. I am so anxious to see you that I cannot help trying to persuade you to spend Wednesday night in Eastbourne. Is this possible? It would give us both great delight. Vivien is still so unwell, that we are having a doctor come to set our minds at rest; but by that time she ought to be much better, and in any case it would be a great satisfaction to us if I could see you.

Failing this, I might possibly be able to come up to town on Wednesday alone, in the hope of having the evening or afternoon with you, leaving Vivien to follow me on Thursday. If you cannot come to Eastbourne, and if you could see me in London, I shall try to do this.

1 – Fearing that Russell and VHE were or might become lovers, Russell's ex-mistress OM wrote to him on 9 Sept., 'I don't think it would *help her* and help towards making the Eliot life happier to let her fall in love with you.' She feared he was 'separating her from Eliot' and 'running a great risk'. BR replied on 10 Sept. that he 'would not for the world have any scandal & as for the Eliots it is the purest philanthropy'. He averred he was 'fond of [TSE], & really anxious to be of use to him'.

Hoping to hear from you, and hoping very much that you can spend Wednesday here,

Sincerely yours
Thomas Stearns Eliot

TO *J. H. Woods*

MS Professor David G. Williams

[11 September? 1915]

c/o British Linen Bank,
Threadneedle St, London E.C.

Dear Professor Woods,

I have returned to England, and have finally decided to remain here for the winter. I found Mrs Eliot in very poor health; the strain upon her this summer has been very great, and I should not wish to expose her to the hardships of a winter in a foreign country under such conditions. And, after looking at the matter from both sides of the ocean, I think that it is better to stick to my original plan. Of course it would be an advantage to work directly under the eye of the department. But as I was so near to coming up for my degree over a year ago, I feel that it would be a proof of incapacity were I to take such an advantage to be a necessary condition of satisfactory work. The headmaster of my school understands my situation, and will make it possible for me to have as much time to myself as I should have had if I had taken on work at Wellesley and at Harvard too.

I shall return to take examinations either in the spring or in the fall. May I send on parts of my thesis, from time to time, for inspection and criticism? I propose to offer Ancient Philosophy (through Aristotle), Modern Philosophy (both parts), Psychology, and out of the second division Logic and either Theory of Knowledge or Ethics. I should very much appreciate the kindness if I might have hints from the examiners in regard to the extent and detail of knowledge expected in these fields.

I hope that you will forgive me if I delay sending you the *de Anima* notes for a time; as I shall be too busy to copy them for a month or two. Of course, if Hardie can send you the Zabarella, you will not want my notes.

I hope that you will sometimes find time to write me a line of news or advice – I want to keep as closely in touch with the department as I can. I am very grateful to you – more than I can tell you – for your advice in the past, and for the interest you have taken in my affairs and the kindness you have shown.

Sincerely yours
Thomas Stearns Eliot

TO *His Father* MS Houghton

27 September 1915

c/o Mrs Toone, Sydney Cottage,
Conegra Road, High Wycombe,
Bucks

My dear Father,

I had been hoping to have letters from you this week, but [as] I infer from your telegraphing to the Haigh-Woods and to Pound that you had not yet received any letter from me, I cannot feel certain of getting one for another week. I supposed that my first cable would let you know that I had found it advisable to stay here. You were prepared, I know, for the possibility, and I felt certain that you would be sure that if I were ill I should send you word. Mr Haigh-Wood telegraphed the cable to me, and I cabled at once to reassure you; but I suppose from your cabling to Pound that you never received my cable. I am sorry that you cabled to him, because he is not the sort of person whom I wish to be intimate with my affairs. He has shown a keen interest in my career; and has been and will be useful; but my acquaintance with him is primarily professional.

You will know by this time what the situation is, and that my course of action is well considered – as I could not have shown in a cable – and the one which promises the most happiness, if present embarrassment is got over. I have had a week of the school work, and am beginning to get into the routine. Tuesday and Thursday I am free for the whole afternoon; Monday, Wednesday and Friday after half-past-four. At the beginning the work demands some thought and planning: and every school has its own system, which has to be learned by being used. I arrive at half past nine; have classes till quarter to one; return here for lunch, and (on the three days) go again to the school for two classes of forty minutes each. The boys are of various ages and abilities; I have found the two upper classes quite good at French, the middle boys indifferent at history; and the small boys capable of being interested. The chief difficulty is the presence in the same class of new boys, some knowing much and some little. Wycombe is a place which will do very well for a time.

I shall have time enough to do my work for the degree, but am at present harassed by the question of money. My deposit is reduced to almost nothing, as it is all that I have at present to live upon. If no money comes from you at the end of a fortnight I shall be forced to cable, as I shall be reduced to the last pound by the time you get this. I hate to *cable* for money; though it could come through the British Linen Bank, to be delivered to me in person. I cannot settle down to work upon the degree without the certainty of at least the necessary minimum. You know that I should but for the degree have devoted my spare time to writing, which would have pieced out my income. So I must make it clear to you exactly how I am placed now, without waiting for your letter.

I am getting this off at once because I wish you to know, when I do cable, that it is because I am absolutely forced to do so.

Always Your Affectionate son
Tom.

Bertrand Russell TO *Charlotte C. Eliot* MS Houghton

3 October 1915 Trinity College, Cambridge

Dear Madam,

I am venturing to write to you, because your son has been consulting me on the subject of his prospects, and I thought you might wish to know what I had said to him. He was one of my best pupils when I was at Harvard a year ago, and already then I felt him a friend as well as a pupil. Since he came to England, I have come to know him better, and have been struck by the seriousness of his moral purpose and his strong wish to live up to every duty. He has asked me what I think of the financial outlook for him if he stays in England. I do not, of course, know what reasons there may be against his staying in England, but on this one point I felt bound to say that I thought the outlook for him in England just as good as in America. His Oxford tutor [Harold Joachim] is, I know, prepared to recommend him warmly, and owing to the war the openings are much more numerous than usual at present, and are likely to remain so for many years. Practically all educated men of military age, except the physically unfit, have felt it their duty to join the army, so that the supply of teachers is at present extraordinarily short. Of those who have gone to fight, a very large proportion, I fear, are sure to be killed or disabled, so that the deficiency will by no means cease with the cessation of the war. Under these circumstances, I think he may rely with considerable confidence upon obtaining suitable work when he has taken his Ph.D.

I inquired carefully into the work he still has to do for his Ph.D., which was all the easier as I had taught him. So far as I can judge, his work at High Wycombe will not prevent him from getting through the necessary preparation, and I understand that the school is willing to let him be absent during the summer term.

I have taken some pains to get to know his wife, who seems to me thoroughly nice, really anxious for his welfare, and very desirous of not hampering his liberty or interfering with whatever he feels to be best. The chief sign of her influence that I have seen is that he is no longer attracted by the people who call themselves 'vorticists', and in that I think her influence is wholly to be applauded.

He seems to me to have considerable literary gifts, and I have hopes of his doing work which will bring him reputation as soon as he is free from worry as to ways and means.

I remain
yours very truly
Bertrand Russell

TO *Bertrand Russell* MS McMaster

11 October [1915] [High Wycombe, Bucks]

Dear Mr Russell

I wrote to Waterlow[1] as you suggested, and he asked me to dine with him last Sunday evening. The consequences were so gratifying to me that I wanted to write and tell you. He has given me Balfour's book[2] to review, and will let me have two thousand words on it. I was quite unprepared for such an important review, but of course snapped at it, and took on another book too. He gives me a month for the Balfour and another month for Wolf's *Nietzsche*.[3] I think that it is worth my while to put in all my time on this reviewing until I have got these two books, at the expense of the thesis. Do you agree with me? It is not worth doing at all unless I do my best: if I do a good review I can afford to do no more for some time; and if I don't put all my strength on it, it's a plain waste of time. Besides, it will (if good) impress the people at Harvard much more than the same amount of work added to put in upon the thesis. And my family will merely know that I have passed the examination; whereas this they will see.

So I wanted to thank you again for introducing me to Waterlow. I find the school work taking less time: this is due chiefly to an adaptation of my

1–Sydney Waterlow (1878–1944), scholar and diplomat, was on the editorial committee of *The International Journal of Ethics*, 1914–16.

2–Arthur Balfour (1848–1930), Conservative politician, Prime Minister 1902–5, was made First Lord of the Admiralty in May 1915; Foreign Secretary in 1916. See TSE's review of his Gifford Lectures, *Theism and Humanism*, in *International Journal of Ethics* 26: 2 (Jan. 1916), 284–9. TSE described the volume as 'a protest against the aesthetics, the ethics, and the epistemology of "Naturalism"'; a 'brilliant book' that would be 'a noteworthy philosophical event at any time'.

3–See TSE on A. Wolf, *The Philosophy of Nietzsche* (1915), in *IJE* 26: 3 (Apr. 1916), 426–7. TSE praised the work as 'an admirable piece of simplification', while regretting the 'omission of Nietzsche's views on art, with the interesting pessimism with respect to the future of art . . .'

ideals of scholarship. I find that it's useless to try really to learn anything just now, that I must make the best of what I do know: if I make the boys work I don't have to work so hard myself; and where work really shows (in the eyes of a headmaster) is in working the boys hard, keeping discipline, and making the red tape run smoothly – as well as being ready to do any odd jobs for him like superintending games or taking a scripture class at five minutes notice.

At the same time, it makes this sort of work much easier to have at the same time some work to do which I can feel justified in putting my best abilities upon, such as they are. The reviewing has cheered me up very much.

I am planning to see you at Garsington,[1] when I come to Oxford, or better on a separate expedition; as I shall probably not try to stay the night at Oxford.

Always yours gratefully
Thomas Stearns Eliot

TO *Harriet Monroe* — MS Houghton

17 October 1915 — 3 Compayne Gdns [London N.W.]

Dear Miss Monroe

I have received the cheque for £3, as well as the two copies of *Poetry*, and wish to thank you.[2]

I am much pleased that you should have liked my 'Portrait of a Lady'.[3]

Sincerely yours,
T. Stearns Eliot

TO *His Mother* — MS Houghton

18 November 1915 — Sydney Cottage, Conegra Road, High Wycombe, Bucks

Darling Mother,

I have had a busy week or so. I finished the review of Balfour's book and got it off to Waterlow. He found it a bit too long, but seems pleased

1 – The Elizabethan manor house bought in 1913 by the Liberal MP Philip Morrell and his wife, Lady Ottoline.

2 – Payment for 'The Boston Evening Transcript', 'Aunt Helen' and 'Cousin Nancy', *Poetry* 7: 1 (Oct. 1915).

3 – *Others* I: 3 (Sept. 1915).

with it, and hopes to get it into the January issue. Russell was in town just before I sent the review away, so I showed it to him, and he liked it very much. As for the book on Nietzsche, I have finished it, and now am reading some of Nietzsche's works which I had not read before, and which I ought to read anyhow before my examinations. The book I am to review is rather slight and unsatisfactory – it is neither a guide to Nietzsche's works for beginners, nor a commentary for advanced students.

Maurice[1] was home for five days leave this week. It was really the first time I had seen anything of him, as he had been away, first at Sandhurst and then with his regiment, almost all the time until he left for France, which was the very day we were married. I was awfully pleased with him, and feel a strong affection for him now, so that I can understand the way his family feel while he is away. He is a very handsome boy, with a great deal of breeding – very aristocratic, and very simple too. It seems very strange that a boy of nineteen should have such experiences – often twelve hours alone in his 'dug-out' in the trenches, and at night, when he cannot sleep, occupying himself by shooting rats with a revolver. What he tells about rats and vermin is incredible – Northern France is swarming, and the rats are as big as cats. His dug-out, where he sleeps, is underground, and gets no sunlight.[2]

I saw him several times. His family had their Christmas dinner when he was here, as he may not be home for another five or six months. It was awfully touching, and a bit melancholy – everyone trying to be gay and cheerful – the immediate family and a few aunts. But everyone was at their best and kindliest, and kept up the usual Christmas diversions. There was cranberry sauce in my honour – they did not know that it ought to be served with the turkey! and had it as a dessert! but I pretended it was right, as they had taken pains with it. The pudding came in blazing properly, with an American flag on it. Mrs Haigh-Wood did everything to show that she was fond of me. I rather expected, naturally, to take a back seat when Maurice was at home, but they all treated me with more cordiality than ever, and I felt very fond of them. The presence of Maurice, his loveableness and goodness, made the evening different from what family parties usually are. I was glad *not* to see him off – it was more painful than

1 – Maurice Haigh-Wood, VHE's brother: see Glossary of Names.
2 – Colonel H. C. Wylly's *History of the Manchester Regiment* (1923), II, 131, records that in this month, 'Another party went out from No. 26 Fire trench, composed of Second Lieutenant Haigh-Wood, Corporal Herbert, and three men. On two bombs being flung into the enemy sap, a heavy fire commenced and Corporal Herbert was at once hit, and was only brought in with great difficulty by his party.'

his first leavings: there were many, I heard both officers and men, at the station, returning: the men mostly drunk, and their women crying; the officers and their women very quiet. Vivien was pretty well knocked out by it, and has had neuralgia in consequence. And unfortunately one of Maurice's best friends was killed just after he had returned from leave.

The weeks seem to go by very quickly now, and I begin to measure the time – four weeks until Christmas. The holidays are nearly five weeks. I love to be in London, especially as I begin to know more people there. I want to know all sorts of people – political and social as well as literary and philosophical.

You will be having Thanksgiving dinner soon – I shall think of you on that day – it is next Thursday.

Always your loving son
Tom

TO *Wyndham Lewis* TS Cornell

[November? 1915] Sydney Cottage, Conegra Road,
High Wycombe, Bucks

Dear Lewis,

Will it suit you equally well to come in Sunday night instead of Saturday night at the same hour, about 8.30? I find we have got to go and dance on Saturday. I hope very much that Sunday will do for you equally well. Let me know and please don't disappoint me. I want to hear about the preface.[1]

I shall be at 34 Russell Chambers, Bury Street, W.C. on Saturday morning.

Yours ever
Eliot

1–WL's preface to H. E. Clifton and James Wood, *Mayvale*, in *Cambridge Magazine* 5: 8 (4 Dec. 1915), 173.

Bertrand Russell TO *Charlotte C. Eliot* MS Houghton

3 December 1915

34 Russell Chambers, Bury Street,
London W.C.

Dear Mrs Eliot

Please accept my very best thanks for your kindness in sending me your biography of Dr William G. Eliot, which has arrived safely, and which I am most glad to possess.[1] I am sending you my *Philosophical Essays* [1910] though I fear most of them are rather uninteresting.

I have continued to see a good deal of your son and his wife. It has been a great pleasure having them staying in my flat, and I am sorry to lose them now that they have a flat of their own. She has done a great deal of work for me, chiefly typing, and consequently I have come to know her well.[2] I have a great respect and liking for her: she has a good mind, and is able to be a real help to a literary career, besides having a rare strength and charm of character.

Tom read me his review of Balfour's Gifford Lectures, which I thought *admirable*, and so did the Editor of the *International Journal of Ethics*. I am glad he is joining the Aristotelian Society.[3] It is a good thing for him to be moving to Highgate,[4] as, besides a slight increase of salary, it makes it easier for him to get to know philosophical people in London. I hope to introduce him to several during the Christmas vacation. It seems to me that he would have every reason to hope for a distinguished philosophical career in this country if it were not for the worry and the great fatigue of his present struggle to make both ends meet. I have an affection for him

1–CCE's biography of her father-in-law: *William Greenleaf Eliot: Minister, Educator, Philanthropist* (Boston and New York, 1904).

2–VHE had helped BR to prepare a collection of his articles, *Justice in War-Time* (1915).

3–The prestigious Aristotelian Society held regular meetings in London; from 1888 it published *Proceedings of the Aristotelian Society*, an important outlet for philosophical debate.

4–After a term at High Wycombe, TSE had accepted a better post (£160 a year with dinner and tea) at Highgate Junior School, where the headmaster kept a place on the staff for young men of literary aspirations who needed to earn some money while trying to make their way. TSE taught French, Latin, lower mathematics, drawing, swimming, geography, history and baseball. John Betjeman, a pupil aged ten, presented 'that dear good man' with some poems headed *The Best of Betjeman*, but TSE never revealed his opinion of Betjeman's work, only laughing when pressed by the author at intervals during their lifelong friendship. In a letter to TSE (17 Dec. 1936), Betjeman wrote: 'I do remember you at Highgate . . . You were known as the American Master and I remember that a boy told me you were a poet but I didn't believe it' (John Betjeman, *Letters*, I, *1926–1951*, ed. Candida Lycett Green, 163).

which has made it a happiness to be able to help him, and I hope opportunities may occur again in the future.[1]

Wishing you the compliments of the season,

I remain
Yours very truly
Bertrand Russell

TO *J. H. Woods*

MS Professor David G. Williams

28 December 1915

3 Compayne Gdns, London N.W.

Dear Professor Woods,

I am very glad to hear from you at last, and I shall be very glad to answer your questions and perform your commissions. But I cannot help thinking that a letter I sent you about two months ago went astray, as you ask a question which I thought I had answered, and do not answer some which I asked.

As for the typewritten notes, they were presented me by a man who borrowed mine to have a copy taken for himself. As I have my illegible original, I presented the copy to you.

I will write to Joachim at once about your inquiry. I have no reason for doubting that he will be in Oxford next year, or J. A. Smith either. These are undoubtedly the two best men in Oxford. Ross[2] I suppose will be back at the end of the war. Beare[3] in Dublin is awfully good of course; but I do not think there is anyone in Oxford to touch Joachim and Smith.

Now as to my own questions. I should like to know as soon as possible whether I could *take my examinations in April*. I have a month's holiday then, and could perhaps be two weeks in Cambridge, if I took the first boat west and the last east. I could not stay longer. Of course I should prefer to come in the summer, and *if it were in any way possible* to take my examinations in August, I should *prefer* to do so. *But I could not* get to America before the first week in August. I hope you can let me know very

1–BR told OM on 10 Nov. that he loved TSE 'as if he were my son'; and he added, 'he is becoming much more of a man. He has a profound & quite unselfish devotion to his wife, & she really is very fond of him, but has impulses of cruelty from time to time' (quoted in Ray Monk, *Bertrand Russell: The Spirit of Solitude* (1996), 444).

2–William Davis Ross (1877–1971), tutor in Philosophy at Oriel College, 1902–29, was in the Ministry of Munitions. TSE's annotated copy of his translation of the *Metaphysica* (1908), purchased 1912, is in his library.

3–John Isaac Beare (1857?–1918), Regius Professor of Greek, University of Dublin, 1902–15, and a translator of Aristotle.

soon what arrangements I can make. I should also *very* much like to know more detail as to reading for the topicals: ancient philosophy to Aristotle, modern to Kant, *especially psychology* and *logic*, and either:

metaphysics
modern phil. *from* Kant
ancient " " Aristotle.

Should you advise me to choose the latter? I have not read any in Greek, except some Plotinus, but I should like to take it.

I should be very grateful if you could answer these questions.

I hope you will send me the Patañjali here. It will revive very pleasant memories.

I should like to write you a more personal letter than this, and tell you of my own affairs and my life for the past three months – but I must postpone it until I write again.

With all best wishes for the New Year to yourself and Mrs Woods.

Very sincerely
Thomas S. Eliot

1916

TO *Conrad Aiken*

MS Huntington

10 January 1916

3 Compayne Gdns, London N.W.
(please forward)

Dear Conrad

I owe you many apologies, but I have been most frightfully busy. The news is that I am to be at Highgate School, near town, next term, that I am starting to rewrite my thesis, that my wife has been very ill, that I have been taken up with the worries of finance and Vivien's health, that my friend Jean Verdenal has been killed,[1] that nothing has been seen of [Martin] Armstrong, who is now a captain in Kitchener's army, that compulsion is coming in,[2] that my putative publisher will probably be conscripted, that we are very blue about the war, that living is going up, and that

King Bolo's big black bassturd kween
 That airy fairy hairy un
She led the dance on Golder's Green
 With Cardinal Bessarian

I am *keen* about rhymes in -een:

King Bolo's big black bassturd kween
 Her taste was kalm and klassic
And as for anything obscene
 She said it made her ass sick.

As for literature, have you seen our Katholick Anthology? (Elk. Matthews).[3] It has not done very well, in spite of the name of Yeats. I have written nothing lately, too much absorbed by practical worries. Your idea of a kwaterly is very attractive but

1–TSE had last seen him in autumn 1911. TSE's *Prufrock and Other Observations* (1917) was to be dedicated 'To Jean Verdenal 1889–1915'; and in *P 1909–1925*, the dedication of 'Prufrock and Other Observations' became 'For Jean Verdenal, 1889–1915. Mort aux Dardanelles'.

2–Prime Minister Herbert Asquith introduced a Bill for the 'compulsory attestation of single men of military age' on 5 Jan., which led to conscription for single men (extended to married men in May).

3–EP claimed that Francis Meynell and other Roman Catholics had protested to Elkin Mathews about the title. Copies were still available in 1936.

King Bolo's big black bassturd kween
Was awf'ly sweet and pure
She interrupted prayers one day
With a shout of Pig's Manure.

But I repeat that

K. B. b. b. b. k.
Was awf'ly sweet and pure
She said 'I don't know what you mean!'
When the chaplain* whistled to her

* Charles, the Chaplain.

But about the *P*[*oetry*] *Journal*, you see I would be thrown out of *Poetry* if I wrote for that, and Poetry pays – which is everything to me. My *only* paying publications are *Poetry* and the *Int. Journal of Ethics*. Do you know anything about some sons of bitches named Sherman French and Co.?[1] They wrote asking me to send them a book, and when I wrote back asking for terms they said they hadn't known I was an Englishman and they could only boom books by native talent. If you are in with them you might tell them to butter their asses and bugger themselves, or something like that on my behalf, that my great-aunt Hannah married a Cabot,[2] and that I have written their name on bumwash.

I *hope* to write, when I have more detachment. But I am having a wonderful life nevertheless. I have *lived* through material for a score of long poems, in the last six months. An entirely different life from that I looked forward to two years ago. Cambridge seems to me a dull nightmare now – but then – it's a good enough life in its way.

Living is going up. Eggs are three pence. Income tax heavy. Still, one can get a good dinner cheap, if one knows where to go. The heaviest item in London is rent – you can't get a good flat much under £65, unless you go well out of town. How is your baby?[3] Paget[4] I see from time to time, and from him I hear that Armstrong says he has 'left the old life behind him' i.e. is a soldier and doesn't care to see his pacific acquaintances. Myers[5] married a Belgian.

1–Sherman French & Co., Beacon St, Boston: publishers of poetry books including Louis Untermeyer's *First Love* (1911).

2–It was in fact TSE's great-aunt Martha Stearns (Hannah's sister) who married Joseph Sebastian Cabot. The Cabots were Boston Brahmins: one of the First Families of the City.

3–Conrad and Jessie Aiken's baby John, b. Oct. 1913.

4–Unidentified.

5–R. H. Myers (1892–1985), music critic and writer, who was involved in postal censorship 1915–18.

I have few ideas, and much work to do. Come to England in the spring? We shall be in London through July.

Yours ever
Tom.

Remember me to Jessie.
Congratters on the New book.[1] Who will have it here? I shall get one.

TO *Bertrand Russell* MS McMaster

Tuesday [11 January 1916] [34 Russell Chambers, Bury St, London W.C.]

Dear Bertie,

This is wonderfully kind of you – really the last straw (so to speak) of generosity.[2] I am very sorry you have to come back – and Vivien says you have been an angel to her – but of course I shall jump at the opportunity with the utmost gratitude. I am sure you have done *everything* possible and handled her in the very best way – better than I. I often wonder how things would have turned out but for you – I believe we shall owe her life to you, even.

I shall take the 10.30, and look forward to a talk with you before you go. Mrs Saich[3] is expecting you. She has made me very comfortable here.

Aff.
Tom

1–Conrad Aiken, *Turns and Movies, and other tales in verse* (Boston, 1916).
2–BR had taken VHE to Devon for a change of air. On 3 Jan. he told OM that he had 'made a valiant attempt to get out of going away with Mrs E', but that 'the whole thing rather amused me, because it was so unlike the way things are conventionally supposed to happen'. He had talked to TSE, and felt 'the responsibility for her health', and that TSE was 'willing to take my place, but reluctant on account of his work (He has to take a Ph.D degree at Harvard, and his only time for preparation is during the school holidays)' (*Selected Letters of Bertrand Russell: The Public Years 1914–1970*, ed. Nicholas Griffin [2001], 51). When BR returned to London, after five days, he invited TSE to join her in Devon at his expense.
3–The charwoman.

TO *His Father* MS Houghton

14 January 1916 Torbay Hotel, Torquay

My dear father

I wrote to mother yesterday, and I want this to go by the same boat, as I have not written to you for so long. This is a very towny seaside place, but *much* more attractive than Eastbourne (Vivien is massaging my head, so my writing will be rather scrawly) with a real bay and a little harbour just in front of the hotel, with boats. It is wonderful to be here at the seaside in January, warm enough to go out without an overcoat. If I had some old clothes I should be inevitably tempted to seize a boat and put to sea – except that Vivien couldn't come with me. There are some signs of war even in this remote western country – a torpedo boat from time to time, and a naval officer at the hotel who goes out in a motor boat, looking for submarines.

The west country is very lovely – rich and green, with bright red soil. We passed through Eliot country getting here – Somerset[1] – quite near.

The post-time has nearly come, and Vivien wants to put in a word, as she hasn't been able to write to you lately

[In Vivien's hand:]

Dear Mr Eliot

This is not a proper letter, only a line, because the post, we have just found, goes out in five minutes. I have wanted to write to you for a long time, but all the time I have been ill writing letters has been such an effort to me. I hope you got my line at Xmas, and also that the little things I sent to Ada, Charlotte and Margaret arrived safely. Will you please thank Mrs Eliot for her nice letters. There are proper grates (for *coal* fires) in all the rooms in our flat, but we had gas stoves fixed in to the two bedrooms, and also a gas *cooker* in the kitchen, because it is much cheaper than coal. But as I was ill, we found that we could not get enough heat from the gas stove in our bedroom, and it is not healthy either, so we had it removed, and burn a *coal* fire there, and also in the sitting room. It is most beautiful here at Torquay, and we are so grateful to Mr Russell for giving us this wonderful holiday.

V. S. E.

1–TSE's ancestor Andrew Eliot (1627–1703), a cordwainer, emigrated in about 1669 from East Coker, near Yeovil, Somerset, to Salem, Massachusetts.

TO *Bertrand Russell* MS McMaster

Friday [14 January 1916] Torbay Hotel, Torquay

Dear Bertie,

I hope you got our wire this afternoon. The MS is here, and Vivien will have it ready for you at the time you want it. I am very anxious to hear all the lectures, and shall certainly be at the first one;[1] but I am not sure about my Tuesday afternoons after that (though I *think* I have a half holiday on Tuesdays) so you had better not give me a ticket now, in any case.

Vivien is not very well today. She felt very well yesterday, and was too active; consequently a bad night, and stomach and headache today, and very tired. As it was a lovely afternoon, however, we took a taxi drive along the shore to the place where one sees the two small islands; as we thought there might not be another such good chance. It is one of the loveliest bits of shore I have ever seen. There was no wind; the water that peculiar clear green blue which I have never seen anywhere else. I was in raptures over it. An atmosphere of perfect peace that nothing but the ocean has. It is wonderful to have come out of town and been bathed in this purity. You could not have chosen a better place for Vivien: it's a sign how badly she needed it, when even under the absolutely *perfect* conditions you have provided for her she is still so weak and fatigued. I am convinced that no one could have been so wise and understanding with her as you. She was very happy. I have felt happier, these few days, than ever in my life.

Vivien hopes you will forgive her for not writing tonight, as she is so very tired. She is all right when she is lying down, but immediately she gets up is very faint.

Thank you very much for the cheque. You think of everything.

I shall see you on Tuesday. I am looking forward to the first lecture.

Affectionately,
Tom

1–The first of Russell's eight Tuesday lectures at Caxton Hall, published as *Principles of Social Reconstruction* (1916), was given on 18 Jan.

TO *Bertrand Russell* MS McMaster

Sunday [16 January 1916] Torbay Hotel, Torquay

Dear Bertie,

Thank you very much for putting me in for Jourdain's[1] work – your efforts have been inexhaustible, and I shall do my best to justify them with Jourdain as well as Waterlow. I wrote to him at once, and I hope I can do something for him. I must do everything I can to earn more money, even with the thesis etc. on my hands. If Jourdain is willing to take something from me, and if I could do it well, I should find it worth while aside from the money, as an introduction. If he wants it soon, I should have no extra time; but I am going to find out if there is any opportunity for tutoring boys a few hours a week – privately, at Highgate, or through the medium of one of the agencies. It pays fairly well.

Vivien is wretched today – another bad night. Yesterday she was fairly well; we walked along the shore for over half an hour; but today very tired and low.

I shall come Tuesday afternoon, and of course Vivien is hoping to come. I don't expect to see you afterwards, or only for a moment – but I want to see you in a few days, if possible for you.

Affectionately,
Tom.

TO *Bertrand Russell* MS McMaster

Monday 7 p.m. [17 January 1916] Torbay Hotel, Torquay

Dear Bertie,

I was awfully sorry to be obliged to postpone the journey till tomorrow, as now it will be impossible for us to get to the lecture; but I was quite sure that Vivien was not well enough to travel today. I was almost convinced of it yesterday but decided to postpone the decision till this morning. *Of course* we are staying this extra night at our own expense; I insist on that. Vivien wanted to stick to the original timetable, but as I let her do rather too much on Saturday, she was quite exhausted yesterday, and was by no means fit today. I am sure that the net results will be definitely on the side of advance, but she will not be fit for much the rest

1–Philip Jourdain (1879–1919), mathematician, had been a student of Russell's at Cambridge and was British editor of *The Monist* and the *International Journal of Ethics*.

of this week. A very strict regimen, with very clear limits of exertion will be imperative for the rest of the winter.

I will write to you tomorrow night, and hope to see you as soon as possible.

Affy
Tom

Charlotte C. Eliot TO *Bertrand Russell* MS McMaster

18 January 1916 4446 Westminster Place, St Louis

Dear Mr Russell,

It was very kind in you to send me a copy of your book: *The Problems of Philosophy*. I have delayed acknowledgement, because I wished first to read it and I have been very busy. I have now read as far as the eleventh chapter. When I have completed the book, I shall re-read it, as thus I can grasp the contents more as a whole. I find the text very lucid – a sort of concentration of light on the important points. I have always been interested in Philosophy, since I studied as a girl what in those days was termed 'Mental Philosophy'. Most of what little knowledge I have was obtained through reading, and is desultory. I am glad to study the *Problems*. I read Bergson's *Creative Evolution*[1] and attended a course of lectures thereon, largely influenced by Tom's enthusiasm, which I think became later a 'diminishing quantity'.[2] In Bergson's emphasis on *life*, its power and indestructibility, I think some persons found an intimation of immortality, which excited their interest.

My personal experience [has] been that the mere reading of Philosophy stimulates the mind and increases its creative power, so that I have sometimes read Philosophy as a preparation for writing. I do not see any reason why if my son makes Philosophy his life work he should not write all the poetry he desires, if not too much of the ephemeral '*vers libre*'. I went yesterday to the Library, to look for Tom's review [of Balfour, *Theism and Humanism*] in the *International Journal of Ethics*. I found and read it. It produced an excellent impression but I am too ignorant to understand

1–Trans. Arthur Mitchell (New York, 1911). TSE's annotated copy survives, with his notes and an essay on Henri Bergson (Houghton).

2–TSE wrote later that his 'only conversion, by the deliberate influence of one individual, was a temporary conversion to Bergsonism' (*A Sermon*, preached in Magdalene College Chapel, Cambridge, 1948, 5). By 1924 he was asking, 'Has not his exciting promise of immortality a somewhat meretricious captivation?' (*Vanity Fair* 21: 6, Feb. 1924, 29).

and appreciate the article. I feel very grateful to you for having obtained for Tom the opportunity to do this work, and am very glad he is to join the Aristotelian Society.

I hope Tom will be able to carry out his purpose of coming on in May to take his degree. The Ph.D. is becoming in America, and presumably also in England, almost an essential for an Academic position and promotion therein. The male teachers in our secondary schools, are as a rule inferior to the women teachers, and they have little social position or distinction. I hope Tom will not undertake such work another year – it is like putting Pegasus in harness.

Tom has always had every reasonable desire gratified, without any thought of ways and means, up to the present time. I am sure his father will do for him all he can as soon as he can. We hope for a return to power of the Republican party, and a consequent revision of the tariff. Mr Eliot thinks after the War is over, we shall be flooded with cheap German goods. I think even England, with her free trade traditions will find she needs protection.

I saw in the *Fortnightly Review* an article by Ezra Pound, in which he mentions Tom as one of two of the most intelligent writers.[1] He is generous in his praise. And a kindly man. Yet I cannot read Pound. His articles seem over-strained, unnatural. As for the *Blast*, Mr Eliot remarked when he saw a copy he did not know there were enough lunatics in the world to support such a magazine.

Yours very truly,
Charlotte C. Eliot

TO *Sydney Waterlow* MS Waterlow

27 January 1916

3 Culworth House, Henry St,
St John's Wood, N.W.

Dear Waterlow

It is very kind of you to forward the compliment and the message, and I shall look up your friend as soon as I can. In spite of your apologies, you have excited my curiosity, and I look forward to meeting him.

1 – 'With the appearance of James Joyce and T. S. Eliot, and the more "normal" part of Mr Wyndham Lewis's narrative writings, one may even hope that intelligence shall once more have its innings in our own stalwart tongue' ('Rémy de Gourmont' [Part I], *Fortnightly Review* 98, 1 Dec. 1915, 1159–66).

I am sending a copy of the Anthology I mentioned to you.[1] I make the same apology for it that you do for your friend! but you have expressed an interest in such stuff, and I hope that some of the contents may amuse you.

Yours sincerely
T. Stearns Eliot

TO *J. H. Woods* MS Professor David G. Williams

20 February 1916 3 Compayne Gdns, London N.W.

Dear Professor Woods,

Thank you very much for writing and for asking the other members of the faculty to write. I will send on my thesis a little ahead, and if it is *not* acceptable I will ask you to *cable* so as to save me the journey.

I shall sail either the 2nd or the 5th of April and thus will have a few days before the week of the 19th and I hope a few days afterward. My examinations will have to be crammed into a very few days, I am sorry to say. I will let you know very shortly just what day I shall arrive.

I enclose two letters from Joachim. I am sure he and Smith (with whom he is hand in glove) will greet you very cordially, and I look forward to having you so near. I hope you will be often in London. If there is anything else I can do for you before you come I am at your disposal –

I am in a great rush tonight. I will write again very shortly.

With many thanks,

Sincerely,
Thomas Stearns Eliot

Bertrand Russell TO *J. H. Woods* MS Harvard

4 March 1916 34 Russell Chambers, Bury St, W.C.

Dear Professor Woods

I am looking forward to your answer as to my lectures[2] next year. I am very anxious to give the sort of course that will be acceptable. But what I want to write about now is Eliot. I hope he is all right for his Doctor's Degree. I have seen a great deal of him since his marriage, and have got to know a new side of him, which I never suspected. He has been poor and

1–*Catholic Anthology* (1915).

2–The lectures were cancelled because the Foreign Office refused BR a passport.

his wife has been ill. He has had to work very hard to make a living, and has spent his spare hours in looking after his wife, with the most amazing devotion and unselfishness. I can't help fearing that he may have grown rusty in his work – but if he has it is not from laziness, quite the reverse. It has driven me almost to despair to see his really fine talents wasting; he is so reserved and modest that I am sure Harvard will never learn anything of his private circumstances from him.

He has here, among all the younger literary men, a very considerable reputation for his poetry. All sorts of cultivated people who have never met him think his work in that line the best work done by any young man. For a long time, I was unable to see any merit in it, but now I agree with them. It takes time to get used to a new style. My view is that he is right to live in Europe because the atmosphere of Europe is better for that sort of work; and that is the sort of work he ought to aim at doing. But my only motive in writing is to recommend him to your kindness, and to let you know something of the struggle he has had – which he would never mention. Except in the one matter of health, his marriage is a very happy one and altogether desirable.

Yours very sincerely
Bertrand Russell

TO *Bertrand Russell* — MS McMaster

Monday [6 March? 1916] 3 Culworth House

Dear Bertie

We went to the dentist this afternoon. I was not able to go with Vivien, but I arrived a few minutes later and talked to the doctor afterwards. Vivien was very much shaken by the interview, and is now in very great pain, both neuralgia and stomach. I think the dentist quite failed in tact, and did not understand what was required, though I had talked to him and also written to him last night. I saw that she had had a shock, and was puzzled when he made light of the matter in talking to me afterwards. He said it could be easily attended to, required no anaesthetic, could wait for some little time, and meant no great pain or risk. He said that there was probably some decay in the crowned tooth, and that the nerve of the other tooth was dead; that the pain it had given was in the process of dying. He told me that he had not told her this – I then found that he *had* told her and also, what he had *not* told me, that there was a possibility of an abscess. He evidently thought that I was the person to be calmed down, and that I had communicated my fears to Vivien, and evidently he had not understood what I had told him. I have no doubt he is a good dentist, but the interview has done no good, and has taken it out of her very much indeed. How much this will postpone her recovery I cannot yet tell. She is very low tonight. I think that the teeth will take care of themselves until she is ready to have them attended to. She is very ill tonight, and I am very very sorry that she went through this. It has been too great a strain upon her will.

I will write to you tomorrow, and see you soon and talk to you.

Yours aff.
Tom

She finished the typing this afternoon before going to the dentist. I am sending it tonight.

The dentist told her that there was a possibility of an abscess forming in the tooth of which the nerve had died. After all however, the consequences are not his fault – he was very kind and did his best. The mistake was in letting her go at all – the effort and the anticipation during the last weeks – which she didn't say anything about, and which have taken every ounce of strength out of her.

Don't expect her to lunch tomorrow. I am sure it will be some days before she can go out to lunch or dinner.

TO *J. H. Woods*

MS Professor David G. Williams

6 March 1916

3 Culworth House, Henry St,
St John's Wood, London N.W.

Dear Professor Woods,

I enclose the form[1] which was sent me by the secretary.

I shall sail, if all goes well, on the first of April. This will I suppose compel me to have all the examinations in the week of April 10th as (I presume) the spring holidays occupy the week of April 17th. I hope that this will not inconvenience the department.

I trust that no international developments will prevent my sailing. If a breach with Germany should occur, either to make it impossible to sail or

1 – The form (postmarked 7 Mar. 1916), which gave notice of his intention to submit his PhD thesis, set out the title: 'The Nature of Objects, with reference to the philosophy of F. H. Bradley'.

to jeopardise my return, I hope such an unfortunate occurrence might be considered only a postponement.

I am sending my thesis in a few days in any case, and will write you a line by the same mail. If it should *not* prove acceptable, there might just be time to cable to me before my sailing; but I hope that it will not be found unsatisfactory.

Sincerely yours
Thomas Stearns Eliot

Cable address: '*LINEN*', *London*.

TO *Harriet Monroe*

MS Chicago

27 March 1916

18 Crawford Mansions,
Crawford St, London W.

Dear Miss Monroe

I hope that I have not seriously inconvenienced you by not writing before in regard to your inquiry about putting my 'Prufrock' into your anthology.[1] I can only excuse myself by saying that I have been busier than most men are in a lifetime – and I find it very hard to keep anything on my mind. I do hope your plans have not been put out by my delay.

I am very much pleased that you want to reprint the poem; but as it has already appeared in the *Catholic Anthology* here, and as it will form the ballast of a *very* small volume in the future, I really feel that I should be making a mistake in reprinting it again in an Anthology before it appears in a book.

If there is anything else of mine which you would care to use instead, I wish you would make use of it. But I suppose you are using only material which has already appeared in *Poetry*, or I should suggest some things of mine which appeared in *Blast* and *Others*.

Thank you for the clippings in regard to the *Dial* episode.[2] Does the battle still go on? I should be glad to participate with a few quotations which the critic would perhaps not identify.

1 – *The New Poetry: An Anthology*, ed. Harriet Monroe and Alice Corbin Henderson (New York, 1917). TSE discussed it in 'Reflections on Contemporary Poetry' [III], *Egoist* 4: 10 (Nov. 1917).

2 – *The Dial* had been attacking Monroe and her anthology, and in its issue of 25 Nov. it condemned her for being negligent in allowing TSE's 'plagiarism', in 'Cousin Nancy', of George Meredith's line 'The army of unalterable law'.

From the 9th to the 22nd April my address will be c/o J. K. Clement Esq.,[1] Wayland, Mass. U.S.A. Otherwise, I have a new London address which you see above.

Yours faithfully,
T. Stearns Eliot

Henry Ware Eliot TO *J. H. Woods*

MS Professor David G. Williams

7 April 1916

Hydraulic-Press Brick Company,
Central National Bank Building,
St Louis, Mo.

My dear Sir:

I thank you for your kind letter of the 3rd. Mrs Eliot and I will use every effort to induce my son to take his examinations later. Doubtless his decision was much influenced by Prof. Russell who cabled to me as follows:

'STRONGLY ADVISE CABLING TOM AGAINST SAILING UNDER PRESENT PECULIARLY DANGEROUS CONDITIONS UNLESS IMMEDIATE DEGREE IS WORTH RISKING LIFE.'[2]

The day following, Tom cabled final decision. I was not greatly pleased with the language of Prof. Russell's cablegram.

I shall send Tom a copy of your letter, which has comforted me much.

Yours truly,
H. W. Eliot

TO *J. H. Woods*

MS Professor David G. Williams

3 May 1916

18 Crawford Mansions,
Crawford St, London W.

Dear Dr Woods

I must apologise for not having written to you before, after my cable. I need not say how disappointed I was not to be able to come, after the winter of work, and after you had made all the arrangements for me.

1–James Clement (1889–1973), Harvard Class of 1911, had married Marguerite C. Burrel in 1913. In later years TSE visited them annually in Geneva.

2–BR had also written to OM on 29 Mar. that VHE's nerves were 'all to pieces. It is the worry of his going that upset her. She was afraid he would be sunk by a submarine' (*Selected Letters of Bertrand Russell: The Public Years*, 56). TSE had been due to sail on 1 Apr.

Transportation has been so irregular during the war that I might have foreseen what occurred – my boat postponed for five days at the last moment. Coming on top of all the difficulties I had encountered, this was a crushing blow and I could not bear for some time to let myself think about it. I am still in a state of mental confusion, but am trying, after a few days in the country, to settle down to writing an article and a review, for which I got the opportunities through Sydney Waterlow and P. E. B. Jourdain. Our holidays were taken up, first with the details of a necessary emigration from one flat to another, and then with a much needed week in the country for both of us.

I hope you will let me know 1. whether my thesis was satisfactory 2. whether it will still hold good at my next opportunity for taking the examinations 3. if satisfactory, with what margin or by what squeak.

I shall come *at the first opportunity*. I hope that the war will be over, as naturally I do not like to leave my wife here, or venture the waves myself, while it is still on.

I do not know whether to urge you to persist in coming to England next winter. I hope that you will – but I should be sorry not to be examined by you in Cambridge. I hope that Mrs Woods's health is not such as to prevent your both coming.

Do accept all my thanks, and my deepest regrets at not being able to see you in Cambridge this April. I hope I shall see you there within a year, unless you will grant me your presence here. Please also thank all the faculty for their kindness in writing to me, and for giving me the chance of taking my degree at an irregular time.

Very sincerely yours
Thomas Stearns Eliot

TO *Scofield Thayer* — MS Beinecke

7 May 1916 — 18 Crawford Mansions

My dear Scofield

Can it be that a year ago you and I were charming the eyes (and ears) of Char-flappers[1] from one virginal punt, I by my voracity for bread and butter and you by Sidneian showers of discourse upon Art, Life, Sex and Philosophy? Yes! I recognise the Scofield of Magdalen, the connoisseur of puberty and lilies, in the Scofield of Washington Square, about to wed the

1 – Presumably an Oxford slang shortening of 'Cherwell-flappers', though the *OED* has no record of it.

Madonna of the mantelpiece,[1] whose praises from your lips I have not forgotten. – So you have hit upon the Fountain of Eternal Youth, not in Florida, but Troy. 'Only the soul can cure the senses, and only the senses can cure the soul'.[2] And the century of sonnets?[3] And have I not St Praxed's ear to pray horses for you, and brown Greek manuscripts?[4] . . . to pray that domestic felicity may not extinguish the amateur, to pray that possession of beauty may not quench that ardour of curiosity and that passionate detachment which your friends admired and your admirers envied.

And I hope that within an interior of dim light drifting through heavy curtains, by a Buhl table holding a Greek figurine, and a volume of Faust bound in green and powdered with gold, with a bust of Dante, and perhaps a screen by Kōrin,[5] a drawing by Watteau – a room heavy with the scent of lilies, you will enshrine such a treasure as that with which you rightly credited me, – a wife who is not wifely.

Treasure me in thy heart, and remember that when Mr and Mrs Scofield Thayer come to visit London, Mr and Mrs Stearns Eliot will be outraged if they are not the first to entertain them.

Yours always
Thomas Stearns Eliot

Vivien Eliot TO *Scofield Thayer* — MS Beinecke

8 May [1916][6] — 18 Crawford Mansions

Dear Scofield,

How nice that you are going to be married! Nothing could be better! Try black silk sheets and pillow covers – they are extraordinarily effective – so long as you are willing to sacrifice *yourself*.

I was never more delighted than when I heard that you have an orange wallpaper. We have one, in our dining room.

1–He married Elaine Eliot Orr on 21 June. After their divorce in the 1920s, she became the first wife of E. E. Cummings.

2–'To cure the soul by means of the senses, and the senses by means of the soul!' (Oscar Wilde, *The Picture of Dorian Gray* [1891], ch. 16).

3–'Rafael made a century of sonnets . . . Else he only used to draw Madonnas' (Browning, 'One Word More', 5–8).

4–'And have I not Saint Praxed's ear to pray / Horses for ye, and brown Greek manuscripts, / And mistresses with great smooth marbly limbs?' (Browning, 'The Bishop Orders his Tomb at Saint Praxed's Church', 73–5).

5–Ogata Kōrin (1658–1716), Japanese artist whose Matsushima screen is in the Boston Museum.

6–The envelope was 'Opened by the censor'.

Do come and see us when you bring her to see Europe. You can do us and the Tower of London on the same day.

With congratulations of the most fervent.

Vivien S-E.

TO *Bertrand Russell* MS McMaster

14 May [1916] 18 Crawford Mansions

Dear Bertie,

Vivien told me about the books. I did not quite know how to thank you, at first. I was awfully touched. This sort of gift is a peculiar sort of symbol, and its position in a future when no one can guess what will have become of all of our lives renders it much more of an attachment, somehow, than if you were ninety and at death's door. There is more kindness in it than people will ever see.

Affectionately

Tom

Vivien has been quite ill all today. She must have eaten something which disagreed with her last night, as she was very ill in the night, and was not fit to do anything today. She meant to write to you, but will write tomorrow. She seems very overdone.

Charlotte C. Eliot TO *Bertrand Russell* MS McMaster

23 May 1916 4446 Westminster Place [St Louis]

Dear Mr Russell,

Your letter relative to a cablegram sent us, was received some little time ago. I write now to thank you for the affection that inspired it. It was natural you should feel as you did with the awful tragedy of the *Sussex*[1] of such recent occurrence. Mr Eliot did not believe it possible that even the Germans, (a synonym for all that is most frightful,) would attack an American liner. It would be manifestly against their interest. Yet I am aware there is still a possibility of war between Germany and America. The more we learn of German methods, open and *secret*, the greater is the moral

1–On 24 Mar. 1916, the London Brighton and South Coast Railway cross-Channel steamer, *Sussex*, was torpedoed off Dieppe with a loss of some fifty lives. Three Americans were among the injured. The sinking of the *Sussex* led to President Wilson's ultimatum to the German government on 18 Apr., condemning Germany's unrestricted submarine warfare in the Atlantic.

indignation of many Americans. I am glad all our ancestors are English with a French ancestry far back on one line. I am sending Tom a copy of a letter written by his Great-great-grandfather in 1811, giving an account of his grandfather (*one* of them) who was born about 1676 – in the county of Devon, England – Christopher Pearse.

I am sure your influence in every way will confirm my son in his choice of Philosophy as a life work. Professor Wood speaks of his thesis as being of exceptional value. I had hoped he would seek a University appointment next year. If he does not I shall feel regret. I have absolute faith in his Philosophy but not in the *vers libres*.

Tom is very grateful to you for your sympathy and kindness. This gratitude I share.

Sincerely yours,
Charlotte C. Eliot

Vivien Eliot TO *Henry Eliot* — MS Houghton

1 June 1916

18 Crawford Mansions,
Crawford St, London W.

Dear Henry

I got your letter from New York only two days ago – so you see I am losing no time in answering. We *both* wish that you would write to us more often – please do! Make a rule of writing once a fortnight, and we will do the same – it is the only way to keep in touch. And I think we all ought to keep in touch – don't you? I am going to buy some films for my camera today, and then we shall send you some photos of ourselves and our flat. We are very proud of this flat. It is the tiniest place imaginable – just a dining room – a drawing room – a large bedroom – a kitchen and a nice bathroom. We have constant hot water, which is a *luxury* in England, and as this building is quite new, we have 'every modern convenience'! I chose all the papers, and we have some rather original effects. We have an *orange* paper in our dining room, (which is also Tom's dressing room and study!) and black and white stripes in the Hall.

I don't know if all these details interest you I'm sure!

We were both interested in your descriptions of the Preparedness procession.[1] But, as Tom says, what are they preparing for? – do they

1 – Preparedness parades were held across the USA in the summer of 1916, to demonstrate America's readiness for war. The *Sunday Star* reported on 27 May that 80,000 people processed through Boston: it was the biggest parade in the city's history.

know? He says they just don't want to feel out of it! There is a good deal of bitter feeling about America, over here. It is horrid, I hate it. I am afraid it will take years before it calms down. People talk in a slighting way about America.

I am enclosing to you a letter from my brother – the latest I've received, just so that you can see the manner of boy he is. And also, his tone is *typically* English – army English. And of course England is *all* army now. The letter is full of foolish little family jokes and references – but you will understand that. You will return it, won't you?

We are glad you have gone to New York – there was no future in St Louis. Tom is *wonderful*. I have never met a man who gets so much pushing and helping and who impresses people so much with the feeling that he is *worth* helping. Just now we are faced with a problem. If he goes on teaching – it means that he must throw away innumerable chances and openings for writing, and just do the little scraps that he has time, and energy, for – after school. And school tires him very much – and chances don't come twice. If he leaves school-mastering (for which he is <u>too</u> good, and *not* fitted) – it is a gamble, at first. He would win in time, but in the first year or two – how should we live?

I can't write more now. T. will write soon. Please write, as soon as you can.

Vivien

My brother is not one of K[itchener]'s army (which by the way, were mostly put in Khaki directly they joined). He is of the regular army – and of course there is some feeling of 'class distinction'.

TO *Harriet Monroe* MS Chicago

7 June 1916 18 Crawford Mansions

Dear Miss Monroe,

Your letter to me sent to the American address has just reached me. I deeply regret not having got it before. But the misadventure was not to be foreseen.

As for the 'Prufrock': you see, I shall probably have a small volume coming out just about the same time as your anthology, in the autumn, in New York. If it were much before or much after I should probably be quite glad to enter 'Prufrock' in both, but it seems to me that to synchronise would be inadvisable. It is so much longer and confessedly so much better, than anything else I have done, that I cannot afford (or so I think) to scatter my forces. If there is anything else that would do, I hope you will accept a substitute; the 'Portrait', or perhaps the 'Figlia che piange' which I believe Pound has sent you. Will you forgive me?

I shall indeed be delighted to contribute a morsel to your prose section whenever you will let me. Would you like (1) comments on some of the theories in Pound's *Gaudier-Brzeska*,[1] or (2) a few comments on several 17th C writers who seem to me of importance for contemporaries (e.g. Webster, Ford) or (3) comments on a few poets whom the age neglects (e.g. Malherbe, Swift, Voltaire, as *poets*). I should be glad to review any new versifier when you want it done. – You see I want to find out what you would be willing to endure.

With all best wishes

believe me
sincerely yours
T. Stearns Eliot

Let us then leave the *Dial* to posterity.

TO *Bertrand Russell* MS McMaster

7 June 1916 18 Crawford Mansions

Dear Bertie

Thanks awfully for the books – the second lot arrived today. They will come in most usefully, and I shall be extremely grateful for them. Jourdain wants another article on Leibniz first – monads again – by July 15, so I shall have to shelve the idealists for a time – He will lend me your book, and Latta and Montgomery[2] (the latter I have however). Do you know of any books – chiefly *historical* – dealing with Leibniz other than those I am acquainted with, which I could get anything out of?

I am glad to hear you like the Nietzsche review. It seemed to me rather inferior at the time. Have not yet heard from the *N. Statesman* as to whether they want the reviews I sent them.[3]

1 – EP, *Gaudier-Brzeska: A Memoir. Including the published writings of the sculptor and a selection from his letters* (1916).
2 – BR, *A Critical Exposition of the Philosophy of Leibniz* (1900); G. W. Leibniz, *The Monadology and Other Philosophical Writings*, trans. Robert Latta (1898); G. W. Leibniz, *Discourse on Metaphysics, Correspondence with Arnauld, and Monadology*, trans. George R. Montgomery (1902).
3 – TSE's reviews of Paul Elmer More, *Aristocracy and Justice* (24 June), and Charles Sarolea, *The French Renascence* (1 July).

I rejoiced to hear such good accounts of your defence.[1] It must have been a great success, in the only way in which you expected or wished it to succeed.

I am glad your term is nearly over. I hope I shall see you next week.

Affectionately
T. S. E.

FROM *J. H. Woods*

TS Harvard

23 June 1916

Department of Philosophy and Psychology, Harvard University

Dear Eliot,

The Division of Philosophy has accepted your thesis without the least hesitation. Prof. Royce[2] regards it as the work of an expert. Prof. Hoernlé[3] has written a criticism which I will send you later. Meantime we will keep the MS. here.[4] I hope that we can arrange some time which will make it more convenient for you to take the rest of the examination. In any case, please let us be reassured that your interest in Philosophy is as strong as before.

With kindest regards to Mrs Eliot and to yourself,

Sincerely yours,
James H. Woods

1–In Apr. 1916 the No-Conscription Fellowship had issued a leaflet in protest at the sentence of two years' hard labour passed on a conscientious objector, Ernest Everett, for refusing to obey military orders as a member of the Non-Combatant Corps. When six men were imprisoned for distributing the leaflet, Russell wrote to *The Times* (17 May), saying he was the author and if anyone was to be prosecuted he was the person primarily responsible. On 5 June he was tried before the Lord Mayor of London on a charge of making, in a printed publication, 'statements likely to prejudice the recruiting discipline of His Majesty's forces'. Russell defended himself and, according to Lytton Strachey who was present with OM, 'spoke for about an hour – quite well – but simply a propaganda speech'. Found guilty, Russell was fined £100 with £10 costs, with the alternative of sixty-one days' imprisonment. When his appeal failed on 29 June he refused to pay the fine so the authorities seized some of his books for public auction, at which a group of his friends bid £100 for the first volume offered and so settled the debt.

2–Josiah Royce (1855–1916), Professor of the History of Philosophy from 1892. TSE had attended his graduate seminar in Comparative Methodology, 1913–14.

3–R. F. Alfred Hoernlé (1880–1943), Assistant Professor of Philosophy, 1914–20, had written to Woods on 13 June: 'He knows his Bradley excellently, and has done a most valuable piece of work in bringing together and treating systematically B's scattered dicta on feeling, experience, thought, etc.'

4–Now at Houghton. Published as *Knowledge and Experience in the Philosophy of F. H. Bradley* (1964).

TO *Conrad Aiken* TS Huntington

21 August 1916 18 Crawford Mansions, Crawford St, London W.

My dear Conrad,

What do you think of me? Have you written to me at all since you sent me your book?[1] If so it went astray, or rather went to a deserted address, and the people at Culworth House, St John's Wood, have not shown themselves over zealous in forwarding mail. Will you accept the present screed for the scramble of pedagogy and journalism (NOT forgetfulness or intentional insult) of the past three months? I am not even sure of your address; but it *was* Chestnut Street, and I hope that if I put on the wrong number the post-office will try every door in the street and then send it on to your aunt Mrs Potter's in Sparks Street, Cambridge.

First to explain myself. You know that my wife has been very ill all the winter. She has been getting gradually better, but very slowly. At present we are at Bosham, near Chichester in Sussex, for most of the holidays, and she has improved a great deal here, so I feel encouraged. But it was a great anxiety all winter and spring, as she kept having incidental troubles like teeth which set her back. I may say that this was not a case of maternity in any degree. Most people imagine so unless I explain. It has been nerves, complicated by physical ailments, and induced largely by the most acute neuralgia. This has been one leading cause for my neglect of correspondence with everybody in America except my immediate family.

Another cause is the mentioned scramble. The school takes up most of my days, and in my spare (*sic*) time I have been writing: philosophy for the *Monist* and the *International Journal of Ethics*, reviews for the *New Statesman*, the *Manchester Guardian* and the *Westminster Gazette*. The first two I got in with through Bertrand Russell, the others through a man named Sidney [*sic*] Waterlow. I am now trying to get an introduction to the *Nation*. The papers are rather hard up for good reviewers at present. On the other hand they are devoting much less space to books than they used to do. I have reviewed some good books and much trash. It is good practice in writing, and teaches one speed both in reading and writing. It is bad in this way, that one acquires an extraordinary appetite for volumes, and exults at the mass of printed matter which one has devoured and evacuated. I crave a new book every few days. The *New Statesman* is rather the best fun to review for. They give me pretty good books, and as

1 – Aiken, *Turns and Movies, and other tales in verse* (1916).

soon as I have time I am going to approach them with an article. I am doing a long review on Charles Péguy[1] for them now. Composing on the typewriter, I find that I am sloughing off all my long sentences which I used to dote upon. Short, staccato, like modern French prose. The typewriter makes for lucidity, but I am not sure that it encourages subtlety.

This autumn will find me busier than ever, as I am preparing a set of six lectures on contemporary intellectual movements in France to deliver under the auspices of Oxford to the general public[2] – mostly, I believe, ladies. If they come off, I ought to be able to secure plenty of lecturing, at least enough to keep us. And I have several distinguished predecessors on the Oxford lecturing circuit – Belloc[3] and F. E. Smith[4] for instance. You will see that I have been very busy grinding axes. Of poetry I have not written a line; I have been far too worried and nervous. I hope that the end of another year will see me in a position to think about verse a bit.

Nearly everyone has faded away from London, or is there very rarely. The vorticists are non-existent. Lewis is a gunner in the R.G.A.,[5] Wadsworth is something in the navy and is out in the Mediterranean, F. M. Hueffer is settled to an army career in the Welsh Guards and is in France,[6] T. E. Hulme has been in France for ages. As for the Hampstead school, I haven't the remotest idea whether Aldington is conscripted or not,[7] and

1–TSE's review of Victor Boudon, *Avec Charles Péguy, de la Lorraine à la Marne (août–septembre, 1914)*, appeared in *NS* 8: 183 (7 Oct. 1916).

2–Between 3 Oct. and 12 Dec., TSE gave afternoon lectures and classes on modern French literature at Ilkley in Yorkshire. The average attendance at each of the lectures was fifty-eight, dropping to fifteen at the discussion classes which followed. In his reports he regretted 'that no papers were offered as I missed this means of observing the reaction of the audience. The subject was difficult and involved, and most of the writers discussed were new to the majority of the students.' Shyness prevented questions being asked 'which might have proved interesting and useful'. Owing to the war there were few men and the local secretary noted the unpopularity of the hour, which meant that most teachers could not attend. Some members were engaged in nursing, while others were 'too busy or too tired to attend regularly or to read'. For this and TSE's other lecture series, see Ronald Schuchard, *Eliot's Dark Angel* (1999), 25–51.

3–Hilaire Belloc (1870–1953), poet, author, and Liberal MP 1906–10.

4–F. E. Smith, created first Earl of Birkenhead in 1919 (1872–1930), lawyer, wit and statesman, had given university extension lectures on modern history.

5–Having volunteered for the Royal Garrison Artillery in Mar., WL spent the rest of the year in military camps in Britain.

6–Ford Madox Hueffer (1873–1939), novelist, memoirist and critic, joined the Welsh Guards in 1915, and fought on the Somme and at Ypres before being invalided out in 1917. The four novels of *Parade's End* (1924–8) drew on his experiences.

7–Though he volunteered at the outbreak of war, RA's enlistment was deferred for medical reasons. He was sent to France in Dec. 1916. See Glossary of Names.

don't care and as a matter of fact have never met him, but I believe H. D.[1] is doing his part of the *Egoist*, and is pegging away at Greek. There are no conscientious objectors among the Vortex, they are all in another set, mostly localised in Bloomsbury. One of them, Gilbert Cannan (novelist)[2] I met down here at Bosham not long ago; a cadaverous silent person. There are a few rather nice people about here – G. Lowes Dickinson[3] is one. Ezra holds out in London, and refuses to rusticate; he has one or two Japs with whom he fences. He has just translated (with untiring energy) Laforgue's 'Salome', and wants me to do the 'Hamlet'[4] to go to make up a volume between us of the *Moralités Légendaires*, and I have done a few pages of it.

We are vegetating and gaining health against the coming term on a backwater [Bosham] near Portsmouth harbour, where the tide is either very much in or very much out; the place alternates between mud and water, and is very charming. I have been working always in the morning, and bathing, boating and bicycling in the afternoon.

I was awfully glad to have your book, and very much pleased at your sending it to me. And now that I have come up from the country for a night, I find it safely locked away from me in a bookcase of which my wife has the key. I marked a number of pages with marks of admiration or disapproval, and meant to quote them to you, but this will probably be at Christmas, as I may not have time for another letter before then. And I am too tired out from a day at the British Museum to flow with ideas at this midnight. All I can say now is that I liked the book, some of the poems very much, some less. It seemed to me a distinct advance in workmanship over the first book. You have gone a good way. I think the title poems on

1–Hilda Doolittle (1886–1961), American-born poet and novelist, who wrote as H. D. at EP's instigation. She moved to London in 1911, and in 1913 she had married RA, assistant editor of *The Egoist*.
2–Gilbert Cannan (1884–1955), novelist and dramatist; a founder of the Manchester Repertory Theatre.
3–Goldsworthy Lowes Dickinson (1862–1932), historian, pacifist, and promoter of the League of Nations; Fellow of King's College, Cambridge; Apostle. OM thought him 'a rare and gentle Pagan Saint . . . by temperament religious and poetical' (*Ottoline at Garsington* [1974], 117–19).
4–Laforgue retold the stories of Salomé and Hamlet in his *Moralités Légendaires* (1887). EP's version of the 'Salomé' appeared as 'Our Tetrarchal Précieuse', *Little Review* 5: 3 (July 1918). TSE's 'few pages' of the 'Hamlet' do not survive, and it is unlikely that he persevered with the task, especially in the light of EP's remark that translations of Laforgue's prose were held up by copyright laws ('Irony, Laforgue, and Some Satire', *Poetry* 11: 2, Nov. 1917). In 'Hamlet and His Problems' TSE wrote: 'The Hamlet of Laforgue is an adolescent; the Hamlet of Shakespeare is not, he has not that explanation and excuse' (*SW*, 102).

the whole by far the best.[1] I don't say that I like them – but you will probably be more flattered by the emotion they did produce. Anything which can provoke as strong nausea with life as those did in me is well done. They affect me like Maupassant. And your whole viewpoint at present, my dear Conrad, what is it? I mean, how do you feel early in the morning and on Sunday afternoons? That is the real test, and I wish you would come out with it in a letter. There is a kind of cynicism in some of the poems (the sequel to *Earth Triumphant* I am thinking of)[2] which I should like to analyse . . . And then your blessed materialism I suppose . . . I am still a relativist, a cracker of small theories like nuts, essentially an egoist perhaps, but I have not the leisure to be cynical, a good thing perhaps, life is always positively something or the opposite, it has a *sens*, if only that[:]

the torch-bearers, advancing from behind the throne which King Artaphernes[3] had just vacated, progressed two by two into the centre of the hall. To the shrill piping of the quowhombom and the muffled rattle of the bass trpaxli mingled with the plaintive wail of the thirty captive kings, they circled thrice forwards and thrice backwards, clockwise and counter-clockwise, according to the sacred ritual of the rpat, and finally when the signal was given by the pswhadi or high priest, they turned a flip flop somersault and disappeared down their own throats, leaving the assembly in darkness.

But if you still believe in my sanity, and receive this letter, write to me. I will write, for I find that this letter contains nothing of the slightest interest.

yours ever
Tom

1–'Turns and Movies' is a narrative and dramatic sequence of fifteen poems about dancers and performers and their amours.

2–*Earth Triumphant* (1914) had been Aiken's first book, and the last poem in *Turns and Movies*, 'This Dance of Life', was subtitled 'Earth Triumphant: Part Two'.

3–Brother of Darius the Great (King of Persia 522–486 BC), King Artaphernes figures in books V and VI of Herodotus' *Histories*. TSE is parodying the ethnography of classical historians.

TO *Eleanor Hinkley* TS Houghton

5 September 1916 18 Crawford Mansions

Dear Eleanor,

You will not believe that this is really the first time that I have been able to write to you! I am in despair at being able to make it clear to everyone how little time I have now. And the more time passes, the better and longer letter one feels that one ought to write, to make up. So in consequence I have been losing my correspondents, except Jim Clement, who writes whether I write or not, though his letters consist chiefly of complaints at my not writing. But then as I have *never* written to you all this year, you have reason to be offended with me. But I hope you will write to me this fall. I used to depend on your letters, and I am hopelessly out of touch with Cambridge gossip, too.

I am writing now because I see no chance of *more* time later. So you will, I hope, accept this scrap as the best I can do. I have just come back to town from our holidays, leaving Vivien behind for a few days to see if she can snatch a little more benefit from the country before the long winter. She had a bad attack of neuralgia just last week, lasting five days, and it undid, I am afraid, most of the good that the previous weeks had done. I am very anxious, as London winters are horrible. I do not know when I shall be able to bring her to America, either from the point of view of time or her health. But I really hope that she will have a somewhat better winter than last.

We enjoyed Bosham very much. It is a tiny fishing village, with no hotels, not on the open sea, but up an inlet at the head of a bay, not very far from Portsmouth. It is very informal, and I lived most of the time in a shirt and flannel trowsers.[1] The chief occupations bathing, boating, and bicycling. There are lovely walks back toward the Sussex downs. The natives are charming, much like New England country people, both in aspect and accent, they use 'sir' rather more, but are equally keen on making money out of visitors. But I must say that only a few days ago, when we were out walking, we stopped in at a farmhouse where we were given as many mushrooms as we could take away for sixpence. We had lodgings, with meals in our own rooms in the usual way, and a bouncing kindly landlady, named Miss Kate Smith, a very good cook. Her brother-in-law, Mr Tillett

1 – 'I shall wear white flannel trowsers, and walk upon the beach' ('The Love Song of J. Alfred Prufrock', 123 (TSE's spelling is the same as in his TSS, and in *Poetry* and *Catholic Anthology*).

(he would be 'Capn' with us), is an authority on the weather, and informed us every night exactly what the prospects for tomorrow would be, but as he always prophesied rain, and also gravely informed me that the barometer in Bosham usually went contrariwise, I came to place very little faith in him. When we had my brother-in-law for a few days (he has been invalided home for insomnia) we had a sail boat twice, a very slow one, but it was the first time I had been in a sail boat for two years, and I enjoyed it as much as Vivien and Maurice. He is a tall, rather stylish boy, with a bristly little moustache, and looks nearer twenty-five than twenty. He is thoroughly WORN OUT and from some of the horrors which he once entertained us with I am not surprised. A boy of nineteen (for he had his twentieth birthday with us) who is quite used to the sight of *disjecta membra* and has spent nights when he couldn't sleep in shooting rats with a revolver, makes me feel comparatively immature. But his life has not made him callous at all. And he is very open minded, much more so really than my own family or our friend Roscoe Thayer[1] of Cambridge, in certain respects.

There were a number of friends of mine at or near Bosham for some time, including a man named Lowes Dickinson, who has just been lecturing in America. So that we were by no means lonely. Then I had a good deal of work to do there, reviewing, which has to be punctual, and some preparation for the course of lectures which I am to give in the winter, or rather in the next three months. I will send you the prospectus[2] for them when it is out, it looks very impressive, but I am wondering how I can acquire knowledge of all the things which I have therein engaged myself to talk about. That is what I have come up for, to read at the British Museum, and write out full analyses of the lectures. It will be rather trying at first, and I am hoping that the attendance will not be large.

Do write to me. There is so much that I want to hear about. Tell me what Frederick is preaching about.[3] Tell me how Emily [Hale] is. And about the aunts and uncles. I *must* try to write to Aunt Mattie.[4] And lastly, tell me a lot about your immediate family and then about yourself. It will take you at least six of your typed pages. Remember that you are going to

1–William Roscoe Thayer (1859–1923), Harvard-educated author and editor.

2–TSE's lectures at Ilkley, Yorkshire, from 3 Oct. to 12 Dec.: 'Syllabus of a Course of Six Lectures on Modern French Literature by T. Stearns Eliot, MA (Harvard)'. See Schuchard, 'In the Lecture Halls', *Eliot's Dark Angel*, 27–32.

3–TSE's cousin Frederick Eliot was Associate Unitarian Minister of the First Parish in Cambridge, Massachusetts, 1915–17. TSE remarked in a later year, 'some Eliots are wiser than others, and my cousin Frederick . . . is an ass' (quoted in Mary Trevelyan, 'The Pope of Russell Square').

4–Martha Laurens Stearns (1849–1919), unmarried younger sister of TSE's mother.

see me again as soon as I can come, and that I hate to lose contact in the meantime. Give my love to Aunt Susie, and Believe me

Your affectionate cousin

Tom

I enclose a picture – made for my Identity Book, to go to Sussex. Do I look the same?

Remember that this and all letters are read by the censors. Give my affection to Harry Child, if you see him.

TO *His Mother* TS Houghton

6 September 1916 18 Crawford Mansions

Dearest Mother,

Before I mention anything else I must speak of the letter which you enclosed to me, else I shall forget it. It is quite true that there is a picture which I forgot, in the scramble and confusion, to deliver. It is a small water colour of Oriel College, and is wrapped in brown paper, addressed to E. D. Keith, Phoenix Mills, North Brookfield. It should be in a drawer of my bureau at Gloucester, or else on the shelf of the closet. If you do not find it in either place it might be in the drawer of the little smelley table, or in the steamer trunk which I took and left behind. I hope you will be able to find it, as I feel very much ashamed at having failed in the commission. If you do find it, will you send it on for me to E. D. Keith, 'Plumstead', North Brookfield, Mass.? I will write to him as well. He was a nice fellow, and roomed at Miss Carroll's on my floor. He has been married since.

Another thing to mention is your offer of sending books. It is ever so kind of you, dear mother, but I think I can do without any. Fifteen dollars is a great deal to pay, and the few books I absolutely need I can buy. But I may make out a list of a *few*, perhaps three or four dollars worth, for Shef to send. Thank you very much. *New* philosophic books that I want I do not need to buy, as I can usually get them from the *Monist* or the *Westminster*. Jourdain (the *Monist* and the *I. J. Ethics*) is the most satisfactory employer I could wish. I have only to suggest an article and he clamours for it, and any book I see advertised and want to review he will send for, for me. Most papers only give you books which have been sent to them, and do not trouble to send to publishers unless the publishers send to them. The *Westminster* have given [me] some novels to do.[1] At

1 – Many of its reviews were unsigned, but none is thought to be by TSE.

first sight they do not appear to pay much, as it is only half a crown (60¢) per each short notice of six or eight lines. But the editress[1] told me that she could read and review *six* novels in an evening! and encouraged me to do the same. Vivien can do some of them for me, and the editress also informed me that I could sell the novels (published at 6s) for 2s each. At that rate one would rake in £1 7s for an evening's work, which is not bad. I am learning something of the ins and outs of journalism, you see. These short notices are invaluable to the publishers, as they get from them all the little phrases, such as 'enthralling', 'good workmanship', 'a book of wide appeal', et cetera, which, with the name of a good newspaper after them, constitutes an important part of advertisement. This is Fleet Street!

I am working on my lectures now. The syllabus will be out in a few days, and it will look very imposing, with T. S. ELIOT M.A. (HARVARD) on it. I shall send you one directly. There is a good deal of reading to be done, and I want to be well prepared for the discussion which will follow every lecture.

I enclose, among several other things, (chess problems[2] and a rather amusing letter of an autograph fiend), a review of the *Catholic Anthology* printed in the *Nation*.[3] It is the best review I have had yet. Bertie thinks it is due to the fact that Massingham,[4] the editor, visited Lady Ottoline Morrell[5] lately, and probably had the things called to his attention there. Anyway, I am hoping that it will be of some help to me in getting work from the *Nation*.

I have begun this letter upside down. The facts are that I came up from Bosham yesterday, leaving Vivien there to try to squeeze a few more days benefit out of the seaside before the winter. I do not know how long she can stand it alone, but I hope that she can be induced to stay a week without me, as it is very good for her. We enjoyed our month immensely, and it did us both a world of good. Unfortunately, Vivien had the ill luck to have a very bad attack of neuralgia last week. It lasted the whole week, and discouraged her fearfully, as she felt that she had lost all the benefit of

1–Naomi Royde-Smith (1875–1964), journalist and novelist, was literary editor of the *Westminster Gazette*, 1912–22.

2–TSE played chess by post with his father.

3–See [Anon.], 'Fragmenta Aurea', *N.*, 26 Aug. 1916, 670–2: 'Mr. T. S. Eliot's work is far and away the best . . . [Prufrock] is . . . brilliant . . . freely executed, and here and there premising a richer and more mature sense of beauty.'

4–H. W. Massingham (1860–1924) was editor of *The Nation*, 1907–23.

5–Lady Ottoline Morrell, wealthy and eccentric hostess, whose manor house from 1915, Garsington, was an important retreat for writers, artists and opponents of the Great War; see Glossary of Names.

the previous weeks. These attacks always weaken her very much. It was aggravated, I think, by the fact that we had to move into different rooms (in the same house) as the landlady had let the ones we were in. The new rooms were unused and the sitting room very damp; I think this protracted the neuralgia. At any rate it gave us both mild attacks of rheumatism, mine in the left leg. Hers is nearer to gout, which she gets in the feet. It remains to be seen when she comes back what the net result of the seaside was. I hated to leave Bosham; it seems like a beautiful dream. The villagers all know us now, and we felt quite at home there. They are very much like New England fishing people, but rather more complete in their way. The old men are the typical old sailors of pictures, with great rings of white beard around their faces, play bowls on the green in the evening (it calls itself the Bosham Bowling club, Members Only) and arguefy in the *Anchor Tavern* in the evening and on Sunday after church. There is also the village idiot, the village drunkard ('a splendid workman afore the drink got him'), the curate, et cetera. It is idyllic.

You are so good and kind with offers of help that I should like to work night and day without stopping to make up for it, but I know I never can. How splendid you and father are! I do appreciate it all, and so does Vivien. We shall, as you say, probably need some help before Christmas, but I hope not much. I have only recently paid the Oxford bill: the Linen Bank sent the cheque back to St Louis before crediting me with the money.

I must stop now. Good-night!

Your loving son
Tom.

TO *Henry Eliot*

TS Houghton

6 September 1916 — 18 Crawford Mansions

Dear Henry,

It is nearly 12 o'clock, and I am very tired, but I must write you just a line, because I shall never have more time than I have now. I enclose a photograph which I had taken for my Identity Book to go into the country; it is rather good, I think. Therefore I shall send this letter to someone to forward to you, as I am not sure that your address is 7 Fifth Avenue or some other number, it sounds too simple to be true. I am also going to get you a *Catholic Anthology* tomorrow. I had a very good review in the London *Nation* which I will send you. I feel a sort of posthumous pleasure in it. I often feel that 'J.A.P.' is a swan song, but I never mention the fact because Vivien is so exceedingly anxious that I shall equal it, and would be bitterly disappointed if I do not. So do not suggest to anyone how I feel. The present year has been, in some respects, the most awful nightmare of anxiety that the mind of man could conceive, but at least it is not dull, and it has its compensations. You have been awfully good to send us so much money, and we do appreciate it. I am always glad when you write to Vivien, for she is very fond of you. I have left her at Bosham for a few days longer; meanwhile I am working at my lectures. I will send you the syllabus when it is out. I cannot write more, but I will try to write a few lines from time to time.

Affectionately
Tom

TO *Mary Hutchinson*[1] — TS Texas

6 September 1916 — 18 Crawford Mansions

Dear Mrs Hutchinson

I was very sorry to miss the opportunity of seeing you when you wrote to me at Bosham, but as I suddenly discovered [Roger] Fry's[2] plans for taking you on the water, I thought that it would be a pity to interfere with them. When I returned to Bosham, I found that you had left – after I had been occupied for several days with a brother-in-law who turned up from France. Had I known that I should have no other opportunity I might not have been so generous as to yield precedence to the boating party. But I hope that I may see you when you return to town.

Sincerely yours
T. Stearns Eliot

TO *J. H. Woods* — TS Professor David G. Williams

7 September 1916 — 18 Crawford Mansions

Dear Professor Woods,

I must apologise for not having answered your exceedingly kind letter sooner, but I can only say that I have been under very great pressure. I want

1 – Mary Hutchinson, hostess and patron of the arts; see Glossary of Names.

2 – Roger Fry (1866–1934), artist and art critic; champion of Cézanne and organiser of the London Post-Impressionist exhibition of 1911, he also founded the Omega Workshops with Vanessa Bell and Duncan Grant in 1912. Author of *Vision and Design* (1920) and *Civilization* (1928).

to tell you how keenly I appreciate your kindness and that of the department in regard to my thesis, and that I shall try to justify its acceptance by passing a good examination when I come. I do not know at all when that can be. My plans are very subject to alteration still, and I have so much on foot that it is difficult for me to make plans for my visit to America. This autumn I am to give a course of six lectures in Yorkshire on Social, Philosophical and Religious Problems in Contemporary France (the syllabus is given as 'Literature' and the course is advertised as 'Contemporary France', but this is what it really is). If I can establish myself in this Oxford Extension Lecturing I shall abandon teaching, and shall also have a clear six months a year for whatever else I wish to do.

I have been very busy in Fleet Street journalism as well. I am doing considerable reviewing for the *Westminster Gazette* – all sorts of things from Durkheim[1] and Boutroux[2] down to *Village Government in India* and even H. de Vere Stacpoole's novels.[3] I got hold of their Indian books by telling them that I was a student of Sanskrit and Pali – whereupon they gave me several books on contemporary Indian politics. I have been doing some work for the *New Statesman* as well,[4] Jourdain has been very kind to me, and gives me practically any book I want to review for the *Monist*, besides articles. He will have two articles, I believe, in the October *Monist* – the Leibniz number – one on Leibniz and Bradley,[5] the other on Leibniz and Aristotle.[6] He wants me to do a series on English idealists of the last generation (Green, Caird etc.),[7] but I fear it will progress very slowly, as I have so little time. He has also given me an introduction to Stout,[8] in the hope of getting reviews for *Mind*. I was so busy, and so much taken up and concerned about my wife's health, this last winter, that I was able to attend but very few meetings of the Aristotelian society, much less read the papers beforehand, but I hope to pay more attention to it this year.

I have just returned from a holiday with my wife at the village of Bosham, on the coast near Portsmouth. We had a delightful month, though

1–TSE, 'Durkheim', rev. of Émile Durkheim, *The Elementary Forms of the Religious Life: A Study in Religious Sociology*, trans. J. W. Swain, in *Westminster Gazette*, 19 Aug. 1916.
2–TSE, review of *Philosophy and War* by Émile Boutroux, in *IJE* 27: 1 (Oct. 1916), 128.
3–Not reviewed.
4–TSE, 'An American Critic' (rev. of Charles Sarolea, *The French Renascence*), *NS* 7: 168 (24 June 1916); and a review of L. M. Bristol, *Social Adaptation*, in *NS* 7: 173 (29 July 1916).
5–TSE, 'Leibniz's Monads and Bradley's Finite Centers', *The Monist* 26: 4 (Oct. 1916), 566–76.
6–TSE, 'The Development of Leibniz's Monadism', *The Monist* 26: 4 (Oct. 1916), 534–6.
7–Not written.
8–G. F. Stout (1860–1944), Professor of Logic and Metaphysics at St Andrews University, was editor of *Mind*, 1891–1920, but TSE did not contribute to it.

disturbed for my wife by an attack of neuralgia at the end, which I fear will retract some of the benefit of her holiday. Part of the time we had the company of Lowes Dickinson. I have seen a good deal of BR, but it is impossible to report much news of him, for obvious reasons.[1]

I am still clamouring for Patañjali. Please give my affectionate regards to Lanman when you see him.

Sincerely yours
T. S. Eliot

TO *Harriet Monroe*

TS Chicago

7 September 1916 — 18 Crawford Mansions

Dear Miss Monroe,

Many thanks for your kind letter. The title you have given will do excellently.[2] The proof is all right except that I am T. S., not T. R. There is only one 'T. R.' I hope![3]

I wonder if you have yet received my review of H. D.'s *Iphigenia*?[4] I sent it about the middle of August, but being in the country I did not have the address of *Poetry* by me, and I remembered the number as *345* Cass Street.[5] However, if there is any intelligence in the Chicago post-office, the letter ought to reach you. If it does not, I have another copy of the review. I must apologise for the delay in any case. I also have been over-worked.

I am glad that you have taken the 'Portrait'. All success to your anthology!

Thank you for your suggestions. I shall certainly try a note or two on you, 750 words or so. As I have not time, I am glad that you have not space, for anything long.

I shall be most interested to see the October *Poetry*.

I am interested in what you say about the *Dial*. Is there any chance for *us* with it now? It would be poetic justice if we could capture its columns.

1–In June, after BR was convicted of impeding recruitment on account of his support for the No-Conscription Fellowship, he was sacked from his lectureship at Trinity College, Cambridge.

2–'Conversation Galante', 'La Figlia Che Piange', 'Mr Apollinax', and 'Morning at the Window' appeared under the heading 'Observations', *Poetry* 8: 6 (Sept. 1916), 292–5.

3–Theodore Roosevelt (1858–1919), President of the United States, 1901–9. This letter arrived after the magazine had been printed, so the initial was not corrected.

4–TSE, 'Classics in English', *Poetry* 9: 2 (Nov. 1916), 101–4, a review of The Poets' Translation Series, I–VI, of which *Iphigenia* was III.

5–The correct address was 543 Cass Street.

If you notice any signs of improvement in it, I should consider it a great kindness if you could let me see a copy.

Sincerely yours
T. S. Eliot

TO *Harriet Monroe* MS Houghton

28 September 1916 18 Crawford Mansions

Dear Miss Monroe,

Thank you very much for the cheque for £5, which I received by the last mail. I hope to send you an attempt in prose before long.[1] I shall be most interested to see a copy of the Anthology as soon as it appears.[2] Will you send me one? With all best wishes for its success

Sincerely yours
T. S. Eliot

I like the new cover of *Poetry* very much.

Vivien Eliot TO *Henry Eliot* MS Houghton

Wed[nesday] 11 Oct[ober 1916] 18 Crawford Mansions

Dear Henry –

I am writing this in the train on my way to Manchester. I am going to stay with friends at a place called Hale, which is about ten miles the other side of Manchester. This girl I have known all my life. She married a year before I did, and she has got two children. I have never seen her since I was married. I am only going to stay a week, or perhaps ten days. I know I shall hate it. I know my Father was <is> a Lancashire <and Yorkshire> man, and I was born in Lancs. altho' I only lived there three weeks! but we have a number of old friends who live in Lancashire and in North Wales. They are most dreadful people really – very very rich manufacturing people – so provincial that my American friends tell me they are very much like Americans!! Tom has just met a few at Ilkley (in Yorkshire) when he went for his first lecture – and he says the same – he was struck with how much more like Americans they are than the South of England people. I rather

1–This suggests that 'Eeldrop and Appleplex' may have been submitted to *Poetry* before appearing in *Little Review*, May and Sept. 1917.
2–*The New Poetry*, ed. Harriet Monroe and Alice Corbin (New York, 1917), which TSE would review in *Egoist* 4: 11 (Dec. 1917).

dread this visit, because I have got out of the way of these people now – (not that I ever was in the way – having lived in London and in such a different set all my life) but I was more used to them when we used to go every year to spend our summer hols. at the country houses of one or another of them. They have the most beautiful country places you can imagine. I have not been up to the North for just two years now, and so much has happened in between – I feel a different person to the girl who sat in this train just exactly two years ago, going to be bridesmaid at the wedding of this girl I am now going to stay with.

I wanted to answer your letter before I left home but hadn't time. Really Henry I am quite sure you *cannot* afford these constant five poundses. I *shall* thank you whatever you say – and I tell you I think you are nobly adorably generous and kind. It was very very welcome because we are very low at present – we have only got ~~about~~ £22 in the bank, and Tom won't get any more till Christmas – so you can see we are in a fairly tight place. Unfortunately it has meant writing to your Father for help again. I can't bear to do that. I should never have arranged to go on this visit if I had known how low we should be – for it has entailed getting more clothes than I should have needed otherwise – but I promised in July to go now, so I really could not back out. I liked your letter to me – thank you. I shan't have my sinus trouble touched until I simply have to. I still hope to live it down. Did T. tell you they sent me to see a doctor three weeks ago? It was chiefly for my headaches (I don't mean the sinus pain, these headaches are something quite separate and much *more* horrible!) So I went and he said I was chiefly starved! The headaches are called hemicranial migraine, and they are really 'nerve storms' affecting one whole side of me – they make me sick and feverish and they always last 15–24 hours – and I rise up weak and white as if I had been through some long and dreadful illness. He explained that they are caused in me by starvation – I do not eat enough to nourish my nervous system – and brain. They are rather rare, these headaches – *no drug touches* them. I have taken (before I knew the futility of it) 15–20 grains of phenacetin without having the slightest relief). However he gave me some medicine to take regularly, and told me not to economise – and I have certainly had them less often since. But it will take a long time, he said. I must have been iller last winter than I thought. I hope all this does not bore you. I have really a lot to say to you in this letter. Tom got your letter about two days ago – as he was out I opened and read it (we always do this with *family* letters) so that I read the postscript which you did not intend me to see. I had read it all sort of in one glance – so that by the time I'd realised it was private I had seen it all. However, it does not matter, Tom knows perfectly well that I share his feeling over the poetry – in fact, he knows that of the two of us perhaps I worry most – and rather more often get despondent. I look upon Tom's poetry as real genius – I *do* think he is made to be a great writer – *a* poet. His prose is very good – but I think it will never be *so* good as his poetry. Anyhow, it is a *constant* canker with me that it is at a standstill – and every time that thought is in Tom's mind I see it. I know how he feels – he has told me more than once – he feels *dried up* – not a bit as if he could write poetry even if he had the leisure and circumstances.

For this – I feel *very* strongly that Journalism is bad for Tom. It is. If he was not a poet it would be excellent for him. He loves it. But I am sure and certain that it will be the *ruin* of his poetry – if it goes on. For him – he ought never *to have to write*. For you – I daresay it would not be at all a bad thing for you to have to write. I believe too, that you would be infinitely happier, doing journalism.

This brings me to what I had decided to speak to you about. After Tom got your last letter, he and I have talked about you, and thoroughly discussed the whole matter of you and your work and your life!! I hope you don't mind. But even if you do I am going to tell you what conclusion Tom and I came to. Now please this is *quite* serious, and it is *Tom's* just as much as *my* idea. Well, we want you to come and live in England. You are not doing well in your business – in America. It is a business you could do here – you might do much *better* here, – anyhow you couldn't do much worse. You would have references and could get introductions. *But, chiefly*, you could fill out your life by writing. You say you long to write, and we believe you. We both think you could do well at journalism. Now directly Tom gets sufficient lectures[1] to keep us, he will do no more *journalism*. He will keep on writing for *The Monist*, and will certainly write on Philosophy. He is, by the way, more interested in Philosophy than he was a year ago. The reaction against it is passing. But all his journalistic work you could take over. He could put you in to *more* than you could do, even now. I must stop now, and will continue again before you answer this. So wait. But Tom said he thought your life would be much more

1 – Concurrently with his Yorkshire lectures, TSE had begun the first year (at £60 with £3 expense allowance) of a three-year course in Modern English Literature at Southall, Middlesex. The classes were held on Monday evenings for twenty-four weeks in the autumn and winter. Each session lasted for two hours, divided between a lecture and a discussion. The sixteen-part syllabus had been published in Sept., under the auspices of the University of London Joint Committee for the Promotion of Higher Education of Working People. TSE actually devoted all the classes to Victorian literature: see Schuchard, *Eliot's Dark Angel*, 32–9. During the first term he continued to teach at Highgate School.

worth while if you were living earning less than you are now, and *writing*, and living over here – than it can ever be as you are. You could risk it – you have no one to keep. Tom took on a much larger risk than that would be – a year ago – and I can swear he has never regretted it. Of course he has had me to shove him – I supply the motive power, and I *do* shove. If you were here I should shove you! Tom is writing to you about this.

I arrived here yesterday. I hate it. It is poisonous. I shall leave as soon as I decently can.

Until the next instalment –

Yrs.
Vivien

TO *Alfred Zimmern*[1]

MS Bodleian

27 October 1916 18 Crawford Mansions

Dear Mr Zimmern,

I find that I owe you a great debt of gratitude: Ramage of the W.E.A. [Workers' Educational Association] said that you have mentioned my name to him not long ago. The result is a tutorial class at Southall, which promises to be a success. I had already decided that both my health and my interests advocated resigning from my school, and this windfall supplies me with more justification. It is therefore, you see, a very important event to me and I am deeply indebted to you.

I must also thank you for the introduction to Graham Wallas:[2] I went to see him not long ago, and hope that I may be able to see him often.

Again with my warmest thanks

Sincerely yours
T. Stearns Eliot.

Perhaps when you – and myself! – have some leisure, I may have the pleasure of seeking you out again? I am doing about fourteen hours work a day at present, including Sundays, with the Oxford Extension work, the W.E.A., and various reviewing.

1–Alfred Zimmern (1879–1957), classical scholar, and co-founder in 1919 of the Institute of International Affairs. Knighted in 1936. Later first Secretary General of UNESCO, 1945.
2–See letter to Wallas of 23 Mar. 1917.

TO *Henry Eliot* MS Houghton

5 November 1916 18 Crawford Mansions

Dear Henry

As usual, I cannot write more than a page, but I am looking forward to acknowledging your generosity more adequately after Christmas with letters of respectable size. I don't think Vivien and I would ever get used to this sort of kindness – every new act recalls all the past. I have certainly reason to be proud of my family: the way they have accepted the responsibility of helping me, without a single murmur, has been wonderful. You don't know how keen Vivien is to meet mother and father and you, and how bitterly she regrets the separation in space. We do long for you to come to London.

I hope that a year from now I may be self-supporting. I am basing most of the hope on lectures, of course. You know that I am giving up the school at Christmas, as I find that I am losing in every way. I have not time to pursue my literary connections, and overwork is telling on the quality of my production. After Christmas, I hope to see people and drum up trade.

Vivien was afraid that you might be offended by what she wrote to you about coming to London. I am sure that you won't be, but I am not sure that you will realise quite how seriously we meant it, or that we had thought a good deal about it before it was mentioned. It wasn't just a momentary fancy, or expression of sentiment, nor is it completely chimerical. Of course I don't propose dropping something for nothing, or simply walking about the streets of London. But I do think that if one makes up one's mind what one wants, then sooner or later an occasion will come when it is possible to seize it, for I think everybody gets the kind of life he wants, and that if he doesn't know, or doesn't want strongly enough, he will never get anything satisfactory. The only recklessness, I think, consists in taking a risk when your will is not strong enough in that direction to carry you through. But at least, if you really made up your mind that you hated your present life, and wanted to come here, then when an opening did appear, if it were only a pinhole, you would be prepared to perceive it. Whereas if you were not sure what you wanted, you would not even see the opportunity when it came. I am becoming more and more superstitious about luck and fortune – or rather, I call it the deeper reality behind ordinary superstition.

Father writes very despondently about finances. I suppose it is partly because of the doubtful election prospects. I am doubtful myself – though in ignorance – whether the election of Hughes[1] would make so much difference to his affairs as he thinks; but I should also like to know whether these are as bad as he thinks. He was speaking of my life insurance, and warned me that this was probably all that there would be for Vivien. Of course I am very anxious about her future in the event of my death. $5,000, (insurance), at any possible interest, would not be enough to keep her. While I hope soon to be self-supporting, I don't know whether I shall ever earn enough money to leave her to live upon after my death. *What do you know about his affairs at present?*

It is another superstition of mine that if you *don't* face any possibility of disaster it is much more likely to happen. Besides your own interest, and besides the *comfort* it would be to have you here, it would be a great deal to me to know that there was someone near who would look out for Vivien in case I died. It is very hard, and harder for her than for me, to have all my family at a distance. I want her to seem quite real to you, literally one of my own family, and I should not trust her care to anyone but one of my own family.

I must stop now. Always affectionately

Tom.

But whether you were here or not, I should like you to be the person to make yourself responsible for her in my stead. *Will you do that?*

I want *all* of my family to take the sort of interest in her which would persist after my death; but I depend *especially* on you.

1 – Charles Evans Hughes (1862–1948), an Associate Justice of the Supreme Court, was the Republican candidate for the US Presidency. On 7 Nov., he was defeated by Woodrow Wilson, Democrat, by 277 electoral votes to 254.

1917

TO *Mary Hutchinson* MS Texas

1 January 1917 18 Crawford Mansions

Dear Mrs Hutchinson

I am glad to be able to accept your invitation for Twelfth Night,[1] and will come with great pleasure. Thank you for the map. I am very dependent upon such aids; it was only by a lucky accident that I found the house before.

Sincerely yours
T. S. Eliot

TO *His Father* MS Houghton

Monday 5 February 1917 18 Crawford Mansions

My dear Father,

In view of the present circumstances I shall write this letter now for the Wednesday boat and again by the Saturday boat. At present I am particularly concerned over possible interruption of mails. I wrote to ask you a week or two ago whether you could send six months rent. I should like, if it were possible, to have a year's rent now, as it may become very difficult and precarious to send any communication from America to England. It would be a safeguard, I think, if you can spare the money. The rent has got to be paid anyhow, and I have calculated that absolutely nothing would be saved – supposing that we ran short – by sub-letting the flat (furnished) and boarding in rooms. The cost of boarding would be so great, at best, as to eat up the slight profit on sub-letting, we should merely be depriving ourselves to no advantage. So that if the rent were not forthcoming we should be in a very awkward position.

I suppose that the boats will sail regularly for the present. The situation has unsettled and disturbed me. I thoroughly approve of Wilson's action,[2] and support it with full sympathy. I am waiting for the occasion of actual

1–A Twelfth Night party, 5 Jan.

2–On 3 Feb. 1917, the United States had broken off diplomatic relations with Germany.

declaration of war, as nothing seems to be gained now by any other course. I don't think it necessary yet to consider what America would attempt to do. If she put an army into the field (impractical as this seems to me) I should have to think over my position carefully. Altogether, one does not know what to look forward to. At present, I simply want to protect ourselves as far as possible against risks, and knowing that the rent can be paid will go a great way. In case the mails seem to be going to be seriously imperilled, I shall wire you asking you to wire money.

I will write a short letter to Mother, and again by Saturday's boat.

Your loving son
Tom

TO *His Father* — TS Houghton

1 March 1917 — 18 Crawford Mansions

My dear father,

My last letter, a week ago, was broken off rather abruptly to catch the mail. Since then you have cabled me $100, and Tuesday came a number of letters from mother, one of them including the cheque for $75. I had had no letters from America for over a month, and of course had no means of knowing that a draft had been sent. It is a great relief to me to have the money, as I had got down to the end of my current account, and was about to draw on the $250 which I have laid aside in a deposit account.

I ended the last letter in telling you how the war had blocked the best possible opportunities and openings. If anything else had done it I might not feel justified in going on; if there had been no opportunities or openings, or if I had proved incompetent to make the most of them. But this has not been the case; setting the war aside, I have succeeded in what I have undertaken. And the opportunities are still there, and I feel justified in waiting for them, and not chucking away all the capital of work that I have put into them, and which will remain good to my credit if I can hang on to it. This is why I feel justified in hanging on through the rest of the war with any employment I can get. In fact, I should feel wrong in giving up now what I have already gained. I hope to get some sort of employment before long which enables us to face out the rest of the war with some security.

I am sorry that it is impossible to send you my contributions as they appear in the papers. I have an article in the *New Statesman*,[1] I believe

1 – 'Reflections on Vers Libre', *NS* 8 (3 Mar. 1917), 518–19.

coming out on Saturday. Such articles and reviews as appear in the *Monist* and [*International*] *Journal of Ethics* you can see in America.

I shall write to mother by the next mail and answer all her sweet letters. I have never been so glad to get letters; the interval seemed as if it would never end.

Vivien is a little better, and is gaining, but worries over our affairs have ~~pulled her down~~ held her back a great deal. When she worries she bleeds internally, in a metaphorical sense, as well as other internal pains, like migraine and stomach trouble, in a literal sense. It is some comfort to think of our difficulties as impersonal – that is, that thousands of other people, in a good many countries, are suffering worse from the same cause, and that the whole world is going to find living harder after the war.

I anticipate that there will be at least one beneficial change, however, and that is that there will be much more activity in the Workers Educational Movement after the war. There is much discussion of educational reforms now, and this is one of the branches which ought to profit. If so, I ought to be in on the rake off, for I am giving the only literature class now going in the whole London district, and the authorities seem to be very well pleased with it. One of the class told me that I was the best literature tutor they had ever had in that class. I enjoy it immensely, and the Monday evening is one of the moments of the week that I look forward to. The class is very keen and very appreciative, and very anxious to learn and to think. These people are the most hopeful sign in England, to me.

We had a very nice letter from Charlotte, and two photographs which Henry took at Christmas of the children. Chardy must be very pretty now, though of course I should like to see Theodora more.[1] They are very nice children.

I must post this now.

Always your devoted son
Tom

1–TSE's sister Charlotte and her husband George Smith had two daughters, Theodora and Charlotte (Chardy).

Vivien Eliot TO *Charlotte C. Eliot* MS Houghton

8 March 1917 18 Crawford Mansions

Dear Mrs Eliot,

At last I am replying to your two nice letters of Jan. 30 and 31. I am so glad you understand the sort of brain that needs a great amount of sleep – you say my temperament must be like your own, and I believe it is. I worry a great deal, and my brain is always restless and active. Often when I lie down to sleep I feel that a wheel is going round in my head, and although my body is dead tired my brain gets more and more excited.

We are not sleeping quite so much now – but I still am doing about eight or nine hours – but my migraines are coming back and I dont feel nearly so well. Tom sleeps about seven or eight hours – he did not get over that influenza for *weeks* – in fact, I can say that it is only for the last five or six *days* that he has seemed like himself. Up till then he was most gloomy and depressed and very irritable and I knew he felt that life was simply not worth going on with. It is hard <u>not</u> to feel that here, when every day the strain and difficulty is a *little* increased, and the screw turned a little tighter. First it is one thing, then another. Now we are threatened with '*no* papers'[1] (from Tom! if that comes it will just ruin all literary men) ~~and there are no~~ – perhaps I had better not continue this subject.

Tom did *not* get a new suit, *or* new flannels. I am ashamed to say it. His old underwear is still thick and in <u>fair</u> condition however, but it needs *incessant darning*. Darning alone takes me hours out of the week. He needs a suit, and I think *must* have one. His pyjamas too are all very old and want constant mending. I often wish we were in America, there are very heavy storms yet in front of us – and we are a bit worn down by all that has been already.

With love to you and Mr Eliot. Affectly *Vivien*

N.B. New postal address is – 18 Crawford Mansions Crawford Street. London. <u>W.1</u>

I *would* get Tom some new vests myself but I really *do* think the old ones are quite good for the rest of this winter – and he is wearing his flannel shirts all the time – *under protest!*

1 – On 23 Feb., *The Times* reported that, in response to paper shortages, the government was considering restricting halfpenny newspapers to four pages, and penny newspapers to eight.

TO *Bertrand Russell* MS McMaster

13 March 1917 [London]

Dear Bertie,

Thank you for reading my article[1] and returning it so promptly. I think that what you say about it is probably correct, and I am so keenly aware of its deficiencies that I shall probably keep it in my drawer for a year or two. The questions involved are so difficult that it seems impossible under present conditions to treat them adequately, and I have no desire to do either your point of view or my own an injustice. One's philosophy is bound to be based on temperament, but it certainly ought to be 'reasoned' as well, and my article is I feel too scattered and incoherent.

I made no positive objection to the principle of 'reverence'[2] – it merely seems to me inadequate. My chief objection is to the passage on p. 165.[3]

Aff.
T. S. E.

TO *Bertrand Russell* MS McMaster

Thursday [15? March 1917] 18 Crawford Mansions

Dear Bertie,

Thanks for your letter, which was very good of you. Nevertheless, I feel that the article is not satisfactory to me. I feel that I have put either too

1–Evidently TSE had written a critique of BR's *Principles of Social Reconstruction* (1917), though neither the article nor BR's response has been found.

2–BR, in his chapter on 'Education' (*Principles of Social Reconstruction*, 146), argued: 'A man who is to educate really well, and is to make the young grow and develop into their full stature, must be filled through and through with the spirit of reverence.' However, he declared too, 'It is not in a spirit of reverence that education is conducted by States and Chambers and the great institutions that are subservient to them' (148).

3–'It will be said that the joy of mental adventure must be rare, that there are few who can appreciate it, and that ordinary education can take no account of so aristocratic a good. I do not believe this. The joy of mental adventure is far commoner in the young than in grown men and women. Among children it is very common, and grows naturally out of the period of make-believe and fancy. It is rare in later life because everything is done to kill it during education. Men fear thought as they fear nothing else on earth – more than ruin, more even than death. Thought is subversive and revolutionary, destructive and terrible; thought is merciless to privilege, established institutions, and comfortable habits; thought is anarchic and lawless, indifferent to authority, careless of the well-tried wisdom of the ages. Thought looks into the pit of hell and is not afraid. It sees man, a feeble speck, surrounded by unfathomable depths of silence; [overleaf] yet it bears itself proudly, as unmoved as if it were lord of the universe. Thought is great and swift and free, the light of the world, and the chief glory of man.'

much or too little into it. I should prefer to discuss Authority and Reverence.[1] I think what I have said is in appearance too negative and perhaps looks obscurantist. I am convinced that there is something beneath Authority in its historical forms which needs to be asserted clearly without reasserting impossible forms of political and religious organisation which have become impossible. But this is a task which needs impulse and hope, and without more peace of mind and contentedness, better nerves and more conviction in regard to my future, I do not feel capable of satisfying myself.

Yours aff.
Tom

TO *His Mother*

MS Houghton

21 March 1917

18 Crawford Mansions,
Crawford St, W.1 *Note* W.1

My dearest mother,

You will not have heard from me for some time, so I hope this will arrive quickly. You know that I have spent a large part of my time hunting for work to stop the gap, and I can assure you that nothing takes more time. Now I have found it, and I am in much better spirits than I have been for some time past. A friend of the Haigh-Woods is a very successful banker,[2] and he gave me an introduction to Lloyds Bank, one of the biggest banks in London. I am now earning £2 10s a week for sitting in an office from 9.15 to 5 with an hour for lunch, and tea served in the office.[3] This of course is not a princely salary, but there are good prospects of a rise as I become more useful. Perhaps it will surprise you to hear that I enjoy the work. It is not nearly so fatiguing as schoolteaching, and is more interesting. I have a desk and a filing cabinet in a small room with another man. The filing cabinet is my province, for it contains balance sheets of all the foreign banks with which Lloyds does business. These balances I file and tabulate in such a way as to show the progress or decline of every bank from year to year. The work had lapsed for some time, and I am filling in last year's balances; when that is completed, I should be able to

1–For Russell on Authority, see *Principles*, 27, 33ff, 167ff; for Reverence, 146, 227.
2–E. L. Thomas was Chief General Manager of the National Provincial Bank.
3–TSE began work on 19 Mar. in the Colonial and Foreign Department, 'at £120 a year and no food . . . on the false pretence of being a linguist' (Harvard College Class of 1910, Twenty-fifth Anniversary Report, 219).

draft a little report on any bank when needed. French and Italian I find useful, and shall have to pick up a little Spanish, Danish, Swedish, and Norwegian as well. The work is very interesting to me, and also, when 5 o'clock comes it is over, and I can think about my writing for Jourdain, or the *New Statesman*, or my class, with a free mind.

Of course there is no engagement to give more than a week's notice so the place is not a trap. I hope for more evening work next winter. My article in the *New Statesman* was a great success, and I shall probably be able to get articles in very often. That is the best thing possible for me, as it will get my name known. Squire (the editor of the *New Statesman*)[1] urged me to begin at once writing articles for American periodicals, and offered me an introduction to the *Century* and the *Dial*. Russell could introduce me to the *Atlantic* [*Monthly*]. I shall be rather busy for Jourdain too, as he has decided to increase the reviewing on the *Monist*, and as it is difficult now to get competent people to review technical books for a technical paper, we are to do almost all of it between us – I to do philosophy, theology, biology and anthropology.

It is a great satisfaction to me to have regular work, and I can do my own work much the better for it. Even when circumstances stand in my way as they do at present, I should not feel that I was doing all I could if I did only what writing and lecturing there is to be done. Besides, Vivien is very anxious to give up her charwoman as soon as the weather is a little warmer, and I insist that she must not. She has not got over the laryngitis yet by any means; the work would take all her time and the strength which should go to building up; and I am afraid she cannot have as good a holiday as last summer. I want her to go away in July and August, as I think she can get another girl to accompany her. I might be able to get a short vacation, but I think we could live almost as cheaply, she in the country I here, during the hottest period, as we do now. Besides, for the present, I do not feel comfortable for her never to have anyone in the flat while I am out all day. Of course, when I think of all the clothes she needs – she has not had any for a long time, and I have my new suit – I see advantages in giving up the woman, but I do not like it.

The war must end sometime. Do write me about the health and activities of all the family. I have not had a letter from Henry for a long time. I hope he will find his present post good enough to keep, as I feel that it is not good to move about so much.[2]

1 – See TSE's letter to him of 29 Mar.

2 – HWE was a partner in the Chicago advertising agency Husband & Thomas (later the Buchen Company), 1917–29.

I think of you and wonder what you are doing very often.

Always your devoted son
Tom

TO *Charlotte Eliot Smith* MS Houghton

21 March 1917

18 Crawford Mansions,
Crawford St, W.1 *Note.* W.1

My dear Charlotte,

We were delighted to get the pictures from you, and still more when two more came from Henry, for the little head of Chardy is by far the best of the lot. Vivien is going to have it passe-partout'd. All of the pictures of Chardy are good. Theodora does not 'take' so easily, and the picture of her as Tunisienne does not do her justice – though it looks extraordinarily like Marion. It was jolly to see the Christmas party, too. I get the impression that Theodora is extremely tall, already, and probably will be tall. I should like to have helped bring in the greens.

As you say, political topics are barred in letters: it is a great annoyance to me, as I am violently interested in the subject at present. However, one can 'lay down' bottles to be opened when the vintage has ripened. I quite believe that you do not find much intelligent discussion among your friends or our relations. The war has at least brought *variety* into our lives. I am at present combining the activities of journalist, lecturer, and financier. During the daytime I am now employed at Lloyds Bank as a stop-gap. Lloyds is one of the banks with largest foreign connections, and I am busy tabulating balance-sheets of foreign banks to see how they are prospering. My ideal is to know the assets and liabilities (of every bank abroad that Lloyds deals with) for ten years past! You will be surprised to hear of me in this capacity, but I enjoy it. Incidentally, I shall pick up scraps of the Spanish, Portuguese, Danish, Swedish, and Norwegian languages. Russians, fortunately, manage to produce their reports in English or French. Anything to do with money – especially foreign money – is fascinating, and I hope to learn a little about finance while I am there.

This engagement, of course, is due to the fact that under war conditions it is impossible to make an all-the-year-round living by writing and lecturing. I hope to have more lecturing next winter. My literature (working people's) class has been a great success, and I am enthusiastic about the work. These people, who meet once a week for my lecture and discussion, and write papers, are very anxious to improve themselves, though there is not the slightest chance of its helping them to make a better living. In America there would, I think, be less chance for this sort of class. Education is so diffused, and it is so easy for almost anyone to get a so-called 'college education', that education is less prized. A young man who will work himself to death to 'go through college' usually works himself to death making money afterwards. The idea of people studying all their lives is unknown, as also among the more prosperous classes in England. But my class is entirely *disinterested* in its devotion to study and thought.

I really ought not to write any more. I have several letters to write, and a pile of books to review for the *Monist*, and I ought to write an article for the *New Statesman*.

Vivien sends you her love, and adds her thanks for the pictures. She has continued to suffer from her larynx – you know she had a bad attack of laryngitis some weeks ago, and her voice is very weak. The protracted cold weather has made matters more difficult. She is very anxious to do without the charwoman when the weather is warmer, but I am sure that would be unwise. What she needs is another summer at the seaside.

With much love to you all from both of us

Your affectionate brother,
Tom

TO *Graham Wallas*[1] — MS LSE

23 March 1917

18 Crawford Mansions,
Crawford St, W.

Dear Mr Wallas,

I am writing to inform you of my having at last hooked something – a very small fish, it is true. I am now in the Foreign department of Lloyds bank, living in hopes of a rise in salary. Anyway, it is a relief to be no longer on the hunt, and a nuisance to everyone I know. The work is neither difficult nor exhausting nor uninteresting; it is done under very comfortable conditions, and leaves me less fatigued than teaching, so that I can read and write in the evenings. I should like to think that I shall come to learn something of that extraordinary science of banking, if I can grasp any of it.

1 – Graham Wallas (1858–1932), Professor of Political Science, London School of Economics, 1914–23. An early Fabian, he had protested against the war in 1914. His writings included *Human Nature in Politics* (1908) and *The Great Society* (1914).

Mr Boas[1] has been very kind to me, and hopes to get me some evening work next autumn. What I should like especially would be another tutorial class, but there seems faint hope of that. Thank you again for getting me into contact with Mr Boas.

I hope I may see you again soon.

With kind regards to Mrs Wallas and your daughter.

Sincerely yours
T. S. Eliot

And after all I forgot to thank you for writing to Hobhouse.[2] I was much disappointed over the *Manchester Guardian*, but apparently the place has been filled.

TO *Eleanor Hinkley* TS Houghton

23 March 1917

18 Crawford Mansions,
Crawford St, W.1

Dear Eleanor,

I am seizing a spare moment to write a page to you, as always if I wait to write a letter it is never written. I have wondered often whether you ever received a longish letter from me last summer from Bosham, as I have not heard from you since. There has never been a time in the last two years when I have not had to leave as many things undone as I have done, and much of what I have done has been at the expense of more or less of one's lawful amount of sleep every night, so you will understand my not writing oftener.

At present – as both writing and lecturing are so restricted and precarious under present conditions – I am working at Lloyds Bank (not to be confused with the shipping people) during the day, and doing my writing in the evening. I sit in a small office with a mahogany desk and a tall filing cabinet, and feel much more important than my salary warrants, as I have charge of all the balance sheets of their foreign correspondents, filing and tabulating and reporting on them. Not that I know anything

1–F. S. Boas (1862–1957), Divisional Inspector for Higher Education for London County Council from 1905; scholar of Elizabethan and Jacobean drama; Professor of English Literature, Queen's College, Belfast, 1901–5; author of *Shakespeare and his Predecessors* (1902).

2–L. T. Hobhouse (1846–1929), first Professor of Sociology, London University, 1907–29. Previously on the staff of the *Manchester Guardian*, he was a friend of the editor, C. P. Scott (1864–1932).

about banking, but the business is so huge that I don't suppose more than half a dozen men in the bank know more than their own little corner of it. I share an office with Mr McKnight,[1] who lives in a suburb, cultivates a kitchen garden out of hours, polishes his silk hat with great care when he goes out, and talks about his eldest boy.

My greatest pleasure however is my workingmen's class in English Literature on Monday evenings. I have steered them through Browning (who arouses great enthusiasm), Carlyle, Meredith, Arnold, and am now conducting them through Ruskin. There are not many working *men* at present, except one very intelligent grocer who reads Ruskin behind his counter; most of them are (female) elementary schoolteachers, who work very hard with large classes of refractory children all day but come with unabated eagerness to get culture in the evening (stimulated, I hope, by my personal magnetism). I sit at the head of a table flanked by Mrs Howells and Mrs Sloggett. Both are mad. Mrs Howells is a spiritualist, and wanted to give me mental treatment for a cold in the head. She writes articles on the New Mysticism etc., for a paper called the *Superman*,[2] and presents them to me. Mrs Sloggett writes me letters beginning Dear Teacher, Philosopher and Friend,[3] and her special interests are astrology and politics. She has written a character study of me (very flattering) which I should like to send you; and spends some of her time writing letters to cabinet ministers. Still, at the present time she does not seem to me much madder than most people. The rest of the class are quite sane, and some of them are remarkably clever, and I have to do my best to keep up with them in discussion. This class of person is really the most attractive in England, in many ways; it is not so petrified in snobbism and prejudice as the middle classes, and yet is very humble. To an American, the English working classes are impressive because of their fundamental conservatism; they are not, as a whole, aggressive and insolent like the same people in America.

You will perhaps be interested to hear whom I met about a fortnight ago. I was at a gathering of a curious zoo of people known as the Omega

1 – TSE said to Valerie Eliot that he based the character Eggerson, in *The Confidential Clerk*, on Mr McKnight.

2 – First published in Mar. 1915 as *Man: all about him from his horoscope, hands, head, face, handwriting etc.*, this monthly magazine continued (from Apr. 1915) as *Superman*, and ran, with a gap of six months, until Oct. 1916.

3 – 'Shall then this verse to future age pretend / Thou wert my guide, philosopher, and friend?' (Pope, *Essay on Man* IV, 390).

Club,[1] and was sitting on a mat (as is the custom in such circles) discussing psychical research with William Butler Yeats (the only thing he ever talks about, except Dublin gossip)[2] when a red-faced, sprucely dressed man with an air of impertinent prosperity and the aspect of a successful wholesale grocer came up and interrupted us with a most disagreeable Cockney accent (and you may hear accents in Amurka but the lower middle class cockney beats them all). I was so irritated by the man that I left for another part of the room almost at once – later I found out that it was Arnold Bennett.[3]

I must stop now; I have written far more than I expected to. Do write to me some time. Give my love to Aunt Susie, and believe me

Always affectionately
Tom

TO *J. H. Woods* MS Professor David G. Williams

23 March 1917 18 Crawford Mansions

Dear Dr Woods,

It was very good to hear from you at last. I was afraid that my letter had never reached you, and was on the point of writing again. I have been hoping that you might turn up in London, and still hope so, as I cannot possibly come to France.[4] I am very sorry indeed to hear that Mrs Woods has been ill; I can sympathise with you fully, as my wife has suffered so much. I suppose you will stay with her during the Easter holidays: could you not come over here in July or August?

1–Founded in Feb. or Mar. 1917, the Omega Club (an offshoot of Roger Fry's Omega Workshops begun in 1913) met on Thursday evenings in Fitzroy Square. VW wrote on 26 Apr. to her sister Vanessa Bell: 'I hear from Lytton that the Omega Club is doomed – very few go, and only the dullest' (*Letters of Virginia Woolf*, Vol. 2, *1912–22: The Question of Things Happening*, ed. Nigel Nicolson [1976], 150).

2–According to Arnold Bennett's *Journal*, WBY, with Roger Fry and Bennett himself, had attended a spiritualist séance at Mme Van der Velde's on 8 Feb. Roy Foster reports that WBY had at this time 'embarked upon one of his most bizarre and credulous involvements yet' in psychical research. The episode involved a 'mildly deranged chemist' who had invented a machine for communicating with the spirit world: this was investigated by the Society for Psychical Research, and declared by WBY to be 'the greatest discovery of the modern world' (*Yeats: A Life: The Arch-Poet*, 2003, 74).

3–Arnold Bennett (1867–1931), novelist, playwright and diarist; author of *The Old Wives' Tale* (1908) and *The Clayhanger Trilogy* (1910–16).

4–Woods was in France on an exchange professorship, and as organiser of the American University Union in Paris.

First of all, let me report on C. E. B.[1] Russell says of him

> 'B. is alright. A little supercilious, but no harm in him. Very scholarly and learned, not profoundly original but more or less so.'

Joachim says

> 'I only met B. once and B. R. knows him much better than I do. My impression of him is that he is so fearfully competent that he makes me feel very incompetent. However, on reflection out of his presence I don't think I am so feeble after all. He is perhaps rather lacking in "intuition". His views on things like war and friendship and logic are very sympathetic to me, and he has always been most flattering when he wrote about me. So I am most grateful to him, but still on intellectual matters I manage to look up to him!'

This is all I have gathered. I know one or two other people who might know him, but probably not well.

I will finish the *Organon*. I should have done so ere now but that I did not know where to send it. There is not very much to add. The *de Anima* is a more difficult question. The notes are on interleaves and in such small writing (mostly in the original Latin to boot) that I fear no one could possibly decipher them but myself. I do not quite like to trust the fruit of so much labour to the submarines in the Channel, but perhaps I can offer it as an inducement to you to come and fetch it, until I can transcribe it. I will send you a copy of an article I wrote for the *Monist* – I fear not a very good one, done under trying conditions – on Leibniz and Aristotle. I promised Jourdain some months ago an article comparing Leibniz' logic to Aristotle's, for *Scientia*, but I have had no time for such a gigantic undertaking.[2] Also, I projected a series for him on Green and other Victorian idealists, not a word of which is yet written.[3] I am doing a good deal of reviewing for him; he is enlarging the reviewing of the *Monist*; he takes charge of mathematics, chemistry and physics, and I of philosophy, religion, biology, and anthropology.

I am also writing more or less for the *New Statesman*. As for my poems, I believe they will be published; it is a question as to whether the printer

1 – Despite the middle initial, C. E. B. was probably Charles Dunbar Broad (1887–1971), who had studied under Russell, and was now a fellow of Trinity College and lecturer in logic at St Andrews. He was Knightsbridge Professor of Moral Philosophy at Cambridge, 1933–53.
2 – The article was never written.
3 – TSE's interest in T. H. Green (1826–1882) – political and religious philosopher, philosophy tutor at Balliol College, Oxford; later Whyte's Professor of Moral Philosophy; leading member of the British Idealist movement – was probably a product of his work on F. H. Bradley, who was taught by Green. Other notable British Idealists included Harold Joachim and J. M. E. McTaggart.

can do it for £15, which is all the publisher is prepared to spend. I shall of course send you a copy if the book appears. The other book (the *Catholic Anthology*) got me a very favourable notice from the (London) *Nation*.

I have an evening class in English literature (mostly social and religious topics, Arnold, Ruskin, etc.) under London University, a class of working people, which I enjoy very much. This class of people is the most agreeable in England to me – you see I am by way of being a Labourite in England, though a conservative at home. The middle class – including most of the people one knows, or at least their families, is hopelessly stupid. Its family life is hideous. When of sufficient means, the middle classes want their sons to go to public schools; but the only motive is snobism, and the lack of respect for education is amazing . . . Some day I shall write a book on the English; it is my impression that no one in America knows anything about them. They are in fact very different from ourselves.

Have you seen B. R.'s book?[1] It is very weak. I don't know now when I shall be able to go to America for my exams. It doesn't look like it at present, and if we go to war, I shall want the government to give me something to do. Now I am working by day in Lloyds Bank as a stop-gap. Literature and journalistic work is not in great demand, nor is lecturing or teaching, except school teaching, which I refuse to return to – it is altogether too exhausting. So I have charge of the balance-sheets of the foreign correspondents of Lloyds. It is not uninteresting, and it is pleasant to work in a bank where tea is served at 4 p.m., but I wish it were more remunerative.

Life here simply consists in waiting for the war to stop – if one thought of that too much it would have the same effect as Chancery on Richard Carstone in *Bleak House*.[2] What is the use of plans? one thinks often.

I must stop. Do give my and my wife's sympathy to Mrs Woods, and let me hear from you soon again.

Yours ever
Thomas S. Eliot

1 – *Why Men Fight*, the US edition of *Principles of Social Reconstruction*, had been published in Jan.

2 – Richard Carstone is destroyed by his obsession with a case in the Court of Chancery. TSE later called *Bleak House* Dickens's 'best novel' ('Wilkie Collins and Dickens', *SE*, 461).

TO *Henry Eliot* TS Houghton

23 March 1917 18 Crawford Mansions, Crawford St, W.1 W.1

Dear Henry,

This is only a short note, but it is perhaps better than nothing. I have never written to thank you for the draft of £10 which you sent at a very opportune moment, just in the nick of time to save me from withdrawing my £50 which I have managed to tuck away in a deposit account. Later, father sent me some money. He has been wonderfully good, but it does go against the grain for me to take it; I have taken so much and so thoughtlessly in the past. Just now I am earning £2 10s a week filing balance sheets in Lloyds bank; the work is not exhausting, and the pay may improve; besides, I have my evening class and what writing I do. I sent you a copy of the *New Statesman*;[1] I am trying to think of another article now.

Remember that every letter you write helps to keep me in touch with America, and that it is fully appreciated by both of us. The world seems a complete nightmare at times; nothing that could happen would be surprising. I wonder if there will ever come a time when we shall look back and find that the period we are living through seems quite unreal in retrospect.

I hope you will not go to Chicago unless you are quite certain it is a better thing. But you might, on the whole, prefer to be back there to living permanently in New York, wouldn't you?

I shall not write any more, because I want to get into the habit of writing single pages like this more often.

Very affectionately,
Tom

TO *Mary Hutchinson* MS Texas

28 March 1917 18 Crawford Mansions

Dear Mrs Hutchinson

I must apologize very deeply for not having answered your letter before. I was away when it came, and so could not answer before the afternoons

1–He was probably referring here to 'Reflections on Vers Libre' (3 Mar. 1917), although the issue of 17 Mar. carried his unsigned review of 'Diderot's Early Philosophical Works'.

you suggested; and I have been meaning to write to ask if I could come another time. I should like very much to come to see you soon. I am now at Lloyds Bank all day, and cannot leave till 5. I have no idea how long it takes from Cannon Street to Ravenscourt Park – perhaps you know better than I. But will you let me know whether I may come on a Saturday, or in the evening, if the afternoon is too late?

I was very sorry to hear that you have been ill. The weather must have handicapped you severely, but I hope you are very much better by now.

Sincerely yours
T. S. Eliot

TO *J. C. Squire*[1] MS Texas

29 March 1917 18 Crawford Mansions

Dear Squire,

Here is another contribution, which I submit for your approval.[2]

I should like to drop in and see you, but I am at present working in Lloyds Bank from 9.15 till 5. I have been there for the past ten days. It is not bad work, and much more comfortable and less wearing than schoolmastering, though (so far) even less remunerative. But I hope to preserve some energy for writing.

I shall try the *Dial* shortly, and then the *Century*, but have nothing on hand yet.

Sincerely
T. S. Eliot

Are you ever in town on Saturday at lunch time? I am free then.

Vivien Eliot TO *Charlotte Eliot Smith* MS Houghton

4 April 1917 18 Crawford Mansions

Dear Charlotte

I feel very much ashamed of not having written sooner to thank you for sending the photos. We were delighted with them – they are such jolly

1–J. C. Squire (1884–1958), poet and critic; literary editor of *NS* 1913–19, where he wrote as 'Solomon Eagle'; later founding editor of *The London Mercury*, 1919–34.

2–Probably the unsigned review of Gamaliel Bradford, *Union Portraits*, in *NS* 9 (21 Apr. 1917); he would send a copy of the book to his mother for Christmas.

ones. I am quite proud of my nieces (it seems so odd to have nieces.) I think that big head of the little one – Charlotte – is most artistic. I am having it framed. I like the way she has her hair cut. I am always threatening Tom to cut my hair like that! But he won't let me. I am writing on the eventful day of American's declaration of war.[1] No news *seems* so thrilling as it used to, as we are no longer allowed posters – But today's news is very exciting – rather unpleasant but exciting to me personally. You said a few things in yr. last letter that made me think you may feel sympathetically about the war – or war. I am sure you will hate the thought of yr. husband's possibly going to fight. But I suppose, and hope and pray, that the married men will not be conscripted for a long time – and if one dared to think that the war ever ever will be over one wd. hope it wd. be over before that. I can't help feeling, indeed I *know* that many of you in America simply don't know what war means – I mean what this war means. I don't suppose you ever will, as we have known it. This sounds a depressing letter, but I have got a bad sore throat, and it does not help towards looking on the bright side of things, if there is such a side!

Tom and I live a scrambling, over worked, hand-to-mouth sort of existence, which I know it wd, be quite useless to describe to *anyone* who does not see us living it. We muddle along somehow, and time flies. I should like you to see our flat. It is the one thing I do really take a pride in – I mean seem to have succeeded in. It means an extraordinary lot to me – I am a person who simply does not exist without a home, and am always fussing with it. Well, please excuse a very dull letter – most of what one wd. like to say one can't.

Affectly Vivien

Vivien Eliot TO *Charlotte C. Eliot* MS Houghton

Easter Sunday 8 April [1917] 18 Crawford Mansions

My dear Mrs Eliot

We have just been home to lunch and tea. We nearly always go on Sundays. We got back here at 6. Today the time has been changed.[2] We all had to put our clocks on one hour. It is such a good idea, I think. So now, although by our new time it is 7.30 p.m. it is broad daylight. In another

1 – President Wilson had addressed Congress seeking a declaration of war on 2 Apr. but the USA's formal declaration of war on Germany did not in fact follow until 6 Apr.
2 – British Summer Time was introduced as a wartime measure in 1916.

month it will be light up till nearly 9. ocl. I love long days. But summer is so pitifully short, and winter so hideously long. I never can quite enjoy the summer, because I can't forget the terrible winter that has gone, and the terrible one so soon to come. Life rushes by – with us. Somehow it all seems a long scramble, and *effort*, and one scarcely has time to think. A good thing, perhaps. Please excuse pencil. I cannot write in ink except on the smoothest paper. The *act* of writing is a terrible effort to me. My mind is full of things to say, but my hand will not obey my mind. I write laboriously and illegibly.

Tom is going on smoothly at the Bank. His health is *much* improved since he went there. There is a marked change in him. Everyone notices it. His nerves are so much better – he does not have those black silent moods, and the irritability. Those months when he was entirely at home were very very trying. He *writes* better, feels better and happier and has better health when he knows that money (however *little*) is *assured*, and coming in regularly – even tho' he has only a few hours a day to write in, than when he has *all* day – and nothing settled, nothing *sure*. I am so *thankful* this work is congenial to him. I never thought it would be. It was quite a surprise to me to find he liked it.

I long for the end of the war (such an expression is most futile to express my longing) and when we can come to America. The fact that America has declared war is rather terrible to me. I so dread that Tom might have, some day, to fight. And yet I think he would almost like to. You, over there, do not realise the bad and dreadful effect war has on the characters of young men (and old men). If they are nervous and highly strung, (as Tom is, and also my brother) they become quite changed. A sort of desperation, and demoralisation of their minds, brains, and character. I have seen it so, so often. It is one of the most dreadful things. But how can they help it?

I must stop now. I am very tired.

Affectly,
Vivien

TO *His Mother* — MS Houghton

11 April 1917 — 18 Crawford Mansions

Dearest Mother

I have been wondering very much what you think now, and am looking forward to your letters. Do you like [President Woodrow] Wilson any better? I am sure that it was the right thing, and had been expecting it for some little time. It ought to make his two messages more important in the eyes of those who were not inclined to take them very seriously at the time. The German declaration that American armed liners would be considered as pirates was the last touch. I am pleased for several reasons, but chiefly because I think the war was so momentous as it was, that winding it up as a world war will be the best chance now for a satisfactory conclusion. I wish that our country might have a chance to refresh its memory as to what war really is like, – now that it is such a very vivid thing to Europe. On the other hand I hope now that it will not last long enough for that. You will be having all the excitement and bustle of war without the horrors and despairs – except those which will follow from taxation. It will be very interesting to hear from you how St Louis is taking the affair (I take the society meetings, national anthems, etc. for granted – I mean what the different nationalities really feel, and what the lower classes think). I can imagine the mob breaking the windows of Faust's Restaurant, and sacking the Anhaüser-Busch,[1] and Mr Busch giving a million dollars toward national defense.

I wonder what the Service Act will be.[2] I don't suppose persons like myself would be called up for a couple of years, and it will be over before that. Peters[3] and Little[4] (Leon) are no doubt patrolling the seas – they were in the naval reserve; and various others who were in the Troop or the Battery – George Parker[5] you remember, our cousin – are now in camp. I don't envy them. I certainly do not feel in a position to go until 'called out', though Vivien has been rather troubled – I should go then, but not till then.

I am getting on nicely in my work at the bank, and like it. It is wonderful to find something to do in wartime which is less fatiguing than teaching, and the men at the bank are very pleasant. I want to find out something about the science of money while I am at it: it is an extraordinarily interesting subject. Besides, Vivien was very anxious about my health while I was at home – it seemed to get worse and worse; and now I am better and more cheerful she is much happier. Then too I have felt more creative lately.

1 – Faust's was a German-owned restaurant, Anheuser-Busch a big brewery: both in St Louis.
2 – The Selective Service Act, introduced on 18 May, required the registration of all men aged 21–30 (later extended to 18–45). Exemptions from service were granted to those with dependent families, indispensable duties at home, or physical disabilities.
3 – Harold Peters, TSE's Harvard room-mate and sailing companion; see Glossary of Names.
4 – Leon Little (1887–1968), a Harvard classmate, served as a lieutenant and was awarded the Navy Cross.
5 – George Alanson Parker (1887–1966), lawyer and classmate; he was descended, like TSE, from Colonel Charles Cushing (1744–1809).

Besides my lectures, which are now on Ruskin and involve some reading in political economy, and considerable reviewing for Jourdain (mostly anthropology and biology lately)[1] I have been doing some writing – mostly in French,[2] curiously enough it has taken me that way – and some poems in French which will come out in the *Little Review*[3] in Chicago. I shall probably appear in that every month. I start with a sort of dialogue serial (prose) which will be continued.[4] Besides, I have some ideas for an Article on Introspective Consciousness.[5] My essay in the *Statesman*,[6] which should have reached you by this time, brought me several compliments.

The weather has been fearful lately, snowing every day, and melting into slush. Poor Vivien has felt it in several ways, including *neuralgia*, rheumatism and catarrh. On the whole she is much better, but for the weather. I look forward to your seeing her well and happy, – one does not dare say next summer, but one hopes it. She has taken a most positive affection for you, and talks of you very often.

I must stop now.

With very much love

Your devoted son
Tom

TO *His Father* MS Houghton

18 April 1917 18 Crawford Mansions

My dear father

Yes, your clippings arrived, and give much pleasure; one doesn't see much of that sort of picture here. I remember the Emmons as a topic of

1 – Reviews of William Temple's *Mens Creatrix* (1917) and R. G. Collingwood's *Religion and Phillosophy* (1916), in *IJE*, July 1917.

2 – 'I thought I'd dried up completely. I hadn't written anything for some time and was rather desperate. I started writing a few things in French and found I *could* . . . I think it was that when I was writing in French I didn't take the poems so seriously, and that not taking them seriously, I wasn't so worried about not being able to write. I did these things as a sort of *tour de force* to see what I could do. That went on for some months . . . then I suddenly began writing in English again and lost all desire to go on with French. I think it was just something that helped me get started again' ('The Art of Poetry, 1: T. S. Eliot', *Paris Review* 21 [Spring/Summer 1959], 47–70).

3 – 'Le directeur', 'Mélange adultère de tout', 'Lune de miel' and 'The Hippopotamus', were to be published in *Little Review* 4: 3 (July 1917). Margaret C. Anderson (1890–1973) had founded the *Little Review* in 1914. EP was its foreign editor, 1917–19.

4 – 'Eeldrop and Appleplex', *Little Review* 4: 1 (May 1917), 7–11.

5 – Probably never written.

6 – 'Reflections on Vers Libre'.

conversation in the family; I seem to remember that the family used to come to the office and pester the life out of you. Wasn't there a boy at Eton, and various expenses of that sort?

I am very busy now as I wrote in my last. In a fortnight's time I hope to be somewhat less so, as my working class will be over. That usually takes Saturday afternoon and Sunday in preparation, especially lately, as I am doing Ruskin and have to read up economics. I amused the class last time by reading out a passage of Ruskin in which he cursed out America, because he said he detested liberty.[1] He was a great friend of Charles Eliot Norton,[2] who I imagine was equally crusty. Did you ever have anything to do with him? One of the class is a middle-aged woman who is quite cracked, and keeps writing me letters (which I do not encourage) beginning 'dear teacher, philosopher and friend'. She wants to cast my horoscope – I declined.

I am absorbed during the daytime by the balance sheets of foreign banks. It is a peaceful, but very interesting pursuit, and involves some use of reasoning powers. The system is this: the annual reports are entered (by me) on large cards, with spaces: 'Cash in hand', 'Correspondents', 'Investments', 'Advances', 'Discounts' etc., so that by looking at the card one can get an idea of the banks' progress for some years past. Foreign banks give much fuller reports than American banks, some of them almost volumes; some of the balance sheets much more subdivided than others, and a great variety of items. I get, let us say, the report of the Crédit Foncier d'Algiers, and I find a large item called 'Property acquired by expropriation'. The question is, should this be classed under our heading 'bank premises'. I find after enquiry that the chief business of this bank is lending money to farmers on real estate, and that much property falls into their hands by the failure to meet these obligations. Therefore this property (to be sold at auction) must have a separate column. Or an Australian bank has an item 'Advances under Government Wheat Scheme', and I must find out whether this is an ordinary advance, or the money guaranteed by the Government. Or the Russian-Asiatic bank holds a large capital for the Chinese Government, and I want to find out whether this is to be classed as part of the capital of that bank. All this has made me want to find out something about the theory of banking, and especially Foreign Exchange. Incidentally, tea is served at four.

1 – *Time and Tide* (1867), Letter XXII, para. 141: see the library edn of Ruskin, ed. E. T. Cook and A. D. O. Wedderburn, Vol. XVII (1905), 432, n.3.

2 – Charles Eliot Norton (1827–1908), co-editor of the *North American Review* 1864–8; a founder and co-editor of *The Nation*, 1865; and Professor of the History of Fine Art at Harvard, 1873–98.

At the Embassy, everyone is very busy, but no one knows anything about America's plans. The stars and stripes over the Smith Premier Building is the only sign of our activity. I hope fixedly for the war to end in the autumn. We keep well, and fairly cheerful. Vivien is pretty tired, from doing the housework and cooking. She is a good cook.

I must do a bit of reading now. There is nothing important in this letter, I find: I like your letters, short and often. Do write every week. I shall write to mother by next mail, and thank her for the prescription.

With much love

Your devoted son
Tom

Vivien Eliot TO *Charlotte C. Eliot* — MS Houghton

30 April [1917]

18 Crawford Mansions,
Crawford St, London W.1 (*one*)

Dear Mrs Eliot,

At 12 o'clock last night I asked Tom how much longer his work would take him – and he said about two hours. 'And then', he said, 'I am going to write to my mother'. He looked *so* tired that I begged him to let me write to you this week instead. I said I knew you would prefer it rather than that he should curtail his sleep still more. And so he agreed to let me, although he wanted very much to write to you himself.

He was working all yesterday and last night on his last lecture to the working people – it is the last one today, of this course. The lecture is on George Borrow. Tom has made a great success of his Class, and has kept up the numbers so well that it has been a surprise to everyone. Most of the other classes of the same sort have fallen off dreadfully in numbers this year. Of course it has been almost impossible to prevent it. But Tom has done really well – and he feels it I know. His people are most obviously fond of him. I have wished he could get more of the same sort of work. But I am not sure *now* that he is particularly anxious to – although of course he will be glad to have this same class for two years more. (When he took it up, it was to be for *three winters*). Now that Tom has taken so extraordinarily to the City (we call the business and commercial part of London 'the City') he is considering, to my *great* astonishment, taking up Banking as his *money-making* career! We are all very much surprised at this development, but not one of his friends has failed to see, and to remark upon, the great change in Tom's health, appearance, spirits, and literary productiveness since he went in for Banking. So far, it has obviously suited him. He is *extremely* interested in finance, and I believe has a good deal of hitherto unsuspected ability in that direction. If he can push on in Banking, and in the course of a year or two secure a sufficient income from it, there is no reason why he should not obtain through it his greatest ambition: viz: a congenial and *separate* money-making occupation – *of a sort* that will leave his mind and brain fresh enough to produce good literature, and *not to have to depend on writing for money at all*. This is what he has *always* been hoping for – he has never altered. The difficulty has been to *find* the money-making career which would *not* exhaust his brain and faculties. So far, the Bank *seems* to be the thing. No one could be more surprised than I am. I shed *tears* over the thought of Tom going into a Bank! I thought it was the most horrible catastrophe. Most of Tom's friends agreed with me. We all wrung our hands and lamented. And it took more than Tom's protestations to convince us that it was no tragedy. Only when he began to be more bright and happy and boyish than I've known him to be for nearly two years, did *I* feel convinced – and only when he has written *five*, most *excellent* poems in the course of one week, did Ezra Pound and many others, believe it possible.

As far as I am concerned of course I have never had the remotest connection with business in my life – I mean all my family and most of the people I've known have always been professionals, so I had no idea at all what it was like! I imagined that Tom would either have to stand behind the counter – or else sit at a desk in a room with lots of others, doing drudgery all day.

Will you please tell Mr Eliot that Tom was *very* much pleased and stimulated by the cheery little letter Mr Eliot wrote saying he was pleased about T's Bank work. It is nice that he approves.

I have had a most awful cold, and it has left me with one of the worst coughs I've ever had. I feel *full* of catarrh – nose – chest – everywhere. There are many things I should like to write about, but one is never sure as to what is allowed. But we *both hope that you will take* every opportunity of finding out all you can of how we are getting on.

With much love,
Vivien

TO *His Mother* MS Houghton

13 May[1] 1917 18 Crawford Mansions

My dearest Mother,

I have had a very busy week, and the sudden hot weather which has suddenly given London the atmosphere of a conservatory – after the frigid spring – has been rather upsetting to both of us. You will be glad to know that I have ordered my suit – a very pretty grey, and of very substantial material.

Lately, having brought up to date the piece of work I was doing at the bank, I have been set to watch another man and have him explain his work to me. I have had about a week of this. On Thursday morning he was reading me a letter from his brother in France, when someone came in and said that a lady wanted to speak to him outside. He was out of the room for about five minutes, and when he came in said briefly 'My brother's been killed'. He was awfully cut up about it, and was absent from the office for the rest of the week. Meanwhile I had to do his work for him, and as it is rather important, I felt the responsibility rather heavy on me. However, I referred all doubtful points to a superior, and I think I got through without making any mistakes; if so it ought to redound to my credit. But coming so suddenly it was quite exhausting.

My review of the work on Wilson came out in the *Statesman* on Saturday.[2] As my proof had been sent to Ireland by mistake, it was not revised, and the form did not quite satisfy me. I often make substantial alterations in the proof. I also sent off a batch of reviews to Jourdain.

I am going to undertake a 'contributing editor' job with a monthly paper called *The Egoist*[3] – the same which is publishing my poems (next week, I hope).[4] It will not take much time, and accordingly will not bring in much money – not more than a pound a month, but it will add to my notoriety. At present it is run mostly by old maids,[5] and I may be a beneficial

1–His mother has altered April to May.

2–TSE, unsigned review of H. Wilson Harris, *President Wilson: His Problems and His Policy*, *NS* 9: 214 (12 May 1917), 140.

3–On RA's departure for military service, EP had suggested that TSE should replace him as Assistant Editor from June, and secretly provided a third of the £36-a-year salary.

4–*Prufrock and Other Observations* was published in June at 1s, in an edition of 500 copies. Without TSE's knowledge, EP put £5 towards the printing cost, and was repaid later: see Jane Lidderdale and Mary Nicholson, *Dear Miss Weaver: Harriet Shaw Weaver 1876–1961* (1970).

5–Dora Marsden (1882–1960) and Harriet Shaw Weaver (for Weaver, see Glossary of Names). Marsden had founded and edited the *New Freewoman*, 'an individualist review',

influence. This is due to Ezra Pound. How I can find time to take up Spanish, which I am anxious to do both for its own sake and for its use in banking, I don't know.

I am hoping to get two weeks holiday this summer, as we both need it, and Vivien isn't willing to go away alone. If I get a fortnight, however, I could send her away a week or so earlier, and join her. We have neither of us been out of town since September, and we need a change very badly.

I hope you will not let the war interfere with your going to Gloucester. I cannot see the slightest reason for fearing the seaside, if you have that in mind. You cannot realise what it is to live in the midst of alarms of war! Besides the brother of the man I mentioned, there was killed last week the fiancé of one of Vivien's friends, and the next day I heard that one of my Oxford friends – the man who went to the seaside with me that Christmas – was critically wounded and may not live.[1] If the war goes on I shall be losing American friends too. I should like to know where Leon and Harold Peters are stationed now.

I have had no news from Henry since he went to Chicago. How does he like it?

I am glad to say that Maurice is still in England.

I must go to bed now, and get ready for another week.

With much love to both of you

Your devoted son
Tom

TO *His Mother* MS Houghton

Sunday 20 May 1917 18 Crawford Mansions

My dearest Mother,

We have plunged from winter into August weather, and the close damp heat is most trying, though to me any kind of heat is stimulating and agreeable. The streets are filled as always at this time of year with spring

—

which appeared twice monthly from 15 June to 15 Dec. 1913. In Jan. 1914 the name was changed to *The Egoist*, and Weaver succeeded her as editor in mid-year.

1–Karl Culpin, a second lieutenant in the Gloucestershire Regiment, died two days after this letter was written. TSE was to recall, in a letter to the secretary of the Merton Society, 24 June 1963: 'My closest friend at Merton, whose name was Culpin, was taken late because of bad eyesight and was killed, I think, on his first day in the trenches.'

flowers for sale, narcissus, daffodils, tulips, lilac, roses, all for a few pence – about the only things which remain at the same price.

I am going to have a sort of promotion tomorrow – whether it will bring any immediate rise of salary I don't know. I said that I had been put on to help another man at his work. Now he is to do something else, and I am to do what he was doing. It is quite an interesting post, and involves the handling of bills and cheques often for very large amounts, and receiving and sending of money by cable. The work during the day is rather irregular – often for an hour or more in the morning there is nothing to do at all, and I pull out a Spanish grammar which I keep by me and study away at that (when I get to read Spanish easily I think I will take up Danish or Portuguese). Then from half past one things begin coming in, and as all the money has to be 'cleared' by three o'clock, there is a rush. After that there is the cabling, and the letter writing, and after four one can usually take it easy again. I don't know that it is etiquette for me to go into any further details. The bank is so shorthanded now that there is a good chance of moving about the office and learning various branches of the business.

Another article of mine came out in the *New Statesman* on Saturday.[1] It is inferior to the other, but I will send it to you. My third article is not yet finished. I am now fully established as assistant editor of the *Egoist*. I will send you the June issue when it comes out, though I don't know whether it will have anything of mine in it or not. My colleagues are a Miss Weaver,[2] a funny little spinster, but quite nice, and I believe quite intelligent, and a Mrs Aldington, better known as 'H. D.', a poetess, who like most, or a good half of the world of art and letters in London, is an American. I went to see her this afternoon for the first time, and found her very agreeable and disposed to look upon me, for some reason, as a great authority upon Greek language and literature. London is an amazing place – one is constantly discovering new quarters; this woman lives in a most beautiful dilapidated old square, which I had never heard of before; a square in the middle of town, near King's Cross Station, but with spacious old gardens about it.[3]

I am expecting my book to be out in a few days. An offer came from a rich man in New York named John Quinn,[4] a patron of letters, to print it

1–'The Borderline of Prose'. *NS* 9 (12 May 1917), 157–9.

2–Harriet Shaw Weaver, editor of the *Egoist*.

3–H. D and her husband RA rented a large room at 44 Mecklenburgh Square. In *Bid Me to Live* (1960), H. D. gave a fictional account of her life there after the departure of RA.

4–John Quinn, wealthy New York lawyer and literary patron: see Glossary of Names. On 11 Aug. 1915, EP had written to him about TSE: 'I have more or less discovered him . . . I think young Eliot is the first person I should like to have confer with you. He has more entrails than might appear from his quiet exterior, I think.'

at his own expense in case the *Egoist* did not have funds. Of course it was unnecessary, but it was pleasant, nevertheless; and he will probably review it in *Vanity Fair*,[1] which, whatever else may be said for the paper, would bring notoriety.

The air is full of thunder and lightning this evening. Vivien is like Marion and Grandma Faraway[2] with thunderstorms – or I believe Marion used to be until the house was struck.

I am glad you are going to Gloucester after all. I could not bear to think of your not being there in the summer. When I come home after the war I should like to be able to go straight to Gloucester – though that will be May, I presume. This year I do not expect to get any holiday until late in the autumn. The Haigh-Woods are going away soon for a fortnight and we are to have the house for that time – they will keep the servant there and pay her and pay for her food. It is very nice of them. They live in Hampstead, which is on the edge of London, and the air is better than it is here. Besides, there is a garden, at the back. Vivien needs a holiday badly.

I must stop now. I had a letter from Henry from Chicago. He did not say what he was paid, but apparently is not so hard worked as in New York. I hope his employers are as pleasant as mine.

Always with very much love

Your devoted son

Tom

All your news of St Louis always interests me.

TO *His Mother*

MS Houghton

28 May 1917 — 18 Crawford Mansions

Dearest Mother,

This is a 'bank holiday' in London: that is to say, yesterday, being Whitsunday (Pentecost) was a Religious Feast, and the next day is a holiday. So I have been sitting at home writing an article for the *New Statesman*.[3] It is very warm and bright; the gramophones across the court have been going without intermission, and the streets are full of people. As soon as I finish this letter for the mail, we are going out walking. It is also Vivien's [twenty-ninth] birthday. We had two very nice letters from you

1 – He did not do so.

2 – Grandmother Stearns had lived in North Lexington, Massachusetts.

3 – Apparently not completed or not published.

and one from father this morning. One of them was *open*, the one which also contained a comic picture from the newspaper and Roger Amory's bill.[1] There was nothing else in it, was there? The other contained the receipt to the above. Thank you very much for paying it; though I hate to think of the money going to that purpose.

I daresay the hernia might make a difference, though there is no indication of its still being open. The doctor told me at the time that there was usually a family predisposition in such cases. I don't believe that Henry would be accepted for anything. He seems very anxious to go; I am afraid that is largely dissatisfaction with himself and his present life; but I think that the best thing he can do is to stay in one place long enough to have a really settled life. He ought, of course, as everyone has always said, to be married; being a very affectionate domestic person without great or absorbing ambitions. He *was*, of course, the sort who would be quite as likely to marry the wrong woman as the right, but that might not be so likely now.

I am sorry to hear about Marian's throat but very likely the change of climate will do her good. St Louis is very smoky. And Millis[2] ought to be very pleasant now.

We have not been very well lately. It is partly the sudden and extreme change in the weather. I must send this letter off now or it will not catch the boat. I will write by next mail.

Very devotedly
your son
Tom.

TO *His Father* MS Houghton

13 June 1917 18 Crawford Mansions

My dear father,

I resume communication after not having written for some time. I have been getting your letters regularly, with enclosures, and have heard more regularly from Henry than for some time past. He seems very restless and unsettled and longing for a chance to escape at any price. The trouble is

1–Roger Amory (1887–1960), Harvard class of 1910, became Class Treasurer in 1916; later president of the Consolidated Investment Trust.

2–Millis, Massachusetts, is a rural town in Norfolk County, about thirty miles south-west of Boston, where TSE's sister Charlotte and her family lived.

that he has never been in contact with any but one sort of reality – that of the most disagreeable business experience – and that he is still longing for experience in general – which makes him seem in a way very immature. Perhaps the same thing is true of many young or even almost middle-aged business men. I think it is this feeling as much as anything which makes him so anxious to come abroad.[1] It might of course freshen him up and give him more satisfaction with his existence; on the other hand it might not make him any happier to return to what he has been doing. I think everyone sooner or later must come to a point – in order to be happy at all – where one is simply content to cultivate one's garden and do one's work in peace and a certain security.

To me all this war *enthusiasm* seems a bit unreal, because of the mixture of motives. But I see the war partly through the eyes of men who have been and returned, and who view it, even when convinced of the rightness of the cause, in a very different way: as something very sordid and disagreeable which must be put through. That would be my spirit.

I have been particularly busy at the bank this week, and in the excessive humid heat it has been rather tiring. The man who taught me my job has gone on his holiday, and I have full control over it now. All the money coming in *for* foreign banks ('Correspondents') passes through my hands, and I also have charge of documents (bills of lading etc.) to be delivered against payment (one for fifty bales of *old clothes* imported from Rotterdam, over which I had some correspondence with a Jewish lady in Whitechapel). I have had to find a good many things out for myself. At a time like the present one has much more opportunity of stepping into important work and having an interesting job. The foreign work is I believe the most interesting part of banking, especially at the present time, when one can from time to time see very big things happening in which one plays a small part without really knowing what is going on.

To turn from banking to literature. I have been too tired the last few hot days to do much. My book [*Prufrock and Other Observations*] is out, and you will probably get a copy by the time this arrives. The cover is not all that I desire, but one must take what one can get in times like these, and I am lucky to get it printed at all without cost to myself. There ought to be a few reviews in a few weeks.

The *Egoist* I believe you can get in Boston, at one or two shops, but I will enquire.

1–HWE did not travel outside the USA until he visited England with his mother in 1921.

We are going to the Jourdains[1] on Sunday, with the Waterlows. We are dreading it a bit, as it means a train journey of over an hour and a long walk from the station, but Jourdain has been so kind to me that I thought I ought to accept, for both of us. Vivien will be very tired afterwards. We are going to occupy her parents' house for a time, as they have gone away. They will pay and feed the servant, and we shall have only our own expenses, with a change of air. I long for the country or rather the seaside now; the City (as the business district is called) is full of flowers for sale very cheap.

I must stop now. I like to think of you at Gloucester soon. The submarines won't go there! I long to see you, every day.

Your devoted son
Tom

TO *The Editor of* The Nation[2]

Published 23 June 1917

Sir –

I enclose herewith an extract from a letter lately received from a young officer which I hope may interest some of your readers. I may add that the officer in question entered the Army directly from a public school, and began his service in the trenches before he was nineteen.[3] – Yours etc.,

T. S. Eliot
18 Crawford Mansions, Crawford Street, W.1.
June 17th, 1917.

'June 8th, 1917

'Dear ———, There is rather a good article in *The Nation* this last week called "On Leave".[4] You should read it. I have often heard it said that the curious thing about those who have been to the front is their complete indifference. They appear to be practically untouched by what they have seen and gone through, they talk of war in a callous and humorous way, they even joke about its horrors. The impression one has from them is that it is, on the whole, a dreary and unpleasant business,

1–The Jourdains lived in Crookham, Hampshire.
2–The magazine ran a series of letters from the trenches.
3–VHE's brother Maurice Haigh-Wood.
4–By H. M. T[omlinson], 2 June 1917, describing London as seen by a soldier home from the front.

with its anxious moments and its bright moments, but not nearly such a hell as one really knows it to be.

'In the case of the vast majority, however, this is an attitude, a screen – I speak of educated, thinking men – and it is not granted to many who have not shared the same experiences to see behind the screen. The reason for this, as the article points out, is the practical impossibility of the uninitiated to realize or imagine even dimly the actual conditions of war. And a man who has been through it and seen and taken part in the unspeakable tragedies that are the ordinary routine, feels that he has something, possesses something, which others can never possess.

'It is morally impossible for him to talk seriously of these things to people who cannot even approach comprehension. It is hideously exasperating to hear people talking the glib commonplaces about the war and distributing cheap sympathy to its victims.

'Perhaps you are tempted to give them a picture of a leprous earth, scattered with the swollen and blackening corpses of hundreds of young men. The appalling stench of rotting carrion mingled with the sickening smell of exploded lyddite and ammonal. Mud like porridge, trenches like shallow and sloping cracks in the porridge – porridge that stinks in the sun. Swarms of flies and bluebottles clustering on the pits of offal. Wounded men lying in the shell holes among the decaying corpses: helpless under the scorching sun and bitter nights, under repeated shelling. Men with bowels dropping out, lungs shot away, with blinded, smashed faces, or limbs blown into space. Men screaming and gibbering. Wounded men hanging in agony on the barbed wire, until a friendly spout of liquid fire shrivels them up like a fly in a candle. But these are only words, and probably only convey a fraction of their meaning to their hearers. They shudder, and it is forgotten. . . .

'I need hardly say that on a great number of men war does produce this effect; of these the old regular army officer is a type – blunt, kindly, jolly good fellows – who have never stopped to think in their lives.'

TO *His Mother* — MS Houghton

27 June 1917 — [3 Compayne Gdns, London N.W.]

My dearest mother,

This will be only a line, even after not having written for *ever* so long – I think a fortnight. For I am very busy and very tired; I have been going to bed very early lately and am consequently behindhand in my work. I have been frightfully tired lately for some reason. I think I have told you about the things I have been working on.

We have not heard from you for over a *fortnight* – I hope for a letter tomorrow. One of us usually goes into Crawford Mansions every day for the mail.

We have been thankful to be here during the hot weather – and in a month we shall be going away. I love to think of you as being at Gloucester. I imagine how everything looks and think of the summers when I was at Gloucester before you and saw you and father coming across the path with your luggage, and climbing over the stone wall where it is broken down; and going to meet you. The only thing I don't like to think of is the *Elsa*.[1]

We are going to have tennis on Saturday – I am, that is. Vivien is going to write to you tomorrow. I only wrote tonight at bedtime to say how often I thought of you.

Your devoted son Tom –

Vivien Eliot TO *Charlotte C. Eliot* — MS Houghton

28 June 1917 — 3 Compayne Gdns, London N.W.6

Dear Mrs Eliot

I am putting this letter in with Tom's, which he left open for me. He was so desperately tired – he wanted badly to write a longer letter – but he was too tired. I wish he was going to have a long holiday with you at Eastern Point, or with me, at Bosham. I worry very much about his health – it seems he has not average strength – and added to that he lives as no average man does. The incessant, never ending grind, day and evening – and always *too* much to do, so that he is always behind hand, never up to date – therefore always tormented – and if *forced* to rest or stop a minute it only torments him the more to feel that inexorable pile of work piling up against him.

He got your letter this *morning* – dated June 3rd, and was glad of it.

I wrote you a *long* time ago thanking you for the birthday present you sent me. I do hope you got it in the end.

I also told you about Tom's new suit. He has had it about a month. I also bought him two pairs of pyjamas, and one shirt, and six prs. of socks. These were absolute necessities.

1 – TSE's catboat (EVE); see plate 21. Catboats were originally East Coast fishing boats, with gaff-rigged sails, but adapted for racing and cruising around the turn of the nineteenth century: see Stan Grayson, *Cape Cod Catboats* (Marblehead, Mass., 2002).

Tom enjoys and revels in the *large* and airy rooms in this house, the peace and quiet of the neighbourhood, and the green-ness of the open square behind and the creeper-covered houses in front. My mother's two servants are very efficient and nice girls, and everything works so smoothly and quietly. It would be ideal if we did not find that it does cost us considerably more to just live here, *even though* Father pays us £1 a week for the servants' food. The reason of this is that they are used to a more liberal way of living here, and not being *my* servants, I cannot possibly change the ways, and adopt here my own *rigid*, locking-up-everything principles – which I have had to evolve since my marriage. In the flat, if we have a woman, I lock up every mortal thing, and not a grain of rice or a crust of bread is eaten without my knowledge. Naturally one does not enjoy having to practise such parsimonious ways – but when it is a choice between that and practically starvating as it has been with us – there is of course no question. It seems strange to me, very strange, to be back here in this home of mine, with Tom, living here, after these two years of noisy struggle. I had almost forgotten that life could be so pleasant, so smooth. It is the old tale, I suppose, of no-one's ever appreciating anything until they have lost it. I was also going to add that life in a suburb is *more* expensive than it is nearer the heart of town, because the shops are dearer, and all of one standard – and one is in their hands. Also, life is more conventional – there are people one knows, or who know one, about – one has to keep up appearances. Living where *we* do (Crawford Mansions) in a little noisy corner, with slums and low streets and poor shops close around us – (and *yet* within a stone's throw of great squares with big houses and one of the most expensive residential districts) it is like being in a wilderness, we are just two waifs who live perched up in our little flat – no-one around us knows us, or sees us, or bothers to care how we live or what we do, or whether we live or not. Tom says, Americans who have never been here cannot and never do realise how *vast* London is. It is so enormous – well, you can't imagine it and all the differences – I know.

Food prices are, as you say, extremely high, and, we are constantly told, will go on rising. In fact they *do* rise, week by week, and it becomes more and more difficult and harassing to procure proper nourishment on the money which Tom is earning. It is almost impossible. I think that Tom most certainly *ought* to be getting a larger salary. £2.10 a week, for the work he is doing, seems to me absurd. He is now doing far more difficult work than he did at first – and has quite a position. I dont know what will happen if he does not get a rise soon.

I must stop now, I ought to write to Henry and to my friend Lucy Thayer. With much love to you all

Vivien

TO *His Mother* MS Houghton

1 July 1917

18 Crawford Mansions,
Crawford St, W.1

Dearest Mother,

I was more than glad to get your two letters after not having heard for so long, but disappointed to find that father's letter in spite of its vast size, contained no letter, but only enclosures, though I was interested and approved Lodge's speech.[1] I was particularly interested in your Colonial Dames[2] circular which I thought very well written and a model of its kind. You must have been very busy about these things, and I hope you will take a rest now at Gloucester.

I am sure that I acknowledged your cheque, but in any case I will do so again now, in duplicate, for both Vivien's and my own, with very grateful thanks. My suit I have had for some time; it is very satisfactory, and I believe will last very well.

It is as you say very hard to keep house on small means now. I suppose conditions are the same all over the world. I do not think that anyone could manage more economically than Vivien. She finds it somewhat more expensive here (Hampstead) than at Crawford Mansions, partly because provisions cost more than they do near us, and partly because she has to use another person's servant and another person's method. But the Haigh-Woods send money to cover the servant's food, and of course her pay. V. has our Rose at Crawford Mansions very well in hand, and keeps the provisions locked up, doling out from day to day, which makes a great difference.

We are both better for being here. We had some tennis yesterday – myself and Maurice, and Ezra Pound and a man named Dakyns,[3] a friend of ours. Maurice has come back from Lincolnshire and is going to have a three

1–Henry Cabot Lodge (1850–1924), a leading Republican senator. TSE is probably referring to his 'Speech delivered in the Senate on the declaration of war with Germany, 4 April 1917', reprinted in *War Addresses 1915–17* (1917); also distributed as a government offprint.

2–Mrs Eliot was a charter member, and successively Secretary, Vice-President and President of the Missouri Society of the Colonial Dames of America. At this period she was serving as chairman of the War Work committee.

3–Arthur Dakyns (1883–1941), barrister-at-law, worked at the Ministry of Labour 1917–20; later Lecturer in Public Administration, Manchester University, 1926–36.

weeks 'course' at Chelsea Barracks (London) so he will be near us for that time. It is a course given to select officers who have already had experience in France. We are very glad to have him here.

I have done three pieces of work lately – part of a dialogue for the *Little Review*, a review for the *Egoist*, and a review for the *New Statesman*.[1] I am to get £3 per month from the *Egoist*, and £2 per month from the *Little Review*. The best I can hope at present is to see my income rise at the same rate as the cost of living!

I have been very busy at the bank – an enormous foreign mail lately. I have a dozen letters to dictate early tomorrow. So I think I will go to bed and write again on Wednesday. I like to address letters 'Eastern Point'.

With very fond love
Tom

TO *Mary Hutchinson* MS Texas

2 July 1917 3 Compayne Gdns London N.W.

Dear Mrs Hutchinson,

Your letter was finally forwarded to me here, where we are staying for the present. My wife was just on the point of writing to explain why we were so rude as not to acknowledge your card of the week before, and so I will answer both in one. The truth is that she read the card 'July 25', and as we were not sure about that far off date we did not see the card again until too late. We were very much mortified.

It would be very nice to dine with you this week, but we find we cannot fit it in at all. The only free evening is one when my wife has a dancing practice so late as to make it impossible to appear anywhere afterwards. We hope we can come to see you some time before long. In any case will you not be at Wittering this summer? We shall be at Bosham for a time at the end of July – not as long as last summer, unfortunately.

It is good of you to speak well of *Prufrock* – I fear it will simply appear a *réchauffée* to most of my friends – they are growing tired of waiting for something better from me.

With many regrets

Sincerely yours
T. S. Eliot

1–TSE, 'Eeldrop and Appleplex' [I], *Little Review*, May 1917; a review of *Passages from the Letters of John Butler Yeats*, ed. EP, *Egoist*, July 1917; and a review of Paul Bourget's *Lazarine*, *NS*, 25 Aug. 1917.

TO *Eleanor Hinkley* TS Houghton

23 July 1917 18 Crawford Mansions,
Crawford St, W.1

Dear Eleanor,

I was delighted to get your letter this evening, and felt as if telegraphic communications with the transpontine continent had at last been repaired. In fact I had thought several times of writing to you briefly and brusquely to ask if it was a fact that both my letters had been sunk or engulphed in the censor's office; or if not to ask you to state succinctly exactly why you hated me. You have just stopped a crisp epistle.

You have given me a long arrears of news. I am surprised to hear that so little has changed. Life moves so rapidly over here that one never hears twice of the same person as being in the same place or doing quite the same thing. It is either killed or wounded, or fever, or going to gaol, or being let out of gaol, or being tried, or summoned before a tribunal of some kind. I have been living in one of Dostoevsky's novels, you see, not in one of Jane Austen's.[1] If I have not seen the battlefield, I have seen other strange things, and I have signed a cheque for £200,000 while bombs fell about me. I have dined with a princess and with a man who expected two years hard labour; and it all seems like a dream. The most real thing was a little dance we went to a few days ago, something like yours used to be, in a studio with a gramophone;[2] I am sure you would have liked it and the people there.

At present I work from 9.15 till 5.30 in Lloyds Bank Limited, Foreign Department, consigning vast sums of money to various destinations, writing letters to banks in such places as Toronto, Japan, Copenhagen, Mauritius, or Buenos Aires. I feel very important, and should feel more so if I got more money from it. My other occupations are editing the *Egoist* (assistant) of which I will send you a copy, writing for the *Little Review*, for the *New Statesman* (and also helping the editor thereof to read proof, while he listens at the telephone for the latest news from the House of Commons).[3] My book seems to have sold pretty well, although it has not

1–TSE is alluding to the Austen-inspired sketch in which he had acted with Hinkley in 1913.
2–Though not writing of this occasion, Stella Bowen remembered 'our flattered pleasure when T. S. Eliot turned up, with his gentle, benevolent smile and a black satin chest protector, at some of our beer and gramophone parties' (*Drawn from the Life: Reminiscences* [1941], 61).
3–J. C. Squire, a founder member of the Fabian Society, had been a parliamentary reporter until 1912, and stood unsuccessfully as the Labour candidate for Cambridge in the election of 1918.

been much reviewed yet. I also go to the dentist. My teeth are falling to pieces, I have to wear spectacles to read, and from time to time I am contorted with rheumatism – otherwise I am pretty well. I managed to play a game of tennis Saturday.

I hope that Sohier[1] will let us know when he gets to England. He will surely come to London. I don't know whether I shall be called up in the course of time or not; perhaps I shall be if things go to pieces in Russia.[2] But I am not sure that I should pass the medical examination.

I am delighted to hear of your dramatic triumphs. I am sure that I could never write a play. I wish that I could see yours.[3]

I have a small Jewish messenger boy named Joseph, in brass buttons. He said today: 'I know what I should do if I had £5000'. This precocious creature is about eleven. 'What would you do?' 'I'd invest it in Canadian Pacific preferred.[4] But not now', continued the loquacious youth, 'this is not a good time. If I had it now, I'd have a good dinner – duckling and green peas, gooseberry tart and cream. Duckling is nicer than duck, the bones are tenderer'. Such is the society I move in in the City. My typist is Mrs Lord, whose husband is a captain in the regular army – she carries his D.S.O. medal about.

Write soon again, and give my love to your mother.

Always affectionately
Tom

TO *Robert Nichols*[5] TS Mrs Charlton

8 August 1917 18 Crawford Mansions

Dear Mr Nichols,

It was a very great pleasure to me to receive your letter. I found it yesterday on my return from a short holiday. Oddly enough, I had seen

1 – Her brother-in-law, Edward Sohier Welch.

2 – Following its disastrous June offensive, the Russian Army was collapsing, and there were fears that Russia would withdraw from the war, making American support for the Western Allies essential to prevent a German victory. The Bolshevik Revolution was to begin in November.

3 – She had completed *The Clam Digger*, a tragedy in three acts, in the spring, and *Their Flesh and Blood*, an earlier comedy in four acts, was to be produced later in the year in the 47 Workshop.

4 – 'The Empire's Greatest Railway' had been in the news, having taken over the Allan Line shipping company.

5 – Robert Nichols (1893–1944), war poet, novelist and playwright. He joined the Royal Field Artillery in Oct. 1914, fought at the Battle of Loos in 1915, and was invalided out with shell-shock. Professor of English, Imperial University, Tokyo, 1921–4.

St John Hutchinson[1] in Sussex the day before, and he had spoken of you. I also know of you of course from Aldous Huxley and (if you do not mind my mentioning it!) from the *Times*. So I am sure that there is enough basis for correspondence! I sincerely hope that when you are next in London you will not find it too much trouble to look me up – or even to let me know in advance – as I can always be found at this address. It would be a pleasant anticipation for me.

Your more than appreciative praise gave me great pleasure. I have heard very little of my book, since it was published, and have ceased to look for reviews. Still I fear that I have had too much appreciation rather than too little. I am not anxious to write more – or rather I feel that the best promise of continuing is for one to be able to forget, in a way, what one has written already; to be able to detach it completely from one's present self and begin quite afresh, with only the technical experience preserved. This struggle to preserve the advantages of practice and at the same time to defecate the emotions one has expressed already is one of the hardest I know. I wonder if you will agree with me.

I remember getting hold of Laforgue years ago at Harvard, purely through reading Symons,[2] and then sending to Paris for the texts. I puzzled it out as best I could, not finding half the words in my dictionary, and it was several years later before I came across anyone who had read him or could be persuaded to read him.[3] I do feel more grateful to him than to anyone else, and I do not think that I have come across any other writer since who has meant so much to me as he did at that particular moment, or that particular year.

Let me say that I do not think you have any more reason to be downcast at being praised by the *Times* than I have for not being. I have not yet seen your book; I hope that I may do so.[4]

With every hope of meeting you

Yours sincerely
T. S. Eliot

1–St John 'Jack' Hutchinson (1884–1942), barrister-at-law; husband of MH.
2–*The Symbolist Movement in Literature* (1899) by Arthur Symons (1867–1945). 'But for having read his book, I should not, in the year 1908, have heard of Laforgue or Rimbaud: I should probably not have begun to read Verlaine; and but for reading Verlaine, I should not have heard of Corbière. So the Symons book is one of those which have affected the course of my life' (review of Peter Quennell, *Baudelaire and the Symbolists*, in *NC* 9 [Jan. 1930], 357).
3–While TSE was in Paris in 1910–11, his friend and French teacher Alain-Fournier discussed Laforgue several times in his literary column in *Paris-Journal*.
4–Nichols's *Ardours and Endurances* (1917) received a glowing review: 'Nothing can prevent poetry like this from taking its place among those permanent possessions of the race which will remain to tell the great-grandchildren of our soldiers to what pure heights of the spirit

TO *His Mother* TS Houghton

8 August 1917 18 Crawford Mansions

Dearest Mother,

This must be a very short letter, as it is late; several business letters I had to write took much longer than I expected. I got back from Bosham Monday night, after a very rainy week. We went out every day however, and got soaked on the water – there was very little wind and much rain, and we had to row home always – and I think got benefit out of the holiday. Bosham is not as good harbour as [East] Gloucester, as there is a narrow channel and a strong tide, but sailing is the same thing everywhere. We had a delightful sail Sunday. The morning was very bright, and we sailed about ten miles down the harbour to have lunch with some friends who have a house in a remote spot. The wind brought us most of the way back, then it began to rain and we had to row. Bosham is less beautiful naturally than Gloucester, but more picturesque; the village is much prettier. The natives are much the same, and have a curious middle-western twang.

I am *sure* that I acknowledged that $12 long ago! In fact, I remember the letter – I think it was in May. I am very sorry you have had so much trouble over it, and that I did not write again to thank you. I have the suit, as you know.

I wrote to father for money several weeks ago. I presume he will cable it to 'Linen'.

Now I *must* stop and write again on Sunday. I will tell you more about Bosham.

With very much love
your devoted son
Tom

TO *Eleanor Hinkley* TS Houghton

8 August 1917 18 Crawford Mansions

Dear Eleanor,

I wrote you a brief but rather dull letter about ten days ago; as it occurred to me that it was just possible the letter might never reach you,

—

Englishmen rose out of the great war's horror of waste and ugliness, noise and pain and death!' (*TLS*, 12 July).

and as I have a moment spare before going to bed, I am writing you a still briefer one to let you know that I have already written. I sometimes think it is better to write brief letters – unless one had one particular thing to say at some length; one sits down to write a 'good long letter' and becomes conscientiously dull – I do, I am sure you don't! Short letters are sometimes more personal. I remember Jean Verdenal saying to me when I left Paris that Space more than Time would separate us.[1] I think one feels space less in a short letter.

I should like to write oftener, just to be able to feel more certain that we should recognise each other and have more or less a common language when we meet again. I don't imagine you as changed at all – I am sure that I don't want to! – as for myself, I think that in some ways I have improved (somewhat less selfish and more considerate), also hardened a bit. However, we shall see eventually.

My plan is that when I come over after the war you and Aunt Susie will come back with me for a visit.

I have just returned from a week at the seashore, splashing about in a boat. Vivien is staying on for a few days, and so I am alone till Monday. I meant to write a long review this evening, but my time has been taken up with letters.

Affectionately
Tom

TO *His Mother* — MS Houghton

Sunday 2 September[2] 1917 [London]

My dearest mother,

It is a long time since I have written. I have thought of you all the oftener for not writing, however. I have in the last two weeks – I think it is ten days or more since I wrote – done two articles for the *Egoist*, and two for the *New Statesman*, and have nearly finished a longer one. I must now begin at once to prepare my two sets of lectures; which will involve reading a number of authors of whom I know very little: Brontë, George Eliot, Emerson, Charles Reade, Kingsley, Huxley, Spencer, Samuel Butler. I should slip a prospectus of one of my two sets of lectures into this letter, but I know that enclosures are not allowed. While I enjoy these lectures very much in

1 – See Verdenal's letter of 5 Feb. 1912.
2 – Misdated August.

a way, I shall be very glad when I can give them up altogether, for they take a great deal of time that I want to devote to work of a more permanent nature. Just at present they form a very important addition to my income,[1] but at my present rate of increase of salary I can reasonably look forward to a time when they will be unnecessary, and I shall be able to spend *all* my spare time exactly as I please. When I can earn all the money I need out of one thing, and be able to read and write in the rest of my time without thinking of the financial reward for what I do, then I shall be satisfied. The lecturing really takes more out of me than the bank work during the day. Vivien is staying on for a few days more at Bosham; and I have been for the past five days with my friends the Dakyns's, who live about ten minutes walk from us. It is an economy, and they leave me quite to myself for working, and going out or coming in when I like; and they have a large house with a good library, so that I am quite comfortable. I shall go home again in a day or two, not to abuse their hospitality too long.

I wonder how much longer you are staying at Gloucester. I like to think of you being there until October, but perhaps it will be cold by then. I see that the first draft is being called up soon.

I must get back to work. It is Sunday, and I must make the most of it. After all, without working very hard, I think the times we live in would be unendurable.

Always your very devoted son
Tom

Vivien Eliot TO *Mary Hutchinson* — MS Texas

Saturday [8? September 1917] South View, Bosham

Dear Mrs Hutchinson

I am not sending back your story[2] today because I want you to let me show it to my husband – will you? I know he would be so interested, and I enjoyed it immensely – it is so vivid and amusing. You *must* let me show it to him. Please write me a line and say yes. I will take great care of it – and you shall have it back as quickly as possible.

I must really go back on Monday – there are ever so many reasons. So write to 18 Crawford Mansions (W.1) to say if I may show it. Of course I will not until I hear.

1 – TSE was to receive a flat fee of £1 per lecture.
2 – MH's story 'War' was to be published by TSE in *Egoist* 4: 10 (Dec. 1917).

I enjoyed our talk. I hope I shall see you in London.

Yours
Vivien Eliot

TO *His Mother* MS Houghton

12 September 1917 [18 Crawford Mansions]

My dearest Mother,

I have begun to be very busy the last few days preparing my lectures. One set covers very much the same ground as my lectures at Southall last year, but more broadly, beginning with 'The Makers of 19th Century Ideas', lectures on Carlyle, Mill, Arnold, Huxley, Spencer, Ruskin, Morris – then the poets, and then the novelists.[1] I have never read much of George Eliot, the Brontës, Charles Reade, or the Kingsleys. I have read *The Mill on the Floss* and *Wuthering Heights* last week. The other course is a continuation of last year's;[2] they want me to start with Emerson, go on to Samuel Butler and Wm. Morris, then the Pre-Raphaelites, and so on. Both of these courses depend for their continuance upon the enrolment at the first few lectures, so I am waiting anxiously. The first lecture is on the 28th. The preparation keeps me fairly well occupied, along with the *Egoist*, the *New Statesman*, the Spanish Irregular verbs, and the subject of Foreign Exchange, which I find very knotty in the books on the subject. I am behindhand with Jourdain too. I have been trying to read May Sinclair's *Defence of Idealism* to review for the *Statesman* and Jourdain.[3] She is better known as a novelist. Did you ever hear of her? She is a pleasant little person; I have met her several times.

Vivien will be back in a day or two, and will no doubt begin cleaning at once. I have been looking after myself, and the rooms have not been cleaned for ever so long. I make oatmeal overnight and warm it in the

1–Starting on 28 Sept., TSE was to give a course of twenty-five lectures on Victorian Literature at the County Secondary School, Sydenham, under the auspices of the London County Council.

2–See TSE, 'Syllabus for a Tutorial Class in Modern English Literature, Second Year's Work' (1917); in Schuchard, *Eliot's Dark Angel*, 41–4. His salary was raised to £70 for the year.

3–TSE's unsigned review appeared in *NS*, 22 Sept. 1917, but he did not succeed in placing a second notice either in Jourdain's philosophical journals or in the *Egoist* (letter to EP, 23 Sept.). Already a fellow of the Royal Society of Literature, May Sinclair (1863–1946), author of *The Three Sisters* (1914), became the first woman member of the Aristotelian Society after publication of *A Defence of Idealism*, and was among the first novelists to use ideas from psychoanalysis. TSE was to publish her story 'The Victim' in C. 1: 1 (Oct. 1922).

morning. She is going to bring up quantities of blackberries to make jam.

London has been having perfect weather lately; I only hope you have had as good. I am sorry you intend to leave Gloucester early, but I suppose as you say it is very expensive. You have had Charlotte and the children for a long time; it must be fatiguing at times. I should like to know what Theodora is like now. I suppose very tall.

When I was at Bosham I wished that I could take you out sailing there. I don't regret all the sailing that you and I and father did together, I assure you!

Your devoted son
Tom

I am sorry Henry does not get away.
I should like some ice cream.

Vivien Eliot TO *Mary Hutchinson* MS Texas

Wednesday [12? September 1917] 18 Crawford Mansions

Dear Mrs Hutchinson,

Here is your story – and my husband is ever so pleased with it. He is going to write to tell you so. I admire you very much.

Yes, please do what you can to find me a cottage – it is the one thing I want. But I forgot to tell you it must be unfurnished. I have so much furniture I want to get rid of from here. Besides, I shd. hate other people's furniture.

It would have been nice to have stayed a few days with you. I wish I could have.

It really is not bad to be back again. It is nice to see people once more, when I am away I am apt to forget that people – friends – really *are* important.

Let me know when you come back, and you *must* come here and see us. We shall both like that. Meanwhile let me hear the minute you can, about the cottage, and do go on writing!

Yrs.
Vivien Eliot

TO *His Mother* — MS Houghton

19 September 1917 [London]

Dearest Mother,

I shall send this to St Louis, as I am sure that you will be there by the time this arrives. It has seemed like winter here today. The clocks have been put back to solar time, so that what *was* half past six last week is half past five now; so it seems dark much earlier; and today has been a rainy dark day like winter. Saturday still seemed summer; it was hot and cloudless; I spent the afternoon on the river with a man in the bank[1] who owns a 'sailing canoe'; they are tiny little boats like toys. You sit on the edge of the cockpit with your knees up to your chin. A breath makes them move, but they are very steady. There was no wind, and the water was covered with rowboats and punts and canoes; still, it seemed like sailing.

Vivien came back Monday afternoon, after a very crowded and tiring journey; with a quantity of blackberries, which she has made into delicious jam, working all day yesterday; so she is now quite exhausted. She is better on the whole, I think, but she had a severe migraine today in consequence of her efforts.

I had a pleasant evening with Professor Hocking of Harvard a few days ago. He was just returning. He is a very nice man, but not very intelligent. He had been invited (among others) to come over and inspect conditions here and report them in America – saying of course whatever he likes. He did not impress me as having learned much. I should like to see [James] Woods. He is much more alert.

I am busy reading Emerson. He strikes me as very wordy. He has something to say often, but he spreads it out and uses very general terms; it seems more oratory than literature. His biography is interesting, and contains many familiar names.

I must stop now. It is late.

Your very devoted son
Tom

No letter from you so far this week.

1–James de Vine Aylward (1871–1966) had been a painter of horses and a pupil of Bouguereau (1825–1905) before the war. He was to publish a monograph, *The Small-Sword in England* (1945; rev. edn, 1960), as well as *The House of Angelo* (1953) and *The English Master* (1956). Fluent in French and German, he became TSE's assistant in the Foreign Intelligence Bureau at Lloyds Bank, and was a great support during his domestic problems.

TO *Julian Huxley*[1] MS Fondren

19 September 1917 18 Crawford Mansions

Dear Huxley,

It is very pleasant to hear that you are back in London, for a time at least. Certainly we shall meet, so far as it depends on me, but probably I shall not lunch with you or anyone else for thirty-five years – *except* on Saturdays. Are you free on that day, or do you go out of town? I could be depended on for 1.30; all other days I snatch half an hour in Cheapside. Otherwise, we must arrange another hour. I should like you to come here as soon as our autumn cleaning is over; my wife has just got back from the country and as I have been doing some cooking in her absence there is some filth.

Hoping to see you soon,

Sincerely,
T. S. Eliot

Is Aldous[2] at Garsington? I have not heard from him.

TO *Mary Hutchinson* MS Texas

19 September 1917 18 Crawford Mansions

Dear Mrs Hutchinson,

Vivien showed me your story ['War'], but unfortunately through misunderstanding sent it back before I meant her to. I enjoyed it very much. It may seem gratuitous for me to give any opinion when I haven't been asked – and I have never written a story in my life. I thought yours was *very* well written. There were only a few phrases I should have dared to question (I think the words 'sharp' and 'incisive' and one or two others – I wish I had it here). The descriptive part seemed to me the best *written* – the more mature and final choice of words; but the situation seemed to me very firmly grasped and handled, and it doesn't suggest any literary precedent that I know. The only fault I find (and I am not sure that the fault is present, or even that it is a fault) is – it struck me (I have only read

1–Julian Huxley (1887–1975), zoologist, writer, philosopher and administrator. After enlisting in the spring he had been commissioned into the Intelligence Unit of the Army Service Corps. After WW1, he would return to his career as a zoologist: his works include *Essays of a Biologist* (1923).

2–While still at Balliol College, Julian's brother Aldous was a frequent visitor to Garsington. After Oxford, he taught at Eton for a year, starting this month.

it twice) that you had got thoroughly *inside* the feelings, but hadn't quite got *out* again. I like to feel that a writer is perfectly cool and detached, regarding other people's feelings or his own, like a God who has got beyond them; or a person who has dived very deep and comes up holding firmly some hitherto unseen submarine creature. But this sort of cold detachment is so *very* rare – and *stupid* detachment is so much the rule, that it may be only a particular taste.

It is temeritous of me to ask for contributions for the *Egoist*, as I have above me a nice but timid person[1] who likes to stick to old standbys, or else take the remains of Arthur Symons and Yone Noguchi,[2] and with very small space we have two novels on our hands – Lewis's now and Joyce's next book next – but if you were willing to let me have the manuscript in January say, I should like to try to get it in, and I think I could. Will you let me know if you are willing?

I hope we shall see you before very long.

Yours sincerely,
T. S. Eliot

TO *Ezra Pound* MS Beinecke

23 September 1917 18 Crawford Mansions

Dear Ezra

Forgive me. Lecture tomorrow night, also Weaver on my path. Lecture Friday & Appleplex on the brain.[3] Shall make no engagements hereafter, but may try to find time after business one day, taking chances.

Should like to do a short notice on May Sinclair's book for the *Egoist*. I wish Dora did not have to have the very front,[4] as I should like to do monthly series of pungent paragraphs (not necessarily all by one hand) instead of my articles, which I feel have been of inferior quality. One could easily turn out a number of them in four weeks, whereas one does an article all at one go.

1–Harriet Shaw Weaver.

2–Yone Noguchi (1875–1947), poet and essayist who wrote in English and Japanese, and had been acclaimed by Symons.

3–EP was pressing TSE to submit the second part of his experimental dialogue 'Eeldrop and Appleplex', which was to be published in *Little Review* 4: 5 (Sept. 1917).

4–Each issue of *Egoist* began with a philosophical essay by contributing editor Dora Marsden.

Weaver is sending for James.[1] Thursday – I thought too many women – it lowers the tone: not up to the Café Magry: perhaps there should be a special evening for males only, as well as this. Eeldrop on the feminisation of modern society.

Yrs.
T.

TO *Julian Huxley* MS Fondren

23 September 1917 18 Crawford Mansions

Dear Huxley

I got away from the City at 1.15, but under the impression that Waterloo Bridge was near Waterloo Place I did not find my way to Lancaster Place till 1.45. As I could not identify any of the offices as yours I hung about in the hall for some time and then decided that you had gone. It is most deplorable that I should have missed you as Saturday seems to be the only day available and I may be out of town next Saturday. Perhaps you would drop in some evening for coffee?

Yours
T. S. Eliot

TO *His Mother* MS Houghton

3 October[2] 1917 18 Crawford Mansions

My dearest Mother,

I have several letters to thank you for. First for the letter enclosing the birthday cheque, which shall be devoted to the purpose for which you intended it. I shall let you know as soon as I have purchased the flannels. Then for two letters dated September 2 and September 14, one about Rupture. I had forgotten that it was congenital – I thought it was due to an early accident.

I suppose you are back in St Louis now.

We are going to try to find rooms outside of London, not too far for me to come up every day. It is absolutely imperative; we cannot stand the

1–TSE was preparing a special 'Henry James' issue of *Egoist* (Jan. 1918), to which EP contributed a review of *The Middle Years: Autobiographical Reminiscences* (1917).
2–Misdated September.

strain of moonlight nights in London.[1] Last week was a great strain. We spent Saturday and Sunday night in the country, and I persuaded Vivien to spend Monday night there too, as I had to go out to lecture. Now the weather has changed to stormy, so we feel a bit easier; still, we should prefer to be west of London, and I am sure you will agree.

My old course of lectures at Southall has started off on its second year with very good promise; the new course is still inchoate.

Don't talk about not seeing me again; it is too painful, and besides you *shall* see me again. I remember all those occasions you mention, and a great many more, usually beginning with the 'little Tailor' and the firelight on the ceiling.[2] But you must not doubt that you will see me directly the war is over.

I *must* go to bed now.

Vivien is going to write tomorrow. She has simply not been able to write letters, and she has had all the housework and part of the washing to do for some time.

Your very devoted son
Tom

Vivien Eliot TO *Mary Hutchinson* — MS Texas

9 October [1917] — 18 Crawford Mansions

Thanks so much for yr. letter. I made Tom ring up Malleson[3] (before I heard from you) – I was glad I did as they seemed rather sour about it! I went [house-hunting] to Chesham and Wendover but never found Cholesbury, and I had the most depressing and damping experiences at both those places. They were filled with the East End of London. Horrible Jews in plush coats by the million.

I haven't done anything since, out of sheer inertia – and also my time has been *entirely* occupied in washing up greasy dishes. You have no idea the sort of feelings that take possession of me on discovering, at 11.30 at night, that the bed is not made!! But I believe I have got a woman now. Anyhow she *said* she would come tomorrow, but I don't trust her.

Bertie now says he wants to go shares in a country cottage. That will probably mean being out of the frying pan but *in* the fire! However as

1 – When the danger of German bombing raids was greatest.

2 – TSE returns to memories of this song in a letter to his mother of 12 Jan. 1919.

3 – Miles Malleson (1888–1969), actor and director, whose wife Lady Constance (1895–1975) used the stage name Colette O'Neil.

I have NO money, and insufficient energy, the plan has its merits. We are going forth to hunt, in a few days.

Huxley[1] was here on Saturday and spoke very nicely of you – he quoted a saying of Gertler's[2] that rather amused us – viz. that the Mallesons might be said to keep '*open bed*'. It's true, from all I hear!

I *do* hope you are finding servants. I would offer to help, but it would be a farce. If I *do* get this cottage or house, you will come, won't you, and bring people? It will be so funny.

I go on looking forward to seeing you when you come back.

Yours
Vivien Eliot

TO *His Mother* — MS Houghton

14 October 1917 [London]

My dearest Mother

I have not written to you or heard from you for ever so long, and it is winter, now that I am writing to St Louis again. I always think of return to St Louis as meaning Concord grapes on the table[3] in the blue fruit basket, and Stephen[4] washing the brick side walk, and the smell of new school books, Latin and Greek and Geometry. But enough of the smell of school books since then! I am always thankful to be done with teaching. My work has been very light lately. Both my courses of lectures are, I think, assured; as enough members have enrolled for each; whereat I am much rejoiced, as it is rather a compliment to a class to exist at all at the present time, and also, we shall need the money very much this winter. So I shall have my hands just as full as I expected; and it is a good thing to be so busy that one cannot take time to worry much about the present condition of the world and the future of civilisation. Also I take a great deal of pleasure in *The Egoist*; struggling as it is, it is known to some of the most intelligent people, and it stands for something which needs to be kept going; the fact

1–AH wrote to OM that he had gone to town and 'found Eliot crouching with Bertie Russell over a dying fire. Our conversation consisted of long silences occasionally interrupted by Bertie saying something, like "How good it would be to exterminate the whole human race."' (Texas)

2–Mark Gertler (1891–1939), artist.

3–'In the smell of grapes on the autumn table' (*The Dry Salvages*, l. 13).

4–Stephen was the janitor who used to tease TSE when he was a small boy by holding a piece of bread to the fire between his toes and pretending to fall asleep. As TSE danced agitatedly about, Stephen would open an eye and murmur: 'Some nigger's foot's burnin'.'

that it is practically the only publication, except perhaps technical ones, which makes no reference to politics or the war, and that it can keep on its way determined to assert the perpetual importance of other things, is itself important; even though it is possible to get only a small number of the good contributors who were possible a few years ago. I ought to be pretty well satisfied with my life then, in a way, seeing that I can name almost no one whose life has not been thoroughly disorganised in the last three years. Besides, everything I do is interesting, in different ways; the only permanent good I get out of the lectures however is a vast amount of miscellaneous reading and a certain practice in public speaking.

I must stop now. We have had no luck in finding rooms in the country – everything near London is taken – I doubt whether we shall get out of London at all. I am anxious, of course, but these are not matters we can ~~speak~~ write about.

We have had an excellent woman to come in the last few days, which I am very glad of, as Vivien has been doing all the work, including the washing, and it is really beyond her strength, and leaves her neither strength nor time for anything else, even for her own clothes.

Your devoted son
Tom.

Vivien Eliot TO *Charlotte C. Eliot* — MS Houghton

22 October 1917 — Sewhurst Farm, Abinger Common, Surrey

Dear Mrs Eliot

I hope you got my short letter written last week. I thanked you for the money for Tom's underwear. It is not spent yet, as I had a great rush and life was very difficult for the last few weeks. But it shall be spent to the best advantage. So far we have not needed to go into thicker clothes as the weather has been wonderfully good all this month. *Too* good, as you will perhaps have read in the papers. The weather always does seem to favour the Germans, in an extraordinary way! It is always wet when we are trying to advance, in France, and beautiful and cloudless at the times of full moon, when they get their chance to make our lives in London a misery to us.

I told you that we had decided to search (probably in vain) for a tiny cottage, somewhere within very easy reach of town. The only way to do that is to take some neighbourhood as a centre and to stay there for a time, hunting all around. I spent much time and money in correspondence, trying to get rooms near enough for Tom to go up and down each day while I hunted but of sixteen addresses I had not one could take us, except this one – which we discovered, *when* we arrived, to be six miles from the nearest station!! It was a great disappointment, for of course it means that Tom can only be here at weekends. We came on the 20th and had a lovely weekend, and Tom left early this morning. Each day I am going to walk, or go short distances by train, and to do my utmost to discover a small cottage or hut. This is, in my opinion, and in Tom's too, now – the most beautiful country in England. It is all hills and miles and miles of pine forests – with stretches of heath – heather and bracken and bushes – in between. It is very wild although so near to London, and very *very* healthy. If only I could find something in this part! But the more I hear the more improbable it seems – in this part or in any other. You will of course know that we should not be contemplating this thing if it did not seem essential, and likely to become *more* so. We always are, and have been, very careful of what we put in our letters, for of course it is necessary that the censorship about some things must be very strict. Besides, one doesn't care to have one's letters destroyed! But it is rather hard not to be able to explain things in detail to you. I am sure if you were here you would urge us to try to find something in the country. You see we are bound to keep on the flat, for several reasons. If it were not that Tom considers it absolutely necessary to have all his books about him, (and it *is* necessary) we could wander about and not be so fixed. But we can't wander with fifty or 100 books – to say nothing of papers – typewriters, and all the other business! Tom now gives two lectures a week, as I expect he has told you, on Mondays and Fridays, and that *necessitates* those two nights being spent in London at least. The lectures are both in outlying districts – at opposite ends of London. He never gets back before 11. Another point is that it is very difficult indeed to let a flat now – almost impossible I think. And ours, you see, is nearly a top one. So the only thing to do, if one does anything, is to get some cheap cottage to spend as much time as possible at. My people were in the country nearly all the summer, they are just at home now for a fortnight, but are leaving again this week. I have had a great deal of country myself in the last four months – about eight weeks on and off! and I am so *much* better for it. I have not felt so well since we were married. You see, after I got back from Bosham, I had only been at home a week when I got a very severe attack of influenza, from a germ. The doctor said there was a slight epidemic of it just then, and you know what I am when influenza is about! Well, I had a good deal of fever, and was very bad for some days. I had to get in a strange woman – and she only stayed two days, as she caught it from me. Then I had no one. The doctor meanwhile had sternly forbidden me to get out of bed. But while it was still at its height there were two air raids – the first a bad one. So I had to get out of bed each night and go down in the cellars for an hour or two – and the wonder to me is that I got over that attack as quickly as I did. Directly I was able my parents wired for me to go to them (in Sussex) and so I was back in the country two weeks after I left Bosham. I stayed with them for a week, and Tom came for two days. Then I came back and had everything to put in order again, and got on with my interrupted cleaning of the flat. After so much absence, and coming and going, and Tom there alone, it was much more than filthy. Then we decided on this plan – and I thought I had better get hold of a good woman, temporarily. Tom's health *does* suffer by our not keeping a woman if I have to be away. While I was at Bosham he was invited by some very good friends of ours who live quite close to us, to make his home with them. They begged him to stay on a *long* visit – promised to leave him alone and undisturbed, put a sitting room at his disposal, and did all they could about it. The result was that Tom stayed for three days, under pressure, and then insisted on returning to the empty flat, saying he could not work anywhere else. He was very thin when I got back, and of course the truth is that he *is* over worked, and it needs colossal efforts to keep him averagely well. So, seeing that to find this cottage I should have to be coming and going – and as a most remarkable servant was *sent* to me without any effort of mine, in a curious way – I instantly decided to engage her, *temporarily*. She was installed for ten days before we came here, and I found her a most wonderful person. I have never had anyone like her, she is clean and hard-working, an excellent cook and a most finished servant altogether. Also I could see she had common sense, and is very economical. I feel now *perfectly* confident that Tom is at any rate well looked after and fed, when he is at home.

I do hope you and Mr Eliot are keeping well. Please do not worry over Tom too much – we shall be quite allright, we are very cautious people, and Tom is really getting on awfully well. One can't help feeling proud of him – he is doing so well at the Bank, and everyone there likes him so and they seem anxious to advance him. He is giving very interesting lectures this year, I enjoy them immensely, especially the Southall ones (the same people as last year). If only the war were over and we could all come together – I am looking forward so much to going to America. You can see I have a great deal there to draw me – all Tom's family, and his friends, and my one and only great friend, Lucy Thayer, whom you met. Next to my family she is most important to me, and she is not able to get back to me here.

This farm is quite ideal, a sort of fairy tale farm. An old house, of course, right on the steep side of a high hill – surrounded by pine trees. Only a cart track leads up to it. How I wish I could send you some pictures of it.

Hoping you will write soon.

Affectly
Vivien

TO *His Mother*

MS Houghton

24 October 1917

The Egoist, Oakley House,
Bloomsbury St, London, W.C.

My dearest Mother,

I just wanted to write you a line as I did not by the last mail, though it is now late. I was very glad to get your letter and father's this morning, and to have a little news. You made me reflect that I am most often very inexpressive in my letters. But I am constantly thinking of you and picturing you in past scenes, and trying to picture me in the present. There are so many things I don't like to think of, because I think often that I used to be very selfish and self-indulgent in many ways, and quite unappreciative of your and father's kindness and generosity. Now, of course, when the time has gone by, I think of these things, and there is nothing I can do – I cannot even write letters as often as I want to.

We spent last Sunday in a most delightful farm, hidden away in the Surrey hills, about an hour and a half from town. There is a very nice farmer and his wife who do not take lodgers regularly, but they had formerly been gardeners to Lord Russell and to the Trevelyans, and so they took us in. The farm is in a little hollow in the hills, very high, surrounded by a ring of pine woods, broken only by a little narrow yellow winding road that wanders down into the valley. It is four miles from a village, completely in a forest; but you can walk about two miles and emerge suddenly on the top of Leith Hill, precipitous on the other side, with a view wide over the downs of Surrey and Sussex. We had beautiful weather too. I took down books and prepared my lecture on William Morris. I no longer *write* them–I set down about three pages of notes. Vivien says I am getting better and better as a lecturer.

Tonight it is raining torrents, which rejoices me. I must go to bed now.

with Very much love
your devoted son
Tom

TO *His Father* TS Houghton

31 October 1917

18 Crawford Mansions,
Crawford St, W.1

My dear father,

I have had two nice letters from you and mother this week, from St Louis. I wish there was one day when I could always look forward to getting your letters, but the mails are irregular, and I never know when they will turn up. Still, it is always a surprise. I am very busy with my lectures, as I give one on Fridays and one on Mondays, I have hardly finished one before I begin to think of the next. But they cost me far less in effort and time than they used to; I only make a couple of pages of notes now, and I can talk away for an hour or more. When I began, I used to try to get too much into the time, which I believe made the lectures difficult to follow; now I make them very thin, and press a few simple ideas without many qualifications, and my audience keeps awake. I never thought that I should ever be even a passable public speaker, but now I believe I could almost speak extempore. The feeling of power which you get by speaking from very brief notes is pleasant. I remember that the first lecture I gave, in Yorkshire,[1] I had written all out and tried to memorise, and when I came to deliver it I found that I had quite enough for two hours talk!

As you know, Vivien has been in Surrey, which suits her very well, and I have been with her over weekends. This will be the last. We shall be very sorry, as the country there is very beautiful, and the climate delightful, and the farmer's family very kind, and the home made butter and fresh eggs and home killed fowl very good.

Most of my spare time after lectures goes in to the *Egoist* editing. It is good practice editing a small paper, but very difficult under present conditions, when there are so few people to write, and those mostly poor stuff. I struggle to keep the writing as much as possible in Male hands, as I distrust the Feminine in literature, and also, once a woman has had anything printed in your paper, it is very difficult to make her see why you should not print everything she sends in. It is bad enough in a bank. My typist is in a bad temper now because I gave a couple of letters to do to someone else who happened to have nothing to do at the moment. The trouble is in some cases (as my typist) that the women in business don't have to work, but if the men are away and they have no children or are

1 – At Ilkley. Asked for their opinion of the lecturer the class is reported to have said that he seemed a nice young man but he would fiddle with his watchchain (Valerie Eliot).

unmarried they want something to do; so not being wholly dependent on their salary they are rather *in*dependent, and sometimes irritating to men who *are* dependent on their salary. Of course such women are a minority, as there are very few incomes which don't need supplementing nowadays, but there is a certain number.

I am going on with Spanish, mostly at lunch times; and they let me have all the Spanish and Italian and Portuguese financial papers for myself.

I must stop now. Write soon again please.

Your very affectionate son
Tom

TO *Eleanor Hinkley* TS Houghton

31 October 1917 18 Crawford Mansions

My dear Eleanor,

This is I believe only a short note, to acknowledge and thank you for your two letters, both of which I very much enjoyed. This is not the first Sunday of the Month, but on that date I hope to be in Surrey (the garden of England). Vivien has been there for a fortnight, and I have joined her on Sundays. It is really a part of England which you must see some time. It is only an hour or so from London, but some of the most beautiful country that I have seen in England. It is mostly large estates, and very lonely from Dorking on. We have been at a farm two miles from Abinger Common, and Abinger Common is three miles from Abinger Hammer, and the latter is a mile from the nearest station, Gomshall, so you see how remote it is. The farmer happened to have been a gardener in the family of some people we know, and he does not take lodgers regularly. His farm is very high up, the lane is steep, between tall pines, all the way from the station, the farm in a little hollow of the highest hill, with a ring of pinetrees all about it, and a little rivulet trickling down into the valley. The pigs play about, and we can have fresh milk, and home made butter. Two miles away is Leith Hill, which looks for miles over the downs of Surrey and Sussex. It is the sort of country where old farmers touch their hats and call you 'gentry'.

I have not time to write much at present, and my regular work for the *Egoist* takes up most of that. I am trying to make up a Henry James number at present, as three of his posthumous works have just appeared.[1]

1–Henry James, *The Sense of the Past*, *The Ivory Tower* and *The Middle Years*. The 'Henry James' number of the *Egoist* (Jan. 1918) was to open with TSE's 'In Memory of Henry James'.

But there are very few people to write nowadays; all the old lot is broken up, and only drivellers left. I am just writing to ask May Sinclair for something, but I don't believe she will. I have just been invited by a certain Madame Vandervelde,[1] a very dull woman, to contribute to a reading of poets, and what a poor lot they are! the only one who has any merit is a youth named Siegfried Sassoon (semitic) and his stuff is better politics than poetry.[2]

I must stop now. I told you it was only a note of acknowledgment. As I write during business hours, 'trusting to hear from you in due course'.

Affectionately
Tom.

TO *Ezra Pound* — TS Beinecke

31 October 1917 [London]

My dear Ezra,

I return the enclosed card or memo. Would you oblige with further particulars? WHO is Lynch? Irish? WHAT female talent, besides Weaver?

MR Pallister's communication shall be used. I had overlooked the Anglo-French Society, Ltd., you read the papers more thoroughly than I do. Burnham is a Jew merchant, named Lawson (*sc.* Levi-sohn?)[3]

Upward[4] answers on Club paper and asks me for the one day when I said I could not come. Businesslike?

I have been invited by female VANDERVELDE to contribute to a reading of pOETS: big wigs, OSWALD and EDITH Shitwell,[5] Graves[6]

1-Lalla Vandervelde (1870–1964), wife of Emile Vandervelde, Belgian Socialist politician.

2-Siegfried Sassoon (1886–1967), poet and memoirist, had joined the Royal Welch Fusiliers in 1915, but returned to England to convalesce in Apr. 1917, and published his war poems, *The Old Huntsman*, in May. With BR and JMM, he then drafted a public statement denouncing the war which was circulated in July. As a result he was sent to Craiglockhart sanatorium in Scotland, where he befriended and encouraged Wilfred Owen.

3-In the *Egoist* (Dec.), T. H. Pallister recorded the founding of the Anglo-French Society in London. Its president was Harry Levy-Lawson (2nd Baron Burnham, 1916; Viscount Burnham, 1919), proprietor of the *Daily Telegraph*, whose grandfather, Joseph Moses Levy, had originally been the newspaper's printer.

4-Allen Upward (1863–1926), barrister, author of *The Divine Mystery* (1913).

5-Between 1916 and 1921, the Sitwells – Edith (1887–1964), and her brothers Osbert (1892–1969) and Sacheverell (1897–1988) – each published their poems in the annual *Wheels* anthologies.

6-Robert Graves (1895–1985), poet, novelist and critic. Having joined the Royal Welch Fusiliers in 1914, he was convalescing in England after being wounded in France in June 1917.

(query, George?) Nichols, and OTHERS. Shall I oblige them with our old friend COLUMBO? or Bolo, since famous?

One day Columbo went below
To see the ship's physician:
'It's this way, doc' he said said he
I just cant stop a-pissin' . . .

or

King Bolo's big black kukquheen
Was fresh as ocean breezes.
She burst aboard Columbo's ship
With a cry of gentle Jesus.

After all, you say nothing about the Dear old Men,[1] so I suppose you want to get Out of it.

Yrs ever
TSE

TO *His Mother*

MS Houghton

15 November 1917

The Egoist, Oakley House,
Bloomsbury St, W.C.

My dearest Mother,

I have your letter of October 22, and feel very sad at not having written on your birthday [22 Oct.]. And I can hardly believe that you are seventy-four. No one would know it. You are certainly the most wonderful woman of seventy-four I have ever heard of, and I am very proud of you. I should be glad to think of having half your force and youth at that age. You don't know how much satisfaction it has been to me through the last two years to think that I have parents whom I can be so convincedly proud of, who represent to me absolutely the best that America can produce; and by right of whom I feel that I can claim equality with anybody. Just to have ordinary good commonplace parents would be inconceivably depressing – would destroy one's confidence in all directions.

Vivien has been trying to get a place (against my wishes) in a government office, and she has failed; they tell her that having married an American is a complete bar. I am only sorry because I am afraid she will now want to

1 – EP's 'I Vecchii' ('Mœurs Contemporains' VII) opens: 'They will come no more, / The old men with beautiful manners', and alludes to Henry James. TSE is reminding EP of his promise to review *The Middle Years.*

look elsewhere, and would take something where the people are less agreeable and the hours longer than in a Government office. I do not think she could stand the sort of work she would be given to do in a Bank; the hours are too long, she would have to arrive at the same time, 9, every day in spite of sleepless nights and headaches, work probably in a noisy office. It would be much harder on her than on me, even if she had my health; I am in a particularly nice department where I am rather petted. She is possessed with the idea that she ought to earn money, and if she had average health and could find congenial work, I should not object. But I should be very much alarmed, as it is.

I don't think I have anything else of importance to mention this time. I am writing at the Bank, having hurried back from Lunch to do so.

I am much interested in the letter you have from the Mayor of Remilly.[1]

Your very loving son
Tom.

TO *Mary Hutchinson* MS Texas

15 November 1917

18 Crawford Mansions,
Crawford St, W.1

Dear Mrs Hutchinson,

I have been meaning to write to tell you about your 'War', but I had looked forward to seeing you on Sunday, and so postponed it. The Weaver found that she did not have room, and printed a rather bad story instead.[2] It turns out that your story is longish and will occupy about three pages, so we are taking the liberty of printing it in December; when there will be more room, as *Tarr* is at an end this month.[3] The number will be sent you 'in due course'. We are very grateful to have your story for the December number, as it is otherwise vacuous; and the January number is devoted to Henry James, and after that we hope to have some of Joyce's new novel on hand.[4]

I am looking forward to discussing the story with you in detail.

Vivien is very anxious about a 'shabby old pin' which she thinks she left at your house. It was given her by a Russian anarchist, and precious by

1 – CCE's letter does not survive.
2 – Iris Barry, 'Pay Agatha Penrhys . . .', *Egoist* 4: 10 (Nov. 1917), 157–8.
3 – The *Egoist* was to serialise *Tarr*, by WL.
4 – The *Egoist* published episodes II, III, VI and X of *Ulysses*.

associations. A sort of flat oblong head and the pin part very bent. If you find it she would like you to keep it until she sees you again.

Sincerely yours
T. S. Eliot

I will ask Weaver to send you the proofs, but it usually demurs – however I shall insist. But if you make changes besides corrections, Weaver will have fits, as all changes have to be paid for.

TO *Bertrand Russell* MS McMaster

Sunday [November 1917?] The Dolphin Hotel, Chichester

Dear Bertie

Have just found that they have two single rooms at this hotel, so thought I had better book them. I found I could let you know by post instead of wiring, as post leaves at 10 p.m. If you object to this better wire at once. V. has quite worn herself out trying to find a place – there is not an inch of room anywhere. Fearful crowds.

Yrs
Tom.

TO *His Father* MS Houghton

22 November 1917 *The Egoist*, Oakley House,
Bloomsbury St, London, W.C.

My dear Father,

I have just half an hour now at the end of the day, and can write a letter I should have written last night had I not had to finish an article I was writing. We were as a matter of fact supposed to go to a small dance last night, but when the time came Vivien had caught a chill and I had other things to do, and we did not go. H. G. Wells and a lot of people of that sort were to be there. Vivien has not been very well ever since she got back from the country. She was very anxious to get into a government office; and she had applied, and had an interview with a Board which asked her all sorts of questions, then kept her in suspense some days and then flatly rejected her. She was very much disappointed. But I disapproved of the plan from the first, as I am sure she could not stand it. She is ever so much healthier in the country, and I should be delighted if we could find a small cottage, such as she and Miss Thayer had before quite near town at 8/-

(eight shillings) a week. And of course at the present time she is very nervous in town.

I suppose everyone is busy at home with knitting. After reading the poem you sent, I suggest that you should do what my old head master Mr Kelly[1] at Highgate did. He had a small lathe, and turned crutches beautifully, and you could make just as good ones. He made them long, to be cut to size afterwards. The wood (old broomsticks) was provided by some red cross agency. Other people made splints, and bedtables, and other things. However, I think you have done as much as anyone can be expected to do in one lifetime.

I must stop now, or I shall be turned out of the Bank by the cleaners. You mentioned money. I find I have had £55 from you this year, and if I could have the other £10 of the rent I should be very grateful. I shall run pretty low shortly (on my current account) and the rise in my salary and the first instalment on my lectures does not come until January. I have a sneaking hope they may raise me more than they said they would; the manager told me the other day that I had done extremely well with a difficult job; but reason tells me that the larger increase will not be for another six months.

With very much love
Your devoted son
Tom.

Will you cable the money?

Vivien Eliot TO *Charlotte C. Eliot* — MS Houghton

Thursday 22 November 1917 — 18 Crawford Mansions, Crawford St, W.1

Dear Mrs Eliot

At last I can send you an account of the money you sent for T.'s underclothing. I waited for Mother to be able to go with me, and so far the weather has been, and *is*, so unusually warm that neither Tom nor I have made any change in our underclothing since the summer! It is a good thing in a way, but it is *very* damp and enervating at present. I hope you will not be disappointed that the money only reached to so few things. The fact is that *woollens* of all kinds are just double (at least) what they were, and are getting ever more expensive. We went carefully thro' all Tom's winter underwear, and found that the *vests* he has are very much thicker and also much less worn than the pants. (I think you call them 'underdrawers' – Tom

1–E. H. Kelly was Master of Highgate Junior School, 1903–23.

objects to the word 'pants', but it is always used here!) The vests, with some more darning are quite good for another winter, but the pants are all thin and almost beyond further mending. So we thought we had better get just two good pairs of pants – and have done so. They are very thick and good quality. *I enclose receipts*. There was just 6d over – and it was no use getting one of anything, so Mother advised getting this chest protector – as Tom always has a tickling cough in the winter. The chest protector is quilted satin, and fits round the neck and has a double breasted chest part. It is particularly valuable for when he goes out in evening dress – which leaves the chest much less protected than in day clothes. My father has one of these, and Maurice did when he wore civilian clothes – ('civvies', as they are called).

So I hope you will think the money was made good use of. Tom has a good stock of socks, for I bought him some a few months ago, and many of his old thick ones are still very good. He is still worse provided with pyjamas than anything, although I got him two pairs in the summer. The others, the old ones, are now nearly all in rags. He is very rough with his pyjamas, and shirts – tears them unmercifully! I should have liked him to have a new winter suit, but he is wearing his old dark brown one, and altho' very shabby it is still intact. His overcoats are very shabby too. However, he need not be *cold* this winter.

I was so sorry when I heard that I had missed your birthday. I should have liked to send you something. For Xmas I shall send you a little crochet lace I have made myself – I am afraid it is rather useless –

I cannot find a country cottage anywhere. The rush out of London has been incredible. It is a pity, as B. R. has promised to go shares with us in the rent of it, as he needs some quiet place of refuge himself. We did not intend it *instead* of living in town. Tom finds it essential to have his headquarters in London, we simply longed for a refuge, somewhere we *could* go to at any time when things are bad in town. For weekends, too. But I am afraid the scheme must be abandoned. I have already spent more money than I could spare on going about to look for such a place.

I do so often wish we were in America. The very minute the war is over we shall do our utmost to come, but the 'end of the war' seems further off than ever.

Tom has told you that I tried to get work but was refused on account of my 'nationality'.

With love to you and Mr Eliot,

Affectionately
Vivien

I hope you received my letter from the country, a few weeks ago.

To The Editor of The Egoist[1]

Published December 1917

Your writer on 'Elizabethan Classicists'[2] struck me, if I may say so without offence, as straining with youthful zeal after original opinions. His attempted rehabilitation of Ovid merely shows that the true taste for the Classics has gone out with the old classical curriculum; and as for his belittling of Milton[3] – well, I do not believe that he could get a single one of the living Masters of criticism (Mr Edmund Gosse, for example, or Sir Sidney Colvin) to even entertain such views.

J. A. D. Spence
Thridlingston Grammar School.

. . . I have, I pride myself, kept abreast of the times in literature; at least, if I have not, the times have moved very speedily indeed. I was therefore surprised, in what was otherwise an intelligent review (so far as I can judge, without having read the authors mentioned), to find Rupert Brooke dismissed abruptly with the words 'He is not absent.'[4] Brooke's early poems exhibit a youthful exuberance of passion, and an occasional coarseness of utterance, which offended finer tastes; but these were but dross which, as his last sonnets show, was purged away (if I may be permitted this word) in the fire of the Great Ordeal which is proving the well-spring of a Renaissance of English poetry.

Helen B. Trundlett
Batton, Kent.

. . . There was a serious and instructive article on Constantinople by a Mr Symons which I greatly enjoyed.[5] It is good for us to keep our minds open and liberal by contemplation of foreign ways, and though the *danse du ventre* is repellent to the British imagination, we ought to know that these things exist. I cannot speak so pleasantly of Mr Lewis's . . .

Charles James Grimble
The Vicarage, Leays.

1 – Masquerading as readers' letters, these 'excerpts' were written as fillers by TSE.

2 – EP had been contributing a monthly series, 'Elizabethan Classicists', since Sept.

3 – EP argued that Milton merely followed in the rhetorical wake of the dramatists, 'adding to their high-soundingness his passion for latinization, the latinization of a language peculiarly unfitted for his sort of latinization . . . His real place is nearer to Drummond of Hawthornden than to "Shakespear" and "Dante"' (Nov. 1917).

4 – 'Rupert Brooke is not absent' had been TSE's terse comment in his review of Monroe and Henderson's *The New Poetry* (*Egoist* 4: 10, Nov. 1917, 151).

5 – Arthur Symons, 'Notes taken in Constantinople and Sofia' (*Egoist* 4: 10, Nov. 1917, 153).

. . . The philosophical articles interest me enormously; though they make me reflect that much water has flowed under many bridges since the days of my dear old Oxford tutor, Thomas Hill Green. And I am accustomed to more documentation; I like to know where writers get their ideas from . . .

Charles Augustus Conybeare
The Carlton Club, Liverpool.

. . . Is not Mr Lewis's objection to the Grin[1] really a slur upon the cheery philosophy of our brave boys in the trenches, which has been so happily caught by the witty pen of Captain Bairnsfather?[2] And we all know that a little nonsense now and then . . .

Muriel A. Schwarz
60 Alexandra Gdns, Hampstead, N.W.

Vivien Eliot TO *Mary Hutchinson* — MS Texas

[December 1917?] — 18 Crawford Mansions, Crawford St, W.1

Dear Mrs Hutchinson,

I had a very exciting time with you on Thursday. In fact, I have been ill ever since! I gave you lots of false impressions, but I hope I shall be able to put them right some day.

There seem to be some difficulties about having a dance at Dakyns' house – but as I shall not see him until tomorrow night I am not sure about it. If he won't I wish you would have one! I can imagine it being a wonderful occasion. You *must* like dancing.[3]

And, as your husband likes 'crowds', you'd be doing him such a good turn too!

1 – 'The Englishman should become ashamed of his Grin as he is at present ashamed of solemnity . . . he should cease to be ashamed of his "feelings": then he would automatically become less proud of his Grin' (WL, 'Epilogue' to *Tarr*, *Egoist* 4: 10, Nov. 1917).

2 – While hospitalised for shell-shock in 1915, Bruce Bairnsfather (1888–1959) was commissioned by *The Bystander* magazine to draw weekly cartoons, which became immensely popular. TSE wrote later that the 'savage comic humour' of Marlowe had 'nothing in common with J. M. Barrie, Captain Bairnsfather, or *Punch*' ('Some Notes on the Blank Verse of Christopher Marlowe', *Art & Letters* 2: 4, Autumn 1919; *SW*).

3 – BR told OM in 1916: 'The passion of her life is dancing & ever since I have known her I have paid for her to have dancing lessons whenever she has been well enough. I don't suppose she will ever be any good, because of her health, but it is such a passion that I can't bear to baulk it' (Texas; quoted in Ray Monk, *Bertrand Russell: The Spirit of Solitude* [1996], 469).

We are going to a dance tonight at a Studio in Kensington. Also one on Wednesday night.

Most of this week I shall spend looking for a cottage. I do think you and I both *ought* to have one – it would be the only way we could live.

I will write when I have seen Dakyns. Thank you for keeping my pin.

Yrs.
V. H. E.

Vivien Eliot TO *Mary Hutchinson* — MS Texas

[December 1917?] — 18 Crawford Mansions

My dear Mrs Hutchinson,

I am writing quickly to say that I do not think I had better come to see you next Thursday, because I am coming up on that day for a lesson, and I should be tired and the time limited and so I am sure it would not be satisfactory. I would far rather come up one day just to see you and nothing else. That would have to be the week after, and I will leave you to fix a day. Will you? Meanwhile, *will* you be nice and come to tea next Saturday (tomorrow week)? You have never been to see us, and we want you to. Saturday is Tom's only afternoon at home. I should like to ask a few other people if you came, and I wonder if it would amuse you at all to meet the Pounds, or if you'd rather not? You might just mention that when you write. O I do hope this will not be the weekend you go away, but I expect it will! I shall be wretched, if so.

We both positively loved your party, and I was furious at being torn away. And also I must tell you that I have seldom seen Tom so stimulated by anything as he was last night. I am so glad I got the little china man cut of the ham pie.

I liked Miss Sitwell much better yesterday, so I take it back (I told you I did not like her).

Hoping you will write and say you will come.

Yrs.
Vivien Eliot

Vivien Eliot TO *Mary Hutchinson* MS Texas

Tuesday [December? 1917] The Flat [18 Crawford Mansions]

I am so glad you are coming on Saturday, and thank you for that very nice letter. I have thought of this flat as a 'remote tower', somehow it seems so secret and shut off, all the street noises.

You know I have loved this flat, and I think I shall never like the Marlow house so much. But somehow I think I shall like it more if you will really come there. You must come alone sometimes, when it is very *hot*, and we can be just three by ourselves. And then I keep thinking of and planning a very ripping weekend party, if only people won't mind the scarcity of the furniture *and* the food. We could go on the river in punts in the day, and perhaps we should dance in the evening. Do nice things that one *plans* ever really happen, now?

It was stupid of me not to say both of you for lunch on Saturday, I meant to. But you are *both* coming aren't you?

I actually secured Ezra by himself! This is extraordinary and the first time in years. I seized on a moment of discontent with 'them' as he calls his wife!

The Sitwells were here today, and Osbert said I must tell you that *he* says you are to give a dance. One day you really must try Tom's Negro rag-time.[1] I know you'd love it.

Lunch is at 2.15 on Saturday I am sorry it is so late but it has to be. Until then – Yrs.

V. H. E.

TO *His Mother* MS Virginia

[December 1917] [18 Crawford Mansions]

Dear Mother,

I don't know whether you saw this book when it came out in America, but if not I hope it will interest you.[2]

With a very merry Christmas
and infinite love
Tom.

1–For TSE and ragtime, see David Chinitz, *T. S. Eliot and the Cultural Divide* (2003), 8–52.
2–Gamaliel Bradford, *Union Portraits* (1916), which TSE had reviewed, anonymously, in *NS*, 21 Apr. 1917.

Vivien Eliot TO *Mary Hutchinson* MS Texas

[late December 1917] 18 Crawford Mansions

Dear Mrs Hutchinson

I am so sorry I have not answered your invitation sooner. We shall be glad to come on Thursday night, if Tom is well enough. Thank you very much for asking us.

Tom has been rather ill in the last few days – he is overworked and tired of living. I wish he could break his leg, it is the only way out of this that I can think of.

I have been quite busy and happy lately with my new house and my suburban performances.

Hoping to see you on Thursday. We will bring our gifts.

Yrs.
Vivien Eliot

TO *His Mother* MS Houghton

22 December 1917 18 Crawford Mansions

My dearest Mother,

I wanted to write you and father Christmas letters, and here it is nearly Christmas Day, and I have not written for three weeks. Life has been very rushed and confused in these weeks, more than I can ever explain until I see you again, but not so rushed that I have not thought of you continually. In the first place, there is the grey sweater to thank you for. It has been *most* useful; the weather has been bitterly cold, with one or two snowfalls; and I have been very glad of the sweater in unheated lecture rooms. It is beautifully made, and I sometimes picture you when you were knitting it. Then there are the two small envelopes which of course we have not opened yet; they shall go into our stockings with the things we get each other, and we shall thank you for them after Christmas. This will not be a very merry Christmas. Last year Maurice was in England. We have not heard from him for weeks, and no one knows where he is, so his parents are rather anxious. Of course everything is much sadder this year, but I shall not give details about that. The only pleasant feature is the approaching rise in my salary.

I assisted in a poetry reading last week at the house of some rich person for the benefit of something.[1] A hundred and fifty people were induced to

1 – The poetry reading was held by Sibyl Colefax (1874–1950) at her house in Onslow Square on 12 Dec. The poets included the Sitwells, AH and Robert Nichols. Osbert Sitwell

pay 10/6 each, so it was rather a rich audience. Edmund Gosse[1] presided, and a number of 'young poets' of whom I believe I was the oldest, read. It was rather amusing, as the audience and most of the poets were very solemn, and I read some light satirical stuff,[2] and some of them didn't know what to make of it. I think the more intelligent appreciated it, and a number of people asked to be introduced to me afterwards, including several women who said they were Americans, one very nice one, a Mrs Lavery.[3] One or two of the 'poets' were quite nice persons, and I may be able to interest them in the *Egoist*, which I want to extend.

I am distressed about George.[4] His action seems to me quite irresponsible. A man well over forty, with two children, ought to know better. Even at the most excited period here no one would have expected a man in such a position to enlist. I can't see what good it will do him; no one will give him work for being 'patriotic', as he is not going into the firing line, in such work as he hopes to do. Five years from now everyone will have forgotten whether he was in France or not. The motive seems a very trifling one. Charlotte will have a very heavy burden, and you a heavy responsibility. I am very sorry indeed.

I must stop now. I shall write to father by this same mail. I hope you will have just the most cheerful Christmas possible, and I shall think of you all day.

Your devoted son
Tom

(who met TSE for the first time only on 11 Dec.) recorded: 'When Eliot arrived a few minutes late, he was rebuked publicly by Sir Edmund Gosse (though in fact the young man had come straight from the bank where he was then working) . . . [H]e showed no trace of annoyance at being reproved: for . . . he never allowed his companions to suspect the fatigue he must have been suffering.' Sitwell saw TSE as 'a most striking being, having peculiarly luminous, light yellow, more than tawny eyes: the eyes, they might have been, of one of the greater cats' (*Laughter in the Next Room* [1949], 32–3).

1–Edmund Gosse (1849–1928), man of letters, author of *Father and Son* (1907); from 1904 librarian of the House of Lords.

2–'The best thing for me was "Hippopotamus",' noted Arnold Bennett in his Journal.

3–Hazel Martyn of Chicago was a widow when in 1910 she married the painter John Lavery (1856–1941).

4–His brother-in-law George Lawrence Smith had volunteered for active service (though in fact he was assigned to assist engineers Stone & Webster at the US Army base in nearby South Boston).

TO *His Father* — MS Houghton

23 December 1917 — 18 Crawford Mansions

My dear Father

Thank you very much for the £10 which arrived Saturday via the Midland Bank. It came at a very useful time, as I shall not be paid my rise until I get my January salary at the end of that month. I shall be paid for the first part of my lecture courses then too.

For the next two or three weeks I shall have a much desired respite from lecturing, and an opportunity to catch up a little on some of my writing. The lectures do take a great deal of time, and it seems really a Christmas holiday not to be doing them, though the only holiday I get from the Bank is Christmas Day and the day after. I wish I had longer, so we could go into the country out of the nervous strain for a few days. Vivien will not go without me, and she only went for that two weeks in the autumn at my earnest solicitation. Of course the excellent servant we have makes it quite possible, as she is so efficient, and likes responsibility, but Vivien will not go.

I suppose this will be a sad Christmas for you too, but I hope you will have Henry with you.

It seems strange that I should have so busy a life and so little to tell about it. But I think that it is just because it is so busy and rushed that there is so little; – because I don't have time, and no one has time, to stop and enjoy life and tell about it. Besides, everyone's individual ~~fortunes~~ lives are so swallowed up in the one great tragedy, that one almost ceases to have personal experiences or emotions, and such as one has seem so unimportant! – where before it would have seemed interesting even to tell about a lunch of bread and cheese. It's only very dull people who feel they have 'more in their lives' now – other people have too much. I have a lot of things to write about if the time ever comes when people will attend to them.

But I think about you very much.

Your loving son
Tom.

I should like American papers.

TO *His Mother* — MS Houghton

30 December 1917 — 18 Crawford Mansions

My dearest Mother,

The first letters came yesterday that we have had for a long time: none from you, but one from father and one from Henry. We had our envelopes on Christmas day, in stockings as usual, and thanked you again. I have deposited mine, but will of course spend it on clothing: I have not yet decided what clothing I need most. Another nice present arrived – Henry's portfolio. I had no idea that all these pictures existed; some of them I did not remember having seen before; some I remembered quite well. The only member of the family I missed was the *Elsa*, and I should have liked some views of Gloucester. I was very glad to have those of you and father at the Westminster breakfast table,[1] and there was a very good one of Henry there too which I had never seen. I like especially one of you writing at your desk in your bedroom.[2] It gives one a strange feeling that Time is not before and after, but all at once, present and future and all the periods of the past,[3] an album like this. I have been showing the pictures with great pride.

Our Christmas was very quiet but unexpectedly pleasant. The Haigh-Woods had two letters from Maurice that morning, the first in several weeks. He is in Italy now, on the Staff, and I expect is having a very exciting time. He did awfully well to get this post, having passed some examinations with very high rank; and we are very proud of him. He ought to be a Captain before long.

The weather has been very bad, windy and cold; needless to say we prefer it so; but we both have bad coughs and use quantities of handkerchiefs; and the winter in England seems very long. You never know when it is over; finally June comes and you decide to call it summer.

I hope you have a servant now. They are no longer easy to get in England and must be still more difficult to get in America – I hate to think of your having to do your own work.

Tomorrow night is New Year's Eve. I hope you will be thinking of us then, as we shall be thinking of you, and hoping that this may be better for all of us than the last.

Your devoted son
Tom.

Vivien is anxious to write, but has not had time by this mail.

1 – Their St Louis address was 4446 Westminster Place.

2 – See Plates 19A and 23.

3 – 'Time present and time past / Are both perhaps present in time future / And time future contained in time past' (*Burnt Norton* 1–3).

TO *Henry Eliot* MS Houghton

30 December 1917 18 Crawford Mansions

My dear Henry,

This will be a poor sort of letter, as it is very late, and I have a bad cold, and ought to be in bed. Your portfolio arrived several days before Christmas, but of course I did not open it until the day itself. It has given me a lot of pleasure, some of it of a pathetic (but pleasant) sort, and I have enjoyed showing it to people. I am always glad to think it is there, too, as it makes me feel that I have something of the people and the places over here. And it is certainly beautifully done.

Your cheque arrived yesterday. I can only repeat how very generous and good you are. Half shall be spent on Vivien and half on me – mostly on clothes I fancy, which are of course expensive now, and on comforts which one has learned to regard as luxuries nowadays. I am rather better off now than I have been; my rise to £200 a year is of the first of January, and I am promised something more in the middle of the year. The manager has undoubtedly pushed me on fast. The work is interesting, though occasionally trying.

We are neither of us very well at present – colds and coughs – weather bad, and we have reason to be glad when it is.

I should have been delighted personally if you could have got a chance to come over, and had been secretly hoping to see you; but you would certainly have cracked up with your constitution and ears. I think to stay at home and have to go through all the popular silliness there must be very trying. Somehow I have not felt since last March that I ever wanted to see America again. Certainly at the present time I think I should feel like an adult among children. Probably I shall get over this dread in time.

I must go to bed soon. I will send you a copy of the *Egoist* – I take a good deal of interest in the paper.

With much love from both of us

Affectionately
Tom.

TO *Eleanor Hinkley* MS Houghton

31 December 1917 18 Crawford Mansions

Dear Eleanor,

This is just a scrawl at the end of the year to thank you for your last letter of I don't know how long ago! and to recall myself to you, and to combine Christmas and New Year's wishes. I cannot tell you how pleased I was to hear of the success of your play.[1] You deserve it. I wish you would send me one of the printed copies – if there are any – and I should tell you just what I think of it. Of course it is the branch of literature which I know least about.

I will send you a copy of the Henry James number of the *Egoist*[2] when it appears. The idea is mine, and I have a great admiration for him. Not so much the later stuff, but read *The Europeans* and *The American*, and *Washington Square*, and *Daisy Miller*. The first especially is a wonderful criticism of New England. I have been reading Turgenev with great delight – he is one of the very greatest.[3] While you are about it, you ought to read Stendhal – *Le Rouge et le Noir*, and *La Chartreuse de Parme*.

I suppose most of our friends are playing tin soldiers now. The breezes whisper to me that I should not enjoy America at the present moment. But I wish it were all over and you could come and have a winter in London. We shall manage to make it worth your while, even in post-war conditions.

With love and best wishes to you and Aunt Susie.

Affectionately
Tom.

1–*Their Flesh and Blood*, a comedy in four acts, was produced in the 47 Workshop, Dec. 1917.

2–The issue of Jan. 1918 carried TSE's 'In Memory of Henry James': 'I do not suppose that any one who is not an American can *properly* understand Henry James.'

3–TSE reviewed Edward Garnett, *Turgenev*, with foreword by Joseph Conrad, in *Egoist* 4: 11 (Dec. 1917).

1918

Vivien Eliot to *Charlotte C. Eliot* TS Houghton

6 January 1918 18 Crawford Mansions

Dear Mrs Eliot

Thank you very much indeed for the £1 you sent me for Xmas. It was very good of you. I hope you all had a nice Xmas. We had a fairly nice one. We had our Xmas dinner at my home, in the middle of the day, because of air raids! There was no raid as it turned out, but being a full moon it was rather expected. Tom and I went to the country in the late afternoon, and had just two days' holiday. It was nice. We enjoyed looking at Henry's photographs. It was a very nice present for Tom to get, and pleased him immensely. It was good of Henry, and must have taken him a long time to do.

We hear from Charlotte that we may be seeing her husband before long. That would be very nice. I hope, if he does get to France, that he will spend his first leave with us. It will be exciting to see one of the family, although I wish it could be a real Eliot. You are naturally upset at his leaving Charlotte to manage the farm, but she appears to want him to go, and it is apparently to his advantage, so I suppose she will prefer it that way. He will not be running any particular risk if his job is what she says. In one of your letters you seemed to be under the impression that I was away in the country for a very long time in the autumn. I only went for a fortnight, and Tom came for both weekends. When he gets away in the country for his weekends, his health is good. When he stays for a long unbroken period in town, it is not. I am therefore trying to get him away as often as possible. Life in London, at the present time, is much more than trying. About the work in the Government office which I tried for, you will have received Tom's letter in which he told you why I was rejected. Although I have never been to America I am, by law, an 'American born' citizen – and therefore not eligible. The work I now intend to do is tilling the soil, and raising the 'natural fruits of the earth.'

Hoping that you and Mr Eliot are both well, and with our very best wishes that you may have a happy and healthy New Year,

Affectionately,
Vivien

TO *Osbert Sitwell* MS Mugar

10 January 1918 18 Crawford Mansions

I am very glad you can both come. I imagine that the colds will be universal, so you will find sympathetic company. I find however that I should have said *2.15 not* 2, as I may not be home much before that. I hope you don't mind it so late. Accept my apologies for the error.

[unsigned]

TO *Julian Huxley* MS Fondren

16 January 1918[1] 18 Crawford Mansions

Dear Huxley,

I am writing this to you, as I feared that Aldous might possibly have returned to Eton. I did not get his letter, unfortunately, in time to let him know that I could not come on Saturday, and was leaving for the weekend. Since then I have been hoping to find time but have not.

Can we not fix some evening next week? I am always away weekends now (I hope you will come and visit us at Marlow when we are settled). Would *Tuesday* do?

I shall be disappointed if Aldous has already gone. If he is still here but going shortly tell him to drop in if he can tomorrow evening (or both of you). If he has left I will write at once to Eton.

Yours
T. S. Eliot

Or lunch tomorrow at the George and Vulture,[2] if either of you should be in the city by 12. If he is going this week I hope he can manage either lunch or evening –

TO *His Mother* MS Houghton

17 January 1918 [London]

Dearest Mother,

I am writing this after hours, and hope to get it posted in time to reach Saturday's boat. I have not written for a fortnight, I think. Nothing of

1–Dated '16. i. 17' by TSE.
2–The George and Vulture pub was in George Street.

much moment has happened in that time. I have ordered my suit – of course they are more expensive now, and I have to pay £5 – but I think it will be a good one. Also at Vivien's earnest solicitation, I am laying in a light overcoat, as an investment. The prices are rising so and material getting so scarce that I may get a spring suit this year, though I should not wear it at all. This £5 suit would have been £3 10s three years ago. I am buying a pair of shoes too. Then I shall feel well supplied for the future.

I am lecturing again, and the attendance keeps up well. As I started earlier this year, the classes will be over by Easter, which will be welcome. As it is, I can do nothing but these and the *Egoist* and occasional philosophy for Jourdain. There is a very flattering article on me by May Sinclair in the last *Little Review*.[1] I must write and thank her. She was going to try to get it into the *Fortnightly Review* as well. I had to write most of the Henry James number of the *Egoist* myself.

The weather has been frightfully cold for England, and we both suffer from chilblains, and V. from neuralgia in this weather.

I must cut this short or I will not get to the post by 5.30. Everyone has gone and the cleaners want to get into my room.

Your devoted son
Tom.

TO *His Mother* — MS Houghton

6 February 1918 — 18 Crawford Mansions

My dearest Mother,

I have not written to you for so long that I am cabling to let you know that nothing is wrong. The weeks rush by, and at every mail I have felt so tired that I want to wait for the next and write a really good letter, but the really good letter never is written, and this is all I do – but it is at least an affectionate one! Your letters are always a great pleasure and comfort to me, though often a week goes by and two come together. I have not only been very busy and tired, but a slight touch of influenza made it impossible for me to do anything for several days. But I was well nursed through it, and I think am none the worse. It was largely the end of the winter exhaustion, come a bit earlier than usual.

1–May Sinclair, '*Prufrock: And Other Observations:* A Criticism', *Little Review* 4: 8 (Dec. 1917), 8–14. Sinclair's piece did not appear in the *Fortnightly Review*.

1 TSE aged about three, holding Toby

2A The Revd William Greenleaf Eliot, TSE's grandfather

2B TSE's birthplace, 2635 Locust Street, St Louis, which no longer exists

3 His parents at different ages

4A Ada with Henry

4B Henry with TSE

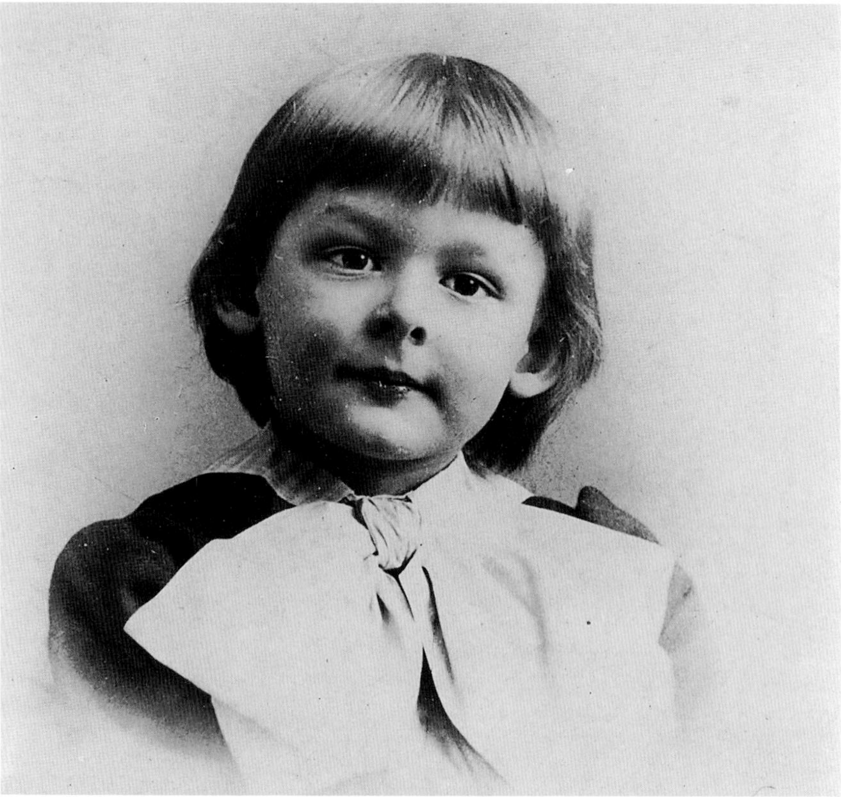

4C 'A baby face with golden promise fraught.' TSE aged about four

5 Daguerreotype of TSE with his sister Margaret

6 With his Irish nursemaid, Annie Dunne, *c.*1895

7A With his mother at East Gloucester, 1895

7B In the schoolyard at
the Mary Institute, St Louis, 1896

8A On the porch at Eastern Point, 1896

8B With T. L. McKittrick, a future President of the World Bank, 1896

9A With his Hinkley cousins and their nannies on the beach at East Gloucester, 1896

9B Eleanor and Barbara Hinkley with TSE in 1897

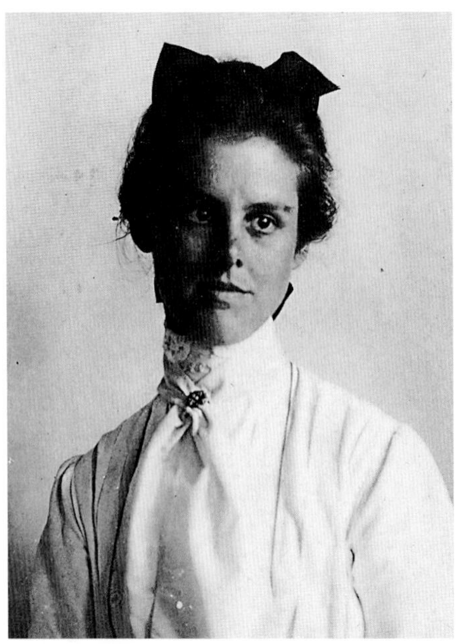

10A Charlotte, the sister who painted his portrait

10B His sister Marian

10C At the front gate of 2635 on the morning after the cyclone of 27 May 1896, with his mother and, *left*, cousin Henrietta and sister Margaret. Marian is hidden

11A With his father, 1895

11B And in 1898

12 TSE in his bedroom at St Louis, *c.*1900

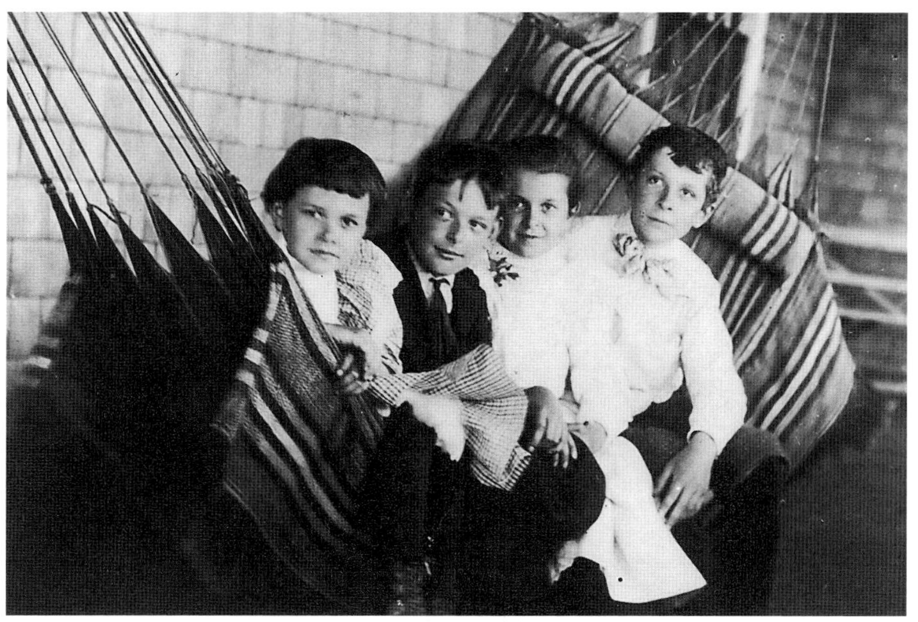

13A With his cousins Abigail, Martha and Frederick Eliot

13B At the piano, *c.*1899

13C One of his father's cat drawings

14A His mother's bedroom at Locust Street

14B Interior of the house at Eastern Point

15 Charlotte's oil portrait (18 x 23 in) *c.*1900–1.
TSE is reading a volume of his red Shakespeare set, which remains in his library

16 Aged about twelve

Your beautiful muffler came the other day, and it is just what I wanted. It is wonderfully soft and warm, and much nicer than any one could buy at any price. With this and the sweater and a new suit and overcoat I am quite set up. I only need a new pair of shoes, which are fearfully expensive now. I shall always think of all the work you put into it whenever I wear it, and wonder when and where you did any particular stitch. My new suit is very nice, very dark gray, almost black.

We get along as everyone else does. I suppose food is a serious problem even in America. It is very hard on anyone who is delicate, and cannot digest many of the things that most people fall back on. Vivien was best off some years ago when a doctor put her on a diet of meat and milk puddings alone, so you can see the difficulty. It would be nice to have a little Orange Pekoe, or a box of Gorton's Boneless Cod!

I have had a great deal to do. Lately I have been at a point in my lectures where the material was unfamiliar to me: I have had to get up the Brontës for one course and Stevenson for the other. Of course I have developed a knack of acquiring superficial information at short notice, and they think me a prodigy of information. But some of the old ladies are extraordinarily learned, and know all sorts of things about the private life of worthies, where they went to school, and why their elder brother failed in business, which I have never bothered my head about. But I am looking forward to lecturing on Dickens. I found *Jane Eyre* and *Wuthering Heights* amazingly good stuff, but I cannot endure George Eliot.

I have three philosophy books on hand for the *New Statesman* which I have not touched, and Bertie's new book *Mysticism and Logic* for the *Nation*.[1] And when I have finished this letter I must do my article for the *Egoist*, on two collections of recent verse.[2] As some of the worst of it is by friends of mine the article will be rather difficult. I shall be glad when Easter comes, and both courses of lectures are over.

I must go to work now. This has at least been words on paper, if not a letter. I hope I can write a better one on Sunday!

With much love to both of you

Your devoted son
Tom

1–TSE, unsigned rev. of BR, *Mysticism and Logic*, *N.* 22 (Mar. 1918), 768–9.

2–T. S. Apteryx (TSE), 'Verse Pleasant and Unpleasant' – on *Georgian Poetry 1916–1917*, ed. Edward Marsh, and *Wheels 1917: A Second Cycle*, ed. Edith Sitwell – *Egoist* 5: 3 (Mar. 1918).

TO *His Mother* MS Houghton

14 February 1918 [London]

My dearest Mother,

I hope this will be legible by the time it reaches you. I am writing in business hours which accounts for the form of my letter. There is very little to do today, and I see no reason why I should not take some of my spare time to write to you. I am still very tired and feeling the effect of a spring season two months too early – the weather has been very warm and muggy. I count [the] days until Easter. I did not have time to do anything for the *Egoist* this month – the first time that has happened. I should like to get B. R.'s new book *Mysticism and Logic* reviewed, but I cannot see my way to it for several days.

I was glad to get the American papers, though I have not had time to more than look at them yet. They are the first I have seen for a very long time, and they seemed very strange and also wasteful of paper on an infinity of trivial matters. The part that usually interests me the most is the sporting news. I am thinking of sending you a paper called *Common Sense*[1] from time to time, as I do not suppose that you see any English news.

I must get back to my work now as some has just turned up. I don't know whether I shall have time to write any more so I will close this off and perhaps make a postscript later.

Always your devoted son
Tom.

TO *His Mother* TS Houghton

4 March 1918 18 Crawford Mansions

Dearest mother,

The last few days have been very cold again, after a warm spell which brought all the buds out; but I do not think that anything has been frostbitten. Today clouded over, after several bright cold days, and tonight it has begun to rain, and may turn to snow. Vivien and indeed most English people suffer in such weather, but I find it rather bracing – at least out of doors, for English houses have not the heating or close-fitted doors that

1 – *Common Sense* was published weekly from Oct. 1916 to June 1921, when it was incorporated into the *Manchester Guardian Commercial*.

ours have. Today (Sunday) I have not been out, but have worked all day for the *Egoist*. You know that I was too tired to do anything for the February number, so I have done more than usual for this. An article on two anthologies of poetry, one mostly by some young friends of mine [the Sitwells], two young Guards officers with literary aspirations; an article on a very foolish book by Amy Lowell,[1] sister of Lawrence Lowell, and one on a literary lawsuit[2] in New York. I am becoming quite adept at reviewing books by people I know – a difficult art.

I have been cramming George Eliot for the last two weeks in preparation for a lecture on her on last Friday. I was surprised to enjoy her so much. Of course there is a great deal of endless prosing, and I think my memory of pleasure is based chiefly on one story – *Amos Barton* – which struck me as far and away ahead of the rest. I read the *Mill on the Floss, Scenes of Clerical Life, Adam Bede* and *Romola* in preparation for this one lecture. This week is Meredith, whom I have lectured on before. The attendance keeps up pretty well, considering the conditions, nine or ten each evening, but it would not at all surprise me if there were no lectures at all given next year.

I appreciate the papers father sends, and hope he will continue. And I must thank you very much for the little parcel of tea you sent; it was very welcome, and helped out our small store very much. I think that it loses a little flavour on the way, still it is Orange Pekoe, and I had not had any for a long time.

Everything looks more black and dismal than ever, I think. The whole world simply lives from day to day; I haven't any idea of what I shall be doing in a year, and one can make no plans. The only thing is to try to fill one's mind with the things in which one is interested.

I must stop now.

Always your very loving and devoted son

Tom

1–TSE, 'Disjecta Membra', a review of Amy Lowell, *Tendencies in Modern American Poetry* (1917), in *Egoist* 5: 4 (Apr. 1918).

2–The Oct. 1917 issue of *Little Review* had been suppressed because it carried WL's story 'Cantleman's Spring-Mate'. John Quinn appeared for the defence, but the case went against the magazine. TSE, in 'Literature and the American Courts', lamented that as a result of the ruling, 'In America the small number of people who are sensitive to good literature are now forbidden to read one of the finest pieces of prose in the language' (*Egoist* 5: 3, Mar. 1918).

TO *John Quinn*[1] TS NYPL (MS)

4 March 1918 18 Crawford Mansions

Dear Mr Quinn,

I am told by Pound that you expressed satisfaction with the brochure on his work.[2] I am very glad if this is so, because I wrote it under considerable pressure of time, and was very much aware of its shortcomings; I lamented not being able to have sight of the proofs. I only hope that it will serve the desired purpose, and shall be very glad if it induces any one unacquainted with Pound's stuff to buy and read his books.

I wish more particularly to express my gratitude to you for your activity on my behalf against the Pirates.[3] I appreciated it the more because I knew you had recently undergone a serious operation: I do not think that there are many people who under such conditions would bestir themselves so actively even for personal friends, still less for a man who was personally unknown to them.

I cannot see how these publishers can find a leg to stand on. As most of the poems have been published in America, they could be within their rights only in printing the 'Rhapsody on a Windy Night', and the 'Preludes' – hardly sufficient for a profitable volume.

I wish that I had enough material for a volume of suitable size for the American public.[4] I am afraid that it will be some time before I have

1–John Quinn, American lawyer and patron of the arts: see Glossary of Names.
2–TSE's pamphlet, published anonymously, was *Ezra Pound: His Metric and Poetry* (New York: Knopf, 1918). On 9 Sept. 1917, EP had told Quinn, who donated $80 towards the publication, that TSE had 'made an excellent job' and that it should 'at least choke off the imbeciles' (*Selected Letters of Ezra Pound to John Quinn, 1915–1924*, ed. Timothy Materer [1991], 129).
3–Quinn investigated an unfounded rumour, started by the editors of the *Little Review*, that Boni & Liveright planned to pirate *Prufrock*. Soon, on 25 Mar., Albert Boni wrote to Quinn's associate Justus Sheffield, 'Regarding *Prufrock* by T. S. Eliot, will you kindly advise Mr. Quinn that I am under the impression that these poems have not been published as yet in book form in the States. If he cares to arrange for their American publication, I should be pleased to take up the matter with him or anyone else authorized to conclude arrangements.' On 19 Apr., Quinn sent a copy of this note to TSE, adding: 'They are a new firm, young Jews, and are sort of making a business of republishing uncopyrighted things or standard works on which copyright has expired . . . I don't think you want to hook up with them. When you get enough material for a volume of suitable size for the American public, I don't think there will be much difficulty about arranging for a publisher.'
4–The publisher Alfred Knopf (see Glossary of Names) had been worried about length when Quinn first recommended TSE to him on 6 Aug. 1917. All the same, Quinn sent the book, and Knopf replied on 17 Aug.: 'I have read Eliot's little book of poems with immense enjoyment. I do not know whether it is great poetry or not. I do know that it is great fun and I like it. I surely hope that he writes some more of it so that we can make a book of him over

enough material to double the size of my small book. I have only written half a dozen small poems in the last year, and the last I have been unable to finish. I regret still more that I have been unable to do anything this winter for *The Little Review*. The cause has been chiefly the simple reason of lack of time, and in the second place I have been too tired to do any original work. I spend a sufficiently fatiguing day in a Bank, and during this winter have supplemented my income by giving two lectures a week, involving considerable preparation, in the evenings to working people. Then also I have *The Egoist* to look after; having an official connection with it I must perform my share each month. At about Easter my courses of lectures will be finished, and I hope then to find time and energy to write. I have been very keenly interested in the success of *The Little Review*, and Pound's enthusiasm on the subject is infectious. I hope to continue my dialogue[1] (not that I was at all satisfied with the first two parts), and if I do any verse Pound shall have it.

Pound showed me a letter a few days ago which he had from Miss Monroe declining his last poems.[2] Although I knew that she had shown herself obtuse on the subject of the *Cantos* I was very much surprised; her tone was offensively patronising. I had gone over these poems carefully before Pound sent them; and had applauded them. The Provençal stuff was amazingly well done, and in two or three of the modern poems I was sure that he had gone some distance beyond the modern poems in *Lustra* [1915]. Anyway, they were first-rate, and it never occurred to me that Harriet would be able to find any excuse for rejecting them. I suppose there were mixed motives, but probably she was jealous of the attention Pound was giving to *The Little Review*.[3]

---

here. You see the present volume consists of only 32 pages of poetry, and it would be quite impossible to do anything with such a thing over here, except to give it away as an advertisement' (NYPL).

1–'Eeldrop and Appleplex': Part II had been published in Sept. 1917, but TSE never continued it.

2–'Homage à la Langue d'Oc' and 'Mœurs Contemporaines' appeared in the *Little Review* in May. TSE included both in EP's *Selected Poems* (1928): 'One of Pound's most indubitable claims to genuine originality' was his 'revivification of the Provençal and the early Italian poetry' (xii).

3–EP became Foreign Editor of the *Little Review* in Mar. 1917 without informing Harriet Monroe (he was already 'Foreign Correspondent' for her magazine *Poetry*). In the *Little Review* (May) he compounded the offence: '*Poetry* has shown an unflagging courtesy to a lot of old fools and fogies whom I would have told to go to hell *tout pleinment* and *bonnement*.' See *A History of 'Poetry' in Letters: The First Fifty Years*, ed. Joseph Parisi and Stephen Young (2002), 198–206.

I am really very glad the crisis occurred. Personally, I cannot forget the length of time that elapsed before Pound succeeded in persuading Miss Monroe to print 'Prufrock' for me, nor do I forget that [in *Poetry*, Sept. 1916] she expunged, in another poem, a whole line containing the word 'foetus'[1] without asking my permission. But what is the important point is that Pound is I think very glad to feel no further responsibility toward *Poetry*. He is deprived of the price of his rent, I believe, but I think that he is delighted at being able to devote all his attention to *The Little Review*. I saw him a few days ago, in very good spirits, and I think morally sustained and stimulated by the subsidy which you have assembled. It will be a great thing to get *all* his serious prose and verse for the *L.R.* from now on.

You see I value his verse far higher than that of any other living poet. And he and Wyndham Lewis are the only men in England of my acquaintance, I believe, who have not in any respect allowed the war to demoralise them.

I am putting a short notice of the Cantleman trial in this month's *Egoist*. I think the typical American attitude in such matters is like that of Miss Amy Lowell, who is always decrying abstract Puritanism, but who when faced with some particular work of art offensive to Puritan taste curls up like a hedgehog. The American Liberal Varnish. I am sure that everyone who knows about the case here is very grateful to you for your part in it.

Again with thanks for your action against Boni, and best wishes for your rapid convalescence, I am

Sincerely yours
T. S. Eliot

Vivien Eliot TO *Charlotte C. Eliot* — MS Houghton

11 March 1918 — 18 Crawford Mansions

Dear Mrs Eliot

I hope that you will not get tired of seeing my writing instead of Tom's – at least I *think* it is instead of Tom's this week. He may have managed to write a line at the Bank, but I know that all yesterday he never moved out of his chair except for meals. Writing incessantly, until very late at night. There is so much else to do, that the lectures always get put off till the last minute, and Sundays and Thursdays, being the days before the lectures, are

1 – 'He laughed like an irresponsible foetus' ('Mr. Apollinax').

always terrible days. Tom looks very white and thin. The winter has tried him beyond endurance. I feel that he must not ever do this lecturing again. It is too much. It is more than one can endure to see a young man so worn and old-looking, and it is always through fretting that he has no time to do the only thing he wants to do, the only thing he likes. That is the truth of it – it is a good half of it sheer over work, and the other half is fretting. It wears me out to see him. I only wish we were near someone of his own family. Of course you must know how he longs to see you. Poetry and literature are the very only things Tom cares for or has the faintest interest in. And *not* the kind of Poetry or literature which *earns money*. He hates to write for money. The Banking frets and irks him *less* than all his other work, because it is so quite different and separate from what he cares about so intensely.

I wish Henry could come over here. Do you not think it would be good for Henry? I *know* it would be good for Tom. We are both pretty sure that Henry could find war work *once he got here*. There is a great deal to do with transport etc. Also the health standards for Red Cross are here *much lower*.

We have had beautiful spring weather this last week, quite hot and brilliant sunshine. But it is not very welcome I assure you. Thank you *so much* for the *tea*. It was a delight – do, if you can, send some more. Tom does so appreciate good tea. For myself unless I have china tea I never can drink it at all. It is difficult now to get any tea but the most inferior kinds.

Affectly,
Vivien.

Tom has got *two* new suits – one very dark and thick – the other a lightish one. Also a very jolly-looking over-coat. Also a new hat.

We have received all the parcels now and are most grateful.

Sweater
Muffler (this is very useful)
Pyjamas
Tea

Vivien Eliot TO *Mary Hutchinson* — MS Texas

Wed[nesday] 13 March 1918 — Flat [18 Crawford Mansions]

My dear Mrs Hutchinson

It was awfully good of you to ask us to this dance. I have really *never* disliked having to refuse an invitation so much as I did that. It was so tempting to me. Dances are so few, and as you know, they mean a lot to me. I am trying to earn an honest (for a change) penny, by cinema acting, and have attained an unexpected success. I had to refuse the Sitwells – last night – for the same reason.

I do not like it. But one must do something, and I have been spending recklessly lately. I get so fearfully tired, for I am really a wretched crock, and always have been, but I hate to own it. So I can never do two things, but only one at a time. I have been envying you tonight.

I have lots to say to you, and I do so want to see you. It was really nice of you to ask us. I appreciated it. Will you come to *lunch*, at 2 o'clock, on *Saturday week? Please* do. I do *want* you to. It is the first time we have free. Please let me know, and do say yes.

Tom is impossible at present – very American and obstinate! Let me know about Sat. week – and do not say no. I have wanted a talk with you for a long time.

I had the delight of seeing Ottoline enter Selfridges today! It was wonderful. Write *here* and say *yes* to Saturday.

Yrs
V.E.

TO *The Editor of* The Egoist

Published March 1918 Little Tichester,[1] Bucks

Madam,

I shall be grateful if you will allow me to state in your columns (in response to numerous inquiries) that to the best of my knowledge and belief Captain Arthur Eliot, joint author of *The Better 'Ole*,[2] is not, roughly speaking, a member of my family.

Yours, etc.,
T. S. Eliot

1 – The fake address alludes to the music-hall comedian Little Tich (1867–1928), whose acts TSE later described as 'an orgy of parody of the human race' ('In Memoriam: Marie Lloyd', C. 1: 2, Jan. 1923, 193).

2 – *The Better 'Ole*, 'A Fragment from France', by Bruce Bairnsfather and Arthur Eliot, with music by Herman Darewski, opened at the Oxford Theatre, London, on 4 Aug. 1917. It ran for 811 performances, and was made into a silent film in 1918. Osbert Sitwell recorded that in the 1920s, visitors to TSE's flat, 38 Burleigh Mansions, were told by TSE to ask at the lodge for 'Captain Eliot'.

TO *His Mother* MS Houghton

24 March 1918

18 Crawford Mansions,
Crawford St, W.1

My dearest Mother,

I should be very much pained if you thought it was not worthwhile to write so often, just because you hear from me so seldom. I always look forward to your letters; of course they do not arrive so regularly as they are written, but I like to think of you, writing every Sunday. And I am always interested in what you have to say, and it doesn't matter what you write about. It *is*, of course a check to one in writing, always finding oneself running up against subjects which it is wiser not to mention, and everything seems to lead to such subjects now. Do you remember the letters I wrote at the beginning of the war? I used to enjoy describing the appearances of London then. And even if one wrote so freely now, one would do it only as a kind of duty of letting people at a distance know.

The spring has come very early and very warm and dry. Yesterday was a boiling day for this time of year, the sky absolutely cloudless. We had five people to lunch, the most ambitious attempt we have ever made, and our small dining-library was packed. But it went off very well; we are excellent hosts, I think; and our servant did admirably. It is easier to have people to lunch than to dinner, of course, because of the impossibility of serving meat; at lunch fish and spaghetti suffice. Of course, entertaining is in some respects cheaper because of the restrictions.

This week brings me two holidays, Good Friday and the Monday after Easter. Also, after tomorrow, no lectures for a fortnight; and then only two weeks more of lectures after that. Then I shall be able to do something for the *Little Review*. I will send you a number of the *Egoist*. If you see the *Nation*, there is a review of mine (*Mysticism and Logic*) in this week's (Sat. 23d Mch) issue.[1]

I had a nice letter from Ada this week, enclosing their wedding present. Has Shef had any rise in salary? She does not say so.

I look forward always to your next letter. In the last you mention sending the pyjamas. In case my letter went astray, I acknowledge them again, with much thanks. They will be very nice for Summer.

Goodbye, dear Mother
Your devoted son
Tom.

1–TSE, 'Style and Thought', unsigned review of BR, *Mysticism and Logic* (1917). On 17 June, Russell wrote to Miss Rinder of the No-Conscription Fellowship: 'Much the best review

TO *Eleanor Hinkley* TS Houghton

1 April 1918 18 Crawford Mansions

Dear Eleanor,

I just received your charming letter this morning, and as today is a bank-holiday, I felt that I ought to try to make a more adequate return to it than the scrap I sent off to you yesterday. So you will be astonished to receive two letters at once.

I like your letters, especially lately, (if I can speak of your last before this as 'lately') because they give me more positively than anyone's else from America the impression that everything is the same, and at the same time the impression that you are interestingly changing. You always begin by conjuring up the exact image of a Sunday afternoon and evening with baked beans and toast and cocoa and other nice things and firelight, quite as it always was, and conversation about little odd new people whom we had just met. But what is larger, your letter gave me the impression of your being quite untouched by the war, and as pursuing your own way quietly and persistently. Perhaps you think it was simply an accident or because the subject is depressing that you omitted all reference, and perhaps you hardly realise consciously yet what the effort to keep oneself unaffected by the war means, but I think it was instinctive force of character. Everyone else in America who writes to me is quite lost in the war and become quite uninteresting, and it makes me feel much more remote from them than if they lived in an oasis where the war had never been heard of. Most people cease to develop, or develop only in the same unpleasant way as each other. Of course in England the sentimental heroic phase is gone, but there are very few people who have been able quite to preserve values and stick to their own business. I think that the play writing has probably done a lot for you. I imagine that you have changed a great deal since I knew you, but changed in ways that I should like and understand; and I fancy that when I see you again it will be like making a new and interesting friend and at the same time an understood old one, I am looking to the hope that you will come over here for a long stay after the war, and I shall gladly take the responsibility of its being worth your while.

You appear to have been making a good many acquaintances. I think one ought always to be meeting new people, and indeed to spend more time with them than with one's old friends, for various reasons – partly

—

of *Mysticism*, the only one with distinction, was Eliot's in *Nation*' (quoted in Ray Monk, *Bertrand Russell: The Spirit of Solitude*, 519).

that they demand more of one, (the former) and that one mustn't lose one's curiosity and adaptability.

I am very glad you like James. You have read some of the best. I believe that the *Aspern Papers*, the *American Scene*, and the *Middle Years* are very good. He is a wonderful conscientious artist, one of the very few, and more European than most English or Americans. I think he has about the keenest sense of Situation of any novelist, and his always alert intelligence is a perpetual delight. As a critic of America he is certainly unique. I am reading *R[oderick] Hudson* now in preparation for an article for the James number of the *Little Review* [August 1918]. I am writing on the Hawthorne influence on James, which comes out at the end in an astonishing unfinished book *The Sense of the Past* (read the scenario at the end). *Hudson* I find dull and stilted and old fashioned; but it is a very early one. I think you might like Turgenev. I admire him as much as any novelist, but especially in the *Sportsman's Sketches*. His method looks simple and slight, but he is a consummate master with it. *A House of Gentlefolk* is good. I come more and more to demand that novels should be well written, and perceive more clearly the virtue and defects of the Victorians. George Eliot had a great talent, and wrote one great story, *Amos Barton*, and went steadily down hill afterwards.[1] Her best stunt was just this exact realism of country life, as good in its way as anything in Russian, and she thought her business was philosophic tragedy. *Romola* is the most inartistic novel I have ever read. Every novelist has a knack for doing some one stunt, and the Victorians none of them were selfconscious enough. Thackeray could do the *Yellowplush Papers* and the Steyne part of *Vanity Fair*, but he had a picture of himself as a kindly satirist. Not at all, he hadn't brains enough, nor courage enough to find out really what he could do well, which was high society sordidness, and do it. Standards of good writing in English are deplorably low. Meredith knew what he was doing, but unfortunately it wasn't worth doing, don't read him. *The Way of All Flesh* was written by a man who was not an artist and had no sense of style; it is too long, and the beginning of the book and the adventures of Ernest are dull, but the character of Christina is amazing. Butler <read his *Notebooks*> just happened to know this phase of English life particularly well; Christina is one of the finest pieces of dissection of mental dishonesty that I know anywhere; Butler pursues her relentlessly to her death. It is a book you must read.

1–TSE wrote in 'The Hawthorne Aspect' that all of George Eliot's 'genuine feeling went into the visual realism of *Amos Barton*' (*Little Review* 5: 4, Aug. 1918).

But one simply must read French; let there be no nonsense about that; it is the most serious modern literature.[1] Both for prose and poetry. It is hard work, and one will never know the language thoroughly, but no one can ever have a really trained taste with English alone. English writing is mostly very careless. When you can afford it I think you ought to subscribe to the *Little Review*. I would send it to you but it is published in New York. There is a good deal about it that is offensively aggressive, but it will keep one's brain active. Make them send you back numbers for several months, so as to have James Joyce's novel complete and you ought to have the February number, which is a most valuable collection and guide to modern French verse.[2] Your account of Shef's criticism is amusing. Of course Shef is wholly a schoolmaster, and a very good one, but with little or no literary critical sense. No, he has more than that; I am unjust; he has extremely good 'native perceptions'; but nothing does more harm to these perceptions than the profession of teaching; the conscientiousness which comes with responsibility toward young people. He is terribly conscientious. He has not preserved any wildness, any liberty.[3]

I must really stop now. Thank you for your letter!

Affectionately
Tom

TO *Bertrand Russell* MS McMaster

13 April 1918 [London]

Dear Bertie,

I wanted to write you a line before Tuesday – as I should not, of course, be able to be present, as unfortunately on previous occasions.[4] I am glad

1 – In 'Contemporanea' (on anthologies of French poetry), TSE professed: 'any one who is writing or seriously criticizing indigenous verse should know the French' (*Egoist* 5: 6, June–July 1918).

2 – The first episode of *Ulysses* had appeared in the Mar. issue; EP's 'A Study in French Poets' came out in Feb.

3 – TSE's brother-in-law Alfred Sheffield. On 13 Nov. 1917, Robert Frost, who had been taught by him at Harvard, wrote to his daughter Lesley Frost, who was taught by him at Wellesley: 'Sheffield is a clever cut-and-dried mind, but he is a survival. Remember how he drove me out of Harvard.'

4 – BR was coming to the end of a course of eight lectures on 'The Philosophy of Logical Atomism', which were printed in *The Monist* between Oct. 1918 and July 1919, and collected in *Logic and Knowledge: Essays 1901–1950*, ed. Robert C. Marsh (1956).

to hear that Bosanquet and others have turned out so well[1] – I think that is awfully gratifying. Demos[2] told me that he had been giving you bibliography on behaviourism. I am not convinced that Watson[3] and those people are really very important. But the avenue of investigation which you suggested to me in a conversation a few weeks ago impressed me very deeply, and I hope you will go in for it very hard. It struck me as important as anything to be done; besides, it would be very amusing to stand the biological sciences on their heads that way.

With all sincerest good wishes.

Yours as ever
Tom

TO *His Mother* — MS Houghton

28 April 1918 — 18 Crawford Mansions

Dearest Mother,

I received a letter from you and two newspapers by the last mail. I was very glad to get both. The newspapers, however, made me think that while America is very conscientiously 'conserving foodstuffs' etc. she is as wasteful of paper as ever. I fear it would take very serious privation indeed to make Americans realise the wastefulness of such huge papers filled with nonsense and personalities. But can nothing be said? Will you not tell people that all through Europe the greatest economy is now exercised in the use of paper; that newspapers are reduced to the smallest possible

1 – Writing in a weekly newspaper, *The Tribunal*, on 3 Jan., BR alleged that American soldiers would be employed as strike-breakers in England, 'an occupation to which [they were] accustomed when at home'. He was charged at Bow Street on 10 Feb. with 'having in a printed publication made certain statements likely to prejudice His Majesty's relations with the United States of America', found guilty, and sentenced to six months' imprisonment in the Second Division. Wishing to continue his work in Brixton, and to enjoy maximum privileges, he sought a transfer to the First Division by asking 'eminent philosophers', including Bernard Bosanquet (1848–1923), to petition the Home Secretary. The appeal was successful, and TSE was able to visit him in prison.

2 – Raphael Demos (1892–1968), philosopher, had reached Harvard from Asia Minor in 1913, and worked as a waiter to pay his doctoral fees. An assistant in philosophy, 1916–17, he was planning to spend a year at Cambridge before returning to Harvard as an instructor. While in England he would call on TSE at the bank, and assist him with modern Greek translation. He was ultimately to become Professor of Philosophy at Harvard, 1919–62; author of *The Philosophy of Plato* (1939).

3 – John Watson (1878–1958), American psychologist and founder of behaviourism; author of *Behavior: An Introduction to Comparative Psychology* (1914). BR attacked him in *The Analysis of Mind* (1921).

compass, and that the public has lost nothing thereby? The forests won't hold out indefinitely in any case; and if less pulp were wasted on newspapers, good books could perhaps be printed more cheaply.

Judging from American newspapers, the war seems to have affected the country not very seriously yet. I don't mean that it is not the chief subject of interest, but that it is *simply* the chief subject of interest, and not the obsessing nightmare that it is to Europe. And we can't make you realise three thousand miles away all that that means. Even with all your privations and difficulties. Your papers talk about the 'fight for civilisation'; do they realise either what civilisation means or what the fight for it means? We are all immeasurably and irremediably altered over here by the last three years.

Harold Peters has been in Scotland lately; I have been hoping that he can get up to London. That would be very interesting.

We should be glad of anything you can send, but I do not know what things are possible.

My courses are over, I am glad to say. Both classes want me back next year, one for a course on Elizabethan Literature, the other for a course on the Development of English Poetry. I shall keep up the first one, if it continues, but the other class, the one which started this year, I do not think will be worth my while. They paid me one pound per lecture, but out of that travelling expenses and a dinner in town (not having time to go back) always took 3/-, and the time, by no means inconsiderable, of preparation must be counted too. So I might devote my time more profitably to other things.

The spring is getting on, but we have had no truly warm weather yet, though the trees and bushes are well out.

I hope to write more regularly now.

Your very affectionate son
Tom

TO *Mary Hutchinson* MS Texas

1 May 1918 [Marlow]

Dear Mrs Hutchinson

I only got your note late last night just as I was going to Marlow and did not have time to answer. I should love to come but had arranged sometime ahead to dine with Pound and some others on Thursday. It is annoying because we are at Marlow now and it limits our chances of seeing anyone.

I am very sorry to hear that you are going to Wittering so soon, but I hope that you do not mean what you say, and that it will be only intermittent. Surely you will be up for a little while in June.

Yours
T. S. Eliot

I hope the book will amuse [incomplete: the margin of the paper is torn]

TO *His Mother* MS Houghton

10 May 1918 [18 Crawford Mansions]

Dearest Mother,

In your last letter received Saturday you ask me whether I got the $10 you sent me for my suit. I did, and I am sure that you will have got my letter thanking you for it by this time, but I will thank you again to be sure.

I shall soon have ten days holiday, in the middle of June, and I have two days at 'Whitsuntide' next week, which will be very welcome. The weather is beginning to be settled and warm now – we had a thunder shower with hail this morning, and everything is very green.

I am trying to do some writing now – an article on Henry James for the *Little Review*, and trying to write verse again. I am glad to have some leisure for reading also, as all my reading last winter was for the courses. My Southall people want to do Elizabethan Literature next year which would interest me more than what we have done before, and would be of some use to me too, as I want to write some essays on the dramatists, who have never been properly criticised.

I have taken up the rudiments of both Spanish and Danish this winter, but have not got very far with either. I can read a Spanish newspaper pretty easily.

I was dining with May Sinclair (the novelist) the other day and met a woman named Robbins [*sic*][1] who said she was a cousin of the Macks in Portland. She seems to write popular novels and to know a good many people here. Did you ever hear of her?

Vivien will write again and give you news. She has been glad to have a letter from you lately, and would have written more often, but that it is

1–Elizabeth Robins (1865–1952), American actress and novelist. She later described her experience of creating Ibsen roles in *Ibsen and the Actress* (1928), and edited the letters written to her by Henry James, *Theatre and Friendship* (1932).

very fatiguing to her and she did not know whether it was of any interest to you to hear from her.

I do hope you are going to Gloucester. I really think it would break you both up not to go. Please do.

Your devoted son
Tom.

TO *His Mother* MS Houghton

22 May 1918 [18 Crawford Mansions]

Dearest Mother,

I have letters from you and father. It is now ten o'clock in the evening, and we have just turned on the lights – daylight saving and a northern latitude. I suppose it will be light till 11 in the middle of June, when I take a holiday. The weather has been very beautiful lately; clear, hot days. In the country wistaria and the golden laburnum are in full bloom.

I am glad you found the article in the *Nation*; but I am surprised and sorry you cannot get the book.[1] It would make the article more intelligible. If the Mercantile Library takes the *English Review* you will find an article in the May issue, mostly about me, by Edgar Jepson,[2] 'Recent United States Poetry'.[3] I was reviewed quite favourably in the *New Republic* some months ago.[4]

It is *Lloyds Bank*, which has no connection with Lloyds Insurance. It is the second largest bank in England. Banks here are different from in America, where a bank is purely local. There are about a dozen very large banks with head offices in London and branches in the country and sometimes abroad. Lloyds Bank has about 900 branches and four or five in France. Of course I have to do only with foreign business. The address is 17 Cornhill, E.C.3., in the heart of the 'City', and opposite the 'Bank' (of England). I have half of a room, two girls, and half of a typist. I share a typist with someone else.

I am very grateful to father for enquiring about the Policy. It sets my mind at rest.

You don't say anything about Gloucester in this letter. But I should feel rather anxious if you were to try to spend a summer in St Louis now.

1 – Russell, *Mysticism and Logic* (1917).
2 – For Edgar Jepson see TSE's postcard of 5 Feb. 1919.
3 – Edgar Jepson, 'Recent United States Poetry', *English Review* 26 (May 1918).
4 – [Babette Deutsch], 'Another Impressionist', *New Republic* 14 (16 Feb. 1918).

We are both feeling the combined effect of sudden hot weather and the strain of a long winter.

Always your loving son
Tom.

TO *His Mother* MS Houghton

2 June 1918 [18 Crawford Mansions]

My dearest Mother,

I have not heard from you or father, I think, since I wrote last. I have been wondering if it has been as hot or hotter in St Louis than it has here. It is really midsummer; often in England August is much colder than June. We have had perfect cloudless days and nights. I am very much afraid that if it were as hot as it sometimes is in St Louis from July to September, in 'spells', you would suffer very much. I thrive on hot weather, and today I have done a lot of work, including a number of necessary business letters. I have written several poems lately, which will be published eventually, and wrote a review today of three philosophy books[1] for the *New Statesman*. I am now preparing to write an article on Henry James and Hawthorne;[2] I read James's little book on Hawthorne [*Hawthorne*, 1879] yesterday – very good. James was a fine writer – his book of impressions of America, written about 1907 I think, is wonderfully well written.[3] There are so very few people who will take the trouble to write well. It is full of acute criticism too.

Then I am reading, and rereading the poets and dramatists of the time of Shakespeare and immediately after. My Southall class is going to take up that period next year, if we are allowed to continue, and I am looking forward to it, as I prefer it infinitely to the 19th Century – to any periods in English Literature.

We are feeling the strain of this trying time very much – when you get this letter you will have to look back to see what time it was. One can hardly think or talk – only wait.

Your devoted son
Tom.

1 – [TSE], 'New Philosophers', unsigned review of J. S. Mackenzie, *Elements of Constructive Philosophy*; DeWitt H. Parker, *The Self and Nature*; James Gibson, *Locke's Theory of Knowledge*, in *NS* 11 (13 July 1918).

2 – TSE, 'The Hawthorne Aspect', *Little Review* 5: 4 (Aug. 1918).

3 – Henry James, *The American Scene* (1907).

TO *His Mother* MS Houghton

9 June 1918 31 West St,[1] Marlow, Bucks

My dearest Mother,

It is a very long time since I have heard from you. I wonder if you have been waiting the same length of time to hear from me; I have not missed a week in writing since a couple of months, to the best of my knowledge and belief. But possibly some letter has not been forwarded yet. You will see by the address above that we have finally (like all our friends) come out of London. There are several reasons – you know we had contemplated it before; but finally we both were in very poor health after the winter, and the doctor said that I ought to be out in the country, for the summer anyway. So we are staying out here, on the Thames, a charming old little town, in the street where Shelley used to live.[2] And I feel much better already, mentally and physically. The relief of being out of London, getting quite away from it at the end of the day, is very great. The train journey is restful too. Of course it adds to the expenses, principally through the cost of a season ticket to go up and down every day, but it is fully worth it, even if it necessitates, as it does, more sacrifices in other directions. The suburban traffic of London is tremendous – most 'city workers' people in offices, live out of town and commute every day, and I am sure that it is much better for one. I think I am a little bit fatter – you know I have lost 15lbs. since leaving Oxford. Vivien is of course much better here too. I wish you could see an English county town in summer. You will find this on the map. I have been sitting out in a back garden all day writing about Henry James and Hawthorne.[3] The roses are wonderful.

I have a week's holiday, a few days hence, and I shall take some long walks and go out on the river.

I do hope I shall have a letter from you in a few days, dear mother, as it is over a fortnight. I shall write to father as soon as my holidays begin.

Your devoted son
Tom.

1–VHE had leased the house for five years from 5 Dec. 1917. BR had a financial interest in the arrangement, and provided some of the furniture. On 17 Dec. BR told OM that it would give him 'a quiet peaceful existence in which I can work'; and on 6 Jan. 1918 he said to Colette O'Neil that his 'work-a-day life will be at Marlow, with Mrs. E' (quoted in Monk, *Bertrand Russell*, 515–16).

2–Shelley leased Albion House, West Street, Marlow, in 1817–18.

3–'The Hawthorne Aspect'.

TO *His Mother* TS Houghton

23 June 1918 [London]

Dearest mother,

I have just written to father, but I want to write a short one to you to acknowledge three from you which I have studied attentively. I am relieved that father has so rapidly rallied and only think that he ought to take very good care of himself for the rest of the summer especially if you stay in St Louis. There is something to be said for Millis, even with the increased fares. I am sure you will let me know how he is, and also how you are (but you have *never* done that!) in every letter.

I gave a good many particulars in my letter to father. Now I am writing with yours open in front of me, so that I may not overlook anything that requires an answer. I *did* get the £2 for the suit: it is very strange on this as on one or two other occasions that I have a strong conviction that I acknowledged it at once. Thank you very much indeed; I think I wrote and told you what a nice suit I got, and what a wise investment it was, as prices have been soaring since.

We both had a very painful time at the dentist, and Vivien has also been having much trouble with her eyes, and has had to have some expensive glasses. She fully meant to write to you today, but woke up with a very bad migraine (I think a delayed result of the dentist several days ago) and was so dizzy when she got up that she had to lie down again. We feel sometimes as if we were going to pieces and just being patched up from time to time. The strain of life is very great and I fear it will be for the rest of the lives of anyone now on earth. I am very pessimistic about the world we are going to have to live in after the war.

You type beautifully.

We had a pleasant day yesterday: a young friend of mine, named Huxley, a grandson of the scientist T. H. Huxley, who is a master at Eton not far away, came out to spend the day with us.[1]

I have some poems appearing very soon in the *Little Review*[2] in New York, and also an article which I wrote at the beginning of this holiday on

1–Of his visit to Marlow, AH wrote to his brother: 'Eliot in excellent form and his wife too; I rather like her; she is such a genuine person, vulgar, but with no attempt to conceal her vulgarity, with no snobbery of the kind that makes people say they like things, such as Bach or Cézanne, when they don't' (*Letters of Aldous Huxley*, ed. Grover Smith [1969], 156).

2–Four poems appeared in the *Little Review* 5 (Sept. 1918): 'Sweeney among the Nightingales', 'Whispers of Immortality', 'Dans le Restaurant', and 'Mr Eliot's Sunday Morning Service'.

Henry James and Hawthorne. I have just reviewed some philosophy books for the *New Statesman*, have some more to do, and am commissioned for articles for that and for a paper called *To-Day*,[1] when I can get them done. Also, I have this week done my monthly work for the *Egoist*, including the delicate task of reviewing half a dozen books by men I know. I think I know most of the people in London who write verse, and a fair number of the other men of letters. I have also read this week most of Catullus, and two plays of Ben Jonson.

I think I have given all my news between you and father. We have not heard from Maurice for some time; I expect he is pretty busy just now. He had a few days in Rome about six weeks ago.

Always your devoted son
Tom

TO *Scofield Thayer* — TS Beinecke

30 June 1918 — at 17 Cornhill, London, E.C.3

Dear Scofield,

Delightful to hear from you, both sentimentally and because it is cheering that there should still be someone who preserves in these times the literary standards of epistolary style. I am also delighted that you should be applying your cosmopolitan talents where they are needed, and breasting the full flood of bovine excreta of which the effluvium in occasional gusts attacks my nostril from oversea. I look forward to the receipt of your specimen.[2] Of course, your superior officer is a Lady. They always are. Be PATIENT, I say PATIENT. Be Sly, INSIDIOUS, even UNSCRUPULOUS, Suffering Many Things, Slow to WRATH, concealing the Paw of the Lion, the Fang of the Serpent, the Tail of the Scorpion, beneath the Pelt of the ASS. Under the cloak of imbecility dart forth your scorn and pour the vials of contumely upon the fair flat face of the people. Be Proud, but Genial, Affable, but Inflexible; be to the inhabitants of Greenwich Village a Flail, and to the Intellect of Indianapolis a Scourge. I WILL REPAY, saith the LORD.[3]

I speak from experience, as asst. (I say ASSt) Editor of the *Egoist*, which I will send you, numero specimene, if you do not know it. I am the only male, and three (3) women, incumbents, incunabula, incubae.

1–He published one article in *To-Day* 4: 19 (Sept. 1918): 'A Note on Ezra Pound'.

2–Thayer was planning to support the *Dial* financially.

3–TSE is parodying various biblical proverbs and epistles, as well as *sententiae* in Shakespeare.

Do you see the *Little Review*? I hope so. There you can watch (in bathing) our Friend Ezra, and sometimes myself (*sc.* next July and after), and particularly the superb new novel of Joyce, which I do commend to your attention. You no doubt have read the *Portrait of the Artist* by him. The best living prose writer.

I should be delighted to write for your paper – or rather for any paper with which you are connected. Is Conrad Aiken still to be the Critic?[1] I think that if I composed something in the hope of your printing it I ought to exploit my geographical position rather than send you my projected series on the Jacobean Dramatists. Studies in European Literature, by one on the SPOT! Reflections on American Literature, by one NOT on the spot![2] As *Poetry* said of J. G. Fletcher 'cosmopolitan by education and residence'.[3]

Everything I say is quite serious. I am delighted with your occupation.

Vivien says (and says to tell you) that she is homesick for America.

Adieu. Would I might talk to you. You have as much news of friends here as I. Harwood,[4] I hear (from the charming Aldous Huxley) is in London again, in some Govt. office. Willie King[5] is in London, in [Military] Intelligence Dept, I have seen him occasionally.

Note my address above.

Je t'embrasse sur les deux joues.

Yours ever
T.S.E.

1–Once Thayer took charge of the *Dial*, Aiken was a contributor but never its official critic.
2–TSE, 'American Literature', a review of *A History of American Literature*, vol. 2, by William B. Trent, John Erskine, Stuart P. Sherman and Carl Van Doren, in *A.*, 25 Apr. 1919.
3–John Gould Fletcher (1886–1950), American poet and critic, scion of a wealthy Southern family, dropped out of Harvard and lived for many years in Europe; a friend of EP, he became one of the mainstays of Imagism. His *Selected Poems* won the Pulitzer Prize, 1938. See his autobiography, *Life Is My Song* (1937), which includes a portrait of TSE; and *Selected Letters of John Gould Fletcher*, ed. Leighton Rudolph and Ethel C. Simpson (1996). From 1926 he was to become a frequent contributor to *C.* and he was also one of the first of the Faber poets.
4–Henry Harwood (1893–1964), an Oxford acquaintance who became a journalist.
5–William King (1894–1958), who was to become Deputy Keeper of British and Medieval Antiquities, British Museum, 1952.

TO *Mary Hutchinson* MS Texas

1 July 1918 [London]

I meant to let you know that I had sent your P.O. on. I sent it to Pound as I thought he could let you have the backnumbers at once.[1] The Joyce is quite superb. I should be interested to hear your opinion of it. I wonder if you are in a hammock reading Ste Beuve. I shall want to know what you think of Sachie's poems.[2]

We have not seen anyone for a long time.

Sincerely
T. S. Eliot

TO *Harriet Monroe* MS Houghton

6 July 1918 17 Cornhill, London E.C.3

Dear Miss Monroe,

Thank you for your appreciation of my review.[3] I know how difficult a task you had, and the result is certainly of great interest.

I shall be glad to write on *Rimbaud* and *Tristan Corbière*. I suppose you want about 1000 words apiece? Not more, I take it. I shall I hope send the first in about a month, perhaps less.[4]

Sincerely yours
T. S. Eliot

TO *His Mother* MS Houghton

7 July 1918 17 Cornhill

My dearest Mother,

We have been living on quietly and trying to escape the 'Spanish influenza' so called.[5] A good many men – and women – have been away

1–The postal order was presumably for back numbers of the *Little Review*.
2–Sacheverell Sitwell, *The People's Palace*, was reviewed by TSE in the *Egoist* 5: 6 (June–July).
3–'Reflections on Contemporary Poetry' [III].
4–Though mentioned again to his mother on 7 July, no essay by TSE on Rimbaud or Corbière was published. In *T. S. Eliot et la France* [1951], Edward H. Greene notes TSE told him that after 1912 and his Laforguian period, TSE read Rimbaud several times, mentioning in particular the influence of his 'Cabaret-Vert' and 'Vénus Anadyomene' (62–3). For his poem 'Tristan Corbière', see *IMH*, 88.
5–The 1918–19 influenza epidemic killed some 20 million people worldwide.

from the office lately, with that curious malady, and as a result I have had more to do, helping out. The season has been very dry – whether that has anything to do with it I don't know – and out here in the country everything is done to a crisp. The flowers seem to stand it better than the vegetables, and just now we are very grateful for fresh vegetables – peas and beans and salads. The weather has been very hot, and appropriate to the 4th July, which was celebrated in London. I say 'celebrated' in quotation marks because it was taken so solemnly, more as a very serious act of international courtesy, something of gravity, than the hilarious 4th of boyhood. I think that the appetite for the noisier sort of fireworks should have died out for this generation. I only missed the strawberry icecream and the yacht race. London is very seriously interested in the game of baseball, which is now practised by Americans and Canadians regularly, and of which I am constantly called upon to explain terms.[1] There seem to be many American soldiers about; at least I see officers pretty often, though I have never seen any of my acquaintance. Occasionally some come to the bank with Letters of Credit. I told you how I missed Harold Peters when he was in Glasgow; I have been waiting for him to turn up again.

I have not had a letter from either of you lately. I am waiting eagerly for news of father, and how you manage to stand the heat at this time of year. Have you tried to let Gloucester or is it shut up? It is rather difficult to let a house when you are not on the spot, I fancy, to put it in order for the tenant. Is Marion going to spend most of the summer with Charlotte? We had a letter from Charlotte not very long ago, in which she spoke more cheerfully of George's work. Also one from Aunt Mattie, who said nothing at all, except that she had been very ill for a long time, and that she was no longer at Mrs Sutherland's, but nearby.

I had a letter from Maurice yesterday, of course with nothing definite as to his location – somewhere in Venetia, living in a large villa, with a Colonel and a Major, and finding the weather very hot.

Naturally, we have seen very few people lately, and as a matter of fact nearly everyone has gone out of town for the indefinite future – or enough people so that those who remain remain as scattered individuals. We long for Bosham and the sea – would that it were near enough to London to come up every day.

1 – On 4 July, the US Navy had defeated the US Army at Stamford Bridge in front of 38,000 spectators, including King George V and the Prime Minister, Lloyd George.

I am thinking of getting together a collection of prose and verse to come out in America in the spring. There is a publisher in N.Y. [Alfred Knopf] who wants it. I should have several essays from the *New Statesman* and the *Little Review*, and a good deal from the *Egoist*, and two essays which *Poetry* in Chicago wants me to write on French poets.

And a few more poems besides those in my book.

I must stop now and go to bed. I hope there will be a letter tomorrow.

Many long thoughts and very much love to both of you

Your devoted son

Tom

Vivien's newly filled tooth has a nerve which every now and then *jumps* or seems to take a twist, and nearly takes her out of her chair. I wonder very much what the matter is.

TO *His Mother* MS Houghton

28 July 1918 [Marlow]

My dearest Mother,

I have a nice letter from you dated the 8th July, nineteen days en route – the first for some time. This will be your first from me for some time, as I have not written for nearly a fortnight. The fortnight before I had two letters from you. Perhaps another one will come on Monday. This is wretched paper but paper is very dear now.

Our weather has been constant rain for a month after a long drought. The crops and gardens have certainly benefited by it, but now we are ready for a little hot sun. The gardens of Marlow are brilliant with hollyhocks now, which start after the foxgloves and lupins and larkspur are over. In England there is continuous bloom, one flower to another, from March nearly to December.

Vivien has not been well ever since she went to the dentist. She was not very well then, but there was a piece of work I thought ought to be done. The dentist put his filling too close to the nerve and she [has] had very bad attacks of pain ever since. Then an abscess developed. She has managed to keep it down by being quiet, resting and two days in bed; I hope it will pass off, but one is never sure. I think a week at Bosham would do her much good, and if father sends the money I think we can do it. Last year it put her into shape for the winter, but this has been a much more trying winter than last. I do not know just how long we can stay here, so you had better write always *to the bank* (Lloyds Bank Ltd., 17 Cornhill, E.C.3) as I said.

We have had two interruptions since I wrote – Maurice came back from Italy for a few days, and Harold Peters came for a day. Maurice is pretty well, and in a fairly comfortable and not very dangerous position at present, and we hope he will stay there. I think the war is wearing on him very much – he has had so much of it, and soldiering. I hope it will not injure him for after life; but there is no gaiety in him now. Peters' ship was at a port some distance from London and he managed to get a day off and fly up to see me. He seemed not much changed, except matured by responsibility and authority; was just as nice as ever, and he and Vivien liked each other very much indeed.

I have not seen anything about the Treaty you refer to. Please keep me posted if you see anything but put it on a separate sheet of paper, writing to the Bank. Vivien worries a great deal about me (and I about her, and also about the *financial aspect* of it). The difficulties of living go on increasing every day as it is.

I shall want always to know how you and father are standing the St Louis summer.

Your devoted son
Tom

TO *Wyndham Lewis* MS Cornell

Monday [29 July? 1918] from 3 Compayne Gdns N.W.6

Dear Lewis,

I want to get at Lady Cunard[1] at once if she is in town. I have been having a row with the Navy here and I want to see Admiral Sims personally if there is any human means.[2]

Can you take me to see her immediately? I believe she knows the Admiral.

I'll call in at Hatfield House[3] first thing tomorrow. If you go out first will you leave a note to tell me where and when I can find you?

This accounts for my total disappearance for some weeks. I came in however on the afternoon convened – no one in.

Yours
Eliot

1–Lady Cunard (1872–1948), née Maude Burke, American-born London hostess.

2–Vice-Admiral William S. Sims (1858–1936), Commander of US Naval Forces in Europe. TSE was applying to join the US Navy, a process that took centre stage in the coming months.

3–WL's studio was at 1 Hatfield House, Great Titchfield Street, London W.1.

TO *Mary Hutchinson* MS Texas

4 August 1918 31 West St, Marlow, Bucks

Dear Mrs Hutchinson

Thanks awfully for your letter and wire which arrived about the same time. I only discovered or realised afterwards that in my haste and excitement I had failed to send mine reply paid, which was very rude of me.

I don't know whether Jack is coming up to town on Tuesday or not. If he is, I should like to know how I could get him by telephone. (I shall be at Lloyds Bank as usual). If *not*, would you tell him that I should be very grateful if he would write to his friend the secretary for me? I intend, as you suggest, to have my medical board as soon as possible, and hope to be graded low.

I have one or two other strings out, but they do not seem very promising chances. I am very grateful indeed to you both for your kindness. I should have liked to come down very much, but feel that I ought to stay here on the spot. I will let you know the result of [the] board.

Sincerely yours
T. S. E.

TO *Wyndham Lewis* MS Cornell

5 August 1918 [Marlow]

Dear Lewis,

I have been trying to get hold of you but have so far failed. Am trying to get into U.S. Navy as I find there are one or two possibilities there. This must be settled within next few days. *Could you phone Osbert*,[1] who will explain the situation? He has been seeing Lady Cunard and will see her again.

Yours in haste
T. S. Eliot

He is at Kings Guards [Telephone:] Regent 3753 this p.m. but not, I think, this evening.

1–Osbert Sitwell was helping to gather testimonials in support of TSE's effort to join the Intelligence Corps.

TO *Wyndham Lewis* MS Cornell

11 August 1918 31 West St, Marlow

Dear Lewis,

I am going to see Schick[1] in the morning, and I am *not* going to the bank at all, as I want to get my physical examination tomorrow if possible. I must therefore communicate with you in some other way than arranged. *I will come to Hatfield House about ten:* would you just *leave a note on the door* to say when and where I can find you or ring you up in the afternoon? I can come to Hatfield House or your Studio (I think I can find it) or wherever you say. This is rather a nuisance, I am afraid, but I do not see any other way.

Yours ever
T.S.E.

TO *St John* OR *Mary Hutchinson* MS Texas

15 August 1918 17 Cornhill, E.C.3

Thank you very much for two letters and the wire. I went to see Gunther today, but did not get much help that way, as he did not put me on to anything new or offer his support in any way. At present I am waiting to hear from Col. Schick as to whether there is any chance in the quartermasters corps. The navy seems to be impossible unless the Admiral and Chief of Staff will wire to Washington for permission to give another commission. So I am not very hopeful.

I will let you know of progress, if any – meanwhile, thank you again.

I find it quite impossible to do any work under these conditions.

Sincerely
T. S. Eliot

1–Lt. Col. Jacob Schick (1878–1934) was in charge of the Division of Intelligence and Criminal Investigation of the US Navy in London. After the war, he was the inventor of the 'dry razor', or Schick safety razor.

Vivien Eliot TO *Mary Hutchinson* MS Texas

[Postmark 18 August 1918] Marlow

Dear Mary,

You may have heard or seen by the time you get this that all Americans here are called up, and within eight weeks time must either have gone to America *to enlist*, or be enlisted here presumably as privates. It has come very suddenly, and Tom is – well you know. He would have written, but is rushing about to the embassy etc. I said I wd. write for him. ~~Can you~~ You know we have *no* influence here, American, or English political. Do you think yr. husband could give him any useful introduction, or any help? Or can you? I mean to get him into a job *here* – propaganda, or something. If he goes to America he will not be able to come back while the war lasts. That means years. If he stays here he will be killed, or as good as. If we don't save him he'll never write again. You know how bitter he is *now*. Will you be a friend and communicate at once and with anyone you think cld. help? Get at Tom at the *Bank*—it's quicker. (*17 Cornhill*, E.C.*3*. [Telephone:] *Avenue 6430*).

Tom says please do not let this get round to Ottoline – this is important. Will explain later. Do do *something, please*.

Yrs.
V. E.

Vivien Eliot TO *Mary Hutchinson* MS Texas

Wednesday [21 August 1918] Marlow

Thank you ever so much for your wire which came this morning. I wired the contents to Tom (at the Bank) and in reply received this. *Where* he has wired to 'Jack' I do not know! Because he doesn't know where the Jowitts are and I said in the wire that Jack was with them (for that is what *you* said, isn't it!?) I am so grateful for what you've done. This about Gunther seems really useful. We knew of Gunther before – Ezra approached him but could do nothing (but he thought he was nice). I am too restless and unhappy to write much. It was as a shock to both of us that Tom was graded so high in the Medical exam. I did not realise until then how much I had *counted* on his being passed quite *UNFIT*. I can't understand it. He took a very strong certificate from our doctor, and he had been *fearfully* ill over the weekend so that he was *obviously* in a wretched state. Nothing gets settled[1] but people are being awfully good, the Sitwells and Lewis especially, really *doing* things, and now you! But it is much more difficult than we supposed. I really have not any confidence. There is a lot for me to do, but I forgot to tell you I am ill (I mean I went to a specialist *just* before this happened, as I was getting iller and iller all the summer) he gave me a lot of fearful directions and I am supposed to be under treatment but of course now I don't make the slightest attempt to do any of it. But I only mean that I ought to be up in town *every* day and all day I feel and I *can't* manage it more than around twice a week.

Tom is *fearfully* vague, and one can never trust him to be worldly wise and to say the <inspired> [required?] thing or suppress the unfortunate truth, or to see what a person is getting at. I *write out* what he is to say under every conceivable situation, but it always happens that some unexpected twist occurs which throws him off balance for the entire interview!

I have just read Clive Bell's thing in the *Nation*.[2] I was immensely thrilled at it. That's the sort of being <fantastical> [?] that I surely cannot scorn. I like everything he says so much that I shall be his disciple in life! The unknown disciple.[3]

Did you read *Tarr*?[4] How Lewis does terrify me. Please get Jack to do his *utmost* and do wire him that nothing is any nearer settled than when I first wrote and *anything* either of you can do . . .

Bosham is probably off, but if we come it will be *between* Sep. 7 – 20th. We have *let* this house for the middle of Sept. at a good rent! The only bright spot!

1–The manuscript from here is in pencil and hard to decipher.

2–Clive Bell (1881–1964), art critic; husband of Vanessa Bell (1879–1961) and lover of the Eliots' friend MH; author of *Art* (1914). Bell wrote in a published letter (*N.*, 10 Aug.): 'The Liberal and Conservative parties are dead. They perished with that old aristocratic civilization which received its death-blow with the war . . . henceforth the Labour Party is the Gentleman's Party.'

3–*The Nation* was running a series of 'Letters from an Unknown Disciple'.

4–WL's *Tarr* (Egoist Press, 1918) was reviewed in the same issue of the *Nation*. TSE reviewed it for the *Egoist*, which had also serialised it.

TO *Edmund Dulac*[1] MS Virginia

23 August 1918 31 West St, Marlow

Cher Monsieur Dulac,

I shall not attempt to respond in the language which you use to decorate so beautifully my exaggerated attainments, lest you perceive how far they are below your praises. But I think it was extraordinarily kind of you to reply so quickly to my plea, and also it is remarkable that on such scanty information as you must have received you could have produced exactly what I wanted.

I am trying to get a non-combatant commission either in Quartermasters' or Interpreters' Corps, and am required to send in testimonials. I *hope* to be able to remain in England.

Again with many thanks

Sincerely yours
T. S. Eliot

TO *Henry Eliot* MS Houghton

25 August 1918 c/o British Linen Bank,
Threadneedle St, London E.C.

Dear Henry,

Thank you infinitely for your letter of the 5th August, which arrived yesterday. You have evidently taken no end of pains over this, and I do appreciate your goodness.

It would appear, after examining your report very carefully, that I have as good a chance over here. Since the end of July I have tried several things. There seemed a very good chance for a job, with commission, in the U.S.A. Navy Office here in London. I interviewed several people in the office, and they said they would be very glad of a man like me in the Intelligence Department, and there was another job too, even better, directly under the Admiral. I thought I was pretty certain to get one or the other, and then they got a cable from Washington forbidding them to give any more commissions over here. There was still some prospect of their cabling for special permission in my case, but it is now two weeks and I have heard nothing. I am going once more to enquire, but am not hopeful.

1–Edmund Dulac (1882–1953), naturalised British artist and book illustrator who helped with TSE's French poems of 1917, as TSE later told the *Paris Review*, 56 (*IMH*, 291). 'Dans le Restaurant' was due to appear in *Little Review* 5: 5 (Sept. 1918).

The second thing is that I had an introduction to Col. Schick, Assistant Provost-Marshal, who has been awfully nice to me. I have had a medical examination, passed fit for *limited* service (hernia) and am to send in an application for a commission in the Quartermaster's or Interpreter's Corps. I have been collecting testimonials from the most important people I know; the whole exhibit goes to France, and if approved, I am examined by a board here. Col. Schick thinks I ought to get this. If this fails, I see nothing else at present but to try for exemption. Not being fit for active service, I am much more useful in my present occupation than in any limited service job for which I could be conscripted as a private, and with an invalid dependent wife it is obvious that I should suffer very badly on a private's pay.

I do not suppose that I shall be called up for some time anyway, being in a deferred class, so there will be time to go on trying, but the strain is great. If you hear of any job which I could get *over here without going back* it would be very useful. There *ought* to be places for which a man who knows *England* well, English society, English business, *would be most suitable.*

I am awfully sorry not to have acknowledged the previous remittances of money. It seems awfully ungrateful, but there have been times when I have been so over worked and tired and worried that the idea of writing has been impossible of execution. And at times when one has a great deal more to do than one can do one takes a kind of vicious pleasure in neglecting things and appearing ungrateful and rude and nasty to the people to whom one least wishes to be.

Thank you again and again. I simply cannot write any more, I have written nine letters today and I have two more to write. Vivien will write as soon as she can.

Very affectionately
Tom.

TO *St John Hutchinson* — MS Texas

25 August 1918 — 31 West St, Marlow

Dear Jack

Thanks awfully for your letter, which is a very useful one, and a departure from the usual form of testimonial. I hope it was not a nuisance to you to write at such short notice, but I thought it might be essential to get it off at once. I rang up Schick in the morning, and he said that the difference of a few days would not matter, but that I ought to get as good recommendations to send with it as I possibly could. So I am hoping to see Bennett[1] on Monday, and if he is well inclined to get a letter out of him on the spot; and turn in my application on *Tuesday*.

Schick said this time that what was most important, when the Board was actually appointed here in London, was to find out anyone I knew who knew any member of the Board and get them to write personally. Lady Cunard would in all probability know one of them, or even if she did not, she could write to someone who did, and the letter could be placed before the member, and this would be more influential than a formal testimonial addressed to no one in particular. If she were in town I think it would be much the simplest thing for someone to take me to see her; but as she is out of town would it not be best if I could meet Nancy and explain to her? Do tell me how you think that could be managed.

You see, Lady C. has been approached about my affairs already, and I don't want her to get muddled or tired of them, but want to ask some one perfectly definite thing.

This is the only point at present. Of course, *all* the testimonials or letters I can get to put before the Board will be very useful – what I have said is only about Lady C.

I hope you are not having as wet a weekend at Wittering as we are here. I envy you there. With many thanks

Yours ever
T. S. E.

TO *Mary Hutchinson* — MS Texas

25 August 1918 — 31 West St, Marlow

Dear Mary,

Thank you so much for your letter. I do appreciate such sympathy in the present difficulties, though I hate a situation which makes me force my practical personal affairs upon my friends to the exclusion of everything else. I quite feel as you do about khaki; at the same time I think that this is the moment for getting into it to the best advantage, and that nothing else is of much use until this has been tried. Everything else is insecure, though I shall try if and immediately this present attempt fails. I am almost at the point of feeling that nearly *anything*, *settled* would be less unpleasant than the present incessant strain.

1 – Arnold Bennett.

I think that conditions might arise when Clutton Brock's name would be very useful.[1] At present what I want are names which could carry instant conviction to *anybody* – celebrities, and people with official or social titles. Of course Brock knows a great many people, and he might be able to suggest something. But if it is a question of a formal testimonial I think it might be more useful later. I have met him once or twice. He is a good person to keep in mind; thank you for thinking of him.

As for your proposal that we should come to Wittering – that is very good of you. But the fact is that when everything is so unsettled we could not think of going away from town. I might have to come back at any time, and I should feel very restless. Your barn is a charming place! but I simply could not write *anywhere* at present – it's out of the question. You understand that, I am sure. We should have loved to come had circumstances been different. Thank you very much from both of us.

Yours ever,
T. S.E.

TO *John Rodker*[2]

MS Mrs Burnham Finney

4 September 1918 — 31 West St, Marlow

Dear Rodker,

I return herewith all of your MSS which is in my possession. There is another prose piece which I gave to Weaver and told her she ought to use, and which I expect she will print shortly, and I will ask her if she has anything else. The *Suite* was too long to use under our present limitations, and two other things we judged it useless to try, in view of our mortifying experiences with *Ulysses*. Have you anything on hand that we could have, prose or verse?[3] Also, would you be willing to review a book or two occasionally?

It is true that my affairs have been unsettled, and living in the country as we are, and being absorbed in military matters, I haven't seen anyone except very much on business. But I am coming back to town toward the end of this month, and as any decision of my fate seems to be in the indefinite future, I expect to occupy my flat myself. Otherwise, I should

1 – Arthur Clutton-Brock (1868–1924), essayist, critic and journalist, author of *The Ultimate Belief*, which TSE had reviewed in *IJE*, Oct. 1916.

2 – John Rodker, publisher, poet and novelist: see Glossary of Names.

3 – Rodker contributed 'Hymn to Death, 1914 and On', *Egoist* 5: 10 (Nov.–Dec. 1918).

have been glad of a tenant – though the present one would be glad to keep it on.

I hope I may see something of you this winter.

Cordially
T. S. Eliot

TO *Robert Ross*[1]

4 September 1918 31 West St, Marlow

Dear Mr Ross,

I have just managed to get your address, which I neglected to notice the other day, from Osbert – or I should certainly have written to you before, to thank you for speaking to Bennett. I found him extremely kind and sympathetic, and he wrote a charming letter for me without any hesitation.[2] Your having spoken to him made it much easier for me.

I have not, however, put in my application yet. I have found that the Intelligence Dept. is much more suitable and have just got in touch with them. I was able to produce an excellent showing of testimonials, and the chances are very good, only they want three letters from Americans as well – and I don't know any prominent Americans here. Thanking you again,

Yours very truly
T. S. Eliot

TO *His Father* MS Houghton

8 September 1918 c/o Lloyds Bank, 17 Cornhill, E.C.3

Dear Father,

Your letter with birth certificate came Friday. Thank you very much for your promptness in writing and in writing to Pres. Eliot[3] and to Ada.

1 – Robert Ross (1869–1918), gallery owner and literary executor of Oscar Wilde. Osbert Sitwell had suggested that TSE approach Bennett through Ross. The text here is taken from *Robert Ross: Friend of Friends*, ed. Margery Ross (1952), 337.

2 – See Bennett's testimonial, 28 Aug. 1918: 'I have pleasure in stating that Mr. T. S. Eliot (whom I understand to be a candidate for a commission in the Quartermasters or Interpreters Corps) has an intimate knowledge of the French language. Also that he is a writer of distinguished merit, for whose work personally I have a great admiration. I may mention that it was my admiration for Mr. Eliot's work which led to my acquaintance with him, and not vice versa' (*Letters of Arnold Bennett* III, ed. James Hepburn, 1970, 66).

3 – President Charles William Eliot of Harvard; see letter of 25 July 1919.

I am in touch with a Major Turner of the Intelligence Service (he comes from St Louis but has not lived in America for many years). He thinks he can get me into that work. My testimonials are *very* good – but he says that to apply for a commission – to satisfy the officials who pass upon these things – I *must* have three *American* testimonials. This is all that is holding me up – I ought to have them *now*, and every day delay is affecting my chances. This is *just* the work for a man of my qualifications and I am the sort of man wanted for it, and my physical disabilities (hernia and tachycardia) would not disqualify me.

I am all the more worried because I have a letter from Ada, dated the *25th*, in which she does not refer to having heard from you or from me. I cabled *her* on the same day I cabled *you*, and asked for testimonials from any Harvard people besides Charles Eliot. What can be the matter? I cabled *again* to her on Thursday last, and have had no reply to *that*.

I have everything required except the American testimonials – my friends here have pushed me in every way possible, and I should hate to be disappointed just for the lack of these. If I do not hear from Ada I shall cable you again.

Thank you very much. I am worn out with trying to do my duty at the bank – which has been so kind to me – and rushing hither and thither as well.

I will write by Wednesday if I have any more news.

Your affectionate son
Tom.

TO *John Quinn* — MS NYPL (MS)

8 September 1918 — c/o Lloyds Bank, 17 Cornhill, E.C.3

Dear Mr Quinn,

Pound told me yesterday that he was cabling to you about me, so I am writing now to explain the circumstances. It seemed to me a pretty considerable favour to ask of you, but he was quite sure that it was the thing to do, and I know that your word would carry as much weight as anyone's.

I am trying to get a commission in the Intelligence Department of the Army. Although of draft age (thirty) I am graded as unfit for *active* service (fighting) on account of a hernia, and furthermore my wife (who is an invalid) is entirely dependent on me, which I believe makes a difference. But I should like to get into the service in some way in which my brains and qualifications, such as they are, would be useful, if I could have a rank high enough to support me financially. The Intelligence Department needs men who know Europe and England well, and I *think* there is a chance for me to be very useful there. From what enquiries I have made the work seems comparatively undeveloped yet and there are great possibilities of work for Anglo-American understanding. Major Turner, whom I saw three days ago in the matter, was very much pleased with my English testimonials, but said that it was an invariable rule for an applicant to have at least three American ones as well.[1]

I have been very busy with these and other personal anxieties for several months past – in fact I have had such a busy year in the effort to make a living under wartime conditions, that I think I shall have more leisure for serious work and freedom from anxiety in the Army than out of it. I have not answered your delightful letter of April 19th as I ought to have done. I deeply appreciated your kindness over the Boni affair. I am all the more grateful as it arose at a time when you were just recovering from a serious operation.

I have a book ready for Knopf, not a very big one, but I think big enough – miscellany of prose (mostly criticism) and verse including *Prufrock* and everything of any merit since *Prufrock*, the manuscript of which is almost ready to go over. It is not the book I should have liked. I should prefer to keep the prose and verse apart; and the former, I fear, bears marks of haste in the writing in many places. But it is time I had a volume in America, and this is the only way to do it; and Pound's book[2] will provide a precedent. I hope you will not find the book a wholly journalistic compilation.

I hope the *Little Review* is really gaining subscriptions in America. It must be a great burden to you in certain ways, and it does not seem to me that it could be permanently run on its present constitution, though this is doubtless the only way possible at present.

I hope you are much stronger now, though I gather that you are still under a regimen. No doubt you find it very hard to preserve yourself from claims. I can understand what you say about that – so well that I hate troubling you with *my* personal affairs – here I have written a long letter about nothing else. Forgive me.

Yours very sincerely
T. S. Eliot

1 – Quinn wrote to Turner on TSE's behalf.
2 – EP, *Pavannes and Divisions* (Knopf, June 1918).

FROM *Leonard Woolf*[1] TS Valerie Eliot

19 October 1918 Hogarth House, Paradise Road,
Richmond, S.W.

Dear Mr Eliot,

My wife and I have started a small private Printing Press, and we print and publish privately short works which would not otherwise find a publisher easily. We have been told by Roger Fry that you have some poems which you wish to find a publisher for. We both very much liked your book, *Prufrock*; and I wonder whether you would care to let us look at the poems with a view to printing them.

Yours very truly
Leonard Woolf

I should add that we are amateurs at printing but we could, if you liked, let you see our last production.[2]

Vivien Eliot TO *Henry Eliot* MS Houghton

[Postmark 27 October 1918]

Dear Henry,

I *have* tried to write to you over and over. I feel awful at not having written to any of you for so long. It is largely that I am *always* now in such wretched health, and I am simply ashamed of it. *I don't want them to know*. And then there is a lot we can't tell, and life is so feverish and yet so dreary at the same time, and one is always waiting, waiting for something. Generally waiting for some particular strain to be over. One thinks, when this is over I will write. And then there is something else. For *months* now, I have waited for T. to be settled. I believe that has nearly come, and you will get a cable before this. I am also waiting to be well. I wish something would bring you over here. I do wish it.

Yr.
V.

1–Leonard Woolf (1880–1969): writer and publisher; see Glossary of Names.
2–Katherine Mansfield, *Prelude* (Hogarth Press, 1918).

TO *Henry Eliot* MS Houghton

27 October 1918 *Write* 18 Crawford Mansions,
London W.1 *permanently*

My dear Henry

Thank you very much for your kind letter of Oct. 3d. I am just writing this to say that I have cashed *all* the remittances *viz.*

$50	13th May	=	£10.8.4
50	17th June		10.8.4
52.80	31st July		11. –

The last was drawn on Lloyds Marlow, but I cashed it at Cornhill. I am cabling to this effect tomorrow. Will write by next mail.

Affy yours
Tom.

TO *His Father* TS Houghton

4 November 1918 18 Crawford Mansions

My dearest father,

You will have wondered very much and I fear worried. I have thought most constantly of you and mother and wanted to write every day, but at the same time I have been so paralysed by rapid occurrences and the suspense that I could not write. Also, I kept hoping from day to day that I should have some final definite piece of news to cable you. Now it has not ended yet, so I am writing.

You know I had been trying every quarter to see what I could get into. At first it was the navy, but after saying that they wanted me they told me that I could only come in for the Intelligence work by enlisting as a seaman and taking an examination in a variety of subjects. As this was slow and precarious, and the examination would be difficult and pure waste of time, and also as I could not live for any time on a seaman's pay, I tried the army. The first thing suggested to me was the Quartermaster Corps – my physical rating precludes me from *active* service, and I found that I should have to get testimonials. I gathered in time about sixteen excellent recommendations from various English prominent official people of my acquaintance,[1] and just as I was ready to put them in with an application

1–They included J. C. Squire, Graham Wallas, St John Hutchinson, Philip Jourdain, F. S. Boas and the Dean of Merton.

I met a man who was a Lieutenant engaged in starting a Political Intelligence section for extremely interesting work, and he was quite sure that I was the man he wanted and asked me to wait and see his chief who was coming to town in a few days. Then after a week or so he told me that this was called off, as some department in Washington had interfered and the Intelligence section was not to be started at all. A few days after that I was introduced to a Major in charge of the ordinary Army Intelligence, whose work appeared interesting. He said he thought he could get me a commission, but that I must have at least three *American* testimonials as well as my English ones. Of course I had difficulty there, as I did not know any Americans here whose names would be immediately recognised as carrying weight. Then I cabled to you and Shef. Finally I found a Captain in the Embassy whom I knew slightly at Harvard;[1] I also found the Ex-Dean of Harvard, who finally gave me a very stiff little letter, which was of no use. So I had to wait. Then President Eliot's kind letter came. And the Harvard Certificates, which were not what I wanted at all; I *meant* personal letters from professors, but Shef did not understand. So I had to wait again. Then I ran across an old Harvard Professor[2] here in a government capacity who gave me an enthusiastic letter, and later a letter came from Professor Woods, to whom I had cabled. So I was all ready.

Just then, when I was finally after long delays going to put my application in, the Navy Intelligence *sent for me*. The Commander was very polite, said he had heard of me and thought I was just the man he needed very badly; that unfortunately they were not allowed to give commissions straight off, but that they could make me a Chief Yeoman, with a fairly good salary – enough, with ration allowance, to live upon – put me at an interesting piece of work here in the London office, and that I would probably be given a commission in a few months' time. He asked me if I would come and how soon. So I went to the bank, explained that the Navy wanted me very badly as soon as possible. They were very nice to me at the bank, as they always have been, and said that in consideration of the importance of the work and my fitness for it they would make no objection to my going, and would have my place for me when the war was over. So I arranged to go in two weeks, after I had trained another man to do my work, and told the navy when I was coming. About a week later I went to the navy for the slight medical examination required for the work,

1 – Bronson Cutting (1888–1935), publisher; later a US Senator. A Harvard contemporary of TSE, he was Assistant Military Attaché in London, 1917–18.
2 – G. H. Palmer.

and then learned that they had to cable to Washington for approval of the appointment. I was told that this was done in every case and was merely a formality.

At the appointed time I left the bank, as the other man was doing my work and the bank had no further need for me unless I could stay on. But the approval had not yet come, and I could not be enrolled. Finally, two weeks after the cable had been sent from here to Washington, I had a telegram from the navy

'Approval received as requested – no further difficulty'.

So I went in to be enrolled. They had started to enroll me when they discovered that the cable from Washington read

'Appointment approved . . . if not registered selective service . . .'

They had assumed here that I was *not* registered. But I pointed out to them that under the Convention *every* American of draft age is registered in England, and that Americans who had failed to register are automatically *liable for service in the British Army*, and the American Government has no further claim upon them; that therefore, the cablegram was incomprehensible. They then applied to our Army here, who could cast no light on the matter, and said they had no claim upon me. So then they said they must cable again.

I then pointed out: 'You *sent for* me, asked me to come as soon as possible, and led me to believe that the matter was quite settled. I took you at your word, and arranged accordingly. Through the delay in your cable (and I was not even told that cabling was necessary) I have already been out of work a week, a luxury which I can ill afford. If this cable takes as long as the other, and I wait for it, I shall have been out of work and without pay for a month. Why should I suffer for your mistakes? You made me a definite offer, and you have not fulfilled it'.

However, they cabled very urgently. Last Thursday they received an answer, saying that the matter would have to be referred to the Provost Marshal General in Washington, and asking for my registration number, address of local board, etc. The Navy has cabled back, and there it is. Meanwhile I have been out of work for two weeks, through no fault of my own. Had they even told me that there might be delay I could have arranged otherwise with the bank, instead of teaching another man in a hurry, and might still be at the bank drawing pay.

I was very angry about their having invited me to leave my work without having previously informed themselves accurately as to the conditions on which they could take me. So I cabled to you to try to get an introduction to the Admiral to lay the matter before him personally and explain the injustice. I have tried to get an introduction to him here but not yet succeeded. Lady Cunard gave me a letter to the Chief of Staff. He however was called out just as I came in and turned me over to the chief of the personnel department. He was very nice to me, perhaps as an effect of the effect of the letter on the chief of staff, but he could do nothing except through Washington. *He* was not the person who made the mistake which has been so costly to myself, in any case. Of course it has *not* got through to Washington that I was actually promised the post, nor is it likely to. There might perhaps be a case for a reprimand, if it got very far. The man who first saw me and offered me the job has told me that it was his fault, but that does not do very much good. My losses are:

1. At least two weeks pay, which I shall stand to lose in any case.

2. I have abandoned the attempt to get an army commission. That would take two months, I was told. I cannot wait two months without work, and I cannot ask the bank to take me back for that time. If the bank takes me in now the least I can do is to let them appeal for me and not attempt to get into the army.

3. My Questionnaire had come from St Louis. The Local Board will soon be wondering why they have not heard from me. I cannot fill it in until I know whether I am to be in the navy or not. When I can get it off I shall cable to you to let them know that it has been delayed and is on the way, and why it has been delayed. But I do not think they are likely to call me up before it comes, as the physical examiner recommended me for six months exemption straight off. So that is all for the present. I have not heard from you for a long long time, and am waiting anxiously. But perhaps the letters have gone to Marlow and will come here deviously.

I am so tired with this long explanation that I cannot write more now. I hope now you know the story you will forgive me for not having written. You see at each step it was either a question of cabling, or else I expected to be able to cable and say that I had got something. This constant deferment for three months has told on me very much; I feel years older than I did in July! I feel now that perhaps I am much more useful in the bank than in the army, and that I would have done better not to have bothered about it.

With very much love to both of you, and to all of you,

Your very affectionate son
Tom

I shall simply have to have this settled or go back to the bank this week or I shall be bankrupt. The financial end of it is the most important of all, now.

TO *Henry Eliot* — MS Houghton

4 November 1918 — 18 Crawford Mansions

My dear Henry,

After all your goodness in cabling and working and writing and providing funds it seems very shabby that you should be in doubt because I have not even let you know when I received money from you. As a matter of fact, *all* the money came, as I wrote you last week, so I trust you will advise the banks which stopped payment. I cannot tell you how grateful we both have been for this money, it was providential. Even now, I am in rather a bad way, owing to the fact that the Navy have promised me a job and induced me to leave the bank on a certain date, and have then kept me waiting two weeks (without pay) on account of certain technical difficulties which have involved much cabling to Washington. I feel very sore about it, and it is not settled yet. I have just written explaining in full to father, and I hope he will send the letter on to you, as it took three closely typed pages to explain.

There are a great many things I want to write to you about, but I can't put my mind on them now. Three months of trying for a job, and for a month or so expecting to get it any day, has told on my nerves; and I feel very old at present, and mentally quite exhausted.

I can't help feeling, after seeing more of my fellow countrymen lately than I have for four years – that I get on very much better with [the] English. I am not speaking only of my friends, but of the ordinary people one's in contact with in both countries. Americans now impress me, almost invariably, as very immature.

Can you not take a couple of months, when the war is finally settled and your colleagues are back, and come over here on a holiday? Keep thinking about it.

As always affectionately
Tom.

TO *Mrs Jack Gardner* — MS Gardner Museum

7 November 1918 — 18 Crawford Mansions

Dear Mrs Gardner,

I have been intending throughout the summer to answer your letter of June 2nd. I must have appeared unaccountably rude both to you and to everyone else of my friends in America: even my family have had to cable to me once or twice for assurance of my continued existence. This has been the most terribly exhausting year I have ever known, and one unfortunate event has crowded another. In the first place my wife's health was so affected by the terrible events of the winter that we had to leave London, and the material discomforts, deprivations and expenses of living in the country (I came to town every day) made a considerable total of embarrassment. On top of that I have spent an immense amount of energy, time, and have been at great expense in trying to get into some branch of government work for which I was fitted. As I was declared unfit for active service I tried to get into either the Army or Navy Intelligence, for which it seemed to me that I was highly qualified, but some official difficulty or other has always arisen. It seems an impossibility for a man to secure any position for which he is really fitted. Only lately I was invited by the Navy to come in to their Intelligence; and threw up my position in Lloyds Bank upon their offer. When the time arrived for me to come in they discovered some technical flaw in the process, and have been cabling to Washington ever since. The only result, so far as I am concerned, is that I have lost a considerable amount of money through having given up my position upon the Navy's assurances, and that I have no likelihood of getting this money back. So apparently my only course is to appeal for exemption on the ground of a dependent wife, and being partially unfit physically, and await events. Possibly in the course of time the army will discover that they need me to peel potatoes.

But I do not want to take up this delayed letter with my grievances. I have of course been unable to do any serious work. My contributions to the last two numbers of the *Little Review* (which I hope you will like!) were written in the spring. Of course I have the *Egoist* editing, and a series of lectures on Elizabethan literature, on my hands as well as my daily work in the Foreign Department of Lloyds Bank. The latter will sound odd to you, but it is the most interesting business work there is, and offers a secure livelihood, and enables me to live in London and pursue my interests and see my friends and the bank have been very appreciative and encouraging. So I shall go back to them, after this disastrous fiasco with the navy, if they will take me.

I think there will be a certain literary activity in London after the war. I think that my friends Ezra Pound and Wyndham Lewis are the ablest literary men in London, and I hope we can do something. Do you know any of Lewis's work, either in drawing or painting, or his novel *Tarr*? He is, in my opinion, the most interesting man in London Society. The army has temporarily robbed literature and art to make an artillery officer of him, but he has lately been doing some work for Beaverbrook.[1] I also think that a younger friend of mine named Sacheverell Sitwell has unusual poetic merit. What do you think of Joyce? I admire *Ulysses* immensely. Lytton Strachey[2] has suddenly become a social lion on the strength of his *Eminent Victorians* which is really very entertaining.

I hope I shall be able to write to you again and give more literary and art gossip soon, if I get my own affairs in order. I wish I could state my case in Washington. Please write to me and tell me about yourself, and Boston – if there is anything to say about the latter. I hope you keep that torpid pool stirred up a little!

Sincerely yours,
T. S. Eliot

TO *John Rodker* MS Virginia

7 November 1918 18 Crawford Mansions

Dear Rodker

Would you care to exercise your critical acumen by doing an article[3] of any length or brevity you please *à propos* of a number of volumes of verse (inc. Fletcher, Sitwells, etc.) for the *Egoist*. I hope you will and I will see to getting the books to you.

Our attempts to meet have usually been abortive. I have been engrossed in personal difficulties connected with the Military. But would you care to come here and dine with me solus on Saturday night? I am alone, my wife is still in the country.

Yrs.
T. S. Eliot

1–WL had left the Royal Artillery to join Lord Beaverbrook's 'War Memorials' project, commissioning war artists such as Augustus John and C. R. W. Nevinson to record the part played by Canadians in the war.

2–Lytton Strachey, critic and biographer; see Glossary of Names. *Eminent Victorians* had been published in May. In an undated letter to MH, VHE wrote: 'Tom *would* like to see more of Lytton. And I feel it's been my fault. That was one of my indiscretions. But I know Tom rather wants him. He is lonely. How can he be otherwise? And Lytton is such a dear, and surely they *could* be friends?' (Texas).

3–Apart from a poem, his first contribution was 'Blackwelliana', *Egoist* 6 (Sept. 1919).

TO *Douglas Goldring*[1] MS Virginia

7 November 1918 18 Crawford Mansions

Dear Goldring,

I am writing to tell you that the delay over your manuscript is due to myself. Pound gave it to me and I intended to see Miss Weaver at once and put it in her hands. Owing to complications in my private affairs connected with military service I failed to do so.

I have given her the stuff now and she will be writing to you herself. We shall be very glad to print some or all of what you send; but it is very doubtful whether we should be able to offer any remuneration. The finances are in not a flourishing state, owing to the war, and there is very little cash available, so perhaps you won't consider it worthwhile.

What about the cuttings from *New Ireland*?[2] I enjoyed these very much, as my opinions nearly coincide with yours, and I want to send them on to the Sitwells who have not seen them.

I hope you will be back in this country before long.

I enjoyed the *Fortune*, as my review testified.[3]

Sincerely yours
T. S. Eliot

TO *Harriet Monroe* MS Houghton

7 November 1918 18 Crawford Mansions

Dear Miss Monroe

I have handed your correspondence *re* Mr Jepson to Miss Weaver, who I expect will include it at my request in the next issue of the *Egoist*, deleting the phrases mentioned.[4]

1–Douglas Goldring (1887–1960), novelist and travel writer. Beginning in Nov.–Dec., the *Egoist* carried consecutive articles by him on 'Three Georgian Novelists' (Compton Mackenzie, Hugh Walpole and Gilbert Cannan).

2–Goldring had published anonymously *Dublin: Explorations and Reflections* By An Englishman (1917), in which he mocked *Ireland's Literary Renaissance* (New York, 1916) by the Irish author and journalist Ernest A. Boyd (1887–1946). The two went on sparring for weeks in *The New Ireland*, a Dublin weekly paper, throughout May and June.

3–TSE found the first half of *The Fortune* (Dublin, 1918) 'boring', but thought its portrayal of English Society on the eve of war made it 'unquestionably a brilliant novel' (*Egoist*, Jan. 1918).

4–Monroe was to publish in *Egoist* 5: 10 (Nov.–Dec. 1918) a protest against Edgar Jepson's review, 'Recent United States Poetry' (*English Review*, May 1918); this included related correspondence with Austin Harrison, editor of the *English Review*. Jepson had written with advice from EP: see *Selected Letters of Ezra Pound 1907–1941* [1951], 135.

I confidently hoped that I should be able to send you the article at the time promised, but various personal matters have so broken up my summer that I have done no work at all. I still hope to let you have it this autumn. As for verse – I have so very little nowadays that I have been able to provide enough only for one issue of the *Little Review* in the past year.

With all best wishes for the future success of *Poetry*.

Sincerely yours
T. S. Eliot

TO *The Editor of* The Nation

Published 9 November 1918

Sir,

As an American of some years' residence in this country, I feel impelled to call attention to the conflict actually taking place between President Wilson and his domestic opponents. The information obtainable through English newspapers is meagre and the importance of the issue may easily be overlooked. It bears not only on the coming peace conference, but on future Anglo-American relations.

The Republican party, now the opposition, has for some time past applied itself to the publication of its grievances against the party in power. Many of these grievances, including charges of administrative incompetence, concern the American people alone. Many are quite likely to be well founded; with the exception of a small number of men close to the President, the Democratic party is probably inferior to the Republican in the quality of its leaders. More recently, however, the Republicans have not confined themselves to criticism of internal policy or internal blunders; some of their spokesmen have attacked Mr Wilson's foreign policy, or maintained tenets wholly opposed to that policy.

The effect of this campaign will soon be patent, if it is not already visible, in this country. So long as it was supposed that Mr Wilson was unanimously supported by his own countrymen, his policy was acclaimed with universal approval by the English Press; now that domestic dissension has asserted itself, we may expect to discover who are and who are not Mr Wilson's sincere supporters in England.

You have stated in *The Nation* that 'The old guard of the Republican party, with Senator Lodge at its head, is undoubtedly opposing, as openly as it dare, the whole League of Nations idea.'[1]

1 – 'Events of the Week', *N.* 24 (2 Nov. 1918).

An examination of some of Mr Lodge's speeches confirms the accuracy of this allegation. The attitude of Senator Lodge and his friends will not find favor with those elements in this country which have favored President Wilson's peace programme. My question is, whether it should commend itself to any English opinion whatever.

Henry Cabot Lodge has been senator from Massachusetts for some years, and he has the best connexions in Boston society. He belongs to a section of the American public which has loyally supported Great Britain from the beginning of the war. And his peace programme certainly appears to offer as much material advantage to England as England could ask. He would seem, in short, to be at least as good a friend to England as President Wilson is. But his policy is potentially even more nationalistic than it is at present pro-British.[1] The 'Old Guard' of his party is traditionally associated with a high protective tariff, and Senator Lodge is traditionally associated with the Old Guard. The history and composition of the Republican party and the present emergencies of its more conservative elements do not encourage one to believe that it would sacrifice business interest to international amity.

It would mean universal disaster if the participation of America in the war does not lead to closer friendships and understanding, to freer intercourse of ideas, between America and England. No understanding based on economic interest alone could survive; even the legitimate interests of the two countries may cause delicate situations; the economic interests of America and England are compatible, but not identical; there are difficulties to be solved, and suspicions to be dispelled. Should affairs be simultaneously directed by Extremist factions in both countries, it is hardly to be expected that the extremes would meet.

Nothing but ideas can bind the two countries together. Since the entry of America into the War, the Republican party has not yet succeeded in producing a single idea of importance. The question whether America should not have entered the war earlier is now a dead issue. The policy of President Wilson is the only one which offers any security for the continuance and development of Anglo-American harmony.

Yours, etc.,
T. S. Eliot.

1–Henry Cabot Lodge represented Massachusetts in the US Senate, 1893–1924. As Chair of the Senate Foreign Relations Committee, he successfully led the resistance to US participation in the League of Nations advocated by President Wilson, arguing in 1919 that entanglement 'in the intrigues of Europe' would endanger American moral leadership in the world.

TO *Mary Hutchinson* MS Texas

9 November 1918 18 Crawford Mansions

Dear Mary,

Jack has I hope explained to you that I did not get your letter. I had been away from the bank for two weeks and my letters had not been sent on as I was expected in; and I only found it yesterday.

Under the circumstances, which I will explain, I should probably not have been in a frame of mind to be an acceptable guest, but I hope you will forgive and invite us later! (I forwarded your enclosure to Vivien).

I had been begged by the Navy Intelligence to leave the Bank and join them, as they greatly needed my services. They supposed that they had authority to enroll me, and did not discover that they did not until they came to do so. Then they cabled Washington, kept me hanging about for two weeks – until I cut the matter short by returning to the Bank, as there was no prospect that the Navy would pay me for the lost time. I have got out of them a letter apologising for the blunder, but I was very angry at their incompetence. Perhaps it is too early to say that it was a lucky escape –

I'm glad you like Webster[1] – but *I* think the first of the lot is the best!

Received a v. dull book of poems from Aldous.[2] I wonder what you are doing – in hiding, or with a houseful of visitors. Do you remain enough aloof from politics and war to be able to put your mind on worthy matters? I can't – I have even been 'impelled' to write to the *Nation*. Lewis, who has been trying to regain health in the country, writes me that the medicine he needs is peace. And freedom from interruptions, as I believe! He is really very seedy.

Sincerely
T.S.E.

1 – 'Whispers of Immortality', which opens 'Webster was much possessed by death' (*Little Review*, Sept. 1918). The 'first' of the four poems published there was 'Sweeney among the Nightingales'.
2 – AH, *The Defeat of Youth and Other Poems* (1918).

TO *Hugh Walpole*[1]

MS Valerie Eliot

10 November 1918 — 18 Crawford Mansions

Dear Mr Walpole,

The reason for my not having answered your letter before is simply that it was forwarded to Lloyds Bank. I have not been there for two weeks (until yesterday) as I was on leave of absence trying to get a position promised me by the U.S. Navy – and which, owing to red tape, has not materialised.

So that I hope you have not given me up quite, but are willing to arrange another meeting. I am now taking up some new and rather intricate work at my bank, so that lunch time is brief and unsatisfactory. Would it be possible for us to dine together? Or I could probably arrange lunch on *Saturday*.

My wife is returning to town some time this week, and I know would be very glad if you would dine with us next week (if we cannot meet sooner), as she has just read *The Dark Forest*[2] with great pleasure.

I should be interested to know your opinion of my latest stuff in the *Little Review*. It isn't so much more time that I want – but Peace and peace of mind and freedom.[3]

Sincerely yours
T. S. Eliot

I think *Wednesday* is my best night this week – could you dine here with me?

TO *St John Hutchinson*

MS Texas

10 November 1918 — 18 Crawford Mansions

Dear Hutchinson,

I rang up your office last week, but you were out, so you ought to have no comment to make on *my* absences (which were alleged by the telephone operator – I *never* go out to tea).

I am at work again having given up the Navy as a bad job – this ends my patriotic endeavours.

1–Hugh Walpole (1884–1941), novelist and man of letters.
2–Walpole's novel *The Dark Forest* (1916) drew on his wartime experiences with the Red Cross.
3–The following day was Armistice Day.

I disinterred Mary's letter at the Bank – it had been kept there with others instead of being forwarded, as they expected me in. I am sorry about that and have written to apologise.

What is the chance of seeing you now?

Yrs
T. S. Eliot

TO *Virginia Woolf*[1] MS Berg

12 November 1918 18 Crawford Mansions

Dear Mrs Woolf

Please pardon me for not having responded to your note immediately – on Mondays I never have a moment up till late at night. And I was not furthermore quite sure of being able to come, as I thought that my wife might be arranging to return on Friday evening, but I now hear that she is coming tomorrow.

I shall look forward to Friday with great pleasure.[2]

Sincerely yours
T. S. Eliot

1 – Virginia Woolf, novelist and critic: see Glossary of Names.

2 – In her diary for 15 Nov., VW recorded of this first meeting with TSE: 'Mr Eliot is well expressed by his name – a polished, cultivated, elaborate young American, talking so slow, that each word seems to have special finish allotted it. But beneath the surface, it is fairly evident that he is very intellectual, intolerant, with strong views of his own, & a poetic creed. I am sorry to say that this sets up Ezra Pound & Wyndham Lewis as great poets, or in the current phrase "very interesting" writers. He admires Mr Joyce immensely. He produced 3 or 4 poems for us to look at – the fruit of two years, since he works all day in a Bank, & in his reasonable way thinks regular work good for people of nervous constitutions. I became more or less conscious of a very intricate & highly organised framework of poetic belief; owing to his caution, & his excessive care in the use of language we did not discover much about it. I think he believes in "living phrases" & their difference from dead ones; in writing with extreme care, in observing all syntax & grammar; & so making this new poetry flower in the stem of the oldest' (*Diary of Virginia Woolf*, I: *1915–1919*, ed. Anne Olivier Bell [1977], 218–19). See also VW's letter to Roger Fry (*Letters*, II, 295–6).

TO *John Quinn* TS NYPL (MS)

13 November 1918 18 Crawford Mansions

Dear Mr Quinn,

I have received your letter of September 27th.[1] I must say that your kindness to me, who am personally unknown to you, has been quite extraordinary, and such as I am not likely to forget. I realise also that you are a very busy man, and that you are not yet recovered from a very severe illness.

My vicissitudes in connection with the Army and Navy have been surprising. Everything turned to red tape in my hands. Of course I am glad now, as the war is ended, that I did not get in, but I was very much annoyed at the time. I was, as you know, collecting testimonials with a view to a commission in the Army Intelligence, through Major Turner. Just as I had secured testimonials which should have satisfied anybody, I was *sent for* by the Navy Intelligence, who said that I had been mentioned to them as the most suitable man available for certain work of theirs, and said that if I could join them as soon as possible they would make me a Chief Yeoman and raise me to a commission in a few months. I accordingly abandoned the Army, arranged to leave the bank, and told the Navy that I would come to enrol in two weeks. When I did so they were not ready – they had cabled to Washington, as they said they had to do in any case, as a matter of routine, (though they had not mentioned this fact in the first place) and not received an answer. So I waited about a week, having left the bank. Then they sent word to me that the permission was received, so I went to enrol, and had commenced this ceremony before they discovered that as I had already registered for Military Service (as all citizens are supposed to) they did not have sufficient authority. I pointed out that *all* citizens of military age were registered, or if not that they lost their American rights and were automatically absentees from the British Army, but it was no use, they cabled again. After I had hung about in this way for two weeks, out of a job, I decided that I could not stand the financial loss, especially as I was assured that it would be impossible to get any money out of the Government to cover me for this period, after having given up my work at the bank at the Navy's request. So I returned to the bank, having wasted a month of time and been out of work for two weeks.

1 – Quinn had written, 'You would be exempt in this country because of your hernia, and also because of your dependencies.' On EP's 'instructions', he had sent a letter to Major Turner on TSE's behalf, a copy of which he enclosed.

Then the armistice came, and I was very glad – anyway, it was not my fault that I had not been able to make myself useful to the country.

I am very grateful to you for all the trouble you were at.

I will do as you suggest with regard to Knopf;[1] as yet I have had no acknowledgement from him of having received the manuscript, and possibly he will not want to print it.

I wonder why the *Little Review* does not gain subscriptions in America. I sometimes think that with us (Americans) the serious has to be the pedantic, and that only the pedantic and the cheap are understood: the *Saturday Evening Post*, and the *Dial* or *Atlantic Monthly*. But of course there are many things about the *L. Review* which I do not care for, and I dare say you would agree with me. Anyway, its present existence is that of a Coalition Government, satisfying nobody.

With the most cordial wishes for your improvement in health,

Sincerely yours
T. S. Eliot

TO *His Mother*

TS Houghton

13 November 1918 — 18 Crawford Mansions

My Dearest Mother,

It seems to me months since I have written to you. I never *forget* to write, but as I explained to father in writing a week ago, the experiences I have been through have been paralysing. It has been just like a Chancery suit – dragging on and on and on, and always apparently about to end so that one could write and say definitely. I have realised how sweet and kind you have been all through, and how cleverly you seemed to divine what was going on and what I was feeling, and you never reproached me for not writing. Also you and father have been splendid in trying to help me. I have got both the Sims and Slocum cables. Of course they are too late for the purpose for which I wanted them, all the same I think I will try to present them merely for the pleasure of a social call, and because it is due to the people who signed them.

When I wrote to father the Navy affair was still dragging on. By Thursday I decided that as no answer had been received I must throw the

1 – Quinn had advised TSE to send a statement about himself and 'what the book stands for'; otherwise, Knopf was 'likely to make breaks, particularly with reference to essays and poems', as he had done with EP's *Pavannes and Divisions*.

thing up, as I could not afford the expense. So I secured a letter from the Navy which partially explained and deplored the business, and went to the bank. The Lloyds managers were very sympathetic, and delighted to have me back. So they signed an appeal for my exemption, and I started in to learn some new and more intricate work, and two days later the armistice was signed. So it is really all for the best that I did not get into the Navy. One may be very useful, but it is not the same thing after the fighting has ceased, especially when one is badly needed elsewhere. And the salaries of the whole bank staff are going to be very largely increased all round, and I may get another rise of my own at Christmas, besides.

Anyway, no one can say that I did not try my best to get into Army or Navy.

Now as soon as conditions become normal, it may not be for some months yet, I shall apply for leave of absence (without pay) for an extended time for a visit to America. After that I should hope to come for a visit every summer, but this first time I want plenty of time – of course the sooner the better! – but I doubt if I can be spared before some months – perhaps the summer. Anyway, you may count upon seeing me as soon as it can be arranged – how wonderful that will be.

I have not time to write more now. I will write and tell you about London on Monday last, I was in the middle of it all, in the City.[1]

With very much love and gratitude

Your devoted son
Tom

I cabled you Monday.

TO *J. H. Woods*

TS Professor David G. Williams

20 November 1918 — 18 Crawford Mansions

Dear Professor Woods,

I am extremely grateful to you for your kindness, both in writing a testimonial for me, which I shall prize, and for writing to my mother. The whole affair is now, happily let us say, a dead issue. The Armistice was the conclusion of three very trying months for me. I at least did my best to get into some service. I was graded as unfit for active service, and wanted to

1–The *Daily Mirror* reported how on 11 Nov., Armistice Day, 'Bells burst forth into joyful chimes . . . bands paraded the streets followed by cheering crowds of soldiers and civilians and London generally gave itself up wholeheartedly to rejoicing.'

secure a post in the Intelligence. The Army Intelligence involved making a collection of opinions; I levied eighteen letters of recommendation from English friends, and then had to have a few American ones as well. Just as I received yours I was offered a post in the Navy Intelligence, but after making all my arrangements I found that they did not have the proper authority to enroll me! The affair dragged on for some weeks, and finally I returned to my work at Lloyds Bank, as there seemed to be no prospect of the Navy's reimbursing me for the time I was losing. The Armistice was signed immediately after.

I hope to return to America for a visit in the summer or autumn, as soon as conditions are normal for travel and I can be spared for a time from my Foreign Exchange work. I look forward to seeing you then. I am aware of still having the *Organon* which I will now finish for you with all possible expedition. I hope you will forgive the delay. I shall also see that you get a copy of a small book which I expect to publish in the spring.

I suppose that you have either been doing war work of some kind or else the Department has been so depleted that you have been over-worked, and in either case have had no time for any independent scholarship. You never sent me Patañjali, but I am not in a position to reproach you! I should like to know what work you have in mind to do. It is a great pity that the life of a Harvard Professor is so engrossed with executive work and committees that he has scant time for writing. Oxford dons complain of this too, but they really don't know how bad it can be.

I should like to have news of Lanman sometime. Will you give him my affectionate regards?

With best wishes for Mrs Woods and yourself

Gratefully yours,
Thomas S. Eliot

Vivien Eliot TO *Henry Eliot* — MS Houghton

21 Nov[ember] 1918 — 18 Crawford Mansions

My dear Henry

Thank you *ever* so much for sending me (us) that £20 which arrived two days ago. It was a shame you had to cable it – it costs so much. I expect the mails will be safer now. It was a very unexpected present, and I have reason to thank you, for Tom says I am to get my winter clothes out of it. Having been out of London for *six months* at a stretch, and too ill to think of such things I have also lately arrived at my last rag. Now, the weather is cold, and the prices of clothes and materials are *very* high, higher than they have been at all up till now. I have got a suit in hand already, and shall now be able to get all I need, thanks to you.

How are your ears at present? Your mother wrote that your *good* ear had been giving trouble as well. That is really sickening, but I hope there is nothing in it. Tom gets very deaf, at times, but when he gets the doctor to blow the wax out he is all right again. I think there is nothing actually *wrong* with T's ears, as with yours. My father is *quite* deaf with one ear, but he hears very well with the other, so it doesn't matter much.

The day before yesterday I had a tooth extracted, with gas. I have a great loathing of gas, and am terribly cowardly about it. I scream the whole time! It upsets me very much, but I had a splendid anaesthetist this time and it was not so terrifying. I had an abscess this size at the end of my tooth. It had been giving me great agony at times. My teeth now seem to have gone all to pieces again. There are endless fillings to do, and I think another *might* [have] to come out. Isn't life a hell with bad teeth?

On the morning I was to go and have this done Tom started to have flu, so I went with a heavy heart. He has not been very bad, so far, I am glad to say. I think we took it in time – he is up, but not out, today. Tom takes cold *very* much more easily than I do. Most of *my* colds are caught from him. I think he would be better if he had one side of his nose cauterised, as our doctor advised.

I really have not been able to rejoice much over Peace! In the abstract I do, and I try to make myself *realise* it. But conditions here will be so hard, harder than *ever*, perhaps, for a long long time, and I must say it *is* difficult to feel anything at all. One is too stunned altogether.

Poor Tom's disaster over his Navy job very nearly did for both of us. It was indeed the last straw. I don't *know* how we have weathered that storm. The first thing I am trying to realise is that as soon as I can, I *really must*, I *ought to*, go to America. I say I, but I mean we. Only, of course *now* again, there are such difficulties about Tom. Had he got into the Navy it would have been easy, it would have followed. But now, back at the Bank, and with the Bank's *amazing* kindness and tolerance behind him, he can scarcely begin agitating about something else at once. I should think he could manage to get a *month's* holiday during next summer, if he explained the circumstances, and that could just give time for a flying visit. I think your parents can count on that, and perhaps something will turn up to make a longer visit possible. <If only we could bring them back here!> I should like to stay rather longer myself, for unless my great friend Lucy Thayer has come to Europe by that time I shall want to spend some time with her, as well as seeing all Tom's family.

I can't help feeling it is almost absurd to be writing this, and that I never shall get to America really.

Do write to me soon.

Yrs. ever
Vivien

I am going to enquire if photographs can be sent now. It *has* been forbidden all this time or I should have sent you some.

You see all your drafts *did* arrive, it was dreadful that you should have been left in doubt. We were off our heads all the summer.

TO *John Rodker* MS Virginia

2 December 1918 18 Crawford Mansions

I sent you the books several days ago to deal with as you think fit. Could you let us have article some time next week. Don't need to mention all of them – do as you please. I waited to write because I hoped to suggest a meeting, but I have been ill and now my wife is, so my plans are all suspended.

Yours ever
T.S.E.

FROM *John Quinn* CC NYPL (MS)

3 December 1918 [New York]

Dear Mr Eliot:

I received your letter of the 13th of November this morning.

I am sorry you had the worry between the Army and the Navy matter. I am glad that you were able to return to the bank and that your maximum loss was a month's time.

You at least have the satisfaction of knowing that it was not your fault that you were unable to make yourself useful to the country, and that you were willing to go. That is the main thing.

Personally, I am very sorry for the armistice. I should like to have had the war go on until half a million Germans were captured in warfare or killed. I think there has been a complete misunderstanding of the German psychology. A Hun does not understand kindness or generosity or magnanimity. A blooded horse or a blooded dog does, but not a Hun or a hyena.

What I did for you about the Army was done cheerfully of course, and was very little at that.

I have heard nothing from Knopf about your book. He possibly will talk to me about it. If he decides against it, and if I can be of any help to you in looking for another publisher, I shall be glad to do it. Personally, I think you could do a little better than Knopf, with possibly some such house as Scribner's or the Macmillan Company, for, after all, your work is not quite as revolutionary and as explosive as E. P.'s.

You say that you 'wonder why *The Little Review* does not gain subscriptions in America'. The answer is that 'gaining subscriptions' is a business matter, and that the two women that run *The Little Review* know nothing about business matters, that they are wholly lacking in tact and what I once called the minor amenities of life, what a stenographer <once> transcribed as 'minor nonentities of life'. They have no business sense and no judgment. I wrote to Pound a year ago that they would never make a success of it from the subscription and financial point of view.

I think you quite aptly describe the present condition of *The Little Review* as that of a 'Coalition Government, satisfying nobody'. But I imagine there will be a dissolution very soon, as to which you may consult E. P., to whom I am writing sending him a copy of a letter declining to make any further financial contributions. Two thousand dollars in two years is quite enough. But Pound can tell you that part of it.

The Dial has been moved to New York, and while it is pseudo-socialistic and pseudo-ethologistic and pseudo-Freudistic and pseudo-philosophistic and pseudo-a-lot-of-things, even pseudo-litho literature, it cannot pay much, if anything. But it does not stink as much as the pseudosities of *The New Republic*. I occasionally buy *The New Republic*, but I think too much of my person to use its sheets in the toilet. *The New Republic* reminds me of the story that a friend of mine used to tell of the proper reply to an insulting letter:

> 'Dear Sir:
>
> Your letter of such-a-date is before me. In a moment it will be behind me.'

The Atlantic Monthly is of course academic, but within strictly academic lines it has published some pretty lively things during the last year. *The North American Review* occasionally has an article or two devoted to literature or art, but for the most part the things in it are mere journalism.

Again let me say that if Knopf is not interested in your book I shall be glad to do what I can to get another publisher for it here.

With kind regards, I am,
Sincerely yours,
[unsigned]

TO *His Mother* MS Houghton

8 December 1918

18 Crawford Mansions,
Crawford St, W.1

My dearest Mother,

I was very much relieved to hear from you at last that father had got my first letter and my cable. I had been worrying very much over not having written to either of you during that trying period.

Since the armistice we have had a round of illness. First Vivien had her tooth out and I at the same time had a light attack of what I think must have been influenza, as it left me so very weak afterwards. As soon as I was out again V. caught it in earnest from a friend, was in bed for over a week, and has not been out of doors yet. The worst is that it has affected her nerves so that she can hardly sleep at all. She wanted to get some Christmas presents to send to you in America, but she can't tell when she will be able to do shopping.

Today I thought I was going to have influenza again, having all the symptoms including a splitting head. However, it has quite left me this evening, but I feel very very weak, and have written to postpone my lecture.

I have £360 a year salary now, so that I ought to be practically self-supporting, which would be a great relief to me. It is certainly a great improvement. What I aimed at was to earn enough from the Bank so that I could devote my evenings and Sundays to literary work without thought of gain. There will probably be a number of new periodicals in London soon, and with my extended connections, and becoming more and more well known in London I could keep myself busy with contracts the whole time. But I have come to the conclusion that it would be frittering my mind and energy away. Also, at present I am very tired from a most exhausting year, alarms, illness, movings, and military difficulties. I want first a rest. So I am not going to write for several months, except perhaps a little

[incomplete]

TO *John Rodker* MS Houghton

9 December 1918 18 Crawford Mansions

Dear Rodker,

I have given your review to Weaver for the January issue, and have also forwarded your communication to her.

I shall not be doing any writing for the *Egoist* for some months, as my doctor has advised me to take a rest and merely read for some time. Would you care to deal with any review books that come in from month to month, on the style of your excellent *Egoist* and *L. Review* reviews. In consideration of a fee. I have spoken to Weaver about this, and it is quite definite whether she writes to you or not – I don't know whether she expected to, as I said I was writing to you.

Sincerely
T. S. Eliot

TO *Arnold Bennett* MS Beinecke

14 December 1918 18 Crawford Mansions

Dear Mr Bennett,

I am writing to thank you in retrospect of the kind letter you wrote for me this summer when I was trying to get an American Commission. I can testify to the effect it produced upon more than one official, though I found that no letter or accumulation of letters would have cut the red tape of American bureaucracy at once. Happily the letter remains in my possession, to be realised upon by my heirs at Sothebys; and I remain in civilian life.

I took the liberty of sending you some time ago the *Little Review* with some verse of mine which I hoped you might like.

I trust that you will soon be able to give all your attention to your own work, and perhaps incidentally preserve Government-Office life in wartime for future generations through that medium.[1]

Again with many thanks.

Sincerely yours
T. S. Eliot

1–Bennett had briefly been Director of Propaganda at the Ministry of Information, Oct.–Nov.

TO *Graham Wallas* MS LSE

14 December 1918 18 Crawford Mansions

Dear Professor Wallas,

I am writing, after a long epidemic of domestic influenza, to thank you in retrospect for your testimonial last summer. It is hardly necessary to say that I am still a civilian, but I only missed a Navy place by a hair's breadth. Under the circumstances, I am just as well satisfied. I encountered a great deal of red tape, and met with several disappointments during the summer, and still (as a result of this plus peace plus influenza) feel very tired, and [am] not writing at present.

I wonder if an American friend named Gray,[1] professor of history at Bryn Mawr, and on the Shipping Board over here, presented an introduction to you. I think you would have found him agreeable.

With many thanks and most seasonable wishes to Mrs Wallas and yourself,

Sincerely yours,
T. S. Eliot

Vivien Eliot TO *Charlotte C. Eliot* MS Houghton

15 December [1918] 18 Crawford Mansions

Dear Mrs Eliot

Of course this will arrive very late for Xmas, and I am so sorry. But influenza has prevented my getting anything off in time – even now I have not been well in time to get any little presents for anyone in America. I shall send you something a little later on – and meanwhile I hope so much that you will all have a very happy Xmas. We ought all to have a much happier Xmas than we have had for years. It is disappointing that thousands of people are still separated, but that is inevitable. My brother will not be with us again, he is at home now, as he managed to get a few days leave, but must go back to Italy on December 20. My parents are very disappointed.

It is really difficult to adapt oneself to the new conditions – although the conditions here continue in most ways to make ordinary living difficult and *terribly* expensive. But to realise that at last the fearful weight and horror are over, well, one can hardly understand it.

1–Howard L. Gray, Professor of European History at Bryn Mawr, 1915–40; author of *War Time Control of Industry: The Experience of England* (1918). TSE wrote 'Grey'.

Tom started with influenza, and although he had it extremely slightly it left him very weak. I got it about a week later, and had such a persistent fever that I was kept in bed for a week, and indoors for a fortnight. I am only just getting strong enough to get about again. Since the war stopped and all that period of indecision and anxiety is over Tom's health seems to be very gradually improving. But he has been worrying himself about his mind not acting as it used to do, and a feeling that his writing was falling off. So I felt very strongly that a complete *mental* rest was what he really ought to have. So after a good deal of argument I have got him to sign a contract with me, saying that he will do no writing of any kind, except what is necessary for the one lecture a week which he has to give, and no reading, except poetry and novels and such reading as is necessary for the lectures, for three months from now.[1] Also he has promised to take a walk every day. I am sure you will be glad to hear this. When one's brain is very fatigued, the only thing to do, I think, is to *give up* the attempt to use it. For if one goes on tasking it and it will not respond one feels one's powers are failing and that means despair. I believe if Tom tries now to live healthily and regularly for three months he will find his mind is quite fresh again.

We are now beginning to look forward to going to U.S.A. I expect Tom told you he thinks he can ask for two months off at the end of the summer. It seems a long time to wait, but as Lloyds have behaved with so much appreciation and generosity to him through all that trying time, and always take such interest in him, he feels he cannot ask before that, as business will not be settled down for a long time yet. What we both hope is to bring you both back with us, and perhaps some others of the family too, so that we *might* get a Xmas together next year.

With love and best wishes to you both,

from Vivien

TO *His Mother* — MS Houghton

22 December 1918 — 18 Crawford Mansions

My dearest Mother,

It is some days since I have heard from you. I shall hope to hear that Henry is with you for Christmas and the rest of the week. It would be nice

1–As agreed, TSE published nothing for three months, taking up reviewing again in Apr. 1919.

if he could take a long holiday, when Husband and Thomas get back, and come over here – it is really time that he came abroad, and just now he must be very stale, and depressed to think that the war is ended without his having taken part in it.

When I got father's last letter I cabled to Aunt Susie to express sympathy for Aunt Marian,[1] but I have heard nothing since. I am very anxious for more news, and am very distressed by the possibility of not seeing her again.

I am feeling much better than I did a short time ago, or when I wrote last. The weather had been very rainy, and I had a sharp attack of sciatica for two or three days, but it has now wholly passed off. Vivien is making me take cod liver oil. I think she is on the whole stronger than she was. Last winter was of course very trying, much more so than anyone can realise, and I have never told you yet of all the things that we went through here – I shall when it is prudent to do so. The doctor still prescribes a very careful and regular life for her, and she still has bad migraines whenever she worries or over-exerts herself. I do not understand it, and it worries me.

We have had Maurice here for ten days and he has just returned to Italy. He of course will have to stay there for some time to come, as he is in the regular army and as he is engaged in directing railway operations.

Is Frank[2] still in France? London is extraordinarily crowded, and the shops, tubes, and buses are packed with people. It is very difficult to do any Christmas shopping.

I am having three weeks holiday from lecturing.

I shall think of you and should like to be with you on Christmas morning for the stockings and the tree. I like to think that you still have a tree.

With every Christmas blessing to you both from us

Your loving son
Tom.

1–His father had written that Marian (christened Mary) Stearns (1854–1918) was seriously ill.

2–Frank Munro Eliot (1886–1967), his first cousin. An officer in the 18th US Infantry, he had been gassed at Cantigny but remained in the army.

TO *His Mother* MS Houghton

29 December 1918 18 Crawford Mansions

My dearest mother,

I was very deeply grieved to hear from Henry that Aunt Marian had already died. (Father wrote '*Aunt Mary*' but I presume he meant Aunt Marian.) I expected it to happen from what father said before, as a haemorrhage in the brain sounds almost certainly fatal, but I am sorry that she never got my cable. I was always quite fond of her, and enjoyed talking to her. I had a very pleasant few days with her once in Paris. I shall miss her very much when I revisit Cambridge, and I had also looked forward to entertaining her in London.

I wonder if she left any money to the Hinkleys or Aunt Nellie,[1] or whether she had only a Davis annuity.[2]

I hope you had Henry and Ada for Christmas and should like to know what sort of Christmas you had. I think you were *very* generous in your presents to me and Vivien and we both thank you very deeply. (Vivien is writing separately). Your letter containing the drafts came the day before Christmas. I wanted to cable a Christmas message to you, but the cable companies refused to take any 'greetings messages' this year on account of the pressure of correspondence.

I got a small Christmas tree, though it was impossible to find in the shops any of the usual trinkets to adorn it. We had our stockings as usual with nuts and oranges and such candies as were obtainable, but very scarce. I gave her a coal-scuttle for the drawing room and she gave me some books. Her aunt presented a turkey, and we had Mr and Mrs Haigh-Wood to dinner, instead of going there, as they have been unable to get any servant.

'Boxing Day', the day after Christmas (a holiday here) we went to see President Wilson arrive and drive to Buckingham Palace.[3] There was a huge crowd, and the streets were all hung with American flags. It was really an extraordinary and inspiring occasion. I do not believe that people in America realise how much Wilson's policy has done to inspire respect for America abroad. I think that *all* the nations, allied, hostile, and neutral, *trust* us as they trust no other – everyone with the exception of particular

1–Ellen Farley Reed (1841–1931), the eldest married sister, whose husband died young from wounds received in the Civil War.

2–As a girl she had spent much time with a family named Davis, who left her money.

3–Woodrow Wilson was the first US President to visit Britain while in office, arriving on 26 Dec. as a guest of the King and Queen, and departing after five days.

circles, political or commercial, whose interests are not in common with those of the world at large. I have heard men of several nationalities speak very warmly. I don't think much of the Democratic party, but I hope it will survive long enough to see the satisfaction of the peace negotiations along Wilson lines. America certainly has a more disinterested record of foreign policy (at least from the time of John Hay)[1] than any other country. Politics here are in complete chaos at present,[2] and I am very pessimistic about it. It is most deplorable that men like Asquith, Simon, Runciman, McKenna, Snowden, should have been defeated.[3]

I must stop now. We wish you a very very happy New Year!

Your loving son
Tom.

Vivien Eliot TO *Charlotte C. Eliot* MS Houghton

30 December [1918] 18 Crawford Mansions

Dear Mrs Eliot

It was kind of you to send me £2 this Christmas, and I am very pleased to have it. I feel very ashamed of sending nothing to America, but you understand about the influenza and other difficulties, which lasted right up to Xmas. We had lovely weather on Xmas day and the day after – 'Wilson weather' and certainly London was looking its *most* beautiful when Wilson drove through the streets. Although very tired after Xmas day, Tom and I went early and stood in the best place we could find, for over two hours. Even then we had quite thirty *rows* deep of people in front of us – and I should have seen nothing at all if Tom had not lifted me up just as they passed. It was a most moving and wonderful sight to see him sitting next the King, and having such a glorious welcome. We all follow

1 – John Hay (1838–1905), diplomat; secretary to Abraham Lincoln, friend of Henry Adams; US Ambassador to the UK; Secretary of State 1898–1905. TSE referred to him as 'the great John Hay, who had been engaged in settling the problems of China and Cuba' (*A.*, 23 May 1919).

2 – The 'coupon' election of 14 Dec. resulted in a substantial victory for the wartime coalition of Lloyd George's Liberals, Bonar Law's Conservatives, and a few independent and former Labour MPs, under the premiership of Lloyd George. However, the coalition was widely distrusted.

3 – The defeated Liberals included Sir John Simon (formerly Home Secretary) and Walter Runciman (formerly President of the Board of Trade), as well as Reginald McKenna (formerly Chancellor of the Exchequer), who had opposed conscription. The Labour MP Philip Snowden was a pacifist and champion of conscientious objectors.

American politics now, although before the war I suppose no ordinary English person knew anything about them. Tom has remarked that English people are more generally political than Americans.

Tom's Xmas was rather shadowed by the news of his aunt's death. It greatly upset him, and I too feel it, for Tom had told me about her and I was very much looking forward to meeting her, and perhaps having her here.

Tom was amused to hear of Robert Nichols' activities in America.[1] We saw him just before he left, while we were waiting for an air raid in a café. The story is that when he went out to France he got stuck in a chimney, where he had to hide. The chimney was knocked down and Robert's mental balance has never quite recovered from the shock. If you can get hold of a novel of Hugh Walpole's, called *The Dark Forest*, I wish you would read it. Hugh Walpole is an acquaintance of Tom's.

Will you please thank Marion for her Calendar, which arrived only today. It is a most useful kind of Calendar, and I have not seen one like it. I shall write to her.

London has never been so full. The crowds are so enormous, everywhere, in the streets and public places, theatres restaurants, you cannot possibly imagine. Of course one sees Americans at every turn.

Hoping you and Mr Eliot will have a very healthy and happy New Year.

Yours affectly.
Vivien

1–In 1917 Nichols had been attached to the Foreign Office, and went to New York in 1918 as part of a delegation from the Ministry of Information.

1919

Henry Ware Eliot TO *Thomas Lamb Eliot* MS Reed College

3 January 1919[1] [Hydraulic-Press Brick Company]

Dear Bob,

Thanks for your nice letter of 28th and enclosures which I now return.

Wilson is hurting himself in his own party. I want him to live long enough for the people to discover him in his true character. There will not be any dividend in H.P.B.[2] until we know more about final results abroad and normal conditions in regard to labor and work are assured. However you will be glad to know that the Co is out of bank and owes nothing except the bonds which are due $50,000 – annually and this is easy to pay.

A dividend is the only thing which is keeping me in this parlous world. I have no other work, now that GRE[3] is practically finished. In a week or more I will be ready to send you results.

We are all well and I thank the Lord that I haven't a club foot or hare lip – but I will take them both if the Lord will give me *one* good ear![4]

My Tom is getting along now and has been advanced at the bank so that he is independent of me. Wish I liked his wife, but I don't.

Ever yrs.
H

TO *John Quinn* MS NYPL (MS)

6 January 1919 18 Crawford Mansions,
Crawford St, W.1

Dear Mr Quinn,

Thank you for your letter of the 3d December. You say nothing of your health, so I hope that it is better than it was when I heard from you before.

1 – TSE's father died, aged seventy-five, four days after writing this letter. It is accompanied by a record of the moves in an unfinished postal chess game with his brother.
2 – Hydraulic-Press Brick Company, of which he was president.
3 – The Greenleaf Real Estate Company was being divided up.
4 – He had long suffered from severe deafness.

I have heard nothing at all from Knopf about my manuscript. I cabled him a week ago, or Pound cabled for me. Knopf must have had the manuscript for over two months, but he has not even acknowledged receipt, so I have been worried. I am not at all proud of the book – the prose part consists of articles written under high pressure in the overworked, distracted existence of the last two years, and very rough in form. But it is important to me that it should be published for private reasons. I am coming to America to visit my family some time within the summer or autumn, and I should particularly like to have it appear first. You see I settled over here in the face of strong family opposition, on the claim that I found the environment more favourable to the production of literature. This book is all I have to show for my claim – it would go toward making my parents contented with conditions – and towards satisfying them that I have not made a mess of my life, as they are inclined to believe. The sooner it is out therefore the better, especially in view of my approaching visit.

Forgive these domestic details, but I wanted you to understand why I am so very anxious to get the book printed. I should consequently be extremely grateful to you if you would ring Knopf up and find out what the matter is; and of course if he does not want the manuscript I should be eternally obliged if you could find another publisher, as you so very kindly offered to do.[1]

I think Pound's new plans are very promising: there is certainly an opening here now.

With all best wishes for your health – I have certainly appreciated very deeply the trouble you took for me at a time when you were still very ill, and when you were apparently doing more than a full day's work of your own. I hope you will have opportunity for a long and genuine rest soon.

Very Sincerely
T. S. Eliot

1 – Responding to this letter, and that of 26 Jan. below, Quinn wrote on 29 Apr.: 'About a month ago Pound wrote to me withdrawing the copy for his book *Instigations* from Knopf and also the copy for your book of poetry and prose. A few days ago Knopf wrote me that he would like to publish your poems alone but not the poems with the prose. Pound will have told you that I have had the matter put with Boni & Liveright recently. They have decided definitely to publish Pound's book. They will let me know in a week about your book. But I think they will decide to take it. I spoke very strongly in favor of it . . . I had clearly in mind that it was important to you to have the book printed for private and family reasons.' Quinn received the manuscript from Knopf on 13 Feb., and took it to Boni & Liveright.

TO *His Mother* MS Houghton

12 January 1919 18 Crawford Mansions

My own dear mother,

I was glad to get Henry's cable last night to assure me that you were not ill. I am glad he was with you. Your cable came on Wednesday.[1] You have not been long out of my thoughts since then, I have been over all my childhood. I don't feel like writing anything in this first letter except to say again how much I love you – if only I could have been with you these last few days. I do long for you, I wanted you more for my sake than yours – to sing the Little Tailor to me.

I am impatient to know how you all are.

Your very loving
Tom.

TO *Henry Eliot* MS Houghton

12 January 1919 18 Crawford Mansions

My dear Henry

I received last night your cable reading

'Do not come now plans uncertain mother well'

and thank you very much. The first cable reached me Wednesday – it came in the morning but Vivien wisely withheld it until I got back in the evening. I don't feel yet as if anything was real, but I have a restless feeling that I shall wake up and find the pain intolerable.

I expect a full account from you of all the circumstances. Mother has such unusual character that I am sure she will come through all right, but I think it is better if she goes away from St Louis, as I gather from your words is possible.

Of course I want to know too how she will be financially.

Vivien has felt this very deeply.

I can't write more now – I have several things of importance to say by the next mail, but I don't feel up to it yet.

I am glad you were in St Louis.

Very affectionately
Tom.

1 – Announcing the death of his father on 7 Jan. 'A fearful day and evening', VHE recorded in her diary.

Vivien Eliot TO *Charlotte C. Eliot* MS Houghton

12 January 1919 18 Crawford Mansions

Dear Mrs Eliot,

I cannot attempt to express how shocked and upset I was at Mr Eliot's death. Tom and I are thinking of you all the time, and feeling so dreadfully for you in your loneliness and grief. These days are very awful for Tom, he would give anything to be with you now.

I feel it myself as a personal sorrow, for I had so much looked forward to meeting Mr Eliot, and talking to him. So many things one longed to speak of, to explain, and to understand. Tom, I know has felt the fearful inadequacy of correspondence, as I have. At last, after so long, with so much unsaid and so much unexplained, it began to be a torture to write at all. This loss is doubly painful, as we could at last look forward to meeting, and before very long. Tom was at the Bank when your cable came. (It came about midday). I was fearfully upset, and at first could not make up my mind whether it would be better to take it to the Bank, and bring Tom away, or to wait until he came home. At last I decided on the latter, and he says he is glad I did. But how I passed that afternoon and told him and gave him your cable I really do not know.

We are very anxious to get letters, but I suppose it will be nearly a fortnight yet. What a blessing you have Henry, he is so good.

I will write you some details about Tom in my next letter, very soon. I can't now.

With loving sympathy and all my thoughts. –

Vivien

TO *His Mother* MS Houghton

19 January 1919 18 Crawford Mansions

My dearest Mother,

You will know that my thoughts have been with you every day, though it always seems that little, very little, can ever filter through to pen and ink of what one feels. I am waiting as patiently as I can for letters.

One keeps thinking of little things – I have been longing to have some little drawing of father's that I could keep and have framed. He used to do very funny ones too in letters sometimes. There was a wonderful set of comic animals that he drew long ago, and were kept in an album together – I think he did them for a fair – but I expect you would not want to split the set. I think he had a great deal of talent. I know you will treasure his scrap-books and the fine genealogy he made. I should like to have one of his books (perhaps one of his Latin texts) to keep for myself, sometimes. If I can think at the end of my life that I have been worthy to be his son I shall be happy.

If Henry had advised it I should have gone to my managers and begged a term of leave to have visited you at once. I should however prefer to come later on and should be able to stay longer for this reason: the Bank is very busy now and still very short-handed. They have just taken over another Bank, and they have not got their former Staff men out of the army yet. They have been very kind to me (as well as very flattering) and I should not like to leave them in the lurch just when they need me most. I am not at all overworked, but if I went away it would be very inconvenient for them, besides handicapping me – I hope for another rise of salary in June. If I postpone coming just until things are settled to peace conditions I can stay more comfortably and longer. And after that often.

Dear mother. I do long to see you. And meanwhile I long for your letters. I am sure Henry and my sisters have been very good at this time.

Your very devoted
Tom.

TO *Mary Hutchinson*[1] MS Texas

22 January 1919 18 Crawford Mansions

Dear Mary,

Do forgive me if I ask if you could keep some evening next week (any night after Tuesday) instead of Friday? I know it is impossible for V. to come Friday (but she will explain all about that when she sees you), and as for myself, I really ought to stay at home and devote the rest of my evenings to matters I haven't had time to think about: I had planned to keep these evenings and I thought that we had better see you tonight when we could. We wanted to come Friday, but as I can hope to promise a less petrified mind next week, and V. can't possibly come Friday – I hope you will let us!

Sincerely
T. S. Eliot

1 – This and some subsequent letters have black borders.

TO *John Quinn* MS NYPL (MS)

26 January 1919 18 Crawford Mansions

Dear Mr Quinn

I am taking the liberty of writing again, as you were so kind in your interest in my manuscript. I have had no news from Knopf yet. He must have had the manuscript for about four months. I cabled to him a month ago and have had no answer.

I explained to you when I wrote last how important it was to me for family reasons to get something in the way of a book published in America. Since then my father has died, but this does not weaken the need for a book at all – it really reinforces it – my mother is still alive.

I have been hoping to come to America for a visit soon, but conditions here are still such that it will probably be many months before I can reasonably ask for long enough leave from my bank for that purpose. So I am unable to exercise much personal pressure.

If you could write or speak to Knopf and find out his definite intentions I should be very grateful. If he intends to use the stuff I should like him to get busy on it; if not, I should like him to deliver it into your hands. Perhaps then you would look it over with a view to what publisher might be willing to take it? Really you are the only person I know in New York to whom I would entrust such an affair, and therefore I hope you will not think me very cheeky in proposing it. And of course I don't know that you are not either in very poor health or very overworked, or both.

But a great deal hangs on it for me, and it was already a pressing matter several months ago!

Always gratefully yours
T. S. Eliot

TO *His Mother* MS Houghton

26 January 1919 18 Crawford Mansions

My dearest Mother,

I have had no letter from you for a very long time. Of course I expected there would be an interval when I should not have any letter from you, but you can judge how impatient I am. Until I either hear from you or of you it hardly seems worthwhile to write, especially as I may get a letter tomorrow or next day. Still, I do not like to have a Sunday go by without writing.

My lectures go on – the one course. That was originally an appointment for three years, you know – if the class held together for that length of time. Of course I should not have liked to desert them in any case before the expiry of that time. And the money is still very welcome. I suppose prices will go down later (though not to what they were before the war) but they are very high now. I am lecturing on Elizabethan Lyric verse tomorrow – Shakespeare, Jonson, Campion, Barnfield etc. Then I go on to the Sonnet and afterwards to prose – Sidney, Raleigh, Bacon etc. I think I sent you the syllabus. I hope to get some of the material for a book on Elizabethan blank verse out of the course.

I shall reply just as soon as I hear from you. How long it seems.

Always your devoted son
Tom.

TO *Virginia Woolf* MS Berg

29 January 1919 18 Crawford Mansions

Dear Mrs Woolf,

I return you the proof,[1] which seems to me admirable.

I shall be very glad indeed to dine with you on Sunday, and talk matters over.[2]

Looking forward to seeing you –

Sincerely yours
T. S. Eliot

TO *Bertrand Russell* MS Berg

3 February 1919 18 Crawford Mansions

Dear Bertie,

I shall be glad to see you on the 12th and will keep the evening free. If you come, you will let me know place and time.

It is not the case that Vivien 'won't reply'. I have taken the whole business of Marlow into my own hands, as she cannot have anything to do

1–*Poems* was to be published by the Hogarth Press on 12 May, at 2s 6d. Fewer than 250 copies were printed.
2–Writing to Vanessa Bell at about this time, VW asked for the return of some decorated papers 'before Sunday, as I want to show them to Eliot' (*Letters*, II, 323).

with this or with anything else that would interfere with the success of her doctor's treatment.

Before I heard from you the people in the house had offered to keep it on for some time if they could have it at a considerably lower rent (as they contend that it is not furnished). I naturally agreed to this. I only heard on Saturday that they will leave on March the 29th, so that after that date I shall be able to get at your things.[1]

I will expect to hear from you about the 12th. I have a great deal to talk to you about.

Yours
TSE

TO *Edgar Jepson*[2] PC Beinecke

5 February 1919 18 Crawford Mansions

Thanks for your letter. I shall await the finished product with interest, and hope that it will not be so finished that it will take a long time.

Yours truly,
T. S. Eliot

TO *Bertrand Russell* MS McMaster

14 February 1919 18 Crawford Mansions

Dear Bertie,

When I came home the other night I found that the sick woman [the Eliots' servant] was much worse; the doctor was there and said she had pneumonia. From then on till last night we have not had a chance to think or speak, hardly to eat and drink. Otherwise I should have written you sooner.

Last night was the first opportunity I had of speaking of our meeting to Vivien. I am afraid that that night I was only thinking of my own point of

1–In Jan. 1918, after quarrelling with his mistress Lady Constance Malleson, BR intended to spend more time at Marlow, but he changed his mind after they were reconciled. While BR was in prison in July, TSE had sent word that he was having difficulty finding anyone to share the cost of the house. BR replied that it was unfortunate as he would probably have to withdraw his own support at the end of the year. He was now anxious to recover his possessions.

2–Edgar Jepson, English novelist and autobiographer: see Glossary of Names.

view towards Marlow. The idea of parting with the house altogether had not before occurred to me; with so many worries on my mind I lost sight of how attached Vivien is to the house and garden. When at last I had an opportunity of telling her of our meeting I found she was extraordinarily upset at the thought of parting with it. She worked very hard at it during all the spring and summer and put so much thought and so many hopes into it. – The garden in particular is such a great joy and source of activity to her that now there are so few things she may do, as you know, I am sure it would be a mistake to deprive her of this interest. She is always thinking about the garden and even while tenants have been in the house has been several times to Marlow to look after it. It seems also that she has even now begun to look forward to happier times; she is expecting the return before the end of this year of her friend Lucy Thayer, when all kinds of things will be possible for Vivien that she cannot do now. She will be so much better when she has a companion, we are sure.

So that I think after all we must go on as we are, and hope that there will be fewer misfortunes in the future. But thank you very much indeed for offering to take over the house.

Yours ever,
T.S.E.

I am sending round the small table and some books I still have (I am ashamed not to have returned them.) The other things you shall have in six weeks, as I said.

TO *Henry Eliot* — TS Houghton

27 February 1919 — 18 Crawford Mansions

Dear Henry,

I have not yet answered your long letter of the 11th January, though I have sent one or two messages to you through mother, which I suppose you got, and perhaps she has sent you my letters to peruse. Perhaps also you have been in St Louis.

I am writing now because the doctor has made me take a week at home, mostly in bed. I did not want to do it, because Vivien has had all the housework to do for several weeks past, and is very tired and looks very ill. Nursing the charwoman through the first and the most critical part of pneumonia was very trying for her. The woman (who is now at her cousin's house) is getting on very well, but she will not be able to return to work for weeks, and meanwhile it is quite impossible to get a woman for more than an odd hour or two. There has been a great deal of pneumonic influenza about and if one of us got it he would have to go to a hospital. Vivien's parents have no servants either and have been unable to get any for months. Her mother has been ill in bed and she is out there now to do what she can for her. So you see the situation is a difficult one.

I have simply had a sort of collapse; I slept almost continuously for two days, and now I am up, I feel very weak and easily exhausted.

Thank you very much for your letter. I was very grateful to you for all the detail, and the actions and attitudes of all the persons appeared very characteristic and real. My first thought was that mother must leave St Louis, and I was glad to find that such was her intention. Her first letters cheered me up a good deal about her, and I still think (you will probably agree with me) that she may have a 'new lease of life' in the sense of power over her affairs, and as you say that she may expand and include her relatives outside the immediate family in her interests. She would certainly enjoy Cambridge. But I do not think that this is so certain that it can endure an indefinite postponement: the sooner she leaves St Louis the better. Her mind is of course revolving over and over and occupying itself with questions of the disposal of small personal affairs. She evidently put no end of care into making up some parcels she sent me – father's underwear and a book and a few drawings I asked for. She has been awfully kind to me, and keeps saying 'this has been very hard on you – you were so far away'. I think it was probably more completely unexpected to me than to anyone else, as I was never told that his trouble last summer was heart disease; and all the more recent reports had spoken of his great improvement in health. My mind keeps recurring to little bits of images in the memory, of Locust Street and Gloucester, I imagine much as it does in old age. I wished at first that father could have had more satisfaction out of his children, yet I cannot think (so far as I know) that his life was a very unhappy one, and after all none of his children was made for the kinds of success that he could have appreciated. I don't think that Ada's distinction[1] ever meant very much to him, and he would probably have extracted more satisfaction out of the sort of domestic citizenship you speak of than out of the most brilliant success. I always tried to give as powerful an impression as I could of my position here but it was a prominence essentially too esoteric to be of much use in that way. Now, I find that I think more of his own youthful possibilities that never came to anything:

1–Ada Eliot won distinction in social work in Boston: she was Director of the Research Bureau on Social Case Work, 1919–27. See Glossary of Names.

and yet with a great deal of satisfaction; his old-fashioned scholarship! his flute-playing, his drawing. Two of the Cats that I have seem to me quite remarkable. I feel that both he and mother in spite of the strength of their affection were lonely people, and that he was the more lonely of the two, that he hardly knew himself what he was like. In my experience everyone except the fools seem to me warped or stunted.

My MSS. has not yet found a berth. Knopf, the publisher in New York, wrote to Pound that the success of his book *Pavannes and Divisions* had not been sufficient to warrant his undertaking any new contracts with him or Wyndham Lewis or myself. So I have asked John Quinn, the art patron in New York, to take the MSS. He has been kind to me and had previously offered to find a better publisher for it. You see it is both prose and verse, as I have written so little, I have had so little time to write. Arnold Bennett told me he could get a volume of verse alone published for me, but I haven't enough verse for that. I hope I shall be able to give up lectures next year. There has been so much to worry about that my evening and Sunday and holiday time has never been clear, and often I am too tired. I feel very played out at present. Vivien wants me to take my holidays on the continent this summer, if I can get over there.

Always affectionately
Tom

Write soon.

TO *His Mother* — TS Houghton

Thursday 27 February [1919] [London]

Dearest mother,

I am just writing a line in response to your letter of February 6th although I know you will get my previous one by the same mail. The reason is that I had a little bit of a collapse and did not go out on Monday, so the letter I wrote on Sunday was overlooked. I have been away from business since then, the first two days in bed. We were afraid it might be influenza at first, but it appears to have been only exhaustion. At first I slept almost continuously. I am much better but still feel very weak. I think it is more the result of all the trying events and worries of the past two months than anything else, as I have not been over-working.

I have been and am still afraid of Vivien's breaking down. The care of the sick woman was very fatiguing and unpleasant, and of course we can get no one in to work regularly. Besides the housework and nursing me she has been out this afternoon to nurse her mother, who has no servants and is ill in bed.

I do not suppose that you will sacrifice any of the furniture, books and pictures which is worth taking east with you.[1] Of course the portraits will be a great anxiety in transportation. As for the books, I presume you will take all of any intrinsic value, and as I cannot remember what else there is I can hardly suggest any that I should like to have saved. Perhaps there are a certain number of books of interest as documents of New England civilisation, i.e. sermons of Andrew Eliot, Theodore Parker, anything to do with Emerson and his circle, poems of Cranch or Dawes,[2] or American History. I remember a set of Prescott[3] (I don't mean Marion's Parkman).[4] I have an idea that such of these things as you could save would be of use to me eventually. Of course I should like the Latin and Greek, but I have Aeschylus and Sophocles. I know other voices will be raised to protect the Rollo books![5] I am also strong for the preservation of any family antiquities in the way of books, genealogical works etc.

This has been a very hard winter to get through, and I hope we shall all feel stronger when the mild weather comes. There will soon be signs of spring here.

With very much love

your son
Tom.

I don't know what to say about Jefferson.[6] If it is very bulky I expect you had better let it go. I should be sorry, as father gave it to me, but it is probably not worth the cost of sending about.

1–After her husband's death, Mrs Eliot moved from St Louis to Cambridge, Massachusetts, as TSE had hoped.

2–Rev. Andrew Eliot (1718–78), TSE's great-great-great grandfather, Minister of the New North Church of Boston, and author of works including *An Evil and Adulterous Generation* (1753); Rev. Theodore Parker (1810–60), radical Boston preacher; Rev. Christopher Pearse Cranch (1813–92), TSE's great-uncle, poet and painter, and member of the Transcendental Club; Rev. Rufus Dawes (1803–59), author of volumes of poetry including *Geraldine* (1839), which TSE characterised as an 'emasculated pastiche' of Byron ('Israfel', *N&A* 7 [21 May 1927] 219.

3–William Prescott (1796–1859), *The History of the Conquest of Mexico* (3 vols, 1843).

4–*France and England in the New World* by Francis Parkman (1823–93), US historian.

5–A series of popular children's books, inc. *Rollo at Work* (1839), by Jacob Abbott (1803–79).

6–Presumably Thomas Jefferson, *Writings*, ed. H. A. Washington (9 vols, 1853–4).

TO *Mary Hutchinson* MS Texas

4 March 1919 18 Crawford Mansions

Dear Mary,

Vivien says she is lunching with you on Thursday. Won't you come on later (at 5.45) and dance at a place near Baker Street. They teach the new dances and steps, which I don't know and want to learn. I hope you won't mind my being rather out of date. It is over by half past seven, and we could dine afterwards. I think it would be rather fun, and the people ought to be a source of amusement. Do come.

Sincerely
T.S.E.

TO *Edgar Jepson* MS Beinecke

4 March 1919 18 Crawford Mansions

Dear Mr Jepson,

I shall be very glad to come and hear you on Sunday at 3 (?) and if you leave any opening shall defend the Elizabethans. I am pretty sure I can come.

I had been meaning to write (but had mislaid your address) to acknowledge your bold championship in *The Egoist*. I wonder if Monroe will have anything more to say! It was, by the way, to me that she wrote to ask to have the correspondence printed in *The Egoist*.[1]

Sincerely yours,
T. S. Eliot

1–In 'Recent United States Poetry' (*English Review*, 26 May 1918), Jepson had written dismissively of the poems by Vachel Lindsay, Edgar Lee Masters and Robert Frost to which *Poetry* had awarded prizes. It seemed 'incredible', he said, that in the year when *Poetry* had published TSE's 'La Figlia Che Piange', its first prize should go to 'that lumbering fakement, "All Life in a Life" [by Masters]'. When Austin Harrison, editor of the *English Review*, refused to print Harriet Monroe's indignant response, it appeared in the Nov.–Dec. issue of the *Egoist*, together with his reply and a further letter by her. An unrepentant Jepson intervened in the Jan.–Feb. 1919 number, and was criticised by Monroe and Aiken in Sept. (A condensed form of Jepson's attack in the *Little Review* in May also provoked a reply from William Carlos Williams.)

TO *His Mother* MS Houghton

12 March 1919 18 Crawford Mansions

My dearest Mother

I have had two letters from you since I wrote last, and one enclosing some old letters that father wrote me twenty years ago. I should have written last Sunday but that I have been engrossed in a problem which has come before me; and taking counsel of friends. I have just had a very flattering offer. It will of course be decided in the course of a few days, but while I am writing I might as well tell you about it. I have been asked to become the assistant editor of the *Athenaeum*,[1] on a two years contract, at £500 per annum. It is an old paper, for many years a (purely) literary weekly, with a very high standing in London. More recently it was changed to a monthly, and lost its character, but now it has been bought by a rich man who is turning it into a literary weekly again. The man who is to be editor[2] is very anxious to get me as assistant, and says he would rather have me than anyone in England.

The advantages are:

1. Social Prestige.
2. Probably more leisure.
3. More money at once.

The disadvantages are:

1. It is practically a new paper: it may succeed or fail.
2. In the latter case I should be in difficulties at the end of my contract. Against this, some probability that the distinction of having held the position would assure me getting something else.
3. No assurance that the salary would rise. At the bank I am sure of that.
4. The work *might* be more exhausting than the bank work; and would have no more relation to my own serious work than the bank work has.
5. I have lately been shifted into new and much more interesting work in the bank which is not routine but research – practically economics and in fact am a sort of department or bureau by myself.

I am to see the General Manager about this.

The chief fact militating against the acceptance is the insecurity after two years, and the fact that there would be a lot of drudgery in journalism

1–Founded in 1828, the *Athenaeum* had recently been bought by Arthur Rowntree.

2–John Middleton Murry, critic and editor: see Glossary of Names.

which would be fatiguing. There is of course as much difference between journalism and literature as between teaching and literature.

There it is in brief, but I assure you I have thought hard and am still thinking. I shall decide in a few days – the question is how soon I shall be getting a really good salary at the bank.

Anyway, it is a great compliment.

I am anxious for you to get settled in Cambridge. Then I shall come to visit you and bring you back with me.

Very affectionately
your son Tom.

TO *Edgar Jepson*

MS Beinecke

12 March 1919 — 18 Crawford Mansions

Dear Jepson,

Will you let me have your paper to press on Weaver for the *Egoist*?[1] (I can't swear how long it is, but lost count of time in listening to it). If you will I should like that and would write or attempt some sort of reply. You know you promised another when you had put it in shape, but I have given up hopes of that.

Yrs.
T. S. Eliot

I have just been given a decadent work of sentiment on the 'New Elizabethans'[2] which makes me feel that some of the sewers of the elder period ought to be aired.

Damn Lamb, Swinburne, J. A. Symonds, Dekker, Heywood and domestic tragedy except *Yorkshire Tr*[*agedy*].[3]

Glad you put in a word for Tourneur – he is a great poet. Think you quite wrong on B. Jonson.[4]

1 – TSE had attended a talk on Elizabethan literature by Jepson on 9 Mar. Jepson's paper was not used in the *Egoist*.

2 – TSE wrote an unsigned review of E. B. Osborn, *The New Elizabethans: A First Selection of the Lives of Young Men Who Have Fallen in the Great War*, in *A.*, 4 Apr. 1919.

3 – TSE wrote later, in 'Four Elizabethan Dramatists': 'The accepted attitude toward Elizabethan drama was established on the publication of Charles Lamb's *Specimens* [*of English Dramatic Poets, who Lived about the Time of Shakespeare* (1808)] . . . For the *Specimens* made it possible to read the plays as poetry while neglecting their function on the stage' (*C.* 2: 6, Feb. 1924; *SE*).

4 – TSE had a high regard for Jonson as poet and dramatist: 'Ben Jonson', *TLS*, 13 Nov. 1919; *SE*).

TO *Virginia Woolf*

MS Berg

26 March 1919 18 Crawford Mansions

Dear Mrs Woolf,

Thank you so much for sending me the patterns,[1] and so many of them. I still think that the one originally chosen is the best, and would probably also be best liked by the people who might buy the book. The dark blue one is also good. But these may be rather expensive, so I have chosen one of the others (marked 3) as an alternative, and it is only reasonable to leave the choice between these three to you.

I wonder if your husband got my note. We were very annoyed at having made an engagement for Saturday so far ahead that it could not be broken, but I do hope you will ask us again.

I look forward to seeing you. It is very good of you to have taken so much trouble over the papers.

Sincerely yours
T. S. Eliot

TO *Herbert Read*[2]

MS University of Victoria

26 March 1919 18 Crawford Mansions

Dear Read,

Thanks for your book.[3] I like it. I read most of it in the train this morning, and when I have read it again I should like to discuss it with you.

I want No. 19 of Wadsworth's Landscape in two colours.[4] Framed. Only I can't pay for it till after the 1st of the month.

Shall see you Friday.
Yours
T. S. E.

1–Papers of various designs and textures were used to cover copies of *Poems*, issued on 12 May.
2–Herbert Read, art and literary critic, poet and novelist, friend of TSE: see Glossary of Names.
3–HR had sent his collection, *Naked Warriors* (1919), with a note: 'Here is my gory war-book. You might like "Comeliness".' TSE later called it 'the best war poetry that I can remember having seen' ('Reflections on Contemporary Poetry', *Egoist* 6: 3, July 1919).
4–TSE had seen the picture at Frank Rutter's new Adelphi Gallery, where Edward Wadsworth was exhibiting his drawings and woodcuts. Frank Rutter (1876–1937), art critic and curator, and active supporter of women's suffrage, edited (with HR) the journal *Art & Letters*, 1917–20. He had been editor of *To-Day*, 1902–4, and curator of Leeds City Art Gallery, 1912–18; and he was art critic of the *Sunday Times* from 1903 until his death.

TO *Bertrand Russell* MS McMaster

26 March 1919 18 Crawford Mansions

Dear Bertie,

We had been considering the means of getting your things back to you when your letter came.[1] The people will be leaving at the end of this week. Vivien will not be able to go down on that day, but if the weather moderates so as to make the journey possible for her she will begin to send the things on by the latter part of next week. She will be using the house a good deal this spring; but it does not look as if the weather would permit her to do so for some little time. She will however go down as presently as possible and look after your articles.

Sincerely
T.S.E.

TO *His Mother* MS Houghton

29 March 1919 18 Crawford Mansions

My dearest Mother,

I have neglected you this week, but it is so hard to write about affairs when you know that they will be decided even before the recipient gets the letter. They are decided now. I am staying in the bank. The bank people were very anxious for me to stay. They are organising some new work, a new department, in fact, of a very interesting and important kind – not ordinary bank work at all, but economic work – I cannot go into further details about it, but I am started on it already; and it will be on a large scale, with numerous assistants. There is a man from the Foreign Office coming in too. As for the salary, I shall know in a few days what it will be. It will be better than my present one, and in a few years ought to be beyond the £500 offered by the *Athenaeum*. The work gives opportunity for initiative and is work for which they wish men of higher education. It will give much more responsibility, and therefore more freedom.

I was moved to this conclusion for several reasons. First the insecurity of a paper. A weekly which is *practically* a *new* one, and which must build

1 – Russell had written asking for the return of his belongings from the Marlow cottage. 'You needn't bring the things all at once, if it is easier to bring them by degrees,' he wrote on 19 Mar.; but he wanted the 'tea-table & coffee-grinder as soon as possible', and enclosed a list including 'check trousers, thick overcoat, top hat, fur for neck, long coat or cloak for term, rough coat for country, and day dress for term and day dress for country'.

up a new circulation, is a great venture. If it failed I should have to begin a new struggle – in journalism. I should be *worrying all the time* about whether it would succeed. The bank work offers prospects of a *very* good salary. I know the people and like them, and they like me very much. I know where I am with them.

But there is another argument besides the financial one. I felt that the constant turning out of 'copy' for a weekly paper would exhaust me for genuine creative work. It would *never* be my first interest, any more than finance is. Finance I can get away from at the end of a day; but review writing would stay by me; I should always be toiling to make my work better than it need be for ephemeral reading. I could not turn it out mechanically and then go to my own work.

Then, if I turned out a good deal of second rate stuff it would not in the end add to my reputation – and to make everything first rate would take too much out of me.

As it is, I occupy rather a privileged position. I am out of the intrigues and personal hatreds of journalism, and everyone respects me for working in a bank. My social position is quite as good as it would be as editor of a paper. I only write what I want to – *now* – and everyone knows that anything I do write is good. I can influence London opinion and English literature in a better way. I am known to be disinterested. Even through the *Egoist* I am getting to be looked up to by people who are far better known to the general public than I. There is a small and select public which regards me as the best living critic, as well as the best living poet, in England. I shall of course write for the *Ath.* and keep my finger in it. I am much in sympathy with the editor, who is one of my most cordial admirers. With that and the *Egoist* and a young quarterly review[1] which I am interested in, and which is glad to take anything I will give, I can have more than enough power to satisfy me. I really think that I have far more *influence* on English letters than any other American has ever had, unless it be Henry James. I know a great many people, but there are many more who would like to know me, and I can remain isolated and detached.

All this sounds very conceited, but I am sure it is true, and as there is no outsider from whom you would hear it, and America really knows very little of what goes on in London, I must say it myself. Because it will give you pleasure if you believe it, and it will help to explain my point of view.

1 – *Art & Letters*, 1917–20, was initially edited by Frank Rutter and HR. SS provided finance, edited one issue, and sought TSE's advice on the contents.

I will send you the *Athenaeum* when there are things of mine in it. There will be one on Friday.[1] I suppose it will be in the library too.

I have written this long letter all about myself, but only on one point, and with none of the personal details about ourselves that ought to go into a letter. And of course too I am very anxious for more news from *you*.

But just now I am very busy. I have promised to do a good deal of work for Murry (the editor-in-chief) until he finds someone else, because he has been so kind to me.[2] And with the new bank work, I shall find my hands quite full for a time.

Always your devoted son
Tom

TO *Brigit Patmore*[3] MS Beinecke

[April 1919?] *The Egoist*, Oakley House,
Bloomsbury St, London, W.C.

Dear Brigit

Thank you for your letter, in spite of the first and last sentences. But if you were furious, why didn't you say so? I shouldn't have been frightened. Do you mean furious altogether, or in so far as you were sure I was wrong? You should, in writing, have given a concise summary of what my 'judgment' was, and then for my benefit, separated the chaff from the wheat. As it is, I am in the dark. Then you are wrong about two things. I don't think I judge to the extent of thinking that I understand the whole or even the essential of a person, but merely that certain expressions and ways of acting seem to indicate certain things about them: these inferences are true or false, and people's history is another matter. If I knew more of your history I should of course understand better what I can see of you, and of course without that knowledge I cannot judge. I can only observe, and correct by further observation.

And do you think it is necessary to subdue your personality to that of the person you are with, in order to understand them? It seems to me merely a question of being enough interested to forget oneself, which is very different from subduing oneself. I can't see any reason for subduing

1 – The first of TSE's regular *A.* pieces over the next two years was an unsigned review of Osborn, *The New Elizabethans*: 4 Apr. 1919.
2 – Although he did not accept the post of assistant literary editor, TSE wrote at least fifteen reviews for JMM over the year.
3 – Brigit Patmore (1882–1965), Irish writer and literary hostess: see Glossary of Names.

oneself except for convenience, or simply because one is realised through the other person. The people who seem most curious about understanding others have usually struck me as very positive personalities.

Certainly, the man who is without vanity, or who can recover from an attack on his vanity and profit by it, has some greatness. Perhaps their vanity goes deeper than women's, I don't know. Vanity is so much part of the human passion – love of power, that it is perhaps never absent.

You must not on any account give me credit for being penetrating. I have impressed people that way before, and the result is always disaster. For there eventually comes some word or action which shows them my immense stupidity, and the whole thing goes up in smoke. Always cut what I appear to understand by half.

Don't think I should fail to take account of what your life has been – only, however it interested me, and how much light it threw, it is not, in one way, essential. The question is what goes on in your mind now?

I must finish a review, before I get my things together.

Yours
TSE

TO *St John Hutchinson* — MS Texas

1 April 1919 — 18 Crawford Mansions,
Crawford St, W.1.

Dear Jack

Your hospitality is very unfair but as you urge arguments of convenience I will accede if you will dine with me next week. I am looking forward to Seraglio[1] very keenly. Love to Mary,

Yrs ever
T.S.E.

1 – On 3 Apr. they went to a performance of Mozart's *Die Entführung aus dem Serail* ('The Abduction from the Seraglio'), conducted by Sir Thomas Beecham, at the Theatre Royal, Drury Lane.

TO *Henry Eliot* MS Houghton

6 April 1919 18 Crawford Mansions

My dear Henry

I have not written to you for a long time and there are some matters about which I ought to have written you. I suppose that Mother will have sent you some of my letters. First I must thank you for the cheque in your last letter but one, £10 and for the £21 you cabled. The last I did not know about until you wrote, as the bank did not notify me. We are very grateful for the money. We have got to have some wallpapering and painting done soon, which will be rather expensive, as the flat is in a very dirty condition after three years. We should rather like to change, but it would be almost impossible to find another good flat cheap in a good part of town. This flat is good and cheap, and in a good part of town, but the *immediate* neighbourhood and some of our neighbours, are not what we should like. It is rather noisy.[1] – So we must be here for two years more. Then we shall be able to pay more, and we want a larger flat: we are rather tired of living in three rooms.

What I should have liked to write to you about before is the *Athenaeum*. But it would have been settled before you could have answered. The *Athenaeum* used to be the chief literary weekly in London. Then in the nineties it ran down, and for the past two years was run as a monthly of social reconstruction. Now it has changed hands and the man who is the new editor (it is again a literary weekly) asked me to be his assistant editor at £500. I weighed the matter for some days. My reasons for declining are as follows:

1) I cannot be sure that the paper will succeed. If it failed, I should be in the street at the end of two years. New papers are risky. In the prime of the *Athenaeum* there was no competitor; now there is the *Times Supplement* at second. The *Athenaeum* is sixth.
2) I am not sure that journalistic life would be good for me. It would involve doing a good deal of writing week by week, on books that I should not always be interested in. It might leave me less energy for original work than I have at present. My reputation is built on writing very little, but very good, and I should not add to it by this sort of thing.

1 – Osbert Sitwell reports that two 'actresses' who lived below the flat spent their time 'playing the piano, singing, or putting some particularly loud record on the gramophone', as well as yelling to 'gentlemen friends' in the street. This often went on 'far into the small hours and without interval'. When TSE complained to the landlord, he was told, 'Well, you see, Sir, it's the Artistic Temperament.' Sitwell thought the experience contributed to *SA*, and that he could 'hear the voices of the *Waste Land* [there]'('T. S. Eliot', unpublished memoir, Texas).

3) The bank have not only been very kind to me in the past but have now started me in some new work which promises to be very interesting and to lead to something good. It is economic and statistical. I do not yet know what I shall get to begin with. It won't be anything like what the paper offered but it will eventually be better.

On the paper I should have had no control over the contributors or the policy. I should have been all the more worried if I foresaw at any time that it was not going to succeed.

I probably have more influence and power and distinction *outside* of the journalistic struggle and having no material stake in it.

At any rate I have made the choice and am satisfied with it.

This has absorbed all my time and thought for several weeks, and I am tired out with it.

I hope at least that it will not be necessary for me to give lectures next year.

I want to write more fully about other things too, but I shall wait till next week. I am doing a certain amount of reviewing for the *Athenaeum* to help the editor, and we have also been obliged to dine out and see a great many people lately.

Thank you very much for the photographs. It is a great satisfaction to have them.

Always affectionately
Tom

Vivien Eliot TO *Charlotte C. Eliot* — MS Houghton

7 April 1919 — 18 Crawford Mansions

My dear Mrs Eliot

There is a letter from you for Tom lying on the table, and he will be pleased to find it when he comes in. He will get in about 5.30, and will then have tea and supper together, and go off to his lecture at 6.30. He will get back again at 11 – and have something more to eat. Monday is always a hard day. It is the most beautiful warm Spring day today, and makes one think of the country.

Our woman, who was so very dreadfully ill with influenza and pneumonia, is now back doing a few hours work a day, but cannot do much as she is still weak. She was ill six weeks and her illness cost us a good deal. Did Tom tell you how she was taken suddenly ill here in the flat one Saturday night, just as she was going home? We had to put her to bed on the sofa, (we have no second bed or bedroom) and there she was for five days, getting worse and worse. I nursed her night and day and we thought she would die on our sofa. I cld. get no one to help me as it was in the midst of the influenza epidemic, and even the doctor did'nt come regularly. It was a dreadful time. I have never seen anyone so frightfully ill as she was. It is a terrible illness. The doctor saw that we could'nt help her all through it, so at last she was taken away in an ambulance. I disinfected the whole flat, and the marvel is that we neither of us caught it. I had a septic throat for a week, but that was all.

Tom is now pretty well, although of course always over-worked and over-tired. The winter has been a trying one. I hope he will get three weeks holiday from the Bank during the spring or summer, and I should very much like him to go abroad, to France, if he thinks he can afford it. After being cooped up in England all these years, everyone feels an intense longing to get out of it, and I think it is particularly necessary for Tom to have a *complete change*, and rest for his brain. He has a friend Windham [*sic*] Lewis (you will know his name, I expect) who will be in Brittany all summer, and Tom wd. love to join him for his little holiday. Ezra Pound and his wife are going to France in a week – to Toulouse – *for six months*. His wife's health has suffered during the war and her doctor recommends she shd. get out of England. They are lucky to be able to, lucky to be so free. Mrs Pound is English, and very charming. She has never been to America, and in several ways she and I have much in common. We are friends. Tom and I are very happy in the people we know – it is a pity you have no outsider to tell you things about us. It is difficult to tell you everything ourselves. I remember you have several times said you wished you had some person intimate with us who would give you news. Of course you could at any time have written to my parents, who would have been glad to keep you posted. Tom has a splendid social position here, and we belong to quite the most interesting set. How happy it would make Tom if you would visit England! I should think it would interest you too, although of course I realise only too well what an undertaking it is.

Of course Tom's money-earning activities are of a kind that make it very difficult for him to think of getting away for any length of time for a good while. If he had accepted that very flattering offer of Sub-Editor to the *Athenaeum* he would have been just as tied. I think on the whole he did wisely to stay at the Bank, although I found it hard to think so at the time.

With love, and hoping to hear from you before long

Your affect.
Vivien

TO *Virginia Woolf* MS Berg

12 April 1919 18 Crawford Mansions

Dear Mrs Woolf,

I must apologise for the delay in sending you this list[1] – the only excuse is fatigue. You will have some of these on your list already. Where I have not got the addresses they will mostly be in the telephone directory, I think. I have probably omitted several of the likeliest people, as one does, but I have a copy of the list and will send you any more names as they come to my mind.

We are having workmen in directly after Easter, and as soon as they let us have our flat again we should be so pleased if you and your husband could come and dine with us one evening.[2]

Sincerely yours,
T. S. Eliot

Vivien Eliot TO *Bertrand Russell* MS McMaster

Sunday [13? April 1919] 18 Crawford Mansions

My dear Bertie,

I went to Marlow[3] a week ago and fetched away several small belongings of yours, and packed up the table, but was unable to get anyone to carry it to the station at the last minute. Tomorrow, unless my cold turns to influenza, I am going again and shall bring the table and whatever else I can carry. Then I will try to get this first collection conveyed to your present address.

I am sorry it has been so long, and I am afraid it will take a good many journeys before you have everything. So please have patience!

Do come and see us when you have a free evening.

Yours ever
Vivien.

1 – A list of potential purchasers of his *Poems*.

2 – The Eliots had dined with the Woolfs a few days earlier, on 6 Apr. VW recorded: 'I amused myself by seeing how sharp, narrow, & much of a stick Eliot has come to be, since he took to disliking me. His wife a washed out, elderly & worn looking little woman' (*Diary*, I, 262).

3 – The Eliots relinquished their lease on 15 Nov.

TO *J. H. Woods* MS Professor David G. Williams

21 April 1919 18 Crawford Mansions

My dear Dr Woods,

Your two letters of Feb 15 and Feb 27 have been a long time unanswered, and this must appear very rude of me.[1] Your first letter came, oddly enough, just as I had received another proposal, which, with illness, occupied my time for many weeks after. May I say first of all, how keenly I appreciate your never failing kindness toward me since the very beginning of our acquaintance? Your last letters are only one more proof of it, but one which has touched me very deeply. In the second place of course I feel very much pleased at the honour in such a suggestion – an honour really out of proportion to my attainments in philosophy.

When I first settled in England my material ambitions were toward a literary editorship. I only went into a Bank as a stop gap until I became sufficiently well known to get the sort of offer I wanted. Now that I am well known I have had the offer and find that I don't want it any longer. I have been offered the assistant-editorship of the *Athenaeum* at a very good salary and have declined it. This for two kinds of reason.

The first is that I have got on very well in Banking, and although I have not yet anywhere near as good a salary as the *Athenaeum* offered me I have lately been pushed into a post of some importance which offers fairly lucrative prospects, and interesting work in economics and foreign affairs. I suppose also I take some self-satisfaction in having carried off a *tour de force* in succeeding with an occupation apparently so incongruous. Also I like the men I have to deal with, and they have been kind to me.

The other reason is more ideal. I think that my position in English letters is all the stronger for my not being associated with any periodical as an employee. Journalism is a profession like any other, and it has no more to do with *literary art* than any other occupation. This is a cardinal point. In writing for a paper one is writing for a public, and the best work, the only work that in the end counts, is written for oneself. If one has to earn a living, therefore, the safest occupation is that most remote from the arts.

There are only two ways in which a writer can become important – to write a great deal, and have his writings appear everywhere, or to write very little. It is a question of temperament. I write very little, and I should not become more powerful by increasing my output. My reputation in

1 – Woods still hoped to tempt TSE back to the Harvard Philosophy Department, though his colleagues were unsure about his suitability. See Manju Jain, *T. S. Eliot and American Philosophy*, 33–5.

London is built upon one small volume of verse, and is kept up by printing two or three more poems in a year. The only thing that matters is that these should be perfect in their kind, so that each should be an event.

As to America: I am a much more important person here than I should be at home. I am getting to know and be known by all the intelligent or important people in letters, and I am convinced that I am more useful in the long run by being here. Finally, one changes. I have acquired the habit of a society so different that it is difficult to find common terms to define the difference.

My father died early in the year, and my mother is going to settle in Cambridge as soon as her affairs are in order. I am looking forward to visiting her there at sometime during next winter or spring. Surely you will be there?

I am hoping to hear from you in answer to my last letter, but you are of course waiting for this letter from me. I hope you will reply to this, and provoke another letter from me: one cannot put the process of four years experience clearly on four sheets of paper.

Very gratefully yours
T. S. Eliot

TO *His Mother* — MS Houghton

23 April 1919 — 18 Crawford Mansions

My dearest Mother

It seems a very long time since I have written to you. I have just had a holiday: Friday to Tuesday was a general 'bank holiday' in England this year, but it has gone very quickly. Vivien unfortunately came down with a mild attack of influenza and was in bed the whole time. She is much better now, but weak. We were to have gone to the country, to Lady Ottoline Morrell's. It was just as well, however, that her attack should have come when I could be at home, as our daily woman only stays till 4 o'clock at present, until she is quite strong again. What usually happens after V. has influenza is that I get it and she has to nurse me before she is well, but I took extra precautions this time.

I spent part of my time writing an article for the *Athenaeum*,[1] and was rewarded by a warm letter of appreciation this morning from the editor.

1–TSE, 'A Romantic Patrician', a review of George Wyndham, *Essays in Romantic Literature*, in *A.*, 2 May 1919; collected in *SW*. 'How *very good* is your essay on Wyndham!' wrote JMM. 'I could not have wished it better done. What a great pleasure it is to have you

I will send you the paper when it comes out. When I declined his offer he decided not to have *any* assistant editor, as, he said, he did not know of anyone else in England whose critical judgment he could trust in matters of the literary policy of the paper. That is very flattering, and makes me feel that I ought to do all I can to help the paper: it is the only weekly that I should care to be associated with. As the articles are to be initialled I shall have credit for them among the people who count.

I have been trying the last two afternoons to buy a muzzle for our dog. We have a dog – a very small Yorkshire terrier with hair over its eyes, a waif which followed me in the street.[1] We have had it some time. It is of very good breeding, and was beautifully trained by someone and a good companion for Vivien when she is alone during the day. Lately there was a dog accused of rabies near London, and so all dogs must be muzzled. The shops have been besieged by frantic people wanting muzzles, all bringing their dogs. I waited in a queue for half an hour yesterday and the woman just ahead of me bought *three* – and there were no more of the size. I managed to get one today, and then had to buy a file and a pair of pincers to alter it to fit. The dog hates it, of course.

I enclose the form of receipt for the stick. I think you had better keep it until I come unless there is some very secure way of packing, but I don't want to run any risks with an object of such value. The worst of such a possession is that I shall be afraid ever to use it. You have another stick of mine, silver headed, at Gloucester. The only things I want immediately are a few books which I asked Shef to send, if possible.

The question of leave of absence is rather a difficult one at present. I had hoped that the new department would be organised at once. It is held up at the moment because we are waiting for rooms. Another department is to move away and give place to us. Until they do so, and it may be two or three weeks, we can do nothing, as the work involves a large outfit of filing cabinets, etc. I cannot broach any question of holiday until the department is actually in existence, and then it will be a question of seeing how the work is to be divided up among my colleagues. I shall probably be very busy and have a good deal of responsibility in the initial organisation, and I don't know whether I can get even an ordinary vacation this summer. At any rate, I must get my foot firmly planted first, and then take a rest. I am also hoping (but this is in strict confidence) to

working with me. I only hope that the collaboration will not be interrupted until we have restored criticism.'

1 – They named the dog 'Dinah Brooks'.

be in a position to show that I could do some work in the bank's interest on the other side, and so get part of the expense paid. Very likely nothing will come of this, however. As soon as the work is under way I can size up better what to ask for and when. The more important I am the more time I can beg, but also the more delayed I may be. It would be in the winter or early in the spring. I cannot tell you how anxious I am to come to you, and how much I think about it. If it was the spring do you think it would be any easier for you to help us both to come? Vivien is very anxious to come.

I had a very nice letter from Marion which I hope to answer soon. I must write to Henry.

With very much love

Your affectionate son
Tom.

TO *Mary Hutchinson* MS Texas

Thursday [1? May 1919] 18 Crawford Mansions

Dear Mary,

Are we going to see you before you go away? Vivienne has been ill this week and we have had so much to do getting ready to leave the flat that we have not had time for any social engagements.

If possible, could we not arrange to meet on Sunday or on Saturday afternoon? Do let me know if you are available. It is so long since we have seen you.

Sincerely,
T. S. E.

We are leaving here by Saturday morning so could you just send a line that I should get by then.

TO *His Mother* MS Houghton

4 May 1919 18 Crawford Mansions

Dearest Mother,

I must answer your questions first.

I received everything, chessmen, and pocket chess also, for which I thank you very much. I should very much like to have the bath robe – mine is *very* worn and also I should like to have father's very much indeed: I should like to have it with me. As for Rollo books. I was anxious that they be preserved; I cannot see that I have any claim upon them beyond the fact that I was the last in the family to make use of them. If there is anyone else in the immediate family who would treasure them as much as I (for I think very highly of them) let them have them. It seems a small matter, perhaps, but there might not unnaturally be some feeling against their going out of the country. The only things I want are

1. Things I value and others don't.
2. Things (i.e. certain books) which I could make better use of than anyone else. There it is in brief.

I have still been very busy. Besides the *A.* I have found myself involved in various literary schemes and intrigues, as I seem to get involved nowadays. For one minor thing, Ezra Pound has gone to France, and I am the only person he can depend upon to look after his forthcoming book, and one or two other things.[1] All sorts of literary affairs seem to claim at least my counsel, and there are often jarring interests to be reconciled by diplomacy. It is gratifying in a way but distracting.

My connection with the *A.* seems to have given me a critical notoriety I did not have before. It is pleasant that I find the editor so congenial. I am writing now about a cousin of ours, who has written a very interesting book which you would like to read: *The Education of Henry Adams.*[2] There is a chance of my placing articles at times with the *Quarterly Review*, which would be a triumph, as it attacked me so ferociously two years ago.[3] My lectures come to an end tomorrow, for which I am very thankful; I hope I have done with education; the pay is not bad, but it seems such a waste!

I am very sorry you have had so much trouble in disposing of the houses: I should think that E. Point at least ought to realise very handsomely. It will be very valuable property in time if not too many cheap houses are built.

1–EP corrected proofs for *Quia Pauper Amavi* (London: Egoist Ltd, Oct. 1919) in Toulouse, but was planning further ahead. He had written to RC-S (22 Apr. 1919): 'I am leaving for the continent this afternoon, shall not return before October at earliest; so I shall be unable to talk with you, or to enquire what kind of publisher you intend to be. My *Instigations* will run to 400/600 pages, prose. It is the most important prose work I have done; you can, if you like, discuss terms of publication of it with T. S. Eliot.' However, *Instigations* appeared only in America (Boni & Liveright, 1920).
2–TSE, 'A Sceptical Patrician' (review of *The Education of Henry Adams: An Autobiography*, 1919), *A.*, 23 May 1919, 361–2. TSE was a 'cousin' of the author, Henry Brooks Adams (1838–1918), in that his grandmother, Abigail Adams Eliot, was a niece of John Quincy Adams, the sixth US President, who was Henry Adams's grandfather.
3–Arthur Waugh, in the *Quarterly Review* (Oct. 1916), had described 'The Love Song of J. Alfred Prufrock' as 'the reduction to absurdity' of 'unmetrical, incoherent banalities'. TSE never contributed to the journal.

No more now.
With infinite love. You are much in my thoughts –

Your son
Tom.

TO *Brigit Patmore* MS Beinecke

4 May 1919

from Hotel Constance,[1]
23 Lancaster Gate W.2

Dear Brigit,

That is settled for Wednesday then. V. is to get tickets tomorrow. You will dine with us, please, at the *Restaurant Español*, Dean Street, Soho (it is just opposite a theatre, I forget which, but the only one in Dean Street). You cannot ask us to dinner, as I have asked another man to come (we are not in evening dress), but if you like you may pay for your ticket.

I am distressed to hear of your nervous prostration, though I suspect it may be digestive prostration as a result of the meal we gave you on Tuesday. V. is also on the verge of collapse in consequence of the horrors of moving.

In case your collapse continues so that you can't stir afoot on Wednesday, please communicate with one of us – Vivien is at 39 Inverness Terrace W.2 and as I could not get in there I am at address above.

Points in this letter:

1. Address of Restaurant p. 1. 7 *p.m. Wednesday.*
2. Our addresses in case of collapse (which would not be forgiven).
3. You can pay for ticket but not for dinner.

Do get well.

Sincerely
T.S.E.

TO *Brigit Patmore* MS Beinecke

Wednesday [7 May 1919]

Hotel Constance

Having no ink

Dear Brigit

This week has been a fiasco altogether – here is the sixth letter I have written (to say nothing of a wire and any number of telephone calls) about

1 – The Eliots moved out of Crawford Mansions while their flat was being decorated.

apparently a very simple matter, and all for nothing. The only thing to do is to start quite afresh. Please don't consider us hopeless and please be kind – we tried hard!

If you will be gracious will *Tuesday* do? Don't say you are leaving town at once.

I have got hold of my man finally, and he can come on Tuesday.

Sincerely
T.S.E.

You will be thinking that it is *I* who am muddleheaded. However, I prefer to argue the point of your neutral state later, if the chance offers. I stick to the point that it is fundamentally a question of mental laziness.[1]

Vivien Eliot TO *Mary Hutchinson* MS Texas

Thursday [8 May? 1919][2] 39 Inverness Terrace, W.2

Mary,

What are we to do about this? You know what you were telling me on Sunday? Well, since then I have found out that Tom has for a long time been very much worried, puzzled, and *annoyed* at the Woolfs' behaviour about his poems which they were, as you know, printing. It seems that when we went to dine there, which was *about a month ago* [Sunday, 6 April], the poems were all finished, and Tom was asked to choose the cover. I remember we *did* choose the cover. They then asked Tom for a list of people's addresses for them to send out a circular to, about the book. Tom made the list, and wrote a letter (very nice) with it. Well, that is quite three weeks ago. Since then he has never heard a word, and we know that *no one* has received a circular about the book. This is very awkward for several reasons. One being that he gave them several poems to print which are *not* published elsewhere, and has been counting on this book of the Woolfs' for showing them. I *mean*, certain people are *asking* to see these poems in order to publish them, and Tom has been waiting and waiting for this Woolf book, to show them.

1–Patmore records that while dining with the Eliots and the Hutchinsons, she had murmured 'Melancthon' while beginning her melon. When TSE asked 'What do you know of Melancthon? . . . Why drag him in?', she replied she was 'Just playing with words. We Irish all do it. Joyce didn't begin it.' To which TSE responded: 'Do you know what you are? . . . You're mentally lazy' (*My Friends When Young* [1968], 87).

2–Dated 1 May 1919 in the first edition of these *Letters*.

Now Mary, do you think that, out of revenge,[1] the W.'s are actually going to shelve the whole of those books of Tom's which they have printed? If they do, what a humiliation for Tom! Because *of course* a great many people *knew* that the Woolfs were printing his poems. Now I think the *whole thing* is sure to come out, because I believe Tom actually wrote to Leonard Woolf last night, about it. I feel awful. I do not know what to do. But I feel very unhappy and angry. I almost wish that Tom would get out of this country altogether, and he will too, if this sort of thing goes on. If a man is sensitive, and an artist, he can't stand these people – I can't say more. But we will talk when I come. Will you please now suggest what is to be done? Because if the Woolfs are really going to do as I say, and throw up Tom's book, I really believe I shall go there and have it out with them. Yet, *if I did*, I believe that Tom would never speak to me again. He would *hate* me. He hates and loathes all sordid quarrelling and gossiping and intrigue and jealousy, *so much*, that I have seen him go white and *be ill* at any manifestation of it.

Joyce is lucky to be out of it. Wise man.

Pound was ruined by it. See what he has become. A laughing stock.[2] And his work all bad. Only a person of coarse fibre, a Wyndham Lewis, *can* stick it and remain undamaged.

If I were you Mary I would write to Tom and tell him what happened.

Do not *attempt* to say anything more to Clive. If you do the whole matter will end in a complete estrangement between us, *I know it*. Leave Clive *out of it*. Do not let him know that his conversation has had any results. If you do not do what I say *about this* – I will never be a friend of yours again. I will not.

Goodbye dear Mary I am not angry with *you*, but I am very much worried.

Write to me please Mary dear

[unsigned]

1 – VW wrote to her sister Vanessa Bell on 4 Apr.: 'By the way, Mary rang me up yesterday in great agitation about Eliot, imploring me to say nothing, denying the whole story, and insisting that he only abused Bloomsbury in general, and not me, and that Clive had completely misunderstood!' (*Letters*, II, 344). Clive Bell was MH's lover. Still suspecting a personal attack, VW began to disparage the Eliots. See also TSE to Eleanor Hinkley, 17 June 1919.

2 – VW had written to Roger Fry (18 Nov. 1918), decrying TSE's cult of EP and WL: 'Not that I've read more than 10 words by Ezra Pound by [*sic*] my conviction of his humbug is unalterable' (*Letters*, II, 296).

Vivien Eliot TO *Mary Hutchinson* MS Texas

Saturday [10 May 1919] [en route to Garsington]

Here I am in the train going to Garsington.[1] It is very hot. I don't know how I feel, I have suspended my feelings until I get there. I got your lovely long letter this morning. You were quite right because Woolf did answer T's letter, and sent him the copy of the poems which T. had asked him for (to send to a man called Schiff[2] – have you heard of him? the Sitwells' 'Holy Ghost') Woolf wrote very curtly – I saw the letter. It could not have been curter. He said they had lost the list of names T. had sent them, and would T. send another. I really always rather hate a man who takes up his wife's feuds, don't you?

So that's where we are at present. I shall certainly keep you posted. Also tell you about this weekend. Everyone seems to be hanging on my experiences at G! I have an appointment with Edith [Sitwell] at 4 o'clock on Monday to give her my report.

I believe we are actually going to bring Jack [St John Hutchinson] and 'Brigit' together on Tuesday night. Last time it did not come off.

You interest me about Virginia and Ottoline. I am going to throw out a few feelers while I am at G. [and] try to trap O into saying something to V's disadvantage.[3] I like to go about collecting evidence, which I may not use for years perhaps never.

Dear Mary – I cannot leave town until I go to Bosham. I have so much to be here for and if it were not for you I should never dream of going away in June at all. But we must have all the joys you write of while I am there, (between June 12 and July 12).

But I think, Mary, that if you were to ask Tom to come to you for Whitsun, he would. In fact I am nearly sure.

With a great deal of love

Vivien

1 – TSE and VHE signed the Visitors' Book on 11 May 1919; Lytton Strachey was there too. According to Miranda Seymour (*Life on the Grand Scale: Lady Ottoline Morrell*, 1993), it was at this time that OM added VHE to the list of women she liked best.

2 – Sydney Schiff, patron of the arts, and, writing as 'Stephen Hudson', novelist and translator: see Glossary of Names.

3 – Ironically, VW records that during the following week, she and OM 'talked personalities; investigated the case of Mary Hutch. & Eliot' (*Diary*, I, 272).

TO *Brigit Patmore* TS Beinecke

Monday [12 May 1919] 23 Lancaster Gate, W.2

Dear Brigit,

<Read Carefully> You are to be at the place previously selected – the Restaurant Espagnol in Dean Street Soho OPPOSITE the ROYALTY theatre at 7 o'clock or *not later* than 7.15 tomorrow *Tuesday* (the day you get this note) in order to dine and go to the Alhambra.[1]

What you say about mental paralysis is nonsense. It [is] a very poor excuse for not thinking any more about the matter. You are lazier than I supposed.

Yours etc
T.S.E.

Vivien Eliot TO *Ottoline Morrell* MS Texas

Monday [12 May 1919] 39 Inverness Terrace, W.2

My dear Lady Ottoline

The weekend [at Garsington] was so perfect that when I woke up this morning I couldn't believe it had happened. I shan't try to thank you, it would be hopeless. But you were too wonderful. We were both frightfully happy.

You know how rather frightened one feels after having talked unreservedly about a person. About Bertie, you know he was *extraordinarily generous* to me, I mean in *giving* things.[2] So much so that it will always make me feel very mean for talking against him. I know you understand perfectly. But I think he was more generous to me than he has ever been to anyone. He really made a sacrifice. I shall never forget that, and it makes a lot of difference to *everything*. I have really suffered awfully in the complete collapse of our relationship, for I *was* fond of Bertie (I think I still am). But it is of course *hopeless*, I shall never try to see him again. For the rest, I shall tell everyone who asks me, that we did not mention them at all! It is much the best way! No one believes it, but that doesn't matter. It would be so delightful to have someone to whom one

1–Together with the Hutchinsons they saw *Carnaval*, *The Firebird* and *The Good-Humoured Ladies*, performed by Diaghilev's Company, with Léonide Massine and Lydia Lopokova. Brigit Patmore had been invited to make up for her missing their planned trip the previous week.

2–In her journal over the summer of 1916, OM had recorded: 'I had a long talk with Bertie about Mrs Eliot . . . It seems odd that such a frivolous, silly, little woman should affect him so much, but I think he likes to feel that she depends on him, and she looks up to him as a rich god, for he lavishes presents on her of silk underclothes and all sorts of silly things, and pays for her dancing lessons' (*Ottoline at Garsington* [1974], 120).

could talk quite freely without any fear. Don't you think so? It is so bad for me to be always cautious and mistrustful. I think one often gossips in self-defence, knowing the other person will. But I shall not feel that way about you, if you won't about me?

If you come to London you will see me, won't you? This letter is from Tom too, as he has a week of fearful over-work ahead of him. He was so happy at Garsington! I know all the signs. You asked *just* the right people. The weather too! (and look at it now!) With love and ever so many thanks from us both –

Yrs. ever
Vivien Eliot

TO *Brigit Patmore* — MS Beinecke

Wednesday [14 May 1919] — Hotel Constance,
23 Lancaster Gate, W.2

Dear Brigit

I have been trying again and again to ring you up, but have found it quite hopeless. I felt that I could not rest until I had spoken to you about last night: I want to apologise to you for letting you go off that way alone. I feel terribly cut up about it, because I had rather it had been anyone in the world but you, and I wish I could hope to make clear that the cause is wholly that I lose my head completely on such occasions, and invariably do exactly the thing I should want not to do. From a purely selfish point of view the worst of it is that your opinion means so much to me.

Nearly the whole evening was a disappointment: I, at least, had looked forward to it very keenly. I won't say it was all a disappointment, but it was inadequate – and a good deal was jarring.

It would be easier to write this if I had been able to speak to you on the telephone first. It seems merely impertinent to keep repeating how unhappy I feel about it. I simply want to beg for a line from you: I want anything rather than suspense. Of course I shall in any case feel very miserable until I see you again and can talk to you. Please, let me hear from you, but what I really want is that you should consent to dine with me perhaps next week – simply out of tolerance – because I cannot bear leaving anything in the air.

Yours
Tom.[1]

1 – Patmore recalls in her memoirs that while they were waiting at the restaurant for the Hutchinsons, 'there was a queer feeling of nervousness in Tom. He said what unusual people

TO *Brigit Patmore* MS Beinecke

Friday [16 May 1919] 18 Crawford Mansions,
Crawford St, W.1

Dear Brigit

After all I have not thanked you for your letter, which is only another illustration of my imbecility – but the telephone always appals me anyway. I was very grateful for it and you are very kind and generous.

I think I realised how you feel among strangers, before you mentioned it. I am naturally so self-conscious myself that I feel it in others. Perhaps one never conquers it quite, but one must never capitalise! You see I have left the laziness and gone on to something else. However, we shall test the constraint.

Au revoir till Sunday. If that won't do you must give me an evening when you come back from Marlow. I am very glad you are going: Vivien will enjoy it.

Yours
Tom.

TO *Mary Hutchinson* MS Texas

16 May 1919 18 Crawford Mansions

Dear Mary,

Of course I should be delighted to come to you for Whitsun.[1] I am leaving town for an indefinite number of weeks, in a few days, to go about in the unknown provinces on business of the bank. I don't know how long I shall stay anywhere, and I shall probably be in town every week or so, and this will remain my address. But I shall certainly be able to get away for Whitsun, and can get down to Wittering. Vivien has made arrangements to do something including that time.

—

they were, how exclusive, how supremely cultured. Suddenly I wondered if he thought I might disgrace them by some outrageous behaviour . . . However, all went well at dinner and at the theatre too, until I blotted my copybook by saying I liked Tchaikovsky's music. That was *not* done in those days, but it didn't depress me and when it was time to go, I said goodnight and went home quite happily' (*My Friends when Young*, 87). She goes on to describe receiving this letter from TSE, with its 'worried and self-accusatory apologies', and wondering 'Heavens, what did it matter! . . . In what kind of state can his nerves be?'

1 – Whitsun was on 8 June. On 10 May, VHE had asked MH to invite TSE for Whitsun.

Please don't have anyone else – flattery quite apart! – I should like best to be the only guest. *Don't* have anyone for me, I mean – of course, if you were going to have someone anyway, don't alter your plans.

So you see I can be seduced – I am looking forward to it very keenly.

Yours,
T.S.E.

TO *The Editor of* The Athenaeum

Published 16 May 1919[1]

Sir,

Mr Lytton Strachey informs me that in my review of Kipling's verse last week I referred to the 'Authorized Version' as the 'Revised Version.'[2] I meant the Bible published by direction of King James I, and still in use in my childhood. Mr Strachey says that there is a modern edition called 'The Revised Version.'[3] I admit and apologize for the error.

Yours, etc.,
T.S.E.

TO *John Rodker*

TS Virginia

17 May 1919 — 18 Crawford Mansions

Dear Rodker,

Leonard Woolf's edition of a few of my poems is now on the market, and I understand that yours would not be ready before August, so that is all right.[4] I accordingly authorise, or give you permission, or whatever is the legal phrase, to print your special edition of 250 copies of a book to contain the poems in the Egoist *Prufrock*, the poems in Woolf's small book,

1–A note headed 'Wednesday' reads: 'Dear Strachey Don't be absurd – of course I should answer. Yrs T. S. Eliot' (BL). Presumably it was sent on 14 May, though 'May 21 1919' has been added in pencil.

2–TSE, 'Kipling Redivivus', a review of Kipling's *The Years Between*, in *A.*, 9 May 1919. Some Kipling poems, said TSE, convey a 'touch of the newspapers, of Billy Sunday, and the Revised Version filtered through Rabbi Zeal-of-the-Land Busy'. He remarked too that 'the Revised Version (substantially the same style as all the versions from Tindall) is excellent prose . . . but is not a style into which any significant modern content can be shoved.'

3–The Revised Version, 1881–5, was a revision of the Authorized Version of 1611.

4–Rodker had just started the Ovid Press, and wished to put out a *de luxe* collection of TSE's poems.

and any others that I may send you in a reasonable time. I enclose three new ones.[1] I should like to know when you want to start on this book, as I want to think over such questions as the order of the poems, dedication; also I have two more quotations, a Latin and a Greek one, to go in as headings. Will you be able to do Greek type? There are two other short Greek quotations.

I am going to be out of town most of the time for some weeks on my employer's business; but I shall be up at irregular intervals once a week or so for the night, and as I shall be moving about, this is the only address, and I can answer anything in the course of a few days.

I shall put on [*sc.* out] a cheap edition, with the Egoist, probably, in the spring of next year: in March or April or May; but that will give you enough time, won't it?

Yours
T. S. Eliot

I will send you a copy of Woolf's.

Vivien Eliot TO *Mary Hutchinson* — MS Texas

Sunday [18? May 1919] — 18 Crawford Mansions

Dear Mary,

I love you much more than ever. I turn to you with thoughts of joy and relief after my adventurings. I am fond of you and I think you wonderful. And wonderful you *are*. So Tom is coming to you for Whitsun! I may go with him for part of this preposterous tour. I may not. I *may* see you at Bosham just the same though.

Your devoted friend
Vivien

Heaven to be back here.
Lovely white room.

1 – Presumably 'Burbank with a Baedeker: Bleistein with a Cigar', 'Sweeney Erect' and 'Ode'.

TO *Lytton Strachey*[1] MS BL

Monday 19 May 1919 18 Crawford Mansions

Dear Strachey,

I find that I am being sent on a tour of the provinces, by my bank, as soon as I can get off, and that I shall probably be gone some weeks. So unfortunately there is no possibility of my asking you to dine with me in the near future, as I should have liked to have done.[2] I only fear that when I am settled here again you will be buried in the country. Perhaps you will keep me in touch with your movements, and perhaps you will even let me have your opinions and Revisions of anything of mine you see in print.

Sincerely
T. S. Eliot

This is my only address.

TO *John Rodker* MS Virginia

Wednesday [21 May 1919] 18 Crawford Mansions

Dear Rodker,

Thanks for your letter. I am sorry for the misunderstanding. I don't think there is enough new stuff for more than twenty-five pages, but perhaps I shall have more by the end of June.[3] I hope so. I wonder if thirty or thirty-five pages is worth your while? With hope to see you in a few weeks.

Sincerely,
T. S. Eliot

1–Lytton Strachey (1880–1932), critic and biographer.

2–TSE had seen Strachey at Garsington on 11 May, and dined with him in London the following day. Strachey related to Dora Carrington on 14 May: 'Poet Eliot had dinner with me on Monday – rather ill and rather American: altogether not gay enough for my taste. But by no means to be sniffed at' (*Letters of Lytton Strachey*, ed. Paul Levy, 2005).

3–Rodker's Ovid Press published *Ara Vos Prec* in Feb. 1920. The poems from *Prufrock and Other Observations* occupy twenty-two pages, preceded by twenty pages of more recent work, including the Hogarth Press *Poems* and 'Gerontion'.

TO *His Mother* MS Houghton

25 May 1919 18 Crawford Mansions

My dearest Mother,

I have not had any *letter* from you for a very long time, except little short notes – not that they were not very nice ones, but I assumed that you were too busy or preoccupied to write. I have the dressing gown, and am delighted to have it. Everything you have sent has come safely.

I don't know whether I told you that the lectures were ended, to my great relief. The class seemed to be satisfied with them (though I was not) and presented me with some very nice books[1] to mark the completion of the three years' course. I don't know whether it will be desirable for me to continue them from any point of view, as perhaps I can make more money as well as more reputation from the *Athenaeum*. I have got to give one lecture on Saturday next, at London University; subject: 'the younger poets'.[2] I don't know what to say. It is a delicate subject.

I enclose an article from the *Times* which will interest you. I haven't been able to identify the author. I don't think his critical acumen is very great, though he is flattering. I am not however greatly flattered by the close association with A. H. He is a nice young friend of mine, a grandson of T. H.[3]

I send you my article on Henry Adams, which I hope will reach you.

Vivien and I both feel pretty tired after the long winter. We didn't have much in the way of a holiday last year – the Army–Navy affair killed that. Owing to the delay in the formation of the new work – owing to lack of housing room – I have not been able to arrange my holiday yet, but I insist on Vivien's going for a time to the seaside in June, anyway.

I hope we shall have a longer letter from you soon. I am anxious that you should be able to leave St Louis before the weather gets too hot.

Your devoted son
Tom.

1–TSE's leaving gift included *The Oxford Book of English Verse*, 'with the gratitude and appreciation of the students of the Southall Tutorial Literature Class May 1919'.

2–Not traced.

3–'Experiments in Poetry', *TLS*, 22 May 1919: a review of *Coterie*, in which TSE's 'A Cooking Egg' appeared. The anonymous author was RA, who bracketed TSE's work with the poetry of AH (grandson of the biologist Thomas Henry Huxley).

TO *John Quinn* MS NYPL (MS)

25 May 1919 18 Crawford Mansions

Dear Mr Quinn:

I have your letter of 29 April and am *most* grateful to you. I do think that the pains you have taken over this book of mine are a very unusual thing for anyone to do for anyone.

I am simply writing to express my appreciation and waiting to hear from you further. If it were possible to alter the manuscript I should like to do so, as I have two or three other essays and a very few poems which I should add, and the essays are better than any in the manuscript. I have been writing a good deal for the rejuvenated *Athenaeum* lately, and the articles I have done for this are longer and better than any of those for the *Egoist*.

It would, as you know, be a great satisfaction to me for private reasons to have a book printed in America. I don't need to dwell on that.

I appreciate all that you say about wasting oneself on trifles.[1] It is very easy for a man in my position to do that: working from 9.15 to 5 in a bank, on foreign exchange, I find an infinite number of things to be done in my small leisure. Some of them are very specious and seductive: not only social engagements but various literary enterprises in which one's very devotion to literature seems to demand that one should take a part – I have to keep a firm eye on what is most important for me.

– Yet I had rather be in a bank than be dependent on literature or journalism for a living. I intend not to see anyone but one man for at least a month.

I do hope you will get the holiday. I am sure you will break down very badly unless you do.

Cordially yours
T. S. Eliot

1 – Quinn had written (29 Apr.): 'Take the advice of an older man who has overdone things and do not waste yourself on trivial things . . . The great thing is to save one's self from the unimportant and non-essential things in order to have the leisure and strength to do the bigger and finer and better work.'

TO *Mary Hutchinson* MS Texas

Monday [26 May?] 1919 18 Crawford Mansions

Dear Mary,

I am so sorry about Thursday. It *would* happen that way, but I am glad I have Wittering to look forward to – sunshine and seawater, and laziness – but I hope my brain will be in a condition worthy of the company. If you *will* have someone, by the way, I *should* like to see Roger [Fry].

I haven't thanked you yet for your letter with Virginia's review, which I only read on the train going down – I can't forget Charles' ride in the morning and arrival at the Rouault farm.[1] I shall want to know what you think of me in the next *Ath.*[2] – though it may not interest you. If you ever have time – to write letters – I should get them / it? eventually and be grateful –

Till Pentecost [8 June] –

Yours
T.S.E.

TO *Brigit Patmore* MS Beinecke

Tuesday [27 May? 1919] 18 Crawford Mansions

Dear Brigit,

This is a letter crowded into the end of an evening of writing, and won't amount to much. But I can't see that it is really a question of expression, but simply of complete integrity – if one is quite honest and fair to oneself the personality will be sufficiently there. There is such a difference between seeing the point of view of people one is with and accepting it. And I don't believe there is such a frame of mind as pure receptivity. I think that when one is most alert to impressions one is also doing the most immediate thinking. And I cannot see that there is a contest between reason and intuition – the most intuitive people I have known have also had the clearest minds – if they cannot give a reason for their opinion they can at all events state it clearly. One can be very alive to any person or situation and at the same time go on with one's own mind undisturbed.

1–It is not clear which VW review MH had sent to TSE, but his comment relates to Gustav Flaubert, *Madame Bovary*, ch. 2.

2–TSE, 'Beyle and Balzac', a review of George Saintsbury's *A History of the French Novel, to the Close of the Nineteenth Century*, vol. 2, in *A.*, 30 May 1919, 392–3.

Perhaps all I have to say is that one must develop a hard exterior in order to be spontaneous – one cannot be that unless nothing can touch what is inside.

But then one never does actually understand other people by thinking in this abstract way – understanding is a by-product of seeing them in different situations, talking of particular and concrete things.

Perhaps we could meet before long though it would have to be at rather short notice on my side. I shall join Vivien for this weekend and next also – perhaps you would be free and perhaps I should, one evening next week.

Yrs.
TSE

TO *Mary Hutchinson* MS Texas

1 June 1919 18 Crawford Mansions

Dear Mary

Whatever your doubts as to your epistolary genius on May 29, your Seidlitz powder blue[1] was very welcome when I returned on May 31st to deliver a lecture and pass Sunday trying to write a review. In spite of the stimulus of your real or pretended enjoyment of Adams I was unable to get on very fast:[2] Robert Lynd's collected papers[3] stuck in my throat, or clogged my liver – and in revenge he shan't go in this week, but Murry will provide a disquisition on Gerard Hopkins.[4] So you see it will never be clear whether he or Roger was first over the fence. Anyhow, Father Hopkins (fact) has been dead, I gather from J.M.M., *déjà quelques années* [some years already]. I am glad Roger is coming, and also glad to have an afternoon and evening first: I see you expect accounts of my provincial *amours*, but if you are too prying I shall reveal all the gossip of the tinplate industry. I am off to Manchester. I shall probably not leave there till Friday night or Saturday morning early; there is a train which gets to Chichester at 4.4 Saturday afternoon. There I suppose I charter a taxi to your house, unless I hear other instructions from you. I shall pass by Crawford Mansions on my way; of course I shall have to do so to fetch flannels. You

1 – Effervescent laxative.

2 – TSE, 'A Sceptical Patrician' (on Henry Adams).

3 – TSE, 'Criticism in England', *A.*, 13 June 1919: a review of *Old Men and New Masters* by Robert Lynd (1879–1949), Irish journalist and essayist; literary editor of the *Daily News*.

4 – JMM, 'Gerard Manley Hopkins', *A.*, 6 June 1919: a review of Hopkins, *Poems*, ed. Robert Bridges. The book was not reviewed by Roger Fry.

will be ready to pour out tea when I arrive? I will try to be intelligent more so than usual.

Yours
Tom.

TO *Lytton Strachey*[1]

1 June 1919 [18 Crawford Mansions]

. . . Whether one writes a piece of work well or not seems to me a matter of crystallization – the good sentence, the good word, is only the final stage in the process. One can groan enough over the choice of a word, but there is something much more important to groan over first. It seems to me just the same in poetry – the words come easily enough, in comparison to the core of it – the *tone* – and nobody can help one in the least with that. Anything *I* have picked up about writing is due to having spent (as I once thought, wasted) a year absorbing the style of F. H. Bradley – the finest philosopher in English – *Appearance and Reality* is the *Education Sentimentale* of abstract thought.

You are very – ingenuous – if you can conceive me conversing with rural deans in the cathedral close. I do not go to cathedral towns but to centres of industry. My thoughts are absorbed in questions more important than ever enter the heads of deans – as *why* it is cheaper to buy steel bars from America than from Middlesborough, and the probable effect – the exchange difficulties with Poland – and the appreciation of the rupee. My evenings in Bridge. The effect is to make me regard London with disdain, and divide mankind into supermen, termites and wireworms. I am sojourning among the termites. At any rate that coheres. I feel sufficiently specialized, at present, to inspect or hear any ideas with impunity.

TO *John Rodker* MS Virginia

1 June 1919 18 Crawford Mansions

Dear Rodker,

I have been back over Sunday and leave again tomorrow. It occurred to me after leaving that I had most rudely forgotten to thank you for the

1–Text from Michael Holroyd, *Lytton Strachey*, II, *The Years of Achievement 1910–1932* (1968), 364–5. The letter disappeared from James Strachey's files shortly before his death.

Gaudier.[1] It was good of you to send it to me, and it seems to me very well done. I should have preferred slightly thicker paper.

If you haven't a *Prufrock* I will get Weaver to send you one. I am sending you Virginia Woolf's book which seems to me very well done. There is one other French poem, which is in one of the later *Little Reviews*,[2] along with some others – you have that have you not? These and the three I sent you and one half-finished one[3] are all I have up to date. Oh, also the thing in *Coterie*.[4]

You can put me down for the *L.R.* if you like – *if* they pay for their contributions – but candidly my hands are likely to be pretty full, with the work I am doing for the *Athenaeum*.

Many thanks again for the Gaudier.

Yours
T. S. Eliot

Vivien Eliot TO *Ottoline Morrell* — MS Texas

Wednesday [4 June? 1919] — 18 Crawford Mansions

My dear – the letter you sent to Marlow reached me this morning. There was no one in the house to forward it, and it missed me there by a post, I think. I left there more than a week ago. I didn't mean to when I wrote to you. I felt very upset when I read your letter this morning. But in spite of everything you ought not to say 'that was a quick change etc. affair'. Believe me it wasn't. I know I should have written, even without getting your Marlow letter. But I could not write, not to anyone on earth, and have not. I have been ill in a sort of way, and I had to go into a sort of retirement which is so necessary to me at times that I should die without it. It is a seemingly selfish, closed up, kind of affair, but without something like it at frequent intervals I should cease to exist as a person at all. I am perfectly certain that no one has so little resistance to human contacts as I. I do not expect even you to realise how beaten upon and worn by the most ordinary amount of human intercourse I became. I don't want to bore you but some day I shall insist on forcing you to realise it! Of course I have been thinking about you. That is the worst of it! I had to. By the way you must never never show anyone my letters. But of course you never would.

1 – *Twenty Drawings from the Note-books of H. Gaudier-Brzeska* (Ovid Press, 1919).
2 – 'Dans le Restaurant', *Little Review* 5 (Sept. 1918).
3 – 'Gerontion' was to be completed during the summer.
4 – 'A Cooking Egg', *Coterie* 1 (May 1919).

I am amused by your description of Bertie's weekend at Garsington. He came straight from there to this flat, in the early hours of a Monday morning, to fetch away another instalment of possessions I had fetched from Marlow. He seemed dreadfully out of temper. Unfortunately I was not dressed, so had to shout to him from the bathroom, as cheerfully as I could. But the response was painful. I was sorry, really, I had asked him to come to tea when he fetched them, and I had come up from Marlow specially. I thought we might have talked a little and come to, at any rate, amicable relations. But it is no good. I will make no more attempts at all. But it is strange how one does miss him! Isn't it hard to put him *quite* out of one's mind? Did you get the tulip box, because I did send it back.

Tom is not abroad. Only backwards and forwards to various parts of England, such as Manchester and Birmingham and Cardiff!! But it *is* doing him good, even that. He is better. Do you really love England? I used to, but since the war I cannot feel that I really do. That is very painful. If I had known you were in London for that one night I *should* have come to find you. That would be easier than anything – just to walk, after dark, to that nice old hotel[1] and find you there. Tell me what your new dress is like. I really *should like* to know. Tom's pyjamas are still at Garsington. Do keep them as a hostage! I can wear them when I come.

Until I have been to Bosham I shall be too tired to see anyone, too stupid and boring and hideous altogether. Everyone thinks I am away or dead. But will you write to me? and give me the chance to write to you. Please.

I am going *next* Thursday. So this address until then. With love.

Affectly
Vivien E.

TO *Harriet Shaw Weaver* — MS BL

5 June 1919 — *The Egoist*, Oakley House, Bloomsbury St, London, W.C.

Dear Miss Weaver,

Thank you for your letter and the cheque for £6. I am much pleased by the expression of your and Miss Marsden's wishes. Certainly the *Egoist* will always have all the support I can give it, and you can depend upon me

1 – Garland's Hotel, Suffolk Street, Haymarket (destroyed by bombs in 1943).

as a Contributor.[1] I hope when the time comes I shall be in a position to do at least as much as I have done in the past. Of course my life is further complicated by my regular long contributions to the *Athenaeum*, and I am anxious to find <more> time to devote to independent writing and to verse. But I am still very jaded.

For your other suggestion, I shall probably be able to tell you definitely in July whether I can produce such a book.[2] I have had overtures from a publisher who has also left town, on a holiday, and whom I shall not see till into July, but what I may propose to him is an entirely new book which would take some time to prepare. I do not know when your final number will be out, but I presume in August, which would leave time. I have written to Blackwell for Greene's *Groats-worth of Wit*, so if it comes will you send it to me and I shall use that for my contribution.[3]

I shall meanwhile be in town weekends, but I expect to find it impossible to see people, as I have to answer accumulated correspondence and do my *Athenaeum* article[4] then. So I shall not count on seeing you till early in July.

Sincerely yours
T. S. Eliot

TO *Mary Hutchinson* MS Texas

Tuesday [10 June 1919] 18 Crawford Mansions,
Crawford St, W.1

Dear Mary

About half a mile further the car collapsed completely and at the same moment punctured a tire, in the middle of a vast plain. Nothing passed but two brakes full of boy scouts so I proceeded on foot followed by three ducks, and arrived at Chichester, dusty but triumphant, in time for a glass

1–The printer had refused since Jan. to publish any more of *Ulysses*, robbing Weaver of a prime incentive for continuing her financial support. At the end of May, she found that although the paper was smaller than before, costs had risen, and she was losing as much as ever, so she and Dora Marsden planned to suspend it for a while to enable Marsden to complete her book of philosophy.

2–The final issue of the *Egoist*, Dec. 1919, announced that the Egoist Press promised publication of *The Art of Poetry* by TSE in early spring, and a flyer for 'The Egoist Press Publications' announced it as 'in preparation'. It did not appear.

3–Robert Greene, *Groats-worth of Wit*, reprinted in the Sheldonian Series, 1919. TSE did not write about it.

4–TSE, 'Criticism in England'.

of beer at the Woodman just before the train. I reached C. Mansions at a quarter to 2! However, I enjoyed the Pentecost very much indeed – you were very charming.

Yrs.
Tom

TO *Mary Hutchinson* MS Texas

Sunday [15? June 1919] [18 Crawford Mansions]

Dear Mary,

My scrawl was despatched in some haste on a hurried day, and did not express much of the pleasure with which I am still looking back on the two days at Wittering. I preserve – at least the illusion – that it was not a drifting fog but was rather only something interrupted or suspended. <*Credo, quia impossibile est?*>[1] I wonder what your second impression is. My mind is not very active at the present moment: I have been occupied on another of my furiously laboured articles, perhaps the most laboured of the lot (you don't know how crude and undigested and indigestible they often seem to me when I see them in print). I thought that there was a moment of fog – or which threatened to end that way – on Sunday afternoon – which I thought afterwards had been saved from exercising further influence by our confession of cross purposes almost directly afterwards. It wasn't cleared up, but it did no harm. I am still wanting to know what your dilemma was – though I am sure it will be settled by you, if at all, without anyone's opinion having had the slightest effect. I am not sure that I should see it just as you do, mind. I think you are capable of being quite incomprehensible and unaccountable, except to yourself. There is something odd in you which makes you appear independent and self-sufficient to a degree – at least to the degree of only wanting from *anybody* what you deliberately want to want from them. It is very interesting. <Do you like to be interesting to different people for different reasons, or do you insist on being – a very superior woman?>

I shall send you some of Pound's poems as soon as I can, and hope you will see why I like them so much. <Have you read James's *Finer Grain* (short stories) or the *Ambassadors?*>

1 – 'I believe it because it is impossible', a common variant of Tertullian's rule of faith '*Certum est, quia impossible est*' ('It is certain, because it is impossible').

I must interrupt this at some point –

Yours
Tom.

You haven't written to Vivien –

I have to go to Garsington on my next return –

I wonder who wrote in the last *Times*?[1] He found my joints in one or two places very cleverly.

Lewis is *not* a sham, but a simple natural innocent, like myself.

TO *Brigit Patmore*

MS Beinecke

15 June 1919 [in transit]

Dear Brigit

This is a hasty greeting in the midst of my pilgrimages. I have been in London several times, but neither seen people nor had time to write satisfactory letters to anyone – the only exception a Whitsun visit to some friends in Sussex – the most of my time rushed about in interviews in Birmingham, Manchester and elsewhere. I wonder if you could give a satisfactory account of yourself – but I shan't attack you because I know perfectly well that you are *pleased* to be lectured to – that is what irritates me. It doesn't worry you a bit, and it's not a bit of use. And it's boring.

I have had a very interesting time on the whole, very crowded, especially including an article and correspondence to be done on Sundays. But mostly a very specialised exercise of intelligence, and rather restful – reading nothing but commercial reviews, and seeing new and strange people.

If I can get back by Saturday I have promised to go down to Oxfordshire over Sunday – otherwise I may be here in the middle of the week, and if not then, not until the middle of the following week, possibly. You see what a nomadic life it is! I hope we can meet by July anyway – unless you have disappeared to your country seat by then. Are you still at this address, in case – ?

Yours
T.S.E.

1 – 'Not Here, O Apollo', *TLS* 12 June, was by Arthur Clutton-Brock. 'Mr. Eliot, like Browning, likes [in *Poems*] to display out-of-the-way learning, he likes to surprise you by every trick he can think of' but is 'fatally handicapping himself with his own inhibitions'.

TO *Eleanor Hinkley* MS Houghton

17 June 1919

18 Crawford Mansions,
Crawford St, W.1

Dear Eleanor,

I am rather ahead with my writing this week, so I can at last consecrate an hour to writing to you. It is 10 p.m. I am alone with Dinah Brooks (Yorkshire terrier). It is very hot. Vivien I have left in Bosham (Sussex) for a much needed holiday, and the servant is also taking a fortnight's holiday at Margate, presumably making herself ill on prawns and winkles. But as she says of everything 'it makes a change' (i.e. when she bakes potatoes instead of boiling them).

It was a very nice letter dated April 8 that I had from you, and I wish I could have answered it before. This spring has been, however, a *very* busy one for me. My lectures ended only in May. Then I have been writing long articles for the *Athenaeum* which not only take time but make me more conspicuous and bring indirectly social engagements. Then I have produced a certain amount of copy for a quarterly called *Art & Letters*.[1] Then I have had one small book brought out and am preparing a larger one (limited edition). Then I have been corresponding with a publisher about a possible prose book (I dare say it will fall through). Then several stripling poets want their long poems criticised. Then to show you what social life entails, I will retail or detail one incident:—

I happen to make to a lady I know pretty well named A. some flippant remarks about a lady B. Later I get to know B. and get on with her quite well. B. repeats to others the compliments I paid her on one of her books. Then a sudden coolness. Next C. a mutual friend asks me if I ever said that I disliked B. and thought her book rubbish because B. has been told that I said it, and was much upset. I may remark that B. has occasionally suffered from melancholia. I deny the remarks, but say that some time ago I had made some light comments which might have been twisted that way. C. promises to report to B. Meanwhile A. gets in a funk lest I hear of this and trace it to her, and anxiously confides in Vivien. A. you see hates B. and also is jealous of her. She therefore repeats my remarks to D. a man friend of hers (A.'s) who dislikes me because A. likes me. D. is a connection of B. and when he hears her repeat my compliments, is irritated, and tells her, with alterations, what I said elsewhere. B.'s husband says he is going to

1–'Marivaux' in *Art & Letters* 1 (Spring 1919); 'Burbank with a Baedeker: Bleistein with a Cigar' and 'Sweeney Erect' in 2 (Summer).

tax me with it. A. hearing of this is frightened and rings up B. to say not to tax me with it, as D. may have made a mistake. This leaves the situation with D. more hating me than ever, as he is put in rather an awkward situation, with B. still suspicious, and A. very humble and contrite, although she is not *quite* sure that I know anything about it. This puts me in a position to make A. uncomfortable by innuendoes. I leave B. quite alone. A.'s husband in conversation constantly tries to hint to me how vain and perverse B. is, and tries to make me say something uncomplimentary to her work. I dodge this, and praise her. I also take the trouble to be very good friends with C., E. and F. all close friends of B.

The sequel is this. G. another woman, is jealous of A. She hears that I spent a weekend at A.'s house. She promptly invites me for a weekend and says that B. is coming. This is very clever, for she knows that I have had no opportunity of a *rapprochement* with B. and that I dare not refuse to come for fear of offending B. In either case G. will be pleased: if I don't go, I shall be out with B. forever, and no woman likes one to be on good terms with another; if I do go, she will get back one on A. So I must go smiling on Saturday, knowing that there will be a large party, all knowing all the facts, to see how I shall get on with B. and knowing also that G. will do her best to get me to say something unpleasant about A., and also that A. will want to know later what G. said about her. Meanwhile I believe that D. is spreading the report that I am very conceited, he being annoyed at my having been asked for a weekend to A.'s, where I bathed in the sea and played with the children, and talked about aesthetics with F. And I like A. and B. very much and don't hate even D.[1]

This is an illustration. It will seem to you foolish. But think of this sort of thing as going on continually in a society where everyone is very sensitive, very perceptive and very quick and you will see that a dinner party demands more skill and exercises one's psychological gifts more than the best fencing match or duel.

The first thing one tries to notice in entering a room is everyone's frame of mind and attitude towards everyone else, individually, which may have changed in twenty-four hours! It does use one's brains! Only, one needs to retire from time to time and rest.

1 – The scenario seems to be as follows: A = Mary Hutchinson; B = Virginia Woolf; D = Clive Bell; F = Roger Fry; and G = Ottoline Morrell. For C and E there are several possibilities: C may have been John Middleton Murry and E Lytton Strachey. VW had reported on 17 Apr. that when she visited the Murrys, 'the mystery of Eliot was further thickened by hearing how he praised me to the skies to them' (*Letters*, II, 350); and she had written to Duncan Grant the same day: 'we have a letter asking us to dinner, and I'm determined, in spite of Mary [Hutchinson] to draw the rat from his hole' (*Letters*, II, 350). VHE wrote to MH on 17 June 1919: 'Tom is going to Garsington, think of Virginia, Tom and Ottoline! O think of it.'

I have written to Emily – I hope it was a nice letter. I should, I think, like her to know what a keen interest I take in everything that happens to her.

I like your letters very much. But I *wish* you would send me copies of any of your printed plays, and I should like to know how you look on your work, and its relation to literature, and what experience of life you think is required for it. But I must defer that till another letter. I take it unkindly that you never write.

Always affectionately
Tom

TO *Ottoline Morrell* MS Texas

Monday [23 June 1919] 18 Crawford Mansions

Dear Lady Ottoline,

Finally I have a chance to write and tell you what happened. First of all, I was bitterly disappointed. And will you let me come very soon? I expect to be settled here again after this week, and after that I should love to come for a weekend if you would ask me.

The man [Harold Peters] who turned up so suddenly is a lieutenant with the American navy and he is the oldest and loyalest American friend I have. He was here about two months ago for two nights, and I begged him to come again before he went back to the States. He has been mine sweeping in the Orkneys; now he is suddenly demobilised, and came down from Liverpool entirely to see me before leaving Europe finally tomorrow. I got a wire from him, and when he arrived I realised that I should have to give up my weekend – at first I thought that I could take an earlier train back to town on Sunday, but there wasn't any. And I saw that it would be a bitter blow to him if he could not have me for the whole of the short time. He would never have got over it; he had come from Liverpool only to see me, and he will probably never be in this country again, and he would not have understood, so I gave up. I could not let him think that anything was different from what it was five years ago. He had been almost the only man in my class at Harvard whom I could endure; and we had been through various adventures and physical risks together; I don't feel at all sentimental about it, but I could not let him go back to America thinking that our relations were altered.

So I had to go to the theatre, which I detest, and walked for miles and miles yesterday showing him the East End and the docks; and I feel completely exhausted and especially depressed by my awareness of having lost contact with Americans and their ways, and by the hopelessness of ever making them understand so many things. I could go on indefinitely with this, but it is probably tiresome, and it was only to explain how much I should have preferred sitting on the lawn with you at Garsington, and to justify my proposing myself again after failing in this way. Will you please ask me *soon* after the next weekend? I wish Mrs Woolf could be there too: I have not seen her for a long time.

You said, by the way, about my poems, some of the things I should like people to say, and which none of the reviewers have said. So I naturally choose to believe that you were 'on the right track'!

Sincerely
T. S. Eliot

I am sending some Joyce.

Vivien Eliot TO *Ottoline Morrell* — MS Texas

Wednesday [25? June 1919] — South View, Bosham, Chichester, Sussex

My dear Ottoline

What a fiasco about poor Tom's weekend! I don't expect you have altogether realised the tragedy of it. The man [Harold Peters] who turned up is a friend of Tom's youth, an American with the development of an average boy of ten. *Boring!* He always makes me perfectly ill, – prostrate. He is so devoted to Tom that he has no other thought but to spend every minute of his leaves in just sitting, waiting for the few odd minutes Tom could spare him out of his days. He has been known to sit at the Bank, for *hours*, quite passive and contented, waiting for Tom to come out. This, you see, was his last leave, and he went back to America on Monday, and it would have simply broken his heart if Tom had left him. He knows no one in England, takes no interest in anything, and I *can't see* what he would have done. But of course you will understand, because *you do* admit loyalty and kindness, don't you?

I have thought about you very much while I have been here. You have no idea how I love this place. It is the only place in England, outside London, that really satisfies me. I never get used to it. I am awfully happy here, and never want to go back. It is so nice to have Mary so near, too. We have glorious picnics together.

I wish you were near, and that *we* could have some picnics too. Write and tell me what you have been doing, and reading, and who has been at

Garsington. You spoke of Lowes Dickinson. I've only met him a few times, but I am afraid I like him about as little as I like anyone! It was quite a shock to hear you found him sympathetic!

I hope you are going to ask Tom again, and that you really do understand. But *please*, my dear, don't ask him until *after* the weekend July 5th–7th, as a favour to me, because I do want him to come down here and stay with me. I never see him now.

Do write to me. With love

Affectly
Vivien

TO *His Mother* MS Houghton

29 June 1919 [18 Crawford Mansions]

My dearest Mother,

The reason I did not write last Sunday was this: on the previous Thursday Harold Peters arrived, and staid until Monday, and I had to be with him every minute until he left. I got very tired, but I was very anxious to give him a good time: he had been minesweeping in the Orkneys, and is just demobilised and has sailed for home; he came all the way from Liverpool just to see me. I was going to Lady Ottoline's for Sunday but put it off. I say I got tired: you know what Pete is, and he has no point of contact with any of my interests or thoughts, but he is the most lovable fellow in the world, and I think really devoted to me, and time cannot alter that. So we went to the theatre (at his expense) and to the Zoo', and for a long walk down the river to the docks – and after all I enjoyed him very much. When he goes back he is expecting to go on a sailing vessel, as navigating officer to Hayti. But he would never go away from Boston for very long; he is devoted to his mother.

So that cut up one week, and the first two days of this week I was too tired to be good for anything. Then I did another review, which took two days. Sat. I went to Bosham to see Vivien; Arthur Dakyns came with his motor car; on Sunday we hired a boat and sailed with Sacheverell Sitwell and Mary Hutchinson down Chichester Harbour to Wittering, where the Hutchinsons live. We had lunch there, and Vivien took some pictures, which I hope will be good enough to send you. The sailing was rather disastrous. There is no proper place to land, and we put the boat up on the beach. Going out the wind was dead ahead and we got stuck on a sandbank; the tide receded rapidly and left us high but not very dry.

I broke a boat hook and finally threw out an anchor and we waded ashore – on planks, because the soft mud would suck you up. Vivien is splendid in a boat, she took off her stockings and jumped off and tried to push. We returned very muddy to the Hutchinsons for tea and returned in the motor, just in time for me to catch my train. I expect the boatman will be furious.

I have a busy day tomorrow. After the bank I must call on a publisher [Martin Secker] – another one – who wants me to write a book on Stendhal the French novelist, but he is not so good as the other publisher I spoke of [Sir Algernon Methuen], so I may hold off. Then I must leave some books for Ottoline, who is in hospital, fetch our dog who has been at V.'s aunts, and go to see a doctor about the varicose veins in my legs, which are increasing. Next day to the dentist's.

Dear Mother: I am sending this to Ada's, as I don't know where you are. I am so anxious that the house should be sold. I should like the bath robe. I must stop now. I think of you often. Goodnight.

Your loving son
Tom.

FROM *John Quinn* — Telegram NYPL (MS)

30 June 1919 — New York

SEND ADDITIONAL ESSAYS AND POEMS IMMEDIATELY INDICATING ORDER INSERTION COPY YOUR BOOK

QUINN[1]

1 – In a letter the same day, Quinn wrote that Boni & Liveright had tried to force him to stand guaranty, instead of which he had withdrawn the book and sent it to Jeanne Foster to offer to John Lane. She was to insist that the poems and essays run together, and to guarantee $150. 'P.S. I think the title for your book should be *A Book of Verse and Prose* by T. S. Eliot. I think *Prufrock* is a bad title, one that would hurt the sale of the book. I shall be glad to have you let me know about this when you send the additional essays and poems.'

TO *Mary Hutchinson* MS Texas

Tuesday [1 July 1919] 18 Crawford Mansions,
Crawford St, W.1

Dear Mary,

Thank you for wiring to the ferryman. I shall have to see him about it if I come this week, but I presume he understands that he will be settled with.

I am sending *Personae* – perhaps you will have read some Pound when I see you next.[1] But really I don't know what are your particular points of intensity in poetry, do I? Your discoveries. 'All one can do is to point'[2] but I hope you will find something in this stuff.

I am sorry to have given you this trouble about the boat.

Yours
Tom

TO *Henry Eliot* MS Houghton

2 July 1919 18 Crawford Mansions

Dear Henry,

It is a long time since I have written. My time has been taken up – but I have not written any poetry – though I have acquired some notoriety. Some friends of mine brought out a small book of my recent verse – you have seen it in *Little Review* – and as they are rather influential it has been reviewed at length in the *Times*, in the *Athenaeum*,[3] and I believe in the *Nation*.[4] Mother will show you some of the reviews. Also, as a result of my *Athenaeum* articles, I have had proposals for books from two publishers – Sir Algernon Methuen[5] and Martin Secker[6] – and hope to arrange something with one or the other. Does the *Athenaeum* reach

1–EP, *Personae* (1909).

2–TSE, 'The Education of Taste': 'The instructor has a course which he can follow: he can point to good literature and then be silent' (*A.*, 27 June 1919).

3–'Is This Poetry?', *A.*, 20 June 1919, 491: an unsigned review by LW and VW of *Poems* and JMM's *The Critic in Judgment* (both Hogarth Press books). VW wrote to TSE, 28 July 1920: 'We felt awkward at reviewing our own publications, and agreed to share the guilt: he reviewed you, and I reviewed Murry' (*Letters*, II).

4–No review appeared in *N.*

5–Algernon Methuen (1856–1924), founder of Methuen & Co. in 1889. Baronet 1916.

6–Martin Secker (1872–1978), publisher renowned for fiction and European authors in translation. He had recently published DHL's *New Poems* (1918).

Chicago? I have arranged to have it sent to mother, but it costs £1 10s per annum so if *you* want it you will have to send for it, but you could do good work by forcing it on any clubs, millionaires, etc. as the best literary weekly in the Anglo-Saxon world. *Art & Letters* I will send you. I write in the *Athenaeum* about three weeks out of four.

I must say that your life, as especially in your last letter to Vivien, is depressing. I suppose that the difficulty is that you must keep on good terms with the firm, and the general difficulty is that no one in America has any understanding or respect for the individual. The gregariousness of the life appals me. Here, for instance, if you go to stay with friends in the country, you can say you want to write or read or sit in the garden alone, and no one objects. The only thing required (on a short visit) is to be as brilliant as possible in the evenings – which does not necessarily imply *intellectual*. London is big; most people live alone, and don't see the same friends more than once a week or two. But I don't know how much is in your own hands: you seem to me to spend a great deal of time simply in morbid and fruitless consciousness of your own misery. Can't you insist on being alone – can't you say you are writing a book – can't you find time for reading and thinking? You are really completely alone. You are unfortunate in having a consciousness – though not a clear one – of how barbarous life in America is. If you had, like all other Americans, no consciousness at all, you would be happier.

Don't think that I find it easy to live over here. It is damned hard work to live with a foreign nation and cope with them – one is always coming up against differences of feeling that make one feel humiliated and lonely. One remains always a foreigner – only the lower classes can assimilate. It is like being always on dress parade – one can never relax. It is a great strain. And ~~life~~ society is in a way much *harder*, *not* gentler. People are more aware of you, more critical, and they have no pity for one's mistakes or stupidities. They are more spontaneous, and also more *deliberate*. They seek your company because they expect something particular from you, and if they don't get it, they drop you. They are always intriguing and caballing; one must be very alert. They are sensitive, and easily become enemies. But it is never dull; and the intense awareness of individual personality – when I do meet Americans now, they always irritate me by never *observing* – by having no curiosity about what sort of a person one is.

London is something one has to fight very hard in, in order to survive. What strikes me about all your friends – about my American friends – about any Americans I meet, is their *immaturity of feeling*, childishness.

But really, your letters, some of the things in them, give me a great deal of pain. I am fonder of you than of any man living. We have some of the same faults and weaknesses – what has preserved me – if I am preserved, which I often doubt (you are not in a position to know) is something which has nothing to do with my conscious character (that is weak enough) but is either a very hidden deep force or just luck, or Vivien's assistance, in large part.

Do you know exactly what you want – is it merely a strong but confused dissatisfaction with Chicago and America, or have you any ideas as to the sort of world you want to live in? What do you expect from the people in it? Is it impossible to live in a self-respecting way in Chicago?

You never speak of the possibility of coming here for a *visit*, even a month. Surely you could if you persuaded yourself that you must have it.

It is late now, and I have work to do. I hope to write more frequently – but something is bound to turn up.

Tom.

TO *Mary Hutchinson* MS Texas

Wednesday [9? July? 1919] 18 Crawford Mansions

Dear Mary

Here is the poem for which you asked, out of politeness I dare say.[1] I don't feel at all finally satisfied with it, so please don't let anyone see it, but let me have your candid opinion upon it when you will, and also please on 'Bleistein' in *Art & Letters*. 'Bleistein' (like 'S[weeney] among the Nightingales') is meant to be *very serious*! and 'Hippopotamus' and Webster aren't –

I am not sure whether you thought that Hulme is a really great poet, as I do, or not.[2] I can't think of anything as good as two of his poems since Blake. And of course you are unjust to Pound. One must learn to appreciate his 'literary-appreciative' style as a medium for expressing something of his own. And I think the 'Cathay' and the 'Seafarer' in

1 – 'Gerontion'.

2 – 'The Complete Poetical Works of T. E. Hulme' was published as an appendix to EP's *Ripostes* (1912). In 'Reflections on Vers Libre' (*NS* 8 [3 Mar. 1917], 518–19), TSE quoted Hulme's 'The Embankment' as one of the two instances of successful *vers libre* remarkable for their 'beauty' (the other was by EP); and later maintained that 'the poems of T. E. Hulme only needed to be read aloud to have immediate effect' ('The Function of Criticism', C. 2: 5, Oct. 1923; *SE*).

Ripostes are wonderfully good.[1] I daresay he seems to you derivative. But I can show you in the thing I enclose how I have borrowed from half a dozen sources just as boldly as Shakespeare borrowed from North. But I am as traditionalist as a Chinaman, or a Yankee.

I thought that Sunday was very delightful, though it was broken off at an interesting moment. How could I have said 'superior', and what is a Henry James young woman?

Yours
T.S.E.

TO *John Rodker*

MS Virginia

9 July 1919

18 Crawford Mansions

Dear Rodker,

I have the new poem I spoke of – about seventy-five lines – which will not have appeared anywhere – but I am withholding it until I know you want it, as I may make alterations. It is also quite possible that I may have another about the same length by August 1. So I hope that the book may be more nearly what you had in mind. I think you have all the newer poems: beside the Woolf volume there is a French poem in *L. Review* ('Dans le Restaurant'), 'Bleistein' and 'Sweeney Erect', 'Cooking Egg' – of which I enclose revised version *with* quotations – and this new one, 'Gerontion'.

I hope you are getting on well with the Lewis.[2]

Yours ever
T. S. Eliot

What's this latest row of *L. Review* with American censorship?[3]

1–'"Cathay" will, I believe, rank with the "Sea-Farer" in the future among Mr. Pound's original work' (*Ezra Pound: His Metric and Poetry*, 27; *TCC*, 181).

2–WL, *Fifteen Drawings* (Ovid Press, 1919).

3–In June 1919, the US Post Office determined that the *Little Review* was in violation of Postal Laws and Regulations, due to the 'obscene' content of *Ulysses* which it had started to serialise after the *Egoist* was unable to continue doing so (for similar reasons); it refused to distribute copies.

TO *John Quinn* TS NYPL (MS)

9 July 1919 18 Crawford Mansions

Dear Mr Quinn,

Thank you very much indeed for cabling to me. I enclose the additional MSS. The four poems can go, I think, in the order given. Unfortunately I have lost my list giving the order in which the various poems and articles were to be printed. But I think that these should be put at the head of the new poems – the ones not in the Prufrock volume; and if I have put the new poems in front of the Prufrock ones, then these should head the new book.

The articles enclosed are a selection of what I consider the best of those I have been contributing to the *Athenaeum*, and might *follow* those already in your hands. I have arranged them in the order I thought the best. The two entitled 'A Romantic Patrician' and 'A Sceptical Patrician' I want to go under one heading: 'Two Types' as I and II with the sub-headings as above.

I thought that the Elizabethan article would be suitable because of the American interest in War poets; and that the popularity of Adams's book ought to lend an interest in that essay. I wonder what American opinion would think of my article on Adams, but it is a type that I *ought* to know better than any other. And the article on American literature seemed to me appropriate.

In each case the title of the book reviewed ought to go below as a footnote instead of where it is, at the top.

Also of course I ought to acknowledge obligation

for various poems: to *Poetry*, *Blast*, *Art & Letters*, *The Little Review*.

for prose: *The Egoist*, *The New Statesman*, *The Little Review*, *The Athenaeum*.

If there is enough material otherwise, I should prefer to withdraw the Eeldrop and Appleplexes, which seem to me to be crude stuff. But I don't feel certain about this and I should like to leave it to your judgment whether it is better, even if the stuff is poor, to have some prose which is not purely critical.

I wish that I were anywhere near satisfied with the book.

But of course I don't know yet whether the book has been accepted by Boni or by anyone else, or whether your cable only means that someone wants to see more material. Anyway, I leave it in your hands in all confidence, but with the always stronger feeling that you ought not to accept or have forced upon you so much disinterested labour. My only justification is that I do not know anyone else with either the influence, the intelligence, or the generosity necessary to undertake it. It is quite obvious that without you I should never get anything published in America at all.

I hear that several weeks ago the *New Republic*[1] referred to me in very flattering terms. I have not seen the paper and do not know the date, but it ought to be of influence with a publisher.

* * *

As for my plans over here, John Rodker has undertaken to print for private circulation a limited edition of some of my poems, rather expensive, this summer, with designs by Edward Wadsworth. I shall see that you are sent a copy.

I have had some correspondence with Sir Algernon Methuen (Methuen and Co.), who asks to discuss my next book with me when he returns to town. I do not know what he wants, but I shall propose either a complete edition of poems, or to write a book on Tudor literature, which I have had in mind for a long time. If he does not want the poems, the *Egoist* will print a complete edition next spring, as the Prufrock is sold out;[2] and in any case Miss Weaver wants to reprint some of my essays as a book. Martin Secker has also suggested that I should write a book on Stendhal, which would be very interesting to do, but according to his offer I should only get about £25 out of it which does not seem to me enough for so much fresh work.

I find it very difficult to keep in front of me the things I want to do most and not be distracted by many things that turn up. As it is I must always live under pressure – at least until I have enough income so as not to worry over all of the details of existence. I have greatly appreciated your comments from time to time upon this matter of wasting energy.

* * *

I have just received from Pound in France a copy of your admirable defense of *Ulysses* (May *L. R.*)[3] with the suggestion that it should be printed in the *Egoist* when and if I receive permission from you. I hope to

1 – Conrad Aiken, 'The Ivory Tower', a review of Louis Untermeyer, *The New Era in American Poetry*, in *New Republic* 19 (10 May 1919), 58–60; reprinted in *Scepticisms: Notes on Contemporary Poetry* (1919).

2 – In fact, the final copies of *Prufrock* were sold, autographed, at 10s 6d in 1921.

3 – The May issue of the *Little Review*, containing episode IX of *Ulysses*, 'Scylla and Charybdis', had been stopped by the US Post Office. Judging by his experience of the censorship of WL's 'Cantleman's Spring-Mate', Quinn felt it was pointless to go to court, so instead he sent a brief to the solicitor of the Post Office department in Washington. He sent a copy of this brief to EP, who wrote to him on 6 July that it was 'the best apologia for J. that has been written. It shd. be printed. I am sending it to Eliot with instructions to publish in Egoist *when* he receives your permission' (*Selected Letters of Ezra Pound to John Quinn 1915–1924*, 176). Quinn did not grant permission.

get this permission. The affair is only one more episode in a national scandal. I should like to do everything I can about it over here. The part of *Ulysses* in question struck me as almost the finest I have read: I have lived on it ever since I read it. You know the trouble the *Egoist* came up against with printers in attempting to print *Ulysses* here.

I am sorry to say that I have found it uphill and exasperating work trying to impose Joyce on such 'intellectual' people, or people whose opinion carries weight as I know, in London. He is far from being accepted, yet. I only know two or three people, besides my wife and myself, who are really carried away by him. There is a strong body of critical Brahminism, destructive and conservative in temper, which will not have Joyce. Novelty is no more acceptable here than anywhere else, and the forces of conservatism and obstruction are more intelligent, better educated, and more formidable.

* * *

As for the *Egoist*, the ladies who run it have decided to suspend publication, after the next two numbers, till further notice. I think that from a financial point of view they are right, and if they devote the money at their disposal to book publication, as they propose to do, it may turn out for the best. It robs Pound and me, of course, of any organ where we can express ourselves editorially or air any affair such as this of Joyce. On the other hand, other publications cut in to the *Egoist* to a certain extent, and the <small> public which *I* could bring to it now reads the *Athenaeum* every week. There I am a sort of white boy;[1] I have a longish critical review about three weeks out of four; but don't write editorials. It has brought me a certain notoriety which I should never have got from the *Egoist*. I had always the most pleasant relations with Miss Weaver. I have only met Miss Marsden once, and then (in strict confidence) frothed at the mouth with antipathy. The fact that the paper was primarily a means for getting her philosophical articles into print, and that its appearance was at irregular intervals owing to the length of time it took her to write them, I think militated against the success of the paper with many people who did not want to read them.

I have taken a great deal of your time – if you have read this far – and I ought to apologise for relieving myself at your expense. I can only end by thanking you again and again for all your kindness.

Sincerely yours,
T. S. Eliot

1 – *White boy*: 'A favourite, pet, or darling boy: a term of endearment for a boy or (usually) man' (OED, citing this letter).

TO *His Mother* MS Houghton

10 July 1919 18 Crawford Mansions

My dearest Mother,

I have lately received several parcels from you, and the care and beauty of the packing almost made me cry. What a time it must have taken you! First the books – the set of Dickens which is now on my shelf, and the beloved Rollo books. Then the bathrobe, which is just what I need for this time of year, and the little picture of the carthorse, and the medals; and finally the *beautiful* pen, which you had so nicely engraved – that I shall prize – the medal of the Latin prize, which I should have preferred *you* to keep. Father gave me $25 for winning that, and I stole $2 out of it to buy a copy of Shelley's poems, and no one ever knew it. Also the handsome watch fob and the two spoons. But doesn't the watch fob belong to *Henry*? I seem to remember years ago Henry's being given a fob with a scarab, and a discussion of the best way to mount a scarab. I want to be sure about this. I almost hated to unpack the parcels, I wanted to preserve them because of the care that had gone into them. The spoon was given me by Aunt Cathie, wasn't it? It is odd – I can't remember her married name – what the L. stands for.[1]

You must not think that it bores me to hear about your business affairs; I could just as well say that my literary affairs were tedious to tell about. I had a cable from John Quinn in New York to send him some more poems and articles so I suppose he has arranged finally for my book to be published. Quinn has been very kind to me as he is to all artists and men of letters. He is a successful Irish American lawyer – counsel for the National Bank of Commerce in New York. He interested [himself] on my behalf and prevented my poems from being 'pirated' in New York about a year ago. He tried to get a publisher last summer, and it was a great disappointment to me that they did not come out then. The trouble was that there was not enough verse to make a big book, and publishers are scary about printing books containing *both* verse and prose.

How splendid it would be if you could have sold the real estate this summer and could come across at once. I would gladly do without *any* holiday for three years if that were possible. On the other hand, ocean travel will probably not be easy till next year. One plan would be for me to come across and to bring you and Marian back with me – then we could have such a long time together at once.

1 – A christening present from TSE's great-aunt, Caroline Eliot (Lackland by her second marriage).

I must stop now. I am taking a short holiday in the middle of August, and if I find that the Government's put no obstacles in the way, I intend to go to France. I hear that there is a man in Paris who wants to import my books.

Always devotedly

Your son
Tom

TO *Mary Hutchinson* MS Texas

[11? July 1919] [London]

Dear Mary,

What a charming letter – so that I must write at once – having written nineteen letters in the last two days – to explain that mine was despatched six hours before yours arrived. I am so pleased – I mean something more important than feeling flattered.

I was so glad you had the sail together.[1] What you say will certainly reach Vivien. Your neighbourhood has made a vast difference to her at Bosham – and I think you are the only woman who really interests her. Besides, I think we are both grateful to anyone who is intelligent enough to take us as two individuals – not as one, or the other, or a neutral composition. But perhaps I will reserve this point for conversation. I have a good deal to say which would simply appear as an illegible mass of blottings and scratchings and revisions, on paper.

Perhaps I will say civilised instead of cultivated. I certainly do not mean a mass of chaotic erudition which simply issues in giggling. You can supply instances of this easily enough. And I loathe 'amusing' information. Culture, if it means anything decent, means something personal: one book or painter made one's own rather than a thousand read or looked at. Some people really read too much to be cultivated. I think everyone must estimate his own powers of assimilation. What I feel about much contemporary taste is that people have merely assimilated other people's personal tastes without making them personal – tastes which are essentially personal. One could make a short list

1 – VHE noted in her diary, 9 July: 'Wonderful day with Mary. Started in boat 9.30 . . . sailed to Hayling. Landed at a perfect beach, had lunch, and I bathed. Mary told me her life, she was delightful' (Bodleian).

Byzantine (a little out of date).

Polynesian, African, Hebridean, Chinese, etc. etc. say savage and Oriental art in general, by people who have not the training to know what these have in common with our traditional art –

Stendhal.

Mozart, Bach etc.

Flaubert (yes!)

Russian ballet (when liked by people who know nothing of the art and its relation to Italian).

Russian novels.

Laforgue (really inferior to Corbière at his best).

I think this comprises modern culture. As I like most of these things I am annoyed. They mostly begin as personal enthusiasms *or convictions* of people who know and can give reasons. But in the ordinary mind they are completely unorganised.

I have now got started on a long subject which I have not now either time or energy to carry out – instead of replying simply to a question of civilisation and culture. I think two things are wanted – civilisation which is impersonal, traditional (by 'tradition' I don't mean stopping in the same place) and which forms people unconsciously – I don't think two or half a dozen people can set out by themselves to be civilised – though one can insist on *not* relaxing what civilisation one has in favour of people who are incapable of appreciating it. I mean the 'shouting and bad manners' need not be tolerated – and culture – which is a personal interest and curiosity in *particular* things – I think it is largely the *historical sense*,[1] which is not simply knowledge of history, a sense of balance which does not deaden one's personal taste, but trains one to discriminate one's own passions from objective criticism. It seems that one ought to *read* in two ways: 1) because of particular and personal interest, which makes the thing one's own, regardless of what other people think of the book 2) *to a certain extent*, because it is something one 'ought to have read' but one must be quite clear that this is *why* one is reading. Although my education is very fragmentary I believe I shall do no more of this.

Also, as I said once, I think there are two kinds of intelligence: the intellectual and the sensitive – the first can read a great deal because it schematises and theorises – the second not much, because it requires to

1 – 'Tradition . . . involves, in the first place, the historical sense, which we may call nearly indispensable to anyone who would continue to be a poet beyond his twenty-fifth year' ('Tradition and the Individual Talent' [I], *Egoist* 6, Sept. 1919; *SW*).

get more out of a book than can immediately be put into words. Don't you think you belong to the second? *I* read very little – and *have* read much less than people think – at present I only read Tudor drama, Tudor prose, and Gibbon – over and over – when I have time to read at all. Of course I don't count the countless books I have had to skim for lectures etc.

I don't know whether I think you more complicated than you are – but I have fewer *delusions* about you than you think – but no doubt a great deal of *ignorance*. I certainly don't recognise the portrait you hold up as painted by me. But remember that I am a *metic* – a foreigner, and that I *want* to understand you, and all the background and tradition of you. I shall try to be frank – because the attempt is so very much worthwhile with you – it is very difficult with me – both by inheritance and because of my very suspicious and cowardly disposition. But I may simply prove to be a savage.

But don't think that my ignorance makes me wholly unappreciative – even the ignorant can have a sense of values.

Yes, I should like some Flaubert.

Yrs.
Tom.

It would be lovely to come Aug. 1st. I shall consult V. There are only two objections possible 1) time 2) I have been down so often, and we are engaged to go to Eastbourne next week: the *expense*. This, I am afraid, weighs with me seriously at present.

TO *Edgar Jepson* MS Beinecke

11 July 1919 18 Crawford Mansions

Dear Mr Jepson,

We should have loved to come on Sunday, but unfortunately I have promised to go down to Oxfordshire for the weekend.[1] I do hope you will ask us again later – also the day and the hour suit us beautifully.

With kindest regards to Mrs Jepson and yourself.

Sincerely,
T. S. Eliot

I should be very much interested to have your candid opinion of my verse in the current *Art & Letters*. If you don't see that publication I will send you typed copies.

1–TSE was to spend the weekend of 12–13 July with OM at Garsington.

TO *Sydney Schiff* MS BL

16 July 1919 18 Crawford Mansions

Dear Mr Schiff,

I ought to have written to you long ago, but I have simply felt too ill to do any writing. This is merely to thank you for your letter, and for your great kindness in analysing my poem [the unpublished 'Gerontion'] so carefully. I wish this letter was able to reciprocate – I can just say a few words before we meet. When I wrote last I had not even begun *Richard Kurt*,[1] so your fears were unfounded. Now I have read it once, and with great interest, and hope to have time to go over <at least> part of it again before we meet. Here, *I* am an outsider, and am timid of any judgements I make. I read with sustained interest a book which seemed to me a very accurate study of a *monde* which is almost unknown to me. There are points about it which I hope you will clear up for me, but I don't think in any case that I shall make any criticism more severe than this: that it seemed to me that the canvas was more crowded with events and people than was essential to the effects. Though, as I say, there was *no* moment of boredom for me.

If it is possible for me to get away in time, we should like very much to come down by the 5.20 train [to Eastbourne] Friday afternoon. (The ballet is postponed until next week). I hope this will suit you – it seems odd of me perhaps to ask to come earlier, at such late notice – but we should like to come!

I will let you know of course if I can't come by this train, but I am practically certain.

We are looking forward to seeing you and Mrs Schiff very keenly.

Sincerely yours
T. S. Eliot

Vivien Eliot TO *Mary Hutchinson* MS Texas

Wed. [16 July 1919] Flat [18 Crawford Mansions]

Mary dear

Thank you for letter. This week has been – is – a horrid muddle and disappointment. We were going to the Ballet with the Sitwells on Friday,

1–Stephen Hudson, *Richard Kurt* (1919), the first in SS's sequence of autobiographical novels.

and I hoped to see you. Now they say that the new one is postponed until *Tuesday* – so we are going with them that night.[1] Will you be there? Surely you need not go back, or else you can come up again? *I* wanted to go to the Ballet tonight but Tom is *IM*possible – full of nerves, really not well, very bad cough, very morbid and grumpy. I wish you had him! So we are to go to the Schiffs on Friday evening instead of Saturday morning, (for the weekend). This is entirely Tom altho' I don't expect you to credit it – As things are I can't do anything about the Bank holiday weekend with you. The money trouble is always cropping up, and it is very bad for him to think we are spending too much. V. bad for his work, or for any man's work I suppose. He gets entangled into going to places he does not really want to, or enjoy, and then has to sacrifice the nice things. He gets angry and stubborn. Mary dear the photographs will not be ready for a fortnight. I can't bear to wait so long. I did write to O. M. exactly what I told you I should, and I put it *most* sensibly and friendlily and with all due regard to her hothouse feelings. And behold, she is furious with me! I am cast into outer darkness, so I can join you there.

Absurd creature!

I feel rather uncomfortable writing to Gordon Sq. Please keep my letter to yourself![2]

Our 'day' *was* wonderful – I have such an admiration for you Mary. You are all that [I] admire, and I consider it is flattering to me that I admire you so! You are such a '*civilised*' rebel.

Jack is coming to dinner tomorrow. I shall kiss him.

[unsigned]

1 – Premiere of the Ballets Russes production (22 July) of Falla's *The Three-Cornered Hat*, conducted by Ernst Ansermet, with choreography by Massine (who also danced the role of the Miller), and with curtains, sets and costumes by Picasso. VHE wrote in her diary: 'Went to ballet with Sachie [Sitwell] & party . . . Very interesting & the music very good. Massine really wonderful. But on the whole nothing like the *Boutique Fantastique*. Saw Mary, Clive, Jack, Ottoline (with the Duke), Read, Aldington, Viola, Nina etc. etc. Did not feel well & looked horrible.' TSE also went the following evening with the Hutchinsons to see *The Three-Cornered Hat* for a second time, as well as *Papillons* and *Prince Igor*.

2 – Clive Bell, MH's lover, lived at 46 Gordon Square.

FROM *Richard Aldington*[1] MS Houghton

18 July 1919 Authors' Club,
2 Whitehall Court, S.W.1

Dear Eliot,

I have several times recently felt impelled to write you my admiration for your critical articles and put it off in the hope of meeting you. Your article in the current *Egoist*[2] again stird my admiration and (I admit) my envy. You have a power of apprehension, of analysis, of the dissociation of ideas,[3] with a humour and ease of expression which make you not the best but the only modern writer of prose criticism in English. I read your essays in the *Athenaeum* with the greatest pleasure; I hope that some day you will collect these and other essays into book form.

Having said this much, with complete sincerity, I feel compelled to add that I dislike your poetry very much; it is over-intellectual and afraid of those essential emotions which make poetry.[4]

Excuse the impertinence of all this and its rather heavy style, due to a sort of pious terror.

Yrs
Richard Aldington

TO *Violet Schiff*[5] MS BL

21 July 1919 18 Crawford Mansions,
Crawford St, W.1

Dear Violet,

I must write to tell you how thoroughly we both enjoyed our holiday with you[6] – but I believe Vivien is writing too so I will merely speak for myself. Incidentally, I feel much better for it. I was really glad of the bad

1 – Richard Aldington, author and critic: see Glossary of Names.
2 – TSE, 'Reflections on Contemporary Poetry' [IV], *Egoist* 6: 5 (July 1919), 39–40.
3 – See TSE, 'Marivaux': 'Critics are impersonal people, engaged usefully in dissociating ideas' (*Arts & Letters* 2: 1, Spring 1919).
4 – RA wrote later: 'Mr. Eliot's poetry is often attacked as incomprehensible and heartless, which is simply another way of saying that it is subtle and not sentimental' ('The Poetry of T. S. Eliot', *Outlook* 49, July 1922).
5 – Violet Beddington (1876–1962) married SS as his second wife in May 1911. A gifted musician, she had studied singing under Paolo Tosti.
6 – VHE wrote in her diary on 20 July: 'Rather unsatisfactory weekend. Schiffs very fatiguing and irritating to me. T. got on all right.'

weather as it gave excuse for more conversation – there are very few people to whom one could say that sincerely!

I am very glad you are going to be at Eastbourne when Vivien is there, but I hope you will be in London for a time before you leave the country, so that I can see something of you.

I send the poem back, – as I said, I don't want anyone to see it but yourselves.

By the way, John put a *Napoleon*[1] into my bag by mistake. I noticed another copy, so I hope you won't mind if I keep it a few days in the hope of being able to look at it. I will post it back carefully.

With best wishes to both of you.

Sincerely yours
T. S. Eliot

FROM *Charles W. Eliot*[2] TS Houghton

25 July 1919 Asticon, Maine

Dear Mr Eliot:

Your letter of July 9th from 18 Crawford Mansions, London, reached me July 23rd. I suppose I asked in my letter of January 4th the questions to which you refer in your present letter partly because I felt interested in the career of a member of the Eliot clan, and partly because I always feel much interested in an exceptional or peculiar career of a well-trained Harvard graduate, – especially if that career be literary or scientific.

From what you tell me, I should suppose you had been distinctly successful so far in your efforts to procure a livelihood in foreign parts and at the same time win reputation as a writer. Your employment in a bank recalls the cases of Lamb, Grote, and Lubbock.[3] In a bank or a Government Bureau one can work a few hours a day for a livelihood and yet be fresh several hours a day for literary or scientific labors. Your living in London needs no justification. You are quite within your rights in practicing on your belief that living in London is good for you spiritually

1–*Napoleon*, a play by Herbert Trench (1919), favourably reviewed by JMM, *A.*, 11 July.
2–Charles W. Eliot (1834–1926), President of Harvard University, 1869–1909; a third cousin once removed of TSE's grandfather.
3–The essayist Charles Lamb (1775–1834) was a clerk in the India House; the historian George Grote (1794–1871) worked in his father's bank; and the astronomer and mathematician Sir John Lubbock (1803–65) became a partner in the family bank.

and also leads quicker than by any other route to established success in literature.

It is, nevertheless, quite unintelligible to me how you or any other young American scholar can forego the privilege of living in the genuine American atmosphere – a bright atmosphere of freedom and hope. I have never lived long in England – about six months in all – but I have never got used to the manners and customs of any class in English society, high, middle, or low. After a stay of two weeks or two months in England it has been delightful for me to escape to either France or America; although I have had English and Scotch friends whom I have greatly admired and loved.

Then, too, I have never been able to understand how any American man of letters can forego the privilege of being of use primarily to Americans of the present and future generations, as Emerson, Bryant, Lowell, and Whittier were.[1] Literature seems to me highly climatic and national as yet; and will it not be long before it becomes independent of these local influences, and addresses itself to an international mind?

You mention in your letter the name of Henry James. I knew his father well, and his brother William very well; and I had some conversation with Henry at different times during his life. I have a vivid remembrance of a talk with him during his last visit to America. It seemed to me all along that his English residence for so many years contributed neither to the happy development of his art nor to his personal happiness.

I conceive that you have a real claim on my attention and interest, – hence this letter. My last word is that if you wish to speak through your own work to people of the 'finest New England spirit' you had better not live much longer in the English atmosphere. The New England spirit has been nurtured in the American atmosphere.

Sincerely yours
Charles W. Eliot

1 – TSE had already dismissed 'such men as Bryant and Whittier as absolute plebieans' ('The Hawthorne Aspect', *Little Review*, Aug. 1918, 48). Elsewhere he identified Poe, Whitman and Hawthorne as the 'important' American writers, adding that 'the essays of Emerson are already an incumbrance' ('American Literature', *A.*, 25 Apr. 1919, 237).

TO *Sydney Schiff* MS BL

25 July 1919

18 Crawford Mansions,
Crawford St, W.1

Dear Mr Schiff,

Thank you for your letter, for the *Little Review*, which I will keep for Pound, and for your book. Of course I have not had time even to look into it yet, but I am looking forward to it with much interest. I want to see at what point if any, it joins the curve of development of *Richard Kurt*. I see in *R. K.* a process of crystallisation in the later part of the book which interests me and which I think may in future lead you further away from or *beyond* your theory of the novel than you think.

I am appreciative of your careful study of 'Gerontion' and shall be glad always to hear anything further you may have to say about it. If I have not another poem by the time I will do an article for *A. & L.* [*Art & Letters*] – not on any current book, as I do enough of that for the *Athenaeum*.

I should really much prefer it if *you* would write to Rodker yourself. I am only a contributor, you know! and I am sure he would be quite as likely to send something serviceable if you wrote. His address, if you do not know it, is John Rodker, 43 Belsize Park Gardens, N.W.3.

But I believe that Aldington would be a better person to acquire, and is a good *prose* writer too. He is more *mature* than Rodker and I expect him to become one of the few to count. His tendency is in the right direction – he really seems to me an important person to have. Richard Aldington's address is c/o the Authors' Club, 2 Whitehall Court, S.W.1. I have an article by Pound for your next number which I will send you.

I do not know who Ludovici[1] is. What little I have seen of [D. H.] Lawrence lately makes me think him thoroughly *dégringolé* [run down].

However, I must stop now.

With best wishes

Sincerely
T. S. Eliot

1–A. M. Ludovici (1882–1971), author and illustrator, was serving in Military Intelligence.

TO *John Middleton Murry*[1] MS Northwestern

29 July 1919 [London]

Dear J. M.,

Thank you very much. I think I know which of the poems you mean already, although I have had the book[2] by me only for a day; but you must not give me credit for any more insight than I can prove to you. What I want is to be able to talk them over with you in quiet and leisure after I have had several days with them.

I hardly dare say what some of them seem to me to reveal – for it might seem an impertinence.

Your letter gave me a great deal of pleasure – more than pleasure. You must realise that it has been a great event to me to know you, but you do not know yet the full meaning of this phrase as I write it.

Yrs always
T.S.E.

TO *Harold Monro*[3] MS Texas

5 August 1919 18 Crawford Mansions

My dear Monro,

Your letter arrived this evening. I should have been really very glad indeed to have contributed to such an interesting critical symposium, but I see that you go to press on Sept. 1st.[4] I am just out of bed and on Saturday expect to leave for three weeks in France,[5] returning on the 1st (probably). I shall not be doing any writing during that time, even my usual work for the *Athenaeum*. In fact, I am very much run down and this is my first real rest for two years.

1–John Middleton Murry: see Glossary of Names.

2–JMM, *Poems: 1917–18* (1918).

3–Harold Monro (1879–1932), poet and owner of the Poetry Bookshop: see Glossary of Names.

4–The Sept. issue of *The Chapbook* was meant to contain 'Five Critical Essays on the Present State of English Poetry', but this item was postponed.

5–EP wrote to Quinn, 6 Aug.: 'Expect Eliot here in a weeks time, hope to put him through course of sun, air & sulphur baths & return him to London intact.' TSE left three days later, met EP for a walking tour in Périgueux in the middle of the month, and returned to London on 31 Aug.

So I can only say that I am very sorry that your request should have come at this time. I shall at least look forward to reading the number.

Yours sincerely
T. S. Eliot

TO *Mary Hutchinson* MS Texas

6 August 1919 18 Crawford Mansions

Dear Mary,

Thanks for books received today. How very kind of you. I shall do my best – you know what a slow reader I am, and I shall only take one volume with me.[1] Have you read them all? The amount I read must depend on the state of the weather and the extent of my recuperation. I have crawled out of bed today to go to the dentist and the French consulate, after several days in bed, and feel very languid. I have just strength to observe that groups are at least as intelligent as most so-called individuals and as tolerable. It's when one expects intelligence from the constituents of the groups that one is completely disappointed. If the group is dominated by an individual the *group* does not count; if it is *not*, then its members do not count as individuals. This is not clearly put. Second I don't know what is the 'intellectual intelligence' and 'dandyism in ideas'. I mean simply that the words convey nothing to me. I thought that ideas should be *clarae et distinctae*,[2] and also that they should more or less work: but you *must* show me a sample swanky idea and I will put on my best bombazine to meet it. Have one for me when I get back. Perhaps Flaubert will help me?

IMPORTANT [*Please* send *Gerontion* back to me at once. I leave Saturday night, and I must revise it in France, so *just* put it in an envelope and send it by return.]

I am *very* tired (as you will have seen from this letter) and very glad to be getting out of London. Perhaps I won't ever come back!

Thank you again for Flaubert.

Yours
Tom.

1 – The following day he sent a telegram: 'Vivien says books were gift forgive apparent ingratitude writing from France when address settled Tom.' It is possible that he had returned to MH most of the books she had sent over to him, not realising that they were all a gift outright.

2 – 'clear and distinct', alluding to a phrase in Descartes's *Meditatio* VI, 15.

TO *Lytton Strachey* MS BL

6 August 1919 18 Crawford Mansions

Dear Lytton,

How propitious that you should have written just before I disappear into central France where no letters will reach me. I have not been away, but in London, in my office or among my books or (several times) in bed, and have frequently imagined you sitting on the lawn at Pangbourne or in a garden, conducting your clinic of Queen Victoria with perfect concentration – but I had not imagined you disturbed by my heresies in the *Athenaeum*.[1] You have frightened me, because I always expect you to be right, and because I know I shall never be able to retaliate upon your finely woven fabric. I have lately read an article of yours on Voltaire[2] which made me envious. I was amazed by your statement about Erasmus,[3] but I am sure you can back it. Besides, my dear Lytton, I am a very ill-read person.

I am going to France, to the Dordogne, on Saturday, for three weeks. I wonder if you would write if I sent you a card from there – but perhaps I should have left before you decided to do so, if you did.

Yours ever
T. S. Eliot

TO *Lytton Strachey* PC BL

[25? August 1919] [France]

I have been walking the whole time since I arrived and so have had no address at all. Through Dordogne and the Corrèze, sunburnt – melons, ceps, truffles, eggs, good wine and good cheese and cheerful people. It is a complete relief from London. I hope to get to Ussel.

Yours
T.S.E.

1–The biographies in Strachey's *Eminent Victorians* (1918) were regarded by some as heretical, and he was planning his biography of Queen Victoria. Among TSE's thirteen pieces for *A.* so far in 1919 was 'The Education of Taste' (27 June), a scathing review of J. W. Cunliffe's *English Literature during the Last Half-Century*.

2–Lytton Strachey, 'Voltaire', *A.*, 1 Aug. 1919, 677–9: a review of *Voltaire in his Letters*, trans. S. G. Tallentyre.

3–'Erasmus was a tragic figure. The great revolution in the human mind, of which he had been the presiding genius, ended in failure; he lived to see the tide of barbarism rising once more over the world; and it was left to Voltaire to carry off the final victory.'

FROM *John Quinn* cc NYPL (MS)

26 August 1919 [New York]

My dear Mr Eliot:

I think I sent you a copy of a letter which I dictated Sunday, June 29th, to Liveright,[1] telling of their damned impertinence to me regarding your book and putting me off for two or three months about it. A few days before that I had had a letter from you saying that you had some later work in prose and verse. I cabled you to send the later work, poems and prose, and in my absence Mr Curtin of my office confirmed the cable by letter. The later work came. Meantime I had had the matter submitted to the John Lane Company of this city, telling them that I would be willing to advance $150 toward the setting up of the book and making of plates. Early in August a letter came in apologizing for the delay in sending a reply but stating that the writer had been out of town, and concluding:

> 'Mr Eliot's work is no doubt brilliant, but it is not exactly the kind of material we care to add to our list. Nevertheless, we appreciate your kindness in bringing it to our attention and regret that we cannot give you a favorable reply.'

I then took the matter up with Knopf, telling him of the new poems and that I had come to the conclusion, in view of the new poems, that a book of poems alone would be the best thing for you. He said that he would be glad to look at the new poems. I then sent the whole thing, poems and prose, including the new poems and prose, to Knopf. He telephoned me a few days later that he was willing and anxious to publish the poems in a volume by themselves. I think that you now have enough poems to make one good volume. I think therefore that you should revise your desire to have the poems and prose in one book. Everyone seems to agree that a hybrid book of that sort does not get anywhere. Max Eastman had a small book of prose and verse published and it fell flat,[2] and others have had the same experience. All the publishers are dead against it. It looks too much like the literary 'remains' of a writer, or a writer who is neither one thing nor the other. When your poems and prose were first submitted to Knopf I insisted upon both going together because I thought there were not enough poems for a book. But with the new poems I think you have enough for a separate volume. I agreed with Knopf that the book should

1–Boni & Liveright, New York publishers, founded in 1917.

2–Max Eastman, *The Ballad of Joseph the Nazarene by 'Williams' and A Sermon on Reverence* (1916).

be entitled *Poems by T. S. Eliot*. I dislike, apparently as much as Knopf dislikes, the name *Prufrock* in the title. He thinks that title would hurt the sale. I agree with him. Knopf pays Pound 10% royalty on *Lustra* up to 5,000 copies. I hope Pound and I will live to see the sale of 5,000 copies of *Lustra* but at the present rate of sale that would insure our living a long time. Beyond 5,000 copies I believe Pound is to get 12½%. I got Knopf to agree to increase the royalty to you from 10 to 12% on all copies sold.

It is too late for the fall list. The fall list of books is already out and published. I told Knopf that I would write you urging you to accept Knopf's proposition of a book of poems and ask you to cable me. On receipt of your cable I will sign a contract with Knopf similar to Pound's contract with him for *Lustra*, at 12% royalty, and Knopf will start printing. The volume will have to go in the spring list which will be out in two or three months and the book itself 'will be published early in the year'. In fact the spring list is now about complete. So I had better be cabled one word, 'Accept', either by you or Pound, which I will understand as authorizing me to close with Knopf for the publication of the volume of poems. A separate volume of prose, critical and other prose, may be arranged later.

Now as to time: Assuming that you would want page proofs before final printing, Knopf should have the final copy not later than October 1st. If therefore you have written any new poems which you want to include in the volume, they will have to be sent by the middle of September so as to get here by October 1st.

In a letter that I had from you just before I went away, dated May 25th, you wanted to alter the MS. for the book so as to add two or three other essays, feeling that the new essays were better than any in the MS. But these questions can be dealt with when you come to publish a separate book of prose.

There was received at my office on July 22nd your letter of July 9th enclosing the additional MS. of new poems and prose. I understand where you want the new poems to go, namely, that they should be put at the head of the new poems, the ones not in the *Prufrock* volume, and that if you had put the new poems in front of the *Prufrock* ones then these new poems enclosed in your letter of July 9th should head the new book. Knopf said that he liked the old poems better than the new ones and I am inclined to agree with him, but they are all interesting and it will make a corking book. If you agree to my suggestion that the poems be put in one volume, then there will be more time to discuss the prose and to pass upon the various questions touched upon by you in your letter of July 9, 1919 to me regarding titles, acknowledgments to other publishers, and the possible dropping of the 'Eeldrop and Appleplexes'. You wrote that you wished that you were anywhere near satisfied with the book. I think that putting the poems in one volume and taking more time on the prose will make you more satisfied with the two books. In your letter of July 9th you left it in my hands 'in all confidence', but at the same time I feel it is better to get a cable from you, and if you should have one or two more poems that you want to include please send them to me and I will put them in the book. Even though they get here by October 15th it will be time enough, although Knopf mentioned October 1st.

I had not seen the reference to you in the *New Republic*. I will call it to Knopf's attention and he might be able to use it on the jacket of the book of poems.

Thank you for thinking of sending me a copy of your book of poems when it is printed by Rodker with designs by Wadsworth.

There is no good book on Stendhal in English. If Secker commissions you to write such a book it will be a big job, and I agree with you that £25 does not seem enough for such a big job.

Regarding my defense of *Ulysses*, I shall have to read it again before I can give permission to have it published in the *Egoist*. I dictated that one evening in the office at the close of a hard day's work, and I remember that I had a dinner engagement that evening. I started to dictate it at ten minutes of six and finished the dictation at twenty minutes after seven. So I hesitate to agree that a mere lawyer's brief, on which he has spent just one hour and twenty minutes, should be perpetuated in a paper like the *Egoist* which has published so much real literature. I am sorry that the publishers of the *Egoist* have decided to stop, but from the financial point of view I think they are right to devote the money at their disposal to book publication, even though it does rob Pound and you of an organ where you can express yourselves editorially and freely. I congratulate you upon your work with the *Athenaeum*. Knopf had heard of it.

Your letter of July 9th was forwarded to me in the mountains and it was refreshing to read it. I was delighted with its fine spirit and its hopefulness. The best advice I can give you is to 'play your own game', to think of yourself and your own work and not be carried away by enthusiasms for others unless they are good friends of yours like Pound, and in that way help you to play your own game or advance work that you are interested in in common.

In a note that I had from Pound today from Dordogne he said that he expected you there in a week's time, so I am sending the original of this letter to you in London and a copy of it I am sending in a letter that I am writing to Pound, so that I will get you either way and you can cable me as requested, and if you have any new poems you can send them to me.

This, I believe, covers the whole thing.

I am glad that you are going down there to have long walks and good talks with Pound. It will be a good thing for you to get away from business for three or four weeks.

With kind regards, I am

Sincerely yours,
[unsigned]

TO *His Mother* MS Houghton

3 September 1919

18 Crawford Mansions,
Crawford St, W.1

My dearest Mother,

I got back from France on Sunday night.[1] I did not write you any letters while I was there, but I knew you would understand why I did not: I wrote only cards to Vivien, and did not read at all.[2] I enjoyed my holiday thoroughly, and feel (and look) very well indeed, so you need not be worrying about me. I think I made the most of my time.

I had very little difficulty in getting a passport, and left at 5 p.m. on a Saturday, getting to Havre at 8 the next morning. There the passport stamping took so long that everyone missed the train. By attaching myself to a French couple I found that I could get a train from Trouville, a seaside resort nearby, which might get me to Paris in time to catch the night train for Périgueux. So we boarded the small steamer and proceeded along the coast for an hour's journey on a blazing bright August day, the boat crowded with people going to the races, and men with violins and singers passing their hats. It was all so French and so sudden that I was dazed by it. Trouville is a very expensive and famous resort, a long beach with villas and casinos and big motor cars, and I was not surprised to have to pay 11 francs for a very good lunch. I loafed about till 4.30, and got to Paris at 8.15. My train left there at 9 from a different station, but I dashed through

1–VHE's diary, 31 Aug.: 'Still in bed. Tom came home. Arrived punctually. Sent Molly to meet him. Has begun to grow a beard. Very nice at first, depressed in evening.'

2–VHE had written to MH, 31 Aug.: 'France really has swallowed Tom up. He promised his doctor neither to read nor to write a word while he was away, and he is certainly obeying him!'

the Place de la Concorde in a taxi, and just caught it. The taxi-driver was a very polite person – I was counting out the money slowly, having lost my familiarity with the coinage, and he said 'That's enough' indicating a small tip. So I gave him a bit more, and said 'That's because I have not been in Paris for eight years'; he roared with amusement, and waved to me as he drove off. I looked out of the window most of the way, being too excited to sleep. At 4 we reached Limoges, where I waited an hour for my train. I got into a carriage which had been German, and found myself in the company of two young soldiers on leave, who played the accordion the whole way, looking at me for approval and swaying in unison. It began to be light, and I could see the beautiful landscape of Périgord, hilly and wooded, very different from Northern France. You feel at once that you are in a different country, more exciting, very southern, more like Italy. The South of France is as different from the North as the South and North of England. Finally, at 7.30 in the morning I reached Périgueux very hungry, where I last was in January 1911. And there Pound met me at the station. I spent part of my vacation with him in the village of Excideuil, and part on walking trips alone.

I am going to continue this account in my next letter; if I tried to tell it all at once I should omit parts. Thank you very much indeed for the $50; it helps very much on the expenses. I found Henry's letter at the bank, and yours came yesterday.

Then your cable, which came when I was away. It was very sweet and kind of you, but I am *really* very well and strong now. My holiday did wonders for me. It was a complete change. I shall take care (V. says she will take care) that I don't lose the benefits of it by overwork. I shall not lecture this winter, but will write for the *Athenaeum* instead. I shall not lecture unless the cost of living keeps on advancing – it is difficult in these days to be certain of anything far ahead.

I found Vivien in bed with a serious attack of bronchitis. As her family were in the country she has no one to look after her but our servant, who leaves at 8 in the evening, so that she was always alone at night. She had concealed her illness from me in writing, so as not to diminish my pleasure in the trip. I should like her to go to the seaside for a few days when she gets better, as she has still a nasty cough and is very pale.[1]

1 – Three days later, VHE wrote in her diary (6 Sept.): 'Frightful day of misery. Felt very ill, packed all morning, left for Bosham at 3.40 with Tom. Perfect weather.'

I have a great deal to write about and reply to, but must postpone it till Sunday.

Always your loving son
Tom.

TO *His Mother* MS Houghton

9 September 1919 [London]

My dearest Mother,

I am just writing a line by this mail as I have so much to do, and will continue my letter about France on Sunday.

Our new department[1] is installed, if not exactly started. I have a table at a big front south window looking over the square toward the Mansion House, in a fine impressive room. I believe I shall have a French typist for foreign correspondence.

When I get settled, and have proved my efficiency in the new work, I intend to get leave, within the next six months, and fly over to see you if only for a few days. I may not be able to give you notice, but I shall expect to bring you back with me.

Always your devoted
Tom.

TO *J. C. Squire* MS UCLA

10 September 1919 18 Crawford Mansions

[Dear Squi]re,[2]

[I] have been walking in France, and [your] letter, after being forwarded from Marlow, [came] for me here. I should like to see you [and to hear] about the *Mercury*[3] and its scope, and [I shall] probably come in after tea one day next [week and hope you] are there. I am trying now [to restrict my] periodical writing to one or [two reviews] in order to get material for a [bo]ok, and so I don't know whether I could [f]it you or not. But I should like to talk to you.

Sincerely
T. S. Eliot.

1–The Information Department at Lloyds Bank.

2–The left side of the letter is badly torn; bracketed readings are conjectural.

3–Squire's *London Mercury* first appeared in Nov. 1919. TSE never wrote for it.

TO *Ezra Pound* MS Beinecke

Friday [12? September 1919] [London]

What else was to be expected? I will come in tomorrow (Sat.) p.m. at 8.45 to refresh you for a few moments with the sight of my beard.[1] If you are out, *n'importe* [no matter].

T.

TO *Henry Eliot* MS Houghton

14 September 1919 18 Crawford Mansions

My dear Henry

I am ashamed of not having written sooner after my return. On finding your two letters with the two cheques. I do think it is munificent of you. I have put the money in deposit account, and it will at least be as safe with me as with you, as I don't intend to spend it. When I have more money I shall of course invest, but at present I feel safe with it in a tangible form.

I had a very delightful trip and feel in much better health for it. I have written some account of part of it in one letter to mother, and shall continue it in my next, and you will doubtless see these letters. France was certain to set me up. The relief of getting into another country after five years in one spot, and being able to speak another language, is a great stimulus and tonic. I should like to get to Italy next year, but I am not sure that I can manage. I wrote to mother that I should try to come over for a short visit as early next year as possible, and to do this I may have to forgo my summer holiday; though what I should offer to the bank would be to take three weeks or a month *without salary*. I don't think the visit to America will be exactly a rest. If mother would come over here in the spring I should defer coming to America till the following year; but if she doesn't, I shall nevertheless expect to bring her back to England with me, which would give us quite a long period together. What I am convinced of is that by coming here she would have the chance to rest that she badly needs. I fear that she has done far too much this summer, and that there is no one about her who knows how to check her. I hope I shall be kept better posted about her than I was about father.

1–See RA's account of his anxiety about the possible effect of TSE's beard on Bruce Richmond, editor of the *TLS*, at their first meeting, when TSE arrived wearing 'a derby hat and an Uncle Sam beard': 'he looked perfectly awful, like one of those comic-strip caricatures of Southern hicks' (*Life for Life's Sake: A Book of Reminiscences* [1941], 269). For Richmond, see Glossary of Names.

I have been very busy since I got back. Vivien had a very bad attack of bronchitis while I was away which kept her still in bed for a week after I returned. Then Murry (the editor of the *Athenaeum*) had to take his wife who is consumptive to the Riviera, and asked me to do as much as I could in writing during the month he is gone. So I have just done two long articles, one on Swinburne and the Elizabethan drama and one on *Hamlet*.[1] In the spring I expect to collect my essays into two volumes, one containing essays on criticism and poetry, which the *Egoist* will publish, and in which I mean to put everything I have written about the writing of poetry. The other will be Studies in Renaissance Literature and will be an adaptation of essays in the *Athenaeum*, and this a man named Cobden-Sanderson[2] wants. I shall also have a new edition of poems up to date, and I just hear from John Quinn that he has arranged for Knopf in New York to print the American edition at 12%, also in the spring.

I feel pretty tired now, after a long walk this afternoon with Maurice, and then pursuing *Hamlet*, or I should like to take up your long reply to my long letter. But that will keep. Meanwhile I am glad you have got a pleasant room by yourself, and can I hope at least read undisturbed.

Always very affectionately,
Tom.

Henry Adams's book is more than good. It is unique.

TO *Sydney Schiff* — MS BL

Sunday [14 September 1919] — 18 Crawford Mansions

My dear Schiff,

Thank you for your letter. My trip was a complete success: I feel very much better for it. I have been very busy since my return. Murry has had to take his wife to France, and wants me to do as much as I can during his absence.

I am glad you have found a house you like better, and hope you will find the conditions more favourable to work than the former turned out to be. It is always difficult to know how much of oneself to give to other people.

1–'Swinburne and the Elizabethans', a review of A. C. Swinburne, *Contemporaries of Shakespeare*, ed. Edmund Gosse and T. J. Wise, *A.*, 19 Sept. 1919; repr. as 'Swinburne as Critic' in *SW*. 'Hamlet and His Problems', a review of J. M. Robertson, *The Problem of 'Hamlet'*, *A.*, 26 Sept. 1919; repr. as 'Hamlet' in *SW*.

2–Richard Cobden-Sanderson, printer and publisher: see Glossary of Names.

As you have a good deal of verse, it would be better for me to give you some prose – about the length of the Marivaux. Let me hear from you. Candidly I don't think that prose ought to be paid at the same rate as verse, unless a very unusual story. I don't think Pound has been in communication with Lewis, or that Lewis knew what Pound was paid. It is more likely that I told Lewis what I was given for the poems. If this has made matters difficult for you I am <very> sorry, but you will have to decide what Lewis's contribution is worth.

I trust you intend to get back to London before leaving for Paris.

Always cordially, with best remembrances to your wife,

T. S. Eliot

TO *Edgar Jepson* MS Beinecke

22 September 1919 18 Crawford Mansions

My dear Mr Jepson,

Thank you indeed for your letter. I hope that this autumn and winter we may occasionally meet, and also that I may again have the pleasure of hearing you speak.

I am inclined to agree with you about the poems, though I think the first is much better than the second.[1] I shall be very anxious to have your opinion about two that I am working on now, which are quite different. I am also pleased that you like the [Swinburne] article.

The Sheep's-wool correspondence[2] has afforded me much pleasure, and then [it ended just][3] when I wanted to join in. I think you may justly consider that your essay was a great success.

The Egoist, I am sorry to say, is 'suspended' after the December issue, and the Company will for an indefinite period concentrate upon publishing books. However, I am very desirous that you should let me have the essays, as I am pretty sure that I could place them more conspicuously, (if you will let me) and incidentally perhaps I might have the pleasure of replying to them. I think *Art & Letters* would do it.[4] *Will you let me know?*

Sincerely yours,

T. S. Eliot

1 – 'Burbank with a Baedeker: Bleistein with a Cigar' and 'Sweeney Erect'.

2 – In 'Recent United States Poetry', Jepson had derided Edgar Lee Masters' poem 'All Life in A Life', which included the line 'His hair was black as a sheep's wool that is black.'

3 – Part of the page is torn away.

4 – The Egoist Press did not print Jepson's essays.

TO *Sydney Schiff* MS BL

24 September 1919 [London]

My dear Schiff,

I return herewith your poem, as you perhaps want my opinion at once. I have seen Hy King's[1] name in the *Athenaeum*. This poem[2] strikes me as a clever *gâchis* [hash] of Laforgue, the Elizabethans, several contemporaries, sentiment, and selfconsciousness. A poem should be very good to justify such length. Still, the writer walks nearer to the light than most.

I will let you have my prose attempt[3] by the end of this week. I am glad to hear that you are pleased with the material for this number – Do you mean that there is a *loss* of £400 a year?[4] I cannot understand why it should be so heavy as that, even if subscribers were very few. And there is no other paper to compete with it.

You shall hear from me in a few days.

Always cordially,
T. S. Eliot.

Vivien Eliot TO *Mary Hutchinson* MS Texas

Friday 26 Sep. [1919] (Tom's birthday!) Bosham

My dear Mary

I only hung about Chichester for about three hours, not getting your wire until I got back here, tired and cross!

But I believe yr. visit tired you very much, and so perhaps it is a good thing we did not meet.

I am going home tomorrow Saturday afternoon.[5] The last week has been too wintry, and now I have your complaint, and I want warmth and comfort, and I think *I* shall take to going to bed at these times! But you have so trained yr. household, and I believe my dragon would not be at all pleased if I went to bed 'for nothing'.

This is written in the middle of packing, and with a headache. I suppose you are unaware of the simple fact that to feel relief in mechanical

1 – Apparently neither TSE nor SS knew that 'Henry King' was a pseud. of JMM.

2 – 'The Train Journey', *A.*, 8 Aug. 1919, 713.

3 – 'Some Notes on the Blank Verse of Christopher Marlowe', *Art & Letters* 2 (Autumn 1919).

4 – SS replied on 27 Sept. that subsidising *Art & Letters* cost him £400 'and more'.

5 – VHE wrote in her diary: 'Tom's birthday. Wish I had gone back. Stormy weather. Got blackberries all morning. Felt ill. *Migraine*. Faceache. Swollen face (slightly).'

occupations, and yr. letter says you do just now – means mental fatigue. If I were you, well, of course I couldn't be. But I dont see how you get along with so few brain-resting occupations. Where should I be without my dirty piece of crochet which I have been doing for five years, or my failures of dresses and underclothes? I fly to them with a frenzy of relief and when you are bored, but must not read! How invaluable! While I stayed chez Schiff I made a dress, the whole time, in public!

It was rather a shock to hear you were so exhausted after the night I spent at Wittering. I cant understand it. Of course I expect to be exhausted myself (and I was simply dizzy) but I dont expect you to be.

I have a good store of things ready to be said to you. I shall probably forget most. About Tom and Bloomsbury for instance. Jack got me on to that on Sunday, I agreed with everything he said! But I have thought that out, and I dont think it will come off. I begin to think you (I mean you, Mary) can only like people on two conditions. And then about giving oneself up to people. I had never seen before we spoke how much I have done that with Tom. Also how little *you* were prepared to do it with anyone. Also how much one gains by doing it, how much one loses; and, how much one *loses by not ever doing it.*

'Now the trouble with you is that there's so much you are oblivious to.' I am quoting, but not exact words. *But* I think it is true. I feel at a point now where there is ever so much to say to you, or, we must retire a few paces.

Well look 'ere, will you come to dinner at Crawford Mansions on Tuesday night? And Jack of course? I want you to and I shall be very upset if you will not. You must please. If not, then we must all dine out together on Wednesday. I cant have you to dinner on Wed. because it is Ellen's day off. Please write to the flat *at once. And send me back that one film of mine you still have. Do not dare to forget. If you have lost it— —*

[unsigned]

<Why did you make Barbara write to me? I have sent her a card.>

<What do you think of Joyce now?? I am in trouble. I am *almost* giving him up! He is abominable. Is he laughing?>[1]

1 – 'Episode XI' of *Ulysses* had appeared in *Little Review* 6: 4 & 5 (Aug. & Sept. 1919).

TO *John Quinn* TS NYPL (MS)

28 September 1919

18 Crawford Mansions,
Crawford St, W.1

Dear Mr Quinn,

I cabled you 'Accept' on receipt of your letter. I am very sorry that I failed to confirm this immediately; I had several articles promised that I had to write, and so did not have time to alter the poem which I enclose.[1]

I want first to express my heartfelt thanks and appreciation of all the pains that you have taken, and of your letter, which gave me great pleasure. I do not understand how you manage to accomplish so much on behalf of other people, in the midst of your heavy professional duties, to say nothing of your private affairs.

I am quite satisfied with any contract that you may make for me with Knopf. I understand that I get 12% from all sales, and that Knopf has exclusive rights to the American edition for some definite period of years. That the copyright after that is mine (as in Pound's case) and that my rights to arrange or dispose of any English edition are not restricted in any way by the Knopf contract. You see, I want a fresh edition here in the spring, which would naturally contain any poems I write in the interval. This would give it an advantage over Knopf's book, but of course I should not have any of the English edition exported to America. Weaver will print it, and she would not export any copies without my consent. At present my poems are out of print here.

I think that you now have all the poems, viz:

'Gerontion'
'Burbank with a Baedeker'
'Sweeney Erect'
* 'Sweeney among the Nightingales'
* 'Mr Eliot's Sunday Morning Service'
* 'Whispers of Immortality'
* 'The Hippopotamus'
'A Cooking Egg'
* 'Lune de miel'
'Dans le restaurant'
* 'Le Spectateur'
* 'Mélange adultère de tout'

1 – 'Gerontion'.

The ones marked * being in the small book of the Hogarth Press which I sent you.[1]

I wish I could guess when this will reach you.[2] I shall make enquiries as to whether there is any provision for carrying overseas mails to the boats; this strike threatens at the moment to be a serious affair, and we are in the dark as to its real cause and its probable course. My own views are Liberal and strongly opposed to the Government in almost everything; but I cannot regard this present expression of labour discontent without grave apprehension and distrust.

With repeated expression of thanks for your action and for the encouragement of your letter.

Yours sincerely,
T. S. Eliot

I enclose a letter to Knopf which you may hand them if you think fit.

FROM *John Quinn* — CC NYPL (MS)

29 September 1919 [New York]

Dear Mr Eliot:

On September 17th I received your cable as follows:

'Quinn,
Thirtyone Nassau Street, New York.
Accept.
(Signed) Eliot'

This was in accordance with the word named on page 3 of my letter of August 26th, 1919. I at once communicated with Knopf and told him of your decision. I had one letter from him and a talk with him on the telephone last week. He was going to put the book in a small format of about 5 inches by 3½, similar to one or two other books of the kind, but I objected to it and said that it would be a dumpy book and undignified. Knopf very willingly agreed to change it to 12mo. I am writing him a letter today, of which I enclose you a copy, telling him everything that you mentioned in your letter of July 9, 1919 to me regarding the book of poems. I agreed with Knopf that I would look over the contract between you and him and sign it on your behalf. That is all that remains for me to do. The rest of it is between you and him.

1–Quinn wrote to TSE on 22 Nov.: 'I received no book of the Hogarth Press. I have a recollection of receiving the "Sweeney" poems and the other new ones, but they were not in a book but were on pages that were taken out of a book or what I thought was a magazine.'
2–Delayed by the railway strike of 26 Sept.–5 Oct., it arrived on 31 Oct.

I congratulate you on getting him for a publisher. I think that my recommendation that the book of poems be separated from the prose was a sound one. That will give you more time on the prose. After this book is out, so that you are no longer a new man, then the regular literary agents are the ones for you to deal through, both regarding your magazine or review publication of poems or prose and regarding books. One of the best men I know is a man that used to be John Lane's manager over here, a very decent Englishman. His name is Harold Paget. The following is the name and address of his agency:

The Paget Agency,
500 Fifth Avenue,
New York City.

I was glad to do this pioneer work for you here on this book, but when a man once has one book published pioneer work is no longer necessary from a man like me. Your next book of prose ought to be handled, it seems to me, through an agent over here.

And that reminds me that I have the copy for your prose volume. Perhaps you would think that now that the prose that I have was not enough for a prose volume. Perhaps you would like to have me return it to you by registered post for reconsideration and rearrangement. Or perhaps you would want me to send it to some literary agency like the Paget Agency. I shall be very glad to do whatever you wish to have done.

I hope that you have had some vacation.

You will see from my letter to Knopf that I suggest that he send the page proofs to you but that I have told him that I should be very glad to look over the general format of the book.

My time is so much taken up that I want to end as many outside personal matters as possible before the busy court days of October begin, and they extend through to the end of June. That is why I tried to make my letter to Knopf a final and comprehensive one. But we will have to have a meeting to go over and sign the contract, and that will involve a letter from me to you sending you the contract. But I have tried to deal with the matter fully in this letter to you. I am glad to have been of service in getting your first book of poems published in this country. It will be a book of high distinction.

With kind regards, I am
Sincerely yours,
[unsigned]

PS You will see from my letter to Knopf that I have suggested my stopping in at his place some day to look over the general format of the book. You will also see that in my letter to Knopf I refer to a letter that I had from Lewis a few days ago in which Lewis spoke of your having written a new long poem ['Gerontion'], and that I have suggested to Knopf that perhaps you might be willing to include that new long poem in the volume which Knopf is bringing out, thus increasing not only its size but its interest and importance. So if that new long poem is finished you might send a copy of it to Knopf at once and tell him where it should appear in the volume.

I am sorry that the book of poems won't be out for the autumn but it will be out, as I think I wrote you, early in the year, that is, in February or March. Boni and Liveright played a low trick on me in holding up their decision about this for over two or three months. They are responsible and solely responsible for the delay that there has been and for the fact that the book won't be out this autumn. However, that is past and it does no good to think too much of the past. I am glad to have been able to be of some service to you. As I have said in my letter to Knopf, I will stop in at his office some day and look over the general format of the book to see that the titles are in good taste and so on, and that the style of the book is attractive both inside and outside, and try to get it on as good paper as I can.

With kind regards, I am

Yours very truly,
[unsigned]

TO *His Mother* — MS Houghton

2 October 1919 — 18 Crawford Mansions,
Crawford St, W.1

My dearest mother,

There is supposed to be a mail tomorrow, and although the services are not yet normal, I have hopes that this may reach you by some boat sailing soon. The paper says that the boats are not leaving New York, on account of our strike; I have not heard from you for some time, but a letter reached me today, fortunately, as I expect to have to wait some time for another. As mine have been directed to Saint Louis, you will just have received them. The general opinion, I think, is favorable to the demands of the strikers, but strongly opposed to their summary methods. There is also some evidence of the growing resentment of the bourgeoisie at the continual demands and continual higher wages of the 'working class'. Certainly the bourgeoisie has turned out amazingly quickly to take the strikers' place; all the underground railways, and a surprising number of trains through the country, are running more or less thanks to volunteers. What is also notable is the cheerfulness with which people have insisted on going about their business, walking miles, or even camping out in their offices and shops; I had a four mile walk to work, and back, for three days, but now I can get underground trains. The omnibuses were so crowded that I could not get on. We have suffered other privations – we only get half a pint of milk a day (for three people) and all foods are strictly rationed.

I have had an invitation to lecture this winter but have declined it. It was in a suburb not easy of access. Such work is really a disadvantage to me now as it would consume the time which I can devote to writing which will give me notoriety and in the end more money. I enclose a letter which shows that I have been asked to write for the *Times Literary Supplement*[1] – to write the Leading Article from time to time. This is the highest honour possible in the critical world of literature, and we are pleased. It is certain that I shall have three and possibly four books out next year: one, perhaps two, of essays, a new edition of poems, and as the other enclosed letter shows, an edition in New York. I thought the letter would interest you, and it shows how kind John Quinn has been to me. He is an important lawyer in New York. I cabled my acceptance.

I think you write very well, and was much interested in your letter to the *Herald*.[2] I am not really competent to declare on the merits of the questions; what is going on in the Senate is at present eclipsed in our papers by the strike. But it is certain that at the Peace Conference the one strong figure was Clemenceau, who knew just what he wanted, and that Wilson went down utterly before European diplomacy. It is obviously a bad peace, in which the major European powers tried to get as much as they could, and appease or ingratiate as far as possible the various puppet nationalities which they have

1 – RA wrote to TSE on 23 Sept., 'Mr Richmond, the editor of the *Literary Supplement*, has a great admiration for your critical prose and, I think, would be willing to publish a leading article by you, if you cared to write it.' Bruce Richmond initially feared TSE would find the paper 'too old-fashioned' and would consider himself 'the property of the *Athenaeum*.', but RA reassured him: he arranged for the two men to meet at *The Times* on 29 Sept. (*Richard Aldington: An Autobiography in Letters* ed. Norman T. Gates [1992], 53). In a tribute on Richmond's ninetieth birthday, TSE recalled his first impressions of Richmond: 'There is still a picture of the scene in my mind: the chief figure a man with a kind of bird-like quality, a bird-like alertness of eye, body and mind. I remember his quickness to put the newcomer at ease; and the suggestion in his mien and movement of an underlying strength of character' (*TLS*, 13 Jan. 1961, 17).

2 – Charlotte C. Eliot, 'An Appeal to the Reservations', *Boston Herald*, 27 Aug. 1919.

constituted and will try to dominate. That is exactly what we expected. And I believe that Wilson made a grave mistake in coming to Europe.

I must write you two more letters at once; one for what I have not had time to put into this, and one solely to recount the rest of my holiday, and for nothing else – otherwise, it will never get written!

Always your very loving son
Tom.

TO *John Rodker* PC Typed copy Beinecke[1]

3 October 1919 18 Crawford Mansions

It has just occurred to me that the title ARA VUS PREC[2] would do. For it is non-committal about the newness of the contents, and unintelligible to most people.

Yrs,
T. S. Eliot

Vivien Eliot TO *Mary Hutchinson* MS Texas

Friday night [3 October 1919] Flat [18 Crawford Mansions]

My dear, aren't you sick of staying in at Wittering? I am awfully disappointed about Sat. night. I hope you will excuse me asking you to bring my trunk. But it is rather miserable to be without everything so long. My Monday's adventures were as follows. Awakened at 6 a.m. by faithful follower outside window, who said a motor was leaving Chi: at 10.30 – and a seat in it wd. cost 30s. Would I go?[3] Yes. A thousand yeses – I was so sick and ill with Bosham. Packed up in great hurry, bitterly cold, no breakfast. Cab fetched me and took me to Chichester. Three motors all leaving at once, full of men, great excitement. Refused permission to take trunk! Left it in Chichester station cloakrooms. Wired Tom to meet me at Putney Bridge, as the motors refused to take us into London in case of being commandeered. Wild drive to London with elderly gent, with false

1 – The original postcard was sold by the Gotham Book Mart, New York, 6 Nov. 1936.
2 – 'Now I pray you', *Purg.* XXVI, 145. Not knowing Provençal, TSE relied on the little Temple Classics edition of Dante which he had carried in his pocket since 1911, and this resulted in the error 'Vus' for 'Vos'. When the mistake was discovered, there was only time to correct the label.
3 – Despite the railway strike.

teeth. Arrived Putney Bridge. No Tom. No lunch. Waited two hours. Wept. Came home. No Tom. 7 o'cl. Tom arrived surprised to see me. Had been waiting at London Bridge for 3¾ hours. Why? Thought I meant London Bridge altho' I said Putney. Both wept.

Well now. Surely you are coming on Monday. I hate you being off there, and me here. If you *can* manage to fetch up my trunk I shall feel more than grateful. I think, if you come by train, you may bring as much luggage as you like. I arranged with the man at Chichester that someone might fetch it, and in that case he will give you back the 5/11d I paid for the carriage of it to London, in case it could be sent. If Tom cannot meet you at the time you arrive, I shall be able to. You must not hate Tom, it isn't fair. But I know you won't, always. I see I was rather silly in that unfortunate letter I wrote you from Bosham, Dear Mary.

I am having horrible times at the dentist, and that is one of the things I 'mind'. It is not very nice here. Nothing seems to have begun. One is waiting, waiting for the strike to stop. Just as one waited for the war to stop. But you didn't, did you? There you are again! And there am I again, but this is not a nasty letter.

I want to get clothes, but everything seems so wildly different (fashions, I mean) that I dare not begin. So I have not ordered a single thing. I dont know what will please Jim[1] most either! Directly that horrible Belgian goes to Bermuda you must begin laying foundation stones for me with Jim.

Meanwhile I have no underclothes. Now Mary darling goodnight. Do try to come on Monday. If no train to London you can easily do it now by taking a train to *Brighton*, and then another to London. There are plenty of those I know. You could really have done that today. I hope you are not still unhappy.

Vivien

TO *His Mother* MS Houghton

14 October 1919 18 Crawford Mansions

II

– Périgueux is a town that I like. The last time I was there was at Christmas (1910), and arriving early on an intensely hot August morning it seemed more southern than it had before. It is a small old town, the metropolis of that district. It had taken me thirty-six hours to get there, but I felt that I

1 – Jim Barnes, MH's brother.

had left London – the London of four years of war – and reached the South at one instant – suddenly Roman ruins, and tall white houses, and gorgeous southern shrubs, and warm smells of garlic – donkeys – ox carts. There is a particular excitement about arriving at an exciting place after a sleepless night of travel. We went to the hotel which had that musty smell I have only found in France and Italy, and I fell straight asleep on a bed, only waking for lunch. I stuffed myself with the good French food, which is as good and plentiful as ever, but more expensive. Then we sat out in a garden[1]

TO *Sydney Schiff* MS BL

17 October 1919 18 Crawford Mansions

My dear Schiff,

I was glad to hear from you, as I have just received an extraordinary letter from Osbert Sitwell,[2] with regard to which I should like to consult you. I am afraid I was very tired the other night, but I have had a great deal to worry me. It is good of you to suggest coming in to see me, and I should be very grateful if we could meet that way, much as I hate to impose upon you. Would Monday evening do, could you come in after dinner?

We are very sorry not to have the pleasure of lunching with you on Sunday, but Vivien must go to Marlow tomorrow, as she is writing to explain; and I am not going because I have something to work at all day which I must finish by Sunday night – so I really must deny myself going out.

I saw the review in the *Times*, but it did not strike me as more unjust than one should expect, and indeed for that sort of thing as good as one expects.[3] Anyway, the *Times* treated me far worse, in 1917, as I can show you![4]

1–The manuscript breaks off here at the top of the second page.

2–Sitwell, who was co-editing *Art & Letters* with Frank Rutter, had written to ask if it was true that SS had invited TSE to replace him as second editor.

3–The review adjudged that Stephen Hudson's *Richard Kurt* 'is like living in a hotel. People come and go through its pages, and leave you with no more than a vague impression that there are too many of them, and that they are unpleasant or uninteresting or both' (*TLS*, 16 Oct. 1919, 569).

4–The *TLS* review of *Prufrock and Other Observations* had found TSE 'frequently inarticulate', and judged that 'the things which occurred to the mind of Mr. Eliot' were 'surely of the very smallest importance to anyone – even himself' (June 1917).

Looking forward to seeing you

Sincerely
T. S. Eliot

TO *Osbert Sitwell*[1] MS Valerie Eliot

[19? October 1919]

We ~~hope~~ <look forward> to be able to come to your next party and are glad to hear that you intend to be in London sometime. ~~There will be so much to talk about~~ Meanwhile, Schiff has *not* approached me with a view to my taking any position with the paper. But he writes to me that he has had a letter from you, and that he wants to see me ~~in a day or two~~ and when we meet the rumour will very likely be discussed. ~~Meanwhile~~ I hope you will continue to write ~~any~~ and let me know when you hear any lies about me, as I am getting tired of them.[2] If a pogrom would dispose of all the liars I should heartily join you, but I am afraid there would be a few left.[3]

Do send me your book as soon as it is out.[4]

Yrs – ever –

TO *Sydney Schiff* MS Valerie Eliot

Monday night [20 October 1919] 18 Crawford Mansions

My dear Schiff,

I want to add this word to say that on reviewing this absurd affair after I said goodnight to you, I am convinced that your nephew had nothing to do with it. I strongly suspect that the rumour was started by a Mrs Hutchinson of whom you may have heard, as an innuendo of hers when several people were present has flashed into my mind. – But so far as you

1 – Unaddressed and unsigned draft.

2 – Sitwell had said he could not help fancying it was SS's 'chatterbox of a nephew who starts the rumours' and 'spread[s] it about'. He meant (he declared), 'B – B – B. Beddington B. Behrens' – Sir Edward Beddington-Behrens (1897–1968), later author of *The International Labour Office (League of Nations): A Survey of Certain Problems of International Administration* (1924).

3 – Sitwell wrote (17 Oct.), 'I suggest we both start a pogrom at Oxford'; and on 18 Oct.: 'If I meet him, there will be a pogrom; and I hope you will also be very severe; he might be flayed alive.'

4 – Sitwell, *Argonaut and Juggernaut* (1919), his first book of poetry.

and I are concerned, the matter is, as you say, of no importance. I want you to know that I appreciate the friendship you show me, and can contrast it with all that is not genuine.

Cordially
T. S. Eliot

TO *Mary Hutchinson*

MS Texas

Wednesday [22 Oct? 1919] [18 Crawford Mansions]

My dear Mary,

I am so sorry and hope it is not a very painful attack, for lumbago can be torture. I am disappointed of course and should have rung you up today about tomorrow evening[1] had I not got your note. However, I am glad in a way that you will not be there, as it cannot be a good address in the circumstances. I don't know whether Vivien is better or not; sometimes she seems much better and sometimes worse. I will ring up in a day or two to ask how you are and about Sunday. I shall see you then in any case surely.

Affectionately
Tom.

I have taken your Flaubert lately as my lunch time reading. A nice man, I think. I have enjoyed it.

TO *The Editor of* The Athenaeum

Published 24 October 1919

Sir,

Your correspondents appear to have exhausted their commentary upon the 'Inaccessible Heritage'.[2] There is, however, one important branch of the subject which has not, so far as I know, been explored. The heritage does

1–TSE's lecture 'Modern Tendencies in Poetry' was delivered to the Arts League of Service on Tuesday 28 Oct., as VHE's letter of the 29th confirms, so this may refer to a separate social occasion.

2–In his unsigned leading article 'Our Inaccessible Heritage' (11 July), JMM complained that many English classics, such as the Elizabethan dramatists, were unprocurable, and suggested that the university presses, or failing them the government, should provide cheap reprints. Among the letters that followed, R. W. Chapman at the Clarendon Press felt that the public did not take the opportunity to purchase the classics already available. 'Experience has shown that even the nimble shilling was inadequate to create new appetites . . . the rate of

not include only the books we wish to buy and cannot procure; it includes also the books which we do not wish to buy, but wish to read and cannot reach. The question is whether the British Museum Library ought not to be open to readers in the evening, and on Sunday.

At present the Library can only be used by those whose occupation or lack of occupation permits them to pass their days there. The research of the professional scholar, the curiosity of the affluent, the affliction of the dotard, the idleness of the pauper – these may all be gratified or solaced in the Library; it can also provide a degree of physical warmth for the homeless. But for those who are regularly occupied elsewhere for even six hours of the day, the Library is useless; and among this last class, I believe, are many of those who might most profitably make use of it.

For this class there is one resource, if they can afford it: the London Library. The London Library, for a private library, is surprisingly good; its terms are generous and its manners gracious; but if one wishes to pursue any subject very far, it is, naturally, not inexhaustible. Moreover, there is no need for more than one complete repository of printed matter. The Museum might, as a test, be opened for two nights a week until ten o'clock. Some enlargement of staff would be necessary; if the Museum authorities would inform us of the probable cost of this innovation we should know whether such an expansion of the usefulness of the Library is beyond the means of the nation, which endures expenses of far less general benefit.

I am, Sir,
your obliged obedient servant,
T. S. Eliot

Vivien Eliot TO *Mary Hutchinson* MS Texas

Wednesday 29 October [1919] 18 Crawford Mansions

Thank you, Mary dear, for your nasty letter. I always love to hear from you. I hope your chill is better.

As Tom is not a French artist, or a Flirt, or Amusing or even Rather Fun, your absence from his lecture was no surprise to him. But I should have loved to sit by you and poke you in the ribs. Instead, I played the

---

production cannot be accelerated unless the demand grows in range and volume.' J. M. Dent, publisher of the Temple Classics, found that the works of Fielding, Goldsmith, Sterne, etc. 'hardly had enough buyers to enable us to keep the books in stock'.

Dormouse to Pasha Schiff's and his concubine's March Hare and Mad Hatter. They leaned heavily on either side of me, in the middle of the front row.

Dear Mary, thank you so much for giving me the opportunity of forwarding yr. invitation to my great friend Mrs Aldous Huxley.[1] You have a delicious sense of humour. Tom and I will come to your party with so much pleasure. I need not reply formally? need I?

You did not send me the film, little cat, even now. And I have all the latest photographs to show you, which are *kolossal*. They almost shock me.

I hope I shall see you at Edith's party, – you will know me by my paisley shawl.[2]

Goodnight my dear. When may I come and spend the night? I embrace you.

V.

TO *Edgar Jepson* — MS Beinecke

31 October 1919 — 18 Crawford Mansions

Dear Mr Jepson,

Yes, I should like that, as I don't want that lecture to go to press in this country until it has undergone your criticisms. I fully realised, by the way, that you forebore to press your point the other night, and was grateful, as yours was the one criticism which appeared to me damaging.

Unfortunately, we happen to be going to Marlow this weekend. This is what happened the last time you asked us, so instead of waiting may I ask you if the *following* Sunday would do? If not, we must try again.

Yours sincerely
T. S. Eliot

I am trying your lecture on *A*[*rt*] *&* *L*[*etters*]. If that doesn't come off, may I speak to Weaver about it?

1–AH had proposed to Maria Nys, a Belgian protégée of OM, at Garsington in 1916, and they married on 10 July 1919. MH wrote, in an unpublished memoir: 'Of the two Huxleys – Maria and Aldous – Maria was the one I loved . . . She always seemed to be sweetly scented, oiled and voluptuous' ('Aldous Huxley'; Texas). According to to AH's biographer, during the 1920s Aldous and Maria Huxley and Mary Hutchinson were involved in a *ménage à trois* (Nicholas Murray, *Aldous Huxley: An English Intellectual* [2002], 143).

2–VHE wrote in her diary (31 Oct.), 'Edith Sitwell's party. Wore my shawl dress. Fairly good. Dull party.'

FROM *Leonard Woolf* — TS Valerie Eliot

2 November 1919 — The Hogarth Press, Hogarth House, Richmond, Surrey

Dear Eliot,

I have been meaning to let you know that we have so far sold 140 odd copies of your *Poems*, and they are still selling slowly. The receipts up to date have been £12-14-10 and the cost £5-19-4 leaving a profit of £6-15-6 of which your share is £1-13-10 for which I enclose a cheque.

Yours sincerely
Leonard Woolf

TO *Edgar Jepson* — MS Beinecke

Monday [3 November? 1919] — 18 Crawford Mansions, Crawford St, W.1

Dear Mr Jepson,

I wrote and suggested next Sunday. I have not heard from you – but I now realise that I have an important article to finish by Monday and that I ought to stay in all Sunday to do it.[1] So might we come the week *after* (Sunday week)? I hope this is possible if you can plan for so far ahead, and please accept my apologies for this confusion.

Sincerely yours
T. S. Eliot

TO *John Quinn* — TS NYPL (MS)

5 November 1919 — 18 Crawford Mansions

Dear Mr Quinn:

This is to thank you for your kind letter of the 3rd October, long unanswered.[2]

I am entirely unexperienced in such matters, but I should have accepted any form of contract that you approved; the contract you enclosed is quite satisfactory to me. I have written to Knopf saying that I have received it

1 – 'Ben Jonson', a review of G. Gregory Smith, *Ben Jonson*, in *TLS*, 13 Nov. 1919, 637–8 (*SW*). It was TSE's first piece for the *TLS*, and unsigned (*TLS* practice until 1974).

2 – Quinn enclosed an amended contract for TSE's *Poems*, limiting Knopf's control of the copyright to ten years.

and that I confirm your action in signing on my behalf. I am sorry that I bothered you by an unnecessary letter of instructions which might just as well have gone direct to Knopf. I earnestly hope that my affairs will not take any more of your time and thought; if you took no further interest in them whatever you would still have earned my lifelong gratitude, which, I assure you, you shall have.

At your leisure, you can have the Prose in your possession returned to me. Some of it I shall probably use; some of it I shall certainly suppress; I do not want to use any of it without thorough revision. It is in fact a great relief to me that it will not reach print in the form in which you have it. Some of it I may work into a book which the *Egoist* will print in the spring, and which I think will be a series of connected essays on the Art of Poetry. But the nucleus of the book will be a lecture which I delivered last week for an organisation called the Arts League of Service, on Poetry.[1] It was one of a series in which Lewis spoke on Painting;[2] it was, I believe, successful, and I want to expand and continue this lecture for a small book. If I do something that satisfies me, I do not see why I should not offer *that* to Knopf as my next book; if he turns it down I am quit of obligation to him, and if he takes it I shall be pleased. It was the preparation of this lecture that delayed my writing to you. I am now at work on an article ordered by *The Times*, and when that is off I hope to get started on a poem that I have in mind.[3]

Again with most grateful thanks.

sincerely yours,
T. S. Eliot

TO *The Editor of* The Athenaeum

Published 7 November 1919

Sir,

Mr Pound's letter of last week[4] appears to me quite superfluous. It is perfectly obvious that he must have been indebted to someone, unless he is a Chinese scholar, which nobody supposes; I am perfectly willing to

1–TSE's lecture, given on 28 Oct. at the Conference Hall, Westminster, later appeared as 'Modern Tendencies in Poetry', *Shama'a* I: 1 (1920).
2–WL's extemporised lecture, on 22 Oct., was chaired by Bernard Shaw.
3–*The Waste Land.*
4–EP's letter, headed 'Mr Pound and his Poetry' (*A.*, 31 Oct.), took exception to TSE's review, 'The Method of Mr Pound' (24 Oct. 1919, 1065–6), of EP's *Quia Pauper Amavi.*

believe that his creditor is the late Mr Fenollosa;[1] but the gist of my criticism is that Mr Pound is less indebted to previous translators – Giles[2] and Legge[3] – than subsequent translators are indebted to Mr Pound.

As for his suspicion that I did not enjoy his Propertius,[4] I did not think the question of public interest: *his non plebecula gaudet*.[5]

I am, Sir, yours, etc.,
T.S.E.

TO *John Middleton Murry* TS Northwestern

[November? 1919] [London]

Dear JM,

Lloyds Bank Limited, 75 Lombard Street, (Bank Station), 1st Floor, *Information* Department, at 12.30. It is quite easy to find. Take a bus to the bank.

Will you please bring the Jepson article with you, if as I expect it is of no use to you, as I shall put it into the last *Egoist*.[6]

God from a Cloud to Squire[7] spoke
And breath'd command: take thou this Rod
And smite therewith the living Rock;
And Squire hearken'd unto God.

1 – As literary executor of the American Orientalist scholar Ernest Fenollosa (1853–1908), EP had edited his essay 'The Chinese Written Character as a Medium for Poetry', *Little Review* 6 (Sept.–Dec. 1919). In his letter to the *A.*, EP declared himself 'most decidedly indebted, if not to the Chinese, at any rate to Ernest Fenollosa's profound insight into the Chinese written character as a poetic medium. This debt is so great that I would not have it lightly forgotten.'
2 – H. A. Giles (1845–1935), Professor of Chinese, Cambridge University, 1897–1932; author of *A History of Chinese Literature* (1901) and *Chinese Poetry in English Verse* (1898).
3 – James Legge (1815–97), first Professor of Chinese, Oxford University, 1875–97.
4 – EP's book included the first publication in full of 'Homage to Sextus Propertius'. However, TSE was to omit 'Homage' from EP's *Selected Poems* (1928) on the grounds that it was 'too much a "translation" to be intelligible to any but the accomplished student of Pound's poetry' (xxiii).
5 – 'the common people do not rejoice in these things' (Horace, *Epistles* 2. 1, 186), a rejoinder to the Latin tag in EP's letter, '*Mollia, Pegasides, date vestro serta*' ['Muses, grant a delicate garland to your poet'] (Propertius, III, 19). The quotation from Horace is used as the epigraph to Ben Jonson's *Catiline*, which TSE was reading.
6 – Jepson's article did not appear in the *Egoist*.
7 – TSE adapts his own verses 'Airs of Palestine, No. 2' ('God from a Cloud to Spender spoke'), which probably date from 1917 (*IMH*, 84–5). Cf. Numbers 20.11: 'And Moses lifted up his hand, and with his rod he smote the rock twice: and the water came out abundantly, and the congregation drank, and their beasts also.' J. C. Squire had relinquished his literary editorship of the *New Statesman* to found *The London Mercury*, which he was to edit from

And Squire smote the living Rock,
And Lo! the living Rock was wet –
Whence issue, punctual as the clock
Land and Water,
The New Statesman,
The Owl,
The London Mercury,
And the *Westminster Gazette*

Yrs,
TSE

TO *His Mother* MS Houghton

10 November 1919 [London]

My dear dear Mother,

I wired to you day before yesterday, because I had not written to you for some time. I keep saying to myself that I should write just half a page, but the desire to write a really *good* letter is too strong for me, and I postpone it to the next night. And the trouble is also that I want to write you several letters at once: one about my and our personal affairs, one about literature, one about your affairs, and one just affection.

Now I have not heard from *you* for some time, and I am worrying about strikes in America. From what little is in our papers the situation appears very critical;[1] it is quite impossible here to understand what is going on or the motives of both combatants. But I see it always as it may affect you, both financially and worse than personal inconvenience. I have felt that at such a time I must have you over here where you would be safe. My dearest wish is that you may get rid of the real estate, and get east, and then I can come and fetch you to stay with us for months.

The particular causes of my being so busy have been two, of both of which I sent you notices. My lecture was said to be a great success. There were about three hundred present – the room was full, and a good many

Nov. 1919 until 1934. In addition, he edited *Land & Water* from 1914 until 1920 (when it was incorporated into *The Field*), advised Robert Graves about his short-lived *Owl*, 1919, and contributed to the *Westminster Gazette*.

1 – 'Coming on top of the steel strike, the dock strike in New York, and a large number of lesser strikes in all parts of the union, the coal strike threatens to paralyse the trade and commerce of the country' (*The Times*, 20 Oct. 1919, 13). By early Nov., 435,000 miners had gone on strike.

poets etc. came prepared to ask questions. I had, in a sense, both a hostile chairman and a hostile audience. The chairman, Binyon,[1] is a middle aged poetic celebrity who evidently knew nothing about me except that I was supposed to be the latest rage and he didn't understand it and didn't like it. He did his best, but thought it his duty in his introductory speech to refute – or at least deny – everything he thought I would say. I carefully avoided mentioning any living poet by name, which disappointed the people who had come to hear me praise Pound or condemn Rupert Brooke, or put my foot into it in any of the ways in which I might bring popular fury onto myself. There was a heavy fire of heckling afterward, out of which I managed to escape by the philosophic method of replying to any question by another question.

It took me a long time to prepare the lecture. I have sent it off to the Secretary of the Arts League of Service, who wants it for a Review in India.[2] I am going to develop the various parts of it, divide it into separate essays or chapters, and make a small book of it.

The other thing was a long essay on Ben Jonson for the *Times Literary Supplement*, which I have just finished; about twice as long as an *Athenaeum* review. It should appear on Thursday, and I will send it you. You will therefore be interested in the letter which I enclose.

I must stop now – this is already too long for a short letter! I will write again on Sunday, and I owe letters to Marion, Charlotte, Ada and Shef. The books have arrived, beautifully packed.

Your very loving son
Tom.

TO *Mary Hutchinson* PC Texas

Monday 10 November 1919 Crawford Mansions

Thank you for the card – I was sorry I could not come, but I had saved the whole day to finish an important article which I will send you in time – Just finished at 3 a.m![3] *À bientôt.*

T.S.E.

1 – Laurence Binyon (1869–1943), poet and art historian.
2 – TSE, 'Modern Tendencies in Poetry', *Shama'a*, I: 1 (Apr. 1920), 1–10.
3 – 'Ben Jonson'.

TO *His Mother* MS Houghton

18 November 1919 London

My dearest Mother,

I have sent you my *Times* Article, which the editor was very much pleased with, and you will see that I did another article on Ben Jonson for the *Athenaeum*[1] and one on John Donne[2] for this week, and now I am not going to write at all for a fortnight. I am tired from having to write three articles in rapid succession after the lecture. Vivien is very tired too. Her aunt [Lillia Symes], her father's sister, who lived in a small flat in Eastbourne, died very suddenly last week. They all went down there for the funeral, and as her mother staid on to put things in order, Vivien has had to go out to Compayne Gardens every day to superintend the servant and charwoman and keep house for her father and Maurice. Her aunt's sudden death was a blow to Vivien, who was fond of her, and a great blow to her father, as she was his last surviving relative.

Maurice, by the way, appears to be doing very well in the Ministry of Labour, although he has been there only a short time, and will doubtless become a permanent government official.

I shall do nothing for two evenings except read proof: two sets of proof have come at once, one from New York and one from the man who is printing a limited edition here at 25s. The New York edition will sell at $1.50 – about sixty-five pages.

This is one of my short letters – I am anxious to hear from you, very anxious.

Very much love
Your devoted son
Tom.

The [works of Thomas] Jefferson are lined up in my bookcase.

1–TSE, 'The Comedy of Humours', on G. Gregory Smith, *Ben Jonson* (a second review) and *Ben Jonson's Every Man in His Humour*, ed. Percy Simpson, in *A.*, 14 Nov. 1919, 1180–1.
2–TSE, 'The Preacher as Artist', a review of *Donne's Sermons: Selected Passages*, ed. Logan Pearsall Smith, *A.*, 28 Nov. 1919, 1252–3.

TO *His Mother* MS Houghton

23 November 1919 [London]

My dearest Mother,

I am glad to have had two letters from you lately. You need not be afraid of a collapse. I am still worried about the labour troubles in America, of which you do not say much. I ordered the *Athenaeum* to go to St L. some time ago, but I will enquire. *The Times Literary Supplement* is a good paper, and not expensive, but you must not expect to find me in it very often. I should only do the 'leading article' and no one person writes that more than six times a year. Abigail[1] has not yet turned up. I will send you a copy of my poems when they appear. I do hope the real estate will go, but not at a sacrifice.

Devotedly your son
Tom.

TO *John Rodker* MS Virginia

[Late November? 1919] [London]

Dear Rodker

I am sorry I was out, as you appear to have called or sent by hand. Here is the proof [of *Ara Vos Prec*]. Ezra showed me a page of the final setting up which pleased me: the paper is excellent, the type is good, and the initials have come out very well. I hope you are allowing to let me have a certain number of copies, to keep and to give to people who could not afford to buy the book in any case? inasmuch as I am not expecting to make any money out of it whatever.

I think Anderson[2] ought to pay for the poems if she prints them, tell her they were only given on that explicit understanding. She certainly won't get any more from me if she doesn't. Weaver is the only woman connected with publishing whom it is really easy to get on with.

Yours
T. S. E.

1–TSE's first cousin, Abigail Adams Eliot (1892–1992), sister of Frederick and Martha, was to spend a year at Oxford before enrolling at the Rachel McMillan Nursery School and Training Centre, London.

2–Margaret Anderson, editor of the *Little Review* (in which none of the new poems appeared).

TO *Ottoline Morrell* MS Texas

24 November 1919 18 Crawford Mansions,
Crawford St, W.1

Dear Lady Ottoline,

May we choose the 6th to come to Garsington (that is Saturday week), as you said either the 6th or the 13th would do equally well?[1]

We should like to see you again before then, if you are to be in town. I shall be busy until Sunday with various importunate affairs; but if you can, I hope you will suggest any evening after Saturday, and we could go to the ballet. I hope you are and will be in town. We enjoyed so much seeing you the other evening.[2]

Sincerely yours,
T. S. Eliot

TO *Mary Hutchinson* MS Texas

1 December 1919 18 Crawford Mansions

Dear Mary,

I think I will not come on Wednesday, but would rather you would ask me another time. – Vivien said to tell you not to tell the Sitwells that she is coming; and she hopes you won't ask any other woman. She also said that she very much enjoyed seeing you today. I look forward to seeing you before very long on some other occasion.

Yours
Tom

TO *His Mother* MS Houghton

2 December 1919 18 Crawford Mansions

My dearest Mother,

I have just got your card and have written off at once to the *Athenaeum* to ask for an explanation.

Now you ask several questions. You may give the photographic Natural History to Charlotte's children, with my best compliments. The Audubon is precious to me, and I want to keep it.

1–The Eliots do not appear in the Garsington guest book during the winter season.
2–VHE's diary, 18 Nov.: 'Ottoline to dinner'.

It is very thoughtful of you to send me a cheque £1.8.3. for my cable, which did not come to so much as that.

I thanked you for the Jefferson in a letter some time ago, and thank you now again. They arrived beautifully packed and in perfect order, and are now on my shelves. The freight shipment seems to cost as much as parcels post, as I had to pay 10s cartage on the books from Shef.

I have (from Shef) the remaining volumes of Boswell, and I am glad to hear that the other was not lost.

I am afraid you have subscribed to the wrong *Times*. The weekly that I wrote in you will have received from me: *Literary Supplement*. The other is a digest of news. The *Times* would probably arrange to send you the *Literary* instead – or you may find this interesting enough to continue. In any case I will see that you get everything I write.

'Westminster' is simply the district of London around Westminster Abbey and the Houses of Parliament, as you would say 'Back Bay' [in Boston]; Goosens[1] (Belgian extraction) is a musician, but I have never heard anything of his.

I should love to have pyjamas made by you. I need pyjamas, and it would seem to keep us nearer together.

I am still worried about American affairs insofar as they may affect you, and the sale of real estate.

Devotedly your son
Tom.

I have just had my photograph taken to advertise my book, and shall send you one for Christmas. He is a very swell photographer who charges £10 per dozen.[2] But he will give me a few at reduced prices.

1–Eugène Goossens (1893–1962), English composer and conductor, who had spoken on 'Music' at the Arts League of Service.

2–Emil Otto Hoppé (1878–1972), the best-known photographer of the Edwardian era; later a photojournalist; author of *The Image of London* (1935).

TO *Ezra Pound* PC Lilly

[Postmark 2 December 1919] [London]

'Ελέναυς!' <Who is Tyro?>[1]

I am absorbing this matter slowly. I regret missing you yesterday. Unless I hear to contrary I suppose I am to go direct to the Lady's[2] house (an Uncle Tom for your L'.E.[3]) on Friday and pronounce my name.

T.

TO *Edgar Jepson* MS Beinecke

13 December 1919 18 Crawford Mansions,
Crawford St, W.1

Dear Mr Jepson,

I have been meaning to write to you for some time, but have been very busy indeed. Both Rutter and the *Athenaeum* liked the content of the article,[4] but neither thought it quite suitable. I have now got it back after some delay and propose using it in the last issue of the *Egoist*, if you do not object. As Weaver is in rather a hurry before Christmas will you write immediately to her if you do object? But I should like the *Egoist* to have an article by you to its credit before it suspends. Are you never going to produce a volume of critical essays? (for the Egoist *Limited* to publish?)

Yours ever
T. S. Eliot

TO *Harold Monro* MS Beinecke

Tuesday [16 December 1919][5] 18 Crawford Mansions

My dear Monro,

My intentions were perfect, but here I have been for two days with bronchial cold, and the doctor today tells me not to think of going out till

1–Helenaus, 'destroyer of ships': an epithet applied to Helen of Troy in Aeschylus' *Agamemnon* (689). TSE is referring to EP's Canto VII, 'But *is* she dead as Tyro? In seven years? / Ελέναυς, έλαυδρος, έλέπτολις'. Tyro is a sea-nymph raped by Poseidon, an episode EP recreates in Canto II.

2–Unidentified.

3–The pious slave 'Uncle Tom', and 'Little Eva', a white child who treats her slaves with angelic kindness, feature in Harriet Beecher Stowe's *Uncle Tom's Cabin* (1852).

4–Jepson's 'lecture' on playwrights.

5–Dated by Monro.

Friday. I very much regret not being able to join you. Is there any possibility of your and Aldous H. being able to join *me*, after dinner? Though I cannot go out, I can sit up and drink coffee, and if the exertion is not too much, I should be delighted if you would.[1]

Yours.
T. S. Eliot

TO *Edgar Jepson* — MS Beinecke

Wednesday [17 December? 1919] 18 Crawford Mansions

My dear Jepson,

I enclose the Playwrights [lecture], which I have regretfully rescued from Weaver. But of course, if it is to go into the *English Review* it is better so, as the *Egoist*, in its present and final stage, is, I fear, only a not very decent interment for any article.[2]

We should very much have liked to come to tea on Sunday but that 1. my wife will be out of town and I too if I recover from the bronchial cold which is keeping me at home 2. We do want you to come here before you invite us again! And I hope that will be directly after Christmas.

Yours sincerely
T. S. Eliot

Vivien Eliot TO *Ottoline Morrell* — MS Texas

[December 1919] 18 Crawford Mansions

Dearest Ottoline,

I have been longing to answer your letter these last few days. I have felt so impatient to get a chance to sit down and write to you. I *loved* your letter. I quite see it might have been better to go to Margaret Morris[3] with yr. letter before Xmas but I *could not*. I have been a great deal too busy and I have been overtired and have had two of my migraines, (awful heads) which have taken two days from me. We had to go to Marlow from Sat.–Sunday – it tired me very much, but was rather fun. A man named

1–Monro reported next day that they had had a jolly evening but were too far away to visit TSE.

2–It did not appear in either.

3–Margaret Morris (1891–1980), dance teacher.

Sullivan[1] wrote and asked Tom about our house at Marlow, he wanted it *for a year*. So he and his wife came also, on Sat. to see it. But I will not let them have it. I dallied with the idea, but it is no use, for I should be *wretched* without it. I *do love it*. The idea of it – thinking about it and planning for it. It all means a great deal in my life. It appears you know the Sullivans! Well, I will tell you my impressions when we meet.

About [Wyndham] Lewis *I am sure* it is better for him to see Diaghileff in Paris, a little later, if you give him a letter then.

I was interested to hear about yr. weekend with Maria [Huxley] and Iris Moffatt.[2] Now you know you would like Mary very much if you knew her well, that is, if you like me! Because although you would not think it we are very much alike. Leaving out the sex business, which of course makes a vast difference. What suggested this to me was your saying you did not find much interest in Iris. Mary finds her terribly boring and uninteresting. I shall meet her, at last, next Tuesday at the Hutches, and shall find, I am *sure*, that I do not get on with her.

I wish *ever so much* that I could see you in your Xmas festivities, and that I could help you dance with the tenants, etc. I know how very tiring it must be. I think it is very wonderful of you to do it all. Xmas is awful, *awful*.

We are both longing for you to come to London. I keep saying to Tom 'when Ottoline is here we will do so and so'. I am thinking and planning about it all the time. You do not know how I admire you my dearest Ottoline. I hope we shall always be friends.

Are you better? Don't have people who are a strain and make you ill. *Why should you*? That is the great disadvantage of living in the country, surely. One must have people in great lumps, or not at all. And what risks!

Will you write directly you have time? Goodbye my dear. Be good and well – I mean happy and well!

Write soon. Love from us both

Yrs ever
Vivien

You are right. I dislike Yeats. Also he and Tom are ← → He hates Tom's poetry. His wife is a distant relation of Dorothy Pound's, I *think* Anglo-Indian people.[3] She has a good deal of money.

1–J. W. N. Sullivan (1886–1937), popular scientific writer and literary journalist; a close friend of JMM, and his assistant editor at *A*.

2–Iris Tree (1897–1968), daughter of the actor-manager Sir Herbert Beerbohm-Tree, had married in 1916 the American artist and photographer Curtis Moffat.

3–George Hyde-Lees, who had wed WBY in 1917, was the stepdaughter of Dorothy Pound's uncle. She was also a close friend of Dorothy Pound.

Do you really think Iris Tree's poetry good?[1] O Ottoline! Must we have Iris as a bone of contention as well as Joyce!

TO *His Mother* MS Houghton

[Postmark 18 December 1919] [London]

My dearest Mother,

This letter will, I fear, not reach you till after Christmas. I sent you an advance copy of my portrait in order that you might have it by Christmas. I will send you a finished copy if you will return that one, as Vivien wants to keep one. I wonder where and in what form Knopf intends to publish it!

I have been at home for a few days with a cold on the chest, but shall be out tomorrow. Also, my doctor has given me a special spray for my nose. I have apparently the same trouble that you had, and he says that if this spray does not cure it I ought to have the membrane cauterized. I always sleep on my left side because I breathe more easily.

I have just finished two articles, one for *Art & Letters*[2] and one for the last issue of the *Egoist*,[3] both of which I will send you when they are printed. Murry has been called to Italy to see his wife and I have promised to do two articles for the *Athenaeum* while he is away. But my New Year's Resolution is 'to write a long poem I have had on my mind for a long time and to prepare a small prose book from my lecture on poetry.' I have one or two other schemes but they are more in the air.

It will be Christmas in a very few days, and I wish that this letter might reach you by Christmas day. I shall think of you all day and Christmas eve. We shall spend Christmas here, and dine with Vivien's family in the evening. The following day I shall go to Wiltshire to stay until Monday with the Waterlows. Vivien did not want to go, but she wanted me to go in order to get a change of air. I think I have often mentioned Sydney Waterlow, whom I have known for the past four years. He is a very important official in the Foreign Office now, and was decorated with the Legion of Honour at the Peace Conference.

1–TSE called Iris Tree's contribution to *Wheels: A Second Cycle* (1917) 'the most mature of the lot' ('Verse Pleasant and Unpleasant', *Egoist*, Mar. 1918, 43–4). Her *Poems* were published in 1920.

2–'*The Duchess of Malfi* at the Lyric: and Poetic Drama', *Art & Letters* 3: 1 (Winter 1920), 36–9.

3–'Tradition and the Individual Talent' [II], *Egoist* 6: 5 (Nov.–Dec. 1919, 72–3; *SW*).

The peace treaty seems to be held up indefinitely in America.[1] I hope it will not prevent America from helping in Central Europe; the destitution, especially the starvation in Vienna,[2] appears to be unspeakable. I suppose Americans realise now what a fiasco the reorganisation of nationalities has been: the 'Balkanisation' of Europe.

I am praying to hear that you have sold real estate, and that affairs in America improve. I wish you were here now, for we could certainly keep you warm. You *must* come in the spring.

How do you like the photographs that Vivien sent?

She is in *fairly* good health, but sleeps very badly. We both send New Year's thoughts and much love.

Very affectionately
Your son
Tom.

1–The Treaty of Versailles, signed on 28 June 1919, was not ratified by the USA until Dec. 1921.

2–Lord Haig and others had just written to the newspapers on behalf of the government-backed 'Vienna Emergency Relief Fund', appealing for financial donations: 'The prospect of a city of 2½ million inhabitants being left without adequate means of keeping its women and children alive, or in health, must appeal to every human heart.' *N.* reported on 20 Dec. that 'the task of saving Vienna, one of the first cities of the world, from the horrors of starvation is urgent'.

1920

Vivien Eliot TO *Charlotte Eliot* MS Houghton

5 January 1920 18 Crawford Mansions

Dear Mrs Eliot

First I must thank you very much for sending me such a generous Xmas present (£3). I was surprised and delighted. It was so kind of you. Tom was very touched at your sending him so much, too. I have not written to you for a long time, as I have had a more than usually busy time lately, and a good deal of worry owing to my aunt's death and my Father's very bad health. Thank you for writing to me after the death of my aunt. I appreciated your kind letter. It was so extremely sudden that the shock of it was too much for my Father. His health has been failing very much the last year, and this trouble made him so much worse that we have all been most anxious about him. He had three sisters, all younger than he. And now they are all dead. They were all unmarried. I have very very few relations in the world, scarcely any. It is different to Tom, he has so many. The day before yesterday we had Abigail Eliot to tea. She is the *first* of Tom's relations I have ever seen – it does seem strange, after 4½ years. We both liked her very much. She seems a nice girl, and I hope we shall see more of her.

The next thing is for you and Marion to come! Do try hard. If you could come in *April*, just in time for the most beautiful time of the year in England. You would love the climate then, and the voyage would be less trying. Tom is longing for you. He *could*, we think, get leave from the Bank to come over to you within the next three months, but for so terribly short a time. He would not get more than three weeks altogether, and it would have to be instead of a summer holiday. Now that he is in a more *responsible* position in the Bank it is harder for him to *get away*, although the *work* is easier and more interesting for him.

The pyjamas you sent him are beautifully made. And so very nice. In the winter he really ought to wear rather warmer pyjamas. He has had three pairs of *flanelette* ones, but they are pretty well worn out now. He had to have a new overcoat this winter. It cost £10.10/- and is a very *very* good one. The best cloth, and lined with wool. Would that be dear, or cheap, in America?

With much love from Vivienne.

TO *His Mother* MS Houghton

6 January 1920 [London]

My dearest Mother,

We are shivering in a cold spell that came immediately after the Christmas holidays. Your cheques arrived on Christmas eve, and I thank you very very much for my generous present. I shall save up for a suit in the spring. There are many things to tell you about. We had Christmas at home with stockings and a tiny growing tree as usual. It was very difficult to find anything for Christmas presents this year, everything was either very expensive or non-existent. On the day after Christmas I went to Wiltshire to stay with the Waterlows. Vivien did not go because she knew that she would get very tired going such a distance for a short time; besides, Mrs W. is not very interesting. I am fond of Sydney: he has been very kind to me in the past. Lowes Dickinson was there: I never liked him much, he is very common, at bottom. But the rain held off just enough for walks, and the country there is beautiful, and Desmond MacCarthy,[1] who was living there, is good company. I don't know that it did me very much good, but it is a good thing to get out of town once in a while.

My salary has been raised £65, and as the salary of the bank has been raised all round, it brings my total to about £500. That would have seemed a fortune to me four years ago, but it is worth about what £250 was then. It takes all one's toil, nowadays, to earn enough more money every year to keep in the same place. The doctors have all raised their fees, and I am just paying a dentist bill of £14. Yet I am very fortunate in having got into the bank and being so highly thought of there – not only for the acquirements which they overestimate (I am supposed to be a profound economist, and a special scholar in French, German, Spanish and Norwegian) but in being liked. I was told by a high official that when some of the men who returned from the war presented a petition against the advancement of newer men over their heads, they made an exception of my case.

And then the difficulties of living are universal. The American professors must be having a very bad time. I wonder if America realises how terrible

1–Desmond MacCarthy (1877–1952), literary and dramatic critic.

the condition of central Europe is. I can never ~~forget~~ quite put Vienna out of my mind. And I have seen people who have been in Germany and they are most pessimistic about the future, not only of Germany, but of the world. They say that there is no hope unless the treaty is revised. I believe by the way that J. M. Keynes: *Economic Consequences of the Peace* [1919] is an important book, if you can get hold of it.[1]

Abigail Eliot came to tea Saturday, and we were both much taken with her. She seems intelligent, and has a sense of humour, and charming manners. She and Vivien found each other very congenial. Vivien had always longed to meet an Eliot, and I believe she thinks every day about you.

I shall have to stop this letter soon, so I want to put the most important thing of all. I want you to let me know as soon as you can whether you are going to be able to come with Marian to England this year. Because if *not*, I will come to America *early*, for a *very short visit*, instead of a summer holiday. But I must know in *good time*, in order to arrange. The physical difficulties in my way are, so far as I can see, these: 1. passages are difficult to get, and must be taken long in advance, 2. ships are at present very slow. I should want to come when I could get a fast ship both ways, or else I should have no time at all. I should also prefer to come when you are settled in the East, incidentally saving four days on the train. Also, it is at present much *cheaper* for you to come than for me to come to you, as the pound is worth only about $3.75; you get many pounds for your dollars, but I get few dollars for many pounds.

These are the considerations, but this is the issue: I want *so very much* that you should see us in England some time. *The sooner you come the better*. For *I* can come to America as well next year, or any year, or every year, as I can this. And for the reasons stated, I could come better next year.

But think it out carefully, mother dear, and then write to me fully. I am thinking of it constantly.

With very much love from us.

Your devoted son
Tom.

I am sending a complete photograph. Will you then send me the other one back, for Vivien?

I have not heard from Henry for *months*.

TO *Henry Eliot* MS Houghton

6 January 1920 [18 Crawford Mansions]

Dear Henry,

It is several months since I have had a word from you. Please send me a line of explanation, if no more, before I write to you. I feel as if this was going out into empty space. I depend on hearing from you oftener, and I have been anxious.

Always affectionately
Tom.

TO *Alfred A. Knopf* MS Texas

7 January 1920 18 Crawford Mansions

Dear Mr Knopf,

This is merely to thank you for your two letters – one acknowledging the proof – and to reciprocate your New Year's wishes.

I have no doubt the portrait has reached you by this time. Hoppé took two: the one I chose is very good.

I am glad to hear that the book will be out by March 15,[1] and thank you for the name of the press bureau.

Faithfully yours
T. S. Eliot

TO *Mary Hutchinson* MS Texas

Wednesday [7 January 1920?] 18 Crawford Mansions

Dear Mary,

I am ashamed of the meal you had to share, but I was very happy having you and I hope it will happen again.

This is to wish you *bon chemin* [a good road] for your journey. Don't get tired, and give my love to Lytton.

Yours
Tom.

I had forgotten all about the flat and will do so again.

1 – *Poems*, TSE's first American book, would be published in late Feb.

TO *His Mother* MS Houghton

11 January 1920 18 Crawford Mansions

My dearest Mother,

I have nothing of much importance to tell you this week. I have taken up the Muller system of <physical> exercises[1] before breakfast, and I think they are benefiting me. I have written an article for the *Athenaeum*[2] this week, and I am starting to put my lecture[3] into book form. <See announcement in the *Egoist*.> I dined with Murry night before last, just back from Italy. Next Tuesday we have asked Abigail to dinner with Arthur Dakyns, Sydney Waterlow, and a man named [J. W. N.] Sullivan who writes the science articles in the *Athenaeum*. Vivien has not been at all well lately – very run down – and has been in bed today.

I am sending you the final *Egoist*.

I am counting on your being here in the spring. I am frantically eager to see you. Vivien sends her love.

Your devoted son
Tom.

TO *Sydney Schiff* MS BL

12 January 1920 18 Crawford Mansions

Dear Sydney,

An extremely good postcard set you both vividly before me, but it was not needed for that, as I have had it on my mind for a long time to write to you. Just before Christmas I had a bronchial attack which laid me up for a week, and although I spent the holidays in Wiltshire with the Waterlows, (where it rained the whole time) I do not feel very well yet. Also Vivien got run down largely through nursing me, and she is not at all well. I wish she was in the south. I am hoping to hear that you are ever so much better and fatter than when you left. I hope you have been able to shake off all correspondence with its reminders of affairs in England, and if you are sufficiently rested, to concentrate on your novel. I have been

1 – These exercises 'for everyone from infancy to old age' were devised by Lt J. P. Muller, late of the Danish Tubercular Sanatorium, and endorsed by Roosevelt, Baden-Powell and Conan Doyle.

2 – TSE, 'Swinburne', a review of *Selections from Swinburne*, ed. Edmund Gosse and T. J. Wise, *A.*, 16 Jan. 1919 (repr. as 'Swinburne as Poet', *SW*).

3 – TSE's lecture on poetry, 28 Oct.; published as 'Modern Tendencies in Poetry'.

trying to start work myself, and it is very difficult when *both* people in a household are run down. You know that I have felt for some time that I have been devoting myself too exclusively to weekly article writing, and felt that perhaps I was losing both the energy, and the power of sustained thought necessary for a longer piece of work. Some time ago Miss Weaver suggested to me that I should collect all my *Egoist* articles to make a book. Then I gave my lecture, and the great fault I found with that was that it contained too many headings each imperfectly elucidated, and imperfectly connected one with the other. So I thought that instead of reprinting essays (a form of book making to which I am averse) I would boil down the lecture and the essays together into a small but constructed book. Now that I have got to making a scheme for it, I find that the difficulty will be to keep it small enough. I want it small – 150 pages or so – more if large type – both in order to get it done sooner and in order to make it a single distinct blow. I want to discuss 1. the modern public 2. the technique of poetry 3. the possible social employment of poetry. It strikes me that <if> people ever stopped to ask themselves what they wanted of poetry, the major part of contemporary verse would appear so obviously superfluous that there would be nothing to say about it. We have in modern society a huge journalistic organism <the 'critical' or Review press> which *must* be fed – there simply is not enough, nowhere near enough, good creative work to feed the 'critical' machine, and so reputations are manufactured to feed it, and works born perfectly dead enjoy an illusory life. If the whole journalistic fabric collapsed, as the economic fabric collapsed in Russia, innumerable 'creative' writers would go down with it. There are always a few good books which can stand alone, forever.

At present I see no sign of the journalistic machine collapsing. It is a quite suitable member of modern industrial society. I see no reason why it should not go on for some time developing, unifying and ramifying like Lever Bros. Ltd. Accordingly, you see, I consider a paper like *Art & Letters* a most valuable stand against it –

I saw Rutter the other day and he told me I should have proof soon. I must explain that I wrote the article[1] under great stress to get it in by December 15, the time you mentioned, and I am afraid it is not very good – certainly far inferior to the last. So I hope there will be other things so good that mine will escape notice.

The show which Lewis put on exhibition at Rutter's [Adelphi Gallery], at your suggestion, has some extraordinarily fine drawings in it. I hope it

1–'*The Duchess of Malfi* at the Lyric: and Poetic Drama'.

will attract notice. It is a pity that the room is not bigger. I went on the first day, and there were no visitors. Wadsworth's show at the Leicester Galleries was on the other hand crowded. With many more drawings, and a conspicuous gallery (I believe they are skilful advertisers) and more illustrative subjects – the Black Country – it seems to go well, and might attract more people than Lewis's, which would only interest people who are really interested in art. Not that Wadsworth's work was not very fine – it struck me as far and away in advance of any of his previous work.

Please do not mention to anyone what I have said about the contents of my book – I do not want other people, except yourselves and perhaps one or two whom I may consult, to have any notion of what I want to say.

Don't think you need answer this – you are too conscientious in that way – but do send me a card to say how you are and encourage me to continue this letter. With kindest regards to Violet and yourself from both of us.

Yours always
T. S. Eliot

TO *Mary Hutchinson* MS Texas

Wednesday [14 January 1920] Crawford Mansions

Dear Mary

I am glad to hear that you enjoyed yourself and didn't get tired, and that Lytton's life is so perfect. But it is a jazz-banjorine[1] that I should bring, not a lute. You apparently were sheltered from the tempest which made our lives miserable.

I wish we could come on Sunday, but we are *both* going out of town for the week-end – was it I gave you the Hindu Magazine?[2] But it is *much* more praiseworthy than the *Mercury*. I regret Sunday.

Tom.

1–'The banjorine (or "*banjeaurine*") was a small, high-pitched banjo' (Chinitz, *T. S. Eliot and the Cultural Divide*).
2–*Shama'a*, which carried TSE's 'Modern Tendencies in Poetry'.

TO *Ottoline Morrell* TS Beinecke

Wednesday [14? January 1920] 18 Crawford Mansions

Dear Lady Ottoline,

I understood that you were to be at Bedford Square today and tomorrow; I hope this is so, because I should very much like to see you again before you leave tomorrow. May I come in tomorrow afternoon at tea time, or rather, a little after 5, after I leave the bank? I will telephone to Bedford Square at noon, so that I may know if it is impossible, but I do hope you can.

I saw Wyndham Lewis yesterday, and he told me he was sending you his book.[1] He is leaving town on Friday, and I should like to bring him to call with me, if I may, as he is one of the most intelligent people I know.

Vivienne sends her love, and if she can get away from her wretched Hampstead [missing word] she would like to come too.

Sincerely yours
T. S. Eliot

TO *Mary Hutchinson* MS Texas

Sunday [18? January 1920] 18 Crawford Mansions

Dear Mary

Just found your note. We *thought* we were coming to dinner tomorrow and I trust you continue to expect us. I suppose it is at 8. Vivien will try to get to you about 7, but might possibly be delayed. She sends her love.

Your Tom.

You have a very suspicious nature.

TO *John Rodker* TS Beinecke

20 January 1920 18 Crawford Mansions

Dear Rodker,

I am sorry that I have not had time to answer your letter of the 17th sooner. Your scheme is an interesting one and I shall be very glad to appear as a Director if my name is of any use to you. Thank you for suggesting it.

1–Probably *The Caliph's Design: Architects! Where is your Vortex?* (1919).

I do not see any reason against your announcing that you have Edition de Luxe privileges for my works.[1] I don't suppose it would complicate any future contracts; anyway it is quite informal and merely amounts to my stating that I am pleased with the job you have made of *Ara Vos Prec* and should be glad to entrust my next book to your press – which is perfectly true. So I am quite ready to do what I can to push the Press, if this is any help.

Will you send me six copies when they are ready?

Yours,
T. S. Eliot

TO *John Quinn* — MS NYPL (MS)

25 January 1920 — 18 Crawford Mansions

Dear Mr Quinn,

I am not sure whether I have acknowledged and thanked you for your last letter. I have had a letter from Knopf to say that he expects to bring out my book on March 15th, which will be very satisfactory.

I am working at present on some old essays and a lecture, in order to make with these and other material a small book on the criticism of poetry and the state of poetry at the present time. Miss Weaver has announced it for the spring, and I hope it will be ready by April. I have had it in my mind for so long that I feel that I must get it done in order to be able to get on to something more creative. And I think that it is time some definite public statement were made of standards in the writing of poetry. If Knopf does well with the poems, and if the book has any notice here, I may offer it to him later. But the articles you returned to me I do not think I shall try to reprint at all.

I have just received a copy of the new monthly *Dial*. It struck [me] as exceedingly dull: I don't see why the *Atlantic Monthly* should need a competitor in dullness, and the *Dial* is an exact copy of it. There is far too much in it, and it is all second-rate and exceedingly solemn. The illustrations are appallingly bad. The proprietors sent me by a man who is here on business for Holt and Company a list of English writers from whom they want contributions. But it is hardly worthwhile to ask the best writers to send things over unless they know they will be published and

1–*Ara Vos Prec*, the first Ovid Press book, was issued in an edition of 264 copies at 15s, with initials by Edward Wadsworth.

how soon. The only way would be to have someone here empowered to receive and select.[1]

The *London Mercury*,[2] which started with a great deal of advertisement, will I hope, fail in a few years' time. It is run by a small clique of bad writers. J. C. Squire, the editor, knows nothing about poetry; but he is the cleverest journalist in London. If he succeeds, it will be impossible to get anything good published. His influence controls or affects the literary contents and criticism of five or six periodicals already. The *Times* always more or less apart, the *Athenaeum* (and, of less influence, *Art & Letters*) are the only important reviews outside of the Squire influence. As the majority of the *Athenaeum* contributors belong to a small set that dislikes Pound, this is unfortunate. I used my influence to get Lewis into the *Athenaeum*, and I think he is now pretty safely established.[3] But Pound would be a more difficult matter.[4] The fact is that there is now no organ of any importance in which he can express himself, and he is becoming forgotten. It is not enough for him simply to publish a volume of verse once a year – or no matter how often – for it will simply not be reviewed and will be killed by silence. Here in London a man's first work may always attract attention, because while he is unknown he has no enemies, but later it is essential that he should establish solid connections with at least one important paper. People like Osbert Sitwell are now much more prominent than Pound, simply because they are always reviewed. No one ever praises Osbert Sitwell's poetry, but all the reviewers mention it, and that is the essential.

As I consider that Pound and Lewis are the only writers in London whose work is worth pushing, this worries me. I know that Pound's lack of tact has done him great harm. But I am worried as to what is to become of him. I should at some time – when you have time, if you ever have any time – like very much to know your candid and confidential opinion about

1–The *Dial* had been a fortnightly for three decades, but was now monthly under its new owner–editor, Scofield Thayer, and publisher, James Sibley Watson. The visitor from Holt & Co was Lincoln MacVeagh (1890–1972), who had studied philosophy under Royce at Harvard. The list of desired 'English writers' included TSE, JJ, WL, Strachey and Conrad. See EP to Thayer, 25 Jan. 1920 (*Pound, Thayer, Watson, and The Dial: A Story in Letters*, ed. Walter Sutton, 1994).

2–*London Mercury* ran from 1919 until 1939, when it was incorporated in *Life & Letters*.

3–WL's 'Prevalent Design' appeared in *A.* in four parts from 21 Nov. 1919 to 16 Jan. 1920.

4–In fact, probably on account of TSE's influence, in Mar. 1920 JMM employed EP as theatre critic of *A.*, where he wrote under cover of the initials 'T. J. V.'. EP contributed on a regular basis from 19 Mar. to 21 May, when JMM terminated his contract.

Pound and his future, if you have enough confidence in my discretion to express it.

Osbert Sitwell tells me that Knopf is publishing his poems [*Argonaut and Juggernaut*] in the spring. Did you know this? I hope they do not appear at the same time as mine. Some of them are rather clever imitations of myself and other people.

I have ordered copies of the article and book you ask about (I was almost sure that I had sent you the latter), but as they are slow in coming I enclose the original proof of the article and a copy of the poems, from which I cut one out for Knopf. I will send you a copy of Rodker's edition, which ought to be ready in a few days.[1]

Always gratefully yours
T. S. Eliot

I hope to hear that your health is better, and that you occasionally insist on holidays.

TO *His Mother* — MS Houghton

26 January 1920 [London]

My dearest Mother,

I am very sorry to hear that you had to stay in bed, but I am sure that Marian will keep you there until it is quite safe for you to be up. I have heard that there is an epidemic of influenza in New York and also in Tokyo, so please go to bed on any curious symptoms appearing. The form that influenza has taken here this winter is intestinal. There is no fever or cold, but violent internal pains, extreme weakness, and in some cases that I know of, fainting spells. Vivien had a mild attack last week, and is still very easily fatigued in consequence. So take note of these symptoms.

The mails are still *very* slow. The last letter I have from you was written on the receipt of my picture.

I have just received a copy of the (New York) *Dial* in its new form. It is very dull – just an imitation of the *Atlantic Monthly*, with a few atrocious drawings reproduced. It is owned and run by Scofield Thayer, who was

1 – Quinn wrote on 6 Mar.: 'Thank you for ordering copies of the article ['Ben Jonson'] and book to be sent to me. The only copy that I got of your poems by the Hogarth Press was the one that you sent me recently with the Hippopotamus cut out.' But TSE was probably referring to the omission of 'Ode' from the Knopf book (see letter to HWE, 15 Feb.).

with me at Milton and at Oxford, and who is enormously rich. He has sent me a message asking me to get contributions from certain writers here (Pound, Lewis, Yeats, Russell, Strachey, and several others), but I am not going to complicate my personal relations with these people by asking them for writings unless I have a definite promise to accept what is sent. It is impossible for him to know, at such a distance, who are the right people and how to approach them, and he ought to have a permanent agent here. A paper like the *London Mercury* looks important at a distance, but is despised here. I hear that Hugh Walpole's novels sell well in America. We do not take him seriously; and personally, he is rather a bore.

Lady Ottoline Morrell has taken a house in London for some weeks, and as she is a great friend of Vivien's and has not been in London except for a night or two for some years, we have seen a good deal of her.[1] She is also giving Thursday evening receptions, and there has been a great deal of jealousy and excitement aroused among all the people who were not invited.

I am working on my book and on an essay on Literary Criticism which is to appear with two others in a month's time. After that there may be one or two bigger things that I want to turn my attention to.

I am sending you the photograph, and you can send the other back when you get it.

It seems to me that it would be just as economical for you to take a flat, if not a small house, in Boston as to run that large and expensive house in St Louis. I do not believe that your presence in St L. is essential for the sale of the property, and the present *suspense* and waiting must be very trying. Have you worked out (1) The expense of living in a very modest way in the east and shutting up the St Louis house, as compared with your present life. (2) Whether any of the *important* business requires your presence in St Louis.[2]

Always your very devoted son
Tom.

1–After the Eliots' most recent visit, OM recorded in her diary that VHE made her understand why some women fell in love with their own sex. Of TSE she noted (17 Dec.): 'his mind is so accurate and dissecting and fits in every idea like a Chinese puzzle, and my mind is so vague and floating and I feel he must think me such an ass' (quoted in Seymour, *Life on the Grand Scale*, 315).
2–TSE emphasised the last two sentences with firm marginal lines.

TO *John Rodker*

MS Virginia

1 February 1920 18 Crawford Mansions

Dear Rodker,

The Copies arrived yesterday, and I congratulate you on an admirable book. I do not think that a guinea is at all too much to charge for such a piece of work. I have not noticed any mistakes except in *Apollinax* and of course my own mistake about the title.[1]

Do you send copies to Pound and Lewis as if not I must present them? And I understood from you (didn't I) that Quinn had ordered several copies of all these publications. Still, I think I had better send him one personally from myself.

I notice stated in the back that ten copies are for review. What papers do these go to?

Many thanks for producing such an excellent book.

Yours
T. S. Eliot

When you have the copies ready for signing, let me know where the signature ought to be put. I have numbered the copies you gave me.

TO *John Rodker*

MS Virginia

6 February 1920 18 Crawford Mansions

Dear Rodker,

Thanks for your letter. I will come out and sign the books on Monday evening if nothing hinders, and unless I hear from you to the contrary. If Monday does not suit you, please give me two other evenings to choose from.

No, I don't think that Review Copies need be sent elsewhere, those three seem to me quite enough.

Yours
T. S. Eliot

1 – The title of the poem was misprinted as 'Mr. Appolinax'.

TO *Scofield Thayer* TS Beinecke

14 February 1920 18 Crawford Mansions

Dear Scofield,

I saw Lincoln MacVeagh a fortnight or more ago, and he gave me some copies of the *Dial* and some instructions from you. It struck me that he was far too much occupied with the business on which he had been sent by Holts to be able to accomplish very much; and furthermore that he would not be here long enough to familiarise himself with the London situation; and also that he did not have sufficient authority on behalf of the *Dial*, so I told him that I would write to you myself.

I shall be very glad to do what I can to further your designs. But MacVeagh was unable to be very clear as to what you wanted. Apparently, you would like me to show the *Dial* to the people on the list he gave me, mention the rates of payment, and inform them that you would accept anything they sent – whether appearing also in Europe or not. I know most of the people – at least in England – and could do this. But I should, you see, be incurring a certain responsibility in making such a request of people, and I should prefer to wait until I hear from you exactly what you want and what you offer. So I shall hope to hear from you.

Meanwhile, I have two suggestions to offer. I think, in the first place, that if you wish to make much of your English contributions, that you ought to come and inspect conditions here for yourself, and second that you ought to have a permanent representative here. I mean by the latter a person of discrimination and intimate knowledge of London letters, who would know everybody, and would have authority to fill a certain number of pages every month, and could solicit, accept, and pay for contributions on the spot. I think that this is as necessary for a paper as for a business house. People are much more likely to contribute if the matter can be pushed and settled on the spot.

As to your coming here, I think you would find it worthwhile to get a reorientation. If you only want to get people who have an *American* reputation already, in order to have their names to impress the American public, then of course the only essential is to pay enormous rates. But I rather infer from your list that you would like to have others as well – people who are among the best but not known in America as yet. Only a person on the spot knows just who these people are and their relative rating. It is a question of investment – if you were going to make an investment in English shares you would either come here or consult an English Broker. You have no idea how things have changed in four years since you were here.

I do not think that you ought to form any alliance or appoint a representative until you have been here yourself. For instance, you must understand that writers here are divided into at least two groups, those who appear regularly in the London *Mercury* and those who do not.[1] The *Mercury* has no standing among intelligent people, and the paper appeals wholly to a large semi-educated public. It is socially looked down upon – a point which is difficult to explain at a distance but quite evident here. Not many of the best writers here would care to appear in a paper which was closely associated with it, and some might decline altogether.

I introduced MacVeagh to Murry, who is the editor of the *Athenaeum*. It might be possible to get essays which appear in this: Santayana, Russell, Strachey, Lewis, Virginia Woolf, E. M. Forster, have contributed various series of essays to it.

Hardy and Conrad (to say nothing of France, d'Annunzio, Gorki etc.) have reached a point of distinction where they do not add to the *prestige* of any paper: simply because they are so well on that they cannot be considered by anyone as associating themselves with the policy or taste of a paper, and only occasionally contribute to any younger paper as a kindness to the editors.

I think you would want a similar representation in France. The more important men there would be such as Romains, Duhamel, Vildrac, Cros, Valéry, Vanderpyl, André Salmon[2] . . . But Pound knows much more about them than I do, as he lives in France a good deal now, and knows most of these men personally.

Also, if you want drawings etc. an art representative. Lewis, Wadsworth, John, Roberts, Sickert ought to be glad to have their drawings used. There are of course important people in Paris too: Picasso, Modigliani, Matisse, Marchand[3] etc.

The *Little Review* has been represented here (since Pound withdrew) by John Rodker (who is publishing a limited edition of my poems), and I hear that they are making an effort to collect money to pay English contributors.

But I think, as I say, that it would be worth your while to come and spend several months here, and meet people.

Yours ever,
Tom.

1–This etiquette was not observed by VW (*Diary of Virginia Woolf*, II, *1920–1924*, ed. Anne Olivier Bell [1978], entry for 31 Jan. 1920).

2–Jules Romains (1885–1972); Georges Duhamel (1884–1966); Charles Vildrac (1882–1971), Guy-Charles Cros (1879–1956); Paul Valéry (1871–1945); Fritz Vanderpyl (1876–1950); and André Salmon (1881–1969).

3–Jean Hippolyte Marchand (1883–1940), painter admired by the Bloomsbury Group.

TO *Henry Eliot* TS Houghton

Sunday 15 February 1920 18 Crawford Mansions

Dear Henry,

I sent you a few days ago by registered post a copy of my portrait (the one Knopf is using for advertising) and a copy of my Limited Edition. I have not sent this to Mother or told her about it. I thought of cutting out the page on which occurs a poem called 'Ode' and sending the book as if there had been an error and an extra page put in. Will you read through the new poems and give your opinion. The 'Ode' is *not* in the edition that Knopf is publishing, all the others are. And I suppose she will have to see that book. Do you think that 'Sweeney Erect' will shock her?

Some of the new poems, the Sweeney ones, especially 'Among the Nightingales' and 'Burbank' are intensely serious, and I think these two are among the best that I have ever done. But even here I am considered by the ordinary Newspaper critic as a Wit or satirist, and in America I suppose I shall be thought merely disgusting.

I am grateful to you for giving me so much news of mother. She gives it herself only in a vague and fragmentary form. I am interested in your suggestion that she ought to put the Mercantile Trust Co. in charge. I am always wondering whether it [is] really necessary for her to take so much upon her own shoulders, or whether it is not merely the family temperament – to do everything oneself and to put on climbing irons to mount a molehill. I am not in the least surprised at Uncle Ed, and the sooner she gets good lawyers, brokers, estate agents and bankers and has nothing to do with Ed the better.[1]

I have just written to her: I want her to take her summer holiday here in England instead of in Boston. I can see nothing against it. She will have to leave St Louis anyway for three months. She does not want to come to England until her estate is settled. I cannot believe that she would stand any serious financial loss by a few months absence, with you in Chicago and good agents in St Louis. I cannot believe that the difference between 1200 miles and 3000 miles matters so much as that. I know she wants to come, I am sure that it would do her a world of good, not only seeing me and seeing how I live, but the voyage, the change, the getting away from old scenes. I cannot see that expense, compared with the expense of my coming to America, can count at all. For she would be able to live in comfort here

1–Edward Cranch Eliot (1858–1928), lawyer. The family felt that he should not charge a widowed relative his full professional fees.

for much less than at home – the cost of living is less, and the rate of exchange would make her money go much further. I mean, of course, that Marian should come with her.

The only thing that I think is holding her back is the family Fear and Conscience – the feeling that she ought not to leave her business matters even for a short time lest something (unknown) should happen, and she might then have less to leave to her children. And the same feeling will make her go on postponing and postponing until it is too late.

Consider my position. I am thinking all the time of my desire to see her. I cannot get away from it. Unless I can really *see* her again I shall never be happy. Now if I come to America it will be nothing but haste, worry, and fatigue. I can get, at most, ten or *possibly* fourteen days with her. We should be thinking of the end the whole time. Vivien could not come with me because of the cost of the fare, and mother would never see her. Mother and I would both be simply worn out by it (and of course, it would be my only holiday for a year). Now why should not mother come here while she is physically able, and keep my visit to America until *she* is no longer strong enough to come? I feel sure that if mother could see things in the true perspective, look ahead and not see, in the Eliot way, only the immediate difficulties and details, she would make up her mind at once and come this summer.

I feel that I am struggling not against real material obstacles but against the family temperament. And I seem to see the relatives lifting up their eyes piously and saying that it is *my* duty to come to mother, and not proper for mother to come to me. As if it were filial piety to see her for ten days instead of ten weeks.

What she is likely to do is to wait until she has sold the house, and then wait until she is settled in Cambridge, and then wait until she has provided for Margaret in her absence, and then wait for something else, and like the rest of us, always put the little things in front of the big. The time for her to come is after she has sold the house, or *before* she has found a house in the East. That may take a long time, and why should she not take a holiday first? The point is that there are *always* enough things at *any* moment to prevent one doing *anything* important.

Will you try and look at this in a large perspective, even if no one else will, and then try to help me? This has been the greatest problem on my mind ever since peace.

I must stop now. I will write again soon.

Always affectionately,
yours,
Tom

TO *His Mother* MS Houghton

15 February 1920 18 Crawford Mansions

My dear dear Mother,

The last letter I have from you is one of January 27. It gave me pleasure of course but it did not answer my question. I wanted to know definitely whether you would come to England this year, so as to *arrange my holidays*, which arrangement is made in March. The point is that if *I* come I must *take my holiday* for it. I shall not get another.

I want to see you *soon*, not wait until conditions are perfectly favourable. Now just consider what it will be if I try to come to America:

I shall have to fix my holiday late in the year, so as not to conflict with others <in asking for a little more time>. I shall have to ask for a week or so extra, in order to have at most ten days or two weeks with you, and I shall have to take this *without salary*. I shall then have to hurry back after these *very few* days, having seen just enough of you to make the parting very painful. This hurried visit will have been my *only holiday* for a year, we shall be worried and distracted by the thought of time, and will be completely prostrated at the end.

Now is this worth it, while you are still *physically able* to come here? For you to come and have *time*, settle down for a time and live with us? Unless I can see you once again for something better than the breathless visit I have described, I shall *never* be really happy to the end of my life.

Is anything so important as that? does anything else really matter? Do you want to come?

Have you worked out just what you will lose in money by coming? Have you seriously considered putting your real estate in the hands of the Mercantile Trust Co, or some company like that <, and leaving power to Henry to act if necessary>? I feel that *time* is *more important* in our meeting than in the sale of property. It seems incredible that there is no one you can trust to do these things for you.

You will *have to come east* anyway for the three hot months – your children will not allow you to stay in St Louis as long as you did last year – *and if you can go as far as* Boston, *why not* London? Will just that difference mean financial ruin?

As to the expense. You have only to consider the *fare* – that will be double the cost of my coming to you, because of Marian coming too. That is the *only* difference. The cost of living *here* would be *less* than the cost of a summer in Massachusetts. 1) Because the cost of living is, still, lower than in America 2) Because your dollars would buy many more pounds than in normal times.

So please consider the practical question of a summer *here*, for you and Marian, compared with a summer in Boston. I say nothing about the benefit I think you would both get (after your worries of the past year) from the voyage and the change. I only repeat that if you cannot come, if I can never again see you for more than ten days or two weeks, that I shall never be happy. And if you come, it must be *quickly*, soon.

I do not want to speak of anything else in this letter. I am busy at the Bank, having been put in charge of settling all the pre-War Debts between the Bank and Germans, which is an important appointment, full of interesting legal questions. I shall have several assistants.

Your devoted son
Tom.

TO *Ottoline Morrell* MS Texas

Sunday [15 February 1920] 18 Crawford Mansions

Dear Ottoline,

I found your card on getting back from Marlow this evening. I should have liked so much to come tomorrow night, but I cannot. I am disappointed at having seen so little of you during this very brief visit, in fact, only having made the beginning of seeing you at all. For you, I am sure, the visit to town will have been an unqualified success. I hope we can make the most of Wednesday evening.

Vivien can come tomorrow night, and would like to, very much, but says that if you have anything else you care to do will you please wire to her not to come. She will come unless she hears from you. She is dreading your leaving, too.

Till Wednesday, then –

Yours
Tom.

I enclose the Phoenix letter. You could never go, of course, but if you know any people who you think ought to join, would you let them know? Do you think Miss Sands would take tickets?[1] It seems as if there ought to be enough people in London to fill the Lyric five times a year, who could afford to join the Phoenix.

1 – Ethel Sands (1873–1962), wealthy American-born painter; pupil of Walter Sickert and friend of OM. For the Phoenix Society, see letter to *The Athenaeum*, 27 Feb.

TO *Lytton Strachey* MS BL

17 February 1920 18 Crawford Mansions

Dear Lytton,

It is delightful to hear from you[1] sitting alone in Pangbourne 'like a Sage escaped from the inanity of Life's battle',[2] but I hear that you were lately in town and did not apprise me. So how should I believe you when you say you wish I was in Pangbourne too? Nevertheless I wish you were here. How extraordinarily difficult London is. One bleeds to death very slowly here. I find that Dryden is a very great man, and I am trying to read Clarendon's *History*[3] – is it a good book? Why are you distracted?

Yours
TSE

TO *Mary Hutchinson* MS Texas

21 February 1920 18 Crawford Mansions

Dear Mary,

I will call for you on Tuesday if that is convenient, as I do not see how to find any other time this week. I suppose you mean about 5.30. The only question is whether I might be delayed, and am excessively busy at the Bank; but in that case I should try to ring up 15 Henrietta Street and let you know.

Yours
Tom.

I enclose a letter from the Phoenix, in case you might care to join, and if you could show it to other people. It seems to me a very important thing to support. I am trying to do what I can; it is strange that there is so little interest.

1–Lytton Strachey wrote on 15 Feb.: 'How good, Eliot, your Blake article! It makes me feel the splendour of Poetry'; he was referring to TSE's 'The Naked Man', a review of Charles Gardner, *William Blake the Man*, in *A.*, 13 Feb. 1920; repr. as 'William Blake' in *SE*.

2–Thomas Carlyle, in *Life of John Sterling* (1851), described Coleridge sitting 'on the brow of Highgate Hill like a sage escaped from the inanity of life's battle' (69). Strachey had written to TSE: 'I'm here all alone – a little distressed and distracted – heaven knows why.'

3–Edward Hyde, Earl of Clarendon, *The History of the Rebellion* (1717).

TO *Harold Monro* TS Beinecke

21 February 1920 18 Crawford Mansions

Dear Monro,

Here it is, such as it is.[1] If I had made it any longer I should have found myself repeating things I have used elsewhere.

Will you send me proof?

I hope that you had a successful visit. I shall look forward to seeing you before long.

Yours
T. S. Eliot

TO *His Mother* TS Houghton

Sunday 22 February 1920[2] [London]

Dearest Mother,

I have had a particularly busy week in all ways. In the first place my work on German Debts has been very heavy. Next week I shall have an assistant and a typist to write my letters and do card indexing, but last week I have had to struggle through chaos myself, receiving hundreds of reports from Branches of the bank, classifying them, picking out the points that needed immediate attention, interviewing other banks and Government Departments and trying to elucidate knotty points in that appalling document the Peace Treaty.

My evenings have been busy too. Monday and Tuesday, working on a longish essay on Contemporary Criticism of Poetry which is to go to the printer this week. Wednesday, dined with Vivien at Lady Ottoline Morrell's, Vivien spending the night with her. Thursday, we had Osbert and Sacheverell Sitwell and Aldous Huxley to dinner. Made a bad break referring to Lord Russell's term in prison, as Osbert's mother, Lady Ida,[3] who is not quite right in her head, had the same experience. We went to Ottoline's Thursday evening reception afterwards, where there was a great

1 – 'A Brief Treatise on the Criticism of Poetry', *Chapbook: Three Critical Essays on Modern English Poetry*, 2: 9 (Mar. 1920), 1–10.

2 – Misdated 21 Feb.

3 – Lady Sitwell had been sentenced in 1915 to three months' imprisonment for debt to moneylenders, having been cheated by an unscrupulous middle man.

mass of people, including that charming old man Augustine Birrell.[1] A Japanese in costume got up and did a sort of hara-kiri sword dance, uttering horrid cries and disembowelling himself with a fan, and then sang the most dismal songs and wouldn't stop until some duchess or other who had brought him managed to soothe him with a cup of tea.

Friday went to dine with the Woolfs.[2] Virginia Woolf is a daughter of Sir Leslie Stephen, who knew Charles Norton quite well, and a very charming woman. Sydney Waterlow was there. He has become Lord Robert Cecil's right hand man, apparently, in the Foreign Office, and is very pompous and smokes cigars.

Saturday and today finished the essay I spoke of, wrote to Sir Algernon Methuen in answer to the letter I enclose,[3] and am writing to you. It is beautiful weather again, we have had no winter yet, all the bushes and shrubs are out in bud, and will probably be nipped later. I think I shall consult a specialist about my nose. The spray has done it no good, and I hardly breathe through it at all at night. Perhaps cauterisation will be enough, and perhaps something ought to be cut out. I think it's being stopped up is the cause of the peculiar pressure I often feel in the middle of my forehead. Besides, I think a stoppage in the nose is dangerous to the ears.

I must write a number of letters this evening to try to get subscribers for the Phoenix Society,[4] a society for producing Old Plays (Jonson, Dryden, and the like) on behalf of which I have been trying to fight against William Archer, who is down on it.[5]

This is only a little note. I will not repeat in this letter all that I said in the last, but I shall go on and go all over it next time. In your last letter someone had just come to look at the house.

Very lovingly,
Tom.

1–Augustine Birrell (1850–1933), author and politician. Through his sayings and *Obiter Dicta* (1884, 1887, 1924), his surname passed into the language as 'Birrelling': to comment on life gently, discursively and ironically.

2–VW recorded of the occasion: 'A happy evening. Eliot & Sidney dine' (*Diary*, II,21).

3–Methuen had written on 18 Feb., 'I am not sure whether your Poems would be likely to have a sale that is attractive to a publisher, but I should like very much to consider the possibility of bringing out a volume of your Essays.'

4–The Phoenix Society was founded in 1919 under the auspices of the Stage Society: see next letter.

5–William Archer (1856–1924), Scottish drama critic; champion of Ibsen in England. Of the Phoenix production of *The Duchess of Malfi* (Nov. 1919), he wrote: 'The privilege of listening to the Duchess of Malfi's beauties of diction was felt to be dearly bought at the price of enduring three hours of coarse and sanguinary melodrama' ('John Webster', *Nineteenth Century* 87, Jan. 1920).

TO *The Editor of* The Athenaeum

Published 27 February 1920

Sir,

The Phoenix Society, which has recently produced a play of Webster [*The Duchess of Malfi*] and a play of Dryden [*Marriage à la Mode*], is appealing to its subscribers, of whom I am one, to endeavour to secure more subscribers at reduced rates for the remaining three performances of the season. It appears that the receipts from subscriptions have been inadequate to the expense of the production.

The so-called cultivated and civilised class is not expected to relieve the necessities of either literature or painting. It is assumed that poetry only pays if it is bought by thousands of people one has never heard of; and that painting only pays if it is bought by some rich people whom one is not otherwise anxious to know; but a Society like the Phoenix can appeal only to the *intelligentsia*, and at a price quite within the *intelligentsia*'s means. Here then was an opportunity for the *intelligentsia* to declare its convictions: but the sounds are forced, and the notes very few.

Whether the performances have been good or bad has nothing to do with the matter. Apathy is more flagitious than abuse; we can almost condone the offence of Mr William Archer, whom we never supposed to be a member of the *intelligentsia*; we cannot excuse the torpor of people who would despise Mr Archer. The performance of Dryden's play seemed to me praiseworthy, and the actors had devoted hard work to a production which certainly could not add to their popular notoriety. But the point is that Dryden is a great poet and a great dramatist, and the Civilised Class has not supported the people who would support him, the Civilised Class has not supported Dryden against Archer. If, at the next performance of the Phoenix, the Civilised Class has not taken advantage of the reduced rates, I shall no longer be able to stifle my suspicion that the Civilised Class is a myth.

I am, Sir,
Your obliged obedient servant,
T. S. Eliot

TO *Harold Monro* PC Beinecke

Sunday [1 March 1920] [London]

My article ['A Brief Treatise on the Criticism of Poetry'] was not I fear a very good one and certainly not what it might have been under more favourable conditions; but did you get it?

Posted a week ago.

T.S.E.

TO *Harold Monro* MS Beinecke

[5? March 1920] 18 Crawford Mansions

Dear Monro

Here is a revision. You will infer from its form that it was done under the most unfavourable conditions. My wife being ill. I hope it is legible – I have tried to make it legible. I am fully sensible of its faults, but I don't understand your suggestion that you were 'meant to disagree'[1] with anything – I do not know what your opinions are, and I certainly should not choose this opportunity for attacking them if I did.

I have tried to prolong it.

Yrs.
TSE

TO *His Mother* TS Houghton

16 March 1920 18 Crawford Mansions

My dearest mother,

The mails seem to be very slow. I have your letter of February 8 and your letter of February 15 telling of the sale of the house. It seems very little to get for it; I can only explain it nowadays by supposing that everyone who would pay more for such a house insists on having one much farther out of town. I only hope that you will be able to get one as

1 – While admitting 'the article's full of good things', Monro had continued: 'I disagree of course with the "Campion, Dryden, Coleridge, Gourmont" statements and with some other things – with which, probably, I am meant to disagree.' All the same, since AH had submitted a short piece, he asked TSE to lengthen his by three inches – even though he had already noted 'a little padding' in it, 'or the extra page would look silly'.

warm and sound and comfortable in Boston. And also that in leaving you will not be tempted to dispose of too many things which you may want later.

You say that you will have to board, and that you will not be able to get a house in Boston before midsummer. Well, you evidently have not yet had my long letter about your coming here, as you make no mention of it. And you say in this that you might be able to come here next spring. Now it is certain to me that *this* spring, as soon as ever you can pack, is the time to come. You have no house, nothing but uncomfortable and expensive lodgings, and it would be astonishing if we could not make you more comfortable here. Just now, for a few months, you are free. You say yourself that you can do nothing till late summer. You would have just the best part of the year, the most beautiful season, in England. You will never again find it so cheap in England as it is now, because the value of the pound will rise by next year. And you will not again find it so easy and simple to come.

If I were dangerously ill I believe you would come no matter how inconvenient it was; so why not come when it is convenient even though I am not ill.

I might like, for example, to travel at some time in Spain. But I am perfectly willing to postpone it for a dozen years, or twenty, because meanwhile there are other things I want to do more. But there isn't anything I want more than to see you. If you could not come here, if I could only see you by coming for a few days, to you, I would not hesitate; and another year I shall. But I want to see you at least once for longer than that, for long enough to live together a little bit. And I want you to see England.

The future is always precarious. Something will always *appear* to stand in the way of coming at any particular time. It is only when something really serious does prevent that you will see that nothing serious prevents now. I am so convinced that no time will ever be better than this year that if you do not seize the opportunity I shall give up the hope that you are ever coming.

Yet you will only be one week's distance from me.

You see, you speak very vaguely in your letter about 'next year', as if it did not matter when. I have made clear, I hope, in the letter which you have not yet received, that I must arrange my summer *at once*.

So please consider everything, and read my two letters carefully, and answer. If you have any definite difficulties, please think them out. And then let me hear them. I want at least to have something clear to deal with.

It would be unkind not to give me at least clear reasons that I can understand. But we must not delay about it. I ought to know *now*.[1]

Always your very devoted son,
Tom

FROM *J. H. Woods*

TS Harvard

17 March 1920

Department of Philosophy and Psychology, Harvard University

Dear Eliot:

The time of year for new appointments in the Department is upon us. In spite of what you told me last summer I cannot help lingering over my regret that I cannot think of you. In any case, I should be delighted to have a word from you, and especially if there is even a slight change in your plans. It is quite an unworthy thought to tell you that members of the Faculty receive half as much again as ever before. I do not write this to you to tempt you, but that you may rejoice with the young instructors who are relieved from anxiety and pain.

Another year I must return to Aristotle, and if the remainder of the notes on the *Analytics* is not too great and too costly a demand upon your time, I should be very grateful for the labor which you would expend.

May I hope that perhaps you and Mrs Eliot may decide to visit Cambridge this year? It is possible that I shall go abroad, but I have not yet decided. Meantime, we have appointed Demos and Eaton[2] to instructorships. I am not sure whether they were your contemporaries, but I am sure you know Demos, if not both.

With best regards to you both,

Sincerely yours,
J. H. Woods

1–HWE would write to their mother on 3 May: 'As to going over to England, I have not been able to make up my mind. I thought at first that it would be a tax on your strength, but the ocean trip would probably be restful and I think your mind would be refreshed and taken off its worries by the visit. I have a short letter from Tom almost entirely about the question of your coming; in fact that is about all that he has written about to me for a long time. It seems to me now that the time to do it, if you do it, is before you rent a house in Cambridge . . . Tom seems to be worrying himself sick over the prospect of your not going; it seems to be on his mind all the time.'

2–Ralph M. Eaton (1892–1932), author of *Symbolism and Truth: An Introduction to the Theory of Knowledge* (1925) and *General Logic* (1931).

TO *Wyndham Lewis* MS Cornell

[19? March 1920] [London]

Dear Lewis,

I suppose you will be printing a brief rejoinder to Bell?[1] He has certainly not replied, but merely shaken his finger in the way indicated.

Do you ever see Wilenski? I suppose you are having an article in this week.

But what C. B. says does not amount to anything as a retort, and I understand that your letter gave several people considerable pleasure, so it is only ~~desirable~~ necessary, perhaps, not to let him have the last of it.

Yrs
TSE

TO *Ottoline Morrell* MS Texas

Sunday [21 March 1920] [London]

Dear Ottoline,

We both want to thank you very very much for your letters – they gave very great pleasure and it has only been a pain that we have not been able to reply. But a series of deplorable accidents has kept us from writing, from moment to moment. Vivien has been very ill indeed all this week; her stomach is altogether out of order, and she has never been without pains in the head. We have simply been living from moment to moment. I cannot tell you how worried I am.

You may be sure that we miss you in London, and that we both are glad to think how much better we know you for this winter.

Vivien has shown me your last letter inviting us to Garsington for Easter. You do not need to be assured that we should like that. It is always my difficulty that my holidays are so few and I always find several delightful things to do and have to make some sacrifice. My plan for months past has

1 – Clive Bell had attacked the Exhibition of Imperial War Pictures at Burlington House, for its poor quality and the 'hearty self applause' of the artists who believed their friends' praises ('Wilcoxism', *A.*, 5 Mar. 1920). 'At any given moment the best painter in England is unlikely to be better than a first-rate man in the French second-class', yet the critic R. H. Wilenski (1887–1975) claimed that WL was 'more than a match for Matisse and Derain' and the equal of da Vinci. WL replied (12 Mar.) that since Bell had written that Duncan Grant was greater than Blake or Hogarth, he was impudent to object to Wilenski's assertion that WL 'possesses certain affinities with Leonardo'. Bell repeated the comparison to Ella Wheeler Wilcox, who believed that her obscure friends were literary geniuses (19 Mar.).

been to take Vivien with me to Paris for Easter. I have only just been able to secure leave of absence for the Saturday – it is not a general bank holiday, and have therefore just begun to see about the passports. If it comes off we shall have at most three days there, but I do feel though, that it would be worth it. It is the greatest change we could have. Vivien has not been out of England for six years, and I believe that it would be very good for her. And I feel that the only way I can sustain the London grind, and prevent it from deadening my brain altogether is to take *every* opportunity I can of refreshing it in this way. Because it will be every year the same, and I *must* get into the habit of making the best of it – or rather get out of the mental habits engendered by routine work.

Especially because in order to contemplate going to Paris in this way means an effort of the will which few people not in my position could appreciate.

I have not discussed this with anyone else – do you think I am right?

So very few of one's acquaintance realise what it means to have sold the whole of all of one's days, – except at most a month a year – and old age – to a huge impersonal thing like a Bank.

What do you think of the progress of the Lewis–Bell controversy? To my mind, Bell has shown himself up in a way to excite only horror and disgust. It really makes me shudder. But I am afraid that the majority of people will not see through his 'stale' conjuring tricks, or refuse to take his clumsy affectation of superiority at its face value. What horrifies me [is] the *glaring complete indifference* to the question of Lewis's work. If I had never heard of Lewis before that would be self evident to me – Bell's prostitution of art criticism to vulgar spite. I wish that someone would write and suggest that what we should really like to know is his *opinions* of Lewis's work, his reasons for these opinions, and what works of Lewis he has seen on which to base these opinions. But I really can't bear to talk about it.

I have just finished an article on Dante[1] – under difficulties, as you may imagine: and I feel that anything I can say about such a subject is trivial. I feel so completely inferior in his presence – there seems really nothing to do but to point to him and be silent.

Vivien says to tell you she will write as soon as she can, and we both send love. I do hope you are still better than when you came back from Brighton.

Tom

1–TSE, 'Dante as a "Spiritual Leader"', a review of Henry Dwight Sidgwick, *Dante*, in *A.*, 2 Apr. 1920; repr. with revisions in *SW*.

TO *Sydney Schiff* MS BL

24 March 1920 18 Crawford Mansions,
Crawford St, W.1

Dear Sydney,

This cannot pretend to be an answer to all of your letters since I last wrote. But you must understand that there is no one from whom I more enjoy hearing than yourself, and no one to whom I should write more at length if I could.

All that you say about my work is a great pleasure and encouragement to me.

I only wish that Stephen Hudson appeared to have found Cap Martin[1] a release from preoccupations, and that he could manage for six months to cast them off wholly and write.

Now, I have had your letter of the 16th before me, recounting your difficulties with *A[rt] & L[etters]* which do not in the least surprise me. I know how little there ever is worth printing. I will send Rutter a prose and if possible a short poem as well but I can't promise this. But do <u>not</u> let *my* contributions go toward inducing you to bring out the paper when you have not enough else. I don't know whether you have seen the Sitwells on their way to Italy; but I don't suppose anything is to be expected of them when on their travels. They have left Edith as their literary executor. But unless people write prose as well as verse – or at least write verse of a very wide range of emotion and thought – they cannot exactly provide the backbone of a paper.

Certainly, no new material of any merit has come into my sight lately. The *Little Review* and possibly the *Dial* (which has lately been bought and is being run by a friend of mine) are the only American periodicals I know of where one can ever look in the hope of finding anything. I have no idea what sort of stuff is *sent in* to *Art & Letters*.

You must not mind pressing people. Lewis of course ought to devote himself to painting for some time to come. He has dispersed his energies far too much. His drawings, to my mind, have a *classical* quality, give me a conviction of permanence, that even his best writing does not. I am much interested in your comparison with Mantegna, because I have always felt that. Mantegna is a painter for whom I have a particular admiration – there is none who appeals to me more strongly. Do you know the

1–In his letter of 22 Feb., SS wrote that moving into his new house, 'Villa Violet', at Roquebrune, Cap Martin, had been exhausting. TSE refers to SS in the third person by his *nom-de-plume*, Stephen Hudson.

St Sebastian in the Franchetti's house on the Grand Canal? I imagine somehow that you must know the Franchetti family.

I should like to know how long you intend to stay in Roquebrune. Are you coming north, to Paris, or are you coming to England for the summer season?

With kindest regards to Violet

Affectionately
T. S. Eliot

I met Major Douglas[1] not long ago at Pound's and liked him. His book is interesting, but fearfully difficult and obscurely written.

I agree with what you say about contemporary English periodicals. Be sure that I have it on my mind to do all *I* can for *A&L* and I think I see most of your difficulties pretty well.

The *Chapbook* I am sending is an essay written hastily and spasmodically over considerable time. All I can say is that it contains a few ideas which I want to make better use of later. I shall want to know your opinion of my Dante (*Athenaeum*).

Write to me about Hudson.

I want to write to you a separate letter about Tchehov.

TSE

TO *Mary Hutchinson* MS Texas

Thursday [25 March 1920]

Dear Mary,

I should like very much to meet Tonks,[2] and I shall come to supper on Sunday with great pleasure.

I have had your enquiry in mind and should have answered it before now if I had had time. Perhaps I can answer more intelligibly verbally.

Yrs.
Tom.

And I have a question to ask Jack.
I suppose you are at River House [in London], not at Wittering.

1–C. H. Douglas (1879–1952), a British engineer, conceived the theory of Social Credit, which meant supplementing the amount of money available to consumers to enable them to buy all the goods produced. *Economic Democracy* (1920) was enthusiastically reviewed by EP (*Little Review*, Apr. 1920); and in the 1930s both *New Age* and *New English Weekly* supported Social Credit.

2–Henry Tonks (1862–1937), Professor of Fine Art at the Slade, 1917–30, a champion of traditional drawing who considered Augustus John 'the greatest draughtsman since Michelangelo'. He taught WL, and was a friend of the Hutchinsons (he had exhibited a pastel of MH at the New English Arts Club, 1913).

TO *Scofield Thayer* TS Beinecke

26 March 1920 18 Crawford Mansions

Dear Scofield,

I am appreciative of your thoughtfulness in cabling to me; my reply will have made evident to you that I found your question difficult to answer. I know Cummings[1] only as a contributor to the two numbers of the *Dial* that I have seen, and the writer (in one of them) of a critical article on a man whom I know nothing about.[2] I could have suggested someone in England – Huxley, for example – but that I supposed you would not want the delay of giving the book to an English reviewer. But as you were so astute as to take it away from Untermeyer[3] and not let it be engulphed in a common fate with Osbert Sitwell's, I feel that I am perfectly safe in leaving it to your discretion. In spite of my personal affection for Osbert, I should certainly prefer to be reviewed separately.

I will discuss the matter with Pound and enquire his intentions the next time I see him. I shall willingly let you print anything of mine that appears here that seems to me worth reprinting. I have so little time that I shall not often be able to offer entirely fresh material. I have two sets of essays in contemplation at present; and if you come across anything of mine in any English paper that you would care to reprint either verbatim or in a somewhat altered form, let me know about it.

I am sorry that you cannot come to England this summer, and I hope that the affairs of the *Dial* will take such a direction that you will at least be able to come in the autumn.

Always cordially,
Tom.

1 – Thayer had cabled to say he had asked the poet and artist E. E. Cummings (1894–1962) to review *Poems*. TSE did not realise that Cummings had played Second Footman to his Lord Bantock in *Fanny and the Servant Problem*, 1913 (letter to Eleanor Hinkley, 3 Jan. 1915). However, Cummings, who had been at Harvard at the same time as TSE, remembered that the hero had been brilliantly played by a 'cold and aloof' person. See his review of *Poems*, in *Dial* 68: 6 (June 1920).

2 – Cummings had contributed some poems and drawings to *Dial* 68: 1 (Jan. 1920), and an article on Gaston Lachaise (1882–1935), the French-born American sculptor (who in 1924 would execute a bust of Cummings), to *Dial* 68: 2 (Feb. 1920).

3 – Louis Untermeyer (1885–1977), poet and anthologist. His review of *Poems* showed how Sitwell, in *Argonaut and Juggernaut,* 'frankly models his new quatrains on the plan of "Sweeney Among the Nightingales"' (*Freeman*, 30 June 1920).

TO *Henry Eliot*[1] TS Houghton

26 March 1920 18 Crawford Mansions

Dear Henry,

I have not written to you for some time, except a long letter about mother and my anxiety that she should visit England as soon as possible; to which I hope I shall soon have a reply from you. It has been much more on my mind than you can imagine, and has been infinitely exasperating. Mother's mention of the subject so far has been vague and procrastinating, meanwhile I cannot make any plans or arrangements for our summer, which I ought to have done already, and I see the time slipping by. I told her that when she sold the house and began to move east would be exactly the most suitable time in her whole life to come, and now she has sold the house, and wants to wait until she is settled in Boston. And I have not heard from her for a fortnight now. I wish *you* could make her see that *this* is an opportunity that may not come again. It is almost impossible for any of our family to make up their minds. In a few years she may be too infirm to come, and then she will regret not having come now, and I shall regret it all the rest of my life. Just now she is or should be free – she will never be any freer; and if she would only examine the future, and her own state of mind, she would find I think that the latter exhibits the same procrastination and hesitation that she has deplored in her father and in her children. Will you try to see how I look at the situation?

I am returning the letters which you asked for.[2] At the same time I must say this: that I think, as you had enough confidence in me to write to me so fully once, you ought in fairness to me to write more fully now. If you think that I cared then – and I think you would not have written as you did unless [illegible words] of sympathy you could not have had from anyone else – I think you ought to realise that I still feel and think a great deal about you. If I thought that you had written merely to relieve yourself to somebody, merely to write a letter about you, I should not easily forgive your giving so much pain; but I do not think that.

I have another letter from you, written two years ago shortly after the first, in which you wished to retract much of what you had said. You have never in all the time referred to it again. It has seemed to me that for some time past you have written much less frequently, and much more impersonally when you did write, and without very much curiosity in my

1 – Text taken from an unreliable photocopy of a transcript; the original is mislaid.

2 – On 25 Dec. 1919, HWE had written: 'About February 1, 1918, I sent you a long letter, about 25 pages long, with enclosure of a note. Will you send that back to me?'

affairs. You say that you are ashamed of yourself, because you [are] too 'introspective' and 'garrulous'. On the contrary, I felt rather that I wanted to know more about your life than you told me, because I am always trying to picture and imagine it. What I found was more unhappiness than introspection.[1]

If you interpreted my silence correctly, you saw that it meant that I thought the thing was done with, and if so there was no need for anything more to be said. If it was not done with, I think that you might let me know, and what I want to know now is whether you still see her.

I may say that I have kept quite distinct the impression I got of the person and the impression I got of the affair. And I was sure that giving her every good quality, she was still bad for you, and you could never be good for her, and that the only healthy solution was for it to drop altogether. Nothing shocks me except morbidity, and I know that a morbid relation never becomes a healthy one. I live among a set of people some of whom would probably shock your friends (all of them) terribly by varieties of 'immorality' with no pretense; but these people are capable of being shocked in the way that I am. (They may consider myself and Vivien exceptionally moral, but they do not think any the worse of us for that – it merely seems to them interesting).

[Incomplete]

TO *John Quinn* — MS NYPL (MS)

26 March 1920 — 18 Crawford Mansions

Dear Mr Quinn,

Thank you very much indeed for your letter of the 6th instant, received yesterday.[2] I shall always be conscious of my very great obligations to you, and I shall not forget that but for you the book would never have been published at all.

I am very glad that Thayer is in contact with you and I hope that he will make something good out of the *Dial*. It is free from some of the

1–HWE had written: 'I wish that I might give you a picture of myself, in my present environment (Chicago). I am not sure whether it would interest you, bore you, or puzzle you. Your attitude might be somewhat like that of a naturalist studying a colony of ants. I have a horror of your ceasing altogether to think of me as a sentient, rational, self-conscious being.'

2–Quinn wrote on 6 Mar.: 'Your book of poems was published a week ago. I have already bought 35 copies . . . I read it aloud on two evenings to friends of mine, and made converts of both.'

drawbacks of the *Little Review*; whether it has others of its own I do not know. Certain criticisms came to my mind at once, of course. It struck me as having far too much in it: one cannot keep so bulky a paper up to a very high standard, and the good stuff might easily be swamped. I thought there were too many articles, all flung in on the same footing; and that it ought to be split up into departments to be made more readable. The *London Mercury* is a despicable volume, but it is well arranged and its appearance is attractive. I warned Thayer against taking the *Mercury* seriously, or entering into close relations with it. That would damage the *Dial* in the eyes of the better English writers.

I am glad you suggested Pound. I will ask him about your letter and his intentions. At any rate it will cheer him up a bit. He has just finished a new long poem which I think has some very good things in it.[1]

Thayer has just cabled to me to ask if Cummings should review my book. I cabled back (at his request) to say that I know nothing whatever about Cummings, and I took the liberty of asking him to consult you.[2] I dislike always putting any further burden on your shoulders (I do not understand how you accomplish as much as you do) but I really could not think of anyone else in New York whose opinion I could trust. I could have suggested someone in London. Middleton Murry or Aldous Huxley even – but I thought that probably Thayer wanted the review done at once, and that perhaps having the review appear a month earlier would be an advantage. In any case I suppose the book will be given to someone who likes it. Thayer tells me in a letter I have today that he rescued it from Untermeyer, who wanted to review it with Osbert Sitwell. It seems rather astute of Thayer to have stopped this. I know little of Untermeyer, but Heaven preserve me from being reviewed in the company of Osbert. I may say that any poems of his which appear to have any affinity with any of mine were published *subsequent* to mine.

Rodker told me that you had ordered three signed copies of his edition, so that I thought it might be no particular gratification to you to receive another from me; but I have one that I kept for you, if you wish it.

A serious operation is, I know, something that can upset the nerves for a very long time, and I fear you draw upon your nerves pretty heavily. You

1 – EP, *Hugh Selwyn Mauberley*, published by the Ovid Press in June 1920.
2 – On 24 Sept. 1920, Quinn would tell TSE that Cummings's review in the June *Dial* was 'horrible, a sheer bit of impertinence and not at all likely to help its sale. It is most annoying.'

must have the foundation of a strong constitution, but I hope that you really are regaining strength as well.

Very cordially yours
T. S. Eliot

I am gradually putting a prose book together – I think much more solid than the first attempt; and there is a possibility of getting a good publisher to take it here. But London 'good publishers' are very cautious.

TO *Mary Hutchinson* PC Texas

[Postmark 4 April 1920][1] Paris

Nous y sommes. Quel dommage que vous n'êtes pas ici pour les Pâques. Où passez vous le dimanche? Paris est si *gai*. Nous esperons voir Jack mais le temps est court et nous avons à voir tout.[2] Je pense que nous ne pouvons peut-être pas le voir.

T. S. E.[3]

TO *Ottoline Morrell* MS Texas

Saturday 10 April 1920 [London]

Dear Ottoline,

I opened your letter to Vivien as she is not here. Although we were very happy in Paris, I had the misfortune to get a slight attack of flu, and couldn't get back until Tuesday night. It was very worrying and exhausting to Vivien having me on her hands in Paris, and having to fetch a doctor, get medicines etc., and the journey back was very trying for her. So as she had an opportunity to go away for a few days and rest she went away with some friends. I am really quite right again, except for feeling very weak and low spirited, especially at the thought of having used more than the money I had put aside for the visit with so little profit. But now I shall have to work hard as I have promised to submit a book to a publisher in June, and shall be hard pressed to get it done in time. Please don't mention this to anybody as it is a secret.

1 – Easter Day.
2 – On 21 Mar. TSE told OM that he and VHE would have only three days in Paris.
3 – *Translation*: We are there. What a pity you aren't here for Easter. Where are you spending Sunday? Paris is so *gay*. We hope to see Jack but the time is so short and we want to see everything. I think that perhaps we won't be able to see him. T. S. E.

Vivien will be back I think on Thursday and I expect she will be writing to you. She too will have to stay in town and work after that. I do hope that you will come to town again very soon (and stay the night) as otherwise it will be so difficult to see you for some time.

Yours always
Tom.

TO *Mary Hutchinson* — MS Texas

Monday [12 April 1920]

Mary, how charming of you to ask us to dinner, and how we shall both enjoy seeing you again. Vivien is not here just now and she will grumble if I go without her; *also* this week is very difficult for me – especially after the most depressing adventure which Paris turned out to be – so will you please not be nasty, and invite us for next week and write and mention a day? I had influenza in Paris so please be kind, Mary. Let us come next week and have one of our good talks. Love to Jack.

Tom.

TO *Mary Hutchinson* — MS Texas

Thursday [15 April 1920]

Mary, thank you for suggesting another day but I think Thursday is best after all so we will come *Thursday* if you please. And so will you wear the cotton earrings and look nice and be nice and we will talk a great deal. Looking forward to the outing.

Tom.

I see your friend Toulet has turned up in the *Times*.[1]

1 – Paul-Jean Toulet (1867–1920), journalist, poet and novelist. His novel *La Jeune Fille Verte* was reviewed in the *TLS*, 15 Apr. 1920.

TO *Clement Shorter*[1] MS Beinecke

19 April 1920 18 Crawford Mansions

Dear Mr Shorter,

I am pleased and flattered that you should want my book. The address [of the Ovid Press] is 43 Belsize Park Gardens, N.W.3.

I remember also with pleasure the occasion on which I dined with you.

Sincerely yours
T. S. Eliot

TO *John Middleton Murry* MS Northwestern

[19 April? 1920] [London]

Dear John,

I have not quite finished my article on you;[2] it turns out to be much longer than I expected; but I should have it for you on your return. You have left one or two '*pièces d'identité*' [identity papers] in our hands. I suppose you are going in the morning.

Did I hear you say once you had a Beaumont and Fletcher complete you were willing to dispose of? I should like to buy it from you, or if you want a complete Ford and Massinger I have seen one today which I could post haste to get for you. I need a B & F for my Massinger article and want to own one and can't get one anywhere.[3]

Bonne chance.

TSE

TO *The Editor of* The Times Literary Supplement

Published 22 April 1920

Sir,

Your reviewer of last week handled my Essay on the Criticism of Poetry[4] with more courteous clemency than this defective composition deserved.

1 – Clement Shorter (1857–1926), journalist and author.
2 – 'The Poetic Drama', a review of JMM's *Cinnamon and Angelica*, *A.*, 14 May 1920.
3 – 'Philip Massinger', a review of A. H. Cruickshank, *Philip Massinger*, *TLS*, 27 May 1920 (*SW*).
4 – 'The Criticism of Poetry', *TLS*, 15 Apr. 1920, a review of *Chapbook* 2: 9: *Three Critical Essays* (which included TSE's 'A Brief Treatise on the Criticism of Poetry').

My essay contains much matter that should be erased and much that should be reformed; it is incoherent and inexact. I should therefore not affect amazement at learning that the view of criticism detailed in the first paragraph of your reviewer's article is supposed to be the opposite of mine or at hearing given as my opinion that 'a poet ought not to know what he is doing, but should just do it.' I can only apologise to the reviewer for the obscurity which has induced him to this interpretation.

I must say, however, that your reviewer's notions of criticism are not much more satisfactory to me than my own. I suppose that it will be admitted that, with one or two exceptions in remote antiquity, all the best criticism of poetry is the criticism of poets; and I am not prepared to concede that the criticism of Dryden, or of Coleridge, or even Matthew Arnold has the 'intellectual incoherence' which the reviewer says is the 'innocent defect of art' and apparently the inevitable vice of criticism written by poets. The review's use of the word 'philosopher' seems to point not to Aristotle so much as such persons as Hegel and Croce. I am not sure that your reviewer distinguishes the mind which endeavours to generalise its impressions of literary beauty from the mind which endeavours to support a theory of aesthetics by examples drawn from the arts. Schopenhauer, I seem to remember, admired the Apollo Belvedere because the head – the spiritual residence – appeared to strive to detach itself from the body. In general, philosophers (or professors of philosophy) are as ignorant of poetry as of mathematics; and the fact that they have read much poetry is no more assurance of competence in criticising poetry than their ability to reckon in shillings and pence is of their competence to criticise mathematicians.

It would be helpful if your critic would elucidate his use of the term 'philosophy'. My chief reason for writing this letter is my desire that the problems of critical principles should be more pondered and discussed, and that both critics and readers should apply themselves to consider the nature of criticism.[1]

I am, Sir, your humble servant
T. S. Eliot

1–Unknown to TSE, the reviewer was Arthur Clutton-Brock, who did not respond to this letter. However, in an unsigned article, 'The Function of Criticism' (13 May), JMM disagreed with TSE's assertion that poets are the best critics.

TO *John Middleton Murry* MS Northwestern

Sunday [25? April 1920]

18 Crawford Mansions,
Crawford St, W.1

Dear John,

Thank you *very much*. I have appreciated your thought of me, though I have never said much about it. Well, I have lectured, as you know, and it was very very fatiguing and worrying to me, and this is a provincial university too. If I ever took the plunge, it would be, I suppose, for the freedom of journalism: but just now I feel too tired and depressed to put my mind on it.

This is unsatisfactory to you and will appear ungracious. I would much rather have had a talk with you. I am going, from Tuesday, to live in Marlow for three or four weeks, and hope both to rest and to work. I don't want to be in town for the evening more than I can help. I wish you could lunch with me one day and after I have done two articles we should dine.

Thanks for B & F which I shall take care of and return in due course. I shall want to know how much you enjoyed Stratford. We are looking forward to seeing Katherine [Mansfield; JMM's wife].[1]

Yours aff.
TSE

TO *John Quinn* TS NYPL (MS)

10 May 1920

18 Crawford Mansions

Dear Mr Quinn,

I do not know whether I wrote to thank you for your kind letter about my book. I must repeat my gratitude to you.

I was delighted at your prompt and effective intervention with the *Dial*.[2] I think Pound will make a good job of it. I can testify that it had a great effect in raising his spirits; and when he left for Italy he was most cheerful. In addition, he has just finished what seems to me a very good poem, so my mind is at rest about him.

I have contracted with Methuen, here, for a prose book of essays [*SW*], to be in his hands if possible by the end of June. He is one of the best

1–Katherine Mansfield: see Glossary of Names.

2–*The Dial* was paying EP $750 a year as its agent, and soon he became its Paris correspondent.

London publishers, so I am pleased. In conformity with my contract with Knopf, I put in a clause stating that the option on American sheets should be offered to him, so I suppose that is all right?[1] I presume that if Methuen and Knopf fail to come to terms, that is nothing to do with me, though I should be glad for Knopf to have it.

I hope you will be having a holiday before long. I am feeling rather washed out myself, with practical worries like the impossibility of getting a tolerable flat to live in at a possible price, health, whether I should stick to banking if a good journalistic post turned up, and other such problems.

With sincere good wishes for your health

Yours cordially
T. S. Eliot

TO *John Rodker* — MS Mrs Burnham Finney

16 May 1920 [London]

Dear Rodker,

I have done what I could – you needn't take my word for it, but it does not look promising. M[onro] does not see how he could review such a book for the ordinary public – he doesn't want to curse it and wouldn't venture to praise it.[2] *A fortiori*, the *Times* would be worse.

The best thing from a practical point of view, is to become well known to the review press through some volume or volumes which it can endure, before circulating generally anything like this. If one specialises on this sort of work, the only hope of fame is posthumous. If not, a volume, not *for* ordinary citizens, but of stuff they could tolerate, would make the rest get by afterwards. I feel myself, that with so much worthless verse selling in thousands, it is just as good at the present time to have an audience of 200 as 2000, and perhaps a better investment.

Yours ever
T.S.E.

Send E.P.'s book to the *Ath*[*enaeum*]. I think it will do better generally than *Propertius* did.

1 – The contract for *Poems* gave Knopf 'the first refusal of the Author's next work in verse or prose', but Quinn had advised TSE (3 Oct. 1919) that this meant nothing: 'An author can easily comply with it by making impossible conditions.'

2 – Rodker's Ovid Press published *Hugh Selwyn Mauberley* in an edition of 200 copies.

TO *Ezra Pound* TS Beinecke

30 Maggio [May] 1920 18 Crawford Mansions

Cher E.,

Tengo en mi poder su honrada del 13 cnte.[1] I at last must face the fact that I cannot join you in June, nor, probably, in July. My book is far from forward, but, although it is promised for the end of June, that would not alone have the force to stand in my way. But I am still engaged in pourparlers with my family, and it is likely that I go to America in Oct or Nov, though, if my mother continues to believe that she will come here next May, I shall point out the great expense of two voyages in the family at such a short interval. Furthermore, we are both (i.e. Vivien and myself) in a state bordering on prostration from flathunting, and faced with the prospect of having to pay about 250% above what we pay now, if we get anything at all. However, we must go on with it. Kind friends remark, Why not live a little way out of town . . . No prospect of a job at £1000 a year for anybody. I am mindful of your hint before you left that you would probably not go to Italy next year, and it is therefore great sorrow to me. I will transmit the article to Lewis whom I shall see this week after many moons. He is said to be working, but was lately seen with a new female of suburban appearance (Ealing?) outside Verrey's.[2] Berry is promising everyone soundproof studio flats at a trifling rent in six months' time. Conrad Aiken is here; stupider than I remember him; in fact, stupid. Also Bodenheim, the American Max,[3] who arrived in the steerage on Monday with a wife and a baby which will see the light in a few weeks ('Almost any time, in fact' Mrs B. says). He is a bit upset at not finding Rodker, and is asking for Bosschère.[4] He is not unintelligent, anyhow better than Aiken, and being Semites I suppose they will survive somehow. He reports that Hecht[5] has decided to make a million dollars in a year, and has become press agent for the Baptist Church. When asked could not recall anyone else of intelligence in America. I am sending you article on Bolshevist poetry in the *Morning*

1 – 'I am in receipt of your esteemed letter of the 13th inst.' (Spanish).

2 – Verrey's Café, Regent St, a favourite of WL's.

3 – Max Bodenheim (1893–1954), American poet, novelist and (with Ben Hecht) playwright. He published in *The Egoist* and other little magazines.

4 – Jean de Bosschère (1881–1953), Belgian engraver, poet and novelist.

5 – Ben Hecht (1894–1964), American novelist and dramatist.

Post.[1] Lewis thinks he has discovered a poet named J. J. Adams.[2] O god to be out of England, in June.[3]

yrs affexionately
T.S.E.

I gather that you want me to offer Murry a section of *Moberley* to print. Will act on that and suggest 'Moluccas' but leave choice to him.[4] *Art & Letters* is going out of existence. Schiff (and others) pleased by your Arthur Symons.[5] Schiff here and very depressed about the state of English literature, a gloom which I did nothing to alleviate.

Boston Ev. Transcript says I am An Exotic Poet.[6] ('Closed room . . . stale perfumes . . . memories of lusts . . . open the window').

TO *Ezra Pound* TS Beinecke

[June? 1920] [London]

Dear Ez.,

Your three letters to hand and contents seriously noted. I expect to see murry this week and shall endeavour to guide him to the poems i consider most suitable for him. A person named Boulestin may be writing to you to ask you for a poem for an anglo French anthology he wants to publish.[7] He runs a painted furniture shop in George street portman square. He

1–E. B. Osborne, in 'Certain American Poets: The Bolshevist Touch', *Morning Post* (28 May), claimed that EP was 'capable of clever work', but that 'the best of his stuff' seemed 'like mustard-and-cress grown on a red flannel petticoat in a suburban hothouse'.

2–A mysterious British poet, author of 'Café Cannibale', *Tyro* 1, Apr. 1921.

3–Cf. Browning, 'Home Thoughts, From Abroad': 'Oh to be in England / Now that April's there.'

4–EP's *Mauberley* IV begins 'Scattered Moluccas . . .' JMM did not publish any part of the poem.

5–EP, 'Arthur Symons', *A.*, 21 May 1920, 663–4.

6–A hostile review of *Poems* by W[illiam] S[tanley] B[raithwaite], *Boston Evening Transcript*, 14 Apr. 1920. TSE's volume reprinted his poem 'The Boston Evening Transcript'. HWE wrote to their mother on 27 Apr.: 'I don't know whether it would be well to write to the *Transcript* about that review or not. It would be good advertising for the book; but it might inspire the reviewer to reply. That is, presuming you want a letter to be published in the *Transcript*. I have a copy of the book. I like of course most of the older poems; the later ones I do not understand. All I can see is that there are occasional beautiful lines in them. They are like something in cipher. There is nothing in them that could be called sensual; though occasionally something expressive of a horror of sensuality. The review was mischievously misleading.'

7–*The New Keepsake for the Year 1921* (1920), ed. X. M. Boulestin (1878–1943), would include no contributions from TSE, WL or EP.

offers no money but only the advertisement of appearing with so many distinguished anglo french names. lewis has *promised* him a drawing and I have promised a poem if I write one by the end of the month, that is not a very compromising promise. edition on japanese vellum price eighteen and six illustrated by such people as marie laurencin laboureur texte by max jacob giraudoux salmon[1] and such aldington huxley sitwell.

please write to say how long you will be in paris as vivien may come over in july. will you be there till the end of the month?

Private and confidential:[2]

Bank Lst. 500 including bonus

elsewhere not much at present praps Lst. 50 p.a.

I want Lst. 800 a year at least, and must provide for old age.

I could write at least one article a week if not at bank.

I find lectures (not giving any this year) much *more* fatiguing than banking in proportion to the time.

Should of course like six mo. abroad. But in any case must have a flat in London.

Regards to Dorothy. I may have to take my holiday in August now. Any suggestions as to what to do with them?

Yours ever
T.

TO *Mary Hutchinson* MS Texas

Sunday [Postmark 6 June 1920]

Dear Mary do you think we could have dinner a bit earlier tomorrow as we are now such a long journey from Hammersmith that we shall have to leave very early and it gives so little time for conversation after dinner? I shall be with you by half past seven. with love from

Tom.

1–Marie Laurencin (1883–1956) and Jean-Émile Laboureur (1877–1947), painters; Max Jacob (1876–1944), poet, critic and painter; Jean Giraudoux (1882–1944), dramatist, novelist and diplomat; André Salmon (1881–1969), poet and art critic.

2–EP was trying to establish the terms on which TSE was prepared to leave the Bank.

TO *Conrad Aiken* MS Huntington

9 June 1920 Lloyds

I am very sorry I had unexpectedly to be away yesterday and did not have time to let you know. I shall be here tomorrow if you will do me the favour.

T.S.E.

TO *Conrad Aiken* MS Huntington

Thursday [10 June 1920] 18 Crawford Mansions, Crawford St, W.1

Dear Conrad

Can you come in to tea *tomorrow* <Friday> at 5.15 at this address, and do *bring* [Martin] Armstrong with you, or ask him to come from his office, if he cares to. We should be delighted.

You can't answer of course. It is just off Edgware Road (toward Baker St) just near the end of the Marylebone Road. Do come.

Yrs.
Tom

TO *Herbert Read* MS Victoria

20 June 1920 18 Crawford Mansions

My dear Read,

I had been waiting, since the appearance of your first book, to see what you would do when you demobilised your talents. Not having had that experience myself – I speak not from extreme age but from the advantage or disadvantage of a C2 rating which kept me out of the army – I have been a disinterested spectator of the struggles of others with war and peace. My first impression is that you have managed wisely (for there must be a very large part of conscious management) in conserving your forces (instead of making Kneeshaw go violently to peace,[1] as many would have done) and therefore managed better than some contemporaries. I think I like the first series the best of the book;[2] they support each other and

1–TSE, in 'Reflections on Contemporary Poetry' [IV], had described parts of 'Kneeshaw Goes to War', in HR's second collection *Naked Warriors* (1919), as 'decidedly successful'.
2–HR, *Eclogues, A Book of Poems* (1919). This collection included 'The Sorrow of Unicume'.

produce a cumulative effect, as such still life pieces should do. I might question, from my own point of view, the word 'soul', which is too easy a substitute for any state of consciousness, but I have been an offender myself. Afterwards 'Unicume' interests me, but it is different, and I don't quite understand it.[1]

However, here is one person who has enjoyed your book – so success to it and the next.

Yours sincerely
T. S. Eliot

TO *The Editor of* The Athenaeum

Published 25 June 1920

Sir,

Mr William H. Polack's perplexity (*Athenaeum*, June 18, p. 810) is a spectacle before which it is impossible for me to remain passive.[2] He encourages me by saying that he is anxious to learn; and if the knowledge of what I do not believe is a possession which he would dignify with the name of learning, he is welcome to it.

First, then, I am not in the least 'indifferent as to what is expressed.' If I were, I might have a higher opinion of Massinger; for if Mr Polack has done me the honour of reading that review, he must see that my judgment at that point was simply that Massinger had very little personality – very little to express. This misunderstanding is related to the other. I do not believe that a work of art is *any* 'complete and precise expression of personality'. There are all sorts of expressions of personality, complete or precise or both, which have nothing to do with art; so that the phrase

1–HR replied on 27 June: 'I don't think *Eclogues* is in any sense the "demobilisation of my talents".' Apart from 'Etude' and 'Unicume', the poems 'were all either contemporaneous with or anterior to my war stuff . . . they are a few unconscious scraps gathered over the last few years'. He said too that he had sent the 'silly book' to TSE because he was 'one of the few living people' who gave him 'the feeling of a gradient of thought'; and he hankered to be 'in with' him in some sense.

2–William H. Polack had written in response to TSE's 'The Old Comedy', a review of A. H. Cruickshank, *Philip Massinger*, *A.*, 11 June 1920 (repr. as 'Philip Massinger' [II], *SW*). Dickens had not been mentioned by TSE, but Polack contrasted his views with those expressed by JMM in a leading article on the novelist: 'T.S.E. is indifferent as to what is expressed, provided the expression be complete and precise, whereas M. hints that the point to which criticism should apply itself is the nature of that which is expressed . . . I feel that T.S.E. deplores the fact that Dickens was not an artist, but (perhaps) a man of genius; while M. thanks God for it.'

seems to me of very little use for literary criticism. Mr Polack will notice furthermore that I said in my article 'transformation', *not* 'expression'. Transformation is what I meant: the creation of a work of art is like some other forms of creation, a painful and unpleasant business; it is a sacrifice of the man to the work, it is a kind of death.

I should be glad if Mr Polack would study my quotations from Gourmont in their context in the *Problème du Style*, and also Dujardin's 'Stéphane Mallarmé' (*Mercure de France*).

Mr Polack 'feels that T. S. E. deplores the fact that Dickens was not an artist'. I feel that Mr Polack's feelings have run away with him. (So look'd he once, when in an angry parle He smote . . .)[1] But if Mr Polack is again mistaken, what then?

I am, Sir,
Your obliged obedient servant,
T.S.E.

TO *Harold Monro* — MS Beinecke

1 July 1920 — [London]

Dear Monro,

Thank you very much for your letter of the 25th. I shall be delighted to give you an option on the execution of any idea that comes which appears suitable for the *Chapbook* – which, being *sui generis*, is an extremely useful periodical for any writer to be able to contribute to.

I don't suppose I shall have a single idea until I have my book off my mind and a couple of months rest. But I hope to be replenished later.

Yrs sincerely
T. S. Eliot

I'll write again when I have time and try to have some 'ideas' for you!

TO *Ezra Pound* — TS Beinecke

3 July 1920 — at 31 West St, Marlow

Dear EP

I have not yet received the Benda of which you speak.[2] I recall his name as a colleague of Péguy. Is that the same man? I will try to do it as soon as

1–'. . . the sledded Polacks on the ice' (*Hamlet* I. i. 66).
2–Julien Benda (1867–1956), French critic and essayist; author of *La Trahison des Clercs* (1927).

possible but shall be rushed for the next three or four weeks trying to finish polishing the essays for my book. You appear to have made a pretty clean sweep of Paris, on which I congratulate you. With all this stuff and the best English it ought to be possible to extend the circulation of the *Dial* even into England. I certainly cannot think of any other French writer worth having. I am afraid there won't be so much in this country. I am sending Scofield two articles I have just done on criticism, which I hope he will use soon if at all as I must use them for the book.[1]

I expect to be here until July 25 (about) after which address Crawford Mansions but I expect you will be in this country by that time. I plan to go to France in September. I wish to go to the country for ten days or two weeks (any suggestions for itinerary welcomed) and the rest of the time in Paris, where I should like to see anybody worth seeing. Vivien will probably join me in Paris, and therefore there is now no chance of her going there in July.

Is there any chance of Joyce staying in Paris or coming to London, so that he could be seen?

Bodenheim now says he is returning to New York at the earliest possible opportunity. He has discovered that it is very difficult to make a living in London, Murry after preliminary effusiveness has dropped him altogether, and he has put the backs up against him of most of the native English whom he has met. I don't know that there is anything to be done for him (I fear a contribution toward his travelling expenses will be necessary – Mr B. Mrs B. and Master Max junior). He is in some ways more intelligent than the native Britons and excites hostility in that and other ways. Do you take any interest in this case? Lewis finds him much more tolerable than Rodker. But I can't see any means by which Bodenheim might be made self-supporting here; can you?

I have seen a copy of *Instigations* which was sent to Lewis.[2] It makes a very favourable impression.

I await your further news. Regards to Dorothy, and hope that Paris is not too oppressively hot and humid for her.

Yours

T

I meant to begin with this: I have seen Murry and secured a vague understanding that he would print a few of the poems (I said *not more*

1–TSE's first contributions to the *Dial*: 'The Possibility of Poetic Drama' (Nov. 1920) and 'The Second-Order Mind' (Dec. 1920). The first was reprinted in *SW*; the second formed part of the introduction.

2–EP's essays (New York: Boni & Liveright, 1920).

than five) but he has not read them yet. I must say that he is much more difficult to deal with when K. M. is about, and I have an impression that she terrorises him. He told Ottoline that K. M. was the only living writer of English prose (this is as Ott. reports it). I believe her to be a dangerous WOMAN; and of course two sentimentalists together are more than two times as noxious as one. She is going back to San Remo for the winter, in September.[1]

TO *His Mother* TS Houghton

3 July 1920

18 Crawford Mansions,
Crawford St, W.1

Dearest Mother,

I believe it is over three weeks since I have written to you, not counting enclosures sent you to peruse. I have been first very busy trying to find a flat, and have not succeeded, and second, have been trying to do my book. First then, I have received the power of attorney forms several days ago,[2] and did not have time to attend to them for two or three days. Then I went to my solicitor, Mr Leigh Hunt (of James & James) to do it for me, and he said he would have to get a proper notary for it, but that he would do to identify me. So I am to see him tomorrow, and will cable you the same day. I am sorry for the delay, but I did not know any notary or government official who could swear to my identity, so I am doing it this way.

So long as you hold the shares for me I suppose that you will pay the insurance out of it, keeping the policy there, but if you sold the shares and remitted me the money to invest here, you would send me the policy so that I could pay the premiums myself. I agree with you about not selling at the

1–Although OM had been close to Katherine Mansfield and her husband JMM, there had been rows in 1917 when JMM told his wife that OM was in love with him, and in 1918, when JMM gave a hostile review of Siegfried Sassoon which led OM to write, 'A mighty quarrel is raging between JMM and myself' (Seymour, *Life on the Grand Scale*, 299). It is not clear why TSE felt such hostility towards Mansfield. However, he and VHE had recently dined with JMM and Mansfield, who took a violent dislike to VHE, as she explained in a letter to Violet Schiff on 14 May: 'The Elliots [*sic*] have dined with us tonight. They are just gone – and the whole room is *quivering*. John has gone downstairs to see them off. Mrs E's voice rises "O don't commiserate Tom; he's *quite* happy." I know its extravagant . . . but I dislike her so *immensely*. She really repels me . . . And Elliott, leaning towards her, admiring, listening, making the most of her – really minding whether she disliked the country or not . . . I am so fond of Elliot . . . But this teashop creature . . .' (*Collected Letters of Katherine Mansfield* IV, ed. Vincent O'Sullivan and Margaret Scott, 1966).

2–To enable his mother or brother to sell TSE's stock in the Hydraulic-Press Brick Company.

present time. I hope that the labour over this transfer has not added much to what you must have gone through in leaving St Louis. You must be thoroughly exhausted, and on top of that you have to go househunting. I shall wait anxiously for reports of your health. I know that househunting is the most tiring thing one could do. We have looked at a few houses too. A few were slightly cheaper than some of the flats we have seen, but we calculated that they would be very much more expensive to run. They all needed cleaning, painting, and papering to begin with, they would use much more coal and gas, and an extra servant now and then. We want something that we could manage without any servant if necessary. The flats have run from two to four times what we pay now. In addition, everybody has been waiting for the new rents act to pass Parliament.[1] Rents have been limited during the war, but people have been demanding 'premiums': £200–£500 down on signing the lease, besides the regular rent. They say premiums will be illegal, but prices will certainly go up 40% now. Flats are very much in demand, because English *houses* were constructed when it was easy to get servants very cheap, and are very difficult to run without servants. If we lost the woman we have now, we should have to pay twice as much for another who would probably work shorter hours. And if we move to very far from where we are, she will not be able to come to us from where she lives. So it is a very difficult problem, and we have been utterly tormented. We may *have* to stay where we are. Yet there are flats to be had – only at such prices! And Crawford Mansions we have come to loathe on account of the noise and sordidness.

All this has been very unsettling for taking a vacation. I made enquiries, some time ago, and was told by the Cunard that I could not get a passage to America before November. When I come I shall have to come by that line, because it is much the quickest. This year the boats are crowded with American travellers. So, as we both are so unsettled and homeless, and as I do not like to be far away in case of losing a chance to secure a flat, it seems to me much better to leave it till spring. If you are in a position to come then, that will be the best thing in the world for me; and if not, you will know by February *definitely*, and I will come in March. It must be one or the other. You said in one letter 'don't you want to come to America?' It is not at all that I don't want to come. But I *do* rather dread

1–The Increase of Rent (Amendment) Act would receive Royal Assent by Christmas 1920. Restrictions on raising rents had been imposed in 1915 for the duration of the war, so that housing would be affordable. The new legislation eased the restrictions, but property-owners wanted to raise rents in line with costs, and litigation followed.

coming for such a very very short time, because I know that there will [be] so much pain about seeing you for such a short time. If I could come for six weeks I should be wild with impatience to come. And if I can't see you here next spring I must come, because I should regret it every hour of my life if I did not.

My book is supposed to be out in the autumn, and therefore I must try to get it finished by the end of this month. There will not be much in it that you will not have seen already. But it will be a satisfaction to have a prose book. Methuen suggests that I should follow it up with another on English prose, so I hope that this will succeed so that he will want another. I want to do a book on the Elizabethan era, going in to it rather more profoundly than any of the former critics have done.

I enclose review from the *Dial*. It is very flattering, but silly and pretentious.[1] When I get a scrapbook and paste all my reviews in it I will send it to you to read. If reviews sell a book, mine ought to be a success, but that is not certain.

I am to contribute to the *Dial* when I can. Pound is English editor, and is now in Paris getting French contributors. I have been invited to collaborate in a review in Geneva,[2] and Wyndham Lewis wants me to help him with an art and literature review, *Art & Letters* having gone out of existence. I cannot do all of these things.

I do not accept the interpretation of me which the *Times Literary Supplement* is accustomed to make, elsewhere as well as in the review of Huxley's book which you read. I have a very low opinion of this book. Huxley has, of course, like a number of other young men, borrowed a good deal from my poetry.[3] Aldington is an exception – he does not like my poetry, and says so frankly, but I like him none the less. I do not know why it is, but men five years younger than I seem to me much younger, and if they become my friends I feel a sort of paternal responsibility, yet men five years older seem to me about the same age. Murry is my age, Pound is four years older, Lewis is five years older, and Strachey is nearly forty; so is Sydney Waterlow. But Osbert Sitwell and his brother,

1–E. E. Cummings, in 'T. S. Eliot' (*Dial* 69: 6, June 1920), characterised *Poems* as 'an accurate and incorpulent collection of instupidities', and praised its 'overwhelming sense of technique' and 'delicate and careful murderings . . . of established tempos by oral rhythms'.
2–*La Revue de Genève*.
3–'The Old Grimace', *TLS*, 27 May 1920, a review [by Arthur Clutton-Brock] of AH's *Leda*, noted that many of AH's poems 'remind one, in mood and even in manner, of Mr. T. S. Eliot; they express the fact that to the writer life is absurd in its traditional delights and, for the rest, tiresome' (327).

Aldington, Huxley, Herbert Read, and several Americans whom I only know by correspondence, all seem children almost.

Conrad Aiken is in London – I think you have heard me speak of him, I knew him at Harvard, and he is now quite a flourishing poet in America. He is very nice, but in comparison with Englishmen seems to have had rather a soft and easy intellectual existence – not the hard knocking about that one gets among men of brains here. There is an odd American Jew here named Bodenheim; rather pathetic, although foolish. He is a vagrant poet and man of letters at home, and thought that he could pick up a living just as easily here. He received his first blow when he found that no one had heard of him. I told him my history here, and left him to consider whether an American Jew, of only a common school education and no university degree, with no money, no connections, and no social polish or experience, could make a living in London. Of course I did not say all this; but I made him see that getting recognised in English letters is like breaking open a safe – for an American, and that only about three had ever done it. The worst is that he has a wife – they came in the steerage – and his wife is having a baby, and now he wants to go back, and cannot get a passage, and his wife is not well enough to travel, and I do not believe he has any money. What is one to do! it is very distressing, but I think it is better that he should go back. Yet he has a better mind than most of the people here, though he has never been taught to write properly; a much better mind than Aiken, who gets on much better (he has an independent income too).

I want to know where you are, and what you are doing, and especially how you are. Are you at Millis? I hope it is cool and comfortable there.

With very very much love

your son

Tom

TO *Ezra Pound* PC Beinecke

[Postmark 13 July 1920] [London]

Belphégor[1] received and much pleased with it. If you can procure any other of J. B.'s works I will purchase them from you. Will write shortly.

Yrs.

TSE

1 – *Belphégor: essai sur l'esthetique de la présente société française* (1918) by Julien Benda. EP reviewed it (signing himself 'B. L.'), *A.*, 9 July 1920, and arranged for its publication in the *Dial.*

TO *Lytton Strachey* MS BL

14 July 1920 31 West St, Marlow

Dear Strachey,

I am delighted to hear from you and should have loved to come, but unfortunately I have some people motoring down for Saturday afternoon. Perhaps this is providential, as I ought to work Sunday on a book which is heavy on my conscience. How do you ever write a book! It seems to me a colossal task. *Perhaps* you will ask me again some time? On the assumption (quite unjustified) that I shall have finished by the end of the month, I am going to France in the middle of August. I have heard that you might be in London this winter. I hope so.

Yours ever

T.S.E.

Does that mean that *Q. V.* will be finished?[1]

TO *Conrad Aiken* PC Huntington

20 July 1920

You must get your visa via Southampton–Havre as I have my ticket.

Lv. Waterloo Saturday 14th August abt. 7.30 p.m. Arr. Paris 12 noon.

TSE.

TO *His Mother* MS Houghton

27 July 1920 18 Crawford Mansions,
Crawford St, W.1

My dearest Mother,

I received your cheque for $225 from the H. P. Brick Company and your letter yesterday. You can write to Crawford Mansions as before, because we have not found another dwelling of any kind. If I changed my address suddenly I should cable you, but such an event is I fear very unlikely.

The $900 will certainly be a great boon to me. We find that the cost of living still increases, and even if we stay in this flat we shall shortly have to pay a good 50% more in rent. Then everything else is more expensive all the time.

1 – Strachey's *Queen Victoria* was published the following spring.

As you send a cheque on St Louis I shall have to *sell* it here (or else send it to Saint Louis for collection), and I do not know whether it is more profitable to do that in future or to have the dividends made out to you, or Henry, and have you send me a draft on London. I will find out. The latter would make more trouble for you and you have had quite enough already. I am sorry that you have to attend to all these shares for your children in the midst of finding a house. I do not remember which house is 27 Concord Avenue. I hope that the proximity to the street cars is not likely to make the house noisy.

This again is only a note of acknowledgement, thanks and affection in the midst of my final activities, which are now beginning to look like a book. And then it will be three months before it is out.

Your very loving son
Tom.

TO *Wyndham Lewis* 　　　　MS Cornell

Wednesday [28 July 1920] 　　　　18 Crawford Mansions

Dear Lewis

I am supposed to be ill and have been at home for two days using the time in finishing my book. I shall be back again on Friday. Will you be in London next week? I should like to see you again before either of us goes away. I saw Pound today, and of course did not mention this matter to him; but I feel rather embarrassed about it. Will you not broach it to him before long? I don't think he would take a very keen interest in it, but there are so few intelligent persons as it is. Besides, the longer you wait the more likely he is to throw cold water on it, naturally.[1]

There were one or two things I did not like the other evening on thinking over afterward. I am not sure of the desirability of fiction, at any rate at the start – it might weaken the effect. The idea of a large number of (anonymous) topical paragraphs appealed to me. Surely the prime object of such a paper is to give the effect of a nucleus of intelligent independent and powerful opinion about art, and incidentally about literature and general matters. This could be better dealt with in conversation.

1 – This almost certainly refers to WL's projected journal, *Tyro: A Review of The Arts of Painting, Sculpture and Design* (which would be issued for just two numbers in 1921). EP wrote to WL in an undated letter: 'Can't see that TYRO is of interest outside Bloomsbury' (*Pound/Lewis*, 127).

Pound showed me a letter from Murry saying that he had taken on permanently someone else for the dramatic criticism, but hoped he would review more books. Murry is in a fairly strong position, as Ezra had not been on the job long before leaving the country for three months; though I think Murry's motive was more dislike of turning another man out (i.e. moral laziness) than anything else. E. P. was very low about this; and I shall see Murry and try to get him to send some books.[1]

I shall be at the Schiffs the weekend of the 6th. Try to come then. I should like to see you first.

Yrs.
TSE

FROM *His Mother* — TS Valerie Eliot

1 August 1920 — Millis, Massachusetts

Dearest Son:

I have received two letters from you recently, and right glad I was to get them. The proxies preceded them. I have not yet used them and hope it will not be necessary to do so, except in the event of your desiring to sell your stock and re-invest. I hurried off the dividend checks lest you might not receive them before you left for your vacation. With the assurance of the State St Bank (George's), that you could cash them in London, I felt it would not be necessary to convert them into drafts. If you can cash without disadvantage in London, I will have Mr Baker send directly to you. I may be obliged myself to pay taxes on the dividends in Boston, but there is no tax on stock. I shall copy a long letter on the subject of Hydraulic, just sent me by Henry. The Company pays the tax on Stock.

As to the Insurance Policy, as I have already said, I will send it to you the first of September. You had better have it while I am still living, as it would be sent you in event of my death.

As to Henry's letter it will give you information that will assist you in deciding when to sell your Hydraulic Stock. You will understand it better than I, being in a bank. The larger operations of finance are beyond me. It is as much as I can do to look after my own finances.

I shall be very much relieved to hear when you do get a house or apartments – I presume the latter would be better for you for the reasons

1 – EP wrote weekly theatre reviews for *A.* in Mar.–Apr. (signed 'T. J. V.'), but then took himself off for an extended holiday and was dismissed by JMM.

you give.[1] A house, as you say, requires more in the way of service. For several years now we have had but one <servant>, and indeed the wages of one are more than those of two a few years ago. I could not think it right to employ two. Marian and I do the chamber work. I shall have to pay a cook here at least $12.00 a week – possibly more. Why do all the 'Reverend Damns', as someone calls them, talk so much about democratizing industry. The proletariat are better off than most of the bourgeois. Someone examined marriage statistics in Massachusetts, and found that the last year while the number of marriages among the working (hand) classes, had greatly increased, among clerks and professional men they had greatly *decreased*.

I believe in telepathy. I have been thinking for several days I would ask you about Bertrand Russell when I wrote. I was thinking of him this morning, and when Marian brought me up last night's [*Boston Evening*] *Transcript* which I had not seen, there was an editorial of his on the Russian regime – Lenine and Trotzsky. The testimony against the Soviet comes with greater force from him, because he is inclined to Socialism. I was very sorry that he was a Pacifist, because I so intensely disapproved of and *despised* Pacifism, and I felt that at heart he was a man of high ideals, lofty but perverted. And I have always been grateful to him for his kindness to you, although I have too much confidence in your clear intelligence to think you could agree with him.

Apropos of the *Transcript*, one has to take it here, but I shall never get over my grudge against the paper for its scurrilous attack on you. I suppose they resented your poem. The article in question was not a critique, it was vulgar abuse.

I am sorry rents in London are so high. I am paying almost a third more than I should have had to pay last year, $500 more than the last lessee paid. But it was that house or nothing, and I got that only through friends. I could not stand an ordinary boarding house, and a hotel would be very expensive. It is a double house, which I like. It is, of course, smaller than the St Louis house, and has not all the modern improvements – indeed it is quite old, but pretty. If I had taken a smaller house, it would not have held all our furniture. If you were not so far away I would give you some pieces of furniture and pictures. I think it will be more expensive living in Cambridge than in St Louis.

I want a copy of your book [*SW*] as soon as it comes out. I do not know whether I can buy it at once in this country. If you will send me a copy,

1 – In his letter of 3 July.

I will pay for it. I hope Methuen will want another, and that you will 'follow this up with another book on English prose', and one on the Elizabethan era, 'going into it rather more profoundly than the former critics have done.' You are already recognized in England, as an authority and successful writer on the Elizabethan period. It seems as if it would be well to follow it up. Prof. Lowes[1] has made a speciality of Spenser – not nearly as interesting as the Elizabethans. I wish Methuen would use the picture you had taken. It is very good. It is this minute looking at me, being over the table on which the typewriter stands.

Henry promises to come on for a little visit. I shall try to take some trips with him. We want to go to Plymouth – other places too. I shall ride all I can. I shall probably have to diet somewhat the rest of my life, but under that condition it is said the renal trouble does not shorten life. Bread seems to be the most strictly forbidden, and it has been to me a staff of life. I can eat oatmeal of which I am very fond.

I propose if I can go to London in the spring to leave Margaret in the house, and find someone to stay with her. I shall want in London, rooms in which I can live and get my meals out or at least à la carte. The rooms must be as near you as possible. Then when I take trips, as I would like to do, I shall have only to pay for the rent of rooms. I should want to see London first, and then what I have strength for of England. You may have a vacation before I return, so you could go with us. It would be a great saving if I could close the house, but I am afraid of fire in a frame house.

I should very much like to see the article on your work in the *Times Literary Supplement*. Could you send it and let me return it? Or is it pasted into a book? I do not think much of the *Dial*. Henry writes: 'I picked a volume of Conrad Aiken's poems lately – one called *Senlin*[2] – and the chief thing that struck me was the fact that he imitated Tom's work. Whole phrases were lifted out of *Prufrock* – for instance "music with a dying fall" – and the cast of thought was similar. What strikes me about many of these present-day poets, is that they have exuberant imagination but little thought.'

1–John Livingston Lowes (1867–1945), Professor of English at Harvard University, 1918–39; author of *Convention and Revolt in Poetry* (1919), but now best known for his study of Coleridge's sources, *The Road to Xanadu: a study in the ways of the imagination* (1927), which TSE would discuss in *TUPUC* (1933). He was formerly an English professor and Dean of Arts at Washington University, St Louis (1909–18), where he had become a family friend. In due course, Charlotte Eliot would consult him about publication possibilities for her long poem *Savonarola*. TSE wrote in 'The Frontiers of Criticism' (1956): 'Livingston Lowes was a fine scholar, a good teacher, a lovable man and a man to whom I for one have private reasons to feel very grateful' (*OPP*, 108).
2–Conrad Aiken, *The Charnal Rose, Senlin: A Biography, and Other Poems* (1918).

Again Henry writes: 'Tom's critical articles seem to me vastly more "meaty" and less diffuse than the majority of such writing. He is genuinely interested in ideas, whereas most of the critical writing that one sees is a mere display of literary sophistication and erudition. The ones by J. M. M. of which I spoke in a recent letter, on Tom's critical work, were tediously diffuse. I am not interested in the Elizabethans particularly, but I have an idea that Tom's study of them is a penetrating one, and I should not be surprised to see him publish a book on them which will be adopted by the colleges. Tom's criticisms are always full of concrete examples, which is always illuminating, instead of the vague generalities usually seen.' I find the Elizabethan period one of the very most interesting.

Have I previously answered your letter? It seems as if I had previously referred to the Jew, Bodenheim. It is very bad in me, but I have an instinctive antipathy to Jews, just as I have to certain animals. Of course there are Jews and Jews, and I must be not so much narrow-minded, as narrow in my sympathies. There must be something in them which to me is antipathetic. Father never liked to have business dealings with them, and they took advantage of Henry in the Publishers' Press.

This is a long letter. I will stop now, and copy for you Henry's letter on Hydraulic Stock.

It has just occurred to me that I wrote to Vivian [*sic*] and sent her a small birthday check the 15th of June. Did she receive it? I sent to Lloyds as I thought you might have moved.

Very affectionately,
Mother.

I will finish Henry's letter which I am copying and send tomorrow.

FROM *Leonard Woolf* — TS Valerie Eliot

3 August 1920

Monk's House, Rodmell,
near Lewes, Sussex.

Dear Eliot,

We have sold out the edition of your *Poems*. I wish we had printed more as we still get orders for them. After deducting copies for review &c we had 190 for sale and these have all gone now. There are still however one or two at the Chelsea Book Club on sale or return not accounted for. Since I sent you the 18/8 in April, we have sold 21 copies, and the receipts have been £1-19-4½. I enclose a cheque for 10/- which is your share. The total receipts from all sales have been £18-10-4, and the total expenditure £6-1-10; the net profits are therefore £12-8-6, of which your share has been £3-2-6. I sent you a cheque for £1-13-10 last year, 18/8 last April, and now 10/-, total £3-2-6. I hope this is intelligible and correct.

Yours sincerely
Leonard Woolf

TO *Sydney Schiff* — MS BL

Wednesday [4 August 1920] — 18 Crawford Mansions, Crawford St, W.1

Dear Sydney,

I have not read Bridges (in the *London Mercury*) but I should hardly suppose that he was the man to do it.[1] Sullivan in the *Athenaeum* has hardly said more than that Santayana was worth reading.[2] As for Pearsall Smith, I do not believe that any selections of specimens can give much of a philosopher. I have never liked Santayana myself, because I have always felt that his attitude was essentially feminine, and that his philosophy was a dressing up of himself rather than an interest in things. But still I think one ought to read *Reason in Common Sense*[3] or one other volume. <His *Athenaeum* things were exceptionally bad.>[4] He is not quite like anyone else. Anyway, I should like to know what you think of him.

Vivien has broken down rather badly – you may have observed last time we saw you that she was looking very ill – and has had to go to bed. She has been very run down lately and the damage was completed by a <visit to the country last> weekend ~~visit~~,[5] which she did not feel at all fit for and which I ought to have prevented. I hope she will be able to come but I am not at all certain. She sends much love to Violet and says she so much liked her letter and wants to answer it.

I haven't looked up the train, but it will be the earliest after one o'clock that I can get.

With love from both of us.

Yours ever
T. S. E.

1–Robert Bridges, 'George Santayana', *London Mercury* 2: 10 (Aug. 1920), 409–19: a review of *Little Essays: Drawn from the Writings of George Santayana*, ed. Logan Pearsall Smith. Bridges said he found Santayana's philosophy 'very consonant with my own thought'.

2–See J. W. N. Sullivan, 'The Reasonable Life', *A.*, 30 July 1920: 'the wisest volume of essays that has appeared in our time'.

3–The first of five volumes by Santayana comprising *The Life of Reason* (1905–6).

4–Santayana wrote in *A.*, 1919–20, a series of 'Soliloquies from England': collected in *Soliloquies in England and Later Soliloquies* (1922).

5–They had visited Garsington with the Aldous Huxleys and the painter Mark Gertler.

TO *Conrad Aiken* MS Huntington

Wednesday [4 August 1920] 18 Crawford Mansions

I am much disappointed that you can't come.[1] I wish we could have made arrangements sooner, and perhaps you would have come. Shall we see you before I go? I shall be here till the 14th. Do let me know when you get back to London. I wish you were going to stay this winter.

T.S.E.

TO *The Editor of* The Athenaeum[2]

Published 6 August 1920

Sir,

Mr Hannay doubts whether I have justified my distinction between the critic and the philosopher, and suspects that I am making a distinction between a kind of philosophical criticism of which I approve and another kind of which I disapprove. If I *have* made this distinction between kinds to Mr Hannay's satisfaction, and not merely shown that I like some critical writings and not others, then I ought to be content. The frontier cannot be clearly defined; at all events I trust that Mr Hannay would agree that Hegel's *Philosophy of Art* adds very little to our enjoyment or understanding of art, though it fills a gap in Hegel's philosophy.[3] I have in mind a rather celebrated passage towards the end of Taine's *History of English Literature* (I have not the book by me) in which he compares Tennyson and Musset. Taine is a person for whom I have considerable respect, but this passage does not seem to me to be good as criticism; the comparative vision of French and English life does not seem to me to issue quite ingenuously out of an appreciation of the two poets;[4] I should say that Taine was here philosophizing rather than 'developing his sensibility into a generalized structure.'

I do not understand Mr Hannay's request that I should quote an instance of 'this generalization which is neither itself poetry nor discursive

1–Aiken was due to join TSE for a holiday in France.

2–This letter was written in response to a letter from A. H. Hannay (30 July), questioning TSE's 'The Perfect Critic' (9 and 23 July).

3–G. W. F. Hegel, *The Philosophy of Fine Art*, trans. W. Hastie (1886).

4–The French critic and literary historian Hippolyte Taine (1828–93) wrote in *History of English Literature*: 'The favourite poet of a nation, it seems, is he whose works a man, setting out on a journey, prefers to put in his pocket. Nowadays it would be Tennyson in England and Alfred de Musset in France. The two publics differ: so do their modes of life, their reading, their pleasures' (Bk V, ch. vi).

reasoning.' I find in Chambers (the only dictionary within reach) that 'discursive' means 'desultory', 'rational', or 'proceeding regularly from premises to conclusion'. Surely I have not pretended that criticism should avoid 'discursive reasoning' in this last sense?

As to the question whether my article on 'The Perfect Critic' was itself philosophy or perfect criticism, I need only refer Mr Hannay to the *Principia Mathematica*[1] Chap. II, especially p. 65 (The Theory of Types and the Cretan Liar: 'Hence the statement of Epimenides does not fall within its own scope, and therefore no contradiction emerges').

I am, Sir,
Your obliged obedient servant,
T. S. Eliot

TO *Van Wyck Brooks*[2]

MS Beinecke

9 August 1920 — 18 Crawford Mansions

My dear Van Wyck Brooks,

I remember you very much better than you think, when I was a Freshman at Harvard and you were a prominent man of letters there;[3] and later in New York at a certain French restaurant the name of which I think was *Petitpas*. I did not know that you were connected with the *Freeman* and I had not seen the paper until you sent it to me. It is the most interesting of the New York weeklies now, I should say; interesting enough, I should think, to be regarded unfavourably by the Police.

I have just finished a book, and am going abroad for a fortnight, tired and uninspired. I must explain that I write in the evenings and Sundays left me by a banking existence, and am always tempted to promise much more than I can perform. It's very rare now that I *want* to review any book – unless it is some expensive scholarly work that I happen to covet. I wished last winter that I had had a chance to review Irving Babbitt's book.[4]

1–BR and Alfred North Whitehead, *Principia Mathematica* (3 vols, 1910–13).
2–Van Wyck Brooks (1886–1963), literary historian and critic; author of *The Ordeal of Mark Twain* (1920); associate editor of the *Freeman*, a political and aesthetic magazine, 1920–4.
3–Brooks graduated in 1908, and his first book, *The Wine of the Puritans*, was the occasion of TSE's first review for the *Harvard Advocate*, 7 May 1909: Brooks had exposed, wrote TSE, 'the reasons for the failure of American life (at present)'.
4–Irving Babbitt, *Rousseau and Romanticism* (1919). Irving Babbitt (1865–1933), Professor of French at Harvard, where TSE had taken his course on literary criticism in France. See TSE's 'The Humanism of Irving Babbitt', *Forum* 80: 1 (July 1928); reprinted in *SE*. TSE later wrote that Babbitt's 'ideas are permanently with one, as a measurement and test of one's own' (*Irving Babbitt: Man and Teacher*, 1941, 103–4).

But I should probably write so seldom or so irregularly that it is no use indicating any 'sort of books'. What I have always wanted to do for some American paper is to write occasional London letters.[1] I should like to do, of course, any books by a very small number of people in London (when they appear) whose work I admire. But of course they would have to be published in America before you would want to review them, I suppose?

If you ever see Max Perkins remember me to him.[2] You would do me a service if you gave me Tom Thomas's[3] address. I suppose he still lives in Italy.

Sincerely yours
T. S. Eliot

FROM *His Mother* TS Houghton

[August? 1920]

List of Books, the property of Thomas Stearns Eliot[4]

Robert Browning*	6 Volumes	Baudelaire *
Christopher Marlowe	1 Volume	Rostand
Ben Jonson	3 Volumes	Petronii Saturae†
Chaucer	6 Volumes	Rand's Philosophy
Shakespeare*	38 Volumes	Bakewell's Ancient Philosophy
Meredith's Poems	2 Volumes	Plato, Horatius Comina
Austin Dobson		Anthologia Lyrica
Poe's Poems		Apuleius Metamorphoses†
Shelley		Propertius, Ditto translated*
Rossetti		English Literature, Schofield*
Coleridge (large)		De Heredia*
Robert Browning		Reynolds on Art
Keats		Monologues, Browning

1–In Oct. 1920 TSE would agree to write a monthly 'London Letter' for the *Dial*: his first piece came out in Apr. 1921.

2–Maxwell Perkins (1884–1947), future editor at Charles Scribner's of Scott Fitzgerald, Ernest Hemingway and Thomas Wolfe.

3–Thomas Head Thomas (1881–1963) taught art at Harvard after graduating in 1903, then moved to Europe where he wrote *French Portrait Engraving of the XVII and XVIII Centuries* (1910). A friend of HWE, he saw some of TSE's poems in the *Harvard Advocate* and wrote (said TSE) 'a most enthusiastic letter and cheered me up. And I wish I had his letters still. I was very grateful to him for giving me that encouragement' ('The Art of Poetry').

4–At a later date, TSE has written at the head, 'This memo was sent to TSE by CCE just before she moved from St Louis to Cambridge in 1920 and was returned by him to her, checked.' * = checked by TSE; † = marked by TSE as 'sent'; § = ticked by TSE.

Chestertons
Pope
Helicon
Carew
Wither
Marvell
Campion
Burns
Dryden
Tennyson 1830–1863
Scott's Poems
Milton's Poems
Walter Pater,* 3[1] volumes
Sheridan
Rostand
Theocritus, Bion and Moschus*
Aeschylus†
Goethe's Conversations (Two Volumes)†
Petronius
Aeschylus Tragedies
Benvenuto Cellini
Biographia Literaria, Coleridge
Ebb Tide
Aristophanes, The Birds
Macaulay's Essays
Essay on Comedy
Reading Gaol, Wilde
Hooker's Ecclesiastical Polity
Tolstoy on Shakespeare
Pre-Shakespearean Drama, Manley
Art of Musician, Hanchett
Wood Engraving
Nature and Man, Shaler
Defoe
Spingarn's Renaissance
Drawing (Ruskin)
Sartor Resartus
Religio Medici
Chapman's Birds*[2]
Archer Alexander*[3]
Essays on Addison

Dearest Tom:

This is a list of two boxes of books I packed. I do not know whether it includes all. I wish you would mark all you would like, and I will send them when I can. Are there others?

1 – Corrected to '4' by TSE.
2 – Frank M. Chapman's *Handbook of Birds of Eastern North America* is quoted in the note to *The Waste Land*, l. 356 (misnumbered 357). TSE's copy of the 6th edn (1902) is inscribed 'A much coveted birthday present on my 14th birthday T. S. Eliot. 18 June 1928' (King's).
3 – *The Story of Archer Alexander* (1885) by TSE's grandfather, William Greenleaf Eliot, tells the story of an escaped slave who came to work for him. Charlotte C. Eliot wrote, in *William Greenleaf Eliot*: 'Dr Eliot declared that there is nothing in all the scenes of *Uncle Tom's Cabin* to which he himself could not find a parallel in all he had seen and known in St Louis previous to the war of secession. To such books as *The Life of Archer Alexander* the student of history must turn for reliable information regarding "the peculiar institution".'

[in TSE's hand:]

Marked what I want! Some more in the box Shef sent last year. But there is also

Century Dictionary §
Certain French Books
2 little Sanskrit books. §

There was a set of *La Nouvelle Revue Française*. I do *not* want them. I'd like any *family* photographs (Greenleaf etc) that I had, except any I gave away, to Ada, or others.

TO *His Mother* — MS Houghton

9 August 1920

18 Crawford Mansions,
Crawford St, W.1

My dearest mother,

I hope that you have recovered from your little trouble by this time. I am sure you are well taken care of. I hope you will have a resting spell and enjoy the country before you begin to work. Cambridge can be very hot and oppressive in September, and lovely in October. I am delighted with the situation you have chosen. I wish you had a photograph of the house to show me.

I shall of course send you a copy of my book as soon as it is out – in October or November, but you shall not send me a draft for it. I have posted the Manuscript today – I have been working on it up to now. There will be several things in it that you have not seen before. It is a great relief to have finished it. Methuen is going to offer Knopf the American rights, but it will hardly be published in America for another nine months.

Having got this off, we spent the weekend at Eastbourne, visiting some friends called Schiff – very nice Jews. They had, besides ourselves, an Italian named Emanueli, an important editor in Rome, a Lady Tosti, whose husband was a noted musician,[1] and Wyndham Lewis. So we all talked several languages at once, and went motoring along the cliffs, and the weather was very beautiful. We will send you some photographs of the party.[2] The weather has been hot and brilliant. I am taking two weeks holiday on Saturday. I am going to France, and Wyndham Lewis is to come

1–Sir Francesco Paolo Tosti (1846–1916), Italian composer and music teacher.
2–Now at King's.

with me if he can get a passport in time. If he comes we shall go to the coast, as he wants to paint there, and I shall bathe. Later, in October, I shall have ten days more, and Vivien and I will go away somewhere. I will send you cards from France.

I have cashed the dividend. I find that when the dividend is sent, the bank *sells* it, and puts it to my account *less* income tax at six shillings in the pound. But if your income is small, you can get back part of this from the Government later. So that the only disadvantage of your sending the dividend itself instead of a draft, is that I do not get about £9 of the money for a year! But if it was a draft, I should only have to pay the *smaller* amount of tax myself, later on. This is hard to explain in a few words.

I have never taken much interest in [Robert] Frost's poetry, although I know he is much better than most others.

I am sending enclosed some photographs of Vivien taken by Lady Ottoline Morrell at Garsington, near Oxford. They do not really show her face, but I think they give a very attractive general impression. Lady Ottoline wants Vivien to come and stay with her while I am away.

Abby has been in town, and we took her to the theatre last week. She is a nice girl. She seems very young for her age.[1]

Dear Mother, I am looking forward to seeing you.

Your loving son
Tom

TO *Ezra Pound* — MS Beinecke

[9? August 1920] [London]

Dear E. P.

Many thanks – extraordinary promptitude. Davray[2] has sent pass and a most amiable letter – I shd like to drop in on *Thursday evening* if convenient, with pictures and map and *suitcase*. It is possible that I may change my destination. Vivien has been worrying a good deal about my health and my going walking so far away alone. This question arose also at Schiffs on Sunday and it transpired that Lewis (who was present) wants

1–Writing to CCE on 3 May, HWE reported seeing Abigail Eliot's parents, who said that 'Abby enjoyed tremendously seeing Tom and Vivien, thought she [VHE] was lovely, and that they were so hospitable and delightful and had such charming friends, interesting people' (Houghton).

2–Henry D. Davray (1873–1944), French author, journalist and translator, was responsible for foreign literature at the *Mercure de France*.

to go over about the same time and suggested company if I would come to the coast as he wants to work there. I shd not have thought of going with him if it had not occurred in this way; but in case he misses the train, fails to get a passport in time etc. I want the other plan ready, liking the itinerary suggested.

Please give me Joyce's address.

Yrs.
T.

TO *Scofield Thayer* MS Beinecke

10 August 1920 18 Crawford Mansions

Dear Scofield

I hope you will pardon this long silence, as I have from week to week intended writing at some length. I have finally given Pound two contributions which he seems to think acceptable and if so has forwarded by this time. I have been engrossed (in such time as I can spare from banking, flat- i.e. apartment-hunting, income tax and such petty matters) in a book I have been preparing for Methuen to publish in the autumn.

I think Pound has been doing wonderfully well with his French campaign. The Gourmont stuff is a great scoop,[1] and Benda's book is ripping. I hope you can print it in full.[2] There is nothing like the *Dial* here and I see no reason why it should not have an appreciable English circulation. It is unfortunate that there are not so many good writers here as in France, but there is no reason why you should not get what there are.

That strange Bodenheim has been in London and has now disappeared. I was anxious to help him, but it proved very difficult, as you may imagine, to persuade the English of his merit. Finally, as a result of our missing each other at an appointment, he became suspicious of my good intentions and dropped me altogether. I am very sorry about it, and if you see him, I hope you will persuade him that I am not a crook and was only anxious for further opportunity to assist. He did, as a matter of fact, run up against one or two people who treated him rather shabbily, but even without that London is a tough nut to crack.

1 – Rémy de Gourmont, 'Dust for Sparrows', trans. EP, *Dial*, Sept. 1920, 219–24; the first of seven sections.

2 – 'Bélphegor: An essay on the Aesthetic of Contemporary French Society', a translation of Julien Benda's book, was serialised in four parts in the *Dial* (Sept.–Dec. 1920).

I am just off for a holiday and hope to be able to offer you some verse later. When are you coming?

Yrs ever
T.S.E.

TO *James Joyce*[1]

MS Buffalo

11 August 1920 18 Crawford Mansions

Dear Mr Joyce,

Ezra Pound has given me a package for you. I shall be in Paris Sunday the 15th and shall be leaving on Monday. I shall be at the Hôtel de l'Élysée, 3 rue de Beaune, where Pound was. *I hope you can dine with me that evening. Please.* Can you meet me there about 6.30, or up to 7? You can take the parcel and I should very much like to meet you, at last.[2]

You won't have time to answer. But please come.

Sincerely yours
T. S. Eliot

TO *Edgar Jepson*

MS Beinecke

Saturday [14 August 1920] 18 Crawford Mansions

Dear Mr Jepson

Thank you for your note. I should very much like to know what you think of the book, when you have had time to decide, and in comparison with EP's previous volume.[3]

I shall be sending you a copy of my own prose book in the autumn. I don't expect you to like it – I seem to have an entirely different public for my prose. Still, I wanted to do a prose book, and now I've done it, and Methuen has undertaken to publish it and perhaps I shall try[4] some verse now.

1–James Joyce, Irish novelist and poet: see Glossary of Names.
2–The parcel, which TSE had toted all the way from London, contained a pair of old brown shoes: EP thought JJ had need of them. See WL, *Blasting and Bombardiering* (1937), 270–6.
3–EP, *Hugh Selwyn Mauberley* (1920). EP's *Quia Pauper Amavi* had been issued in 1919.
4–TSE wrote 'try to', then changed 'to' to 'do'.

We should have enjoyed very much coming to tea tomorrow – but I am off to France this afternoon for my holiday. I hope we can arrange to meet after my return; I have wanted to see you for a long time.

Sincerely yours
T. S. Eliot

I am sorry there isn't time to let you know about tomorrow – your letter came in the middle of the morning while I was out. Please remember me kindly to Mrs Jepson.

FROM *Vivien Eliot* — MS Valerie Eliot

Monday night [16? August 1920][1] [18 Crawford Mansions, Crawford St] W.1

My dear

I had not time to *write* to Nantes, so am wiring so that you will get a letter at Vannes (?) Just to say, that you *must* keep me posted (well in advance) of addresses, *so that I can get at you*. I *must write*. I am not very well, but will be allright if I can keep in touch with you, and not have uncertainty and upsets. Don't worry, *cos I am not ill*. I am going to Eastbourne tomorrow, almost certainly.[2] So you see its allright. (I will wire tomorrow to Vannes *in case* I do *not* go to E.)

I had a most incredibly horrible migraine on Sunday, and that has left me so dreadfully shaken and prostrate and unnerved. I think I shall be *better* at E. – I am *glad* to go, and glad it was arranged. If only you will keep me posted and do not let me get upset dearest I shall be allright.

Write to Schiff – very nicely. Must not let him fall into K. M.'s[3] hands.

Yr. most adoring.

V.

Take care.

1–TSE left on 14 Aug. for Paris, from where he set off the following day for a walking tour with WL, visiting Nantes and Vannes in Brittany, and then going on to Saumur and Tours in the Loire.

2–She was going to stay with Sydney and Violet Schiff while TSE was away.

3–Katherine Mansfield.

FROM *Vivien Eliot*

MS Valerie Eliot

20 August [1920] Berrow, Carew Road, Eastbourne

My dearest Wonkypenky

I have had, in all, two wires from you and one postcard. The first wire was in duplicate and getting it made life possible. The second wire has come this morning, and we are all surprised that you are going to Tours, and away from the coast.[1] Why is this? I'm sorry about you missing the sea dear. Well my darling I have been *most* ill but am now *much* better so *dont worry*. I am having an extremely *gay* time, and must say I rather like it, altho' it is too much for me. Still, it makes me realise things, and see how out of things I have become, and see that the less one does the less one can do. Yesterday I felt so ill and despairing that I went to my room and cried and called yr. name. Today I am so much better.

Saturday.

It was impossible to finish this yesterday. One gets not a minute to oneself, and I simply cannot really write to you at all. So just do what I ask and get the utmost pleasure out of your holiday. And the last ounce of health. Do not think about me at all. You know I am like a cat with nine lives. I shall be perfectly happy and content if you come back *absolutely* well, and having enjoyed it. But now you *must* keep me *posted in address*. Directly you get this please *wire to the flat* and give me an address so that I can write and have *time* to write. I fear this wont get you. If only you wd. write a postcard *every* day, and not miss, how much happier for me, and all this wiring saved. Write to old Schiff *just a postcard*. Your loving

Wee

TO *Sydney Schiff*

MS BL

22 August 1920 Saumur

My dear Sydney,

I have intended to write to you ever since I got to France, but as you will have gathered, we have moved about more than we anticipated, and also I wanted to wait until I was a bit rested. I have been somewhat anxious about Vivien, as she looked – and was – very tired and ill – the day

1–TSE and WL had planned a holiday on the Brittany coast at Vannes, but it was so cold when they arrived on 19 Aug. that they retreated to Saumur, eighty-five miles away in the Loire.

I left; but I have every confidence that the stay with you and Violet will have done her good.

We dined with Joyce in Paris, as you will I am sure be interested to know. Fritz Vanderpyl,[1] a friend of Pound and myself, was also present, and I enclose a sketch (by me) of the party. Joyce is a quiet but rather dogmatic man, and has (as I am convinced most superior persons have) a sense of his own importance. He has a sort of gravity which seems more Protestant than Catholic. He is obviously the man who wrote his books – that is, he impresses you as an important enough personage for that. We will talk about him later.

Paris was a great relief after many months of London.

W. L. has been sketching a bit here and I have been roaming about. We are both, I think, a great deal better. I have enjoyed Lewis's company very much, and have had a great many conversations with him – I do not know anyone more profitable to talk to.

You will I hope be back in London by the middle of September, and then I look forward to a long talk with you. There are very few people in London whom one can talk to – you are certainly one of them.

But on a holiday like this I feel too physically tired to write a good letter – just as at other times I am too mentally tired and have too little time – so I suppose that I shall never write any letters!

With kindest regards to Violet.

Yours affectionately
T.S.E.

1 – Fritz Vanderpyl, Belgian poet and novelist; art critic of the *Petit Parisien*, 1919–40.

FROM *Vivien Eliot*[1] — Telegram Valerie Eliot

23 August 1920 — Eastbourne

WELL AND HAPPY WRITE FLAT VIVIENNE =

TO *His Mother* — PC Houghton

[Postmark 24 August 1920] — Tours

Have been having a fortnight in France with Wyndham Lewis. Visited the Breton coast, Nantes, and Saumur. The weather is very cool – too cool for the coast. Dined in Paris with one or two French friends and Jas. Joyce, the Irish novelist; and have enjoyed myself very much. I will write a letter when I get back, in a week.

Much love,
Tom.

Vivien Eliot TO *Mary Hutchinson* — MS Texas

Wednesday [25? August 1920] — Flat [18 Crawford Mansions]

Mary dear, I could not write from Eastbourne. It was quite impossible, there, to write or to think. I had rather a peculiar time, on the whole, so *unlike* my usual life, so different that I was bewildered, and lived like a child, without ever taking stock. I liked it. Now I am ill. I have got influenza: the minute I got back. I am writing this flat on my back, and with a very bad headache. I have just had Jack's letter, but I don't know if he had better come here because of infection. I caught it myself from someone I was with just before I left Eastbourne. I wd. love him to come and eat here if he wd like but anyhow it wouldn't do for him to see me.

I send the films. For God's sake don't lose *one* or let any bad or careless person handle them.

As to Tom – a lot seemed to happen in that time between my leaving Bosham and his going to France. I had rather an affair with him, for one thing. It began when we were staying with the Schiffs for the Peace weekend. Don't you yourself find that staying in people's houses together is very conducive to reviving passion? I am sorry about his unsatisfactory

1 – Delivered to 'Eliot Poste Restante Tours'.

letter to you. I did not see it, or know of it. In future I am going to simply wash my hands of Tom and refuse politely to explain him or interpret him or influence or direct him. I mean to have some sort of individual existence, and Tom must manage his own muddles. This does not mean that I shall be above talking [about] him with you Mary, because that is an exciting joy that I wouldn't be without. And you do stand alone. And I shall see you very soon I hope. I am coming to Bosham next Wednesday, if I am well enough, and I am really counting on a lot of talk with you. I think I can explain everything.

Has Tom enemies? You ask me but I think you know that better than I. Anyhow it doesn't matter, for I think enemies stimulate him. The important point is – friends. I must say I felt rather disillusioned after those three weeks of the 'going out more' and 'seeing more people' attempt. But I must *speak* to you. I can't and won't write any more.

I *swear* the films shall follow this. I haven't been acting piggishly, I've just been giving way (letting out my stays, so to speak) Good-bye darling Mary. I shall not expect Jack unless I hear again.

Sneezing violently –

Vivien

TO *Ezra Pound* PC[1] Beinecke

[Postmark 26 August 1920] [Tours]

This is the best thing I have found, such as it is. Amboise has some of the best Renaissance Gothic I have ever seen if one likes that, and the river there is superb. W. L. having fallen off his bicycle on the road to Chinon has retreated to Dieppe.[2] He believes that he has escaped lockjaw. Shall see Fritz [Vanderpyl] and perhaps Cros[3] in Paris.

Yrs. T.

1 – The card shows the porch of the Collegiate Church of Saint-Ours at Loches.

2 – TSE recalled this episode in 'Wyndham Lewis', *Hudson Review* 10: 2 (Summer 1957).

3 – Guy-Charles Cros (1879–1956), poet.

TO *Wyndham Lewis* MS Cornell

Friday [27 August 1920] [Paris]

I sent Fritz a card to say I would fetch him about 5–6. If he dines with me I will return here before dinner. Or better still, come on to his flat, 13 rue Gay Lussac, between 5–7.

T.S.E.

TO *Sydney Schiff* MS BL

Tuesday 31 August 1920 18 Crawford Mansions

My dear Sydney,

Thank you for your charming letter which did indeed welcome me back. I was, as usual, very loth to leave France. Our change of plans must have appeared odd, especially as it took us so long to reach the coast! But when we *finally* got to the actual sea coast the weather had become suddenly very cold, and we felt we could not stand the dreariness of the Breton landscape, so we rushed back, to Saumur. The Loire is extremely beautiful, and I had never stopped in that part of France before. There was good wine, and Lewis found some delightful old houses to sketch that just suited him, and we enjoyed ourselves thoroughly. He had intended to go to Dieppe or Boulogne after a week or ten days and get hold of some special material there. Unfortunately, we hired bicycles, and his wretched machine collapsed and bruised his hand so as to prevent him from working for some time. I left him in Paris. He is a most excellent companion in travelling and a great comfort intellectually.

We saw Joyce again in Paris – but I feel that I would rather reserve him to talk about than try to give my impressions on paper.

Don't expect too much of the *Dial* at once! I agree with you about Hueffer: he is very readable, but after a time one comes to feel that he is an unpleasant parasite of letters. The article by Aldington was taken by the *Dial*[1] prior to Pound and not through him. I think Aldington and Flint[2] say a good many silly things about verse and prose, and I am hoping for an opportunity to discuss this with Aldington. I think the effect of Pound's editorship will be visible gradually, especially after he gets the form of the paper altered.

1–RA, 'The Art of Poetry', *Dial*, 69: 2 (Aug. 1920), 166–80.
2–F. S. Flint (1885–1960), Imagist poet, translator and civil servant.

I should love to come to Eastbourne again – the weekend party was a great success too! – but candidly I do not feel I can afford the expense of any more weekends at present. *Shall you come straight back to Cambridge Square after the 15th*? I want you to.

Vivien's photographs of you are wonderfully good. You will have to tell me about her success as an actress – she won't admit it.

I have arranged to meet Lewis as soon as he gets back, to discuss the paper. Do write and say when I shall see you. With love from both of us to you and Violet.

Affectionately
T.S.E.

TO *Sydney Schiff* MS BL

Sunday [5 September 1920] 18 Crawford Mansions

My dear Sydney,

After all, if you can have me, I should very much like to come down for next weekend (11th), as I want very much to have a talk with you – and somehow that seems easier in Eastbourne than in the midst of London. I shall also want to show you what I hope to have written by then. If it is not convenient then I shall have to hope for your speedy return. But tell me frankly whether I can come or not.

Affectionately
T. S. E.

TO *Henry Eliot* TS Houghton

13 September 1920 18 Crawford Mansions

My dear Henry,

You will think me a beast not to have written – not to have even acknowledged your very detailed letters about mother's health and about the family finances;[1] and finally, to have left your so generous cheque so long unthanked. It is difficult, especially the more time elapses, to explain the thousand little and big things that interfere with the letter one wants to write. I do not think I shall ever have time to write a letter worth anyone's

1 – HWE had written on 20 July that their mother had been diagnosed with incipient diabetes, and on 4 Aug. that he had sold $800 of Liberty Bonds and was sending money to TSE.

keeping. As the world becomes worse to live in, every month, so the minutiae of existence seem to consume more time and energy; so many of the processes that were formerly almost automatic now demand the thought of a Field-Marshal planning a campaign. And also, as one gets older, one seems to accumulate more responsibilities; toward one's friends, toward younger men who are always wanting help of thought and advice; and literary schemes too, instead of being an exciting game, are one more responsibility. One feels now, at I imagine a much younger age than people ever had to before, a responsibility toward the next, unfortunate generation.

I have consumed much time and worry in the problem of a flat. Just now I am on the verge of taking one; if I take a new one it will be because I have your £90 in the bank, and feel safer in paying a higher rent than before. Rents are fantastic. The 'Rents Act' only really protects those who want to stay where they are; and all the nice (comparatively) cheap flats are occupied by people who will probably hang on to them till they die and then bequeathe them to friends. But I cannot say more in gratitude than that you have made it possible for me to change my flat – if there is another one to be found. I do not think we shall ever have a house; quite apart from the rent (houses are not much dearer than flats!) the cost of running a house now is prohibitive – even if one can get servants to work, at any price.

26th September: I began this letter several days ago and since then my time has been completely and absurdly absorbed in the question of which of two flats to take, or even whether to take neither and wait or even try to stick this one out for another three or five years. We are going round in a few minutes to have a last deciding look at one of them, for we must choose by tomorrow morning. I have just heard that some friends of ours have taken a small house in a disagreeable suburb and have to pay £120 *plus* rates and taxes, which will certainly bring it up to £150 or more, and then they will have higher fares to pay to get into town. So nothing else is better. The *other* flat is only £100 a year, which is very cheap for what it is, but there are expensive fittings, stoves etc., which *must* be bought. So if you don't pay one way you pay another. I go on with all these details just to suggest faintly how such petty elements of life as hiring a place to live in consume all the energy one has. I have not done any writing for months, and now we are both sleeping very badly.

I have finished the proofs of my book with Methuens, that's one thing at least, and it ought to be out in October. I feel maddened now because I want to get settled quietly and write some poetry; there seems no likelihood of it for some weeks at best, as if we take another flat there will be a thousand details of business to occupy both of us. What I (what both of us) would like best of all would be to have a nice easily run very tiny flat quite cheap and also the most insignificant small labourer's cottage in the country, where we could always go for a change or for weekends, and the rent of which wouldn't matter. Such a combination would have been possible before the war. But to live in the country *all* the time would involve great fatigue in coming to town every day, and we should probably never see our friends.

I must write you again as soon as I have any leisure or peace of mind, because there are lots of points to mention in your various letters to me; but I must get this off because it is already scandalous how long I have been unable to thank you for your gift. Thank you again, very very gratefully.

Your affectionate brother
Tom.

Those are charming photographs of Millis you sent. I was very glad to get the one of mother's new house.

TO *Sydney Schiff* TS BL

Friday [17 September 1920][1] [London]

Dear Sydney,

I don't quite know where to send this, but you said you were leaving on the 18th, so I hope it will catch you. You say nothing about dates in your letter, but I trust you will be in London from next week.

I never see the *New Age*.[2] I had the impression that you were rather bored with it, but from what you say it appears to be improving. Certainly there is no other political weekly, at any rate, that is anything but dormitive.

Of course Arnold is tarred with his own brush. He is not really a free man, in the best sense of the word; who in England was, at his time?[3] Who

1 – Tentatively dated a week earlier in the first edition of these *Letters*, but redated in the light of the new letter of 5 Sept.

2 – *The New Age*, which ran from 1909 to 1922, was a Socialist and literary paper edited by A. R. Orage (1873–1934), later founder of the *New English Weekly* and an advocate of Social Credit.

3 – TSE is evidently referring to the Introduction to *SW*, which takes its bearings from *Essays in Criticism* (1865, 1888), by Matthew Arnold (1822–88). TSE observed that 'what makes Arnold seem all the more remarkable is, that if he were our exact contemporary, he would find all his labour to perform again' (ix). The notion of the critic as 'free' recurs in the essay 'The Perfect Critic', where TSE hails 'the free intelligence' as 'that which is wholly devoted to inquiry' (12).

in England is now? I wish someone with more leisure and more scholarship than myself would make a study of the spiritual decadence of England which should not be a web of generalisations about the Puritan revolution etc. but a skilful collocation of facts. But I must not write any more; I have had an immoderately busy week and have not finished getting my proofs into shape. But for that – I have not had a moment free – I should have written to Violet to say how much I enjoyed the weekend. We must not let our theatricals drop!

What is the connexion of Rodker with the *New Age*?[1]

Yours affly.,
T.S.E.

Besides, I am using Arnold a little as a stalking horse, or as a cloak of invisibility-respectability to protect me from the elderly. I wanted him as a scarecrow with a real gun under his arm.

TO *His Mother* — TS Houghton

20 September 1920 [London]

My dearest mother,

I had been expecting a period when I could devote several leisurely evenings to writing a long letter and including an account of my visit to France with Wyndham Lewis. But I came back only to make up my mind to try again to find us a new flat. I think I have found one, it has taken a lot of trouble and will take more before we are in. Of course it is considerably more expensive, but I believe it to be very much more respectable, very much less noisy, and in a better neighbourhood in which not so many people are arrested.[2] In any case, we shall I think be free from the neighbourhood of prostitution. This new flat has absorbed most of my time out of bank hours – seeing the landlord, writing to him, trying to get him to make alterations, etc. I will let you know when to change the address. Also, at the same time the proof for my book turned up and has had to be corrected very rapidly in order to get it through in time for publication this autumn. I got Pound and his wife [Dorothy] also to help

1 – Rodker was only a contributor.

2 – 'There are evil neighbourhoods of noise and evil neighbourhoods of silence, and Eeldrop and Appleplex preferred the latter, as being the more evil . . . From time to time the silence of the street was broken; whenever a malefactor was apprehended, a wave of excitement curled into the street and broke upon the doors of the police station' (TSE, 'Eeldrop and Appleplex' [I]).

in correcting it, but even so it entailed a lot of work, what with all the quotations in various languages which had to be verified and were found to have lots of mistakes in them.

I have another ten days holiday due to me in October, and want to take Vivien away for that period; it may unfortunately fall within the time which we shall have to devote to overseeing preparations and moving. I do not suppose that I shall be properly settled at work again till November; I have several things I want to do; and I want a period of tranquility to do a poem that I have in mind.

I am anxiously waiting to hear that you have got right in your new house. Henry has sent a photograph of it which looks very attractive and quiet. I hope that the street cars will not be a nuisance. You have never lived on a street car line. I hope and expect that you feel perfectly well again.

Abby has left with a friend for a trip in Belgium and Holland before returning to America. She was very anxious to go to Berlin, but we finally dissuaded her from attempting that.

I must write again at the end of the week. It is just striking 12. I am only writing this that you may not get discouraged and stop writing again, for I depend dearly on your letter every week.

your very affectionate son
Tom

TO *Mary Hutchinson* MS Texas

Wednesday [22 September 1920] 18 Crawford Mansions

My dear Mary,

It would be far more reasonable to ask if you had forgotten me, and if something had suddenly recalled me to your memory. If so, what was it? It would be interesting to know. In answer to your questions: 1. I am not well, and am about to have an operation. 2. I have been engaged in activity tending toward a new flat, varied by agreeable weekend visits. 3. My pamphlet will emerge into obscurity during October *hoffentlich* [it is to be hoped]. 4. Am I writing much? Only signing my name to leases and agreements.

I had a very pleasant time with Lewis in France; we started in Brittany and went up the Loire on bicycles. We stopped in Paris long enough to see and dine with Vanderpyl, Croce[1] and Joyce twice. I should like you to meet Joyce.

1–Benedetto Croce (1866–1952), Italian philosopher, critic and senator; author of *The Philosophy of Spirit* (4 vols, 1902–17).

It is very kind of you to invite me to Wittering in October, but I am rather afraid that my operation and the removal will get in the way. I heard from Jack and was very sorry I couldn't arrange to meet him, but am writing to him to suggest a date when he gets back. Please do not dread the winter in London. Why should you? It might be so nice. I can think of ways in which it might be.

Yrs
Thomas Eliot.

TO *John Gould Fletcher*[1]

MS Arkansas

23 September 1920 18 Crawford Mansions

My dear Fletcher,

Thank you very much for writing me so fully. But I hope also that you will let me see or even if possible have a copy of the article when it appears.[2] My article, of course, was (at best) and could only be a partial statement of what I take to be a neglected aspect.[3] Certainly I don't deny the importance of emotion. I often find it present to me when other people find only frigidity – or vice versa.[4] One writes about the world one has experienced: and experience without emotion (of *some* kind) is almost a contradiction. I think there is an important distinction between the emotions which are in the experience which is one's material and the emotion in the writing – the two seem to me very different. But I do not believe that my view is very different from yours. It differs very much from Aiken's.

Have you tried any critical articles on the *Athenaeum*? Your *Chapbook* summary of America seemed to me excellent.[5]

Yours sincerely,
T. S. Eliot

I was appalled by Lindsay.[6]

1–For Fletcher see note to TSE's letter to Scofield Thayer, 30 June 1918, above.

2–Apparently unpublished, this article is not among Fletcher's papers at Arkansas.

3–'The Perfect Critic'. Fletcher preferred the second part.

4–'Emotional people – such as stockbrokers, politicians, men of science – and a few people who pride themselves on being unemotional – detest or applaud great writers such as Spinoza or Stendhal because of their "frigidity"' ('The Perfect Critic' [II]).

5–John Gould Fletcher, 'Some Contemporary American Poets', *Chapbook* 2: 2 (May 1920), 1–31.

6–Vachel Lindsay, 'The Broncho that would not be Broken', ibid., 38–9.

TO *The Editor of* The New Republic[1] MS Princeton

23 September 1920 18 Crawford Mansions

Dear Sirs,

I thank you for your letter of the 24th August. I can only say that I am pleased at being asked to contribute verse to your paper, and, as I have not a shred of verse about me at present, I can only keep your invitation in mind, which I shall do.

Yours faithfully,
T. S. Eliot

TO *Mary Hutchinson* MS Texas

28 September 1920 18 Crawford Mansions

My dear Mary,

My letter had, if no other, the merit of provoking yours. I am more than most people dependent on my friends' good will (though I hate to keep invoking it). Since I have come back I have been too immersed in private affairs of the most trying sort to seek out anyone. So I have only seen a very few people who looked me out. I have assumed that those were the only ones who wanted to see me at all. So I was very much pleased to hear from you and Jack.

But as for not seeing us! You asked us to Wittering for the weekend when I was leaving for France, and so Vivien suggested September instead. Then neither of us heard from you till well into September, after our month was settled. So that is why we have not met.

I quite believe you when you say you like living in the country, but still I wonder if you would like it if you had to choose finally and cut yourself off from town or from country. That is what it has come to for me – for I do not see how I can afford both. One of the things about living in the country is that it simplifies existence (or plays at simplifying it, which is pleasanter still) but for me it only complicates it. *You* seem to me to have obtained so to speak a life lease on the pre-war terms, and to have been guaranteed against the horrible waste of time, energy, life, of the struggle with post-war machinery of life. If you take this as a reproach you will lose the whole point of it: it is merely a statement.

1 – The editor of the *New Republic* was Ridgely Torrence (1875–1950).

I think life in London would be more tolerable if there were more mixing: if there were more people entertaining who were capable of bringing very diverse people together and making them combine well. That is a great point in the Schiffs' favour. They won't have anyone about whom they don't really like: so the atmosphere preserves one from boredom. One result is that everyone is ready to expand and play the fool if necessary. We got up some good acting at Eastbourne and they have started to take a great interest in it and are going to have acting parties at Cambridge Square.

Please let me know when you come back?

Yours affectionately
Thomas Eliot

We are moving in three weeks.

Vivien Eliot TO *Mary Hutchinson* MS Texas

[28? September 1920] [18 Crawford Mansions]

Dear Mary,

I think it is nice of you to have written like that, and very nice to offer us Eleanor.[1] I do not know yet when Tom will have his operation, but I shall know on Thursday. I will write and tell you. I want him to put it off until we have moved, and until we know just *how* ruined we are by the transaction, and until we have decided about Paris. But I suppose he will do just as the doctor advises (on Thursday). We are moving in three weeks.

I think it *would* be good for him to go to Eleanor after the operation, and I hope it may be arranged. But, Mary, I could not possibly go with him. It is a pity, but there are some things I can't do, and that is one of them.

Would there be anyone in the village who could come in and cook his meals?

I do not bear you a grudge – it is not that. But I hope you will come back to London soon, if only for a few days, and see me then. I should like to talk to you.

It would have been nice if you had come to Eastbourne to find me. I wish you had.

Please let me know at once when you will be in London.

V.

Send these photographs back, because they are the *only prints* I have and are destined for America. But if you like either I will have a print done for you.

1 – The Hutchinsons' country house, Eleanor, at West Wittering, Sussex.

TO *His Mother* MS Houghton

6 October 1920 18 Crawford Mansions

My dearest mother,

Our time and thought has been taken up lately by negotiations over a new flat [at 9 Clarence Gate Gardens]. It has been a great worry. Everything is so expensive, so fearfully expensive, that it is bound to cripple one and prevent one from being able to do other things – and it means counting very close at that; and then one is so anxious lest it should prove to have some unexpected drawback when one finally gets into it. We have been worried out of our wits. I have finally agreed to take one – it will cost a great deal for us. But I simply cannot any longer work where we are, or even rest. I have of course been unable to write, or even read and think, for some weeks. Previously, we had practically decided on another one, but dropped it at the last minute partly because the landlord was a very disagreeable person – that took a lot of time. We have to have a flat that could be managed without a servant, for if we lost the one we have we should never get another at anywhere like such low wages and would never attempt to get another. I would do a good deal to keep this one, who has been with us four years; for besides taking low wages she does all sorts of things that no one else would do, and is almost like a trained nurse when either of us is ill. But we must have a flat convenient enough so that we *could* manage to do without her, if the pinch of expense became so tight.

You had better write to the Bank unless you meanwhile hear from me another address.

My book will I hope be out in two or three weeks. We have made all sorts of plans for you when you come in the spring – both for London and visiting other cathedral towns and the country. I am very glad you have got your moving over. I fear the streetcars will be trying for you at first. I am very sorry to hear about Charlotte. It sounds very painful.

I dissuaded Abby from going to Berlin. She went to Holland with a friend, and will soon be in Boston. She wanted Vivien to travel with her, but owing to this question of moving, and the expense, Vivien could not go. It was a pity. I do not know whether we shall ever take the rest of my holiday.

When you come, we shall arrange to let you have our flat and our servant, and we shall go elsewhere for the time. This is much the best plan. You will only have to walk into it.

Harold Peters has reached England; I have a letter from him from Plymouth; he will be in London in a few days.

I should be inclined to recommend English securities rather than French were it not for the income tax, which is *very heavy* here. I will try to find out for you at what rate foreigners not living in England have to pay tax.

I am very tired and must stop now.

Your devoted son
Tom.

TO *Henry Eliot*

TS Houghton

10 October 1920 18 Crawford Mansions

Dear Henry,

I am answering your letter at once, as you request.[1] It is very kind of you indeed to take such infinite trouble and provide such very full information.

I figure that the $22,500 of stock at 4% and 3.60 pays Lst. 250 per annum. If I sold it @ 50 and 3.60 exchange I should get Lst. 3125. This invested in various bonds to yield @ 7% would give Lst. 218 p.a. The rate has fluctuated around 3.50 (a little over) the last few days. If you could sell @ 50 and buy sterling around 3.50 I think it would be a good investment. I have not heard of a projected loan to England in the American market.[2] If you sold 100 shares ($10,000) @ 50 = $5000 and could get sterling @ 3.50 it would produce Lst.1428, which invested @ 7% yield would net me Lst.100 p.a., a loss of only Lst.11 p.a. over 4% on the 100 shares (Lst.111 p.a.). I should not gamble on sterling going much lower.

Apparently I am not liable for any income tax in America on the Brick stock.

I think, in short, that it would be worthwhile to sell half the stock at a ratio of 50 (stock) to 3.50 (exchange) or thereabouts. If the exchange dropped further you could of course sell the stock for less, if necessary; and if the stock rose you could take a less favourable exchange. But I should be surprised if sterling got as high as 4.00 for many months. The present British government is very extravagant, and is likely to stay in power for some time; and on the other hand the accession of a Labour government would very likely be reflected by a depression in the value of sterling.

1–HWE had written on 24 Sept. about TSE's stock in the Hydraulic-Press Brick Company, asking whether to sell the shares immediately so as to profit from the exchange rate.

2–HWE had reported, 'rumor has it that England is planning to float a large loan in the United States with the purpose of establishing here large British credits. If this should be true, the effect upon foreign exchange rates would probably be favorable.'

One is as a matter of fact very much in the dark (even arbitrage men seem to be) as to the immediate future of sterling. You know quite as much as I.

I cannot figure on better than 7% for gilt edged (government) securities.

We shall not let you forget your suggestion that you should come over with mother next year. You ought to have six weeks – that would give you at least three weeks here if you made proper arrangements, and that would be well worth it. In fact, you must come; so don't let yourself think that there is any further doubt about it.

I am sorry you had Margaret on your hands. It must have been torture.[1] I want to write to you again soon about other things.

Always your affectionate brother,
[T. S. E.]

TO *Wyndham Lewis* — MS Cornell

15 October 1920 — 18 Crawford Mansions

Dear Lewis,

Thanks for your address. I should have communicated before but have been in almost hourly consultation with somebody or other about the flat which I am trying to take from an insane she-hyaena. As it is still uncertain what day I can move or whether she will make it impossible for me to move at all I have been able to form no plans and make no engagements. As it appears that I can get you on the telephone I shall ring up at the first moment I find myself free.

Yours
T. S. E.

TO *Edgar Jepson* — MS Beinecke

15 October 1920 — 18 Crawford Mansions

Dear Jepson,

Please forgive my unpardonable delay in replying to your kind invitation – which has been due to pressure of business of the most agonizing

1–HWE had related that their sister Margaret had been to stay with him in Chicago. 'You can have no idea of what acute boredom is unless you have Margaret talk to you for an hour. It is not mere ennui; it is an excruciating pain; it is like being killed by light taps of the bastinado.'

description. I shall be very much pleased if I may come to your supper on Sunday evening.

Sincerely yours
T. S. Eliot

TO *Scofield Thayer* TS Beinecke

17 October 1920 18 Crawford Mansions

Dear Scofield,

Thank you very much for your charming letter, written on my birthday, and also for the interesting cheque enclosed therein, which came to hand at a most opportune moment.[1] I also observe your sagacious consideration in withholding payment until you had raised the rate.

Upon due reflection, and after perusal of Mr Shanks's[2] contributions, I shall be glad to undertake a contribution every other month under the name of 'London Letter', dealing with the literary life of the metropolis. I suppose it will turn out to be mostly an attempt to diagnose the reasons for there not being more life than there is; but I will endeavour to spot any germs of vitality that appear, lest our American public should find the London spectacle too depressing. As soon as my personal affairs, which means at the moment protracted negotiations over a flat, have quieted down a bit, I will compose something to send you.

Mr Shanks, by the way, has just been presented with a silver medal for writing the most beautiful poem for the year 1919,[3] so he will probably retain enough conviction of his own merit to tide him over. I do not suppose that Pound will have any objection to the change.

Meanwhile I will not publish this matter abroad.

I received last night by the post a package bearing a label which indicated that it came from the offices of *The Dial*. When opened, it was found to contain *The House of Dust* by Conrad Aiken, and nothing else.[4] There was no enclosure or inscription to indicate why the volume was sent to me. It occurred to me that it might be intended for review: and if so, I fear it was a piece of naughtiness on your part at Conrad's expense. I have

1–A cheque in payment for 'The Possibility of a Poetic Drama', *Dial* 79: 5 (Nov. 1920).

2–Edward Shanks (1892–1953), English poet, novelist and critic, had written three London Letters for the *Dial* (Apr., June, Aug.), the last on TSE and English criticism. TSE's first London Letter would appear in Apr. 1921.

3–Shanks's *The Queen of China and Other Poems* (1919) was awarded the first Hawthornden Prize.

4–Conrad Aiken, *The House of Dust* (1920).

glanced through the book and it appears to me that the workmen called in to build this house were Swinburne and myself; the Dust being provided by Conrad. I trust that this criticism will not appear egotistic on my part, but I can point to a quotation on page 83.[1] So will you tell me what I am to do with the book? I will forward it to anyone in America or the United Kingdom whom you designate. I have always, of course, had the most friendly relations with Conrad; and I shrink from straining our friendship by reviewing his book.

Vivienne has recently been approached by a certain person of our acquaintance with the request that she should forward to you a manuscript which had already been rejected by Pound. To which she replied that as Pound occupied the position of Foreign Editor of the *Dial*, it would be considered a violation of etiquette. But, she said suavely, that the person was quite at liberty to send the manuscript direct. However, the individual in question has (very wisely, in my opinion) decided not to risk it.

Vivienne sends her love, and thanks you for your letter.

This address will continue to find us until further notice. My cable address in case of need is 'Eliot, Information, Branchage, Stock-London'.

Yours as ever
T. S. E.

TO *Wyndham Lewis* — MS Cornell

18 October 1920 — 18 Crawford Mansions

My dear Lewis,

You may already have left for Hastings, but if not I trust it will do you good and that the strike[2] will not prevent your coming back. Don't let it. It is true that we are having great trouble and I rather doubt if we can move at all. This fills me with despair. Just had a party of Schiff, Ottoline, and Siegfried Sassoon (all accidentally). Come and see us directly you get back.

Write to this address.

Yrs –
T.S.E.

1–Aiken: 'Sometimes, I say, I'm just like John the Baptist – / You have my head before you . . . on a platter' (III, vii, 9–10). TSE: 'Though I have seen my head (grown slightly bald) brought in upon a platter, / I am no prophet – and here's no great matter' ('The Love Song of J. Alfred Prufrock', ll. 82–3).

1–A national miners' strike began on the day of this letter; it was triggered by wage reductions consequent upon the de-controlling of mines on 31 Mar.

TO *Leonard Woolf* TS Berg

23 October 1920 18 Crawford Mansions

My dear Woolf,

I have been most anxious to come out and see you and Mrs Woolf, since you have returned to town; but have been prevented by a series of calamities. I have been engaged in long and most vexing legal negotiations over a new flat, and got partially moved in last week; since then my father-in-law was taken suddenly ill, and I have not been able to attend to anything else. He had to have an operation very suddenly on Friday, and I did not get to bed till Saturday night; he was just at the point of death, and we do not know from hour to hour whether he will survive. My wife has been on the edge of collapse in consequence.

There have been several minor complications too, such as a minor operation on my Nose. But at present my father-in-law's condition is the only concern on my mind, and we have to hold ourselves in readiness at any moment.

I have not forgotten, however, that you promised to review my book, and as the author's copies have just come in, I suppose it will be in the hands of the *Athenaeum*. So I have written to Murry tonight to say that I have asked you to do it, and to ask him to send it to you; and I very much hope he will. I am looking forward with great curiosity to finding out what you think of these essays.[1]

Please tell your wife that I am disappointed at not having seen her since my visit[2] which I enjoyed so much, and disappointed at being now in a position such that I can neither ask you to come and see us, nor come to see you.

Sincerely,
T. S. Eliot

1–LW's review of *SW* appeared as 'Back to Aristotle', *A.*, 17 Dec. 1920.

2–TSE had visited the Woolfs at Rodmell on 18 Sept. VW records in her diary for 19–20 Sept.: 'He is a consistent specimen of his type, which is opposed to ours. Unfortunately the living writers he admires are Wyndham Lewis & Pound. – Joyce too . . . We had some talk after tea . . . about his writing. I suspect him of a good deal of concealed vanity & even anxiety about this.' TSE 'wants to write a verse play in which the 4 characters of Sweeny act the parts. A personal upheaval of some kind came after Prufrock, & turned him aside from his inclination – to develop in the manner of Henry James. Now he wants to describe externals. Joyce gives internals' (*Diary*, II, 67–8).

TO *The Editor of* The Times Literary Supplement

Published 28 October 1920

Sir,

I hope that I am not too late in raising one or two questions suggested by the important article in your issue of September 30 entitled 'A French Romantic'.[1] I have been delayed by personal preoccupations; I am excused for writing now, if I am excused at all, by the importance of the subject, the interest of the article, and the fact that no other correspondent has anticipated me.

I willingly concede the point, contested by Mr Cyril Falls, that M. Maurras is a 'romantic'.[2] M. Maurras has been handled very competently by M. Julien Benda in an appendix to *Belphégor*.[3] So much for M. Maurras. It is in attempting to apprehend your critic's definitions of the terms 'romanticism' and 'classicism' that my intellect is confused and my serenity disturbed. We are told that Lamartine 'floundered in romanticism' partly because 'the sense of the mystery of things remained with him.' Later we learn that 'Romanticism is an excess of emotion'; but we are not informed what balance can be struck between excess of emotion (which is surely a fault) and a sense of the mystery of things (which cannot be altogether a bad sense to have). The writer treats Romanticism on the whole with disapproval until he suddenly declares that the period of classical production in France was also 'a great romantic period'. This period is not the 17th century, which is dismissed as a period of 'formalism': it is a period which is represented by the Cathedrals and by

1–[Basil de Selincourt], 'A French Romantic', a review of Albert Thibaudet, *Les Idées de Charles Maurras* (Paris, 1920), *TLS*, 28 Oct. 1920.

2–Charles Maurras (1868–1952), French poet, critic, political philosopher and polemical journalist, was founding editor of the reactionary and extreme monarchist paper, *L'Action Française* (1908–44). Building on 'three traditions' – classicisim, Catholicism, monarchism – the thrust of Maurras's ideology was to become increasingly right-wing, authoritarian and anti-democratic. TSE later wrote 'The *Action Française*, M. Maurras and Mr. Ward', in *NC* 7: 3 (Mar. 1928), an issue that included his translation of Maurras's essay 'Prologue to an Essay on Criticism'. TSE said he had been 'a reader of the work of M. Maurras for eighteen years', and, far from 'drawing him away from' Christianity – in 1926 Maurras was condemned by the Pope, with five of his books being placed on the Index – it had had the opposite effect. In a later essay, TSE named Maurras as one of the 'three best writers of invective of their time' (*SE*, 499). Cyril Falls, in a letter to the *TLS* (7 Oct.), defended Maurras against the charge of political extremism: he is 'a convinced classicist' who has written 'many denunciations of romanticism'.

3–Benda wrote, 'The eulogies bestowed daily on the high-priest of the *Action Française* for "returning to the manners of the classic style" make us smile when we consider his enthusiasm for his own doctrines, the violence of his arguments, and especially the virulent, contemptuous tone he uses towards his adversary' (*Belphégor*, trans. S. J. I. Lawson [1929], 156).

Jeanne d'Arc (but not, apparently, by Agnes Sorel). I should be interested to know how the 'cathedrals' are more classical, or more romantic either, than Vézelay, St Benoît-sur-Loire, or Périgueux; but that is not the point: the point is, what is meant by applying *both* terms to their elucidation?

I suggest that the difficulties which veil most critics' theories of Romanticism (and I include such writers as Pierre Lasserre[1] and Irving Babbitt) are largely due to two errors. One is that the critic applies the same term 'romantic' to epochs and to individual artists, not perceiving that it assumes a difference of meaning; and the other is that he assumes that the terms 'romantic' and 'classic' are mutually exclusive and even antithetical, without actually enforcing this exclusiveness in the examination of particular works of art.

Another difficulty is that these writers do not always appear to distinguish between *definitions* and *propositions*. Again, your critic introduces unexpected terms which are not defined. I cite 'intellectual and emotional integrity', 'spiritual purpose', and 'larger integration'. The alternatives are to elaborate a rigidly deductive system, or to employ the terms 'romantic' and 'classic' merely as convenient historical tags, never stretching their meaning beyond the acceptance of the intelligent reader. And it would perhaps be beneficial if we employed both terms as little as possible, if we even forgot these terms altogether, and looked steadily for the intelligence and sensibility which each work of art contains.

I am, Sir, your obliged obedient servant,

T. S. Eliot

TO *Mary Hutchinson* PC Texas

[Postmark 30 October 1920] 18 Crawford Mansions

I am so sorry about these postponements. Vivien's father is dangerously ill and was operated upon last night <at two hours notice>.[2] We were up all night and V. has to be with him most of the time: so we simply cannot arrange any plans at all at present.

aff.
T. S. E.

We cannot predict from hour to hour.

1–Pierre Lasserre (1867–1930), literary critic; director of L'École des Hautes-Etudes; author of the first study of Maurras, *Charles Maurras et la Renaissance classique* (Paris, 1902). Lasserre was a friend of Péguy and a disciple of Sorel, who broke with Maurras and the Action Française in 1914.

2–His second emergency operation.

TO *His Mother* TS Houghton

31 October 1920 18 Crawford Mansions

My dearest mother,

I am afraid you will be anxious on account of my not having written for so long. I do not think that I have ever had so many difficult things on my mind at once. For the last ten days Vivien's father has been very ill. It appeared at first to be ptomaine poisoning from some tinned sardines, but they finally decided that the poisoning was only the occasion of something more serious. I was called over Friday afternoon. The specialists had a consultation at half past six, and at quarter past eight they operated in the house. After the operation the surgeon said that he would have been dead in another five or ten minutes. There was an enormous abscess in his abdomen, which was just beginning to break. They were not certain even after the operation that he would live through the night, and none of us got to bed at all.

He had suffered very great agony for days, and was very weak indeed. We had two nurses, but of course there was work all the time for everybody. So far, he has recovered wonderfully well, and in spite of the discomfort of having to sit up in bed with a tube in the wound to draw out the suppuration, is in very good spirits. He has not been told that although the surgeons were able to get out the abscess, they confess themselves quite at a loss to know the cause of the abscess. They say that they will have to operate again, but they hope to be able to postpone it until he is over the shock of this operation and is stronger.

Vivien is now nearly prostrated. The news that the operation was necessary was very sudden, and the doctors held out very little hope of his surviving it. She held out through the night, so long as there was work to do, but she has been in bed with a terrible migraine yesterday, and [is] now very weak. To add to the difficulty Mrs Haigh-Wood's servant (she has only one now) was taken with a bad cold and fever Friday, and had to go home. We have lent them our Ellen for a few days, as Vivien's mother cannot do all the work, help with her father, and cook for the family and two nurses as well. So we are doing our own work and are to go out for meals.

Her father is not strong and we fear a sudden relapse at any time. We are not on the telephone here which makes Vivien very uneasy, as they could not get at us at night, and with the nurses there is nowhere in the house for Vivien to sleep. We shall not be able to breathe freely for weeks; but it is almost miraculous that he should have lasted up to this point.

I should be very grateful to you if you would write to Mrs Haigh-Wood and give her your sympathy.

Vivien is particularly fond of her father; she takes more after him and his side of the family, and understands him better than the others <do>. He has no living relatives except very remote ones. He is a sweet, simple man, perfectly happy when he is in the country painting and drawing. I saw him when he was almost unconscious, but he immediately recognised me and asked when my book was coming out, and when I saw him for a moment yesterday he said he wanted a copy at once.

Previous to this, I have been engaged as I told you, in negotiations over my new flat. The negotiations proved to be much more trying and complicated than there was any reason to expect, and in the end Mr Haigh-Wood (just before he fell ill) had to help me straighten them out. I took the flat over from a very selfish, cranky, and insanely suspicious grasping old spinster, who insisted on all sorts of formalities, made her solicitors draw up elaborate documents to be signed, then objected to the way they were drawn up and began all over again, then stipulated that I should pay her solicitors' fees, charged a prodigious price for the oilcloth and fittings of the flat, which we had to buy, insisted on the money down before signing the lease, insulted us when she left, and maliciously had the electricity, gas, and telephone cut off so as to put me to the trouble of putting them on again. Of course, in the circumstances, I had to employ solicitors too. So the whole thing has come very expensive. But it is a very nice flat, and the actual rent of it will be only £15 more than the rent of Crawford Mansions will be on a new lease. It is a much better block, very respectable looking and in a good neighbourhood. It has one more room than this flat, and the rooms are rather bigger. It will do beautifully for you when you come, it is only one flight up, and there is a lift as well, and anthracite stoves which you can keep going all the time to provide a constant temperature, and constant hot water supply.

Of course I wanted to throw it up on account of the old lady's insolence, but I reasoned that we had lost six months already in hunting, and that it would pay me better to be swindled on the price of the lease, and get settled at once, than to start the hunt anew and not be able to work for several months more. You see, we began looking for a flat in June, and since then I have simply not had the time to do a single piece of work, and when one has in mind a great many things that one wants to do, that irritates the nerves more and more.

Before I embarked on this flat of which I speak, I had very nearly taken another one – not nearly so good – and dropped it finally because I was convinced that the landlord was asking about twice as much for it as he was entitled to. But to prove that and get him punished would have been difficult, and I should have had to take the flat first.

My book is 'out' on Thursday,[1] and I have just received six copies from Methuen. I am sending you one tomorrow. I am pleased with the form they have given it. Knopf, who published my poems in New York, has bought 350 copies, and I suppose it will be reviewed in American papers at the same time.

I have promised to write occasional 'London Letters' for the *Dial*, and also letters of some sort to a weekly called *The Freeman* in New York. I have been asked to send a contribution to the *Evening Post*. Then there is the *Revue de Genève*, and Bruce Richmond, of the *Times* (London), wants something from me when I have time. Wyndham Lewis is projecting a small Art and Literature paper and wants my help. So if I would undertake it, I should have my hands very full. But I want to get to work on a poem I have in mind.

My new address is 9 Clarence Gate Gardens, London, N.W.1.

But anything that comes here will reach me, as we have not quite moved out yet, and I think a friend of Vivien's, Lucy Thayer whom you have met, will be here soon and will occupy it. Her mother died of cancer after several years of torment, and Lucy who looked after her the whole time is to come abroad for a rest.

If you have not yet sent the dividend, you can send it to the new address, but *Registered* mail had better go to the Bank, as there is always a chance of its being delivered when no one is in, and taken away again. The Bank address you know is Lloyds Bank Limited, Information Department, Head Office, 71 Lombard Street, London E.C.3.

I *of course* want the Insurance continued, and I suppose you will pay the Policy out of the dividend before sending it. If I died, this money would be most important for Vivien. She would get £60 a year from the Bank; and I depend on leaving her Insurance, what money I save if I live long enough, and what I may eventually inherit from you (that will, I pray, be a long time ahead) to live upon. What money she will eventually get from her father's

1 – *The Sacred Wood: Essays on Poetry and Criticism* was dedicated to his brother. Of the US edition (Feb. 1921), his mother wrote to HWE, 'I have felt quite badly about it because of the savage criticisms. I do not like the name [and] I think $2.50 is too high a price.' HWE would write to their mother on 22 Mar. 1921: 'When I get out of the wilderness of his allusions to writers of whom I have never heard, I like the book; the style is clear, clean-cut, economical of words; the phrases are clear, exact, not mussy or vague. The thought is hard to follow sometimes, though, not because it is obscure, but because it is subtle or complex.'

estate will not be enough for support. The death duties in this country are very heavy indeed, and the estate is divided equally between her and Maurice. Again, Vivien and Maurice get nothing until *both* her father and her mother are dead; so I have to plan for the contingency of Vivien and one of her parents surviving me. If she had to try to support herself even partially, there is not much she could do; her eyes are so weak that the oculist says she must never again subject them to any continuous strain, either reading, writing or sewing, for more than two hours a day. At one time, before our marriage, she was very successful in tutoring backward children, individually; but young unmarried women always find it easier to obtain such work. Therefore I should not for a moment consider letting the insurance drop.

To add to the confusion, Harold Peters and his friends have been here for a week, their yacht is at Southampton, and they are going to cruise in the Mediterranean. I am very fond of Harold, but this visit has been much more of a strain and a responsibility than a pleasure. I want them to enjoy their stay, but they know no one in London, and could not be combined with the sort of intellectual society that I know, and it would mean giving up a great deal of time.

I must stop now, I have so much to do –

You have not written for some time, I suppose because you did not know where to write. But you can always write to the bank, although I prefer to get letters at home. I am anxiously waiting to hear your latest news.

With very much love,

your devoted son,
Tom

TO *Sir Algernon Methuen* MS Lilly

2 November 1920 18 Crawford Mansions

Dear Sir Algernon Methuen,

Thank you for your letter about your anthology.[1] I should be very pleased to have you use any poem of mine in an anthology. I am only not quite certain whether I have anything suitable for your purpose? I take it for granted, perhaps mistakenly, that you mean to use poems

1 – *An Anthology of Modern Verse*, ed. A[lgernon] M[ethuen] (1921) was to include 'La Figlia Che Piange' (pp. 69–70). Methuen's request for a poem had specified (30 Oct.) that 'it must be of a lyrical and moderately intelligible character. Please forgive this insult . . . the book is not only for the general reader but also for use in schools.'

that have already been published. I have no unpublished verse at the present time.

The only poem that strikes me as possible is one called '*La figlia che piange*'. If you still have the small volume I sent you, you will find it at the end. Many people seem to like it who do not like the other things. <But I should very much like to have your own opinion.>

Sincerely yours
T. S. Eliot

I am very much pleased with the format of the '*Sacred Wood*'.

TO *Walter de la Mare*[1]

MS De la Mare Estate

5 November 1920

18 Crawford Mansions

Dear Mr de la Mare,

Harold Monro gave me your very kind invitation, and I had a faint hope of being able to come. But I have been in bed for three days, and even if I am up it will be impossible. We have had very critical illness in my wife's family lately, and the crisis is not yet past.

I hope you will ask me again before very long, as I should very much like to meet you. Also, when I am settled in the flat into which I am trying to move, I should be delighted if you would do me the honour of coming to dinner.

I have never had the opportunity of meeting you before and am very much disappointed.

Yours sincerely,
T. S. Eliot

Please forgive my posting this without a stamp.[2] But I only heard from Monro definitely this morning, and, not being able to go out I forgot to ask anyone else to get stamps.

1–Walter de la Mare (1873–1956), poet and author. Order of Merit, 1953. In due course, TSE became his publisher at Faber & Faber, issuing *Collected Rhymes and Verses* (1942) and *Collected Poems* (1948); and he wrote 'To Walter de la Mare' for *A Tribute to Walter de la Mare* (1948).

2–De la Mare paid 4d on receipt of the letter.

TO *Harold Monro* MS Beinecke

Friday [5 November 1920] 18 Crawford Mansions

Dear Monro,

I am writing to de la Mare to express my regrets and to say that I want to come to see him when I am better. Also, I want to try to get him, and you, to come and dine at my new flat. It is true that I was doubtful of being able to come, as my father in law has been at the point of death: now I have been in bed for three days with a cold brought on by fatigue. When I am about, and a bit straightened out, I will write and try to get hold of you. But I still hope to be able to come to your party on the 10th.

I am awfully sorry about Sunday.

Yours ever
T. S. E.

TO *Walter de la Mare* MS De la Mare Estate

8 November 1920 18 Crawford Mansions

Dear Mr de la Mare,

I hope you will pardon my curious behaviour – which was due to the fact that I wanted to come. After being laid up with a cold myself, I infected my wife with it, which is a much more serious matter, as it is apt to lead to complications to which I am immune. I tried all the morning to get someone who could stay with her this evening, but without success.

I do not know whether you can ever be tempted to town of an evening, but I shall try to do so. My new flat will be one stop from Baker Street Station. If you will not, I shall invite myself to see you, but I should rather you came to see me first.

Yours sincerely,
T. S. Eliot

TO *Russell Green*[1] PC Texas

[Postmark 16 November 1920] 9 Clarence Gate Gdns

Again I should like to help you, but am involved in personal anxieties which take all my time – I shall not even be able to fulfil my promises made, much less make new. Better luck some other time.

T. S. Eliot

TO *Mrs Dawson Scott*[2] CC BL

16 November 1920 9 Clarence Gate Gdns

Dear Mrs Dawson Scott,

I should be very glad to take the chair for Mr Jepson: I hope you will let me have a reminder in February so that I shall be ready for it in good time. I should also be glad to talk at some time, if you care to have me do so.

Sincerely yours
[T. S. E.]

Vivien Eliot TO *Mary Hutchinson* MS Texas

[17 November 1920] 9 Clarence Gate Gdns
Note new address – !
Telephone. Pad[dington] 3331

Dear Mary,

I hope you have not thought me unfriendly. If you will believe me I have *longed* to see you and talk to you all these horrible weeks. But I see no one, hear of no one, go nowhere. It only amazes me that life *can* be like this, and one goes on. It is just 5 weeks today, and I have been fighting, every minute, a long losing battle against *horrible* illness, unimaginable pain, doctors' mistakes – obstinacy – stupidity – delays – family's blindness. The only thing on *my* side has been my father's courage and determination. But I am afraid we're going to lose after all, and after so much fighting it will be very hard to bear.

1–Russell Green, who had won the Newdigate Prize at Oxford with his poem 'Venice' (1916), was editing the seventh number of *Coterie*. TSE had contributed 'A Cooking Egg' to *Coterie* 1 (May 1919).
2–Fixtures secretary of the Tomorrow Club, which met weekly at Caxton Hall to hear speakers mostly on literary topics.

You see I never can make an engagement more than an hour ahead. There are changes every few hours, and every single complication and misadventure happens. I never go to bed without fear, and to ring up first thing every morning takes all one's courage. If you could, when you have a perfectly free afternoon, *ring me up*, (if you would like to see me) about 2 o'clock, I would come over then and there if it happened to be one of the afternoons when I feel a little security. If I am not in, get Ellen to ring me up and give me your message, because she always knows where I am.

I've been out of 'the great world'[1] so long I am afraid I shall soon fade away altogether.

Your very affect.
Vivien

TO *Sydney Schiff* MS BL

30 November 1920 9 Clarence Gate Gdns, London N.W.1

My dear Sydney,

We were much distressed at hearing of Violet's last misfortune, and wait to hear how serious it will prove. I pray that it will not retard and complicate her recovery from her illness and operation. Do give her our warm sympathy.

Certainly this is the way in which I have <myself> known disasters to follow each other, and always when one has drawn up one's plans with the greatest exactness. Events succeed one another, apparently for the purpose of making one's mind useless to one. There are times, I think, when one must try to seal one's intellect hermetically, to prevent it from being destroyed by circumstances which it cannot mend.

Vivien's father has kept much in the same state, with some improvement but alarming fluctuations which cause great anxiety to the family. The surgeon was called for a consultation today, and Vivien spent the day at Hampstead and is completely exhausted by the agitations. I am much concerned about her health; she manages to keep up and do a great deal, at the price of a migraine once a week, and bad nights. I have not at all been in a mood for work.

What you say about my book gives me great pleasure – but notwithstanding this and the respect I have for your good opinion – it makes me a little apprehensive. I fear that in the course of time you will

1 – Byron, *Don Juan* XI, xlv.

find that it is not quite so remarkable as you had thought, and that you will then cease to find any merit in it: I only hope that you will express your opinion as frankly then as now.

You have no reason for not saying what you think about Murry. His criticism is dictated by emotion, which is *not* the same thing as saying that he feels strongly about the things he criticises. Even when he is right, he is the victim of an emotion, and the rightness seems an accident. He never surrenders himself,[1] but uses what he is talking about as an outlet for some feeling; and this is a sort of irreverence for reason which is hard to bear. It is quite tolerable for an artist, scientist or workman to be an egotist if he will give himself up to the one thing, but Murry I believe is an egotist in that too – hopelessly isolated from <both> persons and causes.

I saw Trench[2] last night, but am sorry that I got no chance to talk to him – at a dinner given by the 'Poetry Circle' of the Lycaeum Club (Ladies).[3] It was an odd gathering – we all (i.e. the speakers) – seemed to be lions of various sizes, from the Dean Inge[4] to Edith Sitwell and myself – but no one seemed very clear as to what we were or what we did.

Are any doctors or nurses ever satisfactory?

With, again, sympathy for you and for Violet, and hoping to hear soon that things are better

Affectionately
T.S.E.

TO *His Mother* TS Houghton

2 December 1920 9 Clarence Gate Gdns

My dearest mother,

You will I know understand why I have not written for such a long time again. Nevertheless I have been thinking about you and wondering about your health a great deal, and I was very glad to get a letter from Marion yesterday which sounded very cheerful and happy. I am delighted to think

1–'What happens is a continual surrender of himself as he is at the moment to something which is more valuable. The progress of the artist is a continual self-sacrifice, a continual extinction of personality' ('Tradition and the Individual Talent'; *SW*, 52–3).
2–Herbert Trench (1865–1923), poet and playwright; author of *Ode from Italy in Time of War* (1915).
3–For further accounts of the occasion, at which he made his first after-dinner speech and met the woman who was to introduce him to the Tarot pack, see both the next letter (to his mother, 2 Dec.) and *Aldous Huxley 1894–1963: A Memorial Volume*, ed. Julian Huxley (1965).
4–W. R. Inge (1860–1954), Dean of St Paul's Cathedral, 1911–34.

that you are seeing so many people and entering into so many activities, and I like to imagine you going about Cambridge. I like seeing many people myself; I even enjoy large crowds and public occasions. And then the most complete solitude to recuperate in.

We have of course been on pins and needles about Vivien's father the whole time. When we think that the surgeon, one of the most skilled in London, was so horrified when he opened him, at the second operation, at what he found inside that he wanted simply to sew him up and let him die in peace – we are absolutely terrified to believe that it is now possible, and even probable, that he will recover. I am really uneasy the whole time, thinking what would happen to Vivien and her mother *now* should a new complication arise – as it might do at a moment's notice. When there seemed no hope they could keep up, because there was always something to be done and they were quite prepared for the worst, but they could not possibly go through it again. Even if things continue for the best, it will take them a long time to recuperate. And there have been all sorts of minor difficulties: the two nurses did not get on together; the two servants Mrs H. had to have are unsatisfactory and don't want to stay in a house with an invalid, and so on.

I went out to see Mr Haigh-Wood this afternoon after the bank, and found him very bright and hopeful and patient.

Vivien has had to be at home most of the time, housekeeping and shopping and so on, and has not seen any friends or been out in the evening for six weeks. I have been out twice lately, once to Leonard and Virginia Woolf's, where I found Lowes Dickinson,[1] and once to a dinner at a Ladies Club called the Lycaeum Club. That was rather amusing. Their 'Poetry Circle' gives a large dinner once a year and invites men of letters to speak. There were seven speakers: Maurice Hewlett,[2] Dean Inge (better known as 'The gloomy dean'), Sturge Moore the poet,[3] St John Irvine (a dramatist), Edith Sitwell, Aldous Huxley, and myself. I had been asked to

1 – Goldsworthy Lowes Dickinson (1862–1932) – affectionately known as 'Goldie' – Fellow of King's College, Cambridge; author, and advocate of a league of nations. His writings include *Letters from John Chinaman* (1901), *A Modern Symposium* (1905), and *The International Anarchy, 1904–1914* (1926). See E. M. Forster, *Goldsworthy Lowes Dickinson* (1973), and *The autobiography of G. Lowes Dickinson and other unpublished writings*, ed. Dennis Proctor (1973). VW wrote in her diary on 5 Dec., 'Eliot & Goldie [Lowes Dickinson] dined here t'other night – a successful party'; and she remarked of TSE that he was 'all caught, pressed, inhibited; but great driving power some where – & my word what concentration of the eye when he argues!' (*Diary*, II, 77).

2 – Maurice Hewlett (1861–1923), English novelist and poet; his poetry includes the well-regarded *The Song of the Plow* (1916).

3 – Thomas Sturge Moore (1870–1944): English poet, playwright, author, engraver.

speak on 'Modern Tendencies of Dramatic Poetry', but when I got there and saw the list I found that the subject was given to someone else, and mine was 'Modern *Audiences* of Dramatic Poetry'. So I had to prepare an entirely new speech while the others were speaking. Then Huxley, who was ahead of me, fainted in the middle of his speech, the atmosphere being rather close, and I had to speak five minutes before I had expected to! However, I described the sort of audience I should like to have, and the sort I should not want to have, if I were having a verse play produced, and it appeared to be received very well.[1] Some of them read their speeches from a manuscript which seems to me a mistake, and the gloomy dean's speech consisted almost wholly of quotations. I sat next to an elderly lady who asked me if I knew a poem called 'The Thin Red Line',[2] so I lied and said yes, and she said she had written it. She was Scotch and believed firmly in ghosts, and invited me to a 'Celtic concert'.

Knopf, who brought out my poems, has bought 350 copies of my book, but I do not know whether bound copies or merely the pages, so I do not know how soon it will be out, but I certainly expect before Christmas. It would be quicker if you wrote yourself to Alfred A. Knopf, Inc., 220 West 42nd Street, and asked him about it, than if I wrote and told you. It has been very well received so far, and I hope it will sell. Several other books of essays have appeared simultaneously, and one, by Clutton-Brock,[3] at the same price and in the same binding; I do not know whether that will affect the sales adversely, but if so it is Methuen's fault, as he published both books. There is one by Murry too.[4]

I am rather tired of the book now, as I am so anxious to get on to new work, and I should more enjoy being praised if I were engaged on something which I thought better or more important. I think I shall be able to do so, soon. Having Peters and his friends on my mind has worried me too a good deal. One of them is ill in a nursing-home and they may be here till nearly Christmas.

Poor Maurice [Haigh-Wood] has been pluckily struggling to prepare for an examination for a new post which he greatly covets, and the examination is tomorrow. He has been under insuperable disadvantages;

1–This impromptu speech was probably akin to 'The Possibility of a Poetic Drama'.
2–'The Thin Red Line' was the title of a famous 1881 painting by Robert Gibb RA depicting a noted action by the British Army's 93rd (Highland) Regiment at the Battle of Balaclava on 25 Oct. 1854, during the Crimean War. Frederick W. O. Ward wrote a poem with the title, in *English Roses* (1899). The anonymous lady's poem is unknown.
3–Arthur Clutton-Brock, *Essays on Books* (1920).
4–JMM, *The Evolution of an Intellectual* (1920).

the nurse is installed in his room and he has not even a room to himself to work in uninterruptedly in the evenings, besides having to run out for medicines and things often, and to do his work at the Ministry of Labour in the daytime.

I must stop now and go to bed. I shall attempt to write to Marion and to Henry in the course of a few days. Mrs Haigh-Wood was delighted with your letter, and so was Mr Haigh-Wood; so it did much good.

Always your devoted son,
Tom

TO *Sydney Schiff* MS BL

6 December 1920 9 Clarence Gate Gdns

My dear Sydney,

I had not heard of Lynd's article until I got your letter, and I have procured the *Nation* today. I am not so affected by Lynd's hostility as I am by your act of friendship – for whether your opinion of the book is modified by friendship or not, the public expression of your opinion *is* an act of friendship, which I value.[1]

It is <a> curious <coincidence> that I should have reviewed a book of Lynd's essays last year, and damned it, I believe, by quoting from it.[2] His combination of slovenly journalese and parsonical zeal <the 'true old enthusiastic breed'[3] of dullness> was particularly depressing as an example of some of the things about the contemporary degeneracy that one loathes.

We *hope to hear* that Violet is progressing, and that weather at Eastbourne is favourable. She must have been very discouraged. Vivien's father has progressed, and has even been lifted into a chair for an hour – but there is a long anxious time still ahead. I may run over to Paris on Saturday – I have a week's holiday due me – I have been trying to write a little and find my brain quite numb, and Vivien wants me to have a change. I am only afraid of the absence of artificial heat in Paris.

Always affectionately,
T.S.E.

1 – Robert Lynd. 'Buried Alive', *N.*, 4 Dec. 1920, 359–60: 'Mr Eliot, in his critical essays, is an undertaker rather than a critic . . . he fails as a critic because he brings us neither light nor delight.' SS's protest was not published.

2 – TSE, 'Criticism in England', *A.*, 13 June 1919.

3 – Dryden, *Absalom and Achitophel*, 530.

TO *Edgar Jepson* TS Beinecke

8 December 1920 9 Clarence Gate Gdns

My dear Jepson,

I am returning your tickets with many regrets. I should not have failed to come to hear you, but I am taking a long deferred week of my holiday on Saturday, and if nothing prevents I shall be in Paris on the date of your lecture. But should anything detain me in London, I should certainly turn up at your lecture and buy my own ticket.

I should very much have liked to come, and I am disappointed. I have, however, promised to take the chair for you at the Tomorrow Club I think in March, and I shall look forward to that. I hope I shall see you and extract from you what you are going to talk about, long before that. I have promised to address that institution myself, and if I had not already engaged myself to chair for you, I should have asked you to do it for me.

I have moved to this address, hence the delay in replying.

Sincerely yours
T. S. Eliot

Miss Ana M. BERRY, I believe, is the person.[1] She is found, or was found – for I have heard nothing of or from her since the summer – at the Arts League of Service, 24 Adelphi Terrace House, Robert Street, Adelphi; and I can't remember the address of her flat. It is in Sloane Court, Sloane Street, I think.

TO *R. C. Trevelyan*[2] TS Trinity College, Cambridge

10 December 1920 9 Clarence Gate Gdns

Dear Trevelyan,

It is a great pleasure to receive such a letter as yours – a greater pleasure than the most flattering review. All human feeling seems to desert a reviewer, whether he be favourably disposed or the reverse.

I admit that I had several motives in saying what little I said, in passing, about Milton.[3] First I find him, *on the whole*, antipathetic. Dante seems to

1–Anabel M Berry, organising secretary of the Arts League of Service (which TSE had addressed on the topic of 'Modern Tendencies in Poetry' in Oct. 1919).

2–R. C. Trevelyan (1872–1951), poet, translator, playwright; son of the historian and statesman Sir George Macaulay Trevelyan (1838–1928) and brother of G. M. Trevelyan (1876–1962).

3–Writing on 7 Dec., Trevelyan described *SW* as 'the most helpful literary criticism of our time', and proposed: 'I wish you would come into the open a little more about Milton. What

me so immeasurably greater in every way, even in control of language, that I am often irritated by Milton's admirers. Then I have certain specific charges to bring against Milton. As I did not have occasion to discuss them at length, I introduced them in a way which I hoped might stimulate the reflective, and which I was not unwilling should vex the thoughtless. I have no great desire to write about him, and I think it is wisest – for me at least – only to write about subjects in connection with which I have strong convictions or enthusiasm about or on behalf of something. The only way I feel at present any desire to write about Milton is in connection with the history of blank verse; and I have been intending, when I had leisure, to do that.

But I was not writing to expatiate upon my intentions, but to thank you for your letter, which gave me, as I said, very keen pleasure.

Sincerely yours,
T. S. Eliot

TO *Ezra Pound* TS Lilly

Wednesday [22 December 1920] 9 Clarence Gate Gdns

Cher Maitre:

I infer that there is no prospect of seeing you. Your letter is extremely obscure, but it appears that you are going South. This is a blow. Please write and explain lucidly what your plans are and for how long. What happens to the *Dial*? Am I expected to receive books for review, in your absence? I will deal with them as directed. I have the opuscule[1] this evening, and observe that you have commenced operations on it.

---

you implied, rather than stated, seems to be of great importance, and I think the whole book would have gained a great deal if you had boldly said what you felt. Some day any how, you should write a history of English blank verse, if only in 20 pages. That would give you your opportunity.

'I was fascinated by what you said about "rhetoric". Rhetoric is out of fashion just now, and no doubt imitative and stupid rhetoric is about the worst of poetic vices. But after all, in a work of any scale, like a play or long poem, something, or rather a number of things have to be done to keep things alive and in movement, and to prevent the design falling flat and dead; and the sum of these things may as well be called rhetoric as anything else' (Houghton).

In 'Notes on the Blank Verse of Christopher Marlowe', TSE contended that 'after the erection of the Chinese Wall of Milton, blank verse has suffered not only arrest but retrogression' (*SW*, 87). Returning to the term 'rhetoric' ('Milton I', 1936; *OPP*, 1957), TSE stated that it was 'not meant to be derogatory'.

1–The *Dial* (Dec.) included 'The Second-Order Mind'. Eight months after EP had 'commenced operations' as foreign agent for the *Dial*, he wrote about the Nov. issue to Thayer (8 Nov.): 'AT LAST a magazine that I can read!!' (*Pound, Thayer, Watson, and The Dial*). 'Opuscule' is a minor literary work. (See 'opusculus', EP letter to Thayer, 7 June 1920.)

If no more, Farewell and Pleasure.

Yours
T.

TO *Leonard Woolf* TS Berg

26 December 1920 9 Clarence Gate Gdns

My dear Woolf,

I read your review[1] when I got back from Paris, and I should have written to you before to thank you, but simply that I have not had the leisure.

I need hardly say that I should feel sufficiently flattered merely by the fact that my book suggested Aristotle to your mind. But it is a much more delicate flattery to feel that you have got, I think, what I am after, whether I have succeeded or not. I feel that there is much in the book which ought to have been completely rewritten, which is unnecessarily difficult or obscure. What I should like would be to have an opportunity of discussing with you, not so much the book, as the general questions of critical method which your article provokes. I hope that may be soon.

We were very disappointed to learn that you are at Rodmell, and cannot come to dinner this week. I trust that we can arrange it soon after you return. Meanwhile, I am sorry to say, my wife's father has only last night taken a turn very much for the worse, and we fear that it is merely a matter of a few days; I am very anxious for my wife's health in consequence.

With best wishes for the new year to both of you,

Sincerely,
T. S. Eliot

1–LW, 'Back to Aristotle', a review of *SW*, *A.*, 17 Dec. 1920, 834–5: 'Mr Eliot means by criticism what Aristotle meant by criticism'; he brings 'us up with a shock against the satisfying, if painful, hardness of the intellect'.

1921

TO *Scofield Thayer* TS Beinecke

1 January 1921 [misdated 1920] 9 Clarence Gate Gdns,
LONDON N.W.1

Dear Scofield,

Wishing you all the compliments of the season:

I have your letter of the 11th and your letter of the 15th ultimo, and thank you, first, for your amiability and mansuetude in not reproaching me for the 'London Letter'. Had I been able to do any writing in the past two months, this would have taken precedence over everything else; and for the present and future it will, as I intend to get it done in the course of the coming week. The fact that Vivien's father has been at the point of death for ten weeks has interfered with every plan that has or could have been made; and a number of difficulties, partly issuing therefrom and partly quite independent, have further embarrassed my activity to a point unknown even in the last five years.

I hope to post you this 'London Letter' in a week.

Now for the other matter. I have turned over in my mind what there is to be done, with a view to seeing what part of it I could compass; for I think it would be quite obvious to you if you were here that the job itself is wholly beyond my powers. I am very desirous that it should be done, but for me it is physically impossible. For one thing, you need a man who can get about, call on merchants and printers etc. and also lunch with the valuable people. As I have to be at an office six days a week, and my hours are 9.30 to 5, you see it is impossible for me to do anything during the day; and for seeing friends and acquaintances, doing my personal business, writing letters, accounts, and finally my reading and writing, I have to divide my evenings and my Sundays among these as best I can. You certainly need a man who can devote a good half of his time for several weeks, merely to obtain the preliminary information; and it is true that the most of this can only be done by personal interviews. If you like, until you can send or find here someone else, I will try to see Mr Ratcliffe; but if I promised to try to do what you need I should simply delay you indefinitely.

Offhand, I can only say that I know the cost of paper and labour to have increased enormously here since five years; I cannot say how it compares, taking into account the rate of exchange, with costs in America. The papers here at all comparable to the *Dial* sell at higher prices; the *London Mercury*, for example, is now 3s, and has no illustrations; but perhaps all these papers aim at a larger profit per copy than the *Dial* does.

Then as to the possibility of working up a subscription list in England. This, I think, will take considerable time. Undoubtedly Americans can make better magazines than the English can, but it takes time to persuade the English, as the fact must be made softly to penetrate their *un*consciousness. *Vogue*, for example, is far better than anything they do themselves in that line, and they know it, but in the first place *Vogue* is not a literary paper, and in the second place it is not conspicuously an importation. There seem to be two things to do: to aim at a circulation only among the sufficiently intelligent, which would be in time three or four hundred; or to produce an English edition, with English theatrical, musical etc. notes instead of American. Perhaps, as the latter is a very big undertaking, the first is more feasible.

I should of course have been very glad to fling myself into this work, even without the fee which you suggest: it is not, however – to return to what I said before – a question of its interfering with what I am doing; it would prevent me from doing *anything* else, and at that it wouldn't, it couldn't possibly, *get done!*

In writing such a long letter as this I am compelled to leap about from one point to another as they occur to me, or I would not get it done at all. There is this: English people, with very few exceptions, are unused to *subscribing* to anything. They either buy things as they see them on bookstalls, or at most they order them from a bookseller, and pay his bill once a quarter. At one time I got quite tired of hearing people say that they 'had been meaning to' subscribe to the *Little Review*. They never did, even when pretending to be very much excited by *Ulysses*. If you want more than the 300 or 400 readers (and that would take time to get) you must have your future manager here arrange for the paper to be visible and handy on every bookstall, at every tube station.

You would have, for your 4000 readers whom you have in mind, to cut the throat of the *Mercury* and perhaps also the *English Review*. I imagine you pay considerably better, but as I have never contributed to either of these I cannot say for certain. I can find out from others. It is not simply, however, a matter of paying more, to get their best contributors away, but of having some busy person on the spot to overcome the inertia of the elder writers. When you are, for example, no longer in a position to *share* an article by Robert Bridges or Conrad or Hardy with the *Mercury*, these people must be persuaded that the *Dial* is more respectable company to appear in.

Another point I have been requested to mention, unrelated to the above. I took a deferred six days holiday in Paris a fortnight ago, and saw Fritz Vanderpyl. He complains of receiving communications from various people on the *Dial* who do not appear to be working quite in concert. He says that he was sent some copies to dispose of on the impression that he had a bookshop, then when he explained he received an apology, but later the enclosed invoice which he asked me to send you. As I do not know the full facts, and am not sure that Vanderpyl is capable of giving them, I pass this on without comment. I thought his article on Vlaminck rather poor journalese,[1] but perhaps that sort of thing goes down. He showed me some poems which were certainly much better than that, and which seemed to me quite good, and I will tell him to send them on unless you are choked up with material at present.

Has, if I may mention it, the question of a more cheerful cover (I dont mean a Christy Girl[2] but something as bright as the *Nouvelle Revue Française*) ever been raised? I think for an English edition a cover which made more prominent some of the names familiar to this public might be well.

The *Dial* is undoubtedly better than any English literary paper I know, and the book reviewing in it far less dull.

If you had someone over here who could fly about, I might be able to make myself useful to him, or even if you nominated some native inhabitant for this preliminary exploration. I understand from Pound that what prevents you from coming at present is that your colleague is temporarily incapacitated from full activity by the labours of a medical degree, in other words taking some examinations. If this is so I suppose you will not be able to come before the summer.

I wish I could give more helpful suggestions, but I am now exhausted by such a long letter. I will write you again in sending the 'Letter', if I can by that time suggest anyone here who would be suitable for your purpose.

Yours ever
T.S.E.

I have not mentioned this matter to anyone.

1–Fritz Vanderpyl, 'Maurice Vlaminck', *Dial*, Dec. 1920.
2–Howard Chandler Christy (1873–1952), American artist. The 'aristocratic and dainty though not always silken-skirted' young woman of his illustrations became known as the Christy Girl.

TO *Maxwell Bodenheim* TS Estate of Enid Goldsmith

2 January 1921 9 Clarence Gate Gdns

Dear Bodenheim,

Your (undated) letter has remained for some time on my table, but only as all the other letters of the same period have remained, finding me still in the midst of practical anxieties which take precedence over not only correspondence but literature. I was, however, very glad to hear from you. My irritation at your imagined grievance against me (even now I am not clear that it was more than your having supposed me to have missed an appointment, which set fire to some stored impersonal suspicion), was at the time considerably tempered by anxiety; and I am greatly relieved, not only to hear that you are pacified, but that you are in New York and apparently living. I only hope that the domestic weepies, which must have tortured you here, can be more readily coped with there.

I of course escape to Paris whenever I can get a bit of holiday, which is not very often. I will agree with you in anything you care to say about the placid smile of imbecility which splits the face of contemporary London, or, more abstractly, the putrescence of English literature and journalism. I am inclined to think that I am slightly more comfortable here than in America, I can get a drink of very bad liquor of any sort when I want it;[1] which is important to me, and several of our little colleagues in America are just as muddleheaded as the English. I have got used to being a foreigner everywhere, and it would fatigue me to be expected to be anything else. I intend to visit America some day, but I don't think it will amuse me. I have, moreover, a certain persistent curiosity about the English and a desire to see whether they can ever be roused to anything like intellectual activity. And I suppose there are more people in America to tell the natives what's what from a European point of view than there are in England. Once there was a civilisation here, I believe, that's a curious and exciting point. This is not conceit, merely a kind of pugnacity.

I am glad to have your poems, and wish I could place them for you lucratively, but the only place where I can sell my own is the *Dial*, and whatever influence, if any, that I ever had with the *Athenaeum* has disappeared. Some day I want to force a rather detailed opinion of your poetry upon you.

1–Prohibition had been introduced in the USA in 1920, and lasted until 1933.

Unfortunately, *Poetry* is never sent to me. I should like to see that one.[1] I should like to hear from you about New York sometimes.

Yours always,
T. S. Eliot

TO *Leonard Woolf* — TS Berg

2 January 1921 [misdated 2 Dec. 1921] 9 Clarence Gate Gdns

My dear Woolf,

I shall be very glad to dine and discuss with you on Sunday the 9th. I should of course enjoy staying the night with you, but as I have to be at my office so early, I fear it is rather impracticable; I should have to be up at peep of day and should not see any more of you that way: but I shall not rush away early unless to spare you fatigue.

By the way, can you keep me a copy of the Gorki–Tolstoi book.[2] I have been meaning daily to get a postal order for it.

With new year's wishes for both of you

Sincerely
T. S. Eliot

TO *Mrs Dawson Scott* — CC BL

2 January 1921 9 Clarence Gate Gdns

Dear Mrs Dawson Scott,

You will think it odd of me not to have let you know about my paper, but I was away for some time till just before Christmas, and then got your circular. I think April 21st will suit me very well; as for the subject, I wish I had provided you with a proper title in good time, but at least the one you have been obliged to give will not, I believe, be misleading.

With best wishes for the new year,

Sincerely yours,
[T. S. E.]

1 – The Dec. issue of *Poetry* included Bodenheim's 'In Defence of Rodker'.

2 – Maxim Gorky, *Reminiscences of Leo Nicolayevitch Tolstoi*, trans. S. S. Koteliansky and LW (1920; repr. Jan. 1921).

Vivien Eliot TO *Mary Hutchinson* MS Texas

5 January 1921 9 Clarence Gate Gdns

Dear Mary

Did you really invite us to dinner on Saturday? If so we shall be delighted to come. It seems a long time since I saw you, and I shall be glad to.

Of course I dread making an engagement. It seems fatally unwise, I have had so many disasters. But there it is. It is nice of you to constantly ask us out of our turn. We want you to fix a day for next week, to come here. Last time was nice, was'nt it.

My father is at present, at the moment, quite comfortable and getting a little stronger. His illness has long ago passed beyond the comprehension of anybody, – of any of the doctors. So one has nothing to go on, and just waits to see what will happen next. He still firmly believes he is going to get well, and is talking about going to the South of France, *next month*!

I have done nothing, of course, but have just bought a copy of Tom's book to send to my lover of the past, anonymously.[1]

Goodbye till Saturday Mary dear

V.

TO *His Mother* MS Houghton

16 January 1921 [misdated 1920] [London]

My dearest Mother

This is just to tell you that I am alive and well, but very tired and postponing writing for a day or two. Vivien's father is getting on miraculously well but now that the strain is somewhat relaxed Vivien is showing signs of breaking up and has been kept in bed all day with a bad migraine.

I was so glad to get your last dear letter.

Your devoted
Tom.

1–VHE's former boyfriend was a schoolteacher named Charles Buckle.

TO *Leonard Woolf* TS Berg

18 January 1921 9 Clarence Gate Gdns

Dear Woolf,

Thank you for your letter of the 11th. We were very sorry that you could not come on Monday, but we hope that we can arrange an evening soon which will be convenient to you both.

I am forwarding your story on to the editor of the *Dial*, asking him to communicate directly with you about it. I will send your friend's story too if you wish, but candidly I had rather you did it yourself. It does not really strike me as good enough; but you know I have no official connexion with the *Dial* whatever, but simply happen to be an old school and college friend of the proprietor. The address is

Scofield Thayer Esqre.,
The *Dial*, 152 West 13th Street,
New York City.

I am glad to hear that you are bringing out a volume in the spring,[1] and please remember that I shall want a copy, as also of the Tchehov Notebooks.[2]

Sincerely,
T. S. Eliot

TO *His Mother* TS Houghton

22 January 1921 9 Clarence Gate Gdns

My dearest Mother,

I have not written you a real letter for a very long time. I have been working this weekend on an overdue article for the *Dial*, the first I have written for many months. It came very hard, and I do not think that it is very good or very well written, but it is a start, and I hope that I shall soon get my hand in again. As you know, I have several commissions for articles for the *Times* and elsewhere. I do not feel any great desire to renew my connexion with the *Athenaeum*. For one thing, the space is too limited to develop a really serious article, and for another thing I and Murry have fallen apart completely. I consider his verse quite negligible, and I don't

1–LW, *Stories of the East* (1921).
2–Maxim Gorky, *The Note-Books of Anton Tchekhov Together with Reminiscences of Tchekhov*, trans. S. S. Koteliansky and LW (1921).

like his prose style; his articles seem to me to become more and more windy, verbose and meaningless. Personally, I think him a man of weak character and great vanity, and I do not trust him; I think he loves both money and being a public figure. He will become more and more a conventional and solemn pundit, quite insincere, hysterical and morbid. Richmond of the *Times* I like very much; and he has the very great advantage of not being himself a writer, so that the element of professional jealousy cannot enter.

Robert Lynd's article in the *Nation* has no importance, except that three columns of such violent abuse may be a good advertisement. He is an utter nonentity; his own literary criticism is wholly worthless; I reviewed one of his books in the *Athenaeum* a year ago, none too favourably, and I do not imagine that he has forgotten the fact.

I am hoping to settle down to work now. Vivien's father is apparently getting on nicely. They had him downstairs for a few hours today; we brought him down and up in a special invalid chair; he can even walk a few steps alone, but of course is very very weak. It is proposed to take him away to a healthy place in the country, with the nurse, in a few weeks. He has become touchingly devoted to Vivien, in consequence of the contact they have had during his illness, and her goodness to him; in fact, I think he is really fonder of her than of anyone else, though he does not know that.

My own health has been much better since my week in Paris before Christmas. It was such a complete change, and I enjoyed myself so thoroughly. I stayed at my old pension Casaubon, you know the old people are all dead, and the grandson is now proprietor. But I was out to most meals. Part of the time I was with Maurice, and mostly with old and new French friends and acquaintances, writers, painters (I got very cheap a drawing for Vivien of one of the best of the modern painters, Raoul Dufy),[1] and the sort of French society that knows such people. I want to get over again in the spring for a short time, just before you come. If I had not met such a number of new people there Paris would be desolate for me with prewar memories of Jean Verdenal and the others. But it is very easy to make new acquaintances, as so many of them have heard of me even if they do not read English. And of course they are very anxious to get articles into English and American papers, as they are, many of the writers, very poor now!

What you wrote me about having tired yourself out worried me very much – not so much for this occasion, but for the future. Do you think that

1–Raoul Dufy (1877–1953), French painter of the Fauvist school.

17A The view from the Eliot home at Eastern Point

17B TSE

17C Henry, 1895

18A 1907

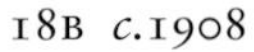

18B *c.*1908

C On other occasions

19A Henry (who is taking the photograph) with his parents at the breakfast table, 4446 Westminster Place, St Louis

19B Henry

19C TSE in 1910

20 Sailing off the Dry Salvages

21A TSE in the *Elsa*

21B At the helm with a friend (probably Harold Peters)

22 Jean Verdenal, January 1915

23 His mother at her bedroom desk
(see letter of 30 December 1917)

24 Etching of Vivien Haigh-Wood as a child, by her father, which she gave to Enid Faber on 23 March 1933

25A Vivien and TSE at 18 Crawford Mansions, 1916

25B In the dining room at Crawford Mansions, July 1916

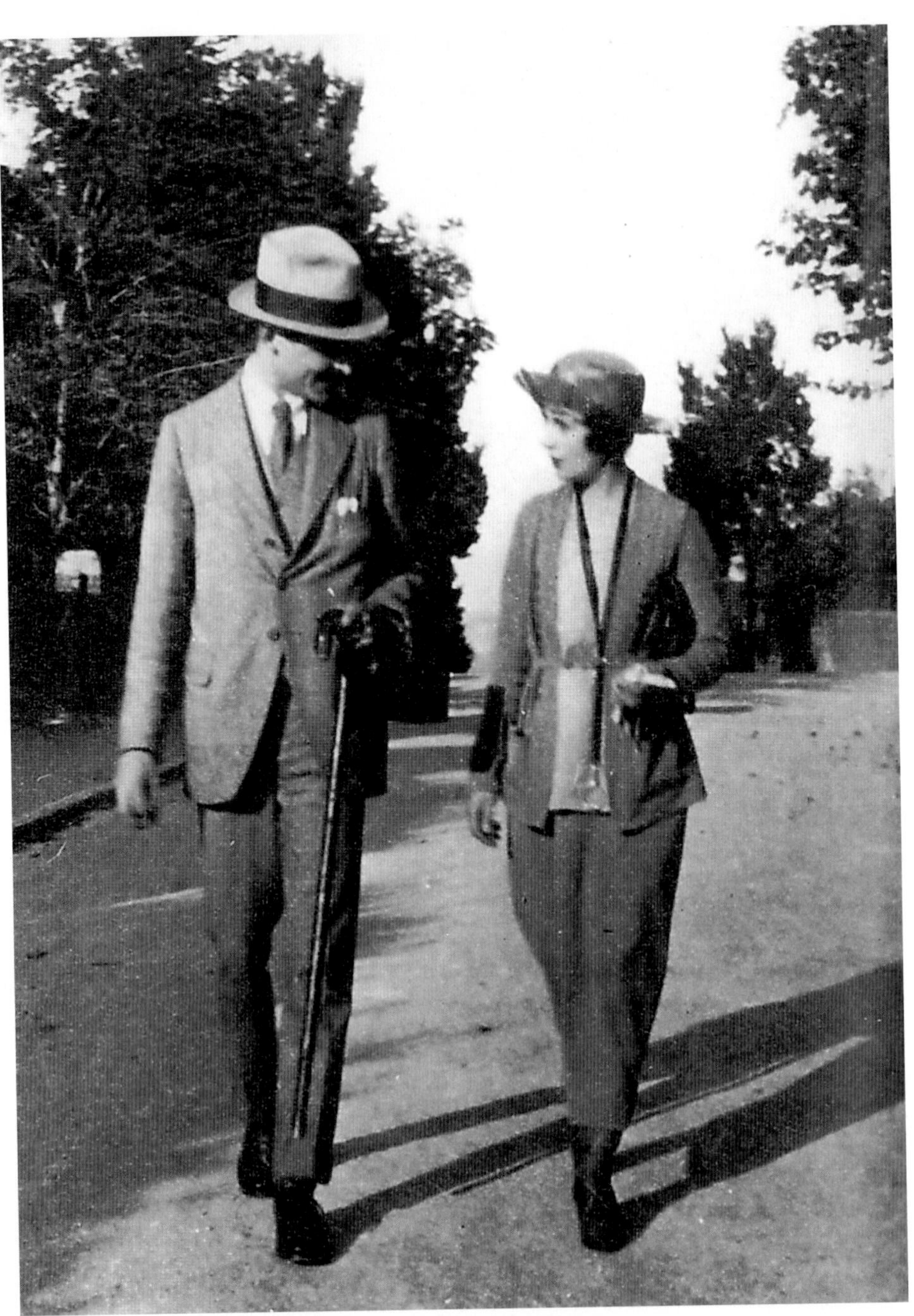

26 Tom and Vivien, *c.*1920

27 TSE with Ottoline Morrell at Garsington, *c.*1920

28A TSE with Maurice Haigh-Wood, Bosham, Sussex, 26 August 1916

28B At the door of South View, Bosham, 1916

29A Vivien, Jeremy and Barbara Hutchinson (on wall). TSE, St John Hutchinson ('Jack'), Sacheverell and Osbert Sitwell, at West Wittering, Sussex, July 1919

29B TSE, Osbert Sitwell, Mary Hutchinson, Jeremy Hutchinson

30 TSE with his mother at Clarence Gate Gardens, summer 1921

31 TSE and Henry at Itchenor, Sussex, 1921

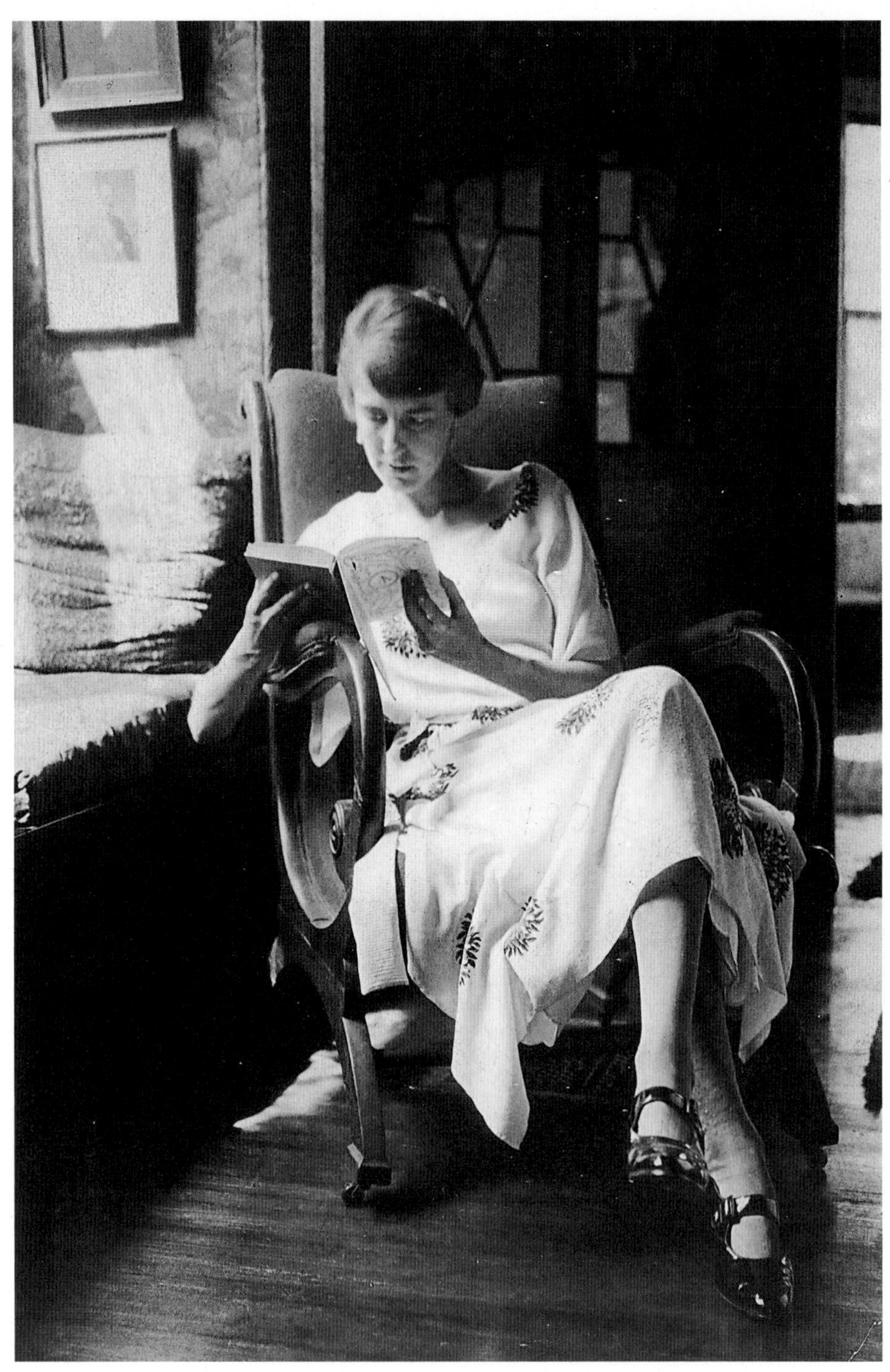

32 Eleanor Hinkley, 1922

you can do things which would tire a woman of thirty? Of course your Christmas dinner was a tremendous thing to do, and I have no doubt that there were a lot of incidental activities, like buying presents for everybody. I can picture you rushing about and not lying down all day, and Marion following up trying to restrain you and wringing her hands and you not allowing her to do anything for you, and she too getting more tired in the end than if you had let her. But seriously, although you say so little about it, this sounds like a piece of pure folly. Besides, I want you to be *very* well in the spring, and I promise you you shall be made to lie down every day for a good long rest.

I am very glad you had Henry with you. I have not heard whether he ever received my book, which I sent him to arrive about Christmas.

I hope to have a more satisfactory report from you in a few days.

Your devoted son,

Tom.

By the way, there is a question I have had in mind to ask you a hundred times. Did you ever pay my bill to those kind German people (Happich)[1] in Marburg early in the war? You know, when I got back to England it was forbidden to send money to Germany, and I asked you to pay it for me. But if you have not, or cannot remember, I will try to get in touch with them, if they are still alive, and pay it. That money, with the interest, would be a little fortune to them now. Please let me know.

Vivien Eliot TO *Charlotte C. Eliot* — MS Houghton

25 January 1921 — 9 Clarence Gate Gdns

My dear Mrs Eliot,

First of all I must thank you for your Xmas present, and for your kind letters, and ask you to excuse my not having written before. I am so very tired that it seems too much to do to write a letter, I have had to reduce my activities to the lowest point. During Father's illness I have given up all attempts to see my friends, or to read, or write. All the same I feel completely exhausted. Father is making a miraculous recovery, and was carried downstairs in a carrying chair on Sunday! We all assembled for tea, and he lay on the sofa for an hour with great pleasure and triumph. His spirit is as young as a schoolboy's and he has a wonderful and sweet character.

1 – TSE had stayed with Herr Superintendent Happich and his wife in July–Aug. 1914.

A letter came to Tom from you this morning, telling of your bad cold. We are very distressed to hear of it, and we are hoping you are really *well* again. The one great thing, almost the only thing, to guard against, is *over fatigue*. If one always kept well within one's strength, I believe there would be very little illness. But of course, one often has no choice.

We like this flat immensely. It is quiet, warm, well ventilated, and in nearly every way satisfactory. Clarence Gate Gardens is really one *huge* block of flats, taking up a whole street, and on both sides of the street. We find it well *managed* and properly controlled and after our experiences at Crawford Mansions, where there was *no* management or control it is a great relief. Tom is *better* than he was at Christmas time. But he is always distressed that he can do so little writing. He gets tired with his long day at the Bank, and feels more inclined for a quiet evening of reading, and early to bed, than to begin the real business of his life, and sit up late.

I want to thank you again for your very generous Xmas present. I shall begin now to look for rooms for you and Marion, and I shall enjoy doing it.

With love, from Vivien

TO *Scofield Thayer* TS Beinecke

30 January 1921 [London]

Dear Scofield,

I enclose a story which Leonard Woolf gave me to send you. He is I consider a very able man, and well known as a writer on political and economic subjects, and was formerly a civil servant in Ceylon. He is the husband of Virginia (Stephen) Woolf, some of whose short stories are extremely good. I have heard his novel (*The Village in the Jungle* [1913]) strongly praised. I confess that I find this story disappointing, but I told him I would send it on to the *Dial* and ask the *Dial* to reply direct.[1] It has not been published here but is in print because he is having a small volume privately printed in the spring.[2] Will you deal with him? his address is

Hogarth House,
Paradise Road,
Richmond,
Surrey.

1 – LW's story was rejected.
2 – LW, *Stories of the East*, was published in Apr. by the Hogarth Press.

If I can get hold of something good by his wife I will get her to send it to you. She is a daughter of old Leslie Stephen.

T.

TO *Scofield Thayer* TS Beinecke

30 January 1921 9 Clarence Gate Gdns

My dear Scofield,

I discover to my consternation that the letter which I thought I had sent off some time before my 'London Letter'[1] which left a week ago is still lying on my table under a mass of refuse and unanswered letters. With my profuse apologies I send it on now. Meanwhile neither Vivien nor I has had any opportunities to make investigations. Meanwhile also the exchange has shown signs of working against your plan, but of course until we know actual prices here it is impossible to say how important the rise from 3.50 to 3.86 (at this date) may be. Had you ever thought of getting it printed on the continent? But I suppose that is fantastic, and also might arouse a storm of patriotic abuse.

My 'London Letter' was I fear a puny result after such delay, but remember it is the first writing of any kind that I have done for six months; and therefore it came very hard. I rewrote it twice, and I think the last draft is the best, anyway. Let me know whether it suits you and whether it is the right length. I suppose it is too late for the February number, and that therefore you will not want another till the middle of March, but if you should want it sooner please send me a cable.[2] I think my affairs are in better order now and I shall be able to get some work done. It will be several months before I have any verse ready for publication, but I shall send you an article. My idea was that in the 'Letter' you would not want so much critiques of books (which in most cases appear in New York as well) but the reverberations of books in London.

Are you coming over in May or June?

yours ever
Tom.

1 – 'London Letter', *Dial*, 70: 4 (Apr. 1921): the first of a bimonthly series by TSE.
2 – Thayer thanked TSE (10 Feb.) for a 'distinguished Letter', adding: 'Why no verse? I serve notice that I do not consider it seemly for the editor of *The Dial* ever again to repeat this question.'

TO *Mary Hutchinson* MS Texas

3 February 1921 9 Clarence Gate Gdns

Dear Mary

Thanks awfully for your letter, which I appreciated and enjoyed. Monday would have suited me capitally for another talk. Most unfortunately, Vivien went out too soon after her attack of the other night, and got a chill and in consequence is now in bed speechless with throat and lungs in a bad state, and of course the danger of bronchitis. Of course she is so fearfully run down that she is liable to get anything at any minute. She is having a perfectly dreadful time lately and I feel very sorry for her. As soon as she gets over this attack she is going away in the country. In the circumstances, would you rather come on Thursday, but if not, do come on Monday if you don't mind Vivien's being shut in her room as before. Anyhow I shall expect you one of those two days. – You have made me want to read Keats's letters: I have not much wanted to read lately – only *after* having written something one wants to read.

Tom.

TO *Mrs Lethbridge*[1] MS copy Valerie Eliot

8 February 1921 9 Clarence Gate Gdns

Dear Mrs Lethbridge,

It was very kind of you to remember to send me *Leutnant Gustl*,[2] which I have been reading today with great pleasure. It recalls the tones of German conversation which I had completely forgotten. When I finish it I shall have to ask you to recommend me something else. I looked at the new German books at Jaschke's[3] the other day: very little, and it seemed to me very costly.

I promise not to keep this an unreasonable time.

Sincerely yours,
T. S. Eliot

1 – Unidentified.
2 – *Leutnant Gustl* (1901), a pioneering stream-of-consciousness novella by the Austrian novelist and dramatist Arthur Schnitzler (1862–1931).
3 – Jaschke's bookshop, Charing Cross Road.

TO *His Mother* TS Houghton

13 February 1921 9 Clarence Gate Gardens

Important

My dearest mother,

I think that I wrote and thanked you for the dividend in my last letter, and for the insurance policy. The document which you said you enclosed by mistake, I did not find; please let me know whether you have found it.

Mr Haigh-Wood has been taken away a day or two ago to Tunbridge Wells, where they will stay for some time. He can walk some steps quite by himself now, and seems securely on the road to health. It is truly miraculous.

Vivien has had a severe attack of influenza lately, which is the reason I have not found time to write for some days, and is very weak. The worst of anything like this is that it retards very much the course of treatment for her stomach, and sets her very far back.

I want however to put only one matter into this letter, so that you may consider it and give me a thought-out reply *at once*. You should now decide on the time at which you wish to come, and should *reserve a passage immediately*. Please let me know

1. When you are coming.
2. How much you are willing to pay (per week) for board and lodging.
3. Whether you wish lodgings, or as I strongly advise, two bedrooms and a sitting room in a hotel.
4. How much of your food requires to be specially prepared. I must know this in order to decide what is the best form of habitation for you.
5. Whether you would consider taking a small furnished flat, if we got a reliable woman to come in and cook for you. I believe that this arrangement might be made no more fatiguing, and perhaps really less troublesome, for Marion, than a hotel or lodgings. I might be able to secure one in our block of flats, which is a very large one.

Please think these over and answer them as soon as you possibly can. I will say no more in this letter, except to thank you for yours (I hope Mr Lowes will like the book)[1] and to send my devoted love,

your son,
Tom.

1 – CCE was giving a copy of *SW* to Professor John Livingston Lowes at Harvard.

PS IMPORTANT

Please let me know also whether it will be only you and Marion or whether there is any chance of Henry coming too. I am not only very anxious to see him (I am always worried about his health and happiness and future) but I know it would do him a world of good, it might be *very* important to him. Also, I think he could manage to get away for long enough to be worth while, and I believe he would if you urged him to do so. The poor fellow has *never* been abroad; he ought sometime to get at least a peep far outside of the commercial life of Chicago among the people he has to mix with there. Do try to make him come, for his own sake.

Tom.

TO *Mrs Lethbridge*

CC

27 February [1921] 9 Clarence Gate Gdns

Dear Mrs Lethbridge,

I am returning you *Leutnant Gustl*, with many thanks. It seems to me a brilliant piece of writing, extremely well sustained, and I am very much obliged to you for acquainting me with it. I should like to find some other book of Schnitzler, as I do not know anything but *Anatol.*[1] I notice that a new play of his, *Reigen*, has been very badly treated by the Berlin public on the grounds of its impropriety![2]

I hope that we may some day have an opportunity of meeting again, and meanwhile, *empfehle mich* [I'll take my leave] –

sincerely yours,
[T. S. E.]

TO *Brigit Patmore*

MS Beinecke

2 March [1921] 9 Clarence Gate Gdns

My dear Brigit,

Alas! this is only another illustration of our life: owing to a crisis in which I want advice I have had to seek out three people, two of whom want to see me tomorrow afternoon. And as Vivien would be able to see

1 – *Anatol* (1893), a series of dramatic sketches about a fashionable philanderer.

2 – *Reigen: Zehn Dialoge,* also known as *La Ronde*, was printed privately and performed in 1900, but its Berlin premiere in Dec. 1920 caused scandal and provoked anti-Semitic riots. Schnitzler subsequently withdrew it from performance.

you or anyone only for a few minutes I hope you will come a little later when she could see you longer, and when *I* should be able to be present also: we speak of you often, and really <u>want</u> to see you. May I write in a few days and suggest? It's a pity you are not on the telephone.

Yours always
T.S.E.

TO *His Mother* — MS Houghton

6 March 1921 — 9 Clarence Gate Gdns

My dearest mother,

I have not yet heard from you in reply to my questions about your time of coming and the arrangements I should make for you, but I have been thinking the matter over very carefully in the meantime. You must admit that we are in a much better position to judge about accommodations in London than you are, and so I trust that you will fall in with our plans for you.

In the first place lodgings are much rarer in London than they used to be. Even if you had lodgings, the landlady *never* does the housekeeping. She cooks the food, but you have to order it. And it is a rare exception to find the cooking good. There are many hotels and boarding houses, of all sorts; no doubt we could find you a good one with good cooking. But everything that you had to have cooked or prepared specially means considerable extra expense, and also you would find it absolutely necessary to have a private sitting room. It would be expensive, and I do not think there is one very near here.

Lucy Thayer, Vivien's American friend, has taken a small but comfortable flat not far away [at 12 Wigmore Street], and would be very glad to take us in, as she could easily do. You could have our comfortable flat and servant. This is the best scheme for *everybody*. You object that you do not wish Marion to have to do housekeeping. This objection more than disappears: Marion would only have to order meals, our servant knows her work and would need no other instructions. She would do the shopping. In lodgings Marion would have to do the same, and in both lodgings and hotels she would have always to see about meals, deal with management and servants, and have constant anxiety of your not being comfortable enough or not getting food prepared right. I know that my scheme would actually be more restful for her than what you propose.

I should see more of you and under better conditions this way. We should often dine here, I should keep my books here and should often work here in the evenings, and should be dropping in of course all the time.

Vivien and I have absolutely the same opinion about this, and she is quite as anxious as I am. We should be perfectly comfortable and would have no responsibility at Lucy Thayer's, simply paying our board.

The only thing is that we want to know *at once*, so do please take what I have said very seriously and make up your mind quite fresh. It would make a great difference to our peace of mind.

Your devoted son
Tom.

TO *Edgar Jepson* PC Beinecke

6 March 1921 9 Clarence Gate Gdns

I see that your address before the Tomorrow Club is on Thursday. I wish you would tell me what you want me to say or give me some hint of the subject, beyond the title, which would help in the introductory eulogy –

Yrs
T. S. Eliot

TO *His Mother* MS Houghton

8 March 1921 9 Clarence Gate Gdns

Dearest mother,

I just have your letter of the 23rd February, and think of cabling you tomorrow to urge you strongly to change your reservation to an earlier date.

Next day: I have cabled this afternoon. You say you have reserved a stateroom for the *Celtic* (*Cedric*?) for the 11th June. This would bring you to Liverpool on the 18th June. The point is that the middle of May to the middle of June is apt to be the *best weather of the year in England*. It is certainly likely to be sunnier and as warm then as later. The time is so short anyway that it is *important* to get the best of the season. You need not dread the cold in May; it is much warmer here in May than in America, although in midsummer it is not nearly so hot. I think the end of August or beginning of September is the best time to return; and you should certainly come in May, to get the good weather and prolong your stay.

Remember that *living* in London will not be expensive, if you do as I tell you to.

I cabled to change your reservation to the *Cedric* or the *Olympic*, both of which sail on May 14, getting you here on the 21st – you will see from the list I enclose that there are several boats sailing in May. Also, it is somewhat better to arrive at *Southampton*, which is 1½ hours from London by express train, than at *Liverpool*, which is 4 hours away.

I have chosen boats of the same line as the one you chose (White Star) in case you have paid part or all of the price, but if you have not, you can of course change to a *Cunard*. Please take my advice in this as in the other matter of habitation, as they both make for the comfort and happiness of everyone concerned. The proposal for taking this flat means also a great *saving in expense*.

I shall expect you by the 21st May, and shall arrange to meet you at the station in London.

You will make a great mistake if you postpone arriving till the 18th June. The best plan is to get three clear months from the 21st May.

Also, you ought to make an attempt to get Henry to come with you. He could return alone before you did, and even if he only had a fortnight here it would be worth it. It is much more desirable that he should come over with you than that he should be able to return with you. With even a month's holiday he could do it, and it would be *absurd* if he could not get that much.

You do not seem to get my letters very quickly, and I almost think one has gone astray, as I thanked you for the dividends and insurance papers some time ago. I also sent you a copy of Desmond MacCarthy's article.[1] I have known him some years, he is literary editor of the *New Statesman*. Bob Trevelyan, of whom you ask, is a member of the same family as the historian, cousin or nephew. His father was named Sir George Trevelyan, I think. He is a country gentleman and minor poet, mostly writes translations from Latin and Greek.

Mr Haigh-Wood appears to be getting on very well, and is now at Eastbourne, recuperating, walks about a little and writes letters. It was a miraculous cure.

---

1 – Desmond MacCarthy, 'New Poets, T. S. Eliot', *NS*, 8 Jan. 1921: a review of *Ara Vos Prec*.

I am very sorry to hear about your real estate troubles. *Surely* the city compensates you for the loss in value and the expense of rebuilding! But you will have to arrange, and well in advance, for your affairs to be looked after while you are away. *Otherwise*, something will turn up at the last moment, and you will say 'I must wait and see to this'. And it is *important* that you should come early and have your first experience of English weather while it is good and settled.

I must go to bed now.

Make your sailing early – the Shipping Companies are used to such alterations, and let me know at once.

Your devoted son
Tom

TO *Brigit Patmore* MS Beinecke

17 March [1921] 9 Clarence Gate Gdns

Dear Brigit

It is pleasant to hear that you have not forgotten us, in this interval. I wish I could reply as I should wish. For the last four days Vivien has been lying in the most dreadful agony with *neuritis* in every nerve, increasingly – arms, hands, legs, feet, back. Have you ever been in such incessant and extreme pain that you felt your sanity going, and that you no longer knew reality from delusion? That's the way she is. The doctors have never seen so bad a case, and hold out no definite hope, and have so far done her no good. Meanwhile she is in screaming agony, and I fear the exhaustion might just snuff her out. She has just enough mind left to send you her love, and say she really would like to see you very much – though she couldn't talk or speak – if you could come in late one afternoon and have a cup of tea with me. Could you, at short notice (it would be)? And *later* I hope to come to tea and meet Collins.[1]

Ever yours
Tom.

1 – Unidentified.

TO *Marianne Moore*[1] MS Rosenbach

3 April 1921 9 Clarence Gate Gdns

Dear Miss Moore,

I am writing to thank you for your review of my essays in the *Dial*.[2] It gave me pleasure, and still more pleasure to be reviewed by you, as I have long delayed writing to you, in fact since the 1917 *Others*, to tell you how much I admire your verse.[3] It interests me, I think, more than that of anyone now writing in America. I wish that you would make a book of it, and I should like to try to get it published here. I wish you would let me try.

Sincerely yours
T. S. Eliot

I have just met McAlmon, who spoke of you, and whom I liked.[4]

TO *His Mother* MS Houghton

3 April 1921 9 Clarence Gate Gdns

My dearest mother,

I have not written lately, being very busy and also there was nothing further to say on the subject most on my mind until I heard from you. I was *very glad* to get your last two letters and to hear that you had changed to June 1st. Also, Southampton is much nearer London than Liverpool. I doubt if I can get to Southampton, but I shall meet you at the station.

Our flat has electricity, gas stoves in bedrooms, anthracite stoves in sitting room. Hot water is supplied constantly from a heater to *all* the building. First floor (i.e. second floor, American style) and lift (elevator) also.

I have Baedekers.

1–Marianne Moore (1887–1972), one of the most distinguished American poets and critics of the century, contributed to *The Egoist* from 1915 and went on to become acting editor of *The Dial*, then editor, 1927–9. In his introduction to her *Selected Poems*, which he was to publish at F&F in 1935, Eliot stated his judgement that her 'poems form part of the small body of durable poetry written in our time'.

2–'In his poetry, he seems to move troutlike through a multiplicity of foreign objects and in his instinctiveness and care as a critic, he appears as a complement to the sheen upon his poetry' (*Dial* 70: 3 [Mar. 1921], 336–9).

3–*Others: An Anthology of the New Verse* (1917) included thirteen of her poems.

4–Robert McAlmon (1896–1956): American poet and publisher; from 1921, an expatriate in Paris; friend and supporter of numerous modern writers. His own publications include stories (*A Hasty Bunch*, 1922), the autobiographical novel *Post-Adolescence* (1923), and *Being Geniuses Together: An Autobiography* (1938). He founded Contact editions which published Hemingway, Stein and others.

Bring hot water bottles each, and heavy and light underwear.

I should like to have as many of my books as possible. Especially the *Century Dictionary*, the heaviest of all! There are also a few photographs I bought in Paris and Italy, and a copy, illuminated, of the Eliot arms. This would have to be taken from its frame. The books should be sent by slow freight to save expense.

I will send you in a day or two my Andrew Marvell article from the *Times*.[1]

You overestimate the cost of cable. But thank you for the cheque.

I have managed to arrange a week's holiday in July, so as to go away with you. I should like to take you to some cathedral town like Exeter, and for a few days into the country. But we shall see how *much* and what you will want to do. I understand that Henry cannot come with you. It is a great pity, but he must come another year.

I shall write again in a few days.

Always your devoted son
Tom.

An old friend of the Thayer family, a Mrs Studt, is coming on the *Adriatic*, so you may meet her.

<I have sent cheque to Fr. Happich.>

TO *Sydney Schiff* MS BL

3 April 1921 9 Clarence Gate Gdns

My dear Schiff,

I hope this note will catch you before you leave Roquebrune. I would have acknowledged your letter before, but besides several pieces of work I had undertaken, I have been occupied with Vivien's illness. You probably have not heard of this, but she was so ill – after her father was out of danger she nearly collapsed, that the only thing was a thorough treatment. So she has been in bed for the last five weeks, at first in a nursing-home, and lately, on account of the expense, at home. We have had a specialist treating her for nervous exhaustion and for her stomach trouble, which became very alarming; and also massage etc. She has not been allowed to see any one,

1 – TSE, 'Andrew Marvell', *TLS*, 31 Mar. 1921, 201–2. This influential article on seventeenth-century poetry memorably defined Marvell's Puritan wit as 'a tough reasonableness beneath the slight lyric grace', and defined literary wit, not as 'erudition', but 'a recognition, implicit in the expression of every experience, of other kinds of experience which are possible' (*SE*, 303).

except myself, or to write letters. When she is up again she will go to the country for a month. I *think* she is better, but of course the immediate effect of taking to bed, and relaxing from the strain, was to increase the symptoms, so that I have had some very anxious moments. In any case she cannot expect to be really well for a year or two, but I hope that with careful living – and occasional treatment – she will improve steadily.

Please explain to Violet that Vivien has been unable to write even a card.

My poem has still so much revision to undergo that I do not want to let anyone see it yet, and also I want to get more of it done – it should be much the longest I have ever written. I hope that by June it will be in something like final form. I have not had the freedom of mind. I have done an 'Andrew Marvell' (just appeared in the *Times*) one or two things for the *Dial*, one for the *Chapbook*, and something for Lewis. I believe the paper is now in the press. He has been doing much painting, and I am looking forward to his exposition next week;[1] I have seen a few canvasses which I liked very much. I like the drawing you gave me more and more; it seems to me one of his best.[2]

I am so sorry to hear of Violet's continued ill health. I suppose of course she will not be able to stand the strain of a journey to Berlin but will remain in Switzerland. You have had, I fear, an unfortunate winter. But I certainly hope you will be able to return to London for a time, this summer.

We both send love.

Yours ever
T.S.E.

TO *Richard Aldington* CC

7 April 1921 [9 Clarence Gate Gdns]

My dear Aldington,

Thank you very much for your letter. The flowers will be a continuous pleasure for days. Of course she would be very happy if you could send some next week, and even a few kingcups buds might last long enough to give delight, as she is very fond of them.

I hope you will write for the *Statesman*. With the downfall of the *Athenaeum* and its more and more complete extinction in the *Nation*,[3] the

1–'Tyros and Portraits, Drawings by Wyndham Lewis', at the Leicester Gallery.

2–Reproduced in Vol. 2 of these *Letters*.

3–In Feb. 1921 the *Athenaeum* was absorbed by the *Nation*, leaving RA temporarily without a job.

Statesman has been coming up in the popular estimation (I mean in the estimation of the 'intellectuals') and is the 'thing' to write for. MacCarthy has a good chance to make something of it.[1] I have known him off and on for some years. I don't know what they pay now, but I believe as well as any weekly; I got Lst.5 each for a couple of articles years ago.[2] I think more intelligent people would see your work in the *N. Statesman* than in any other weekly.

Although we cannot in the least afford it, we are frightfully keen to get a tiny country cottage. It would be very good for both of us. I should be extremely grateful to you if you would find out all you can about any vacant cottages and let me know as soon as you can; rent, price, habitability, size, garden, plumbing, distance from a town or station, whether isolated, terms of tenancy etc. A country cottage might be just the saving of my wife's health. So I should be infinitely grateful to you for the trouble – and I know how much trouble it is.

I fear that in a day or two our communications will be stopped by the strike, for god knows how long.[3] Having only contempt for every existing political party, and profound hatred for democracy, I feel the blackest gloom.

Whatever happens will be another step toward the destruction of 'Europe'. The whole of contemporary politics etc. oppresses me with a continuous physical horror like the feeling of growing madness in one's own brain. It is rather a horror to be sane in the midst of this; it is too dreadful, too huge, for one to have the comforting feeling of superiority. It goes too far for rage.

Yours sincerely
[T. S. E.]

TO *His Mother* — MS Houghton

14 April 1921 — 9 Clarence Gate Gdns

My dearest Mother,

I have your letter of March 27 and am replying now, lest the strike dislocate the mails. It is certain to be settled somehow before you sail.

1 – Desmond MacCarthy was literary editor of the *NS*, 1920–7.
2 – TSE, 'A Victorian Sculptor', *NS*, 23 Mar. 1918; 'New Philosophers', 13 July 1918.
3 – The coal-miners' strike which began on 1 Apr. continued until 1 July.

I am very glad you transferred to the *Adriatic*, June 1st. How glad we shall be when you are safely over. I did not wish to urge you to prolong your stay at the *other* end, as August is a good month on the sea, and June *should* be a good month here.

I suggest that you should have your letter of credit made out so that *either* you or Marian can draw on it, in case of an emergency, and also to save you from going to the City (business part of town) whenever you want money. If you get it from the Old Colony you can have it made out on Lloyds Bank so that I could help you with it.

You will have Henry given the necessary powers to act for you in your absence.

As to Paris, we shall see when the time comes whether you feel up to that. I have made no plans for that holiday, waiting to make them with you. There are all sorts of nice places I have thought of, depending on how far we go, country or town etc. It was advisable to have France on your passports, however.

I do not want you to exert yourself at all over my books. They are not worth one minute of fatigue on your part. Only if Shef could get them ready *at his leisure* I should be very grateful to you.

The other little flat we should use is very cosy and in some respects nicer than ours, so you have no cause to worry about that. It is settled that you are to be here.

I sent you my Marvell a few days ago. I have to give a lecture next week to a literary club [at Caxton Hall]. I am sorry I promised to do so – several months ago. I shall not waste much time on it.

I say this now – please have Henry cable to me when you sail to let me know you have started. Or *just* before. I shall feel more contented to have him come to New York with you in any case. *Do not start fatigued*, and remember that Marian is bound to worry about you, and spare her by doing *much less* than you feel you *can* do.

You are of course to have breakfast in bed every morning, the later the better, for Ellen!

Must stop now.

Your devoted son
Tom.

Vivien would have been not only disappointed but anxious if you were at an hotel.

TO *Wyndham Lewis* MS Cornell

Saturday [16? April 1921] [London]

Dear Lewis,

Thank you very much for the *Tyro*[1] which has just arrived; I am writing at once before reading it as I should like to say some things in reference to the conversation last night. I think the *Tyro* has a very good appearance indeed this time. But my first thought on looking at the reproductions was that it is and has always been a pity that you have associated yourself with so many inferior artists. It seems to me that the idea of a group may have been all right once, but that *now* it is just wrong for you – that you should *dis*sociate yourself, in the public mind, from any group and from all other British painters. I think that this way of making associates of Dobson, Wadsworth etc. gives them a certain power to damage *you* – i.e. you drag them up to your level and give them a kind of chance to repudiate *you*. (*Would I think of contributing to Wheels?* and so give the S[itwells] a lift and the right to sneer at me?) *I* think that you ought to emphasise your isolation.[2] When I looked through the illustrations just now rather carefully I felt that it almost looked as if you were disparaging your own work in putting it alongside that of these people.

Now as to Paris. I can't feel that there is a great deal of hope in your going there permanently. Painting being so much more important in Paris, there are a great many more clever second-rate men there (and the second-rate men are so infinitely *cleverer* than the second-rate men here) to distinguish oneself from. Then you know what ruthless and indefatigable sharpers Frenchmen are; in comparison the methods of Dobson etc. being only schoolboy tricks. Are they likely even to refrain from interfering with you?? If you do go to Paris (for a time) the best way seems to me to live in retirement there and just work and get some things done for an exhibition here. (Your last one was a success in spite of being hurried and had a very good press). I think it is a good thing to get out of people's way and not

1 – *Tyro: A Review of the Arts of Painting, Sculpture and Design* (1921) included TSE's 'Song to the Opherian' (signed Gus Krutzsch) and 'Notes on Current Letters'. In addition to four illustrations by WL, there were reproductions of works by William Roberts, David Bomberg and Frank Dobson.

2 – *Wheels*, a series of annual poetry anthologies, 1916–22, was a platform for the Sitwell trio and friends inc. AH. TSE wrote, in an unsigned review of *Wheels: A Third Cycle*: 'Every one of the writers of *Wheels* must make a choice. They can either hang together, and make a small place for themselves in the history of literature by being the interesting fashion of a day, or they can choose to run the risk of being individuals' ('The Post-Georgians', *A.*, 11 Apr. 1919).

be seen for some time, not see any of the Chelsea people etc. Separate oneself from the 'young' whose company is only a taint on one – but as a matter of fact you could do that as effectively in London as in Paris, and I cannot help feeling that this temporary retirement would at this point be your wisest course.

If you are going away this week let me know in time so that we can arrange a meeting first.

Yours ever
T.S.E.

TO *Edgar Jepson* PC Beinecke

20 April 1921 9 Clarence Gate Gdns

If you cared to take the trouble to come to Caxton Hall tomorrow night I should of course be delighted, but it will be a very poor address, as I have had very little time.

Sincerely
T. S. Eliot

TO *John Middleton Murry* MS Northwestern

22 April 1921 9 Clarence Gate Gdns

My dear John,

I was glad to hear that you will be in England next month, if only for a short time, and send you my new address. I was also glad to have a letter from you, and to get a copy of your article for the *New Republic*[1] for which I thank you. It is on the whole the best review I have had. For one thing it calls attention to the only part of that book which seems to me of any permanent value. I think that the essays on Jonson, Massinger, Marlowe and Dante are the best. 'The Perfect Critic' I should not wish to reprint. I should prefer to reprint the papers that I like in some more homogeneous volume; I envisage 1. An Elizabethan volume. 2. A seventeenth Century volume to Pope with a *Nachblick* [glance] at Collins and Johnson. 3. A volume containing analyses of my favorite poets in French,

1–JMM, 'The Sacred Wood', *New Republic* 26 (13 Apr. 1921), 194–5. 'Mr Eliot possesses a critical intelligence of a high order'; his manner is 'often unfortunate, portentous and disdainful'.

German, Italian and the Classics. 4. Perhaps a volume on the present day. This seems to me at present all the critical prose I shall ever want to do. It is true that I have started a poem. But Vivien has been very ill. Eight weeks in bed so far, and I shall be occupied this summer with my mother who will be here.

I thought I identified an article on Baudelaire as yours.[1] It struck me as the best thing I have seen in English on a poet whom I admire immensely. The Swinburne–Symons illusion of him (more Symons) has taken hold and will be difficult to dislodge, but this article is an important step forward.

I do not know whether you disapproved of me or not, but I was convinced that you had since a certain period lost all desire to see me, and all interest in myself. The reasons for this were a matter of conjecture; it seemed on the surface capricious, but I did not doubt that reasons existed, in your own mind. But we shall soon meet, I trust, and discuss many things. Your idea of a note book strikes me as a very good one, and it ought to be possible to produce such a thing at very small cost. Whether it would sell is another matter. But I think the best thing now would be, if there were several modest periodicals on the market, involving little outlay, which could be left off or transformed at any time. I am too tired to write further at the moment either personally or impersonally. You do not say how long you will be here, but surely you will be in London long enough for one or two satisfactory conversations.

It is possible (not likely) that I may get to Paris for Whitsun, if I can afford it, but only for two or three days. I should not like to miss you.

Yours ever,
TSE.

Do let me know your dates as soon as possible. Will the address be printed?[2]

TO *Edgar Jepson* MS Beinecke

[22 April 1921] 9 Clarence Gate Gdns

Dear Jepson,

In the fatigue of last night I failed to express my thanks afterwards to you for coming and for supporting me so ably.

1 – 'Baudelaire and Decadence', *TLS*, 7 Apr. 1921, 217–18.

2 – JMM was to give six lectures at Oxford, from 16 May; published as *The Problem of Style* (1922).

I know you disapprove of Elizabethan Drama, and this is not the example I should have chosen to convince you, but it may be interesting and well acted and I have this extra ticket as my wife can't go. It's *The Witch of Edmonton* – and Sybil Thorndyke is in it.[1] If you care to use this I shall be glad to see you there.

Sincerely
T. S. Eliot

TO *His Mother* MS Houghton

27 April 1921 9 Clarence Gate Gdns

Dearest Mother,

I have your two letters of the 12th and 15th, the former containing two clippings. I thought Murry's very good; he sent it to me from where he is living in France. He seems to be very anxious to be friendly at present. I thought that Aiken's[2] was rather grudging and not the result of a conscientious study of the book. When I say 'science' he assumes that I mean 'psychology' because he is interested in that superstitious study: and I thought I noted a desire to disparage. There was a review of one of his books of verse in the *Dial* a couple of months ago, showing by parallel passages how much he had borrowed or stolen from me.[3]

I also received a few days ago your registered letter with the Hydraulic cheque in it, for which I thank you. It is good that the Hydraulic has been able to keep on paying dividends in the midst of the industrial depression which is very bad in America as well as here.

Now for your dividends. The simplest and best way is to instruct the company or companies to pay the dividends direct to your bank for your account. This is the *usual* way in England and I suppose it can be done in America. You get a letter of credit, not buying so much English money outright, but of such a kind that the bank debits your banking account as you draw on the letter of credit. <For safety,> you get the Letter of Credit for a much larger sum than you expect to need. You should also provide yourselves with some English money *before* you start – buy it from the

1 – *The Witch of Edmonton* by William Rowley, Thomas Dekker and John Ford, was put on by the Phoenix Society, under the direction of Montague Summers (1880–1948), at the Lyric Theatre, Hammersmith, on 24 Apr.. Sybil Thorndyke (1882–1976) played the witch.

2 – Conrad Aiken, 'The Scientific Critic', a review of *SW*, *Freeman* 2 (2 Mar. 1921), 593–4.

3 – Babette Deutsch, in her review of Aiken's volume *The House of Dust*, set four passages by Aiken against TSE's originals ('Orchestral Poetry', *Dial* 70: 3 [Mar. 1921], 343).

Bank so as not to be cheated. Get some £5 notes, some £1 notes, and some silver and copper, say £20 in all for the two of you.

I have already advised your getting your letter of credit made out so that *either* you or Marian or Henry can draw on it – so that you will not have to go 'down town' or as we say 'to the City' every time you want money. We shall see that your expenses are moderate, once you get here.

I am very glad indeed that Henry can come. It is a unique opportunity and *must* not be missed and I am delighted that you urged him to come. It will do him a world of good at a critical moment. I want him to keep up his drawing all the time.

1. Now mother dear there are *two things I want to impress on you. One* is that you are not to worry any more about being in our flat, or to go on making other plans. We shall arrange for you and for Henry in the way that is best for everyone, and only we who are on the spot can do it or can know what is best and what is feasible. So think no more about it until you get here, for you can do no good by that. *Everything is settled.* <You are to come here.>

2. *The other thing* is that the coal strike will look much more alarming to you than it does from here. It may be settled before you get this letter, but *even if not*, I am sure the boats will run. The danger of a general strike is over. So do not be apprehensive or alter your sailing unless the boats are running differently. The temper of England is not revolutionary – it is only in Scotland that we see some manifestations of that spirit.

I will stop now and write again as soon as I think of more advice.

I have Baedeker's *London* and *Great Britain* etc.

Your devoted son
Tom

TO *John Quinn* — TS NYPL (MS)

9 May 1921 — 9 Clarence Gate Gdns

Dear Mr Quinn,

In a moment's breathing space after a protracted series of private worries extending over some months – for one, my wife has been ill and in bed for eight weeks, and has just gone to the seaside – I have been running over delayed correspondence, and discover that I am still your debtor for a letter received many months ago. This perhaps the worst of the many negligences I have committed in this time. I do not know whether you can easily turn up a copy of that letter, but it was one for which I was very grateful.

You appear, like me, to lead a very exhausting life, with the leisure that you want always a mirage ahead of you, your holidays always disturbed by unforeseen (or foreseen) calamities. But of course your work is far more difficult and worrying than mine. Even what *I* do – I am dealing alone with all the debts and claims of the bank under the various Peace Treaties – sometimes takes a good deal of thought and strength. When my private life is uneventful, that is not serious enough to matter; but when I have private anxieties on my mind, it is too much. Now I am expecting my mother from Boston in a few weeks; as she is seventy-seven, and not so strong as she was when I saw her last, that will be another anxiety as well as a joy.

I have not yet had any practical reason to regret my livelihood, in the circumstances. Had I joined the *Athenaeum*, two years ago, I should now be desperate, as the *Athenaeum* has disappeared, and I am certain that I at least would not have been one of those to find a safe nest in the *Nation*. The chief drawback to my present mode of life is the lack of *continuous* time, not getting more than a few hours together for myself, which breaks the concentration required for turning out a poem of any length.

I see reason in your objection to my punctuation; but I hold that the line itself punctuates, and the addition of a comma, in many places, seems to me to over-emphasise the arrest. That is because I always pause at the end of a line in reading verse, which perhaps you do not.[1]

My book of essays has come out since I wrote to you last. I was under the impression that I sent you a copy, as I seem to remember clearly writing your name in one; but as I do not appear to have heard from you, it is quite possible that under the strain of the effect of my father-in-law's critical illness upon my wife, I have mistaken the intention for the fact. If so, I should like to know, and send you an English copy. It is a very imperfect production, and there are only four or five of the papers which I should like to save for a definitive book. I have no idea whether it has sold either here or in America; the reviews have been various. I am not anxious to produce another for a year or two; and meanwhile have a long poem in mind and partly on paper which I am wishful to finish.

I have had no news whatever from Pound, beyond two postcards with no address, since he left this country. He appears to be avoiding communication with England, and to consider the country hopeless. I hope

1 – Quinn wrote on 24 Sept. 1920, 'Your avoidance of punctuation marks [in certain poems] is obviously studied, but it occurred to me that in some cases the sense, in others the grammar and in others the rhythm required a certain pause that might be indicated by a comma.'

to see him in Paris at some time during the summer or autumn. I hope he and Thayer will not contrive to rub each other the wrong way, and I certainly would do everything I could to smooth both down; but each has his spines. Pound undoubtedly got a great deal of the best stuff in the *Dial;* I wish that I could have replaced him here after he left, but I have been quite incapacitated this winter, and I never did get about or pick up as many people as he did.

Did I tell you that I met Joyce in Paris last autumn? I found him quite charming, and liked him; though I can see that he is certainly a handful, with the true fanatic's conviction that everyone ought to forward the interests of his work. It is however the conviction of the fanatic, and not the artfulness or pertinacity of ordinary push; and the latter part of *Ulysses*, which I have been reading in manuscript, is truly magnificent. I hear that he has captured some of the French literary elite who profess to know enough English. I have promised to reply to an article by Aldington deprecating his influence; but that was in the April *English Review*, and I have not begun.[1]

Lewis I see often, and he is one of the few whom I have seen of late. His recent show ['Tyros and Portraits'] at the Leicester Galleries was too small for the kind of work exposed, but evidently to my mind, an advance on his previous work. They were the first canvasses of his which have much interested me; I have heretofore thought of him as a consummate draughtsman rather than a painter. One of the figures, a large portrait of a woman, called 'Praxitella',[2] was very good, but I am more interested in his caricatures and satires, two or three of the 'Tyros', and a self-portrait in the same vein. It seems to me that he ought to go on and develop this type of work, which no one else practises. At any rate, his show has had very favourable notices and much advertisement.

I objected to Thayer that the *Dial* contained too much, and was not got up brightly enough for the British public; that the print, rubrics, etc., ought to show more diversity and emphasis, and that the most important articles ought to be exhibited more clearly. He replied that the present form was the best for America. I hope his business sense is as good as his intentions. The paper is certainly better than anything of the same bulk in this country.

1–He did not write a reply to 'The Influence of Mr. James Joyce', *English Review*, Apr. 1921.
2–WL's oil portrait of Iris Barry, bought by Edward Wadsworth for £200; now in Leeds Art Gallery.

I should like very much to hear from you at any time, but I have no justification for expecting to do so, and I ought to appreciate, if anyone does, and respect your lack of time.

Sincerely yours,
T. S. Eliot

There is a young American here named Robert MacAlmon (he has been connected with a paper called *Contact* in New York) who seems to me of promising general intelligence and very amiable personality.

TO *His Mother* — MS Houghton

9 May [1921] — 9 Clarence Gate Gdns

Dearest mother,

I thank you very much for the cheque, but I did not want *you* to pay Frau Happich: it is a debt I ought to pay, and that is why I did not tell you how much. It was £10 I sent (MK.2400), so you sent £2.11.11 too much. Today finally I have her acknowledgement.

We wait and pray for your coming. I cannot think just now of any more advice to give. I think of you all the time.

If you want to go to France you must, when you get here, postpone your return till October, which I hope you may do. You will I think easily be able to sell your passage for a later one. Paris is hot, dusty, unhealthy, and crowded in August, and I do not at all approve your going in that month.

Much much love, dear mother –

Tom.

If you can, I should like to have my silver stick and especially the gold one of grandpa's, but *do not burden* yourself with such unnecessary commissions – the only thing essential is you.

TO *Edgar Jepson* — MS Beinecke

18 May 1921 — 9 Clarence Gate Gdns

Dear Jepson,

Thank you very much for sending me your paper, which I have read with much pleasure. I suppose you want it back. Especially agree with the incantation idea, which seems to me quite enough to condemn a large part of what is *called* vers libre. I shall be sending you a copy of the *Chapbook* and would be glad of any comments.[1]

I should love to hear the next part of your series, but I doubt very much whether I shall be able to. Unfortunately, it is probable that my mother will arrive, from America, on the same day, and thus it will be impossible to come or to accept your kind invitation to dinner. But in that case I hope you will let me see the MSS. But I should have preferred to come to the lecture and support you as you supported me, or to the best of my ability. <With best wishes to your wife and you,>

Sincerely yours,
T. S. Eliot

TO *Scofield Thayer* TS Beinecke

21 May 1921 9 Clarence Gate Gdns

My Dear Scofield,

I am glad to hear that my letter was received in time. I shall try to get my next one to you by the middle of June. I am also glad to get your draft for $40.00 for which I thank you. I note with discomfiture that the exchange is, as the phrase ironically puts it, 'moving in England's favour', but that you cannot help.

I have perused the offending paragraph[2] with complete placidity, and find it as correct as reports usually are. I cannot see how a malicious construction could be put upon it, but on the other hand I cannot see that it means anything more than that I invited MacAlmon to dinner. I don't know what the 'Late French Hamper' is, but I don't think anyone else does either, so that's allright. The same criticism applies to your comments on *Contact* in the May *Dial*, which mystify, but do not libel. What on earth does it all mean? I have ventured to tell MacAlmon that it means nothing. I have found him a very charming young man of lively intelligence and amiable personality. But why on earth do you devote so much space and such obscure vaticination to a young writer who might just as well, and who would willingly, remain in privacy until he has performed some

1–*Chapbook* 22 (Apr. 1921) included TSE's 'Verse and Prose'.

2–Thayer proposed to refer to TSE in the *Dial* in a 'facetious manner without malice': 'According to the latest dispatch, Mr. T. S. Eliot (who was wrung through Milton Academy, Harvard College, the University of Paris, and Merton College, Oxford, before coiling down and curling up in his Late French hamper) has bidden Mr. McAlmon to meat.' The matter was dropped.

notable feat? I found *Contact* an interesting little paper, with the exception of the letters of Mr Slinkard, for which there is a sufficient explanation. MacAlmon's remarks about me were in part quite shrewd,[1] and in part based, as I explained to him, on misinformation. But why make an international event out of a private matrimonial union which is only interesting for the parties concerned?

I am sorry to hear of a little embroglio with Aldington. Apart from any question of his importance as a writer, he is an extremely nice man, and I quite believe the account he gave me, of his having wished to spread the *Dial* about here, and of the subsequent discovery that one of the members of his club had been in the habit of purloining parcels of books. He says that this incident has made it impossible for him to offer any more contributions to the *Dial*? Is that so?

I propose, in my next 'Letter', to mention the fact that Strachey's book [*Queen Victoria*] appeared here at about the same moment that it began appearing serially in the *New Republic*. I suppose that publication in New York was delayed to allow the readers of the *New Republic* to enjoy the first taste.

It is not likely that I shall be in Paris until October, but I suppose that you will still be there, and will, I presume, pay a visit to London in the autumn. There is not much reason for coming here in July or August.

I shall receive you with pleasure in the autumn, or as you say, in the fall! Come!

Yours ever,
Tom.

TO *James Joyce*

TS Buffalo

21 May 1921

jetzt[2]. . . . . . 9 Clarence Gate Gdns,
London, N.W.1

My dear Joyce,

I am returning your three manuscripts by registered post as you require, and am exceedingly obliged for a taste of them.[3] I think they are superb – especially the Descent into Hell, which is stupendous. Only, in detail,

1 – TSE 'will become a poor critic', McAlmon had written, 'if he does not relate literature to reality rather than to literature' ('Modern Antiques', *Contact*, Jan. 1921).
2 – 'now'.
3 – 'Circe' (subject of the detailed comments in this paragraph), 'Eumaeus' and 'Oxen of the Sun'.

I object to one or two phrases of Elijah: 'ring up' is English, 'call up' the American; 'trunk line', if applied to the telephone service, is English, the American is, if I remember, 'long distance'. I don't quite like the wording of the coon transformation of Elijah, either, but I cannot suggest any detailed alteration. But otherwise, I have nothing but admiration; in fact, I wish, for my own sake, that I had not read it.

I am delighted to hear that even a limited and very expensive edition is to appear. Has it been properly circularised in England? If not, I might supply a few names. I wish that Miss Beach would bring out a limited edition of my epic ballad on the life of Christopher Columbus and his friend King Bolo, but

Bolo's big black bastard queen
Was *so* obscene
She shocked the folk of Golder's Green.

Aldington's article I only heard of when Miss Weaver sent me a copy ten days ago.[1] He has promised to write to Austin Harrison to ask him to print a letter by me; Aldington is quite a decent person, and I am sure he has done. I wanted this precaution because the next issue of the *English Review* was already out, and as Harrison does not know me at all, he might have declined to print a communication so late, especially since his paper does not print letters as a rule.[2]

I do not expect to get over to Paris until October, as I shall have my mother here most of the summer. I hope very much to find you there then, as I so much enjoyed seeing you in December. I have heard that you were about to move into a new flat, and if so I trust that you will let me have your new address.[3]

Yours always sincerely,
T. S. Eliot

1–RA, 'The Influence of Mr. James Joyce', *English Review* 32 (Apr. 1921), 333–41. RA considered *Ulysses* 'a tremendous libel on humanity' and a damaging influence on young writers.

2–No letter was published. TSE responded in '*Ulysses*, Order and Myth', *Dial* 75: 5 (Nov. 1923), 480–3.

3–On 3 June JJ moved into Valery Larbaud's flat in the rue du Cardinal Lemoine, where he spent four months, rent-free, during its owner's absence.

TO *Robert McAlmon* TS Beinecke

22 May 1921[1] 9 Clarence Gate Gdns

Dear Bob,

I was glad to hear from you. I will go through your poems[2] at leisure if I may, and write you about them in due course. I'm glad to hear that you like Paris; the right way of course is to take it as a place and a tradition, rather than as a congeries of people, who are mostly futile and timewasting, except when you want to pass an evening agreeably in a café. The chief danger about Paris is that it is such a strong stimulus, and like most stimulants incites to rushing about and produces a pleasant illusion of great mental activity rather than the solid results of hard work. When I was living there years ago I had only the genuine stimulus of the place, and not the artificial stimulus of the people, as I knew no one whatever, in the literary and artistic world, as a companion – knew them rather as spectacles, listened to, at rare occasions, but never spoken to. I am sure Julien Benda is worth knowing and possibly Paul Valéry. But Paris is still alive. What is wonderful about French literature is its solidarity: you don't know one part of it, even the most contemporary, unless you know the seventeenth and eighteenth centuries, and more too, in a way in which Pound and [Clive] Bell don't – Pound because he has never taken the trouble, and Bell because he couldn't. Bell is a most agreeable person, if you don't take him seriously, but a great waster of time if you do, or if you expect to get any profound knowledge or original thought out of him, and his Paris is a useless one. If I came to live in Paris the first thing to do would be to cut myself off from it, and not depend upon it. Joyce I admire as a person who seems to be independent of outside stimulus, and who therefore is likely to go on producing first-rate work until he dies.

I should not worry at all about what Thayer says. I thought his witticisms in the May number very tasteless and pointless.[3] Why do our

1 – Misdated 2 May in the first edn. of these *Letters*.

2 – Robert McAlmon, *The Portrait of a Generation* (1926).

3 – In an unsigned 'Comment', Thayer sniped at William Carlos Williams's suggestion that Alfred Kreymborg should be given 'one hundred thousand dollars': 'one hundred thousand dollars! O Hieronimo! Robert Menzies McAlmon, where are you now? Matrimony always was a roundabout way to arrive at anything.' He explained in a footnote that 'Mr McAlmon recently took to wife a young British woman' – on 14 Feb., McAlmon married Winifred Ellerman (1894–1983), daughter of a shipping magnate – and 'forthwith dispatched himself and her to the British capital' with 'the notion of buying print-paper in her country cheap'. The implication was that McAlmon's need for cheap paper for his magazine *Contact* 'antedated' his wedding (*Dial* 70: 5, May 1921, 606–10).

compatriots try so hard to be clever? Furthermore, his language is so opaque, through his cleverness, that it is unintelligible gibberish. Cummings has the same exasperating vice.

But Joyce has form – immensely careful. And as for literary – one of the last things he sent me contains a marvellous parody of nearly every style in English prose from 1600 to the *Daily Mail*.[1] One needs a pretty considerable knowledge of English literature to understand it. No! you can't generalize, in the end it is a question of whether a man has genius and can do what he sets out to do. Small formulas support small people. Aren't the arty aesthetes you mention simply the people without brains?

Write to me again soon, yours,

Tom

TO *Dorothy Pound* TS Lilly

22 May 1921 9 Clarence Gate Gdns

My dear Dorothy,

So you are living at Vivien's old hotel![2] I am delighted to have your address at last, in an official channel, and to know that you are installed so near the ghost of Rémy.[3] Yes, Vivien was in bed for eight or nearly nine weeks, and then had a bad attack of gastric influenza when she got up. I think that not only the anxiety, but the standing so much by her father's bed precipitated internal displacements.

I shall be in Paris for some time in October – probably not before then. Presumably you will not move south until December. My mother will be here in June. I don't suppose that you will betray your mysterious movements, but I shall go to your hotel in October and at least enquire after. Postcards with no address are not really very good means of tracing people.

In October I shall be ready for a little mountain air, after I have finished a little poem which I am at present engaged upon. I see that the mountain air is about to produce *Ulysses*, which I am mightily pleased to know, as the unpublished manuscript is even finer stuff than the printed. Tell Ezra

1 – The first part of Episode XIV of *Ulysses* ('The Oxen of the Sun') had appeared in *Little Review* 7: 3 (Sept.–Dec. 1920), 81–92. JJ wrote to Weaver on 23 Apr. 1921, asking her to 'pass on to Mr Eliot when you have read them the two episodes Mr Pound sent and also the typescript of *Oxen of the Sun*' (*Letters of James Joyce*, III, ed. Richard Ellmann, 1966, 41).
2 – Hôtel du Pas de Calais, 59 rue des Sts Pères, Paris VI.
3 – Rémy de Gourmont (1858–1915), French novelist and critic, had lived at No. 73.

that I am awaiting a testimonial to the ozone in the shape of some considerable opus from his Corona [typewriter], and that the *Dial* appears to be in need of a Paris letter from him.

Yours ever affectionately
T.S.E.

TO *Herbert Read*

TS Victoria

2 June 1921 — 9 Clarence Gate Gdns

My dear Read,

I am humiliated, after such a long silence, to be writing to you on a purely practical subject – but circumstances all this winter and spring – a great deal of anxious illness, not my own – have been very unfavourable to the correspondence I had hoped for. To come to the point, I am looking for a bed-sitting room in this neighbourhood, (Baker Street Station) for my brother, who is to arrive from America next week, and I know that you once, before your marriage, dwelt in Nottingham Terrace, next to Tussaud's.

I have forgotten the address you had then, but is that a place that would be suitable for a single gentleman, bed and breakfast, by the week?

I have been looking at 'Apartments' in the neighbourhood, and find them all dilapidated, and the proprietors unprepossessing.

Are you writing at all now, or only reading? Or do you find that the Treasury work is too exhausting? You have, from what I have heard, been making such a success as a civil servant, that you may find no time or strength left to serve the Muses. I hope that is not so. It would be a great pleasure to hear from you again.

Yours always
T. S. Eliot

On 10 June, TSE's mother, brother and sister Marian arrived in London for a two-month visit. His mother and sister were to occupy the Eliots' flat in Clarence Gate Gardens until 20 August, while TSE and Vivien rented Lucy Thayer's smaller flat at 12 Wigmore Street.

TO *Leonard Woolf* MS Berg

15 June 1921 (post address)
9 Clarence Gate Gdns, N.W.1

My dear Woolf,

I am very sorry to hear that your wife is not well, and hope that it may be nothing serious. I was disappointed that your dinner did not take place. I must apologise for the delay – your card arrived after we had moved out and my mother was moving in, and I only discovered it, among others, two days ago: otherwise I would have accepted for us at once. I hope you will be able to have another and will ask us again, and I hope you can both go to *Bartholomew Fair* on the 26th.[1]

Please give your wife our sympathy and tell her I hope she will soon be well.

Sincerely yours
T. S. Eliot

TO *Mary Hutchinson* MS Texas

[Postmark 16 June 1921] 9 Clarence Gate Gdns

Dear Mary,

I have spotted a telephone at 41 Gordon Square under the name of Alix.[2] Of course it may have been turned off while in Vienna but I rang up Vanessa[3] and arranged to look at the room tomorrow afternoon. If the telephone works the place seems ideal. Do you think the neighbourhood of Oliver Strachey would have a good or bad influence upon young Henry [Eliot]?[4] Henry, a low name in this country, Henery, but still current in America. In any case, I want to get a room at Birrell's for my unhappy brother in July – reply reply, to whom should I apply: Francis Birrell Esqre.? Or Garnett?[5] or someone else.

1 – The first performance of Jonson's play since 1731, by the Phoenix Society at the New Oxford Theatre.

2 – Alix Strachey (*née* Sargant-Florence, 1892–1973), psychoanalyst, had married James Strachey in 1920. They had a flat at 41 Gordon Square, but were currently in Vienna for analysis with Freud.

3 – Vanessa Bell and Duncan Grant lived at 37 Gordon Square.

4 – Oliver Strachey, a musician and civil servant, brother of Lytton and James, lived at 42 Gordon Square.

5 – The critic and journalist Francis Birrell (1889–1935) and the novelist David Garnett (1892–1981) ran the Bloomsbury Bookshop in Taviton Street.

I do not feel that I have really seen you for many weeks, or know about you. Nevertheless, I enjoyed the other evening very much. –

Always affectionately
Tom.

TO *Ottoline Morrell* MS Texas

21 June 1921 9 Clarence Gate Gdns

My dear Ottoline,

We are waiting anxiously to hear how you stood the journey and how you are now. I did sympathise with your desire to get away from the nursing home, but it seems to me that you must have been very weak for a journey. In fact, we were quite frightened.

I hope you will be thoroughly rested before you have my mother and me. May we fix on a date now? If it is possible, I should like to bring her early in August (the 6th or the 13th?) but that is only *if it makes no difference to you* – I believe you mentioned the 9th of July to Vivien and if that suits you better I easily can arrange it. I should bring my mother over from Oxford or else take her there on Sunday evening.[1] But do let me know what suits you best, and at the same time say how you have been.

My mother is very excited at the prospect of Garsington and of meeting you whom she has heard so much about!

Vivien is very tired again and can do nothing at all. She sends quantities of love and sympathy.

Affectionately yours
Tom

TO *Richard Aldington* MS Texas

23 June 1921 Address still 9 Clarence Gate Gdns

My dear Aldington,

I trust you know me well enough by this time to believe that I would have written to you long ago but for circumstances of an unusual character (as my circumstances usually are!). We have moved for the summer to 12 Wigmore Street (but address letters for security as before) in order that my mother and sister, whom I have not seen for six years, might have our flat.

1 – They visited OM at Garsington on 7 Aug.

My brother is here also. These new and yet old relationships involve immense tact and innumerable adjustments. One sees lots of things that one never saw before etc. In addition my wife is here for their benefit against the express command of her specialist, who told her that it was very wrong for her to be in town at all this summer. So I shall not rest until I have got her away again.

I was very distressed by your previous letter. I hope that this can be arranged without its imposing the whole financial burden on you. If so, it is unspeakable. I have no idea whether your sisters are children or grown. You must get them into practical occupations or trades if or as soon as they are old enough, because they will be happier.

I felt on the contrary that it was I who did not support you adequately with Balderston,[1] particularly about Manning.[2] Will B. give him any work? All it seems that I can do is to write to MacCarthy – shall I do that? I do not know the *Nation* people who run the *Athenaeum* now. If however there is anyone else you think it would help if I wrote to, let me know.

You tempt me to undertake more than I can, perhaps – there is so much that one would like to do or be glad to do, and it is so easy to postpone the most important thing. But I *will* keep in mind what you say, and am grateful to you. My Dryden was not good, because only a series of unconnected scraps.[3] How are you now? I am very tired and can hardly drive this pen. With kind regards to your wife.

Yours ever
T.S.E.

Harriet Weaver has just published a book of Marianne Moore's verse.[4] Have you had it? Can anything be done about it? Can you do anything about getting a good review in the *Times*?[5] I am glad if you are going to do something on Cowley. Should like to help with Jackson later.[6]

1–John Lloyd Balderston (1889–1954), American playwright and screenwriter; editor of the *Outlook* (which had published RA's 'The Poetry of T. S. Eliot' on 7 Jan.).
2–Frederic Manning (1882–1935), Australian novelist and poet.
3–TSE's review of Mark Van Doren, *John Dryden*, *TLS*, 9 June 1921 (*SE*).
4–Moore, *Poems* (Egoist Press), was edited without the author's approval by H. D. and 'Bryher', pseud. of Winifred Ellerman (1894–1983), wealthy English writer, philanthropist, and patron of many writers ranging from James Joyce to Edith Sitwell.
5–[Harold Child], *TLS*, 21 July 1921. TSE discussed the book in 'Marianne Moore', *Dial* 75: 6, Dec. 1923.
6–Holbrook Jackson (1874–1948), editor and literary historian, founder-editor of *To-Day*, 1917–23.

TO *Richard Aldington* TS Texas

6 July 1921 9 Clarence Gate Gdns

My dear Aldington,

We very deeply appreciated the kindness of you and your wife in offering us your house for the time you are to be walking, and had circumstances been favourable I should certainly have accepted. I recall it as a Paradise. But I was just getting my wife away to a place in the country on Chichester harbour which I hope she will find agreeable enough to stay in till the end of July, and meanwhile I must be in town to be with my mother. I am going to Warwick (where I have never been) with them on Saturday – my mother proceeding to Stratford and Kenilworth from there. She is terrifyingly energetic for seventy-seven.

Anxieties of several kinds; and the strain of accommodating myself to people who in many ways are now strangers to me, have consumed my time and energy. I have also had another matter to deal with, which I may want to discuss with you at a later opportunity. I am sorry for the pain you must have, as well as for the practical anxiety. Is it clear how much financial, as well as parental, responsibility will fall upon you if no arrangement can be made with your mother? How much more money will you have to make, and how are you going to make it? How much sacrifice is required?

I shall be glad to accept credit at the Poetry Bookshop instead of payment for the Notes:[1] will you signify this to Monro? I have asked several persons to buy their books there.

I am not as much impressed by Manning's *Scenes and Portraits*[2] as I expected to be – it seems to me rather derivative as literature. But I think he is undoubtedly one of the very best prose writers we have, and if literary journalism won't support him it ought not to support anybody. I am writing tonight to MacCarthy, and am also mentioning Miss Moore's poems to him. Do you know what can be done to get the book some favourable reviews? I presume that Miss Weaver has sent you a copy – if not, ask her for it.

I shall be glad to send something to Jackson, as soon as the pot has settled down and I can look through the steam and count my chickens.[3] It might fit in well with my general programme of literary criticism which

1–TSE, 'Prose and Verse', *Chapbook*, Apr. 1921.

2–Frederic Manning, *Scenes and Portraits* (1909).

3–September's *To-Day* published 'Maxims and Precepts', a page of excerpts from TSE.

must by this time be fairly obvious to you, and I hope and believe fairly congenial: I mean that any innuendos I make at the expense of Milton, Keats, Shelley and the nineteenth century in general are part of a plan to help us rectify, so far as *I* can, the immense skew in public opinion toward our pantheon of literature. But I should like to discuss this with you in conversation.

I do hope your holiday will be a happy one. Write to me when you return.

Yours ever
T.S.E.

TO *Ottoline Morrell*

MS Texas

14 July 1921

9 Clarence Gate Gdns
(for letters, but still at Wigmore St)

My dear Ottoline,

I have been wondering for a long time how you have been and should so much like to know. It seems almost incredible that you should really be as well as you appeared the last time I saw you – after such a terrible ordeal.[1] But I have been involved in the most trying complications since then, which have exhausted my time and strength completely. There has been a project for the revival of *Art & Letters*, or rather as it now appears, a quarterly of similar size under a new name. It has undergone various transformations and passed through various hands since it was first broached to me – Schiff has taken part in it, but the person to provide the money is Lady Rothermere.[2] I found myself in a very difficult situation in it, and I am sorry to say was obliged to call Vivien back from the country to help me out. It has called for exceptional tact. Even now Lady R. has not placed the project on a definite basis, and we are no further forward than we were when we started. It is not, in its present form, a scheme that could possibly replace the bank, and indeed what little I should get out of

1–In June 1921, DHL had published *Women in Love*, in which the character of Hermione Crich is based partly upon OM. When she read a typescript in 1917, she claimed to have been libelled and investigated the possibility of legal action, but none was taken.
2–Mary Lilian Harmsworth, née Share (d. 1937): Lady Rothermere. Daughter of George Wade Share, in 1893 she married Harold Sydney Harmsworth, first Viscount Rothermere (1868–1940). It was owing to Scofield Thayer, whom she met in New York, that she became the backer of TSE's periodical *The Criterion*, 1922–5. The first issue (Oct. 1922) was to feature the first UK publication of *The Waste Land*.

it would be no more, I imagine, than any other contributors. But it is something that, once started, one feels could be made something of, in time, and would be an interesting attempt just now when there is *nothing* in London. But I cannot tell you how very exhausting and difficult the business has been – at least, I can tell you better when I see you, and the most fatiguing thing is the lack of definite progress.

I tell you all this *in the strictest confidence*, of course: I particularly don't want it mentioned at present. It is so vague. We have done all we can at present, and Vivien, who has been *invaluable*, is going back to the country at once. She is worn out. I had already got my brother in to live with me (at Wigmore Street) as we did not expect her to come back, and it is very confined and uncomfortable quarters for three people.

Of course I did not expect to do any work while my family were here; but I have not even attended to ordinary and necessary business correspondence.

I am taking a short holiday at the end of next week, till the 2nd. Vivien sends her love and is very anxious about you, and will write soon. I am looking forward to seeing you in August –

Affectionately
Tom.

Vivien Eliot TO *Scofield Thayer* — MS Beinecke

20 July [1921] — 9 Clarence Gate Gdns

Dear Scofield

Tom is so tired and hot, and is busy finishing off various things before he goes away for ten days of his holiday, that I am writing for him, altho' my mind has left me and I am becoming gradually insane.

T. says that there is no reason whatever for your leaving your 103° in the sun for the cool breezes of this island – *because*, so far, nothing in the least definite has been done by Lady Rothermere. She seems to be anxious to postpone any positive action, for private reasons <Excuse the alliteration> of her own, – and nothing at present can be done. (In my own opinion there is nothing in the whole business). However, the one definite utterance I can report, from several sources, is that she does *not* wish or intend to amalgamate in any journal or to spill her cash for the cause of Literature. If she really puts her mind to anything it will be to purchase and run a small paper of her *own*. I am sorry, and Tom is sorry. The other would have been a good idea.

You must excuse Tom for any dilatoriness in writing, he has had his family on his hands since early in June. We have given up our at least cool and civilised flat to them, while we are encamped in an attic with a glass roof. So you see other people have troubles as well as yourself, and I believe you invited me to come and drown myself with you, once. I am ready at any moment. T. says delighted to review Joyce. That at least is definite. Will let you know if anything happens to, or with, Lady R., not that you will have any interest.

Well, go and frizzle – we shall be in Paris in *October*, many D's V.

Yrs.
Vivien

TO *Gilbert Seldes*[1]

MS Timothy and Marian Seldes

6 August 1921

9 Clarence Gate Gdns

Dear Mr Seldes

Thank you very much for the draft £10 10s 6d. I hope my next letter will arrive in better season.[2]

I am glad to find that you also are an admirer of Swift – and an acute one.[3]

Sincerely yours
T. S. Eliot

TO *John Rodker*

MS Mrs Burnham Finney

8 August 1921

9 Clarence Gate Gdns

Dear Rodker,

I am very sorry to hear that the press has had to come to an end, after doing such good (and improving) work. I shan't bother you about the £5.15.9 – I hope you will succeed in emerging from your difficulties. I wish you could put your experience in with someone else who wanted to run a

1 – Gilbert Seldes (1893–1970): American writer and cultural critic; managing editor of *The Dial*; see Glossary of Names.

2 – Payment for TSE's 'London Letter' in *Dial* 71: 2 (Aug. 1921).

3 – Seldes's review of Shaw, *Back to Methuselah*, compared it to *Gulliver's Travels* ('Struldbrugs and Supermen', *Dial* 71: 2).

press. I had been hoping to see *Ulysses* emerge from your press. Is there no chance of your being associated with a printing business again?

Yours
T.S.E.

TO *Hugh Walpole* MS Valerie Eliot

8 August 1921 9 Clarence Gate Gdns

My dear Walpole,

I am sorry. But do come on Thursday at *any* time – but 12.30 is a good time as the restaurants are not so full. I am at Lloyds Bank (Foreign Dept.) 20 King William Street, near either Bank (Central London) or Monument (District) stations. A messenger will lead you to my cave.

Yours always sincerely
T. S. Eliot

TO *Mary Hutchinson* MS Texas

15 August 1921 9 Clarence Gate Gdns

Dear Mary

I should be delighted to come to Wittering, but the 1st October is the first date I can manage. I have had to devote the last two weekends to taking various members of my family to Garsington, and I must simply stay in town for the next month to save expense but chiefly to tackle a special piece of work. Do write and let me know if that date is possible, as I shall be very disappointed as it is. Do we meet in six weeks time?

Yes, it was too bad that you couldn't come down, but I thought you were coming to see Vivien.

Yours affectionately
Tom.

TO *Richard Aldington* MS Texas

16 August 1921 9 Clarence Gate Gdns

Dear R.A.,

Monday will suit me capitally and the *Cock* is excellent. If you could make it 12.*15* so much the better: I can get out as early as I like, but must always *at the latest* be back by 1.30.

I should like to meet [Holbrook] Jackson and think it worthwhile and I appreciate the trouble you take to introduce me to people. As for the *Outlook*, the simple fact is that I have not sent anything: whether, beyond that, we have been outmanoeuvred, I do not know. The only man I know who writes for it regularly is a small fellow named Martin Armstrong, who sometimes comes to lunch with me; he seems quite friendly. However, that is neither here nor there. MacCarthy is of course an Irishman, that is to say he belongs to a race which I cannot understand. He seemed eager to get Manning, and it is quite possible that his attitude is nothing more than vagueness. I had a letter from him asking me formally to contribute and suggesting some books. Unfortunately he said he was immediately leaving for three weeks, so I suppose my reply will be dealt with by someone else. I suggested that you were the most competent person.

What I must explain at this point is, *in strict confidence*, that there is a possibility of a new literary venture, to be financed up to a certain (too certain) point, in which (if it comes off) I shall be deeply involved. This should soon be decided, and I shall then want to discuss it with you at length. But if it is realised, I shall probably have little time for outside writing. It will not yield me much beyond the price of my own contributions, if that, but it might be interesting.

Yours ever
T.S.E.

My family leave on Saturday, and I shall then return to 9 Clarence Gate Gardens.

TO *Dorothy Pound* MS Lilly

21 August 1921 9 Clarence Gate Gdns

Dear Dorothy,

Tuesday is excellent,[1] but Clarence Gate is not, as my family have just vacated it and it is being prepared and cleaned. I am not even there yet.

1–TSE had sent a telegram on 18 Aug.: 'Will you dine on Monday or Tuesday?' (Lilly).

So will you come around to the Kensington Palace Hotel, I think it is, around the corner from Church Street. I will be in the hall at 7.15, Tuesday.

Yours
T.S.E.

TO *His Mother* MS Houghton

[23 August 1921] [9 Clarence Gate Gdns]

Dearest mother,

I am waiting anxiously for next Tuesday to hear of your arrival in Cambridge. But still more I am anxious for the first letters telling how you are. Remember what I said to you before you left about keeping up and keeping strong for your next visit.

We do not move back till the end of the week. We both said we could hardly bear to go back there – the flat seems to belong to you now and is very strange and desolate without you in it.[1] Although it seems as if you had only been here a few days, it is very difficult to realise that you have gone. But I think that the distance will seem less great and less important now, don't you? It was wonderful to have you all with us.

Your devoted son
Tom.

Vivien Eliot TO *Henry Eliot* MS Texas

Tuesday 23 [August 1921] Wigmore St

Dear Henry,

I am writing to you very quickly because we want to thank you at *once* for what I found in the typewriter. It was quite a shock when you opened it. It is *terrible* that you should be so generous. We want to open an account here in your name and put that money away for you so that you

1–CCE would write to HWE on 14 Oct. 1921: 'Now I come to the painful part of my letter. I am enclosing a letter from Tom – a beautiful one. I think he missed us very much. He is devoted to Vivien, too much so I think, for she expects so much. And now as I always expected, he is the one to break down. I am surprised at his saying that when we were in the flat it had a cosiness which it misses now. I think the poor boy misses the affection that makes no demands from him, but longs to help him. Vivien loves Tom, and he her, although I think he is afraid of her. The only time he failed in his beautiful attitude of affection for me was when I did not go to see Vivien two days in succession after she returned from Itchenor, and that was the day I received the deed and was busy. (I went one day, but not the next.)'

shall have a small fund, to which you can contribute occasionally if you like, ready for you when you come back.

And the typewriter?[1] What does that mean please? You can hardly have mistaken them *in* (as Tom insists) the circumstances. But whatever it means, you are shown up as an angel. A bloody angel, as they say over here.

Now I want you to tell me something truly. You are not to lie. Did your mother and sister show, think, say or intimate that I behaved like 'no lady', and just like a wild animal when [we] saw you off? I was perfectly stunned on that occasion. I had no idea what I was doing. I have been more or less stunned for many months now and when I come to, I suppose it seems dreadful, to an American. I have worried all the time since. Tom said it was perfectly allright, etc, but I am sure he has lived here so long he hardly realises how *very* much less English people mind showing their emotions than Americans – or perhaps he does realise it so perfectly. But I was extremely anxious to show no emotion before your family at any time, and then I ended in a fit!

I found the emotionless condition a great strain, all the time. I used to think I should burst out and scream and dance. That's why I used to think you were so terribly failing me. But I won't talk about that now, except to ask you if ever two people made *such* a fearful mess of their obvious possibilities. I don't understand, and I never shall. Twenty-four hours of contact out of two months. Both flats are equally unbearable to us, so we stay here morosely. We miss you dreadfully – for me, especially in the morning and late at night. We have not even had the spirit to buy wine, yet when the evening comes we curse and abuse each other for not having seen we want it all the more now. I believe we shall become pussyfeet. Your roses have lived till now, but are dying so miserably as I write. Sorry about having to scratch out so many words, but you should be flattered that I write to you at all.

Tom has plunged deep into the 'Quarterly' now, and set things going. It *is* going to be the most awful affair, so difficult and tiresome, all the business I mean. I see rocks ahead. However she Lady R. *might* not accept the terms even now, there were two slight alterations in the letter, on father's advice. I have not got near father to give his pipe, but he knows about it, and gave a loud roar, T. says. I had my worst headache, lasting twenty hours, from Saturday night, so haven't pulled up yet.

1–HWE had left his own typewriter and taken TSE's, which was worn out.

See the Marble Halls we *might* have dwelt in this month – this is the Sitwell country house.[1] Show it to your mother because I think it's rather nice. And here's a photograph Otto[line] took. *Keep it*, it is the only one I have.

Write at once and don't wait '*for the mood*'. The mood *comes*, in writing.

Tom will write about the typewriter.

Anyhow we leave on October 1.

Good-bye Henry. And *be personal*, you must be personal, or else it's no good. Nothing's any good.

Vivien

FROM *Lady Rothermere* TS Valerie Eliot copy

23 August 1921 9 Clarence Gate Gdns, N.W.1

Dear Sir,

I beg to confirm the arrangement made between us for your appointment as the sole responsible Editor of the Quarterly Magazine to be called the London Quarterly or some similar title approved by us jointly, which I am about to inaugurate,[2] as follows:-

1. I will provide £600 (six hundred pounds) a year for each of the first three years to meet with any receipts from sales and advertisements the expenses involved in getting up, printing, issuing and advertising the Magazine. You are to be entitled to any surplus which the £600 and any such receipts may give in excess of the expenses as remuneration for your services and/or the extension or improvement of the Magazine as you may think fit, but you are in any event to retain out of each annual instalment of £600, £100 for your services if you think fit. The sums I am to provide will be paid by me in annual instalments of £600 to an account to be opened by you at the Lloyds Bank Limited in your name 'L. Q. Account' at the commencement of each year, the first payment to be made by me immediately on your formal acceptance of this letter. All receipts are to be paid into the same account. The banking account to be operated by you solely, but for the purposes of the Magazine solely.

1–'I dreamt that I dwelt in marble halls / With vassals and serfs at my side' (from Michael Balfe's opera *The Bohemian Girl*, 1843). Enclosed was a photograph of Renishaw Hall, the ancestral home of the Sitwells in Derbyshire.

2–The title of the new periodical was ultimately to be *The Criterion*.

2. The accounts are to be audited by an Accountant nominated by me either annually or semi-annually as I think fit, all facilities for the audit to be afforded by you. If and when the business is in a position to warrant the expense of a business manager, I am to be at liberty to appoint some person selected by me, but approved by you to that post on terms to be agreed with you.

3. Except with my express consent all expenses, including payments to Contributors, are to be met out of the annual sum of £600 provided by me and any such receipts as above mentioned. You are during the three years to have the entire control of the literary contents of the paper and sole authority to solicit and accept and reject contributions but in the event of your withdrawing from the editorship at any time, thereafter the Banking Account is to be operated by me or my appointee.

(Signed) Lilian Rothermere
23d August 1921.

TO *Sydney Schiff* MS BL

25 August 1921 9 Clarence Gate Gdns

My dear Sydney,

I was exceedingly sorry to hear this afternoon that you too have broken down and have been in bed. I am not surprised, with the work and worries you have had. I only hope you will be able to get away to some bracing place in a few days time. I am anxious to have the most accurate reports of both of you.

I should have communicated before, but the whole of last week was engrossed by the departure of my family, and I cannot tell you how exhausting we both found it – the reaction from the strain of it has been paralysing.

I have seen Mr Broad [a solicitor], and have had him draw up a letter which Lady Rothermere has now returned signed. I confess I feel more worried than anything, and shall not get any pleasure from the paper until I have seen enough issues appear to believe it a success.

I shall ring up again and will come to see you as soon as you are fit for it, but I do not wish to bother you until you are able to bear it. I am anxious to know how both Violet and you are. Vivien is not at all well.

Aff.
Tom

We return to Clarence in a few days time.

TO *Mary Hutchinson* MS Texas

1 September 1921 [London]

Dear Mary

Many things have prevented me from writing before – the departure of my family, moving back, and a business which I must ask you not to mention to anyone, as I am not certain whether it will come off. It is a project for a new quarterly, the patron Lady Rothermere, the question whether it can be run on the money which Lady R. can provide. Therefore I am immersed in calculations and estimates, and problems of business management. Do you think, candidly, that a paper the size of *Art & Letters* (or a mite more in it) is (1) possible (2) worthwhile. There are the questions (1) are there enough good contributors (2) are there enough possible subscribers (3) cost (4) whether I am competent and have time enough.

I have only discussed this with two or three people for the sake of technical information which they have, so *please keep it to yourself till I let you know it may be revealed.* You will understand that I have had little time for the amenities of society or even the pleasures of friendship. Also I am feeling completely exhausted – the departure of my family laid us both out – and have had some splitting headaches. To complete my tale of complaint I have had to put my holiday a week earlier, the first October, the day I was to come to you. I should have put it in September if I could, so as to get a rest and then begin my business afterwards. But I had to have as much time *after* my holiday as possible, as, if this is realised, I should want to get a number out in December. As it is, I shall be rushed before and after, and I have one weekend, which, as I shall be here, and accepted it some time ago, I must keep, to the Woolfs. I am hideously annoyed, and disappointed. Is there any chance of your coming up to London before October, and could we meet? Do you know we have not met since April! Do write and comfort me.

Affectionately
Tom

What was your hotel in Paris – Hôtel de Nice? Bd. Montparnasse?

TO *Richard Aldington* MS Texas

Wednesday [7 September 1921] 9 Clarence Gate Gdns, N.W.1

My dear Richard

I am dreadfully sorry that I have not written. I have been burning to do so but my wife has been very ill, we have had to have new consultations, and to make matters worse we have been moving from Wigmore Street back here, and I have had no time or brains to write to you. This is just to tell you that I shall write to you fully on Thursday or Friday – Please wait!

Yours ever affectionately

Tom

TO *Richard Aldington*

TS Texas

8 September 1921 9 Clarence Gate Gdns

Dear R.A.,

I think you and Jackson have done me very handsomely between you; in fact, I have never received any recognition nearly so flattering as this.[1] I hope it will at least come to the notice of Messrs. Methuen, against whom I have no grievance except that they chose 'La figlia che piange' to print in an anthology because it is the mildest of my productions. As for the content of your article, I cannot in the least judge! I can only feel, and be greatly pleased and encouraged by, the spirit of it.

I enjoyed immensely my little weekend with you, and look forward to some week when I can come on a Friday evening. As for a cottage, I think I had better hope for one in Kent, which would bring me to London Bridge or Cannon Street, and make it possible for me to live in the country for a week or two at a stretch. So I cannot help wishing that you were in Kent too.

I have also enjoyed the literature you lent me, which I have been reading at lunch and in trains. The Epstein book[2] is most interesting; I disagree with some important conclusions, but it is a formidable work to attack, and therefore very tonic. Also, he makes his texts – Aragon, Cendrars, Apollinaire etc., – a more serious affair, to be tackled in earnest.[3]

I will write you more about the Hypothetical Review later. With affectionate regards to you and your wife.

T.S.E.

1 – RA described *SW* as 'the most stimulating, the most intelligent, and the most original contribution to our critical literature during the last decade' (*To-Day*, Sept. 1921).

2 – Jean Epstein, *La Poésie d'aujourd'hui* (Paris, 1921).

3 – Louis Aragon (1897–1982), French poet and novelist; Blaise Cendrars (1887–1961), Swiss novelist and poet, naturalised French, 1916; Guillaume Apollinaire (1880–1918), French-speaking poet and art critic.

TO *Richard Aldington* MS Texas

16 September 1921 9 Clarence Gate Gdns

My dear Richard,

I return the depressing letters with my sympathies. I have been looking for the review in the *Dial*, but without success. This is only what one must expect, but that does not make it any the less depressing.

I have quite my share of the universal ignorance and superficiality – I only lay claim to a certain cunning in avoiding direct bluff and dealing chiefly with what I *do* know, only hinting at my pretended knowledge of what I don't know. I have, I confess, always been rather afraid of shocking you by revealing the imperfection of my scholarship in every language, art and science.

It was charming of you to send me that apposite and cheering quotation from Coleridge.[1] I have asked someone who knows [Richard] Cobden-Sanderson the publisher to arrange a meeting. Do you think that it would be any good for me to see Waugh,[2] or is there any better way to approach Chapman and Hall? The only alternative seems to be to employ some sort of business man of the kind that pick up a living by odd journalistic jobs of the sort. At present I am feeling tired and depressed – I don't like you to make your cottage a home for neurasthenics like Manning and myself – you have enough on your mind and shoulders without that.

I have a note from Jackson suggesting dinner some evening next week and saying that he would try to get you too, but I fear that you cannot be persuaded to come. I observe that the last train to Aldermaston is 9.15 and I have a boarder at present, or I should offer you a bed. When I haven't a boarder, you will always be welcome here.

I have just finished an article, unsatisfactory to myself, on the metaphysical poets.[3] The only point made is that the metaphysicals are not, as a group, metaphysical at all, but a perfectly direct and normal development, and that if English verse had not gone to pieces in the eighteenth century after Pope (with reservations) and never recovered the seventeenth century poets might be taken quite naturally and without

1 – RA's letter is lost.

2 – Arthur Waugh (1866–1943) was managing director of Chapman & Hall. In all probability, the matter went no further. Waugh's contempt for *Prufrock*, as expressed in the *Quarterly Review* (Oct. 1916), provoked EP's reply, 'Drunken helots and Mr. Eliot', *Egoist*, June 1917.

3 – TSE, 'The Metaphysical Poets', a review of *Metaphysical Lyrics and Poems of the Seventeenth Century: Donne to Butler*, ed. Herbert J. C. Grierson, *TLS*, 20 Oct. 1921, 669–70 (*SE*).

quaintness. They are quaint because we are unused to the intellectual quality in verse. I am not sure that the greatest nineteenth century *poets* (in your sense!) are not Ruskin and Newman. Do you know them well?

I enclose a letter from MacCarthy which may interest you. I find Apollinaire a little disappointing.

Yours ever
T.S.E.

Do write as often as it is not a burden: it is a great pleasure to me.

TO *Edgar Jepson* MS Beinecke

23 September 1921 9 Clarence Gate Gdns

Dear Jepson,

We have perpetual bad luck – we seem never to be able to meet except when one of us gives a lecture – and not always then. I'm going away for the weekend, having made the engagement about two months ago. I have never met Hueffer, and I should have been delighted to get the chance finally of a talk with you.

This summer was quite taken up by a visit from my family, to whom we gave up this flat.

I expect to go away next week for a holiday, but when I come back I shall try to arrange a Sunday meeting with you?

With many regrets

Yours sincerely
T. S. Eliot

TO *Richard Aldington* MS Texas

[28? September 1921] [9 Clarence Gate Gdns]

My dear Richard

Your letter touched and pleased me more than I can say. If I do not reply immediately it is not because I don't take it seriously or don't feel grateful to you, but for reasons which will let me write in a day or two – i.e. I am seeing a nerve specialist. Please don't mention this to anyone at present.

Ever yours
Tom.

TO *Wyndham Lewis* MS Cornell

Friday [30? September 1921] [London]

Dear Lewis,

Will you please not mention to anybody what I told you this afternoon about the possibility of my going away for two or three months. I don't even know that I shall take this man's advice, and haven't yet mentioned it to the Bank. I expected to be run down and I am – but after all I haven't had a holiday yet and may feel quite different after. So as things are so unsettled, such a rumour of my going away and not going would make me look very foolish. As nobody knows anything about it whatever except the specialist, my wife and yourself, it can go no further if you don't speak of it.

In any case, it would only make a difference of only one issue to the paper. I will let you know what I decide. Meanwhile I hope you will be successful in getting a studio.

Yours,
T.S.E.

I hope we can arrange a dinner soon.

TO *Richard Cobden-Sanderson*[1] MS Beinecke

2 October 1921 9 Clarence Gate Gdns

Dear Mr Cobden-Sanderson,

I should have written to you much sooner, but that my time and thought has been absorbed in private problems of the moment.

As I told you, what I have in mind is a quarterly review, of which we should print 500 copies for the first issue. It would be about the size of the *Nouvelle Revue Française*, or a little bigger, and I want estimates based on 80 pages for the first issue.

What I should like to have from you, if possible, is a statement of the various items of expenditure involved in printing and publication, including the <printing and> despatch of preliminary circulars to possible subscribers, advertisement, office labour, and in fact everything except payment to contributors. I should then work out a scale of payments, and could decide whether the periodical is possible on the funds at my disposal: £600 and the small number of *advance* subscriptions obtainable.

1 – Richard Cobden-Sanderson, printer and publisher: see Glossary of Names.

Of course, the estimate could not be exact, but it would have to be a safe one; as you know, I cannot launch out with impunity, as the funds are clearly defined. Also, it would in any case be impossible to start publication before March, so that we should have to make some alteration in the estimates then; it is to be hoped that costs of some items will be lower. I had hoped to be able to have a number out by January 1st, but I have been ordered away for complete change and rest, by a nerve specialist, and have just been given leave of absence by my employers. This is quite a surprise to me, but simply implies a gap of three months, and no change in future plans.

As I am going away in ten days, is it too much trouble to ask you to look over the enclosed estimates from four printers and let me have them back by the end of the week? If you have not time, would you simply return them, and I will discuss the business afresh with you in January. I simply thought that I should like to have some idea where we were, before I left. I should like to think that we should be able to do something along the lines we discussed.

Looking forward to seeing you again,

sincerely yours,
T. S. Eliot

TO *Henry Eliot* — TS Houghton

3 October 1921 — 9 Clarence Gate Gdns

My dear Henry,

I have been feeling very nervous and shaky lately, and have very little self-control. Vivien wanted me to see a nerve specialist, so she made an appointment and went with me, to the most celebrated specialist in London. He examined me very thoroughly with his own tests, and said I had greatly overdrawn my nervous energy, and must go straight away for three months complete rest and change and must live according to a strict regimen which he has prescribed. The bank have been very kind about it and have given me three months leave without any difficulty at all. So I am going in about a week, as soon as I have trained another man to my work. I am going first, I think, (we have not yet decided) to Eastbourne (by the sea) for a month anyway. After that I might go abroad, if I could find a place cheap and comfortable – of course I could not travel.

I ought to be very grateful for this, as I suppose I should have to have it some time, and having it now, before there is anything really serious wrong with me, ought to set me up for a long time. I confess I dread this enforced rest and solitude (I must be away completely among strangers with no one I know) and expect a period of great depression. It is very terrifying to stop after having gone on for so long. I am told that people always find the first part of such a cure very trying indeed. I wish more than ever that you were here now. Vivien will have to stay here; if possible, I should like her to go abroad. She so terribly needs change and stimulus. She felt very deeply, much more than you can imagine, your all leaving, and life has seemed much sadder since then. It did not seem right or inevitable. We cannot reconcile ourselves to it.

Your having been here seems very real, and your not being here but in Chicago seems as unreal as death.

I was most painfully touched at finding that you had secretly left your typewriter behind instead of my wretched old one, which I hope will not fall to pieces. I have the same feeling whenever I look at it or use it.

Of course I made lighter of my treatment in writing to mother than in writing to you, so please do not let her know that it is more than a fortunate opportunity to rest and recuperate. I have not described to her at all how I feel, and indeed it is almost impossible to describe these feelings even if one wants to.

Vivien was very pleased with your letter, and thinks the photographs simply wonderful; but waited to write to you until I had done so.

I will send you a card from time to time.

Very affectionately
Tom

TO *St John Hutchinson* — MS Texas

3 October 1921 — 9 Clarence Gate Gdns

Dear Jack,

I have an idea. As I am going away in a week, and of course am forbidden to do any writing *whatever*, I shall have to write to the *Dial* and say that I cannot do my London Letter for them. I do this letter every other month. The idea is a sort of chat (which I do very badly) about the intellectual life and the life of the intellectuals in London at the moment – not criticism of new books etc. so much as to communicate to the lonely reader in Chicago or Los Angeles a pleasant comforting sense of being in the know about activities in London. Excellent models are provided in the *Patrician.*[1] *You* would be able to provide that pleasant comforting sense,

1 – The British edition of *Vanity Fair*, launched 1919.

knowing everything and everybody, with a tone of smartness foreign to my heavy pen. You would get £10 more or less, for each article.

May I write to the *Dial* and tell them that I have a distinguished substitute? I would have to be sure that your contribution would be sent off *by the 15th October*. You would be doing me a great favour, and I don't know anyone in London who would do it better. Will you let me know immediately? Please accept.

Yours
Tom.

TO *Richard Aldington* MS Texas

[3? October 1921] 9 Clarence Gate Gdns

My dear Richard,

Forgive my not writing – I have had so much to do, and have felt so ill that it has taken me twice as long to do it. I have seen the specialist (said to be the best in London) who made his tests and said that I must go away *at once* for three months, <quite> alone and away from anyone, not exert my mind at all, and follow his strict rules for every hour of the day. So I have been given leave by the bank for that period, very generously – they continue to pay my salary. I am going in about a week, as soon as I have taught enough knowledge of my work to a substitute.

I did not anticipate such a medical verdict, and the prospect does not fill me with anything but dread. But the only thing is to carry out the doctor's instructions exactly, and refuse to think of the future after the three months.

Perhaps you will think: why not simply chuck the bank, rest, and begin journalism. But I simply feel too ill for that, and I am sure that this would be the worst possible moment for such a change. I should have to brace myself to a new effort, instead of relaxing, and I should worry myself in a short time into a far worse state. So I am sure you will agree with me that the best thing is to follow the doctor's orders for the three months, and not make any plans beyond that date.

So will you guard your intercession in patience and my gratitude will not die! I really feel very shaky, and seem to have gone down rapidly since my family left.

I will let you know (in confidence) where I go and will hope to be cheered by an occasional letter, which will be acknowledged by a postcard, all I may write: I don't want correspondence from the general public of my acquaintance at all. I should have liked to spend a night with you before I go off, but it is contrary to orders, and I ought to lose no time in beginning. Were I not forbidden intercourse I should have liked to go somewhere within a possible distance of you.

I return <regretfully> the Allan papers.[1] It would have been great fun to do Hogarth! or Wren or Inigo Jones (but there are no architects on the list). But [there's] hardly need to answer it, is there? I appreciate also your always wanting to share things! Will you do one or more, and which?

– Yes, I shd. love to write a book on Wren, or at least on the *églises assassinées*[2] of London. But one would have to spend more money in travelling about seeing things than one would ever get out of a book. I long to see Rome and the seventeenth C. architecture there – having been to Vicenza. I shall go to Eastbourne first, perhaps somewhere abroad later, but can't *travel* at all –

About your Murry (returned herewith).[3] I think the title too clearly betrays the nature of the review <and does not apply to Bax?> – I should be inclined to choose some neutral title. I should also be inclined to put the first paragraph (with the necessary alterations) at the *end* of the part about Murry. I like the draw-and-quarterly beginning of the second paragraph – but perhaps this is a counsel of journalistic inadvisability.

Of course, I agree with your estimate. At the same time there is a distinct difference between the baseness of Murry's verse and that of plain stupidity like Shanks, Squire and Turner.[4] It is a distinction which belongs to psychology rather than art, and is not worth one's time, but I am sure that it is there.

Have you got the books? Many thanks for the use, I enjoyed them all.

Would you like me to lend you my Cowley's Poems – apparently complete, four little volumes in an old edition of British poets?

There are many other things, in your recent letters and elsewhere, that I should like to discuss. But I have so much to do in order to get away next week – So take my blessing, and believe me

Yours ever
Tom.

1–Unidentified.
2–'murdered churches'. See Maurice Barrès, *La Grande Pitié des Églises de France* (1914).
3–RA, '"Vaulting Ambition"', a review of JMM, *Poems 1916–1920*, and Clifford Bax, *Antique Pageantry: A Book of Verse Plays*, *NS*, 15 Oct. 1921. RA did not make the suggested changes.
4–W. J. Turner (1889–1946), poet admired by WBY, now better remembered for biographies of Mozart, Beethoven and Berlioz.

Is the Manning work nearly finished?[1] Please explain my disappearance to Jackson, if you ever write to him.

I don't know Cowley's letters at all, I am sorry to say.

TO *St John Hutchinson* MS Texas

[4? October 1921] [London]

Dear Jack

I'm very glad to hear that you consent and am sure it will be excellent. I am sending you a copy of the August *Dial* with my feeble contribution which will at least give you a notion of the length. Don't bother about the *Patrician*, it was only a mild analogy from another sphere of journalism. Of course I should *not* consider your financial proposal.

Thank you very much for your letter which I appreciate. I certainly look forward to seeing you before I go.

Yours
T.

TO *Mary Hutchinson* PC Texas

[Postmark 5 October 1921] 9 Clarence Gate Gdns

Thank you *very much* for your letter. I will come with pleasure on Saturday.

T.S.E.

TO *Richard Aldington* MS Texas

Saturday [8 October 1921] [9 Clarence Gate Gdns]

I wanted to write to you in time for the country post, but was simply so sleepy that I have had to lie down and sleep the whole time. I am writing tomorrow.

Yours
Tom.

1 – In Aug., Frederic Manning had asked RA to help him complete a biography of Sir William White. See Jonathan Marwil, *Frederic Manning: An Unfinished Life* (1988), 218.

TO *Richard Cobden-Sanderson* PC Beinecke

9 October 1921 9 Clarence Gate Gdns

Please excuse card – as I am very rushed and tired. I appreciate the trouble you have taken, and am much pleased with your proposal. I will write to you in January when I get back.

With best wishes
Sincerely
T. S. Eliot

TO *Harold Monro* MS Beinecke

12 October 1921 9 Clarence Gate Gdns

Dear Monro,

You need not apprehend the danger of another edition – if you sell *Ara Vos Prec* at all you will sell it before the poems are reprinted. I am only sorry to hear that your profits are limited to 4½d each.[1] But you can safely put the book into your next catalogue, as I do not propose another edition until the volume can be considerably augmented.

I am sorry that I cannot come in to your party tonight – but the reason is that I am going away tomorrow for three months treatment and rest cure – and should have gone already if there had not been so much to do before I left. I shall be back in January and hope to see you then.

Sincerely
T. S. Eliot

TO *Richard Aldington* TS Texas

[13 October 1921] 9 Clarence Gate Gdns

My dear Richard,

You should know that if I have not written to you more quickly, on such an occasion, it is not that you have not been constantly in my mind. It is almost incredible that such generosity and friendship could exist at all, and

1 – Monro wrote on 8 Oct. that he had bought all the remaining copies of *Ara Vos Prec* – fifty plain and six signed – to be sold for 10s 6d plain and 18s 6d signed, 'and if you find anyone expressing an interest please pass it along to me, as I believe in quick sales. I have had them about five days and so far have sold two to the trade and only made nine pence profit on them.'

I want you to know that the assurance that such friendship does exist, is in itself an immense support. I really cannot say enough – but it is not merely quantity of expression, but impossibility of saying what I feel. I should like to treasure your cheque as a symbol. If I have any notion of what your situation is, and the burdens you have, it is a very great sacrifice. I have not cashed your cheque, and have no immediate intention of doing so. Nor do I wish you to think that the money is where it could not be used by you should some emergency arise in your own life in the meantime. What I propose to do is to keep it in a safe place. Should I be forced to use it, I should write to you and tell you frankly what my condition was; but if, before hearing from me, you have need of it yourself, draw the money, and let me know. I think I could provide myself in any great need elsewhere – though I should prefer to use yours, because of our relations. I hope not to have to use any of it. Of course, I cannot tell what my expenses will be. But when the present crisis is over and I am back at the bank I shall know where I am. Mind you, I shall go back to the bank in any case for long enough to compensate more or less for their consideration and kindness, for they have been good to me – but beyond that I simply do not, at present, look ahead. I shall simply concentrate on getting as well as I can. I am going to Margate tomorrow, and expect to stay at least a month. I am supposed to be alone, but I could [not] bear the idea of starting this treatment quite alone in a strange place, and I have asked my wife to come with me and stay with me as long as she is willing. After that she will return here. I hope that Margate will do her a little good too, as she certainly needs it as much as I do. After that I propose to go abroad, probably to a small cottage with a verandah which Lady Rothermere has offered me, in the mountains back of Monte Carlo (La Turbie). I want Vivien to cross over with me, and go somewhere healthy. If she does, would you be able to house a small cat which we are very fond of? We are having great trouble finding a good home for it for this short time she will be in Margate, and for a longer period I can't think of anywhere it would be safer or happier than with you. We should have to arrange to get it down to you – perhaps Vivien could come down and have lunch with you and leave it. I should not want to put you to any trouble. It is a very good mouser.

My address at present will be Albemarle Hotel, Cliftonville, Margate. I have not betrayed it to anyone but yourself and the Bank, so do not expose it to any person. Do write to me when you can spare the time or have a mind to (I mean when*ever*), and if I only reply by an occasional postcard, believe me, nonetheless, *ton bien dévoué* [your very devoted]

Tom.

And what do you think of *Fanfare*,[1] which quotes our testimonials which appear much more enthusiastic thus extracted than they appeared to the writers, embodied in the letters. I think it was generous of you to give them a poem.[2]

TO *St John Hutchinson* TS Texas

13 October 1921 9 Clarence Gate Gdns

Dear Jack,

I think your [London] Letter is admirable,[3] and very much to the point. There is only one thing that occurred to me afterwards. In the *Dial*'s last note to me acknowledging my October Letter I thought I detected a slight note of disapproval at my having said so much about Shaw's book[4] which had already been reviewed. I had been very hard put about to find enough material for that Letter.[5] It struck me that what you say about George Moore tended toward the review, and I think that for the *Dial*'s purposes it would be better if you could condense or shorten it a bit. One treats books rather from the cover inward, so to speak, and can divagate as much as one likes, but not stop too long over anything. The *Chauve Souris*[6] can serve as a starting point for anything that comes into your head about the theatre –

Anyway, I am sure it will be first rate. We are off tomorrow to Margate. With love to Mary and best wishes

yours ever
T.S.E.

I am very grateful to you for writing this Letter. It's a great help.

1–*Fanfare: A Musical Causerie*, ed. Leigh Henry, ran for seven fortnightly numbers from 1 Oct. 1921 to 1 Jan. 1922. The first issue carried other messages of support for the 'Fanfare Movement' from de Falla, Satie, Dorothy Richardson and Duncan Grant. TSE had written: 'Your venture is extraordinarily interesting; you should have no difficulty in eclipsing the current musical periodicals. I should consider myself most happy to be numbered among your contributors.' He did not subsequently appear in its pages.
2–'At a Gate by the Way', in the first issue.
3–Hutchinson's effort was to be rejected by the *Dial*.
4–Bernard Shaw, *Back to Methuselah* (1921).
5–'This is lively at least and surprisingly tolerant of Shaw,' TSE wrote on Valerie Eliot's copy in 1959.
6–*Le Chauve-Souris*, a Paris review produced by the Russian theatre director Nikita Balieff, was brought to the London Pavilion by C. B. Cochran on 2 Sept. It was extremely successful and moved to the Apollo Theatre on 10 Oct.

Vivien Eliot TO *Scofield Thayer*

MS Beinecke

13 October 1921 9 Clarence Gate Gdns

Dear Scofield,

Tom has had rather a serious breakdown, and has had to stop all work and go away for three months. He has to follow a strict regimen, and may only read (for pleasure, not profit) two hours a day. Before he went he fortunately secured St John Hutchinson to do the London Letter for the *Dial*. I have just written to Mr Seldes to tell him, and also to say that Hutchinson would do the next one if this is satisfactory.

Do you want to wait until February for the review of Marianne Moore's poems? If so, Tom could do it for you in January, and would like to. I forgot to mention this to Mr Seldes, so now I suppose I shall have to write again! Unless you will – you have nothing to do I presume, and look at *my* position. I have not nearly finished my own nervous breakdown yet.

Tom is going to be in England for about a month from now, (he is at Margate) and then will be able to go and occupy Lady Rothermere's villa at La Tourbie [in the Alpes Maritimes]. By this you will see that T. and Lady Rothermere have clicked. A Quarterly had been arranged between them, which Tom was to edit in his 'spare' time, and to get what pickings he could from the inadequate sum laid down by her in the name of Literature. Everything is now postponed until January.

Towards the end of November I *want* to go – somewhere. I don't know yet, and it doesn't much matter, but I must escape from England or it will smother me. Have been trying to escape for five–six years!

I *do* expect to come to London in the spring or perhaps before. Meanwhile I may appear in Vienna.

Vivien

Tom sent his love to you.

TO *Richard Aldington*

PC Texas

[Postmark 15 October 1921] [London]

The review of Murry in *TLS.* is a revolting mess of torrid tastelessness and hypocritical insensibility.[1] I have been further exasperated by insults from the American Consulate, who furthermore wish to collect Income Tax

1 – [Ernest de Selincourt], 'Buried Treasure', a review of JMM's *Poems 1916–1920*, *TLS*, 13 Oct. 1921.

from me. I must get my naturalisation papers in order and wish I knew some prominent person in the Home Office to press it forward. It is difficult to keep calm!

T.

Vivien Eliot TO *Violet Schiff* MS BL

Wed[nesday] 26 October 1921 The Albemarle Hotel, Cliftonville, Margate

My dear Violet,

I have been so anxious to know how you were. I have tried to write each day, but have had so many letters to write for Tom. And it is so difficult to write with people about. The last I heard of you was that you had *another* temperature. I do wish you could have the cause of your temperatures discovered. It would give me hope that mine might one day be fathomed. As you know I have just exactly the same lot as yourself, hateful stupid temperatures for no real reason at all. Do write and let us hear how you *both* are. We wonder every day. You will be pleased to hear that Tom is getting on *amazingly*. It is not quite a fortnight yet, but he looks already younger, and fatter and nicer. He is quite good, and not unhappy, keeping regular hours and being out in this wonderful air nearly all day.

I am going back tomorrow. Tom will stay here at any rate for another two weeks. Please let us hear news of you.

With love,
Yours ever
Vivien

This is such a nice, comfortable, and *inexpensive* little hotel. Very lucky.

TO *Julian Huxley* MS Fondren

26 October 1921 The Albemarle Hotel, Cliftonville

Dear Huxley,

I hope you will not mind my writing to you for advice. I have been ordered away from London for three months by a nerve specialist, and have been here a fortnight. I went to this specialist on account of his great name, which I knew would bear weight with my employers. But since I have been here I have wondered whether he is quite the best man for me, as he is known as a nerve man, and I want rather a specialist in psychological troubles. Ottoline Morrell has strongly advised me to go to Vittoz,[1] in Lausanne, and incidentally mentioned that you had been to him. This is all that I know about him. There are so few good specialists in this line that one wants to have more precise testimony of a man's value before trying him – especially as I cannot afford to go to Switzerland, which is so expensive, unless the benefit is likely to justify the expense.

So would you mind letting me know, as soon as you can, whether you consider that Vittoz benefited you, and how brilliant a physician you think him? I should be *very* grateful indeed.

If you recommend him, perhaps you know also of some moderate priced pension or hotel in Lausanne?

I hope that this address will find you without loss of time. I ought to have confirmed it from Aldous whom I saw just before leaving town, but I did not think seriously about Vittoz till the last few days. I particularly want your opinion of him as a psychologist.

With best wishes,

Sincerely yours,
T. S. Eliot

Vivien Eliot TO *Mary Hutchinson* — MS Texas

Friday 28 October [1921] — The Albemarle Hotel, Cliftonville

My dear Mary,

How are you?

I have started Tom well, and he shows great improvement already. He looks younger and better looking. This is a very nice tiny hotel, *marvellously* comfortable and inexpensive. Margate is rather queer, and we don't dislike it.

I am leaving on Sunday or Monday. I think Tom will do quite well here for another two or three weeks. He is not, so far, unhappy, or minding anything. Do write him a nice letter. He really must not write letters, so perhaps he would only send a short answer but you would understand that.

1 – Dr Roger Vittoz, Swiss psychiatrist, see Glossary of Names. In his copy of the third French edn (1921) of Vittoz's *Traitement des Psychonévroses par la Rééducation du Controle Cérébral*, TSE marked a paragraph concerning '*Aboulie*' ('want of will') (35); the sentence 'There is, in fact, often an excessive excitability which makes the sufferer aware of the slightest noise and is frequently a cause of insomnia' (37); and against 'The muscles are at first more or less contracted and sometimes painful' (47), he wrote 'handwriting'.

I hope you will let me come to tea next week, if you have any time? Did you go to Rothermere's 'intellectual party'? What a woman.

With love, and from Tom

Affect
Vivien

TO *Richard Aldington* PC Texas

[Postmark 29 October 1921] The Albemarle Hotel, Cliftonville

I have done my best, not having seen the book.[1] That makes four: Ezra's *Mauberley*,[2] M. Moore,[3] and Edith Sitwell.[4] I am quite distressed about E. P. I'm afraid MacC is no good.[5] *Thanks for letters*, I have much I should like to say to you.

Yrs. affcty
T.S.E.

Did you do Cazamian's book?[6] Should like to see it some time, though it sounds shallow. Should like to discuss Marivaux[7] with you.

1–TSE had written to Bruce Richmond about the reviewing of poetry in the *TLS*, where notices were all unsigned (see postcard to RA, 3 Nov. 1921 below). RA took offence at a notice by F. T. Dalton (1855–1927), an assistant editor, likening the poems in *Hymen*, by his wife H. D., to 'prose sentences capriciously cut into strips' (27 Oct.). An unsigned review in the *NS* (3 Dec.) retorted: 'At no work could be flung with less justice the customary taunt, "prose cut up into lengths".'

2–See brief notice (author unrecorded) of EP, *Hugh Selwyn Mauberley*, in *TLS*, 1 July 1920, 427: 'The poems in this beautifully printed book have the qualities of structure, rhythm, and sincerity, but they are needlessly obscure . . . If he could forget this enmity [to the semi-artistic public], his poems would be sweeter and more effective. As they are, they have a mathematical charm.'

3–See review [by F. T. Dalton] of Marianne Moore, *Poems*, in *TLS*, 21 July 1921, 471: 'Miss Moore does not seem to have very much to say . . . she has no poetic style.'

4–See review [by Basil de Selincourt] of Edith Sitwell, *The Wooden Pegasus*, in *TLS*, 8 July 1920, 43: 'The paraphernalia of verse are instruments of her disdain, metaphor is the chief mode in which she reveals her alienation from the rest of the world.'

5–*NS* (ed. MacCarthy) did not review the volumes by EP, Moore and Sitwell.

6–[Edgell Rickword], review of Louis Cazamian, *L'Evolution Psychologique et la Littérature en Angleterre 1600–1914*, in *TLS*, 20 Oct. 1921.

7–Pierre de Marivaux (1688–1763), dramatist.

Henry Eliot TO *His Mother* TS Houghton

30 October 1921 1037 Rush St, Chicago

Dear Mother:

It has been rainy today and Saturday, and I have spent a luxurious Sunday reading. It is my intention to move from this flat and find a single room, for the reason (which will be exceedingly difficult to explain to anyone) that I wish to do a lot of regular and serious reading. That idea will be so incomprehensible to most of the people I know that I am sure that they will think I am disappointed in love or that I am a neurotic crank. But I find such social life as I know here very trifling; possibly my travels have given me a new point of view, but I know that I have always wanted to read and never want to go about much. Peckham likes social life but it amazes me that people do not outgrow that sort of thing. It seems to me to belong to one's youth.

Peckham says that the preamble to your will, in which you describe yourself as a citizen of Missouri, is not evidence that you are such. The fact that you were a citizen of Missouri when you made your will, in other words, can easily be disproved by evidence that you have changed your citizenship since. However, I would get legal advice on that, and would do whatever is necessary to settle your status as a citizen of Massachusetts. I cannot believe that Mr Shepley is right. I think it might be well for me to go down to St Louis to see him before you finally decide to change your will. I shall have to go there to get the stock certificates, and I might as well do whatever other business I can while there. How about your Missouri state income tax? Did you make a return, or was it unnecessary? I cannot remember.

Uncle Ed has written asking me to handle the printing of his family history. I was very strongly tempted to write him that our firm would charge him a fee of $200 for the work. Of course Uncle Ed expects me to do the work free, which exasperates me in view of his charges for family work. I have, however, written him that I will do it. I am afraid that if I retaliate in that way he will retaliate further by sending you a bill for consultation. Has he ever sent any additional bill for advice, since he settled the estate? I do not think that I or any of us are in a position to offend him, since we never know when we may want to call upon him for some matter, as he is the only member of the family in St Louis now. I do not think he intends to send you any bill for miscellaneous advice, or for things such as this Mercantile matter.

I do not think the oversight of the printing of this book[1] will be very burdensome or take much time, though it is rather a nuisance. I am also getting a Christmas card printed for Tom Dawes [Eliot].[2] I do not mind things much unless they take my evenings or Sundays. Last Sunday I went to the Harveys for supper – fare $2.80 – staying overnight. I also went to the South Side in the morning to hear a Dr Pulsford preach. I had read one of his sermons and thought it good. He is a friend of Sally Scott's, or rather she is one of his admirers. I had also thought of getting a room in that neighborhood (it is close to Chicago University). Dr Pulsford said that Sally Scott was going to spend the winter taking a course of some sort at the University. Since hearing that, I am not sure that I want to go down there. I am afraid she has a tendency to fasten herself on relatives. The buildings of Chicago University are very beautiful, and the grounds are wide and well kept. It is on the great wide boulevard which was, at the time of the World's Fair, the Midway Plaisance. I should like to take a correspondence course there, and to have access to their library. The buildings, which are of stone and very fine, reminded me, in a way, of Oxford; and the suggestion of books and leisure was delightful. I believe there are a good many very nice people in that neighborhood. I wish I knew people who were interested in books and study. The general atmosphere of this flat is like a college dormitory—no privacy or quiet.

Vivien always recites some account of her migraines and malaises in her letters. But I suppose that is natural; it is a relief to talk about one's pains. I do not think she takes proper care of herself, though. I have seen her drink coffee at midnight. I have a feeling that sub-consciously (or unconsciously) she likes the role of invalid; and that, liking as she does to be petted, 'made a fuss over', condoled and consoled, she unconsciously encourages her breakdowns instead of throwing them off by a sort of nervous resistance. It is hard to tell how much is physical and how much mental and uncontrollable by will power; but I think that if she had more of 'the Will to Be Well' she would have less suffering. To acquire this sort of willpower unaided is something like pulling oneself up by one's boot-straps; but I think some strong impulse from outside, some change in her circumstances, might call forth the necessary willpower to be well. She needs something to take her mind off herself; something to absorb her entire attention. The same, of course, is true of Margaret. Of course, Vivien really suffers pain, and on the other hand, she is not so supine as Margaret.

1–Edward Cranch Eliot, *The Family of William Greenleaf Eliot and Abby Adams Eliot* (1921). After the author's death, HWE was to revise the book for a second edition (1931).
2–A cousin.

A good long period of quiet will do Tom immense good. Of course complete solitude might be depressing, and what he needs, I think, is change more than rest. It may be better for him to have Vivien along for a while, at least better than having no one to talk to, but I think it would be good for him to be with congenial friends without her for a while, too. The great thing is to relax. The idea of going to Lady Rothermere's villa near Monte Carlo sounds fine to me.[1] New and beautiful scenes will be good for him. I hope he can do that.

If you give a Boston lawyer your copy of the will to make a new one from, I think you had better send me a copy of the new will before you sign if, and let me take it to Mr Shepley and see whether it conforms to their notions of their part as 'ancillary administrator' or whatever it is. I should like to write Mr Shepley or see him and find out just what he means by his statements as to Missouri claiming you as citizen. I think he misunderstood.

Your affectionate son,
Henry

Have you a cook or are you still eating outside?

TO *Julian Huxley*

MS Fondren

31 October 1921

Albemarle Hotel, Cliftonville,
Margate

My dear Huxley,

Thank you very much indeed for your very full and satisfactory letter.[2] I shall go to Vittoz. Meanwhile I shall beg your patience for two more questions.

1. How long a course does Vittoz usually give? Is there ordinarily a definite term?
2. Is it best to write to him in advance, in order to make certain of having Vittoz himself? If so, (and in any case) what is his address?

He sounds just the man I want. I am glad you confirm my opinion of English doctors. They seem to specialise either in nerves or insanity!

With thanks, and regret for troubling you again.

Sincerely,
T. S. Eliot

1 – In the event, TSE decided to go to Lausanne instead.
2 – Not preserved.

TO *Henry Eliot* PC Harvard

[Postmark 1 November 1921] Cliftonville, Margate
(But write to C. G. Gdns)

Have been here a 4tnight, & may stay several weeks longer. Very good sea air, and quiet. Will keep you posted.

Yours aff.
T.

Vivien Eliot TO *Bertrand Russell* MS McMaster

1 November 1921 [dated by Russell] 9 Clarence Gate Gdns, N.W.1

Dear Bertie,

It was so nice actually to get a letter from you again. We were both pleased.

As you probably know, Tom is having a bad nervous – or so called – breakdown. He is away, and I am answering all his letters. Otherwise of course he would have written himself. He is at present at Margate, of all cheerful spots! But he seems to like it!

In a short time I hope he will go to Switzerland, to see Dr Vittoz. We have heard so much about him. I think I remember you speaking of him too.

We both send very many congratulations, and Tom says he is quite sure the baby[1] *will* have pointed ears, so you need not be anxious. Even if not pointed at birth, they will sharpen in time.

With love from both, and very glad you are back.

Vivien Eliot

1–John Conrad Russell was born on 16 Nov., 1921 (d. 1987). TSE's poem about BR, 'Mr. Apollinax', mentions 'His pointed ears'.

TO *The Editor of* The Times Literary Supplement

Published 3 November 1921

Sir,

I am obliged to Professor Saintsbury for his suggestions,[1] of which I shall make use, if he will permit me, on some later occasion. As I greatly respect Mr Saintsbury, so I would not be behind him in my testimony of that great neglected poet, great neglected dramatist, and great neglected critic, John Dryden.

I only regret that the conclusion to be drawn from Mr Saintsbury's letter appears to contradict my own conclusions from the study of Caroline verse. Mr Saintsbury appears to believe that these poets represent not merely a generation, but almost a particular theory of poetry. The 'second thoughts' to which he alludes are, I think, and as I tried to point out, frequent in the work of many other poets besides, of other times and other languages.[2] I have mentioned Chapman, and the contemporaries of Dante. I do not believe that the author of *Hamlet* and *Measure for Measure* was invariably satisfied with 'the first simple, obvious, natural thought and expression of thought'; or that the author of the 'Phoenix and Turtle' whistled as he went for want of thought. Nor can I believe that Swinburne thought twice, or even *once*, before he wrote

Time with a gift of tears,
Grief with a glass that ran.[3]

On the subject of Caroline poetry, there is no one to whom so much gratitude is due, or to whom I should listen with as much deference, as Mr Saintsbury.

I am, Sir, your obliged humble

CONTRIBUTOR.

1 – George Saintsbury (1845–1933), editor of *Minor Poets of the Caroline Period* (1905–21), proffered his letter, published on 27 Oct., as 'an annotation' to TSE's 'The Metaphysical Poets'.

2 – Saintsbury argued that Dryden used '"metaphysics" as equivalent to "second thoughts," things that come *after* the natural first; and, once more, this definition would, I think, fit all the poetry commonly called "metaphysical", whether it be amatory, religious, satirical, panegyric, or merely trifling'.

3 – Saintsbury recalled a friend's reaction to hearing these lines from *Atalanta*, 'Don't you see that the fellow just wrote it the other way and turned it round to make fools like you admire?' and added that Swinburne 'here and elsewhere, was "right metaphysical" in his method'.

TO *Richard Aldington* PC Texas

[Postmark 3 November 1921] Albemarle Hotel, Cliftonville, Margate

So R[ichmond] didn't print my letter[1] – perhaps (1) because I had another letter in (2) because he printed yrs.[2] (3) because there wasn't room (4) because I complained that all the verse worth reviewing at all had been treated the same way. <Damned his policy, in fact.> (My first book was done to death this way[3] – they only gave me more notice later, either because I had become a contributor or because the Woolfs published my second book). But I am sorry I can't agree with you about H. D. having seen the book since. It seems to me stucco.

Yrs. aff.
T.

Perhaps he suspected collusion. The envelope [was] addressed to him *personally* so there should be no mistake. Hope to hear from you soon.

TO *Sydney Schiff* MS BL

Friday night [4? November 1921] Albemarle Hotel, Cliftonville

My dear Sydney,

I am so sorry about the MSS – Vivien told me – but as you told me to keep it, and as I am always uneasy in the possession of other people's MSS., I had locked it up in my box at the Bank safes. I will get it out for you when I come up to town, and do hope you will not be grossly inconvenienced by the delay. It will not be very long now.

I hope that your being in town is not bad news, and that you are both making progress. I should have liked to hear from you, but of course did not expect to, knowing that you had much to do and bad health and worries. I have done a rough draft of part of part III [of *The Waste Land*], but do not know whether it will do, and must wait for Vivien's opinion as to whether it is printable. I have done this while sitting in a shelter on the front – as I am out all day except when taking rest. But I have written only

1 – See postcard to RA, 29 Oct., above.

2 – RA claimed that 'H. D. is the greatest living writer of *vers libre*', and that her poems showed 'a poetic personality both original and beautiful'.

3 – *Prufrock* would 'hardly be read by many with enjoyment' (*TLS* review [by F. T. Dalton], 21 June 1917).

some fifty lines, and have read nothing, literally – I sketch the people, after a fashion, and practise scales on the mandoline.

I rather dread being in town at all – one becomes dependent, too, on sea or mountains, which give some sense of security in which one relaxes – and hope to be only a day or two. I hope to have good news of you both from Vivienne – she tells me very little about her own health, in spite of my complaints.

With best love to you and Violet

Yrs aff.
Tom.

TO *Richard Aldington* MS Texas

[5? November 1921] Albemarle Hotel, Cliftonville

Dear Richard,

Just got your article on Cowley.[1] You are doing, I think, very valuable work with this kind of criticism; though its value will hardly be appreciated immediately by more than a dozen people. It makes Manning look pretty cheap.[2] The ignorance about the subject is so universal that the erudition will hardly be noticed. Gassendi,[3] for example, is no more than a name to me, and I know *nothing* of T. de Viau[4] and the others. I hope that eventually you will be able to work your French and English researches into a rather big book, which will make an impression.

In same issue I see myself decried by one S. Magee[5] (¿MacCarthy himself? or only some blood brother?)

Yrs in haste
TSE

1 – RA, 'Cowley and the French Epicureans', *NS* 23 (5 Nov. 1921), 113–14 (repr. in *Literary Studies and Reviews*, 1924).
2 – Apparently undervaluing RA's work, Frederic Manning was dilatory in paying him the agreed £50 for his help with the biography of Sir William White; see note to TSE's letter of 3 Oct., above.
3 – Pierre Gassendi (1592–1655), French philosopher and mathematician.
4 – Théophile de Viau (1590–1626), French poet.
5 – S. Magee, 'On Melody' (*NS* 18 [5 Nov. 1921], 134–5) – or rather the lack of it in the arts – 'because our prudes hate and fear it'. An extract from TSE's 'Ode' is quoted in evidence.

TO *Richard Aldington* MS Texas

6 November 1921 Albemarle Hotel, Cliftonville

My dear Richard,

I am awaiting the reply to a wire I have sent to Lausanne, and if it is favourable I shall leave next week. I shall be going to the Continent within the fortnight anyway, and my wife will come also, though not to Switzerland.

My idea is to consult, and perhaps stay some time under, Vittoz, who is said to be the best mental specialist in Europe – now that I have a unique opportunity for doing so. I am satisfied, since being here, that my 'nerves' are a very mild affair, due, not to overwork, but to an *aboulie*[1] and emotional derangement which has been a lifelong affliction. Nothing wrong with my mind – which should account, mon cher, for the fact that you like my prose and dislike my verse. However the principal point is that from some day next week our flat will be vacant for six weeks. Would it be of any use to you and your wife to occupy it for that period? It would cost you absolutely nothing, the only condition being the retention of our woman, an excellent cook and discreet servant, at a salary of 25s a week. In any case I did not intend to let the flat, so I should be losing nothing by your having it, and you would be doing us the service of keeping our woman while we are away. I thought that a short season in London might be of use to both of you, if it were possible in some way like this. We should be delighted.

If you decide favourably will you write immediately upon your decision? I shall be here till Friday in any case, but after that *may* be at 9 C.G.G.

Again I postpone writing! but I hope to hear from you soon.

Yours aff.
Tom.

When am I to see your notes on Waller? I shall be interested, because I made nothing of him, though I admire Denham and Oldham.

1 – See note to letter to Julian Huxley, 26 Oct., above.

TO *Harold Monro* MS Beinecke

16 November 1921 9 Clarence Gate Gdns, N.W.1

Dear Monro,

Thanks very much for your kind letter. I am just back from Margate, and am off to Switzerland tomorrow. Remember that I shall be back by the middle of January and hope to see you then.

Sincerely,
T. S. Eliot

TO *Sydney Schiff* MS BL

[16? November 1921] [9 Clarence Gate Gdns]

My dear Sydney

I am sending the two stories back because I should be more easy in my mind to have them in your possession. I saw Lewis last night but forgot to give him 'Bestre'[1] so I enclose that also – will you take care of it and give it to him with the same explanation? It may be merely superstition, but I hate to have the responsibility for what is really other people's property while I am away.

I am writing to the *Times*, and hope to receive your book[2] soon in Lausanne. I'll send you address as soon as I have one. Meanwhile I am distressed to hear of Violet's continued ill luck. I need not repeat again how well I know this sort of illness and how miserable it is for her.

I enjoyed Sunday very much and am *very* grateful to you for encouragement.

Yrs always
Tom.

at the last moment in haste

1 – WL's short story 'Bestre', *Tyro*, Mar. 1922 (repr. in *The Wild Body*, 1927).
2 – SS's novel, *Elinor Colhouse* (1921).

TO *Glenway Wescott*[1] MS Beinecke

16 November 1921 9 Clarence Gate Gardens

Dear Mr Westcott,

Thank you for your kind letter, which gave me great pleasure. It is a great disappointment not to see you now. I have had a nervous breakdown and have just returned from the east coast, and am leaving tomorrow for Switzerland. If on your way you pass that country, remember that I shall be in Lausanne, and that a letter in good time to the address above will reach me. I shall be here again by the middle of January.

Sincerely yours
T. S. Eliot

TO *Richard Aldington* TS Texas

17 November 1921 9 Clarence Gate Gdns

My dear Richard,

Your letters find me in transit between Margate – which I was very sorry to leave! – and Lausanne. We leave London tomorrow morning.

Now about your sister. I have been trying to think whom I know might be useful to her; but unfortunately I have only the most casual musical acquaintances, and none who could be likely to help. As to Edith, the situation is this. The only connexion that she has with music and musical people is through her companion, Helen Rootham,[2] an appalling woman who trains and launches young singers. Edith may assist in some small degree in the launching, but I am sure that the only way to enlist that assistance (for what it is worth) is for your sister to take lessons from Helen Rootham. So, although I enclose herewith an introduction, I can hold out no hopes, and do not believe that it is worth your sister's while to make use of it. I am awfully sorry about this.

I should think it would be better if you could first issue a book of criticisms in *London*: what I should like to see would be a fairly heavy

1–Glenway Wescott (1901–87), American novelist, lived in Germany, 1921–2, and was to become a prominent figure in the literary community in Paris, 1925–33. He was the model for 'Robert Prentiss' in Hemingway's novel *The Sun Also Rises*. Although he began his career as a poet, he became best known for later novels inc. *The Pilgrim Hawk: A Love Story* (1940) and *Apartment in Athens* (1945).

2–Helen Rootham (1875–1938), Edith Sitwell's governess and subsequently companion. Osbert Sitwell thought her 'perhaps the finest woman pianist it has ever been my good fortune to hear'. Her translation of Rimbaud's 'Les Illuminations' was set to music by Benjamin Britten (1939).

work including ancient and modern, showing some historical continuity. Is that not possible? Please discuss with me the problem of publishers: you should certainly not give a scholarly work of that sort (such as I have in mind) to Miss Weaver, but should (under the auspices of the *Times*) get some fairly big publisher, Cape or Collins at least. If you can show reason why this should not be carried out, then do it in America; but I should prefer it to be done here first. I do not know Methuen personally, and I do not know what value a letter from me (merely on the fact of his having published my book), would have. I don't even know what he thinks of me (I hope he has seen that Saintsbury and Birrell have spoken well of me). But I am at your disposal.

By the way, have they sent you the *Little Review* (quarterly) in which Ezra (in an otherwise irritating attempted-funny article) speaks of me as the 'Dean of English Letters'?[1] He refers to you also in a common condemnation.

I did not conceal from you that I think you overrate H. D.'s poetry. I do find it fatiguingly monotonous and lacking in the element of surprise. I mean that this last book is inferior to her earlier work; that many words should be expunged and many phrases amended; that the Hellenism lacks vitality; and also morally, I find a neurotic carnality which I dislike. (I imagine you dislike equally the Prudentianism of myself and Mr Joyce, and expect you to abhor the poem on which I have been working and which I am taking away with me!) But our correspondence would be irreparably injured if I did not deliver my opinions. I wish, on the other hand, you would let me know at some time your final opinion on my verse, and tell me frankly why you dislike it.

I think you have said about Waller exactly the sort of thing that there is to be said, and I only wish that the article could have been of a good length (two or three times as much, with quotations).[2] I do think it is worthwhile discussing these questions of derivation, neglected in English criticism, but important for the 'tradition'. I should like to know, however, why it should be Waller, rather than Denham, who seems to me just as smooth and gives a deal more pleasure, who should have had the influence. Can you tell?

Of course I agree with you about Amy Lowell.

I must stop now. Good luck to you, and I will write and send you my address from Lausanne. And please will you get me a copy of the *Times*

1–EP, 'Historical Survey', *Little Review* 8: 1 (Autumn 1921), 39–42. EP disagreed with TSE's statement that 'the greatest poets have been concerned with moral values', and was sarcastic about RA's *English Review* article on JJ.
2–RA, 'A Note on Waller's Poems', *To-Day* 8: 48 (Dec. 1921), 245–8.

with Ronsard[1] in it, as I shall be away, and send it to me later? Do you not agree that Bellay is rather the greater poet of the two?[2]

If you come to Paris, my wife will probably be there and will be glad to see both or either of you.[3] I shall be there for two or three days only in January.

yours affectionately
Tom

PS On second thoughts, I address the letter to Miss Rootham. I believe, by the way, she is a good teacher, and a very pushing and successful *launcher*. Perhaps your sister could not do better.

I am writing to Edith Sitwell also.

TO *Mary Hutchinson* MS Texas

[17 November 1921] [London]

Dear Mary,

This is a farewell note, to tell you how very much I enjoyed seeing you yesterday – it gave me *great* pleasure – and also to thank you again for your sweet and beautiful present.

Au bonheur!
Tom

TO *The Editor of* The Times Literary Supplement

Published 24 November 1921 Lausanne

Sir,

In your last issue I have read a review of an anthology of *Modern American Poetry*;[4] from this review I gather that certain of my verses

1–[RA], 'Pierre de Ronsard' (leading article), *TLS*, 2 Mar. 1922, 129–30.
2–As members of the Pléiade, Ronsard (1524–85) and Joachim du Bellay (*c*.1525–60) led a renaissance of French poetry.
3–HWE wrote to his mother on 1 Dec. 1921: 'I sent you Vivien's cablegram giving her address, 59 rue des Saints Pères. It must be a literary street. I saw in a book that Ernest Renan lived there once. I showed the cablegram to a man named Sherwood Anderson, who was over there this summer, and he said Ezra Pound lived on that street. Vivien does not say how long she will be there, so that one does not know how long to continue sending letters there' (Houghton).
4–*Modern American Poetry* (1921), ed. Louis Untermeyer, included TSE's 'Morning at the Window' and extracts from 'The Love Song of J. Alfred Prufrock' and 'Preludes'.

appear therein. I should be grateful to you if you would make public the fact that I had no knowledge that any of my verse was to be used in this way; that I was not consulted in the choice; and that, in short, the whole production is a surprise to me.

This statement in itself may interest but few of your readers. But I should like to remark that I should have much preferred *not* being included in this anthology. On previous occasions, when compilers of such works have asked my consent, there have always been personal reasons for my willing compliance: here there would have been none.

Some months ago I discussed the general question of anthologies with a poet (of a very different school and tradition from mine) whose name is much more widely known than mine is. We agreed that the work of any poet who has already published a book of verse is likely to be more damaged than aided by anthologies. I hope that other writers may be encouraged to express their opinions.[1]

I am, Sir, your obedient servant,
T. S. Eliot

TO *Ottoline Morrell* — MS Texas

30 November 1921 — Hôtel Ste. Luce, Lausanne

My dear Ottoline,

This is just to tell you that I am here, in your room (so they tell me) and under Vittoz; and that I am very much pleased, with Lausanne, with the pension (the food is *excellent*, and the people make everything easy for one – ordering milk etc.) and with Vittoz. I like him very much personally, and he inspires me with confidence – his diagnosis was good and in short he is, I am sure much more what I want than the man in London. I never did believe in 'nerves', at least for *myself*! He is putting me through the primary exercises very rapidly – so that I seem to have no time for any *continuous* application to anything else. I shall be here till Christmas. So thank *you* very much for Vittoz, and for the pension. Of course I can't tell *much* about the method yet, but at moments I feel

1–TSE was supported the following week (1 Dec.) by Robert Graves – possibly the poet mentioned – who wrote to 'commend heartily' TSE's 'courageous letter'. But Adam L. Gowans, who had not heard of TSE until he read the review, said he would 'certainly purchase his poetical works' if any of his poems in the anthology appealed to him (8 Dec.); and John Haines (15 Dec.) had bought *Prufrock* 'entirely on account of the poems from it contained in *Catholic Anthology*'.

more calm than I have for many many years – since childhood – that may be illusory – we shall see.

Yours always affect.
Tom

TO *Wyndham Lewis* PC Cornell

[Postmark 3 December 1921] Hôtel Ste. Luce, Lausanne

I wish you wd. send me the criticism you said you would write, please.[1] I shall be here till Christmas. Good doctor.

Yrs.
T.S.E.

TO *Mary Hutchinson* PC Texas

[Postmark 4 December 1921] Hôtel Ste. Luce, Lausanne

This is [a] very quiet town, except when the children come downhill on scooters over the cobbles. Mostly banks and chocolate shops. Good orchestra plays 'The Love Nest'.[2] A horse fell down yesterday; one cannot see the mountains, too foggy. How are you? Yrs. aff. T.S.E.

TO *Jacques Rivière*[3] MS Texas

5 December 1921 Hôtel Ste. Luce, Lausanne – Suisse

Dear [?] Monsieur,

Je viens de recevoir votre aimable lettre qu'on m'a expediée de Londres. Je rappelle bien ma promesse, et j'aurais dû vous prévenir de ma situation. Je suis ici jusqu'à Noël, au moins, pour un traitement de psychasthénie – sous la direction d'un célèbre médecin d'ici. Je n'ai rien écris depuis longtemps, et avec la meilleure volonté du monde, je ne crois pas pouvoir

1–WL had perhaps offered to write a critique of drafts of *TWL*, which TSE may also have shown to SS in London (letter of [4? Nov]).

2–From the musical comedy *Mary*, with music by Louis A. Hirsch, and book and lyrics by Otto Harbach and Frank Mandel, which opened at the Knickerbocker Theater, New York, in Oct. 1920.

3–Jacques Rivière (1886–1925): French critic, cultural arbiter, novelist, and director, 1919–25, of *NRF*, which he made into the premier French intellectual review.

un article, si petit que ça soit, pendant deux mois encore.[1] Je suis comblé de regret, et je vous fais toutes mes excuses, et vous prie d'accepter l'expression de mes sentiments les plus cordiaux.

T. S. Eliot[2]

FROM *André Gide*[3] MS Houghton

7 décembre 1921

Cuverville, par Criquetot l'Esneval,
Seine Inférieure

Monsieur,

Permettrez-vous à un lecteur attentif du *Sacred Wood* de vous faire une proposition:

La rubrique des *lettres anglaises*, à la *Nouvelle Revue Française* se trouve à présent sans titulaire. Accepteriez-vous de nous envoyer régulièrement une chronique, qui renseignât les lecteurs français sur l'état de la littérature de votre pays, qui l'éclairât sur la valeur des oeuvres nouvelles et ne lui laisse rien ignorer d'important? – une chronique enfin qui ne permît plus aux Anglais de juger cette époque inférieure à celle de Matthew Arnold.

Jacques Rivière, le directeur de la *Nouvelle Revue Française* se propose de vous écrire, si vous acceptez en principe, au sujet des conditions matérielles, et de la question de traduction.

Je vous fais adresser d'autre part un petit volume de morceaux choisis, où vous reconnaîtrez, je l'espère, ma pensée souvent voisine de la vôtre.

J'apprends indirectement, par Lytton Strachey qui me donne votre adresse, que vous venez d'être souffrant et qu'un repos complet vous est prescrit. Mais il dit aussi son espoir en votre très prochain rétablissement. Je m'autorise de cet espoir pour vous écrire ainsi, tout en m'excusant de venir troubler votre convalescence. Le moindre mot de vous, qui ne serait

1 – TSE's promised letter from England was deferred until the spring, as agreed when he met Rivière in Paris in Jan.; it was published as 'Lettre d'Angleterre', *NRF* 18 (1 May 1922).

2 – *Translation*: Dear Sir, I have received your kind letter which has been sent on to me from London. I remember my promise very well, and I should have warned you about my situation. I am here till Christmas, at least, for treatment for psychoasthenia – under the direction of a celebrated doctor here. I have written nothing for a long time, and with the best will in the world, I don't believe I could do an article, however little, during the next two months. I am extremely sorry, and send all my apologies, and ask you to accept the expression of my warmest regards. T. S. Eliot

3 – André Gide (1869–1951), French essayist, critic, novelist and dramatist. Founding editor of *NRF*, 1909. Nobel Prize for Literature, 1947.

pas un refus, nous permettrait de patienter en attendant votre guérison complète.

Croyez à mes sentiments bien cordiaux.

André Gide[1]

Sydney Schiff TO *Vivien Eliot* TS Alan Clodd

9 December 1921 18 Cambridge Sq, Hyde Park, W.2

My dear Vivienne,

Please forgive a typed letter but I want to answer your letter at once and if I don't do it in this way I am afraid I shall not get to it.

I am delighted that you like *Elinor Colhouse* and am greatly pleased at what you say about it. It is very encouraging to have a spontaneous expression of feeling like yours and I really am grateful.

Violet will reply to your interesting letter to her. I do not think you are wrong when you say that the people who matter most to you in London are ourselves (and another).[2] I put the other in brackets because I am not competent to form an opinion but I dare say you are right. I know those sorts of impressions one gets when one has been with people who are malicious and I do not think I am much surprised that you have found the particular people you allude to inclined to be spiteful but why they should feel so towards Lady R[othermere] I really cannot understand as she has been extraordinarily kind to them and for that matter to everybody else.

1 – *Translation*: Dear Sir, Would you allow an attentive reader of *The Sacred Wood* to make you a proposal:

At the moment, *La Nouvelle Revue Française* has no established contributor dealing with English literature. Would you agree to send us a regular Letter from London, informing the French reader about the state of literature in your country, enlightening him as to the quality of new works and keeping him up to date with all important new developments? – a Letter, in short, that would make it no longer possible for the English [French?] to think the present age inferior to that of Matthew Arnold.

If you agree in principle, Jacques Rivière, the editor of *La Nouvelle Revue Française*, proposes to write to you about the material arrangements and the question of translation.

I am sending you, under separate cover, a little anthology of my writings from which you will recognise, I hope, that my thoughts are often akin to yours.

I learn indirectly, from Lytton Strachey who has given me your address, that you have been ill and have been ordered a complete rest. But he also expresses his hope of your very early recovery. I take advantage of this hope to write to you, while apologising for troubling you during your convalescence. The merest response from you, provided it were not a refusal, would allow us to bide our time until your complete return to health.

With my most cordial regards, André Gide.

2 – MH: see VHE's letter to MH, [20? Dec. 1921], below.

It has been my experience though that kindness is no shield against vicious propensities.

This short letter is no indication of my thought of you and of Tom. I value you both very much and care greatly that you shall both fulfil your destinies and express yourselves as you have a right to. Incidentally if you can get happiness all the better, but I do not think I quite know what happiness is. Certainly it is not a static condition and the term is so loosely used that I always hesitate to employ it.

I have had a long characteristic letter from K. M. [Katherine Mansfield] which gave me pleasure for it is full of her personality and her personality is a fascinating one. She talks of getting away from Switzerland but I think she alludes to her soul rather than to her body for, poor little thing, her health will not allow her to escape from the mountains which I dare say by now weigh rather heavily upon her. However she and J. M. M. seem to be mutually pleased with each other and that, after all, is a very important consideration.

By the way, your letter reads exactly as though you were talking, which is a very good sign. Your natural sincerity is one of your fine qualities.

Believe me with much affection

Yours always
Sydney S.

We have no *Lit. Sup.* here at the moment but have ordered a copy and will send you a cutting on.

Henry Eliot TO *His Mother* TS Houghton

12 December 1921 1037 Rush St, Chicago

Dear Mother:

The New York Edison Co. First Lien 6½%'s are O.K. Moody rates them Aa. They are certainly sound. They yield you 6.1% (current yield) at the price of 106½. I have not wired you because I doubt if they will go higher right away, at least not before the new year; yesterday's paper quotes them at 106. Try to get them at 106 – though after all that is only $10 difference on the two bonds, and not worth haggling over.

I enclose clipping on Liberty bonds. The 6 Liberty 2d's that you bought in September at about 90 are now 96.82. The three Liberty 3d's which you bought at 93 are now 97½. The Western Unions that you bought at something like 102½ (plus accrued interest) are now 107¼, and the Edison Brooklyns must have gained the same number of points, though I do not see them quoted in that paper. It is pleasant to make a profit so quickly – about $750 in two months.

I think your inscription is beautiful. It is poetry. I hope you or he will send it right on. When will the tablet be made?

I do not think Tom's work has deteriorated, though I think his later poems much less inspired than his earlier ones. I attribute that, however, to a too great consciousness of his audience. I think that what he needs, both for his mental health and for the sake of his poetry, is solitude for a while. Tom seemed to me last summer to be going on his nerve. In the first place, he was overworking; in the second place, he had three interests – the bank, the magazine, and his own writings, which are properly two separate interests, the critical and the poetical. All the time what weighed on his mind was a craving for the last of these – poetical composition – and a sort of frantic state of mind at never being able to get around to it. If he could rest thoroughly, and then get a little time to gratify his desire to do creative writing, he would get over his nervous state. I am afraid he finds it impossible to do creative work (other than the critical) at home. Vivien demands a good deal of attention, and I imagine is easily offended if she does not get it well buttered with graciousness and sympathy. She has a keen sense of the practical side of getting ahead in the literary world, or as she puts it, 'what is the use of being famous after you're dead?' in which she may be partly right, but it can be overdone. Tom had a heavy social correspondence to write sometimes in the evening after getting back from Clarence Gate. The strain of going out among people who after all are foreigners to him, and, I believe, always must be to an American – even Henry James never became a complete Englishman – has, I think, been to him pretty heavy. I remember a year or more ago, in a letter to me, he spoke of always having to be keyed up, alert to the importance of appearances, always wearing a mask among people. To me he seemed like a man playing a part. He has got to relax. I almost think it would be well for him to come to this country for a short while, for the sake of the change. The two weeks on the water would do him good.

I thought the essay on the Metaphysical Poets excellent, and so wrote him. I think I will write him another letter. Is it Poste Restante, Lausanne, Switzerland? or shall I send it to the rue des Saints Pères? or c/o Lloyds? I will send it to you to forward.

Your affectionate son,
Henry

TO *Henry Eliot* MS Houghton

13 December 1921 [Hôtel Ste Luce] Lausanne

My dear Henry,

This is a Christmas letter – I dare say you may be in Cambridge, but you will find this on your return. I do not appear to have answered your letter of October 20 which is *shameful*, as you enclosed a cheque for £25 which was *very* useful and comforting in this emergency. I only worry whether you spend what money you have wisely – i.e. upon yourself. I have never known anyone who had less notion of hygiene, of taking care of health, than you – Vivien says you are worse than I in that respect – at least now that she has taught me – and I do things like taking cod liver oil in winter, and cure a cold at once etc. And I find that I worry less about my health, as a result of looking after it, so that is time saved.

I have not gone into any details with mother about my health, so do not do so yourself. It is not in fact serious. The great thing I am trying to learn is how to use all my energy without waste, to be *calm* when there is nothing to be gained by worry, and to concentrate without effort. I hope that I shall place less strain upon Vivien, who has had to do so much *thinking* for me. I realise that our family never was taught mental, any more than physical hygiene, and so we are a seedy lot. I should like to *talk* about these things with you. I felt that I got, or was beginning to know you better – when there exists any difficulty in speaking, it is never so great as between near relatives. I only hope that we can keep the new connexion alive by writing, and at least begin where we left off, when we meet again.

I am very much better, and not miserable here – at least there are people of many nationalities, which I always like, and I like talking French better than English, though I think English is a better language to write in. I am certainly well enough to be working on a poem!

Do write to me to London (I shall be there before the middle of January). Don't forget England, even if it makes you miserable. If you keep it in mind, you will come back.

With much affection
Tom.

TO *André Gide* MS Mme Catherine Gide

14 December 1921 Hôtel Ste Luce, Lausanne

Monsieur,

Je viens de recevoir votre gracieuse lettre, que vous m'avez adressée à Londres. Puisque vous saviez déjà que j'ai été souffrant, j'espère que vous aurez tiré la conclusion – en attendant une réponse – que je n'étais plus chez moi: donc, que vous ne m'en voulez pas à cause du délai.

Certes, je tiens votre proposition pour un compliment du premier ordre, et je serais ravi de collaborer à *La Nouvelle Revue Française*. A ce moment, malheureusement, je ne suis pas à même de vous donner la réponse que je voudrais. Jusqu'à ce que je reprenne ma vie normale, je ne sais pas ce que seront mes forces ou mes loisirs. Je rentre à Londres vers le *15 janvier*.

Ce n'est pas à moi de poser des conditions – si la *N.R.F.* est content d'attendre, je serai bien interessé de continuer des pourparlers (Je voudrais bien savoir 1. combien d'articles par an 2. l'étendue de chaque article – S'il s'agit seulement de livres de quelque valeur littéraire, je ne crois pas qu'il y ait de quoi rédiger un article tous les mois). – Si la *N.R.F.* ne peut pas attendre, je n'ai qu'à exprimer mon regret trés vif.

Je passerai plusieurs jours à Paris vers le 5 janvier. Si vous ne serez pas à Paris, je pourrai peut-être voir M. Rivière. Mais j'espère me pouvoir donner le plaisir de faire votre connaissance un de ces jours.

Je serai bien content de recevoir le livre, quoique je connais de vos oeuvres depuis onze ans. Si vous ne me connaissez que par le *Sacred Wood* j'aurai envie de vous envoyer mes poésies, qui sont au moins supérieures à mes proses!

Je quitte Lausanne à Noël; après, la seule adresse que je puisse vous donner c'est Hôtel du Pas de Calais, 59 rue des Sts Pères, Paris jusqu'à ce que je rentre à Londres.

Je vous prie, Monsieur, d'accepter l'expression de mes sentiments les plus distingués.

T. S. Eliot[1]

1 – *Translation*: Dear Sir, I have just received your kind letter, which you sent to my London address. Since you already knew I was ill, I hope you concluded – while waiting for a reply – that I was not at home, and so do not hold the delay against me.

Indeed, I consider your invitation as a compliment of the highest order, and I should be delighted to contribute to *La Nouvelle Revue Française*. At the moment, however, I am not in a position to reply as I would like. Until I take up my normal life again, I do not know how much energy or leisure I shall have. I go back to London around *15 January*.

It is not for me to state conditions. If the *NRF* is prepared to wait, I shall be very interested to continue negotiations (I should very much like to know 1. how many articles a year

FROM *Scofield Thayer* MS Beinecke

18 December 1921 1, Habsburgergasse 2, Vienna.

Dear Tom,

I was glad to hear from Pound that you looked not badly when he saw you in Paris.

I am sorry to receive a letter from Mr Seldes in regard to 'a lad named St John Hutchinson whom I used to know at the Foreign Office'. Mr Seldes writes further: 'He is a charming lad and a great gossip. And he sent us a horrid and vulgar and tedious and totally impossible London Letter. Not knowing how close his connection with Eliot may be, Watson[1] and I decided to send him a small cheque for the article. We sent him $25 which was about 2/3 of the actual amount it came to as 1/3 of it was so out of date that we felt justified in refusing to consider it. But this $25 is pure loss and we do not feel justified in printing the article at all. I managed to explain that the article came too late to be printed in the current number and to prevent the man from sending any more. Arrangements for a substitute we have not yet made, but we must have something before March which is the earliest date of restoration of Eliot's correspondence.'

You see I believe in frankness and hope you understand that Mr Seldes, Mr Watson and Mr Thayer are all very sorry indeed that the charming lad was not delivered of so charming a letter as his friend Mr Eliot and as we Mr Eliot's friends had hoped.

I am writing Raymond Mortimer[2] asking him to let us have a London Letter. But I do hope we shall have a new London Letter from you soon

—

2. the length of each article – if it is a question of dealing only with books of a certain literary standard, I don't think there will be enough material for an article every month.) – If the *NRF* cannot wait, I can only express my keen regret.

I shall be spending several days in Paris around 5 January. If you are not going to be in Paris, I could perhaps see M. Rivière. But I hope I shall be able to have the pleasure of making your acquaintance one of these days.

I shall be very pleased to receive the book, although some of your works have been known to me for the last eleven years. If you know me only through *The Sacred Wood*, I should like to send you my poems, which are at least superior to my prose writings!

I leave Lausanne at Christmas; after that, the only address I can give you is Hôtel du Pas de Calais, 59 rue des Saints-Pères, Paris, until I return to London.

Yours most sincerely, T. S. Eliot

1–James Sibley Watson (1894–1982), doctor, inventor of early internal X-ray procedures, silent film maker, and co-owner of *The Dial*.

2–Raymond Mortimer (1895–1980), critic and writer, whom TSE had known at Oxford. After writing his first 'London Letter', he went on to succeed TSE as London correspondent of the *Dial* at the end of the year. Literary editor of *NS*, 1935–47.

and howsoever good your next London Letter may be the best thing about it will for me at least be that it will indicate that you are well again.

Merry Christmas!

[unsigned]

TO *Sydney Waterlow* — MS Waterlow

19 December 1921 — Lausanne (leaving Saturday)

My dear Sydney,

Thanks awfully for writing to me – this is a dull place, and I am grateful for letters. Yes, I am feeling much better. I have been under Vittoz, who is not a psychoanalyst, but more useful for my purpose; I was aware that the principal trouble was that I have been losing power of concentration and attention, as well as becoming a prey to habitual worry and dread of the future: consequently, wasting far more energy than I used, and wearing myself out continuously. And I *think* I am getting over that.

I shall not stay in this *carte-postale colorée* [picture postcard] country any longer than necessary – its chief recommendation is that it is full of foreigners – American countesses, Russian princesses, Rumanians, Greeks and Scandinavians, Czecho counts, Belgian punks etc. I am not quite certain whether I shall immediately rejoin Vivien in Paris, or go south first. Apparently all of Western Europe is equally expensive. I'm delighted to hear that your holiday was such a success – you sent me p. cards, but no address on them. It's also delightful to know that you will be as near as Holland Park. I shall return sometime in January and hope to find you installed. I don't think you will regret it.

No, I don't expect to visit Montana.[1] I had a letter from J. M. just before leaving England – so curious that it was quite impossible to reply at all.[2] Its bearings are also curious. But more of that later.

I am trying to finish a poem – about 800 or 1000 lines. *Je ne sais pas si ça tient.* [I do not know if it will work.]

Yours ever
T.S.E.

1–Montana-Sierre in Switzerland, where Katherine Mansfield had been living since May, and where JMM had now joined her.
2–The letter from JMM has not survived.

Vivien Eliot TO *Mary Hutchinson*[1] MS Texas

Tuesday [20? December 1921] Hôtel du Pas-de-Calais,
59 rue des Saints-Pères, Paris

Mary!

Paris was too much for me, and for the first three weeks I was stunned. I wrote to no-one. I could not remember England. I felt so strange. It comes of having been shut up in England for about seven years. It is bad for one. It is very painful, being torn up by the roots, and thrown, hurled, alone and stunned, into such a strange way of living. The first weeks were really painful. I was so *absolutely* alone. I was almost frightened. All the French I knew deserted me. I *did* things, but they made no impression, were no good. Only very gradually, and not fully yet, I have begun actually to *live* here. The first few days with Tom were very perfect, and it was only after I saw him climb into that dreadful Swiss train, and me left on the platform, at 9.20 in the evening, that I felt someone had taken a broomstick and knocked me on the head. After that I forgot London and everything and everyone, and became absorbed in getting a clutch on Paris. Do you see? I have even forgotten Tom. No-one seems at all real to me. At the end of ten days I decided to go to Cologne. I knew a man there. It took me four days to arrange passports and visas, and at the end of that the mark dropped 500, and I got a cold. The man was returning to Paris in a fortnight. So I wired, and said I would not go. Just at that time I saw Roger [Fry], in the post office. He did not seem at ease, or pleased to see me, and escaped hastily. What makes life difficult is the awful expense. I am paying for this myself. I live in a high up little room, and have meals *en pension* which I loathe, to save money – but everything is too incredibly dear. It costs *fortunes*.

The Pounds have a most exquisite Studio (with two rooms) not far from here! Only £75 a year. Now if I could secure such a thing, or even two or three rooms, I would certainly take them, for on the whole I think I would prefer to live here. For Tom, I am *convinced, Paris*!

I have an awful down on London, which increases. That last evening – ! at the Huxleys. *What* a last impression of London. And that has stuck in my mind. The monotony, the *drivel* of the whole stupid round. Here of course you will disagree. I have seen Joyce several times and find him a most unsympathetic personality. Vain!! egoist! Unseeing.

1–TSE added his seasonal greetings on a card on 23 Dec: 'Pour vous souhaiter la bonne année' ['To wish you a happy new year'].

Now, my dear, *dear* Mary, there are only three people in London I can bear the thought of seeing. The first, *of course* is you.[1] I do miss you fearfully. You would almost force me to go back, if I knew I should not see you otherwise. I adore the thought of you. Are you coming here? Write to me, please forgive me – tell me everything. About Tom – I *don't know* I don't know. About that maid you sent me I am too ashamed to speak. *I forgot it all!* Does she think she is engaged? O Lord. Tom kept on Ellen. *He would.* I may not go back for ages. What has happened? Are you angry? Have I behaved even worse than usual? Please write, and do not frighten me.

Ever,
V.

The man from Cologne arrives tomorrow – will stay with me. After that I don't know. If I really engaged that maid I will have her. Have *both*. But she would have to wait till I return.

TO *Alfred A. Knopf* — MS Texas

25 December 1921 — Lausanne

Dear Mr Knopf,

I have your letter of the 5th instant. I am sorry to have given you the impression of criticising any action of yours within the contract. I merely wrote to ask whether this use of my verse had had *your* approval, before taking any further action. I had assumed, perhaps quite unreasonably, that I should be informally, at least, notified when any of my verse was to be used, or that I should receive a copy of the volume in which they appeared.

Furthermore, as I have been away for nearly three months by ill-health, and could not consult my contract, I was unaware that the contract included rights of publication of selections in *Great Britain*. When I return I shall consult the contract, and shall have pleasure in confirming your statements.

With best wishes,

Yours faithfully,
T. S. Eliot

Not having seen the book, I cannot have any opinion on the actual selection.

1–The others were Sydney and Violet Schiff: see SS's letter to VHE, 9 Dec.

His Mother TO *Henry Eliot*[1] Fragmentary TS Valerie Eliot

29 December 1921

I received yesterday a cheerful letter from Tom following the Christmas cablegram of the previous day. Both with a letter dated Lausanne. 'I shall soon rejoin Vivien in Paris . . . where there are so many people I want to see. I am ever so much better, my concentration improves and I am beginning to feel full of energy. I am working at a poem too.'

59 Rue des Saints-Pères.

1 – The full text of this letter, and the letters and cablegram from TSE to which CCE refers, have not been found. On 12 Nov., HWE had written to his mother: 'I think probably Tom is too tired to write about business matters, perhaps his physician has told him not to. In any case his not writing is probably caused by his travelling about and being at places like Margate. He may be feeling depressed, though I should think his vacation would benefit his spirits' (Houghton).

1922

At the beginning of January 1922 TSE rejoined Vivien in Paris, where Pound introduced them to the American publisher Horace Liveright and they all dined with James Joyce. During the next ten days or so, TSE and Pound worked over the drafts of The Waste Land. *In mid-January TSE returned to London alone while Vivien went to Lyons. Pound's work was not yet finished, however, as he had yet to put the poem a third time 'through the sieve'. Responding to a further draft, presumably sent from London, he thought the poem 'MUCH improved', and gave final guidance in an exchange (misdated in the first edition of these* Letters*) which began on 24 January.*

Over the next few months, TSE revealed the poem to other friends – Richard Aldington, Edgar Jepson, Aldous Huxley, the Woolfs and the Hutchinsons – but when offering it to potential publishers such as Knopf or Maurice Firuski he seemed reluctant to show or even name it. Thayer wrote on 29 January offering $150, sight unseen, for publication in The Dial, *but because of a misunderstanding TSE turned this down on 8 March. Pound's suggestion to Thayer that TSE might be awarded the $2,000* Dial *Prize came just too late. Liveright had already expressed interest, and by 3 April he had offered '$150 against 15 per cent royalties', again sight unseen. This time TSE accepted, but when the contract arrived in June he was dissatisfied and asked Quinn to act on his behalf in rewriting it. Meanwhile, he was making arrangements for* The Criterion, *in which* The Waste Land *was to be published for British readers.*

With publication in Britain and America apparently settled, TSE agreed to type the poem out again for Pound's confidential use, adding that he now had no objection to its being shown to James Watson or Scofield Thayer. Watson was in Paris, and although he was not initially impressed by the poem, The Dial *made another bid for it, with a hint to TSE that the* Dial *Prize would be part of the remuneration. At first TSE said he would accept this with Liveright's approval, but then decided he could not trouble Liveright and Quinn any further and wrote on 21 August to Watson (who was en route to New York) saying that it was too late. He also wrote to Quinn, mentioning that he had had 'an attractive proposal'.*

The Dial was undeterred, and Gilbert Seldes approached Liveright with a suggestion for generous terms. Finally Quinn invited Seldes and Liveright to his office on 7 September, by which time Liveright already had the poem in proof. Quinn dictated letters from each to the other which sealed the agreement that resulted in the poem's publication in The Dial *during October and as a book from Boni and Liveright in December.*

Vivien Eliot TO *Mary Hutchinson* MS Texas

Thursday 12 Jan[uary 1922]

Hôtel du Bon Lafontaine,
64 & 66 rue des Saints-Pères, Paris

Mary dear

What a *wonderful* letter to add to my collection! And thank you for the book of Clive's *Poems*,[1] which I am indeed very glad to have.

Forgive my not writing sooner. I have so much to tell you and complain – but as I should be back in London in less than a fortnight, I would rather talk it than write it.

I long to see you again, and to have a long talk with you.

Indeed you are right about Paris, and French people. I don't want to live in Paris, *but*—

Tom has been here ten days. I think he is much better. You must judge for yourself. I know he is looking forward to seeing you, and not very many others. He will be back on Monday. I am going to Lyons for about a week on Saturday and then Paris again for a few days, then London. I won't *try* to write anything.

My love to you, and to Jack.

I hope I am still your 'greatest friend.'

Vivien

1–Clive Bell, *Poems* (1921).

TO *Scofield Thayer* TS Beinecke

20 January 1922 9 Clarence Gate Gdns, London N.W.1

Dear Scofield,

I now have your letter of the 18th ulto. and am in bed with influenza. I regret that my action – as you make it painfully evident – has precipitated an embarrassing situation for Mr Hutchinson, *The Dial*, and myself.[1] I am sure that you and Mr Seldes will agree that his letter was as good as mine have been. Your account leaves nothing obscure, and you may inform the business manager that I wish him to deduct $25 from the next payment, if any, that may ever become due to me. I trust that this may be if any before the next general meeting of shareholders, in order that there may be no inconvenient questions.

The next letter possible from me would be for the April number. In response to a hint from Mr Seldes, I should no longer analyse particular books, but should perform more general rumination on London (would the Señor like soliloquies in London) by the gentleman with a vacuum-cleaner. But if you find Mortimer more satisfactory, you need not make another change.

I understand that I am to prepare a few words about Miss Moore. I shall shortly have ready a poem of about 450 lines, in four parts, and should like to know whether the *Dial* wishes to print it (*not* to appear in any periodical on this side) and if so approximately what the *Dial* would offer.[2] I should like to know quickly as I shall postpone all arrangements for publication until I hear. It could easily divide to go into four issues, if you like, but not more. It will have been three times through the sieve by Pound as well as myself so should be in final form.

I trust that you [are] gaining spiritual and physical benefit from Vienna,[3] give my best respects to Schnitzler.

I think something conclusive should be done to Murry.

Yours
Tom

1–Having rejected St John Hutchinson's trial 'London Letter', the *Dial* paid him a kill fee of $25.

2–At the head of the letter are Thayer's sums dividing 450 by 35 and by 40 (the approximate number of lines per page), with '12pp. 120'.

3–Thayer was undergoing analysis with Sigmund Freud in Vienna.

TO *André Gide* MS Mme Catherine Gide

24 January 1922 9 Clarence Gate Gdns

Cher monsieur,

J'ai été désolé de ne pas pouvoir vous voir à Paris. M. Rivière me dit que vous étiez chez lui une demi-heure avant mon arrivée. Le jour après, le samedi, je suis allé vous chercher à Auteuil, mais apparemment vous fûtes déjà parti pour Bruxelles. J'espère toujours ce plaisir de faire votre connaissance à ma prochaine visite à Paris.

J'ai peur que votre volume de morceaux choisis ne fût égaré, puisque je ne l'ai pas trouvé ici. Je veux le commander d'une librairie, pourtant il m'aurait été un grand plaisir d'en avoir un exemplaire qui fût présenté par vous.

Je suis heureux de constater que M. Rivière et moi, nous nous sommes entendus très bien et que j'enverrai un chronique à la *N.R.F.* au mois de février.

Je vous prie, cher monsieur, de recevoir encore l'expression de mes hommages sincères.

T. S. Eliot[1]

TO *Richard Cobden-Sanderson* MS Beinecke

24 January 1922 9 Clarence Gate Gdns

Dear Mr Cobden-Sanderson

I am very glad to hear from you. I have only been back ten days, and have been laid up with flu all that time. At the present moment everything is still in the air, therefore, and I have not yet seen Lady Rothermere.[2] I will

1 – *Translation*: Dear Sir, I was extremely sorry not to be able to see you in Paris. M. Rivière tells me that you were with him only half an hour before my arrival. The following day, Saturday, I went to look for you in Auteuil, but you had apparently already left for Brussels. I am still hoping to have the pleasure of making your acquaintance during my next visit to Paris.

I am afraid the anthology [*Morceaux choisis*, ed. Gide (1921)] must have gone astray, since it was not waiting for me here. I will order it from a bookshop, but I would have had great pleasure in owning a copy presented by you. [A copy inscribed by Gide to TSE is now at Houghton.]

I am happy to note that M. Rivière and I reached a very satisfactory agreement, and that I shall be sending a London Letter to the *NRF* in February.

Once again with my respectful regards. T. S. Eliot

2 – TSE had approached RC-S about the possibility of his becoming publisher of the new magazine to be financed by Lady Rothermere and edited by TSE.

write to you a little later and tell you how things stand, and shall hope to see you before very long.

Sincerely yours
T. S. Eliot

FROM *Ezra Pound* TS Houghton

24 Saturnus An I [24 January 1922][1] [Paris]

Caro mio [My dear]:

MUCH improved. I think your instinct had led you to put the remaining superfluities at the end.[2] I think you had better leave 'em, abolish 'em altogether or for the present.

IF you MUST keep 'em, put em at the beginng before the April cruelest month. The POEM ends with the Shantih, shantih, shantih.

One test is whether anything wd. be lacking if the last three were omitted. I dont think it wd.

The song has only two lines which you can use in the body of the poem.[3] The other two, at least the first, does not advance on earlier stuff. And even the sovegna doesnt hold with the rest;[4] which does hold.

(It also, to yr. horror probably, reads aloud very well. Mouthing out his OOOOOOze.[)]

I doubt if Conrad is weighty enough to stand the citation.[5]

1–This date was interpreted as 24 Dec. 1921 in *Letters of Ezra Pound, 1907–1941* (1951), ed. D. D. Paige, which was followed in the first edition of TSE's *Letters*. However, given the calendar that EP published in the *Little Review* (Spring 1922), Hugh Kenner reinterpreted it ('The Urban Apocalypse', in *Eliot in His Time*, ed. Walton Litz [1973], 44n). EP wrote to H. L. Mencken, 22 Mar. 1922: 'The Christian Era ended at midnight on Oct. 29–30 of last year. You are now in the year 1 p.s.U [post scriptum *Ulysses*].'

2–The superfluities run to seventeen pages in all (*TWL: Facs*, 90–123). Of these, EP annotated three typescripts, 'Song [for the Opherion]', 'Exequy', and the two pages of 'The Death of the Duchess', plus one manuscript, the fair copy of 'Dirge'. This letter mentions the first two, and EP's enclosed poem 'Sage Homme' alludes to 'Dirge', so these were probably the 'last three' still being considered for inclusion by TSE. However, EP's annotation, 'cadence reproduction from Pr[ufrock] or Por[trait of a Lady]', suggests that it was perhaps 'The Death of the Duchess' that did not 'advance on earlier stuff'.

3–A marginal bracket by EP on the typescript of 'Song [for the Opherion]', interpreted by Valerie Eliot as covering four lines, perhaps spanned only 'When the surface of the blackened river / Is a face that sweats with tears?' (10–11): *TWL: Facs*, 98–9.

4–'Exequy' at one time ended 'SOVEGNA VOS AL TEMPS DE MON DOLOR' ('be mindful in due time of my pain', *Purg*. XXVI, 147; *TWL: Facs*, 100–1). TSE retained Dante's next line (*TWL*, 427), and quoted this passage in the Notes and elsewhere.

5–TSE had proposed to use an epigraph from Conrad's *Heart of Darkness*, ending 'The horror! the horror!' (*TWL: Facs*, 2–3).

The thing now runs from April . . . to shantih without break. That is nineteen pages, and let us say the longest poem in the Englisch langwidge. Dont try to bust all records by prolonging it three pages further.
The bad nerves is O.K. as now led up to.[1]
////
My squibs are now an bloody impertinence. I send 'em as requested;[2] but dont use 'em with Waste land.

You can tack 'em onto a collected edtn, or use 'em somewhere where they wd. be decently hidden and swamped by the bulk of accompan[y]ing matter. They'd merely be an extra and [w]rong note with the nineteen-page version.
Complimenti, you bitch. I am wracked by the seven jealousies, and cogitating an excuse for always exuding my deformative secretions in my own stuff, and never getting an outline. I go into nacre and objets d'art. Some day I shall lose my temper, blaspheme Flaubert, lie like a shit-arse and say 'Art shd. embellish the umbelicus.'

SAGE HOMME[3]

These are the Poems of Eliot
By the Uranian Muse begot;
A Man their Mother was,
A Muse their Sire.

How did the printed Infancies result
From Nuptuals thus doubly difficult?

If you must needs enquire
Know diligent Reader
That on each Occasion
Ezra performed the caesarean Operation.
E.P.

//////////////

1–*TWL*, 111.
2–Presumably in a letter not preserved.
3–'Wise man'; but also a pun on '*sage femme*', meaning 'midwife'.

Caul and grave clothes he brings
Fortune's outrageous stings,
About which odour clings
        Of putrifaction,
Bleichstein's dank rotting clothes
Affect the dainty nose,
He speaks of common woes

                Deploring action.

He writes of A.B.Cs.
And flaxseed poultices,
Observing fate's hard decrees
        Sans satisfaction;
Breedings of animals
Humans and canibals,
But above all else of smells
        Without attraction.

Vates cum fistula [1]

E. P.

E. P. hopeless and unhelped

Enthroned in the[2] marmorean skies
His verse omits realities,
Angelic hands with mother of pearl
Retouch the strapping servant girl,

The barman is to blinded him
Silenus bubling at the brim,   (or burbling)
The glasses turn to chalices
In his fumbling analysis
And holy hosts of hellenists
Have numbed and honied his cervic cysts,
His follows Yeats into the mists
Despite his hebrew eulogists.

1 – 'Poet with a fistula (or ulcer)'.
2 – He typed 'in the The'.

Balls and balls and balls again
Can not touch his fellow men.
His foaming and abundant cream
~~Has moulded this world~~
Has coated his world ~~with~~ . The coat of a dream;
Or say that the upjut of his sperm
Has rendered his senses pachyderm.

Grudge not the oyster his stiff saliva
Envy not the diligent diver. Et in aeternitate

It is after all a grrrreat litttterary period
Thanks for the Aggymemnon.

[unsigned]

TO *Ezra Pound* TS Houghton

[26? January 1922][1] [London]

Cher maitre,

Criticisms accepted so far as understood, with thanks.

Glowed on the marble, where the glass
Sustained by standards wrought with fruited vines
Wherefrom . . . ???[2] **OK**

Footsteps shuffled on the stair . . . [3] **OK**

A closed car. I cant use taxi more than once.[4] **OK**

Departed, *have* left no addresses . . . ???[5] **OK**

1 – Tentatively dated [24? Jan. 1922] in the first edition of these *Letters*, but evidently a reply to EP's letter of that day. EP added the comments in bold and returned the letter, presumably with the next, which answers the remaining points.
2 – This version of *TWL* 78–80, which does not exactly match the surviving drafts or printed text, is probably a response to EP's comment on the typescript '*3 lines* Too tum-pum at a stretch' (*TWL: Facs*, 10–11). 'Wherefrom' appears in the unpublished typescripts in Thayer's papers (Beinecke) and Watson's papers (Berg), and in *C.*, though not in the *Dial*, Boni & Liveright or Hogarth Press printings.
3 – The first appearance in final form of *TWL*, l. 107.
4 – The first appearance in final form of this phrase in *TWL*, l. 136. EP had written '1880' against the anachronistic 'closed carriage' in the TS (*TWL: Facs*, 12–13), but TSE wished to keep 'the human engine waits / Like a taxi throbbing', 216–17.
5 – The first appearance in final form of *TWL*, l. 181. No TS of ll. 173–82 survives in the drafts, but EP had presumably objected to the manuscript reading, 'Departed, and left no addresses' (*TWL: Facs*, ll. 24–5).

What does THENCE mean (To luncheon at the Cannon St Hotel)???[1]

Would D[orothy Pound]'s difficulty be solved by inverting to

Drifting logs
The barges wash . . . ???[2]

1. Do you advise printing Gerontion as prelude in book or pamphlet form?
2. Perhaps better omit Phlebas also???[3]
3. Wish to use caesarean operation in italics in front.
4. Certainly omit miscellaneous pieces. **Those at end**
5. Do you mean not use Conrad quot. or simply not put Conrad's name to it? It is much the most appropriate I can find, and somewhat elucidative.

Complimenti appreciated, as have been excessively depressed. V. sends you her love and says that if she had realised how bloody England is she would not have returned.

I would have sent Aeschyle[4] before but have been in bed with flu, now out, but miserable.

Would you advise working sweats with tears etc. into nerves monologue; only place where it can go?[5]

1–'To luncheon at the Cannon Street Hotel / Followed by a weekend at the Metropole' (*TWL*, ll. 213–14. EP must have written 'THENCE' on a draft that is now lost. On both the TS and its carbon, EP had objected to the word 'perhaps' in 'And perhaps a weekend at the Metropole' (*TWL: Facs*, 30–1, 42–3).
2–*TWL*, ll. 273–4. No pertinent TS survives among the drafts, so Dorothy Pound's difficulty is unknown, but these lines were restored to their original order.
3–EP had cut eighty-two lines of 'Death by Water', leaving only the ten lines about Phlebas (*TWL: Facs*, 62–9).
4–It is not clear what 'Aeschyle' refers to, but possibly EP and TSE had thought to make a translation. In an earlier year, EP had written on 'Aeschylus' in *Egoist* 6: 1 (Jan.–Feb. 1919) and 6: 2 (Mar.–Apr. 1919): see 'Translators of Greek', *Literary Essays of Ezra Pound*, ed. with an Introduction by TSE (1954), 267–75. See also EP, 'Jean Cocteau *Sociologist*', *New English Weekly*, 10 Jan. 1935, repr. in EP, *Selected Prose 1909–1965*, ed. with an Introduction by William Cookson (1973), 405–6: 'As to Greek drama, before Cocteau had published any, Eliot and I looked over the ground. This is no place to say what we thought of it. But it is, permissably, a place to register the fact that we DID nothing about it, except possibly form a few critical opinions that we wouldn't have had, if we hadn't prodded and poked at Father Aeschylus.'
5–TSE is asking what to do with the lines bracketed by EP in 'Song [for the Opherion]': 'When the surface of the blackened river / Is a face that sweats with tears?' (*TWL: Facs*, 98–9).

Have writ to Thayer asking what he can offer for this.

Trying to read Aristophane.

[unsigned, perhaps incomplete]

FROM *Ezra Pound* TS Houghton

[28? January 1922][1] [Paris]

Filio dilecto mihi:[2]

I merely queried the dialect of 'thence'; dare say it is o.k.[3]

D. was fussing about some natural phenomenon, but I thought I had crossed out her queery. The wake of barges washes <andc.>, and the barges may perfectly well be said to wash.

I shd. leave it as it is, and NOT invert.

I do *not* advise printing Gerontion as preface. One dont miss it AT all as the thing now stands. To be more lucid still, let me say that I advise you NOT to print Gerontion as prelude.

I DO advise keeping Phlebas. In fact I more'n advise. Phlebas is an integral part of the poem; the card pack introduces him, the drowned phoen. sailor, and he is needed ABSoloootly where he is. <Must stay in.>

Do as you like about my obstetric effort.

Ditto re the Conrad; who am I to grudge him his laurel crown.[4]

Aeschylus not so good as I had hoped, but haven't had time to improve him, yet.

I dare say the sweats with tears will wait.

Aristophanes probably depressing, and the native negro phoque melodies of Dixee more calculated to lift the ball-encumbered phallus of man to the proper 8.30, 9.30 or even ten thirty level now counted as the crowning and alarse too often katachrestical summit of human achievement.

I enclose further tracings of an inscription discovered recently in the buildings (?) outworks of the city hall jo-house at Charleston S.C.[5]

1 – This letter was tentatively dated '[27? Jan. 1922]' in the first edition of these *Letters*. 'Say early in 1922 TSE', is written in crayon at the head in TSE's hand.

2 – 'Hic est Filius meus dilectus in quo mihi conplacui': 'This is my beloved Son, in whom I am well pleased' (Matthew 3:17).

3 – EP writes as though 'thence' had been TSE's word, not his own. In the TS of 'Death by Water', he had changed 'descends / Illicit backstreet stairs, to reappear' to 'descends / Illicit stairs, thence to reappear' (*TWL: Facs*, 62–3), but those lines were cut.

4 – Valerie Eliot remarked, in a BBC broadcast (2 Nov. 1971): 'Pound left the decision to him, so he omitted the passage, a fact which he later regretted.'

5 – Enclosure no longer present.

May your erection never grow less. I had intended to speak to you seriously on the subject, but you seemed so mountany gay while here in the midst of Paris that the matter slipped my foreskin.

You can forward the Bolo to Joyce if you think it wont unhinge his somewhat sabbatarian mind. On the hole he might be saved the shock, shaved the sock.

You will remember (or if not remind me of) the occasion when the whole company arose as one man and burst out singing 'Gawd save the Queen'. The ante-lynch law (postlude of mediaeval right to scortum ante mortem)[1] has I see been passed to the great glee of the negro spectators in the congressional art gallery.[2]

Dere z also de stoory ob the poker game, if you hab forgotten it.

[unsigned, perhaps incomplete]

TO *Richard Cobden-Sanderson* MS Beinecke

29 January 1922 9 Clarence Gate Gdns, N.W.1

Dear Mr Cobden-Sanderson

If you are free on *Thursday* or *Friday* evening could you come to Lady Rothermere's after dinner and discuss matters with her directly? I have shown her your letter and she is much interested. I hope one of these nights is possible. I will let her know as soon as I hear from you which.

Sincerely yours
T. S. Eliot

She lives at 58 Circus Road which should not be far from you?

FROM *Scofield Thayer* MS Beinecke

29 January 1922 1, Habsburgergasse 2, Vienna

Dear Tom,

It is good to know that you have again taken up the old-fashioned custom of answering letters. I hope I shall not have to await another case of influenza before receiving another letter. I also hope you have now recovered from this case of influenza.

1 – 'Whoring before death'.

2 – The House of Representatives had passed an anti-lynching Bill, but Southern Senators blocked it with a 21-day filibuster.

You seem to take ill my frankness in re the lad Hutchinson. I informed you of the details merely because I felt that unless you knew *The Dial*'s grounds for not publishing you would in conjunction with Mr Hutchinson in all probability judge this delinquency upon *The Dial*'s part harshly. The shareholders of *The Dial* are happy to be able after protracted deliberations to inform you that provided you are agreeable to receiving $25 more than you otherwise would receive for your next London Letter the Board of shareholders on its part will be agreeable to the deduction from this sum of $25. Then you and Mr Hutchinson and *The Dial* and Mr Seldes and the mad hatter will no doubt be *tutti contenti*.

I note that the next Letter possible from you will be for the April number and therefore take this opportunity to beseech you to endeavour, the god of influenza permitting, to get off this Letter soon. Mortimer, in sending me a copy of his London Letter spoke of his profound admiration for you and of his hesitation at supplying so exalted a position even for one Letter. 'I feel it a presumption to replace Eliot, whom I admire greatly, even for an instant.' Also allow me to state that you are *The Dial*'s favorite foreign correspondent not excepting the indefatigable Ezra. Write about what you damn well please.

Yes we await your 'few words' à propos Miss Moore.

Of course I am most interested to hear about the long poem. I thought you were aware that we pay fixed rates always and that therefore it is not for us to bargain. We pay for prose that has been unpublished anywhere 2 cents the word. We pay for verse that has been unpublished anywhere $10 the page which is something more than double our rates for prose. Four hundred and fifty lines will take something more than 11 pages. *The Dial* allows itself when dealing with famous writers to offer round sums rather than split figures. Can we have the poem? *The Dial* would pay $150. The fact that the poem has been sieved three times by your great colleague should sufficiently ensure against any impropriety which might otherwise have got by your own censor. Can you not send me here a copy of the poem?

Dr Schnitzler is acquainted with your name though not inappropriately enough with your *longest* and most shall I say Viennese poem.

Poor Murry! With London, Paris and Vienna all out to get him one wonders what the future holds for this sparse husband of England's latest short-story prima-donna!

Valentinian love to Vivien and yourself!

[unsigned]

TO *Mary Hutchinson* MS Texas

[late Jan 1922?] [9 Clarence Gate Gdns, N.W.1]

Dear Mary,

I am very much disturbed by your note. I had wondered – you must tell me all about it, because we can't leave things like this. You know I am working on my lecture up to Wednesday the 8th so that I cannot make any appointments, so will you have dinner with me the following Thursday, or if you are alone any night after that let me come to you, if you prefer it, and let me hear as soon as possible.

Tom

TO *Richard Cobden-Sanderson* MS Beinecke

30 January 1922 9 Clarence Gate Gdns

Dear Mr Cobden-Sanderson,

Since writing to you I have heard from Lady Rothermere who says that she is only free on *Thursday*. I hope you can come then. She also wishes me to ask you if you will come to dinner on that night? Will you let me know if you will, or whether you prefer to come in afterwards? I will meet you there.

Sincerely yours
T. S. Eliot

TO *Richard Cobden-Sanderson* MS Beinecke

Wednesday [1 February 1922] 9 Clarence Gate Gdns

Dear Mr Cobden-Sanderson,

Lady Rothermere dines at 8. I shall wear a dinner jacket myself. I think I told you her address is 58 Circus Road, St John's Wood. I look forward to seeing you again.

Sincerely
T. S. Eliot

TO *John Rodker* MS Virginia

Sunday [5? February 1922] 9 Clarence Gate Gdns

Dear Rodker,

I should have communicated with you before but we have had flu simultaneously and successively ever since getting back. I have finally seen Lady Rothermere and had a long discussion about the paper, and the result is that it is to be *her* paper not mine and she is to do it her own way. I am thankful to get rid of the responsibility of it, which has been a weight on my mind. I have agreed to take charge of the contributions, though not of the payment for them: – I shall try however to see that it is the maximum possible.

In this capacity, may I ask you to contribute either (as best suits you) the article on cinema you thought of writing, *or* (preferably) a shorter *regular* continued chronicle on cinema and music hall? Apart, of course, from other contributions, which will be welcome?[1] I want to do my best to get enough good stuff from the start to keep out bad, that's quite enough of a function to occupy *my* time.

I hope I shall see you at Lady R.'s on Wednesday – if not, I will write to you later in the hope of arranging a meeting. I have been busy with the enclosed.[2]

Yours
T. S. Eliot

1 – In the event, despite TSE's willingness to accommodate an article on the cinema, Rodker was not to contribute to *C*. As the years moved on, TSE tended to take an anxious view of the cinema; in a blurb for a study by Peter Mayer, *Sociology of Cinema* (1946), he sounded this note: 'this book represents a piece of pioneer work on the most serious of all film problems . . . What is the effect upon the mass of the population who attend a cinema once or twice a week, or more, of the films that they see? And particularly urgent is the question, what is the effect upon the children of the nation? Mr Mayer's conclusions are by no means reassuring. This book ought to be widely read and seriously pondered. Its readers may well differ as to what ought to be done, but they will agree that the situation cannot be left to look after itself.' See also David Trotter, 'T. S. Eliot and Cinema', *Modernism/modernity* 13: 2 (Apr. 2006), 237–65; and on TSE and the music hall, Ron Schuchard, 'In the Music Halls', *Eliot's Dark Angel* (1999); David Chinitz, *T. S. Eliot and the Cultural Divide* (2003).
2 – TSE was now showing *TWL* to friends.

TO *Clifford Bax*[1] TS Texas

6 February 1922 9 Clarence Gate Gdns

Dear Mr Bax,

I must apologise for not replying immediately to your kind letter. I am flattered by your compliment, and impressed by the tone of your letter, which augurs well for the duration of the review. My situation is briefly this: I have very little time for writing, and am committed to several regular engagements and connexions. Except for special reasons, therefore, I have to select periodicals by the simple rule of the highest pay. Would you kindly let me know, as soon as your terms are fixed, what your rates will be?

At the present moment I have but recently returned to London after a three months holiday in pursuit of health, and I have several promises to fulfil. A little later I may be able to speak more definitely – please forgive my vagueness in this letter.

Sincerely yours,
T. S. Eliot

TO *Henry Dugdale Sykes*[2] MS Private collection

17 February 1922 9 Clarence Gate Gdns

Dear Sir,

Your letter, as well as your remarks the other night, gave me great pleasure, and were quite enough to reward me for the trouble of preparing a lecture. If I print the paper in this or a revised form, I will send it to you. I have not seen Stoll's book,[3] but I have an essay of his on *Hamlet*.[4]

I find myself still of the opinion that Tourneur's A.T. precedes R.T.,[5] though this opinion is that only of a poetical practitioner, not of a scholar.

1–Clifford Bax (1886–1962), prolific writer; editor of *The Golden Hind*, a quarterly magazine of art and literature, Oct. 1922–July 1924. TSE did not contribute to it.

2–H. D. Sykes (1874?–1932), author of *Sidelights on Shakespeare* (1919), and later of *Sidelights on Elizabethan Drama: a series of studies dealing with the authorship of sixteenth and seventeenth century plays* (1924). He had published an essay on the dating and attribution of Tourneur's plays (*Notes & Queries* 96, Sept. 1919). TSE later called him 'our greatest authority on the texts of Tourneur and Middleton' ('Cyril Tourneur', *TLS*, 13 Nov. 1930; *SE*, 186).

3–E. E. Stoll, *John Webster: The Periods of his Work as Determined by his Relations to the Drama of his Day* (1905), to which Sykes had referred in his letter.

4–E. E. Stoll, *Hamlet: An Historical and Comparative Study* (1919), is mentioned by TSE in 'Hamlet and His Problems' (*SE*, 141).

5–Both Stoll and Sykes believed that *The Atheist's Tragedy* (pub. 1611) was written later than *The Revenger's Tragedy* (pub. 1607). The quotations TSE cites in the rest of this paragraph are from Sykes's essay.

Everything that denotes development as a poet, I find in R.T. in contrast to A.T. I cannot think that the 'more sparing use of rhyme' is an argument.[1] The question is does the R.T. use rhyme as the earlier Elizabethan plays did? It has many rhymes in the body of a paragraph, not simply to close them off: i.e. T. uses rhyme *freely*, not in a convention. The fact that the 'diction of A.T. is much more elaborate and stilted' seems to me also in my favour. Also, A.T. is much more *imitative* (see grave diggers' scene). The Vere poem does present something definite.[2] But from what I can see, this was an occasional poem for which T's genius was far from suited, and it would not be surprising if, in order to do it all, he had to adopt a style he had outgrown, – even putting aside the conjecture that he had his tongue in his cheek.

I shall try to get hold of your articles. I think I shall, on rereading the plays you mention, agree with you on their authorships.[3]

Excuse this haste. I should very much like to continue this discussion with you at leisure.

With many thanks

Yours very truly
T. S. Eliot

TO *Richard Aldington* — MS Texas

Saturday 17 February 1922 — 9 Clarence Gate Gdns

My dear Richard

You will excuse me, I hope, for not answering your letter before. What you say about my poem gave me great pleasure and gratification. I was engrossed with my lecture, then with several social obligations postponed by the lecture, and then with an article for the *N.R.F.* and now with a letter for the *Dial*.[4] I enclose a copy of the lecture, excuse certain weaknesses of style etc. which I altered on the other copy. It went off successfully – I think

1 – According to Sykes, Stoll argued that 'the more sparing use of rhyme' and the 'more elaborate and stilted diction' are evidence that *The Atheist's Tragedy* came at a 'later stage of Tourneur's metrical technique' than *The Revenger's Tragedy*; Sykes had 'no doubt that Dr Stoll is right'.

2 – Cyril Tourneur, *A Funeral Poem upon the Death of . . . Sir Francis Vere, Knight* (1609), which Sykes cited to help establish the date of *The Revenger's Tragedy*.

3 – Sykes argued for Tourneur's authorship of *The Second Maiden's Tragedy*.

4 – 'Lettre d'Angleterre', *NRF* 18 (1 May 1922); 'London Letter', *Dial* 72 (May 1922).

of working up the relevant paragraphs into the three articles on Blank Verse that Richmond wants. What do you think?[1]

Tell me details of your reception with *Outlook* and *N. Statesman*; I shd. like to know for my own benefit. Also want to know how to join authors' society[2] and whether they wd. do anything for me about the piracy in the Untermeyer book, anthology.[3]

I have been hesitating over the *Dial*'s offer of $150

[unsigned, presumably incomplete]

TO *John Middleton Murry* MS Valerie Eliot

Tuesday night [21 February 1922][4] [London]

My dear John,

I enjoyed my weekend with you more than I can tell you, though you must have realised something of my satisfaction. And I think the circumstances were ideal for persons like ourselves.

Vivien is very ill, and has today gone to a nursing home outside of London at her doctor's urgent request. She may not stay very long, but I expect three weeks at least. There was nothing else to be done at the moment. She must be made to sleep.

I have sent your letter on to her but I am afraid she will not be able to write letters.

Yours always
Tom.

1–These articles were never to be written, though TSE would write 'Four Elizabethan Dramatists', C. 2: 5 (Oct. 1923). See letter to J. M. Robertson, 4 Sept., below.

2–The Society of Authors, London, was founded in 1884.

3–*Modern American Poetry* (1921), ed. Louis Untermeyer.

4–Misdated '20 Feb.' by JMM.

TO *Maurice Firuski*[1] MS Williams College

26 February 1922 9 Clarence Gate Gdns

Dear Sir,

Your name has been given me by Mr Conrad Aiken, who has also shown me a volume of poems by Mr John Freeman, recently published by you, with the appearance of which I was very much pleased.[2]

I have now ready a poem for which that form of publication seems to me the most suitable. I understand that you issue these books in limited editions, and that for the volumes you take for this series give a sum down in advance royalty.

My poem is of 435 lines; with certain spacings essential to the sense, 475 book lines; furthermore it consists of five parts, which would increase the space necessary; and with title pages, some notes that I propose to add, etc., I guess that it would run to from twenty-eight to thirty-two pages.

I have had a good offer for the publication of it in a periodical. But it is, I think, much the best poem I have ever written, and I think it would make a much more distinct impression and attract much more attention if published as a book.

If you are interested in this, I should be glad to hear from you what terms you would be prepared to offer for it, at your earliest convenience, as the other offers for it cannot be held in suspense very long.[3]

I am,
yours faithfully,
T. S. Eliot

1–Maurice Firuski was proprietor of the Dunster House Press, Cambridge, Massachusetts.
2–John Freeman, *The Red Path, and The Wounded Bird* (1921), designed by Bruce Rogers. When TSE told Aiken over lunch on 14 Feb. about 'a poem, 450 lines long', Aiken recommended Dunster House. The following day, Aiken wrote to Firuski: 'He seeks a publisher who will produce it nicely, and in America, and in a small edition. Firuski! cried I, and there you are. When I elucidated, mentioning Rogers and 450 copies and two years exclusive right and a possible hundred dollars and a beautifully produced book, his eyes glowed with a tawny light like fierce doubloons . . . I have not seen the poem. It may or may not be good, or intelligible. But, reflect: Eliot has a real reputation; a poem of that length by him will be a real curiosity, even perhaps an event; and he assumes that you will have of course, the English as well as the American market' (Chapin Library, Williams College).
3–Firuski replied on 11 Mar. that he usually paid 'about one hundred dollars for a work of this kind' and that if TSE sent a copy of the poem, he would decide promptly.

TO *Alfred A. Knopf* MS Texas

4 March 1922 9 Clarence Gate Gdns

Dear Mr Knopf,

Thank you for your letter of the 20th ultimo. I have no disposition to interfere with any arrangement you may have made. If my namesake is Mr Harold Stearns[1] he should be a competent person. I should only protest if he proposed to make an extract from a poem. I should be glad to see a copy of the anthology. Thank you for advising me.

Yours very truly
T. S. Eliot

TO *Scofield Thayer*[2] Telegram Beinecke

8 March 1922 9 Clarence Gate Gdns

CANNOT ACCEPT UNDER !8!56 POUNDS = ELIOT +

Ezra Pound TO *Scofield Thayer* TS Beinecke

9–10 March 1922 [Paris]

Dear Thayer:

Here's the Galligan,[3] I dare say it is a fluke. He seems to have changed his mind the week after; any how. And ENNY how I did not say I was 'sathisfied', I merely said it was . . . . . oh what did I say . . . . 'at least a review by a literate person'.

(Liveright writes that it hasn't sold a copy, so thaaaat's thaaat . . . . . Richard evidently wd.nt. add to the *Dial*'s influence.

And ANNY how, you are certainly right in regarding him with suspicion.

///

1–Harold Stearns (1891–1943), an editor at the *Dial* until 1919; author of *Liberalism in America* (1919), and editor of *Civilization in the United States* (1922). The anthology referred to may be *The Little Book of Society Verse*, ed. Stearns and Claude Fuess.

2–This garbled telegram was sent to Thayer in Vienna in response to his offer to pay $150 for publishing *TWL* in the *Dial*.

3–A warm review of EP's *Poems 1918–21* by Richard Le Gallienne, *New York Times*, 5 Feb. 1922.

I am afraid Eliot has merely gone to pieces again. Abuleia, simply the physical impossibility of correlating his muscles sufficiently to write a letter or get up and move across a room.

It is most 'undiplomatic', I dare say you and I have more reasons for wanting to wring his neck than any one else has; I mean we wd. have, or wd. have had, if it were not definitely a pathological state, due to condition of his endocrines.

His poem is as good in its way as Ulysses in its way—and there is so DAMN little genius, so DAMN little work that one can take hold of and say 'this at any rate stands, and makes a definite part of literature'.[1]

I wish to Christ he had had the December award [from the *Dial*], or even that you wd. chuck the *Dial* and pension him off, to get him out of his bank. (Inconvenience of such a course to me wd. be considerable . . . but there it is.[)]

I don't know whether a loan wd. cover the case. Damn him for not sending you the mss. And curse his family; they are the absolute punk of punk <mother brother sister>

Dont bother to return the Galligan review

Next Morning.

I wonder, cd. Eliot be got into some sort of job on the *Century* or *Atlantic*. (God knows he is not an affirming revolutionary, and he dont, as I at moments, get mistaken for a labour-leader or bolshy bomb-thrower

I wonder wd. he take a professorship. Probably not.

Some bloody college had given FROST a job with no duties.[2] It's a long, Chrrrist its a L O N G way to Tipperary.

Three months off and he got that poem done. I think he is being in that bank is the greatest waste now going on in letters, ANYWHERE. Joyce is provided for, at least he now has a steady income only somewhat too small. Wd. be AMPLE if he hadn't two offspring, which I can't see that he has any business to have.

Anyhow, he and I are tougher than Thomas. I dont know whether strong editorial statement of this waste, wd. be any use.

1–EP had written to Thayer on 8 Feb: 'Eliot's poem is very important, almost enough to make everyone else shut up shop . . . The Eliot, as you have probably decided, is a whole and oughtn't to be divided'; and would write to Quinn on 21 Feb.: 'Eliot came back from his Lausanne specialist looking O.K.; and with a damn good poem (19 pages) in his suit case, same finished up here; and shd. be out in Dial soon, if Thayer isn't utterly nutty. Wadsworth in yesterday on way to Marseilles reported that Eliot was again ill. About enough, Eliot's poem, to make the rest of us shut up shop.'

2–Robert Frost was poet in residence at the University of Michigan, 1921–3.

You and Watson are certainly doing your share of upkeep <(of Am. Lit.)>. So is Quinn.

Whether printed statement, backed by fact that prize has been favourably commented on, wd. rouse some latent capitalist! I suppose they cant want literature until they have some idea what it is.

yrs. ever
Ezra Pound

TO *Ezra Pound* — TS Lilly

12 March 1922 → 12 Wigmore St, W.1[1]

Cher maitre:

I have substituted for the J. Conrad the following, or something like it:

Nam Sibyllam quidam Cumis ego ipse meis oculis vidi, in ampulla pendere, et ubi pueri dicerent, ‘Σίβυλλα τί θέλεις; respondebat illa, αποθανε[ι]ν θέλω.’[2]

I received your message from the young man. The facts are that Thayer (in a letter not distinguished by urbanity) offered me $150, which did not strike me as good pay for a year's work when I shall not do anything else of that size for two or three years, and shortly after I was told on very good authority that George Moore got £100 for a story,[3] by someone who had been told by George himself. I think these people should learn to recognise Merit instead of Senility, and I think it is an outrage that we should be paid less merely because Thayer thinks we will take less and be thankful for it, and I thought that somebody ought to take steps to point this out. Had he offered the 150 with more graciousness instead of as if he were doing me a great favour I might have felt more yielding. As it is I wired him some days ago that I would take £50 and no less. Liveright[4] wrote to say he wanted it, and I have written asking what he wants to give and telling him the exact length, and I have other plans also if Thayer doesn't cough out.

1–For a second time, TSE and VHE moved out of Clarence Gate Gardens and into the flat at 12 Wigmore Street leased by Lucy Thayer, who was away on the Continent: they sublet their flat in Clarence Gate Gardens, and did not return there until late June.

2–This quotation from Petronius, *Satiricon*, was corrected before appearing as the epigraph to *TWL*.

3–George Moore, 'Peronnik the Fool', *Dial* 71 (Nov. 1921) 497–533.

4–Horace B. Liveright (1884–1933), partner in the publishing firm of Boni & Liveright.

Now there is this in which your cooperation is necessary. I have now arranged with Lady Rothermere about the quarterly review, have decided on quite a good small format and paper, neat but no extravagance and not arty, to be published probably by Cobden-Sanderson, in such a way that I shall have only to select the contributions. She will finance it for three years anyhow, there is enough money to pay contributors at £10 per 5000 words and proportionately (should be 80 pages) and I don't see why it shouldn't be tried and the right people as far as possible (i.e. as far as they can be enlisted) get the money regardless of consequences. Lady R. is a particular admirer of yours and especially anxious for your collaboration, as of course I also consider it an essential condition. Also, my credit with her would suffer seriously if you did not. Will you therefore consider

1. A Paris letter every quarter as per *Dial*, say 1500 words.
2. Of course cantos etc. except that I suppose you would get more by putting them in the *Dial*, but I shall hope to arrange much higher rates for verse.
3. Sending over contributions by the best people. I am particularly anxious to obtain Picabia,[1] for whom I have much respect. None of these people can get printed in England otherwise. When you translate, translator's fee also.

It is of course clear that the selection of contributions is entirely in my hands. If Lady R. goes in for illustrations later, which I discouraged for the present, I should with your permission suggest that you should for a fitting consideration be given a free hand to make up special numbers devoted to the work of one man each. Otherwise illustrations do more harm than good, and she warmly admires the Brancusi no. of *Little Review*.[2]

[Wyndham] Lewis has not got a portrait out of Lady R. and is in an extremely pessimistic mood, as you will find when you see him. Do not allow this to affect you. I want the paper to be good while it lasts, and if at any time I could not have my own way with it I should drop out and publish the fact. But I see no reason for anticipating this. Any suggestions from you as to people anywhere on the continent to be approached would be cordially welcome, but I should take anything from Picabia, Cocteau, etc. that you approved provided the space permitted.

1–Francis Picabia (1879–1953), French avant-garde painter and writer. He never contributed to C.

2–The 'Brancusi Number', *Little Review* 8 (Autumn 1921), included EP's essays 'Brancusi' (3–7) and 'Historical Survey' (39–42).

I thought it would be a good idea to get Larbaud to send me his lecture on Joyce.[1] I also see no reason why some things should not appear in this and in the *Little Review* concurrently. Please consider that this venture is impossible without your collaboration, and let me hear from you as soon as possible.

Best sympathies to D. and enquiries after Agamemnon.

T.S.E.

TO *Valery Larbaud*[2]

TS Vichy

12 March 1922

12 Wigmore St, London W.1
temporary address for two months

Dear M. Larbaud,

I am initiating a new quarterly review, and am writing in the hope of enlisting your support. It will be small and modest in form but I think that what contents it has will be the best in London. It is guaranteed for three years and if I can get enough material of the best quality will persist for at least that time.

I hope, for instance, that you will let me have your lecture on James Joyce. I want to get work by the best writers on the continent, as other reviews here publish very little by foreign authors. There is, in fact, as you very well know, no literary periodical here of cosmopolitan tendencies and international standards. I am not at present aiming at a very large public, but at the most enlightened part of the British public – there are, I think, at least a thousand people in England who are aware of the low state of literary journalism here.

At present the review can only offer at the rate of £10 per 5,000 words, and cannot use anything much longer than that, but if there is sufficient demand for the paper, these conditions can be altered.

I mentioned the Joyce Lecture because I know that it exists and because if we could have it this year it would be timely, but of course any contribution from you would be very welcome. I should not desire French or other contributors to write specially for the English public, or to consult any other motive than the subjects they were interested in writing about;

1–Larbaud's 'James Joyce' – *NRF* 18 (Apr. 1922), 385–409 – had been delivered first of all as a lecture at 'la Maison des Amis des Livres' in Paris, Dec. 1921. For Larbaud see note below.

2–Valery Larbaud (1881–1957), French novelist and man of letters, whose lecture 'The "Ulysses" of James Joyce' would appear (in part) in C. 1: 1 (Oct. 1922), 94–103.

but of course, with you, there are also many subjects in English literature about which you may be writing, or want to write, and of which you are much better qualified to speak than anyone in this country.

As a postscript, I should like to say that I should be very happy if you could suggest or put me in touch with any writers in Spain whose work ought to be better known in this country. I remember that the last time I saw you you mentioned several with approbation.

I do not know where you are at present, but I trust that this letter will be forwarded to you and that I may soon hear from you in a favourable sense.

Sincerely yours,
T. S. Eliot

FROM *Scofield Thayer*

MS Beinecke

12 March 1922

1, Habsburgergasse 2, Vienna.

Dear Tom,

I have received from you a wire as follows, 'Cannot accept under 856 pounds – Eliot'.

I presume there is some error upon the part of the telegraphic service.

Were you to let me see the poem and to know why it is you feel that *The Dial* should make an exception in this case to its general rule, I should be happy to consider the matter further. But in the meantime I have had to notify *The Dial* that we are apparently not to receive the poem.

I presume you know that Mr Watson and I are running *The Dial* with a very large annual deficit: we have had to make personal sacrifices to keep it going. It would not be possible for us to pay higher rates than we already pay to our contributors and to continue in existence. I thought you would be in sympathy with us in our attempt to pay all contributors famous and unknown at the same rates.

I trust your review of Miss Moore and your London Letter are now arriving in New York.

Salutations!
[unsigned]

TO *Hermann Hesse*[1] TS Schiller-Nationalmuseum

13 March 1922 12 Wigmore St, London W.1

Monsieur,

Pendant un voyage récent dans la Suisse j'ai fait la connaissance de votre *Blick ins Chaos*,[2] pour lequel j'ai conçu une grande admiration. J'ai porté ce livre à la connaissance d'un ami d'ici, M. Sydney Schiff, qui a dans la suite écrit à votre éditeurs, visant à une traduction anglaise.[3]

Maintenant, je suis chargé de l'initiation d'une nouvelle revue sérieuse, à Londres, qui sera, en tout cas, plus importante que les revues existantes, et beaucoup plus accueillante à la pensée étrangère. D'abord, je me suis proposé de demander une ou deux des parties de *Blick ins Chaos*. Malheureusement, le 'Karamazof' est trop long pour un seul numéro (qui ne comportera que quatre-vingts pages) et puisque la revue ne paraîtra que tous les trois mois, nous ne pouvons guère découper. Et le 'Muishkine', je pense, ne devrait pas être séparé de l'autre. Mais je suis certain que vous aurez beaucoup d'autres choses, également importantes, que je voudrais bien être le premier à présenter au public anglais.[4]

Je peux vous assurer que dans cette revue vos écrits atteindraient l'élite des lecteurs anglais. A présent, nous ne pouvons offrir aux contribuants que la somme de £10 les 5000 mots, et proportionellement; seulement un article ne devrait pas dépasser les 5000 mots environ.

Je veux que la pensée allemande soit bien représentée dans cette revue, et je voudrais bien me renseigner sur les écrivains allemands d'après-guerre qui jouissent de votre approbation.

Je trouve votre *Blick ins Chaos* d'un sérieux qui n'est pas encore arrivé en Angleterre, et je voudrais en répandre la réputation.

Vous ne me connaissez pas du tout: je me présente comme collaborateur au *Times Literary Supplement*, ancien collaborateur de l'*Athenaeum*, et correspondant anglais du *Dial* de New-York et de la *Nouvelle Revue Française*; en outre l'auteur de plusieurs volumes de vers and d'un volume de critique.

1–Hermann Hesse (1877–1962), German novelist and poet; Nobel laureate 1947. TSE would visit him at Montagnola, near Lugano, on 28 May 1922.

2–Hesse, *Blick ins Chaos* (Berne, 1920). TSE's copy, dated by him 'Berne Dec. 1921', is at King's. He quoted from the novel in his Notes to *TWL*, ll. 366–76.

3–See *In Sight of Chaos*, trans. by SS as 'Stephen Hudson' (Zurich, 1923). Thanks to TSE, the *Dial* ran passages from SS's translation in June and Aug.

4–Hesse contributed 'Recent German Poetry' to C. 1: 1 (Oct. 1922), 89–93.

Je n'ai pas parlé ou écrit l'allemand depuis huit ans; par conséquent je n'osais pas vous adresser dans cette langue; mais je le lis encore très couramment. J'espère bientôt revisiter l'Allemagne.

En esperant de reçevoir de vos nouvelles, je vous prie, monsieur, de croire à mes hommages sincères.

T. S. Eliot[1]

TO *Richard Cobden-Sanderson* TS Beinecke

13 March 1922 12 Wigmore St

Dear Cobden-Sanderson,

Forgive me for not having acknowledged your supplementary estimate, which arrived just as I was going to see Lady Rothermere. I have been overwhelmed with the labours of moving, for the last two weeks, having let my flat for two or three months, and am now at the address above, irritable and exhausted.

1 – *Translation*: Dear Sir, During a recent visit to Switzerland, I came across your book *Blick ins Chaos*, which filled me with admiration. I brought it to the attention of a friend of mine here, Mr Sydney Schiff, who subsequently wrote to your publishers about the possibility of an English translation.

I have now been entrusted with the founding, in London, of a new, serious review, which will, at any rate, be more important than the existing ones, and much more welcoming to ideas from abroad. My first thought was to ask for one or two sections of *Blick ins Chaos*. Unfortunately, the 'Karamazov' section is too long for a single issue (only eighty pages in all), and since the review is to appear only once every three months, we can hardly subdivide the text. And the 'Muishkine' section, I think, should not be separated from the other. But I am sure that you must have many other equally important writings, that I should very much like to be the first to present to the British public.

I can assure you that, through this review, your writings would reach the élite of British readers. For the time being, we can pay contributors only at the rate of £10 per 5000 words; but no article should exceed 5000 words approximately.

I want German thought to be well represented in the review, and I should very much like to know about those post-war German writers who meet with your approval.

I find in your *Blick ins Chaos* a seriousness the like of which has not yet occurred in England, and I am keen to spread the reputation of the book.

Since I am quite unknown to you, let me introduce myself as a contributor to *The Times Literary Supplement*, a former contributor to *The Athenaeum*, and English correspondent to the New York *Dial* and the *Nouvelle Revue Française*; in addition, I am the author of several volumes of poetry and a volume of criticism.

I have not spoken or written German for eight years; consequently, I have not presumed to address you in that language; but I still read it very fluently. I hope to visit Germany again soon.

Hoping to hear from you soon, I beg you, Sir, to be assured of my sincere admiration. T. S. Eliot.

Lady Rothermere was quite pleased with the paper, the form and the type, and agreed to the figures which I submitted to her. The next step is of course the throwing out [of] hooks to desirable contributors, which I am now engaged in doing. That will occupy some days before I can get a good idea of the probable amount of support on that side, especially as some of my letters are to people abroad. If the returns are fairly satisfactory I will let you know as soon as possible and arrange a meeting with you. I will then give you some notes for a letter to Liveright.

Sincerely yours, and thanking you for all the trouble you have taken,

T. S. Eliot

FROM *Ezra Pound* — cc Lilly

14 Mars [1922]

70 bis, rue Notre Dame des Champs
Paris vi^{e}

Cher T:

Willing to do anything I can for you personally, but do consider the following points: I have not the slightest interest in England. I have published nothing there since I left (a year and a quarter ago). I know absolutely nothing to England's credit. The *Morning Post* is the real voice of England, and the most concentrated and persistent will toward evil in Europe.[1]

I am not the least interested in the fortunes of any writer in England save yourself, and you omit to mention the essential point: What salary are you receiving as editor?

I absolutely refused to have anything to do with another projected English review (only last week) unless they wd. guarantee to provide you with enough to get you out of your bank. I am not the least interested in any scheme <concerning you> which has not that for its aim.

No Englishman's word is worth a damn, I dont know whether the ladies are any more precise. When Hueffer sold the old *English Review* to Mond[2]

1 – *The Morning Post*, a Conservative daily paper edited by Howell Arthur Gwynne (1865–1950), ran a series of hysterically anti-Semitic articles in 1920 (repr. as *The Cause of World Unrest*). A boycott among Jewish advertisers started a long decline, and the paper was ultimately bought out by the *Daily Telegraph* in 1937.

2 – Sir Alfred Mond, later the first Baron Melchett (1868–1930), industrialist, financier and politician; mentioned in TSE's poem 'A Cooking Egg'. Ford Madox Hueffer (later Ford) founded the *English Review* in 1908 and edited it for just one year; he sold it in 1909 to Mond, who invited Austin Harrison (1873–1928) to become editor.

it was with the understanding that he was to remain Editor, as he was dealing with the titlocracy he didn't bother to get the matter in writing, and Mond turned him out at the end of four months.

Do remember that I know nothing whatever about Lady Rothermere, save that she, by her name, appears to have married into a family which is NOT interested in good literature. I am interested in civilization, but I cant see that England has anything to do with any future civilization. I consider it a waste of my time to write Paris letters for the *Dial*, but the *Dial* pays from £10–£15 per cent letter, and takes the rest of my stuff, when there is any at a rate which, taking the lot, permits me some mental ease during the year.

I dont, demme, see why I should write a letter to London for £3/. It certainly will not serve to put up my rates. I am not sure, since you cite a contemporary case of injustice, that it is fair to Thayer <for me> to sell the same stuff elsewhere at a third of the rate he pays.

Remember I have beggared myself, and kept down my rates for years by contributing to every free and idealistic magazine that has appeared.

Also I dont see what claim Lady R. has to my free services as unpaid foreign editor and scout. Thayer paid me for just that sort of work during a year and a half.

I cant see that England deserves a good review.

Of course if Lady R. is willing to cooperate with me in a larger scheme which wd. mean getting you out of your bank, and allowing you to give up your whole time to writing, I might reconsider these points.

You may show her this letter. In fact that is the simplest way for you to present the matter to her. I am willing to do anything I can to further your own production. I cant see that editing a quarterly will give you any more leisure to write poetry.

I have absolutely no animosity against Lady R. whom I have never laid eyes on; but I have an absolute mistrust of anything English, particularly of any 'upper class' english interest in literature. I can not use the term 'aristocracy' of a lot of illiterate motor owners, whether English or other. In the main I think these people like to talk, to express sympathy, and then to waste the artist's time. As I think I have told you, I found it less interruption to my work to write for the *New Age* at £1/1 an article, than to keep up ones intercourse with Mayfair.

I have published nothing in England since I left, the last book of mine to be printed there was printed privately.[1] (In a few days you will say 'yes,

1 – EP, *Hugh Selwyn Mauberley* (Ovid Press, 1920).

but there is an article of his in the *New Age*'.[1] That one exception is made because I wanted to get the matter recorded in print, before a rather indiscreet letter of mine reached someone in the U.S. . . . but no matter. <I hadn't time to translate and arrange french publication.>)

I dont want to appear in England. I have no belief in their capacity to understand anything. They still want what I was doing in 1908. They want immitations and dilutations.

I dont see what company I should be in, apart from your own, and if you try to do editorials as well as spend your days in Lloyds, I dont know that they will be very enlightening.

Dont think I am writing an ultimatum; I am only trying to be clear.

(1) I consider any participation in the proposed review would be a waste of my time; the rates are not high enough to buy one any leisure, they wd. merely pay ones expenses while one was doing a hurried piece of hack work.

(2) I want definitely to know that you have an agreement in writing re/

(a) your salary, of which I want to know the amount

(b) that you are to have absolute controll of the contents, choice unimpeded, of what goes into the review.

(c) guarantee of three years duration of the review under these conditions.

(3) I want to hear direct from Lady Rothermere, that she will help me in my endeavour to get you out of Lloyds and to make proper arrangements for providing you with suitable leisure for writing.

It is rather odd your writing at just this time. I had not intended to say anything to you about the scheme until I had got it working. However . . . Exhibit B. detailed refusal to another magazine proposition recd. week before last. (Please return)

1–EP, 'Credit and the Fine Arts . . . A Practical Application' (*New Age*, 30 Mar. 1922), was about 'Bel Esprit', EP's scheme to find thirty guarantors of £10 a year, to enable TSE to leave the bank. A private circular in the same month stated: '[TSE] certainly is not asking favours, our plan was concocted without his knowledge. The facts are that his bank work has diminished his output of poetry, and that his prose has grown tired. Last winter he broke down and was sent off for three months' rest. During that time he wrote *Waste Land*, a series of poems, possibly the finest that the modern movement in English has produced, at any rate as good as anything that has been done since 1900, and which certainly loses nothing by comparison with the best work of Keats, Browning or Shelley' (*Letters of Ezra Pound*, 241). EP had written to Quinn on 8 Nov. 1920: 'The suggestion that you and several other[s] should subsidize me is very noble, and I appreciate your spirit in making the tentative suggestion; but I think Eliot is the first man to be taken off the wreckage. After all, I am a free man; not incarcerated for the greater part of the day, all day and every day' (NYPL).

Whereas illiterate motorists have never been averse from wasting the time of artists and writers, and recognizing that persons of 'social standing' usually want a writer to stop doing his own job in order to amuse them and that when they buy pictures they usually buy those of people who have invented nothing etc. n.b. during the war they went in for this sort of thing; and noting that they usually find out five years later that they've been 'ad, and then forswear the arts. Also noting that practical men have never been averse from exploiting men of letters (or anyone else) remembering that 'England' means Gifford against Keats,[1] that the Fleet St system means the union of as many mediocrities as possible against the man with even a spark of genius; remembering the history of English literature as shown in her exiles: Landor in Italy, Keats, Shelley, Byron, Beddoes out of England, Browning in Italy and Tennyson in Buckingham Palace; and having no reason to suppose that anything is yet altered in that Island. I set down the following as the minimum conditions for my collaboration in proposed 'review':

1. That T. S. Eliot be endowed for life, at such rate per year as will enable him to leave his job in Lloyds bank, and give his entire time to literature, and that this shall imply no lien whatever on his time.

   Note: the problem before the writer in our time is how to live without turning out rubbish that will sell. The greatest waste in ang-sax letters at the moment is the waste of Eliot's talent; this wd. not be remedied if he left Lloyds and were compelled to spend his time doing journalism, or to review books etc. etc. He must have *complete* liberty.

   Note continued: I have no reasons to suppose that anyone in England is interested in literature or in anything save their own personal aggrandisment. I place this condition re/Eliot as a minimum test of the sincerity on the part of promoters.

2. The review is to have an Editor, who shall receive a salary, not necessarily large, but guaranteed to be regular.

   2a. That he shall be at liberty to choose the contents of the section of the review, say 50% of its pages, placed in his care.

3. That there be a board of associate 'editors' who shall have no voice in choosing the contents of the main editor's part of the magazine, but who shall have complete liberty to write and print *whatever* they like in their own sections.

1 – The infamous attack on Keats's *Endymion* (*Quarterly Review*, 1818) was written by John Croker Wilson, though it was widely believed to be by the editor, William Gifford.

3b. that these associates be not more than ten in number, and that so far as possible they shall not be selected from the idiot, cretin, or myxodemic sections of the community.

4. That I shall have complete liberty to fill ten pages per month, as I see fit, with no interference from any one. That it shall not be considered a breach of contract if I do not fill these ten pages, or any part of them. That I be paid at a rate not less than current rates of the *Dial*. <That this not promise or be construed to mean the offer of any other contribution to the review.>

5. That there be a business and make-up editor, who shall receive a proper salary, and be responsible for regular appearance of the review.

Rider: I imagine that this project will go the way of similar projects in England; that it will end in there being a new periodical devoted to mediocrity, and that good men of business like Bennett and W. L. George[1] will net a certain profit; that free speech will remain, as at present, in abeyance; and that good writers will gain neither cash nor leisure from the enterprise.

[unsigned]

TO *Scofield Thayer* TS Beinecke

16 March 1922 12 Wigmore St, W.1

Dear Scofield,

Please excuse my not replying sooner to your letter, except by my wire; but I have had a good deal of trouble over letting my flat furnished and moving here, where I shall be till the 20th June. In addition, there have been engrossing personal affairs, and I have been prevented from dealing with any correspondence.

I also took some days to think about your offer, during which time I happened to hear on good authority that you had paid £100 to George Moore for a short story, and I must confess that this influenced me in declining $150 for a poem which has taken me a year to write and which is my biggest work. To have it first published in a journal was not in any case the way I should choose for bringing it out; and certainly if I am to be offered only £30–£35 for such a publication it is out of the question.

1–W. L. George (1882–1926), journalist and prolific short-story writer.

I have written to Ezra Pound to explain my reasons for refusing to dispose of the poem to the *Dial* at that price and he concurs with me.

I sent a London letter, assuming that it would be for the April number, but as Mortimer's has just come out in March I infer that mine is not wanted until the May number, so that I am sending Mr Seldes one or two alterations to bring it up to date.

You have asked me several times to give you the first refusal of any new work of mine, and I gave you the first refusal of this poem.[1]

Sincerely,
Tom.

TO *Wyndham Lewis* — MS Cornell

16 March 1922 — 12 Wigmore St

Dear Lewis,

I have been absolutely taken up the last ten days with the hell of moving etc., am very tired and depressed. Vivien has been in bed with fever, and life has been horrible generally. I have heard from Pound. Will you let me know where you are? if you have gone or if you have not. Can we arrange a meeting? Please write. Not on telephone here. I have been too busy to write, but have been anxious to know about you.

Yours ever
T.S.E.

FROM *André Gide* — MS Houghton

16 mars 1922 — [Paris]

Cher Monsieur Eliot

Ma sympathie vous est toute acquise et déjà je vous envoie mes voeux pour la réussite de votre projet.

Ma collaboration . . . ? Elle vous est acquise en principe; mais je ne puis la rendre effective avant de connaître quelques précisions:– Au sujet de la question matérielle, vous restez bien vague; mais le change permet des conditions avantageuses pour nous sans être désobligeantes pour vous. Au surplus cette question m'importe moins que celle de la composition de votre premier No., que le choix de vos collaborateurs – tant anglais

1–At this point Thayer has written 'Not submitted'.

qu'étrangers. J'attends d'être fixé sur ces points; et sans doute pourrai-je ensuite, me rendre compte du genre de collaboration qui serait la plus opportune.

Au revoir cher Monsieur

Croyez à mes sentiments bien cordiaux

André Gide[1]

TO *Valery Larbaud* TS Vichy

20 March 1922 12 Wigmore St, W.1

Dear M. Larbaud,

I am very much gratified at receiving your gracious letter of the 18th, and look forward with keen pleasure toward reading your critique of Joyce. But I should be particularly pleased at having the honour of publishing first something of yours on Landor; that would also be a happy rebuke to the English literati for their neglect of a great poet and prose author.[2] Certainly, I hope that you will write those articles in English, as there is inevitably some loss in translation. But I shall do my best, and exercise my own supervision, for what that is worth, to secure for you a good translation of the Joyce.

I am also very much obliged for the names of Spanish writers. None of them, I regret to say, is known to me, but I have no hesitation in accepting your judgement, and shall write to them.

I will send you details of the contents of early numbers as soon as possible. I hope that later it may be possible to improve the rates of payment, so I invite the first contributors for the honour they will do the review, and not for their personal advantage.

Very sincerely yours,

T. S. Eliot

1 – *Translation*: Dear Mr Eliot, I am completely at one with you in your enterprise, and I hasten to send you my best wishes for success.

As for my contributing . . . ? I can readily agree in principle; but before doing so in practice, I should need further information on certain points. As regards the material question, you remain rather vague; but the exchange rate works at present in our favour without putting undue strain on you. Besides this consideration is less important for me than that of the make-up of the first issue, and the choice of your contributors, both English and foreign. I wait to hear from you on these points; and after that I shall no doubt be able to see what kind of contribution would be most appropriate.

Hoping to hear from you again, With my most cordial regards, André Gide

2 – Larbaud had translated Walter Savage Landor's *High and Low Life in Italy* in 1911, and had written that he was contemplating a series about him.

TO *Hermann Hesse* PC Schiller-Nationalmuseum

27 March 1922 12 Wigmore St

I have your manuscript today[1] and thank you very much. I will write to you in a week or two. I am delighted to receive something from you.

Mit herzlichem Gruss [With warmest regards]

T. S. Eliot

TO *Scofield Thayer* MS Beinecke

27 March 1922 12 Wigmore St

Dear Scofield,

I discovered when in Switzerland a very admirable essay entitled *Blick ins Chaos* by Hermann Hesse. Mr Stephen Hudson has made a translation of this and is sending it to you. I think that you will find it an interesting work.

Sincerely yours,
T. S. Eliot

TO *Harold Monro* MS Beinecke

[April? 1922] [London]

My dear Monro,

It was a great pleasure to me to receive your book,[2] especially with your name in it, and I am looking forward to putting it into my pocket to read at lunch time, when most of my reading is done!

I hope we may meet at some fortunate date. <I am sorry to have seen you so little for so long.>

Yours ever
T. S. Eliot

1–Hesse, 'Recent German Poetry' (trans. by F. S. Flint), *C.* I: I (Oct. 1922), 89–93.
2–Harold Monro, *Real Property* (1920).

TO *Sydney Schiff* TS BL

3 April 1922 12 Wigmore St

Dear Sydney,

I have written to Joyce, and enclose a note to [Fritz] Vanderpyl. You will infer therefrom that he plumes himself on being as well as an art critic (in the *Petit Parisien*) and a poet (not at all bad), an archimage in the arts of eating and drinking. He can probably introduce you to good restaurants. He writes very learned articles on Cuisine for the *Petit Parisien*. I should like to get some of them published in this country.

I hope that the weather is not quite so vile as it is here, and that you are really finding the atmosphere an elixir. Do let me hear from you as soon as you are rested and have assembled impressions.

with love to both,
yours always,
Tom

TO *T. Sturge Moore*[1] TS Texas

3 April 1922 12 Wigmore St

Sir,

I applied to my friend Richard Aldington for your address. I have undertaken the task of finding and selecting the contributors for a modest quarterly review which is subsidised to a moderate extent for three years. I propose that the quarterly should be simple and severe in appearance, without illustrations, and my only ambition is that it should unite the best critical opinion in England, together with the work of the best critics whom I can find from other countries. Whilst I should admit other writing in very small quantity, I wish to make it primarily a critical review. To its ultimate financial success I am comparatively indifferent; but while it lasts, under my direction, I shall make its aim the maintenance of critical standards and the concentration of intelligent critical opinion; also, the

1 – Thomas Sturge Moore (1870–1944), English poet, playwright, author and wood engraver, published his first book of poems, *The Vinedresser and Other Poems*, in 1899. His brother was the philosopher G. E. Moore. A respected acquaintance of many writers, including A. E. Housman and AH, he also designed bookplates and bookbindings for WBY. See *W. B. Yeats and T. Sturge Moore: Their Correspondence, 1901–1937*, ed. Ursula Bridge (1953).

diffusion of such funds as can be mustered, among the proper persons as contributors.

I have a great respect for your judgement and taste, and count it of the highest importance to secure your support. I think that you would appear in as respectable company as there is, and a company which would feel itself dignified by your presence. Would you be willing to contribute an essay of say five thousand words, or more or less, to an early number? I should be delighted, for instance, to publish anything by you on the subject of Flaubert (versus Mr Middleton Murry's opinions) or if you chose to dissect Murry's Oxford lectures, *The Problem of Style*, I would obtain it for you.[1]

I should like to start publication in June, but am not certain whether it will be possible until autumn, as I am not disposed to launch this paper until I am certain of the right contributors for the first four numbers. At present the review can only offer at the rate of £10 per 5000 words, but my first endeavour would be to improve these terms. In the hope of hearing from you favourably, I remain,

your obliged obedient servant,
T. S. Eliot

TO *Alfred A. Knopf*

TS Texas

3 April 1922 — 12 Wigmore St

Dear Mr Knopf,

According to the terms of our contract for *Poems*, you will remember, I was to offer you my next two books, i.e. *The Sacred Wood* and the next thereafter. I have now a poem of about 450 lines which I wish to publish as a small book, of about thirty pages. It is, I think, a good one.

I have no desire to evade or withdraw from the terms of the contract, but I have already received an unsolicited offer of $150 down against 15 per cent royalty from Mr Liveright, whom I met in Paris, for publication in the autumn. This is what I should have asked in any case. If you do not care to take the poem will you let me know immediately? Also, if you do. I am anxious to get the poem published as soon as possible. Perhaps you would

1–In his reply (n. d.), Moore declined Flaubert and JMM, but offered to write on *SW*, 'the critical work which has most interested me since Santayana's *Poetry of Barbarism*'.

prefer an option on the next prose book, when it is ready, which will not be for a year or so.[1]

With kind regards,

your very truly,
T. S. Eliot

TO *Lucy Thayer* cc Valerie Eliot

3 April 1922 12 Wigmore St

Dear Lucy,

I am enclosing (1) receipt for gasbill for the December quarter: this I paid some time ago, as I found it here on arrival, and thought it best, as it was overdue, to pay it and collect it from you afterwards; (2) John's bill for electricity for the same quarter, which seems pretty late; if you have paid it already send me the receipt and I will take the matter up with him; (3) John's rent due March 25th. I understood from Vivien that you said you had sent the money to him already; in that case let me know.

In writing to John will you let him know that you are not taking the flat on, and *also* will you please tell him that I will see to the disposition of the furniture at the end of the lease? I don't want him to wonder why I am taking the furniture out when the time comes.

I would have written before, and sent this gasbill, but have been very over busy, and also Vivien was very ill indeed from the moment we arrived. I hope that there is some prospect of your returning to Europe – especially now that Vivien is so much at home on the continent, and evidently really needs to get away from London and from England for long periods together.

I hope that your father's health is not now a cause for anxiety.

Very sincerely,
[T. S. E.]

1 – On 1 May, Knopf replied that 'in view of the fact that you are anxious to have the new book out at once, it is best for you to accept Mr Liveright's offer'. But he looked forward eagerly to TSE's 'next prose book, option on which you were good enough to offer me in exchange for the *Poems*'.

TO *Sylvia Beach*[1] TS Princeton

4 April 1922 12 Wigmore St

Dear Miss Beach,

Thank you very much for sending the beautiful *broché* copy of *Ulysses* on faith; it also comes most opportunely in that it provides me with wrapping for returning you the unbound sheets. I am sorry that I have cut some of the pages; I was expecting to have it bound here. I am posting you the sheets, registered, tomorrow.

I am distressed and indignant at this news. If you cared to entrust me with the names of the mentioned literary critics I could make, gradually, discreet investigations about the conspiracy. I presume you have documentary evidence of their having *asked* for the book, in the form of letters to yourself. I might be in a position later to give publicity to the affair, if that were possible and desirable.[2] Perhaps, however, you prefer to keep these secrets to yourself. I thank you for the enclosure, which I will preserve. In any case, believe me,

your obliged obedient servant,
T. S. Eliot

1–Sylvia Beach (1887–1962), American expatriate who in Nov. 1919 opened Shakespeare & Company, a bookshop and lending library, at 8 rue Dupuytren, Paris, moving two years later to 12 rue de l'Odéon. Her customers included JJ (she published *Ulysses*), Gide, Maurois, Valéry, EP, Hemingway and Gertrude Stein. TSE wrote in a tribute ('Miss Sylvia Beach', *The Times*, 13 Oct. 1962), 'I made the acquaintance of Sylvia Beach, and at the same time of her friend Adrienne Monnier, on a visit to Paris early in the nineteen twenties, and thereafter saw them frequently during that decade. Only the scattered survivors of the Franco-Anglo-American literary world of Paris of that period, and a few others like myself who made frequent excursions across the Channel, know how important a part these two women played in the artistic and intellectual life of those years.'

2–Though there was probably no 'conspiracy', the dearth of British reviews of *Ulysses* made JJ suspicious too. He wrote to Harriet Shaw Weaver on 10 Apr., 'There is a rumour here that certain critics who had asked for press copies and obtained them had decided to boycott the book. I am inclined to believe it' (*Letters*, I, ed. Stuart Gilbert, 1957). TSE wrote later ('Miss Sylvia Beach'), 'No tribute to Sylvia Beach would do her justice that did not stress her services to James Joyce. But for two generous and devoted women – Harriet Weaver and Sylvia Beach – I do not know how Joyce could have survived or how his works could have got published.'

TO *Antonio Marichalar*[1] ? TS

5 April 1922 12 Wigmore St

Monsieur,

M. Valery Larbaud m'a donné votre adresse, et en vous écrivant je me mets sous sa protection.

Je me suis chargé de l'initiation d'une nouvelle revue littéraire à Londres, qui devrait paraître par trimestre. Dans cette revue je voudrais présenter à l'élite parmi les amateurs anglais des belles lettres les représentants les plus importants de la pensée étrangère; à present, on ne connaît, et très mal d'ailleurs, que la pensée française. Je voudrais canaliser vers Londres les courants étrangers les plus profonds. Ainsi, je veux me mettre en rapport avec les écrivains et les redacteurs de revues les plus illustres de l'étranger.

Si vous regardez mon projet d'un oeil favorable, j'ose espérer que vous daignerez me laisser souhaiter un article de vous; nous serions tout heureux de pouvoir vous présenter aux lecteurs anglais les plus accueillants. Nous comptons faire paraître le premier numéro au mois de juin, ou au mois de septembre au plus tard.

La revue sera subventionée par Viscountess Rothermere; à present nous ne pouvons offrir que la somme modeste de £10 les 5000 mots; et un article ne devrait pas dépasser par beaucoup cette étendue; naturellement, nous accepterions aussi des morceaux plus courts. Nous nous chargerions du travail de traduction.

En comptant beaucoup sur votre appui, je vous prie, Monsieur, de recevoir l'expression de mes sentiments les plus distingués.

T. S. Eliot[2]

1–Antonio Marichalar (1893–1973), Spanish literary critic; contributor to *El Sol* and *La Revista de Occidente* (edited by José Ortega y Gasset). He was to write on 'Contemporary Spanish Literature' in *C.* 1: 1 (Oct. 1922), and took responsibility for the regular 'Madrid Chronicle' and 'Spanish Chronicle', 1926–38.

2–*Translation*: Sir, M. Valery Larbaud gave me your address, and in writing to you I place myself under his protection.

I am responsible for starting a new literary review in London, which should appear quarterly. In this review I would like to introduce an elite readership of English letters to the most important representatives of foreign thought; at present only French thought is known about, and poorly at that. I would like to channel towards London the deepest foreign currents. With this in mind, I want to put myself in contact with the most distinguished writers and editors of reviews from abroad.

If you look favourably on my project, I hope you will be willing to offer an article of your own; we would be very happy to introduce your work to the most receptive English readership. We are counting on the first number appearing in June, or in the month of September at the latest.

The review will be financed by Viscountess Rothermere; at present we are only able to offer the sum of £10 per 5000 words, and an article should not go much beyond that limit;

TO *Sydney Schiff* MS BL

[6? April 1922] [London]

Dear Sydney

The only person I have to whom I can give you a note is Vanderpyl. I will send it to Foyot,[1] as I have had to be out all evening and just got in before the post. I do hope you will find what you want in Paris and both be much better for it. In haste

Yrs aff.
Tom.

Directly I have time I will send a line to Joyce about you.

TO *T. Sturge Moore* MS Texas

10 April 1922 12 Wigmore St

Dear Mr Sturge Moore,

Thank you very much for your letter which encourages me to hope that you may have something for me by September 1st. If and as soon as you are moved I hope you will let me know, and what the subject is. I only suggested Murry as a sort of stalking horse, and because I was exasperated to hear that a letter of yours about his filthy[2] Flaubert article[3] had been omitted from *The Times*. I am very much flattered by what you say of my book (which was disliked by the Right and the Left) but of course, if (as I hope) you contribute to a very early number, it might be more fitting to have some other subject. But please be sure of the very high importance I attach to securing something from you; and I shall importune you soon again.

Yours sincerely
T. S. Eliot

---

naturally we also accept shorter pieces. We would be responsible for the work of translation.

Counting very much on your support, I beg you to accept my deepest respects. T. S. Eliot

1 – The Hotel Foyot, rue de Tournon, Paris, where the Schiffs lived for many months, and where they would seek to entertain Proust. See also Richard Davenport-Hines, *A Night at the Majestic: Proust and the Great Modernist Dinner Party of 1922* (2006).

2 – At TSE's request this 'deplorable' adjective was burnt from the holograph before his letters to Sturge Moore were sold. He did not remember the content 'but there seems to me no excuse for applying' the word to it. 'This is not only immoderate but is a very loose and inaccurate use of . . . "filthy", since I cannot believe there was anything obscene in an article by Murry, or, indeed in anything appearing in those days in the *Times Literary Supplement*' (letter to Mrs Ursula Bridge, 25 Mar. 1959).

3 – JMM, 'Gustave Flaubert', *TLS*, 15 Dec. 1921, 833–4.

TO *Sydney Schiff* MS BL

10 April 1922 12 Wigmore St

Dear Sydney,

I am writing to tell you for Vivien who is very tired from her journey home with a temperature of 100, among fearful crowds: so much so that three trains were run. I think she was most wise to make up her mind as she did, so quickly, to cut her losses and come home, ill as she was. She stood no chance of getting well quickly in a Paris hotel. I regret now that I urged her to go. If you remember, she had been so ill here up to the last and had not really recovered. She sends you both her love, and it is not necessary to say how much she regrets having had no opportunity to see a good deal of you in Paris, which you know she had looked forward to for so long.

Ever yrs. affectionately
Tom.

I shall write in answer to your letter in a few days time.

TO *Mary Hutchinson* MS Texas

Wednesday [12? April 1922] 12 Wigmore St

My dear Mary,

I rang you up tonight but you were said to be out – I find from the doctor that Vivien's temperature has kept steadily about 100, and he says that she must keep very quiet for the next day or so and ought not to see anyone or talk, as the first thing is to get her temperature down. She is frightfully vexed, but it can't be helped: she mustn't see you tomorrow; she told me to tell you that the moment she was allowed to see anyone, she should send someone to telephone to you to try to arrange if you can come. She said to tell you that she had several most *important* matters to discuss with you, so she wants to lose no time in seeing you.

I enjoyed last evening very much, for my part, I assure you – I was afraid that I was tired and not in good form – but I hope I can do better soon – and see you before your party.

affectionately
Tom.

TO *Sydney Waterlow* MS Professor Waterlow

Monday [17 April? 1922] 12 Wigmore St

My dear Sydney,

I was very glad to hear from you and to know both that you are settled and that you are not going to Genoa. That is very good. I have been laid up for the past week with a chill and a temperature which I have not been able quite to get rid of, and hardly expect to find it wise to get out in the evening for some days. I shall I hope be able to come on the following Thursday.

I rather want to see J. M.'s book. Vivien read it and gave me a pretty good idea of it. According to her there are passages where one would say that it was – Sullivan speaking. But one or two good things. I shall certainly read the book on style.[1]

It hardly seems to me worthwhile for one to say anything about *Ulysses* for six months at least – until all the imbeciles who like and dislike it for insincere reasons have tired themselves. But when you've finished it I should like to discuss it with you.

Please give Margery my kindest regards.

Yours ever
T.S.E.

TO *Mary Hutchinson* PC Texas

Wednesday [19 April 1922]

Thank you for your suggestion. Come to the Piccadilly at 5.15 and I will look out for you – inside the Regent St entrance. That will be the best place for me as I too shall be on my way somewhere.

T.S.E.

1 – JMM had published two books in Mar.: *The Things We Are* (a novel) and *The Problem of Style*.

TO *Sydney Schiff* MS BL

20 April 1922 12 Wigmore St

My dear Sydney,

I return herewith the letter from Squire[1] which I think ought to be preserved. You have all my sympathy for having had to receive such an insult. It is much worse even than I should have expected. You see, don't you, that no truce is possible with such people when anything out of the ordinary merely provokes a sneer, in the very first sentence. I like his saying that it doesn't 'bowl us over'! Please look at the sort of thing they '*find room for*' in the last number. I know how you must feel about it.

I am glad to hear that you are finding Paris profitable, with new people of interest as well as old friends; and it is very satisfactory to know that *Elinor Colhouse* is to be translated into French. Had I not fallen ill, I should have written to ask you, as I had in mind, whether you wished Vanderpyl to know that you are a writer.

It has been rather difficult, as Vivien has had a bad time recovering herself and has had me on her hands as well. I am behindhand with a lot of work – a week in bed is a serious loss for a man in my position – and am about ready to chuck up literature altogether and retire; I don't see why I should go on for ever fighting a rearguard action against time, fatigue and illness and complete lack of recognition of these three facts.

Always yours aff.
T.S.E.

TO *Edgar Jepson* MS Beinecke

20 April 1922 12 Wigmore St

It is very pleasant to hear from you again. O dear, I should have liked to come to supper on Sunday, but I have been laid up for several days with a chill, and shan't be out in the evening anyway. Is there any chance of a subsequent Sunday?

Yours sincerely
T. S. Eliot

1 – The letter from J. C. Squire does not survive.

Ezra Pound TO *Scofield Thayer* TS Beinecke

23 April 1922

Dear Thayer:

Thanks for permission to use Turk. Night.

I shd. be very glad to use The Hungarian Night; as it appeared in The Dial = but I'm afraid the damn technicalities of my contract oblige me to make a new translation.[1] it is a waste = but I have done it. Have done it here where I cdn't compare it to the anonymous Dial version. I don't think I have improved on it.

Will of course make due acknowledgments to Dial.

Re. Eliot. he is again ill, I hear.

Order of facts in face of anomaly.

1. I tried to get him to finish poem & send it to you from Paris (in January I think)

   1a. Wrote to Eliot to send poem.
2. I wrote to X to <persuade him> see that T. S. E. sent poem to you.
3. Spoke with friend, returning to London saying he shd persuade T. S. E. to send poem.
4. Eliot writes me (as I think I mentioned in a p.s.) that Geo Moore is getting special rates from the Dial. (also S. Anderson)
5. That being the case I can hardly reprove Eliot – if you have put the thing on a commercial basis, for holding out for as high a price as he can get. i.e. if the Dial is a business house, it gets business treatment. If the Dial is a patron of literature T. contends it should not pay extra rates for 'mere senility'. All of which is extreme theory-ism, perhaps, on his part.

I do not concur in his refusing to let you publish the poem. (In fact I have emphatically dis-concurred with a number of his recent movements re/ another matter.)

I don't from your note, know precicely what he thinks I concur in, or what he has led you to think I concur in.

I cannot relish being paid less than a senile bunch of tripes like Geo. Moore, any more than does Eliot. But then you and I haven't the long personal background, that you and he have and I am possibly less mercurial in these matters. – my health is better than his.

1–Paul Morand's 'Turkish Night', trans. by EP, *Dial*, Sept. 1921, and 'Hungarian Night', *Dial*, Nov. 1920. An English edition was envisaged but not achieved.

I happen to think his poem worth more than a whole vol. or six vols. of Geo. M. – especially since the old souse has taken to gingerbread fake antiques.

I shd. prefer one good review to several less good ones.

I have, as I think you know, always wanted to see a concentration of the authors I believe in, in one review.

The Dial perhaps looks better to me than it does to Eliot. (life in general does.)

However if you and Lady R. and the 'Times' want him I can't but concur in his holding out for the highest bid. (Though I think it is a little rough of him to drag me into the auction rooms – where I have no desire to be.[)]

I have, I must have, bored you to death reiterating my belief that the way to make a literature is to provide the few men capable of producing it, with leisure.

This 'few' does not, alas, include all of your contributors.

It would mean in a perfect state of things, very high payment for a piece of real work. If you haven't even seen the *mss.* it is rather unreasonable of Tom to expect you to believe that it is a masterpiece.

But as I'm not au courant with Geo. M's prices, etc. etc. etc. I cannot go into details about price. I have never I think, gone much into details about my own prices (am perhaps an awful warning to T.) & I cannot be expected to go into details about other peoples prices. THERE IS MORE OF THIS LETTER TO COME[1]

Yours
Ezra Pound *over* for P.S.

Have recd. two letters from America mentioning the Dial, one thought it was improving. Tother complained that Dial readers were probably too 'Sherwood-Andersonized' to take in any extraneous idea. – but then I hardly hear from anyone who isn't more or less on my side of the fences: international high vs. localism. E. P.

1–Thayer replied to EP on 30 Apr. that TSE's letter of 16 Mar. had accused him of lying about the rates paid by the *Dial*. 'In offering to accept his poem without having seen it and in offering to pay him a round sum for it I went beyond the limit of what an editor should do. And in answer I received a telegram which I could take only as an insult' (*Pound, Thayer, Watson, and The Dial*).

TO *Ottoline Morrell* MS Texas

26 April 1922 12 Wigmore St, W.1

My dear Ottoline,

I was so glad to get your letter – I was just on the point of writing to you too. Vivien sends you her love. We have both had incessant illness since a week before Easter – neither of us has seen anyone for some time. What we want is to go for a few weeks somewhere near enough for me to get up to town, as I can't get any holiday just now. We want to get braced up. We have never been to Brighton, and I know you know it and I should be very grateful if you could recommend a hotel there to start with. Even if it was expensive for us, it would not matter so much, as we could look about for a cheaper one when we got there. Brighton is a very easy journey with good early trains. It is no use my wasting time looking about – so could you tell me of the hotels you know there?

We should both love to come to Garsington as soon as we are back and recuperated. If we stayed away as long as three weeks the 20th would be too soon, but might we fix the week or the fortnight afterwards? I will get [Wyndham] Lewis – I have not seen him for a number of weeks. Unless he is particularly interested in Eights Week!

I did enjoy seeing you, so much, that brief afternoon, and you *looked* so well – I hope you are. Vivien will write very soon, and longs to see you; she had been intending to write for some days, but not up to it.

Have you read Murry's books? I cannot get up enough interest at the moment.

Yours always affectionately
Tom.

TO *Mary Hutchinson* MS Texas

Thursday [27 April 1922] [12 Wigmore St]

My dear Mary

Be it so – I trust your judgment. I hope your news of Massine[1] at the Coliseum is true, as I have been to see him and thought him more brilliant and beautiful than ever – if what you said was sincere it is I consider a

1 – Léonide Massine (1896–1979), Russian dancer and choreographer, joined Diaghilev and the Ballet Russe de Monte Carlo. TSE called him 'the greatest mimetic dancer in the world' ('Commentary', C. 3: 9, Oct. 1924, 5).

great compliment, as I (having never been so close before) quite fell in love with him. I want to meet him more than ever, and he is a genius.

About us to dinner – we are both so run down that I am writing to one or two places near London with a view to our going away for two or three weeks, where I can get up to town. We should try to get away toward the end of the week, or sooner if possible, so we can make no engagements at the moment. We should have loved to come, but – and this Wigmore [Street flat] is a difficult place to live in, and we can't get back till June, and are both *very* seedy, so I think it is a good idea. But I hope to see Massine with you. I enjoyed our Piccadilly tea so much.

Yrs ever aff
T.

Will ring you up early in the week.

TO *Leonard Woolf*

MS Berg

6 May 1922 — 12 Wigmore St

Dear Leonard

I am so sorry and anxious to hear that Virginia is ill again.[1] I pray that it is not serious, and hope to hear of her progress. Do give her my sincere sympathy: we know what constant illness is, and I think very few people do.[2] I hope that I shall see you both soon.

Sincerely yours
T. S. Eliot

TO *Charles du Bos*[3]

MS Texas

7 May 1922 — 12 Wigmore St

Monsieur,

I am writing to express my thanks for your admirable translation of my chronicle.[4] It is not simply that you have been faithful to the sense, but

1–VW had told Roger Fry on 6 Apr. that she had 'the most violent cold in the whole parish' (*Letters*, II, 525).

2–He was to publish her essay 'On Being Ill', *NC* 4: 1 (Jan. 1926).

3–Charles du Bos (1882–1939), French man of letters.

4–'Lettre d'Angleterre', *NRF* 18 (May 1922), 617–24. Jacques Rivière also said the *chronique* was excellent (4 Mar. 1922). A revised English text appeared, as 'A Preface to Modern Literature: Being a Conspectus Chiefly of English Poetry, Addressed to an Intelligent and Inquiring Foreigner', in *Vanity Fair* 21: 3 (Nov. 1923), 44, 118.

that you have improved the expression; so that the article is actually *better written* than it was in English. I have compared the text, and note several pleonasms and bad phrases which you have ingeniously removed. Your knowledge of English must be quite remarkable, and I shall hope and trust that anything I write will pass through your hands.

I hope also that we may meet on my next visit to Paris.

Je vous prie, Monsieur, d'accepter l'expression de mes sentiments empressés.[1]

T. S. Eliot

TO *Richard Aldington* — PC Texas

[Postmark 12 May 1922] Castle Hotel, Tunbridge Wells

Thanks very much for your two letters, will answer on Sunday. Have retired here for a needed change of air, coming up every day – Very grateful thanks.

Aff.
T.

TO *Ottoline Morrell* — MS Texas

[17? May 1922] Castle Hotel, Tunbridge Wells [Kent]

My dear Ottoline

You see we have finally come to Tunbridge Wells. We had to give up the idea of Brighton because it proved to be too far for me to come up every day. Lewis rang me up on Saturday and said that you wished to change our visit to the 16th June. That will suit us very well, and is a happy coincidence. I have just had an invitation from my father-in-law to spend a fortnight in Italy, and have just arranged to get away for a fortnight of my holiday at the end of the week so I should have been writing to you today in any case. So I shall be away from the 20th May till the *4th June*, and shall look forward to seeing you the following weekend. Vivien is here with me; she cannot decide whether to take the opportunity to come as far as Paris with me and stay there while I am in Italy, or to go miserably to the seaside in further search of health. She is very seedy, and also in the middle of an attack of your kind of neuralgia. She sends you her love, and

1 – 'I beg you, sir, to accept an assurance of my attentive regards.'

says that in any case she will be back in time for the weekend at Garsington.

I think this visit to Italy will just save me from another breakdown, which I felt was impending.

Yours affectionately
Tom.

TO *Richard Aldington* MS Texas

17 May 1922 Castle Hotel, Tunbridge Wells

My dear Richard,

I am very much beholden to you for your last two letters, so far unanswered, which have given me pleasure. I think you must have written a clear and business-like letter to Richmond (and I divine a good scheme behind it)[1] as he wrote a clear and business-like reply. Richmond has been unfailingly kind to me, and about my repeated delays in producing an article on Seneca has been angelic.[2]

I simply do not know what Ezra has in mind, except what his letters tell me. I have had another letter from him, not referring to Bel Esprit, but a very nice one, about the Review. But that will keep till I see you. Meanwhile I am off on Saturday to Lugano for a fortnight's rest; I hope to cross over into Italy and see Ezra for a few days. I will write you from there. My brain has run down, so that at present I have to flog it for hours to produce the feeblest result, and my last effort, before going away, is to fulfill my engagement to the *Dial* for a *July* Letter. Tell me candidly what you think of my chronicles in the *N.R.F.* and the current *Dial*. I never know when this sort of job passes muster and when not.

The Lit. [*TLS*] page is a miserable affair, but are *you* getting any money out of it?

1–RA wrote to Amy Lowell on 5 May: 'T. S. Eliot is very ill, will die if he doesn't get proper and complete rest for a long time. A scheme is on foot to raise the money by asking a selected number of people to contribute £10 a year towards the nucleus of an income for him. About £80 has been promised already in England and more is hoped for; also I have a guarantee from the *Literary Supplement* that they will take at least £100 a year's worth of articles from him.' After EP had published 'Credit and the Fine Arts . . . A Practical Application', RA wrote again to Lowell on 7 July: 'I had a long talk with Eliot, who pointed out that we were all being made ridiculous and that he could not possibly accept such hare-brained propositions as Ezra's scheme involved. I quite agreed with him, but I still thought then that my private scheme might have worked out independent of Ezra' (*Richard Aldington: An Autobiography in Letters*, ed. Norman T. Gates [1992], 67–9).

2–TSE's article on Seneca never appeared.

I have felt a little better for being here. Vivien will be writing to your wife in reply to her very kind letter. I add my thanks to hers in advance. I must say at once however, that even from here, with a perfect and quick train service, and at a hotel only one step from the station, I find that the journey minimises the benefit. I know of old, that if there is the slightest uncertainty or anxiety about catching trains, I get no benefit out of the country. From here I arrive at Cannon Street, from Aldermaston I should have a further journey from Paddington to the Bank, and I should have to get up in the morning about 6.30. Of course I should have loved being at Aldermaston, and of course Vivien would, but it would be very unwise for me to attempt it. Could I have had a holiday at that time, it would have been perfect for us. I am going to Italy at the invitation and expense of my father-in-law, and by good luck this next fortnight was possible – so it was all arranged very quickly. I needed the holiday now, and the offer of a fortnight in Italy without expense came at the right time.

We are very grateful to you both – You do not know how valuable your encouragement has always been to me, *en outre* [besides]. I hope to see you in June – you leave the day I return – but as soon as you are back.

Yrs ever aff.
Tom

TO *Edgar Jepson* — MS Beinecke

19 May 1922 — 12 Wigmore St, W.1

My dear Jepson,

I am very glad to have your book,[1] and I very highly appreciate your sending it to me. I have read it and shall read it again, and I like it very much. It also seems to me well written and perfectly sincere – which seems to me a very great compliment indeed! I should like to discuss parts of it with you at leisure. I am off tomorrow for a fortnight's <needed> holiday, having been invited to spend it at Lugano. I hope to see Pound while there, as he is in Italy, and I hope to see you very soon after my return.

With grateful thanks,
Yours sincerely,
T. S. Eliot

1–Probably *The Religion of the Life Force* (written under the pseudonym R. Edison Page); reviewed in the *TLS*, 18 May 1922, 327: 'perhaps the best thing about this little book is its optimism. Mr. Page believes that man, "the Life Force at its highest and most powerful," is developing into "a final superhuman race".'

I am also looking forward to showing you a poem I have written this winter, and getting your judgment.

TO *Antonio Marichalar* MS Real Academia de la Historia

20 May 1922 12 Wigmore St

Monsieur,[1]

Je vous prie d'accepter toutes mes excuses; je n'ai pas répondu à votre gracieuse lettre du 11 avril, ma santé m'ayant empêché de m'occuper de mes affaires. Je vous serais bien reconnaissant de votre collaboration. Naturellement, la choix du sujet est à vous, mais au début, un essai critique sur la littérature espagnole contemporaine serait bien à propos.

Puisque la revue ne peut pas paraître avant le mois de septembre ou octobre, je vous écrirai plus tard pour vous rappeler votre promesse.

Croyez, monsieur, que nous sommes très fiers de votre collaboration, et agréez l'expression de toute ma sympathie.

T. S. Eliot

J'attends avec un grand intérêt le numéro de *Indice*.[2] Vous trouverez un petit chronique de moi dans la *Nouvelle Revue Française* pour le mois de mai.[3]

TO *Gilbert Seldes* MS Beinecke

20 May 1922 12 Wigmore St

My dear Mr Seldes,

Thank you for your letter of the 4th inst. Yes, I have got *Ulysses*, and am toiling over it fitfully, and hope to produce a 'full dress' review in a month

1 – *Translation*: Dear Sir, Please accept my sincere apologies; I did not reply to your kind letter of 11 April, my health preventing me from tackling any business. I will be very glad of your participation. Naturally, the choice of subject is up to you, but at the outset, a critical essay on contemporary Spanish literature would be most appropriate.

Since the review cannot appear before September or October, I will write later to remind you of your promise.

Believe me, dear Sir, that we are very proud of your participation, and I send my very best wishes. T. S. Eliot

I look forward with great interest to the issue of *Indice*. You will find a little chronicle by me in the May *Nouvelle Revue Française*.

2 – *Indice*: Spanish review edited by Juan Ramón Jimenez.

3 – TSE, 'Lettre d'Angleterre', *NRF* 18 (1 May 1922).

or so. It is a big job. I also have under way a long delayed article on Marianne Moore.

I apologise for the enclosed 'Letter' (July) for two reasons. First, my health having given out again, I have been living at a hotel outside of town and have written this (the only thing I have written for two months) under great difficulties, so I hope you will excuse MSS. instead of typescript. I should feel less apologetic about this if I thought it a good 'Letter'. You were kind enough to say that the last had a good press – I was not satisfied with it myself, and I am sure that this is inferior. It has been accomplished under great strain, but that will not excuse its shortcomings.

I am writing on the eve of a 4t nights holiday, but please address me here until June. On June 20th I return to 9 Clarence Gate Gardens N.W.1.

I think the last number, barring my 'Letter', is a *very good one*.

Sincerely yours
T. S. Eliot

I *hope* my writing can be read!

I apologise and am keenly aware both of the excessive brevity and the inferiority. I have been out of touch with things, and my mind is in a very deteriorated state, due to illness and worry. Had it been possible to withhold this over my holiday, I should not be sending it, and if you think it too poor to use, do not scruple to throw it in the basket.

TO *Richard Cobden-Sanderson* MS Texas

20 May 1922 12 Wigmore St

Dear Cobden-Sanderson,

I have not been idle during the last two months, although I have been handicapped by a good deal of illness and worry. This is just to tell you that I have copied out a list of about six hundred names and addresses from the Hogarth Press, but I think I had better type it out so that your staff can read it. I am just off for a fortnight's holiday which I badly need, being rather run down, and hope you will be in town at the beginning of June. I will ring you up immediately on my return, so that we can arrange an early meeting.

With best wishes for your health.

Sincerely
T. S. Eliot

TO *Alfred A. Knopf* MS Texas

20 May 1922 12 Wigmore St

Dear Mr Knopf,

Thank you for your kind letter of the 1st inst. It is true that I am most anxious to publish my poem in America in the autumn, on account of copyright. I shall hope within a year or so to have a prose book to offer you.

With best wishes, I am
Yours faithfully,
T. S. Eliot

TO *Leonard Woolf* MS Princeton

20 May 1922 12 Wigmore St

Dear Woolf,

Your letter and MS. arrived just in time, as I am just leaving for a 4tnight's holiday. I am delighted to have this Dostoevski, and should like very much to know how much more there is or will be of this chapter, and whether the rest cd be printed in subsequent issues [of the *Criterion*].[1] Also how soon are you anxious to bring it out as a book. I cannot use this till October as it is impossible to start in June.

The paper would pay, by the way, at first at the rate of £10 per 5000 words, and it would not be *lower* than that, later.

I have been invited to Lugano for a fortnight and shall be back early in June. I should be glad to hear that Virginia is well again: it takes some time for a person to pull up again after these high temperatures –.

With many thanks
Yours
T. S. Eliot

Poste Restante – Lugano

1–See F. M. Dostoevsky, 'Plan of the Novel, "The Life of a Great Sinner"' (trans. S. S. Koteliansky and VW), *C.* 1: 1 (Oct. 1922), 16–33.

TO *Hermann Hesse* MS Schweizerisches Literaturachiv

24 May 1922 Hotel Bristol, Lugano [Switzerland]

Lieber u. geehrter Herr Hesse,

Sie werden sich erinnern, dass ich Ihnen aus London geschrieben habe. Jetzt bin ich nach Lugano gekommen, und bleibe noch zehn Tage. Es wäre mir eine grosse Ehre und Vergnügen, wenn ich Sie besuchen möchte, und mit dem Verfasser von 'Blick ins Chaos' sprechen. Ich habe ganz klar gestgestellt, dass ich nur wening wenig deutsch kann hier ohne Wörterbuch oder Dolmetscher! Jedenfalls würde ich mit Ihnen eine Unterhaltung haben.

Möchte ich Sie einladen, auf Frietag oder Samstag Thee zu nehmen?

Empfangen Sie, lieber Herr Hesse, der Austruck meiner besonderer Hochachtung.

T. S. Eliot[1]

TO *Mary Hutchinson* PC Texas

[Postmark 27 May 1922] Lugano

Specialità Asti Spumante fresca Barolo Lagrima Christi PILSNER URQUELLE oggi sera festa di lago illuminazione del lido fuochi di artifice.

Soit que tu vives près de Dieu
Ou aux Champs Elysées, adieu,
Adieu 1000 fois, adieu Marie . . .[2]

1 – *Translation*: Dear and esteemed Herr Hesse, You will remember that I wrote to you from London. I have now arrived in Lugano and am staying here for another ten days. It would be a great honour and pleasure if I could visit you and speak with the author of *In Sight of Chaos*. I have made it clear that I know only a little German here without a dictionary or interpreter! Nevertheless I would love to have a conversation with you.

Could I invite you to have tea on either Friday or Sunday?

Please accept, Herr Hesse, the expression of my greatest respects. T. S. Eliot

2 – Sent from Italian-speaking Switzerland, this polyglot postcard can be loosely translated: 'Specialities fresh Asti Spumante Barolo Lachrima Christi PILSNER URQUELLE today there's a lake festival the lido in lights fireworks.

Whether you live near God
Or the Champs Elysées, adieu
A thousand times adieu, Marie . . .'

TO *Ottoline Morrell* PC Texas

28 May 1922 Lugano

I wonder if you know this lake – it is very beautiful, though too much hotels, casino, and American trippers. But smothered in roses and wisteria. I shd like six months of Italy and heat and sunshine, and have never felt quite so lazy and languid.

Ever affectionately
T.S.E.

TO *Conrad Aiken* PC Huntington

[Postmark 31 May 1922] [Lugano]

I recommend this place as comfortably warm, with good bathing, and free from the picture galleries etc. which are such a nuisance in Italy proper. Back some time next week. Hope you are both well.

T.S.E.

TO *Hermann Hesse* PC Schweizerisches Literaturarchiv

[Postmark 31 May 1922] [Lugano]

Ich empfange Ihre Dichtung mit Freude und herzlichen Dank. Ich werde sie bei meiner Reise nach Mailand lesen. Sonntag fahr ich nach London – 6. Ich erinnere ich mich immer an meinem Besuch bei Ihnen.

T. S. Eliot[1]

TO *Sydney Schiff* MS BL

[Early June 1922] [London]

My dear Sydney,

I am very glad to hear that you are back. Your letter to the Bank finally reached me, and I was sorry not to have seen you in Paris; but I did not stop there at all, as my time was so limited and my holiday was for the

1 – *Translation*: I received your book with pleasure and many thanks. I will read it on my journey to Milan. I return to London on Sunday – 6th. I am still full of memories of my visit to you. T. S. Eliot

purpose of health. I was feeling very low indeed and had completely given up writing letters to anybody. Lugano was delightful – Hesse was there too – and walking and boating and bathing were good for me, and I also went to Verona and saw Pound. Now I am plunging into work on Lady Rothermere's review – and shall be immersed in that for many weeks. But I hope to see you and have a talk soon – I will come in on *Saturday* at 5 if I don't hear to the contrary. We have missed you.

Yours aff.
T.S.E.

TO *Jacques Rivière*[1]

TS Texas

10 June 1922 9 Clarence Gate Gdns, London N.W.1

Cher monsieur,

Je viens de rentrer à Londres après une vacance en Italie, et je m'empresse de vous répondre. Je n'ai pas du tout oublié ma promesse, mais me voici à ce moment écrasé par des devoirs manqués et par des affaires personnelles. Aurez-vous la patience de me permettre de renouveler la promesse à l'échéance? Mon portefeuille est vide, j'ai très peu écris – sauf quelques poésies – depuis six mois. Vous ne voulez que de la prose?

Je suis occupé d'une nouvelle revue qui va paraître à Londres, dont je vous enverrai un exemplaire lors de sa parution.

Wyndham Lewis est un de nos meilleurs écrivains (et certainement notre meilleur peintre); peut-être il pourrait vous envoyer un conte.[2] Adresse:

Lee Studio
Adam and Eve Mews
Allen Street
Kensington
London, W.8

Agréez, cher monsieur, l'expression des mes sentiments très distingués.

T. S. Eliot[3]

1 – The original letter has no addressee, but is presumably addressed to Jacques Rivière to whom TSE had earlier promised another piece for *Nouvelle Revue Française*.

2 – Nothing by WL was published in *NRF* in the following year.

3 – *Translation*: 'Dear Sir, I have just got back to London after a holiday in Italy, and I am replying immediately. I have by no means forgotten my promise, but at the moment I am overwhelmed by deferred business and personal matters. Would you have the patience to allow me to renew the promise at its maturity? My portfolio is empty – I have written very little – except some poems – since six months ago. Do you only want prose?

I am busy with a new review which is going to appear in London, a copy of which I will send you on its publication.

TO *Leonard Woolf* MS Princeton

10 June 1922 12 Wigmore St, London W.1

Dear Woolf,

I should very much like to publish the Dostoevski, but am thinking over the matter carefully – [1]

If you and Koteliansky[2] could have ready by the 1st September or the 1st November (i.e. for the first or second number) some of either of the other writers, I think this would be better. For the reason that it would obviously [be] impossible to print the whole of the Dostoevski chapter. There is also this point, that the Dostoevski is coming out in the *Nouvelle Revue Française*.[3]

But if it is unlikely that you could have either of the other writers in time, I should certainly consider using the first part alone. I should prefer Rosanov or the correspondence, but in any case could you let me know soon whether you <and K.> could promise it, as I shall want to advertise some of the principal contents of the first two numbers in advance.

Sincerely yours
T. S. Eliot

TO *T. Sturge Moore* MS Texas

11 June 1922 12 Wigmore St

Dear Mr Sturge Moore

It would be quite possible, I think, to publish in the quarterly such an essay as you outline, as it appears to fall into two distinct parts – so that

—

Wyndham Lewis is one of our best writers (and certainly our best painter). Perhaps he would be able to send you a story. Address:

[etc.]

Accept, my dear sir, my most sincere good wishes. T. S. Eliot

1 – LW sent the translation on 25 May, adding that Koteliansky was also offering to translate either the correspondence between 'the best living Russian poet and the best living Russian critic' or the *pensées* of V. V. Razanov (1856–1919), a reactionary avant-garde writer (*Letters of Leonard Woolf*, ed. Frederic Spotts, 1990, 282–3).

2 – Born in a Jewish shtetl in the Ukraine, S. S. Koteliansky (1882–1955), 'Kot', as he was known to friends, moved in 1911 to London where he befriended DHL, LW, VW, JMM, and Katherine Mansfield (whom he adored), and the artist Mark Gertler. In 1923–4, he was business manager of *The Adelphi*. He translated into English several Russian writers including Dostoevsky and Chekhov. See further: John Carswell, *Lives and Letters: A. R. Orage, Beatrice Hastings, Katherine Mansfield, John Middleton Murry, S. S. Koteliansky: 1906–1957* (1978).

3 – Dostoievski, 'La Confession de Stavroguine', published in *NRF* in two parts: 18 (June 1922), 647–65; 19 (July 1922), 30–57.

the lapse of three months would not seriously matter. I must express my great pleasure at hearing that my hope of support from you is so near to being realised. Could you let me know the title of the essay and the probable length of each part – also when the first part is likely to be ready?[1]

I only hope that you will have reason to be satisfied with the company in which your work will appear.

Yours very truly
T. S. Eliot

TO *Richard Cobden-Sanderson* MS Beinecke

12 June 1922 12 Wigmore St

Dear Cobden-Sanderson,

I trust that you are back in town now. Will you come and see me as soon as possible? Could you dine with me on *Thursday*, say at the Cock – or if more convenient I could come to see you at 5.30 or could meet in the evening.

Sincerely yours
T. S. Eliot

TO *Ottoline Morrell* MS Texas

15 June 1922 12 Wigmore St

My dear Ottoline,

I am afraid there has been a misunderstanding about the weekend. Vivien I find was under the impression that I had arranged about it with you at dinner. For she knew that I had already told her that I could not leave London for a weekend until she went to Bosham in July. Perhaps I have not sufficiently explained to you or to anyone that through my ill health and inability to cope with anything I have kept Lady Rothermere waiting to bring out her Review, for a whole year. That is one of the reasons why I took my holiday early, to prepare myself for the next three months of entire concentration on this one object. Lady Rothermere has

1 – T. Sturge Moore, 'The Story of Tristram and Isolt in Modern Poetry': I. Narrative Versions (C. 1: 1, Oct. 1922, 39–49); 'The Story of Tristram and Isolt in English Poetry': II. Dramatic Versions (C. 1: 2, Jan. 1923, 171–87).

been so extraordinarily good about all this delay that I now owe it to her to push the Review forward with the greatest possible speed. I shall not go out anywhere and must not contemplate any weekends. I wish we could have come at the same time as Lewis, as was previously arranged. If I was a man of leisure and had not three weeks only of holiday a year, how many nice things I could do – but one is always disliked for one's hardships I find!

Vivien asks me to tell you that she has, since seeing you, and greatly on account of your having urged it, gone to a wholly new specialist, who immediately diagnosed her whole trouble as *glands*. Most of her glands are not working at all. In addition to this there is poisoning from colitis. These two things more than account, the specialist says, for all her symptoms. He has outlined for her a perfectly new and violent cure, which she has already begun. She is to have the glands of animals, but of course this at present is purely experimental, and it may take a long time before they find the right glands. In addition to that she is to have a very strong internal disinfection, going without food *completely* for two days a week.

She sends you her best love and hopes this cure will prove scientific enough.

We can only look forward to seeing you again.

Yours affectionately
Tom.

TO *Wyndham Lewis* TS Cornell

18 June 1922[1] 12 Wigmore St

Dear Lewis,

I am very sorry to find that tomorrow afternoon will be impossible – we are getting in – or starting to get in to Clarence Gate on Tuesday, and I have got to see a furniture remover here tomorrow, and that is my only time to do it. Do forgive me, I hope not to have to move again for some time, and will *Tuesday* be possible for you – if not perhaps Wednesday? I want particularly to see you as soon as possible. Will you let me know about Tuesday, and I hope I have not deranged any plans of yours.

Yours ever
T.S.E.

1 – TSE wrote '18. vi. 21'.

TO *John Quinn* TELEGRAM NYPL (MS)

21 June 1922

DISSATISFIED LIVERIGHTS CONTRACT POEM MAY I ASK YOUR ASSISTANCE APOLOGIES WRITING ELIOT.

FROM *John Quinn* TELEGRAM NYPL (MS)

22 June 1922

GLAD TO ASSIST EVERYWAY POSSIBLE YOUR CONTRACT CABLE WHETHER SHALL SEE LIVERIGHT OR AWAIT YOUR LETTER QUINN.[1]

TO *Mary Hutchinson* MS Texas

Friday [23 June 1922] 9 Clarence Gate Gdns, N.W.1

Dear Mary,

I want to write this note just to tell you how much I enjoyed the evening. I liked Massine very much indeed – with no disappointment – and hope that I shall see him again. He was much as I expected him to be. I enjoyed the whole evening and thought it perfect. It was very sweet of you to have arranged it. I am sorry to hear that you *expected* me to dinner – I thought it was left that I could either come to dinner or pick you up afterwards. As a matter of fact, I was having a sitting with Lewis for a drawing and did not get home till nearly eight; so I just had time to wash and change and eat something and reach the restaurant by 9.30. Of course I was disappointed not to have dinner with you as well; I expected at least to arrive early enough to find you in the middle of dinner.

I am rather tired – I went out to a dinner and a dance last night, while Vivien starved; and enjoyed myself, and got off with the Aga Khan, and finished up the evening at Wigmore Street where I ended the vermouth and packed my clothes, rather fun. I hope I shall see you next week.

With love,
Tom.

1 – Quinn followed up with a letter the same day: 'you don't have to tie up with Liveright. I could easily arrange for your next book with another publisher', adding that he had heard from EP 'that you had finished a very fine poem of, I think, some twenty pages, which would shortly appear in the *Dial*'.

Do you think Massine liked me? and would he come and see me, do you think?

TO *John Quinn* TS NYPL (MS)

25 June 1922 Clarence Gate Gdns

Dear Mr Quinn,

I was overjoyed to get your cable last night, generously giving me your help. I must say to begin with that I was very loath to trouble you in this affair, as the original book with Knopf had given you such endless difficulty and taken so much of your time. Had I not had this in mind, I should have consulted you at the very beginning of the negotiations with Liveright. It is only that I now see no other possible way of settling the matter, that I have appealed to you; and I thank you from the depth of my heart for your kindness.

I have written, mostly when I was at Lausanne for treatment last winter, a long poem of about 450 lines,[1] which, with notes that I am adding, will make a book of thirty or forty pages. I think it is the best I have ever done, and Pound thinks so too. Pound introduced me to Liveright in Paris, and Liveright made me the offer of 15 per cent royalty and $150 in advance. I thought I ought to give Knopf the option, and did so; but Knopf said that it was too late for his autumn list this year, and Liveright offered to publish it this autumn, so I cabled to him to say he could have it. I then received the letter and memoranda of agreement which I enclose, and after some days deliberation decided to cable to you.

I think you will agree that the form of agreement is extremely vague and gives all the advantage to the publisher. I wish exactly the same terms that you made for me with Knopf: i.e. American (and Canadian) rights only, *book* rights only, copyright in author's name, and contents to belong to me when this book is out of print. As I read Liveright's form, it practically gives him world rights, translation rights, periodical rights, anthology rights, and seems tantamount to selling him the book outright for $150. I do not know the 'term of the standard contract of the Authors' League of America', and it seems to me that the question of what matters are 'not specifically covered' might involve litigation.

1–TSE typed 'words'.

I am writing to Liveright to say that I am placing the agreement in your hand, that you have Power of Attorney to act for me, and that I am leaving the entire question of the terms of contract to you.

I cannot see any reason why he should not give a proper formal contract, and if he will not make the same terms as Knopf I authorise you to withdraw the poem from him altogether.

I am sending you as quickly as possible a copy of the poem merely for your own interest, and I shall send you later the complete typescript with the notes, in the form to be handed to the publisher. Liveright said he would print it for the autumn if he had the poem by the end of July.

There are other matters which I have been waiting for an opportunity to write to you about, but I will write of them later, as it would take much space and time. The last nine months have been months of illness and anxiety and worry; otherwise there are several letters that I should have written you. I am ashamed to be writing now only to ask another sacrifice of time and thought from a man who has far too many demands upon him. But there is simply no one else in ~~New York~~ America whom I can ask, or trust, in a matter like this.

With my very great gratitude,

sincerely yours,
T. S. Eliot

TO *Sydney Schiff* TS BL

25 June 1922 9 Clarence Gate Gdns

Dear Sydney,

Thank you very much for your letter. It is very good of you to offer me 'The Thief', which you know I liked particularly. I should be exceedingly glad to have it. Of course I do not want to interfere with your arrangements with the *Dial*; and it is difficult to make appearance in a quarterly coincide with that in a monthly; but if the *Dial* could use the other sketches first I should be very glad indeed. I should like to use 'The Thief' in the second number (December),[1] as I have a great deal of material which I have promised to put in the first, and I am afraid I shall have to postpone some of that. After the first number it will be easier fitting things in.

And of course it would be a help if I could have it as soon as possible, as I am trying to make up the two numbers as exactly as possible now.

1–SS's story 'The Thief' was to be published in *C.* 1: 2 (Jan. 1923), 188–91.

Vivien sends her love to you and Violet, and would have rung Violet up today for a talk, but knew your Sundays were always very much occupied. She is dreadfully tired by the moving and as we are now not quite satisfied with the result of this new treatment she is seeing another doctor tomorrow or the next day and had better keep quiet till after that. Although we feel that we have got on the right direction now, the starvation is producing other symptoms which make me feel that some modification is necessary; and we have heard of another man who uses the same treatment but very much better. She says she will ring up directly this wretched time of uncertainty is over.

Yours always affectionately,
T.S.E.

TO *John Quinn* TELEGRAM NYPL (MS)

26 June 1922

VERY GRATEFUL PLEASE WAIT LETTER ELIOT

Vivien Eliot TO *Ezra Pound* TS Lilly

27 June 1922 9 Clarence Gate Gdns

Dear Ezra,

Tom reported your conversation to me about glands a little while after he got home. I was very much interested, and I have been trying to write to you ever since, but have had a great many practical things to do in the way of moving from Wigmore Street to here for instance, and have also been in very much worse health for the last month than for a very long time. I could not even write now but for having someone to take it down for me.

I was forced to go to a specialist about a fortnight ago for my skin, and he mentioned glands as being the probable cause of some of my troubles. I must say I have often thought of this as a possibility myself. This doctor also found Colitis which of course I knew I had, and has given me a very violent treatment which I do not think will be of any use. He gave me some glands to take called Ovarian Opocaps and told me that this was a 'shot in the dark'. I think that English doctors are more fond of 'shots in the dark' than any treatment based on scientific knowledge. It appeals to the 'sporting' side of the English character. I have taken these glands (they are in cachets) for a fortnight, and so far of course have not noticed any result whatever. I shall go on with them for a month as he told me to. Meanwhile I should be more than glad if you could make enquiries as you suggested to Tom, and so I will now give you a list of symptoms.

First of all, Colitis. This is, I am told, a symptom in itself. It may apparently be a symptom of anything, nobody seems to know what.

Temperature. I very often have a temperature of 99.4 for two or three weeks at a time for no obvious reason.

Increasing mental incapacity. I have a horror of using my mind and spend most of my time in trying to avoid contact with people or anything that will force me to use my mind.

Physical Exhaustion.

Insomnia. This has been going on for eight years.

Migraines.

I cannot think of anything else at the moment, but I should think this should be enough to go on with.

I should have great faith in anything you suggest, and I only hope you are still as interested in the subject of glands as you were when Tom saw you in Italy. It is so dreadful to be stuck in ill-health as I am, and one becomes at last dull and hopeless about it.

This is an extremely stupid letter.

Unless any disaster prevents it I am going to Paris on September 29th with Tom who will then take a week's holiday. I hope I shall see you then. If I am no better by then I shall be prepared to go on to Switzerland or Germany, or any place with intelligent doctors. I have taken a cottage in the country for two months and am going there in a fortnight. Give my love to Dorothy.

Tom received a sort of memorandum from Liveright which was extremely vague and unsatisfactory, so much so that Tom decided that he could not sign it. He thought the best thing to do would be cable to Quinn and put the whole matter of the contract into his hands. He has done this and Quinn has replied that he will gladly see to it and take all responsibility.

Yours ever
Vivien

[In TSE's hand:]

Vivien has shown me this letter and I think it is *quite inadequate* as a description of her case, but she is *very* ill and exhausted and I do not think she can do any better now. I will write to you a little later and go much more into detail and the history of her illness, as I am sure there is a lot more you would like to know.

Yrs always
T.

TO *Richard Cobden-Sanderson* TS Beinecke

27 June 1922 9 Clarence Gate Gdns

Dear Cobden-Sanderson,

I have delayed answering your letter of the 23rd June until after discussing the matter with Lady Rothermere.

We both think that owing to the delays which the 'Review' has suffered and the current rumours of its having been abandoned, that it is highly desirable that an announcement should appear as soon as possible, and I think that I explained to you my personal reasons for believing that this would be a good step.

Of course, neither Lady Rothermere or myself knows what the expense of such a circular would be. As soon as I can get a copy for the circular into your hands, would it be possible for you to obtain an estimate in the course of a few days? I think that the circular should be out by the middle of July. Of course it would be only a preliminary announcement and a more detailed circular would follow in September. As you say, the first circular may not have much effect upon the general recipients, but I think that the effect upon certain groups in London should justify its existence.

I gather that you do not think that the preliminary circular would actually have an injurious effect, but it is simply, from a publishing point of view, a superfluity?

I raised with Lady Rothermere the question of the title and brought out the points upon which you and I agreed that 'London Review' was a weak name.

We have finally decided upon *The Criterion*, a title suggested by my wife which I think combines the various advantages which we sought. Do you not think so?

I will let you have the copy for the circular quickly and if necessary will arrange to see you at once with regard to any points about it that need discussion.

Meanwhile I hope to hear from you, and hope to get you to dine with me as soon as my affairs are in order.

Yours sincerely,
T. S. Eliot

Thank you very much for your letter.

TO *T. Sturge Moore* TS Texas

27 June 1922 9 Clarence Gate Gdns

Dear Mr Sturge Moore,

Thank you for your letter of the 22nd June.

I am very sorry to ask any contributor and especially yourself to condense his work, and I hope that as the review develops this will cease to be necessary. Of course I should not wish you to omit any important part of the essay, but I fear that it will be impossible at present to exceed very far the limit of 5000 words inasmuch as the total contents of the review will probably not exceed 30,000 words. It is entirely a question of the means at our disposal.

I am very glad to have your title and look forward to reading the first part of your essay as soon as it is ready. Do you think it would be possible for you to have the first part for me by the 1st of August?

Yours sincerely,
T. S. Eliot

TO *Richard Aldington* TS Texas

30 June 1922 9 Clarence Gate Gdns

My dear Richard,

It has been one of my first desires to write to you fully ever since I got back, but there have been very great preoccupations.

As for myself, my holiday in Switzerland was extremely successful as the weather was perfect and I passed my time in boating, bathing, eating, sleeping and making little trips about the lake. It is sufficient to say that I continue to be in very much better health than before I left; in fact in better physical health than I was when I came back from Switzerland in January.

During the last three weeks we have had all the horrors of moving back to this flat involving a great deal of detail, and also quarrelling with the landlord of the other flat as well as the labour of extracting damages from the tenant I had in this flat. At the same time my wife's health has got very much worse, no doubt accelerated in its decline by removing, during which process she has had the fatigue and strain of interviewing two Harley Street men. The first one prescribed two days complete starvation which only had the effect of weakening her resources still further. The other one decided against the starvation and has given considerable useful advice, but no explanation. They agreed that she is a very bad case of Colitis, and one of them considers that there is also a defective secretion of glands.

We have taken a very small cottage near Bosham, but of course I shall only be able to go at weekends. If we can get a satisfactory woman to come in by the day I am sure that the country would be beneficial.

When my wife received your letter enclosing Ezra's while I was away she immediately wired to you to ask for Ezra's address. She did not however get your letter for several days as she was at Eastbourne, and that is the reason why she wired instead of writing. I cannot understand why the wire was never received.

As you probably know, I went to Verona and had about two days with Ezra. He was extremely delightful, but I must say that the scheme which we discussed is at present in such a nebulous state that the time has not yet come either for accusing me of excessive cautiousness or of endeavouring to bring influence upon me through my wife who has felt quite rightly that she could not accept the responsibility of endeavouring to influence me.

You see, she was at the time very much in favour of me accepting the post which Murry offered me on the *Athenaeum*, and as I rejected that offer upon my own instinct, and as my instinct proved entirely correct, she would be all the more hesitant on a second occasion.

Ezra says that the kind of subscribers whom he is likely to get in France and in America are people of small means who could not afford to put down bonds; in fact he says that some of them have only guaranteed a subscription for five years. He was very vague as to the methods being used in America. He appears to have delegated two or three women in New York and had also written to Quinn but had not yet received his reply.[1] He expressed himself as approving the conditions I laid down so far as it was possible to obtain subscribers of sufficient means.[2] He intended to take no part in a campaign in this country and considers the whole thing here should be left in your hands, and that Wyndham Lewis, Schiff, or anyone else in this country should communicate with you, and act only in concert with you. He kept saying that the principal feature of the Bel Esprit was its extreme flexibility so that people in each country could keep their own methods. His idea of the financial machinery seems to be that people in America should send cheques to him and that he should pass them on to me as received.

1–Quinn pledged $300 per annum for five years.

2–In his efforts to liberate TSE from Lloyds Bank, EP was seeking thirty guarantors of £10 a year for an indefinite period.

Altogether the whole thing is very unsatisfactory, and unless a dignified committee can be formed immediately I see no hope for it whatever. Of course until some definite and reasonable estimate can be formed both of the income, tenure and security, there is nothing that I can either accept or reject. I see no advantage for myself in an indefinite income for five or ten years only.

I say all this without having been in communication with you for many weeks. The situation is embarrassing and fatiguing to me in spite of the motives, which I appreciate. I don't want to find myself in the end offered some unsatisfactory solution. I think you will agree with me on many points and also that the method proposed by Ezra is rather bordering on the precarious and slightly undignified charity. At the bank I am at least independent of the people whom I know, and a doubtful income, which I should be obliged to attempt to double by literary work, would not be of the slightest advantage from anyone's point of view.

I am sorry to recur to this subject which I wish was not necessary for me to mention.

I was very much interested by your leader in the *Times*[1] and I thought that the verses quoted had considerable beauty.

Can you do me an article by the first of August? I want to have all the contributions for my first number in by this date as the printers estimate will be based upon them. I depend upon you for the first number and I hope you will lead off by an article reviving the past traditions of criticism. I do not want to launch in a campaign against Murry or [Clutton-]Brock; in fact I wish to be very careful especially at first, not to appear to use the paper as a weapon. I should like to have from you for your first article some piece of criticism of quite a contemporary application rather than the more historical work which I hope you will let me have later. I am putting in the first two sections of my poem and the rest in the second number. Sturge Moore has promised a long essay in two parts.

This has been rather an impersonal letter and there are many more things I should like to say to you.

I hope you will answer all the enquiries about yourself which you know I would make and I shall write to you again very soon.

Yours affectionately,
Tom

I am now forced to employ a typist for a couple of hours twice a week, and I have dictated this letter to her – hence any peculiarities of forced style!

1–RA, 'Cyrano de Bergerac', *TLS*, 29 June 1922, 417–18.

TO *Leonard Woolf* TS Princeton

1 July 1922 9 Clarence Gate Gdns

Dear Leonard,

I am waiting hopefully to know whether the Dostoevski plan or the Tolstoi letters are possible;[1] as I want to send one advance circular to the printer in a few days time, I should very much like to know. Either, of course, would be extremely valuable; I would publish them as soon as was desirable for your own purposes, or give you as long as need be for their preparation.

I do not want to bother Virginia, who I hope is better than she was, but I should like to remind her that she promised me a title.[2] If time worries her, I could just manage until January, but I should like to promise the public that something of hers would appear in an early number. I hope your silence does not mean that she has not been so well. My own faith in the omniscience of physicians has been very much disturbed in the last year or two.

Sincerely yours,
T. S. Eliot

If you see Roger Fry, tell him that I very much hope for something from him soon.

Could you also let me know the name of the woman [Mrs Green] you spoke of who translates from German, as I have not yet found anyone else? I should like to try her on something in the first number.

TO *Sydney Schiff* TS/MS BL

4 July 1922 9 Clarence Gate Gdns

My dear ~~Schiff~~ Sydney,

I have your two notices and Violet's postcard. I am very grateful to you for having written to Proust at once as I realise how difficult it is to turn to such a task in the midst of preparations for departure. I have also written to him, and as you suggested have sent it to his private address. I await consequences eagerly.

1–TSE's hopes were to be realised with the publication of 'A Few Extracts from Letters exchanged between Leo Nicolayevich Tolstoy and N. N. Strakhov relating to F. M. Dostoevsky', trans. S. S. Koteliansky, in C. 3: 10 (Jan. 1925), 164–9.
2–VW had written on 14 Apr. to say she would try to write something of 'less than 5,000 words' by 15 Aug.; she would 'very much like to be edited' by TSE. VW's story 'In the Orchard' was to appear in C. 1: 3 (Apr. 1923).

In my letter I said that I did not know of anyone but yourself who was competent to translate him into English, but that you had volunteered to do it if he was willing to let something of his appear.

I will send the books to Einstein as you suggest. We hope to hear soon that you are benefiting from Crowborough and getting a great deal of work done there.

Affectionately yours,
Tom.

Vivien wishes me to say that she does greatly appreciate and realise the interest which you and Violet take in her health and welfare. She also is grateful for your understanding of her circumstances, a thing which she never even expects from anyone else.

As the review draws near I find my correspondence in connection with it so overwhelming, moreover as I cannot altogether drop my attempts to make money by writing, that I have been absolutely forced to employ a shorthand typist two evenings a week for correspondence. Hence anything strained or impersonal you may notice in my letters.

TO *Richard Aldington* TS Texas

4 July 1922 9 Clarence Gate Gdns

My dear Richard,

I was very glad indeed to get your two long letters and the typed translation, which I have not yet had time to examine and which I want to discuss with you later. Probably the only question about it will be the question that arises first – whether it is possible to include a contribution of such length into a periodical of the small dimensions to which we shall be limited at first, – but the dimensions after the first two numbers will depend on the sales and on the contributions.

I subscribe light heartedly to your terms. All of the subjects you mention sound delightful, but if for the first number of you can think of something of a more immediate pertinence I shall be grateful. I think that £10 was rather a meagre payment but I may have told you that I had some friction with the *Dial* on the question of payment which I thought inadequate for my poem, considering the amount of work I had put into it and also considering the vast amount of verse, which in comparison with most writers, I refrained from writing. I subsequently arranged for publication as a book with Liveright, but I am not pleased with his form of contract and I have now put the whole matter in the hands of Quinn.

Be sure that I fully appreciate all of the difficulties you experience in struggling to accomplish something for me. It certainly cannot interfere with our relations – that is an absurd suggestion – but I only fear that the sporadic activities bursting up unexpectedly in various parts of the world will completely block the progress of the main scheme and everybody concerned be made ridiculous.

I shall henceforward be going down to Bosham for my weekends. I only hope that there is some prospect of your being in town for a night in the immediate future?

I am anxious now to find reliable and not too expensive translators for various languages; at the moment French, German and Spanish, but later I shall probably want Italian and Scandinavian as well. Do you think that [Bruce] Richmond can put me on to anybody? I mean from among the people who write short notices on books in various foreign languages in the Supplement [*TLS*]. And also would you have time and would it be worth your while to do from time to time a certain amount of translation (at the translator's rates to be fixed) from French and Italian?

Yours affectionately,
Tom.

<Have decided on *The Criterion* – Vivien's suggestion.>

TO *Leonard Woolf* — MS Princeton

5 July 1922 — 9 Clarence Gate Gdns

Dear Leonard,

Thank you for your letter of the 3d. I am disappointed over the Tolstoi, and should still like to believe that I might have a few [of Tolstoi's letters] to publish at least just before you published the lot as a book. Do you not think that there might be a few suitable for the review, at least by November 1st? My first number should be out by October 1st.

Of course, failing these, and the Dostoevski plan, I should like to have the Stavrogine. Can you tell me (1) whether the version you would offer me would be the one you already showed me or the other (2) when your other version would appear (3) which is longer? I suppose that either version would occupy two numbers.

Please thank Virginia for her title ['In the Orchard'], which of course she will be at liberty to change; but I trust that will not be necessary. I do hope that Rodmell will be enough to set the doctors' suspicions at rest;

and tell her that when she can write again, I hope that this will be the first thing she will do.

Yours
T. S. Eliot

Roger Fry has promised to get something done on his return.[1]

TO *Ezra Pound* MS Lilly

9 July 1922 9 Clarence Gate Gdns

Caro Ezra,

The title of the Review is *The Criterion.* This title was suggested by Vivien, as *The London Review* seemed colourless and perhaps misleading, and had just been accepted and approved; and your letter arrived as a most auspicious confirmation. <V. had never heard that you had conceived of this title for yours.> I told Lady R. that you had suggested the same title as had been agreed upon two days before, and she was mightily pleased.

Thanks also for your notes on the slave trade,[2] which I am keeping by me, but don't think it is quite the thing to make an impression in an early number – the meaning or implications being too subtle to strike the subscribing public. What about the article on Impressionism which you promised[3] (no need to *boost* joyce as I am reprinting part of Larbaud's essay[4] as testimony that the Review approves of J. J.)? Are you to be relied upon to promise this *by Nov. 1*?

About the '2 Worlds',[5] please let me know about the organisers of it and who the probable star and second star or planetary contributors will be? Is it run and edited by women? Does it approve of the Baroness? <What stuff will it have that I cd use?>

I don't ask for Cantos simply because I know you can get more money from the *Dial*, and I don't want at present to use things which appear *previously* in the *Dial*, and it is difficult to arrange for simultaneous

1 – Roger Fry, 'Mallarmé's "Herodiade"', *C.* 1: 2 (Jan. 1923), 119–26.

2 – Not found.

3 – EP responded: '*On me demande l'histoire de l'impressionisme littéraire en Albion le perfide*' ['I have been asked for a history of literary impressionism in perfidious Albion']. See EP, 'On Criticism in General', *C.* 1: 2 (Jan. 1923), 143–56.

4 – Valery Larbaud, 'The "Ulysses" of James Joyce'.

5 – There may have been plans to launch Samuel Roth's magazine *Two Worlds* (New York), but it did not appear until Sept. 1925 (it ran for eight issues, until Sept. 1926).

publication in a monthly and a quarterly. Otherwise they would be most particularly sought after.[1]

I shall be glad to have a conversation with Berman[2] if he arrives in this country.

I am now waiting to hear whether Quinn has managed to screw Liveright down to a legal contract or not. I hear from other sources that Liveright is an excellent publisher if you have him pinned down by every legal written safeguard – and that he is quite merciless if you don't. Quinn seemed quite willing, and I have had a very amiable letter from him.

Do you recommend anybody in France for the *Criterion*? Also, have you come across anyone who is [at] all informed about Scandinavia? I am *not* anxious to get many French people for the *first two* numbers, more anxious to get other (foreign) nationalities: the French business is so usual (in London) that it doesn't raise a quiver; the only name worth getting is *Proust*, whom I am fishing for. But later, yes, any French stuff that is really *good* no matter who signs it; after two or three numbers could perhaps even afford e.g. Picabia and Benda in the same number. Do you know where Benda is now?

Until the next, if you answer at least some of my questions, O student of the Kama-Sutra [. . .][3] grow fat and libidinous.

Yours ever

T.

Have you ever heard of a man in England named *Hogben*,[4] in connexion with glands?

Vivien is being treated (and the doctor seems to have supplied a very sensible regimen) for colitis, which she has a bad case of; but the doctor himself says that colitis is not a disease but a symptom, and that it may be

1–C. did in fact publish the next instalment of EP's *magnum opus*, 'Malatesta Cantos', in July 1923.

2–Dr Louis Berman (1893–1946), New York endocrinologist; author of *The Glands Regulating Personality* (1921). EP wrote about his glandular medicine in 'The New Therapy' (*New Age*, Mar. 1922). On 4 July, EP told Quinn: 'Eliot has always been reserved about his domestic situation, so much so that I thought Mrs. E. had syph . . . Last time I saw him I got down to brass tacks, and find the girl really has a long complication of things, tuberculosis in infancy, *supposed* to have been cured. Symptoms, so far as I now see, point to pituitary trouble, Berman, author of that gland book, turned up here on Sunday, on his way to a medical conference in Edinburgh. I am sending him to Eliot, and hope he will get best gland specialists onto the job' (*Selected Letters of Ezra Pound to John Quinn, 1915–1924*, ed. Timothy Materer).

3–TSE has tried his hand at कामसूत्र, the Devanagari script for Kāma-Sūtra. His pencilled transcription is too faint to reproduce.

4–Lancelot Hogben (1895–1975), biologist and writer.

a symptom of all sorts of more deep seated maladies, and there seems no reason why colitis also should not be a symptom of glandular trouble. Meanwhile she continues to take animal gland capsules thrice daily.

TO *E. R. Curtius*[1] TS Bonn

9 July 1922 9 Clarence Gate Gdns

Sehr geehrter Herr!

Ich gestatte mich, Ihnen zu schreiben, in der Hoffnung dass Sie mitarbeiten werden, an einer neuen Rundschau in London worauf ich Redakteur bin. Diese Rundschau wird erst im Monat Oktober erscheinen, und danach vierteljährlich.

Ich wunsche, in dieser Rundschau das Werk der bedeutendsten Schriftsteller des Auslands neben dem Werk der besten englischen Schriftsteller[n] vorzustellen. Der Charakter der Rundschau wird literarisch und international sein. Aus Frankreich und Spanien hat mein Bestreben schon guten Erfolg – z.B. Gomez de la Serna und A. Marichalar [*Ich bin englischer Korrespondent der 'Nouvelle Revue Française'.* added in ink in margin] – aber ich hege hauptsächlich die Hoffnung, engere Beziehungen zwischen der englischen and der deutschen Literatur der Gegenwart zu verknüpfen. Mein Freund Hermann Hesse hat einige Beiträge gegeben; aber ich begehre vorzüglich auch Ihr [cancelled: es following Ihr] Werk auch in England bekannt zu machen.

Darf ich sagen, dass ich schreibe, nicht nur wegen Ihrer Zelebrität, sondern weil ich Ihr 'Literarische Wegbereiter des neuen Frankreichs'[2] hoch schätze.

Die Übersetzung wäre hier besorgt von jemand der deutsche sehr gut kann, viel besser als ich!

Ich bewundere auch Ihren Aufsatz über Proust.[3] Von Proust auch hoffe ich im nächsten Jahr etwas herauszugeben.

Vorläufig können wir nur Pf. 10 für 5000 Wörter bezahlen, hoffentlich zu einem besseren Preis später. Vorläufig können wir nur Aufsätze um höchstens 5000 Wörter gebrauchen, vorzüglich kurzere.

1 – Ernst Robert Curtius (1886–1956), German scholar, literary critic and philologist; professor of German at Marburg University since 1920.

2 – Curtius, *Die literarischen Wegbereiter des neuen Frankreich* ['Literary Precursors of the New France'] (1919).

3 – Curtius, 'On the Style of Marcel Proust', C. 2: 7 (Apr. 1924).

Ich kann versichern, Sie würden unter unseren Leser[n] eine sympathische und gebildete Audienz betreffen.

Erlauben Sie mir zu hoffen an Ihre baldige und günstige Nachrichten; ich zeichne mich, mit vorzüglicher Hochachtung,

T.S. Eliot

Die Rundschau wird *THE CRITERION* heissen.[1]

TO *Richard Aldington* TS Texas

10 July 1922 9 Clarence Gate Gardens

My dear Richard,

Thank you very much for your letter[2] and the article you have sent. I much appreciate the loyalty of your support and of which the present prompt contribution is only one of many evidences. I shall write to you about this article again.

Thank you for recommending to me Flint, to whom I am writing. Do you know enough of the usual scale of payment to be able to suggest at what rate you think we should pay for translations, in view of the rate of £10 per 5000 words which we give for original contributions.

1 – *Translation*: Dear Sir, I am taking the liberty of writing to you, in the hope that you might take part in a new review in London of which I am editor. This journal will appear first in the month of October and then quarterly.

I want in this review to place the work of the most important writers from abroad beside that of the best English writers. The character of the review will be literary and international. In France and Spain my attempts have had happy results – for example Gomez de la Serna and A. Marichalar – but my principal hope is to bring about closer relationships between contemporary English and German literature. My friend Herman Hesse has given me an essay; I would also very much like to make your work known in England.

May I say that I am writing, not only on account of your fame, but because I particularly prize your *Literary Precursors of the New France*.

The translation will be taken care of here by someone with good German, much better than mine!

I wonder about your essay on Proust. Next year I also hope to publish something of Proust's.

For the moment, we are only able to pay a maximum of £10 per 5000 words, hopefully a better remuneration later. For the moment we can only use essays of up to 5000 words, preferably shorter.

I can assure you that you will find a sympathetic and educated audience.

Permit me to hope for a prompt and favourable response from you; I sign myself, with deepest respect, T. S. Eliot

The review will be called *The Criterion*.

2 – Not found.

As for French, of course you know I would rather have translations from you than from anybody.

As for publication in America, we should raise no objection to subsequent publication there or indeed to simultaneous publication if the publication *is* simultaneous. The difficulty is in arranging simultaneous publication in a quarterly and in a weekly or monthly. We should like of course to build up an American circulation, but at present the rates of payment are so low that it would obviously be more than unreasonable to ask contributors not to use their contributions in America.

In haste,
Yours affectionately,
Tom

TO *John Rodker* TS Virginia

10 July 1922 9 Clarence Gate Gdns

Dear Rodker,

You will remember that some time ago I suggested that you should contribute to the new quarterly, a rubric on cinema and music halls. I have had to forego rubrics for the reason that the space at the present is so limited that I think that the Review will be much more effective if it consists of entirely signed articles. I therefore revert to another suggestion and ask if you will do a single article on the cinema which you thought would take about 3,000 words. I am trying to make up several numbers ahead as owing again to the limited space, it is rather difficult to fit in all the shapes and sizes of article. Therefore I should be very glad if you will do it for me as soon as you can and let me have it, so that I might use it for the first or second number.

I hope that you still want to write it, and look forward to reading it with great interest.[1]

Can you let me have it, do you think, by the 10th August?

Yours,
T. S. Eliot

Starts October 1st.

1–Rodker duly wrote a 'Note on the Cinema', but it was never to appear in C.

TO *Sydney Schiff* MS BL

11 July [1922] 9 Clarence Gate Gdns

My dear Sydney

I have been waiting every day to hear from Proust, but have heard nothing. I am very disappointed. I must send in the copy for this first circular (there will be a fuller one in September) at once, so will you let me know if he has replied in either sense?

Yours always affectionately
Tom

TO *Richard Cobden-Sanderson* TS Beinecke

13 July 1922 9 Clarence Gate Gdns

Dear Cobden-Sanderson,

I send you herewith the copy for the advance circular. The first thing is to get an estimate of the cost for one thousand, and I will get Lady Rothermere's approval at once. I leave the formulation of the subscription form to you.

The type of the specimen page which you submitted is so excellent that I think it would be a pity not to adopt the same type, or larger or smaller sizes of it to suit, throughout.

That is one of the objections to the cover and also to the letter paper, which I return herewith. I have scribbled my objections on it. I think now that RED and black will look best, and the vertical type for the title as on the specimen page. Also, all of the lettering, except the title, should be much smaller, leaving much more white space.

Sincerely
T. S. Eliot

TO *F. S. Flint* TS Texas

13 July 1922 9 Clarence Gate Gdns

My dear Flint,

I am starting in the autumn for Lady Rothermere, a new quarterly review toward which Richard Aldington is giving me a good deal of help. (It will not, I may say, be an illustrated or art quarterly, but will consist of rather long essays, chiefly literary and critical). I am intending to include a larger proportion of foreign writers than is found in any of the reviews in existence, and in this respect Richard tells me that you can, if you will, be of the greatest use. It is very difficult, as you know, to find people who both know foreign languages well and have literary merit and knowledge of English. I want if possible, not to have to have translations done by ordinary hacks but by men of letters. As our rates of payment must at present be low – £10 per 5,000 words – so we can only offer at present the usual rate of 15/- per 1,000 words to translators. But I set great store on having translations done by the right people.

Will you undertake a certain amount, or as much as you can do, of this work? There will not after all be very much, as the paper is a quarterly; and I think that the material to be translated will be such as you would find interesting. I have at the moment two things which I want to be in the first number: an essay in Spanish by Ramón Gómez de la Serna,[1] and an essay in German by Hermann Hesse.[2] Both of these are very good people indeed, and have the additional interest of being quite unknown in this country; and if you will undertake this piece of work I should like very much to send you the manuscripts at once.

I need hardly say that I hope you will sometimes be tempted to send in original contributions as well.

Yours truly,
T. S. Eliot

TO *Richard Aldington* TS Texas

13 July 1922 9 Clarence Gate Gdns

My dear Richard,

Thank you again for the information about translators' rates. I have written to Flint.

I have undertaken to reprint the *Ulysses* section of Larbaud's Joyce. The reprinting of anything that has already appeared in a review is of course against my principles, but I thought that in this case as the section in question is not very long, I might well make an exception.

Would you agree to translate it for me?

The first number will appear either the 1st or the 15th of October, so that you can arrange for publication in America any time after the middle

1–Ramón Gómez de la Serna (1883–1963), avant-garde novelist, critic, dramatist and aphorist. 'From "The New Museum"', C. 1: 2 (Jan. 1923), was translated by Flint.
2–Hesse, 'Recent German Poetry'.

of that month. I do not want you to think that I do not value your article or that I am excessively captious about contributions! If I should seem so you will realise that it is because the success of this review, at least from the point of view of its contents, if not from that of circulation, means a very serious stake to me. You know that I have no persecution mania, but that I am quite aware how obnoxious I am to perhaps the larger part of the literary world of London and that there will be a great many jackals swarming about waiting for my bones. If this falls flat I shall not only have gained nothing but will have lost immensely in prestige and usefulness and shall have to retire to obscurity or Paris like Ezra. But you know all this as well as I do.

All that I have to criticize in your article is this; that I know you are holding yourself in from prudence in my interest, desiring not to write anything which can arouse hostility toward the review. For that reason I think, your article lacks the bite of, for instance, your article on Joyce,[1] and also I think it suffers from not being sufficiently concrete. I am perfectly aware of your reasons for avoiding mention of names or quotations of examples.

Yours always affectionately,
Tom.

When will you be in London?

My circulars are now being prepared and I will certainly very gratefully send you some and every additional subscriber will be a blessing. Let me know when you are coming to London – I want to see you very much.

TO *Sydney Schiff* TS BL

13 July 1922 9 Clarence Gate Gdns

My dear Sydney,

Thank you very much for your letter of the 12th, and for troubling to send it express. I am of course very disappointed that no reply has yet come, but I still have hope that Proust will yield to your persuasion if to anybody's.[2] Of course it would have been much better if I could have asked

1–RA, 'The Influence of Mr. James Joyce', *English Review*, Apr. 1921, 333–41.

2–Proust was wary of responding to a request from TSE that was associated with SS's solicitations: 'this Eliot question is all mixed up with the more delicate Schiff question', wrote Proust (cited in Davenport-Hines, *A Night at the Majestic*, 269). A devout admirer, SS had begun translating Proust in 1919 and was proposing himself to the author as the only suitable translator. In the event, Proust's 'The Death of Albertine' came out in C. 2: 8 (July 1924,

you to do this earlier. But I have not been in a position to discuss the review, and indeed have not been discussing it intimately with anyone. Also I had originally intended not to ask Proust until there was a tangible number of the review in existence to reassure him about the company in which he would find himself; it was in fact all that you told me about him after you came back from Paris, and knowing that you had come to know him so well, that made me venture to try to secure his support before the appearance of the first number.

With many thanks and best wishes to you both from both of us,

Yours affectionately,
Tom

TO *Leonard Woolf* — TS Princeton

13 July 1922 — 9 Clarence Gate Gdns

Dear Woolf,

Thank you for your letter of the 8th, and for the trouble you have taken.

I shall still hope that Koteliansky will agree to our publishing <the> 'Plan', but otherwise I should like to publish <the> 'Confession', if it can be arranged so that the first half of it appeared in the review before the other version appears in book form. The review will appear either the 1st or the 15th of October. Is there any possibility that you might not publish the book before the middle of that month? If Koteliansky remains obdurate about the 'Plan' will you let me have 'Confession' again in order that I may make up the number?

Yours always,
T. S. Eliot

—

376–94), in the translation by C. K. Scott Moncrieff; this was an extract from the penultimate book, *La Fugitive* or Second Part of *Sodome et Gomorrhe*, published as *The Captive* (1927). After Scott Moncrieff's death in 1930, the translation was completed by SS with *Time Regained* (1931).

Vivien Eliot TO *Richard Aldington* MS Texas

Saturday morning [15? July 1922] 9 Clarence Gate Gdns

Dear Richard Aldington,

Tom always leaves his letters behind for me to read, and this morning among others I have just read yours.[1] It is not easy for me to write to you in this way but I feel for once I must come out of my obscurity and say something. I think your letter is unkind, and not friendly. It is exactly the letter to upset Tom, and to harden his pride, and to help to precipitate the disasters we all foresee and which you cheerfully say he is asking for.

At this moment I know he *cannot stand* a letter like this from anyone he actually *did* look upon as his friend. You might have said nearly all you did say, but in such a different tone, if you were really the friend I have thought you were to Tom. It looks to me as though you are definitely angry and resentful against him for some reason, and are taking it out of him all round. Quarrel with me if you like, and send me any kind of letter, or no letter at all – to show your scorn for my interference.

The article in the [July] *Dial* that you speak of was written just before Tom went to Lugano. He was in a state of collapse – so *ill – he asked me what he should say*. And I told him what to say, and he just wrote it down, *anything*, not caring, for he felt too ill and in despair. So the article is more mine than his. I would be glad if everyone knew that.

And as for the title – the *Criterion*, I am responsible for that too. It would be nice if you had offered some good suggestion for the title yourself in time. Perhaps you do not know how many were tried and discarded, and how much worry and bother even the stupid naming of the Review caused us. Anyhow, I thought of the *Criterion* out of my own head simply because I liked the word, and I gave no thought to the meaning. Lady Rothermere liked it too, and Tom, too tired – *too tired* to bother very greatly once an apparently harmless title had been found, which pleased Lady Rothermere, agreed, and was glad to get the matter settled.

I don't suppose he thought of it the way you have put it, because he has *so many other things to think of*. Now, after your letter, I feel the title must once more be changed, although the notices are now being printed, and the letter paper. And Lady R. will be annoyed. I don't see what to do. – Tom won't care, he will say let the wolves get him. You little understand his state of mind.

1–Not found, but TSE addresses RA's complaints in his letter to EP, 19 July 1922.

I am English, and once I liked England – once I fought like mad to keep Tom here and stopped his going back to America. I thought I could not marry him unless I was able to keep him here, in England. Now I hate it. I hate the word. I hate the people whom you explain so well and so truly. I think Ezra is lucky and wise to have got out. And it is an everlasting stain on the English that he did get out. I hope Tom will soon get out. Tom will never know I have sent this letter unless you tell him. You know I am ill and an endless drag on him.

I know you have been very good, and a friend to Tom. I have, I must say, always thought of you as his real friend. But the test is now, when Tom is apparently doing, or has done, something you do not like.

He does stand or fall by this review. Can't you understand it? Each person who gives him a push now gives him a push out of England. And that will be damned England's loss.

Vivien Eliot

TO *Richard Aldington* — TS Texas

17 July 1922 — 9 Clarence Gate Gdns

Dear Richard,

I am surprised at your letter. My criticism of your article for the *Criterion* was extremely mild compared to criticism you have often made of what I have written. I did not intend you to imagine that I was unwilling to print your article and I think you have taken a very exaggerated ~~view~~ tone about the whole matter. It is odd that the first time I have ever offered anything but praise of your work it should cause you such great offense, considering the many times you have objected to writings of mine.

I want to print your article (of course) and as you have promised me that I shall have it for the first number I shall take it that I may print the article before it appears elsewhere, unless I hear from you by return of post (as I am making up the paper now).

Yours always,
Tom.

TO *Dorothy Pound* MS Lilly

Monday [17 July 1922] 9 Clarence Gate Gdns

Dear Dorothy,

I have just come back from Bosham. Will you have tea with me on Wednesday at the Carlton at 5.30? That is the easiest place for me to get to from the bank. I hope you can.

Yours always,
T.S.E.

TO *F. S. Flint* TS Texas

18 July 1922 9 Clarence Gate Gdns

My dear Flint,

Thank you very much for your letter and for your good wishes. I am delighted to have your consent and am sending you tomorrow the two manuscripts by registered post. Gómez wrote that this manuscript was the only one in existence and implored me to take good care of it and return it to him when the translation was made. I have had no time to read it, especially as I am not enough of a Spanish scholar to read very hurried writing with ease, but whether it is worth his solicitude or not, it is, he says, the only copy.

I am very sorry that the rates are so low at present, and I can only say that the first endeavour of the review will be to increase its rates and to show more respect to the art of translation which is so painfully underrated in this country.

I am sorry that you did not take the last remarks in my letter as they were intended. I really should very much like to have a contribution from you, and should have asked for it in any case at this moment.

Will you bear this in mind and at least propose a subject if you have nothing more tangible at present?

Yours sincerely,
T. S. Eliot

TO *Ottoline Morrell* TS Texas

18 July 1922 9 Clarence Gate Gdns

My dear Ottoline,

I should have written to you before, but as you know I am head over heels in work, and we have also started occupation of the little cottage where I spend my weekends. I am dreadfully sorry to hear that you have had to put yourself into the hands of the specialists again and I do hope that the consultation has not shown the necessity for an operation. You know I have a great antipathy to operations and I hope, if you have not already had an operation in consequence of this examination, that you will not do so. Please write soon and tell me what has happened. I have so little time for seeing people now that I shall not know about it until you write.

We hope that the cottage [at Bosham, near Chichester] will be a success. It is certainly attractive although the conditions are primitive. Vivien has already benefited a great deal in some ways, but at the same time the cure is so drastic that it makes her feel extremely ill and indeed causes her a great deal of pain. In two or three weeks I hope we shall know definitely how sound the treatment is.

Yours ever affectionately,
Tom

TO *Herbert Read* TS Victoria

18 July 1922 9 Clarence Gate Gdns

My dear Read,

I estimate that you ought to be back in London by this time, although I have not heard from you, and I hope that your travels in Italy have been in every way successful.

I am writing now to tell you definitely that I am undertaking for Lady Rothermere the entire choice of contributors for a quarterly review, of which the first number will appear in October. The review will differ from *Art & Letters* in that it will not be illustrated and that it will contain a much smaller proportion of verse and fiction. There will also be room for longer articles than was possible in *Art & Letters*, although I am at present more in need of shorter ones from 1500 to 2500 words. It will be mainly critical and reflective.

Although I will not publish regular or complete reviewing, it is always open to chosen contributors to use any new book or books as a foundation for an article as in the quarterly review of a hundred years ago.

I have been particularly anxious since it has been settled finally that the review is to appear, to obtain something from you for an early number. Do not disappoint me. Let me know what you are writing or wish to write about and let us arrange to meet and discuss these matters, as soon as I know that you are back in London.

Yours sincerely,
T. S. Eliot

TO *Richard Cobden-Sanderson* — TS Beinecke

18 July 1922 — 9 Clarence Gate Gdns

Dear Cobden-Sanderson,

Thank you very much for your letter of the 17th inst. I hope to be able to place the list in your hands within a few days, and I think it would certainly be worth while to send a circular to most of the people on your list. There are also three or four people to whom I want to send ten or a dozen copies each for distribution.

I quite agree with you that it is better to have the envelopes plain and I agree with your previous suggestion that they should be of a rather large size.

Yours sincerely,
T. S. Eliot

Will you add the name Ernst Robert Curtius in alphabetical order to the list in the circular. He is one of the best Germans.

TO *Leonard Woolf* — TS Princeton

18 July 1922 — 9 Clarence Gate Gdns

Dear Woolf,

Thank you very much for your efforts and their success. You know that I shall be delighted to publish <the> 'Plan' and that it will be most valuable to the Review.

The only question is how early in October you must bring out your book. If you will let me know definitely I can prepare to bring out the review slightly in advance. I should certainly put in a note to say that you were publishing it together with the unpublished Chapter. I shall take this contribution as definitely settled, and please remember that any other parts of books or shorter pieces will always be most welcome.

Is this Plan done by you or by Virginia?

Yours,
T. S. Eliot

Vivien Eliot TO *Mary Hutchinson* — MS Texas

Tuesday [18 July 1922] — 9 Clarence Gate Gdns

My dear Mary

I came back here yesterday and as the dentist can't see me this week, I find, I am going back tomorrow and so I cannot have lunch with you, for I want to get the 1.40. I am very very sorry not to see you for so long. I want to see you – badly. I would have stayed here till Thursday in order to see you but I do feel I ought to go back and start there properly, without delaying any more, especially as I shall probably have to come up again next week.

The weekend was rather ghastly as we had no woman, but I have engaged *two*! – one in the mornings and one for the evenings. It is quite a nice cottage, but inconceivably tiny.

If only if *only* I could find an unfurnished cottage there and put my furniture in [it], how happy I should be! Bosham seemed so lovely. Even although Tom may be leaving the Bank at Xmas and us going to live in Paris, it would be worthwhile – for there is no country I like better than English country. Don't you think it is the best? But should quite cheerfully exchange Paris for London, I think.

Write to me!

My love
VE

TO *John Quinn* — TS NYPL (MS)

19 July 1922 — 9 Clarence Gate Gdns

Dear Mr Quinn,

Thank you very much for your letter of the 22nd ultimo. By this time you will have my letter of explanation, as I have yesterday a mild letter from Liveright which sounds as if he would come to terms. As it is now so late I am enclosing the typescript to hand to him when the contract is complete, or to hold if he does not complete. I had wished to type it out fair, but I did not wish to delay it any longer. This will do for him to get on with, and I shall rush forward the notes to go at the end. I only hope the printers are not allowed to bitch the punctuation and the spacing, as that is very important for the sense. I am not sure that you will approve of the punctuation, but I very much hope you will like the poem, as it seems to me the best I have ever done, and I am anxious to hear.

I did get your draft for £10,[1] and am distressed to hear that I did not acknowledge it and thank you at the time. Rodker owed me £5 so I kept the whole and discharged his debt, with which he was quite satisfied. I should like to present you the manuscript of *The Waste Land*, if you would care to have it – when I say manuscript, I mean that it is partly manuscript and partly typescript, with Ezra's and my alterations scrawled all over it.

It is true that I had three months leave from Lloyds Bank in the winter, and was in Lausanne under a nerve specialist, a very good man. Physically, I was in very poor shape even after that, until I had two weeks holiday in Lugano (and a visit to Pound in Verona), and since then I have been very much better. My wife also has been very ill with colitis, and has only just found a treatment which seems to be doing her some good.

I expect to write to you again within a fortnight, on other matters, and meanwhile I pray that my affair with Liveright will not give you a great deal of trouble. And meanwhile you will be spared the nuisance of a long letter from me.

Yours always gratefully,
T. S. Eliot

TO *Ezra Pound* TS Lilly

19 July 1922 9 Clarence Gate Gdns

Cher Ezra,

I have seen Dorothy this afternoon and she has handed me the draft for Lir. 4246.50 on Rome.[2] As I have no immediate crying need to spend the money and havnt time for a three days debooch, I shall bank it or invest

1–Quinn sent the money on 25 May 1921 as payment for a copy of *Ara Vos Prec* on vellum.
2–From 'Bel Esprit' funds.

it temporarily in some appreciable security. As you have not mentioned the address of the Club and as Dorothy <didn't know it> says that you beg me to do nothing more than acknowledge formally without consulting you, I await your further advices.

I hear good report of the progress of Cantose. If the *Dial* refuses please let me inspect, but probably unwise to make the paper too conspicuous at first, if the rape of the bishop is an integral part. I have decided not to put any manifestoe in the 1st number, but adopt a protective colour for a time until suspicion is lulled. What do you think of 'The Possum' for a title?

The reason why I did not send Vivien over to Paris is that first she is extremely run down, at a very low point where all weak spots break out – neuralgia, neuritis, eye trouble etc., and second that she has just been started on a new diet for colitis (of the colitis there is no doubt whatever) which involves great care in the preparation of food – all meat to be minced in a machine three times, milk to be the best sealed medical milk, certain proportions of vitamines and proteids daily; the diet seems to be the best so far and really doing her good. I didnt want to run the risk of upsetting her improvement at the start by letting her break the diet by Duval or even the Voltaire. But if Berman comes to London I should be delighted. Ask him does he know of a man named Hogben who is writing a book on hormones, in England. What I want to know and what I do not get from Berman's book is what treatment he gives after he has diagnosed. Both of the doctors Vivien has seen lately have examined her teeth with great care and were disappointed to find nothing wrong. I should like to put her into your hands but think that from present appearances Paris should be postponed till October.

I have just had a little difficulty with Richard over an article he contributed, and which I ventured to criticise mildly (at his request) and which he immediately sent to the *XIXth Century*[1] without asking permission. As he has not proposed to send me anything else to take its place I am annoyed. He improved the occasion to (1) reprove me for 'expressing contempt (in the *Dial*) for eminent writers in language so defective' (2) say that the *Criterion* is a very dangerous title and 'somewhat pretentious': 'I wonder' he says 'if you quite understand the profound english repulsion for everything which seems to be assuming superiority? It is a very subtle thing.' (3) says that everyone says that I am getting bitter and hypercritical.

1 – RA's article was not published.

Insultos

Also evidently regards Bel Esprit as entirely a personal favour toward me. I dont want personal favours, I want it to be purely a question of the production of verse, a small, a very small, but still a public utility of work.

I Dont think 300 a year however is a living income for me, especially with vagueish guarantees, unless some very definite way is shown me of getting another 300 by not too close or bestial labour. I shall not stand in the way of your finding out just how much money can be got and how many people will give it for the arts in any form, *only* I do not at present find 600 a penny too much and cannot accept one bed room as being liberty in comparison with my present life. I only say this not to pledge myself now and finally to accept the terms when they are finally drawn up in black and white: while the matter has been in this nebular state I should have been a fool if I discouraged it but also fool if I pledged myself . . . however have met Orage[1] and liked him

Lady Rothermere is coming to Paris and wishes to meet you. She will be there next week at Hotel Westminster. I like her. You might put Berman on to her after a time, but I dont think he would find many weak glands. I shall give her your address and she will probably communicate with you.

I trust Quinn is not having too much trouble with Liveright.

Good fucking, brother.

[unsigned]

TO *E. R. Curtius* — TS Bonn

21 July 1922 — 9 Clarence Gate Gdns

My dear Sir,

Thank you for your letter of the 14th inst., I am very much delighted at the prospect of receiving an early contribution from you and at having the distinction of being the first editor to introduce your work in this country. I should like very much to have from you, not simply a 'chronique' of contemporary literary activity in Germany, but a piece of your individual criticism, whether dealing with modern literature or with the writers of the nineteenth century. The subject which you suggest of fixing contemporary valuation of the older writers is very attractive.

As I am very much pressed both for time and for space with the first number I should be very glad if you could promise me an article by the first

1 – A. R. Orage, editor of the *New Age*.

of November at the latest, for the second number, in which I shall be able to give you the full space of 5,000 words if you wish it.

You ask about the programme of the review. The first number will contain contributions by myself, Mr George Saintsbury, Mr T. Sturge-Moore, Miss May Sinclair and Mr Richard Aldington in this country, and two or three foreign contributions – Gómez de la Serna, Valery Larbaud, and Hermann Hesse.

In general it will consist of a small number of critical and reflective essays and an occasional poem or story. We are also publishing a translation of a Plan of a novel by Dostoevski.

Its great aim is to raise the standard of thought and writing in this country by both international and historical comparison. Among English writers I am combining those of the older generation who have any vitality and enterprise, with the more serious of the younger generation, no matter how advanced, for instance Mr Wyndham Lewis and Mr Ezra Pound.

Now that I know you are an English scholar I shall have pleasure in sending you a book of critical essays [*SW*] of my own, which although it contains many statements which I have come to question or even repudiate, is still representative.

I am also interested to know that you live in Marburg, where I was myself living in 1914, and of which I have the pleasantest memories.

Be assured that any contributions you send will be highly appreciated and the sooner you send them the better I shall be pleased.

With many thanks, believe me,

Sincerely yours,
T. S. Eliot

TO *The Editor of* The Dial — TS Beinecke

28 July 1922 — 9 Clarence Gate Gdns, London N.W.1

Dear Sir,

I cabled you to the effect that I had sent you my letter on the 24th saying that it amounted to about 1,000 words. I did this in the hope that it would enable you to publish the letter in your September number if you were depending upon it.

I have had it very much on my conscience that for some time my letters have only reached you at the last possible moment. What is more important, as I told you in my last letter to you, is that I am quite aware that they have not been very good stuff. This is not only my own opinion but that of others. I do not like to think that I have been providing you with poor material, and I should always like to do my best work for the *Dial;* I now feel that the sort of letters which I have been sending you, are not only damaging to myself, but perhaps also to the *Dial.* This has been due to unfortunate circumstances and pressure of a great deal of business of other kinds. I therefore wish to say frankly that I think it would be to your interest to have some other correspondent, one who would have time both to get about more and know what is going on in London, and also to produce a more finished article. I therefore offer you this opportunity of changing your correspondent, as I am sure you must concur with me in my opinion of the work I have been doing.

I have two pieces of work still to do for you which I have undertaken, and I shall always prefer contributing to the *Dial* than to almost anything else, but I do not like contributing anything but the best I can do.

Yours very truly,
T. S. Eliot

TO *Ezra Pound* TS Lilly

28 July 1922 9 Clarence Gate Gdns

Dear Ezra,

I have this evening your letter with the typed script of the prose of your unknown friend which I shall peruse carefully over the weekend, hoping that I shall see the point to which you refer. Your letter, as frequently, is extremely obscure; I do not understand the point of the pug dog nor the apparently more significant allusion of the storming of the bastille. Perhaps you will kindly explain this latter point to me as it might prove a useful piece of knowledge?

I will let you have a copy of the *Waste Land* for confidential use as soon as I can make one. Of the two available copies, one has gone to Quinn to present to Liveright on completion of the contract, and the other is the only one I possess. I infer from your remarks that Watson is at present in Paris. I have no objection to either his or Thayer's seeing the manuscript.

As for the circular I do not suppose that you wish any comments from me and I suppose that it is already in circulation. If so I trust that it will, as it requests, be circulated privately only; if I was doing such a thing myself I should have omitted the name of Lloyds Bank.[1] The other point

1–Printed by Rodker, the 'Bel Esprit' circular opened: 'In order that T. S. Eliot may leave his work in Lloyd's Bank and devote his whole time to literature, we are raising a fund, to be

that occurs to me is that the less of my private circumstances that need be issued, so much the better; even when such private circumstance are accurately reported. Particularly I do not want any rumour to get into circulation, especially in America, to the effect that I have a family which *should* be providing for my support. As I have already informed you what my Mother's means are, you will be in a position to deny any such rumor. I do not know why the suspicion should have come into my head, but I do conceive that it is the sort of sensational falsehood which might well be supported by hysterical and sympathetic persons in the United States.

The presenting of Neophytes however commendable they may be will not absolve you from the liability of contributing yourself. I have put your name down in the circular and I think that the second number will be a suitable time for you to make your appearance. That number should be out early in January, and therefore we must fix November 1st as the last date on which you should send it, and it will be more preferable for me to have it locked up in my care long before even that date. I do not want to concentrate the jailbirds too much at the beginning and I think that if the *Waste Land* bursts out in the first number and you contribute to the second, that Lewis must remain behind the scenes until the third. Of course one can throw in always a few people whose names are entirely unknown.

I wait in hope that Berman is coming to this country.

I understood from Dorothy that a translation of Rémy's *Physique* with either an essay or supplement by yourself was soon to appear in New York.[1] Am I to receive a copy or am I to order it myself through Messrs. Jones and Evans in Cheapside?

I am glad that you have lunched with my friend and that she has your approval.

Yrs. fraternally

T.

If this Circular has not gone out, will you please delete *Lloyds Bank*, to the mention of which I *strongly object*. If it is stated so positively that Lloyds Bank interfered with literature, Lloyds Bank would have a perfect right to infer that literature interfered with Lloyds Bank. *Please see my position* – I *cannot* jeopardise my position at the Bank before I know what is best. They would certainly object if they saw this. If this business has any

—

£300 annually.' EP wrote to Quinn on 10 Aug.: 'if you reprint Bel Esprit private circular, *please omit name of LLOYD'S bank*.'

1 – Rémy de Gourmont, *Physique de l'Amour: Essai sur l'instinct sexuel* (Paris, 1903), trans. by EP as *The Natural Philosophy of Love* (Boni & Liveright, 1922).

more publicity I shall be forced to make a public repudiation of it and refuse to have anything more to do with it.

TO *T. Sturge Moore* PC Texas

[Postmark 28 July 1922] 9 Clarence Gate Gdns

I have your MSS. and am looking forward to reading it over the weekend. I am very grateful for your punctuality – it is of the greatest assistance.

With many thanks,

Yours sincerely
T. S. Eliot

TO *T. Sturge Moore* MS Texas

29 July 1922 9 Clarence Gate Gdns

Dear Mr Sturge Moore,

I have read your essay with great pleasure and interest: it would certainly give distinction to any review in which it appeared. On the first reading I seem to find myself wholly in agreement with you. I did not know that [Laurence] Binyon was so good: I have never read anything of his.[1]

With many thanks

Sincerely yours
T. S. Eliot

FROM *John Quinn* TELEGRAM photocopy Valerie Eliot

29 July 1922 [New York]

LIVERIGHT EXECUTED CONTRACT PREPARED BY ME TYPESCRIPT RECEIVED TODAY SUGGEST MAIL LIVERIGHT NEW YORK BRIEF DESCRIPTION FOR CATALOGUE GLAD EVERYTHING SATISFACTORILY ARRANGED BEFORE GOING MY VACATION TOMORROW WRITING[2]

QUINN

1 – Moore, in his critical treatment of Tristram and Isolt in English poetry, praised Laurence Binyon's *Odes* (1901, rev. 1913).

2 – Quinn's letter details his activity over several days: 'I dictated the contract between you and Liveright, based upon your Knopf contract, late yesterday . . . you did not give the name of the book. But fortunately, in a postscript in one of his recent letters to me Pound gave me the

TO *Ottoline Morrell* TS Texas

[end July? 1922] 9 Clarence Gate Gdns

My dear Ottoline,

I was very glad to hear from you, and to know that you are now a little better; though your letter is a sad one, and I had not known what a bad time you had been having. I do indeed sympathise with you. I have just returned from a weekend in the country: Vivien is better, but the difficulties of living in the country are so great under such conditions, when it is impossible to get exactly the food necessary for the regime, and impossible to get it properly prepared, and when the weather is so bad – that I cannot feel quite certain that the benefit is enough to compensate for the privations. And she keeps having attacks of the neuritis in her right arm.

I have, too, been buried in correspondence over the review, of which I suppose you have received a notice; and its success must of course be the first thing in my mind at present, and the most important thing to me. But

—

name' (28 July). '[Y]our letter of July 19th, with the typescript of the poem, came today [and I told Liveright that] you would "rush forward the notes to go at the end" . . . I have asked one of the careful stenographers in the office to make a copy of the poem from the typescript. I'll send the typescript to Liveright on Monday morning. When I told him I had it, he asked me to give my opinion of it. I told him that I would read it over Sunday. You wrote that that copy would do for Liveright "to get on with". But you said nothing about proofs or reading proofs. In a small book, where style and form of printing and the format of the book generally have such a part, I should think you would insist upon having page proofs and not galley proofs. I dare say there will not be time for Liveright to send you first galley proofs and have you correct those galley proofs and return them to him, and then have Liveright send you page proofs and have you correct these and return them to him. So I suggest that you cable him that you want page proofs or write that to him. If the notes that go at the end come to me, I'll send them at once to Liveright' (29 July). 'I received this morning in the mail from Liveright, without letter, a duplicate of the contract signed by him . . . I am writing to Mr. Liveright this morning sending him (a) the original typescript of the poems, which was received from you last Friday, and (b) a careful copy of it. I read the poems last night between 11:50 and 12:30 . . . *Waste Land* is one of the best things you have done, though I imagine that Liveright may be a little disappointed at it, but I think he will go through with it. It is for the elect or the remnant or the select few or the superior guys, or any word that you may choose, for the small number of readers that it is certain to have' (31 July). '[Liveright] may be disappointed in the size of the book. Frankly, if you could add four or five more poems to it, even if it meant delaying the publication of it for a month, I should be inclined to recommend that you do so. But that is only a suggestion. I don't know how lengthy the notes are, or how many pages they will take, so I am writing a little in the dark. I give you my impression, though, that people are likely to think that the book is a little thin and to compare it with your first volume of poems published by Knopf . . . You won't mind my suggestion' (1 Aug). (See Charles Egleston, *The House of Boni & Liveright, 1917–1933: A Documentary Volume* [*Dictionary of Literary Biography* vol. 288, 2004], 264–7.)

also I have preferred not to think much about the Bel Esprit. I have been very much impressed by the kindness of my friends and their untiring efforts, but of course the publicity is painful, and I cannot help feeling that I cannot have anything to do with it myself, and in fact must pretend to know nothing about it. Sometimes I simply want to escape from the whole thing and run away. I am sure that you will understand why I feel this way, and why I cannot say anything about a committee or any other details. And why I cannot criticise Pound; and, even though I may not care for some of his methods, I appreciate that it has been part of his method to try to keep me out of the business as much as possible. I am sure you will understand my feelings about this matter, though I put them very lamely. Thank you very much for your letter – I wish that I could answer it and write fully and leisurely.

Always yours affectionately,
[Unsigned.]

I need hardly say that this is a *confidential* letter – what I have said would be certain to be *misunderstood* by most people and would give the impression that I was ungracious and ungrateful. The last thing I want to do is to offend against or hurt the feelings of my good friends who have toiled so hard and disinterestedly for me. But I am sure you will understand that appreciation of this kindness is part of the pain and embarrassment that I feel; and I am sure that you will understand my feelings on this matter if anyone will. – The committee would, I am sure, make the project much more impressive to the public. I started this letter on Monday! and have had to put it aside for work on the review: difficulties start up quite unexpectedly now and then.

TO *Sydney Schiff* — CC Valerie Eliot

2 August 1922 — 9 Clarence Gate Gdns

My dear Sydney,

Thank you for your letter[1] and enclosures. Your view of the matter is very similar to mine, which I have already expressed, and unfortunately is not that of those who are accustomed to small and precarious incomes and therefore cannot take my circumstances into account and realise why

1 – SS wrote on 1 Aug., 'Admirable as the intention of your admirers is, so far as I know the facts, their method has not been practical . . . For me a guarantee is worthless unless it is based upon a forfeitable material value and a signature guarantees only that which the law, *when invoked*, can enforce.'

I should need more money or more security. About the precise sum needed they are as free to differ with me as I am to decline; but about the guarantee I see no room for doubt. The sum of £300 is based upon the assumption that I shall make £300 more out of periodical writing; so that even upon their own figures an absolute guarantee of the fund is necessary. I see no evidence that this guarantee is forthcoming.

You will of course understand that I am in a difficult position; I cannot take any part in the affair beyond expressing my opinion to Pound and Aldington. At the same time, if the affair becomes public in such a way as to jeopardise my present position or make me ridiculous, I shall be forced publicly to discountenance it. As it is, no one could find it agreeable to have his private needs and way of life a subject of public scrutiny and criticism, however devoted it shows his friends to be.

I subscribe to your attitude in the enclosed letters. I appreciate warmly the trouble you have taken.

Yours always affectionately,
[T. S. E.]

TO *Dorothy Pound* — MS Lilly

Friday [4 August 1922] — 9 Clarence Gate Gdns

My dear Dorothy

It is very sweet of you to send the lavender – of which we are both very fond. Mine is now buried in shirts, Vivien's I am taking down to her tomorrow. She has been better as to colitis, but still has bad neuritis in the right arm. She hopes to get strong enough to see you in Paris in October, if, as is probable, she does not come up to town again for some weeks.

I hope Dartmoor is doing you good, but you looked too well to need it.

Yours ever
T.S.E.

TO *Alec Randall*[1] TS Tulsa

9 August 1922 9 Clarence Gate Gdns

Dear Mr Randall,

Thank you very much for your letter. Your offer is most valuable, and I should like to see you as soon as I can and discuss Germanic matters with you. I will write to you next week and see if we can fix a date. I am unfortunately confined to the City, in fact to E.C.3, at lunchtime; perhaps you could come to see me some evening?

The review aims at gathering the best foreign writers, but of course it is at present very small, and as the majority of the contributions must of course be English, not more than one of any one foreign nationality can appear in each number. For the first two, I have Hermann Hesse – whom I know – and Ernst Curtius. I want also to get at the best Scandinavians. Preferably men who are unknown here but ought to be known: rather than men like Hamsun[2] and Couperus[3] who are already known here.

Do you know Alfred Kerr?[4] I find his style difficult and his vocabulary impossible, but Germans have spoken to me of him very highly.

Sincerely yours,
T. S. Eliot

I enclose a circular for your guidance –

TO *Richard Cobden-Sanderson* TS Beinecke

9 August 1922 9 Clarence Gate Gdns

Dear Cobden-Sanderson,

I enclose cheque for 12s from Mr F. S. Flint for a year's subscription. Will you kindly send him a receipt.

The letter paper and envelopes seem to me excellent. I notice that the red lettering is a little blurred, but I presume that the type will be quite clear in the finished work. Will you have the paper printed as soon as possible?

1–Alec (later Sir Alec) Randall (1892–1977), diplomat, entered the Foreign Office in 1920. In the early 1920s he was Second Secretary to the Holy See. He ended his career as Ambassador to Denmark, 1947–52. He became a regular reviewer of German literature for both C. and the *TLS*.

2–Knut Hamsun (1859–1952), Norwegian writer. Nobel Prize for Literature, 1920.

3–Louis Couperus (1863–1923), Dutch writer whose novel *The Hidden Force* (1900) was published in English in 1922.

4–Alfred Kerr, né Kempner (1867–1948), theatre critic who championed naturalistic drama.

For myself I should like a slightly larger envelope of the same shape and I should prefer it to be quite plain with no printing on it.

I think that I can send you nearly all of the material by the beginning of the week. I will indicate the order in which the contributions are to be printed. As I said it is all going in sooner or later and until it is set up I am quite in the dark as to whether we have too much or too little for our pages.

I have seen one or two people who have already received the circular and they appear to be quite pleased with its appearance.

I think that as soon as you get back it would be well if we could meet and discuss the questions you raise of mutual responsibility and we can then make notes about any points which we desire to make explicit.

Yours ever,
T. S. Eliot

TO *Dorothy Pound* MS Lilly

Wednesday [9 August 1922] 9 Clarence Gate Gdns

My dear D. P.

I arrived back from my weekend at Bosham, last night, went to the doctor about my cold, tonight had to have a shorthand typist in for correspondence (she comes twice a week) so is there any hope of my finding you tomorrow, of your not leaving town till Friday? If *so*, will you send me a line to Eliot, Information Branchage, Stock, London and I will come in. I hope so. If not, when?[1]

Booklets – about what? I have asked Orage, but he says he writes no more, and I am told is taken up by the Gotcheff system.[2] I shd like to get him. Novels – difficult in a quarterly – unless short – and one does not wish to commit oneself until one knows how good it is. Has anyone seen it?

Shall be disappointed if impossible to see you before you go to Paris.

Yours ever
T.

1 – Dorothy Pound could not make any of the days TSE suggested, so he wrote again on 12 Aug.: 'I am indeed very disappointed, but do let me know as soon as you return. TSE.' (Lilly).
2 – After fifteen years as editor of the *New Age*, A. R. Orage had stepped down to follow George Gurdjieff in the summer of 1922. See Carswell, *Lives and Letters*.

TO *Sydney Schiff* CC

9 August 1922 9 Clarence Gate Gdns

My dear Sydney,

I have several letters from you which I am anxious to answer, but I have been away over the weekend and I was also suffering from a heavy cold with neuralgia, and therefore have arrears to make up.

I will write you on Sunday. In the meanwhile I have forwarded your letter to Conrad Aiken and fully concur with your opinion of his review.

I will take up the point about Austin Harrison[1] when I write you. These things are very vexing.

Yours always affectionately,
[T. S. E.]

TO *Antonio Marichalar* TS Real Academia de la Historia

9 August 1922 9 Clarence Gate Gdns

Cher Monsieur,

Je m'empresse de vous accuser réception de votre très intéressante étude;[2] recevez mes vifs remerciements. Puisque c'est un genre d'article dans lequel j'ai moi-même fait des tentatifs, j'apprécie fort bien que l'auteur se sacrifie à ses collègues; et j'espère recevoir de vous plus tard quelque chose où vous vous 'raconterez' (dans le sens de Gourmont) plutôt que vos contemporains; et je n'ai aucun doute que le public anglais desirera vous connaître davantage.

Votre article paraîtra dans le second numéro; on vous enverra la petite bonification au mois de novembre. Je vous ferai parvenir un exemplaire de *The Criterion* dès le début; et j'espère que vous continuerez de m'envoyer *Indice*, que je trouve (en dépit de ma connaissance exiguë de la langue espagnole) d'un très grand intérêt. Votre article me poussera à recommencer mes études espagnoles.

Le premier numéro contiendra des contributions de Larbaud, G. Saintsbury, Sturge Moore, Gómez de la Serna, Hermann Hesse, moi-même,

1 – Austin Harrison, editor of the *English Review*. SS wrote on 3 Aug.: 'Austin Harrison has printed my translation of Hesse's first essay "The downfall of Europe" without acknowledging or mentioning me as translator . . . I had no little difficulty in getting Harrison to take it. He now places it *first* in the August number <It is singled out for notice in *The Times*.> as though he had discovered Hesse or as though Hesse had selected the *English Review* in which to make his bow to the English public . . .'

2 – Antonio Marichalar, 'Contemporary Spanish Literature', C. 1: 1 (Oct. 1922).

et un inédit de Dostoevski.[1] Dans le second, Ernst Curtius et Marcel Proust ou Paul Valéry.

Merci de vos compliments gentils, et croyez-moi votre dévoué

T. S. Eliot[2]

James Sibley Watson TO *Scofield Thayer* MS Beinecke

12 August [1922] Hotel Continental, Paris

Cher S. T.

Eliot seems in a conciliatory mood. The poem is <better than> not so bad. Shall I try to persuade him to sell us the poem at our regular rate with the award in view? We should have to ask ~~him~~ <any prospective recipient> in advance whether he would accept it unless we wanted to run the risk of being turned down – as the king by John Galsworthy.[3] It seems to me the award is a more important matter than the poem anyway, and I should favor giving Eliot the prize even without the poem, magnanimity not of course for me entering into the transaction. *The Dial* would then demonstrate its likeness to the Russian steam-roller – shining that is upon the just and unjust – at once impartial and relentless. *And* you could write comment on Eliot – *and* Gilbert [Seldes]'s publicity <campaign in the midwestern press> would make him squirm like any conger eel. In fact a whole muster of peacocks could be done in at one shot. (Do I quote?)

Failing which I must say I favor Pound as second choice – ill as we get along.

1 – The list of authors largely matches those in the first *C.* On 16 Sept., TSE would send Marichalar a revised list of the contributions to the first two numbers, while thanking him for his kind letter and '*bénédiction*'.

2 – *Translation*: Dear Sir, I hasten to acknowledge receipt of your very interesting article; receive my hearty thanks. Since it is the sort of piece that I have sometimes tried to write myself, I appreciate very well how the author has to sacrifice himself in the interest of his colleagues; and I hope later to get something from you in which you 'talk about yourself' (in the sense Gourmont uses the expression), rather than about your contemporaries; and I have no doubt that the English public will be keen to know you better.

Your article will appear in the second number; the small fee will be despatched in November. I will send you a copy of *The Criterion* as soon as it appears; and I hope that you will continue to send me *Indice*, which, despite my meagre knowledge of the Spanish language, I find very interesting. Your article will push me to take up the study of Spanish again.

The first number will contain contributions by Larbaud, G. Saintsbury, Sturge Moore, Gómez de la Serna, Herman Hesse, myself, and an unpublished Dostoevsky text. In the second, Ernst Curtius and Marcel Proust or Paul Valéry.

Thank you for your kind words. Sincerely yours, T. S. Eliot

3 – The novelist John Galsworthy had declined a knighthood.

Somehow the idea of E. E. C. [E. E. Cummings] as recipient grows less and less supportable. First it would probably make Cummings sore. Second it would probably be the most unpopular choice we could hit upon. You may be right about *The Enormous Room*'s popularity, however. I shall be better able to tell about that when I get back to Gilbert.

It is said that Eliot has sold Liveright the first publication rights, but I am certain Gilbert could get round Liveright if necessary.

S. W.

Telegraph me care 'Francheul Paris' if you want me to try persuading Eliot. I sail Aug 19th.[1]

TO *E. R. Curtius* TS Bonn

14 August 1922 9 Clarence Gate Gdns, N.W.1

My dear Herrn Curtius,

Thank you for your letter of the 10th instant. I should be very glad to have the essay on 'Balzac and the magical tradition', and look forward to receiving it by the 1st November with great pleasure.[2] And for a later number I should certainly be very glad to have the essay on Hölderlin and/or George.[3]

Allow us to hope that we may some day see a work from you on English literature comparable to your book on contemporary France.[4] Such work seems to me of very great value. You shall receive the *Criterion* regularly. I should very much like to know whether you think that [there] would be an English-reading public in Germany, no matter how small, which would care to buy the *Criterion* provided that we could sell it in Germany at a possible price. It would of course have to be a price from which we could expect no profit, and I shall have to discuss with the publisher at what price we could afford to supply it to Germany; but the project seems to me

1–Four days later, Watson wrote again: 'In response to Pound's letter Eliot has assumed a more conciliatory attitude and has sent on a copy of *Waste Land* for our perusal. I am forwarding it to you. I am sorry that Pound's vagueness in writing caused Eliot to send the copy to Paris instead of to you direct, but I suppose it will do for a starter. Anyway I wrote him more plainly about the prize and await his answer. I found the poem disappointing on first reading but after a third shot I think it up to his usual – all the styles are there, somewhat toned down in language <(adjectives!)> and theatricalized in sentiment – at least I thought so . . . If Eliot accepts the prize and sells us the poem politely at our regular rate – and you aren't satisfied I suppose I shall bloody well have to come out with 2000 to bel esprit.'

2–See E. R. Curtius, 'Balzac', *C.* 1: 1 (Jan. 1923).

3–The German poets Friedrich Hölderlin (1770–1843) and Stefan George (1868–1933).

4–Curtius, *Die literarischen Wegbereiter des neuen Frankreich*.

a worthy one, and I should be very grateful if you would let me know what you think of it. The difficulties of international communication are very great: in fact, even German books are sold here in England at prices beyond *my* means, and are only obtained after a long delay.

Please give my kind regards to M. Gide, and believe me,

yours very cordially,
T. S. Eliot

I shall then expect your essay by November 1.

TO *Gilbert Seldes*[1]

TS Beinecke

14 August 1922 — 9 Clarence Gate Gdns

Dear Mr Seldes,

On looking over my letter to you on the 9th inst.,[2] I think that I may have expressed myself obscurely or ambiguously and I wish to make the issue quite clear.

Personally, as I have told you, I feel that my London Letters have been of very poor quality. I should myself prefer to write articles for you such as the one you suggest, but I do not think that it is within my powers, considering how little time I have, to do both such articles and a regular London Letter. If however the *Dial* considers that it would lose more by my ceasing to write London Letters than by my not writing anything else, I am quite prepared to go on with London Letters in the same way.

The point is that I cannot undertake to do both. Putting aside my personal preference I should like the *Dial* to consider simply its own interest and let me know what it wants me to do.

Thanking you again for your kind letter,

I am,
Yours faithfully,
T. S. Eliot

1 – Passing this letter to Thayer, Seldes wrote on it, 'Note form and substance.'
2 – TSE's letter of 9 Aug. has not been found, but see his letter of 28 July to the *Dial*.

TO *Edmund Wilson*[1] TS Beinecke

14 August 1922 9 Clarence Gate Gdns

My dear Sir,

Thank you for your letter of the 1st inst. I should be very glad to do for you such an article as you suggest.[2] For the next two months I shall be far too busy to attempt such a thing, but I think that I should be able to provide one during October or November if that is satisfactory to you. As for a poem, I am afraid that it is quite impossible at present as I only have one for which I have already contracted.

Will you kindly let me know whether you would be glad to have an article in November?

I will look into the question of a photograph. Mr Wyndham Lewis has recently done a drawing of me of which I wish to have a photograph made, and this might suit you as well as a direct photograph. But an excellent photograph was taken years ago by Mr E. O. Hoppé and I will see if he can have a print made and sent to his agent in New York for you.

Yours sincerely,
T. S. Eliot

TO *F. S. Flint* TS Texas

15 August 1922 9 Clarence Gate Gdns

Dear Flint,

I am indeed sorry that you have been so harassed. While I am not sure, without longer study, that I quite share your opinion of the author, I am

1–Edmund Wilson (1895–1972), American journalist, literary and social critic and novelist; author of *Axel's Castle: A Study of Imaginative Literature 1890–1930* (1931) among other books; managing editor of *Vanity Fair* from July 1922 to May 1923. EP had written to Jeanne Foster on 6 May, 'What wd. Vanity Fair pay Eliot for "Waste Land"[?]', and suggested that John Peale Bishop write to TSE. Bishop met EP in Paris on 3 Aug., and on 5 Aug. he reported to Wilson: 'Eliot is starting a quarterly review: he is to run "Waste Land," the new series of lyrics in the first number: he and Thayer have split and the *Dial* will not publish it. Perhaps you might want to arrange for the American publication. Pound says they are as fine as anything written in English since 1900.'

2–TSE's contribution was to be 'Contemporary English Prose: A Discussion of the Development of English Prose from Hobbes and Sir Thomas Browne to Joyce and D. H. Lawrence' – a translation of 'Lettre d'Angleterre', *NRF* 19: 3 (1 Dec. 1922), 751–6 – in *Vanity Fair* 20: 5 (July 1923). Wilson was to write to TSE on 26 Feb. 1923: 'I have just seen your thing on English prose in the *Nouvelle Revue Française* and I wish you could let us reprint it in *Vanity Fair* . . . I think it is so admirable that it would be a great pity for it not to appear in English. We could pay you about $75.'

at least doubtful whether it is quite what we want for the first number. We will therefore hold it up for the time.[1] Whether it is printed or not, I will give you my word that the payment will be forthcoming for what has been done, not later than the appearance of the first number.

I have another Spanish contribution, typed, a perfectly simple and straightforward *chronique* of Spanish letters,[2] which I propose to substitute for the Gómez. (He devotes several paragraphs to Gómez). I should venture to ask you if you would do this, but I gather that you are leaving for a holiday, so unless I hear from you *by return* I shall offer it to a Spaniard who has been recommended to me.

You say nothing about the Unities, but perhaps refreshed by your vacation you will assault them?

Sincerely yours,
T. S. Eliot

TO *James Sibley Watson* — TS Berg

15 August 1922 — 9 Clarence Gate Gdns

Dear Mr Watson,

Thank you for your charming letter of the 14th. I am indeed heartily sorry that there has been this difficulty; I only wish that the full explanation which you give could have reached me at the time. I should have accepted Thayer's offer when it was made, but that he told me categorically that the *Dial* paid the same rates to everybody, and I knew on very good authority that Moore had received a considerably larger sum. My objection was, therefore, a protest against discrimination in favour of a writer whose work I cannot believe to have any permanent value, and whom I knew to be in no financial want. Unfortunately my letter to Thayer about Moore seems to have crossed one from him again denying that the *Dial* discriminated between its writers, so that neither of us was inclined to continue the correspondence. I also had in mind, perhaps, that what I offered and had always in fact given was *exclusive* serial publication, whereas numerous writers have placed their work both in the *Dial* and in London too.

1 – Gómez de la Serna's 'From "The New Museum"' was held over until the second issue of C. (Jan. 1923), 196–201.

2 – Antonio Marichalar's contribution appeared, in a translation by S. A. Middleton, as 'Contemporary Spanish Literature', C. I: 3 (Apr. 1923), 277–92.

It is true that I have not only given Mr Liveright the first publication (book) rights, but also have executed the Contract, under which he is to pay me $150 on publication. I suppose that the poem is now going to press. For my part, I should be quite willing (out of loyalty to the *Dial*) to let you publish it first, in that event of course I should expect to forego the $150 advance from Mr Liveright, and should receive it from you instead of from him. What I could not do is to give you exclusive rights now, as the poem will appear in London in October in the *Criterion*. But I will put it this way:

Subject to Mr Liveright's consent, I would let the *Dial* publish the poem for $150, not before November 1st. In this event, I would forego the $150 advance from Mr Liveright, and he would delay publication as a book until the new year. Possibly he would be glad to do this, on the possibility of the book's getting the prize, which might increase the sales. If so, the only alteration in my contract with him would be to delete the clause giving me $150 in advance, and alter the date fixed for publication. It would be necessary to get Mr Quinn to act for me on the legal side, though he has done so much for me already that I dislike to trouble him.

The periodical in which the poem appears here will in any case not be circulated in America.

If you receive this letter, will you let me hear from you before you sail?

With all best wishes,

Sincerely yours,
T. S. Eliot

You will understand of course that I am legally bound to Mr Liveright.[1]

TO *Sydney Schiff* TS BL

15 August 1922 9 Clarence Gate Gdns

My dear Sydney,

I have been very rushed with correspondence but must manage to write to you as I have been wanting to do so for so long. I am very sorry to hear that you are finding it difficult to get on with your work; I have been through the same ordeal often and know how agonising it is. But a moment comes when the thing comes out almost automatically; I think

1 – Watson conveyed this to Thayer on 19 Aug.: 'Got a letter from Eliot regretting his haste in thinking we were trying to rob him, and offering us the right of publishing his poem simultaneously with its pub. in the *Criterion*.'

that it is partly the anxiety and desire to express it exactly that form the obstacle; then a moment of self-forgetfulness arrives and releases the inspiration. I imagine that all writers who have arrived at a degree of consciousness in their mental activity suffer in this way.

Aldington's reply is what I should have expected.[1] I wish that I could see you to talk, as there is so much one cannot explain in any other way, so until I do I cannot explain everything I want to explain. Possibly I could spend the Saturday night and Sunday with you at Crowborough the weekend after next: I could let you know definitely by the Monday next, and meanwhile you will let me know if it would be inconvenient. Vivien is writing to Violet as soon as she can; I was down there over Sunday (one night). I think she is better, but I see that it is very difficult for her to take her cure properly and attend to all the details of it anywhere but in her own home; and I am not at all sure that the country air and out of door life balance the discomforts and the imperfections of diet etc. If she could have a house of her own in the country, and have Ellen to look after her, it might be quite a different matter. She has to do so many more things for herself, as well as plan so much more, in the country. I must stop now, I have written ten letters tonight.

Yours ever aff,
Tom

If you know of any persons who might subscribe, I should be glad to have more circulars sent you. It was good of you to subscribe three times.

When you get back to London, I should like to have a photograph made of the Lewis drawing to send to my mother. May I?

1–In answer to an enquiry from SS, RA had responded on 2 Aug.: 'I consider a subsidy of £300 a year adequate, in view of the fact that an additional £100 a year is promised by a large literary paper in London in exchange for a very small amount of work, that from other sources Mr. Eliot can easily count upon at least another £100 a year.

'The security for the £300 is the honour of the subscribers who have guaranteed their subscription in writing. I am asking subscribers for an annual banker's order so as to take from them the great labour of writing an annual cheque.

'There is a certain amount of risk in this of course, but a man who will take no risks for a big object is not worth considering. About £200 a year is now promised; and several additional subscriptions of £10 a year are in sight. Since Mr Eliot's health will probably force him to leave the bank in a year or so he may be glad of our little fund even if it is inadequate and ill-secured.'

SS responded to RA (7 Aug.): 'I can only reply that if Eliot is prepared to give up his present post in return for the promised subsidy of £300 a year you are confident of obtaining, I shall certainly supplement it by an annual subscription.

'I am very sorry you are so apprehensive about his health. Should your fears be so unhappily justified there would arise a different and more serious situation which I prefer not to anticipate.'

TO *F. S. Flint* TS Texas

17 August 1922 9 Clarence Gate Gdns

Dear Flint,

Our views about Gómez are not widely divergent.

Let me hear from you upon your return, and perhaps we can meet and discuss what is to be done with him, and with the unities?

Sincerely,
T. S. Eliot

TO *Paul Valéry* TS Bibliothèque Nationale

17 August 1922 9 Clarence Gate Gdns

Monsieur,

J'ai reçu avec un vif plaisir la traduction du *Serpent* faite par M. Wardle.[1] La traduction me paraît excellente; néanmoins, je me suis muni de vos 'Charmes'[2] et j'en ferai une vérification détaillée et minutieuse.

The Criterion (je vous envoie une annonce qui pourrait vous intéresser) est fier de publier en Angleterre une oeuvre d'une telle importance, et je regrette seulement que nous n'avons pas reçu la bonne nouvelle à temps d'illustrer notre annonce de votre nom, qui a une distinction particulière parmi l'élite du public auquel nous visons.

Permettez-moi d'espérer que nous recevrons plus tard quelques proses inédites aussi?

Croyez, Monsieur, à l'hommage sincère d'un de vos admirateurs les plus dévoués.

T. S. Eliot[3]

1 – Mark Wardle's translation of Valéry's 'The Serpent' appeared in *C.* 1: 3 (Apr. 1923), 267–76. TSE wrote 'A Brief Introduction to the Method of Paul Valéry' for the subsequent book, *Le Serpent par Paul Valéry* (London: Cobden-Sanderson, 1924).

2 – Paul Valéry, *Charmes* (1922), the collection that included 'Le Serpent'.

3 – *Translation*: Dear Sir, I have received with great pleasure the translation of the *Serpent* done by Mr Wardle. The translation strikes me as excellent; nevertheless, I have equipped myself with a copy of your *Charmes*, and shall check it carefully and in detail.

The Criterion (I am enclosing a publicity leaflet which might interest you) is proud to bring out a work of such importance in England, and I only regret that we did not receive the good news in time to enhance our publicity with your name, which enjoys particular distinction among the élite of the public we are aiming at.

Allow me to hope that we may later receive some unpublished prose texts as well?

Please accept the sincere tribute of one of your most devoted admirers. T. S. Eliot.

TO *James Sibley Watson* TELEGRAM TS Berg

17 August 1922

PLEASE TAKE NO STEPS AWAIT NEW LETTER ELIOT[1]

TO *Sydney Schiff* TS BL

20 August 1922 9 Clarence Gate Gdns

My dear Sydney,

I am surprised to hear that you are leaving Crowborough so soon; it would seem to show that your period in the country has not been any more enjoyable than many people's experience seems to have been this year; I am sorry for that.

I was going to ask you whether it would be convenient for me to come the following weekend instead of the 26th, for the reason that a young cousin of mine [Abigail Eliot] is in England at the moment and is leaving early next week. I had already written to ask her to come to Bosham, so that she could see Vivien before she leaves; and next weekend turns out to be the only time at which she can come. As you will be in London so soon you will probably not think it worthwhile to have me the following weekend, as we should meet so soon in town, but if you are staying longer than you now think I should be able to spend the weekend after next at Crowborough.

I am sorry that you are dissatisfied about your book but perhaps you will talk to me about it when we meet.[2]

Considering that Vivien has only been in the country a fortnight, in a four roomed labourer's cottage, and having incessant bad weather, she has made considerable progress. I don't think she is more of a 'townbird' than any of us, in fact I think she gets more out of solitary country life than anyone I know.

1 – Watson wrote to Thayer on 19 Aug., while sailing back to the USA: 'Got a letter from Eliot regretting his haste in thinking we were trying to rob him, and offering us the right of publishing his poem simultaneously with its pub. in the *Criterion* . . . But the next day I got a telegram saying "don't act till you receive a second letter." Haven't received it yet, though it may come on board tonight when we touch at Plymouth. So the matter is still in the air. Please don't do anything definitive without letting me know first. I reach New York probably August 26.'

2 – Probably SS's novel *Prince Hempseed* (1923).

I am very very busy still, but in a few weeks I hope that the pressure of the first number will be abated.

Always affectionately
T.S.E.

TO *John Quinn*

TS NYPL (MS)

21 August 1922

9 Clarence Gate Gdns

Dear Mr Quinn,

In reply to your letter of the 28th ultimo, I cannot thank you enough for the great pains you have taken on my behalf.

The contract seems to me as perfect as it is possible for a contract to be.

I certainly cannot accept your proposal to purchase the manuscript at your own price,[1] and if you will not accept it in recognition of what you have done for me lately and in the past, it will not be any pleasure to me to sell it to you. I therefore hope that you will accept it. But as I feel that perhaps you like some of my early poems best I should be glad, for example, to send you the manuscript of 'Prufrock' instead, and I hope you will let me do this.

I hope that Liveright will not be disappointed at the length of the poem.

A few days ago I had an attractive proposal from Mr Watson of the *Dial* who was very anxious to publish it; but I think between ourselves that the *Dial* are rather unbusinesslike people and that there is a lack of coordination.

They suggested getting Liveright to postpone the date of publication as a book, but I have written to them to say that it seemed to me too late to be proper to make any change now and that I should not care to trouble either Mr Liveright or particularly yourself with any questions of alterations in the contract.

I cannot go into details about the proposal as it was stated to be confidential and of course you will not mention it to anyone else.

I have been exceedingly busy for some weeks with the preparation of a quarterly review of which I send you a circular for your amusement.

1–After TSE's offer to let Quinn have the drafts (19 July), Quinn had replied (on the eleventh page of his letter of 28 July–1 Aug.): 'I shall be glad to have the MS. of *Waste Land* but I shan't let you "present it to me". When you finish the whole thing, poetry and prose, if you will send the MS. or the MSS. to me, I shall be glad to have it, but you must agree to the condition that I send you a draft for what I think it is worth.'

One never knows whether any public activity of this sort is worthwhile but it is interesting to make such an attempt at least once in one's life; if it succeeds – as far as anything of the sort can be expected to succeed – it will be of satisfaction to me; meanwhile it is a kind of experience. If it succeeds I shall have to delegate a great deal of the work which I am myself doing for the first few numbers; if it does not succeed in the sense of justifying its continuation, I hope at least that it will make an interesting volume or two in the literary history of our epoch.

I hope that you will write to me at the end of your holiday and let me know how you are inasmuch as I feel partially responsible for your needing it as much as you do.

Again with most cordial thanks.

Yours sincerely,
T. S. Eliot

TO *James Sibley Watson* — TS Berg

21 August 1922 — 9 Clarence Gate Gdns

Dear Mr Watson,

I am very sorry that your wire did not arrive in time for me to write to you at Plymouth, but I hope that this letter will reach you very soon after your arrival in New York.[1]

I answered your first charming letter in haste and without having thought over the matter very thoroughly. But now it seems to me that it is far too late and that matters have gone too far for me to change my plans.

It would involve altering the contract with Mr Liveright in which business I should again have to invoke the aid of Mr Quinn and I think it would be quite unjustifiable for me to give any further worry to either Mr Quinn or Mr Liveright, quite aside from the fact that I myself am so busy for many weeks to come that I shall have no time to devote to any additional business.

You of course were not able to approach me in the matter earlier, but had it been possible or had Thayer explained the difficulty to me as you have done instead of leaving it in complete silence, I should of course have

1 – Watson had telegraphed from Paris on 18 Aug. that he had not received TSE's second letter, but that communications 'addressed Steamship *La France* touching Plymouth Saturday night will reach me'. The next day, he sent a letter: 'I hope we shall be able to have the poem at your terms. Please let me know in care of the *Dial* 152 W. 13th St, etc. I am eager to start persuading Mr. Liveright and also to settle the matter of the *Dial* award.'

fallen in with your proposal. But as things are I should not feel justified in troubling Mr Quinn in any case, and I should not feel justified in troubling Mr Liveright unless the alteration were to his advantage as well as mine. Furthermore to put the matter frankly, the advantage to me would be nil unless the receipt of the prize were to form the basis of a contract which of course you would not be likely to give.

Let us hope that on a future occasion, if I survive to write another poem, no such difficulty will arise.

Believe me, with all best wishes,

Yours very sincerely,
T. S. Eliot

TO *Edmund Wilson* TS Beinecke

21 August 1922 9 Clarence Gate Gdns

Dear Sir,

Referring to my letter of the 14th, I have spoken to the Secretary of Mr E. O. Hoppé, the photographer, who has promised to send you a photograph of me immediately. If you do not receive it perhaps you will let me know.

Sincerely yours,
T. S. Eliot

TO *Herbert Read* TS Victoria

23 August 1922 9 Clarence Gate Gdns

Dear Read,

Thank you for your postcard with a nice window. I should have returned your brief with comments before, but have been so very busy. What I have written on it are therefore only jottings which I intended to make into a letter, and may be largely unintelligible, but take them for what they are worth to you. I am looking forward to the article with great interest, but you don't need to feel pressed for time.[1] My great

1–HR's 'The Nature of Metaphysical Poetry' was to be held over to C. 1: 3 (Apr. 1923). TSE's jottings on HR's typescript draft included the two observations: (i) 'Some philosophies are in themselves incoherent & emotional (e.g. B. Russell) and therefore useless for poetry. Bradley more useful than Russell.' (ii) 'Function of poetry is to express as a whole of feeling a digestion of *all* experiences in a mind. The more complicated & comprehensive the mind the better. Also the mind should be *continuous* with *all* (or as much possible) previous mind. Peel the onion.' (Victoria)

difficulty, I find today, is that contributions are too long for my ninety-six pages; I overestimated the capacity of ninety-six pages, and I am having to postpone one or two things for the first number. So if you can be *under* 5000 words an embarrassed editor will appreciate it. I think your essay will be a good one!

Yours ever,
T. S. Eliot

TO *Richard Aldington* PC Texas

[Postmark 23 August 1922]

I will be in Monday evening 28th by 9 – is that convenient for you? Let me know.

T.S.E.

TO *Dorothy Pound* PC Lilly

[Postmark 23 August 1922] [London]

I am delighted to hear you are back.[1] I am *rushed* this week, may I come in on *Tuesday* afternoon and see sketches?

Yrs. ever
T.S.E.

TO *Richard Cobden-Sanderson* PC Texas

[Postmark 23 August 1922] [London]

I will answer yr. letter in a day or two – I have my hands full trying to get the French translation finished.[2] Excuse delay.

T. S. Eliot

1 – She had been on holiday on Dartmoor.
2 – TSE's translation of Larbaud's lecture, 'The "Ulysses" of James Joyce'.

FROM *His Mother*

TS copy Valerie Eliot

23 August 1922

24 Concord Avenue, Cambridge
[Massachusetts]

Dearest Son:

Aunt Susie was here last evening with Eleanor and I read to them the prospectus of *The Criterion*. Aunt Susie said she would subscribe, so will you have the prospectus sent to her? and will you fill out the address on all copies sent to America, for I do not think just Holborn is enough from this side of the water. Have you sent to any of the Harvard professors? And do you think it would be well to do so? I have sent to the University for a list of the professors in the Department of Literature, and will forward to you to use or not as you think best. I do not know whether you would send them to Harvard University or to their residences. There is Professor Lowes, he is lovely. I gave him a copy of your *Sacred Wood*, and Mrs Lowes brought a copy to me of his *Convention and Revolt in Poetry*.[1] Henry read it when at home and was delighted with it. He talked of sending you a copy. If you would like it I will send you my copy.

Professor Lowes's address is: John L. Lowes, 983 Charles River Road, Cambridge, Mass. Professor Kittredge's is: Prof. George L. Kittredge, 8 Hilliard St, and Professor Grandgent's: Charles H. Grandgent, 107 Walker Street.

I would also like another copy of the prospectus, two or three copies, with address filled out.

I suppose Vivien is still at Bosham. I addressed to her my note of thanks to Clarence Gate Gardens, and you will take to her as I suppose she will not leave Bosham for a while yet. I judge from the tone of your last letter she was better. It was very sweet in her to send me the lavender. Barbara thought she looked far from well, and said she felt very sorry for her. But I hope she will soon be better. I am glad to hear you say you are well, and hope you will remain so. Let me know what I can do for *The Criterion*.

Ever yours with love,
Mother.

1–John Livingston Lowes, *Convention and Revolt in Poetry* (1919).

TO *E. R. Curtius* TS Bonn

28 August 1922 9 Clarence Gate Gdns, N.W.1

My dear Herrn Curtius,

Thank you very much for your kind letter. I shall look forward toward having your Essay by the 1st November, and later, I hope for something on some subject in contemporary, or nineteenth century, German literature. But my purpose is not so much to give the readers information *about* German literature, as to give them a direct acquaintance with German writers; so that you will see that almost any subject about which you care to write will suit us equally well.

I am very much pleased by your wanting to reciprocate by a German book. I do not know what books you have published, except the *Literarische*[*n*] *Wegbereiter* which I already possess, but if you have published any other, that would be my first choice. And if you have *not*, then I should prefer *you* to choose something which you think I ought to become acquainted with. Beyond your book and that of Hesse, and a few things of Spengler and Keyserling,[1] I know almost nothing of German literature since 1914.

The problem of selling the *Criterion* in Germany is at the moment a very difficult one. It will be sold here at 3s 6d, for export we might reduce it to the bare cost of printing, that is 2s, which with the mark at eight thousand to the pound, would be eight hundred marks per copy, to say nothing of the profit wanted by whatever German bookseller, of course, who might act as agent. I should like to know, at your leisure, at what price you think such a review could be *sold* in Germany to the public.

There is another point on which I beg your tolerance. I should like to exchange copies with foreign reviews, with a view, later, to having a '*revue des revues*' in each number, as soon as the *Criterion* can be enlarged to that extent. What German reviews do you think would do this with me? I have noted the names of *Die Neue Rundschau, Die Neue Markur* [*sc. Merkur*], *Der Sturm* and *Die Aktion*. I want, of course, reviews as nearly as possible of similar aims, limitations, and sympathies as our own. Are these suitable? Like books, the German reviews are difficult to obtain here and expensive.

1–Oswald Spengler (1880–1936), philosopher of history; author of *Der Untergang des Abendlandes* ('The Decline of the West', 1919). Hermann Keyserling (1880–1946), cultural philosopher.

I want to thank you also most heartily and appreciatively for your generous offer to notice the *Criterion* in the *Frankfurter Zeitung*.

Always yours cordially,
T. S. Eliot

TO *Herbert Read*[1] PC Victoria

[Postmark 29 August 1922] [London]

I agree that there is both in Guido and the others, and Italian poetry seems to me to retain a debased form of the metaphysics after the psychology is gone. But I think the distinction, in one and the same author, is worth drawing . . . But I do not know these early Italians well – only in selections. You may know them a good a deal better than I.

Also important not to confuse the 'literary' with the 'philosophical' senses of *Metaphy*. and *Psych*.

yours,
T.S.E.

TO *Ezra Pound* TS Lilly

30 August 1922 *The Criterion*,
9 Clarence Gate Gdns, N.W.1

Cher Ezra,

Yes, it is quite true that one does not want to write any prose, and I never feel quite justified in doing so myself, nevertheless one does. I can't myself see what good it does, and the effort of persuading oneself that it is worthwhile writing at all is only just about enough to cover one's verse and nothing over. 99% of the people who 'appreciate' what one writes are undisguisable shits and that's that. Your notes, epistolary, telegraphic, etc. are cordially appreciated and after I have corrected the speling will in due time appear and in due time be paid for. With most grateful thanks yours always sincerely, faithfully. I received a letter from your friend Watson most amiable in tone

1–The advice concerns HR's 'The Nature of Metaphysical Poetry', for C. 1: 3, Apr. 1923. 'Guido' is Guido Cavalcanti (*c*.1255–1300), friend of Dante.

For below a voice did answer, sweet in its youthful tone,
The sea-dog with difficulty descended, for he had a manly bone.
(From 'The Fall of Admiral Barry').[1]

offering $150 for the 'Waste Land' (not 'Waste Land', please, but '*The* Waste Land', and (in the strictest confidence) the award for virtue also. Unfortunately, it seemed considerably too late, as I had the preceding day got the contract, signed by Liveright and Quinn, book to be out by Nov. 1st, etc.) I can't bother Quinn any more about it, I don't see why Liveright should find it to his advantage to postpone publication in order to let the *Dial* kill the sale by printing it first, and there has been so much fluster and business about this contract that I don't want to start the whole thing up again, so I see nothing but to hope that the *Dial* will be more businesslike with other people. Watson's manner was charming, if Thayer had behaved in the same way the *Dial* might have published it long ago, instead of pretending that I had given him the lie as if he was *ehrenfähig* [capable of honour] anyhow. Anyway, it's my loss I suppose; if Watson wants to try to fix it up with Liveright I suppose he can, that's his affair. I suppose the move was entirely due to your beneficent and pacific efforts, which are appreciated. Dam but why don't they give the prize to you?

More presently.

King Bolo's big black basstart kuwheen,
That plastic and elastic one,
Would frisk it on the village green,
Enjoying her fantastikon.

T.

TO *Richard Cobden-Sanderson* — TS Beinecke

31 August 1922 — *The Criterion*, 9 Clarence Gate Gdns

Dear Cobden-Sanderson,

Thank you for your letter of to-day's date, which I have been working over this evening. The plan suggested has certain disadvantages; it limits the foreign contribution to one (short one), it reduces the number of contributions to six, and it provides proportionately too large a space to be filled by editorial matter. Also, by leaving the Larbaud over as well as the Spaniards I shall be faced with the same difficulty in the following issue.

My alternative is this, if my calculations are not quite incorrect. I find that the original estimate with which your printers provided you gives the

1–See letter to EP of 22 Oct. 1922 and note.

cost of 600 copies of 96 pages as £59 2s, and the cost of 600 copies of *128* pages as £75 2s 6d. I therefore assume that 600 copies of *112* pages would cost around £67.

I calculate also that with the matter on which the printers have furnished this last estimate of space, and the *rest* of *The Waste Land*, we should almost fill the 112 pages, leaving the one to three pages probably for editorials, and I do not want more than four. (ten out of ninety-six would be far too much a one-man show).[1] That is, the number would include

Saintsbury
Dostoevski
Sturge Moore
May Sinclair
Hesse
Eliot
Larbaud
(Editorials)

I enclose the rest of *The Waste Land* again, and would be grateful if you would find out from the printers (1) cost of extra sixteen pages (2) estimate of space the rest of *Waste Land* needs. If there were in the end a few pages over I suppose they could be left blank as fly-leaves.

Of course, the sooner we can get the material into galley-proof, and get it to the printers and back again, the better.*

I am still waiting for Lady Rothermere's address, but if the 112 pages can be done I undertake it on my own responsibility.

Yours ever
T. S. Eliot

* Saintsbury has returned completed the copy I sent him. So that's all ready.

TO *J. M. Robertson*[2] — TS Valerie Eliot

31 August 1922 — *The Criterion*, 9 Clarence Gate Gdns

Sir,

I take this opportunity of acknowledging an indebtedness, extending over many years, to your work, in connexion with the Elizabethan studies

1–Parts I and II of *The Waste Land* ran to six pages. (In the event, the poem took up fifteen of the 104 pp. of the first issue of C.; the contents were as listed, with no editorial.)
2–J. M. Robertson (1856–1933), Scottish critic, rationalist and politician, whose books included *Elizabethan Literature* (1914) and *Shakespeare and Chapman* (1917).

which have always formed one of my strongest interests. It is with the justification of paying this tribute that I venture to solicit from you the honour of a contribution, at any time within the next six or nine months, of any piece of unpublished manuscript.

The enclosed circular gives some description of this quarterly. Besides general literary contributions, I am anxious to secure occasionally contributions from writers who have both literary distinction and more exact scholarship than the majority of those whose names you see. From my point of view anything from you on the subject of Elizabethan or Jacobean literature would fill a place which cannot be supplied by anyone else, and I hope that your point of view will not be unfavourable to mine. I am aware, of course, of the favour I am asking from anyone so preoccupied as you must be; I only hope that you may have, or may at some time wish to write, something which would appear more suitably in this review, and find a more select and judicious audience, than elsewhere.

We are at present limited to essays of about 5000 words in length; the present rates of payment are insignificant, being only £10 the 5000 words.

I fear that my name may be known to you only in a connexion which will hardly dispose you in my favour. I must say that I am quite aware that certain critics have chosen to make you responsible, in a way, for theories of mine which were certainly encouraged by your arguments, but which are by no means the inevitable conclusion from your arguments.[1] I am sorry that this has involved you in attack, and even abuse, which was primarily aimed at myself. They have thoroughly mistaken my meaning and perverted my words, as they have yours; but I am afraid that persons who are incapable of following an argument, or of distinguishing an argument intended to prove one thing from a theory intended to suggest the possibility of something on a wholly different plane, and who are guided entirely by their emotions, would be impenetrable to any explanations which I could give.

I am, Sir,

Your Obliged Obedient Servant,
T. S. Eliot

1–TSE's 'Hamlet and His Problems', which began as a review of Robertson's *The Problem of 'Hamlet'* (1919), had been met with some adverse critical comment. Robert Lynd, in 'Buried Alive', *N.* 18 (4 Dec. 1920), spoke of TSE coming to 'bury Hamlet, not to praise him'. Likewise, Arthur Clutton-Brock took TSE to task for his account of *Hamlet* as 'an artistic failure'. TSE's arguments, said Clutton-Brock, 'are partly taken from Mr Robertson, though not stated with his accuracy, and partly Mr. Eliot's own' ('The Case against "Hamlet"', in *Shakespeare's 'Hamlet'* [1922], 14–32).

Gilbert Seldes TO *James Sibley Watson* CC Beinecke

31 August 1922 152 West 13th St, New York

Dear Doctor:

Quinn is out of town and the enclosed is my letter to him. You have already received Eliot's letter, but I think that we are doing the right thing to go ahead. With Liveright I have arranged as follows. We pay them nothing and we publish the poem without the notes in our November issue. They bring out the book after our date of publication and we send them an order for 350 copies of the book at our usual discount (about 40%) and in connection with our advertising contract with them. We take the financial settlement by that time. (The idea, of course, is that we will push the book mightily in connection with our subscriptions. The book sells for $2 so that if it remains a total loss on our hands we will be paying about $350.) I have suggested that they number all the copies of the first edition, giving a bibliographical value to it, and they have promised to use no publicity mentioning the award until we release it. They do not ask for a refund of the first publication rights payment, and we can, as a matter of fact, pay Eliot our regular rate if that is considered necessary. That I did not mention to Quinn, as you notice.

We must assume that Eliot O.K.'s publication in *The Dial* without the notes. The one thing which troubles me in addition is Eliot's remark about making the award the basis of a contract. It seems to me that he means something a little more definite than what you take it to mean, because he surely could not imagine bad faith on our part. I speculate: does he mean that he ought to have a more favourable contract with Liveright because he gets the award? It sounds unreasonable, because he gets the two thousand. Does he mean that he wants some sort of contract with us for the future? I shall, of course, not cable him until I hear from Quinn, so you have time to answer this letter. If cabling becomes necessary owing to delays it would certainly be in such terms as to make him realize that tentative conversations have led both Liveright and Quinn to be enthusiastic and that we will undertake any reasonable contract and ask permission to publish in November.[1]

1 – These terms were confirmed at Quinn's office on 7 Sept. and in letters between Seldes and Liveright, both dictated by Quinn. On the same day Quinn advised TSE: 'The arrangement insures you (a) $150 from Liveright on publication under his contract, (b) the $2,000 award, and (c) the royalties for the publication of the poem in *The Dial*, which ought to be at least $10 a page . . . It was a close shave, and when the papers were all signed up, and I took Liveright and Seldes out to lunch, Seldes went to telephone to *The Dial* giving them notice about the publication of the poem in the next number.'

The notes, by the way, are exceedingly interesting and add much to the poem, but don't become interested in them because we simply cannot have them. Please write.

Faithfully yours,
[unsigned]

PS I have bought a Yeats play and as we had no definite rate for plays I said we would pay at a page rate of $8 a page, which is about what a page of prose comes to. The advantage of this is that we can use the small type and still not lose money by doing so. Please decide whether this small type is a good hunch or not, as I wrote to Thayer about it some time ago and have had no reply.[1]

TO *J. M. Robertson* TS Valerie Eliot

4 September 1922 *The Criterion*, 9 Clarence Gate Gdns

My dear Mr Robertson,

I am very happy to have your kind letter of the 3d and trust that you will not allow your search through your manuscripts to flag. Had you merely said 'more than 5000 words' I should not have been daunted (by your Shakespeare studies) but as you say '*far* more' I suppose I must wait until you find something shorter. I accepted, and shall print, one manuscript of 8000 words for the first number, but without having realised the extent to which it was to disturb the arrangement of the other contents.[2]

Please remember that the choice of subject rests entirely with you; if it is 'off' the Shakespeare field, I shall undoubtedly return to you later for something 'on' it; and if it is 'on', I shall appeal to you later for something 'off'. The study of Elizabethan blank verse development would suit me admirably. It is precisely a subject on which I have been supposed to be writing a set of articles for the *Times*, for the past year; but life and vicissitudes have intervened; and now that I hear you have dealt with the subject, I am humbly thankful that I did not venture in before you.[3] Or alternatively, your reference to having once hoped to establish a decent method in criticism suggests a very valuable essay. I must say that I have shared your hope, and share your despondency.

1–*The Player Queen* was printed in small type immediately after *The Waste Land*.

2–See Robertson, 'Gustave Flaubert', C. 1: 2 (Jan. 1923), 105–18.

3–J. M. Robertson, 'The Evolution of Blank Verse', C. 2: 6 (Feb. 1924). (TSE's projected pieces for the *TLS* were not written.)

May I be precise and say that I should like to receive something from you either by the 1st November or by the 1st February (but of course preferably the earlier date)? I like to allow good time in order to be able to insist upon accurate composition by the printers.

One justification for 'exoticism' is that at the present epoch it is necessary to summon aid from the whole of Europe, in order to muster enough good brains to make possible even a *quarterly* review.

I have good reason to believe that the review signed 'C. B.' was written by Mr Clive Bell the art critic. One reason is that he has conceived Hamlet in what he believes to be his own image, but I have others. I am told that Mr [Clutton-]Brock showed him his manuscript before publication.[1] It is needless to say that I am immensely interested in both of your forthcoming volumes.[2]

With the most cordial thanks I remain,

Your Obedient Servant,
T. S. Eliot

TO *Richard Cobden-Sanderson* MS Texas

7 September 1922 *The Criterion*, 9 Clarence Gate Gdns

Dear Cobden-Sanderson,

I am very sorry indeed to hear your bad news.[3] I will not trouble you either with business or expressions of sympathy, but will write to you on Monday.

Yours cordially
T. S. Eliot

1 – 'The Case against *Hamlet*', the *TLS* leading article of 18 May 1922 (which was written by John Cann Bailey, not by Clive Bell), discussed Robertson and TSE as well as the book they 'provoked', Arthur Clutton-Brock, *Shakespeare's 'Hamlet'* (1922).

2 – J. M. Robertson, *The Shakespearian Canon* (1922), and *Explorations: Essays in Literature and Philosophy* (1923).

3 – RC-S's father, the printer T. J. Cobden-Sanderson, died on 7 Sept. 1922, aged eighty-two.

Gilbert Seldes TO *Horace B. Liveright* TS copy NYPL

7 September 1922 [New York]

Dear Mr Liveright:

This is to confirm the understanding between me as Managing Editor of *The Dial* and yourself with reference to the publication in *The Dial* of Mr Eliot's poem *The Waste Land* as follows:

We are to publish the text of the poem, without the notes, in the November *Dial*, which will be published about October 20th. We will not publish the prose notes in our publication of the poem. The poem will be copyrighted together with other literary matter in *The Dial*.

In consideration of your consent and agreement to the above publication of the poem, we agree to purchase from you, on publication, 350 copies of the book at the usual forty per cent. discount of the retail price. We will pay for the books purchased within six months of their delivery, and this arrangement regarding the purchase of said books from you shall not apply to or be considered part of our separate arrangement regarding advertisements and book purchases.

I have no hesitation in saying to you personally that *The Dial*, on the merits of Mr Eliot's work as a whole, intends to give to Mr Eliot its this year's annual award of two thousand dollars ($2,000) for services to the cause of letters.

In connection with our publication of the poem in *The Dial* we will announce its publication in book form by your firm with notes.

It is our understanding that your contract with Mr Eliot for the publication of the book, both as to time and so forth, will be modified in order to perform this arrangement.

Will you kindly confirm the foregoing.

Yours very truly,
The Dial
by [ ] Managing Editor.

TO *Richard Cobden-Sanderson* MS Beinecke

10 September 1922 *The Criterion*, 9 Clarence Gate Gdns

Dear Cobden-Sanderson

I am sorry to delay you. I had to go out of town for the weekend on Friday afternoon and did not return home and found your letter tonight on my return.

We will stick to the *ninety-six pages*, and leave out Parts III, IV and V of *The Waste Land*, if the printer's estimate (returned herewith) leaves room for title and note about contributions subscriptions etc and a note stating that the Dostoevsky will come out in a book (it will only be a sentence, and I will send it tomorrow). Will you let me know this.

The sooner we can send the estimates to Lady Rothermere the better; I have her address now.

Yours (to catch the last post) ever
T. S. Eliot.

Sample very nice

TO *J. M. Robertson*

TS Valerie Eliot

12 September 1922

The Criterion, 9 Clarence Gate Gdns

My dear Mr Robertson,

I have read your essay on Flaubert with great interest and am in accord with you, <I think on all points.>

I have not estimated the number of words but I think with the omission indicated that it will fit in quite well.

When I read Murry's article in the *Times* I was, like several other people, very much irritated.[1] An additional reason for my irritation was the fact that he had obviously borrowed several very useful ideas from an essay by Marcel Proust which was published in Paris about a year before, and borrowed them without acknowledgment.[2] His estimate of the value of Flaubert's work however, was very different from that of M. Proust.

At one time I knew Mr Murry very well indeed, when I was working with him on the *Athenaeum*. Since then differences of temperament have divided us and he has treated me in his published writings, with either open patronage or disguised innuendo.[3]

1–JMM, 'Gustave Flaubert', *TLS*, 15 Dec. 1921. Robertson's essay began by engaging with JMM's published essay.

2–JMM borrowed from Marcel Proust, 'À propos du "style" de Flaubert', *NRF* (Jan. 1920). RA had written to Sturge Moore on 30 Dec. 1921: 'Did you observe that a paragraph in the 2nd column, 2nd page (about Flaubert's sense of time) was taken from an article by Marcel Proust in *La Nouvelle Revue Français*?' (Senate House).

3–JMM, in a review of *SW* (*New Republic*, 13 Apr. 1921), wrote that TSE possessed 'a critical intelligence of a high order', but found his manner 'portentous and disdainful', his writing 'often stiff and hidebound'. On 7 June 1921, VW recorded TSE in conversation apropos JMM: '"When we first knew each other we seemed to be becoming very friendly; but then we realised that we were fundamentally antagonistic"' (*Diary*, II, 124).

It is however on wholly impersonal grounds that I have not yet invited him to contribute to this Review.

I think it would be interesting to mention in a footnote that your essay is one of a proposed series unless you preferred that I did not do so.

I hope that the publication of this essay will only remind you more strongly that I very much hope to have the honour of publishing your paper on Elizabethan blank verse at a later date. I should be sorry to forego the latter, but your paper on Flaubert is so appropriate and desirable that we must use it as soon as possible which will be in the second issue, to appear on January 15th.

You will receive proof in due course.

With very many thanks, believe me,

Sincerely Yours,
T. S. Eliot

<Please forgive an inexperienced secretary.>[1]

Horace B. Liveright TO *Gilbert Seldes* TS copy NYPL

12 September 1922 [New York]

Dear Seldes:

I have yours of the 8th and it is understood between us that we are not to publish *The Waste Land* previous to its appearance in *The Dial* and that the retail price will not exceed $2.00.

I don't think that we'll publish it before January, so you need have no worry about this. I also think that it would be a good idea to number the copies in the first edition whatever its size may be. Naturally, I'll be glad to take back copies of the book as I need them.

Faithfully,
Horace B. Liveright

1 – TSE corrected a number of errors by hand.

TO *Mary Hutchinson* MS Texas

13 September 1922 9 Clarence Gate Gdns, N.W.1

Dear Mary,

I was really dreadfully sorry to have to upset the picnic last Saturday. There was a bungalow to be sold which seemed exactly what we wanted.[1] I went in the morning to see it and found there would be no one there till late in the afternoon, and then only for an hour or two. I felt we must see it, as we were leaving the next day, and we are so anxious to get something permanently in the neighbourhood. Unfortunately, it was no good, for it wanted a great deal of money to put it into repair, and also the price was absurdly high. We were both disappointed. Vivien wanted to move right in somewhere. She hated leaving the country. She says she will send you back the book tomorrow.

We look forward to seeing you in London as soon as the country releases you. It was a shame we had no picnics this year. If we could only get a cottage in the neighbourhood!

Affectionately
Tom.

TO *Ezra Pound* TS Lilly

15 September 1922 9 Clarence Gate Gdns

My dear Ezra,

The fact that I have not written for some time or made any comment on your letter is no evidence of dilatoriness. I have a great deal to say but for reasons which I do not pretend are reasonable, I prefer to wait until after you have seen Richard as I presume you will on his way back from Rome. Richard has not recently been (using the word in the most exact sense) sympathetic; for that matter I do not think that Richard and yourself have much more in common than a disapproval of my way of life up to the present. I, or both of us, may be in Paris in October; this is not absolutely certain as I may not want at that time to go so far for so few days; but if I do come, I may wait and discuss matters with you fully in person. If not, I will write you fully as early as possible. Please do not mention to Richard what I have said as I do not want to widen the breach or to have any quarrel with him.

1 – They were no longer able to rent the seaside cottage at Bosham for their holidays, and so hoped to find something else near the Hutchinsons in nearby West Wittering.

Your contribution is quite admirable and will form a conspicuous adornment of the second number.[1]

Please give my apologies and regrets to Dorothy. As it happened I went to the country on Friday and got leave at the last moment to stay over until Monday night. I wired to her on Tuesday but my wire was returned undelivered with the report that she had already left for Paris. We shall see her I trust if we come to Paris in October.

Yours ever,
Ts.

Liveright's proof is excellent.

Vivien Eliot TO *Ottoline Morrell* — TS Texas

15 September 1922 — 9 Clarence Gate Gdns

Dearest Ottoline,

I was dreadfully sorry to miss you when you were in London, as I am so anxious to see and talk to you. I came back just after and I was very sorry to leave the country, but I had to give up the cottage then. I feel more and more that I should like to live in the country, London is so horrible.

Thank you so much for your letter and for what you say about the 'Bel Esprit' scheme. I have a lot to say on that subject, more than I can write in a letter at present. As for giving you a list of names of people who would be likely to be interested, I do not know of one person outside of those who have already been approached (or who I suppose have been approached) who would be likely to take the slightest interest in the scheme. Anyhow, I do so long for T. to have a freer life and a less ugly one.

T. had dinner with Murry the night before last and enjoyed seeing him again. I certainly do wish that there was not so much hatred, and when one gets right away from everybody one cannot see what it is all about.

I do wish you were in better health – you must have had a horrible summer. I am feeling very ill again just now but I hope it will pass.

With so much love to you, dearest Ottoline,

Your affectionate friend,
Vivien

1–EP, 'On Criticism in General', C. 1: 2 (Jan. 1923), 143–56.

TO *Antonio Marichalar* TS Real Academia de la Historia

16 September 1922 9 Clarence Gate Gardens

Cher Monsieur,

Merci de votre aimable lettre, et de vôtre bénédiction! Je vous envois ci-inclus une annonce corrigée avec la liste des principaux collaborateurs. Le premier numéro contiendra:

George Saintsbury:	'Dullness'
Dostoevski:	Plan of an Unfinished Novel
(translated by S. Koteliansky and Virginia Woolf)	
T. Sturge Moore:	The legend of Tristram and Iseult, I
T. S. Eliot:	The Waste Land (poem) I–II
May Sinclair:	The Victim
Hermann Hesse:	German Poetry of To-day
Valery Larbaud:	Ulysses

Second numéro (probablement):[1]

Rt. Hon. J. M. Robertson:	Flaubert
Paul Valéry:	Le Serpent (and translation by M. Wardle)
J. W. N. Sullivan:	The Literary Papers of Galileo
Ernst Curtius:	Balzac and the Occult Tradition
Stephen Hudson:	The Thief
Antonio Marichalar:	Spanish Literature of To-day
Ezra Pound:	Impressionism
T. Sturge Moore:	Tristram and Iseult, II.
T. S. Eliot:	The Waste Land, III–V.
Gómez de la Serna:	Bric-à-brac.

et ainsi de suite!

Recevez, Monsieur, l'assurance de ma sympathie loyale.

T. S. Eliot[2]

1 – EP's essay was renamed 'On Criticism in General', and Gómez de la Serna's story became 'From "The New Museum"'. J. W. N. Sullivan's piece on the papers of Gallileo never appeared, but Pirandello's 'The Shrine' and Roger Fry's 'Mallarmé's "Herodiade"' were added.

2 – *Translation*: Dear Sir, Thank you for your lovely letter, and your blessing! I am sending you enclosed a corrected announcement of the list of the main contributors. The first number will contain [etc].

The second number (probably) [etc].

and so on!

Please accept, Sir, my loyal affection. T. S. Eliot

TO *John Quinn* TS NYPL (MS)

21 September 1922 9 Clarence Gate Gdns

My dear Mr Quinn,

I am quite overwhelmed by your letter,[1] by all that you have done for me, by the results that have been effected, and by your endless kindness. In fact, the greatest pleasure of all that it has given me is the thought that there should be anybody in the world who would take such an immense amount of pains on my behalf. The thought of this will be a permanent satisfaction to me.

Of course I am entirely satisfied with the arrangements that you have made. It is exactly what I should have liked; only I did not see how it could be done, if it was to be done at all, without calling upon you once more, which, after all you had already accomplished, I was absolutely determined not to do. I also feel that it would be in the nature of asking a favour from Liveright, and also I was loath to ask you to do this on my behalf. I gather that Liveright is quite satisfied that the arrangement will be ultimately to his advantage, and certainly the *Dial* have behaved very handsomely.

My only regret (which may seem in the circumstances either ungracious or hypocritical) is that this award should come to me before it has been given to Pound.[2] I feel that he deserves the recognition much more than I do, certainly 'for his services to Letters' and I feel that I ought to have been made to wait until after he had received this public testimony. In the manuscript of *The Waste Land* which I am sending you, you will see the evidences of his work, and I think that this manuscript is worth preserving in its present form solely for the reason that it is the only evidence of the difference which his criticism has made to this poem. I am glad that you at least will have the opportunity of judging of this for yourself. Naturally, I hope that the portions which I have suppressed will never appear in print and in sending them to you I am sending the only copies of these parts.

I have gathered together all of the manuscript in existence.[3] The leather bound notebook is one which I started in 1909 and in which I entered all

1–On 7 Sept., Quinn wrote that he had invited Seldes and Liveright to his office that morning, and they had come to an agreement. Liveright would allow the *Dial* prior publication of the poem, without notes, in return for which the magazine would buy 350 copies of the book and give its $2,000 award to TSE. 'So everything is all right . . . it was a pleasure to do this little job for you today.' Instead of quarrelling about the manuscript of *The Waste Land*, Quinn would accept it 'as a mark of friendship', on condition that he would allowed to purchase the manuscripts of the early poems that TSE had mentioned. TSE eventually received $140 (£29 14s 10d) from Quinn.

2–EP did not receive a *Dial* award until 1928.

3–These materials were to be posthumously published in *IMH* (1996).

my work of that time as I wrote it, so that it is the only original manuscript barring of course rough scraps and notes, which were destroyed at the time, in existence. You will find a great many sets of verse which have never been printed and which I am sure you will agree never ought to be printed, and in putting them in your hands, I beg you fervently to keep them to yourself and see that they never are printed.

I do not think that this manuscript is of any great value, especially as the large[r] part is really typescript for which no manuscript except scattered lines, ever existed. It is understood that in the valuation you speak of *The Waste Land* is not to be included and the rest must be valued at its actual market value and not at any value which it may (or may not) acquire in course of time.

I think it is very good of you to have subscribed for three copies of the *Criterion*, and I also appreciate to the full your action in writing to [Richard Cobden-]Sanderson. Your letter is wonderfully concise and to the point, and there is certainly nothing in it which could possibly give offence. About the American agencies, I want to put the question before you. I am publishing *The Waste Land* in two sections in the first and second numbers in the hope that it might bring in a few more readers, and because I thought it wiser not to appear myself as a prose essayist in the early numbers. It would therefore have been extremely ungracious to Liveright (although we gave him only the book rights) and now much more so to the *Dial*, if these two first numbers were circulated in America. I therefore propose to wait until copies of the first number or two can be sent to American Agents or Publishers as specimens.

Sanderson I may say in confidence, desires to approach Liveright on the subject to see if Liveright would undertake to have say two or three hundred copies regularly in the form of sheets to publish in America under his own name. He has had dealings with Liveright before and suggested Liveright to me before he knew that I had any relations with him myself. It is hardly necessary to say that whenever you can spare the time I should be extremely grateful for any suggestions or advice from you in this matter.

I think it might be possible for *The Criterion* to secure a small circulation in America and I do not see why it should interfere with the success of the *Dial*. Of course I should not want to compete with the *Dial* in any way but I think that the two papers will be so different in form and appearance that there should be no risk of this. I wish that the *Dial* could secure some circulation in this country, but that seems to me a much more difficult matter. For one thing it is a monthly and the more often periodicals appear the less easily they can be transplanted. For another thing it contains a great deal of local matter and in order to make it really successful in another country, the editors would have to give it form which perhaps would make it less valuable at home. If the *Criterion* were a monthly, we could of course work a good deal together in exclusive fields, but of course it would be impossible for me to edit a *monthly* magazine unless it were to provide enough income for me to devote myself to that and no other regular work. I may say that at present I am not taking a penny from it except a fee for my poem. If it succeeds I shall of course receive a corresponding remuneration. As it is I think I can say that it will look a much more expensive production than it is.

I have been extraordinarily successful in getting hold of the people whom I want to write for it and in order to do justice to these people if for no other reason, I should like to have the paper secure an adequate circulation and publicity. I have no doubt that the paper will appear too conservative to some and too radical to others, but I have gone on the principle of trying to secure the best people of each generation and type. I think that the trouble with the *Little Review* at its best was that its second-rate stuff was so appallingly bad; and my theory is that the best of the most advanced writing of our time (which of course means a very small number of writers) will really appear to better advantage among the really respectable and serious writers of the older type than among their own third-rate and vulgar imitators.

I am very glad to hear that you have had even a month of rest. I know so very well all of the symptoms that you describe that I know you should have had much more time. Whenever I get very tired or worried I recognise all the old symptoms ready to appear, with half a chance, and find myself under the continuous strain of trying to suppress a vague but intensely acute horror and apprehension. Perhaps the greatest curse of my life is noise and the associations which imagination immediately suggests with various noises. It is abominable to live in a town flat unless one can afford a very expensive one, for the reason that one can never forget the lives and disagreeable personalities of one's neighbours; but I find myself in the position where a house in London is just beyond my means.

I must stop this very long letter. Thanking you again and again.

Sincerely yours,
T. S. Eliot

I am dissatisfied with this letter, it does not express either my gratitude or the great interest I have in your health and affairs. I dictated it with a bad headache and under stress of haste to catch the first mail. I will write again.

T.S.E.

TO *F. S. Flint*

MS Texas

22 September 1922

Dear Flint,

Can you manage to return this[1] to the printers, getting it off by *Monday night*? I am *very* sorry to press you but there have been delays. The printers are

Hazell, Watson and Viney Ltd
Aylesbury
Bucks

I am instructing them to *add your name* (unless you prefer not I prefer to have it).

In haste,

apologetically
T. S. Eliot

FROM *Virginia Woolf*

MS Valerie Eliot

25 September 1922 — Monks House, Rodmell, Lewes

Dear Tom,

I hope you will forgive me for what I feel to be an impertinence on my part, but circumstances compel me to risk annoying you.

I think it best to explain to you openly that Ottoline asked me some time ago to join Mr Aldington's Committee for what they call the Eliot Fellowship Fund. I did not altogether agree with their proposals, particularly as I could not make out that they knew what your views were. But I agreed to join. From what you said on Sunday I gathered that – as I had thought – the scheme was impracticable from your point of view. Today Ottoline has sent me a revised version of the scheme which is still less satisfactory than the first. I feel therefore that I must explain the position to her and must ask you therefore whether I am right in understanding you to say that

1) £500 a year is the least sum that would make it worth your while to leave the Bank.

2) that you do not consider the pledges to pay a yearly contribution are a sufficient security to warrant you in giving up your present work.

1–The proofs of Hesse, 'Recent German Poetry', translated (though unsigned) by Flint.

If you simply put 'Yes' on a postcard I shall take it to mean that I am right on both points.

(Perhaps I may add that Leonard and I entirely agree with you, if these are your views).

Yours ever
Virginia Woolf[1]

TO *Richard Cobden-Sanderson* MS Beinecke

Tuesday [26 September 1922] *The Criterion*, 9 Clarence Gate Gdns

Dear Sanderson,

I enclose proof. Saintsbury, Miss Sinclair, and Flint (Hesse) I told to return direct to [the printers at] Aylesbury. I hope that was not wrong. I will send you cover copy and final note tonight.

In haste
T.S.E.

TO *Richard Cobden-Sanderson* TS Beinecke

27 September 1922 *The Criterion*, 9 Clarence Gate Gdns

Dear Sanderson,

I am returning herewith your letter of the 22nd., of August to Lady Rothermere, which I understand you will alter, in respect of the one point of responsibility for payment, and send to her in duplicate at Claridges Hotel, Paris. I am also sending you the manuscript and the Proof of the first part of my poem, so that you may have a record of the undesired alterations made by the printers. You will observe that the translator's name is given only in the case of the Dostoevsky, and that it should be in brackets underneath. Finally I enclose a note re manuscript etc.

1 – On the same day, VW wrote to OM: 'I wired to you to day to stop sending out the circular because I cant agree to the scheme which is now proposed, and – what is far more important – I find that Tom himself, (who was here yesterday) is not ready to accept the original scheme, let alone this one . . . Anything less than £500 would, he says, throw him into journalism, and he prefers the Bank. But now I see from the revised circular that we are trying to get only £300 a year for a period of not less than five years, and this depends upon pledges to contribute yearly . . . It is a thousand pities that Pound and Aldington didn't get Tom to explain his views before they launched the scheme. Let alone the worry to Tom himself – and I'm afraid he takes it all much to heart and feels his position most awkward – the scheme once muddled will be very hard to start again' (*Letters*, II, 561).

I am to send you in a day or two the copy for advertisements, and a list of Periodicals in order; also the copy of a new circular for insertion.

Lady Rothermere is to send you from Paris, some names of people to whom circulars should be sent.

Yours
T. S. Eliot

TO *Richard Cobden-Sanderson* MS Beinecke

28 September 1922 *The Criterion*, 9 Clarence Gate Gdns

Dear Cobden-Sanderson,

Enclosed circular. I do not think I can abbreviate much, I suppose that if a somewhat smaller type is used than for the last it can be brought down to the size to fit into the Review?

Enclose also advert. Only question: can it all go in to the small size space in daily papers? If not, list of contributors must then be omitted, but these should go into *Times Lit Supp* double advert.[1] I give list of papers in what seems order of importance. Will you let me know *how many* can be done for £40?

I tried to telephone three times in afternoon. I will ring your office up at 12 tomorrow in case there is anything pressing.

Times Lit. Supp
Times
Morning Post
Observer
Nation
New Statesman
Manchester Guardian
Yorkshire Post
Birmingham Post
Southport Guardian

I don't of course suppose *all* of these can be done, but this is the *order*, subject to your judgment; and perhaps some are comparatively cheap?

Yrs. ever
T. S. Eliot

1–The two-column announcement of the *Criterion* (*TLS*, 19 Oct. 1922) listed the contents of the first number, including *The Waste Land*, and future contributors including E. M. Forster, Roger Fry, WL, JMM, EP, Marcel Proust, HR, Paul Valéry, CW and VW.

FROM *Virginia Woolf* TS Valerie Eliot

30 September [1922] Monks House, Rodmell

My dear Tom,

Of course I understand how difficult your position is, and only regret that I was forced to open the question again, for it must be a torment to you.

I have had a very reasonable letter from Ottoline, and no harm has been done. She will wait until she hears from me again.

Please come and see us, for that will be much better than writing. We go back on Thursday. Will you dine on Sunday, (the 8th, I think.) Dinner is at seven thirty, but come earlier if you will, for we shall be in anyhow.

I am extremely sorry to hear such bad news of your wife. Please give her my sympathy. I can't imagine any fate more odious. Indeed, you have had a frightful time of it.

Ever yours,
Virginia Woolf[1]

1 – On the same day, VW wrote to OM: 'I have just heard from Tom who writes – "I should like to be able to answer your questions as you ask them, but when I force myself to put my mind on it I know that the whole matter is or has become so very difficult and complicated that I cannot without going into it from top to bottom. I have had to keep my mind off this matter as much as possible and concentrate on what I must do from hour to hour. It has been an incessant strain, knowing that this business was going on; I have been assailed from all sides, and the situation has been made in some quarters very difficult. When no definite offer has been made one cannot let one's imagination run on what one might do in one set of circumstances or another. I find the only way to live at all is to fix my attention on the particular work of the moment. If I may come and see you as soon as you get back to Richmond, I should like to discuss every aspect thoroughly with you, and I think I can make clear why it is so difficult. I am sure however that you will understand my present attitude; so do you mind waiting until I see you? I hope it will not put you in a difficult position." So we have asked him to come next week, and I will let you know whatever I can make out from him . . . I should like to be able to tell Tom exactly how the matter stands so that he may not be in the dark any longer. So could you let me hear before Sunday . . . And he says that Mrs Eliot has now been ordered to undergo treatment at some remote place for several months – another expense I suppose' (*Letters*, II, 563–4).

TO *Richard Cobden-Sanderson* TS Beinecke

1 Oct[ober] 1922 *The Criterion*, 9 Clarence Gate Gdns, London N.W.1

Dear Sanderson,

I agree that the best way to publish the circular is to print it like the previous one and have it folded, I do not think that I can reduce its size any further. Beside the six hundred copies to be enclosed I think that enough should be printed to send to all the persons on our list who received the first circular, and have not subscribed as well as a few for trade purposes. Will you let me know what it will cost to print thirteen or fourteen hundred?

I hope to hear from you the cost of printing the display cards which I had mentioned in our conversation. How many do you think we can dispose of? The only question is whether we should use enough to justify the cost of printing.

I received last night a part of the page proofs, which look very well, and I am posting it back to-night. I suppose that I shall now receive parts from day to day.

Yours ever,
T. S. Eliot

TO *Edmund Wilson* TS Beinecke

1 October 1922 9 Clarence Gate Gdns

Dear Mr Wilson,

Thank you very much for your letter of the 20th of August, and for your kind expressions which are very welcome.[1] Mr Hoppé has promised* to send you my photograph either direct or through his New York office, and if you have not yet received it by the time you get this letter please let me know and I will remind him again.

Yours sincerely,
T. S. Eliot

* some weeks ago.

1 – Wilson, 'The Poetry of Drouth', *The Dial* 73: 6 (Dec. 1922), 611–16; repr. in *T. S. Eliot: The Critical Heritage*, I, ed. Michael Grant (1982), 138–44.

TO *Richard Cobden-Sanderson* TS Beinecke

3 October 1922 *The Criterion*, 9 Clarence Gate Gdns

Dear Cobden-Sanderson,

Thank you for two letters. I return the proof of circular herewith. Your estimate for the advertisements, including the *Southport Guardian*, is quite satisfactory.

I have had the full proof sheets today and am returning them tonight. It is extremely satisfactory.

You will see that I am enclosing the corrected proof of the rest of *The Waste Land*. I shall ring you up tomorrow morning at about 11 and will explain why I have done so. I particularly regret that I have someone coming to see me at five-thirty, but if necessary I could look in at 12. I hope you can manage to be there at 11, as I particularly want to get you.

I will send a list of the Press and of complimentary copies in a day or two.

Yours ever,
T. S. Eliot

TO *John Middleton Murry* TS Northwestern

3 October 1922 *The Criterion*, 9 Clarence Gate Gdns

Dear John,

I had been hoping that it might be possible to see you again soon after our dinner, but I have heard that you are at East Grinstead and therefore difficult of access for persons like me, so I must write to you instead; and perhaps, when you are in town for the day, you will come and lunch in the City, at least. The first number of the *Criterion* has involved endless detail, and a great deal of the side of the venture that is least interesting. You, if no one else, will I hope sympathise with the worries of even a paper which is to appear only quarterly. I have hesitated, considering the exiguity of both emolument and public, to press upon you the claims of an unborn quarterly of unknown qualities – but you must know what my ideal of a 'critical quarterly' is – and no other interests me. Are there in existence any parts or fragments of the work on Shakespeare,[1] that you would allow to appear in such a form? I say Shakespeare, because I imagined you might be working on it, and I do not want to ask you to go out of your way;

1–JMM, *Keats and Shakespeare* (1925).

besides, I think it is more interesting to get writers to give what they are working on in any case. But if not, you surely have set down, or want to set down, some meditations which might be too difficult for any other vehicle. *The Criterion* will fail of its purpose unless it can get what the stomachs of coarser periodicals fail to digest.

May I now proceed to the blunter question: on what date? if my hopes have any foundation.

When shall I see you again?

Yours ever,
T.S.E.

TO *Valery Larbaud* TS Vichy

5 October 1922 *The Criterion*, 9 Clarence Gate Gdns

Dear Mr Larbaud,

You will receive on or about the 16th a copy of the first number of the *Criterion* containing the translation of your lecture on *Ulysses*. Of this there are two things to be said. I was obliged to my great regret to omit the part of your lecture which dealt with the other works of Joyce, although these parts are not only of equal interest but of equal importance, for the understanding of the last part. But I found that several of our contributors had considerably exceeded the number of words allotted to them, and it was necessary to keep the size of the review within certain limits on account of the expense.

My other point is the cause for an apology. The translator who was to have taken charge of your lecture, who is an eminently competent person, disappointed me at the last moment, so that I had no alternative but to set to work under great pressure and translate it myself. This I was extremely loth to do, because I had never attempted any translation before, and in consequence I am afraid that you will find that the translation hardly does justice to the original. This is only one of the unhappy unforeseen accidents that arise during the preparation of the first number of a new periodical.

You will shortly receive from the publisher the scanty emolument.

While the *Criterion* is greatly honoured by the inclusion of this essay I want to speak rather of an indefinite promise with which you excited me.

[incomplete]

TO *Richard Cobden-Sanderson* MS Texas

6 October 1922 *The Criterion*, 9 Clarence Gate Gdns

Dear Sanderson,

I will let you have press list by Monday. Wrapper is *excellent*. I see nothing wrong with dummy exc. cover as discussed and a few corrections already shown in *page proofs* returned to Aylesbury. Don't send new dummy to my office; I couldn't look at it till evening anyhow – send them here.

Everything very good so far.

Yours ever
T. S. Eliot

TO *Mary Hutchinson* TS Texas

Friday [6 October 1922] 9 Clarence Gate Gdns

Dear Mary,

Vivienne has been very ill this week with bronchitis, which her doctor was afraid would turn to bronchial pneumonia. <But he says that the danger is now past.> He has been every day; thinks she has strained her heart in some way, and is keeping her in bed and very quiet, trying to reduce the blood pressure. So it will be quite impossible for her to see anybody for several days. She is very depressed and disappointed. Will you and Jack do me the honour of dining with me at the Café Royal instead, *Monday* at 8. I want very much indeed to see you, both – don't disappoint me – I will wait at the Regent St entrance for you.

Yours ever aff.
Tom.

TO *Henry Eliot* TS Houghton

11 October 1922 9 Clarence Gate Gdns

My Dear Henry,

I have of course been meaning to write to you for a very long time; and I am painfully aware that my recent letters have been concerned mainly with my own business, or with the barest mention of events, and that they may have seemed cold and fatigued. You will have understood, I hope, why this has been, and if you do not know now I can never explain to you better. I have not had the leisure to write a satisfactory and personal letter for years, and it is a recreation at which I am painfully out of practice.

Thank you very much indeed for the welcome cable. It was very good of you to telegraph the news. The dividend will of course be exceedingly welcome to me myself, under present conditions, but I am still more glad because it somewhat relieves my anxiety about mother. For myself, the important point is that Hydraulic should rise and give me an opportunity to sell when Sterling is low: it looks as if Sterling might fall a few points before very long. Do you think that Hydraulic will continue to pay dividends for the next year or so? if so, it ought to have reached a good point for selling by the middle of next summer. I have seen a few days ago a late Harvard friend of mine, whom you may remember – Howard Morris[1] – who is now a very successful Bond Broker in New York. His opinion is that Industrial Securities will rise for the next nine months or so and that then there will be another slump. So I want to look out for an opportunity to dispose of the Hydraulic Stock by next summer.

What is its present quotation after the dividend?

I hope that you will use this slight prosperity as an argument to encourage mother to look forward to another visit to England in the Spring. You must know how anxious I am that she should come once more and also how valuable it is for her to be encouraged to look forward to another visit. I am sure that the next visit would be an even greater success than the last from every point of view. We should also keep her much quieter, and should take her into the country for a longer time and under proper conditions. Vivien's diet is so very exacting for her that we have very high standards of hygiene, much higher as you must know yourself than the family have at home. I also feel convinced that a Summer in England under our care would be very much safer for Mother than a Summer in Cambridge. So do keep reminding her that she is to come.

I have been very anxious lately about her health. She mentioned in a very vague way some ailment, of which she made very light, but which, knowing the family ignorance in matters of health, I cannot take so lightly. She has not even told me what it is so that until I have definite news from somebody I shall continue to be very uneasy.

Thank you very much for the book by Cabell[2] which you have sent me. I have read nearly all of it, and am very much more favourably impressed than I was by some quotations from his work, which I have seen in

1–Howard Morris (1887–1954). They met at Milton Academy and shared rooms in their second year at Harvard.

2–James Branch Cabell, *Beyond Life: Dizain des Démiurges* (1919).

Reviews. I got the impression that his style was extremely stilted, derivative, literary and affected. I still think it somewhat literary and pompous, but I find him extremely agreeable. I also think that there is a good deal to be said for the theory of romance which he expounds; largely because of the abuse to which the word 'realism' has been subjected in our generation. Cabell's argument is of course rather an exaggerated persuasion to the other extreme; but if he put the matter in a wholly balanced and judicial manner not two dozen people would care to read his book or weigh his opinions. I have sometimes thought of taking up myself in a much drier and more legal style, the only style that I can muster, these questions of the cant words 'realism' and 'impressionism'. It would be possible to do so in connection with James Joyce, about whom I have to write an article for the *Dial*; but I do not intend to let myself go on this highly contentious subject at the present time; people who admire Joyce to excess would only abuse me, and the people who detest him would only abuse both Joyce and myself.

I am very sorry to know that you think that as one grows older the affections seem less important. I find myself that the reverse is true. I do not find that young people are capable of any real affection, just as they are incapable of any real understanding. They are interested only in themselves and they care only for people who affect them in the way they like to be affected. They enjoy their own feelings and are indifferent to the individuality of the people for whom they care. As one grows older one clings more and more – so I find – to the few genuine affections which it is possible to have, and one does not become any more indifferent or insensitive to difficulties in the way of understanding and affection.

I could go on very much longer, but in another letter, but I can write no more now. The *Criterion* is to appear next Monday, and you will doubtless receive your copy almost as soon as this letter. It has been a heavier undertaking than I anticipated, but I think that the result, so far as the first number is concerned, is satisfactory. And whatever you think of my Poem, which appears there and also in the *Dial*, I do not think that you can have wholly the same opinion of it that you have of my last work.

Always affectionately,

Your brother,
Tom

If mother comes next Spring, it would be tremendously worth your while to come too, even if you could get only four weeks holiday. You must come.

TO *Richard Cobden-Sanderson* TS Beinecke

13 October 1922 *The Criterion*, 9 Clarence Gate Gdns

Dear Cobden-Sanderson,

I have your letter of today which I imagine was written before I telephoned to you. I shall be writing to Lady Rothermere shortly.

Thank you for the circulars and for the proof of the *Times* advertisement which I return. You will see that unfortunately several of the most important names were omitted because of their having been given higher up in the circular and they are so important that it is essential that they should be added. As I left word on the telephone, Middleton Murry's name is also to go in. Otherwise the advertisement looks very neat.

I am sending you herewith your periodical list marked for review copies. But if you notice the omission of any papers to which it is desirable to send, please send to these papers also.

Yours ever,
T.S.E.

TO *John Middleton Murry* TS Northwestern

13 October 1922 *The Criterion*, 9 Clarence Gate Gdns

Dear John,

I am very happy to have your promise to write, and have immediately written off to see that your name shall go to distinguish the advertisement of the *Criterion*. I appreciate your undertaking the promise so cheerfully, especially considering the fact that your mind is at present engrossed by a book. (May I ask what it is?) I had hesitated to ask you, knowing so well that it is only the review, and not yourself, that will be the gainer by your contributing.

January 31 will be just right; I will not bother you about the matter again until Christmas. Your support will certainly be of the greatest value; and I think I am safe in believing that you will be in sympathy with the paper's aims (which are partially expressed in this circular). I am sure that you will have a flow of fresh ideas immediately this book is off your mind.

I should like very much indeed to spend a weekend with you. I am going away for ten days or a fortnight at the end of next week for a rest, and until I come back my plans are unsettled. But I shall choose a weekend to suit your convenience, considering the work you are engaged upon. My wife wants me to thank you very much; she would have liked to come too, and wants me to explain that she is under such a strict regimen, including a very severe diet, that it is impossible for her to visit, travel, or stop at hotels, and so I must regretfully decline for her.

The Waste Land will appear (without notes) in the *Criterion* No. 1 and in the *Dial*; it will be published as a book, with notes, in January or February, by Liveright in New York[1] and by the Hogarth Press[2] here. I will send you a copy; and I should like to show you the notes first, after you see it in the *Criterion*. I particularly want you to get a fair impression of it, as I am anxious to know your opinion.

I hope the necessity of getting a book done to time does not worry you too much; I look forward to seeing it.

yours ever,
T.S.E.

TO *Richard Cobden-Sanderson* — MS Beinecke

15 October 1922 — *The Criterion*, 9 Clarence Gate Gdns

Dear Cobden-Sanderson,

I rang you up on Saturday, simply to know whether there was anything to discuss, but you had gone. You will of course be sending Lady Rothermere at least one copy at once, and unless she has already asked, will you ask her how many she wants?

Will you please send a copy to:

Ecc. Sig. Giovanni Papini,[3]
Via Colletta, 10
Florence, Italy.

Unless it is now too late, I should like his name <G. Papini> to be added to the list of contributors in the advertisements in which the names are given; you will have added those I mentioned in my letter of Friday night.

1 – *The Waste Land* (New York: Liveright) was published on 15 Dec. 1922, in an edition of 1,000 copies at $1.50.

2 – The Hogarth Press edition was to be issued on 12 Sept. 1923, in an edition of 460 copies at 4s 6d.

3 – Giovanni Papini (1881–1956), journalist, critic, poet and novelist. In early years, a vehement critic of Christianity, he converted to Roman Catholicism in 1920 and wrote a best-selling novel, *Storia di Cristo* (1921; *The Life of Christ*, 1923). Other works included an autobiographical novel, *Un Uomo Finito* (1912; *A Man – Finished*, 1924). In the 1930s he became a supporter of Fascism, which won him conspicuous advancement. He dedicated his *Storia della Letteratura Italiana* ('History of Italian Literature', 1937) to '*il Duce, friend of poetry and of the poets*'.

Will you also send a copy to
The Editor,
The Dial,
152 West 13th Street,
NEW YORK CITY

marked for 'Review'. Would it not be a good idea to have a few slips printed with the words 'For Review' on them, for future press copies?

Yours ever,
T. S. Eliot

TO *Richard Cobden-Sanderson* MS Beinecke

16 October 1922 *The Criterion*, 9 Clarence Gate Gdns

Dear Sanderson,

Thank you for your letter, and for the six copies. The appearance of the paper is all that I could have desired; it is a model. I hope that the appearance and a few favourable notices will double the subscriptions!

Yours ever
T. S. Eliot

TO *Sydney Schiff* MS BL

Monday [16 October 1922] *The Criterion*, 9 Clarence Gate Gdns

Dear Sydney,

Thank you very deeply for your letter. You could not have used words which would have given me more pleasure or have so persuaded me that the poem may possibly communicate something of what it intends. But I cannot expect to find many critics so sympathetic.

Gratefully
Tom.

Vivien Eliot TO *Sydney Schiff* MS BL

Monday [16 October 1922] 9 Clarence Gate Gdns

Dear Mr Schiff,

Tom has shown me your letter to him, and I want to thank you on my own account for showing such real and true appreciation of *The Waste*

THREE SHILLINGS & SIXPENCE NET

THE CRITERION

A QUARTERLY REVIEW

VOL. I OCTOBER 1922 No. 1

CONTENTS

PUBLISHED BY
R. COBDEN-SANDERSON
17 THAVIES INN, LONDON, E.C.1

Land. Perhaps not even you can imagine with what emotions I saw *The Waste Land* go out into the world. It means to me a great deal of what you have exactly described, and it has become a part of me (or I of it) this last year. It was a terrible thing, somehow, when the time came at last for it to be published. I have been distracted these last two days. Yours is the first word that has reached us, and your letter was unexpectedly moving.

I am glad, too, that you like the *Criterion*. It seems to me an achievement, by a man who has only his evenings, tired out by eight hours in the City, and who fills hot water bottles, and makes invalid food for his wretchedly unhealthy wife, in between writing!

I hope I'll see you both before I go away.

Very much love to Violet
Yrs. ever
Vivien.

TO *Richard Cobden-Sanderson* TS Beinecke

18 October 1922 *The Criterion*, 9 Clarence Gate Gdns

Dear Cobden-Sanderson,

Here are the names and addresses of two reviews to which a German correspondent has strongly recommended sending review copies:–

1. *Der Neue Merkur*,
Munchen,
Theresienstrasse, 12,
Germany.
2. *Die Neue Rundschau*,
Berlin W.,
Bulowstrasse, 90,
Germany.

The copies should be marked 'For review and exchange', and I will write to these people later separately. I think it might be well to send a copy in the same manner to:–

Il Convegno,
Via Canova, 25,
Milan,
Italy,

as I understand it is one of the most intelligent of the Italian Reviews.

I am going away at the end of the week for about a fortnight's rest. I shall not give out my address as I do not want to be bothered by correspondence, but I will let you know where I am in order that you may communicate with me if necessary. I hope things are going well both with the *Criterion* and with your private affairs; I sincerely hope that you do not feel as tired as I do.

Yours ever,
T. S. Eliot

This was written last night. I have your letters. I think Lady R's objections boil down to very little; do not concern yourself but leave it to me. They are mostly points for which I was responsible and which I have not changed my mind about. I shall write as soon as she replies to my letter.

TO *F. S. Flint* — TS Texas

18 October 1922 — *The Criterion*, 9 Clarence Gate Gdns

Dear Flint,

I have had to devote all my attention up to the present date to the labour of getting out the first number; so that it has been quite impossible for me even to think about what to do with Gómez.[1] When I come back I will send you back the papers and discuss with you what is to be done. I hope that we can meet and talk things over.

Yours sincerely,
T. S. Eliot

TO *Ezra Pound* — TS Lilly

22 October 1922 — 9 Clarence Gate Gdns

My dear Ezra,

I am glad to receive your expression of approbation of the first number. Of course I should be delighted to have a few poems of Yeats, but so far I have had to go on the principle of asking people whom for one reason or another I felt pretty sure of getting, and as Yeats does not particularly like me, I believe, there appeared no reason why he should consent if I wrote to him direct. Could you do anything in the matter? About Heuffer [*sic*] I have already explained to you my difficulties. I certainly do not want him for several numbers yet because there are a great many other people beside myself who do not like him: the difficulty, if I asked him, would be to get

1–Ramón Gómez de la Serna, 'From "The New Museum"', was eventually published in C. I: 2 (Jan. 1923), 196–201.

some of his really best work but not simply his egotistical meanderings about his own services to English literature. If you happen to hear however of his having done anything praiseworthy you might let me know.

I think it is particularly important to reserve the *verse* contributions to the really first-rate people. For that reason I should very much like to get Yeats. There ought of course to be some other less formal periodical in existence which would serve as a kindergarten for meritorious youth but I do not think that the *Criterion* can afford to print verse, for the present at least, except by people who really know their job. Hence my desire to get hold of Yeats. I do not see why we should not arrange later on to print some of your cantos in the same month in which they appear in the *Dial*. That is to say, if the *Dial* would print on the 25th of the month before one of our quarterly numbers it would be all right. <They wd have it *first*, and I don't suppose they insist on *exclusive*?>

You will possibly observe in the list of contributors a few passengers who will have to walk the plank as soon as the ship gets out of sight of land.

Re the Dostoevski. Lady Rothermere has some early Swinburne manuscripts, one of which is quite good. I should like to print it in the next number.[1] Have you any suspicion as to whether it would be necessary to get the consent of Gosse. Gosse is certainly the last person in England to give me any assistance if he could avoid it.

I presume you have heard from Quinn about the poem. Seldes and Watson have behaved extremely nicely and Quinn has been invaluable. I declined the *Dial*'s proposal when Watson made it to me direct for the reason that I did not want to put Quinn to the slightest further trouble after he had taken so much pains to make out a perfect contract for me with Liveright, so that the matter would never have been carried off unless it had been taken over my head.

Has anything been heard of Proust? I see that the *Nouvelle Revue Française* announce what appears to be a fragment from a new volume, to appear in their monthly magazine.[2] Is this to be available for the *Criterion*?

I am off tomorrow for ten days at the seaside. I feel much too tired for the journey to Paris and simply want to get away to some dull place and 'have left no addresses'.[3] Will write on my return.

Yours,
T.

1–The Swinburne MSS did not appear in *C*.
2–Marcel Proust, 'La Regarder Dormir', *NRF* 19 (Nov. 1922), 513–22.
3–*The Waste Land*, l. 181.

I regret profoundly not seeing you, otherwise I have no particular desire to go to Paris just now.

'In old Manila harbour, the Yankee wardogs lay,
'The stars and stripes streamed overhead, & the band began to play;
'The band struck up the strains of the old Salvation Rag,
And from the ~~quarter~~ mizzentop there flew REAR ADMIRAL BARRY'S flag.'[1]

Vivien Eliot TO *Mary Hutchinson* MS Texas

[late 1922?]

Mary,

I have been thinking about our talk, and sounding Tom a little. I see now that if a small sum was, unconditionally, offered to him by the fund, and *guaranteed*, and if the *Criterion* then became a success *or showed that it would ultimately become* a success, Tom would automatically leave the Bank.

I am sure of this. But I think that any forcing or pressure to *make* him leave the Bank at *this point* would be very tactless, and bad policy.

So much depends on the *Criterion*.

As to the other question of the Left and Right – in my case I think I could, by a bold stroke, combine their forces. In this way – the Right, being in the ascendent, tolerates the Left, and recognises its *usefulness*. The Left admires and reveres the Right with its whole heart. Why not therefore, later, start a communal life with the Right and the Left, and perhaps a George, or even an adopted child – all together?

T. wants *very much* to ask Lytton but does not think Lytton would be at *all* likely to consent to write for the *Criterion*. But he will ask him I hope.

All this is *private*.

If you give me away on any point, I will *never* speak to you again, of course.

[Unsigned]

1 – Rear Admiral Edward B. Barry (1849–1938) became commander of the US Pacific Fleet, 2nd Division, in 1899. His flagship, the USS *West Virginia*, docked in Manila Harbour in Oct.–Nov. 1909. He was forced to resign after forty-five years' service in 1911, following an alleged liaison with a cabin boy. EP had suggested printing TSE's verses about King Bolo, and wrote to him on 29 Aug.: 'your admirer [John Peale] Bishop thinks of collecting Bawdy Ballads, of War and Peace. (the real folk litterchure, including "She Was Pore but she wuz honest" and others that ought n't be left longer to the incertitudes of verbal tradition[)].'

TO *Georges Jean-Aubry*[1] MS Texas

1 November 1922 9 Clarence Gate Gdns

Mon cher Jean-Aubry

Je viens de rentrer – je trouve votre aimable lettre, mais je reviens trop tard pour paraître chez Lady Colefax.[2] Voulez-vous dire à Valéry que je suis navré, c'est un *grand chagrin* de ne pas le voir – je le chercherai à Paris au printemps. Dites aussi que Charles Whibley[3] (à Jesus College, Cambridge) aurait voulu le voir aussi. Si j'avais pu venir à Londres, j'aurais eu le dessin de donner un petit déjeuner – vous, Valéry, Whibley, et moi. Rendez à Valéry mes regrets et mes hommages sincères au premier poète de la France.

Merci de l'envoi de l'intéressante pièce suédoise. Envoyez-moi, je vous en prie, *votre adresse*, afin que je puisse vous en parler. Et quand pouvez-vous me montrer votre Conrad?[4] Ça pourrait se découper en 2 morceaux, ou vous pourriez l'abréger un peu, non?

Yours always,
T. S. Eliot

Rappelez moi à Madame Alvar, s'il vous plaît.

Je ferai expédier un numéro du *Criterion* à Valéry.[5]

1–Georges Jean-Aubry (1882–1950), critic of art, music and literature; author of *La Musique Française d'aujourd'hui* (1916), and *Valery Larbaud: Sa vie et son oeuvre* (1949).

2–Paul Valéry gave a talk on 'La poésie et la langage' ('Poetry and Language') at Argyll House, 211 King's Road (with the permission of Lady Colefax), on 31 Oct. 1922. For Valéry's visit to London in Oct. 1922, see Michel Jarrety, *Paul Valéry* (2008), 529–31.

3–Charles Whibley (1859–1930), scholar, critic and journalist, whose friendship was valuable to TSE. His 'Bolingbroke' was to appear in C. in Apr. and July 1923.

4–Nothing by Aubry was to appear in C.

5–*Translation*: My dear Jean-Aubry, I have just returned – I find your lovely letter but I'm back too late to appear at Lady Colefax's. Would you tell Valéry that I am terribly disappointed, and that it is a *great pity* not to see him – I will look him up in Paris in the spring. Tell him also that Charles Whibley (of Jesus College, Cambridge) would have liked to see him too. If I had been able to come to London, I would have planned to give a small lunch – for you, Valéry, Whibley and myself. Please give Valéry my regrets and my sincere homage to the premier poet of France.

Thanks for sending the interesting Swedish piece. Please send me *your address*, so we can talk about it. And when can you show me your Conrad? It could be cut into two pieces or you could shorten it a bit, couldn't you?

Yours always, T. S. Eliot

Remember me to Madame Alvar, please.

I will send a copy of the *Criterion* to Valéry.

Vivien Eliot TO *Ezra Pound*

MS Lilly

2 November [1922] 9 Clarence Gate Gdns

Dear Ezra,

1) T. is running down again. He keeps trying to write to you I know but in the meanwhile I am writing and this letter is PRIVATE.

2) – *and most important* – the Rothermere woman has been and is being offensive to T. about the *Criterion*. She has written three offensive letters and I am afraid this is going to bring about an awful crisis unless someone can be clever about it – *in time*. She is coming to London about the 15th and if when she sees T. she behaves in the same way as her letters I don't see that he can do anything but throw up the *Criterion* – *and I believe that is what she wants*. She is unhinged – one of those beastly raving women who are the most dangerous. She is now in that asylum for the insane called La Prieuré[1] where she does religious dances naked with Katherine Mansfield. 'K. M.', she says in every letter – 'is *the most intelligent* woman I have *ever* met.' K. M. is pouring poison in her ear (of course) for K. M. hates T. more than anyone.

3) Can you get for T. this money (Bel Esp.) which you speak of in yr. letter,[2] without the condition that he leaves the Bank *immediately*? If so – could he not buy the *Criterion* from Rothermere? Not using his own name in the transaction. I am sure a few people here would help in *that*, with small sums. She *might* be glad to sell it, *now*, for it may be that she is just furious at having promised the money for something she now hates and is bored with. She would *not sell it later on* if it began to *pay*. Do you think this is a *possible* idea? If so, how shall we do it – and *can you get that money*? T. would of course leave the Bank ultimately – and I know he

1–A former Carmelite monastery at Fontainebleau where George Gurdjieff (1872–1949), a Russian mystic of Greek parentage who had left Russia about 1920, had re-established (with financial support from Lady Rothermere and others) his Institute for the Harmonious Development of Man, originally founded in Moscow in 1914. His followers participated in stylised dancing in order to attain a greater degree of consciousness. Katherine Mansfield was to die at La Prieuré on 9 Jan. 1923.

2–EP's letter to TSE, dated '1 Hephaistos' (1 Nov.), explained that 'Bel Esprit' had so far collected pledges of £230 for five years (including permanent pledges for £120), and Liveright's pledge was yet to come. In all, £345 had been raised for the first year. EP concluded optimistically: 'Seems a fair chance that one cd. proceed at same rate. You will have the Dial 2000 in case of any utter emergency . . . All I can add is that I am ready to use my best endeavours to keep the subsidy at £300 a year.'

could make the *Criterion* a success. I could provide £500 (it wd halve my income) – and wd gladly. Write at once.

VE

It could not be run *at all* under £400 a year.

TO *Ezra Pound*

MS Lilly

[3 November 1922] [London]

Cher Ezra

Vivien wrote to you yesterday about the position I am in. Lady Rothermere has been getting increasingly offensive ever since the *Criterion* came out, and especially since she entered her retreat for maniacs. I wish you could see her before she leaves Paris and tell her bluntly that the *Criterion* is a SUCCESS. I have had nothing but good notices. Nearly all the copies are sold (600 printed). But this woman will shipwreck it.

V's idea is to get the money somehow and buy the paper from her – before she has time or opportunity to make my position such that I must throw it up, on her hands. V. thinks she would take £500 for it *now*, especially if my name was kept out of it, and we could find some American who would allow us to use his name in the purchase.

Can you not come over to London for a weekend and see me, as you *know* I cannot come to you.

If you and I could get the *Criterion* into our own hands and could only find the money to run it for a couple of years, it would be the thing of our lives.

Try to get over here to see me, and meanwhile *don't let a soul suspect that* everything is not absolutely right between me and Rothermere.

T.

FROM *Ezra Pound*

TS Valerie Eliot

4 November [1922] 70 bis, N. D. des Champs, Paris VIe

Cher T:

This shd. reach you on the anniversary of the Guy Fawks plot.

I answered V's note last night, but had no means of knowing whether her letter was a familial consortium or her own impressions.[1]

1 – EP wrote to VHE: 'Dear Vivian, Your bomb to hand . . . CERTAINLY do NOT fork out £500. We are trying to build up yr. bloomin income, NOT to blow it in wild speculation . . .

I have this a.m. written to Lady R. asking for an interview. Last time I saw her she was affable, and said she was coming to tea, whereafter she vanished, and I did not know she was still in Paris. I wish you'd be specific. What is she trying to force into the Crit.

Of course if she says it looks like a corpse, she's right, mon POSSUM, do you expect her to see what is scarce discernable to the naked eye, that it is *supposed* to be PLAYIN' POSSUM

I think both you and V. are in delirium, thinking of payin £500 for the privilege of having worked six months. Bring out another number. Put in all our own stuff. IF, ever IF the bills have been and are being paid. £500 for a review that has run one issue?? Gees she'd be SOME financier if she cd. work that dimereena

Dear ole SON. You jess set and hev a quiet draw at youh cawn-kob.

The only asset of the Crit. is YOU, youh-sellf. If you quit, *it* quits. You'll have been euchred for a free start that is the common fate of all mankind, them as boosts periodicals they dont own.

Run one more number.   at least.   Announce your resignation therein, if necessary. Pay your patient friends. and announce the opening of the 'New Effigy', 'The Golden Vanity' (there's fine title for for a really sumptuous work). <dont give this one away>

But sink money into a liability, that wd. stay a liability for some years. *Nevairrrrrrrr!* For the privilige of disguising oneself to look like a member of the Athenaeum Club.   Mon gibletts.   Mon Gosh, Mon chienggggg.

If you can trust my discretion, send me the correspondence between you and L. R. and I'll try to get a clear idea of the matter.

£500 is bunk. If she is scared of the prospect of expenses she'll give the damn thing away. Chrissssttttt cant you see that *you are* the Criterion. If you go it collapses. Have you . . . got a contract? Not that English contracts are worth a damn, but on the chance that she may not know that no english contract is binding.

I dont see that one story by Katherine M. wd. queer the review. Print the Adams in the next number,[1] and the Mansfield in the third. That will hold things calm over the interval. Tell her you had already accepted the

—

Do understand that I take no interest in England or English magazines. I dont think the island matters a damn, I shd. like to get T. out of it into a decent climate. If he likes to print Stsbury, Stg Moore, Binyon, etc. that's his affair. He has got out a damn good quarterly for the purpose, i.e. of being feasible in a damned country, where any more active manifestation wd. be doomed to extinction. BUT . . . . buy it? NO.'

1–B. M. Goold-Adams, 'The Obsequies', C. 1: 3 (Apr. 1923), 293–302.

Obsequies for the 2nd number. I dare say K. M. IS the most intelligent female she has ever met. So long as she dont include Middleton M., I dont mind. Personally I find it no worse to conciliate the K. M. faction than to conciliate the [Laurence] Binyon faction. When I first met Lady R. she seemed rather more ready to burn the Bastile than you are.

Air yew sure, mon cher, that she is being *intentionally* offensive. Remember that she is not one who has started at the social apex and descended. People of a slightly lower social order than we are . . . . . apt to be offensive when they are only, in their own eye, being frank, hearty and outspoken.

especially in your present exhausted and enerve condition . . . . perhaps a slight magnification takes place.

At any rate, consider hanging on for another three months. Let us get our own money back out of it. At least divide what spoils there are, IF there are any. I hope you haven't undertaken printing expenses on yr. own???

IF you're going to chuck it, you at least have the chance of launching a few explosives, or a few new authors before you abandon the deck. Print my article,[1] and blame the demise on me.

et tu exageres. NO periodical cd. be the '~~affair~~ thing of our lives'

As I said in note to V. Bill Bird who is doing the 3 Mts Press[2] is ready to print a review at his expense.

IF you cant stick the Crit. let it go out in glory and seek then the southern shore. more anon. must keep an appointment.[3]

E

1 – EP, 'On Criticism in General'.

2 – William Bird (1889–1963), an American, had founded the Three Mountains Press in Paris in 1921, and published four of EP's books, 1923–8. On 29 Aug. 1922, EP had told TSE of planned limited editions by Ford Madox Hueffer, William Carlos Williams, Hemingway, and others, and invited a contribution 'in yr. non-academic vein', perhaps the Bolo poems. 'The plan seems to me to solve the question of free expression, better than the Little Review did; and better than the necessary caution of heavier periodicals, like the Dial and the Crit. can afford.'

3 – A further six-page letter in the same vein followed the same day.

TO *John Middleton Murry* MS Northwestern

5 November 1922 9 Clarence Gate Gdns, N.W.1

Dear John

I should like very much to spend the weekend of the 25th with you. I was just on the point of writing to suggest a meeting soon.

I wonder if you know the work of a German critic named Curtius. I have sent him your *Problem of Style* [1922], and as I happen to have two copies of his book on modern France, it seemed appropriate that I should send you one, unless you know it already.[1] I look forward to seeing you on the 25th.

Yours ever
T.S.E.

TO *F. S. Flint* TS Texas

6 November 1922 *The Criterion*, 9 Clarence Gate Gdns

Dear Flint,

I am now back in town and am sending you back the Gómez manuscripts and your translations. Do you think you could lick some of these into English by the 1st December? If you cannot, I do not know who can, as this is not a problem for the ordinary translator at all. I do not want very much, only two or three of those which you think can be made most presentable. At any rate they will provide relief for the lighter-minded of our readers who find the review too dull and indigestible. I shall be awfully grateful to you if you will exercise your talents upon this material.

Would you care to tackle a critical essay on Balzac, written in German, by Ernst Curtius[2] which I hope to receive in a few days? He is quite an intelligent German and has written an essay on Proust which Proust is highly pleased with.[3] It ought to prove more interesting to you than the Gómez.

I may say that the payments for the first number have been delayed by the fact that Sanderson and myself have been single-handed and have had a great many unexpected details to attend to, but this matter will be dealt with this week.

1–E. R. Curtius, *Die literarischen Wegbereiter des neuen Frankreich*.
2–See Ernst Robert Curtius, 'Balzac', C. 1: 2 (Jan. 1923), 105–18.
3–Curtius, 'Marcel Proust', *Neue Merkur*, Feb. 1922.

I am much obliged to you for letting me see the story. It struck me that the writer has distinct ability and ought to be encouraged, and I shall write to her to express the hope that she will go on. I do not think that I shall be able to use this one because we shall only publish, as a rule, one piece of fiction in each number and I have already secured fiction for two or three numbers ahead; so that I should prefer to wait as I think – for what my opinion is worth – that your friend will easily surpass it before very long.

Yours ever,
T. S. Eliot

TO *Ezra Pound* CC

7 November 1922 9 Clarence Gate Gdns

Cher Ezra,

In answer to your question: yes, of course I have a contract for three years, prepared for me by an able solicitor, as binding and clear as possible, and OF COURSE I know that a contract would be no damb use if she wanted to chuck the paper or give it to someone else. Even with the contract the TITLE, which we presented, belongs to her, and the title is the paper.

So far the point is not the number of lunatics whom she wants included. She objects (1) to the whole getup and printing of the paper without specifying anything good about it, and I have with difficulty persuaded the publisher not to throw it all up at once; which would mean the trouble for me of getting another publisher if possible, lot of trouble, and she would probably insult him too (this in STRICT confidence); also her only comment on the contents is that it is Dull and that Saintsbury is bad.[1]

I am not running the paper for Binyon any more than for K. Mansfield. Of course I dont mind printing a story by K. Mansfield, though I prefer Binyon and have no use for either. I will however suggest to Lady R. that she should secure a story from K. Mansfield. I myself should much prefer to have something from Murry; he is at least in every way preferable to his wife. The latter is not by any means the most intelligent woman Lady R. has ever met. She is simply one of the most persistent and thickskinned toadies and one of the vulgarest women Lady R. has ever met and is also a sentimental crank.

1 – Saintsbury's article 'Dullness' was the first item in C. 1: 1 (Oct. 1922), 1–15.

I notice that the *Criterion* is generally reckoned as a source of income when Bel Esprit income is calculated, but is useless and hopeless on other occasions. I am not entitled to want more than £300 stipend, but am expected to edit a review for which there is no need or use and to write articles for the *Times* which are also of no use and furthermore are said to damage my brain. My dear Ezra, I dont want to write articles for the *Times* or for anything else, I dont want to write articles at all, I dont want to write, no sensible man does who wants to write verse. But I dont see how I am supposed to be selfsupporting in five years except by an enormous output of useless articles, literary rubbish etc. instead of the small number by which I have hitherto supplemented my income. It is preferable to run a review and be paid for letting other people write than to write oneself, but if the situation for a review is as hopeless as you make out I dont see any reason for bothering about that either. (I thought you said it 'might become a property').

Of course I do not see England exactly as you do, it comes largely from having spent so much of my time among commercial people and not mixing with literary people as much as you have done; it also comes from a belief that nothing matters about a country except being let alone, climate, chemists, and the character of the lower classes: of course England is deficient in some of these qualities.

My own idea is that the way to make a review is to make it as unliterary as possible: there are only half a dozen men of letters (and no women) worth printing, better get good people from other occupations who at least write about something they know something about. (This is NOT for publication to Lady R. or anyone else.) I want Sir J. Frazer, Trotter, Eddington, Sherrington or people like that.[1] Also historians if they can write. (Hence Whibley on Bolingbroke).

Unless I can edit a paper that pays, or else that is so 'important' in some way or other that rich ignoramuses will feel that they MUST subsidise it, I dont see how I can ever earn more than £150 per year maximum.

Lady R. is (so far as I can make out her address) at La Prieuré, Avon, Fontainebleau. Only thing is to congratulate her on the review as if ignorant of what I have told you, to counteract influence of K. M. who has presumably told [her] that it is bad.

[T. S. E.]

1–Sir James Frazer (1854–1941), anthropologist; Wilfred Trotter (1872–1939), neurosurgeon and psychologist; Sir Arthur Eddington (1882–1944), astronomer; Sir Charles Sherrington (1857–1952), physiologist – none of whom contributed to C.

TO *Richard Cobden-Sanderson* TS Beinecke

8 November 1922 *The Criterion*, 9 Clarence Gate Gdns

Dear Sanderson,

I think that we should now settle the payment due to the contributors as early as possible, and give you hereunder the schedule with the number of words computed by Messrs Hazell, Watson and Viney. I have estimated the payment at £10 per 5000 words accordingly. Will you check my figures?

Dullness	5,304 words	...........£10. 6. 0
Story of Tristram and Isolt ...	4,720 words	.............8. 14. 0
F. M. Dostoevsky	4,548 words	.............8. 11. 0
Recent German Poetry	1,484 words	.............2. 10. 0
The Victim	8,000 words	............16. 0. 0
Ulysses of James Joyce	3,520 words	.... 6. 10. 0

I think that you have the addresses of all the writers to whom to send cheques. The cheque for the Dostoevsky should be made out to Mrs Virginia Woolf, and I will ask her to settle the indebtedness between Koteliansky and herself.

Yours sincerely,
T. S. Eliot

Have you figures handy for the total cost of No. 1? I should like them ready for Lady R.

TO *Richard Aldington* TS Texas

8 November 1922 9 Clarence Gate Gdns

Dear Richard,

I have only a few days ago returned from Worthing where I have been having a fortnight's rest, the remainder of my holiday. I was sure that you would understand that I was not writing a single letter while I was there and that you would hear from me upon my return. I hope that your holiday in Rome was in every way a satisfactory one and that it has had a stimulating effect. It is very good news to hear that you are doing an essay which will be very welcome. I shall count upon you for the third number, in which I know you will not find Whibley's 'Bolingbroke' an unwelcome neighbour. I am looking forward to reading your further news in the literary review.

I do not think that Larbaud's article can be taken as criticism at all. It is merely an introduction to the subject, and I think it is useful to anyone who is going to read the book. I am struggling with a notice of *Ulysses* myself which I have promised long since to the *Dial*; I find it extremely difficult to put my opinion of the book intelligently, inasmuch as I have little sympathy with the majority of either its admirers or its detractors.

The *Criterion* has kept me very fully occupied and still does. I should very much like to know who wrote the extremely amiable and, as *I* thought, intelligent notice in the *Times*?[1]

Is there any prospect of seeing you in London in the near future?

Yours ever,
T. S. E.

TO *Valery Larbaud* — TS Vichy

8 November 1922 — 9 Clarence Gate Gdns

Dear Larbaud,

Thank you for your letter of the 29 ulto. I hope that you found the translation of your essay as satisfactory as you pretend; I can only say that it hardly does justice to the original. I am very sorry to hear that you have been ill and overworked. I had intended to come to Paris for a few days last month, but I was so tired that I merely went to the seaside instead and I am afraid that I am not likely to be in Paris again until the spring. Your essay on Landor sounds *extremely* desirable and I hope also that you can include Landor's unpublished letters.[2] I have complete faith in the excellence of your English, but if you wish, I will read it through carefully with an eye to possible solecisms. Can you tell me how long it is likely to be and when you can promise it to me, or at least promise the first part of it?

It is high time that some justice should be done to Landor in this country.

I will try to find or procure a spare copy of my paper on Andrew Marvell for you. I have had the design of ultimately polishing it up for a projected volume of essays on the English seventeenth century.

Yours very sincerely,
T. S. Eliot

1 – [Harold Child], in *TLS*, 26 Oct. 1922, praised both C. and *TWL*: 'We know of no other modern poet who can more adequately and movingly reveal to us the inextricable tangle of the sordid and the beautiful that make up life.' Repr. in *T. S. Eliot*, ed. Grant, 134–5.

2 – Larbaud had offered an article on 'Landor and Italy', which would include letters by Landor that he had discovered in Florence, but it did not appear.

TO *Edmund Wilson* TS Beinecke

8 November 1922 9 Clarence Gate Gdns

Dear Mr Wilson,

I have received your letter of the 17th ulto. and have written strongly to Mr Hoppé [about his photograph of TSE] protesting against the carelessness in his office. I am also sending you shortly a copy of the Wyndham-Lewis drawing. I am very sorry that you have had the trouble of writing again. Of course I shall be very glad to let you have an article as soon as I can fulfil one or two long outstanding obligations.

Yours sincerely,
T. S. Eliot

FROM *Ezra Pound* TS copy Valerie Eliot

[9? November 1922] 70 bis, N.D. de C. [Paris]

Cher T:

A. I have written to lady R. (as per request) several days ago, stating that the *Crit.* was a masterpiece of editing.

She is right about its being dull; and UTTERLY wrong in disapproving the format.

I cant judge of the relative intelligence of her female friends, never having met K[atherine] M[ansfield]. *If* she *hasn't suggested* printing K. M.; I shdnt. and if she hasn't committed any greater crime than saying the review is dull and expressing a divergent taste in formats, I don't see that the insult is very deadly.

///

As to my other inconsistencies. A half dozen articles for the *Times*, WHILE you are working in bank, is a vastly different thing, i.e. computed in mental strain, to same or even larger number of said articles done in comparative leisure.

///

The *Crit.* is a £100/ a year as long as you stick to it. As I wrote V. yesterday, it may become a property, but that process of *werden* [becoming] implies Lady R's initial outlay; to become a property means, as I used the phrase, to have the prospect of paying its expenses <plus>, IN TIME.

You are entitled to want any income you can get. Six articles to *Times*, plus Review, plus £300, plus incidentals.

I certainly agree that it is preferable to run a review to writing too much.

Saintsbury is a meritorious old dodo, if he had had any more pep he wdnt. be where he is. Oh well.

Can I lucidify further. The *Criterion* is 'good' so long as it is a tube down which Lady R.'s or someone elses funds flow toward YOU.

As a hole into which our funds < = or funds to be raised by us>, wd. have to be poured to feed IT, it is *not* good. It is another printer to feed.

It is estimable as a high court of letters, position now held by the *Dial*, against which there is no appeal save to you (or possibly to the Three Mts. Press) *incontrastabile* [*sic*] *e gravoso*.[1]

It is merely a question of whether the bank is more exhausting than *Crit.* plus 6 *Times* articles, plus six squibs for *Dial*. Plus any further or more lucrative sinches you cd. devise.

Lady R. is a natural force, to be exploited. One does not ask reason (ratio), rationationation of the ocean currents.

As next move, I suggest that you write to her, admitting dullness, saying that Stsby. is the best of a set of necessary evils. That the format is universally commended. That I have tried to communicate with her and have written to you to know her whereabouts.

Is she paying the bills? to date?? As long as she goes on doing that

Ask not for roses
Ask not for wreathèd crowns,
Owners are hell
Complain not of her frowns

Who pays. I tremble, friend to think
What Quinn had said

Were this price on his head;
If from his purse the price
were drawn to stipendate
Old Stsbury and old Stg Moore

Or if decorum, neath such staid device
Trundled across the sward, where we of late

Did BLAST, and mocked the Times,
used 'merde' to tip our rhymes
et cetera

1 – 'Giudicio incontastabile gravoso' ['judgment severe and incontestible'], Dante, 'Morte villana, di pietà nemica', 3 (*Vita Nuova* VIII).

What can a bunch of skirts
against the cob
Of Sweeney? belittle hence thy hurts
and buck the job.
Bigob.

Seems to me easier (IF the cash will continue to flow from Lady R.) to keep her tolerating a 'politic' dullness, holding her to bait of greater liveliness at a steadily disappearing future,

THAN to find new capital. ANY other owner wd. have ideas about the magazine, and probably want to WRITE in it, and have his or her friends in greater numbers.

The last subscriber to B[el] E[sprit] (new this week) talked of starting a magazine with Hem.[1] (upon which Hem brought him to me) but he wdn't stand the *Crit.* for ten minutes. he'd want Sandburg or Lindsey, or possibly Sterling[2] (he don't admire the latter's poesy, but thinks him the best fooker in California.) says 'George is a great boy.'

I can't see ANY capital for a conservative quarterly. Apart from Thayer and Lady R. all the capital I know wd. prefer my position to yours.

I dont see a 'jeunes' magazine. Hueffer and I cdnt. see a 'jeunes' magazine two years ago. Hence the 3 Mts. brochures. Minimum expense on printing. For maximum meaning.

When I say I want you out of bank I mean I want you relieved of strain before you *crever* [burst].

I agree with Lenin, that those who have lived under the old dispensation are no good; only hope of a node of civilization lies in bringing in new blood.

Hem. is more intelligent than Saintsbury. I dont expect anyone save me and Linc. Steffens,[3] and Soiseau [Bird], and Hem's present boss to think so, YET. For purposes of an Eng. Quarterly, Stsb. is more opportune.

You did ? get the fact that I approved of yr. editing; of the editorial feat of No. 1. Crit. Misunderstanding seems to lie in interpretation [of] my loose phrase 'become a property', used at a time when I was ignorant and wholly unsuspicious of a rift in the Eliot–Rothermere lute, thinking the £1200 of opening expenses guaranteed by Lady R.

1–Ernest Hemingway.
2–Carl Sandburg (1878–1967), poet and biographer; Vachel Lindsay (1879–1931), poet known as the 'Prairie Troubadour'; George Sterling (1869–1926), prolific poet and mentor of Robinson Jeffers.
3–Lincoln Steffens (1866–1936), American journalist, best known for his statement after a visit to the Soviet Union in 1921, 'I've been over into the future, and it works.'

Has she seen the favourable press notices? and does she know edtn. is nearly sold out?

I think youre right about ole Fraser, never heard of the other ole blokes. Whibley is a complete shit who used to write horsepiss in the *Daily Mail*, but is said to have written good 17th century essays at one time.

Have I, caro mio, have I protested against anything except the expenditure of £500, for the shadow of a name, substance of which cd. be had for the grabbing.??

Vale et me ama [farewell and with my love]

E.[1]

FROM *Ezra Pound* TS copy Valerie Eliot

10 November [1922] 70 bis, N.D. de C.

Cher T:

I enclose communique from that hot bitch Lady R., somewhat lacking, perhaps in veracity,[2]

1 – On the verso of the last sheet, VHE wrote: 'Would like to go over this letter with you. *Send a line*, and promise to write fully in a week. The man needs dealing with now. Send a line *at once*, and say drily that you have seen D[orothy] twice.'

2 – Headed '"Claridges", Paris. 8th Nov. 1922', Lady Rothermere's letter reads:

'I am seriously disturbed to hear from you that Eliot is in such a bad state of health.

'You write however of the editorship of *The Criterion* as if it were a large monthly review or even a weekly one instead of a slender quarterly! The production of *The Criterion* is not *at all a vital* matter to me.

'I offered to be responsible for the financial support of it because several friends of mine assured me under the direction of Eliot such a quarterly would do much towards the furtherance of the influence of Eliot and others, which would also be an excellent thing for English literature.

'Several months after Eliot had undertaken to produce *The Criterion*, I wrote and assured him that he was in no way ever morally bound to see the thing through, and he replied that he was wholly interested in it heart and soul.

'I have the greatest possible friendship and esteem for Eliot and consider that he has most successfully produced the first number. If this extra work can in any way be injuring Eliot as you think I would infinitely prefer that the production should cease.

'However I do not believe honestly that the appearance of *The Criterion* is in any way responsible for Eliot's present state of health. Don't you think you exaggerate a little?

'I believe Eliot is nervous and run down because of the effect of years of lack of fresh air, exercise and proper nourishment on a delicate constitution. With regard to the suggestion that he should leave the bank I really do not think that it is *anyone's business but Eliot's* and my impression is that he likes the work even if it is exacting.

'I am leaving for London in a few days and shall certainly see Eliot and hope to find his state of health less grave than you think.'

She was in the summer ready to raise funds for your release. She SAID she had got a donation of 1000 dollars down. I shd. like to have that transferred to B[el] E[sprit] treasury, or to you, before the explosion.

/ / /

She SAID she had a plan to propose, when I met her with Higgins; she also parted saying she wd. call in two days. Then exit. she disappeared.

/ / /

I dont, of course, know what upset her.

Possibly the appearance of Waste Land in *Dial* may be not unalien to the row. She said in the summer that the *Dial* could NOT have it, because it was to go into the *Crit.*

That may be the fly in her cunt-salve.

/ / /

However I supply you with all possible data. She, as per enclosed, has highest esteem for you, and considers the 1st number of *Crit.* successful. <we have that in writing – keep the letter in case of court proceedings>

I suggest that <with her> you take the position that you wish to leave the bank, as soon as suitable arrangements can be made, and that relieved of that onus, give the air and exercise you so need (vide enclosure), your soul, much enlarged wd. be even more entirely 'in' the *Criterion* and the endeavour benefit english letters, to say nothing of french.

I don't see any other line that will gather up that 1000 dollars (which for all of me, may be transferred to you at once, without waiting for B. E. [Bel Esprit] subsidy.)

I dont see that anything is to be gained by having her continue in the idea that you consider the bank a pleasure 'even if it is exhausting'.

I think she hates Thayer and Watson, especially the former. The latter hates her. and that she is possibly wroth over the *Dial* coup. However that is four times as much in yr. pocket as you wd. get from her in a year, and Watson at any rate is a better proposition than she is. I am inclined to prefer S. T. to her, in the light of present events. Her present illumination seems to confirm their versioni of her N.Y. escapade. escapade = eschaper.

Of curse, Caro mio, I have, by the herein enclosed epistle of yr. friend, been 'deeply insulted,' I the distinguished man of letters, etc. by a lowbrowed ranting bitch (as V. so aptly calls her).

Now, carino, do be sensible, do not be disturbed by Lady R., consider the course of the moon, watch the day of the month on which her frothings occurr.

Raveth she one way on the first day, she will rave again on the 29th. day, thus with regular or irregular intervals according as to the processes of her endocrines.

Brewster hath said, 'Never treat with the female client, save in the presence of the male relative'.

and Jackson hath said 'For three days in every month is every woman a stark raving lunatic.'

Considering which things, I who have nothing to gain from her Bitchshipp have replied to her with a courteous letter, employing soft words, yea even now, O Tomasso.

I have said that you are 'heart and soul' in the *Crit.* and that I believe you wd. leave the bank, under suitable circumstances.

I think you can assume that position, at least until the 1000 bones, have been transferred, either to you, or to Richard [Aldington]'s formally organized committee of trustees. (or at least till we have *tried* to get it shifted.)

If you wd. keep me more au courrant, I might play this game of halma a bit better. but if you are too tired to write, dont bother.

Tu ne reponds rien, rien, rien, rien, à mes questions, tu le sais, cochon!!! ???> Jam-, jam-, jHDammais.[1]

Did I say that another solid B. E. subscription had come in? and that the secretary of the Persian legation in Washington also approves. Do you want a job on the Persian finance commission?

Have you any kick ref my article in Nov. *Dial*?? If so shoot it along. I'm a glutton for punishment.

Only dont take Lilian [Rothermere] to heart, be not wroth with a menstrous woman.

yours
E

TO *Richard Cobden-Sanderson* MS Beinecke

12 November 1922 — *The Criterion*, 9 Clarence Gate Gdns, London N.W.1

Dear Cobden-Sanderson,

As I just told you on the telephone I forgot to include the payment due to F. S. Flint for translating the German article [by Hermann Hesse]. The article is 1484 words which for this purpose I will call 1500 and at the

1 – 'You tell me nothing, nothing, nothing, nothing in response to my questions, as you know, pig! Nev-, nev-, never.'

usual rate of 15/- per 1000 we therefore owe to him £1.2.6. You have his address, as he is a subscriber.

Yours,
T. S. Eliot

Have you any news from Paget about placing American copies? This ought to be hurried on, so that we can know how many of No 2 to print.

I notice that the Agencies who send MSS. to you do not usually send stamps. What do they expect?

TO *Gilbert Seldes* — TS Timothy and Marian Seldes

12 November 1922 — *The Criterion*, 9 Clarence Gate Gdns

Dear Mr Seldes,

I am afraid that I have not thanked you for your cheque of $130. This is due to the fact that it arrived while I was at the seaside taking a much-needed rest, and while I was there I neither received nor wrote any letters. I must also thank you for your letter of the 10th ulto. and for your review of *Ulysses* in the *Nation* which I think extremely interesting and valuable and which I should have liked to see in its complete form. It is on the whole much more satisfactory than any other review of the book that I have seen and I shall find it still more difficult to say anything about the book myself.[1]

I am sending you a few circulars of the *Criterion*, and I trust you have received the first number which I had sent to you. Now sold out. So far, no steps have been taken toward acquiring American subscribers. This is owing to the appearance of my poem in the first number; I do not want the first number to be put upon the American market as it would have been unfair in view of the almost simultaneous appearance of the poem in the *Dial*. I am looking forward to receiving the Nov. no.; Liveright's proof was on the whole very good indeed and I have no doubt that the appearance in the *Dial* will be equally good.

I hope that you received my cable in time to make use of my valedictory letter on Marie Lloyd for the December number.[2]

Yours always sincerely,
T. S. Eliot

1–Seldes described *Ulysses* (*Nation* [NY], 30 Aug. 1922, 211–12) as a 'monstrous and magnificent travesty', and called JJ 'possibly the most formidable writer of our time'. TSE's review, '*Ulysses*, Order and Myth', came out in *Dial* 75: 5 (Nov. 1923), 480–3.

2–'London Letter', *Dial* 73: 6 (Dec. 1922); repr., with revision, as 'In memoriam: Marie Lloyd', C. 1: 2 (Jan. 1923), 192–5, and as 'Marie Lloyd' (*SE*).

November number just received. Poem admirably printed. I see some remarks by you which I find very flattering[1] – But I find this poem as far behind me as 'Prufrock' now: my present ideas are very different. Thanks for hint: I want to deal with the 'intellectual love of God' later.[2]

TO *Richard Cobden-Sanderson* PC Beinecke

13 November 1922 [London]

Thank you for your letter and statement of disbursements. I hope that you can manage Thursday: if *not*, can you let me know definitely by Thursday *morning*, if I telephone you about noon?

Yrs,
T.S.E.

Can give you larger part of MSS. on Thursday.

TO *Ezra Pound* PC Lilly

14 November 1922 [London]

I sat down to write to you tonight but am so very tired that I cannot. I will try again tomorrow –

Yrs. ever
T. S. E.

TO *Richard Aldington* TS Texas

15 November 1922 9 Clarence Gate Gardens, N.W.1

Dear Richard,

I was very glad to get your letter and enclosures. As for my health, I am very tired, but this is not unusual. As for *The Waste Land*, that is a thing

1 – Seldes wrote, 'Until I had read *The Waste Land* by Mr Eliot I believed that *Ulysses* was the only complete expression of the spirit which will be "modern" for the next generation' ('Nineties – Twenties – Thirties', *Dial* 73: 5, Nov. 1922, 577).

2 – Seldes's paragraph about TSE and JJ concluded: 'That infinite intellectual love which God has for himself, according to Spinoza, is perhaps the last remaining contact of this age with what is divine.' In 'The Perfect Critic' (*SW*), which also invokes Spinoza, TSE had written: 'without a labour which is largely a labour of the intelligence, we are unable to attain that stage of vision *amor intellectualis Dei*'.

of the past so far as I am concerned and I am now feeling toward a new form and style.

I do not know how the *Dial* separated the prefix of 'Apothanein';[1] I spelt it out carefully enough for them.

Ezra's Paris Letter is certainly excellent.[2] As for the *Phoenix and the Turtle* I do not see what you mean by a parody of Donne; I wish you would quote me phrases of Donne of which it seems to you reminiscent.[3] I expect that the person who praised it was Murry; I do not know of anyone else except myself who has ever expressed admiration for it.

Your notice of the *Criterion* ought certainly to boost its circulation in America.

Your poem I much enjoyed; I can pay it the compliment of saying that it makes one realise how far this excellent instrument of the seventeenth century is deteriorated in the hands of Georgian versifiers. Have you studied with any care Bishop King in Saintsbury's collection? He seems to me one of the finest and I have long desired to write a short paper about him.[4] I want to write something about Cowley[5] also, undeterred by the fact that you preceded me and probably know a great deal more about him.

As I hoped, your visit to Italy seems to have stimulated you; I think your article on Pastoral Drama might be a valuable one,[6] and I hope you will write it. I know nothing about these people, but the verses which you quote give me pleasure. Do write it.

Yours ever,
T. S. E.

May I keep poem or not?

1–In the epigraph to *The Waste Land* 'ἀποθανεῖν' was printed 'ἀπο θανεῖν'.

2–EP, *Dial*, Nov. 1922, partly about Bel Esprit.

3–In 'A Romantic Patrician' (*A.*, 2 May 1919), TSE had written: 'We should not gather from [George] Wyndham's essay that the "Phoenix and Turtle" is a great poem, far finer than "Venus and Adonis".' TSE borrowed Shakespeare's 'defunctive music' for 'Burbank with a Baedeker: Bleistein with a Cigar'. RA wrote to Amy Lowell on 1 Apr. 1922: 'there is a craze for the "Phoenix and the Turtle" just now and I am very much looked down upon because I suggest that it is only the divine William making fun of Donne' (*Richard Aldington: An Autobiography in Letters*, 67).

4–The poems of Henry King (1592–1669), Bishop of Chichester, had been included in Saintsbury's *Minor Poets of the Caroline Period*, III (1921). TSE, in 'The Metaphysical Poets', hailed King's 'Exequy' as 'one of the finest poems of the age'. His paper on King was never written.

5–See, for example, TSE's articles 'The Minor Metaphysicals: From Cowley to Dryden', *Listener* 3 (9 Apr. 1930), 641–2; and 'A Note on Two Odes of Cowley', in *Seventeenth Century Studies Presented to Sir Herbert Grierson* (1938), 235–42.

6–RA, 'Et Ego in Arcadia', C. 1: 3 (July 1923), 409–40.

TO *Ezra Pound* MS Lilly

Wednesday [15 November 1922] [London]

Dear Ezra

As you want me to reply about Bel Esprit, I will now make time to tell you exactly how the matter is with me.

1. Of course I want to leave the Bank, and of course the prospect of staying there for the rest of my life is abominable to me. It ought not to be necessary to say this.

2. Of course I have *not* got the money from Lady Rothermere, and of course I have never spoken to her about it. I understood that you and Richard were the agents in the matter. There is more reason why I should ask you why *you* didn't get it from her. I can't go about passing the hat for myself – besides, I could hardly go to her and say 'I hear you have 10000 fc. for me: please give it to me'.

3. I am *not* thinking of buying the *Criterion*, *but* it will be a great disaster to me if it comes to an end. Thank you for writing to Lady Rothermere on my behalf, but if you call her answer an insult, I don't think you know what insults are: I should like you to see a few of her notes to me.

Now about Bel Esprit. What I have to say has always seemed to me so obvious that there was no need to say it . . . but perhaps I was wrong. In the case of you and Dorothy this situation has never come up, so perhaps your imagination has not stretched so far. Dorothy has comparatively good health, a family who can help her, and prospects of enough money to live on afterwards. Vivien has none of these things. Her father's property, such as it is, is practically all tied up in Irish real estate, which <he has been trying to sell all his life,> has never paid much, now pays less, and can't be got rid of; which will be an encumbrance to her and her brother for the rest of their lives. Finally, at the most optimistic view, she will *never* be strong enough to earn her own living. If I had only myself to consider, I should not bother about guarantees for a moment: I could always earn my own living. But I am responsible toward her in more than the ordinary way. I have made a great many mistakes, which are largely the cause of her present catastrophic state of health, and also it must be remembered that she kept me from returning to America where I should have become a professor and probably never written another line of poetry, <so that in that respect she should be endowed>.

At the end of five years, unless all the guarantees are renewed, where should I be? I should have to start all over again. I couldn't even get a job in a bank – who would want a man of forty? – and if I did I should have to start again at the bottom, at £150 a year. And if I died meanwhile, what then? In the bank, I am assured £500 a year and perhaps more, and in case of death a widow's pension increasing according to the size of salary.

I will leave the Bank as soon as I have such guarantees – for my life or *for Vivien's life* – as would satisfy a solicitor. If the contributors cannot give such guarantees, then they are people who ought not to be in such an enterprise at all; but I think that *if my situation were clearly put to them*, they would consider me an imbecile not to require the guarantees.

Although I have much more to say to you, I am very tired and it is after 1 o'clock. I have not yet seen Lady R. I am looking forward with horror to seeing her tomorrow and will write to you afterwards.

Yours ever

T.

PS You might send any reply dealing with this subject to me at Lloyds Bank Ltd., Information Dept., 71 Lombard Street, London E.C.3.

TO *Mary Hutchinson* PC Texas

[Postmark 16 Nov 1922]

Yes my dear thank you. I shall write to you tomorrow. In great haste

T.

TO *Richard Aldington* TS Texas

18 November 1922 9 Clarence Gate Gardens, N.W.1

My dear Richard,

I am enclosing a copy of a cutting from the *Liverpool Post*[1] which I received tonight as you ought to see it at once. This is not altogether a

1–Brother Savage, 'Books and Bookmen', *Liverpool Daily Post and Echo*, 16 Nov. 1922: 'The first number of a quarterly review, *The Criterion*, just issued by Mr. Cobden Sanderson, includes a long poem by Mr. T. S. Eliot, *The Waste Land*, which is attracting considerable attention. Despite that Mr. Eliot's friends endeavoured strenuously to keep the affair a secret, it has come to light (by way of America) that the author of "Mr. Prufrock" is the first beneficiary under a unique scheme through which a co-operation of English, French, and American enthusiasts, known as "Bel Esprit," pledged themselves to give $50 per year for life or as long as the author needs it. The only gift we can make to an artist, their private manifesto declared, is leisure in which to work, leisure, moreover, while he is young enough to profit by it. The practicability of the scheme is assured by the fact that, with backers to the number of ten and upwards, the dangers arising out of individual patronage are eliminated;

surprise to me as I have suspected for some time that something of the sort might happen. I am putting the matter into the hands of my solicitors to take immediate action and I am sure that you will support me by your testimony in this very serious matter. I need not point out to you how calamitous such falsehoods might be for me if allowed to pass uncontradicted. I will write to you again after I have seen my solicitors.

Yours ever,

Tom.

You should realise as well as I what has made possible the appearance of such a libel and you ought TO know as well as I FROM what source it is likely TO have emanated. As I want TO *track it down* and not merely secure an apology FROM the *L'pool Post*, please DO NOT MENTION THIS TO A SINGLE PERSON *until I have seen my solicitor and written you again*. I pledge you TO secrecy. I shall write you again immediately I have seen my solicitor.

TO *Ezra Pound*

MS Lilly

18 November 1922 9 Clarence Gate Gdns

Dear Ezra,

I am enclosing a copy of a cutting from the *Liverpool Post* which I have received tonight and which I shall place in the hands of my solicitors for immediate action. I may say this is not a surprise to me and I have suspected for some little time that something was on foot. You should realise as well as I what has made possible the appearance of such a libel and you ought to know as well as I from what sources it is likely to have

—

and there is sufficient difference of taste assured to prevent any single subscriber from trying to force the artist's work into any mould or mode not his own.

'Until quite recently Mr. Eliot was earning his livelihood in a London bank. Attempts had previously been made by his admirers to persuade him to give himself up to literature, and they pointed to his poetry and *The Sacred Wood*, a book of criticism, as work which substantiated their claim for him as an author with a future. Actually, as the amusing tale went at the time, the sum of £800 was collected and presented to Mr. Eliot there and then. The joke was that he accepted the gift calmly, and replied: "Thank you all very much; I shall make good use of the money, but I like the bank!" That was two years ago, and he held out until last spring, when he suffered a severe nervous breakdown which necessitated a three months' leave of absence. Thereupon the society of "Bel Esprit" was hatched in secret and carried through, the poet's own wishes not being consulted. The poem in *The Criterion* is the initial result of what must be regarded as a considerate and generous scheme, with excellent possibilities.'

emanated.[1] You will of course support me in any statements which it is necessary to make. I do not propose to let this matter rest with an apology from the *Liverpool Post*, but to track them to their source.

Yours,
T.

I need not point out how calamitous these statements may be for me. Please be thinking this over but do not make any investigations and do not reveal this to a single person until I have seen my solicitor and written you again. Keep absolutely quiet about it.

TO *Richard Aldington* MS Texas

Monday [20 November 1922] [London]

Look here, my dear Richard, why do you never give me the benefit of the doubt? You know perfectly well that I would never refuse permission to you and give it to Read, and that if I had any notion that Read was going to write about the *Criterion* I should have warned him. I don't want anyone to write of me as the editor, and am very angry that he has done so.[2]

I am seeing my solicitor and have nothing more to add at present except that this libel business is still a *secret* and confidential.

Yrs.
T.S.E.

TO *Daniel Halévy*[3] TS Alan Clodd

27 November 1922 *The Criterion*, 9 Clarence Gate Gdns

Monsieur,

Je vous remercie de votre lettre du 20 courant. Je pense bien que la préface[4] dont vous me notifiez serait bien intéressante pour nous. J'entends

1–TSE was referring to RA.
2–HR wrote about C. in a paragraph at the close of his 'Notes from England' in *Écrits du Nord* 1: 2 (Nov. 1922), 35–8. The same issue carried an advertisement for TSE's new periodical, naming the contributors but not the editor.
3–Daniel Halévy (1872–1962), French social historian, essayist and biographer; acute and dispassionate chronicler of the Third Republic; the editor of the *Cahiers Verts* in which Julien Benda's novel *La Croix des Roses* ('The Cross of Roses') appeared. See Alain Silvera, *Daniel Halévy and His Times* (1966).
4–Julien Benda, 'A Preface', appeared in C. 1: 3 (Apr. 1923). This was written in the form of a dialogue with Benda's *La Croix des Roses*, which had just appeared in the *Cahiers Verts* edited by Halévy.

de ce que vous me dites que la traduction est déjà en train et qu'elle sera faite en peu de temps. Voulez-vous bien me dire vers quelle date vous pourriez me l'envoyer et à peu près combien de mots cette préface contient?

Je crois avoir déjà expliqué à Monsieur Benda que les conditions pécuniaires sont £10 les 5000 mots et que l'article ne devrait pas dépasser par beaucoup cette longueur.

Est-ce que le dialogue avec préface va paraître à Paris dans une revue ou dans une volume?

En attendant de vos nouvelles, je vous prie, Monsieur, d'agréer l'expression de mes sentiments très distingués.

T. S. Eliot

Pardonnez la dactylographe –[1]

TO *Richard Cobden-Sanderson* TS Texas

27 November 1922 *The Criterion*, 9 Clarence Gate Gdns

Dear Sanderson,

I should have rung you up to discuss your last two letters with you but have been far too busy. I have carefully gone over the terms of Hachette which you sent me.[2] It is not quite clear to me just what advantages the *Criterion* gains in compensation for the rights given but I shall get you to explain that to me when we next meet. I return to you the circular which I have altered only to the extent of adding a few names which of course should be inserted in alphabetical order. It seems to me that Hachette ought to print this circular at their own expense and it seems to me still more cheeky of them if they suggest that the *Criterion* should pay for the insertion of an advertisement in a paper which is merely an organ of their own house. Do you not agree with me?

I hope I can find time to come in one afternoon this week and discuss these questions with you.

1 – *Translation*: Sir, Thank you for your letter of the 20th inst. I definitely think the preface you mention would be of interest to us. I understand from what you say that the translation is already under way and that it will be completed shortly. Would you please tell me what date you could send it to me by and about how many words this preface contains?

I think I have already explained to M. Benda that the pecuniary conditions are £10 per 5000 words and that the article should not go much beyond this length.

Is the dialogue with the preface going to appear in Paris in a review or volume?

While waiting news from you, please accept this expression of my deepest respects, T. S. Eliot

Forgive the typist [added in pen as postscript to typed letter]

2 – Hachette was the French distributor.

Does Lady Rothermere propose to have a proper contract with Hachette and if so for how long does she propose to commit the paper to this arrangement?

I think it would be worthwhile to try to get Gyldendal[1] as well for distribution in Denmark and Norway. I have the names of two or three good Swedish publishers which I will give you for that country, as I do not suppose that Gyldendal are very powerful in Sweden.

I do not in the least understand what Lady Rothermere means by wanting my photograph and Miss Sinclair's and Saintsbury's and I am not at all sure that the latter will care to have their photographs in the *Daily Mirror*. I will try to ring you up for a word tomorrow and hope to see you later in the week. I am writing to the two people in question to remind them about the copy.

Yours ever,
T.S.E.

TO *Scofield Thayer* TS Beinecke

27 November 1922 9 Clarence Gate Gdns

Dear Scofield,

I am very glad to see from your letter that your peregrinations have brought you back again to Vienna which seems a more suitable habitat for your subtle and cynical spirit than the commercial turmoil of New York. I am glad to hear that the succession of the London Letter is to fall upon Mortimer whose single essay in that line exhibited a knowledge of events which put me into shade. I am sure that everybody will be satisfied with the transference, and I hope to be able to present *The Dial* with specimens of the heavy sort of work of which I am less incompetent.

I must congratulate you upon the maintained quality and increasing reputation of *The Dial*. The issues up to date certainly constitute an achievement of which you and your colleagues may well be very proud. I think that the Viennese stuff you have had is first-rate and I think you have made a particularly good stroke in securing the collaboration of Hofmannsthal.[2] I am trying to dig out a few good writers in various parts

1–Denmark's largest publisher, founded 1770.

2–Hugo von Hofmannsthal (1874–1929), Austrian playwright, poet, essayist, and librettist for Richard Strauss. The *Dial* had printed stories by him (July and Aug.), and a 'Letter from Vienna' (Oct.).

of Europe for *The Criterion* and I hope that if any of them strike you as interesting you will share them with me.

The Dial is gradually establishing itself in London but so far only among the people who make it their business to find out what is good. I think that if you could have a London office or even simply a London Agency to which English subscribers could address themselves, and if you could advertise a bit in some of the best English papers, that your circulation would be greatly increased. For example, two of my friends who order *The Dial* regularly from a London bookseller were unable to get a November number, and were actually informed by the bookseller that *The Dial* had collapsed and ceased publication.[1] If you had a London office or an active business agent here such mistakes would not happen.

Sincerely yours,
T.S.E.

TO *The Editor of* The Liverpool Daily Post and Mercury

Published 30 November 1922   9 Clarence Gate Gdns, N.W.1

Sir,

My attention has been called to two paragraphs about myself in the issue of the *Liverpool Post* of the 16th of this month. The two paragraphs contain a number of statements which are quite untrue.

No such collection or presentation as that mentioned ever took place, and I never made the statement attributed to me. I have not received £800 or any part of such sum, nor have I received any sum from 'Bel Esprit', nor have I left the bank. The 'Bel Esprit' scheme in the manifesto referred to by your correspondent is not in existence with my consent or approval. Finally, the appearance of my poem in the *Criterion* is not the result of any scheme whatever.

The circulation of untrue stories of this kind causes me profound astonishment and annoyance and may also do me considerable harm. They

1–The previous day, HWE had written to Charlotte Eliot: 'Did you say you had the *New York Times*' review of *The Waste Land*? I have one if you would like it. The *Dial* sends a postal asking subscribers to return copies and offering them the next two copies (Dec. and Jan.) in exchange, the demand for the November number having been tremendous. I think they said they had about a thousand unfilled orders.'

are a reflection on me and on my dealings with my friends. I trust that you will take immediate steps to put this matter right.

Yours etc.,
T. S. Eliot[1]

TO *Richard Cobden-Sanderson* TS Texas

1 December 1922 *The Criterion*, 9 Clarence Gate Gdns

Dear Cobden-Sanderson,

I rang you up today to tell you that I have the manuscript of two more articles for you. Had I been able I should have taken them with me and left them at your office myself, as I do not like to entrust them to the post. If your man is free and if it is desirable to save the time, the envelope will be here tomorrow morning if he calls for it any time after 10.30.

J. W. N. Sullivan has been unable to finish the article he promised me, for private reasons beyond his control. I shall therefore choose over the weekend something to take its place and will let you have it by Monday. I have several papers to choose from, and if there is a little space over I have a short thing of my own if necessary.

I have received from the Atlantic Literary Agency translation of a story by Pirandello which I think is quite good and which I wish to accept.[2] Is it safe to assume that these people have the proper translation rights and publication rights in this country, or should I ask them for an explicit statement to this effect before accepting the story?

Yours ever,
T.S.E.

PS I return herewith a postcard in very bad French from a gentleman in Spain named Torre. Will you send him a copy and I will write and ask him to send me copies of any papers in which he notices the *Criterion*. We need not continue to send it to him if the results do not justify it.

Will you write to Lady R. (I can't as she did not mention it to me) and say that I have no copies of my photograph, but a London photographer

1–The editor signed his name to this canny apology, printed beneath TSE's letter: 'We are extremely sorry that our contributor should have fallen into the mistake which Mr. Eliot specifies. We are quite sure that nothing except a tribute to Mr. Eliot's high position as a critic and poet was intended in what our contributor wrote. But clearly he was misinformed, and we must express to Mr. Eliot our sincere regret that anything calculated to give him pain or annoyance should have appeared in our columns.'

2–See 'The Shrine', *C.* 1: 2 (Jan. 1923), by Luigi Pirandello (1867–1936), author of *Six Characters in Search of an Author* (1921).

has a very good one which he will sell if she authorises the expense: and ask her (TACTFULLY NOT TRUCULENTLY)!! *where* she wants to use it and in what way?

I hope your legal difficulties are clearing themselves up.

See *Liverpool Post* for 30 November 1922. I will send you a copy.

TO *Mary Hutchinson* MS Texas

Friday [1 December 1922] 9 Clarence Gate Gdns

Dear Mary,

I was <u>very</u> sorry not to see you. I was in a very deep sleep, and my secretary was coming at 8, and as my nights are seldom more than five hours I usually take a nap before dinner. Vivienne was delighted with the beautiful flowers and wants me to say that she will write to you, and is not averse to seeing you at the end of next week.

Affectionately
Tom

She was out at the hairdressers' when you came, or she wd have rushed out in the hall to greet you.

TO *Gilbert Seldes* CC Valerie Eliot

1 December 1922 [London]

My dear Mr Seldes,

I presume that the announcement of the *Dial* prize is now made public,[1] as the December number must be out, but I think it is just as well that I should let you know that the award has leaked out and reached this country several weeks ago. I should have written to you before but my time has been engrossed by another matter of which I shall tell you. A friend of mine congratulated me a fortnight ago on having received the *Dial* prize, and when I expressed astonishment, he gave me the following information. He told me that Alfred Kreymborg[2] had given him the information with the remark that it was confidential, but that several days later Kreymborg and John Gould Fletcher had lunch with him and had discussed the award quite openly, as an accomplished fact, in the presence of one or two other people,

1 – *The New York Times Book Review* had announced the *Dial* award (to 'Thomas Seymour Eliot') on 26 Nov. 1922, 12; repr. in *T. S. Eliot*, ed. Grant, 135–6.

2 – Alfred Kreymborg (1883–1966), poet, playwright and puppeteer.

and without any mention of secrecy. I of course, on the understanding I had with you, had not mentioned the matter to anyone, and I am sure that it was not your desire that the award should be known before the public announcement was made in the *Dial*. I was therefore very much embarrassed on being told of it, and stated that I had only informal knowledge of the matter; and I asked my friend to mention it to no one else. But as there were several other people present on the occasion on which it was discussed, it is very likely now known to a good many.

I have no idea how Fletcher or Kreymborg came by the knowledge and had I had the time during the past fortnight I should have attempted to see one of them and investigate his sources. I understand that Kreymborg has now returned to New York, and I daresay that you will be in a better position to find out who betrayed your confidence than I am. It might have been, and for all I know may still be, very annoying in its consequences for both the *Dial* and myself.

I think it is always as well to trace rumours to their source. I enclose for your private and confidential information two cuttings from *The Liverpool Post*, one issuing a libellous falsehood about me, and the other retracting the statement. I also enclose a copy of a letter which I have addressed to *The Liverpool Post*. This matter has given me considerable trouble and I have taken a good deal of expensive legal advice. As I have neither the time nor the private means of conducting a protracted lawsuit, I shall not pursue the matter any farther. I have no knowledge of the source from which this story emanated, but it is obviously a malicious attack from some concealed enemy in London, not necessarily the writer of the paragraph, although it is bad enough to repeat such a story with no foundation. Please do not mention this matter to anyone, as I shall only communicate it gradually to certain persons. But I should be very much obliged if you could keep your eye open for the appearance of this or any similar libel in America. It is possible that the story may be copied by some American paper, and it is also possible that the same person may try to circulate it direct in America where I have not the same means for arresting its spread.

I hope that you got my article in time for the December number;[1] if not, I am very sorry, and you must console yourself with the thought that it is the last time that you will be worried by my unpunctuality. I hope to send you something quite soon but the date of its publication will be at your convenience.

Yours always sincerely,
[T. S. E.]

1–TSE's 'London Letter' on Marie Lloyd, repr. with revision in *C.* 1: 2, Jan. 1923 (*SE*).

TO *Virginia Woolf* TS Berg

4 December 1922 *The Criterion*, 9 Clarence Gate Gdns

Dear Virginia,

I was on the point of writing to you over a fortnight ago when an incident occurred which has not left me leisure to write or even enough time to read the *Daily Mail*. I am enclosing two cuttings from the *Liverpool Post* one of the 16th November and the other of the 30th, and you will understand that in the time between these two cuttings my mind has been wholly occupied and my time consumed with taking legal advice and writing difficult letters. I have had to see my solicitors a number of times and have also taken advice from a K.C.[1] The amount of worry and fatigue, to say nothing of the complete loss of time, involved in a thing like this is incalculable. The length of time between the original paragraph and the apology is explained by the fact that after writing to the *Liverpool Post* and waiting several days with no reply, I asked their London editor to wire to Liverpool, who replied that my letter had never been received. Some days were thus wasted, and I had to send the letter again and wait, presumably while the editor consulted his contributor and found to his satisfaction that the libel had no foundation. I have been extremely anxious to avoid the necessity of a libel action, because of the expense, because of the protracted and immense strain which such action involves, and the utter impossibility of carrying on my own work at the same time. However, I do not consider that the reparation offered by the *Liverpool Post* is at all adequate considering the grossness of the accusation.

I have also received an anonymous letter, stating that the author has heard that a collection is being made for me and that although the author's means are very small, no one has ever appealed to his charity in vain. He therefore enclosed four three-halfpenny stamps and subscribes himself 'Your Wellwisher'.

I started to read *Jacob's Room*[2] before this nasty business began and am now starting again and I hope that I shall have time to read it thoroughly before some new attack is made which will require all the same business over again. It will not be a surprise to you to be told that it is a book which requires very careful reading – I should say compels very careful reading because there is a great deal of excitement in reading it. I can only say so far it seems to me that you have really accomplished what you set out to

1–King's Counsel, a senior barrister.

2–Her *Monday or Tuesday* (stories) had appeared the previous year.

do in this book, and that you have freed yourself from any compromise between the traditional novel and your original gift. It seems to me that you have bridged a certain gap which existed between your other novels and the experimental prose of *Monday or Tuesday* and that you have made a remarkable success. But I hope that I shall have more interesting and more detailed observations to make after I consider that I have really mastered the book.

I should like to have the title[1] of the story you are giving me in order that it may be mentioned in the list of contents of No. 3 which I am putting into No. 2. I should also be very glad to have the story itself as soon as you can let me have it; it could be set up at once and also it would be a very great help in enabling me to gauge how much space to allow to other contributors.

I hope that you and Leonard are both well and I hope that I may see you before very long.

I have not mentioned this business of the *Liverpool Post* to anyone except the few people I have consulted; please do not divulge it to anybody. I am very tired indeed at present, and I only hope that I may be able to get a little comparative rest for a few weeks.

Yours always,
Tom.

I *rely* upon neither you nor Leonard mentioning this *Liverpool Post* affair to anybody.

TO *Thomas Lamb Eliot* — TS Reed College

4 December 1922 — 9 Clarence Gate Gdns

Dear Uncle Tom,

I received from mother the day before yesterday a draft for the equivalent of $10 and a copy of a letter which you had written to her. I am writing first of all to thank you very warmly for the gift, and also to tell you how very much touched and pleased I am at the memorial of which it forms a part. All of father's children had such deep admiration for him that I am sure they will all, like myself, be more pleased at reading your letter and thinking of the feelings which dictated it than they will be even at receiving the gift. It has always been a source of great regret to me that father's benefactions to the city of St Louis should have been performed in

1–VW, 'In the Orchard', *C.* 1: 3 (Apr. 1923), 243–5.

such a modest way that his memory will not endure there longer than the lives of a few friends and his descendants. Your remembrance and your letter have I am sure given as much pleasure to me as they can have done to anybody.

I hope that you and all the family are in very good health and will be for many years to come; I hope that we may meet again perhaps in England and perhaps in America. You must come over and see us!

With very many thanks and with the keenest pleasure in your letter. Vivien sends her kind regards –

I am,
Always sincerely your nephew,
Tom.

TO *Sydney Schiff* TS BL

4 December 1922 9 Clarence Gate Gdns

Dear Sydney,

Vivien has reported to me a conversation which she had today with Violet on the telephone. As I understand that you have now a positive attitude in the matter of the anonymous letter, I have decided to let you know about an affair which is indicated by the enclosed cuttings. Please keep these cuttings by you in order that you may refer to them if occasion arises.

This affair has caused me intense worry for a fortnight and has occupied the whole of my time. As you will see at once the question of taking legal proceedings has had to be gone into carefully and with no delay. All of my time has been spent in difficult and harassing correspondence and in consulting my legal advisers. Needless to say we do not consider this reparation adequate.

I have not yet revealed this affair to anyone except those people whom I have consulted legally. *I must ask you not to mention it to anyone.* If any conversation arises in your presence, as some day it no doubt will, you will have certain of the facts at your disposal and therefore no misunderstandings can occur when you are present.

Yours always,
Tom.

TO *Richard Aldington* TS Texas

7 December 1922 9 Clarence Gate Gdns

Dear Richard,

You will not I know think I have neglected you. I should have written to you at the weekend to tell you how things were getting on but that one event has followed another so rapidly that I have had no time to write or to keep you in touch. I find myself very worn out with this affair and have had to spend today in bed.

I think that I have not written to you since receiving the first cutting from the *Liverpool Post*. I immediately took the matter up with my solicitor and also invoked the aid of Bruce Richmond who has been most extraordinarily kind and helpful. The letter that you see in the enclosed cutting is the combined result of his, my solicitor's, a K.C.'s, and my own labours. After sending the letter I waited four days and having no response I went to the London office of the *Liverpool Post* and had them wire to Liverpool who replied that no letter had been received from me. It is most extraordinary as the letter was expressed and posted in my own hand. There was nothing to do but to send another copy which I did and received an acknowledgment. After two days more the letter which you see appeared. I have since written, again taking advice, to find out that the motive which they ascribe to their contributor is incompatible with such a story.

No sooner had the copy of the *Liverpool Post* arrived than I received an anonymous letter signed 'Your Wellwisher' stating that the writer had heard that a collection was being taken up for me and that although the writer's means were small no claim on his charity was ever in vain and he therefore enclosed four postage stamps with the hope that this would help to strengthen my poetry until I became poet laureate!

These things have made a complete interruption in my work for several weeks as well as leaving me with a feeling of utter exhaustion. I will write again as soon as I have time, with so much work in arrears.

Yours ever
Tom.

FROM *Richard Aldington* MS Valerie Eliot

7 December 1922 Malthouse Cottage, Padworth,
Near Reading, Bucks.

Dear Tom,

The news in your letter fills me with indignation and I waste my imagination in wondering who could be so petty, so base, so disgusting as to send you that anonymous letter. I feel conscience-stricken at the part I have unwittingly played in making this possible, yet I do not know how to express to you my sorrow that all this should have happened to annoy you, from an impulse which was meant very differently. Truly, may you reflect that indiscreet friends are a hundred times more dangerous than open enemies. As to 'Bel Esprit', I cut off from its public manifestations months ago – but that doesn't help you.

I wish I might console you for these *déboires* [annoyances]. If I say they are the common lot of men of genius you will feel the implied compliment inadequate to cover the affront to your honour. If I declare that an anonymous insult is no insult, because it comes from a coward, that will not take away from your headache. And if I send you a few rags from the wardrobe of Zeno and Epicurus, I carry coals to Newcastle. Try to think though that persecution precedes its opposite, that venom exerts itself always against what is noblest and finest, and do not turn the fine edge of your mind by hacking with it.

Such thoughts probably come merely as an additional irritant, since they proceed from the tranquillity of one whose withers are unwrung. But let me repeat that I will sign and make public any announcement or disclaimer you like to dictate. Beyond this I do not know what I can propose; if there is anything, suggest it.

Meanwhile, I hope your rest will enable you to get this business out of your head and to regain tranquillity.

I am sending you later a copy of Jackson's *To-Day*, which has a pleasant air of good-fellowship about it.

Yours as always
Richard.

TO *Henry Eliot* TS Houghton

8 December 1922 9 Clarence Gate Gardens, N.W.1

Dear Henry,

It was kind of you to send your wire of congratulations although I gathered from your letter of the 11th November that you are more pleased with the Prize than with the work for which it is bestowed. I am sorry that you did not really like the poem. There is a good deal about it that I do not like myself, but I do not think that my own reasons for finding it short of what I want to do are reasons which are likely to occur to any of its critics. It is very difficult to anticipate what particular kind of misunderstanding will become current about anything one writes. I consider my Sweeney poems as serious as anything I have ever written, in fact much more serious as well as more mature than the early poems but I do not know anybody who agrees with me on this point except Vivien and William Butler Yeats who have both said much the same thing about them. You say you are trying to be honest and you ask me to give you the benefit of the doubt if you seem malicious. I confess that your attitude toward literature often seems to me unnecessarily complicated by the motives which you impute to the author, for example what you say about Saintsbury as well as what you say about myself. I think that you do not take things (even things such as my own which do not seem at all simple) simply enough, and I think that a simple person who is not worried as to whether they ought to like a thing or not and does not approach a thing with an attitude of suspicion frequently gets a truer impression than the more sophisticated who are constantly occupying their minds in dissecting art and the impressions it makes on them. But such simple sensitive natures, especially in this age of great chatter and great consumption of printed chatter, are very rare. I have a long letter to write to you on this and other subjects, but I must defer it for the present. I must write again about the Hydraulic Stock, because it is more important for me to choose the right moment for getting rid of it and it is for reasons which I will explain later most important that I should be able to convert it into something which would bring a certain if considerably diminished return.

I hope you will write again soon about this and about everything else. Meanwhile receive our very best wishes for Christmas which I hope you will be able to spend at home.

Always your affectionate brother,

Tom.

I held this letter back because I have so much to talk about that I could not let it go without mentioning one or two other things. Mother has told me that the Hydraulic are announcing a dividend both in December and January. I hope that the prosperity will last until the middle of the year, but I want your advice on this point for so far as it affects me the important question is how high to count on the stock going in order to sell. I have a feeling not perhaps wholly justified that six or nine months of industrial prosperity may be followed by another depression. Do you not think that it would be wise to sell out at least half of my stock at 60 or 65? Now so far as this affects you (and affects us indirectly) *will this not lead you to consider another visit to England next summer*? As you know I am very keen for mother to come and for you to come too. Even if you could not come for so long as she you could come over later, and take perhaps a little time in Paris, and return with her. *I feel sure that you can manage to get the time for this if you want to, and I beg you to take it seriously.*

I have been harassed lately by two episodes, one a libellous remark in a provincial paper stating that I had been offered £800 two years ago to leave the bank and that I accepted the money and declined to keep my promise, and the other an anonymous insulting letter offering me sixpence for the collection which the writer had heard was being taken up for me. I have had to pursue both these matters and it has involved a great deal of consultation with friends, with legal advisers and a great deal of correspondence. It has been very bad for Vivien to have this strain, especially two such attacks on me coming at once and it has greatly impaired for the time being the good effects of the regime which she has been pursuing. We are both completely worn out. It is as much the damage that these things have done in impairing the four months of dogged and persistent efforts she has made as anything else about the matter, that makes me angry. But of course I should in any case have had to take action about the libel as persistence of such reports might eventually cause a catastrophe to my position at the bank, and for this reason they could more easily ruin me than they might many people. With a very happy Christmas to you from both of us. *We are longing to see you again.*

T.

TO *Wyndham Lewis* TS Cornell

8 December 1922 9 Clarence Gate Gdns

Dear Lewis,

I should like to see you on a matter of business: Can you meet me on Sunday evening at 9 o'clock at Verrey's [in Regent Street] as that is the only time I have over the weekend? Do not telephone unless it is impossible for you to manage this; *If I do not hear from you I shall be there.*

Sincerely,
T.S.E.

TO *Ezra Pound* TS Lilly

12 December 1922 9 Clarence Gate Gdns

My dear Ezra,

Enclosed is a copy of your proof. I have already, in order to save time, corrected (so far as necessary) one copy and returned it to the printer, so I hope and trust that you will not require any alteration beyond such printers' errors as I have not spotted. I have seen Yeats and passed a very agreeable afternoon with him and he has promised a contribution in prose for the following.[1]

Now as to the Obsequies [by B. M. Goold-Adams]. I couldn't have got it in to this number because I had already accepted for that purpose some time ago a short sketch which you will see, and which I think is good of its kind. For the next number I have got Virginia Woolf, also arranged some time ago. There will be no number therefore before July, so please let me know when you wish to produce the lady's book. It seems to me very good, although not emphatically a work of genius. I have been offered a story by Pirandello, do you know anything about him?

I enclose copy of my published word and the newspaper's retraction of the story which I reported to you. This has given me a devil of a lot of trouble, conferences, consultation with solicitors and a K.C. and letter-writing. At the same time I have had the nuisance of an anonymous letter from a 'Wellwisher' offering me 6d in stamps toward the 'collection' which is being made for me. This letter I found upon diligent enquiry was composed at a tea-party in the Bosschère[2] household obviously inspired by a person of whose name I have as yet no statement.

1–WBY, 'A Biographical Fragment', *C.* 1: 4 (July 1923), 315–21.
2–The Belgian writer and poet Jean de Bosschère.

The net result of these *affaires* has been three weeks of no work done and a state of exceptional fatigue but it is obvious to the meanest eye that a person in my position must take the trouble to protect himself against such attacks when made.

I think I must have a number of other things to discuss, but I have had to wait so long to write this that they have got lodged somewhere inside my brain.

I will write again soon. Benedictions.

Yours ever,
T.

TO *Ottoline Morrell* — TS Texas

12 December 1922 — 9 Clarence Gate Gdns

Dear Ottoline,

I have been wanting to write and tell you that I wired to Yeats after hearing from you and consequently lunched with him at the Savile Club. I enjoyed seeing him immensely; I had not seen him for six or seven years and this was really the first time that I have ever talked to him for any length of time alone. He is really one of a very small number of people with whom one can talk profitably about poetry, and I found him altogether stimulating.

I have been also far too busy with two very nasty little personal affairs which have taken the whole of my time: one an anonymous letter enclosing 6d in stamps for the 'collection' which the writer had heard was being made for me, and the other a bit of personal gossip in the *Liverpool Post*, giving a good deal of information evidently taken direct out of the circular which 'Bel Esprit' issued in America and incorporating the story that two years ago I had been offered £800 to leave the bank and had accepted the money on those grounds and then failed to fulfill my promise. My legal advisers held no doubt that the allegations were libellous at law, but they advised me to obtain an apology from the paper inasmuch as no damages I might get would ever compensate for the strain and worry of fighting the case. The most dangerous aspect of the matter was of course the possibility of such a malicious lie getting to the ears of the bank. It involved two or three weeks of intense strain and during that time gave me no interval for anything else.

I have only mentioned this matter to a very few persons and they have all promised not to discuss it, or mention it, and as I think it is best that it should not be talked about publicly I rely on your keeping it absolutely to yourself.

This has been a very great strain for Vivien as well as she has been sleeping worse than I have ever known her to do before. She has been quite too ill with these matters to write or to do anything.

Thank you again for my meeting with Yeats. I hope we may have good news of you soon.

Always affectionately,
Tom

TO *Antonio Marichalar* TS Real Academia de la Historia

12 December 1922 *The Criterion*, 9 Clarence Gate Gdns

Cher Monsieur

Merci de votre lettre du 2 courant. Certainement, j'indiquerai la date de vôtre article![1] C'est grand dommage que nous n'avons pas pu l'insérer plus tôt, mais la tache de rédiger une revue d'une étendue si étroite, et qui ne paraît que trimestriellement, est très ennuyeuse. Je voudrais bien recevoir votre petite note sur Benavente.[2] J'espère quand même que son talent est à un niveau supérieur à ceux de la plupart des gens auxquels les prix sont cernés (exception faite d'Anatole France).[3] La bonification sera rendue au commencement du mois d'avril.

Bien cordialement,

Vôtre
T. S. Eliot

Indice[4] va-t-il reparaître bientôt?[5]

1–When Marichalar's article on 'Contemporary Spanish Literature' appeared in *C.* 1: 3 (Apr. 1923), it was dated 'August 1922'.

2–The Spanish dramatist Jacinto Benavente (1866–1954) was awarded the Nobel Prize for Literature in 1922. Marichalar appended a brief note on Benavente to his essay in *C.*, recording that the award of the prize had caused as much surprise 'within his own country' as abroad.

3–The French writer Anatole France (1844–1924) had been awarded the Nobel Prize in 1921.

4–On 20 May TSE had asked Marichalar to send him a copy of the Spanish review *Indice*.

5–*Translation*: Dear Sir – Thank you for your letter of the 2nd inst. Certainly, I will indicate the date of your article: it is a great pity that we have not been able to get it in earlier, but the task of editing a review on such a small scale, and which only appears quarterly, is very tedious. I would be very glad to receive your little note on Benavente. I hope, however, that his talent is on a superior level to that of the majority of the people to whom prizes are given (with the exception of Anatole France). Payment will be made in April.

Yours cordially, TSE.

Will *Indice* reappear soon?

TO *Ezra Pound* MS Lilly

15 December 1922 *The Criterion*, 9 Clarence Gate Gdns

Dear Ezra,

I sent you cutting from *Lpool Post*. That is ended so far as the paper is concerned – though their apology is a meagre one – remains to find out the author. The other affair – the anonymous letter – was hatched in the Bosschère household – Madame d'E. says *she* wrote it – both shuffling and unconvincing, but I am sure it was inspired by another person – anyway, I have of course had to drop Bosschère.

It may appear that in the disturbance and exasperation of these and such affairs – which are perhaps a much greater strain and wear upon me than on almost anyone else – I overlook the intentions, thought and labour of my friends for many months past. This is not the case. If I did not attempt to expose the difficulties of my situation to you I should appear (& be) much more unreasonable. It has been a great annoyance to me that I have not been able simply to express appreciation. I have however a faint but consistent notion of the amount of time, thought and energy you must have spent on this matter, and I don't underestimate this or take it for granted – I think it's wonderful.

Yours ever
T.

PS Your letter received. Lawd how you cuss and rave. I have reread your Preface – praps you've forgotten what it is, but I see nothing in it violent enough to warrant complete expurgation (I only think 'damn their eyes' weakens an otherwise forcible remark). It appeared detached from the rest, and it was a question of space. I have turned in some bad copy of mine own, and with your Preface will now have 104 pp. as before instead of 96. So chaw yore old corn cob & think of God & Maise Huffer.[1]

However, in my opinion, it is *not* the *bite* of the thing – the bite is 'criticism is a preliminary excitement'.[2]

Now if your goin on cussin cuss to me at Lloyds Bank, 71 Lombard St E.C.3.

1 – The phrase 'damn their eyes' was cut from the brief preface to EP's 'On Criticism in General', in C. 1: 2 (Jan. 1923) – the issue runs to 96 pp. – which discusses his debt to Hueffer (Ford Madox Ford).

2 – EP wrote in his piece: 'I consider criticism merely a preliminary excitement, a statement of things a writer has to clear up in his own head sometime or other, probably antecedent to writing; of no value unless it come to fruit in the created work later.'

TO *Richard Aldington* MS Texas

15 December 1922 *The Criterion*, 9 Clarence Gate Gdns

My dear Richard,

Thank you very much for your letter. Do not think that I suppose that these attacks are the consequences of any activities of yours; because I do not. Likewise I want to say that these misfortunes, and any other worries and vexations which have been by-products of Bel Esprit, have not for a moment obscured my appreciation of your great and ceaseless toil on my behalf. God knows how many hours you have spent on it. One's appreciation is a continuous feeling: the worries and anxieties and deliberations may appear at any particular moment more instant and pressing. When I have discussed this business with you, they have had to come first, if it was to be discussed at all. But I assure you now that I recognise your part in this and am not in the least blinded to it by the serious anxieties I have had.

One would like to be able to write letters, real letters – if there were time.

When are you coming to fetch Plautus? And why not, for a change! tell me how your life is going on?

With heartiest good wishes for Christmas

Yours ever
T.S.E.

TO *Scofield Thayer* TS Beinecke

18 December 1922 9 Clarence Gate Gdns

Dear Scofield,

I am very glad to hear from you once again and to receive your expression of approbation of the *Criterion*. I am also glad to know that you (who must now be an authority on the subject), consider Hesse's article to be not unjust toward his contemporaries.[1]

I shall look forward with great interest to reading more of the German stuff that you have got hold of. I have heard of Thomas Mann from Curtius and mean when I have time to look into the subject.[2] But I find that I have at present very little time for reading which is rather a handicap

1–Hesse, 'Recent German Poetry'.
2–C. would print articles by Thomas Mann in 1931 and 1933.

as one likes to be able to know something about people before asking them to contribute.

Your offer of Hofmannsthal is extremely generous. I should certainly be glad if you would put in a word for us with him and should like his essay on his visit to Greece if it is not more than 5000 words.[1] Preferably less, as I find it more difficult to get good short contributions than good long ones. You may tell him that our rates are £10 per 5000 words, and like the *Dial* we make no distinction of persons. (You need not emphasise the latter part!) Of course, foreign contributions cost us more as we have to pay the regular rates to translators as well. I should be very grateful if you would make this proposal to him.

Referring again to the difficulty which my friends had in getting the *Dial* in London, I also would remark that I have not yet myself received a copy of the December number which I imagine appears on the 25th of November. I am only querulous about this for the reason that I always look forward so keenly to reading it. I gather, from cuttings which have reached me from New York, that it also announces that the *Dial* prize has been awarded to me. Although accordingly I have not received exactly official intimation I trust that I may express my profound appreciation of the honour which the *Dial* has bestowed upon me and hasten to add my assurances that I hope I shall be able to do my little bit in helping the future success of the *Dial* by always giving it a refusal of whatever I consider to be my best work. <What a sentence! (dictated)>

Possibly I may be tempted to make a flying visit to Germany some time next year and if so I hope that we may meet somewhere on the Continent. Meanwhile accept my most cordial good wishes of the season, and many thanks.

Yours ever,
T.S.E.

I am told that a writer named Ernst Bertram[2] is very good.

1–Hugo von Hofmannsthal, 'Greece', C. 2: 5 (Oct. 1923), 95–102.

2–Ernst Bertram (1884–1957), poet; Professor of German Literature, Cologne University, 1922–46.

TO *Richard Cobden-Sanderson* MS Beinecke

26 December 1922 *The Criterion*, 9 Clarence Gate Gdns

Dear Sanderson

I have returned the *complete* page proof to Aylesbury. I suppose you have instructed them about cover and *margins*. It came to 97 pp. so I told them to put the contributors' note etc. on p. 98 and have fly leaf in *front* only, making 100 pp. altogether. Should not Hachette's name and address be below yours on cover, in small type?

I hope you are enjoying yourself and look forward to dining next week. In haste

Yrs –
T. S. Eliot

TO *John Quinn* TS NYPL (MS)

27 December 1922 9 Clarence Gate Gdns

Dear Mr Quinn,

Thank you very much for your kind letter of the 4th. It contained a filing card from the Copyright Office of the Library of Congress, certifying that *The Waste Land* was Copyright in my name.[1] I repeat this merely because the letter was stamped 'Received unsealed' and was officially sealed by the post office department, so that I want to be quite certain that there was no other enclosure except of course a copy of your letter to Gilbert Seldes. I am perpetually grateful for your continuous and unremitting devotion to my interests, in the midst I am sure, of innumerable other duties apart from your own affairs; and I am immensely grateful always for your continued support and encouragement.

What I particularly want to mention, in a letter which must be a very brief one, is to ask you whether you have received the manuscript of all my poems which I sent you some weeks ago. I sent it by registered post and it should have reached you long since.[2] If you have not received it please let me know so that I may institute inquiries at once. If it has gone astray, my only but very deep regret will be that it was my only means of expressing my gratitude for all that you have done for me.

1 – 'For the first term of 28 years'.

2 – The *March Hare* notebook and the drafts of *The Waste Land* reached Quinn on 17 Jan. 1923.

I am very glad that you like the *Criterion*.[1] It has taken a great deal of time and thought, and the approval of my friends is the only reward that I can at present expect. I hope that we can make the thing a real success. I shall ask Cobden-Sanderson to get into touch with Liveright. I am not sure that he has not already made some temporary arrangement with Brentano,[2] but if a pushing publisher like Liveright would take hold of the thing I have no doubt that it would be more satisfactory in the long run. I am very much obliged to you for having spoken to Liveright about it.

I hope to write to you again soon – but you will think that I live perpetually in the hope of writing and never fulfill my promises.

I trust that you are able this winter to take a little better care of your health and not sacrifice it to all the calls that are made upon you.

Yours very sincerely,
T. S. Eliot

TO *Herbert Read* — TS Victoria

27 December 1922 — *The Criterion*, 9 Clarence Gate Gdns

My dear Read,

I have at last had time over the holidays to read pretty carefully your essay[3] although it is very solid reading, and I am going to read it again; and I must tell you that I like it very much indeed. I had been considering whether it would be possible to divide it into two parts but I am anxious if possible to avoid mutilating it in this fashion and it does appear as far as I can make out that we shall be able to publish it entire in No. 3. This depends of course on two or three contributors keeping their word and confining themselves to the limits which they promised. If it is necessary to print the article in two I shall of course ask your permission and leave it to you to indicate the division, but as I say I am anxious to respect the construction of your article.

I hope for an opportunity to discuss it with you at more length. Forgive this hasty and tardy acknowledgement and thanks,

Yours ever,
T. S. Eliot

1 – Quinn called the first issue (he had been sent a 'sample editorial' copy on 13 Dec.) a 'beautiful thing, beautifully printed'. He had discussed American distribution with Liveright, who 'might consider it if the thing was presented to him', and suggested that RC-S approach Liveright directly.

2 – The New York bookseller.

3 – 'The Nature of Metaphysical Poetry', C. 1: 3 (Apr. 1923), 246–66.

TO *Gilbert Seldes* TS Timothy and Marian Seldes

27 December 1922 9 Clarence Gate Gdns

My dear Mr Seldes,

I thank you very much for your letter of the 14th December. Although I gather from your letter that you are going to be absent, presumably for a needed holiday, I am addressing one more letter to you. This is merely to acknowledge the December *Dial* and your article in the *Nation* which has reached me.[1] I can say without flattery that I prefer your remarks about *The Waste Land* to those of Mr Wilson which are somewhat more sensational in tone. I do not mean that I do not like his article, but that the whole thing was just a little too highly coloured. At the same time, he made some rather acute remarks which showed me how people may be affected by certain elements in the poem that I do not myself very much like. I do not think that I can put this any more clearly at present.

While I wish to express my appreciation of Mr Wilson's praise, there is one point in Mr Wilson's article to which I must strongly take exception. I do very much object to be made use of by anyone for the purpose of disparaging the work of Ezra Pound.[2] I am infinitely in his debt as a poet, as well as a personal friend, and I do resent being praised at his expense. Besides, what Mr Wilson said of him was most unfair. I sincerely consider Ezra Pound the most important living poet in the English language. And you will see that in view of my great debt to him in literature it is most painful to me to have such comments made.

I have always on my mind the articles which I am to write for you and be assured that the delay has been through no fault of mine.

By the way, in response to your earlier question, there are a certain number of copies of the first number of *The Criterion* available and you will be able to get one from Brentano. If not, I have two of my own, and I can save one for you.

1–The *Dial* 75: 6 (Dec. 1922) included both TSE's final 'London Letter' and Edmund Wilson's 'The Poetry of Drouth', a review of *TWL* ('So Mr Eliot hears in his own parched cry the voices of all the thirsty men of the past – of the author of Ecclesiastes in majestic bitterness at life's futility, of the Children of Israel weeping for Zion by the unrefreshing rivers of Babylon, of the disciples after the Crucifixion meeting the phantom of Christ on their journey; of . . . Dante's astonishment at the weary hordes of Hell, and of the sinister dirge with which Webster blessed the "friendless bodies of unburied men"'). Seldes's 'T. S. Eliot' appeared in *Nation* [NY]. 115 (6 Dec. 1922); repr. in *T. S. Eliot*, ed. Grant, 144–51.

2–Wilson criticised the 'extremely ill-focussed Eight Cantos of [Eliot's] imitator Mr. Ezra Pound'.

I am very deeply aware of the honour which *The Dial* has bestowed upon me as well as of the financial assistance which will be a very great help at a difficult time. May I be able to give *The Dial* still better work in the future!

With many thanks for your letter

Yours always sincerely,
T. S. Eliot

TO *Lady Ottoline Morrell* MS Texas

29 December 1922 9 Clarence Gate Gdns

My dear Ottoline,

Thank you so much for your present which surprised me on Christmas morning – the beautiful little diary is now in my pocket waiting for the new year – through which it will remind me of you as well as of my engagements – and I hope that your name will occur in it from time to time. I hope that next year will have a brighter record of engagements than this!

Vivien is longing to write to you, and will, soon, to thank you and to answer your letter. But this week has brought her a fresh attack of neuritis alternating with neuralgia, and she has been quite used up since Christmas. It's wonderful how keen her mind keeps with such pain. With love and best wishes from both of us.

Yours affectionately
Tom

TO *Richard Cobden-Sanderson* TS Beinecke

31 December 1922 *The Criterion*, 9 Clarence Gate Gdns

Dear Cobden-Sanderson,

Thanks for your letter of the 27th inst. I trust that you have had a satisfactory holiday in spite of the miserable weather, and greet you on your return with the compliments of the season. I am looking forward to seeing you on Tuesday and hope that you will not object on this occasion to dining *here* with me instead of my going to your club. Will you accept my hospitality at 7?.

About the Hachettes' name I thought that you had arranged that in some way with Lady Rothermere. I think it would be a good thing if their name as French agents appeared somewhere in the paper. 800 seems to me definitely the maximum that we ought to print. But we can talk this matter over and also discuss the question of the amount of advertising to be done when we meet.

Yours ever,
T. S. Eliot

PS Did I ask you to send a press copy to *Les Ecrits du Nord*, 1385, Chaussée de Waterloo, Uccle, Brussels, Belgium. I thought I had done so but I have heard from the Editor who says that he has not received it. This can wait however until No. 2 is out and I will give you a fresh list of foreign press copies.

There is a parcel of rejected MSS. ready for your man.

TO *Henry Eliot* TS Houghton

31 December 1922 9 Clarence Gate Gdns

My dear Henry,

Your very nice letter of the 3rd December arrived just before Christmas with your drafts and we were overwhelmed at your kindness and generosity. I hope that you have received the shirt from me and the book from Vivien undamaged.

I have been infernally busy with the *Criterion* which takes up more time than in the circumstances I should wish to give to it. Of course the hope is that in a year's time it may have got on to such a footing as to provide a certain amount of income for me; if it can be made absolutely solid, and either self-supporting (but that would take very much longer than one year) or else important enough and with a large enough circulation and sphere of influence to attract more support it might provide at least a partial way out of my problem of living a double or triple life. If the paper did not arrive at something like this point within a year it would obviously be folly for me to go on with it indefinitely. In any case if I can get out a year or so of really good numbers so as obviously to make it the best paper of its kind in England it will give me standing as an editor and perhaps invite other openings. So you see I have perfectly practical aims and motives for undertaking the work. If it were not for these possibilities, it would be only a curse, for even the interest of the work and contact with interesting people would not justify my almost complete inability to do any writing of my own which the *Criterion* enforces. All this of course is only for your private consideration and not to be mentioned to anyone else.

The *Dial* prize also may improve my standing and add to the circulation of my books and perhaps make my work of all kinds more sought after. But of course under present conditions I could not make use of such advantages because I have not the time to do so. I sometimes envy you for having an occasional evening in which you can sit down and read a book; for at least I am sure that you have read much more than I have done in the past year. I know in a general way what is going on and glance at contemporary work with a view to finding new contributors but what I particularly long for is time to fill in the innumerable gaps in my education in past literature and history. There is very little contemporary writing that affords me any satisfaction whatever; there is certainly no contemporary novelist except D. H. Lawrence and of course Joyce in his way, whom I care to read. But there are all the things that I ought to have read long ago and so much that I should like to know in the various sciences.

Does your work keep you very long hours now and do you find it very fatiguing? And if circumstances improved sufficiently, do you intend to leave Rush Street and find rooms by yourself?

Vivien has been very tired since Christmas. She sat up to dinner in the evening on that day for the first time in months. As I have said before, she has been living since last July under the severest and most spartan regimen that I have ever known, which has been much more difficult than any regimen in a nursing home or sanatorium because living it in the midst of ordinary life imposes much more responsibility on her and requires infinite tenacity of purpose; she has not been able to deviate in the slightest from the most limited and particular diet, and she has not been able to take ordinary exercise, only the special exercises prescribed for her and she has hardly seen anybody. I have never known anybody stick to a thing with such persistence and courage, often with relapses which made her feel that the whole thing was useless. She has certainly made great gains by it, but I think that the strain of such a mode of life is beginning to tell on her, and lately she has been sleeping very badly indeed. If I were not tied to the bank I could have gone abroad with her for a time; as it is she is not only under the strain of her own treatment but the strain of our very tense and always rushed and overworked mode of life.

We thought of you a great deal on Christmas day and wished that you were here. Do write again very soon and tell me also in what health you find the family in Cambridge.

Always affectionately
Tom.

V. has read me some bits of *Babbitt*.[1] It has some good things in it.

1–Sinclair Lewis, *Babbitt* (1922), a novel.

GLOSSARY OF NAMES

Conrad Aiken (1889–1973): American poet and critic. Though he and Eliot were a year apart at Harvard, they became close friends, and fellow editors of *The Harvard Advocate*. TSE said he had 'gone in for psychoanalysis with a Swinburnian equipment' and did not 'escape the fatal American introspectiveness' ('Reflections on Contemporary Poetry', *Egoist* 6: 3, July 1919). Aiken wrote a witty memoir of their times together, 'King Bolo and Others', in *T. S. Eliot: A Symposium*, ed. Richard Marsh and Tambimuttu (1948), describing how they revelled in the comic strips of 'Krazy Kat, and Mutt and Jeff' and in 'American slang'. His writings include volumes of poetry among them *Earth Triumphant* (1914); the Eliot-influenced *House of Dust* (1921); and *Selected Poems* (1929), which won the Pulitzer Prize 1930; editions of *Modern American Poets* (1922), and *Selected Poems of Emily Dickinson* (1924); and essays gathered up in *Scepticisms* (1923) and *Collected Criticism* (1968). His eccentric autobiographical novel *Ushant: An Essay* (1952) provides a satirical portrait of TSE as 'Tsetse'.

Richard Aldington (1892–1962): poet, critic, translator, biographer, novelist. A friend of Ezra Pound, he was one of the founders of the Imagist movement; a contributor to *Des Imagistes* (1914); and assistant editor of *The Egoist*. In 1913 he married the American poet H. D., though they were soon estranged. In 1914 he volunteered for WW1, but his enlistment was deferred for medical reasons; he went on active service in June 1916 and was sent to France in December (TSE replaced him as literary editor of *The Egoist*). During the war, he rose from the ranks to be an acting captain in the Royal Sussex Regiment. He drew on his experiences in the poems of *Images of War* (1919) and the novel *Death of a Hero* (1929). After WW1, he became friends with TSE, working as his assistant on the *Criterion* and introducing him to Bruce Richmond, editor of the *TLS* (for which TSE wrote some of his finest essays). From 1919 Aldington himself was a regular reviewer of French literature for the *TLS*. In 1928 he went to live in France, where, except for a period in the USA (1935–47), he spent the rest of his life. He is best known for his early Imagist poetry and translations. In 1931, he published *Stepping Heavenward*, a lampoon of

TSE – who is portrayed as 'Blessed Jeremy Cibber': 'Father Cibber, O.S.B.' – and Vivien (as 'Adele Palaeologue'). This ended their friendship. His growing estrangement from Eliot was further publicised in an essay written in the 1930s but published only in 1954, *Ezra Pound and T. S Eliot: A Lecture*, which takes both poets to task for their putatively plagiaristic poetry. He also wrote an autobiography, *Life for Life's Sake* (1941), controversial biographies of D. H. Lawrence and T. E. Lawrence; and *Complete Poems* (1948). See also *Richard Aldington: An Intimate Portrait*, ed. Alister Kershaw and Frédéric-Jacques Temple (1965), which includes a brief tribute by Eliot; 'Richard Aldington's Letters to Herbert Read', ed. David S. Thatcher, *The Malahat Review* 15 (July 1970), 5–44; Charles Doyle, *Richard Aldington: A Biography* (1989); *Richard Aldington: A Life in Letters*, ed. Norman T. Gates (1992); *Richard Aldington & H. D.: Their lives in letters 1918–61*, ed. Caroline Zilboorg (2003).

Richard Cobden-Sanderson (1884–1964), printer and publisher, was the son of the bookbinder and printer, T. J. Cobden-Sanderson (1840–1922), who was Bertrand Russell's godfather; and grandson of the politician and economist Richard Cobden (1804–65). He became the publisher of the *Criterion* from its first number in October 1922 until it was taken over by Faber & Gwyer in 1925. He also published three books with introductions by TSE: *Le Serpent* by Paul Valéry (1924), Charlotte Eliot's *Savonarola* (1926), and Harold Monro's *Collected Poems* (1933). In addition, his firm produced books by Edmund Blunden and David Gascoyne, editions of Shelley, and volumes illustrated by Rex Whistler. He became a dependable friend as well as a colleague of TSE.

Ada Eliot (1869–1943): Eliot's eldest sister – whom he liked to describe as the Mycroft to his Sherlock Holmes – and wife of Alfred Dwight Sheffield. A prominent Boston social worker, she was a graduate of the Mary Institute, St Louis, Missouri, and went on to further study at Radcliffe College, Cambridge, Massachusetts. She was district secretary of the Family Welfare Society, Boston, 1897–1900; Secretary of the Dependent Children's Committee, New York Charity Organization Society, 1900–1. She served too in many other capacities: Probation Officer, New York City, 1901–4; Massachusetts State Board of Charities, 1909–14; President of the Society for Aiding Destitute Mothers and Infants, Boston, 1914–18; Director of the Research Bureau on Social Case Work, 1919–27; member of the Advisory Board of the Massachusetts Public Welfare Commission, 1919–34; and member of the Board of the Boston Children's Mission,

1927–39. Her writings included 'The Social Case History' (1920); 'Case Study Possibilities' (1922); and 'Social Insight in Case Situations' (1937).

Charlotte Eliot (1874–1926), TSE's third eldest sister, married George Lawrence Smith, an architect, in September 1903. She studied art at college in St Louis and then in Boston, with sculpture being her especial interest.

Charlotte Champe Stearns Eliot (1843–1929), the poet's mother, was born on 22 October in Baltimore, Maryland, the second child and second daughter of Thomas Stearns (1811–96) and Charlotte Blood Stearns (1818–93). She went first to private schools in Boston and Sandwich, followed by three years at the State Normal School, Framingham, Massachusetts, from which she graduated in 1862. After teaching for a while at private schools in West Chester, Pennsylvania, and Milwaukee, Wisconsin, she spent two years with a Quaker family in Coatesville, Pennsylvania. She then taught at Antioch College, Ohio, 1865–7; at her Framingham School; and at St Louis Normal School. It was while she was at the last post that she met Henry Ware Eliot, entrepreneur, whom she married on 27 October 1868. She was secretary of the Mission Free School of the Church of the Messiah for many years. As her youngest child (TSE) was growing up, she became more thoroughly involved in social work through the Humanity Club of St Louis, whose members were disturbed by knowing that young offenders awaiting trial were being held for long periods with adults. In 1899, a committee of two was appointed, with Mrs Eliot as chairman, to bring about reform. It was in large part due to her campaigning and persistence over several years that the Probation Law of 1901 was approved; and in 1903, by mandate of the Juvenile Court Law, a juvenile court was established with its own probation officer and a separate place of detention. As a girl, Charlotte had nursed literary ambitions, and throughout her life wrote poems, some of which (such as 'Easter Songs' and 'Poems on the Apostles') were printed in the *Christian Register*. In 1904 she published *William Greenleaf Eliot: Minister, Educator, Philanthropist*, a memoir of her beloved father-in-law; and it came as a great joy to her when TSE arranged for the publication of her *Savonarola: A Dramatic Poem*, with an introduction by himself (London, 1926). When she was shown the issue of *Smith Academy Record* containing TSE's 'A Lyric' (1905), she said (as TSE would remember) 'that she thought it better than anything in verse she had ever written'. TSE reflected on that fine declaration: 'I knew what her verse meant to her. We did not discuss the matter further.' Inspired by a keen ethic of public service, she was a member of both the Wednesday Club of St Louis and the Missouri Society of the Colonial Dames of America, serving successively as secretary, vice-president, and president. She chaired a committee to award a Washington University scholarship that required the beneficiary to do a certain amount of patriotic work; and in 1917–18 she did further service as chair of the War Work Committee of the Colonial Dames. After the death of her husband in January 1919, she moved home to Cambridge, Massachusetts.

Henry Ware Eliot Snr (1843–1919), the poet's father, was the son of the Rev. William Greenleaf Eliot (1811–87) and Abby Adams Cranch (1817–1908). Born on 25 November 1843, he was educated at Washington University, St Louis. To his father's disappointment, he eschewed the ministry – 'too much pudding choked the dog', he maintained in his unpublished memoirs 'The Reminiscences of a Simpleton' (1910-11) – in favour of a business career. After several years with a grocery firm, Reed and Green, he went into partnership as a manufacturing chemist, Eliot and Larkin. When flood and fire contributed to the firm's failure, he borrowed money from his father to meet his debts, later repaying the money tenfold. In 1868 he met Charlotte Champe Stearns, whom he married on 27 October that year. They had seven children and settled at 2653 Locust Street, St Louis. In 1874 he became Secretary of the Hydraulic-Press Brick Company and subsequently its President and Treasurer. On his retirement at seventy, he was appointed Chairman and attended the office until his death. From 1877 to 1919 he was a member of the board of directors of Washington University. As a consequence of scarlet fever as a boy, he was handicapped by deafness: Eliot said he had such an acute sense of smell that he could identify which of his daughters owned a stray handkerchief.

Henry Ware Eliot, Jr (1879–1947), TSE's elder brother, went to school at Smith Academy, and then passed two years at Washington University, St Louis, before progressing to Harvard. At Harvard, he displayed a gift for light verse in *Harvard Celebrities* (Cambridge, Mass., 1901), illustrated with 'Caricatures and Decorative Drawings' by two fellow undergraduates. After graduating, he spent a year at law school, but subsequently followed a career in printing, publishing and advertising. He attained a partnership in Husband & Thomas (later the Buchen Company), a Chicago advertising agency, from 1917 to 1929, during which time he gave financial assistance to TSE and advised him on investments. He accompanied their mother on her visit to London in the summer of 1921, his first trip away from the

USA. In February 1926, he married Theresa Anne Garrett (1884–1981), and later the same year the couple went on holiday to Italy along with TSE and Vivien. He was one of TSE's most regular and trusted correspondents. It was not until late in life that he found his true calling, as a research fellow in anthropology at the Peabody Museum, Harvard. He was instrumental in building up the T. S. Eliot collection at Eliot House. Of slighter build than his brother – who remarked upon his 'Fred Astaire figure' – Henry suffered from deafness owing to scarlet fever as a child, and this may have contributed to his diffidence. Unselfishly devoted to TSE, whose growing up he movingly recorded with his camera, Henry took him to his first Broadway musical, *The Merry Widow*, which remained a favourite. It was with his brother in mind that TSE wrote: 'The notion of some infinitely gentle / Infinitely suffering thing' ('Preludes' IV).

Margaret Dawes Eliot (1871–1956): the second child in the Eliot family.

Marion Cushing Eliot (1877–1964), the fourth child of Henry Ware and Charlotte Champe Eliot, studied at Miss Folsom's school for social service in Boston. She was Eliot's favourite sister and visited him in London with his mother in 1921.

Vivien Eliot, née Haigh-Wood (1888–1947). Born in Lancashire, she was brought up in Hampstead from the age of three. Having met TSE in company with Scofield Thayer in Oxford in the spring of 1915, she and TSE hastened to be married just a few weeks later, on 26 June 1915. She developed close friendships with Mary Hutchinson, Ottoline Morrell and others in TSE's circle. Despite chronic personal and medical difficulties, they remained together until 1933, when TSE finally resolved to separate from her during his visit to America. She was never reconciled to their separation, became increasingly ill and unhappy, and in 1938 was confined to a psychiatric hospital, where she died in 1947. She is the dedicatee of *Ash Wednesday* (1930). She published a number of sketches and stories in the *Criterion* (under various pseudonyms with the initials 'F. M.'), and collaborated with TSE on the *Criterion* and other works. See Carole Seymour-Smith, *Painted Shadow: The Life of Vivienne Eliot* (2001).

Charles Haigh-Wood (1854–1927): TSE's father-in-law. Born Charles Haigh Wood, in Bury, Lancashire, the son of a carver and gilder who prospered, he was educated privately, at the local grammar school, and (from 1873) the Royal Academy School in London. He started exhibiting in the Academy three years later. He became a member of the RA, and pursued a successful career as a minor portrait and genre painter. On his mother's death, he inherited her properties in Kingstown (Dún Laoghaire) in Ireland, as well as Eglinton House, and thereafter he was supported by the rents of his tenants. In 1885 he married Rose Esther Robinson (1861–1941). They moved to Hampstead in 1891, settling at 3 Compayne Gardens, where they lived for the rest of his life. According to TSE (Oct. 1920), Vivien was 'particularly fond of her father; she takes more after him and his side of the family, and understands him better than the others do'.

Maurice Haigh-Wood (1896–1980): TSE's brother-in-law. He was six years younger than his sister Vivien, and after attending Ovingdean prep school and Malvern School, trained at Sandhurst Military Academy, before receiving his commission on 11 May 1915 as a second lieutenant in the 2nd Battalion, the Manchester Regiment. He served in the infantry for the war, and on regular visits home gave TSE his closest contact with the nightmare of life in the trenches. After the war, he found it difficult to get himself established, but became a stockbroker, and he remained friendly with, and respectful towards, TSE even after his separation from Vivien in 1933. In 1930 he married a 25-year-old American dancer, Ahmé Hoagland, and they had two children.

Emily Hale (1891–1969) came from a similar Bostonian milieu to the Eliot family. Her father was an architect turned Unitarian preacher who taught at Harvard Divinity School, and her uncle was a music critic for the *Boston Herald*. Her mother was a mental invalid from early in life. Eliot met Emily at the home of his cousin Eleanor Hinkley in 1912, and in an unpublished memoir wrote that he fell in love with her before leaving for Europe in 1914. However, after his marriage in 1915, he did not see her again for many years. Although she did not go to college, a fact which handicapped her career, Emily was a passionate theatre-goer, amateur actor and director, and was to forge a career as a drama teacher. In 1921 she took a post as administrator and drama tutor at Milwaukee-Downer College, a private women's school, and later taught at Smith College, Concord Academy, and Abbott Academy. During the 1930s and 1940s, Eliot once again took up his relationship with her, and they saw a lot of one another both in England, where they visited Burnt Norton together in 1934–5, and during his trips to the USA. Following Vivien's death in 1947, Emily was disappointed that Eliot did not want to marry her, and there was a cooling of their friendship. Towards the end of his life Eliot apparently ordered her letters to him to be destroyed, while his letters to her are at Princeton, where they are sealed until 2020. See Lyndall Gordon, *T. S. Eliot: An Imperfect Life* (1998).

Eleanor Holmes Hinkley (1891–1971): Eliot's cousin, the second daughter of Susan Heywood Stearns (1860–1948) – Eliot's mother's sister – and Holmes Hinkley (1853–91), a scholar 'of rare modesty and delicacy of temperament', who died shortly before her birth. Eleanor studied at Radcliffe College in Cambridge, Massachusetts. Among the advanced courses she took there was Professor George Baker's 47 Workshop. She went on to act with Baker's group as well as write a number of plays for it: see *Plays of 47 Workshop* (New York, 1920). One of these, *Dear Jane*, a comedy about Jane Austen in three acts, was to be produced by Eva Le Gallienne at the Civic Repertory Theater, New York, in 1932. It was through amateur theatricals held at her family home, 1 Berkeley Place, Cambridge, Mass., that Eliot met and fell in love with Emily Hale in 1912. According to Valerie Eliot, there was always an affectionate understanding between the cousins and he appreciated her joyous sense of the absurd. Eliot's correspondence with her is full of humour and playful social observation, and it shows a shared love of theatre.

Mary Hutchinson, née Barnes (1889–1977): a half-cousin of Lytton Strachey, married St John ('Jack') Hutchinson in 1910. A prominent Bloomsbury hostess, she was for several years the acknowledged mistress of the art critic, Clive Bell, and became a close, supportive friend of both TSE and Vivien. TSE published one of her stories ('War') in the *Egoist*, and she later brought out a book of sketches, *Fugitive Pieces* (1927) under the imprint of the Hogarth Press. She wrote a short unpublished memoir of TSE (Harry Ransom Humanities Research Center, Austin) and was for a time in the late 1910s a very intimate friend of his. See David Bradshaw '"Those Extraordinary Parakeets": Clive Bell and Mary Hutchinson', *The Charleston Magazine* 1997/1998, 16 & 17.

Edgar Jepson (1863–1938), English novelist and journalist, and author of two volumes of autobiography, *Memoirs of a Victorian* (1933) and *Memoirs of an Edwardian* (1937). He studied Greats at Oxford, under Benjamin Jowett (1817–1893), taught for a while in Barbados, and in the absence of Frank Harris edited *Vanity Fair* for six months. He wrote novels, including detective stories and supernatural and fantastic fictions, and children's stories including *The Second Pollyooly Book* (1914). He was a friend and champion of Pound and Eliot, and in his essay 'Recent United States Poetry' (*The English Review*, 26 May 1918) he praised their work at the expense of their American contemporaries.

Harold Joachim (1868–1938): fellow and tutor in philosophy in Merton College, Oxford, 1897–1919; British Idealist philosopher and follower of F. H. Bradley; author of *The Nature of Truth* (1906), an influential account of the 'coherence theory' of truth. TSE recalled buying Joachim's *The Nature of Truth* at Harvard, and taking it with him in 1914 to Oxford, where Joachim was his tutor. According to Brand Blanshard, it was claimed that 'if you started any sentence in the *Nichomachean Ethics* of Aristotle, Joachim could complete it for you, of course in Greek' ('Eliot at Oxford', in *T. S. Eliot: Essays from the Southern Review*, ed. James Olney, 1988). TSE wrote an obituary letter in *The Times* (4 Aug. 1938; 'to his criticism of my papers I owe an appreciation of the fact that good writing is impossible without clear and distinct ideas'), and also paid tribute to him in the introduction to *Knowledge and Experience in the Philosophy of F. H. Bradley* (1964). In a late letter, he said 'he taught me more about how to write good prose than any other teacher I have ever had' as well as revealing 'the importance of punctuation in the interpretation of a text such as that of the *Posterior Analytics*' (24 June 1963: TS Merton College). TSE's systematic notes on Joachim's lectures on Aristotle's *Nichomachean Ethics* at Oxford 1914–15 are at Houghton.

James Joyce (1882–1941), expatriate Irish novelist, playwright and poet. Having lived in Zurich and Trieste, Joyce moved to Paris in 1920, where he became a centre of expatriate writers, including Pound and Stein. In *Blasting and Bombadiering* (1937), Wyndham Lewis recounts his and TSE's first encounter with Joyce there in August 1920 when bringing him a parcel of shoes. Joyce's *A Portrait of the Artist* was serialised in the *Egoist*, and *Ulysses* in the *Little Review* up to 1920. When *Ulysses* appeared in book form in 1922, the same year as *The Waste Land*, TSE called it 'the most important expression which the present age has found' – 'a book to which we are all indebted, and from which none of us can escape' ('*Ulysses*, Order and Myth', *Dial* 75: 5, November 1923). TSE published in the *Criterion* a number of pieces by and about Joyce, and at Faber he was responsible for the publication of *Finnegans Wake* (1940). See *The Letters of James Joyce*, ed. Stuart Gilbert and Richard Ellmann (3 vols, 1957, 1966); Richard Ellmann, *James Joyce* (2nd edn, 1982).

Alfred Knopf (1892–1984), New York publisher; founded Alfred A. Knopf Inc. in 1915. He was responsible for publishing in the USA numerous important European authors, and he was to bring out not only Eliot's *Ezra Pound: His Metric and Poetry* (1917) but also *Poems* (1920) and *The Sacred Wood: Essays on Poetry and Criticism* (1921).

Wyndham Lewis (1882–1957) was a painter, portraitist, novelist, philosopher and critic; and one of the major modernist writers. A friend of Ezra Pound, Lewis was the leading artist associated with Vorticism, and editor of *BLAST*, the movement's journal, 1914–15, in which TSE's 'Preludes' and 'Rhapsody on a windy night' appeared (in issue 2, July 1915). Lewis served as a bombardier and war-artist on the Western Front, 1916–18, and later wrote memorable accounts of the period in his memoir *Blasting and Bombardiering* (1937), including brilliant portraits of TSE, Pound and Joyce, and wartime and modernist London. TSE reviewed Lewis's first novel *Tarr* (1918) in the *Egoist* 5: 8 (Sept. 1918), describing him as 'the most fascinating personality of our time', in whose work 'we recognize the thought of the modern and the energy of the cave-man'. Lewis considered Eliot 'the most interesting man in London society' (7 Nov. 1918). TSE went on to publish Lewis in the *Criterion* and, even though Lewis was notoriously querulous, carried on a lifetime's friendship and correspondence with him. Lewis did a number of drawings of TSE, one of which hung in Eliot's flat, and his portrait of TSE is in the National Portrait Gallery. On Lewis's death, TSE wrote 'The Importance of Wyndham Lewis' in the *Sunday Times* (10 March 1957), and a memoir in *Hudson Review* X: 2 (Summer 1957): 'He was . . . a highly strung, nervous man, who was conscious of his own abilities, and sensitive to slight or neglect . . . He was independent, outspoken, and difficult. Temperament and circumstances combined to make him a great satirist . . . I remember Lewis, at the time when I first knew him, and for some years thereafter, as incomparably witty and amusing in company . . .' See *The Letters of Wyndham Lewis*, ed. W. K. Rose (1963), and Paul O'Keeffe, *Some Sort of Genius: A Life of Wyndham Lewis* (2000).

Katherine Mansfield (1888–1923), short-story writer, was born in New Zealand. Her first stories were published in A. R. Orage's periodical *The New Age and* collected in *In a German Pension* (1911). She met John Middleton Murry in 1911, and presently became friends with many writers of the day including D. H. Lawrence and his wife Frieda, and Virginia Woolf (who published *Prelude* in 1918), and hovered on the fringes of the

Bloomsbury Group. She married Murry in 1918, and went on to publish *Bliss* (1920) and *The Garden Party* (1922). After her death from tuberculosis at the Gurdjieff Institute at Fontainebleau, Murry published two collections of her stories, and her *Journal* (1927) and *Letters* (1928). See Claire Tomalin, *Katherine Mansfield: A Secret Life* (1987).

Harold Monro (1879–1932): poet, editor and publisher. In 1913 he founded the Poetry Bookshop at 35 Devonshire Street, London, where poets would meet and give readings and lectures. In 1912 he briefly edited the *Poetry Review* for the Poetry Society; then his own periodicals, *Poetry and Drama*, 1913–14, and the *Chapbook* (originally the *Monthly Chapbook*), 1919–25. From the Poetry Bookshop, Monro published the five volumes of *Georgian Poetry*, ed. Edward Marsh (1872–1953), between 1912 and 1922, and the first volumes of poetry by writers including Richard Aldington and Robert Graves, and some of his own collections including *Children of Love* (1915) and *Strange Meetings* (1917). He married in 1920 Alida Klemantaski (daughter of a Polish-Jewish trader), with whom he never cohabited but who remained loving, loyal and supportive to him; both endeared themselves to Eliot, who would often use the premises of the Poetry Bookshop for meetings with contributors to the *Criterion*. After his death, TSE wrote a 'Critical Note' to *The Collected Poems of Harold Monro* (1933). See Joy Grant, *Harold Monro and the Poetry Bookshop* (1967); Dominic Hibberd, *Harold Monro: Poet of the New Age* (2001).

Harriet Monroe (1860–1936): American poet and editor, based in Chicago. Monroe was the editor of *Poetry: A Magazine of Verse*, which she founded in 1912 – when she was already over fifty – and continued to edit until 1936. It provided a crucial launching place for many modern poets, including Eliot (whose 'Prufrock' was published there in 1915), Ezra Pound, Wallace Stevens, William Carlos Williams, Marianne Moore, W. B. Yeats and Robert Frost. She was co-editor, with Alice Corbin Henderson (first associate editor of *Poetry*), of *The New Poetry: An Anthology* (New York, 1917), which TSE reviewed in *Egoist* 4: 9 (Oct. 1917). Her autobiography, *A Poet's Life: Seventy Years in a Changing World*, appeared posthumously in 1937. See also *A History of Poetry in Letters*, ed. Joseph Parisi and Stephen Young (2002).

Lady Ottoline Morrell (1873–1938): daughter of Lieutenant-General Arthur Bentinck and half-sister to the Duke of Portland. In 1902 she married Philip Morrell (1870–1941), Liberal MP for South Oxfordshire

1902–18. A patron of the arts, she entertained a notable literary and artistic circle, first at 44 Bedford Square, then at Garsington Manor, nr. Oxford, where she moved in 1915. She was a lover of Bertrand Russell, who introduced her to TSE, and her many friends included Lytton Strachey, D. H. Lawrence, Aldous Huxley, Siegfried Sassoon, the Woolfs, and the Eliots. Her memoirs (ed. Robert Gathorne-Hardy) appeared as *Ottoline* (1963) and *Ottoline at Garsington* (1974). See Miranda Seymour, *Life on the Grand Scale: Lady Ottoline Morrell* (1992, 1998).

John Middleton Murry (1889–1957): influential English writer, critic and editor, founded the magazine *Rhythm*, 1911–13, and worked as a reviewer for the *Westminster Gazette*, 1912–14, and the *Times Literary Supplement*, 1914–18, before becoming editor from 1919 to 1921 of the *Athenaeum*, which he turned for a time into a lively cultural forum – in a letter of 2 July 1919, TSE called it 'the best literary weekly in the Anglo-Saxon world'. In a 'London Letter' in *Dial* 72: 5 (May 1921), Eliot said he considered Murry as editor 'genuinely studious to maintain a serious criticism', but he disagreed with his 'particular tastes, as well as his general statements'. After the demise of the *Athenaeum*, Murry went on to edit the *Adelphi*. 1923–48. In 1918, he married Katherine Mansfield, who died in 1923. He was friend and biographer of D. H. Lawrence; and as an editor he provided a platform for writers as various as George Santayana, Paul Valéry, D. H. Lawrence, Aldous Huxley, Virginia Woolf, and TSE. His first notable critical work was *Dostoevsky* (1916); his most influential critical study, *The Problem of Style* (1922). Though as a Romanticist he was an intellectual opponent of the avowedly 'Classicist' Eliot, Murry offered Eliot in 1919 the post of assistant editor on the *Athenaeum* (which Eliot had to decline); in addition, he recommended him to be the Clark lecturer at Cambridge in 1926, and was a steadfast friend to both TSE and his wife Vivien. See F. A. Lea, *The Life of John Middleton Murry* (1959); and David Goldie, *A Critical Difference: T. S. Eliot and John Middleton Murry in English Literary Criticism, 1919–1928* (1998).

Brigit Patmore, née Ethel Elizabeth Morrison-Scott (1882–1965): Irish author who married John Deighton Patmore (grandson of the poet Coventry Patmore), and became a popular hostess in London. Her friends included Ezra Pound, Richard Aldington and H. D. She wrote novels including *The Impassioned Onlooker* (1926), as well as a memoir, *My Friends When Young* (1968), which offers a sympathetic picture of Vivien Eliot.

Harold Peters (1888–1941): friend and sailing companion of Eliot at Harvard. After graduation, he went into real estate, and served in the Massachusetts Naval Militia during WW1, and on leaving the navy spent most of the rest of his life at sea. L. M. Little records that at Harvard Eliot and Peters 'were an odd and very interesting pair', and that 'it was Peters who chided [Eliot] about his frail physique', thus prompting Eliot's regular attendance at August's Gymnasium, as well as his boxing lessons, rowing and 'small-boat cruising'. Peters and Eliot would spend many happy and dangerous hours sailing together, sometimes in thick fog, off the Dry Salvages. In 1932, Peters sailed round the world for two years as skipper of an 85-foot auxiliary schooner, having previously participated in the transatlantic race from Newport to Plymouth, and the Fastnet Race. In 1941 he died after falling from a hoisted motor-boat into a dry dock at Marblehead.

Ezra Pound (1885–1972), American poet and critic, was one of the prime impresarios of the modernist movement in London and Paris, and played a major part in launching Eliot – as well as Joyce, Lewis, and many other modernists. Eliot called on him at 5 Holland Place Chambers, Kensington, on 22 Sept. 1914, with an introduction from Conrad Aiken. On 30 Sept. 1914, Pound hailed 'Prufrock' as 'the best poem I have yet had or seen from an American'; and on 3 October called Eliot 'the last intelligent man I've found – a young American T. S. Eliot . . . worth watching – mind "not primitive"' (*Selected Letters of Ezra Pound*, 40–1). Pound was instrumental in arranging for 'Prufrock' to be published in *Poetry* in 1915, and helped to shape *The Waste Land* (1922), which Eliot dedicated to him as '*il miglior fabbro*'. After their first meeting, the poets became friends, and remained in loyal correspondence for the rest of their lives. Having initially dismissed Pound's poetry (to Aiken, 30 Sept. 1914) as 'well-meaning but touchingly incompetent', Eliot went on to champion his work, writing to Gilbert Seldes (27 Dec. 1922): 'I sincerely consider Ezra Pound the most important living poet in the English language.' He wrote an early study of Pound, *Ezra Pound: His Metric and Poetry* (1917), and went on, as editor of the *Criterion* and publisher at Faber & Faber, to publish most of Pound's work in the UK, including *Selected Shorter Poems*, *The Cantos* and *Selected Literary Essays*. After his move to Italy in the 1920s, Pound became increasingly sceptical about the direction of TSE's convictions and poetry, but they continued to correspond. After Eliot's death, Pound said of him: 'His was the true Dantescan voice – not honoured enough, and deserving more than I ever gave him.' See A. David

Moody, *Ezra Pound: Poet: A Portrait of the Man and his Work* I: *The Young Genius 1885–1920* (2007), Humphrey Carpenter, *A Serious Character* (1988), and *The Selected Letters of Ezra Pound 1907–1941*, ed. D. D. Paige (1950).

John Quinn (1870–1924): Irish-American corporate lawyer in New York; major patron of modernist writers and artists; and collector of manuscripts. He afforded generous support, both financial and legal, to writers including Conrad, Yeats, Joyce and Ezra Pound. TSE began corresponding with him at the urgent prompting of Pound, who had read about him as a patron, in the *New Age* in January 1915: the correspondence ran until Quinn's death. Pound urged TSE's importance upon Quinn ('I have more or less discovered him,' he proclaimed). Quinn bought from TSE (for a fair price) the drafts of *The Waste Land*, which he later bequeathed to the New York Public Library. Though a supporter of the Irish nationalist cause, he worked for the British intelligence services, helping to report upon *agents provocateurs* who were working in the USA to mobilise anti-British groups of Irish and Germans. See B. L. Reid, *The Man from New York: John Quinn and His Friends* (1969).

Herbert Read (1893–1968): English poet and literary critic, and one of the most influential art critics of the century. Son of a tenant farmer, Read spent his first years in rural Yorkshire; at sixteen, he went to work as a bank clerk, then studied law and economics at Leeds University; later still, he joined the Civil Service, working first in the Ministry of Labour and then at the Treasury. During his years of service in WW1, he rose to be a captain in a Yorkshire regiment, the Green Howards (his war poems were published in *Naked Warriors*, 1919); and when on leave to receive the Military Cross in 1917, he arranged to dine with TSE at the Monico Restaurant in Piccadilly Circus. This launched a life-long friendship which he was to recall in 'T. S. E. – A Memoir', in *T. S. Eliot: The Man and his Work*, ed. Allen Tate (1966). Within the year, he had also become acquainted with the Sitwells, Ezra Pound, Wyndham Lewis, Richard Aldington and Ford Madox Ford. He co-founded the journal *Art & Letters*, 1917–20, and wrote essays too for A. R. Orage, editor of the *New Age*. In 1922 he was appointed a curator in the department of ceramics and glass at the Victoria and Albert Museum; and in later years he was to work for the publishers Routledge & Kegan Paul, and as editor of the *Burlington Magazine*, 1933–9. By 1923 he was writing for the *Criterion*: he was to be one of Eliot's regular leading contributors and a reliable ally and advisor. In 1924 he edited T. E. Hulme's posthumous *Speculations*. His later works include *Art Now* (1933); the introduction to the catalogue of the International Surrealist Exhibition held at the New Burlington Galleries, London, 1936; *Art and Society* (1937); *Education through Art* (1943); and *A Concise History of Modern Painting* (1959). In 1947 he founded (with Roland Penrose) the Institute of Contemporary Art; and in 1953 he was knighted for services to literature. Eliot, he was to recall (perhaps only half in jest), was 'rather like a gloomy priest presiding over my affections and spontaneity'. See Herbert Read, *Annals of Innocence and Experience* (1940); James King, *The Last Modern: A Life of Herbert Read* (1990); *Herbert Read Reassessed*, ed. D. Goodway (1998); and Jason Harding (*The* 'Criterion': *Cultural Politics and Periodical Networks in Inter-War Britain* [2002]), who states that Read contributed sixty-eight book reviews, four articles, and five poems to the *Criterion*.

Bruce Richmond (1871–1964), editor, was educated at Winchester and New College, Oxford, and called to the Bar in 1897. However, he never practised as a barrister. Instead, George Buckle, editor of *The Times*, appointed him an assistant editor in 1899, and in 1902 he assumed the editorship of the fledgling *Times Literary Supplement*, which he commanded for thirty-five years. During this period, the *TLS* established itself as the premier academic and critical periodical in Britain. He was knighted in 1935. TSE, who was introduced to Richmond by Richard Aldington in 1919, enthused to his mother that year that writing the leading article for the *TLS* was the highest honour 'in the critical world of literature'. In a tribute, he recalled Richmond as possessing 'a bird-like alertness of eye, body and mind . . . It was from Bruce Richmond that I learnt editorial standards . . . I learnt from him that it is the business of an editor to know his contributors personally, to keep in touch with them and to make suggestions to them. I tried [at the *Criterion*] to form a nucleus of writers (some of them, indeed, recruited from the *Times Literary Supplement*, and introduced to me by Richmond) on whom I could depend, differing from each other in many things, but not in love of literature and seriousness of purpose. And I learnt from Richmond that I must read every word of what was to appear in print . . . It is a final tribute to Richmond's genius as an editor that some of his troupe of regular contributors (I am thinking of myself as well as of others) produced some of their most distinguished critical essays as leaders for the *Literary Supplement* . . . Good literary criticism requires good editors as well as good critics. And Bruce Richmond was a great editor' ('Bruce Lyttelton Richmond', *TLS*, 13 Jan. 1961, 17).

John Rodker (1894–1955): poet, novelist and publisher. Born in Manchester, of an immigrant Jewish family, he published his *Poems* in 1914. During WW1, Rodker was a conscientious objector, and after going on the run, sheltering with the poet R. C. Trevelyan, he was imprisoned in Dartmoor Prison. In 1919 he started up the Ovid Press (a small press which lasted about a year), and published TSE's *Poems* (1920), Ezra Pound's *Hugh Selwyn Mauberley*, and his own *Hymns* (1920), as well as portfolios of drawings by Wyndham Lewis, Henri Gaudier-Brzeska, and Edward Wadsworth. In 1919, he took over briefly from Pound as foreign editor of the *Little Review*. In the 1920s he spent time in Paris on the second edition of Joyce's *Ulysses* and set up the Casanova Press. He published his *Collected Poems, 1912–1925* (1930), and later worked with Anna Freud on the Imago Press in order to publish translations of Freud.

Bertrand Russell (1872–1970): one of the most influential twentieth-century British philosophers; co-author (with Alfred North Whitehead) of *Principia Mathematica* (1910–13), and author of innumerable other books including the popular *Problems of Philosophy* (1912), *Mysticism and Logic* (1918) – which was reviewed by TSE in 'Style and Thought' (*Nation* 22, 23 March 1918) – and *History of Western Philosophy* (1945). In 1914, Russell gave the Lowell Lectures on 'Our Knowledge of the External World' at Harvard, where he encountered Eliot. On 27 March 1914, Russell described Eliot as 'very well dressed and polished, with manners of the finest Etonian type'. He later characterised him as 'proficient in Plato, intimate with French literature from Villon to Vildrach, and capable of exquisiteness of appreciation, but lacking in the crude insistent passion that one must have in order to achieve anything'. After their accidental meeting in 1914, Russell played an important role in introducing TSE to British intellectual life, as well as getting him launched as a reviewer for *International Journal of Ethics* and the *Monist*. However, it has been alleged that, not long after TSE's marriage, Russell may have had a brief affair with his wife Vivien. The three friends shared lodgings for a while at Russell's flat in London. Russell was a conscientious objector and vocal opponent of WW1, which led to a brief prison sentence in Wandsworth. In later years, TSE saw little of his one-time professor and friend, and he later attacked Russell's philosophical and ethical views, in his

'Commentary' in the *Criterion* (April 1924), and elsewhere. Russell provides a partial account of his relationship with the Eliots in *The Autobiography of Bertrand Russell* II: *1914–1944* (1968). See also Ray Monk, *Bertrand Russell: The Spirit of Solitude* (1996).

George Santayana (1863–1952), Spanish-born American philosopher, studied at Harvard under William James and Josiah Royce, and was author of many philosophical, literary and autobiographical books, including *The Sense of Beauty* (1896), *The Life of Reason* (1905), and *Three Philosophical Poets: Lucretius, Dante, and Goethe* (1910). At Harvard, Eliot took his courses in the History of Modern Philosophy, 1907-8, and the Philosophy of History ('Ideals of Society, Religion, Art, and Science, in their historical development'), 1909-10. Following his mother's death in 1912, Santayana moved to Europe and lived in Paris and Oxford before settling in Italy. Conrad Aiken called him 'that Merlin, that Prospero, with his wizard mantle from Spain'; and he was hugely influential in Harvard philosophy during Eliot's time there. The *Harvard Monthly* declared in March 1912 that Santayana had 'attained a following which in enthusiasm and intensity . . . is impossible to parallel'. In 1918 Eliot remarked upon the 'imperial and slightly amused gaze of Mr. Santayana', while in *The Varieties of Metaphysical Poetry* he observed that, though *Three Philosophical Poets* was 'one of the most brilliant' of his books, Santayana was 'more interested in poetical philosophy than philosophical poetry'.

Sydney Schiff (1868–1944): novelist and translator, and patron of the arts. In 1911 Schiff married his second wife Violet Zillah Beddington (1874–1962), sister of Oscar Wilde's friend Ada Leverson, and a gifted musician who had studied singing under Paolo Tosti. Schiff soon began writing fiction and engaging in patronage of the arts. His first novel, *Concessions* (1913), was published under his own name, but *War-Time Silhouettes* (1916) and later novels appeared under the *nom-de-plume* 'Stephen Hudson'. The pseudonym was adopted in anticipation of the appearance of *Richard Kurt* (1919), the first of a sequence of autobiographical novels – the series would be gathered up in a volume advisedly called *A True Story* (1930). Schiff came from a wealthy Jewish family (his father having been a successful stockbroker), and he chose to support Isaac Rosenberg among other writers and artists; he would subsidise the short-lived but notable periodical *Art & Letters* (1918–20), as well as contributing to it and editing one issue. He was a major champion of Marcel Proust (and he would ultimately translate *Le temps retrouvé*), a friend of several other writers (Vivien Eliot dubbed him 'the Sitwells' Holy Ghost'), and a supporter of Wyndham Lewis (who painted a commissioned portrait of him and then went on to satirise him in *The Apes of God*). He and his wife were to become close friends of the Eliots: his first surviving letter to TSE dates from 3 May 1919. Though always ready to salute greater talents than his own, Schiff was still his own man, with decidedly independent views: he was for example prompt to dispute with TSE the value of the posthumously collected writings of the philosopher T. E. Hulme. On the death of Violet Schiff, TSE wrote in tribute to the couple: 'In the 1920s the Schiffs' hospitality, generosity, and encouragement meant much to a number of young artists and writers of whom I was one. The Schiffs' acquaintance was cosmopolitan, and their interests embraced all the arts. At their house I met, for example, Delius and Arthur Symons, and the first Viscountess Rothermere, who founded the *Criterion* under my editorship. Middleton Murry and Katherine Mansfield knew their house, and Wyndham Lewis and Charles Scott-Moncrieff, and many others . . . I write primarily to pay homage to a beloved friend, but also in the hope that some future chronicler of the history of art and letters in our time may give to Sydney and Violet Schiff the place which is their due.' (See 'Mrs Violet Schiff: All-Embracing Interest in the Arts', *The Times*, 9 July 1962.) See also Richard Davenport-Hines, *A Night at the Majestic: Proust and the Great Modernist Dinner Party of 1922* (2006).

Gilbert Seldes (1893–1970), journalist, editor and critic, graduated from Harvard in 1914 and was a war correspondent before becoming for a while editor of the *Dial*, 1920–3. His works include the influential study *The 7 Lively Arts* (1924) – on popular arts, embracing the comic strip and popular songs as well as cinema and vaudeville – and *The Stammering Century* (1928). In later years he was prolific as an essayist; he also wrote for the Broadway theatre, and became the first director of TV programmes for CBS News, and the founding Dean of the Annenberg School for Communication at the University of Pennsylvania. See Michael G. Kammen, *The Lively Arts: Gilbert Seldes and the Transformation of Cultural Criticism in the United States* (1996).

Alfred Dwight ('Shef') Sheffield (1871–1961), husband of TSE's eldest sister Ada, taught English at University School, Cleveland, Ohio, and was an English instructor, and later a Professor, of Group Work at Wellesley College. His publications include *Lectures on the Harvard Classics: Confucianism* (1909), and *Grammar and Thinking: a study of the working* *conceptions in syntax* (1912). He later joined the editorial staff of *Webster's International Dictionary*.

Scofield Thayer (1890–1982): American poet and publisher; pioneering editor of the *Dial*. Thayer came from a wealthy Massachusetts family, which enabled him to travel and act as a patron of the arts. He was a friend of TSE from Milton Academy, where he was his junior by a year. Like TSE, he went on to Harvard and Oxford, where from 1914 he spent two years studying philosophy at Magdalen College: it was at his rooms there that TSE met Vivien Haigh-Wood in 1915. From 1919 to 1925 he was editor of the *Dial*, having joined forces with Dr James Sibley Watson (who became president of the magazine) to save it from closure. Re-launched as a monthly in January 1920, the *Dial* became the most enterprising and innovative cultural and arts magazine in the USA. It published TSE's 'London Letters' and *The Waste Land* as well as important essays by him such as '*Ulysses*, Order and Myth'; Yeats, Pound, cummings, Joyce and others of the most important Anglophone modernists; and influential European writers including Mann, Hofmannsthal and Valéry. A meeting with Lady Rothermere prompted her to finance the *Criterion*, with Eliot as editor. In 1921, Thayer settled in Vienna, where, while continuing remotely to edit the *Dial*, he underwent analysis with Sigmund Freud. He suffered a series of mental breakdowns, resigning from the magazine in June 1926. Certified in 1930, he spent the remainder of his life in care. Watson kept going with the *Dial*, and Marianne Moore took over as editor until its final issue in 1929. Moore judged Thayer to be 'very quiet friendly polished and amusing', and 'in his discernment and interplay of metaphor . . . very brilliant' (*Selected Letters of Marianne Moore*, ed. Bonnie Costello [1998]). See also Nicholas Joost, *Scofield Thayer and 'The Dial'* (1964).

Jean Jules Verdenal (1890–1915), the son of a French doctor, was born on 11 May 1890 at Pau in the French Pyrenees. He became a medical student in Paris, where he and Eliot met as fellow lodgers at Mme Causabon's *pension*, 151 bis rue St Jacques. During the academic year 1910–11 they became close friends, sharing many literary and cultural interests. Although they continued to correspond after Eliot's return to America in the autumn of 1911, they were never to meet again. Renouncing his deferment from military service, on 18 March 1913 Verdenal joined the 18th Infantry Regiment and served on the Western Front from 2 August 1914 to February 1915, being appointed an assistant medical officer in November 1914. He was killed in the Dardanelles on 2 May 1915. Eliot dedicated to Verdenal 'The Love Song of J. Alfred Prufrock', with an epigraph from Dante opening '*Or puoi la quantitate / comprender dell'amor ch'a te me scalda*' ('Now can you understand / the measure of love which warms me towards you'). In an autobiographical note in *Criterion* 13 (April 1934), Eliot evoked 'the memory of a friend coming across the Luxembourg Garden in the later afternoon, waving a branch of lilac, a friend who was later (as far as I could find out) to be mixed with the mud of Gallipoli'. See George Watson, 'Quest of a Frenchman', *Sewanee Review* (Summer 1976).

Dr Roger Vittoz (1863–1925): Swiss psychiatrist recommended to TSE by Ottoline Morrell. He published one book, *Traitement des psychonévroses par la rééducation du controle cérébral* (Paris, 1911), of which there was an English translation by H. B. Brooke, *Treatment of Neurasthenia by Means of Brain Control* (2nd edn., 1913). Morrell, who was treated for neurasthenia, wrote of him: 'He taught his patients a system of mental control and concentration, and a kind of organisation of mind, which had a great effect on steadying and developing me . . . The man himself impressed me by his extraordinary poise and goodness. Part of the treatment was the formation of the habit of eliminating unnecessary thoughts and worries from one's mind, and to do this one had to practise eliminating letters from words, or one number from a set of numbers' (*Ottoline: The Early Memoirs*, 237). Other patients of Vittoz included William James, Joseph Conrad and Julian Huxley. See R. Dupond, *La Cure des Psychonevroses par la Méthode de Dr. Vittoz* (Paris, 1934); H. Lefebvre, *Un 'Sauveur': Le Docteur Vittoz* (Paris, 1951); and Adam Piette, 'Eliot's Breakdown and Dr. Vittoz', *ELN* 33: 1 (Sept. 1995), 35–8.

Harriet Shaw Weaver (1876–1961): English editor and publisher, and political activist, whom Virginia Woolf described as 'modest judicious & decorous' (*Diary*, 13 April 1918). In 1912, Weaver began by giving financial support to the *Freewoman*, a radical periodical founded and edited by Dora Marsden, which was renamed in 1913 (at the suggestion of Ezra Pound) *The Egoist*. Weaver became editor in 1914, turning it into a 'little magazine' with a big influence in the history of literary modernism. Following in the footsteps of Richard Aldington and H. D., TSE became assistant editor in 1917 (having been nominated by Pound) and remained so until it closed in 1919. When Joyce could not secure a publisher for *A Portrait of the Artist as a Young Man*, Weaver in 1917 converted the *Egoist* into a press to publish it. She went on to publish TSE's first book,

Prufrock and Other Observations (1917), Pound's *Dialogues of Fontenelle* and *Quia Pauper Amavi*, Wyndham Lewis's novel *Tarr*, and Marianne Moore's *Poems*, and other notable books. (She played a major role as Joyce's patron and confidante, and went on to be his literary executor and to help to put together *The Letters of James Joyce*.) TSE wrote in tribute in 1962: 'Miss Harriet Shaw Weaver . . . was so modest and self-effacing a woman that her generous patronage of men of letters was hardly known beyond the circle of those who benefited by it . . . Miss Weaver's support, once given, remained steadfast. Her great disappointment was her failure to persuade any printer in this country to take the risk of printing *Ulysses*; her subsequent generosity to James Joyce, and her solicitude for his welfare and that of his family, knew no bounds . . . [Working for her at the *Egoist*] was all great fun, my first experience of editorship. In 1932 I dedicated my *Selected Essays* to this good, kind, unassuming, courageous and lovable woman, to whom I owe so much. What other publisher in 1917 (the Hogarth Press was not yet in existence) would, I wonder, have taken *Prufrock*?' See also Jane Lidderdale and Mary Nicholson, *Dear Miss Weaver: Harriet Shaw Weaver, 1876–1961* (1970).

James Haughton Woods (1864–1935): Professor of Philosophy at Harvard, 1913-34, and chairman of the department, 1914–16. He introduced courses in Indian philosophy to the University, and his *Yoga System of Patanjali* (1914) was the first American scholarly study of Indian philosophy. Eliot studied Greek Philosophy with him in 1911–12, and 'Philosophical Sanskrit' in 1912–13. After Eliot submitted his thesis, Woods told him he wanted to create a 'berth' for him in the Philosophy Department at Harvard. Eliot recorded later that 'a year in the mazes of Patanjali's metaphysics under the guidance of James Woods left me in a state of enlightened mystification' (*ASG*, 40). Eliot's lecture notes on Woods's lectures in 1911–12 are in the Eliot Collection, Houghton Library.

Leonard Woolf (1880–1969): writer and publisher, and husband of Virginia Woolf, whom he married in 1912. A friend of Lytton Strachey and J. M. Keynes at Cambridge, he played a central part in the Bloomsbury Group. He wrote a number of novels, including *The Village and the Jungle* (1913), as well as political studies, including *Socialism and Co-operation* (1919) and *Imperialism and Civilization* (1928). As editor, with Virginia Woolf, of the Hogarth Press, he was responsible for publishing TSE's *Poems* (1919) and *The Waste Land* (1922). In 1923 he became literary editor of the *Nation & Athenaeum* (after TSE had turned it down), commissioning numerous reviews from him, and remained a friend. See *An Autobiography* (2 vols, 1980); *Letters of Leonard Woolf*, ed. Frederic Spotts (1990); and Victoria Glendinning, *Leonard Woolf: A Life* (2006).

Virginia Woolf (1882–1941), English novelist, essayist and critic, was the author of *Jacob's Room* (1922), *Mrs Dalloway* (1925), and *To the Lighthouse* (1927), among many experimental and influential novels, as well as of *A Room of One's Own* (1928), a classic of modern feminist criticism, and *The Common Reader* and other collections of essays. Daughter of the biographer and editor Leslie Stephen (1832–1904), she married Leonard Woolf in 1912, published her first novel *The Voyage Out* in 1915, and founded the Hogarth Press with her husband in 1917. The Hogarth Press published TSE's *Poems* (1919), *The Waste Land* (1923), and *Homage to John Dryden* (1923). For his part, TSE published in the *Criterion* Woolf's essays and talks including 'Kew Gardens', 'Character in Fiction', and 'On Being Ill'. In addition to being his publisher, Woolf became a friend and correspondent; and her diaries and letters give a detailed first-hand portrait of him. See Hermione Lee, *Virginia Woolf* (1996).

INDEX OF CORRESPONDENTS AND RECIPIENTS

CORRESPONDENTS

RECIPIENTS

GENERAL INDEX

Page references in **bold** indicate a biographical note, those in *italics* an illustration